DEBTOR AND CREDITOR

M.J. TREBILCOCK
B.J. REITER
J.B. LASKIN

Debtor and Creditor:
Cases, Notes, and Materials

UNIVERSITY OF TORONTO PRESS
Toronto Buffalo London

© University of Toronto Press 1979
Toronto   Buffalo   London
Printed in Canada
Reprinted in 2018
ISBN 978-1-4875-8565-5 (paper)

Canadian Cataloguing in Publication Data

Trebilcock, Michael J
  Debtor and creditor

ISBN 0-8020-2331-2

1. Debtor and creditor – Canada – Cases.
I. Reiter, Barry J.   II. Laskin, J.B.
III. Title.

KE1030.A7T74   346′.71′077   C79-094234-8

Preface

These materials provide an introduction to the legal relationships between debtors and unsecured creditors. While in this field, more than in almost any other, practice and personal experience are extremely important, the book does not purport to be a guide to those aspects of the debt-collection process. The practical skills are occasionally referred to, but they are better learned elsewhere. Nevertheless, the book should be of value to practitioners, both as a basic research tool and as a source of additional lines of legal argument.

The book begins with materials bearing upon the setting in which debt-collection takes place: the nature of a debt and of the credit market, the characteristics of debtors and of creditors, the importance of credit in society, and the policy choices involved in determining how debts may be enforced.

It then proceeds to an examination of the common law and legislation which prescribe and delimit the remedies available to creditors and the protection afforded to debtors. In this it does not pretend to be exhaustive; there are many rarely used common law doctrines and statutes of narrow scope. However, the book does contain a fair sampling of substantive materials, both for their own sake and for the opportunity which they provide to apply the broader concerns reflected in the materials with which the book begins. The traditional collection techniques are cnavassed – execution, garnishment, equitable execution – and priorities among creditors considered, together with some of the proposals which have been advanced for drastic reworking of the enforcement system. After a discussion of mechanics' lien legislation, which makes a distinctive set of remedies available to creditors engaged in construction, and the rights of creditors to impeach transactions made to defeat debt enforcement, the book concludes with a series of chapters on bankruptcy.

Because significant bankruptcy reforms have been anticipated for several years, we experienced some difficulty in selecting material for inclusion in the bankruptcy chapters. In the end, we chose to use the proposed new Bankruptcy Act (Bill s-14, first reading 27 February 1979) as the major statutory reference point, in the expectation (we hope realistic) that it or a substantially similar bill will shortly be enacted. In the remainder of the book, where provincial statutes are relevant, our normal course has been to use Ontario legislation as the focus for discussion, though that of other provinces is referred to where comparisons are instructive.

A great many people have assisted in the preparation of these materials, and we gratefully acknowledge their help. Former students Hugh Ryan, Paul Lindsay, Phil Zylberberg, and Michael Wolfish, and present student Patricia Loughlan, have all provided invaluable research assistance. Our secretaries, Alice Ng, Kathy O'Rourke, and Verna Percival, have had to put up with endless changes. Our former colleague,

T.E.J. McDonnell, contributed suggestions for reorganizing the materials, and Professor C.R.B. Dunlop of the University of Alberta Faculty of Law gave us many helpful ideas and corrected errors in earlier editions. Finally, Sheriff P.J. Ambrose of the Judicial District of York kindly supplied us with the forms which appear in Chapter 15.

We would also like to thank our publishers for their assistance and encouragement.

M.J.T.
B.J.R.
J.B.L.
Toronto, March 1979

Acknowledgments

Permission to reproduce material already in print has been granted by the following authors and publishers, for whose courtesy we are grateful. The material is listed in the order in which it appears, or first appears, in the book.

Salmond and Williams, *The Law of Contract* (1945), pp 577–8, 589–90
Permission of Sweet & Maxwell Ltd.

Ison, *Materials on Debt Collection* (1972), pp 10, 18, 224–25.
Permission of T.G. Ison

Canadian Consumer Loan Association and Federated Council of Sales Finance Companies, *Canadian Consumer Credit Factbook* (1974), Exhibit 40
Permission of Association of Canadian Financial Corporations

Trebilcock and Shulman, 'The Pathology of Credit Breakdown' (1976), 22 *McGill L.J.* 415
Permission of Fred B. Rothman & Co.

Caplovitz, *Consumers in Trouble* (1974), pp 53, 170, 171, 301–6
Reprinted with permission of Macmillan Publishing Co., Inc. from *Consumers in Trouble* by David Caplovitz. Copyright © 1974 by The Free Press, a Division of Macmillan Publishing Co., Inc.

Small Claims Court Referee, *Statistical Report* (1977)
Permission of C.G. Femia

Leff, 'Injury, Ignorance and Spite – The Dynamics of Coercive Collection' (1970), 80 *Yale L.J.* 1
Reprinted by permission of The Yale Law Journal Company and Fred B. Rothman & Company from *The Yale Law Journal*, Vol. 80, pp 1–46. A.A. Leff

Ison, 'Small Claims' (1972), 35 *Mod. L. Rev.* 18
Permission of T.G. Ison

Cayne and Trebilcock, 'Market Considerations in the Formulation of Consumer Protection Policy' (1973) 23 *U.T.L.J.* 396
Permission of University of Toronto Press

viii Acknowledgments

Department of Communications and of Justice, *Privacy and Computers* (1971), pp 55–7, 62–4
Reproduced by permission of the Minister of Supply and Services Canada

Equifax Services, 'Sample Management Selection Report'
Permission of Equifax Inc.

Sharp, *Credit Reporting and Privacy* (1970), pp 107–98
Permission of Butterworth & Co. (Canada) Ltd.

Ziegel, 'The Case for a Credit Register Deserves to be Fully Examined', *The Globe and Mail*, 2 October 1970
Permission of J.S. Ziegel, The Gobe and Mail, Toronto

Law Reform Commission of British Columbia *Report on Debtor-Creditor Relationships*, Part 1 (1971), pp 6–10
Permission of Law Reform Commission of British Columbia

Report of the Committee on the Enforcement of Judgement Debts, Cmnd. 3909 (1969), pp 86–9, 319–21
Reproduced with the permission of Her Majesty's Stationery Office

Rock, *Making People Pay* (1973)
Permission of Routledge & Kegan Paul Ltd.

Law Society of Upper Canada, *Creditors' and Debtors' Rights, Bar Admission Course 1977–78*, pp 127–8, 129–30
Permission of Law Society of Upper Canada

Dunlop, *Exemptions of Income and Assets from Execution* (1974), pp 4–7
Permission of Law Reform Commission of British Columbia

Karlen, 'Exemptions from Execution', (1967), 22 *The Business Lawyer* 1167
Permission of The Business Lawyer

LaForest, 'Some Aspects of the Writ of Fieri Facias' (1959), 12 *U.N.B. L.J.* 39
Permission of University of New Brunswick Law Journal

Dunlop, 'Execution Against Personal Property in England and British Columbia' (1972), 7 *U.B.C. L. Rev.* 171
Permission of C.R.B. Dunlop

'Despite orders, jailing of debtors is ignored', *The Globe and Mail*, 5 August 1975
Permission of The Globe and Mail, Toronto

Gordon 'Case and Comment' (1954), 32 *Can. Bar Rev.* 1141
Permission of The Canadian Bar Association

'Garnishment – Property Subject to Garnishment – Joint Account Depositor has Burden of Proving this Ownership of Funds to Prevent Their Garnishment for Debts of Other Depositor – *Leaf* v *McGowan* (1957)' (1958), 71 *Harv. L. Rev.* 557
Harvard Law Review Association. Copyright 1958 by the Harvard Law Review Association

Ellis, 'The Charging Order–A Neglected Means of Enforcement?' (1962), 20 *U. of T. Faculty of Law Rev.* 35
Permission of Students' Law Society, University of Toronto Faculty of Law

Report of the Study Committee on Bankruptcy and Insolvency Legislation Canada 1970
Reproduced by permission of the Minister of Supply and Services Canada

Wallace, 'The Logic of Consumer Credit Reform' (1973), 82 *Yale L.J.* 461
Reprinted by permission of The Yale Law Journal Company and Fred B. Rothman and Company from *The Yale Law Journal*, Vol. 82, pp 461–82. G.J. Wallace

Canadian Construction Documents Committee 'Standard Form of Stipulated Price Construction Contract'
Permission of Canadian Construction Documents Committee

Ontario Law Reform Commission, *Report on the Non-Possessory Repairman's Lien* (1972), pp 7–12
Permission of Ontario Law Reform Commission

Consumer and Corporate Affairs Canada, *Background Papers for the Bankruptcy and Insolvency Bill (1978)*
Permission of Consumer and Corporate Affairs Canada

Comments from Canadian Bankruptcy Reports
Permission of The Carswell Company Limited

'The Growing Popularity of Personal Bankruptcy', *Moneysworth*, 14 June 1971
Ralph Ginzburg © Ralph Ginzburg 1971

Duncan and Honsburger, *Bankruptcy in Canada* (3rd ed. 1971), pp 469–71, 479, 484
Reproduced with the permission of Canada Law Book Limited, 80 Cowdray Court, Agincourt, Ontario M1S 1S5

Contents

CHAPTER 6: THE EFFECT OF JUDGMENT AND INTEREST UPON JUDGMENT

CHAPTER 7: EXAMINATION OF THE JUDGMENT DEBTOR

CHAPTER 8: EXEMPTIONS FROM THE EXECUTION PROCESS

CHAPTER 9: EXECUTION

CHAPTER 10: GARNISHMENT

CHAPTER 17: IMPEACHABLE TRANSACTIONS

CHAPTER 18: INTRODUCTION TO BANKRUPTCY

CHAPTER 21: THE PROPERTY OF THE BANKRUPT

CHAPTER 22: DISTRIBUTING THE ESTATE AND DISCHARGE

DEBTOR AND CREDITOR

1
The Nature of a Debt

INTRODUCTION

This chapter examines the distinction between debt and damages claims, pointing out
the procedural advantages of a creditor being able to sue in debt rather than damages,
for example, the ability to enter default judgment without proof of the quantum of the
claim. Substantive advantages of a debt claim are also explored, including, arguably,
the absence of any duty to mitigate, as exemplified in the well-known case of *White
and Carter Councils Ltd* v *McGregor*, and, more arguably, the inapplicability of the
doctrine of penalties, as canvassed in *Bridge* v *Campbell Discount Co Ltd*. On the
question of the discharge of a debt claim, special attention is paid to the problem of part
payment and the potential application of the doctrine of promissory estoppel. The
impact of section 16 of the Ontario Mercantile Law Amendment Act on part payment
by way of discharge of a larger debt claim is also examined.

I THE PROCEDURAL DISTINCTION BETWEEN DEBT AND DAMAGES

Salmond and Williams, *Law of Contracts* (2nd ed, 1945) pp 577–8, 589–90 (footnotes
omitted)

Debt is the remedy in respect of such promises to pay a liquidated sum of money as the common
law enforces specifically. The common law compels the promisor to do the very thing (albeit
somewhat tardily) which he has promised, *viz.*, pay the specified amount of money. Damages
are the common law remedy in respect of all other promises and of warranties. In such cases the
common law does not compel the undertaking party specifically to perform his undertaking but
compels him to pay a pecuniary substitute for such performance. In cases where the principal
remedy is debt, damages, which according to the circumstances may be either substantial in the
form of interest or nominal, may sometimes be awarded in respect of the failure of the debtor to
make punctual payment ...

The breach of a contract to pay a liquidated sum of money is sometimes remedied by the
award of damages ascertained on the principle of *Hadley* v *Baxendale*. More frequently,
however, the remedy is not damages assessed on this principle but debt (*i.e.*, a judgment for the
very sum which was promised). As an incident of a claim in debt, damages, being either nominal
or substantial in the shape of interest according to the circumstances, may sometimes be
awarded in respect of the breach of contract constituted by the failure to pay on time.

When, then, is the remedy for failure to perform a contract to pay a liquidated sum of money in
damages only and when in debt? The answer appears to be that the remedy is in debt whenever
the promise to pay is unconditional and is not a promise to pay by way of loan. When the promise
to pay is conditional or is to advance money as a loan the remedy is exclusively in damages ...

2 THE ADVANTAGES OF SUING IN DEBT

Ison, *Materials on Debt Collections* (Queen's University 1972) p 10

A plaintiff whose action is in debt may have an easier time both procedurally and substantively than someone claiming in damages. Consider the following advantages:

1 / An action for debt in the High Court can be commenced by a specially endorsed writ, making documentation simpler than in a claim for damages.

2 / With a specially endorsed writ, a motion for summary judgment can be made before any defence is filed. This cannot be done in a claim for damages.

3 / Where no appearance is entered or no defence is filed on a debt claim, the plaintiff can enter final judgment for the amount claimed, but if the claim is for damages, he can only enter interlocutory judgment and must then have a hearing to prove his amount of damages.

4 / Despite the theory that damages are supposed to be a full indemnity, there is often a tendency to scale down and courts frequently award less than a full indemnity on a claim for damages even when the defendant has been wholly at fault. There is no such risk on a debt claim, because there is no severance of quantum from liability.

5 / The rules relating to the assessment of damages, for example remoteness, are not generally applicable on a claim for debt. In particular, the rule that a plaintiff must mitigate his loss is not applicable on a debt claim.

3 THE SUBSTANTIVE DISTINCTION BETWEEN DEBT AND DAMAGES

a / *White & Carter (Councils) Ltd* v *McGregor* [1962] A.C. 413 (H.L)

[The plaintiffs (appellants) were suppliers of litter bins to which advertisements were attached. The defendant's (respondent's) sales manager contracted with the plaintiffs to advertise the defendant's business on a number of bins for a period of three years. Because the sales manager had been given no specific authority to make the contract, the defendant wrote to cancel the contract on the same day on which it had been made. The plaintiffs refused to accept the cancellation and carried out the terms of the contract. The plaintiffs sued in debt for the whole sum due for the three years, relying on a clause of the contract which provided that 'in the event of an instalment or part thereof being due for payment, and remaining unpaid for a period of four weeks ... then the whole amount due for the 156 weeks ... shall immediately become due and payable'. The defendant's position was that the contract had been repudiated before anything had been done under it, and as such, the plaintiffs' only remedy was damages, which would have imposed a duty upon the plaintiffs to mitigate their losses.

In a 3-2 decision, the House of Lords permitted the appellants to refuse to accept the repudiation and to go ahead with the work against the wishes of the respondent, and then to recover in debt with all the ensuing advantages flowing therefrom. Lord Hodson, with whom Lord Tucker agreed (Lord Reid having written a separate concurring judgment), gave the majority judgment:]

The true position is that the contract survives and does so not only where specific implement is available. When the assistance of the court is not required the innocent party can choose whether he will accept repudiation and sue for damages for anticipatory breach or await the date of performance by the guilty party. Then, if there is failure in performance, his rights are preserved.

It may be unfortunate that the appellants have saddled themselves with an unwanted contract causing an apparent waste of time and money. No doubt this aspect impressed the Court of Session but there is no equity which can assist the respondent. It is trite that equity will not rewrite an improvident contract where there is no disability on either side. There is no duty laid upon a party to a subsisting contract to vary it at the behest of the other party so as to deprive himself of the benefit given to him by the contract. To hold otherwise would be to introduce a novel equitable doctrine that a party was not to be held to his contract unless the court in a given instance thought it reasonable so to do. In this case it would make an action for debt a claim for a discretionary remedy. This would introduce an uncertainty into the field of contract which appears to be unsupported by authority either in English or Scottish law save for the one case upon which the Court of Session founded its opinion and which must, in my judgment, be taken to have been wrongly decided.

[In a concurring judgment, Lord Reid, while agreeing with the result, more narrowly stated the proposition advanced by Lord Hodson:] It may well be that, if it can be shown that a person has no legitimate interest, financial or otherwise, in performing the contract rather than claiming damages, he ought not to be allowed to saddle the other party with an additional burden with no benefit to himself. If a party has no interest to enforce a stipulation, he cannot in general enforce it: so it might be said that, if a party has no interest to insist on a particular remedy, he ought not to be allowed to insist on it. And, just as a party is not allowed to enforce a penalty, so he ought not to be allowed to penalise the other party by taking one course when another is equally advantageous to him. If I may revert to the example which I gave of a company engaging an expert to prepare an elaborate report and then repudiating before anything was done, it might be that the company could show that the expert had no substantial or legitimate interest in carrying out the work rather than accepting damages: I would think that the de minimis principle would apply in determining whether his interest was substantial, and that he might have a legitimate interest other than an immediate financial interest. But if the expert had no such interest then that might be regarded as a proper case for the exercise of the general equitable jurisdiction of the court. But that is not this case. Here the respondent did not set out to prove that the appellants had no legitimate interest in completing the contract and claiming the contract price rather than claiming damages; there is nothing in the findings of fact to support such a case, and it seems improbable that any such case could have been proved.

NOTE The dissenting judgments of Lord Morton of Henryton and Lord Keith of Avonholm were based on two propositions: first, while the contract in question was not one for which specific performance was obtainable (since the defendant's only obligation under the contract was the payment of a sum of money for services to be rendered), to allow the plaintiffs to insist on performing their part of the contract, and then to force the defendant to pay the contract price for unwanted services, would be, in effect, an indirect form of specific performance. Second, repudiation of a contract is really a breach of contract. As such, the party complaining of the breach has a duty to mitigate the damage he has suffered. The case has been applied in Canada: see *Tanenbaum and Downsview Meadows* v *Wright Winston Ltd* (1965), 49 D.L.R. (2d) 386 (Ont. C.A.). It was also distinguished by the Ontario Court of Appeal in *Finelli* v *Dee* (1968), 67 D.L.R. (2d) 393. In the latter case, a homeowner cancelled a contract to pave his driveway. The contractor, nevertheless, completed it, and billed him for the debt. The court refused to allow the action. It distinguished *White & Carter (Councils) Ltd*, stating that in that case the contract could be completed with no further action or co-operation from the defendant; in *Finelli*, the contractor's work required access to the property of the defendant and hence his co-operation. The rule in United States' jurisdictions differs. After repudiation the innocent party may not continue to perform the contract and recover the whole sum. The duty to mitigate is the same, whether the claim be characterized as a claim for damages or debt: *Western Advertising Co* v *Mid-west Laundries Inc* (1933) 61 s.w. 2d 251 (Missouri).

QUESTIONS Does the decision in *White & Carter (Councils) Ltd* make commercial or economic sense with respect to the efficient allocation of resources? If the claim had been characterized as a damages claim how would the plaintiffs' position have been affected? Is the distinction suggested in *Finelli* logical?

b / *Bridge* v *Campbell Discount Co, Ltd* [1962] 1 All E.R. 385 (H.L.) (reversing *sub nom Campbell Discount Co Ltd* v *Bridge* [1961] 2 All E.R. 97 (C.A.)

[Pursuant to a hire-purchase agreement made on 20 July 1959, the Appellant, Mr Bridge, took possession of a used automobile owned by the respondent company. The total price of £482 10s was payable as follows: (a) the appellant was to pay £105 immediately in the form of cash and trade-in of his present automobile; (b) the appellant undertook to pay the balance by way of thirty-six consecutive monthly payments of £10 9s 2d starting from 20 August 1959; (c) at the conclusion of the payments, the appellant was to have the option of purchasing the automobile for the sum of £1.

The standard-form contract contained numerous clauses delineating various conditions and undertakings by which the 'hirer' was to be bound. Clause 6 gave the hirer the option of terminating the hiring by giving written notice to the owners, whereupon the provisions of clause 9 were brought into effect. Clause 7 gave the owners the right to terminate the hiring agreement and retake possession of the car immediately upon the failure of the hirer to make any of the payments due under the agreement or to observe any of the other stipulations contained therein. Clause 9 provided that if for any reason the contract was terminated before the vehicle became the property of the hirer, the hirer should forthwith, inter alia, '… pay to the owners the arrears of rent due and unpaid at the date of termination of the hiring together with interest thereon … and by way of compensation for depreciation of the vehicle such further sum as may be necessary to make the rental paid and payable hereunder equal to two-thirds of the hire-purchase price …'

The hirer paid the first monthly instalment, but the next month he wrote the following letter to the respondents: 'Dear Sir, Owing to unforeseen personal circumstances I am very sorry but I will not be able to pay any more payments on the Bedford Dormobile. Will you please let me know when and where I will have to return the car. I am very sorry regarding this but I have no alternative.' He then returned the car to the dealer, whereupon the respondents sued him for the amount of two-thirds of the hire-purchase price less the deposit and the first instalment.]

Lord Morton of Henryton: The learned county court judge, after hearing the solicitors for both parties, recorded his judgment as follows: 'Hold penalty. Claims dismissed.' From this judgment, the respondents appealed. The Court of Appeal allowed the appeal and gave judgment for the respondents for £206 3s. 4d. with costs. The court, holding that the appellant had exercised his option to terminate the hiring under cl. 6 of the agreement, followed the decision of the Court of Appeal in *Associated Distributors, Ltd.* v *Hall*, [1938] 1 All e.r. 511 at 513, where Slesser, l.j., said: 'This is a case where the hirer has elected to terminate the hiring. He has exercised an option, and the terms on which he may exercise the option are those set out in cl. 7. The question, therefore, whether these payments constitute liquidated damages or penalty does not arise in the present case for determination.'

My Lords, in my opinion *Associated Distributors, Ltd.* v *Hall* was rightly decided, and, if I had thought that, in the present case, the appellant exercised his option under cl 6 of the agreement of July 20, 1959, I should have agreed with the decision of the Court of Appeal in the present case. In that event, the appellant would have been bound to pay the stipulated sum of £206 3s. 4d., not by way of penalty or liquidated damages, but simply because payment of that sum was one of the terms on which the option could be exercised. I am of opinion, however, that the appellant never had the slightest intention of exercising the option contained in cl 6, and the terms of his letter show that he did not have cl 6 in mind. He frankly and simply informs the respondents that 'I will not be able to pay any more payments on the Bedford Dormobile.' There is no reference to any option, and I cannot reconcile the statement just quoted with the view that he intended to exercise an option, the terms whereof put him under an immediate obligation to pay a further large sum to the respondents. To my mind, the letter means that the writer feels reluctantly compelled to break his agreement, and the apologetic terms of the letter confirm me in this view. Why should the hirer apologise so humbly, twice, if he thought that he was merely exercising an option given to him by the agreement? Another indication that he never thought of the option is the fact that he returned the car to the dealers, whereas, under the clear terms of the option, he was bound to return it to the respondents.

The respondents contended in this House that the defence of the appellant, already set out, amounted to an admission that he had exercised his option under cl 6. My Lords, I cannot agree. The date mentioned in the defence is Sept. 14, 1959, when the car was returned to the dealers. If the appellant 'terminated the agreement' under the option, he must have done so on Sept. 3, when he gave the 'notice in writing' required by cl 6. The defence alleges that the termination was effected by an act, namely the return of the vehicle, and not by any notice in writing. For these reasons, I think that no admission was made. Moreover, in the Court of Appeal, counsel for the appellant argued that he had not exercised the option and no objection was raised to his so arguing.

My Lords, if I am right so far, the appellant has clearly committed a breach of the hire-purchase agreement by failing to pay the subsequent instalments, and it becomes necessary to consider whether the payment stipulated in cl 9 (b) of the agreement was a penalty or liquidated damages. 'The essence of a penalty is a payment of money stipulated as in terrorem of the offending party; the essence of liquidated damages is a genuine covenanted pre-estimate of damage.' See per Lord Dunedin in *Dunlop Pneumatic Tyre Co., Ltd.* v *New Garage & Motor Co., Ltd.* [1915] a.c. at p 86. I find it impossible to regard the sum stipulated in cl. 9 as a genuine pre-estimate of the loss which would be suffered by the respondents in the events specified in the same clause. One reason will suffice, though others might be given. This was a second-hand car when the appellant took it over on hire-purchase. The depreciation in its value would naturally become greater the longer it remained in the appellant's hands. Yet the sum to be paid under cl. 9 (b) is largest when, as in the present case, the car is returned after it has been in the hirer's possession for a very short time, and gets progressively smaller as time goes on. This could not possibly be the result of a genuine pre-estimate of the loss. Further, in my view, the provisions of cl. 9 were 'stipulated as in terrorem' of the appellant. As counsel for the appellant put it: 'They are intended to secure that the hirer will not determine the agreement until at least two-thirds of the price has been paid.' The result is that the appellant is entitled to relief in accordance with the principles laid down by Lord Thurlow, L.C., in *Sloman* v. *Walter*.

LORD RADCLIFFE: [His lordship was of the opinion that the hirer's letter and return of the automobile was not an exercise of option to terminate, but rather was a breach of contract which would enable the Court to invoke the doctrine of penalties to vitiate the effect of Clause 9. He continued:] Having regard to the view that your Lordships have taken as to the true facts of the case, our decision does not, I take it, conclude the question of an owner's rights under such agreements, when the hiring is determined under a hirer's option or by an event specified in the contract but not involving a breach. Such questions are closely related to what we have to consider here, but it does not follow that the legal arguments that sustain the hirer, when he is sued on breach, would be capable of sustaining him in these other situations. Indeed, although I wish to decide nothing, I appreciate that the doctrine of penalties can only be applied to those situations by the construction of almost a new set of arguments that would not arise naturally out of the arguments and considerations that have prevailed with courts, either of equity or of common law, when relieving against penalties in the past. 'Unconscionable' must not be taken to be a panacea for adjusting any contract between competent persons when it shows a rough edge to one side or the other, and equity lawyers are, I notice, sometimes both surprised and discomfited by the plentitude of jurisdiction and the imprecision of rules that are attributed to 'equity' by their more enthusiastic colleagues. Since the courts of equity never undertook to serve as a general adjuster of men's bargains, it was inevitable that they should, in course of time, evolve definite rules as to the circumstances in which, and the conditions under which, relief would be given, and I do not think that it would be at all an easy task, and I am not certain that it would be a desirable achievement, to try to reconcile all the rules under some simple general formula. Even such masters of equity as Lord Eldon and Sir George Jessel, M.R., it must be remembered, were highly sceptical of the court's duty to apply the epithet 'unconscionable' or its consequences to contracts made between persons of full age in circumstances that did not fall within the familiar categories of fraud, surprise, accident, etc., even though such contracts involved the payment of a larger sum of money on breach of an obligation to pay a smaller (see the latter's judgment in *Wallis* v *Smith* (1882) 21 CH. D. 243). But I do not speculate what principles they would have thought applicable to a hire-purchase contract, in which the hirer, I dare say willingly enough, transacts only with a dealer who is not the agent of the owner and, if he signs up at all, signs up to an elaborate fixed menu of stipulations and conditions, which he probably does not bother himself to read and very likely does not or cannot understand.

I agree that the appeal should be allowed.

LORD DENNING: My Lords, in order to determine this case it is as well to remember what is the nature of a hire-purchase transaction. It is in effect, though not in law, a mortgage of goods. Just as a man who buys land may raise part of the price by a mortgage of it, so, also, a man who buys goods may raise part of the price by hire-purchase of them. And just as the old mortgage of land was not what it appeared to be, so, also, the modern hire-purchase of goods is not what it seems to be. One might well say of a hire-purchase transaction what Maitland said of a mortgage deed: 'This is the worst of our mortgage deed ... it is one long suppressio veri and suggestio falsi': see his Lectures on Equity (2nd Edn.) (1949), p. 182. Take this present transaction. If you were able to strip off the legal trappings in which it has been dressed and see it in its native simplicity, you would discover that the appellant agreed to buy a car from a dealer for £405 but he could only find £105 towards it. So he borrowed the other £300 from a finance house and got them to pay it to the dealer, and he gave the finance house a charge on the car as security for repayment. But if you tried to express the transaction in those simple terms, you would soon fall into troubles of all sorts under the Bills of Sale Acts, the Sale of Goods Act, and the Moneylenders Acts. In order to avoid these legal obstacles, the finance house has to discard the role of a lender of money on security and it has to become an owner of goods who lets them out on hire: see *Re Robertson, Ex p. Crawcour*, (1878), 9 CH. D. 419, *McEntire v Crossley Brothers, Ltd*, [1895] A.C. 457. So it buys the goods from the dealer and lets them out on hire to the appellant. The appellant has to discard the role of a man who has agreed to buy goods, and he has to become a man who takes on hire with only an option to purchase: see *Helby v Matthews* [1895] A.C. 471. And when these new roles have been assumed, the finance house is not a moneylender but a hire-purchase company free of the trammels of the Moneylenders Acts: see *Transport & General Credit Corpn. Ltd. v Morgan* [1939] 2 All E.R. at 28. So you arrive at the modern hire-purchase transaction whereby (i) the dealer sells the goods to a finance house for cash; and (ii) the finance house lets them out on hire to a hirer in return for rentals which are so calculated as to ensure that the finance house is eventually repaid the cash with interest; and (iii) when the finance house is repaid, the hirer has the option of purchasing the car for a nominal sum. The dealer is the intermediary who arranges it all. The finance house supplies him with the printed forms, and he gets them signed. In the result, the finance house buys a car it has never seen, and lets it to a hirer it has never met, and the dealer seemingly drops out.

When hire-purchase transactions were first validated by this House in 1895 in *Helby v Matthews*, the contract of hire had most of the features of an ordinary hiring. In particular, the hirer was at liberty to terminate the hiring at any time without paying any penalty. He could return the goods and not be liable to make any further payments beyond the monthly sum then due. There was no clog on his right to terminate. And this was one of the reasons why the House saw nothing wrong with the transaction. Lord Macnaghten in characteristic fashion pointed out what a benefit this was to the hirer: '... if a coveted treasure is becoming a burthen and an encumbrance it is something, surely, to know that the transaction may be closed at once *without further liability and without the payment of any forfeit*.' Since that time, however, the finance houses have imposed a serious clog on the hirer's right to terminate the hiring. They have introduced into their printed forms a 'minimum-payment' clause such as never appeared in *Helby v Matthews* [1895] A.C. at 482. The clause in this case is a good example. The minimum payment is *two-thirds* of the hire-purchase price. The respondents stipulate that, if the hiring be terminated for any reason before the car has become the property of the hirer, then the hirer must deliver up the car in proper condition and also make up the payments to £321 13s. 4d. in all. Now the appellant only had this car for eight weeks. He had already paid £115 10s. He delivered it up in good condition. So the respondents have the car back. Yet they claim another £206 3s. 4d. from him, so as to make up £321 13s. 4d. altogether. In the result, it means that he must pay £321 13s. 4d. for eight weeks use of the car.

What possible justification have the finance houses for inserting this 'minimum-payment' clause? They call it 'agreed compensation for depreciation'. But it is no such thing. It is not 'agreed'. Nor is it 'compensation for depreciation'. There is not the slightest evidence that the appellant ever agreed it, and I do not suppose for a moment that he did. He simply signed the printed form. And as for 'depreciation', everyone knows that a car depreciates more and more as it gets older and older, but this sum gets less and less. It is obvious that the initial rental of £105 (which was one-quarter of the cash price) would compensate at once for a twenty-five per cent. depreciation; and the monthly rentals covered any remaining depreciation over the next three years. The truth is that this minimum-payment is not so much compensation for depreciation but rather compensation for loss of the future instalments which the respondents expected to receive, but which they had no right to receive. It is a penal sum which they exact because the hiring is terminated before two-thirds has been paid. In cases when the hiring is terminated, as it was here, within a few weeks, it is beyond doubt oppressive and unjust. Is not, this, then, a classic case for equity to intervene? The contract is contained in a printed form. Not one hirer in a thousand reads it, let alone understands it. He takes it on trust and signs it. It is binding at law but, when it comes to be examined, it is found to contain a penalty which is oppressive and unjust. It seems to me that such a case comes within the very first principles on which equity intervenes to grant relief. 'The whole system of equity jurisprudence proceeds upon the ground that a party, having a legal right, shall not be permitted to avail himself of it for the purposes of injustice, or fraud, or oppression, or harsh and vindictive injury', see Story's Commentaries on Equity Jurisprudence (1839), Vol. II, p 508.

The Court of Appeal acknowledge that, in some cases, there is room for the intervention of equity. They accept that, where the hiring is terminated because the hirer is in breach, equity will relieve him from payment of the penalty: see *Cooden Engineering Co., Ltd.* v *Stanford* [1952] 2 All E.R. 915. But they say that, when it is terminated for any other reason, as, for instance, if the hirer gives notice of termination himself, or if he dies, there is no equity to relieve him or his executors from the rigours of the law: see *Associated Distributors, Ltd.* v *Hall* [1938] 1 All E.R. 511. The jurisdiction of equity is confined, they say, to relief against penalties for breach of contract and does not extend further. Applied to this case it means this: If the appellant, after a few weeks, finds himself unable to keep up the instalments and, being a conscientious man, gives notice of termination and returns the car, without falling into arrear, he is liable to pay the penal sum of £206 3s. 4d. without relief of any kind; but if he is an unconscientious man who falls into arrear without saying a word, so that the respondents re-take the car for his default, he will be relieved from payment of the penalty. Let no one mistake the injustice of this. It means that equity commits itself to this absurd paradox: It will grant relief to a man who breaks his contract but will penalise the man who keeps it. If this be the state of equity today, then it is in sore need of an overhaul so as to restore its first principles. But I am quite satisfied that such is not the state of equity today. This case can be brought within long-established principles without recourse to any new equity. From the very earliest times, equity has relieved not only against penalties for breach of contract, but also against penalties for non-performance of a condition. And the stipulation for a 'minimum-payment' was, it seems to me, a penalty which was payable on non-performance of a condition. The respondents said to the appellant: 'If the hiring is terminated for any reason before you have paid £321 13s. 4d., then you must make up the payments to that sum'. The condition was designed to ensure that he should pay a minimum sum of £321 13s. 4d. If he fulfilled that condition, he was not liable to pay any penalty; but, if he did not perform it, he had to pay the difference. The principal object was to secure a minimum payment of £321 13s. 4d. The condition was the means of achieving it.

To prove this point, I need not dwell on the cases of penalties for breach of contract. Their name is legion, and no one disputed them before your Lordships. A good instance is *Sloman* v

Walter (1783) 1 Bro. C.C. 418, to which your Lordships were referred. But I must draw attention to the cases of penalties for non-performance of a condition. They, too, are legion. Take mortgages for instance. At law, the mortgagor was subject to a penalty for non-performance of this condition: 'If you repay the money on this day six months, you shall have the land back: but if you do not repay it by that date, you shall lose it for ever', see Coke on Littleton, s 332. The court of equity always relieved the mortgagor in case of non-performance of this condition, and it did so, not by reason of any specialty about mortgages, but in pursuance of its general power to relieve against penalties: see *Kreglinger* v *New Patagonia Meat & Cold Storage Co., Ltd.* [1914] A.C. at p 35 by Viscount Haldane, L. C. Take next the common penalty bond. It was taken in order to secure that something should be done by the obligor, such as to be of good behaviour (or to pay an annuity, or anything else). The obligor bound himself by his bond to pay a specified sum, say £20, on some such condition as this: 'If you are of good behaviour (or pay the annuity or whatever else it might be), this obligation shall be void: but if you do not do so, then this obligation shall be of full force and effect.' In many of those cases, there was no covenant by the obligor to perform the condition; no covenant by him to be of good behaviour (or to pay the annuity or to do anything else); no covenant on which he could be sued at law; but simply a bond that, if he did not perform the condition, he would pay the specified sum. There was thus no breach of contract for which he could be sued at law for damages, but only non-performance of a condition which exposed him to payment of the sum specified in the bond. Yet equity always granted relief in such cases if the sum was a penalty: see, for instance, *Tall* v *Ryland* (1670), 1 Cas. in Ch. at p 184. *Collins* v *Collins* (1759), 2 Burr at p 826) and the very learned note by Mr. Evans in his appendix to Pothier on The Law of Obligations (1806), p 92; and it did so not by reason of any specialty about penalty bonds, but in pursuance of its general power to relieve against penalties. It would restrain the obligee from suing at law on the bond so long as the obligor was ready to pay him the damage he had really sustained. Likewise, even when the sum had already been paid over in the shape of a deposit to secure performance, equity would be prepared to grant restitution if it was a penal sum: see *Benson* v *Gibson* (1746) 3 Atr. 395 by Lord Hardwicke, L.C., *Steedman* v *Drinkle* [1916] 1 A.C. 275 by Viscount Haldane.

In my judgment, therefore, the courts have power to grant relief against the penal sum contained in this 'minimum-payment' clause, no matter for what reason the hiring is terminated. The 'minimum-payment' clause is single and indivisible, and no just distinction can be drawn between the cases where the hirer is in breach and where he is not. I find myself in entire agreement with the judgment of Lord MacDermott, C.J., in *Lombank, Ltd.* v *Kennedy, Lombank, Ltd.* v *Crossan* (1961) (N. 1) (C.A., unreported) from which I have profited much. I do not think that *Associated Distributors, Ltd.* v *Hall* [1938] 1 All E.R. 511 was rightly decided ...

I would, therefore, allow this appeal and remit the case to the county court judge so that he may determine the amount of damage, if any, which the respondents have sustained, and give judgment for that sum only.

[Lord Devlin concurred with Lord Denning. His judgment is omitted.]

Appeal allowed; case remitted to County Court.

NOTE Several years after the decision in *Bridge* v *Campbell Discount Co Ltd* the English Court of Appeal had to consider a case involving a hire-purchase agreement which contained an almost identical minimum-payment clause. In *United Dominions Trust (Commercial), Ltd* v *Ennis*, [1967] 2 All E.R. 345 the hirer had not paid even the first instalment when he informed the finance company that he could not afford to pay any of the instalments. The finance company's representative thereupon dictated the following letter to the hirer, which he subsequently signed: 'Dear Sir, I am writing to inform you I wish to terminate my agreement with you as I cannot fulfil the terms stated.' All three of their lordships were of the opinion that this letter was not an exercise of the hirer's right to terminate the contract, but rather was a breach of contract. It was thus open to the court to find that the minimum-payment clause was a penalty clause and therefore not enforceable. Denning LJ was still of the opinion that such clauses could not be enforced in any circumstances. However, he went on to give these comments:

Accepting for the moment that *Associated Distributors, Ltd* v *Hall* is good law and that a hirer, by exercising the option, does commit himself to paying this large sum, then I say this; a hirer is not to be taken to exercise such an option unless he does so consciously, knowing of the consequences, and avowedly in exercise of the option. If this were not so, the document would be an absolute trap set to catch him. Not one hirer in a thousand reads these small printed clauses. Even if he did, he would not understand them. When he returns the car, he naturally assumes that is the end of the hiring, and in consequence, an end of the instalments. He should not be held bound to make in addition this tremendous payment – as the price of termination – unless he knows what he is doing. In order to bind him to it, knowledge of it must be brought home to him in fact so as to amount to a new agreement by him to pay the sum. (at p 348)

More recently, in *Granor Finance Limited* v *Liquidator of Eastmore Limited* [1974] S.L.T. 296, The Scottish Outer House (Lord Keith) had to consider a hire-purchase agreement containing a provision that upon the hirer-company going into voluntary liquidation, the finance company could repossess the hired goods, the contract would be terminated and the hirer would be liable to pay two-thirds of the total contract price pursuant to the minimum payment clause. The court followed *Bell Brothers (H.P.) Ltd* v *Aitken*, [1939] S.C. 577, [1939] S.L.T. 453, a Scottish decision which came to the same conclusions as *Associated Distributors, Ltd* v *Hall*, [1938] 1 All E.R. 511 (C.A.), and followed the reasoning of Viscount Simonds and Lord Morton of Henryton in *Campbell Discount* in holding that the doctrine of penalties is not applicable except in cases involving breach of contract. For a detailed analysis of those issues in England, see Ziegel, 'The Minimum Payment Clause Muddle,' [1964] *Camb. L.J.* 108.

Bridge v *Campbell Discount* has been applied in Canada in *C.A.C.* v *Regent Park Butcher Shop* (1969) 67 W.W.R. 297, 3 D.L.R. (3d) 304 (Man. C.A.), a case involving an equipment lease. See also *Neonoex International Ltd* v *Wassill*, [1974] 1 W.W.R. 587 (Sask. D. Ct), which treated an acceleration clause in a lease as a penalty. Both *Regent Park* and *Neonoex* were followed in *Powell & Co* v *C.N.R.* (1975), 13 N.S.R. (2d) 713 (S.C.A.D.). However, in *Security Leasing Co. Ltd* v *Balkan Restaurant Ltd*, [1976] 5 W.W.R. 590 (B.C. Co. Ct), in an action for the balance of a rental due under an acceleration clause in a fixed-term cash-register lease the court deviated from this line of cases. Cashman Co. Ct J held that a provision which provided for the acceleration of rent payments was not a penalty, and should be enforceable just as a provision accelerating the due dates of monthly rentals of land appeared to be enforceable.

The lessor was entitled to the balance of the rent due. See also *Direct Leasing Ltd v Chu* (1976), 1 B.C.L.R. 166, [1976] 6 W.W.R. 587 (B.C.S.C.) And see *Pacific Leasing Corp Ltd v Fire Valley Land & Cattle Co Ltd et al* (1969), 4 D.L.R. (3d) 454 (B.C.S.C.).

QUESTION Suppose that a conditional sales contract contains a minimum-payment clause similar to the one contained in the hire-purchase agreement considered in *Campbell Discount*. In addition, it also contains the following clause: 'Should the conditional buyer breach any term, condition, or stipulation of this agreement, he shall be deemed to have exercised his option to terminate the contract, and in consideration thereof, he shall be deemed to have agreed to pay the amount so stipulated in the said minimum payment clause.' What result?

NOTE: THE DEVELOPING DOCTRINE OF UNCONSCIONABILITY In the light of recent developments in the doctrine of unconscionability, even if the traditional view enunciated in *Associated Distributors Ltd v Hall* that the doctrine of penalties is only applicable in cases of breach of contract, is accepted, it may still be possible to negate the effect of minimum payment clauses in situations where inequality of bargaining power exists. In recent years, Anglo-Canadian courts have been increasingly willing to void contracts in clear cases of unconscionability. The following cases are relevant: *A. Schroeder Music Publishing Co v Macaulay*, [1974] 3 All E.R. 616 (H. of L.); *Lloyds Bank Ltd v Bundy*, [1974] 3 All E.R. 757 (Eng. C.A.); *Clifford Davis Management Ltd v W.E.A. Records Ltd*, [1975] 1 All E.R. 237 (Eng. C.A.). In *Lloyds Bank Ltd v Bundy*, Lord Denning subsumed the various legal categories into which equitable relief falls – duress, undue influence, breach of fiduciary duty, illegality – and sought to apply a unifying principle which he found to be 'inequality of bargaining power.'

He stated (at p 765): 'Gathering all [these categories] together, I would suggest that through all these instances there runs a single thread. They rest on "inequality of bargaining power". By virtue of it, the English law gives relief to one who, without independent advice, enters into a contract which is grossly inadequate, when his bargaining power is grievously impaired by reason of his own needs or desires, or by his own ignorance or infirmity, coupled with undue influences or pressures brought to bear on him by or for the benefit of the other. When I use the word "undue" I do not mean to suggest that the principle depends on any proof of wrongdoing. The one who stipulates for an unfair advantage may be moved solely by his own self-interest, unconscious of the distress he is bringing to the other. One who is in extreme need may knowingly consent to a most improvident bargain, solely to relieve the straits in which he finds himself ...'

Recent decisions of Canadian courts suggest that the doctrine of unconscionability is being given an increasingly significant role in the regulation of inequality of bargaining power: See, for example, *Morrison v Coast Finance Ltd. and Vancouver Associated Car Markets Ltd.* (1966), 54 W.W.R. 257, 55 D.L.R. (2d) 710 (B.C.C.A.); *W.W. Distributors & Co. Ltd. v Thorsteinson* (1960), 33 W.W.R. 669, 26 D.L.R. (2d) 365 (Man. C.A.); *Gaertner v Fiesta Dance Studios Ltd. et al.* (1973), 32 D.L.R. (3d) 639 (B.C.S.C.); *McKenzie v Bank of Montreal et al.* (1975), 7 O.R. (2d) 521 (H.C.J.), affirmed (1976) 12 O.R. (2d) 719 (C.A.); *Beach v Eames* (1976) 18 O.R. (2d) 486 (Co.Ct.).

14 Debtor and Creditor

For an economic analysis of the doctrine of inequality of bargaining power (unconscionability), see Trebilcock, 'The Doctrine of Inequality of Bargaining Power' (1976) 26 *U.T.L.J.* 359.

4 THE DISCHARGING OF DEBTS: THE SPECIAL PROBLEM OF PART PAYMENT

a / Ison, *Materials on Debt Collections* (Queen's University 1972) p 18

A debt may discharged in any of the following legal ways:
1 Payment
2 Release
3 Consensual recission
4 Novation
5 Accord and satisfaction
6 Breach of contract entitling the party who would otherwise be indebted to treat the contract as terminated by breach
7 Bankruptcy
8 Avoidance of the contract on any ground upon which the party who would otherwise be indebted may be entitled to treat the contract as void, e.g. for deceit

An important question arises if a debtor succeeds in persuading his creditor to accept part payment of a debt and to forgive the rest. Can the creditor subsequently sue for and recover the remainder? The common law had trouble with this problem. Note particularly the judgment of Lord Denning MR in the following case:

b / *D & C Builders* v *Rees* [1966] 2 Q.B. 617 (C.A.)

[The plaintiffs, jobbing builders, claimed £182 13s. 1d. from the defendant as the balance due for work and labour done and goods and materials supplied in respect of alterations and repairs to the defendant's shop in May and June, 1964. In July 1964, when there was no dispute as to the work done, the sum of £482 13s. 1d. had been owing to the plaintiffs, but the defendant had not paid. On November 13, 1964 when the plaintiffs were in desperate financial straits, the defendant, through his wife, offered to pay the plaintiffs £300 if they would accept it in settlement, stating in effect that if the plaintiffs did not accept it they would get nothing. The plaintiffs told the defendant's wife that they had no choice but to accept and on November 14, 1964, they received a cheque for £300 in exchange for a receipt stating that the sum was received 'in completion of the account.' On the plaintiff's claim for the balance, the defendant set up a defence of bad workmanship and also that there was a binding settlement, a question which was tried as a preliminary issue. Judge Trapnell held that there was no consideration to support the agreement of November 13 and 14 and decided the preliminary issue in favour of the plaintiffs. On appeal by the defendant:]

LORD DENNING, M.R.: ...
This case is of some consequence: for it is a daily occurrence that a merchant or tradesman, who is owed a sum of money, is asked to take less. The debtor says he is in difficulties. He offers a lesser sum in settlement, cash down. He says he cannot pay more. The creditor is considerate. He accepts the proffered sum and forgives him the rest of the debt. The question arises: Is the

settlement binding on the creditor? The answer is that, in point of law, the creditor is not bound
by the settlement. He can the next day sue the debtor for the balance: and get judgment. The law
was so stated in 1602 by Lord Coke in *Pinnel's* Case (1602) 5 Co. Rep 117a – and accepted in 1889
by the House of Lords in *Foakes* v *Beer* (1884) 9 App. Cas. 605.

Now, suppose that the debtor, instead of paying the lesser sum in cash, pays it by cheque. He
makes out a cheque for the amount. The creditor accepts the cheque and cashes it. Is the
position any different? I think not. No sensible distinction can be taken between payment of a
lesser sum by cash and payment of it by cheque. The cheque, when given, is conditional
payment. When honoured, it is actual payment. It is then just the same as cash. If a creditor is
not bound when he receives payment by cash, he should not be bound when he receives
payment by cheque. This view is supported by the leading case of *Cumber* v *Wane* (1721) 1 Sta.
426, which has suffered many vicissitudes but was, I think, rightly decided in point of law.

In point of law payment of a lesser sum, whether by cash or by cheque, is no discharge of a
greater sum.

This doctrine of the common law has come under heavy fire. It was ridiculed by Sir George
Jessel in *Couldery* v *Bartram* (1881) 19 Ch. D. 394, 399. It was said to be mistaken by Lord
Blackburn in *Foakes* v *Beer*. It was condemned by the Law Revision Committee (1945 Cmd.
5449), paras. 20 and 21. But a remedy has been found. The harshness of the common law has
been relieved. Equity has stretched out a merciful hand to help the debtor. The courts have
invoked the broad principle stated by Lord Cairns in *Hughes* v *Metropolitan Railway Co* (1877)
2 App. Cas 439, 448.

'It is the first principle upon which all courts of equity proceed, that if parties, who have
entered into definite and distinct terms involving certain legal results, afterwards by their own
act or with their own consent enter upon a course of negotiation which has the effect of leading
one of the parties to suppose that *the strict rights arising under the contract will not be enforced,*
or will be kept in suspense, or held in abeyance, the person who otherwise might have enforced
those rights *will not be allowed to enforce them when it would be inequitable having regard to
the dealings which have taken place between the parties.*'

It is worth noticing that the principle may be applied, not only so as to suspend strict legal rights,
but also so as to preclude the enforcement of them.

This principle has been applied to cases where a creditor agrees to accept a lesser sum in
discharge of a greater. So much so that we can now say that, when a creditor and a debtor enter
upon a course of negotiation, which leads the debtor to suppose that, on payment of the lesser
sum, the creditor will not enforce payment of the balance, and on the faith thereof the debtor
pays the lesser sum and the creditor accepts it as satisfaction: then the creditor will not be
allowed to enforce payment of the balance when it would be inequitable to do so. This was well
illustrated during the last war. Tenants went away to escape the bombs and left their houses
unoccupied. The landlords accepted a reduced rent for the time they were empty. It was held
that the landlords could not afterwards turn round and sue for the balance, see *Central London
Property Trust Ltd.* v *High Trees House Ltd* [1947] 1 K.B. 130. This caused at the time some
eyebrows to be raised in high places. But they have been lowered since. The solution was so
obviously just that no one could well gainsay it.

In applying this principle, however, we must note the qualification: The creditor is only
barred from his legal rights when it would be *inequitable* for him to insist upon them. Where
there has been a *true accord*, under which the creditor voluntarily agrees to accept a lesser sum

in satisfaction, and the debtor *acts upon* that accord by paying the lesser sum and the creditor accepts it, then it is inequitable for the creditor afterwards to insist on the balance. But he is not bound unless there has been truly an accord between them.

In the present case, on the fact as found by the judge, it seems to me that there was no true accord. The debtor's wife held the creditor to ransom. The creditor was in need of money to meet his own commitments, and she knew it. When the creditor asked for payment of the £480 due to him, she said to him in effect: 'We cannot pay you the £480. But we will pay you £300 if you will accept it in settlement. If you do not accept it on those terms, you well get nothing. £300 is better than nothing.' She had no right to say any such thing. She could properly have said: 'We cannot pay you more than £300. Please accept it on account.' But she had no right to insist on his taking it in settlement. When she said: 'We will pay you nothing unless you accept £300 in settlement,' she was putting undue pressure on the creditor. She was making a threat to break the contract (by paying nothing) and she was doing it so as to compel the creditor to do what he was unwilling to do (to accept £300 in settlement): and she succeeded. He complied with her demand. That was on recent authority a case of intimidation: see *Rookes* v *Barnard* [1964] A.C. 1129 and *Stratford (J.T.) & Son Ltd.* v *Lindley* [1964] 2 W.L.R. 1002 1015. In these circumstances there was no true accord so as to found a defence of accord and satisfaction: see *Day* v *McLea* (1889) 22 Q.B.D. 610. There is also no equity in the defendant to warrant any departure from the due course of law. No person can insist on a settlement procured by intimidation.

In my opinion there is no reason in law or equity why the creditor should not enforce the full amount of the debt due to him. I would, therefore, dismiss this appeal.

DANCKWERTS L.J.: I agree with the judgment of the Master of the Rolls. *Foakes* v *Beer*, applying the decision in *Pinnel's Case*, settled definitely the rule of law that payment of a lesser sum than the amount of a debt due cannot be a satisfaction of the debt, unless there is some benefit to the creditor added so that there is an accord and satisfaction.

In *Foakes* v *Beer*, Lord Selborne, while approving *Cumber* v *Wane*, did not overrule the cases which appear to differ from *Cumber* v *Wane*, saying:

All the authorities subsequent to *Cumber* v *Wane*, which were relied upon by the appellant at your Lordships' Bar (such as *Sibree* v *Tripp* 15 M.W. 23, *Curlewis* v *Clark* (1849) 3 Exch. 375, and *Goddard* v *O'Brien* 9 Q.B.D. 37)) have proceeded upon the distinction, that, by giving negotiable paper or otherwise there had been some new consideration for a new agreement, distinct from mere money payments in or towards discharge of the original liability.

Lord Selborne was distinguishing those cases from the case before the House.

But the giving of a cheque of the debtor for a smaller amount than the sum due is very different from 'the gift of a horse, hawk, or robe, etc.' mentioned in *Pinnel's Case*. I accept that the cheque of some other person than the debtor, in appropriate circumstances, may be the basis of an accord and satisfaction, but I cannot see how in the year 1965 the debtor's own cheque for a smaller sum can be better than payment of the whole amount of the debt in cash. The cheque is only conditional payment, it may be difficult to cash, or it may be returned by the bank with the letters 'R.D.' upon it, unpaid. I think that *Goddard* v *O'Brien*, either was wrongly decided or should not be followed in the circumstances of today.

I agree also that, in the circumstances of the present case, there was no true accord. The Rees really behaved very badly. They knew of the plaintiffs' financial difficulties and used their

awkward situation to intimidate them. The plaintiffs did not wish to accept the sum of £300 in
discharge of the debt of £482, but were desperate to get some money. It would appear also that
the defendant and his wife misled the plaintiffs as to their own financial position. Rees, in his
evidence, said: 'In June (1964) I could have paid £700 odd. I could have settled the whole bill.'
There is no evidence that by August, or even by November, their financial situation had
deteriorated so that they could not pay the £482.

 Nor does it appear that their position was altered to their detriment by reason of the receipt
given by the plaintiffs. The receipt was given on November 14, 1964. On November 23, 1964, the
plaintiffs' solicitors wrote a letter making it clear that the payment of £300 was being treated as a
payment on account. I cannot see any ground in this case for treating the payment as a
satisfaction on equitable principles.

In my view the county court judge was right in applying the rule in *Foakes* v *Beer*, and I would
dismiss the appeal.

WINN LJ [Discussion of facts omitted]: The question to be decided may be stated thus: Did the
defendant's agreement to give his own cheque for £300 in full settlement of his existing debt to
the plaintiffs of £482 and the plaintiff's agreement to accept it in full payment of that debt,
followed by delivery and due payment of such a cheque, constitute a valid accord and satisfaction discharging the debt in law?

Apart altogether from any decided cases bearing upon the matter, there might be a good deal
to be said, as a matter of policy, in favour of holding any creditor bound by his promise to
discharge a debtor on his paying some amount less than the debt due: some judges no doubt so
thought when they held readily that acceptance by the creditor of something of a different nature
from that to which he was entitled was a satisfaction of the liability; cf. *Pinnel's Case* (1854) 3
E&B. 83, *Smith* v *Trowsdale, Cooper* v *Parker* (1855) 15 C.B. 822. A like approach might at some
time in the past have been adopted by the courts to all serious assurances of agreement, but as
English law developed, it does not now permit in general of such treatment of mere promises. In
the more specific field of discharge of monetary debt there has been some conflict of judicial
opinion.

Where a cheque for a smaller sum than the amount due is drawn by a person other than the
debtor and delivered in satisfaction of his debt, it is clear that the debt is discharged if the cheque
be accepted on that basis and duly paid; cf. *Hirachand Punamchand* v *Temple* [1911] 2 K.B. 330.

In the instant case the debtor's own cheque was accepted, though not stipulated for by the
creditor, as the equivalent of cash, conditionally of course upon its being duly paid on presentation: such is the modern usage in respect of payments of money due, common, though not yet
universal, in domestic no less than commercial transactions. This court must now decide the
effect of that transaction.

[Discussion of cases omitted.]

In my judgment it is an essential element of a valid accord and satisfaction that the agreement
which constitutes the accord should itself be binding in law, and I do not think that any such
agreement can be so binding unless it is either made under seal or supported by consideration.
Satisfaction, viz., performance, of an agreement of accord, does not provide retroactive validity
to the accord, but depends for its effect upon the legal validity of the accord as a binding contract
at the time when it is made: this I think is apparent when it is remembered that, albeit rarely,
existing obligations of debt may be replaced effectively by a contractually binding substitution
of a new obligation.

In my judgment this court should now decline to follow the decision in *Goddard* v *O'Brien* and should hold that where a debtor's own cheque for a lesser amount than he indisputably owes to his creditor is accepted by the creditor in full satisfaction of the debt, the creditor is to be regarded, in any case where he has not required the payment to be made by cheque rather than in cash, as having received the cheque merely as conditional payment of part of what he was entitled to receive: he is free in law, if not in good commercial conscience, to insist upon payment of the balance of the amount due to him from the debtor.

I would dismiss this appeal.

Appeal dismissed with costs.

NOTE For a general analysis of *D & C Builders* see Baker, 'Satisfaction of a Debt,' (1966), 116 *New L.J.* 715. For comments on the 'economic duress' aspects of the case see W.R. Cornish (1966), 29 *Mod. L. Rev.* 428 and W.H.O. Windes (1966), *L.Q. Rev.* 165. Generally, see Hogg, 'In Support of *Foakes* v *Beer*' (1966), 4 *V.U.W.L. Rev.*; Gordon, 'Creditors' Promises to Forego Rights' [1963] *Camb. L.J.* 222.

In *D & C Builders*, Lord Denning MR comments on a situation in which one party threatens another with an unlawful act unless the other, to avoid execution of the threat, complies with his demand. These comments were applied in *Central Canada Potash* v *A.G. Sask.*, [1975] 5 W.W.R. 193 (Sask. Q.B.), at 307. However, on appeal, the Saskatchewan Court of Appeal held that the tort of intimidation does not extend to such situations and overruled the trial judge's award of damages, an award which was based on an application of *Rookes* v *Barnard*, [1964] A.C. 1129, [1964] 1 All E.R. 367: see *Central Canada Potash* v *Govt of Sask.*, [1977] 1 W.W.R. 487, at 519.

D & C Builders was applied in *J. Clark & Son* v *Finnamore* (1973), 6 N.B.R. (2d) 837, in deciding whether an accord and satisfaction had been reached in a claim for damages in a motor vehicle accident.

QUESTIONS When Lord Denning MR and Danckwerts LJ speak of 'no true accord' are they referring to 'accord and satisfaction' or 'promissory estoppel'? Does it matter?

What sorts of economic pressure on the part of the debtor are acceptable so as not to negate the voluntary nature of the accord and satisfaction? Would the situation have been different had the debtor thought there was faulty workmanship when in fact this was not the case?

c / Economic Duress

Where consent to an agreement has been coerced, the doctrine of duress may be invoked to invalidate the agreement. For example, the rule has been applied to the recovery of money paid to release property unlawfully detained: *Astley* v *Reynolds* (1731), 2 Str. 915. Perhaps one of the more important developments of the doctrine has been in the concept of 'economic duress,' in which the exercise of superior economic bargaining power to impose unfair contractual conditions may be called into question. Thus the doctrine has been applied in situations of threatened breach of contract or refusal to perform a contract: *Nixon* v *Furphy* (1925), 25 S.R. (N.S.W.) 151; *Knutson* v *The Bourkes Syndicate*, [1941] S.C.R. 419. While the doctrine of economic duress has not yet been fully accepted in Anglo-Canadian jurisprudence as a justification for invalidating a contract, US courts have shown a greater willingness to apply it where both the element of coercion and total lack of consideration are present: see, for example, *Hochman* v *Zigler's Incorporated* (1946), 50 A 2d 97, (N.J. Ct of Chancery); *Leeper* v *Beltrami* (1959), 333 P. 2d 402 (S.C. of Calif.).

Generally, see Windes, 'The Equitable Doctrine of Pressure' (1966), 82 *L.Q. Rev.* 165; Cornish, 'Economic Duress' (1966), 29 *Mod. L. Rev.* 428.

d / Promissory Estoppel

If accord and satisfaction cannot be established, it may still be possible for the debtor to assert the doctrine of promissory estoppel as a defence. However, the scope of the application of the doctrine to the part payment situation has not yet been defined authoritatively. After *D & C Builders* two important questions remain unanswered.

First, must detrimental reliance be proved before the doctrine can be applied? While it is clear that one party must have been led to 'alter his position' it is still an open question as to whether he must have altered his position for the worse. In *D & C Builders*, Danckwerts LJ was of the opinion that detrimental reliance is a necessary element of promissory estoppel ([1966] 2 Q.B. 616, at 627). On the other hand, Lord Denning MR has more recently declared that in his opinion detrimental reliance is not required, so long as the one party in fact acted on the belief induced by the other party (*W.J. Alan & Co. Ltd* v *El Nasr. Export & Import*, [1972] 2 All E.R. 127, at 140). If detrimental reliance is required, then it may be very difficult for the debtor to assert promissory estoppel in the part payment situation: can it ever be said that there is a detriment in paying part of a larger debt owed? (See *D. & C. Builders* v *Rees*, at 627, per Lord Danckwerts.) The authors of *Halsbury's Laws of England* suggest, in this respect, that one situation in which detrimental reliance might be found is if the debtor, in reliance on the representation, spends the money owed on something else (4th ed, vol 9, para 578).

The second question still outstanding is whether, by the operation of promissory estoppel, part payment can ever, as a matter of principle, be a complete discharge of the debt. It has been held that in general, the effect of promissory estoppel is to suspend the enforcement of the creditor's strict legal rights. Upon giving the debtor reasonable notice, the creditor may seek to enforce these rights at a later date, unless it becomes impossible in law for the debtor to revert to his original position, in which case the estoppel may become permanently binding and the contractual obligation extinguished (*Ajayi* v *Briscoe*, [1964] 3 All E.R. 556, and *Birmingham & District Land Co* v *London & North Western Ry Co* (1888), 40 Ch. D. 268 (C.A.), at 286 per Bowen LJ). While it may be difficult to find situations where performance of a promise to pay money can ever be impossible in law, *dicta* of Lord Denning in *D & C Builders* indicate that 'where the creditor has led the debtor to undertake a new commitment which would make full payment of the debt onerous to him and thereby inequitable, promissory estoppel will have a permanent effect, even though, strictly speaking, impossibility to pay cannot be shown.' (9 *Halsbury's Laws of England* (4th ed) para 579). Whether this attitude will prevail over the general rule in *Foakes* v *Beer* ((1884), 9 App. Cao. 605 (H.L.))remains to be seen. It should be noted that in situations in which s 16 of The Mercantile Law Amendment Act obtains, there is no doubt that the obligation to pay is extinguished.

Finally, the Supreme Court of Canada in *John Burrows Ltd* v *Subsurface Surveys Ltd* ((1968), 68 D.L.R. (2d) 354) seems to have attenuated the scope of the doctrine by requiring strict proof of a course of negotiations from which it can be inferred that the 'promisor' intended to alter the legal relations created by the contract. For a critical comment on the case see George Glover Jr, (1969), 27 *U.T. Fac. L.R.* 142; generally B.J. Reiter, 'Courts, Consideration, and Common Sense' (1977), 27 *U.T.L.J.* 439.

e / The Mercantile Law Amendment Act, R.S.O. 1970, c 272, s 16

16. Part performance of an obligation either before or after a breach thereof when expressly accepted by the creditor in satisfaction or rendered in pursuance of an agreement for that purpose, though without any new consideration, shall be held to extinguish the obligation.

NOTE This section, first passed in 1885 in Ontario, is similar to other provisions existing in other Canadian provinces: British Columbia: Laws Declaratory Act R.S.B.C. 1960, c 213, s 2(33); Manitoba: The Mercantile Law Amendment Act, C.C.S.M., c 162, s 6; Saskatchewan: The Queen's Bench Act R.S.S. 1965, c 73, s 45(7). To the extent that it is applied by the courts, it avoids the type of problem found in *D & C Builders* v *Rees*. However, there are three problems the section raises that may limit its usefulness.

First, it provides that part performance only extinguishes the obligation where there is an 'agreement' to that effect. If interpreted solely against the common law background this may be of little help to the debtor, as 'agreements' require consideration or a seal to be binding at common law. This view was adopted by Gregory J in *Bell* v *Quagliotti* (1918), 25 B.C.R. 466, but has been rejected in a long series of other decisions starting with *Bank of Commerce* v *Jenkins* (1888), 16 O.R. 215, and continuing to today: eg *Rommerill* v *Gardener* (1962), 35 D.L.R. (2d) 717 (B.C.C.A.)

Second, the section states that 'part performance' extinguishes the old obligation. What if the creditor revokes the agreement to accept less before the 'part' is actually 'performed'? Can he unilaterally force the debtor to accept the old obligation? There are contradictory cases on this point. In the early decision of *Bank of Commerce* v *Jenkins*, supra, Rose J thought he could not revoke, while MacMahon J was uncertain. The latter's scepticism is also shown by a Manitoba court in *Mackiw* v *Rutherford*, [1921] 2 W.W.R. 329, while Rose J's analysis was confirmed by the Alberta Court of Appeal in *Hoolahan* v *Hivon*, [1944] 4 D.L.R. 405.

Third, there is the problem of onus. How difficult is it for the debtor to prove that section 16 has been complied with? For a recent answer, see the *Beaupre* case below.

f / *Champlain Ready-Mixed Concrete* v *Beaupre* [1971] 3 O.R. 568 (C.A.)

[Appeal from a judgment of a Division Court dismissing a claim alleged to have been discharged by satisfaction.]

JESSUP, JA (orally): This is an appeal from a judgment rendered in the Sixth Division Court of the County of Simcoe dismissing the plaintiff's action with costs.

The facts can be stated quite briefly. The defendant was indebted to the plaintiff in the amount of $930.85 for concrete supplied by the plaintiff to the defendant. In February of 1970 the defendant wrote to the plaintiff advising that he was in financial difficulties and stating that he proposed a settlement with his creditors on the basis of 50 cents on the dollar. Subsequently, there was a discussion by telephone with a representative of the plaintiff in which the representative of the plaintiff said he would look into the situation with other creditors of the defendant. Having done so, the representative of the plaintiff had another telephone discussion with the defendant in which he advised the defendant that the proposal was not acceptable.

Shortly afterwards the defendant sent to the plaintiff a cheque for $500 on the reverse of which he had typed the following endorsement '$500.00 has been accepted by Mr. Coldwell as payment in full'. When the cheque was received by the plaintiff, Mr. Coldwell for the plaintiff 'x'd' out by typewriter the words 'in full' and added to the endorsement made by the defendant the words 'on account, balance $430.85'.

There was evidence given on behalf of the plaintiff that subsequently some two weeks later a bill was sent to the defendant for the balance owing on the account of $430.85. The defendant said that he heard nothing with respect to the balance he owed until he received the Division Court summons. The plaintiff, of course, cashed the cheque after altering the endorsement, as I have mentioned, and the action in the Division Court was for the sum of $400 representing the balance of $430.85 with an abandonment of the $30.85 which was in excess of jurisdiction.

In these circumstances, the rights of the parties are governed by s 16 of the *Mercantile Law Amendment Act*, R.S.O. 1960, C 238 [now R.S.O. 1970, C 272], which provides:

16. Part performance of an obligation either before or after a breach thereof when expressly accepted by the creditor in satisfaction or rendered in pursuance of an agreement for that purpose, though without any new consideration, shall be held to extinguish the obligation.

It is quite clear on the facts that the cheque for $500 was not rendered in pursuance to an agreement for part performance within the meaning of s 16 and the only question, therefore, is whether on the evidence it can be held that there was an express acceptance by the plaintiff of the cheque in partial payment tendered by the defendant.

In the course of his judgment the learned trial Judge said:

In my view, if a party receives a cheque marked 'payment in full', the cheque may be cashed and a claim made for the balance owing, but it is incumbent upon the creditor to forthwith write the debtor and advise him that the cheque is not being accepted as payment in full.

With the greatest respect for the learned trial Judge, I do not find support in the authorities for that statement of law. It is a question of fact in every case, whether or not there has been express acceptance of part performance in satisfaction of an obligation; and while the silence of a creditor may be some evidence which is to be considered with all the other evidence in deciding whether or not there has been express acceptance, in my view it is not a factor which is singly governing the rights of the parties.

In any event, in this case the evidence of the plaintiff was that a revised billing had been sent out at the end of the month and the endorsement on the cheque having been altered, its alteration would have necessarily come to the attention of the defendant when the cheque was returned to him from his bank. A defendant, pleading s 16 of the *Mercantile Law Amendment Act*, has in my opinion a heavy onus. He must prove an express acceptance of part performance. In my view, on the facts of this case, that onus was not met.

In the result, I think the appeal must be allowed and the judgment below set aside. In its place a judgment will go for the plantiff for $400 and costs to include a counsel fee of $25. The plaintiff is entitled to its costs of this appeal.

Appeal allowed; judgment for plaintiff.

2
The Economics of Debt Collection

This chapter begins with some comments on the nature of the consumer credit market. Some statistical material on the nature of credit use is included, together with material on the respective market shares of different categories of consumer credit grantors in Canada. Trebilcock and Shulman, in their article 'The Pathology of Credit Break-down', provide a profile of the overcommitted debtor.

The remainder of the chapter provides different views on the economics of credit default. This section begins with an important article by Professor A.A. Leff on the concept of transaction costs. Transaction costs are those costs which are directly or indirectly generated by the collection process. Professor Leff argues that the dynamics of the collection process are largely governed by the form and extent of these costs and these explain why the collection processes in the merchant v consumer, merchant v merchant, and consumer v merchant collections settings widely differ in practice. Professor Leff argues that collection problems would be radically reduced if the information flows between debtor and creditor were improved both at the time that credit is granted and at the time default occurs. In the latter case, Leff argues that if each side were apprised of the transaction costs he is likely to incur if the collection process proceeds further, many debt claims which are presently enforced through the courts would be non-coercively settled. He develops a proposal for the intervention of a neutral 'referee' following credit break-down to improve information flows to both creditor and debtor on transaction costs.

Professor Ison, in the extract from his article on 'Small Claims', takes a much more radical position and argues that the merchant-consumer debt relationship may not be susceptible to evenhanded treatment in a judicial/coercive collection setting and develops an argument for the abolition of judicially enforceable consumer debt claims. Professors Cayne and Trebilcock in their article sound a cautionary note pointing out the economic imperatives that govern debtor/creditor relations and emphasize that any extensive attack on existing creditors' remedies will produce certain predictable economic consequences in terms of the cost of credit, who has access to credit, and the possibility of black markets in credit developing to supply the needs of those who cannot qualify for credit in the legal credit market.

Professor Caplovitz advances several alternative systems for the regulation of the consumer credit market and is inclined to favour a system where credit black-listing becomes the principal form of sanction for default. The thrust of this analysis also calls for an evaluation of the economic considerations raised by Cayne and Trebilcock, together with privacy considerations addressed in the next chapter.

23 The Economics of Debt Collection

This chapter concludes with a survey of existing schemes designed to provide some measure of protection and rehabilitation for the over-committed debtor. How effective these schemes are in achieving either of these objectives in part depends on one's view of the economic considerations canvassed earlier in the chapter.

I CREDIT USERS AND GRANTORS: COSTS AND BENEFITS

a / Credit Users

In the Report of the US National Commission on Consumer Finance (1972), the Commission traced the development of consumer credit. They found that there were several reasons for the dramatic growth of consumer credit which are directly attributable to recent socio-economic changes. It is clear that consumers' ability to assume obligations to repay their debts depends largely upon the expected size and variability of their incomes. Generally, real incomes are higher and more stable than in earlier years. Increased urbanization and the changing age distribution of the population have encouraged consumers' use of credit. Today's young married consumers, born in the post-war baby boom, are heavy users of credit. There is a greater willingness to incur debt, which is concomitant with a shift to asset ownership. Consumers have added substantially to their ownership of durable consumer goods through their use of credit in the post-World War II period. An important reason for the shift to asset ownership has been the increase in ownership of homes. Another factor is the decision by consumers to substitute the use of consumer-owned capital goods for the use of commercially owned capital goods, i.e. owning cars and televisions instead of riding the bus and going to movies. The Commission also found that the trend to asset ownership was fueled by the movement of women into the labour force.

Figures released for the year 1973 by a major Canadian consumer loan company revealed that almost 42% of all loans were made to consolidate consumer debts. The next largest categories were automobile loans and travel and vacation loans, each of which comprised only 8% of the total number of loans. On the other hand, the personal loans made in 1974 by a major Canadian Bank were made for vastly different purposes. Automobile loans comprised 30% of all loans and 16% of the loans went towards home improvements. Only 7% were made for the purpose of debt consolidation.

The following tables are taken from M.J. Trebilcock and Arthur Shulman, 'The Pathology of Credit Breakdown' (1976), 22 *McGill Law Journal* 415, at pp 424–5, table 4. (See p 24.)

TABLE 4
A A Major Canadian Consumer Loan Company: Reasons for Loans, 1973

B A Major Canadian Bank: Reasons for Personal Loans, 1974

Reason	Percent of Total Number	Reason	Percent of Total Number
Consolidation of Debt	41.9%	Vans, Trucks, School Buses, Mobile Homes	6.69%
Refinancing Miscellaneous Debt	4.2%	Debt Consolidation	7.25%
Clothing	2.2%	Loan Liquidation	4.05%
Fuel	.1%	Taxes, Real Estate Mortgages, *etc.*	2.42%
Rent	.3%	Travel and Education	7.32%
Medical Expense	.3%	Home Improvement, Furnishings	16.45%
Automobile	8.2%	Motor Cars	30.42%
Tax Service Loan	1.0%	Purchase of Real Estate	4.80%
Cash Voucher	.4%	Boats, Airplanes, Snowmobiles	3.78%
Travel and Vacation	7.9%	Sundry, Including Refinancing	17.00%
Education	.3%		100.00
Investment	.9%		
Repair	4.7%		
Furniture	3.3%		
Taxes	.7%		
Assisting Relatives	.9%		
Insurance Premiums	.6%		
Moving Expense	.6%		
Mortgage and Interest	.2%		
Adjust Contracts	.9%		
Miscellaneous	15.6%		
Unknown	4.8%		
	100.0		

b / Credit Grantors
The table on p 25, top, is taken from the *Canadian Consumer Credit Factbook*, Canadian Consumer Loan Association and Federated Council of Sales Finance Companies, 1974, exhibit 40.

c / The Costs and Benefits of Credit
M.J. Trebilcock with Arthur Shulman, excerpted from 'The Pathology of Credit Breakdown', (1976) 22 *McGill L.J.* 415, at 415 (footnotes omitted)

INTRODUCTION: PERSPECTIVES ON THE ECONOMIC AND
SOCIAL ROLE OF CONSUMER CREDIT

Social attitudes to the virtues of credit have changed markedly over recent years. There was a time when a consumer who borrowed to buy goods was widely regarded with disdain as one whose interests society should not be too solicitous to protect. Either he was a pauper, and thus a social failure, or he was attempting to live beyond his means, in which case the lack of discipline would prove destructive of his character. To believers in the Protestant Ethic, solid

Banks now hold more than half the total market

Cash Credit
A Chartered Banks
B Consumer Loan Companies
C Credit Union
D Others

Purchase Credit
E Sales Finance Companies
F Retailers
G Department Stores

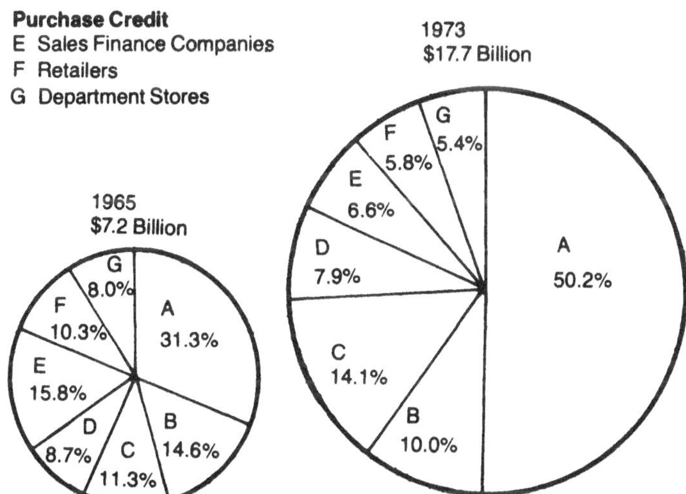

citizens worked hard, saved up, and then, as an invariable principle, paid cash. This cynicism towards the wisdom of using credit is well-reflected in the oft-quoted observation of an English County Court Judge that a great part of his time on the Bench had been concerned with 'people who are persuaded by persons they do not know to enter into contracts they do not understand to purchase goods they do not want with money they have not got'.

However, reflecting the dramatic change in social attitudes, consumer credit outstanding in Canada has risen from $1 billion in 1949 ($77 *per capita*) to $19 billion in 1975 ($825 *per capita*). Today a majority of families sooner or later have occasion to use consumer credit. Why do these families borrow?

1 / Benefits
In some cases, measurable economic benefits can be obtained through the use of consumer credit in the same way that businesses can, in particular cases, maximize profits by borrowing. For example, to buy a television set on credit and reduce outside entertainment expenditures may produce a net saving for a family. Similarly, a washing machine bought on credit may eliminate outside laundromat charges.

There are administrative conveniences to the use of credit. This applies particularly to credit card types of credit which may obviate the necessity of carrying around large amounts of cash, avoid the possibility of being 'caught short' without ready access to a bank, and provide documentary records of transactions.

Using credit may also provide a family with a form of budgetary constraint which will ensure that the family regularly devotes a proportion of its budget to acquiring reasonably enduring assets. If consumers were required to save up and pay cash for all items purchased, many would find the austerity required too much for them. Thus, in the case of these consumers, the use of consumer credit operates as a form of compulsory saving.

The most important advantage of the use of consumer credit is the least measurable in objective terms: consumer credit enables a consumer to maximize the satisfactions that he can obtain from his available resources.

In the case of business credit, this issue poses few problems. Satisfaction is measured in terms of monetary profit, and if the use of credit better maximizes this, clearly its use can be regarded as justified. Thus, there is an objective criterion against which to measure marginal satisfaction derived from the use of business credit. On the other hand, in the case of consumer credit, satisfactions are often physical and aesthetic and thus almost entirely subjective and unmeasurable. Will a man derive more satisfaction from buying a car or appliance for his family now on credit, thus committing future income, or saving up, doing without for five years and then buying it for cash?

Studies indicate that the greatest use of credit is made by young families in the middle income brackets (with rising income expectations, for the most part). This is what one would expect. By using consumer credit prudently, consumers are able to level out peaks in their needs and resources, which otherwise might not coincide. A young married couple with a family will obviously have the greatest needs now for accommodation, home appliances, transportation and educational "investments". The peak earning capacity of the family is likely to occur at some later time when the couple has moved to higher income brackets. Consumer credit thus enables them, perfectly rationally, to meet present needs out of future income, and thus to maximize the benefits which flow from that income:

[I]t would be rational to argue that a consumer should use consumer credit up to the point where his marginal satisfaction from the goods and services so acquired is equal to the marginal cost of credit needed to acquire them within the constraints imposed on him by his income and net worth. Certainly on an *a priori* basis it is as easy to visualize a consumer using too little consumer credit as too much

While the question of what is a prudent use of consumer credit is a difficult one, due to the many subjective factors, it is a central one to framing regulatory laws in the area. Until one arrives at some concept of what is a prudent use of credit, it is difficult to frame legislation along lines that prevent consumer abuses and encourage greater consumer rationality.

2 / Costs

The most notable social cost of the use of consumer credit is overcommitment. Consumer credit is especially dangerous in this respect. Because one buys now and pays later, the pleasures of possession are immediate while the pains of payment are remote, and a proper balancing of both considerations is often not undertaken. With the rapidly rising burden of debt, it is argued that the social damage caused by people taking on commitments they cannot meet is being gravely compounded. If a consumer defaults in payment of his debts he is liable to have his wages garnished (and perhaps as a result lose his job), or his possessions seized in execution, or be forced into bankruptcy. In any of these circumstances his welfare and that of his family may be severely impaired. Even if he manages to meet his commitments and avoid a formal default, it may be at the expense of better food, housing or education, and may cause family division or disintegration:

One wonders, inevitably, about the tensions associated with debt collection on such a massive scale. The legacy of wants, which are themselves inspired, are the bills which descend like the winter snow on those who are buying on the instalment plan. By millions of hearths throughout the land, it is known that when these harbingers arrive, the repossession man cannot be far behind. Can the bill collector be the central figure in the good society?

While it is impossible to quantify overcommitment the figures reported in annual reports by the Federal Superintendent of Insurance regularly disclose that 25% of the accounts of Canada's consumer loan companies are running at least a month or more behind their repayment schedules. These figures, of course, include mutually agreed advance reschedulings, but nevertheless they indicate a degree of marginality amongst a high proportion of borrowers from this category of consumer credit grantor. However, in the Montreal study discussed later in this article, a nation-wide department store informed us that 18–20% of their credit accounts were 30 days or more in arrears, and an oil company credit card department told us that 33% of their accounts were 30 days past due.

Opposing arguments stress, however, the trifling incidence of total defaults. Bad debt write-offs in the consumer credit industry generally average less than 2% of total credit extensions.

The use of consumer credit has strengthened the net worth position of consumers enormously. 'The average net worth [the difference between total assets and total indebtedness] of all families and unattached individuals in the spring of 1969 amounted to $14,369 compared to $8,430 in 1964 – a rise of 70 percent.' Using inflation-proof figures, in 1964, 25% of all families and unattached individuals had debts as great as, or greater than, their total assets. By 1969, this percentage had fallen to 16%. In 1956, 27% of all families and unattached individuals held no assets as compared to 4% in 1969.

Neither has consumer credit discouraged prudence in maintaining a steady level of savings. Indeed, personal savings as a ratio of personal disposable income rose from 4.7% in the early sixties to 7.4% in 1973.

The percentage of non-farm families and unattached individuals using some consumer credit has remained relatively static, increasing slightly from 48.6% in 1956 to 50.8% in 1970, perhaps suggesting, as Neufeld hypothesizes, that some consumers are in fact under-utilizing consumer credit (although the figures may also suggest that an increasing number of *existing* users are over-utilizing credit).

In addition many defaults are explained by quite unforeseeable contingencies such as lengthy sickness or unemployment of the consumer which in no way reflect laxness on the part of the credit grantor in extending the credit. For credit grantors to eliminate all possibility of defaults would involve depriving a number of potentially good credit risks of credit. As the use of credit becomes more widespread consumers will educate themselves as to its possibilities and limitations, just as commercial borrowers have done. In other words, they too will become 'professional' borrowers.

A wider criticism of the phenomenon of consumer credit sees private enterprise promoting the consumption ethic and subverting the sovereignty of the consumer over his own wants which in classic free market economics is essential to the proper operation of a competitive market-place. Galbraith in *The Affluent Society* and *The New Industrial State* argues that most consumer wants today are artificially contrived by the process of production itself, either by emulation and suggestion or by advertising and salesmanship. The conventional theory that holds that production must be maximized so as to cater to existing consumer wants is alleged to be fallacious once it is shown that the process of production creates its own wants.

Defenders of the existing consumer market-place argue that Galbraith attributes far too much influence to advertising. It has not been demonstrated, so it is argued, that advertising raises the general level of consumption. Instead, it may simply reflect pre-existent social tastes and values and only divert consumer expenditures from one product to another. Moreover, even if present consumer wants are contrived, there is no way of altering this through State intervention without imposing another ethic.

Given the diversity of opinion, a fundamental policy issue must be resolved before regulatory laws in the area of consumer credit can be drafted: What is the legimate social function of consumer credit? A similar question, formulated in terms of an individual consumer, was posed earlier: *When is an individual making a prudent use of credit?* The answer to one is dependent upon the other. Of course, any evaluation of existing and prospective forms of regulation of consumer credit implies an examination of the very basic social issues to which they are a response.

2 RELIEF FOR THE OVERCOMMITTED DEBTOR

a / Who Is the Overcommitted Debtor?

M.J. Trebilcock with Arthur Shulman, excerpted from 'The Pathology of Credit Breakdown', (1976) 22 *McGill Law Journal* 415, at pp 426–32 (footnotes omitted)
[The 'Debtor Survey' refers to a 1972 study undertaken by the authors involving interviews of over one hundred judgment debtors, chosen at random from Montreal court records, who had had personal property seized or wages garnished.

The 'Court File Survey' refers to another study undertaken by the authors involving an analysis of five hundred closed courts files, selected at random from files held by the Montreal Provincial Court.

The 'University of Montreal Study' refers to an empirical analysis of some 378 files of debtors under the Lacombe Law and 201 files of debtors in the small debtors bankruptcy programme in Montreal. (Masse, Mackaay, Herand, *Vivre ou Exister?*, University of Montreal, 1974).

The 'Alberta Study' refers to an unpublished 1973 research study of the Alberta Debtors Assistance Board which analysed 636 current files of debtors under Part x of the Bankruptcy Act (see below Chapter 19).

The 'British Columbia Study' was a study undertaken at the University of B.C. Faculty of Law which examined the files of all British Columbia residents granted consolidation orders during the first year of the operation of Part X of the Bankruptcy Act: see Gallins 'The Operation of Part x of the Bankruptcy Act in British Columbia', (1971), 6 *U.B.C.L. Rev.* 419.] ...

The Debtor Survey showed that 19.5% of the respondents fell into the 18–29 years age range, 54.8% in the 30–45 age range, 24.3% in the 46–64 age range, 1.2% in the over 65 age range. Hence, fully 80% of the sample were 30 years or older. Both the University of Montreal and Alberta studies of wage earner and small debtor bankruptcy programmes show a higher percentage of debtors in the lower age ranges. In the University of Montreal study, 37.3% of debtors in both programmes were younger than 29, 32.1% were in the 30–39 age range, 18.2% 40–49, 9.4% 50–59 and 3% older than 60. The Alberta study of Orderly Payment of Debt orders shows 51.87% of debtors in the 0–30 year range, 30.17% in the 31–40 range, 13.51% 41–50, 2.8% 51–60, .62% over 60, and .62% unknown. A major Canadian consumer loan company provided us with the following figures for age of borrower for its Canada-wide personal loan operations for 1973: 0–29 years 40.3%, 30–39 25.6%, 40–49 19.3%, 50–59 11.7%, 60 and over 3.1%. A major Canadian bank provided us with their figures for age of borrower (for 1974) in its personal loan operations across Canada: 0–29 48.85%, 30–39 24.32%, 40–49 16.11%, 50 and over 10.72%.

The Debtor Survey showed that 84.5% of the sample were male, 15.5% female. The Court File Survey showed that 88.4% of defendants were male, 11.6% female. The University of Montreal showed 83.5% male and the Alberta study, 90.88% male.

In terms of the number of people being wholly supported by the debtor, the Debtor Survey showed that 21.6% had no dependents, 9.4% had one dependent, 11.3% two dependents, 49% between three and five dependents, 8.4% more than five dependents. Thus, 57% of the sample had three or more dependents. The University of Montreal study showed 25.5% of the debtors with no dependent, 51.9% between one and three dependents, 20.1% four to six dependents and 2.3% more than six dependents. The Alberta study showed 10.39% of debtors with no dependents, 13.67% with one, 19.37% with two, 23.14% with three, 14.81% with four, 9.60% with five and 9.43% with more than five.

In the Debtor Survey, 14.1% of the debtors were single, 67.9% were married, 16% were separated or divorced and 1.8% were living common law. Thus a majority of the debtors were married and a signficant percentage (16%) had experienced marriage break-down. The University of Montreal study found that 25.5% of debtors under Lacombe Law or in the small debtors bankruptcy programme were either divorded or separated. While Statistics Canada only publishes statistics on the number of people divorced as a percentage of the population and not those separated, the figures for Montreal in 1972 show divorcees as 1.6% of the population contrasted with 8.5% in the University of Montreal study. The Alberta study showed that 10.52% of the debtors were either separated or divorced, and the U.B.C. study found that 20% of the debtors were separated or divorced (compared to a claimed figure of 10% in B.C. generally).

In answer to the question 'Are you presently employed?', 74.7% of debtors in the Debtor Survey said they were, 25.2% reported that they were not. The University of Montreal study found that 34.7% of debtors under the Lacombe Law or in the small debtors bankruptcy programme had no job at the time their files were opened and 67.6% had experienced some period of unemployment during the three years that preceded the survey. Of those debtors who were unemployed at the time their files were opened, 67.7% had been unemployed for periods greater than three months. The average rate of unemployment in Montreal in 1972 was about 7%. The Alberta study found that 41.67% of the debtors had experienced some unemployment during the twelve months prior to the Orderly Payment of Debts order, 38.79% for periods of greater than one month. The U.B.C. study found that only 45% of the debtors granted Orderly Payment of Debts orders were continuously employed during the twelve months prior to filing. Fifty per cent of those who were unemployed at the date of filing were unemployed for a period of more than six months prior to this time.

In terms of usual occupation, 21.4% of respondents in the Debtor Survey described themselves as business or professional people, 16.6% as skilled tradesmen, and 61.9% as unskilled labourers. In the Court File Survey, in the 110 cases where an occupation for the defendant appeared in the court documents 17.2% were business or professional people, 18.1% were skilled tradespeople, and 64.5% were unskilled labourers. Table 5 of the Alberta study shows the occupational break-down among Orderly Payment of Debts debtors.

In terms of occupational distribution among people who use consumer credit generally, a major Canadian consumer loan company and a major Canadian bank supplied us with the figures in Table 6.

TABLE 5
Alberta O.P.D. Debtors

	Males	Female Clients
Skilled Labour	18.51%	6.81%
Unskilled Labour	46.01%	10.41%
Clerical	5.19%	62.06%
Professional	3.80%	3.44%
Student	1.38%	—
Unemployed	5.70%	10.44%
Medical	2.59%	3.44%
Managerial	4.13%	—
Sales	6.05%	3.44%
Armed Forces	2.76%	—
Other	3.58%	—

TABLE 6
Consumer Loan Company (1973)

Occupation	% of Total
Skilled, Semi-Skilled	73.2
Unskilled	9.2
Service Workers	1.5
Sales Persons	1.8
Clerks, Kindred Workers	4.3
School Teachers	.5
Fed., St, County, City Emp.	3.2
Armed Forces	.7
Managers, Officials, Exec.	2.2
Proprietors	1.4
Farmers	.4
Pensioned, Independent	.8
Miscellaneous	.3
Professionals	.5
	100.0

Bank (Personal Loans 1974)

	% of Total
Manual	46.21
Office Workers	19.20
Managers, Foremen	15.29
School Teachers & Professional People	8.78
Salesmen, etc.	10.52
	100.0

In terms of residential and job mobility, 29.8% of the respondents in the Debtor Survey had not changed addresses in the previous five years, 31.9% had changed addresses once, 28.8% had changed addresses two or three times, 9.2% had changed addresses four or more times. Thus,

TABLE 7
Canadian Consumer Loan Company (1973)

Annual Income	% of Total
$ 2,000– 3,000	1.6
3,000– 4,000	6.4
4,000– 5,000	12.8
5,000– 6,000	24.8
6,000– 7,000	10.6
7,000– 7,500	8.7
7,500– 8,000	4.8
8,000– 8,500	5.2
8,500– 9,000	3.7
9,000– 9,500	2.4
9,500–10,000	4.8
10,000–11,000	4.8
11,000–12,000	2.5
12,000–13,000	3.1
13,000–14,000	1.2
14,000–15,000	1.0
15,000 and Over	1.6
	100.0

Canadian Bank (Personal Loans 1974)

Annual Income	% of Total
Under $5,000	5.90
$5,000/$5,999	6.79
$6,000/$6,999	8.88
$7,000/$7,999	10.46
$8,000/$8,999	10.96
$9,000 and Over	57.01
	100.0

69.9% of the respondents had moved homes at least once during the previous five years. Forty-six point five percent of the respondents had not changed jobs in the previous five years, 17.4% had changed jobs once, 25.5% two or three times, and 10.4% four or more times. Thus over 53% of the respondents had changed jobs at least once during the previous five years.

The distribution of the level of educational achievement in the Debtor Survey showed that 28.5% had elementary school education only, 31.8% some high school education, 17.5% were high school graduates, 5.4% were trade school graduates, and 16.4% were university graduates. Thus, over 60% of the sample had less than a full high school education. The University of Montreal study found that 37.2% of debtors in the two programmes had elementary education only, 45.6% some high school education, and 17.2% some post-secondary education.

Figures on the annual family income of debtors in the Debtor Survey show that 12% earned less than $3,000, 28% $3,000–$5,999, 25% $6,000–$7,499, 21% $7,500–$11,999, 14% $12,000 or more. Thus, 40% of the *families* earned less than the average income for *individuals* in Canada in 1972 ($5,828) and about 80% of the *families* less than the average *family* income ($11,300).

TABLE 8 [University of Montreal Study]

Number of Members of the Family Unit	Poverty Level for 1972	Poverty Level for 1973
1	$ 2,580	$ 2,740
2	4,270	4,520
3	5,160	5,470
4	5,990	6,340
5	6,850	7,250
6	8,120	8,720
7	8,540	9,140
8	9,400	10,010
9	10,260	10,880
10	11,120	11,750

TABLE 9 [University of Montreal Study]

Number of Members of the Family Unit	Number of Participants	Average Situation Relative to Poverty Level
1	51 (21.7%)	+35%
2	42 (17.8%)	−17.5%
3	39 (16.6%)	−32.5%
4	53 (22.5%)	−30%
5	24 (10.2%)	−50%
6	16 (6.8%)	−52%
7	4 (1.7%)	−67%
8	6 (2.5%)	−32.5%
TOTAL	235 (100%)	−17.5%

The University of Montreal study found that 32.7% of debtors in the two programmes had no income, 4.8% less than $3,000 gross income a year, 20.3% $3,000–$4,999, 24.4% $5,000–$6,999, 12.6% $7,000–$8,999, 4.8% more than $9,000. The Alberta Orderly Payment of Debts study found that 2.10% of debtors had total net family income a year of less than 2,400, 10.51% $2,412–$3,600, 26.37% $3,612–$4,800, 26.69% $4,812–$6,000, 16.34% $6,012–$7,200, 10.82% $7,212–$8,400, 4.04% $8,412–$9,600, 3.07% over $9,600. It may be useful to compare these figures on debtors in default with figures (Table 7) supplied to us by a major Canadian consumer loan company and bank respectively on incomes of personal loan customers generally.

The University of Montreal study related the income of debtors inscribed under the Lacombe Law between June 1972 and December 1973 to the definition of poverty by the Special Senate Committee in *Poverty in Canada*. Projections to 1972 and 1973 of the Senate Committee poverty lines by family size, as calculated in the University of Montreal study, are shown in Table 8.

The relationship between the income of debtors in the programme and these poverty lines is indicated in Table 9, taken from the University of Montreal study.

The asset position of debtors was also explored in the Debtor Survey. Only 35% of the debtors owned their own homes; the other 65% rented homes or apartments. The Alberta Orderly Payment of Debt study found that 87.42% of the debtors did not own their own homes. The U.B.C. study found that 76% of debtors did not own their own homes. The Debtor Survey found that 53.6% of the debtors possessed cars, 62% black and white televisions, 26% colour televisions and 11% had no television, 56% possessed washers and/or dryers, 66% refrigerators and/or stoves, 49% stereo sets and/or tape-recorders, 60% major furniture items such as living-room or dining room suites, 17% leisure goods such as a vacation cottage, boat or snowmobile. Thirty-six percent reported that they had some savings (including insurance); the remaining 64% said they had no savings at all.

b/ Reasons for Default

From D. Caplovitz *Consumers in Trouble*, (New York, Free Press, 1974), pp 53, 170, 171.

Major Categories of Reasons for Default (percent)

	first reason	second reason	third reason	total reasons	total individuals
Debtor's mishaps and shortcomings					
Loss of income	43	18	10	24	48
Voluntary overextension	13	23	32	17	25
Involuntary overextension	5	12	7	7	11
Marital instability	6	4	5	5	8
Debtor's third parties	8	4	6	6	9
Debtor irresponsibility	4	2	—	4	5
Creditor may be implicated					
Fraud, deception	14	13	15	14	19
Payment misunderstandings	7	3	—	6	8
Partial late payments	—	15	6	5	7
Item returned to creditor	[a]	6	14	2	4
Harassment by creditor	—	1	5	1	1
All other (miscellaneous)	1	—	—	[a]	[a]
Total percent	101	101	100	101	145
N	(1,320)	(570)	(110)	(2,000)	(1,326)

[a] Signifies less than ½ of 1 percent.

Income turns out to be more closely connected to reasons for default than either city or ethnicity. As might be expected, loss of income was a much greater hardship for the relatively poor and contributed to their defaults more often than those of higher income. Conversely, payment misunderstandings were more common among the more well-to-do than among the poor. These patterns are shown in Table 9.3.

Another notable pattern is that voluntary overextension, the mark of the imprudent debtor, turns out to be a more frequent reason for default among those of middle and high income than among those of low income. (The more well-to-do are twice as likely as the poor to give this reason.) This would suggest that persons of low income are in some respects better money

TABLE 9.3
Primary Reason for Default by Income (percent)

	under $4,000	$4,000–$7,999	$8,000 and over
Debtor's mishaps and shortcomings			
Loss of income	49	43	37
Voluntary overextension	7	16	14
Involuntary overextension	5	5	7
Marital instability	7	6	5
Debtor's third parties	8	7	9
Debtor irresponsibility	3	3	4
Creditor implicated			
Allegations of fraud	15	14	12
Payment misunderstandings	6	5	12
Total percent	100	99	100
Summary			
Debtor's mishaps	79	80	76
Creditor implicated	21	20	24
Total percent	100	100	100
N	(327)	(642)	(257)

managers than those of higher income. At least they are more likely to resist the temptations that lead to overextension. The poor tend to default not only because they suffer income reversals, but also because they are slightly more likely to be victims of fraud. These categories together account for 63 percent of the defaults of the poor but for only 47 percent of the defaults of those of high income.

[In Professor Trebilcock's Montreal Debtor Survey ('The Pathology of Credit Breakdown', above) it was found that with respect to the debtor's perceived reasons for default, 61.2% gave as the reason financial difficulties resulting in simple inability to pay. 6% connected their default directly with a failure by the seller or lender to live up to the agreement (e.g. by supplying defective merchandise). 17.5% said they had defaulted either because they were unable to locate the creditor or more usually because they did not think that they owed any money. Some percentage of those cases presumably involved a degree of fault on the part of the creditor through billing misunderstandings, etc. 15.5% appeared to be wilful defaulters, who simply said they were unwilling, although able, to pay.]

c / Extent of Indebtedness
Trebilcock and Shulman, 'The Pathology of Credit Breakdown' (1976), 22 *McGill L.J.* 415, at 432–3 (Footnotes omitted).

In terms of outstanding credit commitments, 16.6% of the debtors in the Debtor Survey reported total debts in the range 0–$499, 8.9% in the range $500–$999, 21.7% in the range $1,000–$1,999, 15.3% in the range $2,000–$3,499, and 37.1% reported debts in excess of $3,500. Thus, over half the respondents had debts in excess of $2,000. The level of overcommitment becomes

TABLE 10

Debt/Programme	Lacombe Law	Bankruptcy	Total
Less than	140	32	172
$3,000	(40.4%)	(16.0%)	(31.5%)
$3,000	171	139	310
to	(49.4%)	(69.5%)	(56.7%)
$9,000	35	29	64
More than	(10.1%)	(14.5%)	(11.7%)
$9,000	346	200	546
Total	(63.3%)	(36.7%)	(100.0%)

TABLE 11

Less than $1,000	.31%
$1,001–$1,500	2.99%
$1,501–$2,000	5.35%
$2,001–$2,500	7.87%
$2,501–$3,000	7.55%
$3,001–$3,500	11.33%
$3,501–$4,000	11.81%
$4,001–$4,500	8.02%
$4,501–$5,000	6.92%
$5,001–$5,500	7.08%

progressively more serious in the case of debtors under Lacombe Law or in the small debtors bankruptcy programme. Table 10 shows the levels of indebtedness found by the University of Montreal study.

The average debt of Lacombe Law debtors was $4,658, and of small debtor bankruptcy debtors, $6,265.

The levels of debt, at the time of making Orderly Payment of Debts orders, found by the Alberta Study are shown in Table 11.

At the order date, three out of every four debtors in the Alberta study were therefore more than $3,000 in debt, with more debtors being represented in the $3,000–$4,000 category than any other.

The Small Claims Court Referee in Toronto reports that for the year 1974 the average debt commitment per debtor interviewed was $5,840. This figure is closely in line with that reported by the Credit Counselling Service of Metropolitan Toronto for 1974. The U.B.C. study found that approximately two-thirds of the debtors under Part x in 1970–71 had debts in excess of $3,000.

Figures from the Debtor Survey on the size of the particular debt on which garnishment or seizure proceedings had been taken show that 28.8% of the debts fell in the range $0–$99, 24% $100–$249, 27.8% $250–$749, 11.5% $750–$1,499, and 7.6% of the debts were in excess of $1,500. The Court File analysis of the same question showed that 32% of the debts fell into the $0–$99 range, 26.8% $100–$249, 25.8% $250–$749, 9% $750–$1,499, 6.2% were in excess of $1,500.

36 Debtor and Creditor

d / Small Claims Court Referee Ontario: Data

for the Twelve Month Period
January 1 to December 31, 1977

1	Number of interviews conducted	1,815
2	Number of persons interviewed – Male 1,303	
	Female 757	2,060
3	Total debt declared in 1,815 interviews (item 1)	$12,843,419.00
4	Average debt per interview	$7,076.27
5	Number of creditors declared in 1,815 interviews	9,460
6	Average number of creditors per interview	5.22
7	Number of credit cards reported	2,434
8	Number of finance company creditors reported	1,646
9	Number of bank loans reported	1,285
10	Number of assignments of wages to credit unions being used to attach wages	22
11	Number of item 10 withdrawn through intervention of Referee	17
12	Average age of heads of family interviewed	38.45
13	Number of female heads of one-parent family interviewed	202
14	Average education (maximum grade attained) of heads of family interviewed	10.62
15	Average number of children per interview	1.59
16	Average gross weekly income (wages, commission, pension, unemployment insurance, workmen's compensation)	
	Male	$218.58
	Female	$174.56
17	Average monthly rent or mortgage payments reported per interview	$249.00
18	Percentage (of 1,815) buying homes	14.44
	renting houses	16.97
	renting apartments	64.80
	having free accommodation	1.77

3 THE NATURE OF TRANSACTION COSTS

A.A. Leff, 'Injury, Ignorance and Spite – The Dynamics of Coercive Collection'
(1970), 80 *Yale L.J.* 1 (footnotes omitted).

Whenever one person does something in the expectation that another will then do something
else, there arises, given the nature of people and time, a potential problem: the other person

might not. Both this expectation and its defeat are life experiences which transcend any legal context. In no society, so far as I know, is it expected that all such expectations will be or even ought to be fulfilled, certainly not through the application of social force. If you love in order to be loved, for instance, you will have to bear, without even much in the way of clucking sympathy, your inevitable disappointments.

In a modern trading society like ours, however, where there are numerous credit transactions, where numberless persons do things in exchange for others' promises to do something else thereafter, there necessarily grow up mechanisms to deal coercively with failed reciprocations. It is the basic point of this essay that the present American collection mechanisms and institutions are grossly inefficient, engendering huge amounts of unnecessary grief and loss for all participants. Only after the anatomy of this malfunction is understood can one expect changes to be made in present collection practices which will eliminate some of this waste.

My plan, therefore, is very generally to describe the operation of the American collection system, indicating first how it would operate if collection transactions were cost-free. I will then consider the effects on such a system of collection costs, with special emphasis on how such transaction costs and the effects of those costs vary depending upon who is trying to collect what from whom. Thereafter, I will assay the role of information in the system, both as a weapon in a coercive collection process and as a method of avoiding it. And finally, I will consider collection as a separate and gravely flawed 'market' and suggest at least the general direction of desirable change.

I COLLECTION IN EDEN: TRANSACTION COSTS IN THE COOPERATIVE MODE
Consider the following situation. At a particular point in time (P_0), one party (call him 'C' for creditor, which he soon will be) has total wealth amounting to v, while another party (call him 'D' for debtor) has zero wealth. At a later point (P_1), c transfers v to D, who promises to reconvey v or its equivalent to c at a still later point in time (P_2). The wealth positions of c and D at the relevant points in time, assuming that the value of v remains constant, may be represented as follows:

	C	D
P_0	v	0
P_1	0	v
P_2	v	0

The simplicity of this result depends on at least one important assumption, that the transactions at times P_1 and P_2 are cost-free. But in fact no transaction is cost-free. Everything one does is attended by some transaction cost, even if that cost is only (and it never is only) an opportunity cost. Thus if the results of the above transactions are to be presented more accurately, the chart ought to read as follows (with 't_{c_1}' standing for the creditor's transactions costs at point P_1, and so on, and 't_{d_1}' standing for the debtor's):

	C	D
P_0	v	0
P_1	$0 - t_{c_1}$	$v - t_{d_1}$
P_2	$v - (t_{c_1} + t_{c_2})$	$0 - (t_{d_1} + t_{d_2})$

All this means, however, is that if one stipulates a system within which something of the value v is to be moved to and fro, at the end of the to, and even more at the end of the fro, there will be a progressive shrinkage of the amount of v left in the system; something will be expended in the moving which redounds to the benefit of neither party.

For the economist this undeniable fact presents few theoretical difficulties. Transaction costs are to economics what friction is to classical mechanics, that which transforms pure science into engineering. For most purposes, a transaction cost is like any other cost and requires no extraordinary fuss. When an economist is speaking *qua* physicist rather than as an engineer he will, after noting the practical importance of transaction costs, exclude them from his theoretical model. Thus the 'economics of transacting' has rarely been subjected to extended consideration by economists. Similarly, to the businessman transaction costs merit no special consideration. The costs of lending and collecting money, for instance, are part of the administrative cost of any credit business and are reflected as are any business costs in the price charged. This understandable lack of theoretical interest should not, however, cause anyone to overlook the fact that the source, shape, magnitude and impact of transaction costs are vitally important to understanding the transactions themselves. To the extent that transaction costs are understood by the participants, they may significantly affect their choice of collection strategies and the overall efficiency of the collection process.

Those transactions in which agreed and undisputed payments are made according to an agreed and undisputed schedule come very cheap. If one takes as the paradigm of efficient collection the check mailed on a fixed date to pay an obligation known by the obligor then to accrue, the total cost is the creditor's bookkeeping and the debtor's labor, check, envelope and stamp. The information component of the collection system – what to pay, when and to whom – has been supplied at the time the contract was entered into and has added almost nothing to the collection cost: the 'medium' of the agreement having already been created, the cost of adding these other messages (given the width of the channel) is close to nil.

This efficiency depends on a 'frictionless' accord between the parties: they agree on the facts of past performance and present obligation. Using the term advisedly, they 'cooperate.' This very arcady of the General Will is, oddly enough, widely existent. Most debts are paid and most obligations are carried out without confusion or coercion. But even in this mode, some transactions are more perfect than others, the declinations, as usual with trouble in Paradise, being associated with failures of knowledge and will. Some people forget and have to be reminded. Some do not forget and have to be reminded. Errors creep into the stating and recalling of the price, some accidental, some not. Creditors with enough transactions to make statistical treatment feasible structure their business relations so as to make provision for these variations within the cooperative mode. If volume justifies differentiation, the effort may be made to counter the 'losses' of delay with differential pricing: the '2% ten-days, 30-days-net' provisions and their ilk are one such procedure, as is the common retailing device of a free period followed by a finance charge. More generally, in seeking to predict the cost of collection, the businessman averages the 'cooperative' paying patterns of his clients (their rate of payment, the administrative costs of reminding and threatening them), and tucks the predicted result into his credit price pattern. He also tucks into that pattern a summation of the effect on his profits of the occasional expulsions from Eden – what it will cost him on the average when people with whom he deals refuse to pay at all, or only under coercion. Individual transactions thus priced on the basis of an average of many past transactions are individually underpriced if they in fact require collection-transaction costs above the average.

If the debtor will not cooperatively carry out his obligation, the creditor must resort to coercion if he is not to be deprived totally of the v involved. Although there are several methods of coercion open to a creditor facing an obdurate debtor, the most visible is the judicial-coercive mode, going to law to enforce one's right to repayment.

II COLLECTION IN AMERICA: TRANSACTION COSTS IN A JUDICIAL-COERCION GAME

A Introduction: The Creditor's Dilemma

Under the American law of contracts, after the other party has fully performed his obligations it is absolutely irrational for you fully to perform yours. If you, D, refuse voluntarily to repay v in full, c would always be better off accepting from you some lesser performance, $v - x$, so long as $(v - x) > (v - t_c)$. Thus if v were 1000, and if D could force c in recovering v to expend a t_c of 100 while suffering no t_d himself, it would be rational for both c and D not to allow the coercive collection process to go to completion, but instead to settle on a repayment of anything between 901 and 999, that is, at any point on $L-L_1$ on the following graph:

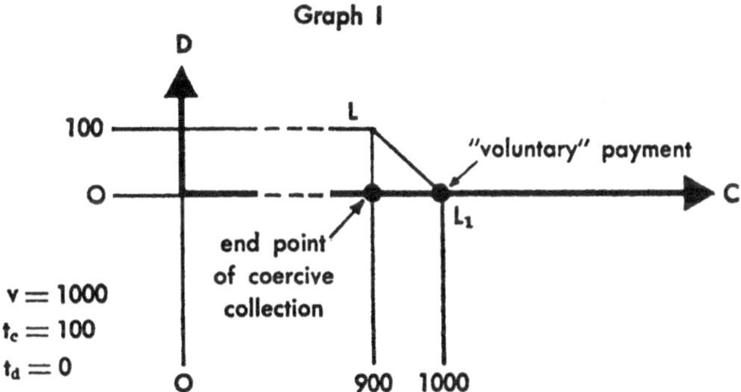

For what $L-L_1$ represents is the locus of all points the sum value of which is 1000, that is, all points which, while no worse than the end point of a completed coercive collection for either party, totally conserve the v for division between c and D. No wealth is 'wasted' on t. If one views coercive collection as a two-person game, and one takes account of the costs of playing it, it is not a two-person zero-sum game, but a two-person minus-sum game, and the parties can both gain by avoiding the play altogether, agreeing instead on an $L-L_1$ settlement.

When D has no t_d, he is comparatively indifferent as to whether the game is played or not; playing cannot make him worse off than not playing can. But what if D were forced to suffer, as part of the same coercive transaction which generated the t_c of 100, a t_d, perhaps one in excess of 100? That, pictorialized, might look like this:

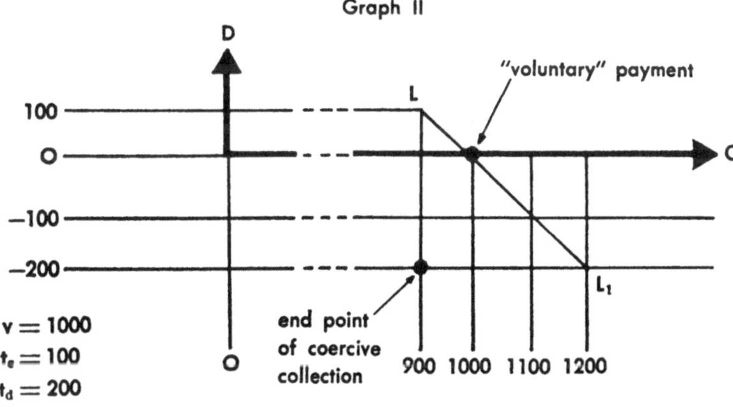

Again, playing the coercion game to completion would be minus-sum, and again both c and D would be well advised to find some point on $L-L_1$ at which to settle. But in this case D would no longer be indifferent as to whether the game were played or not, for a completed game, while hurting c, would hurt D more. Thus the ultimate settlement point on $L-L_1$ would tend to move further southeast, that is, more to the taste of c. And if t_d could be made great enough relative to t_c, D might well decide to pay all of v in order to avoid the threatened playing of the game. Thus the actual posture of the parties will depend largely on the relative quantities of t_c and t_d which, in any particular context, coercive collection will predictably generate.

B The Content of t_c

A claim for or with respect to something of value against a party in possession of it can arise only in a society which recognizes the critical distinction between possession and right to possession. Ours does. In fact, most claims about goods in our society are variations on the simple declarative statement 'You have something which belongs to me,' ordinarily fleshed out with some chronicle of how such an odd state of affairs came about. It is not so much that possession is nine points of the law, but that the legal problem is usually with the remaining point.

It is relatively rare in our society for one to be able to transfer things of value from another's possession to one's own solely by the use of one's own labor, without the other's cooperation, or exceedingly ostentatious assent. It is, in fact, at precisely the moment that one asserts in oneself a right to possession which is superior to another's actual possession that the requirement ordinarily attaches that one purchase a third-party source of information and force, the 'law.' But the 'law,' at least as embodied in legal process, is a very expensive mechanism for generating and channeling information and force.

One must to some extent be Hobbesian about it. If paid for and played from beginning to end, this expensive game does result in the acquisition of an immense bundle of power; behind every final judgment procured in any court in this country stands, ultimately, the United States Army, but even the intermediate mercenaries one buys – sheriffs, marshalls, judges – are usually sufficient unto the day. If someone has something that 'belongs to' you and 'the law' finally says so, so far as power can get it to you, that power will suffice. But the price one is supposed to pay for harnessing the Leviathan to one's cause is, essentially, the cost of moving it according to its own rather arcane principles, that is, the cost of due process.

The cost of due process is high for at least four reasons. First, due process demands that at the outset the court and its officers be wholly ignorant of what happened and it is expensive to educate them, at least using the pleading-and-playlet format of the common law. Second, the process of education cannot proceed on a generalized (mass-produced) basis; each case is theoretically hand-crafted. Third, save in a court of small claims it is usually specialists (e.g., lawyers) who do the crafting. fourth, because the courts do not allocate docket space by competitive bidding between plaintiffs, the creditor with the largest claim at stake must take his place in a 'queue' behind plaintiffs with smaller claims.

In reality, however, the practice is not quite as hard as all that. Fact finding and rule applying does tend to get stylized, and some of the specialists, through repetition, learn their jobs well. But there is another factor involved in using 'the law' with respect to half-executed contracts which tends to increase the transaction costs of the party who has performed: the risk of wrongly losing, and of losing all. Assume again that c has done all that he promised D while D has done none. If nothing else were to happen at that point, c would be out v and D would be ahead v, for something 'belonging to' c is at that point in D's hands. Now, assume further that D refuses to pay, and that c must go to law. Even if the law functions properly (that is, in accord with the assumed facts) the maximum that C can recover is $v - t_c$. But if the law miscarries and a 'wrong' decision is made, C's post-litigation status could be as bad as $0 - t_c$. This, of course, is C's maximum exposure. Though the law does tend to formulate as many transactions as possible in yes-no terms, it is not always that rigid. While C might not get v, he might still get an amount greater than zero. But there are nonetheless innumerable accidents in legal proceedings which lead to status quo results, and for C any result which retains the status quo is more than a total loss.

What makes this risk-of-status-quo factor particularly interesting is that it is proportional to the magnitude of v. It is ordinarily less irrational to spend any given quantity of t_c as the amount of v to be recovered (which would be abandoned by abjuring the expenditure) increases. But the risk component of t_c increases as the amount of v being put in jeopardy by the litigative system increases. So long as v is not thrown into the judicial-coercive system with its power to transform C's property finally into D's, there is always hope. As soon as the final writ is executed, however, no further bargaining about v is possible; whoever it objectively belonged to, it now belongs to whoever won. Thus the greater the value of v, the more C may be irrevocably out-of-pocket, and the more dangerous it is for him to risk the irrevocable loss.

As we shall see, not all kinds of C's need bear this due-process t_c to any material extent. But some do, and to the extent that they do it is significant, sometimes determinative, in their collection-strategy decisions.

C The Content of t_d

The judicial-coercive process is so designed that C may have to go through a number of steps, none cost free, even though D remains totally passive. Unless one counts the cost of tearing up and throwing away an occasional summons, the process can be free for D all the way from institution of the action to execution of the judgment. C's mercenaries will have little difficult or dangerous work to do if D chooses this course of inaction, and the resultant t_c will be low, but the choice is D's. In order to increase C's costs over the bare minimum for commencing a lawsuit and taking it through to judgement, D can expend some money and effort. But the critical point is that in most cases of breach, C will be forced to spend some t_c before D need even decide whether he will spend any t_d.

Were this where the story ended, the irrationality of paying one's debts would not be merely apparent. But we all know that not fully carrying out one's obligations can bring with it a retribution that is hardly limited to social disapprobation, a guilty conscience, or an unpleasant afterlife. Translated into our formal terms, there are components of t_d in addition to those which our analysis has heretofore taken into account. Most of these components do not take the form of a direct transfer payment from D to C, but a typical one does involve such a shift. Not only do the courts regularly enforce contractual clauses providing that the creditor who sues successfully also recover the expenses of collection, even in the absence of any specific provision certain costs of collection are allocated to the defaulting buyer. This particular transfer payment simultaneously decreases t_c and increases t_d. A complete transfer of t_c to D will not be possible because C still must bear the risk component of his t_c, that is, the same miscarriage that would bereave C of v rightfully his will deny him that portion of t_c he would have been awarded had his suit been successful. But this is only to say that these cost-shifting devices may not by themselves be sufficient to force D into a position where it would be wholly irrational to breach, where, that is, $t_c = 0$ and $t_d > 0$.

Beyond these procedures for shifting the cost of coercive collection to D, there are for C even more powerful and threatening devices which involve no transfer payment at all. They function not as payments to c, but as mere destruction of d's wealth. But that too acts to coerce d. In a sense, of course, all t_d is like that; it hurts d without directly helping c. But some kinds of t_d, the costs of defense, for example, can be avoided by raising none. The components of t_d to be considered next cannot be avoided merely by remaining passive. Indeed such a response is likely to increase the injury.

When d has defaulted in the performance he owes to c, there are two courses open to c under modern sales law. He may attempt via self-help to get back what he gave d, or he may at law attempt to get what d promised to give him. In some situations he may reclaim goods delivered under a contract (so far as that is physically feasible) and then, to the extent that that does not get him to where he would have been had the transaction gone through as planned, he may attempt to get additional things of value from d to make up the deficiency.

The attractiveness of the self-help process is obvious: it sometimes permits c to recover some large portion of v without incurring the usual expenses of going to law. It is, in effect, an opportunity to use state-of-nature power to get out of the c position without having either to buy off, or buy in, the Leviathan. It is not, of course, cost free; night work with tow trucks (or even with duplicate keys) entails expense, but seldom as much as a litigated lawsuit and subsequent execution. Moreover, it is possible in this way for c to recover all. This depends on the value to c of the goods seized and the amount of the debt outstanding at the time of the repossession, but given a high enough down payment and a low enough rate of depreciation for the goods, c may be made whole solely by retaking the goods.

But there are significant additional injuries inherent in self-help or judicially-ordered repossession which do not directly inure to c's benefit but which may so increase t_d as to inhibit d's breach. First is the loss which comes solely from being deprived of a good's use. Obvious examples are the repossessed fabricating machine, the padlocked plant and (in the context of non-business 'productive' assets) the automobile which is the only access to work. This harm can be visited on d even if c does not get use and/or resale rights in the item, as the garageman's and lawyer's liens amply illustrate. Once deprivation is coupled with a power of resale, however, d's loss increases and becomes more permanent. There are numerous things in the world that are worth much more to one person than they are to any other person. Consider the situation of a man owning a drill press which he uses in his business. He bought the press ten years ago and has used it since, not without problems, but by and large successfully. It has a slight tendency to yaw to the left and thus the operator must keep up a constant countervailing pressure. When used at top speed it tends to burn out its bearings. After some bitter experience, all that is now known and integrated into its use pattern. What is also known and integrated is that it has no other material peculiarities; make but these few adjustments in use and it will drill press away to one's perfect satisfaction. The price of discovery has been spent. But put such a press up for sale, even in an honest, open auction market, and the sound buyer will discount his bid by the possibility of disaster. After all, it is a 'ten-year-old press' of this manufacture and that appearance. It is a mystery. It may functionally be worth as much as it is, but it may be worth almost nothing.

When there are added to this 'normal' depreciation factor all the other factors which may lower the price fetched by used goods in an aftermarket, for example, restricted buyer pools approaching minimonopsonies, insufficient sale advertising, unenthusiastic and incompetent selling, title uncertainties, and the lack of price-maximizing incentives, the potential loss in value to an ex-possessor becomes substantial. With consumer goods, yet another factor enters further to drive this value-destruction vector: non-functional depreciation, the loss in value consumer goods suffer when they move from the category 'new' to the category 'used.' To use the classic example, the ten odometer miles between pier and Hondling Harry's has no effect on market value; the ten miles from Harry's to the buyer's home costs a fortune. Part of this depreciation is an averaging out of the dangers of mystery: 'if it's so great a car, why didn't he keep it.' The major reason for the loss in value, however, is largely inscrutable: buying a new car is different from buying a used car and market values reflect that difference. In any event, for a variety of reasons, when a creditor repossesses goods and transfers their valuation base from 'value to possessor' to 'market value' the value of the goods involved will tend to decrease absolutely.

Mere value destruction, of course, cannot do c any direct good. If his claim is properly for more than the repossession-resale will realize, it may do him actual harm, assuming he cannot get the deficiency from D at all, or at least without suffering unreasonable additional costs. But the threat of this value destruction is a threat of serious injury available at a cost relatively low in comparison to the magnitude of the injury inflicted. It is an increase in the applicable t_d.

The potentiality of repossession and resale to increase strikingly the ratio of t_d to t_c by destroying value in D's hands is manifest, often to a greater degree, in the operation of the other common execution technique, garnishment. But the attractiveness of garnishment from a creditor's point of view does not lie solely in its excitingly abusive possibilities. In theory, and often in practice, garnishment would be a lovely remedy to have even if it threatened no excess injury to the debtor. The way it is supposed to work is that the faucet whence liquid cash flows periodically to your debtor is directed to divert at least a little rivulet to you, at the faucet's cost and risk, until your cup runneth over. No need to grab possession of things, store them, manipulate them, push and shove them about until they turn into usable dereified value. No need to follow-up, time after time, the vicissitudes of sheriffs and auctioneers. Just wait, and to you all things will be given, slowly perhaps, but with interest. Indeed, from a creditor's point of view, garnishment is one of the most effective techniques for the non-cooperative collection of debts ever devised.

But at least in certain circumstances, garnishment is additionally capable of inflicting grievous injuries upon a recalcitrant debtor that are frequently far in excess of the 'injury' which paying the debt might entail. For though garnishment, like any lien, will interfere with the use of any liened property (a lien on a businessman's bank account will seriously interfere with his use of those liquid assets), the damaging impact of garnishment will likely be greatest if the debtor is a wage earner and the assets liened are his wages. One of the explanations for this is that a wage earner is likely to have a greater practical need for every penny of his wages than a businessman is likely to have for any particular liened asset; on the average, even with respect to equal-size garnishments there is a factor of differential marginal utility of money at work.

If, however, that were the only source of additional injury in wage garnishment it would be sufficient to do what has heretofore been done, severely limit the garnishable portion of a paycheck. The primary injury factor in wage garnishment lies elsewhere, however, in the effect of that legal process upon employer-employee relations. The trouble is that garnishment imposes transaction costs upon the employer. No one doubts that the mere processing of the writ costs the employer some money; the only dispute is about the amount. In addition there is always the risk of error in processing the writ and responding to it. Thus the garnished employer may find himself obligated to pay the same wages twice. In fact, it is precisely the cheapness and efficiency of the process from the creditor's (and even the debtor's) point of view which makes it so annoying to the employer. The reason it is so cheap is that it is the employer who organizes it, administers it, and risks its occasional errors.

In addition to these direct costs, the employer also suffers derivative losses. Insofar as something is deducted from a worker's paycheck (and increasingly as the amount increases) the motivation of the worker to perform well also decreases. He is just not as interested in doing his job as well. That may have a nasty effect, not only on the debtor's productivity, but on the morale of the shop. Moreover, beyond these obvious economic effects lie the equally powerful psychic effects on the employer. One study indicates that many employers are outraged at the debtor's apparent improvidence, and might react to it even if there were no costs involved in processing the garnishment. The offense is moral, and as usual with morality, the employer's response may be impervious to rationality, social or economic. After all, the unfairness is so patent. Here is a transaction between c and d. Either d is improvident, or c is at fault, or both, but of the three parties involved in a garnishment proceeding, who gets the cost, the risk, and annoyance and the anxiety? The only one who had nothing to do with the whole transaction, the employer ...

Taking all these aspects of garnishment together, it is not surprising that employers frequently seek to dissociate themselves from the whole mess. Given the legal situation which makes reaction against the creditor difficult, if indeed at all possible, the employer is likely to take some kind of action against the employee-debtor. That does not mean that the garnished employer will always fire his employee. Frequently, one might guess, he acts by threatening the employee and pressuring him to extricate both of them by paying up. This is the course the creditor would prefer, at least as an economic matter. Or one can also imagine an employer taking the employee's part, either in fighting the claim with the employee or in supplying the wherewithal to settle it. But also with some frequency, the employer will fire the employee just to extricate himself from the whole garnishment *schreck*. And the same factors which militate in favor of such a decision simultaneously tend to maximize the brutal economic effect of any such discharge.

Leaving aside total irrationalities, on the no-guy-who-doesn't-pay-his-bills-can-work-for-me level, the decision whether to fire a garnisheed employee would seem to involve some calculation of comparative costs. If the employee is valuable and hard to replace (at least at his wages), then one would not lightly discharge him. As the labor market tightens, that is, as fewer workers are easily and cheaply available, the higher becomes the value of the one already employed. But the reverse is also true. The less specially skilled and competent the employee, the more easily he can be replaced. Thus it is more likely that the employer will discharge him rather than put up with even moderate economic and psychic costs. But it is just these marginal, easily replaceable workers, pushed out into a loose labor market, who will find it most difficult to find a new job. Thus not only will that group be hit with the cost of being discharged with greater frequency, the intensity and duration of that loss will likely be much greater for them than for any less marginal group.

In brief, if one considers the losses to a debtor who is fired because his employer is garnisheed to be part of the t_d of that collection game, that component is likely to be very high, sometimes far in excess of the creditor's total claim. The threat of garnishment, therefore, is a very effective weapon against a worker who justifiably fears the wrath of his employer. Especially if it can continue to be used even before and without a judgment (for instance, post-*Sniadach*, in the guise of a wage assignment), it will often easily bring an insecure debtor to heel, because it is clear that putting that 'punishment' mechanism into motion is close to cost-free for the creditor, at least as far as enforcement costs are concerned.

It is important to note again that as with repossession value-shrinkage, the injury to the debtor is not simultaneously an equal direct gain to the creditor. In both cases, the loss amounts initially to mere destruction of value in the hands of the debtor. In fact, in both cases, the side effects of actually using the collection procedure decrease the likelihood that the creditor will eventually get all of his v out of the debtor. In both cases the source of the creditor's surcease, the things of value 'owned' by the debtor, are diminished by the act of seizure. Of course distribution of the net loss between the parties differs; in these cases it ordinarily falls much harder on the debtor-employee than on his creditor. And that is what makes the procedure such a potent threat. But when the threats to repossess or to garnish are actually carried out, either through ignorance or to establish credibility it may fairly be said that the system is behaving 'spitefully,' that is, in a manner harmful to both the central participants.

D Spite: A Value Secreted in 'Transaction Costs'
Up to now we have assumed that all t decreases the amount of v left in the system. But this assumption is often untrue in practice; t may also represent the price of additional 'goods' purchased by the two parties for themselves. The most important of these, which is as real and valuable as cars and coats, is spite.

The nature of spite can be exposed most starkly by reference to an illegal but common subspecies of collection, the protection racket. Consider an extortioner approaching a potential victim with the following proposition: 'Give me $100 or I will break the plateglass window of your store.' Assume that (a) the plateglass window in uninsured; (b) it can be replaced for $100; (c) the crook 's cost of breaking it is $10; and (d) breaking the window once is within the crook's power, but no further depredations against the victim are. Obviously, it would make no economic difference to the victim whether he paid $100 and kept the window intact, or refused to pay, had his window broken, and replaced it at a cost of $100. In either case he is out $100.

To the extortioner, however, what the store-owner decides makes a great deal of difference. If the victim pays, his yield is $100. If the victim does not, the crook's assets may be decreased by the cost of breaking the window ($10). Thus while the cost of 'cooperative' payment is zero ($100 of value 'belonging to' the victim is merely transferred to the racketeer), the cost of coercion is $110, $100 of which represents absolutely destroyed value (the difference between a window and a pile of glass fragments) and $10 of which represents the crook's additional labor costs.

Naturally, the crook would strongly prefer that the store-owner pay rather than suffer the asset destruction. But to increase the chances of this outcome, the extortioner must offer some incentive. At a minimum, his proposition ought to be: 'Pay me $99 or I will break your window.' If the victim decides to pay, he will be $1 better off than he would be if the game were played. But the victim has the power to inflict harm on his tormentor. He can deprive the crook of any payment. If the crook decides nonetheless to engage in his game of destruction, the victim will have forced him into an actual out-of-pocket loss. Of course, to bring this about the victim must also hurt himself. He must insist upon an end-point for the confrontation more expensive for himself than the one proposed by the extortioner. What some economic analysis might overlook is that he is nevertheless very likely to do it. People do it all the time. The fulfillment of an urge to spite seems no different from the fulfillment of any other human desire. People pay to satisfy lust, hate, ambition and greed. They also pay for this. As with any other good, of course, the demand for spite is never totally inelastic, and its value is never infinite. While it has some value for almost everyone, the more it costs the less likely it is to be bought.

E Power Over Transaction Costs: The Professional and the Consumer
Up to now, by using the abstract constructs 'c' and 'd' as if there were no material differences among the various kinds of parties to half-executed contracts, I have falsified the reality of collection practice. Abstraction, for all its usefulness, almost always does that. I shall now, so to

speak, 'decompose' the concepts c and d, into recognizable subclasses, so as better to describe the variable impact of various collection strategies in different 'typical' collection situations.

There are three fact bundles which together account for most contract collection problems. In one, interestingly enough, a consumer is in the position of c, having fully or substantially performed while the merchant has not. The second finds the professional as c, having sold on credit or loaned money to a defaulting consumer. In the third major area of collection conflict, no consumers are involved, the underlying transaction having been within the production-distribution stream, not at its estuary. In each of these situations the costs, including the information costs, of the various collection transactions operate in importantly different ways.

1 The Consumer as Creditor: Picture a consumer who has just bought a color television set from a retailer for $500 in cash. The consumer takes the set home, tries it, and finds that it is defective to the tune of $50, that is, that it would cost $50 to bring the television up to warranty. In these circumstances the consumer is a creditor; the retailer has possession of $50 of parts and services 'belonging to' him. The consumer approaches the retailer and asks him to repair the set. The retailer refuses. This leaves the consumer with only coercive collection if he is to recover the $50. But legal action may not be for him a realistic alternative; the t_c of such a move, the cost of hiring a lawyer, filing papers and so on, it likely to be in excess of the $50 at issue, while the merchant need not until then expend any t_d.

Some consumers in this position would disregard the economic disadvantages of going to the law and would sue the seller out of spite. But even assuming that a consumer were so inclined, he would likely find his purpose frustrated, for much of the potential destructiveness locked into repossession and garnishment hardly affects professional debtors at all. A merchant faced with an adverse judgment is better able than a consumer in a similar situation to interdict property execution, by paying the judgment or posting a bond, or at least by showing up at the execution sale to restrict the frigidity of any 'chill.' And if a consumer were to garnish a seller because of his post-judgment obstinacy it would not be wage garnishment, with all its threatened injuries. If the garnishee is the retailer's bank (the most likely target, since it is his most solvent and notorious debtor), the ramifications on the retailer are likely to be minimal; he is unlikely to be 'fired,' even from his account. Thus our hypothetical businessman can allow the consumer to pursue his legal remedies with relative impunity, for none of the consumer's options can force a risk of much more than the $50 claim. That is not much satisfaction for the consumer to buy – merely preventing a windfall. It ordinarily demands 'superspite,' that is, infliction by the consumer of greater harm on himself than he can inflict on his enemy. It may still be done; the history of law is filled with cranks (lawyers or clients, it's often hard to tell) who spend large and unrecoverable sums to assuage feelings of outrage, moral or economic. But it is not bloody likely. We thus have a classic and unhappy creditor situation: the consumer as creditor can officially recover through judicial coercion no more than the amount by which d is in default, but to recover anything he must expend some t_c, perhaps more than the v in issue, while to cause that initial expenditure d need spend no t_d. If the ultimate t_d of a full coercive collection is also low compared to the t_c necessarily involved, and the t_c will not be borne by d even if c eventually wins, then it is usually economically rational for c just to abandon his claim.

2 The Professional As Creditor: When c is in the credit business, however, the impact of the factors noted above changes materially. Perhaps the largest components of t_c are the administrative and risk costs inherent in the due-process 'adjudication' phase of the collection process. Naturally, it is to the creditor's advantage to avoid these if possible. Certainly he can avoid them

by not playing the judicial-coercion game at all, by attempting to collect what he is owed by direct contact with the debtor. But as noted earlier, to avoid judicial coercion altogether is to fail to get the power of the State, the ultimate in civil puissance, on the creditor's side. Thus, if the creditor can get to the execution phase without the costs and risks of an adjudication, it is tempting to try to do so. This can be done most inexpensively if the other party fails to show up and the judgment, that pass-key to judical coercion, is procured by default. There are a number of ways to encourage default, but there are indications that consumers need very little encouragement. Largely because of the prevalence of default judgments against consumers, the cost of the initial adjudication-phase t_c is remarkably small in the vast majority of cases in which businessmen are creditors and consumers are debtors.

That does not mean that a default judgment is cost-free. But efficiency in the legal context is like efficiency elsewhere, it is in large part a function of standardization and repetition. The lawsuit will ordinarily require an attorney, but at the summons and complaint stage he needs relatively little extra time or effort to file two suits rather than one, or eight, or sixteen for that matter. In fact, in businesses which combine large volume collection with no concern about the effects of indiscriminate and excessive behavior on business reputation, it may be cheaper overall to standardize all activities and 'go to law' immediately in every case, without regard to the specific facts of the specific debtor's problem.

In addition to reaping benefit from specialization and standardization, professional creditors may be in a position to externalize a great many more of their costs than can consumers. First, for all cs there is subsidization by the State of some of the costs of recourse to the judicial system. That which the State takes in payment for the use of its information-generating and force-applying mechanisms is ordinarily less than its expense in supplying those services. Second, when one gets to the point of execution one often finds instances of administrative costs being shifted to persons who had nothing to do with either the debt-generating or debt-defaulting transactions. As noted earlier, this is notably the case with respect to garnishment where the employer rather than the creditor or employee-debtor must expend the cost of organizing an installment payment plan. Third, both by 'agreement' and by operation of law much of c's administrative expense, which would ordinarily be part of his t, may be transferred to d. This simultaneously decreases t_c and increases t_d, thereby giving super-leverage to the move as a species of coercion. Insofar as this shift depends on contracts it will vastly favor the drafter of the contract, who is likely to be the professional.

Thus the merchant-creditor has far greater opportunities than does the consumer-creditor to decrease t_c by externalizing or shifting some portion of it, a move which under our earlier analysis should massively increase c's power to force a settlement agreeable to him. But the merchant-creditor's compensatory weapons do not stop there. He also has a very much greater power than a consumer-creditor to increase t_d. One need not here repeat all that has been said previously about the destruction-of-value aspects of property execution and garnishment. They form a clear 'cost' to a d who goes through the whole coercive collection game. Even if, therefore, spite is beneath a presumably rational businessman, and credibility and reputation are ambiguous 'assets' in this context, the combination of (a) the merchant-creditor's power to limit his own t_c, (b) his power to shift it, and (c) his power to increase his opponent's t_d weighs very heavily against there being any substantial practical effect, as to him, of the paradoxical disadvantage of being a creditor under American law.

3 Professionals On Both Ends: There is a third very common situation in which one party fully performs before the other completes his performance: transactions between businessmen.

When those transactions lead to dispute, businessmen avoid the judicial-coercive system, that very flower of Western common law, like some rare Asiatic plague. They go to law only under very special circumstances and as a last resort.

For any two businessmen the components of both t_c and t_d are likely to be roughly the same. Both parties are likely already to have established mechanisms for dealing with disputes. Whatever economies come from the differential between their scales of operation are likely to be small. Except when a businessman is *in extremis*, those gross harms that may be visited on him by carrying out legal execution are harder to inflict; he usually has more room to maneuver and pay up prior to being sold out. The risk-of-loss-of-v factor still favors the businessman who in the particular instance occupies the D chair, but a careful c who is willing to spend for representation can usually soften the risk of total loss. In general, then, t_c and t_d are not likely to be wildly different.

But considerably more important for avoiding the coercive collection game is the availability of a strikingly effective alternative procedure, one which while not abjuring threat and coercion, avoids the costs and dangers of the official varieties. It depends not on force, but on the exchange of information. The 'solution' to many of the divers disputes between businessmen takes the form of some variation on one of the following scenarios. The scene of each is simple: split screen, two telephones:

1 Buyer: Hello, Morris? Those widgets you sent us. They're breaking every minute. You want me to pay for such junk?

    Seller: Look, if your men don't know how to use widgets right, what do you want from me? They're just what you ordered, Grade A-2 stainless steel widgets.

    Buyer: Stainless steel they're not. Swiss cheese maybe, orange-crate wood, but not steel.

    Seller: Look, Kevin, maybe we've been having a little quality control problem – just temporary. Do the best you can and we'll make it up next time.

    Buyer: OK, but don't forget. The noise of popping widgets my partner doesn't have to hear.

2 Seller: Hello, Kevin? So what's with our last bill?

    Buyer: My bookkeeper's been sick.

    Seller: Uh huh. Your hand cramps when you pick up a pen?

    Buyer: Soon, Morris.

    Seller: How soon? Tomorrow?

    Buyer: Come on, Morris; did I make such a stink when you were shipping out those cardboard widgets?

    Seller: OK, OK, Maybe I'll give you a couple of weeks more. You're not *really* in trouble are you?

    Buyer: Absolutely not. I got plenty of orders. Go check with some of the other guys.

    Seller: Don't worry. I already did. OK, take a couple of weeks. Give my get-wells to your bookkeeper.

    Buyer: Hah!

3 Seller: So Kevin? Morris. Where's the money?

    Buyer: Soon.

    Seller: It's been soon a long time. Now it's now.

    Buyer: Look Morris, I could have gotten the stuff from Acme or Nadir cheaper. I gave you the trade.

    Seller: Now you're giving me the business. Now! Or there'll be trouble.

Buyer: Tell you what I'll do. I'll pay you today, right now, what I could've got the merchandise for from Acme.
Seller: Tell you what I'll do. I'll break your head is what I'll do. We got a goddam contract Kevin, and you pay the goddam contract price.
Buyer: Morris, you don't like my deal, sue me with your contract.
Seller: I may and I may not. But one thing I know I'll do: anyone asks me if you pay your bills *the answer is no*. [The last clause is delivered in a high-pitched shriek of absolute credibility.]
Buyer: Morris? Half today, the rest at the end of the month?
Seller: OK.
Buyer: My best to Ethel.
Seller: You too. Remember me at home.

It would be folly to characterize these solutions as 'coercive' or 'cooperative;' *they are deals* and like all deals partake of both elements. But one thing is perfectly clear: this form of solution depends upon the generation, transmission and communication of information and threats of information. And another thing is also clear: until one begins to understand this method of collection, one understands nothing.

III COMMUNICATION AND COLLECTION: INFORMATION AS POWER

The importance of information in collection practice depends upon its peculiar power to supplement force, and frequently to supplant it. To the extent that actualized coercion is a source of waste in the coercive collection game, its replacement by successfully communicated information offers the prospect of greater efficiency, and, depending on one's definition, perhaps more justice.

A Reputation: The Past As Property

If parties had perfect information about each other, the nature of collection law, perhaps even its existence, would be irrelevant. Picture a world without collection law, a peculiar exercise, but one not beyond the purview of useful analytic fantasy. After all, all one must do is imagine a society in which not only had *Slade's Case* not yet been decided, but also in which the law did not enforce partly performed contracts at all, recognizing no claims on things of value except possession, or removal from possession by force or stealth. Would such an apparently massive change in American law make any difference? At first glance it would seem so, for in such a world the end-point of any collection game would seem to be identical with the walk-away point. In such a legal universe, it would appear at first glance to be irrational for sellers to enter into any credit transaction. Commerce would have to operate wholly through carefully planned instantaneous exchanges.

But that's silly. The decision about entrusting would still be made not on the basis of the *law's* effect on the rate of repayment, but on the basis of total experience with the *actual* rate of repayment, the shaping of which is a function of coercive law to only a limited extent. Partially executed contracts would for a variety of reasons continue to be completed some of the time despite the apparent legal and economic absurdity of such activity. Most people carry out their agreements because they carry out their agreements, not because awful things will happen to them if they don't. But equally important, even within an imaginary society which had credit transactions but no legal enforcement, there would still be a powerful source of non-ethical, rational impetus toward repayment. Assuming that trades involving temporal performance differentials are functional in the society, the power to take part in such transactions has value. It follows that exclusion from that system, or a disproportionally high entrance cost, both of which would follow from a reputation for default, is a species of rational economic coercion. That is, even if one's present purse is trash, one's good name may represent a large portion of any hope for a future purse.

'Reputation,' then, for these purposes, may be defined as a measure of a particular person's positive or negative predicted deviation from the other party's average predicted t of collecting from him. If information about a person's reputation were perfect, there would be no such thing as a collection problem. The sole 'collection' practice would be precise pricing of the initial transaction. The end-point of every individual credit transaction being identical with the price, no longer would any cheerfully quick repayer subsidize the slow, slovenly or evasive borrower.

Such prediction-perfecting information is impossible as a practical matter; generating it without cost is impossible even in theory. Even if such a state could eventually be approached by methods so efficient in gathering, correlating, evaluating and communicating information that the cost justified the expenditure, it might still be objectionable to do so on non-economic grounds: the loss of privacy and autonomy might itself be too high a 'price' (on another but equally 'real' scale) to pay. But that it is hopeless and maybe horrible to contemplate a world in which every individual's reputation was perfectly known hardly means that less than total information is valueless, or that it is not an important factor in collection strategy and efficiency. Since reputation has an effect upon the price at which one can deal on credit in the future, it is an asset subject to value fluctuation. Since reputation is a species of information, it can be modified by other information. Thus anyone who can deliver information which will modify a reputation, and communicate that reputation as modified to others, has the power to change the value of an item of another's property. Not only, then, can c threaten absolutely to decrease the value of d's goods by repossessing them, or of his labor by garnishing his wages, but he can also threaten to depreciate the value of his reputation by communicating his displeasure.

But just because here as elsewhere we are all at each other's mercy, it does not follow here either that jeopardy is equal. There are two major jobs involved in effectively deploying information for this purpose: (1) collecting, collating and cumulating the 'bits' of input out of which the reputational messages are constructed; and (2) transmitting those messages to interested listeners. Because of differences implicit among our three paradigm dispute situations, especially with respect to the kinds of information involved in each situation and the organizational status of the different classes, the costs of these operations, and thus their efficiency and effectiveness, vary materially.

The critical factor about businessmen is that they have at their disposal for the exchange of information about each other preexisting communication networks. These channels, necessary for the exchange or orders and instructions for trading, are hardly overloaded by those messages, and reputational data can be added at a low marginal cost. Moreover, these channels are directionally precise. They are built in a network which links people who trade with each other, to whom information about each other is certain to be of interest. A jobber's default is to a goods distribution industry what a man's shampoo is to Playboy Magazine: the number of random or uninterested readers it 'reaches' is kept to a minimum. In addition, the previous information which has been carried on the network makes it easier for additional bits to be linked accurately. One prime rating problem, for instance, tying adverse information to a particular party for use in future transactions (a problem cognate to establishing the good will or bad will of a trade name), is mitigated in industries where participants know not only corporate names but principal's names; Cupcake Custom Cutters may go out of business, or change its trade style, but its owners, if known, will be quickly recognized under any new avatar.

Information among merchants about consumers – their so-called credit ratings – profits less from these institutional efficiencies. The chief constraint is the size of the group to be known. Consumers too can move, change their names, buy under other names. But more than that, any particular merchant is likely to have but a few trades with any particular consumer. The information, to be of any real value, will have to be collected and collated with other transaction reports to give any kind of usable picture. Further, any individual transaction with a consumer is likely to form only a small element in a merchant's total business. When the total possible loss is small, charges for credit information bulk large.

Despite these considerations, the gross volume and risk still seem to justify the creation and maintenance of organizations organized and specialized for collection, collation, and transmission of credit information. These organizations have access to a large audience of individuals willing to tell, and to pay to know. Moreover, they are able to exclude those who will not pay with money and their own information. Moreover, the transaction costs of the subscribers in modifying the debtor's reputations are less than those of the subjects. Picturing credit information as the memory core of a computer, the subscribers have better and cheaper access to both the input and output stations. They can get their versions of reality in and the computer's view of reality out much more efficiently than can the subjects.

As computers render these processes cheaper per unit, as one starts to approach the reality of a 'cashless society,' the usefulness of this device will continue to increase. It will never be perfect, of course, but the threat to damage a credit rating will become increasingly effective as more and more information about past transactions can be economically delivered to a larger and larger number of persons who might enter into future transactions.

When c is a consumer, however, and d is a professional merchant or lender, the power of any threat to reputation is diluted. That does not mean that such a threat, express or implied, is without effect; it is cumulatively the most powerful and frequently a perfectly sufficient ground to assure full and fair performance by merchants. To believe otherwise is to believe that a good reputation is not an important business asset – and if you can believe that, you can believe anything. There is no doubt that a discontented consumer can inflict *some* harm on a merchant he comes to hate – he can refuse to deal with him any more. Moreover, to the extent that he can communicate his perception of the merchant and his products to other potential customers, he will be able to increase the harm he does.

There are several good reasons, however, why the consumer-to-consumer information network about merchants and products functions poorly, certainly less efficiently than the same mechanism among merchants. First, it is of no obvious economic value to any consumer to deliver adverse information about a seller to any other consumer. He may be otherwise motivated to do so – spite, pique, even conversational void – but these motives are not conventionally economic. Insofar as it costs him nothing to do so, for instance in casual conversation, he may affect reputation with his adverse commentary. If consumers were self-consciously a class, like tradesmen in the same trade, they might spend money on such discipline, for it is a benefit to all consumers to drive the wicked and nasty out of business. But at any given moment the act of spending money to convey the adverse information, since not necessarily followed by others' spending to inform, or to support an information-collating institution, seems to the individual consumer like a conferral of a gift. Thus the transmission of this adverse information is likely to stay unorganized, with no pre-existing, pre-paid channels available for its transmission.

In the absence of such specialized information-organizing institutions, the consumer must distribute the adverse information himself. His media for that communications effort does not transcend his normal communications network – talking to people with whom he has an otherwise established relationship. But these others to whom he might deprecate the merchant-offender do not necessarily have any pre-existing interest in his information; not everyone is contemplating the purchase of a new television set at the time the reporter's discontent over the one he just bought is articulated. In other words, he is not quite as bad off as one who advertises Enovid in the *Diocesan Weekly*, but neither is he as well off as an abortionist taking a column or two in *Women's Liberation Now*, or even as well off as a merchant talking to another about a third. While the merchant need check only the consumers in whom he is interested, when he becomes so, the consumer who hears evil of a seller usually must store the information for a period of time. There is, therefore, a good deal of random noise.

In addition, there is a time lag in all information. If a merchant can get in and out quickly enough, he may make a killing before his bad reputation catches up with him. And in any event 'he' is likely to be 'it,' a corporation, the destruction of which through adverse comment is likely to entail only the loss of the promoters' cash investment (around $3.86) and rarely any 'bad will' for the promoters themselves. Their identity is hidden from future marks, as it is not from other professionals, by their trade-name corporate shell. For the general purchasing public, they will frequently be able to 'die,' only to arise elsewhere in a new incarnation, like a vulture from the ashes.

When the failure in performance is a failure in the quality of goods, moreover, it is even easier for a manufacturer to blunt the impact of bad quality by changing model names, styles and numbers. By so doing he destroys that *sine qua non* of competition, comparability. One of the unmentioned advantages of frequent new models is that a lemon of a 1967 is not necessarily presagent of a bomb of a 1968. And when the defect is one of the quality of goods, the information is notably more complex. Whereas the seller need only say (and hear) 'didn't pay up,' the shopping buyer must deal with all kinds of complex information in trying to decide if the product is a 'bad' one. Anyone who has tried to use *Consumer Reports* has experienced the frustration of deciding between a superb Frammis with a shock hazard and a not-so-fine Wudgis without. It is hard, that is, for a consumer to be a purchasing expert with respect to the full panoply of things he may from time to time buy. To evaluate all information is to invite sensory overload and a final tendency toward impulse buying.

I do not want to overstate this, however. Threats not to deal in the future, and to make known one's discontent are effective, at least against businesses cherishing long life and good reputation. In addition, there are information brokers working on behalf of consumers; department store buyers, for instance, are purchasing experts, and for very good economic reasons of their own prefer to sell the goods of sellers whose goods perform. In addition, competitors of the offending merchant should be willing to pass on adverse information from consumers about other sellers as part of their selling campaign (though they do so with startling infrequency). In general then, while generating bad reputation for merchant-DS is the consumer's best weapon, it is less efficient than the merchant-C's comparable weapon, credit rating destruction.

B Credibility: Reputation As a Factor in Negotiated Settlement

There is one special subcategory of information which deserves treatment: in terms of my graphics, data about the likelihood of a party's going to a coercive-play end-point rather than settling at some point on L–L$_1$. Except when spite is being purchased, the purpose of allowing the parties to inflict various injuries on each other is to facilitate threatening. But the magnitude of the injury is merely one factor in the effectiveness of the threat, the other being the likelihood of its coming to pass. Once again to put the situation into the simpler protection-racket context, if the victim continues to refuse to pay despite any threat the crook might make, then within the single-play context of that particular confrontation it is totally irrational for the extortioner to go through with any of his threats. The extortioner starts with zero. If he walks away, his end-point is zero. If he carries out his threats, he ends up at $-t$.

But that t also buys something else which has value: other victims (and this victim next time) are more likely to believe his threats in the future. To a racketeer this is a capital asset; call it 'credibility.' Possessing it, he knows that future victims are less likely to behave so 'irrationally' as to reject his generous offer to settle for less than the replacement cost of the window.

Lifting this lesson out of the context of extortion into that of 'legitimate' debt collection, however, requires a few important shifts. First, a creditor (as opposed to a racketeer) cannot walk away cost-free. By hypothesis, if he walks away he forfeits v in the debtor's hands. Unless $t_c > v$, c must play if he is to recoup any of his loss. Even when $t_c = v$, he should definitely play; his net recovery will be zero within the game, but he will gain in credibility. But the demand for credibility is not totally inelastic, any more than it is for spite; if $t_c > v$ by too much, the extra credibility may just not be worth buying in that particular play.

There is, however, another difference between extortioners and creditors which further complicates the credibility-purchase factor. In extortion the 'business,' the whole business, is collection. The relationship between the parties is one imposed by the extortioner. Every evidence (including wanton destructiveness) of his intransigence – even at great risk and cost – ought to serve to increase the amount of his collections. A reputation for swinish persistence and conscienceless destructiveness is the principal 'good will' item on his balance sheet. But in business, the relationship between the parties which gave rise to the initial transfer of v must be consensual. If we define 'good will' as an established, reliable momentum of use which increases the wealth production of the components (capital, labor) of an organization of those components, then the information that one will not walk away, but will spend to vindicate one's rights, buys both good will and bad will. It increases yield in dispute situations, but also to some extent discourages anybody from dealing in the first place. Thus any enthusiastic collector who is also a seller must temper his collection devices by knowledge of their possible effect on his future gross volume. It follows that if a seller can keep much of the produce of threatening and nasty collection behavior while deflecting a large portion of the hostility such procedures may engender, it will pay him to do so. Hence this is an additional factor encouraging the use of collection agencies and negotiable-note third-party financiers. The seller gets some of the fruits of the aggression, but the collector gets most of the hostility, that is, the reputation for thoroughly rotten pertinacity is externalized from the seller to the collector. But the collector is not selling anything to the class of persons who come to hate him; as to them, he is in the position of an extortioner, selling them only freedom from his own behavior. They cannot discipline him by refusing to deal in the future, for dealing with him is not consensual anyway. To the extent the collector gets the reputation of being a son-of-a-bitch it is a good reputation, useful with the victims and with those who might hire his services. Thus, the 'bad will' component of aggressive collection practice, by being deflected into another business where unreasonable stubbornness is an asset, becomes all good will. There is thus a magical transformation of liability to asset as 'credibility' moves between organizations each specialized to service only half of a unitary transaction (sale and repayment).

Here again, it is more difficult for individual consumer-creditors to establish a reputation for credibility. Because the merchant has greater access to and control over the consumer's reputation than he himself has, the consumer's intransigence will be reported in the merchant's terms. A successful set-off for breach of warranty may well show up as 'resisted payment' and little else. Moreover, as stated earlier the t_c/v and t_c/t_d ratios tend to be much greater for consumer-cs than for merchant-cs; thus, it is inherently less credible that the consumer-c will play the game to the bitter end and it will therefore cost him more to establish his credibility. Moreover, it is very hard for a consumer-c to hide from or externalize the bad-will aspects of his activities. For a consumer to go out of business is to die, and identity changing is quite difficult. Most important, there are for him no available institutional scapegoats (except perhaps 'outside agitators'); there are no 'payment agencies' cognate to collection agencies, nor is there a complainer-in-due-course doctrine.

IV COMMUNICATION AND COLLECTION: INFORMATION AS KNOWLEDGE

A Predicted Ability to Pay

There is one source of extremely high probability that an end-point (rather than a point on $L-L_1$) will be the finish to a collection confrontation, which has nothing to do with spite, ignorance or credibility buying. That is the inability of D to perform. Now, 'can't' and 'won't' often are not easily distinguishable categories. But there is vast difference between one who will not pay because the goods he bought disintegrated to his touch, and another who will not pay because he is trying to steal from the seller, and between one who cannot pay because he has just been laid off from his job, one who cannot pay because he lost the wherewithal on a bad tip on a worse horse, and one who cannot pay because he doesn't want to borrow from his in-laws. A debtor who cannot in fact pay will not be enabled to do so by even the perfectly sufficient communication of a perfectly dreadful image of what will certainly happen to him if he does not. A threat is a method of redistributing things of value, not of creating them. Even letting a turnip know that a pot of boiling water is inexorably in its future will not get any blood out of it, and actually boiling it will merely turn a viable plant into a short and mean meal.

If a victim-pool contains only a few absolutely unable to pay, it might be administratively efficient to treat the whole pool as able to pay anyway, since any kind of differentiation often involves substantial administrative costs. But if a large proportion of defaulting debtors do not pay because they can't, and if the differentiation can be made at reasonable cost, the efficiency of the operation obviously increases. One would then spend to collect from and injure only those able to pay, and that policy if communicated would build a credibility more precisely of the type one would like to have as a professional creditor – potent but not spiteful. And equally important, one could also more efficiently expend his resources with respect to those who cannot pay, not on punishing them, but on arranging to maximize the amount they eventually will be able to pay.

In general, therefore, the more information one can gather about the status of the particular debtor in the particular situation, the better the answer that can be framed to the critical question: do I coerce or cooperate? To coerce the helpless is to waste money and effort; to cooperate with the deadbeat is to risk total loss. If, in fact, the majority of Ds, especially consumer Ds are in the can't-pay category, then any method which takes collection out of a coercive mode (judicial coercive or informational-coercive) and into a cooperative mode (where more time is given, earning potential is not interfered with and asset values are not destroyed) is likely to enhance the efficiency of the whole collection system, and benefit both cs and Ds. But that demands particular information about individual situations. It demands, in effect, a different kind of communication, not among cs and Ds about each other, but between an individual c and an individual D about their current situation. The economic, institutional and organizational constraints upon the efficiency of that form of communication will be the subject of the next section.

B Increasing Knowledge to Minimize Transaction Costs

Insofar as modern retail market allocations are imperfect, it is substantially because the distribution of the produce of mass production does not lend itself to individual bargains based on individualized information. If one views modern collection practice as another species of mass transaction, it becomes quite clear that the same economic constraints lead to most of its imperfections: it is too expensive, given the current institutional framework, for collection transactions as currently designed to be handled individually on the basis of the peculiar needs of particular parties in particular instances. That is what the litigation system attempts to do; its failures illustrate the fact that one cannot easily customize dispute resolution any more than one can customize manufacture or distribution for a mass market.

A perfectly rational collection law, would be that process which produces, in each individual case, a settlement at that point on L–L_1 which represents the actual exchange originally agreed upon between the parties. Because of the ubiquity of t, there is never an end-point of any coercive collection play which is north or east (that is, better for D or C) of any point on L–L_1; the best either can find is a point no worse, and then only under extraordinary circumstances, for instance when C actually recovers t_c from D. In the ordinary case, the entire length of L–L_1 is northeast of, that is, better than, the end-point of any coercive play. Thus the failure of the parties to reach some settlement point on L–L_1 is a typical kind of market breakdown, one which stems from an institutional insufficiency which blocks the efficient exchange of information.

Let us look again at the common coercive-collection situation illustrated by Graph II where t_c and t_d are both > 0, and $t_d > t_c$. Once again it is plain that the most important feature of the diagram is the blank space between the end-point (900/—200) and the points on L–L_1. But this time let us look at that space in a new way, as the pictorialization of a failure in communication, like the '——| |——' on a wiring diagram. For that is exactly what it is, a failure in the transmission of information. If the end-point were known and appreciated, it and every other point within the triangle described by points L, L_1 and the coercive-play end-point would be eschewed.

One of the aims of any collection system ought to be to bridge that gap by turning the ——| |—— into —— \——. This can be accomplished by supplying at reasonable cost a switch for the system which will allow the complex but relevant information to flow.

At the moment of default, the final resting place of the C–D relationship is a function of at least the following factors which must be accurately predicted by *both* C and D if a rational calculation is to be made by them: (1) what the Leviathan will do if solicited; (2) the costs to C and D of the State proceeding; (3) the values of spite, reputation and credibility for C and D; (4) the ability of the parties, both financial and organizational, to adopt certain courses, for example, paying in full, accepting less; and (5) the level of accuracy with which the other party is able to calculate each of the above. Ignorance of these factors by either of the parties is likely to produce, in any given instance, a competitive and bargaining disadvantage. As we have seen, however, not all ignorance that disadvantages one party will necessarily benefit the other; it may instead lead to the absolute loss of value within the two-party system. Consider, for instance, ignorance of the amount of harm that C can inflict upon D by going through the coercive game. Assume that C knows (as indeed he is likely to) that if he repossesses an item and resells it, the item will bring less in the open market than it is worth to D as possessor. This 'destroyed' value may have to be recouped, if at all, as part of a subsequent deficiency judgement against D. Assume further that D could pay for the item as agreed, but he decides for one reason or another to be recalcitrant. So long as the likelihood and extent of t_d is not communicated to D, he is likely to undervalue the cost of recalcitrance when weighing it against the inconvenience of payment; and this tendency will be accelerated if D places a high value on spite. In such a situation, D might decide to go through the coercive collection practice even though full knowledge on his part would impel him rationally, even calculating his spite value, to compromise or even to pay at the voluntary payment point, so as to avoid coercive collection. If in partial ignorance of the true situation (factual and legal) D forces C to resort to coercive collection to recover v, he will have converted a zero-sum game into a minus-sum game, and it is only small comfort to C that most of the destroyed value falls on D.

Or consider a case which involves a misperception by C about D's power to avert a punishing play. Assume that C believes that D is a deadbeat, that is, that D could pay if he wanted to but doesn't want to because he thinks he can get away with it. Such a perception may lead C to place a very high value on both spite and credibility. He will tend to overrate his chance of success in enlisting the power of the State on his behalf. He may, for these reasons, feel justified in expending substantial t_c (in court and/or for private harrassment), and he may have a corresponding willingness to inflict as much judicial and private t_d on his unfortunate debtor as possible. But if C's assessment of D turns out to be incorrect – that is, if D turns out to be unable rather than unwilling to pay – C will have inappropriately spent for credibility (getting a reputation as one who punishes the helpless), for spite (harming himself to harm an unfortunate rather than a true enemy), and for the power of the State (getting an uncollectible judgment).

It is frequently, therefore, also in the interest of both parties to increase each other's level of accurate information, and to facilitate the efficient mutual use of that information. As noted earlier, when the disputants are businessmen in a relatively cohesive industry the channels of information are likely to be relatively well-developed. But when one of the parties is a consumer, the situation almost always resembles the least hopeful of the merchant-merchant set-tos. It is still worthwhile for the disputants to spend to educate each other. In consumer transactions, however, that educational process is exceedingly inefficient, in the quite strict sense of costing a lot for a little bit of result. The first limitation upon efficiency is the absence of regular communication channels between individual seller/lenders and individual consumers. This has been discussed earlier. But even if there were more precise channels of communication open between the specific parties, it is very silly for cs and Ds who have no extensive shared past to trust each other. For while it is sometimes to the benefit of one party to educate the other about the 'real' situation, it is frequently more valuable to keep him wrong or make him wronger. It pays to exaggerate how much 'the law' favors you, how much harm you can do to the other party (via the law or without its help), how intransigent you always are (that is, how much spite is worth to you, and how very much t you are always willing to spend). As in any case where you can sell fantasy (which has no cost-of-goods-sold entry) in place of less favorable fact, it pays to lie – at least in the short run. This applies between businessmen, but much more when one of the parties, a consumer, has less experience with what the truth is likely to be. Thus the party being educated is likely to discount the value of the educator's message if he is simultaneously the opponent in the transaction.

But more important, insofar as there is 'communication' in merchant-consumer coercive collection, it resembles two chutes separated in space and time. A message triggers a reply. A reply, or a failure to reply, triggers another message, or another more coercive move. It is a game, and that's the trouble, for it is not a conversation or a deal. The institutional arrangements – courts, lawyers, and sheriffs, credit reports and collection agencies – are such that assertion, denial, threat and counterthreat are fostered, but conversation and negotiation, both of which demand continuous interaction, are not. This is exacerbated when one of the parties is bureaucratized, with fine differentiation of function within the bureaucracy, or when collection is contracted out. It is, so to speak, exacerbatissimus when one of the parties is a computer with, to say the least, strong constraints upon its creative problem-solving powers.

The point is that getting to $L–L_1$, and finding a sensible point on it demands learning particular reality and shaping to it a particular response. But modern mass collecting is presently no more adapted to bargaining than is the modern mass selling and lending which gives rise to the bulk of coercive collections. Assuming that such post-default individualized collection might better achieve individual-case fairness and efficiency, the question is whether an innovative system can be devised which will foster it without an undue increase in costs. It is no accident that much current collection practice is handled in a relatively rigid, stylized and automatic manner, based on stereotypes and game-like statistical strategies. Just as there are economies in mass production and mass distribution, there are at least apparent economies in mass collection. Customized, individualized communication costs money. There does come a point where the additional costs of having personalized transactions may be too great; a little injustice may be a social good. The real question is still whether changes in current practice can be designed which will simultaneously increase fairness and efficiency.

The problem of improving the flow of trustworthy and usable information in this market seems to me to be essentially one of legal institutions rather than of legal rules. There are, of course, some manipulations of the substantive law which would conduce toward more efficient post-default bargaining, but in the main even those changes are of secondary importance. Of greater moment is so reshaping the institutional framework as to get for the merchant-consumer collection imbroglio some of the apparent advantages of the current merchant-merchant system.

One way to bring this about would have the government supply, in addition to the umpired killing ground of the current judicial-coercive system, an impartial source of particularized reality and a conversation pit. There would be two key elements in this new mechanism. First, every effort would be made to assure that the parties be forced actually to confront each other to discuss their dispute before recourse to more coercive collection practices could be had. I would interdict the two chutes, at least as a sole communication medium. Notices would be sent in such a form and manner as to have a fighting chance at reaching the addressee. Meetings would be so scheduled as to maximize the chance that the parties could, without undue inconvenience, actually attend. Naturally the parties could attend by agent, but only by ones authorized to act bindingly on their behalf.

Second, an impartial 'referee' would be injected into the negotiations to assist the disputants. The referee's role would be to supply for this system much of the more trustable information that makes the merchant-merchant collection system feasible. One of his primary jobs, for instance, would be to make known to the parties what the legal situation is. He would in effect be charged with delivering to the debtor the collection-law equivalent of a *Miranda* warning, telling him he has no duty to settle, that if he doesn't have a lawyer he can get one, that he has certain possible defenses like breach of warranty and fraud (describing them briefly), and that the creditor cannot do anything to him prior to judgment. The referee, however, would also be charged with communicating to the debtor that if he does not have any valid defense, the creditor has at his disposal various legal devices which can have nasty consequences beyond the amount of the debt involved. And then, having communicated the applicable legal reality, the referee would attempt tactfully to act as midwife to the birth of a sensible plan of action for both parties.

Carrying out the referee's job with fairness and competence may be beyond the powers of mankind. The critical danger is that the referee would either fall into the trap of trying to settle everything, no matter how outrageous the creditor or debtor conduct, or decide that absolute 'justice' demanded the exercise of all possible 'rights' to the full. These difficulties are not to be lightly dismissed. After all, this is hardly the first time that a mediation role has been suggested as an innovative grafting onto a conflict model, and the results in other contexts are, to say the least, ambiguous.

Moreover, it is almost in bad taste to describe the waste-making propensities of transaction costs in esurient detail and then suggest, as a possible cure, an additional layer of transactions. The only justification for such a bizarre course is the hope that its costs will be more modest than it might appear, and in any event will be more than compensated for by the way it avoids other costs and losses. A compromise payment plan, if carried out, would transform the payment procedure back to the voluntary mode from the coercive mode. Assuming that the payment plan were acceptable and feasible, the risk component of t_c would decrease dramatically. Moreover, to the extent that the systemic spite of the collection process were not at work destroying value, the likelihood of actual payment would be enhanced. One could also avoid both the bad will of intransigence and the costs of 'contracting-out' collection, and the process would tend to decrease the parties' value for spite. Most important, paying for accurate particularized information would lessen the chance of an unnecessary coercion game being played solely because of the parties' ignorance of the realities of the situation. It is even possible that the gross costs of collection would decrease, that the costs and losses not only to the C-D 'team' but even to CS as a group, even to merchant CS as a group, are greater under the current system than they would be if more precise information were 'bought.'

Much more detailed shaping and planning of an actual system, and perhaps even some operational testing, would be necessary before one could finally assess whether any real benefits inhere in this proposal, and if so, whether its cost can be economically justified. It is at least feasible that important cost-justified gains do exist. It may, of course, turn out that the nastiness and inefficiency of the current system is not remediable in this way. But they are certainly there, and it would be better if somehow they could be made to go away.

[Professor Leff's article has provoked spirited debate in many academic circles. A collection of four specific responses to Leff's analysis can be found in 'Symposium: 1971 A.A.L.S. Bankruptcy Round Table Papers' (1972), 33 *Univ. of Pitt. L. Rev.* 667.]

QUESTIONS
1 In Leff's model of collection in Eden – the cooperative mode – transaction costs are minimal. What consequences would follow if the only mode of collection permitted by the legal system were the cooperative mode, wherein all forms of collection by coercive means were prohibited? Is there anything objectionable in the hypothesis that the creditor would simply estimate the average pattern of default in payments and price his credit accordingly?
2 Leff argues that coercive collection is a two-party minus-sum game in which the parties can both gain by refusing to play altogether and by agreeing instead on a settlement somewhere between the total value of the 'wealth' transferred from the creditor to the debtor and the total value of the 'wealth' minus the sum of the creditor's and the debtor's transaction costs. Why then do creditors ever sue or debtors ever allow themselves to be sued?
3 If information about a person's reputation were perfect, would it follow, as Leff suggests, that there would be no such thing as a collection problem?

4 If the present system of coercive collection is as wasteful as Leff claims why have not creditors, as good profit maximizers, adopted a more discriminating, individualized collection approach?

5 Given the apparently high costs of debt collection in the current coercive system, can transaction costs be reduced within the context of a coercive system – as Leff suggests – or is a completely different model required? How do you evaluate the usefulness of Leff's mandatory information exchange interposed between delinquency and formal enforcement, in contrast to alternative approaches advanced by people like Caplovitz and Ison (see below) which would simply curtail creditor's remedies? Would it be useful to strengthen Leff's proposals by requiring the creditor to apply to a referee for approval of the method to be used to execute his judgment, in order to remove the choice from the creditor of what steps may be taken to collect his debt?

4 SMALL CLAIMS COURT AS A MECHANISM OF COLLECTION

T. Ison, 'Small Claims' (1972), 35 *Mod. L. Rev.* 18.

SHOULD SMALL CLAIMS EXIST?

The need to hold down cost makes it extremely difficult to devise a just and efficient system for handling small claims. It is pertinent, therefore, to consider the nature of small claims to determine whether they should exist at all, and if so, what volume and types of claims must be processed. This is vital because it seems extremely unlikely that a just system will ever be developed for small claims unless the volume can be reduced to a more manageable size.

As mentioned above, the largest category of small claims brought in the courts is debt claims arising out of retail transactions. A strong argument can be made that these claims should be abolished.

The arguments for the suggestion are:

(1) What the courts are doing is contrary to policies pursued by other branches of government. It is surely desirable to prevent abuses in marketing, particularly fraud, high pressure techniques, and the deliberate sale of defective goods. By enforcing the claims of credit grantors without inquiry into their legitimacy, the courts are promoting the marketing of goods on credit by fraudulent and predatory practices. It is extremely difficult to prevent these abuses by direct controls and the policing of selling behaviour. But we can at least make them unprofitable by ensuring that claims resulting from credit sales by such tactics are not enforced by the courts. If it is impossible or uneconomic to devise a system of adjudication case by case, the alternative is to aim at what might be called a just balance of power overall between sellers and buyers. In other words, the aim should be a system in which creditors' remedies are strong enough to make credit marketing feasible, but not strong enough to make it profitable to embark on fraudulent schemes, high pressure techniques, or the deliberate sale of defective goods. It is suggested that this balance of power could be achieved if retailers' claims for debt are abolished, leaving repossession and an adverse credit report as the sanctions against non-payment. Moreover, making the seller more dependent on the security in the goods would reduce the incentive to sell shoddy or defective goods.

(2) There is obviously a direct correlation between the strength of creditors' remedies and the perimeters of consumer credit. For some years now we have had one branch of government (*i.e.*

the courts) expanding the perimeters of consumer credit by the systematic enforcement of debt claims while executive departments of government have been seeking to control inflation. To reduce creditors' remedies would surely be more effective as an anti-inflationary measure than the more direct controls that have been used, such as the Hire-Purchase Control Orders. With the abolition of debt claims, sellers could be expected to limit consumer credit by excluding the poorer risks, *i.e.*, those who could not enhance the seller's security in the goods by paying a substantial deposit.

(3) There is a wide variety of ways in which a seller may default on a contract, and it can be very difficult for a buyer to protect himself in advance. For a seller, on the other hand, there is generally only one grievance that he can suffer, *i.e.* not being paid. This is a risk against which he can protect himself in several ways without having to rely on court proceedings. Moreover it is not essential to the well-being of a retailer that he should be guaranteed the enforcement of all his claims. It is enough that he can achieve a satisfactory outcome in the vast majority of his transactions. A seller does not have it exclusively within his power to determine the result of each transaction, but through adjustments in his credit policy he does have it within his power to determine over time what his bad debt ratio is going to be.

(4) The extension of credit would be done with greater care. Credit by retailers would be limited to families that can repay with ease, and there would be no incentive to push credit on those who can only be made to repay by the threat of wage garnishment. Sellers would be more cautious about checking credit reports, and about security in the goods. Hence the social problems of consumer insolvency would be mitigated.

(5) For marginal credit risks, there would be a reduction of sales financing and some diversion to loan financing. The plan would permit debt claims to continue for cash loans, as long as the loans are not arranged by the seller. This diversion to loan financing would have two advantages. First, the customer would be under no illusion about the cost of credit. Secondly, going to another place to arrange the loan would make a brief period available for contemplation during which the buyer would be released from the hypnotic influence of the sales pitch. To allow buyers a chance to think before they buy, and to think in the absence of the salesman, would be a valuable step in the prevention of fraud and high pressure tactics.

(6) If it is too difficult or too expensive to develop a system that would give full effect to buyers' rights, we ought not to be enforcing sellers' claims regardless of their merits. In other words, if we are unwilling or unable to develop a proper system of adjudication for consumer cases, we ought not to be giving judgment at all. (This argument for the proposal would, of course, vanish if a just procedure for small claims could be found. but the failure to abolish debt claims in retail transactions would make it, in my view, unlikely that a just procedure would be implemented. The volume would be too large. Moreover the other arguments for abolishing debt claims in retail transactions would still be there.)

(7) The social problems of wage garnishment would be avoided.

(8) By making such a substantial cut in the volume of small claims to be processed, the remainder would be reduced to a more manageable size.

There is, of course, scope for refinement in defining the category of claims for which the action at law would be abolished. The essence of the proposal is that debt claims should be abolished for the price of goods sold at retail. The abolition would extend to cash loans when made for a specific purchase or by arrangement with the retailer or in the presence of the retailer, and to claims by credit card companies, at least in so far as they arise out of sales transactions. But claims for the repayment of ordinary cash loans would survive, and so too would claims for payment for services.

Ten years ago, the suggestion might have seemed untenable. No doubt it would have been said that to abolish debt claims would stifle consumer credit. But much has changed since then. In particular, the development of credit reporting has given an additional sanction to credit grantors, and the risk of an adverse credit report may now be as valuable for collection purposes as the threat of a judgment. If so, to abolish debt claims would simply be restoring the strength of creditors' remedies, and their influence on the perimeters of consumer credit, to the same position as a few years ago. That the extension of credit has gone byond healthy grounds is evident from the increasing incidence of consumer insolvency. Moreover the development of teenage credit, and the continuation of credit marketing in Saskatchewan (where debt claims on many consumer credit transactions have been abolished) suggest that the retraction of consumer credit that would result from the abolition of debt claims would not be more than marginal. The hope is that the margin would be a fairly wide one, and that it would include specifically the deceptive sales and defective goods cases.

Of course retailers would suffer occasional losses from malevolent buyers who refused to pay (indeed they do now). But it is probably safe to assume that the total cost to society of establishing a just system of adjudication for retail debt claims would be far greater than the cost of not allowing such claims to be brought.

Another major category of small claims, perhaps the second largest, is those for personal injury and property damage arising out of accidents. I have argued elsewhere that these claims should be abolished.

But whatever reforms are undertaken to reduce the volume or range of small claims, a residual category must remain. This may include, for example, disputes over a seller's right to repossession, claims by a cash buyer for fraud or defective goods, claims by lenders for the repayment of cash debts, claims by a landlord for damage to property, etc. For this category at least, substantial procedural reform is needed.

QUESTION In economic terms, how would creditors be likely to react to Ison's proposals? Would this reaction be in the consumer's interest (see Cayne and Trebilcock below)?

5 MARKET CONSIDERATIONS

a / David Cayne and M.J. Trebilcock, 'Market Considerations in the Formulation of Consumer Protection Policy' (1973), 23 *U. of T. L.J.* 396.

RESTRICTIONS ON CREDITORS' REMEDIES

Many commentators and policy makers concerned with the protection of low-income consumers also endorse the limitation of creditors' remedies. In particular, they advocate the abolition of deficiency judgments after repossession, and contend that repossession itself should be subject to judicial control, that both salary and property seizures be abolished or that exemptions from seizure be substantially raised and that credit-blacklisting be strictly controlled.

Clearly, the exercise by a creditor of his remedies against a debtor for default are some of the most visible and distressing symptoms of over-commitment and it is natural enough, as a first instinct, to respond to these symptoms by advocating their removal. But, as in many other contexts, the symptoms of a problem are not its cause and to remove the symptoms does not eliminate the cause but more often than not merely gives rise to new symptoms. Once again, policy makers must accept the immutable economic imperative that lenders will only extend credit if they can do so on a profitable basis; and it is equally axiomatic that restrictions on remedies will give rise to correspondingly higher interest rates to the extent that they increase bad-debt write-offs. As a result, a certain number of borrowers, unable to absorb the interest rate exacted, will be excluded from the market. More significantly, degenerative consequences will result where interest ceilings prevent the lender from charging rates consistent with restrictions legislatively imposed. In these circumstances, high-risk consumers whom these lenders would otherwise have served must withdraw from the market place (which, admittedly, some proponents explicitly adopt as their objective), or, alternatively, enter the illegal money market where informal day and night harassment, or even the baseball bat, replace the writ of seizure.

Clearly, the extent to which such legislation initiates exclusionary or degenerative processes will depend upon both the severity of the restrictions imposed and the elasticity or inelasticity of the demand for credit. No one restriction could in itself produce substantially adverse effects and hence one commentator would seem to have taken a rather extreme view in questioning whether '... our economy [would] survive' the abolition of deficiency judgments. Pursuing our assumption of workable competition, market imperfections will always temper the exclusionary consequences of such rules. For example, creditors might respond to the elimination or restriction of deficiency claims and garnishments by relying more heavily on remedies not contemplated by the legislation. Thus, in Pennsylvania, the attachment of a debtor's home became commonplace after that jurisdiction prohibited garnishments. Other potential responses might include greater reliance upon threats of execution against a debtor's personal property as a form of harassment, third-party guarantees, and credit black-listing.

The legislator would be unwise, however, to impose a series of restrictions without regard to their economic effects, for each new limitation imposes additional expenses upon the lender. In the first place, it would seem a fair generalization that the alternate remedies which creditors might invoke are less efficient, and hence more expensive, than the remedies legislatively curtailed. This common cost influence will require all competing lenders to increase the cost of credit in order to compensate for their use of less efficient collection techniques. Secondly, and more significantly, the continuous erosion of remedies will ultimately divest the creditor of any alternate remedies. In these circumstances, he will be compelled to respond with a substantial increase in interest rates giving rise to serious exclusionary or degenerative consequences, depending, as we have seen, upon both demand elasticity and prevailing interest ceilings ...

Conclusion

The central contention which emerges from this analysis is that consumer protection rules should, in the absence of the compelling social reasons to which we have earlier referred, be limited to remedying the imbalance in bargaining power which frequently characterizes consumer transactions. Such imbalances may be the result of either structural inadequacies in the relevant market or serious informational deficiencies. As we have already seen, these potential causes are to some extent interdependent because, as a general rule, effective competition will ensure effective disclosure. Hence the policy maker might rationally attempt to alleviate consumer difficulties by supporting programs which will make imperfect markets work more efficiently. In this context, it would be appropriate to rely upon anti-trust legislation, tariff reductions, controls upon excessive advertising which gives rise to important entry barriers, rules prohibiting misleading advertising and sales practices, full disclosure requirements, better access to the legal system to enforce existing rights, and consumer education programs.

For a variety of reasons, however, certain markets cannot be rendered truly competitive; scale economies, for example, may be compatible with only one or two market participants. In these circumstances rules which impose restrictions upon the scope or consequences of contractual rights may be rationally relied upon to place excess profits, the correlative of monopoly or oligopoly, into consumer hands. Conversely, legislative attempts to initiate redistribution processes in structurally sound markets where, *ex hypothesi*, there are no excess profits to redistribute, will give rise to exclusionary or degenerative consequences. They will 'protect' the consumer by eliminating him from the legal market place; they will not protect him by remedying an imbalance in bargaining power. We do not object to legislatively imposed restrictions upon consumer freedom per se, and it is for this reason that we have incorporated a caveat into our normative definition of consumer protection rules. The merits of a rule designed to meet the 'compelling social reasons' to which the definition refers must, however, be evaluated in relation to the number of persons who would be eliminated from the market place, and hence the policy maker must engage in a delicate balancing of competing policy considerations. For example, should automobile manufacturers be required to double the existing braking capacity of cars if the consequential costs preclude 50,000 consumers from purchasing a new car? Is it appropriate to increase exemptions from seizure if a substantial number of low-income debtors will thereby be denied access to the legal credit market? Although no hard and fast lines can be drawn, questions such as these, examined within a framework such as that proposed, must be answered when the merits of contemplated legislation are being assessed.

Hence the policy maker must evaluate the prevailing conditions in the particular markets to which a consumer protection rule would apply, if enacted, for in this way only can the effects of that rule be measured. It is true that some of the most sophisticated analysts contend that market processes are increasingly inoperative. It is also true that Canadian markets, being significantly smaller than their American counterparts, are characterized by higher levels of concentration. Notwithstanding the correspondingly greater need for redistributive rules in the Canadian context, the extent to which market processes have been undermined is still a matter of considerable debate; furthermore, there is no doubt that intense competition still prevails within many sectors of the economy, and hence specific structural conditions retain an overriding relevance for the formulation of consumer protection policies. Rules producing redistributive effects in certain markets might give rise to exclusionary or degenerative consequences in others where competition prevails, and hence the policy maker will not make substantial gains by superimposing a rule upon a variety of different markets without regard to the economic environment of each. This, of course, emphasizes the difficulty of formulating effective general consumer protection rules.

It is in this context that the central weakness in the thinking of many contemporary commentators emerges: some merely give their unqualified support to any legislation which purports to protect the consumer without so much as a passing reference to its economic effects, while others tend to infer structural deficiencies whenever consumer difficulties of any nature occur in the market place. There appears to be an optimistic but naive assumption that legislation designed to redistribute resources to the consumer will in some undefined manner achieve its purpose irrespective of market conditions. As we have seen, this predisposition is particularly manifest in relation to the problems which beset the low-income consumer.

The unyielding nature of the constraints imposed on policy-making by market considerations are graphically dramatized by the progressive shifts in thinking of Professor Caplovitz, as an acceptance of the stark economic realities emphasized in this article has been forced upon him. In the concluding chapter of his book [*The Poor Pay More*] he advances a number of suggestions for restricting the activities of ghetto merchants. These, and other similar proposals, have been evaluated in the latter part of our analysis. Curiously, in a 'throw-away' paragraph at the end of this chapter, Caplovitz rather laconically acknowledges some apprehensions about his proposals:

It is possible, however, that even if such laws were feasible, they would not fully accomplish their intended objectives. Instead of forcing poor risks to curtail their consumption because the merchants would no longer extend them credit, such laws might only stimulate deviant patterns worse than those now in effect. For example, as their credit in local stores dried up, more families would probably turn to the peddlars, who depend almost entirely upon personal, rather than legal, controls. Enforcing laws pertaining to peddlars is not an easy matter, for these men are highly mobile and not readily apprehended. Also, some families might turn to loan sharks for the money that would enable them to buy for cash. Obviously, there is no simple solution to the ills of the low-income marketing system. But this should not deter efforts to reduce the abuses of the system through legislation.

One would have thought that if legislation may possibly produce deviant patterns as drastically unintended as this, one should not enact the legislation just for the sake of having assumed to have done something about the problem.

Professor Caplovitz seems to have had even more serious second thoughts by the time he came to write the preface to the 1967 edition of his book:

A new printing of a book provides the author with the opportunity to evaluate his own work and to share whatever second thoughts he has with the reader. Needless to say, second thoughts have been prompted by greater experience with the subject matter and the wisdom of hindsight. The first of these has to do with the neighbourhood credit merchant who is cast pretty much as the villain in this book. I think it is a mistake to see the credit merchant only as a notorious exploiter of the poor. A more thorough analysis than I undertook in this book would have to examine the economic constraints that operate on these men. In some respects the local merchants charge more for the simple reason that it costs them more to operate ...

Later in 1967, second thoughts seemed to have crystallized further. That year, before a congressional committee, Caplovitz *opposed* the enactment of a consumer bill abolishing wage garnishments.

... I am not yet convinced that doing away with garnishment is either feasible at this time or would have the desired effects even if it were possible to pass such a law.

For example, garnishment is not permitted in Pennsylvania and yet credit merchants are thriving in that state and consumer fraud is just as prevalent there as elsewhere. The creditors in Pennsylvania do not hesitate to attach both personal and real property and sheriff's sales of furniture and even homes are quite common. To lose one's home because of a consumer debt is certainly as harsh a consequence as losing one's job ...

Caplovitz' intellectual agonizing zig-zagged again in 1970 when in testimony before the National Commission on Consumer Finance he advocated the complete abolition of all creditor's remedies to be accompanied by a free market approach to the granting of credit with no restrictions on the right of entry into the business of credit granting and no restrictions on interest rates, which would be left to be determined by the market mechanism. With poor risks, said Caplovitz, 'an interest rate of say 100 per cent ... does not strike me as particularly shocking.' The sole sanction for non-payment under this system would be an adverse credit rating. This proposal is an intriguing combination of drastic interference with existing creditors' rights and acceptance of a free market in credit. Whether a credit-rating system could ever be made comprehensive enough to cover all creditors and debtors, whether debtors could be adequately protected against inaccurate credit ratings, the relative efficiency of this sanction compared to existing sanctions, which factor may reflect itself in the cost of granting credit, the consequences of receiving an adverse credit rating (exclusionary or degenerative), are all considerations that would need to be evaluated in order to determine the total social and economic impact of this proposal.

However, in the final paragraph of his book, Caplovitz comes close to stating the real truth of the matter:

In the final analysis, the consumer problems of low-income families cannot be divorced from other problems facing them. Until society can find ways of raising their occupational opportunities, increasing their income, and reducing the discrimination against them – in short, until poverty itself is eradicated – only limited solutions to their problems as consumers can be found.

A principal thesis of this article is that, outside the general social and economic policies elaborated by Caplovitz in this paragraph, few solutions, limited or otherwise, can be found to the consumer problems of the poor by ad hoc restrictions on the flow of market forces. The consumer problems of the poor are an inherent consequence of paucity of resources and can only be remedied by augmenting those resources, that is, by making the poor not poor. They are not for the most part a result of aberrations in the market process and, beyond making it freer, cannot be cured by ad hoc interferences with it. We have attempted to show that to try to solve the problems of the poor, and indeed any class of consumer, in this way in fact usually makes them worse. We have too often in the past yielded to the temptation to look for scapegoats to whom to attribute the unpleasant consequences of poverty. The somewhat unromantic and visible figures of the ghetto merchant, slum landlord, peddlar, and loan shark have proved easy, although irrelevant, targets. Ease of formulation and painlessness of execution (especially for the proponents) should not be the criteria by which solutions to these problems are selected. In framing relevant responses to the costs exacted by poverty in the market place, it is surely time that the myth that the ghetto merchant and his confrères are the major causes of the problems, and that we can escape being part of their solution, was finally buried.

QUESTION Is this analysis of the economics of the debt collection process correct? In the light of your answer, what should be the broad policy objectives of legislation regulating the process?

b / David Caplovitz, *Consumers in Trouble*, (1974), pp 301–6.

ALTERNATIVE SYSTEMS OF CONSUMER CREDIT

Reforming the present system of consumer credit is not the only solution to the problems posed in this book. Entirely different systems, if enacted, might prove to be even more just than reforms of the old system. As background for considering such alternative systems, it is necessary to note the peculiarities that now surround the money market in our free enterprise economy. Although merchants of automobiles, TV sets, clothing, food, and a thousand other products and services are expected to respond to the laws of supply and demand and compete with other companies in their industry for their share of the market, the institutions that symbolize the essence of capitalism, the financial institutions (whether they be banks, small loan companies, finance companies, or merchants extending credit) are not required to live by these principles of free enterprise. On the contrary, laws protect lending institutions from competition and permit even inefficient lenders to remain in business. These laws state who may enter the business of lending money and the amount that they can charge for their product. We are accustomed to thinking that price fixing in a capitalistic society is an extreme measure that is reasonable only in times of total mobilization for a war effort, as in World War II. But such government regulation is the norm of the money market. Ceilings are imposed on interest rates for loans and for sales made on the installment plan as part of an old tradition of usury laws. Moreover, not everyone with money to lend is allowed to enter this business. Government has established criteria of fitness and need that sharply curtail entry into the lending business. If a community has a lending institution, then another potentially rival lender may be denied the right to set up business in that community. These constraints stem from well-intentioned efforts to protect the public interest against bank failures and usury, but they have had the consequence of creating a banking and lending industry that has many of the attributes of public utilities rather than an industry responding to the dynamics of free enterprise.

The Free Market Model

The most critical features of the UCCC [Uniform Consumer Credit Code] are those designed to make the lending industry conform to the principles of the free market economy.

The UCCC would do this in two ways. First, it proposes a sharp increase in the legal ceilings on consumer loans, including goods bought on time. Second, the UCCC advocates free entry to the business of selling money. Thus, if a department store wants to make loans as well as sell merchandise, it would be able to do so, and no restrictions would be placed on the number of lenders who could be located in a given territory. Through these devices, the drafters of the UCCC envision a system in which the price of loans will be regulated by the free market. By raising the ceilings and allowing all to enter the industry, the drafters assume that competition alone will keep interest rates at a reasonable level and that efficient lenders will drive inefficient (that is, more costly lenders) out of business. Many consumer advocates argue that raising interest ceilings means only that the ceiling will become the floor, as all lenders will charge the highest possible rate and will not compete with each other in terms of rate. There is little evidence to support either position. The consumer advocates note that loans have always been made at the ceiling, no matter what the ceiling has been. The advocates of the free market model counter by pointing out that the ceilings have always been too low and, besides, the constraints on free entry restricted competition.

Unfortunately, the drafters of the UCCC who wish to regulate the money market by the dynamics of free competition nonetheless hedge their position by relying on the state ultimately to regulate the system by sanctioning breaches of contract through the devices of repossession, deficiency judgments, garnishment, and executions against real and personal property. What would happen if the credit industry gave up these harsh remedies, which amount to the big stick method of control, and instead shifted to the 'carrot' of rewarding prompt payers with low rates, 'punishing' poor risks with high rates, and ultimately controlling the system by banishing the deadbeats from the credit market? What is being suggested is a model in which would-be debtors are charged interest according to the risk they represent, and that the ultimate weapon at the disposal of the creditor would be to prevent debtors with a history of defaults from again becoming borrowers. This latter element in the model places a great burden on the systems of information exchange that the credit industry has developed – credit bureaus. Were creditors forced to relinquish their clubs, they may well spend more time investigating the would-be debtor and exercising greater caution in their extension of credit. Moreover, by charging different rates of interest on the basis of the debtor's past performance, creditors would be using the carrot to motivate prompt payments by their debtors. This might be illustrated by imagining a hypothetical world in which persons who reach a certain age, say, eighteen, are allowed to become debtors at a maximum rate of interest, say, 100 percent, irrespective of their income. Should these new debtors prove to be prompt and reliable payers, they would become eligible for a reduced interest rate on their next loan, say 50 percent, and so forth, until they earn the right to pay the low rate of say 6 or 7 percent. Those who perform poorly or default would be punished by having to pay higher rates of interest or by being excluded entirely from the credit game. The latter punishment should not be treated lightly. The economy of America is predicated on consumer credit, and the use of consumer credit is so pervasive that one can truly identify America in the latter third of the twentieth century as a credit society. In such a world, the individual's life chances, his ability to buy an automobile, a home, to finance his vacations, to pay for his education, to marry and start a family early rather than late, all depend on his credit rating. A person's credit rating thus emerges as a new dimension of social stratification and as a new form of what Charles Reich has called the 'new property.' To have one's credit rating drop can be a severe blow to one's happiness, and this alone might serve as sufficient control of the credit system. But to view a credit rating as 'new property' raises further difficulties. Credit bureaus would have to be regulated to ensure that their information is correct. The notion of credit rating as property conjures up the doctrine of 'due process.' The radical proposal of self-regulation and the free market model for the credit industry thus comes up against the thorny issues of 'due process' and 'invasion of privacy' (the open credit file). But these potential problems aside, there is some merit to thinking the unthinkable and forcing debate on such a radical proposal as the carrot rather than the big stick approach to consumer credit. Consumer advocates might well be unhappy with such a proposal, for they would consider it unconscionable for the poor to pay extraordinarily high rates of interest, say 100 percent. But this criticism loses much force in light of the fact that the poor already pay extraordinarily high hidden interest rates, as merchants in low-income areas circumvent the ceilings by having exorbitant markups on their goods. Bound by law not to charge more than 18 percent interest on a credit sale, the ghetto merchant does not hesitate to mark up his goods by one, two , or even three numbers, each number, in this quaint jargon of the trade, representing a 100 percent increase of the wholesale price. Given these evasions of ceilings in the form of unconscionable markups, the imposition by government of ceilings on interest is a rather ephemeral and pointless exercise. On the other hand, the credit industry is bound to object to this proposal, for it is convinced that most debtors are would-be deadbeats who would not pay unless forced to do so by the threat of the big stick. In taking this position, the credit industry strongly underestimates the basic goodwill of most debtors, the forces, for example, that led most Nebraska debtors to continue paying their creditors even when the State Supreme Court declared that they had no legal obligation to make such payments. Moreover, such a view does not take full cognizance of the importance of one's credit rating in this credit society and of the reluctance of most people to injure this 'property.'

One advantage of eliminating creditor's remedies, especially garnishment, is that it would further discourage the unscrupulous creditor, the firm that fails to carry out a credit check before extending credit because it knows that it can garnishee the debtor's wages. All too often, the last firm that piles on, and in so doing, pushes the debtor over the brink, is the first to attach his wages, with the result that the more conservative creditors who behaved more responsibly are forced to wait in line before they can exert their claim against the debtor's income.

Credit Insurance Plans

One flaw in the free market model presented above is that it tacitly assumes that debtors default only because they are unwilling to pay, that is, because they are deadbeats. But we have seen that the great majority of debtors default because they are unable to pay, and most in this position were unable to pay because they suffered sudden reversals in income due to illness or unemployment (rather than by imprudently taking on more obligations than they could manage). These victims of the vicissitudes of life who constitute the bulk of default-debtors would suffer blows to their credit rating for reasons beyond their control. To protect these debtors and their creditors, it has been suggested that insurance systems, either public or private, be established to guarantee consumer loans. It should be noted that there are now several types of private insurance that debtors are often forced to buy as part of the transaction, insurance ranging from credit life to credit health insurance. These private insurance arrangements have been heavily criticized as having exorbitant charges and multiple escape clauses that result in debtors continuing to be liable even though they purchased the policy. In this study we encountered several debtors who thought that they had bought health insurance policies in connection with their debt obligation but who found themselves being sued even though their default stemmed from illness. The advocates of private insurance have in mind a quite different system. One proposal well exemplifies the possibilities of private credit insurance. Each debtor would be issued a 'credit limit card,' which, in this world of computers, would be presented to the creditor at the time of a would-be credit transaction. The creditor would plug the card into his remote terminal and would learn instantly from the computer the debtor's credit limit and whether he has approached or overextended it. In short, the computer would instruct the creditor on the probability that the debtor would be able to repay the loan. Creditors who extend credit only to those who have not exceeded their credit limit would be insured against loss. This insurance would be paid by the creditors rather than the debtors. For example, suppose that a major department store now loses $5 million dollars a year on bad debts. It would pay for this department store to cut its losses by subscribing to the credit limit plan at a cost of say $3 million a year. This model of private insurance not only assumes a high level of computer technology, but it also assumes that creditors want to extend credit only to those who will repay them. Should such a plan be institutionalized, the unscrupulous merchant eager to extend credit regardless of the debtor's ability to pay would be driven out of business since his customers would not qualify for further credit. In this model, the merchant's only redress would be the insurance policy rather than the current mechanisms of law suits, judgments, and garnishments, and he would be eligible for the insurance claim only if he respected the debtor's credit limit. Obviously this somewhat pie-in-the-sky model also places a heavy burden on systems of information exchange about debt obligations. Like the free market model, it assumes that all creditors will feed information on their credit transactions into the local credit bureau, which may be nothing more than the local computer.

The plan of having government provide the insurance for consumer loans also involves the idea of regulating creditors and debtors. The government certainly would hesitate to extend insurance to unscrupulous creditors or debtors. Thus any insurance scheme involves some control over the credit industry as the insuring party moves to eliminate dishonest participants in the credit game. For this reason alone, insurance systems should probably be encouraged.

ALTERING THE MARKETING STRUCTURE

We have speculated about alternative systems for extending credit to consumers, systems based on a free market model for the sale of money and insurance systems to protect the lenders from unexpected hardships to the borrowers. Apart from these radical proposals, much can be done to improve the plight of debtors and remove blatant injustices in the current credit marketplace by regulating the conditions under which consumer credit transactions occur. For example ... we saw that a disproportionate number of these transactions that went awry involved door-to-door sales of expensive merchandise on credit. It is virtually impossible for these sales not to involve high-pressure tactics, deception, and exorbitant markups. For one thing, the salesman's effort, especially his readiness to enter ghetto communities, places a heavy tax on the sales price in the form of the salesman's commission. Merchants accused of unconscionable markups on such items as burglar alarm systems, watches, and deep freezers that are sold door to door at many times the wholesale price or even the retail store price defend their pricing policies by pointing out the extraordinary premium they must pay the salesmen. In addition, the salesmen in these transactions are prepared to tell falsehoods to get the customer's signature on the contract. The various constraints based on repeated sales, familiarity between debtor and seller, the creditor's concern for his reputation, and even the debtor's readiness to shop around are completely absent in these 'con-man' transactions. To call door-to-door salesmen 'con men' might seem at first a harsh indictment, but an examination of their techniques (for example, 'bait and switch,' 'referral sales,' 'free gifts,' and out-and-out misrepresentation such as telling the customer that the freezer comes free with the food plan or that the burglar alarm system is plugged into the police station when it is not) shows that these salesmen are indeed con men and that the border between the illegitimate con man and the legitimate one is extremely thin. Even if the carrot model of consumer credit cannot be instituted, a great deal can be done to reform the present system by simply abolishing door-to-door sales of expensive merchandise on credit. In view of the abuses associated with this method of selling, why cannot Congress further the public good by making it illegal to sell outside the merchant's place of business any item on credit that costs, say, $50 or more? (The $50 cutting point would probably eliminate all these sales, since the salesman would not be able to realize a commission that would make the transaction worthwhile.)

Eliminating door-to-door sales is perhaps the most dramatic example of regulating the transaction. Others include prohibiting small loan companies from making loans outside their places of business, one of several criteria for eliminating dealer-arranged loans, or regulations that would eliminate the practice of referral sales and bait-and-switch selling practices. No doubt other controls over the initial transaction might prove fruitful. The key point is that an alternative to reforming the system at the end point when the transaction has broken down and the creditor invokes harsh collection practices is to regulate it at the outset so that shady transactions conducive to default do not occur.

6 CHANGING THE RULES OF THE GAME

Trebilcock and Shulman, 'The Pathology of Credit Breakdown' (1976), 22 *McGill L.J.* 415, at 449–50, 451–7 (footnotes omitted)

POSSIBLE POLICY DIRECTIONS

1 Irrelevant prescriptions
It is perhaps useful at the outset to dispose of certain ill-conceived policy solutions sometimes proposed for treating problems of over-commitment.

a Censoring credit advertising: The Quebec Minister of Financial Institutions, in a speech to an Interprovincial Conference on Consumer Affairs in Banff, May 15, 1974, announced that he was considering legislation which would prevent cash credit grantors (*e.g.,* banks and finance companies) from advertising the purposes for which they were prepared to extend credit. The object of this exercise would apparently be to stop banks and finance companies from 'over-selling' credit through the medium of glossy travel or automobile advertisements. Vendor credit grantors would also be prevented from emphasizing the availability of credit in advertisements for their merchandise.

It will be obvious from our studies that very few debtors become involved in serious problems of overcommitment because they are seduced by credit advertising into buying red Cadillac convertibles or spending expensive weekends in the Bahamas. Secondly, even if this were so, it is difficult to see how this would justify a discriminatory attack on credit grantors' advertising. If the premise underlying these proposals is correct, presumably all advertising encourages over-buying. Placing the issue against this broader setting, the Galbraithian view of advertising is not so well settled as to justify legislation.

The one proposal in this area that may be deserving of serious consideration would require all lender and vendor credit grantors in all advertisements which refer to the availability of credit to include the average effective annual interest rate charged to their customers. In this way, the pleasures and pains of utilizing credit would be more obvious than at present.

b Interest rate ceilings: The practice of prescribing maximum interest rates chargeable on loans is of respectable antiquity and is reflected in Canada principally in the federal *Small Loans Act*, which regulates the level of interest charges on loans up to $1,500.

As one of the authors, with Professor David Cayne, has elsewhere pointed out, depending on market conditions, at best rate ceilings set above or at the market rate will be irrelevant. At worst, vendor credit ceilings set below market rates will be unenforceable; excess credit charges can be buried in the cash price. Similarly lender credit ceilings will exclude certain risks from the market who, depending on the elasticity of their demand for credit, may be forced into the illegal money market. Interest rate ceilings improve credit terms for virtually no one and many borrowers are actually prejudiced.

The furthest that legislation can reasonably go is to proscribe 'unconscionable' credit transactions, where interest charges bear no relation to the risk involved, as has been done in article 1040(c) of the Quebec Civil Code and provincial Unconscionable Transaction Relief Acts. Perhaps this legislation could incorporate rebuttable statutory presumptions, as exemplified in the U.K. *Money Lenders Act*, providing that rates in excess of stipulated rates on loans of certain sizes are presumed to be unconscionable unless the contrary is proved. Legislation attempting to stipulate firm ceilings will always be too crude and arbitrary to reflect the myriad of risks dealt with in the credit market.

c Minimum deposit requirements: The proponents of minimum deposit requirements argue that the provision of the required deposit is some evidence of credit-worthiness, and provides an inducement to the consumer to protect his equity in the goods by completing the agreement.

We see some force in the second argument but little in the first. Whether a person is credit-worthy depends, obviously enough, on his present and future income, his present and future commitments and various contingencies such as overtime and sickness. The provision of a deposit says nothing about these factors and the requirement of a deposit may well preclude consideration of them.

Minimum deposit requirements have the disadvantage of being virtually unenforceable. By 'jacking-up' trade-in allowances, dealers can readily make it appear that the required deposit has been provided and, except in extreme cases, this practice is difficult to police and prosecute.

d A full-scale curtailment of creditors' remedies: Extreme critics of current credit practices have advocated everything from abolition of wage garnishment to abolition of all formal creditors' collection remedies.

We believe that this approach, while no doubt well-intentioned, is seriously misconceived and naive in its disregard of the economic imperatives operating in the market-place.

2 Proposals for consideration

a The income problem: Unquestionably, for a very large percentage of debtors surveyed in our study, a deficiency of income is the major reason for over-commitment, and only policy responses that address this issue are likely to have any effect. Rational use of consumer credit is generally predicated on fairly rapidly rising income expectations where present needs can be financed out of future income. But for debtors without those expectations, the use of credit becomes a form of income supplement which must ultimately erode buying power and create financial distress.

To discourage the use of credit as a subsistence income supplement requires policies that promote stable economic growth and employment conditions, that provide adequate educational and employment opportunities for all social and economic classes and, ultimately, a guaranteed annual income. Regulation of the debtor-creditor relationship will not touch the heart of the problem of overcommitment: insufficient income.

The remaining suggestions are no more than ancillary to this central proposition.

b Improving the exchange of information between debtor and creditor: Professor Arthur Allen Leff in an important and impressive economic analysis of the formal debt collection process traces the transaction costs incurred by both creditor and debtor. He argues that if each party could be made aware of the costs involved in continuing the formal collection process, invariably, the parties would settle the claim as early as possible to avoid mounting costs. Merchant to merchant debt relations proceed on this basis but rarely merchant-consumer relations. Leff recommends the presence of an impartial referee to assist negotiations between the disputants by supplying trustworthy 'information that makes the [generally cooperative] merchant-merchant collection system feasible'. The referee would inform the debtor of the prospective transaction costs he faces if he allows the collection process to proceed further; he would also inform the creditor of the debtor's true circumstances to avoid needless transaction costs on the part of the creditor in collecting against a debtor with limited or no present ability to pay the full claim.

The intent of this proposal is to induce more cooperative accords on debt claims and avoid the waste built into the present formal collection system. Leff's proposal has much merit and essentially reflects the thinking underlying the creation of the Debtors' Assistance Board in Alberta, the Credit Referee's Office in British Columbia, and the Small Claims Court Referee's

Office in Toronto. These offices, in addition to offering budget counselling services, will attempt to make *pro rate* arrangements with a debtor's creditors, recommend consolidation and instalment orders to the Court where a debtor faces several judgments, recommend variations of garnishment exemptions to the court, process Part x Orderly Payment of Debt applications (in Alberta and British Columbia) and if necessary, counsel personal bankruptcy.

It is clear, for a start, from our Montreal study that these schemes need to be vigorously advertised if the appalling ignorance on the part of debtors in distress is to be overcome. This may require sending out a statutory brochure detailing the agency's services with every enforcement process. In order to interdict the process, it should be possible for a debtor simply to fill in a part of the process documents invoking the agency's assistance and suspending execution pending recommendations to the court by the agency.

This would give the neutral referee more leverage than envisaged in Leff's proposal, which ignores the individual creditor's point of view. It will rarely, if ever, be worth his while to engage in voluntary collective decision-making with other creditors when the possibility is still open of his obtaining a larger payment at the expense of existing creditors or by inducing the debtor to borrow from a new creditor to liquidate the first creditor's debt. Each of the creditors individually will try to avoid a collective arrangement (a type of 'hold-out' problem, in economic terms).

However, despite the considerable merits of proposals like Leff's that would interdict the formal collection process at a relatively early stage and force negotiations between the parties through a neutral intermediary, we believe that this, in terms of policy priorities, is looking at the wrong end of the stick.

Leff states earlier in his article that '[i]f information about a person's reputation were perfect, there would be no such thing as a collection problem. The sole 'collection' practice would be [the] precise pricing of the initial transaction. The end-point of every individual credit transaction being identical with the price, no longer would any cheerfully quick repayer subsidize the slow, slovenly or evasive borrower'. He then, in a few lines in a long article, dismisses this as 'impossible even in theory' and probably objectionable on non-economic grounds such as loss of privacy.

While we accept that complete information is an unattainable ideal, we argue that the present structures could be changed to create stronger incentives for creditors to obtain reliable information and to discourage consumers from supplying misinformation. It is important to clarify the respective positions of creditor and debtor at the time when the credit is granted, not after the credit relationship has broken down and the options are much less inviting.

Reliable information alone will not solve the collection problem. Often collection problems arise because contingencies unforeseen, and sometimes unforeseeable, materialize after credit has been granted. To the extent that these possibilities have not been accurately reflected in the cost of the transaction, the creditor still faces a collection problem if he is to avoid forcing other clients to subsidize credit defaulters.

Present priority rules, as reflected in provincial Creditors Relief Acts, the Lacombe Law and federal Bankruptcy legislation, which permit all unsecured creditors, irrespective of the time at which they granted credit, to share *pro rata* on a distribution, in our view, seriously subvert the objective of improving the exchange of information at the time credit is granted. These rules enable later creditors to unilaterally and retrospectively falsify the information on which an earlier creditor granted credit by subsequently creating competing debt claims. The incentive to search out the best available information on the credit risk to whom a creditor is considering extending credit is reduced, as is the incentive of a later creditor to make a similar search. Neither creditor will have priority.

In recognition of this problem, several commentators have proposed the creation of a public credit register where all major, unsecured debt claims must be registered if creditors are to preserve their priorities. Priorities would be determined by order of registration and unregistered debt claims would be subordinated, obviously, to all registered claims.

In the light of the Ontario Government's continuing efforts at implementing *The Personal Property Security Act, 1967*, by setting up a central registry system for secured debt claims, one may question where a public registry is the key to the proposed priority system. If on a distribution on an execution under the *Creditors Relief Act* or a distribution under a Part x type scheme or a consumer bankruptcy, creditors were simply ranked in order of the date of granting credit, the substantial objective of this proposal would be achieved. No one would risk granting any significant amount of credit without making a serious effort to ascertain a debtor's existing commitments. The need for this information would itself provoke an appropriate response in the private sector, through the further expansion of credit rating bureaux. Privacy and considerations of accuracy of information would seem to be adequately protected through credit reporting legislation of the type already in force in most provinces.

Some problems of detail would remain to be resolved, such as the back-dating of contracts by creditors to improve their priority position, and the ranking of different credit grantors who grant credit on the same day, especially 'line' creditors, such as credit card companies and revolving credit store account operations.

While it is already a criminal offence for a person to obtain credit by fraud, the precedent of section 57 of the South Australia *Consumer Credit Act 1972*, which makes it a specific offence for a consumer knowingly to provide false information in a credit application, would seem a useful complementary reform, so that consumers can have impressed upon them explicitly in credit applications the importance of providing accurate information. It is as much in their interests as a creditor's that credit not be imprudently granted. And, in any event, deliberate misrepresentation is indefensible from whichever side of the market-place it comes.

The Montreal study showed a significant incidence (about 10%) of credit breakdowns arising from transactions involving bait and switch selling of carpet in the home, health studio 'packages', and door-to-door sales of magazine subscriptions and encyclopedias. The abuses that abound in these areas can be reduced through 'cooling-off' periods in door-to-door sales and more vigorous policing of misleading advertising laws. Apart from incidences of outright deception and merchant defaults, a good deal of credit delinquency could be avoided by a vigorous information programme conducted by various government agencies which presently receive and mediate consumer complaints. The complaints records of firms, including name, product and service sector, could be collated and disseminated widely to the public. In effect, existing complaints agencies would operate as business rating bureaux for consumers paralleling the function that credit rating bureaux perform for merchants. While problems of privacy and accuracy of information would need to be resolved, these are not substantially different from problems faced by consumers with credit rating bureaux and now the subject of special legislation.

3 The externalities problem

a Exemption from execution: The exemptions from execution in force in the various provinces of Canada, especially the exemptions from wage garnishment, for the most part, are extremely modest. For example, Alberta [until recently] permitted a married debtor to retain $200 per month plus $40 for each child, and $100 a month in the case of single debtors. While some other

TABLE 20

Situation Poverty Line	Situation before making the Deposit	Situation after making the Deposit
Above the Poverty Line	61.7% (145)	26.8% (63)
Below the Poverty Line	38.3% (90)	73.2% (172)
Total	235	235

provinces are relatively more generous, including Quebec, the fact remains that time and again in our interviews with debtors who had been subjected to garnishment, we were told that following garnishment, they quit their jobs and went on welfare or unemployment insurance. The difference between the level of public welfare benefits and the allowable exemption from garnishment was so small that it was not worth working for the difference. For example, in our Debtor Survey we interviewed a woman aged 26 with two small children left by her recently deceased common law husband. She had been working as a telephone operator but when her wages were garnished she quit and went on welfare. She told us bluntly that the only realistic employment alternative for her was prostitution (where garnishment would be impractical) but had decided against it (rather pragmatically) for fear of contracting venereal disease. Table 20 from the University of Montreal study of Lacombe Law debtors dramatically underscores this point.

The exemption levels in other, less generous, provinces would necessarily reinforce the reaction of debtors similarly circumstanced to those we interviewed. This represents a perfectly rational economic calculation on the debtor's part. The results are that the costs of credit breakdown are passed on to the public at large, and the purpose of the garnishment procedure is, perhaps counter-intuitively, subverted by the very illiberality of the exemptions. Clearly, wage garnishment exemptions cannot be set below, at, or ever marginally above, the relevant welfare entitlements claimable by a garnished debtor if the purpose of the law is to encourage him to continue working and to pay off his creditor over time. The exemptions must be set *significantly* above the relevant welfare entitlements so that a *significant* incentive to work remains. The details are no doubt difficult to ascertain, but the guiding principle is surely clear. Any exemption formula should also provide for regular adjustments to take account of changes in the cost of living and for variations in the exemption in particular cases to take account of any special circumstances of the debtor.

The same observations apply, in principle, to exemptions from execution against personal property. For example, in terms of household effects, New Brunswick exempts only bedding, clothing and food for 3 months not exceeding $100 in value. Newfoundland and Nova Scotia and Prince Edward Island exempt bedding, clothing and necessary cooking utensils. As many debtors subject to seizure in our survey told us, and as is borne out by the extraordinarily high percentage of claim settlements after seizure and before sale, the only way of avoiding being divested of assets necessary for even subsistence living is to borrow the amount of the creditor's claim from someone else – perhaps a finance company from whom the facts are concealed, a friend, or the neighbourhood loan-shark. The debt problem is not solved; it is simply swept under another carpet.

b Costs of wage garnishments to employers: The costs entailed for employers in administering wage garnishments are clearly a major reason why some employers fire employees who are subject to garnishment. One American study found that 53.1% of employers who discharged employees on account of garnishment gave costs as the reason. Other American studies show that an employer's costs in administering a single garnishment deduction run between $15 and $35.

In Quebec employers are not permitted to make any deductions for payments on a garnishment to defray expenses of administration. This again involves a case of the creditor and debtor following credit break-down being permitted by the law to transfer part of the costs to an innocent, involuntary third party, who, of course, reacts predictably. It is not fair to the employer; ultimately, it is not in the interests of the debtor, who stands to suffer from an adverse reaction by the employer; and it is not in the interests of the creditor who also suffers in the event of the debtor being fired. The employer should be permitted to deduct a realistic sum from garnishment payments to cover costs and these should be absorbed by the collection process like other costs.

4 Transaction costs

There are several issues involved in the transaction costs generated for creditors and debtors by the collection process.

Firstly, can these costs be reduced? Does all service of process need to be personal? Why should service not be required by registered post in the first instance, and personal service only permitted where service by post proves impossible? All sales following seizure by unsecured creditors and perhaps some sales following repossession by secured creditors (in the absence of recourse agreements with the dealer) should be held at a well-advertised, accessible place and time each month to maximize the number of buyers attending sales and reduce the needless 'value destruction' that invariably occurs. In those common law provinces which still require separate wage garnishments to be filed against a debtor each pay day or each pay period, a single garnishment against a given employer having continuing effect until the debt is liquidated should be permitted.

More difficult issues are raised by the question of state subsidization of transaction costs. Many provinces permit creditors to sue in provincial Small Claims Courts where process costs are nominal. The rationale for subsidization of litigation costs in Small Claims Courts is a desire to provide roughly equal access to the courts for both business and non-business litigants by attempting to compensate non-business litigants for the scale economies available to business litigants. Why the subsidy should be extended to the latter is not clear and even though higher costs engendered in other courts will often be passed on to the debtor, it may be that in the present context this position provides a more desirable regime of incentives and disincentives to the formal coercive collection processes.

If the true costs of coercive collection are concealed through state subsidies of the collection process, both creditors and debtors have less incentive to exchange the information which might prevent unnecessary court costs. Public subsidies for the costs of credit breakdown would be better directed to the income security problem so that improper use of credit is discouraged at the outset. In addition, our earlier proposal allowing a debtor to invoke the intervention of a Credit Referee or Debtors Assistance Board before coercive enforcement of a judgment proceeds would operate to mitigate normal litigation costs, although involving some public subsidy.

5 Due process

The constitutional debates that are currently raging in the United States over a debtor's constitutional right to due process before his property can be adversely affected, have clear policy implications for Canada. A compelling policy argument grounded simply in considerations of equity (quite apart from constitutional considerations) can be made out for a requirement of due process in certain cases: prejudgment garnishments, utility cut-offs by statutory monopolies such as gas, hydro, and telephone utilities where there is no alternative source of supply, self-help repossession by secured creditors.

An actual hearing, rather than a reasonable opportunity for a hearing, is not necessary in every case. Due process requirements would seem sufficiently met if the debtor were able to fill out a portion of the process form in each case where he desires a hearing; the process should be suspended pending the hearing. In the case of self-help repossession where in many common law provinces no formal process is required, prior notice of repossession should be required and this notice could then be framed so as to permit a request for a hearing. The procedure here suggested is closely modelled on the provisions of the Saskatchewan *Limitation of Civil Rights Act* which also empower the judge on the hearing, irrespective of the validity of the creditor's claim, to make a number of discretionary orders, including suspension of repossession and rescheduled instalment payments. This seems a useful ancillary power and may avoid needless destruction of the value of the debtor's property.

6 Defects in statutory rehabilitative schemes

The Part x wage earner scheme under the federal *Bankruptcy Act*, the Quebec Lacombe Law variant thereof, and proposals contained in the new federal *Bankruptcy Bill* for amending Part x, all suffer from certain common defects given the ostensible rehabilitative objectives of the legislation.

The first problem pertains to secured creditors. One of the attractions for a debtor to enter into a Part x scheme rather than to go bankrupt is that he is able to keep his property in return for an undertaking to pay off his debts in full over a period of time (3 years under Part x). Secured creditors are, however, exempted from Part x with the result that many debtors whose major assets are subject to security will find it more rational to go bankrupt where the assets are still lost but three years of payments can be avoided. To make the discipline involved in making three years' payments an attractive alternative to personal bankruptcy, which is prejudicial both to the debtor and his creditors generally, secured creditors should be subject to Part x, thus freezing their security during the duration of a scheme, payments to them being subject to the same rate of deferment as that applied to other creditors. On the termination of the scheme (if it is a composition as proposed in the Bankruptcy Bill), the unpaid residue of their claims should revive, payable at the contract rate, with their security then realizable in the event of further default. Without such restrictions on the rights of secured creditors, they will be in a position to subvert many Part x type schemes by destroying any incentive for the debtor to enter into such a scheme and prevent creditors generally from obtaining the benefit of the debtor's payments, a benefit which disappears, of course, once bankruptcy occurs.

It is, no doubt, true that these proposals will have some impact on secured creditors' lending and pricing policies. These costs may be outweighed by the rehabilitative virtues of Part x where a debtor is forced to adjust to an imposed form of budgetary discipline, the value destruction inherent in bankruptcy is avoided, and unsecured creditors, who almost always lose in a bankruptcy, are satisfied.

The second problem is that of after-acquired creditors. Under a Part x scheme, the debtor is entitled to retain a reasonable living allowance out of his wages (under the Lacombe Law, the non-garnishable portion of his wages). Because this exemption is fixed, a debtor under the scheme has little or no incentive not to run up further debts, as he suffers no immediate consequences. If further creditors are simply brought under the scheme, the short-run, terminal

TABLE 21

RATE OF ANNUAL PAYMENTS

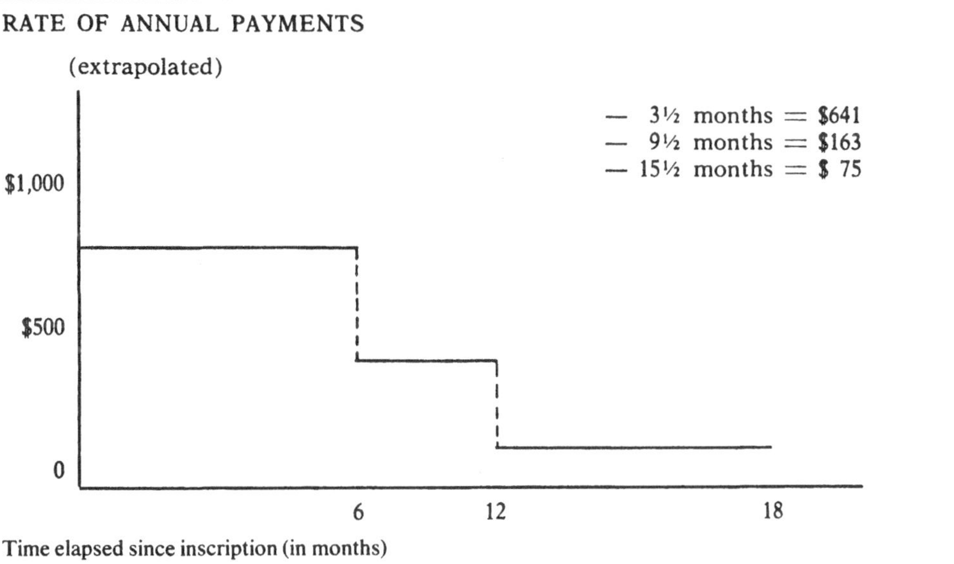

rehabilitative purpose of the scheme instead becomes a permanent way of life encouraging greater financial irresponsibility. As we have already pointed out, improved exchange of information at the time that credit is granted should ensure that future creditors are more frequently aware of the debtor's circumstances before they extend credit. Secondly, it might perhaps be made a criminal offence for a debtor to obtain further credit while under the scheme. Thirdly, if credit is in fact so obtained, this should be treated as terminating the scheme in the sense that creditors then become free again to invoke their normal collection remedies while the debtor may consider personal bankruptcy.

The third problem with Part x and similar schemes is the principle of voluntarism in regard to payments adopted in the legislation. In general, the initiative rests with the debtor to make the appropriate payments into court each pay day. The consequences are predictable. They are indicated in Table 21 from the University of Montreal study of Lacombe Law debtors.

Table 22 from the University of Montreal study, projects the periods of payments that would be required for debtors to liquidate their debts considering both the deposits already made and the debts to be liquidated.

This pattern is reinforced by the Alberta study of Part x debtors, where over 50% were in arrears in their monthly payments, 41.67% being 90 days or more in arrears.

The reasons for this seem obvious. Firstly, debtors suffering from a chronic income deficiency, caused by unstable employment, sickness or high day-to-day family financial outgoings, simply cannot pay anything. They have no discretionary income from which to make payments. Wage earner plans can be of no use to them. Secondly, to the extent that the exempted portion of a debtor's wage is lower than welfare entitlements, he will simply stop working, as in the case of garnishments. Thirdly, the reason why many debtors are financially distressed is that they lack budgetary self-discipline. To expect them to develop it overnight and maintain it over a period of several years is simply naive. We argue that, *provided the exemptions are realistic*, a debtor's payments under Part x or the Lacombe Law or indeed any instalment or consolidation order made by a court, should be deducted at source as in the case of a garnishment.

TABLE 22

Inscription: Periods of Payments Necessary	6 to 12 months 1972	1 to 5 months 1973	6 to 12 months 1973	Total
No Possibility	19 (16.3%)	28 (25.6%)	35 (27.3%)	82 (23.2%)
More than 20 years	21 (18.1%)	17 (15.6%)	12 (9.3%)	50 (14.1%)
From 15–20 Years	10 (8.6%)	5 (4.5%)	0 (0.0%)	15 (4.2%)
From 10–15 years	20 (17.2%)	6 (5.5%)	7 (5.4%)	33 (9.3%)
From 5–10 years	12 (10.3%)	13 (12.0%)	15 (11.7%)	40 (11.3%)
From 0–5 years	24 (20.6%)	30 (27.5%)	41 (32.0%)	95 (27.0%)
No Claims	10 (8.6%)	10 (9.1%)	18 (14.0%)	38 (10.7%)
Total	116 (32.8%)	109 (30.8%)	128 (36.2%)	353 (100.0%)

Moreover, if creditors are expected to forego their normal collection rights for an extended period, as Part x entails, it seems reasonable that there be some assurance of continuity of benefits to them under the scheme. Deduction at source is an accepted principle for all kinds of other imposts, and again provided the exemptions are realistic and provision is made for variation in the event of unforeseeable changes of circumstances, it is hard to see what objection can be made against it.

The final issue raised by the Part x type wage earner scheme is its relationship to personal bankruptcy. It is now widely argued that the bankruptcy process should serve a rehabilitative function as well as providing a collection tool for creditors.

On the one hand one might argue that for a debtor who is hopelessly overcommitted, any prospect of being able to lift himself out of his financial mire and start afresh dictates bankruptcy where, in return for surrendering his non-exempt assets to his creditors, he is permitted to unload his debts and obtain a discharge within a very short period. However, on the other hand, a readily available bankruptcy regime, which is not restricted in its availability to debtors of the kind above described, encourages not rehabilitation but financial irresponsibility. Curiously, neither the existing *Bankruptcy Act*, the Study Committee's proposals for a new Bankruptcy law nor the new Bankruptcy Bill itself attach any significant conditions to a debtor's right of access to bankruptcy. For example, one might have thought that one precondition on which the Bankruptcy Court should be required to be satisfied before accepting a debtor's assignment is that a wage earner plan under Part x is not feasible because of the scale of overcommitment relative to the debtor's projected income stream. If it is feasible for a debtor over, say three years to pay off all or a substantial portion of his debts, is there any case for making bankruptcy available to him? Again, to return to Leff's point, if cooperative (collective) accords between a debtor and his creditors generally produce the most mutually advantageous settlements of claims, and creditors are to be discouraged from unilateral use of coercive collection remedies, should debtors have total freedom to repudiate unilaterally, through bankruptcy, their obligations to their creditors?

7 Discriminatory regulation

Collection agencies are state licensed and regulated in every province in Canada and certain collection practices prohibited. It is difficult to justify singling out collection agents for regulation. If a collection practice is offensive and unacceptable, then it is offensive and unacceptable whether it is engaged in by collection agents, bailiffs, lawyers acting for creditors or collection agents, or by the creditor himself. Only British Columbia in its Debt Collection Act and Manitoba in its Consumer Protection Act have accepted the logic of this. It is important in legislation proscribing certain collection practices that civil consequences be attached to the use of these practices (e.g. unenforceability of the debt claim) so that enforcement resources, public and private, are optimized, and all enforcement initiatives do not rest with a typically under-resourced state agency.

In the case of bailiffs in Quebec, their position both as official court officers and as entre-preneurs working directly for creditors on a piecework basis involves a hopeless conflict of interest. One of two solutions seems open. The first is to make them full-time salaried employees of the court, like other court officials, as is the case in many other jurisdictions. If this is thought likely to be less efficient than an entrepreneurial bailiff system, then at least bailiffs should be recognized for what they presently are: collection agents for creditors. If this is to be the case their self-regulating status should be completely withdrawn. They should be licensed and regulated by an independent state authority, as in the case of other collection agents.

8 The process of reform

Over the past fifteen years, the area of consumer credit has attracted more legislation than any other area of consumer protection. Western jurisdictions have accumulated a great deal of experience in judging the efficacy of different legislative approaches. It is surely time to review and consolidate that experience, abandoning the intuitive method that has characterized public policy-making up to now.

The goal in Canada might well be a uniform provincial Consumer Credit Code. As a first, and urgent, step towards this goal, the task of improving our data collections on critical questions must be embarked upon. The various debtors' assistance courts and agencies dealing with debt problems should be encouraged, across all jurisdictions, to develop common indicators for collecting and reporting relevant data. We make no claims to have performed this task in our very modest study; this is just a beginning. Without hard, empirically unassailable facts, policy-making in the regulation of the consumer credit market will remain what it has always been – at best an exercise in accidental wisdom.

3
Debt and the Invasion of Privacy

With the greatly expanded use of credit data banks and credit reporting agencies, a major sanction for non-payment of debts has become an adverse credit rating. Various issues arising out of the use of credit ratings are canvassed in this chapter: the accuracy of credit information; threats to privacy posed by the storage and dissemination of the information; methods of obtaining information; permissible sources of information; the ability of the debtor to know that such information is being used when a credit decision is taken and his ability to verify the source and accuracy of the information.

The chapter concludes with a novel proposal by Professor Ziegel that even unsecured debt claims should be required to be registered in a public registry and should be ranked in order of registration. The premise of this proposal is that it will improve the quality of the information available to the creditor when he makes his decision to grant or not to grant credit and will prevent subsequent creditors, who at present under our execution and bankruptcy laws rank on an equal basis with earlier creditors, from, in effect, subverting the position of the earlier creditor who made his decision to grant credit on the basis of a situation which subsequent creditors are in a position to change unilaterally.

I THE NATURE OF THE PROBLEM

a / Departments of Communications and of Justice, *Privacy and Computers* (1971), pp 55–7, 62–4.

CREDIT GRANTERS

We live in an economy which depends heavily on the granting of credit for its proper operation. Although an evaluation and judgment of the societal effects of this situation, or of possible alternatives, is beyond the scope of this Report, there is certainly no sign of slackening in the move towards greater dependence on credit. The amount of consumer credit outstanding in Canada has multiplied by more than five in the past two decades, to some $9 billion in 1971. Types of credit include real-estate and chattel mortgages, small loans, bank cards, travel and entertainment cards, oil-company credit cards, and department-store charge accounts. Because of the dominant role played by the banks, they have been considered separately in the next chapter.

Taking the massive existence of a credit industry as self-evident, two of its characteristics were of particular interest to the Task Force. First, most of those who give credit endeavour to obtain detailed information about those who seek it before credit is granted. Second, individuals who consume on credit instead of using cash leave behind them a visible trail of purchases: evenings spent at a night club or hotel, trips out of town, money raised, or houses bought. Information is both the foundation of the credit industry and its principal by-product.

The search for credit involves a classic give and receive relationship. As the Royal Bank of Canada explained in its brief to the Task Force: 'When a person applies to a bank for a loan he gives up a certain amount of privacy in providing the basic personal data and financial history which is required to provide a full assessment of his credit-worthiness. Any information provided to a bank is regarded as "privileged" between bank and customer. It is considered as the "property" of the customer.'

Some lenders make decisions regarding loan eligibility on the basis of information available within their own organizations, but most use the services of some outside agency. These outside agencies include in-file credit-reporting agencies, central registries of indebtedness, and credit-card monitoring services. Investigative credit-reporting agencies are used much less frequently.

Some provincial Attorneys-General have established computer-based systems for the registration of real and personal property and securities, primarily to prevent the fraudulent sale of property subject to liens. Most entries concern people buying cars on credit. Access is open to anyone willing to pay the fee of $2 per entry.

Small-loan companies maintain a lenders' information-exchange through the Canadian Consumer Loan Association, which maintains records on current debtors (to ensure that their credit limit is not exceeded), and on debt defaulters. The Credit Index, located in Morristown, New Jersey, and accessible by teletype, contains information on nine million people who have collectively defaulted on half a billion dollars of debt; 8,500 people in the index have Canadian addresses.

Banks generally rely on their own record of experience with particular customers in deciding on loan applications, although information from other bank managers, from credit bureaux, and from the customer's employer is not infrequently used. Banks have a strict policy of non-disclosure of customer-information except in well defined circumstances which can generally be categorized as being either under compulsion of law or with the express or implied consent of the customer. However, a bank will provide to a credit bureau, upon request, a credit reference with regard to unsecured personal loans. Such reports divulge the maximum credit, payment experience, existing loan position, and length of experience with the customer.

Under common law the relationship between a banker and his depositors is confidential, and the former may be sued for breach of confidentiality should he disclose the contents of the latter's account, although material damage must be proven before the individual can obtain a favourable judgment.

Credit-card operations such as Chargex, the oil-company credit cards, and American Express rely heavily on computers to provide up-to-date accounting information and to help prevent credit card frauds of various kinds. Many provide immediate access to computerized files by persons authorized to accept credit cards. The computer output normally provides information only as to whether or not credit is good, and whether or not the credit card has been stolen.

Many credit cards are accepted throughout North America, and the credit-checking system reflects this situation in that much of the data-processing for Canadian credit-card holders takes place in the United States. Thus information on many Canadian oil-company credit-card holders is stored in a computer owned by the National Data Corporation of Atlanta, Georgia, and is accessible through a terminal in Toronto.

American Express appears to maintain the largest credit data-bank on Canadians in the

United States, with approximately 130,000 Canadian credit card holders on file. Information is almost entirely of an accounting nature. Diners Club (with approximately 75,000 Canadian accounts), Carte Blanche (with about 14,000 Canadian subscribers) and America Airlines (with about 1,500 Canadian subscribers mostly in the Toronto area) run similar operations.

It has frequently been pointed out that extensive use of a credit card by an individual can result in his leaving a fairly complete record of his activities. This record can be useful to the police as well as to others. It is not unknown for criminals to be apprehended as a direct result of using a credit card ...

IN-FILE CREDIT BUREAUX

The term 'credit bureau' is used to describe two businesses of different nature: investigative credit bureaux and in-file credit bureaux. The words 'credit bureau' when applied to the investigative organizations are misleading, since their major customers are not primarily the credit granters, but are more likely to be life, fire, or car-insurance companies, or prospective employers, although mortgage companies and travel-and-entertainment card granters are not infrequent users.

In-file credit bureaux do not normally become involved in investigative activities, but depend largely on information given to them by their customers, who are primarily department stores, small-loan companies, and small businesses which extend credit. To a lesser extent, the services are used by banks and oil companies. Although the in-file bureaux are not, strictly speaking, administrators, they do provide a kind of centralized administrative service, and for this reason they have been included in this chapter.

The in-file credit-bureau industry consists of a number of independent credit bureaux, most of which (151) belong to the Associated Credit Bureaux of Canada (ACB of C), a voluntary association. Over-all, it is estimated that the Canadian industry grosses $12–15 million annually, and employs about 2,000 people. The average charge for a credit report is $1.35.

Members of the ACB of C subscribe to a code of ethics, and to explicit policies to protect privacy. Many of the consumer rights provided for in the United States Fair Credit Reporting Act of 1970 are included in the code of ethics and associated policies. This is not altogether surprising in view of the links between the Assocated Credit Bureaux Inc. in the United States and ACB of C. This linkage permits credit files to migrate with the individual almost anywhere in the United States and Canada.

Although no Canadian credit bureaux are yet computerized, the question is under serious consideration, since the bureaux are under strong pressure to provide more complete and up-to-date service. The principal obstacle to computerization is the high cost of conversion, a cost which is difficult to justify in relation to the relatively small volume of business. Several United States bureaux have already computerized their files (e.g., Credit Data, Retail Credit Corp.), and there is a possibility that the Canadian bureaux may want to rent a software system from a United States company and run it on a computer in Canada. Even with an imported software system, however, the file-conversion costs would be high. If the credit bureaux do not convert to computerized records, there is a danger that current customers will turn to other sources of information.

Retail Credit of Canada, a subsidiary of the Retail Credit Corporation of Atlanta, Georgia, which is primarily an investigative credit bureau, has been diversifying into in-file operations. Approximately 30% of the in-file credit business in Canada is now under its control.

A common suggestion is that credit bureaux should be required to notify a person every time his file has been consulted. The credit bureaux oppose this on the grounds, first, that most people who apply for credit know that their file in the credit bureau is likely to be consulted, and second, that the extra cost would be prohibitive. Even a cost increase of 10% (or 14 cents per enquiry), it is argued, would be enough to affect business significantly, because many customers would start using the more expensive but more complete files of the investigative credit bureaux (about $5 per enquiry) or else start granting credit according to an arbitrary set of rules based on such criteria as age, occupation, and length of residence. They therefore concluded that the consumer would either be forced to pay a higher price for credit or be refused credit for arbitrary reasons.

This argument is worth noting. However, the contention that most people know, when they ask for credit, that a credit bureau file about them can be consulted is open to dispute. Even more open to dispute is the implication that they know how to go about finding their file if they should want to look at it.

It may well be expensive if credit bureaux are forced to alert an individual each time his file is consulted, but an obvious compromise would be an initial notification the first time the file is used (to alert the individual that his file exists), and the subsequent maintenance of a record of use which could be examined on request. Any right to examine the file should carry with it a corollary right to correct inaccuracies and include a procedure for resolving disputed facts. Members of the ACB of C do in fact permit inspection and correction of files by the individual concerned.

b / A Specimen Employment Report
See pages 84–5 for report.

2 THE LEGAL RESPONSE

a / Note
Most of the important forms of action in tort were shaped long before the growth of consumer credit as we know it today. Thus, both practical and conceptual difficulties may lie in the path of a person suffering harm on account of an incorrect credit report. An inaccurate credit report is of concern not only to the consumer, but also to the credit reporter's customer who might suffer loss by relying on incorrect information contained in the report. Thus the lender might grant credit to a person to whom it ought not to be granted or to refuse to grant credit to a person who is perfectly credit worthy.

In this context, several torts may be relevant:

1 Defamation: The elements of defamation are well known and it would seem that many erroneous reports could be defamatory. One obvious practical difficulty for many potential plaintiffs is ascertaining that a report has been made. In this regard, note the provisions of the Consumer Reporting Act, below at p. 90.

The most important substantive issue raised by the nature of the credit reporting business is that of qualified privilege. If such privilege is granted to the reporters, not only must the report be false in order to be actionable, but there must be evidence of malice or abuse. The privilege is normally granted on occasions 'where the person who makes a communication had an interest or duty, legal, social or moral, to make it to the person to whom it is made, and the person to whom it is made has a corresponding interest or duty to receive it.' (*Adam* v *Ward*, [1917] A.C. 309 at 334.)

The leading English case is *Macintosh and Another* v *Dun*, [1908] A.C. 390 (P.C.).

Equifax Services, Sample Employment Report (See page 83)

equifax
services

An Employment Service

Management Selection ____ **REPORT**

Caution to Customers Under terms of our agreement, this report is submitted with the understanding that it is to be held in Strict Confidence. Except where required by law, no information in this report may be revealed directly or indirectly to any person except to one whose official duties require him to pass on the transaction in relation to which this report was ordered. This report contains information pertinent to personnel selection and was prepared for that purpose only.

Account No. 212-313 File No. or Requestor D. Brown
Date 4-30-78 29 28
Name MORTON, CHRISTOPHER M.
Address Chicago, IL., 6437 Thomaston St.

Position Applied for Consultant
Date of Birth 12-19-41
Soc. Sec. or Soc. Ins. No. 202-94-0867

Office Chicago

Report From_______________ ___________________
(If not city in heading) (State whether former addr., etc.)

Scope of Background Check: Show total number of locations, total number of current sources and longest time known. Separately list previous report sources showing no. and longest time known. List any records checked showing location and type.

3 locations, 4 sources, covering 6 yrs.
Cook County criminal court records

sample

Other offices reporting:

Branch   Locations Covered

Directing office: If transferred, show date___________________

9-1-77 to present   Christopher Michael Morton is an employment consultant for
Top-Notch Talent   Top-Notch Talent, an employment agency. He interviews people
#1245 17 E. 27th   looking for work and arranges appointments for them with em-
Chicago, IL.   ployers that have openings. We did not contact this employer
as per your instructions. A source knowing the applicant personally said that this
is an interim job the applicant took until he can find a position equal to his abilities.

3-1-76 to 8-31-77   The applicant was employed as Vice President of Personnel for
Telectron, Inc.   Telectron, a manufacturer of closed circuit television equip-
North Industrial Way ment for use in security systems. He supervised a department
Chicago, IL.   with 25 employees, 3 of whom were in management. Under his
direction the department operated effectively and efficiently. The staff was reduced
25% through his modifying and eliminating procedures. He also developed an improved
salary administration program and installed an affirmative action plan, both of which
are still functioning successfully. His department budget was $400,000 per year and
he kept within it consistently. He was hired as Personnel Director, but they upgraded
his job and promoted him to Vice President on 1-1-77 in recognition of his achieve-
ments. His attendance record was good, and he worked an average of 9-10 hours a day.
He frequently addressed groups of employees and on occasions would represent the
company with the media and business groups. Employees trusted him and would confide
in him on personal work-related problems. He was a forthright and honest person.
His salary was $2600 a month. In mid-1977 Telectron lost a major government contract
and a 40% reduction in staff was required. The applicant's position was eliminated.
He is eligible for rehire.

Equifax Inc.
Equifax Services Inc.
Equifax Services Ltd.
Form 263—3-77 U.S.A.   (Over)

This case removed the privilege from a profit-making credit reporter. It seems to have been accepted as law in Canada although a slightly later English case, *London Association for Protection of Trade* v *Greenlands Ltd.*, [1916] A.C. 15 (H.L.) granted the privilege to member-owned reporting agencies.

```
4-1-72 to 2-28-76          Mr. Morton was employed as Personnel Manager for this
Mattern Manufacturing Co.  local firm which manufactures bedding materials.  The
2049 N. Highland           firm employs 300 people.  He started as an assistant
Chicago, IL.               and was promoted to Personnel Manager in 1974.  He
had responsibility for all personnel functions and salary administration.  He
supervised six employees.  He was well regarded as a capable personnel administra-
tor and supervisor.  He improved the efficiency of the department to the extent
that costs were reduced.  He was honest and reliable.  He was seldom absent and
worked 45-50 hours per week.  His salary was $20,000 per year.  He resigned to
take another position because advancement opportunity was limited.  He is eligible
for rehire.

EDUCATION-SPECIAL SKILLS:  Telectron's records show he graduated from Oakmont
College in 1962 with a degree in personnel adminstration.  He has not attended
school here and sources contacted know nothing further about his educational
background.

MANAGEMENT OF PERSONAL FINANCES:  His income from present employment is approx-
imately $12,000 per year.  He has income from investments estimated at $2500 an-
nually.  His wife is a legal secretary with income of $12-$13,000.  His net worth
is estimated at $100,000 consisting of equity in his home of about $50,000 plus
stocks, savings, and personal items.  He has favorable financial reputation and
meets his obligations promptly.  He and his wife live within their income.

HEALTH-HISTORY:  This applicant is healthy, energetic and unimpaired.  He has had
no past illnesses or injuries.

ALCOHOL-DRUGS:  He is a moderate social drinker.  He does not use illegal
drugs.

COMMUNITY STANDING-HONESTY-INTEGRITY:  He is married and lives with his wife and
daughters, 12 and 8.  He has a good personal and business reputation, and is well
regarded.

PUBLIC RECORDS:  Cook County criminal court records were checked and are clear.
```

Macintosh v *Dun* was recently followed in *Gillett* v *Nissen Volkswagen Ltd.*, [1975] 3 w.w.R. 520 (Alta. s.c.). In *Gillett*, the defendant credit company furnished a written report concerning the plaintiff to a company with which the plaintiff was seeking employment. The report was untrue and it was defamatory of the plaintiff. The report had been prepared by the defendant Carn, an employee of the credit company, following an interview between Carn and the defendant Nissen, who had been the plaintiff's previous employer. Nissen's defamation of the plaintiff was actuated by malice. Quigley J held that Nissen was clearly liable for making untrue and defamatory statements about the plaintiff in his answer to Carn's questions. Since Nissen knew that the statements that he had made were untrue, he could not plead qualified privilege. The plea of qualified privilege was not available to the credit company and its employee, either, since the report had been published to the plaintiff's potential employer. Quigley J held that the decision on qualified privilege in *Macintosh* v *Dun* still applied in Canada, and awarded damages to Gillett.

On the other hand, many American jurisdictions recognize the defense of qualified or conditional privilege: *Wetherby* v *Retail Credit Co.* (1964), 201 A. 2d 344 (Md.). See generally, Prosser, *Torts*, p 792 ff (4th ed. 1971). Consider the excerpt from Sharp, *Credit Reporting and Privacy*, reproduced below at p. 88. Does his compromise suggestion make sense in view of the differing economic strengths of the parties?

2 Breach of Confidence: The potential defendant in an action under this head is the source of information supplied to the credit personnel or reporters. Liability depends on the establishment of a confidential relationship between the plaintiff, the injured subject of the report, and the defendant who supplied the information. The fact that the information was true is not a defence since the essence of the tort is the failure to keep the information within the knowledge of the parties to the relationship.

Banks, according to Sharp, *Credit Reporting and Privacy,* commonly pass on loan information to credit reporters; such disclosures may give rise to liability, on the authority of *Tournier* v *National Provincial and Union Bank*, [1924] I K.B. 461 (C.A.).

Note that the reporting agency, which might have actively solicited the information, is not a party to the action. There are obvious conceptual difficulties in attempting to extend this tort to reach the reporting agencies: where, for instance, is the confidential relationship?

3 Invasion of Privacy: The notion that a cause of action should be created by the mere fact of interference with an inviolable sphere of a person's affairs has been accepted in the American common law. The genesis of this notion was a famous article in the Harvard Law Review (Warren and Brandeis, 'The Right to Privacy' (1890), 4 *Harv. L. Rev.* 193), and its subsequent growth is the subject of numerous articles. (See Bloustein, 'Privacy, Tort Law and the Constitution: Is Warren and Brandeis' Tort Petty and Unconstitutional As Well?' (1968), 46 *Tex. L. Rev.* 611; Green, 'Continuing The Privacy Discussion: A Response to Judge Wright and President Bloustein' (1968), 46 *Tex. L. Rev.* 750.

Canadian courts, however, have been reluctant to recognize this tort. This was made clear in a recent Ontario case, *Krouse* v *Chrysler Canada Ltd.* (1974), 40 D.L.R. (3d) 15 (C.A.), reversing (1972), 25 D.L.R. (3d) 49 (H.C.J.). An advertising company had put out on behalf of Chrysler a 'Spotter' with the names and numbers of all players in the football league for the use of home spectators. It contained an action photograph of Krouse, identifiable by his number, and advertising copy relating Chrysler to football. Krouse was in a position to obtain money from promotions because of his popularity with football enthusiasts.

At the trial, Haines J allowed the action. While denying that the tort of invasion of privacy existed, he considered Chrysler's conduct to warrant a 'passing-off' action, since it involved 'an improper appropriation of the plaintiff's reputation'.

The Court of Appeal reversed his judgment. On the evidence, it found one could not raise either an action for 'passing off' or 'invasion of privacy'. However, Estey JA stated on the general subject of creating such a tort in Ontario:

As I have indicated, there may well be circumstances in which the Courts would be justified in holding a defendant liable in damages for appropriation of a plaintiff's personality, amounting to an invasion of his right to exploit his personality by the use of his image, voice, or otherwise with damage to the plaintiff, but after a careful review of the evidence in the present action, I have come to the conclusion that the respondent has not demonstrated any infringement by the appellants of any legal right of the respondent. [at p 241]

In order to remedy the hiatus caused by the reluctance of the common law to recognize a cause of action, British Columbia and Manitoba have passed statutes creating one. In Manitoba, s. 2(1) of the Privacy Act, s.M. 1970, c 74, says simply:

2 (1) A person who substantially, unreasonably, and without claim of right, violates the privacy of another person, commits a tort against that other person.

Section 3 sets out some examples of violation of privacy, including surveillance, wiretapping, unauthorized use of name or likeness for advertising (the *Krouse* situation), or unauthorized use of letters or diaries.

The British Columbia legislation, the Privacy Act, s.B.C. 1968, c 39, has similar provisions, including an explicit provision covering the *Krouse* situation. However, it contains more safeguards for the defendant. For example, unauthorized use of name or portrait for advertising is not a tort unless the defendant specifically intended to refer to the plaintiff or exploit his name or reputation. For the only reported case under the Act, see *Davis* v *McArthur* (1970), 72 w.w.R. 69 (B.C.S.C.) where a private investigator was found liable to pay damages for infringement of the statutory right to privacy. However, on appeal [1971] 2 w.w.R. 142 (B.C.C.A.), the action was dismissed. It was held that the appellant was not in breach of the provisions of the Privacy Act, as he did not carry out his surveillance in an offensive way or so as to attract public attention, and did not go beyond the grounds of reasonability in his investigation.

QUESTIONS: In Ontario, there is no such legislation at present. Should there be? How extensive should it be? Do different policy considerations obtain with respect to the privacy interests of a debtor subject to harassment, as opposed to the interest of a professional football player in protecting his personal economic resources?

A recent case, *Motherwell* v *Motherwell,* [1976] 6 w.w.R. 550, 73 D.L.R. (3d) 62 (Alta. S.C.A.D.) extended the ambit of the tort of nuisance to cover invasion of privacy. The defendant, who was mentally unbalanced, harassed the plaintiffs, her brother, sister-in-law and father, by telephone and mail. The harassment took the form of false accusations and statements about and concerning the plaintiffs. The plaintiffs brought actions against the defendant for invasion of privacy and nuisance, and were successful at trial. On appeal, the trial judgment was upheld.

4 Negligent Misrepresentation: The nature of the work done by a credit reporter is such that the agency could be found to be one of the class persons affected by the principle of *Hedley Byrne and Co. Ltd.* v *Heller and Partners Ltd.*, [1964] A.C. 465 (H.L.). The important elements of the tort for present purposes are: (1) the plaintiff must have relied on a statement made by the defendant, (2) the statement must have been negligently compiled or communicated and (3) the plaintiff must have suffered harm as a result. Evidently, a lender could claim against a credit reporter who negligently misstated the resources of a prospective borrower.

The requirement of reliance on the statement poses a conceptual difficulty for the consumer. Suppose a prospective borrower consented to a credit check. Would this constitute reliance on a representation (implied or otherwise) that the report will be compiled accurately? What about the fact that a consumer is often forced to subject himself to whatever reporting the lender or insurer feels in necessary? Albeit involuntary, is this not still reliance?

b / J.M. Sharp, *Credit Reporting and Privacy* (1970), pp 107–8.

QUALIFIED PRIVILEGE

… There is a difference between the attitudes of the legal systems of Canada and the United States with regard to the granting of qualified (or conditional) privilege to credit reports. As a general rule, in the United States, a credit report – even one prepared purely as a profit-making business – will be entitled to qualified privilege, unless the agency issuing it publishes it wholesale to the public at large, is grossly negligent or is malicious. On the basis of existing precedents, the Canadian attitude seems to be that only such reports exchanged or circulated within a non-profit-making trade protection society or association will be thus privileged, and the credit report issued pursuant to a profit-making business must take its chance *vis-à-vis* the law of defamation with any other derogatory statement.

This difference may create a considerable gulf between the positions of the plaintiff in the United States and of the plaintiff in Canada; the former has the burden of establishing that the agency was malicious, grossly negligent, etc., while the latter, relieved of this burden, may look to the agency to justify itself.

It does seem illogical that, as between two basically similar legal systems (subject to state/provincial variations) and as between two countries with similar experience in this whole matter, there should be an important variation in the law on this point. As the law stands at present, the author would support a homogenization of the law on this point on the lines of the Canadian rule. This attitude springs from the feeling, which grows after immersing oneself in the decided cases of the United States, that the credit reporting profession there both has its cake and eats it, and the consumer may be lucky to gather any crumbs of legal solace to compensate for any loss or damage he incurs. On the other hand, and again adhering to the principle that prevention is better than cure, the author would revise this view and find the American rule acceptable in return for a comprehensive programme of uniform legislation to cover the points raised in this chapter and those which arise incidentally in earlier chapters.

The outcome of this last suggestion would be that the injured consumer would, in all cases, enjoy a very much better chance of keeping a check on what was being said about him, by whom, and how accurately. In return, the *bona fide* reputable credit bureaus (and this embraces the great majority) would enjoy the protection of qualified privilege in all cases so that, unless they had acted maliciously or with a similarly reprehensible degree of illegality, they could correct the record and be free from the threat of legal action for a genuine error.

This suggestion will not meet favour with many readers. The 'hawks' among both the consumers and the profession will attack it; the author, although not a 'dove', and above all *not* advancing this suggestion as a compromise for the sake of compromise, puts it forward as a rational and balanced scheme which, if it could be achieved, could offer justice to both sides in an area where the balancing of conflicting interests is becoming daily more pressing.

c / The Regulatory Response

i The Consumer Reporting Act: In 1973, the Ontario legislature enacted legislation aimed at regulating credit reporting agencies. This Act, The Consumer Reporting Act, is in part reproduced below. The following questions should be considered when reading it:

1 What are the broad objectives of the Act? What other potential objectives are not embraced by the Act?

2 Section 1(1) (a) excludes persons carrying on a business, trade, or profession from the protection of the Act. Do lawyers, small business persons, and farmers also not have an interest deserving protection against inaccurate credit reports?

3 Section 8(1) prescribes to whom reports may be given. Does it restrict the recipients to persons with a legitimate interest? Section 8(1)(d)(iii) allows a report to be given out for employment purposes, while s 8(3) allows information to be given to the governments of Ontario and Canada. Are these legitimate uses of credit information?

4 Section 8(4) prohibits the sale of files to any person other than a registered consumer reporting agency. Is this justified? Is it a sale of goods? If it is a sale of goods, what consequences might follow?

5 The type of information permitted in a report is governed by s 9(3). Should the methods of collecting that information be regulated as well? What does corroboration consist of in s 9(3)(b)? How is a reporting agency to know when a debt is statute barred under s 9(3)(f)? Why are convictions for crimes given uniform treatment in s 9(3)(h) when some crimes may be more relevant than others? Does s 9(3) provide sufficient safeguards to ensure that stored information is both relevant and accurate?

6 Should the prior consent of the consumer always be required before a consumer report is prepared, or do s 10(2), (3), and (4) largely achieve this?

7 Is the scope of s 10(7) too wide? If, because of adverse information received from a source other than a credit reporting agency, a professor denies a student a research job, or a landlord does not let out a room, or a lawyer declines to hire an articling student, ought the source be disclosed? Should the duty of notification be imposed upon all benefit deniers or only upon credit grantors? In this context, what does 'benefit' mean?

8 Section 11 sets out the right to disclosure. Note that the initiative is on the consumer. Note also that the consumer has no right to see the file. Only a general description of the file, the sources of credit (but not personal) information, and copies of reports sent out within a certain period are subject to disclosure. How do you evaluate the argument that sources of personal information would dry up if subject to disclosure?

9 Section 12(1) puts the onus on the consumer reporting agency to correct errors. What is a 'reasonable time'? What is 'in accordance with good practice'?

10 Section 12(2) allows the consumer to designate certain persons to whom corrected versions of the earlier reports should be sent. Why is there a limitation on such persons?

11 Should the Ontario Act contain a provision similar to s 16 of the Manitoba Personal

Investigations Act, S.M. 1971, c 23 which allows both the user of a consumer report and the consumer reporting agency to assert the defence of qualified privilege in a libel action unless the user or reporter ought to have been aware that the information was false or misleading?

12 Some representatives of the credit reporting industry, in opposing legislation such as Ontario's Consumer Reporting Act, have argued that market forces alone are a sufficient protection to the subject of a report; clients soliciting reports have an interest in receiving as high a percentage of accurate and favourable reports as possible, and reporting agencies have a strong incentive to meet this demand. Are there any defects in this argument?

The Consumer Reporting Act, S.O. 1973, c 97

1. (1) In this Act,

(*a*) 'consumer' means a natural person but does not include a person engaging in a transaction, other than relating to employment, in the course of carrying on a business, trade or profession;

(*b*) 'consumer report' means a written, oral or other communication by a consumer reporting agency of credit information or personal information, or both, pertaining to a consumer for consideration in connection with a purpose set out in clause *d* of subsection 1 of section 8;

(*c*) 'consumer reporting agency' means a person who for gain or profit or on a regular co-operative non-profit basis furnishes consumer reports;

(*d*) 'credit information' means information about a consumer as to name, age, occupation, place of residence, previous places of residence, marital status, spouse's name and age, number of dependants, particulars of education or professional qualifications, places of employment, previous places of employment, estimated income, paying habits, outstanding debt obligations, cost of living obligations and assets;

(*e*) 'Director' means the Executive Director of the Business Practices Division of the Ministry;

(*f*) 'employment purposes' means the purposes of taking into employment, granting promotion, reassigning employment duties or retaining as an employee;

(*g*) 'file', when used as a noun, means all of the information pertaining to a consumer that is recorded and retained by a consumer reporting agency, regardless of the manner or form in which the information is stored;

(*h*) 'Minister' means the Minister of Consumer and Commercial Relations;

(*i*) 'person' means a natural person, an association of natural persons, a partnership or a corporation;

(*j*) 'personal information' means information other than credit information about a consumer's character, reputation, health, physical or personal characteristics or mode of living or about any other matter concerning the consumer;

(*k*) 'personal information investigator' means a person who obtains or reports personal information to a consumer reporting agency for hire or reward;

(2) This Act applies notwithstanding any agreement or waiver to the contrary.

3. No person shall conduct or act as a consumer reporting agency or act as a personal information investigator unless he is registered by the Registrar under this Act.

4. (1) An applicant is entitled to registration or renewal of registration as a consumer reporting agency by the Registrar except where,

(*a*) having regard to his financial position, the applicant cannot reasonably be expected to be financially responsible in the conduct of his business; or

(*b*) the past conduct of the applicant affords reasonable grounds for belief that he will not carry on business in accordance with law and with integrity and honesty; or

(*c*) the applicant is a corporation and,

(i) having regard to its financial position, it cannot reasonably be expected to be financially responsible in the conduct of its business, or

(ii) the past conduct of its officers or directors affords reasonable grounds for belief that its business will not be carried on in accordance with law and with integrity and honesty;

or

(*d*) the applicant is carrying on activities that are, or will be, if the applicant is registered, in contravention of this Act or the regulations.

8. (1) No consumer reporting agency and no officer or employee thereof shall knowingly furnish any information from the files of the consumer reporting agency except,

(*a*) in response to the order of a court having jurisdiction to issue such an order;

(*b*) in accordance with the written instructions of the consumer to whom the information relates;

(*c*) in response to an order or direction made under this Act; or

(*d*) in a consumer report given to a person who it has reason to believe,

(i) intends to use the information in connection with the extension of credit to or the purchase or collection of a debt of the consumer to whom the information pertains,

(ii) intends to use the information in connection with the entering into or renewal of a tenancy agreement,

(iii) intends to use the information for employment purposes,

(iv) intends to use the information in connection with the underwriting of insurance involving the consumer,

(v) intends to use the information to determine the consumer's eligibility for any matter under a statute or regulation where the information is relevant to the requirement prescribed by law,

(vi) otherwise has a direct business need for the information in connection with a business or credit transaction involving the consumer, or

(vii) intends to use the information for the purpose of up-dating the information in a consumer report previously given to him for one of the reasons referred to in subclauses i to vi.

(2) No person shall knowingly obtain any information from the files of a consumer reporting agency respecting a consumer except for the purposes referred to in subsection 1.

9. (1) Every consumer reporting agency shall adopt all procedures reasonable for ensuring accuracy and fairness in the contents of its consumer reports.

(2) A consumer reporting agency shall not report,

(*a*) any information that is not stored in a form capable of being produced under section 11;

(*b*) any information that is not extracted from information appearing in files stored or collected in a repository located in Canada regardless of whether or not the information was obtained from a source outside Canada, except where the consumer report is in writing and contains the substance of any prior information orally acquired that conforms to the requirements of this Act.

(3) A consumer reporting agency shall not include in a consumer report,

(a) any credit information based on evidence that is not the best evidence reasonably available;

(b) any unfavourable personal information unless it has made reasonable efforts to corroborate the evidence on which the personal information is based, and the lack of corroboration is noted with and accompanies the information;

(c) information as to judgments after seven years after the judgment was given, unless the creditor or his agent confirms that it remains unpaid in whole or in part, and such confirmation appears in the file;

(d) information as to any judgment against the consumer unless mention is made of the name and, where available, the address of the judgment creditor or his agent as given at the date of entry of the judgment and the amount;

(e) information as to the bankruptcy of the consumer after seven years from the date of the discharge except where the consumer has been bankrupt more than once;

(f) information regarding any judgments, collections or debts that on their face are statute barred unless it is accompanied by evidence appearing in the file that recovery is not barred by the expiration of a limitation period;

(g) information as to the payment or non-payment of taxes or lawfully imposed fines after seven years;

(h) information as to convictions for crimes, after seven years from the date of conviction or, where the conviction resulted in imprisonment, from the date of release or parole, provided information as to convictions for crimes shall not be reported if at any time it is learned that after a conviction an absolute discharge or a full pardon has been granted;

(i) information regarding writs that are more than seven years old or writs that were issued against the consumer more than twelve months prior to the making of the report unless the consumer reporting agency has ascertained the current status of the action and has a record of this on file;

(j) information regarding any criminal charges against the consumer where the charges have been dismissed, set aside or withdrawn;

(k) any other adverse item of information where more than seven years have expired since the information was acquired or last reaffirmed;

(l) information as to race, creed, colour, sex, ancestry, ethnic origin, or political affiliation; or

(m) any information given orally in the consumer report unless the content of the oral report is recorded in the file;

10. (1) Every person shall, where requested by a consumer in writing or personally, inform the consumer whether or not a consumer report respecting him has been or is to be referred to in connection with any specified transaction or matter in which such person is engaged, and, if so, of the name and address of the consumer reporting agency supplying the report.

(2) No person shall procure from a consumer reporting agency or cause it to prepare a consumer report containing personal information respecting a consumer unless he notifies the consumer of the fact in writing before the report is requested and, where the consumer so requests in writing or personally, he shall inform the consumer of the name and address of the consumer reporting agency supplying the report.

(3) Where a person proposes to extend credit to a consumer and a consumer report containing

credit information only is being or may be referred to in connection with the transaction, he shall give notice of the fact to the consumer in writing at the time of the application for credit, or if the application is made orally, orally at the time of the application for credit.

(4) Where, before extending credit, the proposed creditor obtains the acceptance or refusal of an assignment or proposed assignment of the credit transaction by an assignee or proposed assignee, subsection 3 applies to the assignee or proposed assignee in the same manner as to the person proposing to extend credit, but the giving of a notice under subsection 3 by a person proposing to extend credit or under this subsection by his assignee or proposed assignee shall be deemed to be sufficient notice by both.

(5) No person extending credit to a consumer shall divulge to other credit grantors or to a consumer reporting agency any personal information respecting the consumer except with the consent of the consumer or on his referral unless he notifies the consumer in writing at the time of the application for credit that he intends to do so.

(6) Any notice referred to in this section shall be clearly set forth in bold type or underlined and in letters not less than ten point in size.

(7) Where a benefit is denied to a consumer or a charge to a consumer is increased either wholly or partly because of information received from a consumer reporting agency or a person other than a consumer reporting agency the user of such information shall deliver to the consumer at the time such action is communicated to the consumer notice of the fact and, upon the request of the consumer made within sixty days after such notice, shall inform the consumer,

    (a) of the nature and source of the information where the information is furnished by a person other than a consumer reporting agency; or

    (b) of the name and address of the consumer reporting agency, where the information is furnished by a consumer reporting agency,

and the notice required to be given by the user under this subsection shall contain notice of the consumer's right to request the information referred to in clauses *a* and *b* and the time limited therefor.

11. (1) Every consumer reporting agency shall, at the written request of a consumer and during normal business hours, clearly and accurately disclose to the consumer, without charge,

    (a) the nature and substance of all information in its files pertaining to the consumer at the time of the request;

    (b) the sources of credit information;

    (c) the names of the recipients of any consumer report pertaining to the consumer that it has furnished,

        (i) containing personal information, within the one year period preceding the request, and

        (ii) containing credit information, within the six month period preceding the request;

    (d) copies of any written consumer report pertaining to the consumer made to any other person or, where the report was oral, particulars of the content of such oral report, furnished,

        (i) where the report contains personal information, within the one year period preceding the request, and

        (ii) where the report contains credit information, within the six month period preceding the request,

and shall inform the consumer of his right to protest any information contained in the file under sections 12 and 13 and the manner in which a protest may be made.

(2) A consumer reporting agency shall withhold from the disclosures required by subsection 1

any medical information obtained with the written consent of the consumer which the consumer's own physician has specifically requested in writing be withheld from the consumer in his own best interest.

(3) The disclosures required under this section shall be made to the consumer,

(*a*) in person if he appears in person and furnishes proper identification;

(*b*) by telephone if he has made a written request, with sufficient identification, for telephone disclosure and the toll charge, if any, for the telephone call is pre-paid by or charged directly to the consumer.

(4) Every consumer reporting agency shall provide trained personnel to explain to the consumer any information furnished to him under this section.

(5) The consumer shall be permitted to be accompanied by one other person of his choosing to whom the consumer reporting agency may be required by the consumer to disclose his file.

(6) The consumer reporting agency shall permit the consumer to whom information is disclosed under this section to make an abstract thereof.

(7) A consumer reporting agency shall require reasonable identification of the consumer and a person accompanying him before making disclosures under this section.

(8) A consumer reporting agency shall not require a consumer to give any undertaking or waive or release any right as a condition precedent to his access to his file under this section.

12. (1) Where a consumer disputes the accuracy or completeness of any item of information contained in his file, the consumer reporting agency within a reasonable time shall use its best endeavours to confirm or complete the information and shall correct, supplement or delete the information in accordance with good practice.

(2) Where a consumer reporting agency corrects, supplements or deletes information under subsection 1, the consumer reporting agency shall furnish notification of the correction, supplement or deletion to,

(*a*) all persons who have been supplied with a consumer report based on the unamended file within sixty days before the correction, supplement or deletion is made; and

(*b*) the persons specifically designated by the consumer from among those who have been supplied with a consumer report based on the unamended file,

(i) where the report contains personal information, within the one year period preceding the correction, supplement or deletion, and

(ii) where the report contains credit information, within the six month period preceding the correction, supplement or deletion.

13. (1) The Registrar may order a consumer reporting agency to amend or delete any information, or by order restrict or prohibit the use of any information, that in his opinion is inaccurate or incomplete or that does not comply with the provisions of this Act or the regulations.

(2) The Registrar may order a consumer reporting agency to furnish notification to any person who has received a consumer report of any amendments, deletions, restrictions or prohibitions imposed by the Registrar.

(3) Where the consumer or consumer reporting agency considers himself aggrieved by a decision of the Registrar under this section, he may apply to the Tribunal for a hearing and section 6 applies, *mutatis mutandis*, to the decision in the same manner as to a proposal by the Registrar under section 6 and as if the consumer and the consumer reporting agency each were an applicant or registrant, except that an order of the Registrar may be issued and take effect immediately, but the Tribunal may grant a stay until the order becomes final.

(4) At a hearing before the Tribunal for the purposes of subsection 3, the Tribunal may require the consumer reporting agency to disclose the source of any information contained in its files.

20. (1) Where it appears to the Director that any person does not comply with any provision of this Act, the regulations or an order made under this Act, notwithstanding the imposition of any penalty in respect of such non-compliance and in addition to any other rights he may have, the Director may apply to a judge of the High Court for an order directing such person to comply with such provision, and upon the application, the judge may make such order or such other order as the judge thinks fit.

(2) An appeal lies to the Supreme Court from an order made under subsection 1.

21. No person shall knowingly supply false or misleading information to another who is engaged in making a consumer report.

22. (1) Every person who,

(*a*) knowingly, furnishes false information in any application under this Act or in any statement or return required to be furnished under this Act or the regulations;

(*b*) fails to comply with any order, direction or other requirement made under this Act; or

(*c*) contravenes any provision of this Act or the regulations,

and every director or officer of a corporation who knowingly concurs in such furnishing, failure or contravention is guilty of an offence and on summary conviction is liable to a fine of not more than $2,000 or to imprisonment for a term of not more than one year, or to both.

NOTE Similar legislation has been enacted in other Canadian provinces:
Manitoba, The Personal Investigation Act, S.M. 1971, c P 33
Saskatchewan, The Credit Reporting Agencies Act, S.S. 1972, c 23
British Columbia, Personal Information Reporting Act, S.B.C. 1973, c 139
Newfoundland, The Credit Reporting Agencies Act, s. Nfld. 1973, No. 76
Prince Edward Island, Consumer Reporting Act, R.S.P.E.I. 1974, C-18
Quebec, Consumer Protection Act, S.Q. 1971, c 74
Nova Scotia, Consumer Reporting Act, S.N.S. 1973, c 4
For a review of the Canadian legislation see Ziegel, 'Canadian Consumer Reporting Legislation: Trends and Problems' (1973), 11 *Osgoode Hall L.J.* 503.

In the United States, the activities of credit reporters are regulated by the Federal Fair Credit Reporting Act, 84 Stat. 1127; 15 U.S.C.A. ss 1680–1681 (Supp. 1971). For two different perspectives on that legislation see Sen. Wm. Proxmire, 'Privacy the Collateral', and J.L. Spafford, 'Giving Creditors their Due', in (1975), 11 *Trial* at pp 34 and 35 respectively. Generally see: Note, 'Credit Investigations and the Right to Privacy: Quest for a Remedy' (1968–9), 57 *Georgetown Law J.* 509; Note, 'Protecting the Subjects of Credit Reports' (1971), 80 *Yale L.J.* 1035; A.R. Miller, 'Personal Privacy in the Computer Age: The Challenge of a New Technology in an Information-Oriented Society' (1969), 67 *Mich. L. Rev.* 1089; Koon, 'Translating the Fair Credit Reporting Act' (1971), 48 *Denver L.J.* 51; Note, 'The Consumer v. the Credit Bureau: Whom Does the Law Protect?' (1970), 7 *Calif. Western L. Rev.* 216; Note, 'The California Consumer Reporting Act' (1975), 26 *Hastings L.J.* 1219; Posner, 'The Right of Privacy,' (1978) 12 *Georgia L.R.* 393 and comments thereon.

ii Ziegel, 'The Case for a Credit Register,' October 2, 1970 *The Globe and Mail*, Report on Business at p B6

Consumer credit in Canada has grown rapidly since the end of the Second World War. In 1948 the balance outstanding on all forms of consumer credit was $835 million; at the end of 1967 it

was not less than $8,324,000,000 and it is currently running at a rate of well over $10 billion
–more than 12 times the 1948 figure.

In terms of volume, Canadians are the second largest users of consumer credit in the free
world, only U.S. residents being larger users. West Germany, with a population three times the
size of Canada's, uses only about a third of Canada's volume of consumer credit. Canadians are
spending approximately 20 per cent of their net personal disposable income on consumer credit,
compared with 7.5 per cent in 1948.

Given this phenomenal growth it would be surprising if the system did not also have its
casualties. There is, indeed, evidence that the number of debtors with serious debt problems has
grown rapidly during the past decade. One estimate made by an experienced credit manager has
placed the number at 50,000 for Metropolitan Toronto alone. This may be a little on the high
side, but David Scott, Division Court referee in Toronto, has been interviewing up to 7,500
debtors a year with serious debt problems.

There are many reasons why debtors get into trouble. One undoubtedly is that it is too easy for
many individuals to obtain credit. Credit no longer is regarded as a privilege but almost as a right
and credit has become an indispensable marketing technique for a vast number of retail
establishments. Another, and by no means insignificant, reason is that it is very difficult for even
a conscientious credit grantor to obtain a reliable and comprehensive picture of an applicant's
current commitments.

When an application for credit is received, most retailers content themselves with a few
questions about the nature of the applicant's employment, his marital status, the type of
accommodation he occupies, and one or two references. Lenders are usually more searching in
their questions and will often ask for a list of the applicant's current debts. Whether their
questions are few or many, responsible credit grantors will attempt to verify the answers and to
obtain supplementary information. A most important source for both these purposes is the
credit bureau.

Incomplete records: It is here that major difficulties arise. The records of credit bureaus are
seriously incomplete. They will tell the credit grantor whether a debtor has been sued or has
otherwise been in difficulties with the law and they may tell him something about his general
credit rating, but there is no assurance that the rating is reliable.

For one thing, the members of the bureaus are under no general obligation to volunteer
information about their credit customers. For another, important establishments are not members of the credit bureaus but prefer, like the 'lenders' exchange' operated by the finance
companies, to run their own information services. So it may easily transpire that John Doe who
has an A rating with a bureau because he has never been sued or otherwise had known debt
difficulties may in fact be up to his ears in debt and is about to seek relief under Part X of the
federal Bankruptcy Act or to seek the assistance of a credit counselling agency.

In recent years credit grantors have become increasingly concerned about these information
gaps. About two years ago the Retail Council of Canada first recommended the establishment of
a mandatory register of delinquent debtors. Others have renewed the suggestion since then but
without limiting it to delinquent debtors. The suggestion deserves to be taken seriously.

There is nothing novel about the idea. Since 1849 Ontario has required chattel mortgages to be
registered and the requirement was later extended to conditional sale agreements, book debts
and other types of security agreements. Today all the common law provinces impose this
requirement.

The original rationale behind these laws was that secret liens allow a person to hold himself

out as owning goods that in fact he has pledged and thus gives him a false appearance of
solvency. We no longer regard the giving of security as a sign of financial difficulties but we still
deem it important that the fact should be publicized so that interested parties will not be misled.

Precisely the same reasoning justifies requiring the registration of unsecured debts. In fact, it
can be demonstrated that knowing accurately what debts a consumer has incurred is more
important to a credit grantor than knowing whether the debts are secured.

Quantitative change: No doubt it will be argued that the establishment of such a register would
involve a serious encroachment on the individual's right to privacy. It is difficult to see why it
should be thought a greater encroachment than the records, public and private, that already
exist. The change is only quantitative, not qualitative; the claim to privacy is surely waived
when an individual applies for credit. Safeguards to prevent abuses may be necessary, but this is
a problem common to the handling of all forms of information in our computer-conscious age.

Greater difficulties may be encountered in working out the details of the new register, but
none of them should prove insurmountable. Small amounts of credit and short-term credit, other
than credit advanced under a credit card or other revolving form of credit, should be exempt
from the registration requirement. Nor should it be necessary for the creditor to have to file
anything more than a short statement declaring that he was given or intends to give credit to the
particular debtor.

Amounts owing and other particulars about the credit agreement should not have to be
revealed (although under the existing registration statutes the whole agreement is required to be
filed) but a legitimate enquirer should be entitled to obtain this information on applying direct to
the creditor.

The retail council envisaged the new requirement applying only to delinquent debts. In my
opinion, this would be too restrictive and would defeat an important purpose of the register. It
would only tell a creditor whether a consumer was already in difficulties and not whether, by
virtue of the number of his commitments, he potentially could be. A creditor who fails to file
would not be subject to criminal penalties but would be precluded from presenting his claim in
the event of the debtor's insolvency. If he files late he would be subordinated to creditors who
have filed before him.

An important object of the new register should also be to establish an order of priorities among
general creditors. Under our existing federal and provincial laws, with few exceptions all
general creditors are treated alike. This can give rise to serious inequities. A lender makes a loan
to John Doe knowing that he is already indebted to three other creditors. If the loan goes sour, he
should not be entitled to claim equal status with the earlier creditors. He should be lower down
the totem pole. If each of the creditors had taken security, then, generally, this rule would be
applied to the claims against the security.

There is no adequate reason why a different rule should be applied to the personal claims
against a debtor. In fact, the existing rule encourages irresponsible credit practices. So long as
there is no reliable method of ascertaining outstanding debts the later creditor has a valid
excuse. The establishment of a register would eliminate this excuse – and hopefully improve the
over-all standard of credit granting.

4
Self-Help Collection

INTRODUCTION

While most legal treatments of debtor-creditor relations have in the past tended to focus almost exclusively on formal collection processes, most delinquent debts are collected by informal methods. This chapter surveys the informal collection methods often used by creditors and their agents and examines some of the recent attempts by legislatures to recognize the realities of the collection process and to regulate its excesses.

I THE SCOPE OF THE PROBLEM

a / Law Reform Commission of British Columbia, *Report on Debtor Creditor Relationships, Part I, Debt Collection and Collection Agents* (1971), pp 6–10 (Footnotes omitted)

PART ONE / INTRODUCTION

1 The earliest legislation in Canada dealing directly with debt collections was the Ontario *Debt Collectors Act* of 1896. That Act contained only one section, which penalized any person printing or publishing 'any notice or form which is an imitation, or a colourable imitation of any of the forms appended to the *Division Courts Act*, and which is calculated to deceive the public by inducing the belief that such notice or form is a notice or form from the said court, or is part of the process of a division court,' and also anyone 'who issues or makes use of any such notice or form in connection with any collection agency or otherwise.' Violations were punishable with a fine of $20 under the *Summary Convictions Act*. In 1927, the prohibition of the *Debt Collectors Act* was broadened to cover the publication or use of imitations or colourable imitations of 'other legal process.'

2 The *Debt Collectors Act* remains on the statute book in Ontario. It has no precise equivalent in the statutes of British Columbia, though there is a comparable prohibition, applying to collection agents and bailiffs only, in section 22 (g) of the *Collection Agents Act, 1967*, which is reproduced as Appendix A to this Report. Legislation broadly comparable to this latter statute exists in a number of other provinces.

3 The general structure of most of the modern legislation is similar, and is based upon a pattern first reflected in a statute of Nova Scotia in 1921. Despite their structural similarity, however, there are a number of differences between the various provincial statutes. In 1933, at a time when six provinces had collection agents legislation, the Conference of Commissioners on Uniformity of Legislation in Canada considered the desirability of preparing a uniform Collec-

tion Agents Act, but, acting on the advice of the Ontario Commissioners, decided against proceeding further.

4 British Columbia was among the first provinces to enact legislation, with the *Collection Agents' Licensing Act, 1930*. That statute was progressively amended between 1930 and 1959, and in 1967 it was repealed and replaced by the *Collection Agents Act*.

5 Despite this history of fairly continuous scrutiny, however, and despite the growing concern with consumer credit and consumer protection, the debt-collection process itself has been largely ignored. In particular, the legislative emphasis upon collection agents has tended to obscure the fact that a substantial proportion, perhaps the majority, of debts are collected directly by creditors, and not through the medium of collection agents. Such legal controls as do exist over debt collection are widely scattered across the entire body of the law. Accordingly, the Commission decided, as part of its Project No. 2 on Debtor-Creditor Relations, to examine these controls, as they affect both collection agents and others.

PART TWO / DEBT COLLECTION GENERALLY

(a) The dimensions of the problem

8 The Special Joint Committee of the Senate and the House of Commons on Consumer Credit stated in its 1967 Report that 'collection agency practices sometimes harass the poor and unsophisticated.' Studies done in Ontario and Quebec have produced a good deal of information about alleged unscrupulous tactics employed by creditors and collection agents. The Payne Committee on the Enforcement of Judgment Debts in Great Britain stated in its 1969 Report that 'some creditors are prepared to use any method and to go to unacceptable lengths in order to collect their debt.' The Report includes examples of the sort of harassing tactics reported to the Committee.

9 The Commission has not conducted its own field studies in order to determine the incidence of harassment in British Columbia. It is, nevertheless, satisfied that it does occur, and in a sufficient volume to warrant remedial action. Information obtained from the Inspector of Collection Agents, the Consumer Affairs Officer, the Consumer Services Branch of the Department of Corporate and Consumer Affairs in Ottawa, the Better Business Bureau in Vancouver, and those responsible for the 'Action Line' column in the Vancouver *Province*, among others, reveal a fairly large volume of complaints of harassment and intimidation.

10 There are a number of categories of complaint that seem to recur. It is frequently alleged, for example, that the wrong person has been contacted by a creditor or collector, because of a similarity of names and a lack of detailed research prior to making contact with the alleged debtor, although in a number of cases it was alleged that the creditor or collector was notified of the error.

11 Another common complaint involves charges of repeated telephone calls to an alleged debtor, and of the use of rude, abusive, and threatening tactics on the telephone. In one case, reported to the Better Business Bureau in Vancouver, it was charged that a collector had suggested to the wife of an alleged debtor who was seriously ill that she should commit robbery, if necessary, in order to pay an alleged debt. In another case, obtained from the same source, it was claimed that a collector had telephoned an alleged debtor on 20 separate occasions during the course of a single day. The Director of the Vancouver Community Lawyer Program reported a case to the Commission in which a middle-aged and sick lady, who had three children and had been deserted by her husband, was telephoned at 2 a.m. with a demand for full payment of a loan by noon the same day. The same collector is reported to have told the lady that 'by the

time we are finished with you, we are going to make the Nazis look like nuns.' Recently, in Alberta, a collector was convicted on a charge that he had told a man in a telephone conversation that he was a city detective, and that if a certain bill was not promptly paid, the man and his wife would be arrested.

12 A third group of complaints relates to allegations that creditors or collectors contact friends, neighbours, or members of an alleged debtor's family, either in person or by telephone, and discuss his financial affairs with them.

13 Another frequent complaint is that creditors and collectors contact the employer of the alleged debtor and inform him of the indebtedness, or visit him at his place of work and discuss his affairs with him in the presence of others, or leave embarrassing or compromising telephone messages for him there. In one case, reported to the Better Business Bureau in Vancouver, a telephone message was left for an employee at his place of work stating that a particular collection agency (no longer in business) had called and informed the person who took the message that 'they have issued a committal order against you.' The alleged debt was in fact that of the wife, and, on the basis of the available information, it was at least arguable that it was not a debt for which the husband was in law responsible.

14 A further group of complaints relates to situations in which it is claimed that, although a debt has been discharged by payment, the alleged debtor is nevertheless subjected to repeated demands for payment, whether by the creditor himself or by a collector acting on his behalf.

15 In the Commission's opinion there is sufficient evidence of these and similar activities to warrant the conclusion that there is a problem that requires attention. This conclusion should not be taken as a general indictment of creditors or collection agents. The Commission's view would remain unaffected, however, even if it were shown that harassment was the exclusive habit of but a single creditor or agent. To adapt some words used in another context by the Royal Commission on the Cost of Borrowing Money, Cost of Credit, and Related Matters in the Province of Nova Scotia:

To dwell on the question whether some people in these businesses are a set of [rascals] or not is to miss the point completely. The real point is the extent to which inadmissible practices can be allowed to gain widespread acceptance, so as to commend themselves not only to the few who may be depraved but to the many who are not but who simply do not stop to think about them.

16 The Commission should also not be taken as suggesting that, as between alleged debtors and creditors, the former have a monopoly on virtue and the latter on vice. It may be acknowledged that in many cases people have themselves alone to blame for their misfortunes, and in some cases debtors do seek to evade payment of lawful debts. It may also be acknowledged that the problem is aggravated by the fact that, as the Payne Committee put it, 'the relationship of creditor and debtor often engenders antagonism.' It is also affected by the fact that, again to quote the Payne Committee, 'the debtor class includes many who by misfortune or mischance have drifted into debt and they are peculiarly exposed and vulnerable.' Moreover, there are elements in the law affecting creditors' rights and remedies that place a high premium upon speed and decisiveness in the recovery of debts. This is especially true in the case of consumer debt, where the creditor may be unsecured. Nevertheless, to quote the Payne Committee once more, 'it cannot be tolerated that just claims be pursued by unjust methods ... if reasonable methods of collecting debts fail, the proper course for creditors is to invoke the machinery of the Courts.' The Commission agrees.

(b) The existing law on harassment

17 The remedies available to one who claims to be the victim of abusive or intimidatory tactics are scattered across the entire body of criminal and civil law.

18 (i) Criminial liability: Section 330 (3) of the *Criminal Code* provides that 'every one who, without lawful excuse and with intent to harass any person, makes or causes to be made repeated telephone calls to such person is guilty of an offence punishable upon summary conviction.' Section 331 (1) of the Code penalizes 'every one who … by letter, telegram, telephone, cable, radio or otherwise, knowingly utters, conveys or causes any person to receive a threat (*a*) to cause death or injury to any person, or (*b*) to burn, destroy or damage real or personal property, or (*c*) to kill, maim, wound, poison or injure any animal or bird that is the property of any person.'

19 Section 305 (1) of the Code provides that 'every one who, without reasonable justification or excuse and with intent to extort or gain anything, by threats, accusations, menaces or violence induces or attempts to induce any person, whether or not he is the person threatened, accused or menaced or to whom violence is shown, to do anything or to cause anything to be done, is guilty of an indictable offence.' In *R*. v *Natarelli and Volpe* [1968] 1 C.C.C. 154, the Supreme Court of Canada held that to constitute a defence to a charge under section 305, 'there must be reasonable justification or excuse not only for the demand but for the making of the threats or menaces by which the accused sought to compel compliance with the demand.' Mr. Justice Cartwright stated that:

When it is proved that threats have been made for the making of which there could be no justification or excuse, that the threats were made with intent to gain something and were calculated to induce the person threatened to do something, the commission of the crime defined in section 305 is established and it is unnecessary to inquire whether the person making the threats had a lawful right to the thing demanded or entertained an honest belief that he had such a right; that inquiry would be necessary only if the threats were such that there could be reasonable justification or excuse for making them.

By section 305(2), a threat to institute civil proceedings is not a threat for the purposes of section 305(1)

20 Section 129 of the *Criminal Code* provides that 'every one who asks or obtains or agrees to receive or obtain any valuable consideration for himself or any other person by agreeing to compound or conceal an indictable offence' commits an indictable offence. There are a number of cases in which the Courts have expressed the view that a threat to institute criminal proceedings, as a means of compelling the payment of even a lawful debt, is an abuse of the process of the Court. The Professional Conduct Committee of the Law Society of British Columbia has ruled that 'no member shall demand or appear to demand on behalf of a client, a payment of money or any other thing from any person to avoid a prosecution being launched against that person.'

21 Section 333 of the Code provides that 'every one who demands, receives, or otherwise obtains anything, or causes or procures anything to be delivered or paid to any person under, upon, or by virtue of any instrument issued under the authority of law, knowing that it is based on a forged document, is guilty of an indictable offence.' Reference should also be made to the indictable offence of extortion by libel under section 266. Finally, the *Criminal Code* provisions concerning theft (section 283), false pretences (section 320), forgery (section 324), and the use of counterfeit or unauthorized marks or stamps (section 334) should be noted.

22 (ii) Civil liability: Quite apart from criminal sanctions, there are a number of civil causes of action for damages that might, depending upon the circumstances of the case, be relevant to the problem of harassment. They include actions for trespass, assault, and defamation, and possibly actions for the intentional or negligent infliction of nervous shock, abuse of legal process, and an action under the provisions of the recently enacted *Privacy Act*. It is beyond the scope of this Report to examine in detail the requirements of each of these causes of action. It is sufficient to say that trespass and assault will rarely be relevant, while the precise status and scope of actions for damages for intentional infliction of nervous shock and abuse of legal procedure is far from clear. In view of the fact that communication with neighbours, friends, relatives, and employers of alleged debtors is one of the most frequent sources of complaint about extra-judicial collection procedures, however, the two actions of defamation and invasion of privacy will be given more extended consideration.

23 Defamation consists of the publication to a third person of matter containing a false imputation as to the character of another. If the publication takes a permanent form, for example, if it is in writing, it is described as a libel, and as actionable *per se*, that is, the law presumes that the person libelled has suffered loss, without the necessity for any proof by him of such loss. If the publication takes a more transitory form, for example, if it consists of spoken words, it is described as a slander, and is ordinarily only actionable if the person slandered proves that he has suffered some actual loss.

24 It is of the essence of defamation that it consists of a false statement damaging to the character or reputation of another. 'The law will not permit a man to recover damages in respect of an injury to a character which he either does not, *or ought not*, to possess.' It follows that if the statement is in substance true, there is no actionable wrong. The law, however, presumes that every man is of good reputation, and consequently the plaintiff is not required to *prove* the falsity of an alleged defamatory statement. This is assumed in favour of the plaintiff, it being left to the defendant to show that the statement was true (the defence of justification).

25 In so far as allegations of harassment by creditors and collectors are based upon the fact that they communicate *accurate* information to others about a man's alleged indebtedness; therefore, the law of defamation will provide no remedy.

26 On the other hand, the claim of harassment may occasionally be based upon an allegation that false information has been communicated. In this case, the communication may be *prima facie* defamatory. It has long been settled, however, that merely to say falsely of a man that he owes money is not defamatory. As Chief Justice Begbie put it in *Wolfenden* v *Giles* (1892), 2 B.C.R. 284, 'that is to say what is true of every householder ... on most days of the month.' On the other hand, it has been held defamatory to say falsely of a man that he refuses to pay his debts, or is deliberately delaying payment of them, or he is unable to pay them.

27 Even if the statement be defamatory, however, it will not necessarily be actionable. Sometimes even a false statement may give rise to no liability. 'In certain situations, the law allows a man to speak and write without restraint, even at the expense of another's good name and character. These are called Privileged Occasions.' There are two sorts of privileged occasions – those which confer an absolute immunity from suit, and those in which the immunity is a qualified one only. In the present context, only the latter are relevant. They are described as being occasions 'where the person who makes a communication had an interest or duty, legal, social or moral, to make it to the person to whom it is made, and the person to whom it is made has a corresponding interest or duty to receive it.' The statement is only privileged, however, if made pursuant to the purposes for which the privilege is granted. If it was made for other purposes, the privilege is abused, and will be lost. It is for this reason that it is described as a qualified privilege only.

28 There are no Canadian or English authorities directly in point on the question whether a qualified privilege attaches to a communication made by a creditor or collector to an employer as to an alleged indebtedness of an employee. Although in the United States there are authorities going both ways, the better view seems to be that no privilege ordinarily attaches to such a communication, and it is likely that this view would be adopted by Canadian Courts should the matter be litigated here. Here again it should be emphasized, however, that the statement, even if false, and although not subject to any privilege, will only be actionable if capable of a defamatory meaning.

29 It is apparent, then, that the law of defamation provides a remedy for harassment in what are at best a small number of relatively marginal cases of false and defamatory statements.

30 From the point of view of the alleged debtor, however, the point is not that the statement made to his employer is true or false, but rather that the information contained in the statement is really of no legitimate concern to his employer at all. In essence, his position is that it is an invasion of his privacy for his personal finances to be discussed with his employer or anyone else without his consent.

31 The right to protection against invasions of privacy has not been explicitly recognized, as such, at common law. In British Columbia, however, section 2 (1) of the *Privacy Act* provides:

It is a tort, actionable without proof of damage, for a person, wilfully and without a claim of right, to violate the privacy of another.

Section 2 (2) declares:

The nature and degree of privacy to which a person is entitled in any situation or in relation to any matter is that which is reasonable in the circumstances, due regard being given to the lawful interests of others; and in determining whether the act or conduct of a person constitutes a violation of the privacy of another, regard shall be given to the nature, incidence, and occasion of the act or conduct and to the relationship, whether domestic or other, between the parties.

Section 3 (1) provides, *inter alia*, that:

An act or conduct is not a violation of privacy where (*a*) it is consented to by some person entitled to consent; (*b*) the act or conduct was authorized or required by or under a law in force in the Province or by a Court or any process of a Court.

To date this legislation has been the subject of only one reported case, *Davis* v *McArthur* [1971] 2 W.W.R. 142, an action against a private investigator.

32 It will be seen that this statute does not purport to render every invasion of privacy actionable. The defendant's acts must not only be an invasion of the plaintiff's privacy but, in addition, they must have been committed 'without a claim of right' and must fall outside the scope of the protective provisions of section 3 (1) ...

37 The Commission has concluded that the present law is inadequate to deal with harassment of alleged debtors. The criminal law, for the most part, deals only with more extreme forms of intimidatory behaviour. While some forms of harassment doubtless are criminal, there are others which, though unreasonable, harsh, unconscionable, or unscrupulous, are at present beyond the reach of the *Criminal Code*. With the possible exception of section 315 (3), none of the *Criminal Code* provisions is directed to the problem of harassment as such, and the problems of proof under section 315 (3) are likely to be, at the very least, considerable, and in any event are sufficient to warrant a doubt as to its effectiveness as a restraint in the present

context. Moreover, section 315 (3) requires, as an ingredient of the offence, *repeated* telephone calls.

38 The present state of the civil law is also not conducive to confidence in its utility as a curb on the sorts of excesses referred to. The two torts that seem most likely to be serviceable are actions for defamation and invasion of privacy. Both actions must be brought in the Supreme Court, since both the County Court and the Small Claims Division of the Provincial Court are expressly precluded from exercising jurisdiction over actions for defamation, and jurisdiction over actions under the *Privacy Act* is expressly conferred on the Supreme Court by that Act. As a result, the costs of litigation may well be prohibitive to those most likely to be vulnerable to harassment. Moreover, many of those who are unable, for whatever reason, to pay their debts undoubtedly feel a sense of 'moral guilt' and embarrassment at that fact, and are unlikely, therefore, to be enthusiastic about the possibility of a Supreme Court action with its attendant publicity. In the Commission's view these considerations represent a serious limitation upon the practical usefulness of existing remedies in tort as weapons against harassment, except in rare cases.

39 The Commission has, therefore, concluded that the present law is inadequate to deal with harassment of debtors. That conclusion was relatively easily reached. Far more difficult, however, has been the problem of suggesting reforms.

b / Report of the Committee on the Enforcement of Judgment Debts, (Payne Committee), London, 1969, pp. 319–21.

UNREASONABLE HARASSMENT OF DEBTORS

Nature of problem
1230 A creditor is entitled to use all lawful and reasonable measures to obtain payment before taking court proceedings to recover the debt. Indeed it is through such measures that the great majority of debts are collected without recourse to the courts. Most of these measures for exerting extra-judicial pressures to collect overdue debts are reasonable and acceptable. They include such familiar expedients as rendering bills, invoices and accounts of debtors; written and oral reminders; letters by debt collecting agencies and, ultimately, by solicitors and threats of court proceedings unless payment or an offer of payment is immediately forthcoming. Many debtors respond but there remains a residue against whom such measures fail and court proceedings have to be taken. The question arises whether some extra-judicial methods of collecting debts go beyond what is reasonable and should be controlled or forbidden.
1231 This question raises formidable difficulties. Under the present law, so long as no unlawful means are employed, no restrictions are placed upon the creditor or his representative resorting to any device to obtain payment of his debt; and even if the device is unfair, callous or wicked there is no protection for the debtor nor sanction against the creditor. The result is that comparatively little is known about the various reprehensible forms of pressure which are employed or about their harmful effect on debtors and their families.
1232 We have received factual information from the John Hilton Bureau of the *News of the World* which cites several kinds of pressure by debt collectors against readers of that newspaper:
   i   'the blue frightener' i.e. a printed notice of intention to institute proceedings in a county court but printed in black letters on blue paper so as to simulate a county court summons;

ii   'the red frightener' i.e. a printed notice with large red letters on white paper under the rubric 'You have four days in which to reduce your debt';
iii   frequent calls at the home of the debtor leaving threatening cards;
iv   informing neighbours of the debtor about his indebtedness under the guise of seeking information;
v   informing local shopkeepers of the indebtedness of the debtor under the guise of seeking information;
vi   threatening to paint over a motor car with the statement that it is the property of the creditor;
vii   writing to the employer of the debtor about his indebtedness under the guise of avoiding the need for the debtor to absent himself from work to attend court;
viii threats to send a 'Bad Debt Collection Van' i.e. a van with the words 'Bad Debt Collection' painted in large letters on the side, to make a personal call on the debtor at his home or place of employment.

1233 Through the kindness of the Independent Television Authority we saw a documentary film entitled 'Easy Credit Bad Debts' which had been shown as part of the normal Independent Television programme. This film showed two forms of extra-judicial pressure:
i   visiting the home of the debtor in the early hours of the morning, even on a Sunday morning under the guise of collecting chattels let under a hire purchase agreement; and
ii   implied threat to use force under the guise that any force used against the collector would be met by force.

1234 We have also material from other sources showing that other forms of pressure are used. They include visiting the debtor at his place of work, calling on a shopkeeper/debtor and demanding payment in the presence of his customers, calling with an alsatian dog to collect from the debtor, sending obvious demand notes for debts but wrongly addressed to the debtor's neighbours, threatening to paint the debtor's premises, and other similar measures of intimidation.

c / Note: Some Recent Developments in Tort Law

The paucity of tort cases arising in Canada with respect to harassment of debtors perhaps is an indication of the failure of traditional common law tort concepts to come to grips with the very real problems that do exist in this area of the law. One of the few Canadian authorities in this regard is *Bahner* v *Marwest Hotel Co. Ltd. et al.* (1969), 6 D.L.R. (3d) 322 (B.C.S.C.), affirmed (1970), 12 D.L.R. (3d) 646 (B.C.C.A.), where the court awarded $6,000 'aggravated damages' in compensation for the humiliation and degradation to which the debtor was exposed by being falsely imprisoned in an hotel dining room, for refusing to pay for a bottle of wine which he had ordered, but was not able to drink. Wilson CJSC said (at p 329):

But the fact that he was publicly humiliated by detention by the security officer in the hotel in the presence of the staff and a dozen guests, and by subsequent interrogation and arrest by a uniformed policeman was known to a considerable number of people, who have in all probability and very naturally told other persons about it. It is hard to calculate how far news of this kind may spread and what harm it may have done. Few persons who witnessed his arrest are likely to be aware of his subsequent acquittal ... The degradation consequent upon the experience suffered by the plaintiff is sore and not easily forgotten.

Bahner has been followed more recently in *Perry and Galley* v *Fried and Gorman* (1972), 9 N.S.R. (2d) 545 (N.S.S.C.).

Bahner was also applied in *Delta Hotels Ltd.* v *Magrum* (1976), 59 D.L.R. (3d) 126 (B.C.S.C.), in which Mackoff J awarded aggravated and exemplary damages to the patrons and staff of a hotel dining-room who were brutally beaten by two members of the British Columbia Lion Football team.

In contrast to the state of the jurisprudence in Canada, American jurisprudence contains many examples of courts using both traditional as well as innovative concepts of tort law to deal with unreasonable harassment of debtors. For example, in *La Salle Extension University* v *Fogarty* (1934), 253 N.W. 424 (Neb.), the creditor was found liable on the basis of intentional infliction of mental suffering. Where the debtor's claim was based on 'excessive attachment' (e.g. garnisheeing the debtor's bank account before trial in an amount bearing no relation to the actual sum of the creditor's claim), American courts have sometimes found liability on the basis of malicious prosecution (*Clark* v *Nordholt* (1898), 53 P. 400 (Cal.)) or abuse of process (*White Lighting Co.* v *Wolfson* (1968), 438 P. 2d 345 (Cal.)). In *Brents* v *Morgan* (1927), 299 S.W. 967 (Ky.) recovery was allowed on the basis of invasion of privacy where a creditor posted a sign on his shop window declaring the plaintiff's indebtedness. Similarly, see *Trammell* v *Citizens News Co.* (1941), 148 S.W. 2d 708 (Ky.) where the fact of the plaintiff's indebtedness was published in a newspaper.

Reaching beyond traditional categories of tort law, the courts in Texas have developed a separate tort of 'unreasonable collection': *Wright* v *E-Z Finance Co.* (1954), 267 S.W. 2d. 602; *Duty* v *General Finance Co.* (1954), 273 S.W. 2d. 64. The standard used to determine liability is the reasonableness of the methods used in collecting the debt. While some cases have held that actual physical harm must have occurred, there is no necessity to prove malice. The tort recognizes the interests of the debtor to be protected from abuse, even though a just debt is due. It also recognizes the interests of the creditor to collect his debt, but does not give him a license to harm the debtor simply because payment can be demanded in law. See Martin, 'A Creditor's Liability for Unreasonable Collection Efforts: The Evolution of a Tort in Texas' (1967), 9 *S. Tex. L.J.* 127 and Julavits and Stuntebeck, 'Effectively Regulating Extra-Judicial Collection of Debts' (1968), 20 *Maine L. Rev.* 261, at pp 271–82.)

(d) Some Dunning Letters
The following letter, received by a debtor in Great Britain is extracted from Paul Rock, *Making People Pay* (1973):

You have made no payment to the Agency.
We intend to collect if it takes us a Life Time.
None of the steps to be taken are very pleasant.
Our collectors will call by Day and Night.
You will be on the next **BLACK LIST** to go out to **SHOPS**
H.P. Companies, etc.,
If we find, once the Black List is out, that you owe to two or
more creditors a total sum of £50 we will make you
BANKRUPT.

BANKRUPT Receiving Order/Public Examination/Name in
Gazette/The Petition Etc.
REALISATION OF DEBTORS PROPERTY
The only goods we cannot take are your Tools of Trade,
wearing apparel and bedding to the value of £20.
Really the amount involved is not worth all the trouble it can
cause you.
SO LET US HAVE A PAYMENT BY RETURN OF POST
(Premier Debt Recovery Agency.)

The next three letters are taken from Ison, *Materials on Debt Collection*,
(Queens University, 1972) pp 224–5.


```
                                   ... COLLECTION AGENCIES LTD.,
                                          Kingston, Ontario.


Re:
Balance outstanding $__________

People are known by their actions.  This is particularly true in the
credit community.  Your action or rather inaction would lead me to
believe that you are indifferent to your personal credit standing.
Would you for the sake of this one small acccount have this condition
prevail on your credit file indefinitely?  Surely you value your credit
record enough to contact the writer about this obligation.

We pride ourselves on being reasonable people to deal with, will you give
us this opportunity?

Contact this office immediately.

Yours Very Truly,


Branch Manager
```

... COLLECTION AGENCIES LTD.,
Kingston, Ontario.

Re:
Balance outstanding $ _______

Why bother? Why not forget your responsibilities, wouldn't it be wonderful,
or would it, would it be wonderful if our leaders, our businessmen, our
police, our citizens said let's forget our responsibilities. No, it would
not be wonderful it would be disastrous, it would mean looting, robbery,
murder, a complete loss of our whole way of life. Are you forgetting your
responsibilities? It is our job to first remind you of them by letter and
then if this fails by action. You may be much better off to consider
settling this account now rather than face future action.

I trust that I have managed to convey my meaning.

Send full payment immediately by money order or
certified cheque directly to this office.

Yours Very Truly,

Branch Manager

... COLLECTION AGENCIES LTD.,
Kingston, Ontario.

Re:
Balance outstanding $ _______

Your disregard of my last three letters leads me to believe that you are
acting in an irresponsible manner. Irresponsible people have to be governed
by firm methods which may be considered harsh. If you wish to be treated as
a responsible person, act now, and take time to settle this account.

Remit your payment at once.

Yours Very Truly,

Branch Manager

Do either of the following letters violate s 1 of The Debt Collectors Act, R.S.O. 1970, c 106 (reproduced below at p 113), which prohibits any person from publishing a notice calculated to induce the belief that it is part of a process of court?

<pre>
                        INTENTION
                           To
                         Issue
                        SUMMONS

Re:_______________________________
          Balance:_________________

Be Advised That A Statement of Claim has been prepared

Between

                              ____
                                                     Creditor

                              - and -

                              ____
                                                       Debtor

This Summons will be issued within forty-eight (48) hours, for the above
amount not including court costs.
You will undoubtedly be served with these documents by COURT BAILIFF unless
your CERTIFIED CHEQUE or MONEY ORDER is received at this office.

Notify us immediately of your intentions!

                         Agent For the Creditor
                         ... COLLECTION AGENCIES LTD.,
                         Kingston, Ontario.
</pre>

𝕱inal 𝕹otice 𝕭efore 𝕾uit

_______________________ YOU OWE _______________________

CLAIMANT

If Payment is Not Received within Three (3) days at   100 Central Street
Toronto, Ontario

YOU WILL BE SUED

Direct any queries to   **987-6543**

____

CLERK

QUESTIONS

1 In any of the letters set out above is there anything in their contents or character which seems objectionable? Why?

2 What warnings or threats should a creditor be entitled to issue to a defaulting debtor:
   damage to credit rating?
   simulated court forms?
   threatening to send van?
   communicating with the employer?
   threatening criminal action?
   vague threats of drastic or harsh consequences?

3 Apart from the substance of the communication, there is the question of what is an equitable *mode* of communication?
   collect telephone calls & telegrammes?
   call to debtor at employment with message to phone?
   frequent calls at home?
   informing neighbours? local merchants?
   pre-signed lawyer's letters?

4 Given Leff's proposals for an increased flow of information between debtor and creditor as a means of minimizing transaction costs, what is wrong with the creditor informing the debtor of the precise steps he intends to take to enforce payment so that the debor is made aware of the costs of further default?

e / Contacting the Debtor's Employer

The following letter was sent to the employer of a consumer debtor by a vendor involved in collecting his own debts. Prior to this action, the purchaser had received a letter containing the following warnings:

What would your employer say were we to call his attention to the balance you owe us ... and how we tried to persuade you to do what was right? ...
Mail in your payment at once – or come to the office at once. Whichever you may choose, do it now. Tomorrow may be too late.

T O R O N T O   B U D G E T

Household Products Limited

Dear Sir,
    I respectfully call attention to _________________________________
                       , one
                       , one of your employees who is indebted
to the above named company in the amount of \$_____________ for the purchase
of household necessities.

Notwithstanding the fact that letters have been written in regard to this
indebtedness and a Collector has conveniently called each week, payments have
not been made as promised, and the account today is far in arrears.

Our concern has never favoured the policy of garnishing a person's wages
because it greatly increases the amount of the debt and very often results in
the employee being discharged. If the individual is kept working the garnishee
becomes a bother and expense to the payroll department of the employer.

Our purpose in writing you is definitely not to have you act in the
capacity of a collection agency. We only ask your kind co-operation in calling
this matter to the attention of your employee. As further evidence of our
fairness and patience we are willing to disregard all past due payments and
will restore his credit to good standing provided payments of \$ ....
are made to our Collector each week.

Your satisfaction in this matter will be most sincerely appreciated.

                Yours very truly,

                Toronto Budget Household Products Limited
                Limited Credit Manager

NOTE In *Sawatzky* v *Credit Bureau of Edmonton Ltd.* (Unreported, File No. 62766, 19 May 1970, Supreme Court of Alberta), the defendant sent the following letter to the plaintiff's employer:

The above person, whom we understand is in your employ, is indebted to our client.

It is our wish to endeavour to have this account settled with the least possible cost or embarrassment to the debtor. However, despite numerous requests by letter and/or telephone, the debtor has as yet shown no inclination to make satisfactory arrangements for payment.

We feel that possibly a word from you could impress on him the advantage of avoiding legal proceedings and while we dislike bringing the matter to your attention, your assistance could bring about amicable results.

However, this was a case of mistaken identity, and the plaintiff was not the debtor referred to in the letter. The defendant sent the letter in spite of the plaintiff's denial of indebtedness, and when it found out its mistake, did nothing to atone for its error. The plaintiff sued for defamation, and was awarded \$1,000 in damages, an amount which the Court indicated included exemplary damages.

QUESTION Suppose that Mr. Sawatzky had been fired as a result of the creditor's communication with his employer. Would Sawatzky have had a cause of action against his employer? Against the creditor?

In Ontario, The Employment Standards Act, s.o. 1974, c 112, s 9 (infra p 359) prohibits an employer from firing an employee on the grounds that garnishment proceedings are about to take place.

Many cases have risen in US jurisdictions which have attempted to deal with the problem of the creditor's pre-judgment communication to the debtor's employer within the confines of the traditional common law torts of invasion of privacy, libel and intentional infliction of nervous shock. The Supreme Court of Iowa in *Yoder* v *Smith* (1962), 112 N.W. 2d 862 held that communication to an employer of an employee's indebtedness may be an exception to one's absolute right of privacy:

We believe ... that an employer has a natural and proper interest in the facts relative to debts owed by his employees. He is subject to the expense and inconvenience of defending himself in garnishee as well as other creditor proceedings ... He is not in a category with the general public, which of course generally would have no legitimate interest in a private matter between creditor and debtor ... (per Larson J at p 867)

Many other cases have rejected the assertion of invasion of privacy in these circumstances: *Voneye* v *Turner* (1951), 240 s.w. 2d 588 (Ky.); *Patton* v *Jacobs*, (1948) 78 N.E. 2d 789 (Ind.); *McKenzie* v *Huckaby* (1953), 112 F. Supp. 642 (D.C.); *Hawley* v *Professional Credit Bureau* (1956), 76 N.W. 2d. 835 (Mich.).

For an analysis of the American jurisprudence see 'Creditors Pre-Judgment Communication to Debtor's Employer', K.M. Block (1969), 36 *Brooklyn Law Review* 95.

f / Collections by Lawyers

Lawyers will often write one or two demand letters threatening civil proceedings, and then may institute action if instructed. The main limitation on writing threatening letters is the prohibition (reinforced by the *Law Society Professional Conduct and Discipline Committee*) against threatening anything but civil proceedings.

Solicitors should be aware of section 39(2) of The Judicature Act, R.S.O. 1970, c 228 which provides that 'if such sum or debt is payable otherwise than by virtue of a written instrument at a time certain, interest may be allowed from the time when a demand of payment was made in writing, informing the debtor that interest would be claimed from the date of the demand.' A typical demand letter will include a line claiming interest from the date of the letter.

[Note: Utility shut-offs is another form of self-help collection. It will be discussed in greater detail below in Chapter 14: Special Creditors.]

g / Using the Criminal Law to Collect a Debt

It should be noted that as a general proposition of law, the Courts do not look favourably upon a creditor applying pressure on a recalcitrant debtor by threatening to lay criminal charges. For example, in *R.* v *Bell* (1929), 3 D.L.R. 931 the British Columbia Court of Appeal quashed a conviction of concealing property with the intent to defraud creditors. Macdonald CJA (at pp 933–44) made the following comments:

Now while we think the evidence in the circumstances was not such as could be safely acted upon to found a conviction we wish to say in addition that it is apparent to us that the criminal proceedings were manifestly not taken in vindication of public justice but wholly because of appellant's refusal to comply with the demand to 'dig up the money or take the consequences'. The prosecution, was, therefore, an abuse of the process of the magistrate's court which we cannot countenance. We think that the criminal courts are not to be held *in terrorem* over alleged debtors.

(See also *R. v Michigan Central Railroad* (1907), 17 C.C.C. 483; *R. v Thornton* (1926), 46 C.C.C. 249; *R. v LeRoux*, [1928] 3 D.L.R. 688; 'Criminal Law May Not Be Used To Collect Civil Debts,' *Law Society of Upper Canada Gazette*, Vol. 2, 1969.)

An interesting issue arose in *R. v Winning* (1973), 12 C.C.C. 449, where the accused was charged with obtaining credit from a large department store by false pretenses. In her credit application, the accused had given her correct name and address but had made two false statements which related to her credit-worthiness. The Ontario Court of Appeal held that had the store relied on the application form in extending credit to her, she would have been guilty of the offence, *even though she had always paid her account in time*. The evidence showed, however, that the credit grantor in fact had merely relied on the application form for her name and address. Since credit had not been extended in reliance on the application form, but rather in reliance on the store's own independent investigation of her, the accused could not be convicted of the offence.

2 LEGISLATION ON HARASSMENT AND DEBT COLLECTION

a / The Debt Collectors Act, R.S.O. 1970, c 106

1. Every person, whether principal or agent, who prints or publishes a notice or form that is an imitation or a colourable imitation of any of the forms appended to *The Small Claims Courts Act*, or of other legal process, and that is calculated to deceive the public by inducing the belief that such notice or form is a notice or form from a court, or is part of the process of a court, or who issues or makes use of such a notice or form in connection with a collection agency or otherwise, is guilty of an offence and on summary conviction is liable to a fine of not more than $20.

b / The Collection Agencies Act, R.S.O. 1970, c 71, as amended

This Act is the current Ontario legislation regulating collection agencies. It is applicable to persons dealing with a debtor for the purpose of obtaining the payment of money owing to another person (s 19(a)), but does not apply *inter alia* to a solicitor in the regular practice of law (s 2(a)), to an isolated collection (s 2(f)), or to a creditor collecting his own debts. Collection agencies are required to register (s 4). There are also extensive provisions setting out registration requirements aimed at keeping unscrupulous persons out of the field (s 6). There are wide powers of investigation and inspection, mainly directed at determining whether the agency has misused funds held in trust for its customers or for debtors (ss 23–8). It is an offence knowingly to engage the services of an unregistered collection agency.

30. (1) The Registrar may at any time require a collection agency to provide him with copies of any letters, forms, form letters, notices, pamphlets, brochures, advertisements, contracts, agreements or other materials used or proposed to be used by the collection agency in the course of conducting its business.

(2) Where the Registrar believes on reasonable and probable grounds that any of the material referred to in subsection 1 is harsh, false, misleading or deceptive, the Registrar may alter, amend, restrict or prohibit the use of such material, and section 8 applies *mutatis mutandis* to the order in the same manner as to a proposal by the Registrar to refuse registration and the order of the Registrar shall take effect immediately, but the Tribunal may grant a stay until the Registrar's order becomes final.

31. No collection agency or collector shall,

(*a*) collect or attempt to collect for a person for whom it acts any moneys in addition to the amount owing by the debtor;

(*b*) send any telegram or make any telephone call, for which the charges are payable by the addressee or the person to whom the call is made, to a debtor for the purpose of demanding payment of a debt;

(*c*) receive or make an agreement for the additional payment of any money by a debtor of a creditor for whom the collection agency acts, either on its own account or for the creditor and whether as a charge, cost expense or otherwise, in consideration for any forbearance, favour, indulgence, intercession or other conduct by the collection agency;

(*d*) deal with a debtor in a name other than that authorized by the registration.

34. Where the Registrar believes on reasonable and probable grounds that a collection agency is making false, misleading or deceptive statements in any advertisement, circular, pamphlet or similar material, the Registrar may order the immediate cessation of the use of such material, and section 8 applies *mutatis mutandis* to the order in the same manner as to a proposal by the Registrar to refuse registration and the order of the Registrar shall take effect immediately, but the Tribunal may grant a stay until the Registrar's order becomes final.

Recent legislation has been passed in British Columbia that is more extensive than that in Ontario:

c / Debt Collection Act, S.B.C. 1973 (1st), c 26

14. (1) No person shall, in collecting, negotiating, or demanding payment of a debt, or in repossessing, seizing, or distraining upon any chattel, or in evicting any person from property, exert undue, excessive, or unreasonable pressure upon a debtor, or any member of his family or household, or his employer and, without limiting the generality of the foregoing, undue, excessive, or unreasonable pressure shall be deemed to be exerted where a person

(*a*) makes a charge, threat, or promise that pertains to matters other than the collection of the debt; or

(*b*) except for the purpose of verifying the employment of the debtor, communicates, without the consent of the debtor, with his employer;

(*c*) communicates with a debtor, his family, or his employer, in such a manner and in such circumstances that, because of the nature or frequency of the communications, alarm, distress, and humiliation are likely to result; or

(*d*) uses a summons, notice, demand, or other document expressed in a language, style, or purport of a form used in any court or under the authority of any Act of the Province, or printed or written in the general appearance or format of such form; or (*e*) uses, after the director makes known his objection to it, any agreement, document, letter, or other collection practice; or

(*f*) collects or attempts to collect money from any person who is not liable for the debt; or

(*g*) collects or attempts to collect money that exceeds the amount of the debt owing; or

(*h*) is not a licenced collection agent and collects or attempts to collect a debt in a name other than the name in which the debt was contracted or incurred; or

(*i*) who is a collection agent or a collector

  (i) communicates with any person for the purpose of collecting, negotiating, or demanding payment of a debt by such means that the charges or costs of the communication are payable by that person; or

  (ii) communicates with any person for the purpose of collecting, negotiating, or demanding payment of a debt during a day or during the hours of the day when such communications are prohibited by regulations made under this Act.

(2) Where, in the opinion of the director, a person is causing alarm, distress, or humiliation, the director may send to that person written notice of his objection and, thereupon, that person shall not use the practice to which the director has objected. 1967, c 10, s 22; 1969, c 35, s 3; *am.*

The Act has been recently amended by the addition of s 19A which gives a civil cause of action to 'a debtor who has suffered loss, damage or inconvenience as a result of a contravention of this Act' (Attorney-General Statutes Amendment Act, s.B.C. 1975, c 4, s 4.)

The legislation in Manitoba (The Consumer Protection Act, R.S.M. 1970, c C200) and British Columbia both regulate the collection practices of creditors collecting on their own behalf.

The governing statutes in the other provinces are:

Alta: The Collection Agencies Act, R.S.A. 1970, c 55, s 4 (licence required); s 16 (offences)

Sask: The Collection Agents Act, 1968, S.S. 1968, c 11, s 4 (licence required); s 29 (unlawful collection practices), sections 34–6 (offences and penalties)

Man: The Consumer Protection Act, R.S.M. 1970, c C200, Part XII 'Collection Practices' s 100 (prohibited collection practices); s 102 (where creditor collects amount he has no right to collect, debtor may recover 3X the amount collected). The unlawful collection practices extend to creditors collecting on their own behalf.

Que: Collection Agents Act, S.Q. 1974, c 73, s 8 (permit required); ss 26–30 (prohibited practices); s 36 (offences)

N.B.: Collection Agencies Act, R.S.N.B. 1973, c C-8, s 2 (licence required); sections 4 and 5 (offences)

N.S.: Collection Agencies Act, S.N.S. 1975, c 7

P.E.I.: Collecting Agencies Act, R.S.P.E.I. 1974, c C-12, s 3 (licence required); s 18 (offences)

Nfld.: The Collection Agencies Act, s.Nfld. 1973, No. 14, s 10 (registration); s 21 (unlawful collection practices), s 24 (offences)

QUESTIONS Should debt collection agencies exist at all? Could the system work if creditors were required to collect informally in their own name or use the legal process? Should the provisions of collection agency legislation also be applicable to individuals collecting their own debts?

Also see 'Model Consumer Debt Collection Fair Practices Act', (1975) *Commercial L.J.* 184 drafted by the National Conference of Lawyers and Collection Agencies.

d / The Bailiffs Act, R.S.O. 1970, c 38

1. In this Act,
(*a*) 'Bailiff' means a person who acts, assists any person to act or holds himself out as being available to act for or on behalf of any other person in the repossession or seizure of chattels or in any eviction;
3. (1) No person, other than a person appointed as a bailiff under *The Small Claims Courts Act* or a sheriff's bailiff, shall act as a bailiff unless he has been appointed by the Lieutenant Governor on the recommendation of the Minister.
15. (1) Every person who contravenes any provision of this Act is guilty of an offence and on summary conviction is liable to a fine of not more than $1,000.

In *R.* v *Doucette*, [1960] O.R. 407, 25 D.L.R. (2d) 380, the Ontario Court of Appeal held that bailiffs licenced under The Bailiffs Act are not clothed with any official status as peace officers, and as agents for the creditor, enjoy no greater rights in repossessing the creditor's property than the creditor himself. A bailiff therefore has no right to use force to repossess property from a person having colour of right, and therefore may be found guilty of criminal assault and trespass. If a debtor refuses access to goods and chattels which are being repossessed, neither the creditor nor his bailiff may use force or may trespass to effect repossession. An order under The Replevin Act (see p 133 below) is the only recourse available in these circumstances. This rule, of course, is not applicable to sheriffs or bailiffs acting pursuant to a writ of execution or other court order.

3 ASSIGNMENTS TO COLLECTION AGENCIES

Valley Credits Ltd. v *Key* (1977), 75 D.L.R. (3d) 281 (B.C. Prov. Ct.)

BARNETT, PROV. CT. J.: In this action the plaintiff is the assignee of a debt which I find Victoria Key, the defendant, owed to Norberg & Matheson Agencies Ltd. in the amount claimed, $97.
The plaintiff is a collection agency.
The written assignment given to it by Norbert & Matheson Agencies Ltd. reads:

... in consideration of the sum of $1.00, payment of which is acknowledged herewith, we hereby sell, assign, transfer and set over to and unto Valley Credits Ltd. that certain claim of Norberg & Matheson Agencies Ltd. against Victoria Key in the amount of $97.00 and we do hereby authorize Valley Credits Ltd. to bring action or suit in their own name and do any and all things necessary to enforce collection of said claim.

The defendant had proper notice of the assignment.
Mr. Hansen, the manager of the Williams Lake office of the plaintiff, represented the plaintiff at the trial of this action and testified during the course of the trial. He acknowledged that no

money was actually paid by the plaintiff to Norberg & Matheson Agencies Ltd. In fact, and it is no surprise, the assignment is simply a device which is used to give the plaintiff status to sue in its own name.

The claim was placed with the plaintiff by Norberg & Matheson Agencies Ltd. to be collected from Mrs Key on a percentage basis. That situation has not changed. Mr. Hansen acknowledges that a higher percentage of any moneys collected is retained by the plaintiff in cases such as this where Court action has been taken. He provides an explanation for this fact. He says the increased percentage is necessary to cover paper work and Court costs. Mr. Hansen also says that in a case such as this, when moneys are collected, following deduction of the plaintiff's percentage, 'the trust monies are sent back to the creditor'.

The type of arrangement employed here by the plaintiff and Norberg & Matheson Agencies Ltd. is a common one. The question to be answered in this case is: 'Is it a proper one?'

I should perhaps note at this point that in attempting to answer this question I have had the valuable assistance of written briefs prepared by counsel for the plaintiff and by Mr. Barbour of the Legal Aid Society who presented a contrary submission as *amicus curiae*.

The first matter of concern is that the summons herein was not drawn by a solicitor, and that the plaintiff was not represented at the trial of this action by counsel.

In *The Royal Bank of Canada, Chargex Division* v *Misfeldt*, Provincial Court of British Columbia, Vancouver Small Claims Registry No. 5495/74, decided October 15, 1974 (not reported), His Honour Judge O'Donnell denied the plaintiff leave to enter default judgment where a summons had been prepared by a collection agency. The judgment was founded in part upon the proposition that a summons must be drawn by the plaintiff personally or by a solicitor acting on behalf of the plaintiff.

In *Pacific Parts Ltd.* v *Kintyre All Terrain Equipment Ltd.*, County Court of Vancouver, Vancouver Registry No. F762565, decided November 18, 1976 (not reported but digested in the *British Columbia Decisions*: 'Civil Cases – Practice'), His Honour Judge MacKinnon struck an appearance and defence filed on behalf of the defendant company by its president. He accepted the submission that the Rules of Court did not make any provision for a corporation to appear other than by a solicitor.

With respect, I would decline to follow the *Pacific Parts* decision or the *Royal Bank* decision in so far as it depends upon the proposition that a corporation must engage a solicitor to bring Court action on its behalf.

In *Riskey* v *Revelstoke Steel Fabricators Ltd. et al.* (1964), 47 W.W.R. 638 at p. 639, Ruttan, J., of the Supreme Court of British Columbia disagreed with the argument that a company can only enter an appearance through a solicitor and went on to state: 'A certain authority to act or speak for the company is to be implied from the office held by a senior official of a company.' See also *Charles P. Kinnell & Co., Ltd.* v *Harding, Wace & Co.*, [1918] 1 K.B. 405, 87 L.J.K.B. 342; *Northern Homes Ltd.* v *Steel-Space Industries Ltd. et al.* (1975), 57 D.L.R. (3d) 309, [1975] 5 W.W.R. 115, and *R.* v *Williamson*, [1976] W.W.D. 95.

I therefore attach no importance to the mere facts that this action was not instituted by a solicitor and that the plaintiff was not represented during the trial by counsel.

Mr. Barbour next submits that the plaintiff's action is champertous, and must therefore fail. He cites *Colville* v *Small* (1910), 22 O.L.R. 33; affirmed 22 O.L.R. 426, and *George Biro Real Estate Ltd. et al.* v *Sheldon* (1964), 46 D.L.R. (2d) 610 at pp. 615–20, [1965] 1 O.R. 49.

The facts in the *Colville* v *Small* case were essentially similar to those in the present case. Middleton, J., held that the plaintiff's claim was founded upon a champertous assignment, and dismissed the action. His decision was affirmed in the Divisional Court. However, these decisions depend, in part, upon an Ontario statute, still in force, which is found in R.S.O. 1897 as c 327, entitled: 'An Act respecting Champerty.' It provides, *inter alia*:

2 All champertous agreements are forbidden, and invalid.

There is no such legislation in force in British Columbia and in British Columbia it has been held that champertous agreements do not offend any law or public policy: see *Amacher v Erickson* (1963), 40 D.L.R. (2d) 251, 42 W.W.R. 348, and *Monteith v Calladine* (1964), 47 D.L.R. (2d) 332 at pp 341–6, 49 W.W.R. 641 at pp 651–5, *per* Whittaker, J.A.

There are a number of English decisions where defendant debtors have challenged the status of debt collectors to sue in their own names as the holders of claims assigned to them for collection purposes. When considering these cases it is necessary to appreciate that before passage of the *Supreme Court of Judicature Act*, 1873 (U.K.), c 66, s 25(6), a legal chose in action such as a debt could not be transferred at law, and the assignee of a debt was obliged to sue in the name of the assignor: see *Re Westerton, Public Trustee v Gray*, [1919] 2 Ch. 104, and *Dell v Saunders* (1914), 17 D.L.R. 279, 6 W.W.R. 657, 19 B.C.R. 500. In British Columbia s 26 [renumbered by 1973, c 84, s 9(d)] of the *Laws Declaratory Act*, R.S.B.C. 1960, c 213, grants the holder of an absolute assignment of a legal chose in action the right to sue upon the claim in his own name.

The leading English decision is that of the Court of Appeal in *Comfort v Betts*, [1891] 1 Q.B. 737, 60 L.J.Q.B. 656. In that case the plaintiff was the assignee of debts by the defendant to various tradesmen. By the terms of the deed of assignment the plaintiff had agreed to proceed to attempt recovery of the various debts by Court action or otherwise, and upon recovery thereof to pay to the assignors respectively, out of the aggregate amount recovered, such proportionate part of the aggregate sum as was due the various assignors. The plaintiff recovered judgment at trial and the defendant had applied to set the judgment aside. It was argued [at p 738] that 'an assignment by which debts are merely assigned for the purpose of collection and recovery to a person who is not to have any interest in them, is not such an assignment as is contemplated by the Act' (*i.e.*, the *Supreme Court of Judicature Act, 1873*). The Court of Appeal rejected this argument and dismissed the appeal. It is to be noted that in doing so each of the Judges, in separate but consistent reasons, recognized that the effect of the decision might be to open the door to a new course of business – debt collection. Fry, L.J., expressed himself as follows at p 741: 'I am conscious that we may be opening the door to a new course of business; but whether that may be advantageous or not, I do not think it is for us to inquire.' Lord Esher, M.R., delivered the leading judgment in *Comfort v Betts*. His judgment, as it appears in the Queen's Bench Reports reads as follows [at pp 739–40]:

In this case the defendant owed debts to several tradesmen. They have respectively executed a deed which is in terms an absolute assignment by each of them of his respective debt to the plaintiff. It struck me at first that inconveniences might arise from the course here adopted. It appeared to me that, if an assignment could be made of a number of debts to a person for the mere purpose of enabling an action to be brought in the High Court in the name of the assignee on behalf of all the creditors for the aggregate amount of the debts, whereas before such assignment each debt must have been sued for separately in the county court by the creditor in his own name, it might perhaps occasion mischief, especially in university towns, by assisting people who give credit to young men, and are desirous of avoiding the necessity for suing in their own names. Again, it appeared to me that, if a new business of debt collecting in this manner became established, and large numbers of debts were assigned to debt collectors without their having any interest in such debts, and merely for the purpose of their being sued for, it might be that a considerable amount of business would be taken from the county courts, which might perhaps be considered by some an evil. It therefore seemed to me necessary to consider the case with some care. But after all we are bound by the terms of the Act of Parliament, and must determine this case in accordance with those terms. This document is in form an absolute assignment of each of these debts. It is clear that it was intended to be an absolute assignment of the debts, subject to a trust for payment of the money recovered to the creditors. The legal property in the debts was intended to pass, leaving only a trust; therefore there was an assignment which purported to be absolute, and which the parties intended to be so. Then, is there anything in the words of the subsection which enables us to say that such an assignment as this is not within it? I see nothing that enables us to limit the plain words of the Act. I cannot see that any absolute injustice can be done by giving its terms their ordinary meaning; and on further consideration I do not see that any very great inconvenience can arise. Under these circumstances I think that we are bound to give effect to the plain words of the Act, and to hold that this is a valid assignment of these debts within its terms; and, therefore, that it passed the legal property in them to the plaintiff. On these grounds I think that this application must be dismissed.

Lopes, L.J., expressed the belief that [at pp 741–2]: 'I am inclined to think that the defendant here is in a better position than if he were sued in several actions by the different creditors.'

The issues next came before the Court of Appeal for consideration in *Wiesener* v *Rackow* (1897), 76 L.T. 448. In that case foreign residents has assigned a debt owed them by the defendant to the plaintiff who resided in England, in order to enable him to sue in his own name in England, the arrangement being that the plaintiff should deduct his commission and expenses, and pay over the balance to the assignors. The document assigning the claim to the plaintiff recited that it was made 'In consideration of 50*l*. upon the execution hereof paid'. In fact, nothing had been paid. The assignment was attacked as a mere sham and at trial Bruce, J., distinguishing *Comfort* v *Betts*, dismissed the plaintiff's claim and found in favour of the defendant. He said.

Under the circumstances, the transaction was not a transaction of assignment, but it was merely a transaction, under the cover of assignment, to appoint the plaintiff as agent on behalf of the assignors.

Upon appeal from that decision Lord Esher, M.R., rules:

I am of opinion that, if the finding of fact of Bruce, J. coulld be maintained, the plaintiff could not recover in this action. The learned judge came to a conclusion of fact, and the question is whether we can agree with that conclusion. I am very unwilling to overrule the judgment of the learned judge unless I am compelled to do so. It seems to be quite clear that the creditors intended to assign their debt to the plaintiff in order to enable him to sue for that debt in his own name in England on behalf of foreigners. The creditors intended to pass the legal right to that debt, keeping for themselves the equitable right to the money when recovered. That brings the case within the authority of *Comfort* v *Betts* in which it was held that, if that was the real transaction, the Act of Parliament enables the parties to carry it out. Therefore, taking the facts as they ought to be found to be, and applying the law as laid down in *Comfort* v *Betts* I am of opinion that the plaintiff had a right to sue. The judgment of Bruce, J. must be reversed, and this appeal must be allowed.

Lopes, L.J., and Chitty, L.J., delivered brief concurring opinions.

In *Fitzroy* v *Cave* (1905), 74 I J.K.B. 829, the issues once again came before the Court of

Appeal. The plaintiff wished to secure the defendant's removal from the board of directors of a company. To attain this end, he secured assignments to him of various debts owed by the defendant, with the object of making the defendant a bankrupt, and so removing him from the board. The assignments were made in consideration of a covenant by the plaintiff that in case he should be able to recover the amount of the debts he would immediately pay over to the assignors the respective amounts, or so much thereof as he might be able to recover, after payment of all costs necessarily incurred by him. At trial, Lawrance, J., held that as the plaintiff had no direct personal interest in the debts, and procured the assignments solely for the purpose of getting the defendant out of his position as director, the case savoured of maintenance, and the contract was not enforceable as being against public policy. He accordingly gave judgment for the defendant. In the Court of Appeal, it was once again held that the case was governed by the decision in *Comfort* v *Betts*, and the appeal was allowed. Cozens-Hardy, L.J., in whose judgment Mathew, L.J., concurred, said at p 835:

It is not easy to see how the doctrine of maintenance can be applied to a case like the present. The decision of this Court in *Comfort* v *Betts* really proceeds upon this footing, and seems to me to be decisive of the present case. *The Court is not asked to exercise any discretionary jurisdiction.* If the assignment is valid at all, it is valid in all Courts, and the plaintiff is entitled to judgment *ex debito justitiae.* The plaintiff is merely seeking by this action to recover payment of debts admitted to be justly due. It is said that the plaintiff does not really desire to be paid and can take nothing for his own benefit under the judgment. For the reasons above stated I think this is of no moment.

(My emphasis.) Collins, M.R., wrote a separate judgment and concluded [at p 833] 'without ... attempting to grapple with the broader question' that the decision of the Court in *Comfort* v *Betts* was binding.

Having regard to the above authorities from the Courts of British Columbia and England, I have concluded that the plaintiff's claim in the present case cannot be dismissed on the basis that it is champertous or is not really founded upon an absolute assignment of the nature required by s 26 of the *Laws Declaratory Act*.

However, that conclusion does not, in my opinion, dispose of the matter entirely. There are, I believe, matters of fundamental importance which were not considered by the Court in the English decisions and have not, so far as I am able to determine, previously been considered in any reported Canadian decision. These matters have, however, been extensively considered in the United States, both in the periodical literature and the reported decisions of well-regarded Courts.

In the United States it has been held that where a corporate collection agency takes assignments of claims from its customers and then brings Court action upon the assigned claims, in which the customers retain a beneficial interest, the corporation is, in reality, engaged in the unauthorized practice of law and the actions brought by it are contemptuous of the Courts, and therefore cannot succeed.

A leading American decision is that of the Supreme Court of Michigan in *Bay County Bar Ass'n* v *Finance System Inc. et al.* (1956), 76 N.W. 2d 23. In that case a local Bar Association sought an injunction to prevent the unauthorized practice of law by a corporate collection agency which made a business of bringing Court actions in its own name upon assigned claims. The collection agency relied upon a previous decision of the Court which held that an assignee is a 'real party in interest' and thus entitled to sue in its own name, even though the assignment was clearly made for the sole purpose of enabling the assignee to collect the claim for the benefit of the assignors. (That decision, *Kearns v Michigan Iron & Coke Co.* (1954), 66 N.W. 2d 230, is analogous to the decision in *Comfort v Betts, supra.*) The unanimous decision of the Court is reported as follows at p 29:

Defendants admit that the assignors retain an interest in the claims and are entitled to a percentage of collections on them. When defendants bring suit on such claims the rights of the assignors are involved in and affected by the litigation and dependent upon its outcome. Hence, when the defendants herein prosecute such suits, even though as parties plaintiff, they and the laymen or attorneys representing them also represent, and control the interests of, the assignors. Recognizing, as did the Utah and Iowa courts in the above cases the possible propriety of individual and isolated instances of assignments for collection and suit thereon, as in *Kearns*, or of casual assignments for procedural convenience which permit groups of persons collectively to pursue a similar or common right or one of a defendant's creditors to sue in one action on the claims of all his creditors, we cannot escape the conclusion that engaging in the business of representing the interests of assignors and controlling the proceedings to be taken in suits on assigned claims in which assignors retain an interest, as done by defendants, is engaging in the practice of law. *Detroit Bar Ass'n v Union Guardian Trust Co.*, 282 Mich. 216, 276 N.W. 365. When this is done by one not licensed as an attorney it constitutes the unauthorized practice of law whether done by him in person or through his agent, regardless of whether the latter be a layman or a licensed attorney. *Detroit Bar Association v Union Guardian Trust Co., supra*; *Hightower v Detroit Edison Co.*, 262 Mich. 1, 247 N.W. 97, 86 A.L.R. 509; *Nelson v Smith, supra*; *Bump v Barnett, supra.*

The corporate defendant has engaged in the unlawful practice in Bay county and there is no assurance that it will not continue or commence to do so again. The case against it was improperly dismissed.

In reaching its decision the Michigan Court relied principally upon the 'exceedingly well-reasoned' opinion delivered in a Utah case: *Nelson et al. v Smith et al.* (1944), 154 P 2d 634, where that Court said, *inter alia* [at pp 639–40]:

The courts themselves will not permit laymen to appear in court in a representative capacity. The policy of the courts and the legislature in this regard may not be circumvented by the subterfuge of a layman taking an assignment to permit him to carry on the *business* of practicing law.

...

Courts cannot remain blind to the fact that the assignment of the claim to the defendants for collection is not made as a gratuity. The percentage of the amount collected which is allowed to the defendants is given to them for one purpose only; to compensate them for services rendered in the collection thereof. Where the collection practice involves the preparing of legal papers, furnishing legal advice and other legal services, the compensation allowed must be assumed to be in part allowed to pay for the legal services so rendered. No matter how one looks at it, this constitutes the rendering of legal services for others as a regular part of a business carried on for financial gain. This essential fact cannot be hidden by the subterfuge of an assignment ... Though the state will not interfere if an individual desires to conduct his own legal affairs without the aid of counsel, the public interest demands that no person hold himself out to the public as qualified to render legal services for others unless he in fact is so qualified.

The Michigan Court also quoted from the Iowa decision in *Bump et al.* v *Barnett* (1942), 16 N.W. 2d 579 at p 582, where that Court commented upon an argument that by State statute litigants in justice Courts could appear 'in person or by agent' and therefore the practice of collection agencies routinely suing upon assigned claims was not offensive. The Court stated [at pp 582–3]:

The conclusion does not logically follow. The salutary purpose of the statute may not thus be perverted to encourage the growth of a class of 'justice court lawyers,' unfettered by the rules that bind licenced attorneys and without training in law and ethics ...

In considering whether these decisions set forth principles which are relevant and applicable in the Courts of British Columbia, one must necessarily consider the relevant provincial legislation.

The *Debt Collection Act*, 1973 (B.C.), c 26, provides a definition of the term 'collection agent' in s 1 as follows:

'collection agent' means a person, other than a collector who, for remuneration,
  (i) carries on business, or represents to any other person that he is available to carry on business, collecting debts for others;
  (ii) collects, negotiates payments of, or demands payment of a debt for any other person;
  (iii) receives money from a debtor for distribution to any of his creditors;
  (iv) arranges or operates, or represents to any other person that he is available to arrange or operate, a debt-pooling system;
  (v) carries on the business of, or represents to any other person that he is available to carry on the business of, taking an assignment of a debt due to another for the purpose of collecting, negotiating payment of, or demanding payment of it;

(Note: a 'collector' is a person employed by a collection agent.)
Section 13(1) of the *Debt Collection Act* provides:

13. (1) Unless he is licenced under the Act at the time he acts or becomes entitled to charge for collecting a debt, no collection agent shall
  (*a*) attempt to collect; or
  (*b*) bring or maintain an action in any court to collect; or
  (*c*) charge for collecting,
a debt for, on behalf of, or as assignee of, another person.

The *Legal Professions Act*, R.S.B.C. 1960, c 214, defines 'practice of law' in s 1 [repealed 1973, c 84, s 10(a); re-enacted 1974, c 49, s 7(c)] as follows:

'practice of law' includes

  (*a*) appearing as counsel or advocate;
  (*b*) drawing, revising, or settling
    (i) any petition, memorandum of association, articles of association, application, statement, affidavit, minute, resolution, by-law, or other document relating to the incorporation, registration, organization, reorganization, dissolution, or winding-up of a corporate body;
    (ii) any document for use in any proceeding, judicial or extra-judicial;

     (iii) any will, deed of settlement, trust deed, power of attorney, or any document relating to any probate or letters of administration, or the estate of any deceased person;

     (iv) any document relating in any way to proceedings under any Statute of Canada or the Province;

     (v) any instrument relating to real or personal estate which is intended, permitted, or required to be registered, recorded, or filed in any registry or other public office;

(*c*) doing any act or deed or negotiating in any way for the settlement of, or settling, any claim or demand for damages founded in tort;

(*d*) agreeing to place at the disposal of any other person the services of a barrister or solicitor;

(*e*) giving legal advice;

but it does not include any such act if not done for or in expectation of any fee, gain, or reward, direct or indirect, from any other person; and does not include the drawing or preparing of any instrument by a public officer in the course of his duty, or the lawful practice of a Notary Public;

The *Legal Professions Act* further provides:

72. No corporation and no person other than a member of the Society in good standing shall, subject to the *Inferior Courts Practitioners Act*, engage in the practice of law, except that

(*a*) a person may act on his own behalf in a proceeding to which he is a party;

(*b*) as permitted by the *Inferior Courts Practitioners Act*;

76. Save as otherwise provided, a person shall be deemed to engage in the practice of law who

(*a*) does any act included in the definition of the 'practice of law' in section 1; [am. 1976, c 28, s 22]

(*b*) holds himself out in any way as being entitled or qualified to do, or who offers to do, any such act.

The *Inferior Courts Practitioners Act*, R.S.B.C. 1960, c 194, permits persons other than lawyers to appear in the County and Provincial Courts on behalf of other persons in locales where the services of lawyers are not available. It has no application in the present case.

In the *Royal Bank* v *Misfeldt* case, *supra*, it was argued that the proper interpretation of the provisions of the *Debt Collection Act* is that a collection agent licensed under that Act is entitled to bring or maintain an action in any Court to collect a debt, for, on behalf of, or as assignee of, another person. His Honour Judge O'Donnell did not agree with that submission. He concluded:

To determine the proper interpretation of s 13(1) of the *Debt Collection Act*, one must look at the entire Act to determine its intention.

Upon a fair reading of the Act as a whole it would seem that the intention of the Legislature was to regulate and control the activities of collection agencies and to provide for the licensing of businesses in that field. It did not define the powers of a collection agent, nor were any specifically granted.

It appears to me therefore that when faced with a specific prohibition as is the case in s 72 of the *Legal Professions Act*, this Court is not entitled to prefer an interpretation based on an inference drawn from the wording of s 13(1).

I agree with the reasoning of His Honour Judge O'Donnell.

Further, in my opinion, the staute law of British Columbia is entirely consistent with

American decisions such as the *Bay County Bar Ass'n* v *Finance System Inc.* case, *supra*. The reasoning employed in that decision, and those which it is founded upon, impressed me as salutary and sound, and I prepared to adopt it. In doing so I am in no way questioning the authority of the English decisions such as *Comfort* v *Betts, supra*; the issues considered in the *Bay County Bar Ass'n* case were simply not raised or considered in *Comfort* v *Betts, Wiesener* v *Rackow*, or *Fitzroy* v *Cave, supra*. In short, those cases are distinguishable. Moreover, in my opinion the American decisions are essentially consistent with the *ratio* of the English decisions. The remarks which appear in *Comfort* v *Betts* concerning issues of public policy are *dicta*.

In my opinion, adopting the *ratio* of the *Bay County Bar Ass'n* case, the plaintiff in the present case when:

A it wrote to Norberg & Matheson Agencies Ltd. 'Please sign the enclosed assignment forms and return both copies to this office along with a statement of account. Legal action is advised. Thank you' (ex. 2);

B it drew the summons herein;

C it authorized Mr. Hansen to appear at the trial of this action in a representative capacity; did acts which, in reality, constituted the unauthorized practice of law. See cls. (*e*), (*b*)(ii) and (*a*) within the definition of 'practice of law' contained in the *Legal Professions Act* ...

In British Columbia the Law Society of British Columbia is primarily responsible for initiating prosecutions against persons engaged in the unauthorized practice of law. In recent years there have been successful prosecutions of non-lawyers who made a business of incorporating companies for others (Gibson) or giving legal advice to those wishing to present divorce petitions (Hargitt). The Law Society apparently views the activities of collection agencies somewhat more benevolently. Indeed, prompted by the decision in the *Royal Bank* v *Misfeldt* case, the Benchers considered the matter and the minutes of the meeting of the Benchers, February 28, 1975, record the passage of a motion that the Deputy Attorney-General be advised that it would be appropriate to amend the *Debt Collection Act* to permit persons licensed under the Act to issue process and sign default judgment.

One wonders if the scope of the Benchers' resolution was intended to be limited to proceedings in Small Claims Court and one also wonders why the Benchers would endorse the proposition that untrained persons should be granted licence to institute proceedings on behalf of other persons in any Court as a business. The attitude perhaps reflects the perspective of a profession which does not generally participate in the work of the Small Claims Court ...

In 1975 there were 533 actions instituted in the Small Claims Registry at Williams Lake. The present plaintiff was the plaintiff in 49 of those actions.

In 1976 there were 406 actions instituted in the Small Claims Registry at Williams Lake. The present plaintiff was the plaintiff in 62 of those actions.

In conducting its actions in Court the present plaintiff has displayed, at times, a marked lack of understanding of fundamental principles. Thus, in one case it sued in its own name (although it did not hold an assignment) upon the claim of a creditor who had specifically denied the plaintiff authority to commence Court action on his behalf (No. 45/75); in another case it issued a garnishing order on behalf of a judgment creditor and claimed the full amount of the judgment debt although the judgment creditor had advised the half of the judgment debt had previously been paid (No. 573/73); in another case it commenced an action as the assignee of ICBC alleging a claim for *damages* arising out of a motor vehicle accident. The very same cause of action had previously been tried and judgment in a lesser amount than was claimed had been given in favour of ICBC's insured party (No. 218/76); and in still another case it sued as the assignee of the Town of Williams Lake claiming $10 allegedly a debt owing for services rendered. In reality, the claim was for parking meter *fines* (No. 500/75). These examples are representative; not exhaustive. They demonstrate the wisdom of the American decisions which I have quoted.

One final question remains. Does the fact that in bringing the present action the plaintiff has engaged in the unauthorized practice of law afford a basis for dismissal of the claim? In my opinion that question must be answered affirmatively.

In *Davies* v *Davies (Re Isaac Watts, an unqualified person)* (1913), 29 T.L.R. 513, Watts, an unqualified person, had applied to the Court seeking to have a decree of divorce made absolute. A writ of attachment was sought against him by the Law Society. He was found guilty of contempt of Court and received a jail sentence.

In the United States it has been held that the unauthorized practice of law in the manner of the plaintiff in the present case constitutes a contempt of Court, punishable by contempt proceedings or by injunction: see *Bump et al.* v *District Court of Polk County* (1942), 5 N.W. 2d 914, and also *People* v *Securities Discount Corp.* (1935), 198 N.E. 681.

In Canada it has been held that Courts, including the Provincial Courts, which are, of course, Courts of inferior jurisdiction have inherent power to prevent the abuse of their process by staying or dismissing actions. This is a jurisdiction that ought to be exercised very sparingly and only in very exceptional cases: see *Haggard* v *Pélicier Frères* [1892] A.C. 61, 61 L.J.P.C. 19, and *Re Regina and Rourke* (1975), 62 D.L.R. (3d) 650 at pp 654–5 and pp 658–9, 25 C.C.C. (2d) 555 at pp 560 and 564, [1975] 6 W.W.R. 591.

The present case is, of course, not an exceptional one. Indeed, as I have indicated previously, the cause of action is a simple and modest one and the form of the action is commonplace. But the issues involved have not previously been explored in the Canadian Courts. In my opinion they are of fundamental concern and importance.

The plaintiff's claim, and others like it, cannot be countenanced by this or any other Court.

The plaintiff's claim is therefore dismissed ...

Action dismissed.

QUESTION Should lawyers have a monopoly on collection activities of the kind involved in the foregoing case?

5
Actions Prior to Judgment

The law provides a variety of means through which a creditor can obtain relief prior to or indeed, with no requirement of, a court's deliberation and judgment. Some of these are discussed in this chapter, including seizing property of absconding debtors, arresting debtors about to abscond, pre-judgment garnishment and replevin. Other summary methods of enforcing a debt – e.g., action by an employee under The Employment Standards Act – will be discussed in Chapter 14, Special Creditors.

I THE QUESTION OF DUE PROCESS

In the United States, pre-judgment enforcement procedures have been challenged under the Fourteenth Amendment to the US Constitution, which provides that '[n]o State shall ... deprive any person of life, liberty, or property without due process of law.' Procedural due process is closely related to the common law rules of natural justice; central to both are the requirements of notice and an adequate opportunity to be heard.

The approach taken by the US Supreme Court has been in a state of flux. Prior to 1969, the accepted view was that an opportunity for a hearing and judicial determination at some stage in the collection process – in other words, at the trial of the creditor's action – was sufficient to satisfy due process; see *McKay* v *McInnes* (1929), 279 US 820, aff'g 127 Me. 110 (1928), 141 A. 699. But in *Sniadach* v *Family Finance Corp.* (1969), 395 US 337, the court held that a Wisconsin statute authorizing pre-trial garnishment of wages violated the Fourteenth Amendment: 'due process is afforded only by the kinds of "notice" and "hearing" that are aimed at establishing the validity, or at least the probable validity, of the underlying claim against the alleged debtor *before* he can be deprived of his property or its unrestricted use.'

In *Fuentes* v *Shevin* (1972), 407 US 67, the Supreme Court applied *Sniadach* in holding constitutionally defective Florida and Pennsylvania replevin statutes which allowed pre-trial seizure of goods and chattels on the *ex parte* allegation of a creditor that they were 'wrongfully detained by any other person'. The Court dispelled the notion, based on a narrow reading of *Sniadach*, that the requirement of notice and a prior hearing was confined to wages or other absolute necessities of life: 'Any significant taking of property by the State is within the purview of the Due Process Clause'. Only in 'extraordinary situations', where prompt seizure is 'directly necessary to secure an important governmental or general public interest' and where the person initiating the seizure is a 'government official responsible for determining, under the standards of a narrowly drawn statute, that it was necessary and justified in the particular instance', could the opportunity for a hearing be postponed.

Mitchell v *W.T. Grant Co.* (1974), 416 US 600, signified a retreat from the *Sniadach* and *Fuentes* position. There the Court rejected a constitutional challenge to a Louisiana statute permitting sequestration of property on a creditor's ex parte application to a judge without prior notice or an opportunity to be heard. Without expressly overruling *Fuentes*, the Court distinguished it on the basis that in Louisiana, the creditor must apply for the writ of sequestration before a neutral judicial officer, the application must state 'specific facts' and not just 'bare conclusionary claims of ownership or lien', the only issues to be resolved were the narrow ones of default and the existence of the creditor's lien, and the debtor was provided by the statute with the right to a prompt post-seizure hearing. These procedures, according to the Court, effected 'a constitutional accommodation of the conflicting interests of the parties'; the creditor in this case was an instalment seller holding a security interest in the property under Louisiana law.

The most recent major Supreme Court case on debtors' due process, *North Georgia Finishing, Inc.* v *Di-Chem, Inc.* (1975), 419 US 601, seems to constitute a partial revival of *Fuentes*. In *Di-Chem*, the Court held violative of the Due Process Clause the Georgia pre-judgment garnishment statute under which the petitioner's bank account had been attached. Reaffirming the *Fuentes* view that the Fourteenth Amendment applies to any significant taking of property, the Court found the statute defective in that it denied the debtor the use of its account 'without notice or opportunity for an early hearing and without participation by a judicial officer'; further, it had none of the 'saving characteristics' of the Louisiana statute considered in *Mitchell*. The Court also refused to accept the contention that the protection afforded by *Fuentes* and *Mitchell* was available only to consumer debtors and not in a commercial setting where the bargaining power of the parties was more likely to be equal.

These cases have given rise to a plethora of commentaries in American legal periodicals. For some recent discussion of the issues involved, including the cost and effectiveness of the procedural protection mandated by the Supreme Court, see Catz & Robinson, 'Due Process and Creditor's Remedies: From *Sniadach* and *Fuentes* to *Mitchell, North Georgia* and Beyond,' (1975), 28 *Rutgers L. Rev.* 541; Pearson, 'Due Process and the Debtor: The Impact of *Mitchell* v *W.T. Grant*',(1975) 28 *Okla. L. Rev.* 743, (1976) 29 *Okla. L. Rev.* 227; Scott, 'Constitutional Regulation of Provisional Creditor Remedies: The Cost of Procedural Due Process,' (1975) 61 *Va. L. Rev.* 807.

In Canada, no constitutional provisions exist under which pre-judgment remedies might be attacked. The Canadian Bill of Rights, R.S.C. 1970, App. III, provides in s 2 that no federal law shall be construed so as to deny due process; s 2(e) of the Bill, referring to 'the right to a fair hearing in accordance with the principles of fundamental justice', could also conceivably be applicable. However, most of the relevant legislation is within provincial jurisdiction.

QUESTIONS

1 To the extent that s 56(3) of the Federal Court Act, R.S.C. 1970 (2nd Suppl.), c 10 (below at p 215) incorporates by reference the pre-judgment procedure of the provinces, can it be attacked as a denial of due process?

2 Do the interim alimony provisions of the Divorce Act, R.S.C. 1970, c D-8, s 10 violate the Canadian Bill of Rights? See *Mierens* v *Mierens* (1972), 31 D.L.R. (3d) 284 (Ont.

H.C. Master), answering this question in the negative and holding, as have other Canadian courts, that the requirement of due process means only that the challenged procedures must be 'according to the legal processes recognized by Parliament'.

3 Although provincial legislation may not be attacked on these grounds, the concept of due process still raises policy questions which must be faced. Although recently abolished in Ontario, can pre-judgment garnishment be justified in those provinces which still retain it? Or arresting debtors whose abscondence is feared?

It may be possible to attack pre-trial enforcement procedures on the ground of abuse of process; this route, however, is very difficult. For example, in *Ridgeway Pacific Construction Ltd. v United Contractors Ltd.*, [1974] 6 w.w.r. 662, the trial court rejected such an attack on a pre-trial garnishment order, despite grave hardship to the defendant, on the basis that it had not been shown that the plaintiff's purposes were illegitimate ones such as extortion or harassment, rather than the securing of payment. However, on appeal, [1976] 1 w.w.r. 285 (B.C.C.A.), the garnishment order was set aside on the ground that it had been obtained with a misleading affidavit. The court held that the attachment of debts before judgment is an extraordinary process only to be exercised with 'meticulous observance of the requirements of the governing act.'

Finally, it should be noted that in the US self-help repossession under a security agreement has remained unaffected by the Due Process Clause. Since such repossession is authorized by contract and not by statute, and does not involve the court or any other agent of the state, the government is not sufficiently implicated for there to be the 'state action' which is a prerequisite to the operation of the Fourteenth Amendment. See *Adams v Southern California First National Bank* (1973), 492 F. 2d 324 (9th Cir.), cert. denied (1974), 419 US 1006; and for discussion, Catz & Robinson, 'Due Process and Creditor's Remedies: From *Sniadach* and *Fuentes* to *Mitchell, North Georgia* and Beyond' (1975), 28 *Rutgers L. Rev.* 541, 568–86; Del Duca, 'Pre-Notice, Pre-Hearing, Pre-Judgment Seizure of Assets – Self-Help Repossession under UCC 9-503' (1975), 79 *Dick. L. Rev.* 211; Alexander, 'Cutting the Gordian Knot: State Action and Self-Help Repossession' (1973), 2 *Hastings L.Q.* 893.

In Ontario, the only intrusion into otherwise unregulated self-help procedures is s 35(1) of The Consumer Protection Act, R.S.O. 1970, c 82 which prohibits repossession without a court order if $^2/_3$ or more of the total price of goods has been paid. The Saskatchewan Limitation of Civil Rights Act, R.S.S. 1965, c 103, as amended by s.s. 1970, c 37, s 3, and s.s. 1971, c 50, s 3, strictly regulates prejudgment repossession (see ss 19–22A). Prior to repossession, the secured creditor must give notice to the debtor. The debtor may then apply for a hearing by a judge in which, inter alia, the judge may allow the debtor to retain possession of the property while making regular instalment payments.

2 THE CREDITORS' RELIEF, ACT, R.S.O. 1970, C 97

6. (1) If a debtor permits an execution issued against him under which any of his goods or chattels are seized by a sheriff to remain unsatisfied in the sheriff's hands until within two days of the time fixed by the sheriff for the sale thereof, or for twenty days after the seizure, or allows an execution against his lands to remain unsatisfied for nine months after it has been placed in the sheriff's hands, the proceedings hereinafter authorized may be taken by other creditors or claimants in respect of debts that are overdue.

(2) When a sale has taken place under an execution, the proceedings hereinafter authorized may be taken by any creditor of the execution debtor even though his claim is not then due.

7. (1) An affidavit in Form 2 of the debt and the particulars thereof may be made in duplicate by the creditor, or by one of the creditors in case of a joint debt, or by a person cognizant of the facts.

(2) Before or simultaneously with the filing with the clerk of the county court of the affidavit, there shall be filed with him a certificate of the sheriff, or an affidavit, showing that such proceedings have been had against the debtor as entitle the creditor to proceed under this Act.

(3) The claimant shall serve on the debtor one of the duplicates and a notice in Form 3.

(4) Where the affidavit and notice are to be served out of Ontario, the judge shall by order fix the time after which the next step may be taken by the claimant as hereinafter provided.

9. (1) Where the claim is not contested in the manner hereinafter mentioned, after ten days from the day of service, or after the time mentioned in the order provided for by subsection 4 of section 7, as the case may be, on the application of the claimant and his filing proof of due service of the affidavit and notice, or, where the claim is contested, upon the determination of a dispute in favour of the claimant, either in whole or in part, the clerk of the county court shall deliver to the creditor a certificate in Form 5 and, where the claim is disputed as to a part only, the claimant may elect, by a writing filed with the clerk, to abandon such part and is entitled to a certificate as to the residue.

(2) Upon delivery of the certificate to the sheriff the claimant shall be deemed to be an execution creditor within the meaning of this Act, and is entitled to share in any distribution as if he had delivered an execution to the sheriff, and the certificate binds the lands and goods of the debtor in the same manner as an execution, subject, however, to the debt being afterwards disputed by a creditor as hereinafter provided.

...

(5) On receiving the certificate the sheriff shall make a further seizure of the property of the debtor to the amount of the debt so claimed and the sheriff's fees, and so from time to time in case further certificates are received.

(6) A certificate remains in force for three years from the date thereof, but may from time to time be renewed in the same manner as an execution.

(7) Notwithstanding the expiry of an execution or certificate before the termination of the month during which a notice of money having been levied or received is required to be entered, the execution or certificate, as to any money levied or received during such month, shall be deemed to be in full force and effect.

3 PROCEDURES FOR ATTACHING PROPERTY

a / The Absconding Debtors Act, R.S.O. 1970, c 2

2. (1) Where a person resident in Ontario departs therefrom with intent to defraud his creditors or any of them, or to avoid being arrested or served with process, being then possessed of any real or personal property therein not exempt by law from seizure under execution, he shall be deemed an absconding debtor, and such property may be seized and taken by an order of attachment for the satisfying of his debts.

(2) The order shall be made only in a pending action.

3. (1) Upon affidavit made by a plaintiff or his agent that the defendant is indebted to the plaintiff in a sum exceeding $100, stating the cause of action, and that the deponent has good reason to believe and does believe that such defendant has departed from Ontario and has gone to some place, stating it, to which he is believed to have fled, or that the deponent is unable to obtain any information as to the place to which he has gone, with intent to defraud his creditors or any of them, or to avoid being arrested or served with process, and was, at the time of his so departing, possessed to his own use and benefit of real or personal property in Ontario not exempt by law from seizure under execution, and upon the further affidavit of two other persons that they are well acquainted with the defendant and have good reason to believe and do believe that he has departed from Ontario with intent to defraud his creditors or any of them, or to avoid being arrested or served with process, a judge of the Supreme Court may make an order in the Supreme Court for the attachment of the property of such defendant.

(2) Where the sum claimed is within the jurisdiction of the county court, a judge thereof may in like manner make an order of attachment in that court.

4. A copy of the order shall be served upon the defendant.

5. The order shall remain in force for six months.

7. All the property of an absconding debtor liable to seizure under execution may be attached in the same manner as it might be seized under execution, and the sheriff to whom the order of attachment is directed shall forthwith take into his charge all such property, according to the exigency of the order, and shall be allowed all necessary disbursements for keeping the property, and he shall immediately call to his assistance two substantial freeholders of his county, and with their aid shall make a just and true inventory of all the personal property, evidence of title or debts, books of account, vouchers and papers that he has attached, and shall return such inventory signed by himself and such freeholders, together with the order.

12. (1) Where the defendant or any person on his behalf executes and files in the office from which the order of attachment, or the first order if there are more than one, was issued, a bond to the sheriff with at least two sufficient sureties approved by the proper officer in such office or by the local judge or master, binding the obligors jointly and severally in double the appraised value of the property attached, conditioned that the defendant (*naming him*) will whenever required by order of a judge of the court pay into court the appraised value of the property or so much thereof as will be sufficient to satisfy the claims of all creditors who may be entitled to share in the proceeds of the property, or will produce and deliver to the sheriff the property attached, a judge of the court may direct that such property be restored to the debtor.

(2) If within one month after the property has been attached such bond is not executed and filed, a judge of the court may direct the sheriff to sell any of the goods and chattels that have been attached, except chattels real, upon such terms as the judge considers just.

b / The Small Claims Courts Act, R.S.O. 1970, c 439

164. Where a person indebted in a sum not less than $4, either for debt or damages arising upon a contract, and recoverable in or upon a judgment of a small claims court,

 (*a*) absconds from Ontario, leaving personal property liable to seizure under execution for debt in any county; or

 (*b*) attempts to remove such personal property out of Ontario or from one county to another therein with intent to defraud; or

 (*c*) keeps himself concealed to avoid service of process,

the clerk of any small claims court, upon the application of the creditor and upon his filing an affidavit in the prescribed form made by him, his agent or servant, shall issue a warrant in the prescribed form, directed to the bailiff of the court from which it issued, or to a constable of the county, commanding him to attach, seize, take and safely keep all the personal estate and effects of such person in the county, liable to seizure under execution for debt, or a sufficient part thereof to secure the sum mentioned in the warrant with costs, and to return the warrant forthwith to the court.

c / Note

In *Thomsen* v *Whitman*, [1924] 2 D.L.R. 1012 (Man. K.B.), it was held that where a creditor has obtained a writ of attachment under an absconding debtor statute upon reasonable and probable grounds and without malice, he is not liable in trespass to the debtor by reason of the seizure where the writ is later set aside as unjustified.

d / Pre-Trial Garnishment

Pre-trial garnishment, which was formerly available except as against wages, was abolished in Ontario by The Small Claims Courts Amendment Act, 1977, S.O. 1977, c 52, s 16. The remedy continues to be available, however, in the majority of other provinces.

e / The 'Mareva Injunction'

In recent years, English courts have been willing to consider the granting of an interlocutory injunction to restrain a foreign defendant from removing its assets out of the jurisdiction (and therefore beyond the reach of execution proceedings) pending judgment in the action and payment of any damages recovered. The injunction is designed to ensure that judgment against a defendant who does not reside or carry on business within the jurisdiction can be enforced; its main use has been in maritime disputes, where jurisdiction is often conferred on English courts and the defendant's only asset of substance may be proceeds of insurance.

The basis for the granting of injunction is the English equivalent of s 19 of The Judicature Act, R.S.O. 1970, c 228, which authorizes the issue of an interlocutory injunction wherever it is 'just or convenient' to do so. The procedure has been termed the '*Mareva* injunction', after the name of the case in which it was first upheld by the Court of Appeal: *Mareva Compania Naviera S.A.* v *International Bulk Carriers S.A.*, [1975] 2 Lloyd's Rep. 509. See also *Siskina* v *Distos S.A.*, [1977] 3 All E.R. 803, where the House of Lords discussed the availability of the injunction and held it unavailable in a situation where the plaintiff's substantive claim against the defendant was not justiciable in an English court. To date, there appear to be no reported instances in which Canadian courts have granted injunctions of the *Mareva* type. For a recent case in which such an injunction was refused, see *OSF Industries Ltd.* v *Marc-Jay Investments Inc.* (1978), 88 D.L.R. (3d) 446 (Ont. H.C.J.).

QUESTIONS

1 Is the '*Mareva* injunction' an acceptable solution to the problem with which it attempts to deal? Should it be adopted in Canada?
2 Can the '*Mareva* injunction' be made available in a manner which comports with due process?

4 ARREST

a / The Fraudulent Debtors Arrest Act, R.S.O. 1970, c 183

2. (1) When a person by affidavit of himself or some other person shows to the satisfaction of a judge of the Supreme Court or of a county court that he has a cause of action against a person liable to arrest to the amount of not less than $100, and also such facts and circumstances as satisfy the judge that there is a good and probably cause for believing that such person, unless he be forthwith apprehended, is about to quit Ontario with intent to defraud his creditors generally or the applicant in particular, the judge may order that the person against whom the application is made be arrested and given security for such sum as the judge thinks fit.

(2) A judge of a county court may make an order for arrest in the Supreme Court as well as in his own court.

(3) The order may be made as well before as after the action has been commenced.

(4) Where the order is made before action, unless an action is commenced and notice thereof is given to the sheriff within two days after the date of the order or within such further time as the judge by the order allows, the order shall be superseded and the person against whom it was made is, if under arrest, entitled to be discharged out of custody.

3. An order for arrest shall be in force for two months from its date and no longer, but on its expiration a new order may be obtained in the manner provided by this Act.

21. Where a defendant is taken or detained in custody under an order for arrest in default of giving security, the plaintiff, if he has not already delivered his statement of claim, shall deliver it within one month after the arrest, or within the time prescribed by the rules of the Supreme Court, whichever s the earlier date, otherwise the defendant, unless further time is allowed by the court or a judge, is entitled to be discharged out of custody.

b / *Fleck Bros. Ltd.* v *Petroutsas* (1964), 45 D.L.R. (2d) 190 (B.C.S.C.)

WILSON, C.J.S.C.: The defendant was arrested under the provisions of the *Arrest and Imprisonment for Debt Act*, R.S.B.C. 1960, c 17. What the plaintiff was required to prove was, *vide* s 3 of that Act, that the plaintiff had reasonable cause to believe the defendant was about to quit the Province. I take it that 'quit the Province' means what it says, not a temporary absence, but a final departure and I refer to *Hartney* v *Onderdonk* (1884), 1 B.C.R. Pt. 2, p 88.

On Sunday, March 15th, my brother Ruttan pursuant to the Act above cited ordered that the defendant be held on bail for $1,244.21.

This order was made on the basis of an affidavit of the plaintiff's solicitor which alleged the debt, not a primary debt but a debt under a guarantee, and said that the solicitor had been informed by a constable of the R.C.M.P. that the defendant had reserved a one-way ticket to Athens on a flight due to leave Vancouver at 7:00 p.m. on Sunday, March 15th. On that date, at 6:45 p.m., Mr. Grubb, credit manager for the plaintiff, learned that the reservation to Athens had been cancelled.

On Monday, March 16th, Mr. Grubb was told, again by the R.C.M.P., that the defendant had bought a one-way ticket to New York. This information, it is now revealed, was incorrect, Petroutsas had in fact bought a 21-day return excursion ticket to London.

When this latter fact was brought out before me on the defendant's application to be released, I held that the intention to quit the province had not been proved to have existed at the time of the arrest and ordered the release of the defendant.

The defendant asked for costs. The plaintiff asked that I make an order following *Wehrfritz* v *Russell* (1902), 9 B.C.R. 50, providing that no action should be brought against the plaintiff or the Sheriff for the arrest. Although they were not cited by Hunter, C.J., in his brief judgment it may be assumed that he had in mind two Ontario decisions, *Scane* v *Coffey* (1892), 15 P.R. (Ont.) 112, and *Adams et al.* v *Annett* (1894), 16 P.R. (Ont.) 356. In the first of these judgments, *Scane* v *Coffey*, Street, J., said this [pp 120–1]:

I think that it is within the power of the Court or a Judge, upon an application to discharge a defendant from custody, to impose upon him the terms that he shall bring no action against the plaintiff. The application for discharge is one to the discretion of the Court, to relieve the defendant from the terms of an order which may have been obtained by the plaintiff in the most perfect good faith, and with the fullest belief in the truth of the facts and circumstances laid before the Judge upon the application for the order. It would frequently hamper the Court in such cases in arriving at its conclusion upon an application for discharge, if it were unable to protect the plaintiff against an action as a part of the order discharging the defendant from custody; but at the same time this particular condition should only be imposed where the plaintiff is shewn to have been entirely frank and open in his application for the order for arrest, and to have had reasonable grounds for the statements he has laid before the Judge.

The learned Judge went on to say that he did not find those circumstances to have existed in the case before him.

I next cite the judgment of Falconbridge, J., a formidable authority, in *Adams et al.* v *Annett* at p 363:

I agree. It was within the power of the learned Judge to impose the term on the defendant which he complains of. That term should be imposed only where the plaintiff has been frank and open in his application for the order for arrest, and had reasonable grounds for the statements he laid before the Judge: *Scane* v *Coffey*, 15 P.R. 112.

I assume that the Judge found that the plaintiffs brought themselves within the rule, and I do not think the contrary so plainly appears as to make me disagree with his judgment.

The proposition advanced by the plaintiff and covered by these citations at first gave me some concern. But the authority is there and Hunter, C.J., is no mean authority.

On the evidence before me it is clear that the plaintiff was frank and open and had reasonable cause to believe that the defendant was about to quit the Province.

I award the defendant the costs of his application for release, such costs to be costs in the cause. I direct, following *Wehrfritz* v *Russell, supra*, that 'no action should be brought against the plaintiff or the Sheriff by reason of the *capias* or the arrest.

The $500 which I ordered deposited by the plaintiff may be paid out to it.

If *Wehrfritz* v *Russell* is wrong I think it is for a higher Court to say so.

Application granted.

5 REPLEVIN

a / The Replevin Act, R.S.O. 1970, c 412

1. In this Act, 'sheriff' includes any officer to whom an execution or other process is directed.

2. Where goods, chattels, deeds, bonds, debentures, promissory notes, bills of exchange, books of account, papers, writings, valuable securities or other personal property or effects have been wrongfully distrained or have been otherwise wrongfully taken or detained, the owner or other person capable of maintaining an action for damages therefor may bring an action of replevin for the recovery thereof and of the damages sustained by reason of the distraint, taking or detention.

3. An action of replevin shall not be brought for the recovery of personal property seized under process by and in the custody of a sheriff, or for the recovery of liquor within the meaning of *The Liquor Control Act* seized under any Act of the Legislature.

4. Where a sheriff has in his hands an order of replevin and the property to be replevied or any part of it is reasonably supposed to be secured or concealed in a dwelling house of the defendant or of any other person holding it for him and the sheriff publicly demands at the door of the dwelling house delivery of the property to be replevied and it is not delivered to him within six hours after the demand, he may, and shall, if necessary, but during daylight only, break open the dwelling house for the purpose of replevying the property or any part of it, and, if found therein, shall make replevin according to the order.

5. Where the property to be replevied, or any part of it is reasonably supposed to be secured or concealed in an enclosure other than a dwelling house of the defendant or of any other person holding it for him and the sheriff publicly demands at the enclosure delivery of the property to be replevied and it is not forthwith delivered to him, he may, and shall, if necessary, at once break open the enclosure for the purpose of replevying the property, or any part thereof, and, if found therein, shall make replevin according to the order.

6. Where the property to be replevied or any part of it is reasonably supposed to be concealed either about the person or on the premises of the defendant or of any other person holding it for him and the sheriff demands from the defendant or such other person delivery thereof and delivery is neglected or refused, he may, and, if necessary shall, search amd examine the person, and, subject to sections 4 and 5, the premises of the defendant or other person, for the purpose of replevying the property or any part of it, and, if found, shall make replevin according to the order.

b / Supreme Court of Ontario, Rules of Practice, R.R.O. 1970, Reg. 545

Rule 359
An order of replevin may be obtained,
> (a) on motion therefor, on showing the facts of the wrongful taking or detention complained of, the value and description of the property, and that the person claiming the property is the owner thereof or is lawfully entitled to the possession thereof; ...

Rule 360
The motion shall be on notice to the defendant, unless the special circumstances of the case in the opinion of the court justify the making of an ex parte order, and the court, instead of granting or refusing the order, may direct the sheriff to take a bond in less or more than treble the value of the property, or may direct him, in addition to taking a bond pursuant to rule 362, to take and detain the property until the further order of the court, instead of at once replevying the property to the plaintiff, or may order that the plaintiff, instead of giving a bond, be at liberty to pay into court to the credit of the action, subject to further order, such sum as is proper to stand as security to the defendant in the same manner and to the same extent as any bond that the plaintiff would otherwise be required to give to the sheriff.

Rule 362

(1) Before the sheriff acts on the order, he shall take a bond (Form 139) from the plaintiff with two sufficient sureties in such sum as is prescribed by the order, or, if no special provision has been made, then in treble the value of the property as stated in the order of replevin.

(2) The plaintiff may, instead of giving a bond, pay into court twice the value of the goods as stated in the order, and the sheriff may act upon a certificate of the Accountant that the money has been paid.

6 RECIPROCAL ENFORCEMENT OF JUDGMENTS

At common law, it may be possible to obtain judgment in one jurisdiction and enforce it in another. Detailed discussion of this subject is beyond the scope of these materials. For further reference see: J.G. Castel, *Canadian Conflict of Laws* 403–535 (1975); *Cheshire's Private International Law*, ch. 1 (9th ed. P.M. North 1974).

There is also legislation of limited scope which deals with reciprocal enforcement of judgments; for discussion, see Castel, *Canadian Conflict of Laws* 535–54, 573–93. In Ontario, the following legislation is relevant.

a / The Reciprocal Enforcement of Judgments Act, R.S.O. 1970. c 402

2. (1) Where a judgment has been given in a court in a reciprocating state, the judgment creditor may apply to any court in Ontario having jurisdiction over the subject-matter of the judgment in the place where the debtor resides, or, notwithstanding the subject-matter, to the Supreme Court at any time within six years after the date of the judgment to have the judgment registered in that court, and on any such application the court may, subject to this Act, order the judgment to be registered.

(2) Reasonable notice of the application shall be given to the judgment debtor in all cases in which he was not personally served with process in the original action and did not appear or defend or otherwise submit to the jurisdiction of the original court, but in all cases the order may be made *ex parte*.

(3) The judgment may be registered by filing with the registrar or clerk of the registering court an exemplification or a certified copy of the judgment, together with the order for such registration, whereupon the judgment shall be entered as a judgment of the registering court.

3. No judgment shall be ordered to be registered under this Act if it is shown to the registering court that,

(*a*) the original court acted without jurisdiction; or

(*b*) the judgment debtor, being a person who was neither carrying on business nor ordinarily resident within the jurisdiction of the original court, did not voluntarily appear or otherwise submit during the proceedings to the jurisdiction of that court; or

(*c*) the judgment debtor, being the defendant in the proceedings, was not duly served with the process of the original court and did not appear, notwithstanding that he was ordinarily resident or was carrying on business within the jurisdiction of that court or agreed to submit to the jurisdiction of that court; or

(*d*) the judgment was obtained by fraud; or

(*e*) an appeal is pending, or the judgment debtor is entitled and intends to appeal against the judgment; or (*f*) the judgment was in respect of a cause of action which for reasons of public policy or for some other similar reason would not have been entertained by the registering court; or

(*g*) the judgment debtor would have a good defence if an action were brought on the original judgment.

4. Where a judgment is registered under this Act,

(*a*) the judgment is, as from the date of the registration, of the same force and effect and, subject to this Act, proceedings may be taken thereon as if it had been a judgment originally obtained or entered up in the registering court on the date of the registration; and

(*b*) the registering court has the same control and jurisdiction over the judgment as it has over judgments given by itself; and

(*c*) the reasonable costs of and incidental to the registration of the judgment, including the costs of obtaining an exemplification or certified copy thereof from the original court, and of the application for registration, are recoverable in like manner as if they were sums payable under the judgment, such costs to be first taxed by the proper officer of the registering court, and his certificate thereof endorsed on the order for registration.

5. In all cases in which registration is made upon an *ex parte* order, notice thereof shall be given to the judgment debtor within one month after the registration, and the notice shall be served in the manner provided by the practice of the registering court for service of writs of process, or of notice of proceedings, and no sale under the judgment of any property of the judgment debtor is valid if made prior to the expiration of the period fixed by section 6 or such further period as the court may order.

6. In all cases in which registration is made upon an *ex parte* order, the registering court may on the application of the judgment debtor set aside the registration upon such terms as the court thinks fit, and such application shall be made within one month after the judgment debtor has notice of the registration, and the applicant is entitled to have the registration set aside upon any of the grounds mentioned in section 3.

NOTE As of July 1978, the following were reciprocating states for the purpose of this Act: Alberta, British Columbia, Manitoba, New Brunswick, Newfoundland, Saskatchewan, Northwest Territories and Prince Edward Island.

b / The Reciprocal Enforcement of Maintenance Orders Act, R.S.O. 1970, c 403 as amended

2. (1) Where a maintenance order has been made against a person by a court in a reciprocating state and a certified copy of the order has been transmitted by the proper officer of the reciprocating state to the Minister, the Minister shall send a certified copy of the order for registration to the proper officer of such court in Ontario as is determined by the Minister, and on receipt thereof the order shall be registered.

(2) An order registered under subsection 1 has from the date of its registration the same force and effect and, subject to this Act, all proceedings may be taken thereon as if it had been an order originally obtained in the court in which it was so registered and that court has power to enforce the order and its officers shall take all proper steps so to do.

(3) A copy of an order registered in the Supreme Court under subsection 1 may be filed in the provincial court (family division) having jurisdiction where the person ordered to pay the alimony or maintenance resides and, when so filed, it shall be enforced in the same manner as an order made in that court under Part II of *The Family Law Reform Act, 1978.*

NOTE As of July 1978, the following were reciprocating states for the purpose of this Act:

i   all other provinces and territories of Canada;
ii   the following states of the U.S.A.: Michigan, New York, California, Wisconsin, Colorado, Pennsylvania, New Mexico, North Carolina, Delaware, Arizona and North Dakota;
iii all states and territories of Australia;
iv   United Kingdom;
v   Guernsey, Alderney and Sark;
vi   Isle of Man;
vii Malta and its dependencies;
viii New Zealand and the Cook Islands;
ix   Papua and New Guinea;
x   Southern Rhodesia;
xi   States of Jersey;
xii Union of South Africa;
xiii Republic of Ghana;
xiv Gibraltar

6
The Effect of Judgment and Interest upon Judgment

INTRODUCTION

In Chapter 5, we saw that in certain circumstances it is not necessary for a creditor to wait until judgment is obtained before commencing enforcement proceedings. However, the recovery of judgment, in the course of giving a creditor simpliciter the status of judgment creditor, makes available to him a much wider range of remedies, though it does not, as we shall see, ensure that any of them will prove effective. This chapter discusses the immediate effect of obtaining judgment as a prelude to consideration of judgment creditors' remedies. It also deals with the impact of judgment on the ability of a creditor to recover interest from a debtor for the period before and after judgment intervenes.

I THE EFFECT OF JUDGMENT

a / Note

A common misconception of those unversed in the operation of the collection system is that when judgment is signed against a debtor, payment follows automatically. As a matter of law – and, in many instances, as a matter of experience – nothing could be further from the truth. The judgment merely establishes, irrefutably, the existence of a debt in the stated amount; it is then up to the judgment creditor to attempt to collect the debt found due.

To assist the creditor to execute or enforce the judgment, the law makes available writs of execution. These are directed to court officers, normally the sheriff of the appropriate judicial district or county. Several different types of writs of execution exist; the most common is the writ of *fieri facias*, commanding the sheriff to seize and offer for sale so much of the debtor's exigible property as will yield sufficient funds to pay off the judgment debt. This and other forms of execution will be considered in later chapters.

There are other effects of a common law judgment declaring defendant indebted to plaintiff. While the judgment does not extinguish the pre-judgment debt on which the plaintiff's claim in the action was based, it prevents any further court action based on that pre-existing debt. For instance if x lends y $100, y is indebted to x in the amount of $100. x can sue y for repayment of the debt. When x recovers judgment against y, a judgment debt is created, and although the anterior 'loan debt' is not extinguished, any action by x on it is prevented by the doctrine of merger, discussed below in cases in this chapter. The judgment itself is a new liability giving rise to a fresh cause of action. The plaintiff creditor can later sue on the judgment debt and obtain a new judgment. Although such actions are rare, they may be useful to avoid limitation periods on enforcing a judgment. (Under The Limitations Act, R.S.O. 1970, c 246, a judgment is enforceable for 20 years). Insofar as it orders costs or interest, or insofar as it creates a debt for the first time (e.g. in an action where the cause of action was negligence so that there was no debt, as defined ante page 3, before judgment), the judgment creates a new debt: *Neilson* v *Derko* [1942] 3 D.L.R. 79, infra, p 141.

However, the fact that the cause of action on an anterior debt (where there was one) merges in a judgment does not cause the original debt to change its 'nature'. A claim for wages will still be entitled to statute-granted priority over other claims even after judgment, although the wage claim is now a claim for wages due upon a judgment instead of a claim for wages due upon a simple contract. The effect of the judgment is merely to force the creditor to employ different remedies (the writs of execution) to enforce the claim. The original claim does not lose its identity: *Ball* v *Thorne* (1919), 46 O.L.R. 261, infra, p 141.

An equitable judgment, on the other hand, is a personal command of the court to the defendant; failure to comply with an equitable judgment is per se contempt of court. Thus equitable decrees are enforced indirectly through the court's power to hold in contempt while a common law court enforces its judgments directly, by commanding (e.g.) the sheriff to seize and sell the debtor's property. This direct enforcement, however, will only operate when the creditor takes the initiative. It is he who must issue the appropriate writ of execution, discover what assets the debtor has, discover where they are, and direct officials to satisfy the judgment out of them. The costs involved in the enforcement process are borne by the creditor, but may be added to the judgment debt and thus recouped from the debtor.

The difference between the non-effect of a common law judgment on a debtor and the commanding effect of an equitable decree is now expressly recognized by R. 569 of the Rules of Practice, R.R.O. 1970, Reg. 545. Under the rule, 'a judgment requiring any person to do an act other than the payment of money or to abstain from doing anything may be enforced by attachment or committal.' For a good analysis of the effect of the common law judgment and how it differs from that of the equitable judgment see *Report of the Joint Working Party on the Enforcement of Judgments, Orders and Decrees of the Court of Northern Ireland*, paras. 12–15 (1965).

QUESTIONS Why should a debtor with available funds not be required to pay his just debts found owing by a court of competent jurisdiction? What are the transaction costs involved in the present collection system in which the creditor has the duty to initiate execution, but as well, may choose the methods of execution? Would these costs be less in a system which threatened to jail debtors who can afford to pay but refuse to do so? How are debtors merely unwilling to pay to be sorted out from those unable to do so?

b / *International Harvester Co.* v *Hogan* (1917), 32 D.L.R. 455 (Alta. S.C., A.D.)

Appeal from 30 D.L.R. 790, allowing an appeal on an application for leave to sell goods under execution. Reversed.

The judgment of the Court was delivered by
SCOTT, J.: Upon the hearing of the appeal it was agreed by counsel that it should be heard and determined upon the facts disclosed in the judgment in this case reported in 30 D.L.R. 790.

The material facts are that on April 19, 1916, the day on which the Volunteer and Reservists Relief Act (ch. 6 of 1916) came into force, the plaintiff recovered against the defendant the judgment upon which the execution issued. The defendant became a member of the reserve militia subsequent to the judgment. He claims the protection of the Act, sec. 3 of which provides, *inter alia*, that no person shall, after the passing of the Act, take any action or proceeding against any volunteer or reservist for the enforcement of payment of any debt, liability or obligation incurred before the passing of the Act until 1 year after the termination of the state of war referred to in the Act or until one year after the discharge of such volunteer or reservist whichever shall first happen.

The Master held that though a judgment merges and extinguishes the cause of action in respect of which it is obtained, it does not extinguish the debt, but determines that it exists, that the judgment is the same debt although it gives the judgment creditor a higher remedy, and that a sale under execution upon the judgment would be a proceeding to enforce payment of a debt incurred before the passing of the Act.

In his judgment on appeal from the Master, Ives, J., held that the judgment created a new debt, the old debt being gone by reason of its being merged in the payment, that the new debt is distinct from the original claim, and is not merely the evidence of the original claim, but is the substance of the claim itself, that by it the debtor is freed from the original liability, and is subjected to a new liability, and the creditor has obtained a fresh cause of action. He therefore held that as the judgment was obtained after the passing of the Act the defendant was not entitled to protection under it.

It appears to be well settled in England that upon a judgment recovered in an action for a debt the original cause of action is merged in the judgment.

In *King* v *Hoare*, 13 M. & W. 494, Parke, B., says, at p 504:

If there be a breach of contract, or wrong done, or any other cause of action by one against another, and judgment be recovered in a Court of Record, the judgment is a bar to the original cause of action, because it is thereby reduced to a certainty, and the object of the suit attained, so far as it can be at that stage; and it would be useless and vexatious to subject the defendant to another suit for the purpose of obtaining the same result. Hence the legal maxim '*transit in rem judicatam*' – the cause of action is changed into matter of record, which is of a higher nature, and the inferior remedy is merged in the higher ... The judgment of a Court of record changes the nature of that cause of action, and prevents its being the subject of another suit, and the cause of action, being single, cannot afterwards be divided into two.

See Halsbury, vol. 18, p 209.

The reason for and effect of the rule that the original cause of action is merged in the judgment recovered upon it is plainly stated by Parke, B., in his judgment which I have quoted, viz.: that it reduces the original cause of action to a certainty, that the object of the suit is attained so far as it can be at that stage and that it would be useless and vexatious to subject the defendant to another suit for the same purpose, and I cannot see why the rule should be applicable for any other purpose.

The English cases bearing upon the question which I have been able to find are mainly cases which relate to the question of *res judicata*, and are therefore cases to which the reason for the rule is peculiarly applicable.

The effect of the recovery of judgment in an action is to my mind properly stated in 23 Cyc., p 1105, as follows:

But while the debt or claim in suit becomes merged in the judgment, and the judgment itself becomes thereafter a new liability and a fresh cause of action; yet as to the original debt the judgment neither creates, adds to or detracts from it; its only office is to declare the existence of the debt, fix its amount and secure to the creditor the means of enforcing its payment.

To hold that under the circumstances of the case the defendant is not entitled to the protection of the Act would in my opinion defeat its manifest intention.

I would therefore allow the appeal with costs.

Appeal allowed.

c / *Neilson* v *Derko*, [1942] 3 D.L.R. 79 (Alta. S.C.)

O'CONNOR, J.: This is an appeal from His Honour Judge Dubuc who stayed the plaintiff's application for sale of goods seized under execution until the final disposition of the defendant's proposal under the *Farmers' Creditors Arrangement Act*, 1934 (Can.), c 53.

The plaintiff contends that his debt was incurred after May 1, 1935, and is excluded from the operation of the *Farmers' Creditors Arrangement Act*, 1934, under s 19 [added by 1935, c 20, s 8] which is as follows: '19. The said Act shall not, without the concurrence of the creditor, apply in case of any debt incurred after the first day of May, 1935.'

The defendant on December 8, 1929, made his promissory note in favour of the plaintiff for $560 and interest, and the plaintiff on March 7, 1941, recovered a judgment for $891.62 debt and $47.38 costs, issued execution, procured the defendant's goods to be seized and served notice of motion for sale, whereupon the defendant filed a proposal under the *Farmers' Creditors Arrangement Act*, 1934.

The question at issue is whether the debt 'was incurred after May 1st, 1935.'

[His Lordship cited *International Harvester Co.* v *Hogan* and continued:]

In *Rothschild* v *Fisher*, [1920] 2 K.B. 243, the English Court of Appeal held that notwithstanding a judgment debt recovered after the defendant's marriage on a guarantee executed before marriage there was at the date of the judgment a debt contracted before marriage within s 19 of the *Married Women's Property Act*, 1882 (Imp.), c 75.

Notwithstanding Mr. German's able argument. I am still of the opinion I expressed in *Schaack* v *Nozak*, [1942] 2 D.L.R. 391, that the obtaining of a judgment after May 1, 1935, does not take a debt out of the operation of the *Farmers' Creditors Arrangement Act*, 1934.

It would seem, however, that the costs were a debt incurred after May 1, 1935. In default of payment of the cost of action and execution within 30 days the plaintiff will have an order for sale of sufficient of the goods seized to pay the said costs. If the defendant makes a partial payment within this period and requires further time to pay the balance the application can be spoken to again.

There will be no costs of the appeal.

d / *Ball* v *Thorne* (1919), 46 O.L.R. 261 (C.A.)

The plaintiff sued and recovered a judgment for $195.75 wages due to him by J. Frank Osborne Limited. After the recovery of judgment, the debtor assigned for the benefit of its creditors. Ball then claimed to rank as a preferred creditor, but the defendant, the assignee, contested his claim. This action was then brought to establish his right.

The assignee contends that, upon the recovery of judgment, the cause of action merged, and Ball (the plaintiff) lost the right to a preference which he otherwise would have had. The learned Judge of the County Court held against this contention, and the defendant appealed.

MIDDLETON, J.: The plaintiff's right must be determined upon the true construction of the Wages Act, R.S.O. 1914, ch. 143. This statute gives priority to the claim of the wage-earner for his wages, for the limited period mentioned, in the case of an assignment (sec. 3), in the case of distribution among execution creditors by the Sheriff (sec. 4), in the case of proceedings against absconding debtors (sec. 5), in the administration of estates (sec. 6); and the like preference is given in the case of liquidation and winding-up of a company, by the Companies Act, R.S.O. 1914, ch. 178, sec. 174 (*b*).

Although there can be no doubt that, upon the obtaining of judgment, the original cause of action is changed into matter of record, and no further action can be brought upon the original cause of action, this is by no means conclusive of the question before us. The claim is yet a claim for wages, payable not by virtue of an obligation arising out of simple contract, but by virtue of the judgment upon that contract. There is nothing to prevent our looking behind the judgment to ascertain the nature of the original claim. Indeed, if a record and judgment existed in the old common law form, upon its production the nature of the claim would appear upon its face. The right to the preference is given because the claim is for wages, and the claim remains a claim for wages even after the judgment is obtained. 'It does not merge or extinguish the debt; but it merges the remedy by way of proceeding upon the simple contract ... A man cannot have a remedy by covenant and by assumpsit for the same debt; the two are wholly incompatible and cannot co-exist.' *per* Maule, J., in *Price v Moulton* (1851), 10 C.B. 561, 573.

'The cause of action is changed into matter of record, which is of a higher nature, and the inferior remedy is merged in the higher:' *per* Parke, B., in *King v Hoare* (1844), 13 M. & W. 494, 504. These quotations go to shew that it is the remedy which is merged, and not the right itself.

In the statute in question there is found an indication that the wage-earner's right is not lost by the merging of his claim into a judgment, for the priority is recognised upon a distribution among execution creditors: sec. 4.

Where the Legislature has seen fit to grant a privilege in respect of claims for wages, it is our duty to see that this privilege is not cut down and the intention of the Legislature defeated by an undue application of artificial doctrines. To yield to the arguments pressed upon us would interfere with what was plainly intended. The wage-earner may sue and obtain priority under his execution. If the debtor assigns, he has priority.

It is argued that, by having sued and obtained a judgment which entitles him to priority, he has lost the priority he would otherwise have had under the assignment. This, in the language of Euclid, 'is absurd.'

The appeal should be dismissed with costs.

2 INTEREST

The question of the entitlement of a creditor to interest arises in two contexts. First, the judgment may include an award of interest on the sum of money adjudged owing, by way of compensation to the creditor for the loss of the use of his money up to the date of judgment. Second, the judgment itself may bear interest, so that the creditor is entitled to take enforcement steps to recover not only the amount of the judgment, but also interest on that amount up to the time of full repayment.

a / Pre-Judgment Interest

i NOTE At common law, the right of a successful plaintiff to recover pre-judgment interest is far from clear. Mere non-payment of a debt does not give rise to any claim for interest, though interest may be awarded in certain circumstances in an action for breach of an agreement other than to pay money: *London, Chatham and Dover Ry.* v *South Eastern Ry.*, [1893] A.C. 429.

It is this position which was incorporated into the statute law of Ontario by the former s 38 of The Judicature Act, R.S.O. 1970, c 228 (repealed S.O. 1977, c 51, s 3(1)), which provided for the payment of interest 'in all cases in which it is now payable by law or in which it has been usual for a jury to allow it.' The second branch of this section was held to expand the availability of interest to include cases 'where, in the opinion of the Court, the payment of a just debt has been improperly withheld, and it seems to be fair and equitable that the party in default should make compensation by way of interest': *Toronto Ry. Co.* v *City of Toronto*, [1906] A.C. 117 at 121. However, the reach of this proposition, which depended on the exercise of judicial discretion, was uncertain.

Given the basic contracts principle that a party is to be restored as fully as possible to the position he would have been in had the contract been performed, the common law position on interest is anomalous. The creditor has suffered a loss by being deprived of the use of his money during the period between breach and judgment, and the debtor has had a corresponding benefit. The reasons for the common law position are historical rather than logical; traditional ecclesiastical hostility towards usury was reflected in medieval law and in a persistent negative judicial attitude towards interest. A modern rationale was supplied by Lord Denning in *Trans Trust S.P.R.L.* v *Danubian Trading Co. Ltd.*, [1952] 1 All E.R. 970. He put it in terms of remoteness: interest cannot ordinarily be presumed to be within the contemplation of the parties. Query the accuracy of this assertion in today's debtor-creditor relationships.

One further element of the common law position deserves mention. That is that pre-judgment interest is not generally recoverable where the claim is founded in tort, on the basis that 'where the withholding [of money] merely arises in the ordinary process of ascertaining liability it could not properly be called wrongful': *Borthwick* v *Elderslie SS. Co*, [1905] 2 K.B. 516 at 520–1.

Where interest has been awarded, courts until recently have normally specified a rate of 5% per annum, in apparent reliance on s 3 of the Interest Act, R.S.C. 1970, c I-18 (set out below at p 145). However, in recognition of the fact that the cost of money now far exceeds 5%, there has been an increasing willingness to award interest at higher rates for the time between breach and judgment. See, e.g., *Sidan Investments Ltd.* v *W.B. Sullivan Construction Ltd.* (1974), 44 D.L.R. (3d) 641 (Ont. H.C.J.), and for a recent case in the Supreme Court of Canada, *Prince Albert Pulp Co.* v *Foundation Co. of Canada* (1976), 68 D.L.R. (3d) 283.

The availability and rate of pre-judgment interest in Ontario are now governed by s 38 of The Judicature Act, as re-enacted in 1977. Recent reforms in British Columbia took a slightly different direction: see Prejudgment Interest Act, S.B.C. 1974, c 65.

ii The Judicature Act, R.S.O. 1970, c 228, as amended.

38. (1) In this section, 'prime rate' means the lowest rate of interest quoted by chartered banks to the most credit-worthy borrowers for prime business loans, as determined and published by the Bank of Canada.

(2) For the purposes of establishing the prime rate, the periodic publication entitled the Bank of Canada Review purporting to be published by the Bank of Canada is admissible in evidence as conclusive proof of the prime rate as set out therein, without further proof of the authenticity of the publication.

(3) Subject to subsection 6, a person who is entitled to a judgment for the payment of money is entitled to claim and have included in the judgment an award of interest thereon,

    (*a*) at the prime rate existing for the month preceding the month on which the action was commenced; and

    (*b*) calculated,

        (i) where the judgment is given upon a liquidated claim, from the date the cause of action arose to the date of the judgment, or

        (ii) where the judgment is given upon an unliquidated claim, from the date the person entitled gave notice in writing of his claim to the person liable therefor to the date of the judgment.

(4) Where the judgment includes an amount for special damages, the interest calculated under subsection 3 shall be calculated on the balance of special damages incurred as totalled at the end of each six month period following the notice in writing referred to in subclause ii of clause *b* of subsection 3 and at the date of the judgment.

(5) Interest under this section shall not be awarded,

    (*a*) on exemplary or punitive damages;

    (*b*) on interest accruing under this section;

    (*c*) on an award of costs in the action;

    (*d*) on that part of the judgment that represents pecuniary loss arising after the date of the judgment and that is identified by a finding of the court;

    (*e*) except by consent of the judgment debtor, where the judgment is given on consent; or

    (*f*) where interest is payable by a right other than under this section.

(6) The judge may, where he considers it to be just to do so in all the circumstances,

    (*a*) disallow interest under this section;

    (*b*) fix a rate of interest higher or lower than the prime rate;

    (*c*) allow interest under this section for a period other than that provided,

in respect of the whole or any part of the amount for which judgment is given.

iii The Small Claims Courts Act, R.S.O. 1970, c 439, as amended.

Note: A 1977 amendment added s 54a to The Small Claims Courts Act. This section is identical to s 38 of The Judicature Act, supra.

QUESTIONS

1 To what extent do the new Ontario provisions alleviate the problems of the common law? What problems remain?

2 Given the nature of interest as compensation for the loss of use of money, should the court have any discretion to disallow it? If so, under what circumstances should the discretion be exercised?

3 Would you agree with the proposition that making pre-judgment interest available reduces the likelihood of settlement and increases the likelihood of litigation by adding more to the plaintiff's expected gain from litigation than to the defendant's expected loss? See R.A. Posner, *Economic Analysis of Law* 438 (2nd ed. 1977). If so, how does this affect your decision as to whether pre-judgment interest should be awarded?

b / Post-Judgment Interest

i NOTE As the materials set out below indicate, 'court interest' is 5% per annum. That is, a judgment generally bears interest until the judgment debt is paid in full, and where nothing further is said about the rate of interest, the rate will be 5%: Interest Act, s 3, Rule 548, Form 115; below at pp 145–6.

Such a rate may well be unfair to a judgment creditor. Suppose that the creditor is a consumer loan company. The company will borrow from the bank at a rate of between 9% and 12% yearly. It will lend money to consumers at from 18% to 24% yearly, building its overhead and profits into the 'percentage spread' between the cost of money to it and the price it charges for money. Suppose that the consumer borrower defaults in the timely repayment of its loan, and the lender sues for repayment and recovers judgment. Assume further that it takes one year before the judgment debt is paid in full. If the lender gets only 5% interest during that year, it is losing a great deal of money on its loan. Moreover, the debtor is better off having defaulted on the loan than having paid the debt on time; in fact, given the cost of alternative sources of money, there is an incentive for the debtor (if the less tangible 'costs' of judgment debtor status are not considered) to continue to postpone the date of full repayment.

Lenders have tried to structure their transactions so as to be able to get their contractual rate of interest from the date of lending through to the date of total repayment, whether or not judgment and execution proceedings intervene. The following materials bear on their ability to do so and on the availability and rate of post-judgment interest in general.

ii The Judicature Act, R.S.O. 1970, c 228

40. Unless otherwise ordered by the court, a verdict or judgment bears interest from the time of the rendering of the verdict, or of giving the judgment, as the case may be, notwithstanding that the entry of judgment has been suspended by a proceeding in the action including an appeal.

iii Interest Act, R.S.C. 1970, c I-18

3. Except as to liabilities existing immediately before the 7th day of July 1900, whenever any interest is payable by the agreement of parties or by law, and no rate is fixed by such agreement or by law, the rate of interest shall be five per cent per annum.

iv Supreme Court of Ontario, Rules of Practice, R.R.O. 1970, Reg. 545

Rule 548

548. Every writ of execution for the recovery of money shall be endorsed with a direction to the officer to whom it is directed to levy the money really due and payable and sought to be recovered under the judgment, stating the amount, and also to levy interest thereon at the rate of 5 per cent per annum from the time of the rendering of the verdict or of the giving of the judgment, as the case may be.

Form 115

Writ of Fieri Facias
(Rule 556)

(Court and Cause)

(Seal)

Name and title of Sovereign　　　.

To the Sheriff of . . . . greeting:

We command you that of the goods and chattels and lands and tenements in your bailiwick of *C.D.* you cause to be made the sum of $ . . . and also interest thereon from . . . . . , 19 . ., *(day of the judgment or order, or day on which the money is directed to be paid, or day from which interest is directed by the order to run, as the case may be)*, which sum of money and interest were by a judgment in this action bearing the date of . . . ., 19 . ., adjudged to be paid by the said *C.D.* to *A.B.*, and also the further sum of $ . . . for the taxed costs of the said *A.B.*, mentioned in the said judgment, together with interest at the rate of 5 per cent per annum thereon from . . . . ., 19 . ., *(the date of the certificate of taxation)* and we further command you that so much thereof as you shall have made from the said goods and chattels and lands and tenements be paid out according to law, and if required so to do make appear to our Justices of the Supreme Court of Ontario in what manner you shall have executed this our writ.

In witness whereof this writ is signed for the Supreme Court of Ontario by . . . . (Local) Registrar of the said Court at . . . . this . . day of . . . ., 19 . . .

. . . .
(signature of officer)

v The Small Claims Courts Act, R.S.O. 1970, c 439, as amended.

116. (2) The clerk, at the request of the party prosecuting the judgment or order, shall issue an execution to the bailiff of the court, who by virtue thereof shall levy by distress and sale of the goods and chattels of the party in default such sum and costs, with interest thereon from the date of the order or of the entry of the judgment, as have been ordered to be paid and remain due, and shall pay such sum, costs and interest over to the clerk.

(2a) The interest payable under subsection 2 shall be at the same rate as may be levied under a writ of execution issued out of the Supreme Court, but a judge may order that no interest is payable in respect of moneys owing under a consolidation order that is not in default.

vi *General Credits (Finance) Pty. Ltd.* v *Brush Ford Pty. Ltd.*, [1975] 2 N.S.W.L.R. 786

BEGG J: These are two motions by the plaintiff seeking an order that interest on judgments obtained respectively against the defendants in September 1975 and October 1975 should be at the rate of 16 per cent per annum, in lieu of the present interest rate fixed by the *Supreme Court Rules* 1970, Pt. 40, r 7 (2), which provides as follows: 'The prescribed rate of interest for the purposes of section 95 of the Act is – ... (b) where the judgment or order takes effect after 6 September, 1974 – 10 per cent yearly.'

Section 95 (1) of the *Supreme Court Act*, 1970 provides: 'Where judgment is given or an order is made for the payment of money, interest shall, unless the Court otherwise orders, be payable at the prescribed rate from the date when the judgment or order takes effect on so much of the money as is from time to time unpaid.'

The facts disclosed in each of the motions are that the plaintiffs were mortgagees of certain property and had obtained judgment for the principal sum, interest and costs which would normally carry 10 per cent interest as indicated above. It was stated in the affidavit in support of each motion that the interest rate fixed by the mortgage was 16 per cent per annum and it would be just and equitable for interest to run at that rate rather than the prescribed rate. It was submitted that the Court should thus exercise the discretion given by s 95 (1) and grant the application.

The defendants in neither case appeared to contest the motions, but, as it appeared to me that a somewhat important principle was involved, I reserved my decision to consider the matter. After consideration, I decline to make the orders and dismiss both motions. I state my reasons as follows:

Under s 143 of the *Common Law Procedure Act*, 1899 every judgment and debt carried interest at the rate of 7 per cent per annum from the time of entering up the judgment until the sum was satisfied. It provided that the rate of interest could be varied by rules of court and up to the coming into force of the *Supreme Court Act*, 1970, the rules of court fixed interest at 5 per cent. It will be observed that, as there was no discretion to alter interest in individual cases, a common rule had to be provided.

For the first time in 1970 it became permissible for the Court to vary the prescribed interest rate in individual cases, but the Act did not give any indication as to how the discretion might be exercised.

The subject of interest rates in jurisdictions other than the common law, have been the subject of a considerable number of cases. A number were recently collected by Sheppard J. in *R. W. Miller & Co. Pty. Ltd.* v *The Ship Patris*, [1975] 1 N.S.W. L.R. 704, dealing with the proper interest rate in an Admiralty action. In *Mortlock* v *Hawker* (1942), 65 C.L.R. 473 at p 508, Dixon J., as he then was, referred to the policy of the court in fixing for its purposes a rate which, over a long period, represents a fair or mean rate of return for money and enumerates eight decided cases where the matter was discussed or illustrated. Notwithstanding the somewhat conservative approach heretofore displayed in the use of interest rates, the rule prescribing the current rate of 10 per cent showed a marked jump from 5 per cent to 10 per cent with the object, no doubt, of fixing a rate of interest which was more in keeping with commercial reality.

Having regard to the fact that normally the covenant in a mortgage to pay principal and interest merges in a judgment of the Court, I think that something more than reference to the mere mortgage rate of interest would necessarily have to be shown before the Court would depart from the prescribed rate. Indeed, in the past in England there has been a deal of litigation as to whether the rate of interest payable under a mortgage is to be preferred to the rate prescribed on judgment by the relevant statute in England. The cases are discussed in *Economic Life Assurance Society* v *Usborne*, [1902] A.C. 147, and it is after consideration of those cases that I have come to the conclusion that the present application must fail. The reason for that flows from a consideration of cl 26 of each of the respective mortgages. The relevant parts of those clauses are as follows: 'That the Mortgagor will so long as any moneys shall remain owing on the security of these presents *or on any judgment* or order in which the covenant for payment thereof may be merged pay interest on the principal sum or on so much thereof as shall for the time being remain unpaid at the rate per centum per annum (hereinafter called "the higher rate") formed ... etc.' (emphasis supplied).

I think it is well established that a mortgagee may, by so drafting the terms of the mortgage, prevent the liability under the mortgagor's covenant for the payment of interest merging in a judgment. This was expressed by Fry L.J. in *Ex parte Fewings; Re Sneyd* (1883), 25 Ch. D. 338 at p 355, as follows: 'The first question is simply one of construction. When there is a covenant for the payment of a principal sum, and a judgment has been obtained upon the covenant for that sum, it is plain that the covenant is merged in the judgment, and, if there is a covenant to pay interest which is merely incidental to the covenant to pay the principal debt, that covenant also is merged in a judgment on the covenant to pay the principal debt. Of course a covenant to pay interest may be so expressed as not to merge in a judgment for the principal; for instance, if it was a covenant to pay interest so long as any part of the principal should remain due either on the covenant or on a judgment.'

As a matter of construction on the present mortgage, I am of the opinion that the mortgagor's liability to pay the higher interest rate as specified in the mortgage does not merge in the judgment, and the mortgagee's security will remain alive until the judgment has been satisfied, together with interest at the rate of 10 per cent per annum thereon, together with any additional interest payable under the security. I see no reason, therefore, for making any order varying the interest rate prescribed by the rules of court and the motions are, accordingly, dismissed.

QUESTIONS

1 In *Sidan* v *Sullivan* (1974), 44 D.L.R. (3d) 641 (Ont. H.C.J.), Lerner J, after awarding pre-judgment interest at 8 1/2%, stated that 'thereafter, of course, the judgment is bound by s 40 of The Judicature Act and Rule 548 with respect to interest at 5%.' Do you agree that the rate of interest is necessarily 5% after the date of judgment?
2. Consider the following excerpt from a chattel mortgage:

   Interest at the rate of 2% per month (24% per annum) shall be paid on any unpaid balance hereof which is past due, as well after as before final maturity. Where the holder hereof obtains judgment hereon and the laws applicable in the province in which judgment is obtained permit, interest at the said rate shall be paid on the unpaid portion of such judgment (including taxable legal fees and disbursements) from time to time outstanding.

   How should an Ontario court dispose of a claim by the chattel mortgagee, consequent upon default by the mortgagor, for interest at the rate of 24% per annum from the date of default to the final satisfaction of the judgment?
3. Assume that you are unconstrained by legal technicalities. What rate of interest ought to be allowed on a judgment? (Remember, if you want to play Robin Hood, that lenders are good risk spreaders, and that increasing their costs will likely increase the cost of loans).

vii NOTE: THE PROPOSED BORROWERS AND DEPOSITORS PROTECTION ACT The proposed federal Borrowers and Depositors Protection Act, would, among other things, alter the law as to post-judgment interest. Sections 22 and 23 of the proposed Act would provide that a judgment bears interest at the prime rate unless the court rendering the judgment otherwise orders.

QUESTION Even with interest on judgment debts payable at the prime rate, would there be sufficient incentive for judgment debtors to make prompt payment?

7
Examination of the Judgment Debtor

As we saw in the preceding chapter, mere recovery of a judgment is by no means a guarantee that it will be paid; it is up to the judgment creditor to enforce the judgment debt. In order to have any exigible property owned by the judgment debtor applied to the payment of the debt, the creditor must ascertain its extent, nature and location. The principal means of gaining such knowledge is an examination under oath of the debtor, provided for by the Rules of Practice or The Small Claims Courts Act.

1 NOTE

The fact that the debtor is required to attend (with the concomitant inconvenience) and answer deeply prying questions under oath sometimes acts as a lever to persuade the debtor to pay voluntarily. To this extent, 'transaction costs' of the collection process are substantially reduced. However, the 'hidden costs' of the current system are sometimes attacked.

QUESTIONS
1 Is there any reason why the debtor ought to be forced to take time off work to attend an examination? Consider the problem of a debtor with multiple creditors, each with a right (see Rule 587, infra) to a judgment debtor examination.
2 Why must high-priced legal talent be present to represent both debtor and creditor?
3 After examining the material in this chapter, consider the following proposal.

Once judgment is signed, an assets disclosure sheet would be mailed to the debtor. The sheet would contain all of the questions ordinarily asked on judgment debtor examinations and the veracity of the answers given by the debtor must be solemnly affirmed by him; failure to answer questions would be punishable by imprisonment. The answers would be sent back to a newly-created court official who would send a copy to the creditor (or his lawyer). If requested by the creditor, and if needed for clarification, a viva voce examination of the debtor would be allowed; the examination would be held during evening hours, and would be conducted by the court official; the debtor (or his lawyer) could charge the creditor with substantial costs, to be set off against the judgment debt.
What would be the advantages of such a system? Its costs?

2 PROCEDURE

a / Supreme Court of Ontario, Rules of Practice, R.R.O. 1970, Reg. 545

Rule 587
(1) A judgment creditor may, without an order, examine the judgment debtor upon oath annually before the proper officer of the county in which he resides touching his estate and effects and as to the property and means he had when the debt or liability that the subject of the cause or matter in which judgment has been obtained against him was incurred, or, in the case of a judgment for costs only, at the time, of the commencement of the cause or matter, and as to the property and means he still has of discharging the judgment, and as to the disposal he has made of any property since contracting such debt or incurring such liability, or, in the case of a judgment for costs only, since the commencement of the cause or matter, and as to any and what debts are owing to him.

(2) No further examination shall be had without an order until the expiration of one year from the close of the preceding examination.

Rule 588
Where the judgment is against a corporation, the judgment creditor may in like manner examine any of the officers of the corporation touching the names and addresses of the stockholders in the corporation, the amount and particulars of stock held or owned by each stockholder and the amount paid thereon, and as to what debts are owing to the corporation, and as to the estate and effects of the corporation, and as to the disposal made by it of any property since contracting the debt or liability in respect of which the judgment was obtained, or, in the case of a judgment for costs only, since the commencement of the cause or matter.

Rule 589
The court may order any clerk or employee or former clerk or employee of the judgment debtor, or any person or the officer or officers of any corporation to whom the debtor has made a transfer of his property or effects, exigible under execution, since the date when the liability or debt that was the subject of the action in which judgment was obtained was incurred, or, where the judgment is for costs only, since the commencement of the cause or matter, to submit to being examined upon oath as to the estate and effects of the debtor, and as to the property and means he had when the debt or liability aforesaid was incurred, or, in the case of a judgment for costs only, at the date of the commencement of the cause or matter, and as to the property or means he still has of discharging the judgment, and as to the disposal he has made of any property since contracting the debt or incurring the liability, and as to any and what debts are owing to him.

Rule 590
Where the court is satisfied that there is reasonable ground for supposing that a person or corporation is in possession of any property of the judgment debtor exigible under execution, it may order such person or any officer of the corporation to attend and submit to examination touching the property and means of the judgment debtor.

Rule 591
Where a difficulty arises in or about the execution or enforcement of a judgment, the court may make such order for the attendance and examination of any party or person as seems just.

Rule 592

A person liable to be examined under the preceding rules may be compelled to attend and testify, and to produce books and documents, in the same manner and subject to the same rules of examination, and the same consequences of neglecting to attend or refusing to disclose the matters in respect of which he may be examined, as in the case of a witness.

Rule 593

A person liable to be examined as a judgment debtor or as an officer of a corporation that is a judgment debtor need not be served with a subpoena, but may be served with an appointment, signed by the officer before whom he is to be examined, at least forty-eight hours before the time fixed for his examination, and the person to be examined shall be paid the same travelling expenses as a witness but no witness fees.

Rule 594

Where the judgment debtor does not attend, does not allege a sufficient excuse for not attending, or, if attending, refuses to disclose his property or his transactions, or does not make satisfactory answers respecting the same, or, if it appears from such examination that he has concealed or made away with his property in order to defeat or defraud his creditors or any of them, the court may order the debtor to be committed to the common jail of the county or district in which he resides for a term of not more than twelve months, or that a writ of capias ad satisfaciendum may be issued against the debtor, or, in case the debtor is at large upon bail, may make an order for his committal to close custody, and the sheriff, on due notice of the order, shall forthwith take the debtor and commit him to close custody until he obtains an order allowing him to go out of close custody, on giving the necessary bond in that behalf, or until he is otherwise discharged in due course of law.

Rule 595

Where an officer of a corporation or other person liable to be examined does not attend and does not show a sufficient excuse for not attending, or, if attending, refuses to disclose any of the matters in respect of which he may be examined, the court may order him to be committed to the common jail of the county or district in which he resides for a term of not more than six months.

Rule 596

Where a person has been committed to jail, the court may limit the term of imprisonment or grant such other relief as seems just, but the order does not relieve such person from any civil liability to any other person.

b / The Small Claims Courts Act, R.S.O. 1970, c 439 as amended

131. (1) A party having an unsatisfied judgment may procure a judgment summons from the court out of which execution might issue, if the judgment debtor resides or carries on business within the limits of that court.

(2) Where a judgment debtor resides or carries on business in a city where there are two or more small claims courts having territorial jurisdiction within the limits of the city, a judgment summons may issue out of any such court in which the judgment has been recovered or in which a transcript of judgment has been entered.

(3) Subsection 2 does not apply to small claims courts in The Municipality of Metropolitan Toronto.

(4) Before the summons is issued the judgment creditor, or his agent, shall make and file with the clerk an affidavit stating,

 (a) that the judgment remains unsatisfied in whole or in part; and

 (b) in the case of a second or subsequent summons, that the deponent believes that the judgment debtor sought to be examined is able to pay the amount due in respect of the judgment or some part thereof.

(5) The summons shall be served by mail or, if directed by the judge, personally upon the judgment debtor at least eight days before the return day, and, if he appears, he may be examined upon oath as to any and what debts are owing to him and touching his estate and effects, and the manner and circumstances under which he contracted the debt or incurred the damages or liability that formed the subject of the action, and as to the means and expectation he then had, and as to the property and means he still has of discharging the judgment debt, and as to the disposal he has made of any property.

(6) The party obtaining the summons and all witnesses whom the judge thinks requisite may be examined upon oath, touching the inquiries.

(7) The examination shall not be held in open court unless the judge is satisfied there is good reason to hold it in public.

(8) After the examination or upon written consent signed by the judgment debtor or his solicitor, the judge may make such order as to payment of the judgment and as to the time and manner thereof as he considers proper.

(9) The costs of the summons and of all proceedings thereon shall be costs in the action, unless the judge otherwise directs.

(10) If, after the examination, the judge dismisses the summons, no further judgment summons shall issue out of the same court against the judgment debtor at the suit of the same or any other creditor for a period of six months, except upon an affidavit satisfying the judge that since the examination the party has acquired the means of paying or that he did not then make a full disclosure of his estate, effects and debts upon the examination.

132. (1) A party who has examined a judgment debtor under a judgment summons may procure a show cause summons from the court out of which the judgment summons issued if the judgment creditor or his agent makes and files with the clerk of the court an affidavit deposing,

 (a) the particulars of the judgment and the amount thereof that remains unsatisfied;

 (b) the particulars of the examination upon the judgment summons and of the order for payment that was made; and

 (c) that the judgment debtor is in default under the order for a period of not less than fourteen days and the particulars thereof.

(2) The summons shall be served by mail or, if directed by the judge, personally upon the judgment debtor at least eight days before the return day and, if he appears, he may be examined upon oath as to his default under the order for payment.

(3) Where the circumstances of the debtor have changed, the judge may vary the order made under section 131.

133. If the party summoned,

 (a) does not attend as required by the summons, or at any subsequent date to which the hearing or examination is adjourned, or give a sufficient reason for not attending; or

 (b) attends and refuses to be sworn or to answer such questions as in the opinion of the judge are proper, the judge may order him to be committed to a correctional institution in the county in which he resides or carries on business, for any period not exceeding forty days.

134. A party failing to attend in answer to a judgment summons or show cause summons is not liable to be committed for the default, unless the judge is satisfied that his non-attendance is wilful.

135. (1) Where a judge has ordered a judgment debtor to be committed to a correctional institution, the order shall be enforced by the bailiff, unless the judge directs that the judgment debtor appear before him at a named time and place to explain his contempt, in which case notice thereof shall be sent to the judgment debtor by mail or served personally as directed by the judge.

(2) Where the judgment debtor appears to explain his contempt,

(a) if the judge is of opinion that the default was wilful, he shall order the bailiff to enforce the warrant of commitment; or

(b) if the judge is of opinion that the default was not wilful, he shall order the judgment debtor to attend for examination at the next sittings of the court to be held for the hearing of judgment summonses and, in the event that the judgment debtor does not so attend, the judge presiding at the sittings may order that he be forthwith committed to a correctional institution.

(3) Where the judgment debtor does not appear at the time and place named in the notice, the judge may direct that the warrant of commitment be enforced.

136. Where at the hearing upon a judgment summons or show cause summons it appears to the judge by the examination of the party, or otherwise, that he ought not to have been summoned, or, where the judgment creditor or his agent does not appear, the judge may award the party summoned compensation for his trouble and attendance, to be recovered against the judgment creditor in the same manner as a judgment of the court.

137. (1) Where an order of commitment has been made, the clerk shall issue, under the seal of the court, a warrant of commitment directed to the bailiff of any court in the county and the bailiff may, by virtue of the warrant, take the party and deliver him to the superintendent of the correctional institution in which he has been directed to be imprisoned.

(2) All constables and other peace officers within their respective jurisdictions shall aid in the execution of the warrant, and the superintendent of the correctional institution shall receive and keep the party therein until discharged under this Act, or otherwise in due course of law.

138. A party shall be discharged out of custody,

(a) by order of the judge; or

(b) at the expiration of the time prescribed in the warrant of commitment.

139. (1) The judge may rescind or alter the order for payment made upon a judgment summons or show cause summons and make any further or other order for the payment of the debt or damages recovered and costs forthwith, or by instalments, or in any other manner that he thinks reasonable.

(2) The judge may rescind or alter or stay the operation of any order of commitment made by him, whether or not it has been acted on.

140. (1) A party having an unsatisfied judgment against a corporation may issue a summons calling upon any officer of the corporation to attend before the judge and sumbit to examination as to the property and assets of the corporation and its dealings with them, and, if the person summoned fails to attend or to submit to examination, he is liable to be committed to the correctional institution in the county for any period not exceedings forty days.

(2) The summons shall be issued and served as nearly as may be in the same manner as in the case of a summons to a judgment debtor.

3 SOME CASES

a / *McCart* v *McCart and Adams*, [1948] o.w.n. 441 (Senior Master)

CONANT, SENIOR MASTER [after stating the nature of the application]: By judgment dated 15th January 1936 this defendant was ordered to pay the plaintiff, by way of alimony, $150 per month, and he discharged his obligations under the judgment until 28th February 1945. This defendant has failed to make payments pursuant to the judgment since February 1945. According to the plaintiff's affidavit there was owing the sum of $3,134.71 on four executions issued under the judgment up to 15th October 1947, with interest to 19th November 1947.

This defendant was examined as a judgment debtor on 19th November 1945 and further on 10th December 1945, at considerable length, the examination and re-examination extending to more than 700 questions. Since that examination there have been: an order, dated 24th June 1946, for a receiver to receive the debts owing to this defendant, and an appeal therefrom, which was dismissed: [1946] o.r. 729, [1946] 4 d.l.r. 568 (see also [1947] o.w.n. 48); an application by this defendant, by notice of motion dated 19th February 1946, to reduce the amount of alimony from $150 to $55 per month, which was dismissed, and an appeal from which was also dismissed; a further order, dated 18th June 1947, for a receiver; and four writs of execution. The costs of the proceedings in connection with the first receivership were taxed at $380, those of the proceedings to reduce the alimony at $331.70, and those of the second receivership at $79.80, making a total of more than $790 taxed costs in these proceedings.

Pursuant to the first receivership $1,238.13 was paid to the plaintiff on account of the executions issued under the judgment. The amount paid to the plaintiff from the second receivership is not stated in the plaintiff's affidavit, but from the fact that $3,134.71 was owing to the plaintiff on 19th November 1947 it is manifest that the receiverships were not very fruitful.

After stating the facts above summarized and discussed, the plaintiff, in an affidavit supporting her application, deposes as follows:

'23. The said defendant carries on a practice as a specialist in medicine and surgery of the ear, nose and throat in the Medical Arts Building of the City of Toronto. On his said examination as a judgment debtor the said defendant swore that his gross earnings in the year 1944 were the sum of approximately $18,000.00 and that his estimated gross income in 1945 would be about 25% less than in 1944.

'24. From inquiries I have made and from what various friends of myself and the said defendant have told me I verily believe that the said defendant has as large a practice as he has ever had, and I verily believe that he is well able to pay the amounts due monthly to me under the said judgment if he chose to do so. Having regard to what I verily believe his income to be, I verily believe that a further examination of the said defendant as a judgment debtor is proper and would disclose facts which might enable me to realize upon the said executions.'

The material parts of Rules 580 and 584 read as follows:

'580. A judgment creditor may, without an order, examine the judgment debtor upon oath before the proper officer of the County in which he resides, touching his estate and effects, and as to the property and means he had when the debt or liability which was the subject of the cause or matter in which judgment has been obtained against him was incurred ... and as to the property and means he still has of discharging the judgment, and as to the disposal he has made of any property since contracting such debt or incurring such liability ... and as to any and what debts are owing to him.'

'584. Where a difficulty arises in or about the execution or enforcement of a judgment, the Court may make such order for the attendance and examination of any party or person as may seem just.'

It is well-settled law, as stated in the note of *London and Canadian L. and A. Co. v Merritt* (1882), 2 C.L.T. 260, that: 'although a party entitled to enforce a judgment may, in the first instance, examine the judgment debtor without an order, yet where he desires to examine him a second time he must make a substantive motion for that purpose on notice to the judgment debtor, and show grounds for the order.' It remains to be determined whether in the present case sufficient grounds have been shown.

In *Re Central Bank of Canada; Watson's Case* (1893), 15 P.R. 427, affirmed 16 P.R. 55, Boyd C., allowing an appeal from the Master in Chambers, who had ordered a third examination of a judgment debtor, had this to say, at p 429:

'Very strong and sufficient grounds of fact must be laid to justify further prosecution of a defendant who has fully and fairly answered on two former examinations as to her means. The last examination was had on the 13th March, 1893, and it does not appear that any change in her circumstances has happened since then.'

However, in that case Boyd C. added, rather significantly, the following: 'I do not propose to lay down rules as to what would be sufficient to warrant re-examinations for the third time of execution debtors, but I am clearly of opinion that the present materials ought not so to be acted upon.'

The *ratio* of a change in the circumstances of the judgment debtor indicated in the judgment of Boyd C. should be considered, in the present case, along with the concluding words of Rule 580, which entitle a judgment creditor to examine a judgment debtor 'as to any and what debts are owing to him'.

The judgment debtor was examined at considerable length in November and December 1945, and furnished details of debts owing to him. According to the plaintiff's affidavit the defendant still has a large practice and the plaintiff is entitled to examine him as to debts now owing to him (which, it is reasonable to assume, are different from the debts owing to him when he was previously examined), even if no further information is obtained.

Furthermore, the plaintiff is entitled to examine the defendant under Rule 584, which imposes no requirement that a change in the circumstances of the judgment debtor must be shown, but provides only that the Court may make an order for the examination of any party or person where a difficulty arises in or about the execution or enforcement of a judgment. It is significant that Rule 584 provides for the examination of any 'party', obviously meaning a party to the action, and is not limited to the examination of any person who, in a proper case, may be examined although a stranger to the action.

It would be an understatement to say that in the present case a difficulty arises in or about the execution or enforcement of the plaintiff's judgment. The plaintiff has apparently done everything possible to enforce her judgment. The defendant has been anything but helpful if he has not, in fact, resisted enforcement.

The decision to allow the present application is, I think supported by the observations of Riddell J. in *Beau Monde Ladies' Tailoring Co. v Garrett*, 57 O.L.R. 256, [1925] 3 D.L.R. 957.

Although a judgment debtor is not to be unduly harassed or subjected to inquisition, in the words of Boyd C. in *Watson's Case, supra*, the position of the judgment creditor must also be considered. The embarrassment of the plaintiff because of the defendant's failure to pay the amount owing by him under the judgment may be as great as, or even greater than, any embarrassment the defendant will suffer by reason of a further examination.

An order will go as asked; costs to the plaintiff.
Order accordingly.

The defendant McCart appealed from this order, and the appeal was heard by Wilson J. in chambers at Toronto.

The same counsel appeared.

Judgment was reserved, and on a subsequent day Wilson J. delivered judgment, without written reasons, dismissing the appeal with costs payable forthwith after taxation thereof. Appeal dismissed with costs.

NOTE In *Saddy* v *Prosser*, [1955] O.W.N. 241, the Master held that R. 591 gave him jurisdiction to order the examination of a stranger to the action, in aid of execution. However, he held that notice of the application for leave ought to be given to the stranger, so that the latter could appear and show cause why leave ought not to be granted.

b / *Spiegel* v *Klein*, [1962] O.W.N. 37 (Master)

MASTER (J. R. KIMBER): If the evidence was limited solely to the fact that the debtor is a beneficiary of the estate and that the person to be examined was an executor, I doubt if this would be sufficient to establish, in the words of the Rule, that there is reasonable ground for supposing that the respondent was in possession of any property of the judgment debtor. The father of the judgment debtor died some 13 years ago and the judgment debtor, on her examination, swore that she had already received her full benefits from the estate. However, in this case there is coupled with that the facts relating to the ownership of the house. The judgment debtor states that she pays no rent to the respondent who is her brother, but merely makes the payments on the mortgage.

It is not necessary for the applicant to establish conclusively that the respondent is in possession of property of the judgment debtor, but only that there is reasonable ground for so supposing. If the test were otherwise, there would be little or no need for the examination to be held.

The main purpose of this Rule is to enable the judgment creditor to obtain, by way of examination, sufficient information so that he may decide whether it is worthwhile to institute proceedings against the person examined for a declaration that the property held is the property of the debtor: *Chote* v *Rowan*, [1943] O.W.N. 237.

I am satisfied that, on the review of all the evidence, the application comes within the Rule.

The other objection raised to the holding of the examination was based on the fact that another creditor of the judgment debtor has already commenced an action for a declaration that the residence is held by the respondent in trust for the judgment debtor. It is argued that to permit the examination asked for here would be unfair to the respondent as he would have to submit to cross-examination on matters in issue in the other action.

The Rule is that if the person seeking the examination has already commenced his action, then the purpose of the Rule has been exhausted and all the rights of the creditor are merged in the action: *Chote* v *Rowan*, *supra*, and *Crucible Steel Co. Ffolkes* (1913), 4 O.W.N. 1561.

This Rule, in my view, does not extend to the case where a second creditor wishes to have the examination. The second creditor is entitled to commence his own action and to be represented by his own solicitor in the action, although it may be the Court would make some order directing that the actions be tried together or in some similar manner to avoid the defendant being put to the expense of defending both actions. It would not be proper at this stage to refuse the applicant herein his right to examine, merely on the ground that this would lead to duplication of law suits.

Further, I do not feel that any embarrassment which might arise by the respondent having to submit to the examination herein requested is of any importance. This Rule provides for an unusual procedure in that an individual, who might become a defendant in an action, is liable to be cross-examined before the action is even commenced. The person to be examined may well find this examination embarrassing but the Rule is not concerned with that fact. The fact that there may be more than one examination by different parties may in fact increase the embarrassment but it does not take the second application outside of the Rule.

The order will go as asked. I do not feel that this is a case for costs.

Application granted.

NOTE In *Ideal Electric Ltd.* v *Lepofsky*, [1960] O.W.N. 548, the Master took a restrictive view of the privilege that a solicitor can claim when being examined in aid of execution against his client. The solicitor cannot refuse to answer, on the grounds of the solicitor-client privilege, the question whether a document belonging to his client is in the solicitor's possession. The exact scope of the privilege generally is beyond the ambit of this book; however, a solicitor being examined must be extremely careful since the privilege belongs to his client who alone can waive it. Improper divulging of privileged matters could subject the solicitor to liability to his client.

c / *Beau Monde Ladies' Tailoring Co.* v *Garrett* (1925), 57 O.L.R. 256 (S.C.)

RIDDELL, J.: Judgment was obtained in December, 1922, against the defendant by the plaintiffs for $1,215.75: a *fi. fa.* was returned *nulla bona* by the Sheriff of Toronto.

The defendant was, in February, 1923, examined as a judgment debtor, and on this examination it was sworn by the defendant that he, as agent for his wife, purchased for her and had put in her name certain property in Toronto valued at $4,000 – a first mortgage was placed thereon of $6,000 and a second mortgage given to the vendor of $2,000 in addition to $2,000 paid in money – the defendant admits that he has paid over $1,000 for interest, principal, and taxes since the purchase, his wife having no means to pay the same – he says, however, that the payments were made on her behalf.

The plaintiffs believe and all the circumstances indicate that they have good grounds for suspecting that the purchase was really the debtor's and not the wife's; and that the property is in reality that of the debtor. Of course, the debtor repudiates all interest in it.

Moreover, the defendant stated that he paid his wife's mother, Mrs. Larson, from time to time, large sums of money which he says he had borrowed of her.

The plaintiffs, with a not undue or unnatural curiosity, desired to examine the wife and mother-in-law as to the estate and effects of the debtor, his property and means at the time when the debt was incurred and now, and particularly as to the real estate and moneys expended thereon and as to the payments to the mother-in-law.

They thereupon served a notice of motion, under Rules 583 and 584, for an order for the examination of the two women; and took out an appointment and issued a subpœna *duces tecum* for the examination of the wife for use on the pending motion. The defendant's wife made an application to set aside the appointment and subpœna – the defendant joined in the application – and the Assistant Master granted the motion, with costs, fixed at $18.50, payable forthwith – the order being specifically made 'upon the application of the defendant and Edna Garrett.'

The plaintiffs now appeal, serving both the defendant and his wife.

No written reasons were given for the order appealed from, and neither counsel could inform me of the grounds of the learned Master's decision; the case, however, was fully argued in the light of existing authorities, and I am now able to dispose of the appeal.

The difficulty in the way of compelling an unwilling debtor – and most debtors are unwilling – to pay a judgment against him was notorious and a blemish on the Common Law of England – where personal incarceration failed there was nothing but goods and personal chattels: and the *elegit* of the early Statute of Westminster II. (1285), 13 Edw. I. ch. 18, did not help in most cases, the *medietas terre sue* being generally wanting. Even before the abolition of personal imprisonment for debt under a *ca. sa.*, means were sought to circumvent the debtor who, having means, was evading payment. The 'Lords' Act' (1758), 32 Geo. II. ch. 28, we should now think too drastic – that (sec. 17) permitted the creditors of an execution debtor charged in execution for a debt under £100 to compel the debtor, on pain of transportation for seven years, to make discovery and surrender of his effects for their benefit – this Act was enlarged by (1786) 26 Geo. III. ch. 44; (1793) 33 Geo III. ch. 5; (1799) 39 Geo III. ch. 50. This legislation was not adopted in our Province, but it is the forerunner, prototype, and, in a limited sense, the progenitor, of our system of examination of a debtor after judgment. The value of such examination, of course, largely depends on the lengthened arm of the *fi. fa.* and the provision for attachment of debts.

The provision for the examination of a judgment debtor is now to be found in Rule 580: the proceeding has been found very valuable, and it should not be hampered by undue technicality. It is an examination of the strictest character: *Beattie* v *Barton* (1882), 2 C.L.T. 104; *Re Central Bank of Canada, Watson's Case* (1893), 15 P.R. 427—any question 'fairly pertinent to the subject-matter of the inquiry ... ought to be answered:' *Republic of Costa Rica* v *Strousberg* (1880), 16 Ch.D. 812; *McLean* v *Bruce* (1890), 13 P.R. 504.

The debtor must post himself by reference to books and all other species of records, etc.: *Russell* v *Macdonald* (1888), 12 P.R. 458.

Our law goes farther and provides for the examination of other persons who are able, or who probably are able, to throw light on the debtor's means – the clerk or employee, actual or past, the transferee of property (Rule 582), the person apparently in possession of any of the debtor's property (Rule 583), may be examined – and Rule 584 is still more inclusive: 'Where a difficulty arises in or about the execution or enforcement of a judgment, the Court may make such order for the attendance and examination of any party or person as may seem just.'

In the present case a difficulty has arisen 'in and about the execution or enforcement of a judgment,' and, under this rule, I should without question make the order asked for and have the wife and mother-in-law examined. No honest debtor and no honest relative should object to such an examination.

In England, Order 42 provides for examinations such as are in question here. Order 42, Rule 32 (610), authorises an order to examine a judgment debtor in such cases as those in which we, by Rules 580 and 581, can now examine without an order – then Order 42, Rule 33 (611), is the same as our Rule 584, except that the English rule refers only to judgments or orders other than for the recovery or payment of money – and this distinction it is well to bear in mind.

In *Sturges* v *Countess of Warwick* (1913), 30 Times L.R. 112, the object and import of Order 42, Rule 33, was considered. The language of Vaughan Williams, L.J., at p 114, is not to be taken in too narrow a sense, but simply in connection with the facts of the case he was discussing. 'He took the view that Rule 33' (substantially our Rule 583) 'had reference to a matter which was not new and that the object of that rule was to make orders which had been made under Rule 32' (substantially our Rules 580, 581) 'more efficacious' – I can find nothing in all the legislation or rules indicating that before an order can be made under Rule 584 an examination must have been made under Rule 580 or Rule 581, which required to be made more efficacious. That, however, is not of importance here, as an examination under Rule 580 has been in fact made – and the occasion has undoubtedly occurred which Rule 584 was intended to cover, and some of the subsequent language of the learned Lord Justice is fully applicable: 'The information given here was such that a difficulty had arisen in and about the execution and enforcement of the' judgment ... 'With the information which had been obtained at the first examination, it would have been wrong as well as imprudent for the judgment debtor to seize or realize this property. ... It was impossible to know whether the circumstances were such as to justify the judgment creditor by means of execution in availing himself of the property ...'

If the parties agree I shall turn this motion into a motion for an order for the examination of the wife and mother-in-law under Rule 584, the examination to be unliminited so far as the challenged transactions and the property, past or present, of the debtor are concerned – in which case the order of the Assistant Master will be set aside and the examination will proceed under this order; costs so far to be added by the plaintiffs to their debt.

But, if the parties do not agree, other considerations arise.

Have the plaintiffs the right to examine the wife as a witness on a pending motion?

Rule 228 is perfectly general in its language – although in the former King's Bench Division, the Court, of which I was a member, held that the rule did not apply to a motion against a verdict, I do not find any limitation in respect of such motions as one under Rule 584.

The case of *D* v *W*. (1912), 3 O.W.N. 993, was cited in support of the Assistant Master's order – but that is *nihil ad rem*. There the witness had been sworn but declined to answer certain questions; and my learned brother Middleton held that she was entitled so to decline. That is no authority for the proposition that there was no right to examine at all.

I am making no ruling as to what questions must and what questions need not be answered on an examination to be held. The proper course to pursue was recently laid down by myself in *Trusts and Guarantee Co. v Dodds* (1924), 27 O.W.N. 294 – the witness 'should attend, be sworn, and raise his objections to the questions that are put – if they are objectionable ... The plaintiffs have every opportunity to frame their questions so as to obtain such information as they desire, the solicitor and client have every opportunity to raise objections.'

Trinity College v *Levinter* (1923), 54 O.L.R. 290, may also be looked at.

The appeal should be allowed with costs of the motion before the Assistant Master and of this motion, payable by Edna Garrett and the defendant forthwith after taxation thereof.

d / Note: Adjournment of Judgment Debtor Examinations

In *Hyatt* v *Owens* (1927), 60 O.L.R. 489, the court held that where the creditor had waived the debtor's non-appearance on the day fixed for examination pursuant to their agreement to adjourn, the creditor could not then move to commit the debtor for non-appearance on an agreed-upon subsequent date, since the order required the debtor's attendance only on the originally-named day. The problem created by *Hyatt* is resolved in practice as follows: if an adjournment of the examination is requested by the debtor (or other examinee), the creditor will refuse and obtain a certificate of non-attendance from the special examiner. The creditor will agree with the debtor (examinee) however, that if the debtor appears on a different date (the date to which the parties agree the examination will be 'adjourned') to be examined, the creditor will not bring a motion for committal, under R. 594, supra, based on non-attendance on the originally appointed day.

In any event, the courts are very reluctant to commit a person to jail for failure to attend an examination as appointed. The debtor will almost always be given a second chance to attend: *Thackeray* v *Brown* (1919), 17 O.W.N. 171.

4 SUGGESTED QUESTIONS TO BE ASKED ON JUDGMENT DEBTOR EXAMINA-
TIONS, BAR ADMISSION COURSE (1977–8), LAW SOCIETY OF UPPER
CANADA.

a / Questions to be Asked on Examination of Judgment Debtor

1 What is the debtor's age?
2 Is he single, married, divorced, or living apart from his wife?
3 How many dependants has he?
4 What is his occupation?
5 What is his employer's name and address?
6 What position does he hold?
7 How long has he been in his present position?
8 Does he work full-time?
9 Has he any part-time employment?
10 If out of work what are his prospects of employment?
11 What is his weekly salary?
12 What day is he paid?
13 Has he any other source of income (pensions, family allowances, etc.)?
14 Where does the debtor live?
15 If he rents, how much does he pay, and who is his landlord, and is the landlord any relation to him?
16 Does he own any real estate?
17 When did he last own real estate?
18 Where is the property located?
19 Does his wife own any real estate?
20 Does he drive a car, license number, where is it kept, and is it used by him?
21 When did he last have an automobile?
22 Does his wife have an automobile?
23 If the debtor has an automobile, is there any money owing on it? If so, to whom, and what type of security have they got?
24 Is there any possibility of his inheriting money or getting money together to pay this account?
25 Has he a bank account?
26 If so, where?
27 When did he last have a bank account?
28 Is there any money owing to him? If so, by whom, name and address?
29 Does the debtor have any stocks or bonds?
30 How much money does he owe?
31 What is the cause of his financial difficulties?
32 Has the debtor any other assets of any description?

b / Questions to be Asked of Officer of Limited Company

1 When was the company incorporated?
2 What shares were issued?
3 Were they paid for?
4 Have any loans been made to shareholders?
5 Who were the original shareholders?
6 Who are the present shareholders?
7 Who are the officers of the company?
8 Has the company ever owned real estate?
9 If the company did own real estate,

does it hold a mortgage on any real estate which has been disposed of?

10 What automotive equipment has the company owned?

11 What liens are on the automotive equipment?

12 What bank did the company use?

13 What security does the bank have?

14 How much are the accounts receivable?

15 Are the accounts receivable assigned to the bank or otherwise encumbered?

16 What inventory does the company have?

17 Does the bank have Section 88?

18 What equipment and trade fixtures does the company own?

19 Is there any money owing on equipment and trade fixtures?

20 Is there any office furniture?

21 Is the office furniture encumbered?

22 Where are the books of the company?

23 Where are the bank statements?

24 Where is the minute book?

25 What salaries were paid to officers and directors?

26 Has the company returned any goods to its creditors out of the usual course of business?

8

Exemptions from the Execution Process

At this point, we begin an examination of the actual mechanics of the enforcement process. That is, we assume that the creditor has obtained a judgment and has learned all he can (or all he needs to know) about the assets owned by the debtor. How can the creditor turn those assets into money to be used to satisfy his judgment debt?

From what has gone before, it should be clear that the creditor has a choice of what steps he will take, assuming that he cannot force the debtor to pay 'voluntarily'.

The most common action taken is to procure the issue of a writ of *fieri facias* (*fi.fa.*) from the court which gave judgment for the creditor. The writ is then filed with the sheriff for a judicial district in which the debtor has assets which may be taken in execution. The sheriff then follows the appropriate procedure and seizes and sells assets that he can find; the money produced by the sale is then made available for the satisfaction of the claims of creditors according to their priorities.

Garnishment is another frequently used creditor's remedy. By taking garnishment proceedings, the creditor 'attaches' debts 'owing or accruing due' to his debtor. The debt is thus diverted. Rather than paying the debtor, the garnishee (the debtor's debtor) is required to pay the garnishor (the creditor) or someone on his behalf (court bailiff or sheriff). If he fails to pay as directed and pays the debtor instead, he runs the risk that the garnishor (creditor) may then obtain personal judgment against him for the amount wrongly paid.

Several special means are provided for making particular assets answerable for a person's debts, and these will be given separate treatment infra. However, a particular group of creditor's remedies ought to be mentioned here. These remedies are known as 'equitable execution' and they may be used to satisfy a judgment from assets which are, for some reason, not reachable by execution or garnishment. Briefly, there are three main forms of equitable execution. The court may appoint a receiver, who has power to collect payments which would otherwise be made to the debtor, and to convert the payments to the use of creditors according to their priorities. A second form of equitable execution is the 'charging order'. In making such an order, a court in effect creates a lien on the property charged, much in the nature of a mortgage. Finally, a creditor may procure the issue of a writ of sequestration. Such a writ authorizes the sheriff to enter on the debtor's lands and receive their rents and profits and to seize his chattels and hold them away from the debtor. This remedy, although it produces little money compared to a sale of the lands or chattels under a *fi.fa.*, puts pressure on the debtor to pay by depriving him of the benefits of his property ownership. Execution by way of writ of *fi.fa.* and garnishment are the most effective means of satisfying judgments, and equitable execution is rarely used.

Other pressure tactics which are (rarely) used by a creditor include the writs of attachment and committal. We have already seen an example of the use of these writs – a debtor who fails to appear at a judgment debtor examination may be committed to jail. Although the use of such writs does not produce money, it produces pressure on the debtor to pay more or less voluntarily, or at least to co-operate in being stripped of his assets.

These methods of satisfying judgments will all be considered now. The materials are organized to consider first, in this chapter, what property cannot be taken by creditors by any means. They continue to consider what may be taken by each of the methods outlined above, and the procedures for so doing (Chapters 9 through 11). The recourse available to a debtor wishing to delay execution (or relieve the pressure of it upon him) are discussed in Chapter 12. Chapter 13 considers the distribution of the proceeds of the execution process, and the unusual rights of 'special creditors' are set out in Chapter 14. Finally, Chapter 15 illustrates the operation of the present system for enforcing judgments with some excerpts from a sheriff's file, and considers some of the proposals which have been advanced for wholesale restructuring of the system.

As you read the materials, several general questions might be usefully kept in mind. Are the current mechanisms available for the satisfaction of judgment debts rational and economical, or merely the legacy of times long past? Do the lists of property subject to or exempt from the execution process make any sense? Should there be a general writ of execution allowing all steps permitted by all existing procedures? Should the creditor decide what steps should be taken to satisfy the judgment, or ought some 'official' (government or private) decide which method is best (keeping in mind considerations of cost and justice)? Should all creditors generally be treated equally regardless of the nature of their claim or the recklessness with which they permitted a debt to arise? Are the priorities given to special creditors rational?

2 EXEMPTIONS FROM EXECUTION AND GARNISHMENT

a / History of Exemptions Legislation
C.R.B. Dunlop, *Exemptions of Income and Assets from Execution* 4–7 (prepared for British Columbia Law Reform Commission 1974)

At common law, the general rule was that 'the sheriff might seize and sell all the personal goods and chattels belonging to the defendant that he could find, and which could be sold, with the exception of wearing apparel actually in use, and perhaps goods in the personal possession of the defendant.' The common law rule was interpreted harshly and restrictively: Holt, c.j. observed in 1697 that the sheriff 'may take anything but wearing clothes; nay, if the party hath two gowns, he may take one of them.' As to land, the Statute of Westminster II, in creating the writ of elegit, exempted from its operation the debtor's 'oxen and the beasts of his plow.' It was not until 1845 that legislation was enacted in England exempting from execution 'the wearing apparel and bedding of any judgment debtor, or his family, and the tools and implements of his trade, the value of such apparel, bedding, tools, and implements not exceeding in the whole the value of £5.'

The Canadian and American colonies enacted statutory exemptions well before the 1845 English act, the earliest Canadian legislation being passed in 1786. A prominent feature of the colonial legislation was the liberality with which exemptions were granted to the debtor. The legislation commonly exempted a sizable amount of personal property, frequently specified in much detail, life and other insurance policies and their proceeds, and the matrimonial home or farm. Many American states incorporated exemptions provisions into their state constitutions, thus providing evidence of their importance to the pioneer legislators.

Unfortunately, once the early exemptions legislation was enacted, the tendency in many North American jurisdictions was to fail to keep the provisions up-to-date by regular review and amendment. The result of this legislative neglect was that exemptions legislation in the United States and in Canada today is characterized by extreme obsolescence. Many exemptions statutes currently enforced are geared to the economy of an earlier day. Thus Connecticut confers upon each householder an exemption for 'two tons of coal, two tons of hay, five bushels each of potatoes and turnips, two hundred pounds of wheat flour, two cords of wood, ten bushels each of Indian corn and rye or the meal or flour manufactured therefrom ...' As the economic and social structure of North America has changed, these legislative provisions have increasingly become irrelevant, although the courts have struggled to adapt out-of-date statutes to modern conditions.

Another result of legislative neglect of exemptions legislation has been that monetary limits on exemptions which may have been liberal at the date of enactment, have become increasingly restrictive as the result of inflation. The best example for our purposes is the $500.00 exemption of personal property in section 25 of the British Columbia Execution Act. This financial limit was first enacted in 1873 and must have provided liberal protection in pioneer British Columbia but today it has become ludicrously inadequate as a fair exemption from execution. The $2,500.00 exemption for real property registered under the British Columbia Homesteads Act is of even less significance today partly because of inflation and partly because very few properties are now registered under the Act. The homesteads exemption was last amended in 1867.

(The exemption for personal property in s 25 of the British Columbia Execution Act was raised to $2,500 by S.B.C. 1974, c 87, s 13).

b / Exemptions from Execution

i NOTE: PROVINCIAL LEGISLATION CREATING EXEMPTIONS FROM EXECUTION There is fairly wide variation in the exemptions legislation of the provinces and territories, as to both the type of property rendered exempt and the monetary limits on exemptions. In some instances, the legislation reflects the province's social, cultural or economic characteristics. In Alberta, Manitoba and Saskatchewan, for example, seed grain is exempt; in New Brunswick, both grain and potatoes for planting purposes. Newfoundland exempts fishing skiffs and punts, and Nova Scotia, fishing nets; in Quebec, neither religious artifacts nor works of art placed on public exhibit are subject to execution.

Homestead exemptions are found in the legislation of the provinces west of Manitoba, as well as in the ordinances of the territories. In those jurisdictions the debtor's home up to a fixed value, and sometimes also the surrounding farm land, cannot be taken in execution. Contrast this approach with that of some other provinces including

Ontario where there is no homestead exemption, but execution against all real property interests is restricted by certain special prerequisites: see Ontario Rules of Practice, Rules 540, 561 and 563, infra pp 216, 218.

There are also some common features. Necessary clothing and household furnishings are normally declared exempt, as are tools of the debtor's trade. In some provinces, food and fuel necessary to maintain the debtor and family for a specified period of time are non-exigible as well. These categories of exemptions are open-ended in some jurisdictions; in others, some or all are subject to monetary limits. British Columbia is alone in having a single global limit on the value of exempt personal property.

The relevant legislation in jurisdictions other than Ontario is the following: in Alberta, The Exemptions Act, R.S.A. 1970, c 129, s 2; in British Columbia, Execution Act, R.S.B.C. 1960, c 135, ss 25–9, and Homestead Act, R.S.B.C. 1960, c 175, s 5; in Manitoba, The Executions Act, C.C.S.M., c E160, ss 30–41, and The Judgments Act, C.C.S.M., c J10, ss 13–18; in New Brunswick, Memorials and Executions Act, R.S.N.B. 1973, c M-9, s 33; in Newfoundland, The Judicature Act, R.S.N. 1970, c 187, s 99; in the Northwest Territories, Exemptions Ordinance, R.O.N.W.T. 1974, c E-5, s 3; in Nova Scotia, Judicature Act, S.N.S. 1972, c 2, s 41; in Prince Edward Island, Judgment and Execution Act, R.S.P.E.I. 1974, c J-2, s 25; in Quebec, Code of Civil Procedure, S.Q. 1965, c 80, Vol. II, arts. 552–3; in Saskatchewan, The Exemptions Act, R.S.S. 1965, c 96, ss 2, 9; and in the Yukon, Exemptions Ordinance, R.O.Y.T. 1971, c E-8, s 3.

QUESTIONS

1 Which model of exemptions legislation is preferable: selective and specific exemptions, with a more or less rigid list of exempt property, or lump sum exemptions, with debtor discretion as to which property is to be exempt? Should any lump sum exemptions include a cost of living escalator clause?

2 What considerations should be taken into account in deciding upon a particular model of exemptions legislation?

3 To what extent is it desirable that exemptions legislation be uniform across Canada? Can an argument be made on policy grounds justifying regional disparity in exemptions?

4 Consider the impact on members of the debtor's family when chattels which they use but the debtor owns are seized under a writ of execution. Does existing legislation adequately protect their interests? If not, how might it be improved?

ii The Execution Act, R.S.O. 1970, c 152

2. The following chattels are exempt from seizure under any writ issued out of any court:

1 Necessary and ordinary wearing apparel of the debtor and his family not exceeding $1,000 in value.

2 The household furniture, utensils, equipment, food and fuel that are contained in and form part of the permanent home of the debtor not exceeding $2,000 in value.

3 In the case of a debtor other than a person engaged solely in the tillage of the soil or farming, tools and instruments and other chattels ordinarily used by the debtor in his business, profession or calling not exceeding $2,000 in value.

4 In the case of a person engaged solely in the tillage of the soil or farming, the live stock,

fowl, bees, books, tools and implements and other chattels ordinarily used by the debtor in his business or calling not exceeding $5,000 in value.

5 In the case of a person engaged solely in the tillage of the soil or farming, sufficient seed to seed all his land under cultivation, not exceeding 100 acres, as selected by the debtor, and fourteen bushels of potatoes, and, where seizure is made between the 1st day of October and the 30th day of April, such food and bedding as are necessary to feed and bed the live stock and fowl that are exempt under this section until the 30th day of April next following.

3. (1) Where exemption is claimed for a chattel referred to in paragraph 3 of section 2 that has a sale value in excess of $2,000 plus the costs of the sale and other chattels are not available for seizure and sale, the chattel is subject to seizure and sale under a writ of execution and $2,000 shall be paid to the debtor out of the proceeds of the sale.

(2) The debtor may, in lieu of the chattels referred to in paragraph 4 of section 2, elect to receive the proceeds of the sale thereof up to $5,000, in which case the officer executing the writ shall pay the net proceeds of the sale if they do not exceed $5,000 or, if they exceed $5,000, shall pay that sum to the debtor in satisfaction of the debtor's right to exemption under that paragraph.

4. The sum to which a debtor is entitled under subsection 1 or 2 of section 3 is exempt from attachment or seizure at the instance of a creditor.

5. Chattels exempt from seizure are, after the death of the debtor, exempt from the claims of his creditors, and his widow is entitled to retain them for the benefit of herself and his family, or, if there is no widow, the family of the debtor is entitled to them.

6. The debtor, his widow or family, or, in the case of infants, their guardian, may select out of any larger number the chattels exempt from seizure.

7. (1) The exemptions prescribed in this Act do not apply to exempt any chattel from seizure to satisfy a debt contracted for the purchase of such chattel, except beds, bedding and bedsteads, including cradles in ordinary use by the debtor and his family and the necessary and ordinary wearing apparel of the debtor and his family.

(2) The exemptions prescribed in this Act do not apply to exempt any article from seizure to satisfy a debt for maintenance of a spouse or former spouse or of a child, except tools, instruments and chattels ordinarily used by the debtor in his business profession or calling.

(3) The exemptions prescribed in this Act do not apply to chattels purchased for the purpose of defeating claims of creditors.

(4) The exemptions prescribed in this Act are not available to a corporate debtor.

(5) The exemptions prescribed in this Act bind the Crown.

8. (1) Where a dispute arises as to,

(a) whether or not a chattel is eligible for exemption from seizure under sections 2 to 7; or

(b) whether or not chattels claimed to be exempt exceed the value of the exemption prescribed by section 2,

the debtor or creditor may apply to the county or district court of the county or district in which the chattel is located for the determination of the question, and the court shall determine the question after a hearing upon such notice to such persons as the court directs.

(2) A sheriff may apply to the county or district court of the county or district of which he is the sheriff for direction on any matter arising under sections 2 to 7.

c / Exemptions from Garnishment: Wages

i NOTE All Canadian jurisdictions have legislation creating wage exemptions from garnishment. As with exemptions from execution, approaches and amounts differ.

Some provinces express the exemption in terms of a fixed sum, which may vary with the size of the debtor's family; others exempt a given percentage of the debtor's wages or combine the two approaches. In Prince Edward Island, the exemption is determined by the clerk of the court according to the 'basic needs' of each debtor. New Brunswick is the sole Canadian jurisdiction in which no wage garnishment whatsoever is permitted.

In other provinces and in the territories, provision is commonly made for variation of amounts or percentages in proper circumstances. Some provinces make wage exemptions unavailable in respect of certain debts, such as those arising from family support obligations.

The following is the relevant legislation in jurisdictions other than Ontario: in Alberta, The Execution Creditors Act, R.S.A. 1970, c 128, and Supreme Court Rules of Court, Rules 483–4; in British Columbia, Attachment of Debts Act, R.S.B.C. 1960, c 20; in Manitoba, The Garnishment Act, C.C.S.M., c G20; in New Brunswick, Garnishee Act, R.S.N.B. 1973, c G-2, s 31; in Newfoundland, The Attachment of Wages Act, R.S.N. 1970, c 16; in the Northwest Territories, Judicature Ordinance, R.O.N.W.T. 1974, c J-1; in Nova Scotia, Supreme Court Rules of Court, Rule 53.05(a); in Prince Edward Island, Garnishee Act, R.S.P.E.I. 1974, c G-2, s 17; in Quebec, Code of Civil Procedure, S.Q. 1965, c 80, Vol. II, art. 533; in Saskatchewan, The Attachment of Debts Act, R.S.S. 1965, c 101; and in the Yukon Territory, Garnishment Ordinance, R.O.Y.T. 1971, c G-4.

ii The Wages Act, R.S.O. 1970, c 486.

1. In this Act, 'wages' means wages or salary whether the employment in respect of which the same is payable is by time or by the job or piece or otherwise.

7. (1) Seventy per cent of any debt due or accruing due to any mechanic, workman, labourer, servant, clerk or employee for or in respect of his wages is exempt from seizure or attachment, provided that if a creditor of any such mechanic, workman, labourer, servant, clerk or employee, who has initiated proceedings by way of seizure or attachment of the wages of any such mechanic, workman, labourer, servant, clerk or employee, desires to contend that having regard to the nature of the debt and the circumstances of the debtor, it is unreasonable that as much as 70 per cent of such debtor's wages should be exempt, the judge may in any particular case, upon a hearing of the matter, reduce such percentage of exemption.

(3) If the debtor desires to contend that in the circumstances of any particular case, having regard to the size of his family, the wages he is earning and any other matter or thing that the judge may consider proper to take into account, the exemption allowed by this section should be increased, the judge has power to increase and to make an order providing for an increase of exemption that he may consider just and reasonable under all the circumstances.

(4) Where the creditor intends to apply for a reduction in the amount of the exemption, he shall give notice of the intention to the employer at the time of the service of the notice or other process garnishing or attaching the wages, and if he fails to give the notice, the employer may pay into court so much only of the wages of the debtor as would not be exempt under subsection 1 and may pay the balance of the wages to the debtor.

(5) Subject to subsection 4, the debtor or creditor without waiting for the regular sittings of the court may apply to the judge upon at least five days notice in writing to the other party or his solicitor for an order fixing the amount of the debtor's exemption, and upon the making of the order, if the employer has paid the whole or any part of the wages into court and the amount so

paid in equals or exceeds the amount allowed by way of exemption, such sum shall be forthwith paid out to the debtor, and in case the amount paid in is less than the amount so allowed, the whole amount paid in shall be paid out to the debtor.

(6) Subject to subsection 7, an assignment of wages or any portion thereof to secure payment of a debt whether heretofore or hereafter given is invalid.

(7) A debtor may assign to a credit union to which *The Credit Unions Act* applies such portion of his wages as does not exceed the portion thereof that is liable to attachment or seizure under this section.

8. (1) Where a garnishment order has been made against the debtor, he may apply to the judge for an order for the release of the garnishment and for the payment of the judgment by instalments and, if the judge considers it proper in all the circumstances of the case, he may make the order, fixing therein the amounts and times of payment, and, so long as the debtor is not in default under the order, no further garnishment of the debtor's wages shall be had in respect of the judgment debt.

(2) An order under subsection 1 may be made *ex parte*, but the judge may vary it at any time upon the application of the debtor or creditor with at least two days notice in writing to the other party.

(3) Forthwith after an order is made under subsection 1, a copy thereof shall be sent by prepaid mail by the clerk of the court to the judgment creditor or his agent.

iii Canada Shipping Act, R.S.C. 1970, c S-9

205. (1) With respect to wages due or accruing to a seaman or apprentice the following provisions apply:
(*a*) they are not subject to attachment or arrestment from any court;
(*b*) an assignment or sale thereof made prior to the accruing thereof does not bind the person making the same;
(*c*) a power of attorney or authority for the receipt thereof is not irrevocable; and
(*d*) a payment of wages to the seaman or apprentice is valid in law, notwithstanding any previous sale or assignment of those wages, or any attachment, encumbrance, or arrestment thereof.

iv NOTE: WHAT ARE WAGES? Section 1 of the Ontario Wages Act, supra, defines 'wages' as 'wages or salary in respect of which the same is payable is by time or by the job or piece or otherwise'. Obviously, the question whether any particular debt owed to a judgment debtor is a 'debt in respect of wages' is a question of fact to be determined in each case. However, it is fair to say that the Courts have given a fairly wide construction to the term 'wages'.

In *Craven* v *La Londe*, [1929] 4 D.L.R. 674 (S.C.O.) the manager of a company received a weekly salary and a yearly share of the profits in remuneration for his services. The Court held that the share of profits was 'wages' within the meaning of the Act. Similarly, the Nova Scotia Court of Appeal held in *Swinehammer* v *Sawler* (1895), 27 N.S.R. 448, that a judgment debtor's share in the proceeds of a fishing trip were wages, and therefore not subject to garnishment in the hands of the ship's master. In *Gordon* v *Seabrooke* (1905), 2 W.L.R. 105 (Yukon), it was held that room and board provided by the employer should be regarded as wages, and therefore should be included in the calculation of the exemption.

Two more recent cases are worthy of note. In *Household Finance Corp.* v *Hill*

(1971), 13 D.L.R. (3d) 737 (P.E.I.S.C.) the court was required to construe the wage exemption provisions of the Canada Shipping Act, supra. The provisions of that Act declare that 'wages' includes 'emoluments', a term of wider import than 'wages'. The court held that the wage exemption extends to pension benefit payments owed to a sailor, and that such exemption continues after termination of employment.

Finally, the next case is illustrative of a very interesting problem in attaching wages paid through a payroll account at the employer's bank. Is the case correctly decided?

Holy Spirit Parish Credit Union Society Ltd. v *Kwiatkowski* (1969), 68 W.W.R. 684 (Man. Q.B.).

WILSON, J.: Plaintiff sues in debt; defendants admit creation of the debt but claim it has been fully repaid. Although at issue for some six months, the action had not been set down for trial when the plaintiff issued a garnishing order to attach the proceeds of defendant Stanley Kwiatkowski's bank account.

The issue now before me is whether that garnishing order is subject to the exemption as to wages provided by sec. 6 of *The Garnishment Act*, 1966–67, ch. 18, Stanley Kwiatkowski's wages being paid by way of credit to a bank account opened in his name for the purpose by his employer.

The uncontradicted evidence shows that the established practice of the employer is to pay its employees every two weeks by depositing the wages of each employee into an account opened for the individual employee at the downtown branch of the employer's bank which, incidentally, is not at all in the same locality as the place of employment or of Stanley Kwiatkowski's home.

The employee is offered no option either as to the method of payment or even as to which bank or branch of a bank his wages are to be paid. Indeed, the evidence shows that so long as the employment continues, his wages will be paid in this way in accordance with the settled practice of the employer. The employee receives a wage slip, or pay statement, prepared by the employer, showing calculations of his wages for the concerned pay period and payment by a 'cheque' identified by a number which corresponds with the employee's account number at the bank. The employee is not called upon to endorse a 'cheque,' and what occurs is simply a crediting to his account of the net wages. It is, I think, significant to note that throughout his affidavit the bank manager, in speaking of an employee's account, refers to it as a 'payroll account.'

Stanley Kwiatkowski's only use of his bank account is, within a few days after pay day, to issue a cheque for the full amount paid in. These cheques, drawn in favour of himself as payee, he negotiates for cash and merchandise at his neighbourhood shopping centre, thus sparing himself the trouble of going to the bank to draw out his wages in cash.

When the plaintiff's claim is for a debt or liquidated demand a garnishing order may be had in advance of judgment: Q.B.R. 526 (1) (*b*), but, curiously, not in proceeding in the county court: *The County Courts Act*, RSM, 1954, ch. 50, sec. 27 (1) (*e*). And, because the relationship between banker and client is one of debtor and creditor, garnishment extends to a defendant's bank account, the entire fund on deposit being attachable up to the amount shown in the order.

Even so, where the bank account represents a fund of which defendant is trustee for others, or has been deposited in escrow or otherwise in terms upon a condition not yet satisfied, or the account is held jointly by the defendant with another person equally entitled to make withdrawals, then upon demonstration of the true state of affairs the attaching order will fail. And as in such case the statement of the account – the amount on deposit – may not be read *in vacuo*, divorced from the circumstance whereby the seeming credit came to stand in defendant's name, so here, says Stanley Kwiatkowski, the fortnightly credits to his bank account are to be regarded as being a payment of wages by the bank as agent for the employer, and subject to the exemption in question.

I think this last contention should prevail. For purposes of *The Garnishment Act*, 'wages' do not lose their character as such until they come into the hands of the employee whose earnings they are. Had the applicant taken his wages in cash, or had he drawn a cheque on his 'payroll account,' and deposited that cash or the proceeds of that cheque in another bank account opened by himself, this last account would be attachable without regard to *The Garnishment Act*. And, had Stanley Kwiatkowski adopted the 'payroll account' as his own by making other deposits or making only casual withdrawals, the situation might be different.

But where, as here, the only credits to the account are by way of wages deposited by the employer pursuant to an arrangement which the employee has no option to vary, the entire sum so credited being withdrawn immediately afterwards by the employee and used for his personal needs, then the amount paid into the concerned bank account is, for the purpose of this application, to be viewed as a payment of wages, and so subject to the exemption claimed.

NOTE For a contrary decision under comparable American legislation, see *Dunlop* v *First National Bank of Arizona* (1975), 399 F. Supp. 855.

If, as is widely predicted, payments (including wage payments) increasingly come to be made by electronic transfers direct to payees' bank accounts, the problem illustrated in *Kwiatkowski* is likely to grow even more significant. In this connection, the Law Reform Commission of Canada has proposed that exemptions from garnishment be carried forward into debtors' bank accounts when exempt payments are deposited. The exemptions would remain effective for a reasonable period – the Commission suggests thirty days – following deposit. See *Working Paper 21, Payment by Credit Transfer* 82–3 (1978).

V NOTE: WAGE ASSIGNMENTS The wages which a debtor may receive in the future cannot presently be the subject of execution. The only possible way in which such 'assets' may be reached is through the appointment of a receiver to collect the wages and pay them out to the appropriate creditor(s), but there is doubt whether a receiver will be appointed in respect of such future wages (see Chapter 11, infra). A popular device used by creditors in the past was the wage assignment. A debtor assigned his present and future wages to a lender as security for a present advance. Upon the debtor's default in the repayment of the advance, the assignment would be put to use by the lender's notifying the debtor's employer that the future wages of the debtor-employee be paid to the lender. The wage assignment would remain in effect until the lender was repaid in full. In effect, the wage assignment operated as pre-arranged garnishment and made the assignee a secured creditor. The operation of such assignments is discussed by R.N. Bates, 'The Wage Assignment' (1966), 24 *U. of T. Fac. of L. Rev.* 123.

All forms of wage assignments are void in Alberta (The Wage Assignments Act, R.S.A. 1974, c 61, s 2), New Brunswick (Minimum Employment Standards Act, R.S.N.B. 1973, c M-12, s 15), Nova Scotia (Labour Standard Code, S.N. 1972, c 10, s 85). Only wage assignments made to credit unions are valid in Ontario (The Wages Act, R.S.O. 1970, c 486, s 7(6)) and in Saskatchewan (The Assignment of Wages Act, 1972, s.s. 1972, c 8, ss 5, 6). In Manitoba (The Law of Property Act, c.c.s.m., c L90, s 32(5)) and in Newfoundland (The Attachment of Wages Act, r.s. Nfld. 1970, No. 16, s 8) wage assignments are valid only to the extent of what can be legally garnished. In British Columbia (Payment of Wages Act, s.b.c. 1962, c 45, s 4(2)) only wage assignments made to trade unions, charities, pension plans, medical insurers, banks and credit unions are valid.

The following two cases illustrate difficulties which have arisen in the interpretation of the Ontario legislation.

Regina v *Vannini, Ex parte LeBlanc*, [1970] 1 O.R. 215 (H.C.J.)

WELLS, c.j.h.c.: This is an application resulting from an order made by the District Court Judge of the District of Algoma purporting to be an order made under the *Wages Act*, r.s.o. 1960, c 421, as amended, and for an order removing the proceeding to this Court and for an order quashing the same on the grounds that the Judge lacked jurisdiction to hear the application.

The matter originally came before I.A. Vannini, d.c.j., initiated by an originating notice of motion, and related to an assignment of 30% of his wages by the applicant to the respondent company on the basis that the assignment did not leave enough money to the applicant LeBlanc to provide for his family. The learned District Judge sets this out in his reasons for judgment from which I must say I have largely relied as to most of the facts. What LeBlanc asked for was the raising for a period of time of his exemption of 70% to 100%. The matter in issue appears to be governed largely by definition of the powers given the Court by s 7 of the *Wages Act*.

At the present time all assignments of wages except those to credit unions are invalid. This was achieved by an amendment to s 7 [s-s (6) rep. & sub.] in 1968, c 142, s 1, which substitutes for the provisions set out in the statute in the *Wages Amendment Act*, 1960–61, c 103, s 1, a provision that an assignment of wages or any portion to secure payment of a debt is invalid. There is an exception in s-s (7) as inserted by the Act in this statute of assignments to credit unions which provides that a debtor may assign to a credit union to which the *Credit Unions Act*, r.s.o. 1960, c 79, applies such portion of his wages as does not exceed the portion thereof that is liable to attachment or seizure under this section. As appears by s 7(1) of the statute which I have already quoted, this is 30%. It is provided, however, by s 2 of the amending statute of 1968 that s 1, that sets out new s-ss (6) and (7), does not apply to wage assignments given before this Act came in force. This amendment was assented to in March, 1968, and on the argument before the District Court Judge, counsel admitted that it did not apply to the case in question. In considering the rights of the parties, that is, of the debtor and the creditor, one is consequently thrown back to the rights which are defined by s-s (1) of s 7 which I have already quoted.

... When I come to look at s-s (1) of s 7 of the *Wages Act*, it appears to cover only the case where the debtor in any of the classes of persons named in the subsection has been proceeded against by way of seizure or attachment of wages of any such person by a creditor. Where the creditor contends that the exemption of 70% is too large there is a right given the Judge of the Court in which such proceedings, by way of seizure or attachment of wages, have been taken empowering him to reduce such percentage of exemption. It should be noted, however, that there is a saving clause that the amount of $2.50 for each working day shall always be exempt ... Subsection (4) of s 7 is as follows:

7. (4) Where the creditor intends to apply for a reduction in the amount of the exemption, he shall give notice of the intention to the employer at the time of the service of the notice or other

process garnishing or attaching the wages, and if he fails to give the notice, the employer may pay into court so much only of the wages of the debtor as would not be exempt under subsection 1 and may pay the balance of the wages to the debtor.

In my interpretation of the whole section, this relates only to the process garnishing or attaching the wages of a debtor which is referred to in s-s (1) and this is further borne out by s-s (5) of s 7 which gives both the creditor and the debtor the right to arrange to have the matter determined earlier by applying before the regular sittings of the Court upon five days' notice in writing.

I have examined all the other subsections of s 7 with care and indeed the entire Act. Nowhere can I find any words in the section or in the Act where there appears to be any granting of jurisdiction or power to the Court to deal with wages in any way or by any procedure apart from the ones I have mentioned, that is, procedures by way of seizure or attachment of wages by some creditor ...

The matter came before my brother Lacourciere last November in Weekly Court by way of application by a debtor Dillman who was moving to have his exemption increased to 100% in view of an assignment he had made to the Crescent Finance Corporation Limited. Having made the assignment he found himself unable to live on the 70%. In a considered judgment Lacourciere, J., dealt with the application as follows:

Having considered the cases cited by counsel during the argument, I am of opinion that there is no statutory authority which allows the Court to make an exemption under a wage assignment. The Court cannot, without specific authority, alter the wage assignment made by the debtor.

The application will therefore be dismissed. No one having appeared for the respondent, there will be no costs.

In my opinion, his decision was correct and I should follow it. I agree with what is evidently Judge Vannini's general opinion that it would be most convenient for this legislation to provide for some way of dealing with assignments of wages but I regret that this Act does not seem to make any provision for such. The Act was originally passed in 1885 and it is perfectly obvious that the exemption in any event, of $2.50 per day, is almost meaningless under the present economic conditions. It would, however, I think require an amendment from the Legislature to the Act to give the Court this power by originating notice or any other proceeding by way of attachment or garnishing of wages to deal with the amount of the exemption. I have no power to make such myself.

I have dealt with the matter at this length however because it appears to me that there is no power to deal with the 30% which is the subject of the assignment, as the District Court Judge has done. From some of the judgments cited to me it would appear that certain of the County Court Judges are proceeding as though they possess this jurisdiction which, in my opinion, they do not at the moment have. I think it accordingly appropriate for me to express the views as I have done in the preceding pages.

Order accordingly.

Cangeco (Peterborough) Credit Union Ltd. v *Trentway Bus Lines Ltd.* (1973), 33 D.L.R. (3d) 144 (Ont. C.A.)

The judgment of the Court was delivered orally by

ARNUP, J.A.: The plaintiff appeals from the judgment of His Honour Judge Wren, sitting in the

County Court of the County of Peterborough, dated June 15, 1972, whereby the plaintiff's action was dismissed with costs. The matter proceeded upon an agreed statement of facts and with one addition, which was agreed upon by counsel in this Court, I now state these facts as follows. On September 24, 1968, a promissory note and a wage assignment were executed by Evelyn Bucknell. In June, 1969, she was in arrears in making repayments under the promissory note. She was thereupon sued for the amount then owing and on July 8, 1969, the plaintiff signed judgment against her in the amount of $1,623.93, that action being in the County Court of the County of Peterborough. On February 6, 1971, Evelyn Bucknell made an assignment in bankruptcy. On February 24, 1971, agents of the plaintiff delivered to the defendant, then the employer of Evelyn Bucknell, the wage assignment and demanded payment of 30% of the wages of Evelyn Bucknell under the wage assignment. The defendant complied with this demand for the period only of March 16 to March 22, 1971. On March 24, 1971, Evelyn Bucknell obtained an order signed by His Honour Judge Harry R. Deyman, which order is entitled 'In the First Small Claims Court of the County of Peterborough'. That order purported to increase the exemption of wages subject to attachment to 90% for a period of one year. That order having come to the notice of the defendant, it then proceeded to remit only 10% of the wages of Evelyn Bucknell to the plaintiff in the period of April 7th to October 4, 1971. On October 4, 1971, Evelyn Bucknell was discharged from bankruptcy.

The plaintiff in this action originally sued for the total amount still owing on its debt, namely, $1,238.33. The trial Judge [[1972] 3 O.R. 593, 29 D.L.R. (3d) 55] held that the maximum recovery possible in the circumstances was $556 being the difference between 10% of the wages and 30% of the wages for the period from the delivery of the assignment to the defendant to the date of the discharge from bankruptcy of Evelyn Bucknell. The plaintiff does not claim more than the $556 in this Court. The present action was commenced on February 28, 1972.

The first issue raised on this appeal is whether s 7 [am. 1971, Vol. 2, c 20, s 1] of the *Wages Act*, R.S.O. 1970, c 486, prohibits an assignment of wages to a credit union with respect to wages accruing in the future.

I should first set out what is common ground as being the position prior to the enactment of s 7 in 1968 [c 142, s 1]. That position was dealt with in the Supreme Court of Canada in *Holy Rosary Parish (Thorold) Credit Union Ltd.* v *Premier Trust Co.* (1965), 51 D.L.R. (2d) 591, [1965] S.C.R. 503, 7 C.B.R. (N.S.) 169, and by this Court in *Niagara Falls Railway Employees Credit Union* v *Int'l Nickel Co. Ltd.*, [1960] O.W.N. 42, 23 D.L.R. (2d) 215. In essence those cases hold that an assignment for valuable consideration of property to be obtained in the future is a valid equitable assignment enforceable in equity as soon as the property comes into the possession of the assignor, and that that familiar principle should be applied to the case of a wage assignment. The employer, upon the wages becoming due and payable, holds the assigned portion in trust for the assignee.

We are all of the opinion that there is nothing in s 7 which forbids or in any way interferes with the principle which had been established prior to the enactment of the section, so far as assignments to credit unions are concerned, and that accordingly, by virtue of s 7(7) a debtor may assign to a credit union the relevant portion of his wages, both those which are due at the time of the assignment and those which are to accrue due at some later date.

The next point which requires consideration is the interpretation of s-s (7), and particularly respecting the time as of which the subsection speaks in using the language 'such portion of his wages as does not exceed the portion thereof *that is liable* to attachment or seizure under this section'. In our view, this language relates to the situation as it exists at the time the assignment is taken. On the facts of this case this means that the portion of Evelyn Bucknell's wages that were 'liable to attachment or seizure' under the section (and accordingly capable of assignment to a credit union) was 30%. I should add that, in our view, if an order had been made under s 7(1) prior to the execution and delivery of the assignment of wages decreasing the exemption, or similarly if an order had been made under s 7(3) increasing the exemption, the unexempt portion only, at the time of the assignment, is the maximum amount which is capable of being assigned under s-s (7).

The next question requiring consideration is the effect, if any, of the discharge from bankruptcy of Evelyn Bucknell upon the liability of the defendant to pay in accordance with the terms of the assignment of wages. It is said that the effect of the discharge from bankruptcy, in which bankruptcy the plaintiffs did not prove any claim whatever, was to completely obliterate the debt for which the assignment of wages was security and that the debt having been thus discharged, the security was completely incapable of enforcement in the hands of the plaintiff. We do not agree with this. In our view, the assignment operated in accordance with its terms until the date of the discharge on bankruptcy. We say this because of the position which I have already mentioned, namely, that the assignment effects in equity a transfer of the property to which it relates and that upon the delivery of the assignment to the employer, the employer, as the wages from time to time accrue due, holds the relevant portion thereof in trust for the benefit of the assignee under the assignment.

We agree with the conclusion of Wells, C.J.H.C., in *R. v Vannini. Exp. LeBlanc*, [1970] 1 O.R. 215, 8 D.L.R. (3d) 113, 14 C.B.R. (N.S.) 9 *sub nom. LeBlanc v Associated Finance Co. Ltd.*, that there is no jurisdiction to vary the amount of the exemption from wages upon which a wage assignment can operate except in cases where the wage-earner has been proceeded against by way of seizure or attachment of wages by a judgment creditor (which did not occur here), and as I have already said, such a variation would have to occur before the assignment was made.

In the result, therefore, the appeal should be allowed, the judgment below should be set aside and in lieu thereof there should be judgment entered in favour of the plaintiff for $556 together with the costs of the action. With regard to the costs of this appeal Mr. MacKinnon intimated at the outset that the points involved were of great importance to a large number of credit unions throughout the Province and that so far as this particular defendant was concerned there was no present intention to enforce a judgment even if one were obtained. In those circumstances and having regard to the result which has been reached, there will be no costs of this appeal. Appeal allowed.

QUESTIONS

1 Do you agree that the Court is as restricted (in varying the percentage of wage assigned) as *Vannini* and *Cangeco* suggest? What was the policy behind abolition of the wage assignment? Why are credit unions exempt?

NOTE Persons involved in arranging voluntary pro-rating schemes for debtors in trouble have often asserted that the strongest opponent of such schemes are the credit unions which hold assignments of the debtor's wages. The credit unions are said to be difficult to deal with as they will cling to their wage assignment and refuse to lower voluntarily the percentage they will make so as to leave some part of the wage for periodical partial payments to the other creditors of the debtor.

2 Would you agree with the following suggestion: 'The Wages Act should be amended to allow wage assignments in favour of any person for up to thirty per cent of a debtor's wages, present or future. The court upon application of the debtor at any time would have the power to decrease the percentage of wage validly assigned, and

after such decrease, the assignee would be able to apply at any time to increase the percentage assigned to a maximum of the original percentage assigned?' Why/Why not? Is there a better way to handle the problem posed by wage assignments?

d / Distress for Rent

The Landlord and Tenant Act, R.S.O. 1970, c 236

56. (1) Goods or chattels lying or being in or upon any land leased for life or lives, or term of years, at will, or otherwise are not liable to be taken by virtue of any execution issued out of the Supreme Court or out of a county or district court on any pretence whatsoever, unless the party at whose suit the execution is sued out before the removal of such goods or chattels from the premises by virtue of such execution pays to the landlord or his bailiff all money due for rent of the premises at the time of the taking of such goods or chattels by virtue of such execution if the arrears of rent do not amount to more than one year's rent.

(2) If such arrears exceed one year's rent, the party at whose suit such execution is sued out, on paying the landlord or his bailiff one year's rent, may proceed to execute his judgment.

(3) The sheriff or other officer shall levy and pay to the execution creditor as well the money so paid for rent as the execution money.

57. Where all or any part of the standing crops of the tenant of any land is seized and sold by a sheriff or other officer by virtue of a writ of execution, such crops, so long as they remain on the land in default of sufficient distress of the goods and chattels of the tenant, are liable for the rent that may accrue and become due to the landlord after any such seizure and sale, and to the remedies by distress for recovery of such rent, and that notwithstanding any bargain and sale or assignment that may have been made or executed of such crops by any such sheriff or other officer.

In Alberta see The Exemption Act, supra, and The Seizures Act, R.S.A. 1970, c 338; in British Columbia, the Landlord and Tenant Act, R.S.B.C. 1960, c 207, as amended by S.B.C. 1974, c 45 and the Distress Act, R.S.B.C. 1960, c 115; in Manitoba, The Landlord and Tenant Act, C.C.S.M., c 170, and The Distress Act, C.C.S.M., c D-90; in New Brunswick, the Landlord and Tenant Act, R.S.N.B. 1973, c L-1 and the Memorials and Executions Act, supra; in Newfoundland, The Judicature Act, supra; in Nova Scotia, The Tenancies and Distress for Rent Act R.S.N.S. 1967, c 302, as amended by S.N.S. 1970, c 13; in Prince Edward Island, the Landlord and Tenant Act, R.S.P.E.I. 1974, c L-7, in Saskatchewan, The Landlord and Tenant Act, R.S.S. 1965, c 348 and the Residential Tenancies Act, ss 1973, c 83.

e / Indian Act, R.S.C. 1970, c I-6

89. (1) Subject to this Act, the real and personal property of an Indian or a band situated on a reserve is not subject to charge, pledge, mortgage, attachment, levy, seizure, distress or execution in favour or at the instance of any person other than an Indian.

f / Social Welfare Benefits

i NOTE Most statutes authorizing the payment of social welfare benefits expressly

exempt the benefits from execution, attachment or assignment. Benefits paid under
the following federal acts are so exempt:
  Bank of Canada Act, R.S.C. 1970, C B-2, S 30.
  Canada Pension Plan Act, R.S.C. 1970, C C-5, S 64.
  Canadian Forces Superannuation Act, R.S.C. 1970, C C-9, S 39.
  Central Mortgage and Housing Corp. Act, R.S.C. 1970, C C-16, S 36.
  Companies' Creditors Arrangement Act, R.S.C. 1970, C C-25, S 11.
  Family Allowances Act, S.C. 1973, C 44, S 8.
  Government Annuities Act, R.S.C. 1970, C G-6, S 11.
  National Defence Act, R.S.C. 1970, C N-4, S 225.
  Old Age Security Act, R.S.C. 1970, C O-6, S 21.
  Pension Fund Societies Act, R.S.C. 1970, C P-9, S 15.
  Surplus Crown Assets Act, R.S.C. 1970, C S-20, S 15.
  Unemployment Insurance Act, S.C. 1970–71–72, C 48, S 48.
  War Services Grants Act, R.S.C. 1970, C W-4, S 30.
  War Veterans Allowance Act, R.S.C. 1970, C W-5, S 17.
  Youth Allowances Act, R.S.C. 1970, C Y-1, S 7.
Benefits paid under the following provincial acts are also exempt:
  The Compensation For Victims of Crime Act, S.O. 1971, C 51 as amended.
  The Family Benefits Act, R.S.O. 1970, C 157, as amended.
  The Insurance Act, R.S.O. 1970, C 224, S 170.
  The Old Age Assistance Act, R.S.O. 1960, C 267, S 4 (unconsolidated and unrepealed).
  The Ontario Municipal Employees Retirement System Act, R.S.O. 1970, C 324, S 11.
  The Pension Benefits Act, R.S.O. 1970, C 342, S 24.
  The Public Service Superannuation Act, R.S.O. 1970, C 387, S 322.
  The Teachers' Superannuation Act, R.S.O. 1970, C 455, S 47.
  The Workmen's Compensation Act, R.S.O. 1970, C 505, S 19.

ii Pension Benefits

Bonus Finance Ltd. v *Smith*, [1971] 3 O.R. 732 (H.C.J.)

HOULDEN, J. (orally): This is an application by Crown Trust Company to dismiss garnishee
proceedings taken against it by the respondent Bonus Finance Limited in the Eighth Small
Claims Court of the Judicial District of York. Bonus Finance Ltd. obtained judgment in the
Small Claims Court against one, Wilfred Smith. Mr. Smith is a retired employee of Massey-
Ferguson Industries Limited and is the recipient of a pension paid out of a pension fund
registered pursuant to the *Pension Benefits Act*, 1965 (Ont.), c 96 [now R.S.O. 1970, c 342], as
amended. The applicant Crown Trust Co. is the administrator of the trust fund established
under the plan. Garnishee proceedings were taken by Bonus Finance Ltd. in the Eighth Small
Claims Court of the Judicial District of York for the purpose of seizing or attaching whatever
interest Wilfred Smith may have in the pension moneys.

It is the submission of counsel for Crown Trust Co. that the Court has no jurisdiction to attach
by way of execution, garnishee or otherwise the interest, if any, of Wilfred Smith in the said fund
or in moneys that may be payable to him thereunder. Upon the application of Crown Trust Co.,
Morand, J., concluded that this matter was of great general importance and interest and that

accordingly the garnishee proceeding should be transferred to the Supreme Court of Ontario for determination pursuant to s 62 of the *Small Claims Courts Act*, R.S.O. 1960, c 110 [formerly *Division Courts Act*, renamed by 1970, c 120, s 1 (now R.S.O. 1970, c 439)], as a fit matter to be tried in the Supreme Court.

Section 141 of the *Small Claims Courts Act* provides as follows:

141. For the purposes of garnishment proceedings under this Act,
(*a*) money that is earned or owing, although not yet due or payable, is deemed to be 'owing or accruing'; and
(*b*) a reference to the amount of the judgment creditor's judgment or the plaintiff's claim, or words of like import, is deemed to include the amount of costs that have been incurred.

It is to be observed that the power of garnishment in the Small Claims Court is wider than in the County and Supreme Courts. Under Rule 597 of the Consolidated Rules of Practice, the debt to be garnished must be due absolutely and beyond contingency: *Scully* v *Madigan* (1913), 4 O.W.N. 1003. In the Small Claims Court, it is sufficient if money is earned or owning even though it is not yet due and payable. Section 141 of the *Small Claims Courts Act* was designed to overcome decisions under the Supreme Court Rules to the effect that salary which was only partially earned could not be garnished.

However, the basic right to garnishee is similar both in the Small Claims Court and in the County and Supreme Courts. Section 142 of the *Small Claims Courts Act* provides that, after judgment has been recovered, a clerk of the Court may issue a direction to garnish 'directing that all debts owing or accruing to the judgment debtor be attached'. Rule 597 of the Consolidated Rules of Practice gives the Court the power upon the *ex parte* application of the judgment creditor to 'order that all debts owing or accruing from such third person (hereinafter called the garnishee) to the judgment, debtor, shall be attached'. Speaking of this right. Sedgewick, J., in the case of *Donohoe* v *Hull Bros. & Co.* (1895), 24 S.C.R. 683; reversing 2 Terr. L.R. 52, said (at page 688):

Now one elementary principle runs through all these cases, viz., to enable a judgment creditor to obtain an order compelling a third person (the garnishee) to pay to him a debt which he would otherwise have to pay the judgment debtor, the debtor must be in a position to maintain an action for it against the garnishee, and the debt must be of such a character that it would vest in the debtor's assignee or trustee in bankruptcy if he became insolvent.

Under the *Pension Benefits Act, 1965*, a member of the plan is entitled upon retirement to a deferred life annuity. Section 21 (1) (*b*) of the Act provides that both the pension benefits and the deferred life annuity are not capable of assignment or alienation and do not confer upon the employee any right or interest in the pension benefits or the deferred life annuity capable of being assigned or otherwise alienated. By reason of these provisions it is my opinion that moneys payable by way of pension benefits pursuant to a plan registered under the *Pension Benefits Act, 1965* would not vest in a trustee in bankruptcy if the judgment debtor became insolvent and hence on the basis of *Donohoe* v *Hull Bros. & Co., supra*, would not be capable of being attached by a garnishee order.

Even if I am wrong in this opinion and a garnishee order could be issued in respect of the pension benefits, s 22*b* of the *Pension Benefits Act, 1965* which was enacted in 1967 (1967 c 72, s

1) appears to me to be conclusive that the judgment creditor is not entitled to a garnishee order. Section 22*b* provides:

22*b* Moneys payable under a pension plan shall not be assigned, charged, anticipated or given as security and are exempt from execution, seizure or attachment, and any transaction purporting to assign, charge, anticipate or give as security such moneys is void.

Moneys for the purchase of a pension are paid in small amounts over an extended period of years and are designed to provide for the old age and infirmity of the recipient. In s 22*b* the Legislature has indicated that pension benefits are to be exempt from 'execution, seizure or attachment', and are to be paid to the employee regardless of debts or other obligations that the employee may have incurred. By statute, the payments have been made immune from attachment: *Bell* v *Bell* (1918), 15 O.W.N. 24.

Accordingly, the garnishee proceeding against Crown Trust Co. is dismissed. Counsel for the applicant does not seek costs and accordingly I make no order in that regard.
Application granted.

iii Insurance Benefits

Re Geraci, [1970] 3 O.R. 49 (C.A.)

JESSUP, J.A.: This is an appeal from a judgment of Houlden, J., dismissing an application for a declaration that the bankrupt's designation of his wife as beneficiary of a certain life insurance policy is void against the trustee as a settlement within the meaning of s 60(1) of the *Bankruptcy Act*, R.S.C. 1952, c 14, or, in the alternative, is void as a fraudulent conveyance within the meaning of s 2 of the *Fraudulent Conveyances Act*, R.S.O. 1960, c 154.

For about 13 years the bankrupt had owned a policy of life insurance in which his estate was named as beneficiary. At a time when the bankrupt was clearly insolvent and when the policy had a cash surrender value in excess of $9,000, he designated his wife as beneficiary. The designation was not made as an irrevocable one under s 157(1) of the *Insurance Act*, R.S.O. 1960, c 190, as amended by 1961–62, c 63, s 4. As a result, by force of s 163 of the *Insurance Act*, the bankrupt remained at liberty to deal with the policy to the same extent as if a beneficiary had not been designated. For instance, upon his discharge from bankruptcy, he could surrender the policy for its cash value.

Section 60 of the *Bankruptcy Act* provides that any settlement of property, if the settlor becomes bankrupt within one year after the date of the settlement, is void against the trustee. 'Settlement' is not defined in the statute. Section 39 of the same Act provides that the property of a bankrupt divisible amongst his creditors shall not comprise:

(*a*) property held by the bankrupt in trust for any other person,
(*b*) any property that as against the bankrupt is exempt from execution or seizure under the laws of the province within which the property is situate and within which the bankrupt resides,

Section 156 of the *Insurance Act* as amended permits an insured to designate a beneficiary of a policy of life insurance owned by him. He may from time to time alter or revoke such designation unless it has been made irrevocably under s 157, in which case he may not alter or revoke his designation without the consent of the beneficiary and in which case the insurance money is not

subject to the control of the insured (save as provided in s 163) and 'is not subject to the control
... of his creditors and does not form part of his estate'. Section 162(1) provides that 'Where a
beneficiary is designated', from the time of the happening of the event upon which the insurance
money becomes payable, the insurance money 'is not part of the estate of the insured and is not
subject to the claims of the creditors of the insured'. It is not necessary in this case to decide
whether 'beneficiary' in s 162(1) includes an irrevocably designated beneficiary. Then, s 162(2),
which is crucial to this case, provides:

162. (2) While a designation in favour of a spouse, child, grandchild or parent of a person
whose life is insured, or any of them, is in effect, *the rights and interests of the insured in the
insurance money and in the contract are exempt from execution or seizure.*
(The italics are mine.)

It will be noted that the phrase 'exempt from execution or seizure' appears in s 39(*b*) of the
Bankruptcy Act.
The learned trial Judge held that the designation of the bankrupt's wife as the beneficiary of
his policy of life insurance was a 'settlement of property' within the meaning of s 60(1) of the
Bankruptcy Act, and I agree with him. I think there emerges from the authorities a definition of
the ordinary meaning of 'settlement' that it is a disposition of property to be held, either in
original form or in such form that it can be traced, for the enjoyment of some other person; and
that the designation of a beneficiary of an insurance policy is such a disposition: *Re Player, Ex p.
Harvey, Trustee* (1885), 15 Q.B.D. 682; *Re Bozanich*, [1942] 2 D.L.R. 145, [1942] S.C.R. 130, 23
C.B.R. 234; *Gunner* v *Gunner et al.*, [1949] P. 77; *Lort-Williams* v *Lort-Williams*, [1951] P. 395; *Re
Roddick* (1896), 27 O.R. 537; *Re Benjamin* (1926), 59 O.L.R. 392. Having regard to the wide-
ranging affairs to which the *Bankruptcy Act* applies, I do not think that the word 'settlement' in
s 60(1) of that statute should be given a restricted meaning. The respondent argues that the
designation of the wife as beneficiary of the policy was not a disposition of property because she
would acquire no property rights in or benefit from the policy, unless and until the prior death of
the bankrupt. I think it would be more accurate to say the wife's rights are contingent on the
death of her husband. But the definition of 'property' in s 2(*o*) of the *Bankruptcy Act*, which is in
the widest terms, includes 'every description of estate, interest and profit, present or future,
vested or *contingent*, in, arising out of, or incident to property' (the italics are mine). Moreover,
the circumstance that the wife's contingent interest in the policy may be divested by the
designation of a different beneficiary does not derogate from the fact that she has an interest until
there is divestiture.
While he held that the designation of the wife as beneficiary of the policy was a settlement
within the meaning of s 60(1) of the *Bankruptcy Act*, the learned trial Judge concluded the policy
was not property divisible amongst the bankrupt's creditors by virtue of the combined effect of
s 39(*b*) of that statute and s 162(2) of the *Insurance Act.*
If a settlement of property which comes within s 60(1) of the *Bankruptcy Act*, both as to
substance and as to time, is none the less to be taken as exempt, by virtue of s. 39(*b*), from the
claims of a bankrupt's creditors merely because it would enjoy that exemption under provincial
law apart from s 60(1), the result would be to make s 60(1) completely nugatory. I cannot
conceive that to have been the intent of Parliament. The proper rule of construction is to
harmonize all sections of an enactment and this is achieved in the present case by applying
s 39(*b*) in the light of s 60(1) and not despite s 60(1). I would, therefore, hold that property settled

by a bankrupt within a year before his bankruptcy includes property rendered exempt from execution or seizure, under the laws of the relevant Province, as a result of the settlement.

This holding is in accord with what I consider to be the applicable principle adverted to by Middleton, J., in the passage of his judgment in *Re New York Life Insurance Co. and Fullerton* already quoted, but which bears paraphrase, namely, that a settlement of insurance no less than any other settlement may be attacked as a fraud upon creditors. Hence, where a statute provides for such an attack, as does s 60(1) of the *Bankruptcy Act*, and that statute is competently enacted to that end, provincial legislation of a saving character cannot be invoked to defeat s 60(1) in a bankruptcy situation. The reference to such legislation in the *Bankruptcy Act* must be taken to be a limited one, operable within but not against the scheme of protecting creditors against fraudulent settlements by the bankrupt.

I agree with the learned trial Judge that the declaration made by the bankrupt, changing the beneficiary of his policy of insurance to his wife while he was insolvent, was a fraudulent conveyance within the meaning of s 2 of the *Fraudulent Conveyances Act* and, if it were necessary to do so, I would hold that it was therefore fraudulent and void against his creditors and that such a void designation does not attract the protection against creditors provided by either s 162 or s 157 of the present *Insurance Act*.

The learned trial Judge commended the provision of the Australian *Bankruptcy Act*, 1966, which exempts from property available to creditors, policies of life insurance in respect of the life of the bankrupt or his spouse if the policies have been in force for at least two years before the date of bankruptcy. It does seem unjust that moneys paid in good faith over a period of years to secure a man's wife and children should be available to his creditors and perhaps an exemption similar to the Australian one will recommend itself to both Parliament and the Legislature.

In the result, however, I am impelled to allow the appeal with costs. I would set aside the judgement below and direct that judgment issue making the declaration sought by the trustee on the application before Houlden, J.
Appeal allowed.

QUESTIONS If the designation in *Re Geraci* had been an irrevocable one, what decision would the court have made? What decision should it make on the altered facts? If your answers to these two questions differ, is there an alternate ground for the decision in *Re Geraci* to allow you to answer both questions as you wish?
See *Re Pearson* (1977), 14 O.R. (2d) 453.

g / Matrimonial Benefits

Cairns v St. Amour (1913), 5 W.W.R. 115 (Sask. D. Ct.)

McLORG, D.C.J.: This is an application to set aside a garnishee summons issued at the instance of the plaintiff, on the ground that the debt due the defendant is for alimony and consequently not attachable.

It was conceded by counsel on both sides that no Canadian case dealing with the question could be found, but I was referred to a number of English cases which bear more or less on the subject.

The power of the court to grant alimony is conferred by s 23 of ch. 52 of the Revised Statutes, being *The Judicature Act*, and the affidavits filed on the motion show that there have been two sums attached, $168.35 for arrears of alimony, and $50 for current alimony. These payments are made by virtue of an order of the Supreme Court of July 22, 1913, which provides for payment of $50 per month for interim alimony, pending a further order of the court. It is further shown that the defendant has no means of supporting herself other than this allowance.

A clear distinction appears to be drawn, in the cases which I have been referred to, between permanent and interim alimony. In *Re Robinson* (1884) 27 Ch. D. 160, 53 L.J. Ch. 986, Baggallay, L.J. does not expressly decide whether alimony is inalienable. He says at p 163:

In the Ecclesiastical Court it is the practice to vary or stop the payment of alimony according to the position or conduct of the wife, and if it were necessary to give an opinion on the question, I should be inclined to decide that alimony was not alienable.

Cotton, L.J. says:

But I do not decide this case on that ground (referring to a section of the Divorce Act) because the very nature of alimony is inconsistent with its being capable of assignment. We are familiar with instances of allowances which are not alienable in the case of men, such as the half pay of the officers in the Army and Navy, which are given them in order that they may maintain themselves in a sufficient position in life to enable them to be called out for future service if required. Although alimony is not the same thing, it is governed by the same principle. Alimony is an allowance which, having regard to the means of the husband and wife, the Court thinks right to be paid for her maintenance from time to time, and the Court may alter it or take it away whenever it pleases. It is not in the nature of property, but only money paid by the order of the Court from time to time to provide for the maintenance of the wife. Therefore, it was not assignable by the wife. How far she might dispose of the arrears, or of her savings, is a different matter …

Lord Lindley, on the same page, says:

The question whether alimony is assignable has never been distinctly decided, but the nature of alimony has been often discussed, and there are cases which in my opinion, tend to show that it is not alienable.

On the best consideration I can give this case it appears to me that the policy of the law is that payments made by virtue of an order of the court for the purpose of the wife's support are not attachable. The attaching creditor cannot, I think, stand in any higher position than the defendant. It seems to me that the conclusion I have arrived at may, to a certain extent, be justified by some of the legislation in force here, for instance the provision which exempts $25 a month of the judgment debtor's salary.

I am of opinion, therefore, that the motion is properly brought, and the garnishee proceedings will be set aside with costs, and the money paid into court paid out to the defendant or her solicitors.

QUESTIONS

1 Are Court-ordered payments to men exempt too?

2 Why are allowances of the sort considered in *Cairns* exempt from execution on grounds of public policy, yet taxable in the hands of the recipient?

h / Deposits With Loans and Trust Corporations

The Loan and Trust Corporations Act, R.S.O. 1970, c 254

169. Any amount, not exceeding $300, standing to the credit of a depositor in a registered corporation is not, while in the hands of the corporation or while in course of transmission from the corporation, liable to demand, seizure or detention under legal process as against the depositor or his nominee, assignee or representative, or as against any person to whom the corporation is by sections 170 and 171 authorized to pay such amount.

170. (1) A person who,

(*a*) has on deposit with a corporation a sum not exceeding $600;

(*b*) is the holder of debentures or guaranteed investment certificates issued by a corporation for a sum not exceeding $600; or

(*c*) has on deposit with a corporation a sum and holds debentures or guaranteed investment certificates issued by the corporation, the amounts of which in the aggregate do not exceed $600,

may by a writing, signed by him and deposited with the corporation, nominate any person to receive the amount thereof at his death.

(2) Subject to *The Succession Duty Act*, upon receiving an affidavit as to the death of a person who has made a nomination under subsection 1, the corporation may substitute on its books the name of the nominee in place of the name of such person or may forthwith pay to the nominee the amount due to such person.

171. Subject to *The Succession Duty Act*, where a depositor, debenture holder or holder of a guaranteed investment certificate as described in clause *a*, *b* or *c* of subsection 1 of section 170 dies without making a nomination in accordance with that section, the deposit, debenture or guaranteed investment certificate may, without letters probate or letters of administration being taken out, be paid or transferred to the person who appears to the corporation to be entitled (under the will of such depositor, debenture holder or holder of a guaranteed investment certificate or in the case of an intestacy under the law relating to devolution of property) to receive it, upon receiving an affidavit of the death and that the person claiming is so entitled.

3 PROBLEM SITUATIONS

A number of problems have arisen in connection with exemptions from execution and garnishment, and some of these are considered here. Others which are less general and relate to particular kinds of debtors and creditors are dealt with in Chapter 14, 'Special Creditors.'

a / Attachment of Wages Owed by the Crown to its Employees

i NOTE A creditor whose debtor is a Crown employee may face serious difficulties in attempting to seize wages owed to the employee. At common law, wages paid by the Crown are not subject to garnishment for two reasons: first, a court cannot make an order binding on the Crown (*C.N.R.* v *Croteau*, [1925] S.C.R. 384), and second, wages of Crown employees do not constitute a 'debt' sufficient to permit garnishment (*Lucas* v *Lucas*, [1943] 2 All E.R. 110). These difficulties are commented on in *Royal Bank of Canada* v *Scott* (1971), 20 D.L.R. (3d) 728, infra.

There is a possibility that equitable execution can assist a creditor in this position; he may be able to secure the appointment of a receiver to collect the debtor's wages as they are paid, and hold them for the creditors entitled to them. In *C.N.R.* v *Croteau*, [1925] S.C.R. 384, Duff, J made the following *obiter* comments (at p 388):

Generally speaking, moneys payable by the Crown are subject to equitable execution, the appointment of a receiver operating as an injunction prohibiting the judgment debtor from receiving the fund attached. The process involves no order against the Crown.

There are, however, two problems facing the judgment creditor who seeks the appointment of a receiver in respect of a Crown employee's wages. First, there is the public policy that salaries payable from the Crown from the public treasury should be subject to neither attachment nor any other form of execution: *Paramount Attraction and Sales Co. Ltd.* v *Lust*, [1950] 1 W.W.R. 258 (Alta. S.C.). Recent cases, however, have indicated that this policy is no longer as absolute as it once was: see *Royal Bank of Canada* v *Scott*, below. There is also the 'rule' that future wages are not attachable and a receiver will not be appointed to collect them: *Bedell* v *Gefaell (No. 2)*, [1938] O.R. 726 (C.A.). (We will discuss this second problem in Chapter 11). Thus, unless a receiver is appointed to collect wages currently owed to the debtor-Crown-employee, his wages are probably totally immune from attachment to satisfy a judgment debt, apart from legislation.

Questions are sometimes raised about who is 'the Crown' for the purpose of the rule barring garnishment proceedings. It has been held that a Crown agent, as well as actual government ministries, cannot be subjected to garnishment. In *Canadian Bank of Commerce* v *Monette*, [1972] 1 O.R. 407, Matheson, Co. Ct. J held that as an agency of the Crown, the Board of Governors of a college of Applied Arts and Technology was excluded from garnishment proceedings. Similarly, in *Callow* v *Hick*, [1923] 2 D.L.R. 1185, the British Columbia Court of Appeal held that the B.C. Liquor Control Board was an agent of the Crown. As such, the wages of its employees were exempt from garnishment.

Parliament and the provincial legislatures may, of course, extend the wage exemptions to any class of persons within their respective legislative jurisdictions. For instance, it has been held that it is within Parliament's jurisdiction to exempt the wages of seamen from garnishment under the Canada Shipping Act, supra: *Loughead* v *Shackleton*, [1955] O.W.N. 922, 27 D.L.R. (2d) 610.

ii *Royal Bank of Canada* v *Scott* (1971), 20 D.L.R. (3d) 728 (N.W.T. Terr. Ct.)

MORROW, J.: By garnishee summons issued out of this Court on February 22, 1971, and served personally on S.M. Hodgson, Commissioner of the Northwest Territories, on the same date, the judgment creditor has attempted to attach the salary of the judgment debtor, admitted to be a teacher in the employ of the Government of the Northwest Territories. It was further agreed by counsel that the judgment debtor is in receipt of wages or salary paid out of the Northwest

Territories Consolidated Revenue Fund and that he is a teacher, teaching in a Territorial School at Pine Point and is employed pursuant to the *Public Service Ordinance*, 1965 (N.W.T.) (2nd Sess.), c 9. Counsel also agreed that S.M. Hodgson is the Chief Executive Officer for the Northwest Territories and this office is styled and known as Commissioner of the Northwest Territories. The amount sought to be attached is $1,811.47.

The garnishee filed an answer to the proceedings, taking the position that moneys in the hands of the Commissioner or under his control is not and may not be attachable.

[Six reasons were advanced by the garnishee but only the answers to the second and the fourth reasons are of interest to us. Reason 2 was that 'moneys in the hands of or under control of the Commissioner of the Northwest Territories are funds of Her Majesty the Queen, are public funds and are not subject to attachment.' Morrow, J, dealt with the reason as follows (at 739):]

The control exercised by the Commissioner over moneys from which Mr. Scott would be paid has been discussed above.

It seems to me that this control exercised in the manner and under the authority of the *Northwest Territories Act*, particularly under ss 4 and 19 [rep. & sub. 1966–67, c 22, s 5] thereof, places the Commissioner in the position where he is required by law to handle these moneys as from the 'Royal Purse'. It may be that in actual practice his instructions from the Governor in Council or from the Queen's Minister as set forth in s 4 may be very broad and lacking in specific details so as to make his own decision-making very flexible and appear to be his own but this does not affect the legal position. Such expenditures as he shall make under these powers are as if made on direct instruction from the Crown in the right of the federal or Canadian Government.

The governing legislation makes it clear that the employees or servants of the Territorial Government are not the employees or servants of the Commissioner, although he may hire them and must pay them, but of Her Majesty; the Commissioner as executive officer is not the head of a State or Government independent of Her Majesty but the instrument only (albeit a most important and effective instrument) for relaying or carrying out the instructions that may come down from Her Majesty, the Canadian Government) or to him through the Ordinances passed by the Territorial Council. See also Duff, J., at pp 677–8 in *Lake Champlain & St. Lawrence Ship Canal Co.* v *The King* (1916), 35 D.L.R. 670, 54 S.C.R. 461, for a discussion of 'whether the powers are vested in the Crown to be exercised through the instrumentality of the minister' and my reference to Dicey *infra*, p 744.

Although the Government of the Northwest Territories as presently constituted may give the appearance of a Province and the Commissioner in Council may appear to have much the same powers to legislate as are to be found enumerated in s 92 of the *British North America Act, 1867*, the overriding phrase 'subject to the provisions of this Act and any other Act of the Parliament of Canada' (s 13 of the *Northwest Territories Act*) must in law have the effect of maintaining it in a subordinate position to the Parliament of Canada or in the condition 'of an infant colony', in the words of Wallbridge, C.J., in the *Connor* case, *supra*. All of which in my opinion reinforces the proposition that the funds with which we are concerned retain their legal characteristic of public funds or the 'Royal Purse'.

Under this heading, therefore, I conclude that the moneys in the hands or under the control of the Commissioner are public funds and funds of Her Majesty. The question of attachment will be left for discussion under Q. (4).

[The fourth reason advanced by the garnishee, and the Court's answer to it were as follows:]

4 The judgment debtor is a servant or agent of Her Majesty the Queen and the wages of such servant are not attachable in the hands of the Crown because:

A The Courts cannot make a binding order against the Crown to pay money into Court.

The *Alberta Rules of Court* govern garnishee proceedings in the Northwest Territories by authority of s 25 of the *Judicature Ordinance*. Rules 470 to 482, thereof, govern garnishee proceedings. The effect of Rule 471(1) is to bind the 'debt, due or accruing due from the garnishee to the ... judgment debtor ...' from the time of service of the garnishee summons. The Rules then go on to provide for payment into Court of such moneys. It is clear therefore that if full effect is given to the procedure followed here moneys payable to Mr. Scott from the 'Royal Purse' will be required to be paid into Court. Rule 475(4) provides for judgment to be entered against the garnishee in the event of default in payment. This is of course tantamount to a Court ordering the Crown to pay money into Court.

Under this subheading a great many decisions were referred to by counsel. It will not be necessary to discuss all of them.

The basic principle is well stated by Duff, J., at p 1140 in *C.N.R. Co.* v *Croteau and Cliche*, [1925] 3 D.L.R. 1136, [1925] S.C.R. 384, 30 C.R.C. 350, where he says: 'The real difficulty in attaching monies payable by the Crown to a third person lies in the inability of the Courts to make an order against the Crown.' Again in *The King* v *Central Railway Signal Co., Inc.*, [1933] 4 D.L.R. 737, [1933] S.C.R. 555, the same Judge (now Chief Justice) at p 745 says 'the rule is absolute that no proceeding having for its purpose the issue of any process against His Majesty himself or against any of His Majesty's property is competent in any of His Majesty's Courts'. See also the remarks of Sir Barnes Peacock at p 626 in *Palmer* v *Hutchinson* (1881), C.R. 6 A.C. 619.

It would seem clear to me from these decisions that a Court cannot make a binding order against the Crown, in this case, an order under the garnishee process to pay money into Court.

B Only a presently existing debt is subject to garnishee proceedings and the wages or salary of a public servant are not a debt due and owing from the Crown to such public servant.

Although the conclusion reached under heading (4) (a) above may make it unnecessary to decide the questions in subheadings (b) and (c) herein, because of the possibility of appeal and because of the language in the *Alberta Rules of Court* it is desirable that I cover these questions as well.

Alberta Rule 472 declares that

472 For the purpose of garnishment, wages or salary are deemed to accrue due from day to day; but no employer shall be compelled to pay wages or salary or any part thereof otherwise than in accordance with the terms of the hiring.

The language of the above Rule appears to permit garnishee proceedings to attach moneys on a day to day basis even when the manner of payment may be weekly or monthly or otherwise but I cannot see how such language can circumvent what appears to be the long-recognized privilege that the wages or salary of a public servant are not a debt due from the Crown to the public servant; that such servants of the Crown hold office during the pleasure of the Crown: *Rao* v *Secretary of State for India in Council*, [1937] A.C. 248; *Lucas* v *Lucas and High Com'r for India*, [1943] 2 All E.R. 110.

The language of s 38(3) of the *Financial Administration Ordinance*, 1966 (N.W.T.) (2nd Sess.), c 6, must be considered here. To quote:

38. (3) Notwithstanding subsection (1), any amount due or becoming due by the Territories as or on account of salary, wages, pay or pay and allowances is not assignable and no transaction purporting to be an assignment of any such amount is effective so as to confer on any person any rights or remedies in respect of that amount.

Section 38 deals generally with assignments of Territories Debts and recognizes their validity if the requirements of the section are satisfied. The problem is whether by including s-s (3) in its present form as an exception has the Territorial Government made the salary of its public servants into 'accounts due' or 'becoming due' to the extent that the protection normally afforded servants of the Crown, and as discussed above, has now been lost.

In my opinion this language does not make what was not a 'debt' before into a 'debt' now but is merely declaratory of what cannot be done with assignments of salary, wages, pay or allowances and does not otherwise alter the position.

c It is contrary to public policy to allow the wages or salary of a public servant to be subject to garnishee or assignment.

In the event I may be wrong in my conclusion in holding that in the present case the garnishee order cannot be made as an order against the Crown, it becomes necessary to consider the question of whether another principle or rule of construction would prevent the attachment of Mr. Scott's salary or wages. This remaining argument is as to whether attachment or assignment of the wages of a public servant is to be permitted or not on the grounds of public policy.

One of the leading Canadian cases dealing with this proposition is a decision of the Alberta Court of Appeal, *Hobbs* v *A.-G. Can.* (1914), 18 D.L.R. 395, 7 Alta. L.R. 371, 7 W.W.R. 256. This case involved an attempt to appoint a receiver of moneys owing as pay by the Crown to a member of the Royal North West Mounted Police. Although the Court held there was jurisdiction in the Court to have granted a receiver the receivership was refused on the grounds of public policy. In delivering the judgment of the Court, Beck, J., stated at p 398:

... I think the judgment debtor holds a public office under the Crown, whose remuneration is payable out of national funds, and that it is contrary to the policy of the law that that remuneration, intended to maintain him in a state of usefulness in the [Royal North West Mounted] Police force, should be subject to attachment or other method of execution.

To give only a few further examples to illustrate instances held to be within this rule: In *Central Bank of Canada* v *Ellis* (1893), 20 O.A.R. 364, a Police Magistrate's salary was held to be exempt from attachment as any interference with his salary would be an interference with his office and therefore detrimental to the public service. A Judge's salary could not be assigned for the same reason: *Flarty* v *Odlum* (1790), 3 T.R. 681, 100 E.R. 801; the same with respect to the salary of an assistant parliamentary counsel to the Treasury: *Cooper* v *Reilly* (1829), 2 Sim. 560, 57 E.R. 897.

In the old English case of *Wells* v *Foster* (1841), 8 M. & W. 149, 151 E.R. 987, the reasoning back of this rule of public policy is well expressed.

Lord Abinger, C.B., at p 151 states: 'It is fit that the public servants should retain the means of a decent subsistence, without being exposed to the temptations of poverty.'

Again, at p 153, Parke, B., says

... and that the compensation alloted to him under this act is by way of salary, the object of which is to enable him to maintain such a position in life as will save him from the necessity of risking his character, by incurring those temptations which persons reduced to poverty are necessarily exposed to, and which would render him an unfit person to be again employed as a servant of the Crown. For this purpose, public policy requires that he should not be permitted to assign it away.

In examining the above cases and the many others referred to it is not difficult to see running through all of them a reluctance in the Courts to permit any interference with the remuneration paid to public servants and the reason given in each case is 'public policy'. But counsel for the creditor in the present case argues that 'public policy' is an open or fluid thing and that each case must stand on its own facts, that the cases do not really say that 'all public servants' are so protected but only those particular ones discussed in the cases.

'Public policy' as a guide to a legal decision has been referred to as an 'unruly horse, and when once you get astride of it you never know where it will carry you': *per* Donovan, J., in *Hlibczuk v Minuk*, [1933] 2 W.W.R. 20 at p 23 [quoting Burrough, J., in *Richardson v Mellish* (1824), 2 Bing. 229 at p 252, 130 E.R. 294].

Duff, C.J.C., in *Re Miller*, [1938] 1 D.L.R. 65, [1938] S.C.R. 1, makes a careful analysis of the cases on 'public policy'. At p 66 he states 'there is some lack of unanimity upon the critical point of the jurisdiction of the Courts to proceed under some new head of public policy, that is to say, some principle of public policy not already recognized by judicial decision ...' He goes on to suggest [citing Lord Wright in *Fender v Mildmay*, [1937] 3 All E.R. 402 at p 426], although he does not so decide, that it is not likely that at this day any new head of public policy could be discovered.

It is clear, also, from the above case and the legal decisions reviewed that Courts should be discouraged from extending 'public policy' for fear they may be substituting their opinions or morality for the wishes of the Legislature or Parliament.

In the present case we have a teacher in the pay of the Territorial Government. It is common knowledge that not all teachers in the Northwest Territories are in the Government pay, *viz.*, the teachers in Yellowknife who are in the pay of the local school boards. Can it be said that the mere accident of being an employee of the Government rather than a school board brings 'public policy' to bear. I think I can take judicial notice of the situation that in the Territories today a very high percentage of the salaried employees are Government employees, probably outnumbering 'private enterprise' employees as a class.

As I read and understand the above legal decisions it seems to me that they give rise to a doctrine of public policy based on two main factors – first, a class of employee that had a clear-cut responsibility to the public where harassment by creditors could clearly interfere with his duty to the State, *viz.*, soldiers, Magistrates and so on, and secondly, this doctrine developed in an era when the number of state employees was relatively small in proportion to the total population.

Accordingly under this subheading I do not agree that attachment of this man's salary would be contrary to public policy.

[The garnishee summons served on the Commissioner was set aside for jurisdictional reasons.]

For a case comment on *Royal Bank v Scott*, see Torry (1971–2), 36 *Sask. L. Rev.* 467.

iii NOTE: LEGISLATION REMOVING THE COMMON LAW EXEMPTION On 20 March 1979, the House of Commons gave first reading to Bill C-52, An Act to amend the Financial Administration Act (garnishment and attachment). This bill would abolish the immunity of the federal Crown from garnishment in respect of salaries, fees, and honoraria.

Ontario has adopted a less sweeping solution. Under s 26 of The Public Service Act, R.S.O. 1970, c 386, a creditor whose debtor is an employee of the provincial Crown may apply to have the debt paid out of the salary of the debtor.

The Public Service Act, R.S.O. 1970, c 386

26. Where a debt or money demand of not less than $25, either on a judgment or otherwise and not being a claim for damages, is due and owing by a Crown employee whose salary or wages are paid out of the Consolidated Revenue Fund, and the creditor files with the Treasurer of Ontario,

(*a*) a notice of the debt or money demand; and

(*b*) such proof as the Treasurer may require that the debt or money demand is owing,

the Treasurer may deduct from the salary of the debtor, or from any money owing to him from the Crown and payable out of the Consolidated Revenue Fund, such amount as the Treasurer sees fit in the circumstances and pay the amount to the creditor in discharge or in partial discharge of the debt or money demand.

In administering this Act, the various ministries will generally abide by the seventy percent wage exemption stipulated in The Wages Act, supra, although it seems that they are under no absolute obligation to do so. The process of satisfying a judgment debt from a Provincial Crown employee's wages thus resembles a garnishment of wages, although a slightly different procedure must be used by the creditor applying for payment under The Public Service Act. The procedure under this Act may also cause undue embarrassment to a Crown employee debtor. Standard government procedure upon receipt of an application under s 26 of The Public Service Act involves an interview of the debtor by a supervisor in his ministry to ascertain the causes of the judgment debt, reasonable prospects for its satisfaction, etc.

QUESTIONS Can you justify this specialized treatment for provincial Crown employees? Which approach is preferable: Ontario's or that proposed by the federal government in Bill C-52?

b / The Crown as Debtor and as Creditor

NOTE By statute, the property of the Crown is immune from execution or attachment at the instance of its judgment creditors. To the extent that the Crown pays off a judgment debt, therefore, it does so at its pleasure. The following statutes are relevant:

The Proceedings Against the Crown Act, R.S.O. 1970, c 365

25. No execution or attachment or process in the nature thereof shall be issued out of any court against the Crown.

Federal Court Act, R.S.C. 1970 (2nd suppl.), c 10

56. (5) No execution shall issue on a judgment given by the Court against the Crown.

Crown Liability Act, R.S.C. 1970, c C-38

17. (1) No execution shall issue on a judgment against the Crown given under this Act.

(2) Upon receipt of a certificate of judgment against the Crown issued pursuant to the regulations the Minister of Finance may authorize the payment out of the Consolidated Revenue Fund of any money awarded by the judgment to any person against the Crown under this Act.

The position of the Crown is also different from that of ordinary creditors when the Crown seeks to satisfy a debt owing to it. Besides having various priorities over general creditors (see Chapter 14), the Crown has more of the debtor's property available for the satisfaction of its debt. This result follows from the fact that, generally speaking, statutory exemptions from execution do not affect the rights of the Crown to execute against the lands and chattels of its judgment debtor, because of the principle expressed in s 16 of the federal Interpretation Act:

Interpretation Act, R.S.C. 1970, c I-23

16. No enactment is binding on Her Majesty or affects Her Majesty or Her Majesty's rights or prerogatives in any manner, except only as therein mentioned or referred to.

For a fairly recent example of the operation of a provincial counterpart to this section, see *Straka* v *Straka* (1970), 11 D.L.R. (3d) 733 (Alta. S.C.), where the Alberta statute declaring the debtor's home to be 'exempt from seizure under any writ of execution' was held insufficient to prevent a writ issued at the instance of the Crown from attaching to the property.

There are, however, exceptions to this general rule. For example, while s 225 of the Income Tax Act, S.C. 1970–71–72, c 63, authorizes the seizure of the goods and chattels of taxpayers who have failed to make payment, there is the proviso in s 225(5) that

Such goods and chattels of any person in default as would be exempt from seizure under a writ of execution issued out of a superior court of the province in which the seizure is made are exempt from seizure under this section.

The application of this section was considered in *Re Carolus and M.N.R.* (1976), 70 D.L.R. (3d) 509 (F.C. T.D.)

Similarly, in Ontario, where s 11 of The Interpretation Act, R.S.O. 1970, c 225, states that 'no Act affects the rights of Her Majesty, Her heirs or successors, unless it is expressly stated that Her Majesty is bound thereby', s 7(5) of The Execution Act provides that 'the exemptions prescribed in this Act bind the Crown.' Because s 56(3) of the Federal Court Act, infra, incorporates provincial law as to the enforcement of debts, claims of the federal Crown enforced in Ontario through the Federal Court are also restricted by the exemption provisions of The Execution Act.

Federal Court Act, R.S.C. 1970 (2nd suppl.), c 10

56. (3) All writs of execution or other process against property, as well those prescribed by the Rules as those hereinbefore authorized, shall, unless otherwise provided by the Rules, be executed, as regards the property liable to execution and the mode of seizure and sale, as nearly as possible in the same manner as the manner in which similar writs or process, issued out of the superior courts of the province in which the property to be seized is situated, are, by the law of that province, required to be executed; and such writs or process shall bind property in the same manner as such similar writs or process, and the rights of purchasers thereunder are the same as those of purchasers under such similar writs or process.

c / Property Substituted For Exempt Property

NOTE: Suppose exempt property is destroyed by fire. Can a judgment creditor seize insurance money paid to the debtor in respect of the loss of the exempted chattels? The Ontario Court of Appeal, in *Osler et al.* v *Muter* (1892), 19 O.A.R. 94 at 95 answered that question in the negative:

Here, if the [insurance] company had exercised their right to replace these goods, the exemption would at once apply. [But in this case the insurance company chose to pay the loss at an agreed sum]. If the indemnity money, secured by the thrift of the debtor, can be intercepted by execution, the whole object of indemnity to the debtor under the statute and his care in securing such indemnity are lost. (per Hagarty, CJO at p 95)

Similarly, a more recent case, *Central Mortgage and Housing Corp.* v *Gemmell*, [1975] W.W.D. 61 (Alta.) (Master, in Chambers) held that the proceeds of an exempt homestead sold pursuant to foreclosure proceedings were clothed with the same exempt character. To the same effect, see *Re Williams* (1962), 37 D.L.R. (2d) 575 (Alta. S.C.), and *Royal Trust Co.* v *Dekker*, [1976] 6 W.W.R. 577 (Sask.).

On the other hand, in *Rosmus* v *Bazay*, [1936] 2 W.W.R. 175 the Manitoba Court of Appeal expressly disagreed with *Osler* v *Muter*. The Manitoba Court held that absent clear statutory authority to the contrary, building materials obtained by the debtor to replace an exempt house which had been destroyed by fire were not protected by legislation exempting the family home. Note that the Manitoba Executions Act, C.C.S.M., c E160, s 32, now specifically exempts fire insurance payable in respect of exempt property.

QUESTIONS Which view do you prefer? Why? What considerations are relevant to the interpretation of exemption legislation? Should insurance proceeds be exempt if it can be shown that the debtor has no intention of replacing the exempt property with the funds? What procedural mechanisms could be used to force the debtor to replace the exempt property at the risk of losing the exemption? Should such mechanisms be provided?

d / Chattels 'Ordinarily Used in a Business, Profession or Calling'

i *Langdon* v *Traders Finance Corp.* (1965), 55 D.L.R. (2d) 12 (Ont. C.A.)

The judgment of the Court was delivered by
KELLY, J.A.: The appellant was one of the defendants in this action in which the respondent as plaintiff claimed against the appellant and the Sheriff of the County of Wentworth damages for the wrongful seizure and wrongful conversion of a motor vehicle, and sought damages for the loss of use of the motor vehicle and punitive damages. The seizure and sale were by virtue of an execution in an earlier action, in which the appellant was the judgment creditor and the respondent and his wife were judgment debtors. At trial the respondent recovered judgment against the appellant in the sum of $1,700 and costs, the action against the Sheriff having been discontinued before trial.

The result was based on findings that the motor vehicle seized and sold by the Sheriff was owned by the respondent and was a tool, implement or other chattel necessary to and actually used by the respondent in his business, profession or calling, within the meaning of s 2, para. 5, of the *Execution Act*, R.S.O. 1960, c 126.

To the respondent's claim for damages the corporate appellant set up three defences:

A That the motor vehicle was owned by the wife of the respondent;

B that it was not a tool, implement or other chattel which was exempt from seizure;

C that the appellant was entitled to set off against any amount found due to the respondent the amount of the judgment held by the appellant against the respondent.

As there was evidence to support the finding of the learned trial Judge that the motor vehicle was owned by the respondent, this Court will not interfere with that finding, and only the other issues raised by the defence need be considered.

The facts relevant to these issues are not in dispute.

Prior to December 30, 1961, the respondent and his wife were employees of Diesel Sales Limited, a corporation in which the respondent and his wife had some financial interest. The nature of the respondent's employment by Diesel Sales Ltd. was such that a motor vehicle would not have been 'a tool of his calling'. As has been found by the learned trial Judge, on November 17, 1961, the respondent purchased the motor vehicle in question. This motor vehicle was registered in the name of the respondent's wife, a fact concerning which the respondent alleged he was unaware; at the time of the purchase the respondent borrowed from Keen (Hamilton) Credit Union Limited $1,906 giving as security a chattel mortgage on the motor vehicle.

Diesel Sales Ltd. went into bankruptcy around the end of December, 1961; until about the end of January, 1962, the respondent was employed by the trustee in bankruptcy and after that he was unemployed until about March 1st; at this latter date he became employed by Dyck Duck & Mann Limited as a sales representative on a commission basis and in connection with this activity maintained a small office in the basement of his home.

The respondent's sales territory extends for 25 miles around Hamilton and the product he was engaged in selling was a patented device designed as a component for use in the erection of scaffolding or working platforms; samples of these devices, four in number, were transported by him to building sites where he desired to demonstrate their use to persons engaged in construction work; the set of four samples weighed about 48 to 49 lbs. and the respondent's contention was that the motor vehicle was necessary for the carrying on of this business as a salesman.

The respondent did not use the motor vehicle to deliver articles which he sold; the only use of the motor vehicle which could qualify it for exemption from seizure was the transporting of the respondent and his samples to the places where his prospective customers were.

In January, 1962, the appellant recovered judgment against the respondent and his wife on a guarantee which they had signed with respect to the indebtedness of Diesel Sales Ltd. to the appellant.

On February 22, 1962, the respondent's wife was examined as a judgment debtor and admitted ownership of the motor vehicle, which, later, under instructions from the appellant, the Sheriff seized and sold. On April 6, 1962, subsequent to the seizure the respondent's solicitor wrote to the solicitor for the appellant claiming:

1 That the respondent was the beneficial owner of the motor vehicle;

2 that as 'a tool of his trade' it was exempt from seizure under s 2, para. 5, of the *Execution Act*.

This letter also stated that, if the motor vehicle was not released 'I shall have no alternative but to take interpleader proceedings'. Since the execution under which the seizure was made was issued against the respondent and his wife, the Sheriff could not apply for relief by way of interpleader: Rule 632 limits use of interpleader by the Sheriff to cases where a claim for goods is made by a person other than the person against whom the process issued. Moreover, there is no evidence that the Sheriff was made aware by the respondent of any claim for exemption.

MacKay, J.A., in *Robinson* v *Robinson*, [1965] 1 O.R. 326 at p 327, 48 D.L.R. (2d) 42 at p 43, 7 C.B.R. (N.S.) 209, pointed out the course that was open under similar circumstances, it was available to the plaintiff to have made an application in the original action to determine the ownership of the motor vehicle and whether it was exempt from seizure as 'a tool of his trade'.

However, the respondent chose to bring this action for damages and did not launch any other proceedings. His rights must be considered in the light of the choice he made.

Unless the respondent can establish that the motor vehicle was exempt from seizure as being a tool, implement or other chattel necessary to and actually used by him in his business, profession or calling, the seizure and sale were regular and did not constitute any wrongful act for which the plaintiff is entitled to damages. Since a motor vehicle has been held to fall within the description of a tool, implement or other chattel and since it is beyond question that the respondent actually used the motor vehicle in his business, profession, or calling, the precise question to be determined is whether on the facts of this case the said motor vehicle was necessary to the respondent's business, profession or calling.

As was stated in *Robinson* v *Robinson, supra*, the question as to whether any particular chattel is necessary to the debtor's business, profession or calling, is a question of fact to be decided upon the particular circumstances of each case, but a finding in any particular case must be related to the wording of the statute and in this case to the word 'necessary' and the words qualifying it. The importance of the word 'necessary' in the statute is emphasized by the history of the portion of the Act in which it is now contained. Prior to 1942, the exemption provided by the Act was contained in s 2(*f*) [R.S.O. 1937, c 125] and was framed in these words:

> (*f*) Tools and implements of, or chattels ordinarily used in the debtor's occupation to the
> value of $ ...

Since the amendment enacted in 1942 [1942, c 16, s 1] the wording has been substantially different: the present exemption relates not to tools 'of and ordinarily used in the debtor's occupation' but to 'tools necessary to and actually used in his profession, business or calling'. Accordingly, cases in Ontario decided before the amendment are of little assistance in the interpretation of the present statute.

'Necessary' is defined in the Oxford English Dictionary as 'indispensable, requisite, essential, needful, that cannot be done without'.

To bring himself within the exemption of the *Execution Act*, one claiming exemption must show not only that the 'tool' is such a convenience that his activities in his business, profession or calling would be restricted by its loss but that it is so essential that the business, profession or calling is physically incapable of being carried on without the tool. Following the ratio in *Goldsmith* v *Harris*, something that is 'necessary' to a man's business is something the absence of which would destroy the ability of the man to perform a function the performance of which is essential for his qualification as being engaged in the business.

In the present case there was no evidence that it was a condition of the employment of the plaintiff that he supply his own motor vehicle. Had that fact been proven it would have been one of the circumstances which would have had to be taken into consideration. Similarly, had his employment been such that he was required to carry a stock of a product to make delivery to fill the sales he had made, this would have been a factor to have been considered in determining whether the motor vehicle was necessary for the purpose of his business, profession or calling; but as the facts were brought out there is nothing to show that loss of the motor vehicle would have completely destroyed his ability to make sales, in accordance with the terms of his employment, of the product which the plaintiff was selling. The examples quoted by Dennistoun, J.A., in *Goldsmith* v *Harris*, and the taxi-cab in *Metro Cab Co. Ltd.* v *Munro*, are examples of this essentiality. A taxi-cab operator whose business is the transportation of passengers would cease to be a taxi-cab operator if he were unable to transport passengers as a result of having ceased to have a taxi-cab. A salesman such as the defendant would not cease to be a salesman simply by reason of the fact that a motor vehicle was not available to him to take him and his samples to the place where sales were expected to be made. Understandably, it was beneficial and a great convenience to him and its loss would curtail the extent of his activities. Without it he might not be as financially successful a salesman of his product, but apart from the extent of his activities it is not inconceivable that he should be a salesman of that product without having a motor vehicle to carry himself and his samples to the place where he proposed to conduct his activities as a salesman. While the motor vehicle is *en route* to such a place the respondent was not actually engaged in selling. He was engaged only in going to the place where he hoped to sell and when he got to such a place with his samples the motor vehicle formed no part of the equipment necessary for the carrying on of his business calling as a salesman.

I refrain from expressing any opinion as to what would have been the result if it had been shown that it was a term of the respondent's employment that he himself should provide and maintain a motor vehicle. I confine my opinion to the facts before the Court in this case. Upon these the respondent has failed to establish that the motor vehicle in question owned by him was exempt from seizure under the *Execution Act* as being a tool, implement or other chattel necessary to his business, profession or calling.

If I had come to the conclusion that the respondent had established a right to damages for the seizure and sale of the motor vehicle, it is my opinion that the assessment of damages could not have stood as it proceeded on the wrong principle. The evidence established that the motor vehicle was subject to a chattel mortgage in favour of Keen (Hamilton) Credit Union and that at the time of the seizure and sale, the respondent had no equity in the motor vehicle. If this be the case and the judgment below so finds, the measure of the respondent's damages could not have been greater than the value of his equity in the motor vehicle. The chattel mortgagee was not before the Court as a party but an officer of it was called and gave evidence to the effect that a very substantial sum was still owing by the respondent to the chattel mortgagee. It must be assumed that the chattel mortgagee has not relinquished its claim against the motor vehicle and that it would be entitled, out of the proceeds of the sale of the motor vehicle, to receive the value of its interest in the motor vehicle. If this be the case and the damages stand as assessed by the Court below, the appellant might be called upon to pay to the chattel mortgagee the full amount which was received upon the sale as well as to pay to the respondent the value of the motor vehicle in which the respondent had no equity.

In the result the appeal will be allowed with costs, the judgment below set aside and in its place there shall be judgment dismissing the respondent's action with costs.
Appeal allowed; judgment for defendants.

ii NOTE: BUSINESS USE OF AN AUTOMOBILE The exemption for the business use of an automobile has been considered in many other cases. It was denied in *Goldsmith* v

Harris, [1928] 3 D.L.R. 478 (Man. C.A.) (manager of company); *McLeod* v *Girvin Central Telephone Association*, [1926] 1 D.L.R. 216 (Sask. K.B.) (telephone repair man); *Burns* v *Christianson* (1922), 60 D.L.R. 173 (Alta. C.A.) (chauffeur).

On the other hand, the exemption has been granted in many cases. In *Armstrong* v *Terry* (1967), 61 D.L.R. (2d) 570 (Ont. Co. Ct.), Kelly, Co. Ct. J. held that the automobile of a real estate agent who was required as a condition of employment to have his own car was exempt:

I have no hesitation in believing how difficult it would be for a real estate agent to attempt to carry on his profession, business or calling without the assistance of a motor vehicle. I feel that it would be, for all practical purposes, impossible. It is more than a great convenience to him and I feel that it would greatly destroy his ability to earn his living if he were deprived of the services of a motor vehicle in circumstances such as these. (At p 572)

For other cases in which the exemption has been granted see *Cook* v *Avco Financial Services*, [1976] 6 W.W.R. 756 (Sask. D. Ct.) (travelling salesman); *Delta Acceptance Corporation* v *Schauf* (1965), 50 D.L.R. (2d) 570 (Sask. Q.B.) (trucker owning single truck); *Metro Cab Co.* v *Munro* (1965), 48 D.L.R. (2d) 701 (Ont. C.A.) (one-man taxi service); *Robinson* v *Robinson* (1965), 48 D.L.R. (2d) 42 (Ont. C.A.) (travelling salesman); *Bank of Nova Scotia* v *Jordison* (1964), 42 W.W.R. 433 (Alta. D. Ct.) (salesman); *Hayward Builders Supplies Ltd.* v *MacKenzie* (1956), 20 W.W.R. 591 (Alta. D. Ct.) (tradesman); *Chay* v *Gronius*, [1943] 2 D.L.R. 654 (Man. C.A.) (farmer); *Korycki* v *Korycki*, [1940] 3 D.L.R. 45 (Sask. C.A.) (farmer); *Zelenisky* v *Isfield*, [1935] 2 W.W.R. 45 (Man. C.A.) (fisherman); *Re Lyons*, [1934] 1 D.L.R. 432 (N.S.S.C.) (trucker).

QUESTION Many of the cases cited above were decided under legislation requiring the goods or chattels to be 'necessary' to the business or trade of the debtor. The Ontario Act was amended in 1967 to replace the words 'necessary to and actually used' with the words 'ordinarily used'. Would *Langdon* have been decided differently today?

iii NOTE: WHICH OCCUPATIONS QUALIFY? Questions are sometimes raised about whether a particular occupation will qualify for a business exemption under the relevant statute. In *Rodi & Wienenberger Aktiengesellschaft* v *Kay* (1959), 22 D.L.R. (2d) 258, the Alberta Supreme Court, construing s 2(i) of The Exemptions Act (R.S.A. 1955, c 104), held that wholesale jewellers were not a 'trade or profession' within the meaning of the Act. In *Capaniuk* v *Sluchinski* (1963), 44 W.W.R. 455, the Supreme Court of Alberta (considering the same legislation as that applicable in *Rodi*), held that a sawmill operator was a tradesman and that the onus to disprove this lay on the execution creditor. In *Hayoz* v *Patrick* (1961) 30 D.L.R. (2d) 742, the Saskatchewan Court of Appeal held that 'trade, calling, or profession' did not include a 'business or occupation', but rather was limited to persons coming within the mechanical, craftsman or artisan group. Thus, a person operating a restaurant was held not to be within the scope of the Saskatchewan exempting provisions. On the other hand, in *Bank of Nova Scotia* v *Jordison* (1963), 40 D.L.R. (2d) 790 (Alta. D.Ct.), Tavender DCJ expressly refused to follow the reasoning of the court in *Hayoz*:

I think the clear intention of the legislature is to make exempt such a vehicle when it is required or essential in the debtor's trade, that is, by a mechanic or artisan, or in his calling, that is, by a person in his ordinary occupation or business ... To come to any other conclusion would require me to disregard the use of the word 'calling' and I think I am not entitled to do this. (at p 793)

In *Re Seizures Act* (1966), 57 W.W.R. (N.S.) 178 (Alta. D.C.), the court held that 'because of the very nature and structure of the corporate entity, a corporation cannot have a 'trade or calling' in the context contemplated by the statute. [i.e. in the sense of a tradesman or artisan having a particular skill or craft.] A corporate entity, on the other hand, may conduct a business employing individuals who possess a trade or calling'. (at p 180, per Haddad DCJ)

The Ontario Act should not give rise to this problem, since debtors engaged in 'business' as well as those engaged in callings and professions are given exemptions in s 2 of The Execution Act.

In order to gain the benefit of the exemption granted for tools and instruments used by the debtor in his business the debtor must still be active in the business prior to seizure, or he loses the exemption: *Wright* v *Hollingshead* (1895), 23 O.A.R. 1.; *McRae* v *Frooks*, *Hanna* v *Frooks* (1911), 17 W.L.R. 287 (Y.T.); *McLeod* v *Girvin Central Telephone Association*, [1926] 1 D.L.R. 216 (Sask.).

iv *Re Kreutzweiser*, [1967] 2 O.R. 108 (C.A.)

The judgment of the Court was delivered by
LASKIN, J.A.: The issue in this appeal, taken by the trustee in bankruptcy from an adverse judgment of McDermott, J., of November 7, 1966, is whether certain pool hall equipment, in the main pool and snooker tables, is exempt from seizure under execution pursuant to s 2, para. 5 of the *Execution Act*, R.S.O. 1960, c 126. If it is so exempt, then, to the extent of the exemption, it is by reason of s 39 of the *Bankruptcy Act*, R.S.C. 1952, c 14, excluded from the property of a bankrupt divisible among his creditors.

The bankrupt debtor in this case was, at the time of bankruptcy, owner and operator of a pool hall; and the chattels for which exemption was sought were actually in use by him in connection with the operation of his business when bankruptcy occurred. These chattels included pool and snooker tables, benches, cue racks, ball racks, score boards, display cases and some other things which it is unnecessary to specify. Section 2, para. 5 of the *Execution Act* provides exemption from seizure in the following terms:

5. In the case of a debtor other than a person engaged in the tillage of the soil or farming, live stock, fowl, bees, books, tools and implements and other chattels necessary to and actually in use by the debtor in his business, profession or calling, to the extent of $1,000.

Two points were the subject of contrary contentions by counsel. It was urged and denied that the *ejusdem generis* rule should be applied to the words 'other chattels', as taking their meaning from the preceding words 'tools and implements'. There was, secondly, disagreement on the meaning of the term 'necessary'. Counsel for the trustee submitted that assuming that the pool and snooker tables (and associated paraphernalia) were 'chattels', there must be some uniqueness in them over and above their utilization in the conduct of the pool hall business to justify exemption. For him they were more like stock-in-trade or inventory, rather than, say, a carpenter's tool. The argument suggested that there must be a personal aspect in the claim for exemption as is the case where a professional man or independent artisan is the debtor. To put it another way, the contention was that the chattel must be one used by the debtor himself as opposed to one put at the disposal of or used by or for customers of the business. It would appear that reliance is placed on the taxicab and salesman's car cases in this Court, cited below, in order to found a distinction with apparatus such as, for example, a barber's chair, or a hair dryer in a ladies' beauty parlour, or dry cleaning machinery.

In my opinion, the trustee fails on both points.

The use of the words 'business, profession or calling' makes it clear, if it was not so before when the qualifying term was simply 'occupation', that the exemption in s 2, para. 5 was to have a broad application to many kinds of debtors. Service trades no less than retail trades are embraced in the general reference to 'business'. With such a scope, it would be strange indeed to find a limitation through an antecedent strict construction of the word 'chattels' by referring it to the genus of 'tools and implements'. Indeed, it does not appear that a limitation of this kind could have substance short of reading the word 'chattels' out of the statute. In any event, the course of construction of the word 'tool' in this Court, as is evident from *Robinson* v *Robinson*, [1965] 1 O.R. 326, 48 D.L.R. (2d) 42, 7 C.B.R. (N.S.) 209; *Metro Cab Co. Ltd.* v *Munro*, [1965] 1 O.R. 555, 48 D.L.R. (2d) 701, 7 C.B.R. (N.S.) 294, and *Langdon* v *Traders Finance Corp. Ltd.*, [1966] 1 O.R. 655, 55 D.L.R. (2d) 12, 8 C.B.R. (N.S.) 294, shows that far from the words 'other chattels' being governed in their reach by the preceding words 'tools and implements', they have rather coloured them with their own generality. I agree with my brother Kelly in the *Langdon* case that decisions in Ontario before the 1942 amendment are of limited assistance in construing the present s 2, para. 5; and certainly, in *Re Statham*, [1939] O.W.N. 129, [1939] 2 D.L.R. 764*n*, 20 C.B.R. 196 *sub nom. Re Beulah* v *Statham*, is not to be followed in its adoption of the *ejusdem generis* rule to limit the meaning of the term 'chattels'. At the same time, one can agree with the view in that case that 'stock-in-trade' is outside the exemption, certainly as it is presently expressed. I do not, however, subscribe to the view taken of that term in the *Statham* case.

The question whether the pool and snooker tables (which admittedly were collectively of a value of at least $1,000) were 'necessary to and in actual use' by the debtor in his business is essentially one of fact (as the cited cases in this Court indicate), and is easily answered in the affirmative in this case. In the *Langdon* case it was held that a chattel is necessary to a person's business when its absence [p 660 O.R., p 17 D.L.R.] 'would destroy [his] ability ... to perform a function the performance of which is essential for his qualification as being engaged in the business'. Another way of putting the matter would be to say that chattels are necessary if by their use they permit a debtor in a service trade to carry on his trade conveniently and in the usual manner: see 35 Corp. Jur. Sec., pp 84–6. This, of course, becomes a matter of evidence. That pool and snooker tables are 'necessary' for the carrying on of a pool hall business is not open to doubt. Having regard to the evident purpose of the exemption provisions of the *Execution Act* and to the wide range of debtors included therein, there is no reason to limit the classes of exempt chattels to those that a debtor uses personally; no such restriction can be read into s 2, para. 5.

I would dismiss the appeal with costs.

Appeal dismissed.

V NOTE: SCOPE OF THE EXEMPTION In *Re Statham*, [1939] O.W.N. 129, Urquhart J held that a safe, filing cabinet, adding machine and other office equipment of a debtor engaged in the retail clothing business were stock-in-trade falling outside of the exemption in respect of 'tools, implements or chattels' used in his occupation. His Lordship was of the opinion that articles such as a sewing machine, pressing iron, and large scissors belonging to a tailor were the type of 'tools and implements' intended to be exempted.

Similarly, the court in *Endrizzi* v *Peto and Beckley*, [1917] 1 W.W.R. 1439 (B.C.S.C.) held that a safe, cash register and counter used by a butcher in his business were stock-in-trade outside the scope of the exemption.

In *Davidson* v *Reynolds* (1865), 16 U.C.C.P. 140 (C.A.) the court had to consider the wording of the pre-Confederation Exemption Act, 1860 (Can.) c 25, s 4 the wording of which is substantially the same as the present Ontario exemption for tools, implements and chattels ordinarily used in business. In holding that a horse used by the debtor in his occupation was exempt, Wilson J said (at pp 141–2):

We take the world 'tool' to mean an instrument of manual operation, particularly those used by farmers and mechanics. We think the word 'implement' has a more extensive meaning, including, with tools, utensils of domestic use, instruments of trade and husbandry; but both words, we think, exclude the idea of animals. The word 'chattel' has a legal, well-defined meaning, and is more comprehensive than the other two, and includes animals as well as goods movable and immovable, except such as have the nature of freehold.

QUESTIONS In the *Rodi* case (supra, p 195) the Supreme Court of Alberta held that even if wholesale jewellers were a 'trade or profession' the jewellers could not claim exemption from execution for a typewriter and adding machine as being 'necessary tools or implements of trade.' Do you agree? What decision would you expect from an Ontario Court faced with the facts of *Rodi*?

e / Exemptions – Right or Privilege?

i NOTE If property is declared by statute to be exempt from seizure is it absolutely exempt, or only non-exigible if the debtor claims an exemption? If property is only exempt if exemption is claimed by the debtor, does the sheriff have a duty to inform the debtor of the fact that some property can be exempt, or point out to him property for which exemption may be claimed? Note that the legislation of one province, Quebec (referred to supra p 166), creates two categories of exemptions: some property the debtor may choose to withdraw from execution, while other property is absolutely exempt. Under the Manitoba Executions Act, C.C.S.M., c E160, s 41, every agreement to waive or abandon an exemption is void.

ii *Roy* v *Fortin* (1915), 9 W.W.R. 407 (B.C.C.A.)

MACDONALD, C.J.A.: Defendant made an assignment to the plaintiff pursuant to the *Creditors Trust Deeds Act* of all her property and effects 'which may be seized and sold or attached under execution or the Execution Act or attachments.' She delivered possession thereof to the assignee without making any claim to exemptions under the provisions of the *Homestead Act*. The plaintiff subsequently loaned the defendant certain of the goods and defendant signed a receipt therefor in a form which clearly acknowledges the loan. Several months thereafter she refused to return the goods, claiming them as an exemption, which, but for her ignorance of the law, it is contended, she would have made at the time of the assignment. The plaintiff obtained an order of replevin and from that order defendant appeals.

By amendment (1873) of *The Homestead Ordinance* 1867, it was declared that:

The following personal property shall be exempt from forced seizure or sale by any process of law, or in equity, or from any process in bankruptcy, that is to say, the goods and chattels of any debtor or bankrupt at the option of such debtor or bankrupt or if dead of his personal representative to the value of $500 the same not being homestead property under the provisions of the said Homestead Ordinance 1867.

This section, with certain modifications, is now s 17 of R.S.B.C. 1911, ch. 100. Standing alone it was construed to mean that if the debtor wished to take advantage of the option there given him of claiming an exemption he must make his demand upon the sheriff. In other words, his right to an exemption was declared to be a special privilege which he might insist upon or not at his option. If he insisted upon it, then the sheriff must release the goods selected to the value of $500. *Sehl* v *Humphreys* (1886), 1 B.C. R. Pt. 2, 257. The statute was again amended in 1890 by the addition of several sections which are now ss 18 to 23 both inclusive of the Revised Act. These sections provide the procedure to be followed in the selection of the goods, and, in my opinion, if anything were wanting to make the intention of the legislature clear as to the meaning of the original section, these new sections supply it. It is plainly contemplated that the sheriff may seize all the debtor's goods without setting aside anything by way of exemption, and that if the debtor desires to take advantage of the provision in his favor he must do so within two days after the seizure or after notice thereof, whichever shall be the longest time. It is further provided that in case there should be no dispute as to the value of the goods selected the sheriff shall release the same to the debtor, but that if there shall be a dispute the value shall be appraised, as pointed out in the Act, and when the dispute is adjusted the sheriff shall hand over to the debtor the goods awarded to him. The intention is clear that the debtor is to make his claim at once, and any dispute is to be summarily decided, so that the sheriff may proceed to execute his writ without uncertainty.

The suggestion, that it is made the duty of the sheriff in default of a claim by the debtor to set aside $500 worth of goods as an exemption in favor of the debtor, finds no sanction in any part of the Act and is against the whole tenor of it.

The right to claim an exemption as against an assignee for creditors is founded on the restrictive words used in the Act and in the instrument of assignment which adopts the words of the Act. What are assigned are the assignor's goods which may be seized and sold under execution. Now, all her goods might be seized and sold under execution unless the exemption were claimed in the manner set out in *The Homestead Act*. Hence, if the assignor wished to resort to that right, she should have done so at the time of delivery of possession to the assignee, or at all events, within a reasonable time thereafter. It being her option to claim an exemption or not, her election not to do so would bind her. I think she elected not to claim the goods in question when she borrowed them, and thus recognized the assignee's final ownership of them. She must be presumed to have known the law, and, therefore, it is no excuse to say that at that time she was not aware of her rights.

The construction I have placed upon the sections of *The Homestead Act* in question is consistent with the authorities from *Sehl* v *Humphries, supra*, down to the present time. It was the opinion of Drake, J. in *Pilling* v *Stewart* (1895), 4 B.C.R. 94, and of McColl, C.J. in *Re Ley et al* (1900), 7 B.C.R. 94, and inferentially of the Full Court in *Yorkshire Guarantee & Securities Corporation* v *Cooper* (1903), 10 B.C.R. 65.

I would therefore dismiss the appeal.

McPHILLIPS, J.A. (dissenting): It is impossible upon a careful examination of the evidence and proceedings, to come, in my opinion, to any other conclusion than that the appellant, a married woman, engaged in business was over-reached, in that the attempt is to deprive her of a right which the legislature has accorded to all persons when making an assignment for the benefit of their creditors generally, and accorded to judgment debtors as well, the intention being that persons, who, by misfortune, have become unable to pay their debts in full shall be left something and not be cast upon the community with nothing, penniless with the likelihood of becoming a public charge. The right of exemption must be construed favorably to the class which the legislature plainly intends shall be protected from the undue rapacity of creditors and people are invited to come into the country, a new country, with this statutory guarantee held out to them, and it may be said in passing that the exemption accorded in this Province is slight indeed in comparison to that accorded in other provinces of Canada. All that has taken place earmarks the designing hand of some one conversant with the rightful legal position of the appellant and the attempt is to exploit this lady (the appellant) out of her just rights by having her sign the writing that the goods in question are to be returned. It is idle to contend for a moment that this was not the plain design as it cannot be assumed for a moment that the respondent was not aware of the right of exemption that existed and which the appellant claimed and reserved in the assignment under which he was presuming to act and under which only could he meddle with any of the property of the appellant. The respondent would appear to be an accountant and in some way connected with The Canadian Credit Men's Trust Association, Ltd., and if that association in its business comports in any measure with what might be expected of its name, organic law affecting traders and debtor must be well known to it. In *McPherson* v *Temiskaming Lumber Co. Ltd.*, [1913] A.C. 145, 82 L.J.P.C. 113, Lord Shaw of Dunfermline, delivering the judgment of their Lordships dealing with the facts of that case, said at pp 157, 159:

> What happened in the present case was upon these lines, and without entering upon the matter at large, their Lordships think that the whole series of transactions was simply a juggle to defeat the rights of the execution creditors of McGuire ...
>
> In their Lordship's opinion, the whole circumstances are such as to show that there has been an attempt to defeat the rights of the execution creditors, and that the respondents were aware of this attempt and have pursued a course of conduct with a view to its success.

In my opinion, like observations are applicable in the present case being an attempt to defeat the rights of the appellant.

Upon the whole, therefore, I am of the opinion that the right to exemption upon the facts of the present case is abolute and that right still exists, and even were I wrong in this, and it were a privilege only, that privilege could be exercised in a reasonable time, or at any time before conversion, and that reasonable time would be when affected with knowledge of the right to the exemption and the need to make a selection, and, as in this case, the appellant at the time of the taking possession of the goods in question was unaware of the right to the exemption the giving of the writing to return the goods cannot avail to establish estoppel or waiver; and that upon the facts the claim made by the appellant was within a reasonable time.

It follows that, in my opinion, the appeal must be allowed and the order of the learned judge reversed and set aside with costs to the appellant here and below.

iii *Re Winnicky and Grande Prairie & District Savings & Credit Union Ltd.* (1976), 61 D.L.R. (3d) 559 (Alta. s.c.)

[Winnicky, a full-time life insurance salesman, executed a chattel mortgage on farm machinery which he had purchased, but which was used by his brothers on their farm. After he defaulted, the mortgagee claimed that he was not entitled to an exemption under s 2(d) of The Exemptions Act, R.S.A. 1970, c 129, because he was not a farmer. The exemption was disallowed, and Winnicky appealed from the disallowance].

McDONALD J.: The mortgagee's submission is that because the mortgagor is employed on a full-time basis with a life insurance company, because he was selling his land at the time the motion was heard on April 30th and it therefore was not going to be used in a farming operation, and because there was no evidence that the mortgagor is a farmer, he ought not to be entitled to the exemption provided for in the *Exemptions Act*, R.S.A. 1970, c 129.

The pertinent sections of the Act are as follows:

2. The following real and personal property of an execution debtor is exempt from seizure under any writ of execution: ...

   (*d*) ... farm machinery ... and farm equipment reasonably necessary for the proper and efficient conduct of the execution debtor's agricultural operations for the next 12 months

    ...

4. (1) Notwithstanding anything to the contrary contained in any Act or in any agreement, a person who executes a chattel mortgage of any of the chattels mentioned in section 2 has, in case of seizure under the mortgage, the right to claim as exempt from seizure and from sale any such chattels covered by the mortgage and that cannot be seized or sold without depriving the mortgagor of the number or part of the number of the kind of such chattels that by virtue of section 2 he may hold free from seizure under execution.

1 *If the exemption may be claimed by a mortgagor even if farming is not his principal occupation, does the mortgagor have the onus of satisfying the Court that he is entitled to the exemptions, or does the mortgagee have the onus of satisfying the Court that the mortgagor is not entitled to the exemption?*

In the case of seizures under writs of execution, it was held by Chief Judge Buchanan of the District Court of the District of Northern Alberta, in *Rodi & Wienenberger Aktiengesellschaft* v *Kay* (1959), 22 D.L.R. (2d) 258, 30 W.W.R. 229, that the right to exemption from seizure conferred by s 2 of the *Exemptions Act* is absolute and does not have to be claimed by the debtor.

However, in the District Court of the District of Southern Alberta, Cullen, D.C.J., held in *Re E. T. Marshall Co. Ltd.* v *Fleming* (1965), 55 W.W.R. 11, that *Rodi & Wienenberger Aktiengesellschaft* v *Kay* was incorrect and that the *Exemptions Act* merely confers a right or privilege to claim an exemption which an execution debtor may exercise at his option.

The conflict between these two decisions has never been resolved. I understand that the practice among the Judges of the District Court in Northern Alberta has been to follow the decision of Buchanan, C.J.D.C.; while in Southern Alberta I understand that the Judges of the District Court have followed that of Cullen, D.C.J. ...

The present s 8 reads:

8. (1) A person authorized to execute a seizure shall not seize any goods that appear to him to be exempt from seizure under this Act, but no liability attaches to such a person where in good faith he seizes goods which are later shown to be so exempt.

(2) A creditor, on notice of motion to the debtor, may apply to a judge for an order declaring any specified goods of the debtor to be not exempt from seizure under this Act.

With respect, in my view s 8 is intended to make it clear to a Sheriff's bailiff that he need not seize goods which to him appear to be exempt; affords protection to him if he does seize goods which are later shown to be exempt, and in s-s (2) provides a procedure to enable a creditor to force a bailiff to seize goods which are not exempt if the bailiff has refused to seize them because to him they appear to be exempt. In my view the procedure provided by s-s (2) is restricted to that factual situation. It has no application when the bailiff has seized the goods and the creditor applies for an order for their removal and sale. It does not resolve the conflict between the two decisions. I therefore consider the appeal before me without regard to s 8.

Although it is not necessary to my decision in the present appeal to pass upon the point, in my opinion, the decision of Cullen, D.C.J., in *Re E. T. Marshall Co. Ltd.* v *Fleming* is correct, and I would adopt the reasons given by him.

However, even if, contrary to that view, in the case of an execution debtor the onus rests upon the creditor to prove that the debtor is not entitled to an exemption, that rule would not necessarily apply to the case of a chattel mortgagor. For, as Cormack, D.C.J., pointed out in *Public School Employees' Savings & Credit Union Ltd.* v *Haluschak* (1964), 49 W.W.R. 504, the wording of s 4(1) of the *Exemptions Act* gives the mortgagor a 'right to claim' the exemption. (This is to be contrasted with s 2 which baldly asserts the existence of an exemption for an execution debtor – upon which the reasoning of Buchanan, C.J.D.C., hinged.) From the wording of s 4(1) it is even more arguable that it is for the mortgagor to claim an exemption and that he has the onus of proving that he is entitled to the exemption. That argument was accepted by Cormack, D.C.J.

I agree with Cormack, D.C.J., that s 4(1) is clear that it is for the mortgagor to claim the exemption. Unless he does so, no issue arises as to exemption. It does not necessarily follow that the onus of proof rests upon the mortgagor. If the question of onus were capable of being determined by interpretation of s 4(1), then, if the language of that section were ambiguous resort might be had to s 11 of the *Interpretation Act*, R.S.A. 1970, c 189, which reads:

11. Every enactment shall be deemed remedial, and shall be given such fair, large and liberal construction and interpretation as best ensures the attainment of its objects.

However, the question of onus is not to be determined here by interpretation of the statute. The statute is silent as to onus, and it cannot necessarily be inferred that the obligation which rests upon the mortgagor to assert the claim to exemption imposes the onus of proof upon him.

Although not compelled to Cormack, D.C.J.'s conclusion that the mortgagor should have the onus as a matter of statutory interpretation, nevertheless I reach that conclusion for two other reasons: first, in many cases the mortgagee would find it difficult to prove that the facts were such as not to justify the exemption claimed. Second, to allocate the onus to the mortgagee would place upon him the unusual task of proving a negative. (That these are two vital factors in determining who ought to have the onus is illustrated in a completely different context by Lord Wright in *Joseph Constantine Steamship Line, Ltd* v *Imperial Smelting Corp., Ltd.*, [1942] A.C. 154, [1941] 2 All E.R. 165 at p. 192.)

2 *If the mortgagor has the onus of proving that he is entitled to the exemption, has he proved that fact?*

Of course, it is not apparent from the order made by the learned Judge whether he regarded the mortgagor or the mortgagee as having the onus of proof. Yet it may safely be assumed from the fact that the same Judge in *Public School Employees' Savings & Credit Union Ltd.* v *Haluschak, supra,* held that the onus rested upon the mortgagor, that he approached the present case the same way.

As I have said, I agree that the onus of proof rests upon the mortgagor.

In my opinion the mortgagor has not satisfied the onus which rests upon him. A mere bald assertion that he intends to farm the land and that the farm machinery and equipment which are the security covered by the mortgage 'are reasonably necessary for the proper and efficient conduct of my agricultural operations for the next twelve months' will not usually be sufficient to satisfy the Court of that reasonable necessity. Certainly it is not sufficient to satisfy me that such reasonable necessity exists in the present case. In a case such as this, the mortgagor should by affidavit or *viva voce* evidence satisfy the Court, for example, as to what other farm machinery and farm equipment he has, what crop and what acreage will be seeded, whether he himself or someone else is doing the farming, and as to any other matters which may be pertinent in the circumstances. No effort has been made here to place before the Court any evidence upon which the Court might properly apply the statutory criterion of exemption. It is not for the deponent, or a witness *viva voce*, to say whether the machinery and equipment 'are reasonably necessary for the proper and efficient conduct' of the mortgagor's agricultural operations for the 'next twelve months'. That is a question for the Judge to decide on the basis of proper evidence of facts.

For those reasons, I agree with the disposition of the matter by the learned Chambers Judge. There is, however, one additional ground upon which I would dismiss the appeal:

3 *Can the mortgagor claim an exemption only for goods which were exempt from seizure at the time of execution of the chattel mortgage?*
On reading of s 4(1) of the *Exemptions Act* it appears to me that the chattel mortgagor can successfully claim the exemption from seizure of any chattels referred to in s 2 only where *at the time of the execution of the chattel mortgage* the chattels were among those listed in s 2. This view is based upon the words 'a person who executes a chattel mortgage of *any of the chattels mentioned in section 2*'. To me these words are clear and unambiguous and yield the interpretation I have stated. The words must be given their clear literal meaning if such produces no repugnancy or inconsistency. No repugnancy or inconsistency is created by applying the literal meaning.

To illustrate my conclusion on this point: on the facts of the present case, the mortgagor had the onus of proving, by evidence in sufficient detail, that at the date of execution of the chattel mortgage the chattels were farm machinery and farm equipment reasonably necessary for the proper and efficient conduct of his agricultural operations for the 12 months following that date. Then, in addition, he had to prove that as at the date of seizure they were exempt from seizure on the same ground. This additional obligation is based upon the words

... has, in case of seizure under the mortgage, the right to claim as exempt from seizure and from sale any such chattels covered by the mortgage and that cannot be seized or sold without depriving the mortgagor of the number or part of the number of the kind of such chattels *that by virtue of section 2 he may hold free from seizure under execution.*

(Emphasis added.)

Counsel for the mortgagor, who urges that the only point in time at which the Court need determine whether or not an exemption existed under s 4(1) is the date of seizure, relies on s 11 of the *Interpretation Act*, which I have already quoted. In *Grand Trunk Pacific R. Co.* v *Dearborn* (1919), 47 D.L.R. 27 at p 32, 58 S.C.R. 315, [1919] 1 W.W.R. 1005 at p 1009, Sir Louis Davies, C.J., said of another Alberta statute and obviously with implicit reference to what is now s 11 of the *Interpretation Act*, that

Being a remedial statute ... [the statute being interpreted] should ... be construed, *if its language is doubtful*, liberally and to advance the object the legislature clearly had in view. (Emphasis added.)

It follows that that statutory rule of construction is not applicable where the words used in the statute are clear and unambiguous. I regard the words of s 4(1) as clear and unambiguous. Therefore I do not consider s 11 of the *Interpretation Act* to be applicable.

Therefore, the mortgagor not having satisfied the onus of proving that at the date of execution of the chattel mortgage the chattels were farm machinery and farm equipment reasonably necessary for the proper and efficient conduct of his agricultural operations for the 12 months following that date – indeed the mortgagor having adduced no evidence at all of that fact – the appeal fails on this ground also.

The appeal is dismissed with costs, in col. 3, which will include a fee of $150 for the respondent's written submission.

Appeal dismissed.

Winnicky was followed in *Davis* v *Avco Financial Services*, [1976] W.W.D. 65 (Sask. D. Ct.), and also seems to be in accord with the Ontario position. Recall that in *Langdon* v *Traders Finance Corp.* (p 193, supra) Kelly JA said (55 D.L.R. (2d) at 15) that 'unless the respondent can establish that the motor vehicle was exempt from seizure ... the seizure and sale were regular and did not constitute any wrongful act for which the plaintiff is entitled to damages.'

iv NOTE Some courts have held the statutory exemption to be an absolute right and not a mere privilege. In *Dickenson* v *Roberson* (1905), 11 B.C.R. 155, Hunter CJ said at p 156:

As to the question of the debtor's right of exemption in spite of the cases cited I strongly incline to think that it is absolute, and not a mere privilege to be asserted within the two days on peril of the loss of everything. The effect of the statute is that the debtor may select the $500 worth within the two days, but if he does not the sheriff is to leave $500 worth behind. Suppose the debtor too ill to think of exemptions, was it intended that he should be left destitute, or does the law regard life more than debt? Or suppose he is absent and his notice goes astray, must he go home and find not even a stove to cook his food on?

See also *Spruchs* v *Gregoryk*, [1930] 1 D.L.R. 896 (Man. C.A.). The preponderance of authority, however, holds that the right to exemption is a mere privilege which may be lost if not exercised in the proper manner and within the proper time: *Re Trenwith*, [1922] 3 W.W.R. 1205 (B.C.S.C.); *Carswell* v *Pollard*, [1939] 3 W.W.R. 225 (B.C.S.C.); *Re*

Ley (1900) 7 B.C.R. 94 (S.C.); *Pilling* v *Stewart* (1895), 4 B.C.R. 94 (S.C.); *Johnson* v *Harris* (1878), 1 B.C.R. (pt. 1) 93; *Sehl* v *Humphreys*, (1886) 1 B.C.R. (Pt. 2) 257; *Roberts* v *Gray* (1911), 17 W.L.R. 277 (Sask.); *Pourrier* v *Harding* (1873) 15 N.B.R. 120 (C.A.).

The decision of the Ontario Court of Appeal in *Langdon* v *Traders Finance Corp.* (supra, p 191) poses another serious problem. The creditor who was sued for conversion of an execution-exempt chattel was allowed to set off against the damages awarded against him for conversion, the amount of the judgment debt owed to him by the debtor. If the debt can be set off against the value of the goods, what use is the exemption? Does a creditor face any liability for seizure of exempt property?

Most exemption legislation gives the debtor a right to select exempt goods when the value of goods of an exempt class is more than the amount allowed by statute. (In Ontario, see section 6 of The Execution Act). The extent of the sheriff's duty when confronted with the choice of seizing goods that may or may not be exempt has not been clearly defined. Where the debtor refuses or neglects to make a selection, the sheriff may do so for him and seize the balance: *Cloutier* v *Georgeson*, 13 Man. L.R. 1; *Re Demaurez* (1901), 5 Terr. L.R. 84 (C.A.); *Robin Hood Mills Ltd.* v *Maple Leaf Milling Co.* (1915), 9 W.W.R. 1453 (Man. K.B.) at p 1460 per Mathers, C.J.K.B. On the question of whether or not the sheriff has a duty to leave exempted goods in the absence of a debtor's claim, or has a duty to inform the debtor that certain goods are exempt, the cases are not consistent. Several cases have imposed such a duty: *Purdy* v *Colton* (1908), 7 W.L.R. 820 (Sask. C.A.); *Gould* v *Hope* (1893), 20 O.A.R. 347; *Canadian National Railways* v *Norwegian*, [1971] 1 W.W.R. 766 (N.W.T.T.C.); *Fletcher* v *Pendray* (1916), 27 D.L.R. 637 (B.C.C.A.) In *Fletcher* the Court held that because the sheriff had not informed the debtor that certain goods which he had seized were exempt, the subsequent sale of goods was not merely irregular, but unlawful. As a result, the purchaser of the goods from the sheriff could acquire no title in the goods and could be sued by the debtor in detinue or conversion.

Some courts have been somewhat more understanding of the Sheriff's predicament. In *Johnson* v *Harris* (1878), 1 B.C.R. (Pt. 1) 93, the Court held that where no exemption was claimed by the debtor, the Sheriff could not be held liable for seizing exempt goods. Gray J spoke in these terms (at p 98):

Exemptions under statutes depend upon a great many requisites pointed out in those statutes, many involving very nice points, and requiring the consideration of judicial minds. How is a sheriff – a mere ministerial officer, acting under a positive writ or order of the court – to know whether all the requisites of the statute have been complied with? Why should the onus be upon him? While he is delaying the execution of the Queen's writ, to find out these law points before he acts, the object of his acting may be rendered nugatory. The law says, if a man wants the benefit of a certain privilege which is different from that which men ordinarily possess, let him come forward, claim his right, and prove it before the proper tribunal, and there he shall have the benefit of it. If he waits until it is too late, that is his own fault. He is not to expect all the world to know or believe in his peculiar privileges.

QUESTIONS Which of these views of the sheriff's rights and duties do you prefer? Should the personal characteristics of the typical participants in the execution process play a part in determining the proper role of the sheriff?

4 REFORM OF EXEMPTION LEGISLATION

a / Karlen, 'Exemptions from Execution' (1967), 22 *Bus. Law.* 1167, 1168–70 (footnotes omitted)

'NECESSITY' AND 'VALUE'

Necessity is a frequently recurring concept in describing the kinds of income and property that are exempt from execution. It is seldom defined in the statutory provisions themselves, nor has its meaning been greatly illuminated by judicial decisions. To the extent, however, that courts have dealt with the concept, they have tended to define it in terms of the judgment debtor's accustomed standard of living rather than in terms of the bare minimum needed for survival. It is perfectly possible, therefore, for a judgment debtor accustomed to the 'better things of life' to be protected in his possession of elegant and costly wearing apparel, jewelry and household furnishings, and in his enjoyment of a very large income as against the just claims of a creditor in circumstances far more modest. In addition, the standard remains excessively vague.

UNEQUAL PROTECTION OF THE LAW

Lack of symmetry and coherence is not the worst feature of the laws now under consideration. More serious is the fact that they result in grossly unequal treatment as between rich people and poor people and as between city dwellers and those who live on farms or in the suburbs. Poor people are seldom the beneficiaries of trust or matrimonial awards, or the owners of church pews or private burying grounds. City dwellers seldom have homesteads, domestic animals, teams of horses, stores of food and fuel, or the proceeds of milk sold to dealers.

Vast unevenness also exists from one state to another. In Maryland, a judgment debtor would be lucky if he could salvage $300 worth of property. If he were in Texas, however, he could, if sufficiently ingenious in his investments, enjoy exempt property running into the millions.

POLICY

If, then, the present laws are irrational, unfair, quixotic and antique, what should be the policy and procedure governing exemptions from execution?

As a matter of common sense and fairness, it would seem that the governing policy should be that a man ought to pay his just debts and if he fails or refuses to do so, his property and income should be taken by law and devoted to that purpose. The only qualification to this principle would be that the debtor and his family should not be pauperized and thrown on relief; they should be left enough property and income to keep going and to make a fresh start toward solvency.

If this is a valid governing principle, many of the considerations which feature prominently in the present laws become immaterial. The type of property – whether real or personal, whether a homestead or the site of a shop, whether a radio or television set, whether a team of horses or a truck – ceases to be significant. So also does the character of the judgment creditor; whether he be a domestic servant or a merchant or a banker, he ought to be paid his just debts. So also does the character of the judgment debtor; whether a farmer or a factory worker, a man or a woman, a soldier or a pacifist, his just debts ought to be paid.

Also immaterial are the desires and conditions of third persons not involved in the debtor-creditor relationship. The fact that the settler of a trust wishes to protect an improvident son or nephew ought not to control the rights of third persons when that son or nephew incurs debts which he is unable or unwilling to pay. The fact that a man is so wealthy that he is required to pay steep alimony to his divorced wife ought not to protect her when she lives beyond the standard of living thus provided.

Finally, the standard of living of the judgment debtor ought not to govern the collectibility of the debts he incurs. If it does, a rich wastrel is given the privilege of wallowing in luxury while his less affluent creditor looks on in helpless frustration.

As to the method of selecting the property, that would seem properly to be the prerogative of the judgment debtor in the first instance, subject only to a procedure which would protect the legitimate interests of the judgment creditor. If the judgment debtor were allowed to select the property he wished to retain, he could protect articles of high sentimental value but little intrinsic worth, and he could also choose the items which were most essential to his and his family's vital interests. He, better than any other person, would be likely to know whether the welfare of his family depended more upon an automobile than upon a piece of real estate or some other article. The only protection needed for the judgment creditor would be a fair appraisal of market value of the property chosen. This could be accomplished (if there were any dispute) by appraisers – one chosen by the judgment debtor, one by the judgment creditor and the third by the two previously chosen. The procedure would be administratively simple, avoiding the procedural uncertainties that mar the present laws and vastly reducing, if not eliminating, the time, effort and expense now needed to decide questions of 'value' and 'necessity.'

b / Trebilcock and Shulman, 'The Pathology of Credit Breakdown' (1976), 22 *McGill L.J.* 415, 458–9
[Reread the portion of this article dealing with exemptions, supra pp 73–4.]

QUESTIONS What ought to be the relationship between provincial exemptions from execution and federal exemptions from bankruptcy? What consequences would follow if the bankruptcy exemptions were higher than the relevant executions; the same as execution exemptions; or lower than execution exemptions?

9
Execution

a / Note

Although many 'writs of execution' are available to a judgment creditor, one has emerged as the most effective and most often used. It is the writ of *fieri facias* (*'fi.fa'*) and allows the seizure of almost any of the assets which may be made answerable for a debtor's debts. The issue of a *'fi.fa.'*, and the lodging of it with the Sheriff, are standard first steps in the enforcement process. As will be seen, however, the mere lodging of the writ has a significant immediate effect only on real property. Its effect on personalty really depends on the ability of the creditor to direct the Sheriff to the chattels and to have the chattels sold by the Sheriff.

b / The Execution Act, R.S.O. 1970, c 152.

1. In this Act,

(*a*) 'execution' includes a writ of *fieri facias* and every subsequent writ for giving effect thereto;

(*b*) 'sheriff' includes an officer to whom an execution is directed.

2. The following chattels are exempt from seizure under any writ issued out of any court:

1 Necessary and ordinary wearing apparel of the debtor and his family not exceeding $1,000 in value.

2 The household furniture, utensils, equipment, food and fuel that are contained in and form part of the permanent home of the debtor not exceeding $2,000 in value.

3 In the case of a debtor other than a person engaged solely in the tillage of the soil or farming, tools and instruments and other chattels ordinarily used by the debtor in his business, profession or calling not exceeding $2,000 in value.

4 In the case of a person engaged solely in the tillage of the soil or farming, the live stock, fowl, bees, books, tools and implements and other chattels ordinarily used by the debtor in his business or calling not exceeding $5,000 in value.

5 In the case of a person engaged solely in the tillage of the soil or farming, sufficient seed to seed all his land under cultivation, not exceeding 100 acres, as selected by the debtor, and fourteen bushels of potatoes, and, where seizure is made between the 1st day of October and the 30th day of April, such food and bedding as are necessary to feed and bed the live stock and fowl that are exempt under this section until the 30th day of April next following.

3. (1) Where exemption is claimed for a chattel referred to in paragraph 3 of section 2 that has a sale value in excess of $2,000 plus the costs of the sale and other chattels are not available for seizure and sale, the chattel is subject to seizure and sale under a writ of execution and $2,000 shall be paid to the debtor out of the proceeds of the sale.

(2) The debtor may, in lieu of the chattels referred to in paragraph 4 of section 2, elect to receive the proceeds of the sale thereof up to $5,000, in which case the officer executing the writ shall pay the net proceeds of the sale if they do not exceed $5,000 or, if they exceed $5,000, shall pay that sum to the debtor in satisfaction of the debtor's right to exemption under that paragraph.

4. The sum to which a debtor is entitled under subsection 1 or 2 of section 3 is exempt from attachment or seizure at the instance of a creditor.

5. Chattels exempt from seizure are, after the death of the debtor, exempt from the claims of his creditors, and his widow is entitled to retain them for the benefit of herself and his family, or, if there is no widow, the family of the debtor is entitled to them.

6. The debtor, his widow or family, or, in the case of infants, their guardian, may select out of any larger number the chattels exempt from seizure.

7. (1) The exemptions prescribed in this Act do not apply to exempt any chattel from seizure to satisfy a debt contracted for the purchase of such chattel, except beds, bedding and bedsteads, including cradles in ordinary use by the debtor and his family and the necessary and ordinary wearing apparel of the debtor and his family.

(2) The exemptions prescribed in this Act do not apply to exempt any article from seizure to satisfy a debt for maintenance of a spouse or former spouse or of a child, except tools, instruments and chattels ordinarily used by the debtor in his business, profession or calling.

(3) The exemptions prescribed in this Act do not apply to chattels purchased for the purpose of defeating claims of creditors.

(4) The exemptions prescribed in this Act are not available to a corporate debtor.

(5) The exemptions prescribed in this Act bind the Crown.

8. (1) Where a dispute arises as to,

(a) whether or not a chattel is eligible for exemption from seizure under sections 2 to 7; or

(b) whether or not chattels claimed to be exempt exceed the value of the exemption prescribed by section 2,

the debtor or creditor may apply to the county or district court of the county or district in which the chattel is located for the determination of the question, and the court shall determine the question after a hearing upon such notice to such persons as the court directs.

(2) A sheriff may apply to the county or district court of the county or district of which he is the sheriff for direction on any matter arising under sections 2 to 7.

9. The sheriff to whom a writ of execution against lands is delivered for execution may seize and sell thereunder the lands of the execution debtor, including any lands whereof any other person is seized or possessed in trust for the execution debtor and including any interest of the execution debtor in lands held in joint tenancy.

10. (1) Subject to *The Land Titles Act* and to section 11, a writ of execution binds the goods and lands against which it is issued from the time of the delivery thereof to the sheriff for execution, but save as to bills of sale and chattel mortgages, no writ of execution against goods prejudices the title to such goods acquired by a person in good faith and for valuable consideration unless such person had, at the time when he acquired his title, notice that such writ or any other writ by virtue of which the goods of the execution debtor might be seized or attached has been delivered to the sheriff and remains in his hands unexecuted.

(2) The sheriff shall, upon the receipt of the writ and without fee, endorse thereon the day of the year, the month, the hour and the minute when it was received.

(3) Subsection 1 does not apply to an execution against goods issued out of a small claims court, which binds only from the time of the seizure.

11. (1) Where the name of an execution debtor set out in a writ of execution is not that of a

corporation or the firm name of a partnership, the writ does not bind the lands of the execution debtor unless,

(*a*) the name of the execution debtor set out in the writ includes at least one given name in full; or

(*b*) a statutory declaration of the execution creditor or his solicitor is filed with the sheriff identifying the execution debtor by at least one given name in full.

(2) Subject to subsection 3, where a statutory declaration is filed under clause *b* of subsection 1, the name of the execution debtor set out in the writ shall be deemed to contain the given names affirmed in the declaration and the writ binds land from the time the declaration is filed.

(3) Where a statutory declaration is filed under clause *b* of subsection 1 in respect of a writ of execution of which a copy has been transmitted to the proper master of titles under section 153 of *The Land Titles Act*, the sheriff shall transmit a copy of the declaration to the proper master of titles and the writ does not bind land registered under *The Land Titles Act* until the copy of the declaration has been received by the proper master of titles.

12. Where a writ of execution or renewal thereof of which a copy was transmitted to the proper master of titles under section 153 of *The Land Titles Act* is withdrawn, the sheriff shall forthwith transmit to the proper master of titles a certificate under his hand stating that the writ has been withdrawn.

13. Subject to *The Judicature Act* and the rules of court, land and other hereditaments and real estate belonging to any person indebted are liable to and chargeable with all just debts, duties and demands of whatsoever nature or kind owing by any such person to Her Majesty or to any of her subjects and are assets for the satisfaction thereof and are subject to the like remedies, proceedings and process for seizing, selling or disposing of them towards the satisfaction of such debts, duties and demands, and in like manner as personal estate is seized, sold or disposed of.

14. (1) Shares and dividends and any equitable or other right, property, interest or equity of redemption in or in respect of shares or dividends in a chartered bank or a corporation having transferable shares shall be deemed to be personal property found in the place where notice of the seizure thereof is served, and may be seized under execution and sold thereunder in like manner as other personal property.

(2) The sheriff on being informed on behalf of the execution creditor that the execution debtor has such shares, and on being required to seize them, shall forthwith serve a copy of the execution on the bank or corporation with a notice that all the shares of the execution debtor are seized thereunder, and from the time of service the seizure shall be deemed to be made and no transfer of the shares by the execution debtor is valid unless and until the seizure has been discharged, and every seizure and sale made under the execution shall include all dividends, premiums, bonuses or other pecuniary profits upon the shares seized, and they shall not, after notice as aforesaid, be paid by the bank or corporation to anyone except the person to whom the shares have been sold.

(3) Such seizure may be made and notice given by the sheriff where the bank or corporation has within his bailiwick a place at which service of process may be made, or where a share register is kept.

(4) If the bank or corporation has more than one place where service of process may be made, and there is some place where transfers of shares may be notified to and entered by the bank or corporation, so as to be valid as regards the bank or corporation, or where dividends or profits as aforesaid on stock may be paid other than the place where service of such notice has been made, the notice does not affect any transfer or payment of dividends or profits duly made and entered at any such other place, so as to subject the bank or corporation to pay twice, or so as to affect the rights of a *bona fide* purchaser, until after the expiration of a period from the time of service

sufficient for the transmission of notice of service by post from the place where it has been made to such other place, which notice it is the duty of the bank or corporation to so transmit.

(5) Where any such share is sold, the sheriff shall within ten days after the sale serve upon the bank or corporation at a place where service of process may be made a copy of the execution with his certificate endorsed thereon certifying the sale and the name of the purchaser who shall have the same rights and be under the same obligations as if he had purchased the share from the execution debtor at the time of the service of notice under subsection 2.

(6) Nothing in this Act affects any remedy that the execution creditor might, without this Act, have had against any such share or the dividends, premiums, bonuses or other pecuniary profits in respect thereof, and subsections 1 to 4 apply to such remedy in so far as they can be applied thereto.

15. If a sheriff seizes the shares of an execution debtor in a private company, he shall first offer them for sale to the other shareholders or any one of them in such private company, and if none of them will purchase the shares for a reasonable price, the sheriff may then offer the debtor's interest therein for sale to the public generally and sell and convey to the highest bidder.

16. The procedure for seizure and sale in the case of an equitable or other right, property, interest or equity of redemption in or in respect of a share shall be the same as hereinbefore provided in the case of shares and dividends, and the same shall be held to be personal property found in the place where notice of the seizure is served.

17. (1) All rights under letters patent of invention and any equitable or other right, property, interest or equity of redemption therein shall be deemed to be personal property and may be seized and sold under execution in like manner as other personal property.

(2) Such seizure and sale may be made by the sheriff of any county or district having in his hands to be executed an execution against the property of the debtor who is the owner of or interested in the letters patent.

(3) Notice of the seizure shall forthwith be sent to the Patent Office, Ottawa, and the interest of the debtor shall be bound from the time when the notice is received there.

18. The sheriff may seize and sell any equitable or other right, property, interest or equity of redemption in or in respect of any goods, chattels or personal property, including leasehold interests in any land of the execution debtor, and, except where the sale is under an execution against goods issued out of a small claims court, the sale conveys whatever equitable or other right, property, interest or equity of redemption he had or was entitled to in or in respect of the goods, chattels or personal property at the time of the delivery of the execution to the sheriff for execution, and, where the sale is under an execution against goods issued out of a small claims court, the sale conveys whatever equitable or other right, property, interest or equity of redemption the debtor had or was entitled to in or in respect of the goods, chattels or personal property at the time of the seizure.

19. (1) The sheriff shall seize any money or banknotes, including any surplus of a former execution against the debtor, and any cheques, bills of exchange, promissory notes, bonds, mortgages, specialties or other securities for money belonging to the person against whom the execution has been issued, and, subject to *The Creditors' Relief Act*, shall pay or deliver to the party who sued out the execution the money or banknotes so seized, or a sufficient part thereof, and hold such cheques, bills of exchange, promissory notes, bonds, mortgages, specialties or other securities for money as security for the amount directed to be levied, or so much thereof as has not been otherwise levied or raised, and the sheriff may sue in his own name for the recovery of the sums secured thereby.

(2) The sheriff may seize any book debts and other choses in action of the execution debtor and may sue in his own name for the recovery of the moneys payable in respect thereof.

(3) If it appears to the sheriff that an attempt to collect the book debts, choses in action or the securities for the money referred to in subsections 1 and 2 would be less beneficial to the creditors than a sale thereof, the sheriff may proceed to sell such book debts, choses in action and securities by public auction in the same manner as the debtor's goods may be sold when taken in execution.

(4) The payment to the sheriff by the person liable on such cheque, bill of exchange, promissory note, bond, mortgage, specialty or other security, with or without suit, or recovery from him, discharges him to the extent of such payment or recovery, from his liability thereon.

(5) Subject to *The Creditor's Relief Act*, the sheriff shall pay over to the party who sued out the execution the money so paid or recovered, or a sufficient sum to discharge the amount directed to be levied, and if, after satisfaction thereof and of the fees, poundage and expenses of the sheriff, a surplus remains, it shall be paid to the party against whom the execution issued.

(6) A sheriff is not bound to sue any person liable upon such cheque, bill of exchange, promissory note, bond, mortgage, specialty or other security unless the party who sued out the execution enters into a bond with two sufficient sureties to indemnify the sheriff against all costs and expenses to be incurred in the prosecution of the action, or to which he may become liable in consequence thereof, and the expenses of the bond, not exceeding $5, may be deducted from any money recovered in the action.

20. (1) A sheriff is not, without written instructions and a bond as hereinafter mentioned, obliged to seize property in the possession of a third person claiming it and not in the possession of the debtor against whose property the execution was issued.

(2) The instructions shall specify the property in such a way as to enable the sheriff to identify it.

21. (1) If a sheriff is informed on behalf of the execution creditor that the execution debtor is a mortgagee of land and that the mortgage is registered, or that he is entitled to receive a sum of money charged upon land by virtue of a registered instrument, and, if the sheriff is required on behalf of the execution creditor to seize the mortgage or charge and is furnished in writing with the information necessary to enable him to give the notice hereinafter mentioned, he shall, upon payment of the proper fees, forthwith deliver or transmit to the registrar or master of titles in whose office the mortgage or other instrument is registered, who shall forthwith register it, a notice in the form or to the effect following:

To the Registrar of .... (*or as the case may be*)

By virtue of an execution issued out of the Supreme Court of Ontario .... (*or as the case may be*) whereby I am commanded to levy of the goods and chattels of *A.B.* $......... for debt, and $......... for costs lately adjudged to be paid by *A.B.* to *C.D.*, besides the costs of execution, I have this day seized and taken in execution all the estate, right, title and interest of *A.B.* in a mortgage made by *X.Y.* to *A.B.*, bearing date the .... day of ...., 19......, and registered in the registry office for the County of .... (*or as the case may be*) on the .... day of ...., 19......, as number .... (*or the said mortgage or other instrument may be described in any other manner by reference to dates, parties and the land covered as will enable the notice to be registered against the land therein described*) and in the money secured thereby, and this notice is given for the purpose of binding the interest of *A.B.* under sections 21 to 25 of *The Execution Act*.

Dated this ...... day of ...., 19......

(Signed) ....
Sheriff of the County (*or* District) of ....

(2) Upon registration of the notice, the interest of the execution debtor in the mortgage or other instrument and in the land therein described and in the money thereby secured and in all covenants and stipulations for securing payment thereof is bound by the execution, and such registration is notice of the execution and seizure to all persons who may thereafter in any way acquire an interest in the mortgage, land, money or covenants, and the rights of the sheriff and of the execution creditor have priority over the rights of all such persons subject, as regards the mortgagor or person liable to pay the money secured by the mortgage or charge, to section 22.

22. (1) A notice similar to that mentioned in section 21 shall also be served upon the mortgagor or the person who is liable to pay the money secured by the registered instrument, and after such service the person served shall pay to the sheriff all money then payable and, as it becomes due, all money that may become payable to the execution debtor so far as may be necessary to satisfy the execution.

(2) Service of the notice may be made personally, or by leaving it at the dwelling-house of the person to be served with a grown-up person residing there, or by registered mail to the proper address of the person to be served.

(3) Any payment made after service of the notice or after actual knowledge of the seizure is void as against the sheriff and the execution creditor.

23. In addition to the remedies provided in this Act, the sheriff may bring an action on any mortgage or other instrument seized under this Act for the sale or foreclosure of the land covered by it, and is entitled to a bond of indemnity as in the cases provided for in subsection 6 of section 19.

26. Where an execution debtor is a mortgagee of chattels and the mortgage is registered as required by law, sections 21 to 25 are applicable, except that the notice to be given by the sheriff shall be delivered or transmitted to the clerk of the county or district court or other officer in whose office the chattel mortgage is registered.

27. (1) Where the word 'mortgagor' occurs in this section, it shall be read and construed as if the words 'his heirs, executors, administrators or assigns, or person having the equity of redemption' were inserted immediately after the word 'mortgagor'.

(2) The sheriff to whom an execution against the lands and tenements of a mortgagor is directed may seize, sell and convey all the interest of the mortgagor in any mortgaged lands and tenements.

(3) The equity of redemption in freehold land is saleable under an execution against the lands and tenements of the owner of the equity of redemption in his lifetime, or in the hands of his executors or administrators after his death, subject to the mortgage, in the same manner as land and tenements may now be sold under an execution.

(4) Where more mortgages than one of the same lands have been made to the same mortgagee or to different mortgagees, subsections 2 and 3 apply, and the equity of redemption is saleable under an execution against the lands and tenements of the owner, subject to the mortgages, in the same manner as in the case of land subject to one mortgage only.

(5) The effect of the seizure or taking in execution, sale and conveyance of mortgaged lands and tenements is to vest in the purchaser, his heirs and assigns, all the interest of the mortgagor therein at the time the execution was placed in the hands of the sheriff, as well as at the time of the sale, and to vest in the purchaser, his heirs and assigns, the same rights as the mortgagor would have had if the sale had not taken place, and the purchaser, his heirs or assigns, may pay, remove or satisfy any mortgage, charge or lien that at the time of the sale existed upon the lands or tenements so sold in like manner as the mortgagor might have done, and thereupon the purchaser, his heirs and assigns, acquire the same estate, right and title as the mortgagor would

have acquired in case the payment, removal or satisfaction had been effected by the mortgagor.

(6) A mortgagee of land, or the executors, administrators or assigns of a mortgagee, being or not being the execution creditor, may be the purchaser at the sale and acquire the same estate, interest and rights thereby as any other purchaser, but in that event he or they shall give to the mortgagor a release of the mortgage debt, and if another person becomes the purchaser, and, if the mortgagee, his executors, administrators or assigns enforce payment of the mortgage debt by the mortgagor, the purchaser shall repay the debt and interest to the mortgagor, and, in default of payment thereof within one month after demand, the mortgagor may recover the debt and interest from the purchaser, and has a charge therefor upon the mortgaged land.

28. (1) Any estate, right, title or interest in land which, under section 10 of *The Conveyancing and Law of Property Act* [Section 10 of the Conveyancing and Law and Property Act is excerpted below at p 235], may be conveyed or assigned by any person, or over which he has any disposing power that he may, without the assent of any other person, exercise for his own benefit, is liable to seizure and sale under execution against such person in like manner and on like conditions as land is by law liable to seizure and sale under execution, and the sheriff selling it may convey and assign it to the purchaser in the same manner and with the same effect as the person might himself have done ...

(3) Property over which a deceased person had a general power of appointment exercisable for his own benefit without the assent of any other person where it is appointed by his will may be seized and sold under an execution against the personal representative of such deceased person after the property of the deceased has been exhausted.

29. (1) The interest of a person derived by deed, lease or licence in writing from the churchwardens or other authorities of any church in a pew or sitting, if the interest is assignable by the holder thereof, may be sold under execution at the suit of the churchwardens or other authorities for arrears of rent or other charges to which the pew or sitting is subject, or which the holder thereof may have agreed to pay or for which he may be liable, or at the suit of any creditor of such holder, and the churchwardens or other authorities may become purchasers at such sale on behalf of the church, and may relet or sell the right so acquired ...

30. The title and interest of a testator or intestate in land may be seized and sold under an execution upon a judgment recovered by a creditor of the testator or intestate against his executor or administrator in the same manner and under the same process as upon a judgment against the deceased if he were living ...

c / The Creditors' Relief Act, R.S.O. 1970, c 97

23. Where there is in a court a fund belonging to an execution debtor or to which he is entitled, it or a sufficient part thereof to meet the executions and certificates in the sheriff's hands may, on the application of the sheriff or any person interested, be paid over to the sheriff, and it shall be deemed to be money levied under execution within the meaning of this Act.

25. (1) If the sheriff does not find property of a debtor leviable under the executions and certificates in his hands sufficient to pay the same in full, but finds property or the proceeds thereof in the hands of the bailiff of a small claims court under an execution or attachment against the debtor, the sheriff shall demand and obtain them from the bailiff, who shall forthwith deliver them to the sheriff with a copy of every execution and attachment in his hands against the debtor and a memorandum showing the amount to be levied under the execution, including the bailiff's fees, and the date upon which each execution or attachment was received by him.

(2) If the bailiff fails to deliver any of such property or the proceeds thereof, he shall pay double the value of that which is retained, which may be recovered by the sheriff from him with costs of suit, and shall be accounted for by the sheriff as part of the estate of the debtor.

(3) The costs and disbursements of the bailiff are a first charge upon such property or the proceeds thereof and shall be paid by the sheriff to the bailiff upon demand after being taxed by the small claims court clerk.

(4) The sheriff shall distribute the proceeds among the creditors entitled to share in the distribution, and the small claims court execution creditors are entitled without further proof to stand in the same position as creditors whose executions are in the sheriff's hands.

d / Federal Court Act, R.S.C. 1970 (2d Suppl.) c 10

PROCESS

55. (1) The process of the Court shall run throughout Canada, including its territorial waters, and any other place to which legislation enacted by the Parliament of Canada has been made applicable.

(2) An order for payment of money whether for costs or otherwise may be enforced in the same manner as a judgment.

(3) No attachment as for contempt shall issue for the non-payment of money alone.

(4) A sheriff or marshal shall execute the process of the Court that is directed to him whether or not it requires him to act outside his geographical jurisdiction, and shall perform such other duties as may be expressly or impliedly assigned to him by the Rules ...

56. (1) In addition to any writs of execution or other process that are prescribed by the Rules for enforcement of its judgments or orders, the Court may issue process against the person or the property of any party, of the same tenor and effect as those that may be issued out of any of the superior courts of the province in which any judgment or order is to be executed; and where, by the law of that province, an order of a judge is required for the issue of any process, a judge of the Court may make a similar order, as regards like process to issue out of the Court.

(2) No person shall be taken into custody under process of execution for debt issued out of the Court.

(3) All writs of execution or other process against property, as well as those prescribed by the Rules as those hereinbefore authorized, shall, unless otherwise provided by the Rules, be executed, as regards the property liable to execution and the mode of seizure and sale, as nearly as possible in the same manner as the manner in which similar writs or process, issued out of the superior courts of the province in which the property to be seized is situated, are, by the law of that province, required to be executed; and such writs or process shall bind property in the same manner as such similar writs or process, and the rights of purchasers thereunder are the same as those of purchasers under such similar writs or process.

(4) Every claim made by any person to property seized under a writ of execution or other process issued out of the Court, or to the proceeds of the sale of such property, shall, unless otherwise provided by the Rules, be heard and disposed of as nearly as may be according to the procedure applicable to like claims to property seized under similar writs or process issued out of the courts of the province.

(5) No execution shall issue on a judgment given by the Court against the Crown.

e / Supreme Court of Ontario Rules of Practice

ENFORCEMENT OF JUDGMENTS AND ORDERS GENERALLY

Rule 540

A judgment for the recovery by or payment to a person of money may be enforced by the issue of a writ of execution against the goods and chattels, lands and tenements of the debtor, but, if the amount due on the judgment is less than $200, no execution shall issue against lands and tenements.

Rule 544

Where a party is by a judgment entitled to any relief subject to or upon the fulfilment of a condition or contingency, he may, upon the fulfilment of the condition or contingency, apply for leave to issue execution.

Rule 545

As between the original parties to a judgment, a writ of execution other than a writ of possession may, without leave, issue at any time within six years from the date of the judgment.

Rule 546

Where the six years have elapsed or where a party is entitled to execution upon a judgment of assets in future or where any change has taken place by death or otherwise in the parties entitled or liable to execution, the party alleging himself to be entitled to execution may apply to the court for leave to issue execution.

Rule 547

Every writ of execution shall be endorsed with the name and address of the solicitor issuing it, and, if he issues it as agent for another solicitor, the name and address of such other solicitor shall also be endorsed, and where the writ is issued by a suitor in person, his name and address shall be endorsed.

Rule 548

Every writ of execution for the recovery of money shall be endorsed with a direction to the officer to whom it is directed to levy the money really due and payable and sought to be recovered under the judgment, stating the amount, and also to levy interest thereon at the rate of 5 per cent per annum from the time of the rendering of the verdict or of the giving of the judgment, as the case may be.

Rule 549

The officer issuing the writ or renewal thereof shall endorse upon it a memorandum signed by him of the amount which the party issuing it is entitled to receive for its costs, and any renewal and for any further or other writs or renewals, and no sum not so endorsed is to be collected for such costs.

Rule 550

Upon every execution there may be levied, in addition to the sum recovered by the judgment and interest thereon, the fees and expenses of execution.

Rule 551

(1) Under an execution against one partner, partnership assets shall not be taken in execution, but an order may be made charging the partner's interest in the partnership property and profits with the payment of the amount of the executions in the sheriff's hands, and by the same or a subsequent order a receiver may be appointed of the partner's share of profits whether already declared or accruing and of any other money that may be coming to him in respect of the partnership, and the court may direct all accounts and inquiries and give all such other directions as might be directed or given as if the charge had been given by the partner.

(2) The other partners may redeem the interest charged, or, in the event of a sale, may purchase the same.

Rule 552

The sheriff to whom a writ is directed shall keep a record of all returns thereto and renewals thereof and shall give a certificate thereof when demanded, which certificate shall be deemed a return and shall be in Form 129.

Rule 553

(1) The sheriff, when required to return a writ to the court, shall file the writ or his certificate under rule 552 in the office from which the order to return the writ was issued.

(2) When a writ has been executed or has expired the sheriff shall endorse a memorandum thereof on the writ and return it to the office from which it was issued.

(3) The officer to whom a writ is returned shall endorse thereon the day and hour when it was filed in his office.

(4) Where a writ has been withdrawn, the sheriff shall record the day and hour of such withdrawal and endorse a memorandum thereof on the writ and return it to the party who filed it or to his solicitor.

Rule 554

Where the party who delivered a writ or process to a sheriff to be executed, or any other person entitled to call for a return requires by a demand in writing the sheriff to return the writ, either by returning the writ to the court from which the writ issued or by granting a certificate under rule 552, the sheriff shall, within eight days, return the writ according to the terms of the requisition, and if he fails to do so the party serving the demand may apply to a judge for an order directing the sheriff to comply with such demand.

Rule 555

Where the sheriff is ordered to return a writ and does not make the return within the time specified in the order, the court may order the sheriff to be attached and to pay all costs consequent on his default.

WRITS OF FIERI FACIAS

Rule 556

Every judgment creditor is entitled immediately to issue one or more writs of fieri facias, but, if the judgment is for payment within a period therein mentioned, the writ shall not be issued until after the expiration of such period (Forms 115, 116 and 117).

Rule 557

Where goods or chattels are seized in execution under a writ of fieri facias, the sheriff or his officers acting for him shall, on request, deliver to the owner, his agent or servant, an inventory thereof before they are removed from the premises on which they have been so seized, and no sheriff or other officer shall sell any goods or chattels under a writ of execution until he has previously thereto forwarded a notice of the time and place of the sale to the execution creditor or his solicitor and to the said owner, his agent or servant, by registered mail to the last known address, at least eight days prior to the date of the sale, and by publishing such notice in a newspaper having a general circulation in the county or district where the goods or chattels have been seized.

Rule 558

Where goods are seized by a sheriff under a writ of fieri facias and they remain unsold in his hands for want of buyers, he shall state in his return of 'goods on hand for want of buyers', the time when and the place where such goods were offered for sale by him and the names of at least three persons who were present at the time of such attempted sale, if so many were present, but, if so many were not present, then the names of those who were present, if any, and that there were no others, and, if no person was present, then he shall state that fact.

Rule 559

Where a sheriff makes a return to a writ of fieri facias that he has goods and chattels or lands and tenements on hand for want of buyers, the execution creditor may give written instructions to the sheriff to expose for sale or sell, or cause to be sold, the said goods or lands for the best price that can be obtained for the same and the said writ of fieri facias shall continue in full force and effect as to any residue owing thereunder after such sale.

Rule 560

If the amount authorized to be made and levied under a writ of fieri facias is made and levied thereunder out of goods and chattels, the person issuing the writ is not entitled to the expenses of any seizure or advertisement of lands thereunder, and the return to be made by the sheriff to the writ for sale of lands shall be to the effect that the amount has been so made and levied as aforesaid.

Rule 561

The sheriff shall not expose lands for sale under a writ of fieri facias or sell the lands within less than twelve months from the day on which the writ is filed with him or, after a withdrawal of the writ, within less than twelve months from the day on which the writ is refiled with him.

Rule 562

Where a writ of fieri facias is issued against an absconding debtor in an action in which an order for attachment has been issued, the court may order the sheriff to sell lands of the absconding debtor before the expiration of the twelve months.

Rule 563

A sale of lands shall not be had under any writ of fieri facias until after a return of nulla bona, in whole or in part, in the same action or matter by the sheriff of the same county, or in the case of a small claims court writ of execution, a return of nulla bona by the bailiff of the small claims court from which it was issued.

Rule 564
(1) Before the sale of lands under a writ of fieri facias, the sheriff shall,

(a) forward a notice to the execution creditor or his solicitor and to the execution debtor by registered mail to his last known address at least one month preceding the sale;

(b) publish once in The Ontario Gazette at least one month preceding the sale and in a newspaper having a general circulation in the county or district in which the lands are situate, an advertisement of sale, at least upon one day in each week for two successive weeks, the last of such advertisements to be published not less than one week nor more than three weeks preceding the date of the sale; and

(c) for at least one month preceding the sale put up and continue a notice of such sale in a conspicuous place in his office.

(2) Such notice and advertisement shall specify,

(a) the property to be sold;

(b) the name of the plaintiff and defendant;

(c) the time and place of the intended sale; and

(d) the name of the debtor whose interest is to be sold.

(3) Nothing herein contained shall be taken to prevent an adjournment of the sale to a future day.

Rule 565
The advertisement in The Ontario Gazette of any lands for sale under a writ of fieri facias, during the currency of the writ shall be deemed a sufficient commencement of the execution to enable the writ to be completed by a sale and conveyance of the lands after the writ has become returnable.

Rule 566
(1) A writ of fieri facias remains in force for six years from its issue, unless renewed before its expiration, when it is in force for a further period of six years from the date of such renewal, and so on from time to time, and where the writ is filed with a sheriff, he shall send notice of such expiration by ordinary mail not less than one month nor more than two months prior to such expiration to the person who filed the writ at the last address of such person endorsed thereon.

(2) A writ which is filed with a sheriff may be renewed by filing with him before the writ expires a praecipe (Form 118), and the sheriff shall endorse and sign upon the writ with a memorandum stating the day, month and year of such renewal, and a writ so endorsed shall be entitled to priority according to the time of the last filing thereof.

(3) A writ which is not filed with a sheriff may be renewed by filing the praecipe before the writ expires with the officer who issued the writ, and the officer shall make the same endorsement accordingly.

WRITS OF POSSESSION

Rule 567
(1) A judgment for the recovery or for the delivery of the possession of land may be enforced by writ of possession (Form 122).

(2) Unless otherwise provided by the judgment, a writ of possession shall not be issued except by leave of the court obtained on an ex parte application and such leave shall not be given unless it is shown by affidavit that all persons in actual possession of the whole or any part of the lands and tenements have received sufficient notice of the proceedings in which such judgment was obtained to have enabled them to apply to the court for relief or otherwise.

(3) A second or subsequent writ for recovery of the same property pursuant to the judgment shall not be issued until the prior writ has been returned showing that possession has not been obtained of the whole property recoverable under the judgment.

Rule 568
A writ of possession remains in force for one year from the date of the judgment or order authorizing its issue, and where the writ is filed with a sheriff, no notice of its expiration need be given by him.

WRITS OF DELIVERY

Rule 580
(1) Where a judgment directs the recovery of specific goods, chattels, deeds, securities, documents or any property other than land or money, a writ of delivery may issue directing the sheriff to cause such goods or property to be delivered up in accordance with the judgment (Form 123).

(2) If the goods and property are not delivered up by the judgment debtor and cannot be found and taken by the sheriff, the judgment creditor may apply for an order directing the sheriff to take goods and chattels of the judgment debtor to double the value of the property in question to be kept until the further order of the court to enforce obedience to the judgment.

(3) By leave of the court, such judgment may also be enforced by attachment, committal or sequestration.

WRITS OF ASSIGNMENT OF DOWER

Rule 581
A judgment for the recovery of dower may be enforced by a writ of assignment of dower, directed to the sheriff of the county in which the lands lie, and the writ shall set forth the lands out of which the plaintiff is to recover dower (Forms 127 and 128).

f / The Small Claims Courts Act, R.S.O. 1970, c 439.

102. (1) The judge may order the times and the proportions in which a sum and costs recovered by judgment shall be paid, having regard to section 117.

(2) Unless otherwise ordered, execution shall not issue within fifteen days after the entry of judgment, but the judge may order the amount of the judgment or any instalment thereof to be paid into court.

JUDGMENTS; EXECUTIONS; TRANSCRIPTS

116. (1) Where the judge gives judgment or makes an order for the payment of money and default is made in payment of the whole or of any part thereof, the party in whose favour the order has been made is entitled to execution against the goods and chattels and, subject to section 126, the land of the party in default.

(2) The clerk, at the request of the party prosecuting the judgment or order, shall issue an execution to a bailiff of the court, or to a bailiff of any other court in the county, who by virtue thereof shall levy by distress and sale of the goods and chattels of the party in default such sum and costs, with interest thereon from the date of the order or of the entry of the judgment, as have been ordered to be paid and remain due, and shall pay such sum, costs and interest over to the clerk.

(3) The bailiff of a small claims court has jurisdiction throughout the county to enforce execution and levy by distress and sale of the goods and chattels of the debtor the amount of any judgment and costs and to carry out all other process and proceedings to enforce payment of the judgment, and, where the limits of a small claims court include parts of two counties, such jurisdiction applies throughout both of such counties, but, where a bailiff goes outside the limits of the division for which he is appointed under this subsection, he is not entitled to any mileage allowance in respect of travel outside such division ...

117. Except where a new trial is granted, the issue of execution shall not be postponed for more than fifty days from the service of the summons, without the consent of the party entitled thereto, but, if it is proved to the satisfaction of the judge that a party is unable from sickness or other cause to pay the debt or damages recovered against him, or any instalment thereof ordered to be paid, or that for any other reason the issue of execution should be further postponed, the judge may stay the judgment, order or execution for such time and on such terms as he thinks fit, and so from time to time until it is proved that the cause of disability has ceased.

118. If there are cross judgments between the parties, the party who has obtained judgment for the larger sum shall have execution for the excess and satisfaction for the remainder, and also satisfaction on the judgment for the smaller sum shall be entered, and, if both sums are equal, satisfaction shall be entered upon both judgments.

119. Except in actions brought under section 65, an execution or attachment shall not be executed out of the limits of the county over which the judge of the court from which the execution or attachment issues has jurisdiction.

120. Where the party against whom an execution has been issued pays or tenders to the clerk or to the bailiff, before an actual sale of his goods and chattels, the amount to be levied or so much thereof as the party in whose favour the execution has issued agrees to accept in full of his debt, together with the fees to be levied, the execution shall thereupon be superseded, and the bailiff shall withdraw from possession.

121. (1) The clerk, immediately after a return of *nulla bona* has been made to an execution issued on a transcript of judgment, shall forward by registered mail to the plaintiff and to the clerk who issued the transcript a notice informing them of the date at which the execution issued, the date at which it was returned by the bailiff, and the return made.

(2) The clerk shall file among the papers in the action the post-office certificate of registration, and the absence from among the papers of the certificate is *prima facie* evidence against the clerk that the notice was not forwarded.

122. Where a memorandum of the amount of a judgment or execution or a certificate of a claim within the jurisdiction of a small claims court is filed with a sheriff under *The Creditors' Relief Act*, and the amount is not paid in full, and the sheriff is unable to make the money thereon, the creditor may obtain from the sheriff a return according to the fact and file it with the clerk of the court in which the judgment was recovered, or, in the case of a certificate of a claim, with the clerk of the court of the division where the cause of action arose or where the debtor or one of the debtors, if more than one, resides, and the clerk shall enter the return in his procedure book, and in the latter case the claim thereupon becomes a judgment of the court for the unpaid balance due thereon appearing by the return and may be enforced in the same manner as a judgment of the court ...

124. (1) Every execution against goods shall bear the date of its issue and is returnable immediately after the execution thereof, and, if unexecuted, remains in force for three months, unless renewed, but may be renewed from time to time in the prescribed manner by the clerk at the instance of the execution creditor for six months from the date of the renewal.

(2) The execution so renewed has effect and is entitled to priority according to the time of the original delivery thereof to the bailiff.

125. Where the judge is satisfied by the oath of the execution creditor or by other testimony that he will be in danger of losing the amount of the judgment if compelled to wait until the day appointed for the payment thereof before an execution can issue, the judge may order an execution to issue at such time as he considers just.

126. (1) Where the sum remaining unsatisfied on a judgment amounts to $40 or more, the judgment creditor is entitled to an execution against the land of the judgment debtor, and the clerk, at the request of the party prosecuting the judgment, shall issue an execution against the land of the judgment debtor directed to the sheriff of a county.

(2) The execution has the same force and effect as an execution issued from a county court.

(3) Where an execution against lands has been placed in the hands of the sheriff, he shall give notice thereof to the judgment debtor by registered mail addressed to him at his present or last known residence.

(4) The sheriff shall make a return thereof and pay any money made thereon to the clerk of the court out of which the execution issued.

(5) Until the judgment is fully satisfied, the execution creditor may pursue the same remedy for the recovery thereof as if the judgment had been obtained in the county court.

(6) The writ, if unexecuted, remains in force for three years only from its issue, unless renewed, but may be renewed from time to time in the prescribed manner by the clerk at the instance of the execution creditor for three years from the date of the renewal.

(7) The execution may be renewed by being marked on the margin with a memorandum signed by the clerk stating the day, month and year of the renewal, and a writ so renewed has effect and is entitled to priority according to the time of the original delivery thereof to the sheriff.

(8) The production of an execution purporting to be marked with the memorandum is *prima facie* evidence of its having been renewed.

(9) The sheriff is entitled to the same fees as upon a writ of execution against land issued from a county court.

(10) Where land is on hand for want of buyers, a sheriff to whom the execution is directed may endorse thereon a return of 'land on hand for want of buyers' and shall return a certificate of the endorsement to the clerk of the small claims court from whose office the execution issued in lieu of the writ, and the endorsement and the certificate so returned shall be deemed to be a return of the writ, and thereupon a writ of *venditioni exponas* may be issued by the clerk for the sale of the land, and the original execution remains in force for the residue.

127. The bailiff, after making a seizure under an execution against goods, shall endorse thereon the date of the seizure, and shall immediately and at least eight days before the time appointed for the sale put up at three of the most public places in the division where any property liable to be sold under the execution has been taken, public notice, signed by himself, of the time and place in the division when and where it will be exposed for sale, and the notice shall describe the property taken.

128. The property so taken shall not be sold until the expiration of eight days at least after the seizure thereof, except upon the request in writing under the hand of the party whose property has been seized.

129. Where a bailiff has seized property under an execution or attachment and the action is afterwards settled between the parties, or the defendant makes an assignment for the general benefit of his creditors, the bailiff, until his fees and disbursements are fully satisfied, has a lien therefor upon so much of the property as will reasonably satisfy such fees and disbursements, but, in the event of a dispute as to the proper amount of the fees and disbursements, the amount claimed therefor may be paid into court until the proper amount is certified by the judge, and on such payment into court the lien ceases.

130. (1) The clerk, upon the application of a person having an unsatisfied judgment in his favour, shall prepare a transcript of the judgment in the prescribed form, and shall send it to the clerk of any other small claims court, whether in the same or in any other county, with the certificate at the foot thereof signed by him, sealed with the seal of the court, and addressed to the clerk of the court to whom it is to be sent, stating the amount unpaid upon the judgment, the date at which it was recovered, and the post-office address of the person applying for the transcript, and the clerk to whom the certificate is addressed shall, on the receipt of the transcript and the certificate, enter the transcript and the amount due on the judgment according to the certificate in a book to be kept in his office for the purpose, and all proceedings may be taken for enforcing the judgment in such last-mentioned court.

(2) After a transcript has been issued under this section, no further proceedings shall be had in the court from which the transcript issued without an order from the judge, unless the person who obtained the transcript, or his agent, makes and files with the clerk an affidavit stating,

(*a*) that the judgment remains unsatisfied in whole or in part;

(*b*) that the execution issued out of the court to which the transcript was sent has been returned *nulla bona*, or that he believes the judgment debtor has not sufficient goods in the division of that court to satisfy the judgment,

and, upon the affidavit being filed, the clerk may issue such other process as the applicant is entitled to and may direct.

2 FIERI FACIAS

a / The Binding Effect

i La Forest, 'Some Aspects of the Writ of Fieri Facias,' (1959), 12 *U.N.B.L.J.* 39, at pp 39–40

The writ of *fieri facias* (or *fi. fa.*) is the maid of all work in the law of execution. So much is this so that in ordinary parlance when we speak of issuing execution we mean the *fieri facias*. It commands the sheriff to cause to be made (fieri facias) out of the lands and chattels of a judgment debtor an amount sufficient to pay the judgment creditor with costs. The writ has been the most usual mode of execution for a long time; it is of great antiquity, dating to the earliest days of the common law. This explains many things about the writ. It explains, first of all, its extreme technicality, and, as we shall see, it assists in determining what property of the debtor may be seized under the writ ...

At common law, the writ had effect from its *teste*. As soon as it was issued it bound the goods of the execution debtor into whosoever hands they came. So that if an execution debtor sold his goods after the issue of the writ, the execution creditor had a right to seize them even as against a *bona-fide* purchaser for value without notice. The English Statute of Frauds made an important alteration to this law. It provided, in effect, that the writ should not bind the goods of an execution debtor until it was delivered to the sheriff to be executed.

It should be observed that the provision in the Statute of Frauds merely postpones the time when the writ binds the goods of the execution debtor; it does not otherwise alter the law. So that if a judgment debtor sells goods to an innocent purchaser after the writ has been placed in the hands of the sheriff for execution, the sheriff may seize the goods in the hands of the innocent purchaser.

This blemish on the law was removed in England by section 1 of the Mercantile Law Amendment Act, 1856, which provided that no writ of *fieri facias* should prejudice the right of any person to goods acquired from an execution debtor in good faith, for valuable consideration and without notice. This section and the provision of the Statute of Frauds just mentioned, were re-enacted by section 26 of the English Sale of Goods Act.

NOTE See now sections 10 and 11 of The Execution Act

ii The Land Titles Act, R.S.O. 1970, c 234, s 51(6) and s 153

NOTE Special treatment is given to land governed by The Land Titles Act because the land titles register is intended to reflect the exact state of the title to a given parcel of land.

51. (6) The title of the registered owner for the time being of land or of a charge is subject to enforceable writs of execution against him that have been recorded under section 153, but no writ of execution against a prior registered owner is enforceable in respect of the land or charge unless a note of such writ has been entered in the title register.

153. (1) The sheriff or other officer to whom an execution or other writ, or renewal thereof, affecting registered land is directed, forthwith after its delivery to him, upon written request of the party by whom it was sued, out or renewed, or of his solicitor, but not otherwise, shall deliver or transmit by registered mail to the proper master of titles a copy of the writ or renewal certified under his hand, and no registered land is bound by any such writ until such copy has been received by the proper master of titles and, after the receipt by him of the copy, no transfer or charge by the execution debtor is effectual, except subject to the rights of the execution creditor under the writ.

(2) The proper master of titles shall keep an index or a book in the prescribed form in which shall be entered a record of all writs and renewals, copies of which are received by him from the sheriff or other officer.

(3) No sale or transfer under any such writ is valid as against a person purchasing for valuable consideration before such entry is made, notwithstanding that the purchaser may have had notice of the writ.

(4) Upon production to the proper master of titles of sufficient evidence of the satisfaction of such a writ, he shall cause an entry to be made in the index or book to that effect, and, on such entry, the writ shall be deemed to be satisfied.

(5) Every writ and renewal of a writ shall be presumed to have been spent and the delivery or transmission of a copy thereof ceases to have effect at the expiration of the writ or renewal as appearing on the copy transmitted, but, if there has been a sufficient commencement of the execution to enable it to be completed by the sale and conveyance of the land under the writ and the writ has not been completely executed, the sheriff or officer shall, or the execution creditor may, at any time within one month before the expiration of the writ or renewal as so appearing, file with the proper master of titles a certificate of the sheriff or officer stating that fact, and such certificate shall be noted at the entry of the writ in the index or book, and the writ continues in force for a further period of one year from the filing of the certificate when it ceases to have effect unless another similar certificate is filed that operates in like manner.

(6) Where an execution or other writ is issued against the registered owner under a different name from that under which he is registered, the writ has no effect under this Act unless the person who sues out the writ, or his solicitor, gives a notice to the proper master of titles stating the name under which the execution debtor is registered and otherwise in the form or to the effect prescribed or unless a like notice is written upon the copy of the writ.

(7) Where land is being transferred or charged and where a notice under subsection 6 has not been given, a writ of execution or renewal thereof does not bind the land being transferred or charged as against the transferee or chargee if the proper master of titles decides that the name of the execution debtor appearing in the writ or renewal thereof and the name of the registered owner as it appears in the records of the land titles office do not represent the same person, and he issues a certificate accordingly.

(8) Where a copy of a writ of execution or a renewal thereof is delivered or transmitted to the proper master of titles under subsection 1, the sheriff shall be paid by the person upon whose request the copy is delivered or transmitted a fee of $3 in addition to any other fee payable to the sheriff on the filing of the writ.

(9) No additional fee is payable to the sheriff or to the proper master of titles in respect of a certificate under section 12 of *The Execution Act.*

iii Notice: If a purchaser buys from a debtor who has suffered a writ of *fi. fa.* to be issued and lodged with the Sheriff, what kind of notice will prevent the purchaser's taking title free of the execution creditor's rights? Actual notice? Constructive notice?

In *Young* v *Dencher*, [1923] 1 D.L.R. 439, the Alberta Court of Appeal discussed what kind of notice is required to defeat the title of a bona fide purchaser:

We have discussed the meaning of the provision as to the binding effect of an execution and I am of opinion that the meaning is that the title acquired by a person in good faith and for valuable consideration is good as against the execution unless such person has, at the time he acquired title, notice not only that the execution had been delivered to the sheriff but also that the execution remained unexecuted, that is, not executed, in the sense, I think, that the money had not been made or paid. That, I think is the grammatical sense of the rule. There seem to be no decisions upon the point; but the tendency of legislation, e.g. the Creditors' Relief Act 1910, 2nd sess. (Alta), ch. 4, the Winding-up Act R.S.C. 1906, ch. 144, the Bankruptcy Act 1919 (Can.), ch. 36, is to minimise the effect of an execution, and the purpose of the provision now under consideration is evidently to prevent an execution from interfering with honest commercial transactions made without notice of the execution and to prevent the hampering of such transactions by necessitating the delay which would result if they could not be concluded, except after searching in some public office, the proper particular office being often difficult to ascertain, and of making enquiries of execution creditors or their solicitors as to the condition of an execution of which some kind of notice may have existed. Though a person dealing with the debtor may at one time have known that there was an execution against him in the sheriff's hands if he should either forget it or suppose, by reason of lapse of time or other circumstances, that it has been satisfied or withdrawn, it is not unreasonable that the person so dealing with the debtor should not be prejudiced merely by the fact that at one time he knew of the existence of an execution but that his knowledge should go to the extent the execution was still unsatisfied.

(per Beck, JA at pp 439–40)

b / Issue and Renewal

i Supreme Court of Ontario Rules of Practice, R.R.O. 1970, Reg. 545.
Refer to Rules 545, 546, 566, above at pp 216, 219. Note also Rule 178 which provides that the

... court may from time to time enlarge or abridge the time prescribed by the rules, or by an order, for doing any act or taking any proceeding, and this power may be exercised although the application is not made until after the expiration of the time prescribed.

ii The Limitations Act, R.S.O. 1970, c 246

23. (1) No action shall be brought to recover out of any land or rent any sum of money secured by any mortgage or lien, or otherwise charged upon or payable out of the land or rent, or to recover any legacy, whether it is or is not charged upon land, but within ten years next after a present right to receive it accrued to some person capable of giving a discharge for, or release of it, unless in the meantime some part of the principal money or some interest thereon has been paid, or some acknowledgment in writing of the right thereto signed by the person by whom it is payable, or his agent, has been given to the person entitled thereto or his agent, and in such case no action shall be brought but within ten years after the payment or acknowledgment, or the last of the payments or acknowledgments if more than one, was made or given.

(2) Notwithstanding subsection 1, a lien or charge created by the placing of an execution or other process against land in the hands of the sheriff or other officer to whom it is directed, remains in force so long as the execution or other process remains in the hands of the sheriff or officer for execution and is kept alive by renewal or otherwise.

45. (1) The following actions shall be commenced within and not after the times respectively hereinafter mentioned: ...

(c) an action upon a judgment or recognizance, within twenty years after the cause of action arose:

iii NOTE Under the Rules, generally, a writ of *fi. fa.* must be issued within six years after the date of judgment, and must be renewed within its six year life if it is to continue to 'bind' the estate of the debtor. The problems that arise when a writ is not issued in time or has expired before renewal have been considered many times. It is clear that an alias writ *may* be issued in such circumstances. The procedure to be followed appears to depend on the nature of the defect. If a writ has been issued but not renewed in time, some cases have held that the registrar may extend the time for renewal and issue an alias writ (*Holtite Rubber Co.* v *Sussman*, [1960] O.W.N. 252; *Re Solicitor*, [1959] O.W.N. 8). Others have held that unless the failure to renew in time is the fault of a court officer, an application for leave to extend the time or to issue an alias writ must be brought before a judge in chambers (*Peterboro District Co-op Services* v *Raison*, [1960] O.W.N. 495; see also Rule 209(15)). If a writ has not been issued within six years after judgment, leave to issue an alias writ must be sought pursuant to Rule 546.

There is an apparent contradiction between the requirement that a creditor must have leave to issue execution more than six years after the date of judgment (R. 346) and the right of the creditor to enforce his judgment by action (which includes execution proceedings) for twenty years after the date of judgment. It has been held that the Act predominates so that leave should not be refused on the grounds of hardship to the defendant, if sought within twenty years of judgment. To do otherwise would, in effect, shorten the limitation period provided by statute through interpretation of the (subordinate) rules (*Shmegilsky* v *Slobodzian*, [1964] I O.R. 633).

What happens twenty years after the date of judgment? Older cases held that so long as the writ is regularly renewed within and after the twenty year period, it retains full force and effect. (*Poucher* v *Wilkins* (1915), 33 O.L.R. 125). This rule is now enshrined in s 23(2) of The Limitations Act. However, if the writ is not regularly issued and continually renewed within and beyond the twenty year period, the writ will cease to have any effect after twenty years, and the court loses its jurisdiction to order the issue of execution after twenty years. (*Doel* v *Kerr* (1915), 34 O.L.R. 251.)

The possibility of continuing renewals of a writ of execution may create a dilemma for a solicitor searching the title to land. Consider the following hypothetical chain of title and statutory provisions:

1900　A conveys to B;
1901　X obtains judgment and issues execution against B;
　　　X and his heirs have continually renewed the execution against B to date;
1908　B conveys to C;
1960　C conveys to D;
1975　D proposes to convey to E.

The Registry Act, R.S.O. 1970, c 409

110. In this Part,
(*a*) 'claim' means a right, title, interest, claim or demand of any kind or nature whatsoever affecting land set forth in, based upon or arising out of a registered instrument, and, without limiting the generality of the foregoing, includes mortgages, liens, easements, agreements, contracts, options, charges, annuities, leases, dower rights whether inchoate or otherwise, and restrictions as to the use of land or other encumbrances affecting land ...
111. A person dealing with land shall not be required to show that he is lawfully entitled to the land as owner thereof through a good and sufficient chain of title during a period greater than the forty years immediately preceding the date of such dealing, except in respect of claims referred to in subsection 2 of section 112.

[Subsection 112(3) exempts from s 112(1) certain Crown claims, dower claims, claims imposed by statutory enactments and claims to a freehold interest or equity of redemption shown by the abstract index for the land prior to and continuously during the forty year period.]

It is commonly claimed that The Registry Act provisions relieve solicitors from the obligation of searching for executions filed more than forty years from the date of search. In the hypothetical example above, does the execution obtained by x still affect D's title? Consider, when answering this question, the very briefly reported case of *Re Riggs*, [1938] 3 D.L.R. 745 (Ont. H.C.J.). There, on a motion for directions to settle priorities, the first execution creditor claimed priority over all others when the filing of his execution was followed by a mortgage from the debtor to his wife, after which the other executions were filed. Urquhart J said that 'the Execution Act ... does not mean that by the lodging of an execution, any estate or charge upon the lands is effected,' and held that the first creditor had no prior charge or claim (except as to costs). You might also take account of the general practice of real estate conveyancers, which is *not* to register writs of execution against the title to land in land registry offices when the land is governed by The Registry Act [copies of the writ are customarily filed in Land Registry Offices when the land is subject to The Land Titles Act]. This practice is universal despite the following provisions of The Registry Act:

1. (c) 'instrument' includes every instrument whereby land in Ontario may be transferred, disposed of, charged, encumbered or affected in any other way, and, without limiting the generality of the foregoing, includes any ... certificate of proceedings in any court, judgment or order of foreclosure and every other certificate of judgment or order of any court affecting any interest in or title to land ... every order and proceeding in bankruptcy and insolvency ... and every notice, caution and other instrument registered in compliance with an Act of Canada or Ontario ...

69. (1) After the grant from the Crown of land, and letters patent issued therefor, every instrument affecting the land or any part thereof shall be adjudged fraudulent and void against any subsequent purchaser or mortgagee for valuable consideration without actual notice, unless the instrument is registered before the registration of the instrument under which the subsequent purchaser or mortgagee claims.

See also: *McDonald* v *The Royal Bank of Canada*, [1933] O.R. 418 (C.A.) (reproduced at p 237 below).

c / Exigible Property

i Generally
  1 C.R.B. Dunlop, 'Execution Against Personal Property in England and British Columbia' (1972), 7 *U.B.C. L. Rev.* 171.

The history of the English and Canadian law of creditors' remedies over the past 150 years can be seen as the relationship between two counterbalancing movements, the restriction of remedies against the person and the expansion of remedies against property. Since the English

Judgments Act of 1838, the power of the creditor to imprison his debtor has been steadily cut down, while the kinds of property of the debtor available to execution have been increased.

The policy underlying this historical development is sound. Apart from imprisonment for contempt of court for failing to attend examinations in aid of execution or failing to answer questions in such examinations, it seems wrong that judgment debtors should be visited with a criminal sanction for failing to pay their civil debts. On the other hand, if imprisonment for debt is to be abolished, the law of creditors' remedies must make exigible all of the assets of the judgment debtor, subject to a fair and liberal system of exemptions geared to the basic needs of the judgment debtor and his family.

THE ENGLISH COMMON LAW REGARDING EXIGIBILITY
The interplay between legal and equitable rules and remedies makes a study of English creditors' remedies fascinating and yet treacherous reading. The common law judges here as elsewhere delight in laying down clear and absolute rules, without apparent regard to the fairness or even the common sense of the result. But these common law doctrines must always be seen as part of a greater system in which the courts of equity operated to correct and soften the harshness of the common law. The law of creditors' remedies is an excellent illustration of the *dictum* of Cardozo c.J.: 'Equity follows the law, but not slavishly nor too much.'

The principal remedy available to judgment creditors at common law against the personal property of the judgment debtor was the writ of fieri facias (or fi. fa.), 'the maid of all work in the law of execution.' A textbook on practice, published in 1855, described the writ as follows:

The writ of fieri facias is a judicial writ, that lieth for him who hath recovered any debt or damages in the Queen's Courts. In substance, it is a command to the person to whom it is directed, that, of the goods and chattels of the party, he cause to be made the sum recovered by the judgment, together with interest upon such sum ... and that he have the money and interest and the write itself before the Queen (or before her justices if in the Common Pleas, or her barons if in the Exchequer) at Westminster, immediately after the execution of the writ, or on a day certain in term, to be rendered to the party who sued it out ...

Goods and chattels could also be seized pursuant to the writs of levari facias or the more modern elegit, writs which reached the rents and profits of the judgment debtor's land as well. But as the rules governing exigibility appear to have been the same for all three writs, we can confine ourselves to the writ of fi. fa.

Before 1838, it was clear law that the writ of fieri facias permitted the sheriff to seize tangible goods and chattels, leases, and growing crops. The great limitation on the writ was that it empowered the sheriff to seize only *tangible* goods and chattels, that is, choses in possession as contrasted with choses in action. ...

The writ of fi. fa. was held not to extend to money, bank notes, securities for money, debts owing to the debtor, future earnings of the debtor, either by salary or by payments to the debtor's business, or choses in action generally. Monies and assets in court, in the hands of the sheriff, or otherwise *in custodia legis* were likewise not exigible, except perhaps where the initial execution could be shown to be invalid or fraudulent.

In part, these limitations on the scope of fieri facias are rooted in the medieval origins of the writ and in questions of administrative convenience. The reasons for refusing to permit execution against choses in action, including debts owed to the judgment debtor, are more complex and can be explained in two ways. First, the common law courts seem to have seen the process of seizure as one appropriate only to tangible physical goods, which choses in action are not. Secondly, even if choses in action were capable of a notional seizure, the common law had long taken the view that they were personal relationships between the contracting parties and therefore not assignable or transferable, except in the limited cases of negotiable instruments and obligations entered into by the Crown. Thus the sheriff, and the sheriff's purchaser, could obtain no legal title to a chose in action, and 'nothing can be taken in execution that cannot be sold.' It is true that equity developed a different view of the chose in action as a kind of property and therefore assignable, and there are timid movements late in the common law towards the same objective. But it is the earlier common law view of the chose in action which became a fixed limitation on the scope of fieri facias.

Two principles dominate the common law decisions on execution before 1838. The first is that the sheriff cannot seize a better or greater title than the judgment debtor has. The second rule is that the writ of fi. fa. reaches only legal interests in goods; in general it will not reach equitable interests. The principles are stated repeatedly in the cases, but the actual decisions suggest a somewhat more complex picture.

The rule that the judgment creditor can take no better title than the judgment debtor has was easy to apply to cases where the creditor had seized goods owned by a third party. The courts had more difficulty in the case where the judgment debtor had some legal interest in the goods less than full title, or in the converse case in which the debtor had legal title subject to the interest of some third person. With some hesitation, the common law judges came to the conclusion that partial legal interests in goods were exigible. Thus judgment creditors were permitted to seize goods left with a pawnbroker or redeemable pledges, and goods leased or bailed to the judgment debtor. On the other hand, where the judgment debtor had a lien on goods for work which he had done on them, such a lien interest was held not to be exigible. Parke B said:

A lien is a personal right, which cannot be parted with, and continues only so long as the possessor holds the goods. It is clear, therefore, that the sheriff cannot sell an interest of this description, which is a mere personal interest in the goods. The case is quite different from those referred to, in which goods were let on hire for a certain period, because there the person hiring them has the absolute use of the goods for a particular term, and that interest may be disposed of. Here, the interest cannot be transferred to any other individual; it continues only as long as the holder keeps possession of the subject-matter of the lien, either by himself or his servant. Then, as the sheriff cannot sell, neither, by the general rule of law, can he seize ...

The courts would not permit seizure of goods in the possession of the judgment debtor where the continuance of his possession depended on the discretion of executors or other third persons.

A long and complicated series of cases beginning with *Dean* v *Whittaker et al.* worked out the principles to be applied when an owner of goods placed the goods in the hands of a third person subject to the owner's right of repossession on certain conditions. The problems which arose will be clear if we look at a typical case. In *Beeston* v *Marriott*, a contractor supplied materials to a railway company for the purpose of carrying out his contract. By the terms of the contract it was provided that the materials brought upon the railway should immediately become the absolute property of the company, except that they were to remain under the dominion of the contractor; that, if the contractor should duly complete his contract, the company would give to the contractor as part of his payment the unconsumed materials; and that if, instead of the contractor, the company should use the materials, the company should compensate the contractor in respect of them. Judgment creditors of the railway company executed against the goods, and the contractor obtained an injunction preventing the sheriff from selling his goods. After analyzing the contract, Stuart v.c. concluded that the goods were 'chattels upon the ground of the company dedicated to a particular purpose, in which purpose both the Plaintiff and the Defendants are interested as to the use of the chattels; and as to the surplus, they are ultimately to become the absolute property of the Plaintiff. Chattels in that situation cannot be taken in execution.'

The courts were willing to permit execution against partial interests in personal property, but only where those interests could be clearly delimited and where the judgment debtor either had possession or the immediate right to possession of the goods. This insistence on possession as the touchstone of exigibility in part flowed from the fact that many of the leading cases arose as trover actions brought against the judgment creditor or the sheriff. In part, however, it is evidence of the overriding tendency of the judges to restrict the writ of fieri facias to tangible goods and chattels. The common law judges were prepared to permit fi. fa. to reach partial interests in chattels but only where such interests could be assimilated to tangible goods, that is, where the judgment debtor had possession or the immediate right thereto. The judges were not prepared to expand fi. fa. to reach cases of intangible or non-possessory interests in personalty, or even cases like *Beeston* v *Marriott* where the present possession of the judgment debtor was liable to be defeated immediately by the contractor.

Before the Judicature Acts, it was generally accepted that a writ of fieri facias could not be used to reach equitable interests in goods. This result was consistent with the common law's resistance to execution against intangible interests, and it accorded with the theory that the common law knew nothing about equitable interests in property. As we will discuss later, the courts of equity agreed that such interests were their creation and should be recognized and controlled only by Chancery. But equity drew the further conclusion that it should lend its assistance to a judgment creditor by enabling him to reach equitable interests, even although the creditor had commenced his action and obtained his judgment at law. The theoretical refusal of common law to recognize equitable interests did not mean that such interests were completely exempt from execution, but only that a judgment creditor must seek the aid of equity to reach them.

Towards the end of the century, the clear theoretical distinction between legal and equitable interests in property was blurred in a series of cases which appeared to say that fieri facias could reach an equitable interest in property where the judgment debtor had ''the whole of the equitable and beneficial interest'' and the trustees had a bare legal title. If these cases advanced this rule as a statement of the common law before the Judicature Acts, they are wrong. However the cases can be explained as attempts by post-Judicature Act courts to decide interpleader actions by applying legal and equitable doctrines at once and without the intermediate procedural steps which would have been insisted on before the nineteenth century reforms.

Before 1838, execution at common law was an inadequate remedy which did not reach the intangible personalty of the judgment debtor. The Judgments Act of 1838 was the beginning of English legislative efforts to reform the law of creditors' remedies by restricting remedies against the person and expanding the scope of fieri facias and other types of execution against property. That legislation dealt with many aspects of creditor-debtor law but, for our purposes, it is enough to note that section 12 of the Act made exigible by fieri facias money, bank notes, cheques, bills of exchange, promissory notes, bonds, specialties, and other securities for money, and section 14 created a new remedy, the charging order, against government stock, funds, and annuities, and any stock or shares in public companies in England. Parliament was not the only agency of law reform seeking to overcome the limitations of common law execution; the English creditor, frustrated by the limitations of fieri facias, could also turn to Chancery for assistance.

NOTE For an analysis of the problems presented by attempts to execute against real property generally, see Dunlop, 'Execution Against Real Property in British Columbia', (1973), 8 *U.B.C. L. Rev.* 246.

2 Property Subject to Execution

The Execution Act is the main statute prescribing what property of a debtor may be seized and sold under execution to satisfy creditors. Generally speaking, all forms of property are covered and may be the subject of execution proceedings (subject to the exemptions discussed in Chapter 8, supra). Some additional rights akin to execution rights are given in The Creditors' Relief Act (ss 23, 25) and in The Public Service Act (s 26), supra.

The general legislation governing execution in other Provinces is as follows:

Alberta: The Seizures Act, R.S.A. 1970, c 338
British Columbia: Execution Act, R.S.B.C. 1960, c 135
Manitoba: The Executions Act, C.C.S.M., c E 160
New Brunswick: Memorials and Executions Act, R.S.N.B. 1973, c M-9
Newfoundland: The Judicature Act, R.S. Nfld. 1970, c 187
Prince Edward Island: Judgment and Execution Act, R.S.P.E.I. 1974, c J-2
Quebec: Code of Civil Procedure, S.Q. 1965, c 80, arts. 552–740
Saskatchewan: The Executions Act, R.S.S. 1965, c 97
Nova Scotia: Sale of Land Under Execution Act, R.S.N.S. 1967, c 275.

In Ontario the procedure for executing against specific property varies with the nature of the property (chattels, choses in action, real property). The details of the procedure are contained in The Execution Act and the Rules of Practice (and prescribed forms) supra. Most types of property do not present any difficulty to an executing creditor. If the debtor has an interest in them, that interest is attachable and may be sold. Some unusual interests do cause trouble. The question usually raised is whether the interest which the debtor has in the property is an interest made exigible under the relevant legislation. The materials which follow consider some of these 'problem interests.'

ii Real Estate Transactions

NOTE Real estate transactions in Ontario are usually carried out in two stages. First, an agreement of purchase and sale is entered into by the parties, and a deposit is paid by the purchaser. A fixed closing date is stipulated for completion: on the latter date, the deal is 'closed', the purchaser paying the balance of the purchase price or assuming mortgage obligations, and the vendor conveying title to the property to the purchaser. Land sales contracts are generally considered to be specifically enforceable unless a party has somehow disentitled himself from such relief. To the extent that the contract remains specifically enforceable before the date of closing. Equity 'regards what ought to be done as done', and sees the purchaser as the owner in Equity and the vendor, in a sense, as trustee of the legal estate for the purchaser. This phenomenon is known as the doctrine of equitable conversion.

What happens if an execution is delivered between the date of agreement and the date of closing? If the execution is against the purchaser, the purchaser's interest in the contract (to pay the balance and accept conveyance of the legal estate) may be a valuable asset, especially if the property can be sold for more than the purchaser has agreed to pay (a standard situation in times of soaring inflation and buyer demand in the real estate market). However, the interest of the purchaser has been held not to be exigible (*Kimniak* v *Anderson*, [1929] 2 D.L.R. 704 (Ont. C.A.), infra). The purchaser's interest is solely to have a court of equity decide whether or not to specifically enforce the contract: it is impossible to gauge the extent of the purchaser's interest except after the contract is completed. On the other hand, the interest of the vendor of land is subject to execution (*Robinson* v *Moffat* (1916), 37 O.L.R. 52 (Ont. C.A.), infra p 235).

Kimniak v *Anderson*, [1929] I D.L.R. 904 (Ont. C.A.).

HODGINS, J.A.: The defendant Scharlp has and had an execution against the lands of the plaintiff in the hands of the defendant Anderson, the sheriff of Essex, who thereunder advertised what he understood to be the plaintiff's lands for sale. The plaintiff brought this action to restrain the defendants from proceeding further with the sale.

The plaintiff's case is that his interest in the land is not salable under a writ of *fieri facias* against land.

[Chowats had agreed to purchase land from another party. Before completion, Chowats entered into an agreement of purchase and sale with the plaintiff.]

... Chowats' equitable interest as a purchaser, if transferred to the plaintiff by this agreement, gives the latter no estate in the lands save to the extent to which a Court of Equity would give Chowats specific performance of the agreement with Walker & Sons Ltd., and that interest would be taken by Kimniak as a trust estate as specified in the document.

If Chowats has no salable estate or interest, then the plaintiff has none; but, if Chowats' interest can be sold under a writ of *fieri facias*, so can that of the plaintiff, unless the existing trust imposed on it prevents this.

The trial Judge, in another case, that of *Re Reek & Koven* (1927), 33 O.W.N. 9, has expressed himself as in doubt as to the salability of the interest of a purchaser of land where his right still rests in contract, and refers to the conflict of views on the subject. In *Robinson* v *Moffatt* (1916), 31 D.L.R. 490, at p 492, 37 O.L.R. 52, the Second Divisional Court held that a vendor having the legal estate in the lands under a contract for sale, occupied the position described by Meredith, C.J.C.P.:

'The vendor is a trustee for the purchaser, but bound to convey to him only on fulfilment by the purchaser of all things agreed to be done, on his part, before getting the conveyance. An agreement may never be carried into effect, it may end in nothing by various ways, and it may be that Equity, however measured, may refuse specific performance, and so the vendor may remain owner, unaffected by the agreement, without the aid of any Court. But, whether he does or not, he is still owner and can convey his ownership, subject of course to any equitable right which the purchaser may have: he has none at law except a personal action against the vendor if he should refuse or be unable to carry out his contract.'

This leaves the equitable right of the purchaser undefined, but correctly states the relative positions of vendor and purchaser under a contract for the sale of land and follows the late cases in England on the subject.

[After considering *Central Trust & Safe Deposit Co.* v *Snider* (1915), 22 D.L.R. 75 (P.C.) and other cases, his Lordship continued:]

These modern views of the interest taken by a purchaser under a contract for the sale of land have, I think, completely destroyed the notion that what is acquired can be an equitable estate or interest which vests in a stranger to the contract on a sale under an execution against the purchaser. The difficulties and complications which would arise in working out the rights and interests of vendor, purchaser, and his successor, a stranger to the contract, imposed on the vendor by a sale *in invitum*, are such as to make the original conception of trustee and *cestui que trust* untenable.

In view of the fact that the interest of a purchaser under a contract for the purchase of real estate is expressly subject to what a Court of Equity thinks and decrees that it ought to be, the nature and extent of which cannot be predicated, and that it is also always liable before the Court is seized of it to be lost or to vanish in cases of default, I am of opinion that the interest of such a purchaser is not properly salable under a writ of *fieri facias*, but can only be reached, if it can be reached at all, by way of equitable execution where the Court can protect all parties and exercise or anticipate the rights which would flow from a contract if recognized in Equity as not merely one capable of specific performance but in fact entitled to be so enforced.

The estate which Chowats, if his interest is assignable, handed on to the plaintiff is an interest subject to the uncertainties I have mentioned, and, if assigned or sold under a *fieri facias*, would be in a sense merely the assignment or sale of a law suit or of a right to go to a Court of Equity and there accept whatever it might decree as just and equitable under the circumstances submitted to it when a decision was asked for. This is not the nature or quality of an estate, in my judgment, to which s 34 of the Execution Act, R.S.O. 1927, c 112, applies.

The plaintiff, standing as he must in the shoes of Chowats, has no salable interest vested in him by virtue of exhibit 2, and so the plaintiff is entitled to restrain the intended offering for sale, and the sale itself.

But, apart from that, and if the Chowats interest was such as could be assigned or sold under a *fi. fa.*, there is another ground on which the plaintiff would be entitled to succeed.

Section 8 of the Execution Act, has no application, as the plaintiff is the trustee; no lands are 'held in trust for the execution debtor.'

The plaintiff is a trustee for both Chowats and his wife. He, by ex. 2, has acquired the interest of Chowats in the land to hold in trust to perform certain duties and obligations. This imports a charge on the land until those obligations are discharged, as it is then and then only that his beneficial interest in the land will arise. The Chowats, husband and wife, are entitled to have it held by their obligor on a trust till it is completely performed, while a sale to a third party would deprive them of their security, the transfer of which formed the consideration for the trust and its obligations.

I can find no authority for the proposition that a trust estate can be sold under an execution against a trustee for his own debt, on the ground that if he fully performs the trust, he will at some future time acquire a beneficial interest in the estate. His interest at present is that of a trustee only, and as such it cannot be sold under the Execution Act to pay his liabilities ...

The plaintiff should have judgment setting aside the judgment below and restraining the sale, with costs against the defendant Scharlp, who should also pay the costs of the sheriff. See *Hutchings* v *Ruttan* (1857), 6 U.C.C.P. 452.

Appeal allowed.

QUESTIONS

1 Why would the purchaser's interest not be exigible under s 9 of The Execution Act, which enables the sheriff to seize and sell lands held in trust for the execution debtor?

2 Would the position be different if the purchaser had completed all payments and were in a position to call for an immediate conveyance?
3 Section 28 of The Execution Act renders exigible any interest in land which may be conveyed under s 10 of The Conveyancing and Law of Property Act, R.S.O. 1970, c 85. Section 10 provides that:

'[a] contingent, an executory, and a future interest, and a possibility coupled with an interest in land, ... also a right of entry, whether immediate or future, and whether vested or contingent, into or upon land, may be disposed of by deed, ...'

Why would s 28 have no application to the interest of a purchaser under an agreement of purchase and sale?
4 If a purchaser's interest were exigible, what rights would a third party buying from the Sheriff obtain?

NOTE Most authority seems to support the result reached in *Kimniak*. See:
Re Prittie and Crawford (1889), 9 C.L.T. 45; *Foss* v *Sterling Loan* (1915), 23 D.L.R. 540, affirming (1915), 21 D.L.R. 755, (Sask. C.A.); *C.P.R.* v *Silzer* (1910), 14 W.L.R. 274, 3 Sask. L.R. 162; *Weyerhaeuser* v *Scott*, [1924] 3 D.L.R. 605 (Sask. K.B.). On the other hand, one early Ontario case held the interest of a purchaser to be exigible: *Ward* v *Archer* (1894), 24 O.R. 650. Whether or not a purchaser's equitable interest is exigible pending closing, once the purchase is completed and the purchaser acquires legal title, prior executions against the purchaser take priority over the interest of an assignee of the purchaser: *Ruttle* v *Rowe* (1920), 50 D.L.R. 346 (Sask. C.A.).

The exigibility of the interest of a purchaser of land is still, perhaps uncertain. In *Re Hare and Bellmore Investments Ltd.* (1972), 22 D.L.R. (3d) 139, [1972] 1 O.R. 24 (Ont. H.C.), Haines, J noted the two conflicting lines of authority represented by *Ward* v *Archer* and *Kimniak* v *Anderson*. However, he found it unnecessary to decide between them: the purchaser had previously been declared to have no further rights in respect of a land purchase agreement. Since an execution creditor takes only what the debtor has, the execution in *Hare* would attach no interest in respect of the purchase contract. See also: *J.A.R. Leaseholds Ltd.* v *Tormet* (1965), 48 D.L.R. (2d) 97, [1965] 1 O.R. 347, in which the Ontario Court of Appeal held that *Kimniak* v *Anderson* 'decides no more than a writ of *fieri facias* binds legal estates and interests only and that a trust estate cannot be sold under an execution against a trustee for his own debt ...' (at p 358).

Robinson v *Moffatt* (1916), 31 D.L.R. 490 (Ont. C.A.)

MEREDITH, C.J.C.P.: This motion – which it is to be hoped may bring to an end this prolonged litigation over a simple contract for the sale and purchase of the land in question – is made for the purpose of having a determination of the question whether the vendor can now give to the purchaser that which he sold to him, namely, the land in question in fee simple free from incumbrance.

The purchaser contends that he cannot, for two reasons: ... (2) because of a writ of execution against the goods and lands of the vendor, now in the hands of the sheriff of the county in which the land is, for execution, in full force and virtue. ... On the [second] ground, the contention of the purchaser seems to me to be, plainly, right, that is: that he cannot be compelled to take the land in question until the effect of the *fi. fa.* is removed.

The writ was placed in the sheriff's hands for execution long after the agreement in question was made; but the greater part of the purchase-money is yet unpaid; and the question which seems to have given trouble to the Master, to whom it was referred to ascertain and state whether a conveyance could be made, namely, what effect, if any, the writ of execution has upon the vendor's power to convey, seems to me to be one easily answered, and in respect of which the reason for the answer easily can be given.

Both at law and in equity, the vendor is the owner of the land in the sense of having the lawful title to it; the purchaser has only an equitable right to it; but, to that extent, if the agreement be carried out, is treated in equity as substantially the owner, the real owner, or formal owner, if you choose to call him such, though that would not be strictly accurate; the vendor is a trustee for the purchaser, but bound to convey to him only on fulfilment by the purchaser of all things agreed to be done, on his part, before getting the conveyance. An agreement may never be carried into effect, it may end in nothing by various ways, and it may be that Equity, however measured, may refuse specific performance, and so the vendor may remain owner, unaffected by the agreement, without the aid of any Court. But, whether he does or not, he is still owner and can convey his ownership, subject of course to any equitable right which the purchaser may have: he has none at law except a personal action against the vendor if he should refuse or be unable to carry out his contract.

That being so, on what ground, or with what reason, can it be urged that an execution creditor of the vendor cannot acquire any charge upon the land, though a purchaser from the vendor would acquire right and title? He cannot, of course, acquire any higher right than his debtor had; but why not that much? I have no manner of doubt that the execution creditor, assuming that his execution is valid, has such a right in the land in question, but of course to be worked out in the regular way by sheriff's sale of the judgment debtor's interest in the land. In a case in which the judgment debtor has no real interest in the legal estate in the land, as, for instance, if all the purchase-money had been paid, or validly assigned before the writ took effect, the execution could not stand, substantially, in the way of a conveyance to the purchaser free from incumbrance: and all this seems to me to be quite in accord with the judgment of the Court of Error and Appeal of this Province in the case of *Parke* v *Riley*, 3 E. & A. 215: whilst, if the views of the dissenting Judge in that case could be accepted, the same result should follow now, even if it could not, as he contended, then. That view was that vendor and purchaser must, in all things and inflexibly, be looked upon as mortgagee and mortgagor: and of course in some respects they are in equity substantially the same; and in some cases, for some special purposes, expressly they have been made so, by legislation: see the Mechanics and Wage-Earners Lien Act, R.S.O. 1914, ch. 140, sec. 14 (2). And, since the case of *Parke* v *Riley*, the scope of the Execution Act has been widened from time to time, and is now so comprehensive that the dissenting judgment in that case, even if it had been the judgment of the Court, might not govern the question now involved in this case: see *McPherson* v *Temiskaming Lumber Co. Limited*, [1913] A.C. 145.

This view of the matter is one which makes care on the part of a purchaser of lands, before parting with his purchase-money, necessary: but that is a care which, I have always understood, was and is well-known to be necessary; hence searches in the sheriff's office for executions, which have always, I have thought, been the general practice.

Upon the vendor clearing the way to a conveyance of the land free from all incumbrances, within 10 days, the transaction should be closed; and in that event the vendor should pay all costs subsequent to the judgment for specific performance, to be set off against the costs now payable, under that judgment, by the purchaser to the vendor: otherwise there should be the usual judgment upon the failure to convey after reference; and the vendor should pay all costs subsequent to the judgment for specific performance, but not the costs prior to that, because that judgment was made on the terms of payment of such costs, and these costs should be set off against the costs awarded to the purchaser, and, if there be a balance in the vendor's favour, the amount of it may be deducted from the purchase-money to be returned.

Robinson v *Moffatt* was applied recently in *Re Hal Wright Motor Sales Ltd. and Industrial Development Bank* (1975), 8 O.R. (2d) 76.

NOTE The exigibility of the vendor's interest has been firmly established in many other cases: *Weidman* v *McClary Manufacturing Co.* (1917), 33 D.L.R. 672 (Sask. C.A.); *Morton and Cowell* v *Hoffert*, [1924] 3 D.L.R. 16 (Alta. S.C.); *Adanac Oil Co.* v *Stocks* (1916), 28 D.L.R. 215 (Alta. S.C.).

While the interest of a vendor of land is exigible, it is only exigible to the extent of the vendor's interest at the time of filing of the execution with the Sheriff. Thus, where a vendor who is entitled to unpaid purchase money assigns his interest to a third party, a subsequent execution creditor cannot bind the vendor's interest since there is no longer any interest to which the execution could attach: *Barnes* v *Sharpe*, [1924] 2 D.L.R. 1119 (Alta. C.A.); *Condon* v *Gassall and Drinkle*, [1929] 2 D.L.R. 77 (Sask. C.A.); *Mackenzie* v *Wm. Gray & Sons Co.* (1914), 17 D.L.R. 769 (Sask. S.C.).

Similarly, where the agreement of purchase and sale gives rise to a right of set-off by the purchaser against the vendor to the extent that the purchaser's obligations are extinguished and the vendor has no remaining interest in the land, a writ of execution against the vendor cannot bind the land: *Re Palmer and Southwood* (1976), 67 D.L.R. (3d) 327 (Alta. S.C. A.D.).

The next two cases consider the effect of land registration statutes on the exigibility of the debtor's apparent interest in land.

McDonald v *The Royal Bank of Canada*, [1933] 2 D.L.R. 680 (Ont. C.A.).

MIDDLETON, J.A.: The facts giving rise to this litigation are exceeding simple. In January, 1932, the plaintiff recovered judgment against the said McDonald for $1,208 and costs and placed an execution in the hands of the sheriff of the County of Middlesex, who thereupon made seizures of a mortgage made by one David R. McArthur to the execution debtor. This mortgage was claimed by the Royal Bank to which it had been assigned by the debtor in December, 1925. At the time of the assignment the duplicate original of the mortgage had been delivered to the bank and the mortgagor had been duly notified of the assignment. The bank, however, failed to register this assignment in the Registry Office and the plaintiff had no notice or knowledge of the assignment at the time the sheriff registered the necessary notice of seizure as required by The Execution Act.

By consent of the parties the mortgage money has been released and has been deposited in a special account pending the result of this litigation.

The *bona fides* of the assignment to the bank is not disputed but the learned trial Judge held that the registration of the notice under The Execution Act constituted the execution creditor a *bona fide* purchaser for value without notice and gave him priority over the bank's assignment by virtue of the provisions of The Registry Act.

In this we are all of opinion that the learned Judge erred.

Ever since the decision of the House of Lords in the case of *Eyre* v *McDowell* (1861), 9 H.L.C. 619, the matter is free from doubt. As said by the Chief Justice of Canada in *Jellett* v *Wilkie* (1896), 26 S.C.R. 282, at p 288, 'no proposition of law can be more amply supported by authority than ... that an execution creditor can only sell the property of his debtor subject to all such charges, liens and equities as the same was subject to in the hands of his debtor.'

The case in the House of Lords is singularly parallel to that in hand because it deals not only with the right of the execution creditor but it deals also with the problem presented by the registry of the judgment. The case came from Ireland and under the Irish Statute the judgment could be registered against the lands of the debtor and upon the registration the statute provided that the execution creditor should be deemed to be a purchaser of the lands as under a deed in which the execution debtor was vendor, the execution creditor purchaser and the amount of the execution the consideration for the conveyance. The Irish Court had held that this made the execution creditor after the registration a purchaser for value and as he had no notice of the unregistered conveyance, his title as execution creditor defeated the right of the grantee under the unregistered instrument. This decision was reversed in the Lords by Lord Cranworth, Lord Wensleydale, and Lord Kingsdown after a most exhaustive argument by very eminent counsel. Lord Cranworth gives as the reason for his opinion that apart from the statute the sheriff could only seize the debtor's beneficial interest, that which, if there had been no judgment, the debtor might have appropriated for the payment of the debt. The debtor could not have appropriated the land to the liquidation of his debt without first satisfying the claim of his equitable mortgagee and the statute did not intend to and did not enable the creditor to take that which the debtor could not give.

The effect of the statute was not to vary the rights of the debtor and the creditor by putting them in a position different from that in which they stood apart from the statute. Its intention and effect were that nothing should be transferred except that which the debtor could transfer to a purchaser or mortgagee with notice of all prior titles, that is, that to which the debtor was beneficially entitled. Lord Wensleydale entirely agrees. The provision for registration only affected the debtor's actual interest. It conveys only the real beneficial interest of the debtor and no more. Its effect cannot be increased or lessened by the absence from or presence on the registry of the previous equitable charge.

In the Supreme Court, in the case already referred to, it was held that the registration of an execution did not defeat a prior unregistered transfer made by the debtor even when the land was registered under the Torrens System. It was, however, pointed out that if the sheriff sold under the *fi. fa.* a purchaser from the sheriff would be protected by virtue of the provisions of The Registry Act ...

This is alone sufficient to dispose of the appeal. I would, however, draw attention to the fact that there are other difficulties in the plaintiff's way. The notice of the execution is not an instrument within the meaning of the Registry Act. The Registry Act is plainly concerned with protecting the rights of actual purchasers or mortgagees under registered instruments as against claims under unregistered documents. It does not in any way deal with the rights of creditors.

Furthermore the learned Judge has misinterpreted the Execution Act, R.S.O. 1927, ch. 112. Under sec. 19 the sheriff is only empowered to seize mortgages, &c., 'belonging to the person against whom the execution has been issued.' Section 24 only provides for the mode of taking in execution a mortgage which is made exigible under the earlier section, that is, a mortgage which belongs to the execution debtor.

For these reasons the appeal must be allowed with costs and the action dismissed with costs. Appeal allowed with costs.

See s 69 of The Registry Act, reproduced at p 242 infra.

Davidson v Davidson, [1946] 2 D.L.R. 289 (S.C.C.)

ESTEY J.: The appellant holds against the respondent two judgments registered respectively on July 23, 1943, and March 27, 1944, in the Kamloops Land Registration District in the Province of British Columbia.

The respondent has been, at all times material to these proceedings the registered owner of the lands in question under a certificate of indefeasible title dated November 9, 1936, and issued out of the Kamloops Land Registration District.

The District Registrar at Vancouver has after hearing the interested parties, certified 'that the interest of the said Judgment Debtor liable to be sold under and to satisfy the said Judgment consists of the entire fee, being the entire right, title and interest registered in the name of the Judgment Debtor under the said Certificates of Indefeasible Title and standing in his name upon the records of the said Land Registry Office ...' He then specified the lands in question.

This certificate was confirmed by the Honourable Mr. Justice Wilson, whose decision was reversed in the Court of Appeal. A further appeal is now taken to this Court.

The respondent's contention is that prior to the registration of the judgments he had executed and delivered a transfer of these lands to the Minto Trading & Development Co. in payment of 20,000 shares of stock allotted to him by that company. This instrument of transfer was executed and delivered on June 19, 1935, and as a consequence he contends that since that time he has had no beneficial interest in the said lands. The company has never applied for registration of this transfer, nor does it now indicate any intention with respect thereto.

At common law 'an execution creditor can only sell the property of his debtor subject to all such charges, liens and equities as the same was subject to in the hands of his debtor': *per* Strong C.J.C., *Jellett v Wilkie*, 26 S.C.R. 282 at pp 288–9.

The important issue, therefore, is what interest the judgment debtor had at the time the executions were registered in the Land Registry Office, or more particularly in this case, what is the significance and effect of the delivery by the respondent of the transfer duly executed to the Minto Trading & Development Co. The determination of this question must be had from the provisions of the *Land Registry Act*.

The following section of the *Land Registry Act*, R.S.B.C. 1936, c 140, is relevant:

34. Except as against the person making the same, no instrument ... purporting to transfer, charge, deal with, or affect land or any estate or interest therein, either at law or in equity, on the land ... until the instrument is registered in compliance with the provisions of this Act.

The respondent relies upon the decision of *Entwisle v Lenz*, 14 B.C.R. 51. There the holder of an unregistered transfer brought action to have the judgment registered against the land, since the execution and delivery of the transfer, removed as a cloud upon his title. The learned trial Judge decided under the then s 74 (now s 34 of the *Land Registry Act*) in favour of the execution creditor. His decision was reversed in the Court of Appeal where the learned Judges did not discuss the provisions of the *Land Registry Act*, but rested their decision upon s 3 of the *Judgments Act*, 1899, c 33 (now s 35, *Execution Act*, R.S.B.C. 1936, c 91);

'Immediately upon any judgment being entered or recovered in this Province, the judgment may be registered in any or all of the Land Registry Offices in the Province, and from the time of registering the same the judgment shall form a lien and charge on all the lands of the judgment debtor in the several land registration districts in which the judgment is registered, in the same manner as if charged in writing by the judgment debtor under his hand and seal; and after the registering of the judgment the judgment creditor may, if he wishes to do so, forthwith proceed upon the lien and charge thereby created.'

This section was construed in the *Entwisle* case as effecting no change in the common law. Somewhat similar statutes have been so construed: *Eyre* v *McDowell* (1861), 9 H.L.C. 619, 11 E.R. 871; *Case* v *Bartlett* (1898), 12 Man. R. 280 at p 286.

The *Entwisle* case was criticized but not overruled in *Bk. of Hamilton* v *Hartery*, 45 D.L.R. 638, 58 S.C.R. 338. The criticism was based upon the provisions with respect to the effect of registration under the *Land Registry Act*. In 1921 certain amendments were made to that Act. Counsel for the respondent submits that at least some of these amendments were made, as a consequence of the criticism in this Court, for the purpose of clarifying the statute and continuing the law as laid down in *Entwisle* v *Lenz*. That was the view of the majority of the learned Judges in *Gregg* v *Palmer*, [1932] 3 D.L.R. 640, 45 B.C.R. 267.

One of the 1921 amendments inserted at the beginning of s 34 the words: 'Except as against the person making the same'. The section prior to that amendment read in part: 'No instrument ... purporting to transfer ... shall pass any estate or interest, either at law or in equity, in the land ... until the instrument is registered.'

It is apparent that prior to the insertion of these words the statute emphasized the importance of registration and it provided for what Lord Moulton described as 'the absoluteness of the effect of the registration'. *Loke Yew* v *Port Swettenham Rubber Co.* [1913] A.C. 491 at p 504. It was no doubt the criticism of the *Entwisle* case that brought to the attention of the Legislature this conflict between s 34 and the decision in the *Entwisle* case. This conclusion is strengthened by the fact that s 34 had remained in the statutes without amendment since prior to the *Entwisle* decision in 1908, but immediately following that criticism it was amended.

These words, 'except as against the person making the same' expressly make operative an unregistered instrument against the party making the same. Therefore, the transfer executed by the respondent was operative to transfer to the Minto Trading & Development Co. whatever estate, either at law or in equity, he was in possession of. As a consequence the respondent, as execution debtor, had prior to the registration of this judgment divested himself of his interest in the land here in question. The conclusion, therefore, appears to be well-founded that the Legislature by this amendment has continued the decision in the *Entwisle* case as law in British Columbia.

The Minto Trading & Development Co. is not asking to have the transfer registered under ss 175, 176 and 177 of the *Land Registry Act*, as enacted in 1921. They were, however, enacted at the same time as the words inserted in s 34 and may be helpful in understanding the meaning and effect of these words inserted at the beginning of s 34. Sections 175, 176 and 177 have to do with judgments in relation to those who apply for registration as owner or holder of a charge. A judgment is different from other encumbrances in that as registered it constitutes a blanket charge upon all the lands of the judgment debtor in that Land Registration District. Because of this a different system of registration is adopted and all judgments are listed under the name of the judgment debtor in a 'Register of Judgments'. Under this system questions arise with respect to the identity of owners and judgment debtors for which a summary procedure is essential. But these sections go beyond the decision of such issues. In s 175 it expressly contemplates 'Where application has been made to the Registrar to register the applicant as owner of land ... and there is a judgment registered against the grantor of the fee-simple ....' Then in s 176, 'any judgment creditor ... shall be ... paid ... as costs of investigating the bona fides of the claim of the applicant that he is entitled to priority to the judgment'. Then in s 177 it is provided that where the instrument is entitled 'to priority over the registered judgment' that the Court may nevertheless allow costs to the judgment creditor 'if in the opinion of the Court the judgment creditor was justified under the circumstances ... in requiring the applicant to have judicially established the bona fides and validity of the execution of the instrument under which the applicant claims'. These sections indicate that upon such applications the question of priority shall be determined, a matter which, prior to the amendments of 1921, was settled by the provisions of the sections corresponding to ss 34, 36 and 37. Indeed, the implication appears to be that if the instrument is found to be *bona fide* and validly executed that it is entitled to priority over the judgment creditor under circumstances such as obtain in this case.

These statutory provisions, read as they must be in association with s 34, retain the common law rule with respect to rights of judgment creditors. Under that rule the execution creditor can only attach that interest which exists in the execution debtor. The respondent having disposed of his entire interest before the registration of the judgment, this judgment cannot attach the land in question as certified by the Registrar.

The learned Judge, in confirming the District Registrar's report, based his judgment upon the amendment made to the *Land Registry Act* in 1913 to the then s 22, now s 37. The material portion of that amendment substituted 'conclusive evidence at law and in equity' for the words 'conclusive evidence in all Courts of Justice'. With deference to the learned trial Judge, this amendment does not appear to effect the change which he suggests. All the Courts having to do with these matters apply the rules and principles of both law and equity. Moreover, it appears that the amendments made in 1921 and already discussed deal more specifically with the subject and if s 37 (s 22 in 1913) was intended to effect such a change as suggested by the learned trial Judge, the Legislature would no doubt have further amended that section in 1921.

In my opinion the appeal should be dismissed with costs.

Appeal dismissed.

[The judgment of Kellock J. is omitted.]

QUESTIONS

1 If Minto Trading (the transferee) had claimed that the property was not subject to execution in the hands of the transferor would that claim have been upheld? What if there had been an execution against Minto?

2 What is the point of protecting the maker of the interest by letting him plead that the property has passed to the transferee? As a result of failure to register, the property was exigible in the hands of neither transferor nor transferee.

3 Would the language of The Registry Act, R.S.O. 1970, c 409 or that of The Land Titles Act, R.S.O. 1970, c 234 (infra p 242) change the result reached in *Davidson* if the facts were to recur in Ontario?

The Land Titles Act, R.S.O. 1970, c 234.

75. (1) No person, other than the registered owner, is entitled to transfer or charge registered freehold or leasehold land by a registered disposition.

(2) Subject to the maintenance of the estate and right of the registered owner, a person having a sufficient estate or interest in the land may create estates, rights, interests and equities in the same manner as he might do if the land were not registered.

91. (1) A transfer for valuable consideration of land registered with an absolute title, when registered, confers on the transferee an estate in fee simple in the land transferred, together with all rights, privileges and appurtenances, subject to,

(*a*) the encumbrances, if any, entered or noted on the register; and

(*b*) the liabilities, rights and interests, if any, as are declared for the purposes of this Act not to be encumbrances, unless the contrary is expressed on the register,

and as to such rights, privileges and appurtenances, subject also to any qualifications, limitation or encumbrance to which the same are expressed to be subject in the register, or where such rights, privileges and appurtenances are not registered, then subject to any qualification, limitation or encumbrance to which the same are subject at the time of the transfer, but free from all estates and interests whatsoever, including estates and interests of Her Majesty, that are within the legislative jurisdiction of Ontario.

The Registry Act, R.S.O. 1970, c 409

69. (1) After the grant from the Crown of land, and letters patent issued therefor, every instrument affecting the land or any part thereof shall be adjudged fraudulent and void against any subsequent purchaser or mortgagee for valuable consideration without actual notice, unless the instrument is registered before the registration of the instrument under which the subsequent purchaser or mortgagee claims.

70. Priority of registration prevails unless before the prior registration there has been actual notice of the prior instrument by the person claiming under the prior registration.

71. No equitable lien, charge or interest affecting land is valid as against a registered instrument executed by the same person, his heirs or assigns, and tacking shall not be allowed in any case to prevail against the provisions of this Act.

NOTE As a corollary to the principle that an unregistered mortgage assigned by the judgment debtor prior to the registration of an execution against him is not exigible, it has been held that a prior unregistered lien or mortgage creditor of a debtor takes priority over subsequently registered execution creditors: *Lang* v *MacMillan* (1958), 13 D.L.R. 778 (Ont. H.C.J.); *Yorkshire Guarantee etc. Corp* v *Edmonds* (1900), 7 B.C.R. 348; *Gregg* v *Palmer*, [1932] 3 D.L.R. 640 (B.C.C.A.); *Gregory* v *Princeton Collieries* (1918), 40 D.L.R. 739 (B.C.S.C.); *Sawyer and Massey Co.* v *Waddell* (1904), 6 Terr. L.R. 45; *Kerr* v *Ruttle and Cruickshank*, [1953] 1 D.L.R. 266 (Ont. H.C.J.); *Marshall Wells Alta. Co.* v *Alliance Trust Co.* (1920), 52 D.L.R. 600 (Alta. S.C.); *Pollock* v *Holitski* (1918), 42 D.L.R. 491 (Sask. S.C.).

iii Contingent Interests: The Execution Act (s 28) expressly permits execution against contingent interests in land. An example of the operation of this provision may be seen in *Lawson* v *Lawson*, [1964] 2 O.R. 321 (Ont. H.C.J.), in which the right to a one-third interest in the residue of an estate subject to divestment upon failure to succeed a life tenant was held to be exigible.

iv Mortgages of Land: Sections 21 to 25 prescribe the procedure for seizing the interest of a mortgagee of land.

At common law, the interest of a mortgagee could not be seized by way of a writ of *fi. fa.* The execution creditor had to proceed by way of equitable execution, for example by the appointment of a receiver: *Simpson* v *Smyth* (1846), 1 E & A 9, 172, aff'd 7 Moo. P.C. 205.

Section 21 is not applicable when the judgment debtor no longer owns the mortgage at the time of seizure. Thus where the execution debtor assigns the mortgage prior to the issuance of the writ of *fi. fa.*, the mortgage cannot be seized, notwithstanding the failure of the assignee to register the assignment pursuant to The Registry Act: *McDonald* v *Royal Bank of Canada*, [1933] 2 D.L.R. 680 (Ont. C.A.) (supra at p 237).

v Chattel Mortgages and Conditional Sales

INTEREST OF VENDORS AND MORTGAGEES OF CHATTELS Section 26 of The Execution Act authorizes execution against the interest of a mortgagee of chattels when 'the mortgage is registered as required by law'. The relevant 'law' is now The Personal Property Security Act, R.S.O. 1970, c 344, as amended (proclaimed in force effective April 1, 1976), which applies, in general, to all consensual security interests in personal property. Unlike the formerly applicable Bills of Sale and Chattel Mortgages Act, R.S.O. 1970, c 45, s 8 (repealed by proclamation effective April 1, 1976), the PPSA does not require registration if a chattel mortgage is not to be void as against creditors of the mortgagor and as against subsequent purchasers or mortgagees in good faith for valuable consideration; instead, it is merely the priority of a security interest against competing claims to the chattel that is prejudiced by the failure of the holder of such an interest to perfect it. (PPSA s 22, reproduced below at p 270). This absence of registration as a requirement is unlikely to affect the operation of s 26 of The Execution Act where perfection takes place by registration (see PPSA, s 25).

Since failure to perfect under the PPSA does not render a security interest void, even the unregistered interest of a chattel mortgagee should be exigible as an 'equitable or other right, property, interest ... in goods, chattels or personal property' within the meaning of s 18 of The Execution Act. However, where the chattel mortgage is one which is still governed by The Bills of Sale and Chattel Mortgages Act – see the transitional provisions of the PPSA, ss 64 and 65 as amended – the matter is less clear. If the unregistered mortgage is void as against the persons listed in s 8 of the Act now repealed, there is no interest against which the judgment creditor of the mortgagee may execute; recall *Re Hare and Bellmore Investments Ltd.*, supra p 235. But if there is no one who can assert one of the s 8 'protected interests', the mortgagee may still have an interest which is exigible under s 18 of The Execution Act.

Conditional sales contracts are not specifically mentioned in The Execution Act. However, the interest of a conditional seller would appear to be exigible under s 18.

The difficulty with both conditional sellers' and chattel mortgagees' interests is that these secured creditors do not have the right to possession of the goods – that right is in the buyer or mortgagor. The sheriff cannot seize the goods themselves as he cannot gain any higher right than the right possessed by the debtor, which right excludes the right to possession.

The sheriff is however, not helpless. He can seize the debt owed by the conditional purchaser or chattel mortgagor as a chose in action (s 19(2)), or he can garnish the debt (see Chapter 10, infra). In addition, he can seize the commercial paper involved in the security transaction and sell it.

INTEREST OF PURCHASERS AND MORTGAGORS OF CHATTELS Where goods are 'owned' by a purchaser or mortgagor subject to such security instrument, the rights of the purchaser or mortgagee are subject to seizure under s 18, and the sheriff's sale will convey the interest the purchaser had. There is no problem in regard to chattel mortgages since the debtor has a recognizable interest, an equity of redemption.

However, there is difficulty in the application of s 18 to the interest of conditional purchasers. In *Overby* v *McLean*, [1928] 3 W.W.R. 328 (Man. C.A.), some of their Lordships felt that the interest of a conditional purchaser was not subject to execution since he had 'no interest in the goods', title being elsewhere. More recent cases have taken a different approach. *Overby* was disapproved in *Ruscheinsky* v *A. Spencer & Co. Ltd.*, [1948] 2 W.W.R. 58 (B.C.S.C.), (reproduced immediately below), in which Macfarlane J ruled that the purchaser did have a seizable equitable interest.

Ruscheinsky v *A. Spencer Co. Ltd.*, [1948] 2 W.W.R. 58 (B.C.S.C.)

MACFARLANE, J.: Interpleader by the sheriff of the county of Vancouver. The sheriff pursuant to a writ of execution placed in his hands at the direction of the plaintiff, an execution creditor of the defendant Gim Foon Wong, seized a motor cycle which had been sold to the defendant by Fred Deeley Limited under a conditional-sale agreement. It was duly registered in the proper office. The defendant had made default in payment provided by the conditional-sale agreement amounting to $96.40. The value of the motor cycle is admitted to be under $500. The defendant claims exemption under sec. 25 of the *Execution Act*, R.S.B.C., 1936, ch. 91.

The sheriff's seizure took place on March 17, 1948, and the claim for exemption was filed with him on March 19, 1948. On the day following, notice of seizure was given by Fred Deeley Limited, that is, on March 20, 1948. Both the defendant and Fred Deeley Limited resisted the attempt to sell the motor cycle, the defendant claiming exemption and Fred Deeley Limited claiming that the defendant has no property in the motor cycle and that it is therefore not subject to seizure and sale. The questions arising are:
1 Whether the execution creditor has any right at all to seize and sell the motor cycle in view of the fact that it is held under a conditional-sale agreement which provides that the title to the property shall remain in the vendor until payment in full?
2 If the execution creditor is entitled to seize and sell the interest of the purchaser in the motor cycle, whether the defendant, the purchaser, is then entitled to claim exemption under sec. 25 of the *Execution Act*?

The right to seizure depends, I think, on the construction to be placed on the words, 'may seize and sell *the interest or equity of redemption in any goods or chattels* of the execution debtor' found in sec. 16 of the *Execution Act*. As I have indicated the conditional-sale agreement provides that while the vendor agrees to sell to the purchaser the motor vehicle in question, 'the property is now and shall remain the absolute property of the vendor until after further and complete payment of the purchase price therefor.' To state the question again, it is whether the interest (if any) of the claimant in the motor vehicle is an interest in goods and chattels of the execution debtor, that is, the purchaser under the conditional-sale agreement. The purchaser has a right of possession until default and seizure. He has also a right or option to complete the purchase or title by payment of the balance of the purchase-money. He has a right also of assignment of his interest and also, I think, it has been held a right of charging by way of mortgage that interest. In *Overby* v *McLean*, [1928] 3 w.w.r. 328, at 331, 37 Man R 525, Dennistoun, J.A. says:

The judgment creditor can take only the interest in this motor car that the debtor has, and that is nothing, for the title and right of possession is still in the claimant ...

The claimant there was the vendor under an unregistered conditional-sale agreement. Fullerton, J.A. in the same case says at p 329:

It may be that the execution creditor was entitled under sec. 12 of *The Executions Act*, R.S.M., 1913, ch. 66, to seize and sell the equitable interest which Ratkowski had in the car, but what the execution creditor is here seeking is a sale of the car itself.

It seems to me that the language of Dennistoun, J.A. is perhaps too wide and that it was used in connection with the particular circumstances of that case. I might say that sec. 12 of *The Executions Act* referred to is the same as our sec. 16. It seems to me that in view of the factors which I have mentioned, notwithstanding that the property shall remain the absolute property of the vendor until after full and complete payment, the purchaser has an equitable interest, or an interest in the goods and chattels, being the motor cycle, under sec. 16 of our Act. I think it is clear, of course, that it can only be sold subject to the claim of Deeley Limited, but I think there is here an interest such as is referred to in sec. 16 of the Act.
[The motor cycle was held exigible.]

See contra: *Armbruster Lumber Ltd.* v *Fishburne* (1966), 55 w.w.r. 223.

QUESTIONS Can the decision in *Ruscheinsky* be reconciled with that in *Kimniak* v *Anderson*? Is the position of a purchaser any different depending on whether what is purchased is a house or a motorcycle?

vi Money, Bills of Exchange and Specialties or other Security for Money (s 19(1)): At common law, money could not be taken in execution (*Bradley* v *Hopley* (1828), 1 N.B.R. 147 (C.A.)). Money and banknotes are now specifically exigible under section 19(1). It is fairly frequent practice for a lawyer conducting a judgment debtor examination to ask the debtor if he has any money with him. After further questioning to assure that the debtor has sufficient assets (excluding the money with him) to make the money exigible (i.e. not exempt), the lawyer will wait until a recess in the examination, contact the sheriff and ask the sheriff to come over immediately to seize the debtor's money.

Questions sometimes arise with respect to the exigibility of insurance policies held by the debtor. In *Bank of Montreal* v *McTavish* (1867), 13 Gr. 395, the Court held that money payable under a fire insurance policy under seal was a 'specialty or other security for money' and therefore exigible under the then relevant legislation. Similarly, in *Doull* v *Doelle* (1905), 10 O.L.R. 411, the Ontario Court of Appeal held that the proceeds of a life insurance policy payable to a widow were exigible under execution against the widow.

The Court of Appeal in *The Canadian Mutual Loan and Investment Co.* v *Nisbet* (1900), 31 O.R. 562, held that a paid up life insurance policy was 'security for money' and thereby exigible. But see *Weekes* v *Frawley* (1893), 23 O.R. 235 (C.A.) where the Court held that where premiums on a life insurance policy had not yet been paid up in full, the policy was not exigible.

vii Book Debts and Choses in Action

NOTE At common law book debts could not be seized and sold in execution: *Moore* v *Roper* (1905), 35 S.C.R. 533; *Jobin-Marrin Co.* v *Betts*, (1905), 1 W.L.R. 369 (N.W.T.); *Hudson's Bay Co.* v *Hazlett* (1895), 4 B.C.R. 450 (C.A.). The creditor was forced to collect by means of garnishment proceedings. Section 19(2) of The Execution Act now specifically provides for seizure and sale of book debts.

There was some argument until recently concerning the exigibility of money on deposit at (say) a bank. The difficulties seem to be laid to rest by the decision of the Court of Appeal in *Re A.G. Ont. and Royal Bank of Canada*, reproduced immediately below.

Re A.G. Ont. and Royal Bank of Canada, [1970] 2 O.R. 467 (C.A.)

The judgment of the Court was delivered by
BROOKE, J.A.: The question to de determined by this Court is whether moneys owed by a bank to its customer, being moneys on deposit with or standing to the credit of the customer in his account with the bank, can be taken in execution upon notice of seizure pursuant to the *Execution Act*, R.S.O. 1960, c 126, s 16(2). This question involves not only the interpretation of s 16(2) of the statute but also a consideration of whether or not the form of writ of *fieri facias* directed to the Sheriff pursuant to the Rules, is sufficient to give effect to s 16(2) of the *Execution Act* and, finally, whether s 95 of the *Bank Act*, 1966–67 (Can.), c 87, provides a defence to the respondent bank.

The appeal comes to this Court from an order of Hartt, J., dated June 24, 1969. The facts giving rise to the application before Hartt, J., are not in dispute. Writs of *fieri facias* were issued out of this Court and out of the County Court of the County of York to the Sheriff of the County of York who upon learning that certain sums of money were standing to the credit of the judgment debtors in bank accounts, had his bailiff attempt to seize the bank accounts by serving notice of seizure on the branch office of the respondent's bank where the accounts were located. The respondent bank declined to pay the moneys on deposit in the accounts to the Sheriff contending that a bank account cannot be seized in execution under a writ of *fieri facias*.

In his brief reasons for judgment, Hartt, J., expressed agreement with a judgment of Costello, Co.Ct.J., in *Sheriff of the County of Waterloo* v *Mutual Life Ass'ce Co. of Canada*, [1967] 1 O.R. 131, and disposed of the application declaring that writs of *fieri facias* and notices of seizure served pursuant thereto by the Sheriff could not be used to take into execution moneys due to a customer by his bank or, to put it another way, to seize the debt of the bank to its customer being moneys on deposit in his account.

Sheriff of the County of Waterloo v *Mutual Life Ass'ce Co. of Canada, supra,* was a case in which the life insurance company paid to its insured, the judgment debtor, the cash surrender value of the contract of life insurance after service of a notice of seizure of that debt upon the insurance company pursuant to a writ of *fi. fa.* then in the hands of the Sheriff. Judge Costello held that the writ of *fi. fa.* could not be used to seize the debt but rather the proper procedure was by way of attachment and, accordingly, there was no liability to the Sheriff.

The relevant sections of the *Execution Act* are ss 1 and 16 ...

[His Lordship set out ss 1(a) and 16 and continued:]

It is not questioned in this appeal that the debt of a bank to its customer for moneys on deposit to his credit is a chose in action.

In interpreting s 16(2), Judge Costello looked to what he called a basic principle and stated [at p 132]:

The basic principles of execution, other than seizure of stocks, patents, land and mortgages, the procedure for the seizing of which is specifically set out in the *Execution Act*, R.S.O. 1960, c 126, would seem to me to require that the item seized be in the possession or control of the judgment debtor or his personal representatives. Halsbury, 3rd ed., vol. 16, p 46, says: 'Incorporeal things are generally exempt from seizure under a *fieri facias* ... the debts or other choses in action of the judgment debtor cannot be seized ...'

The cases cited by Halsbury in support of the above quotations are from the first half of the last century and I do not have available to me the statutes in force in England at the time of those decisions to compare with our present *Execution Act*. The principle, as far as I can determine, still is the law if not the practice.

It is in his application of this statement that, in my opinion, the error in His Honour's interpretation of s 16(2) is to be found, since it imports into s 16(2) a condition which is quite inconsistent with choses in action. Section 16(2) found its way into our statutes in 1927. Before that time, and at the time of the decisions referred to in the passage of Halsbury relied upon by Judge Costello, there was no similar statutory provision here or in England. Assuming that Judge Costello has correctly stated the principles applicable at common law, in my view they ought not to be applied in the interpretation of the present s 16(2) so as to change what seems on its face to be the clear intention of the Legislature.

For the purpose of this appeal it is, I think, unnecessary for us to deal with the judgment of Judge Costello as it relates to s 16(1) except to say, having regard to the basic principle as he calls it, as above set out, that he interprets the words 'belonging to' in that section as meaning 'in the possession or control of'. However, the primary problem in this appeal arises when the learned Judge attempts to apply the same interpretation that he has given to the words 'belonging to' in s-s (1) of the word 'of' in s-s (2). It is here that I think that his error becomes manifest. The relevant passage from his judgment is as follows [at p 133]:

Section 16(2) provides for the seizure of book debts and choses in action of the execution debtor and gives the Sheriff the right to sue in his own name for the recovery of the money payable in respect thereof. In the absence of authority to the contrary, I must interpret this to mean physical seizure of documents or other evidence of title or right upon which the suits could be founded and their removal from the control and possession of the execution debtor. This is confirmed by s 16(3) which provides that the book debts and choses in action may be sold, 'in the same manner as the debtor's goods may be sold when taken in execution.' I take s 16(2) to refer to some assignable and saleable document of which the Sheriff is in physical possession. I must find that the *Execution Act* does not provide for the freezing of money owing to the execution debtor but in the hands of a third party by the simple expedient of a notice of the filing of the writ of *fieri facias*. The *Execution Act* provides no penalty for the third party who chooses to ignore such a notice assuming for the moment that the Sheriff does not have the documents on which the execution creditor could base his claim against such third party.

The judgment then proceeds on the basic premise that the only way in which a chose in action can be seized under s 16(2) is by physically taking possession of documents or other evidence of title or right upon which suits could be founded and 'removing them from the control and possession of the debtor'. I agree with counsel for the appellant when he submits that this does violence to the concept of a chose in action. A chose in action (as distinguished from a chose in possession) is an incorporeal right to something not in one's possession and, accordingly, it is not possible for the debtor to have possession of it. In *DiGuilo* v *Boland* [1958] O.R. 384 at p 394, 13 D.L.R. (2d) 510 at p 513, Morden, J.A., in delivering the judgment of the Court of Appeal, said with respect to choses in action:

In *Torkington* v *Magee*, [1902] 2 K.B. 427, Channell, J., said, at p 430:

'Chose in action' is a known legal expression used to describe all personal rights of property which can only be claimed or enforced by action, and not in taking physical possession.

See also Stroud's Judicial Dictionary, 3rd ed., p 478, and Jowitt's, Dictionary of English Law, p 367.

Accordingly, in my view, in holding that in order to seize a chose in action the Sheriff must deprive the judgment debtor of the control and possession of it, Judge Costello was in error on the simple ground that a chose in action is not capable of being rendered into possession.

If, however, I am wrong as to the above being the meaning of the judgment in question and Judge Costello meant simply that to effect seizure of a chose in action under s 16(2), it is necessary to seize physically 'documents or other evidence of title or right' upon which suits could be founded and to remove them 'from the control or possession of the execution debtor', this, of course, would be reading into the section two new conditions and so would be creating a new class of incorporeal rights coming within the scope of the section. In view of the clear wording of the subsection, such an interpretation cannot be supported by resort to the basic principle referred to by Judge Costello or to s 16(3) or otherwise. As to s 16(3) it is no more than permissive, since sale is to be resorted to if, in the judgment of the Sheriff, it would be more beneficial to the creditors than to attempt to collect the debt or chose in action.

In the result, I do not agree with the judgment of Judge Costello and, in my opinion, that judgment ought not to have been applied by Mr. Justice Hartt. Section 16(2) was intended to provide for seizure of incorporeal things which at common law were generally thought not to be the subject of seizure by way of writ of execution. The provisions of the legislation in question are clear, they are not limited in application to a particular class of chose in action or book debt, nor is liability to seizure limited by the condition of the existence in the hands or control of the judgment debtor of documents as evidence of his right. I am aware of the general practice in this Province which is relied upon to obtain payment in satisfaction of a judgment of moneys owing by third persons to the judgment debtor. However, this does not alter my opinion that s 16(2) offers another method by which this may be done.

Were the writs of *fi. fa.* issued out of this Court and out of the County Court of the County of

York such as would by their terms include a chose in action? The writs are, of course, included amongst the material in the Appeal Book and each is a direction to the Sheriff that 'of the goods and chattels, lands and tenements in your bailiwick ... you do cause to be made ...' The notice of the seizure to which it is said a copy of the writ of execution was attached is differently worded and specifies that pursuant to the writ in his hand, the Sheriff now seizes 'all deposits, credits, book debts, accounts receivable, choses in action and all cheques belonging to the judgment debtor and demands payment of the same forthwith'. It is contended by counsel for the respondent that neither a book debt nor chose in action as referred to in s 16(2) is encompassed by the words 'goods and chattels' which the Sheriff was directed by the writ of execution to seize from the third person.

Writs of *fi. fa.* are issued to a Sheriff pursuant to Rule 556 of the Consolidated Rules of Practice of this Court and are in accordance with Form 115. My research reveals that there has been no change in the form of the writ of *fieri facias* since our statute was amended in 1927 to include the provision which is now s 16(2). So far as I am able to discover, the form of writ now used is the same as that that has been resorted to for many years prior to the change in our legislation. In my view, cases decided prior to the amendment in 1927 dealing with the meaning to be attributed to the words 'goods and chattels' and as used in the writ of execution are of limited value. I am aware that the word 'chattel' has in some situations been given a restricted meaning so as to exclude all incorporeal personal property such as debts, shares, copyrights and the right to enforce the payment of a debt: see Jowitt's Dictionary of the Law of England, 2nd ed., p 357; *Hudson's Bay Company* v *Hazlett* (1896), 4 B.C.R. 451; *Adams and Burns* v *Bank of Montreal* (1899), 8 B.C.R. 314; *Yorkshire Guarantee & Securities Corp* v *Cooper* (1903), 10 B.C.R. 65. However, in the cases referred to, the Court was concerned with the meaning to be attributed to words used in the context of particular statutes rather than to the general or broader meaning. In other days, the term 'chattel' or 'chattels personal' often referred only to moveables. Today it may, however, be given the broader meaning so as to include all personal property. In *Robinson* v *Jenkins et al.* (1890), 6 T.L.R. 158 at p 159, Fry, L.J., said:

Order LVII. allowed an interpleader to take place in respect of 'chattels,' which was one of the largest words known to the law, and certainly included choses in action.

Moreover, I think it most important that the words of the writ be interpreted in so far as is possible to give effect to all of the provisions of the statute. The Rules of Practice and forms thereby authorized should be broadly interpreted to give effect to the substantive law: see *Sutt* v *Sutt*, [1968] 2 O.R. 786, [1969] 1 O.R. 169, 70 D.L.R. (2d) 584; affirmed 2 D.L.R. (3d), 33 (C.A.). It is, therefore, my opinion that 'book debts and other choses in action' as dealt with in s 16(2) of the statute should be regarded as included within the term 'goods and chattels' as used in the form of the writ of execution authorized by Form 115 of the Rules of Practice ...

... [S]ervice of a copy of the writ together with a notice of seizure, as was done here, in my view, satisfied the condition of the section and 'affects and binds' the moneys standing to the credit of the customer at the branch of the bank where the writ was served.

In the circumstances, should a bank pay out moneys in satisfaction of its debt to its customer to other than the Sheriff as directed by the writ and notice of seizure, it does so at its peril. While the section does not explicitly authorize a bank to pay the moneys to the Sheriff, I should think the words 'affects and binds' ought to be interpreted as having this meaning. In the case at bar, then, and assuming the bank was indebted to its customer who was the judgment debtor, the bank ought to have complied with the writ and notice of seizure.

In the result then, in my view the appeal must succeed. The order below should be set aside and in its place an order will issue declaring that the writs of *fieri facias* and the notices of seizure served pursuant thereto in these proceedings by the Sheriff of the County of York upon the respondent bank affected and bound the moneys standing to the credit of the judgment debtors at the branch of the bank where the writ or the notice thereof was served.

There will be no costs of the proceedings before Mr. Justice Hartt, the matter really being of first instance. However, the appellant will have the costs of this appeal.

Appeal allowed.

QUESTIONS Are any of the choses in action not capable of being reached by way of *fi. fa.*?

If a chose may be the subject of execution proceedings, why might a creditor use garnishment instead? Defer consideration of this question until you have looked at the sheriff's file in chapter 15, the chapter on garnishment (Chapter 10), and the chapter on priorities of unsecured creditors (Chapter 13).

viii Joint Tenancies

NOTE At common law it was not clear whether or not the interest of one joint tenant was exigible. One line of cases held that such interests were not exigible (see *Re Tully et al.*, [1953] O.W.N. 661 (S.C.)), while other cases supported exigibility (see *Re Craig*, [1929] I D.L.R. 142 (Ont. C.A.); *Toronto Hospital for Consumptives* v *Toronto* (1930), 38 O.W.N. 196 (C.A.), *Re Kates et al.* v *Morrison*, [1951] 4 D.L.R. 260 (S.C.O.), and *Re Klagsbrun* v *Stankiewicz*, [1954] I D.L.R. 593 (S.C.O.)).

Since 1957, s 9 of The Execution Act has provided expressly for the exigibility of an interest in lands held in joint tenancy. If the interest of a joint tenant is so seized and sold by the sheriff, the joint tenancy will be converted into a tenancy in common (between the sheriff's purchaser and the non-debtor joint tenant).

The operation of s 9 itself is straightforward; however, problems may arise because of the right of survivorship incident to a joint tenancy. If a joint tenant dies or transfers away his interest in the joint tenancy after a writ of execution has been lodged with the sheriff but before the completion of sale, does he cease to have an exigible interest in the lands? The answer may depend upon whether the joint tenancy has been severed, as it may be by voluntary act or operation of law. It may further depend upon whether the right of survivorship carries to the survivor the debtor's interest in the joint tenancy free from or subject to the rights of executing creditors. If the joint tenancy is severed by death before 'execution' by the sheriff or perhaps before an advertisement for sale in the *Ontario Gazette* is published (Ontario Supreme Court Rules of Practice, R.R.O. 1970, Reg. 545, Rule 565), the survivor takes the estate by survivorship free of the execution against the deceased's interest. The Ontario Court of Appeal in *Power* v *Grace*, [1932] 2 D.L.R. 793, held that mere delivery of a writ of execution to the sheriff will not effect a severance of the joint tenancy. Thus, where death occurs between delivery of the writ to the sheriff and enforcement of the writ, the survivor takes free of the claims of execution creditors. Delivery of the writ, without more, does not sever the joint tenancy and destroy the right of survivorship. The British Columbia Court of Appeal in *Re Young* (1968), 70 D.L.R. (2d) 594 (immediately below), has held that registration of a judgment against one joint tenant pursuant to section 35 of the

Execution Act, R.S.B.C. 1960, c 135, does not effectively sever the joint tenancy, notwithstanding the words of that Act which say that 'from the time of registering ... the judgment forms a lien and charge on all the lands of the judgment debtor ...'. On the other hand, the debtor cannot, by his own voluntary act, exempt his share of the joint tenancy from execution (*Sirois* v *Breton*, [1967] 2 O.R. 73 (Co. Ct.) (infra p 254)).

Re Young (1968), 70 D.L.R. (2d) 594. (B.C.C.A.)

MACLEAN, J.A.: The appellant, the Public Trustee, applied to a Judge of the Supreme Court in Chambers to discharge a Registrar's caveat filed under s 212 of the *Land Registry Act*, R.S.B.C. 1960, c 208, against the land situate in the City of Vancouver described in certificate of title 561303-L.

The application was refused without written reasons having been given and the Public Trustee now appeals to this Court.

The facts are not in dispute and I set out hereunder the statement of facts taken from the respondents' factum.

On April 17, 1957, Certificate of Title No. 365464-L issued in the Vancouver Land Registry Office concerning Lot 4, except the North Ten (10) feet, now lane, of Lots 1, 2 and 26 to 28, Blocks 10 to 13 and 22 to 25, District Lots 391 and 392, Group 1, New Westminster District, Plan 2149, City of Vancouver; the said lot was registered in the names of Thomas Young and Myrtle Laurel Young as joint tenants.

On January 15, 1964, Judgment No. 18589 registered in the Vancouver Land Registry Office against the lands of Thomas Young, in favour of Ellen Elizabeth Solem and Custer Solem, which was renewed by Judgment 19600 on January 4, 1966, and by Judgment 20774 on January 3, 1968.

The said Thomas Young died on May 31, 1964 and the said Myrtle Laurel Young died intestate on March 3, 1967.

On November 10, 1967, an application for registration and issuance of a Certificate of Title was made under No. 561303-L, which application was made by the Public Trustee as administrator of the estate of Myrtle Laurel Young, deceased.

On the 4th of January, 1968, Caveat No. 7689 was filed in the Vancouver Land Registry Office by the Registrar of the said Land Registry Office, forbidding the registration applied for under Certificate of Title No. 561303-L.

The Public Trustee applied by way of Originating Notice dated the 12th of January, 1968, to the Supreme Court of British Columbia under the provisions of the Land Registry Act, R.S.B.C. 1960 Chapter 208, and amendments thereto, to have the said Caveat No. 7689 discharged.

On January 19, 1968, the matter was heard before the Honourable Mr. Justice Nemetz (as he then was) of the Supreme Court of British Columbia, in Chambers, and the application of the Public Trustee was refused.

The position taken by the appellant, the Public Trustee, representing the estate of the deceased wife, is that the registration of the judgment prior to the wife's death did not sever the joint tenancy, with the consequence that the appellant may now take the property free of the claim of the respondents' judgment creditors.

The respondents, the judgment creditors, submit that the registration of the judgment severed the joint tenancy leaving the property subject to the judgment. In the alternative, the respondents submit that even if the joint tenancy was not severed by the registration of the judgment, the judgment having attached to the interest of the joint tenant who died, it continued to subsist and travelled with the deceased's interest into the hands of the survivor.

I have reached the conclusion that despite the decision of the Supreme Court of British Columbia in *Re Application of Penn*, 4 W.W.R. (N.S.) 452, to the contrary, the registration of a judgment under s 35 of the *Execution Act*, R.S.B.C. 1960, c 135, does not sever a joint tenancy.

The section reads as follows:

35 Immediately upon a judgment being entered or recovered in this Province, the judgment may be registered in any or all of the Land Registry Offices in the Province, and from the time of registering the same the judgment forms a lien and charge on all the lands of the judgment debtor in the several land registration districts in which the judgment is registered, in the same manner as if charged in writing by the judgment debtor under his hand and seal; and after the registering of the judgment the judgment creditor may, if he wishes to do so, forthwith proceed upon the lien and charge thereby created.

In the *Penn* case Farris, C.J.S.C., held that the joint tenancy ceased with the registration of a judgment under s 35 of the *Execution Act* against one of the joint tenants, although in certain circumstances it might be revived. He distinguished the decision of the Ontario Court of Appeal in *Power* v *Grace*, [1932] 2 D.L.R. 793, [1932] O.R. 357. That was a case where it was held that the mere delivery of a writ of *fi. fa.* to a Sheriff is not execution sufficient to sever a joint tenancy.

In *Power* v *Grace*, [1932] 1 D.L.R. 801, Widdifield, Co.Ct.J., said at p 802:

The trend of the authorities is that a mere lien or charge on the land, either by a co-tenant or by operation of law, is not sufficient to sever the joint tenancy; there must be something that amounts to an alienation of title.

This decision was affirmed by the Court of Appeal, *supra*, and the authorities relating to severance of a joint tenancy were extensively reviewed.

Later, in *Re Brooklands Lumber & Hardware Ltd. and Simcoe* (1956), 3 D.L.R. (2d) 762, 64 Man. R. 1, 18 W.W.R. 328, Williams, C.J.Q.B., had occasion to deal with the effect of a registration of judgment under s 3(1) of the *Judgments Act*, R.S.M. 1954, c 129, a provision for all intents and purposes the same as s 35 of our *Execution Act*. The learned Chief Justice said at p 331:

Notwithstanding the judgment in *Penn's* case, *supra*, I have reached the conclusion that the lien and charge given by s 3(1) did not vest an estate in the judgment creditor and the joint tenancy was not severed upon the registration of the certificate of judgment.

In my view the registration of a judgment under s 35 of our *Execution Act* does not sever a joint tenancy and I revert to the words of the trial Judge in the *Power* v *Grace* case (approved by the Court of Appeal) [[1932] 1 D.L.R. at p 892]:

The trend of the authorities is that a mere lien or charge on the land, either by a co-tenant or by operation of law, is not sufficient to sever the joint tenancy; there must be something that amounts to an alienation of title.

I prefer the reasoning in the *Brooklands* case to that appearing in the *Penn* case decided in our own Supreme Court.

Having decided that the registration of the judgment did not sever the joint tenancy, it is now necessary to consider the respondents' alternative submission, that the registration of the judgment suspends the full operation of the *jus accrescendi*, leaving a half interest in the property (equivalent to the interest of the deceased joint tenant) subject to be sold under the judgment.

It will be noted that under s 35 of the *Execution Act* (already quoted) a judgment creditor who registers his judgment in the Land Registry Office becomes the owners of a 'lien and *charge* on all the lands of the judgment debtor in the several land registration districts in which the judgment is registered ...'

'Charge' is defined in the *Land Registry Act* [s 2(1)] as:

... any estate less than the fee-simple, and shall include any equitable interest in land, and any encumbrance upon land, and any estate or interest registered as a charge under section 145;

'Encumbrance' is defined as:

... any Crown debt, judgment, mortgage, lien, or other claim to or upon land created, effected, or given for any purpose whatever, whether by the act of the parties or by or in pursuance of any Statute or law, and whether voluntary or involuntary;

The *Land Registry Act* requires the Registrar of Titles to maintain a register of judgments. The judgment is not noted on the title of the owner such as are mortgages and various other encumbrances, but it appears only in the register of judgments.

The combined effect of the *Land Registry Act* and the *Execution Act* is to make the owner of the registered judgment the owner of a registered 'encumbrance' on the lands of the debtor.

Immediately following the death of the debtor it seems to be beyond question that his interest in the joint tenancy existing prior to his death was extinguished. There still remained entered in the register of judgments an entry made under s 35 of the *Execution Act* indicating the indebtedness of the deceased debtor. As at that moment the legal representative of the judgment debtor had no interest in the lands in question because of the operation of the *jus accrescendi*. The question then is whether the registration of the judgment, a first step in an uncompleted execution, constituted an encroachment upon the surviving joint tenant's rights acquired under the *jus accrescendi*.

Appellant admits that if the execution procedure under ss 33 to 59 of the *Execution Act* had been carried to a point where an order for sale was made, the *jus accrescendi* would have been extinguished. It is not necessary to make a finding on this point here.

It is my view that following the death of the debtor-joint tenant, the judgment creditor had no more than a 'charge' or 'encumbrance' against an interest which no longer existed.

The common law principles relating to real property and conveyancing are still in force except in so far as they are altered by statute. Here we are considering the *Land Registry Act*.

In *Stonehouse* v *A.-G. B.C.* (1960), 26 D.L.R. (2d) 391, 33 W.W.R. 625 [affd in the result 31 D.L.R. (2d) 118, 37 W.W.R. 62, [1962] S.C.R. 103] Davey, J.A. (as he then was), said at p 394:

In my opinion the *Land Registry Act* was never intended to produce a new body of conveyancing and real property law by the fusion of legal principles and the provisions of the *Land Registry Act*. All that it does is to impose a system of recording titles upon the existing real property law and conveyancing practice, making only such changes therein as are expressly provided, or must be necessarily implied to give effect to the Act.

In my view the *Land Registry Act* and the *Execution Act* do not provide a basis for a finding that the rights of the surviving joint tenant under the *jus accrescendi* are so modified or abrogated that he must take subject to a judgment registered under s 35 of the *Execution Act* and on which no further proceedings have been taken.

I think that if I were to hold that the mere registration of a judgment under s 35 of the *Execution Act* constituted an encroachment of the *jus accrescendi*, I would be straying into the legislative field. In my opinion the uncompleted execution gives the judgment creditor no greater rights than the uncompleted execution gave to the judgment creditor in *Power* v *Grace, supra*, where Riddell, J.A., said [1932] 2 D.L.R. at p 794:

In the first place, it has been undoubted law for centuries that where a writ under which an interest in land may be taken by the sheriff has been placed in his hands against a joint-tenant, and the joint-tenant dies before execution, the other joint-tenant surviving holds it discharged of the execution. *Lord Abergavenny's Case*, 6 Co. Rep. 78b, 77 E.R. 373. This law has never been doubted; and the sole question for decision is whether the delivery of the writ to the sheriff is 'execution.'

I would allow the appeal and direct the cancellation of the Registrar's caveat.
[The concurring opinion of McFarlane, JA and the dissenting opinion of Davey, C.J.B.C. have been omitted.]

Sirois v *Breton*, [1967] 2 O.R. 73 (Co. Ct.)

GIBSON, CO.CT.J.: This contest arises out of an application by the Sheriff of the County of Carleton for relief by way of interpleader.

The facts are as follows:

A In February, 1957, Aurèle Breton and his wife Noella Breton became the owners as joint tenants of Lot 546 on the north side of St. Denis St. in the City of Eastview, according to Plan 246.

B About a month later, Aurèle Breton and Noella Breton, as joint tenants, gave a mortgage in the sum of $5,000 to La Caisse Populaire Notre-Dame de Lourdes d'Eastview Limitée, and slightly more than a year later made another mortgage in the sum of $6,250 to Montoro Investments Limited, both secured upon the said lands.

C On April 4, 1960, Aurèle Breton suffered judgment to the judgment creditors in the County Court of the County of Carleton, in connection with which a writ of execution was filed in the hands of the Sheriff on April 22, 1960.

D On August 8, 1960, by deed registered August 9, 1960, S. Aurèle Breton and Noella C. Breton, as joint tenants, conveyed the said lands to Noella C. Breton, subject to the above-mentioned mortgages to La Caisse Populaire Notre-Dame de Lourdes d'Eastview Ltée and Montoro Investments Ltd., and also to arrears of taxes to the City of Eastview.

E On August 25, 1960, by deed registered October 11, 1960, Noella C. Breton conveyed the said lands to the claimants, Thibault Lumber Company Limited, Emco Limited and Gavard Limited as tenants in common, subject to the same three encumbrances.

F On October 7, 1960, by instrument registered November 2, 1960, the second mortgagee Montoro Investments Ltd. granted a discharge of mortgage to S. Aurèle Breton and Noella C. Breton.

G On November 17, 1960, one Manuel de Madeiros and his wife made a mortgage registered January 25, 1961, to one of the claimants, Henri Saint-Jacques.

H On November 24, 1960, the Sheriff of the County of Carleton made a return of *nulla bona* as to the goods and chattels of Aurèle Breton.

I On November 16, 1960, by grant registered February 7, 1961, the three claimants, Thibault Lumber Co. Ltd., Emco Ltd. and Gavard Ltd., conveyed the said lands to Manuel de Madeiros.

J On November 3, 1960, by instrument registered February 8, 1961, Manuel de Madeiros and his wife mortgaged the said lands to the three claimants, Thibault Lumber Co. Ltd., Emco Ltd. and Gavard Ltd.

K On February 2, 1961, a certificate of discharge of mortgage, registered February 8, 1961, was granted by La Caisse Populaire Notre-Dame de Lourdes d'Eastview Ltée to Aurèle Breton and Noella Breton.

L On April 9, 1962, Aurèle Breton made an assignment in bankruptcy, and subsequently received his discharge.

M On April 30, 1962, the judgment creditors filed proof of claim in the bankruptcy of Aurèle Breton in respect of their said judgment claim.

N The assignment of Aurèle Breton in bankruptcy was a voluntary one and no assets became available for distribution before his discharge.

O Eventually, instructions were given on behalf of the judgment creditors to the said Sheriff to levy execution against the said lands, and no steps being taken by the Sheriff in this regard, the judgment creditors served notice of application for a writ of *mandamus* to compel the Sheriff to act. The Sheriff, having received notice of claims of the claimants, applied for an order of interpleader. An order of interpleader was granted on December 3, 1964, and the judgment creditors given carriage of the proceedings ...

The principle seems to be by now clearly established that a joint estate is severable and that the interest of one joint tenant can be sold under execution:
[His Honour cited some cases for this proposition and continued]:
... It is timely at this point to bear in mind that, while a joint estate is severable, the mere filing or delivery of the writ of execution to the Sheriff does not effect a severance. Something more is required by way of action upon the execution on the part of the Sheriff, as by actual seizure or by advertisement in the *Ontario Gazette*, as provided in Rule 571. The principle that the mere delivery of the writ of execution to the Sheriff will not effect or constitute a severance is confirmed and illustrated by the decision that the death of one of two joint tenants after such delivery of the writ of execution to the Sheriff but before action upon such writ of execution at once terminates the joint tenancy in favour of the surviving joint tenant, so that such surviving joint tenant takes free and clear of any claim in the Sheriff's hands against the deceased joint tenant: *Power* v *Grace*, [1932] O.R. 357, [1932] 2 D.L.R. 793.

These principles are all reviewed by Urquhart, J., in a case in bankruptcy, in *Re O'Brien*, [1943] O.W.N. 436, 24 C.B.R. 266. Urquhart, J., however, goes further in speaking of the Rules in *Re Craig* above and *Toronto Hospital* v *City of Toronto* above and *Power* v *Grace* above, wherein he says, 'but this rule only operates, in my opinion, in the case of death'. On that proposition, Urquhart, J., continues and says [pp 437–8 O.R.]:

By s 9(1) of the Execution Act, the writ binds the lands from the time of the delivery thereof, so that if the interest of the joint tenant is *exigible*, as appears to be the case, and the joint tenancy is thereby severable (see also *Re White*, 33 o.w.n. 255; 8 c.b.r. 544, [1928] i d.l.r. 846), then under this section any purchaser from the parties would take subject to the rights of the debtor's execution creditors.

[Italics added.] After some initial difficulty, I now accept completely the opinion of Urquhart, j., when he says, 'but this rule only operates, in my opinion, in the case of death'. My reasoning is that if the death of one of two joint tenants against whom a writ of execution has been filed in the Sheriff's hands occurs within the period of one year from the date of such filing, so that the surviving joint tenant takes free and clear any claim of the judgment creditor against the lands, then that result is brought about by operation of law. To open the door any wider would mean that one of two joint tenants against whom a writ of execution was filed in the Sheriff's hands could defeat the claims of his judgment creditor by his own act of joining in the sale of the lands with his joint tenant. I emphasize the distinction between the judgment creditor being defeated on the one hand by operation of law, and defeated on the other hand by the act of the judgment debtor. In the present case, to repeat the salient facts, Aurèle Breton suffered judgment on April 4, 1960. On August 8, 1960, the judgment debtor and his wife, as joint tenants, conveyed the said lands to the said wife Noella C. Breton. By so doing, they did not, in my opinion, defeat the execution creditor and, to quote again from the judgment of Urquhart, j., in the case of *Re O'Brien* above, 'any purchaser from the parties would take, subject to the rights of the debtor's execution creditor'.

QUESTIONS Section 10 of The Execution Act provides that the delivery of the writ of execution 'binds' the goods and lands of the judgment debtor. Why should the surviving joint tenant take free of the claims of prior execution creditors? If, as a matter of policy, the transferee of the joint interest of the judgment debtor takes subject to a writ of execution in the Sheriff's hands, why should the fortuitous death of one joint tenant exempt the survivor from the binding effect of the writ?

NOTE See also *Sunglo Lumber Ltd.* v *McKenna*, (1975), 48 d.l.r. (3d) 154, in which a British Columbia Court noted that it is as yet unclear what steps must have been taken in the execution process before a joint tenancy is severed. As a matter of policy, how far should the process have gone? Should the existence of an execution against one of the joint tenants ever be allowed to break up the arrangement intended by taking title in joint tenancy in the first place? The hardship possible was illustrated in *Sunglo*. There, a creditor proposed to sell the joint interest of an apparently deserting husband in the matrimonial home. The wife appeared (although she may have had no technical right to do so) and urged that the sale be stayed. The court refused to stay the sale. (See also: *Yuet* v *Louie*, [1973] 3 w.w.r. 574). What will happen to Mrs. McKenna after the sale?

NOTE Sales of joint interest on execution fetch very low prices. The usual prospect facing a purchaser is an action for partition and sale under The Partition Act, r.s.o. 1970, c 338, a time-consuming and costly process. In 1975, the Sheriff of the Judicial District of York sold the interest of a joint tenant of lands for $3,600, the highest bid; the average house price in the City of Toronto was then about $55,000. After the sale, the purchaser discovered that the non-debtor joint tenant had died just after the writ of execution was lodged and before any steps to enforce it had been taken. The purchaser had thus bought all interests in the land for $3,600! Consider the 'transaction costs' involved in this proceeding. Can they be justified?

QUESTION Is the interest of a joint tenant of chattels exigible?

ix Family Assets: In the spring of 1978, the Ontario Legislature enacted The Family Law Reform Act, 1978, S.O. 1978, c 2. The Act substantially revised the property rights *inter se* of spouses and of some cohabiting parties, by initiating a scheme of 'deferred community property'. The Act defines many assets to be 'family assets' and provides for a sharing of these assets upon breakup of the household. As well, spouses are given equal rights to possession of the 'matrimonial home'.

The Act leaves open for debate many questions about the exigibility of 'family assets' and the 'matrimonial home', and about priorities between executing creditors and the non-debtor spouse or co-resident. Consider the questions below in light of the statutory provisions reproduced immediately following them.

QUESTIONS

1 Jacky has a judgment against John. She files an execution against John. John then separates from his wife, Holly, and there is no reasonable prospect of the resumption of cohabitation between them. Jacky directs the sheriff to seize a bank account in John's name, the funds from which have frequently been used for household purposes. John and Holly contend that The Family Law Reform Act renders the funds not exigible. Will their argument succeed?

2 Would the answer to Q1 differ if Holly had commenced an action to declare the money in the account a 'family asset'? If the court had declared it to be a 'family asset'? If the court ordered that Holly was entitled to a 70% interest in the ('family asset') account?

3 Would your answers to Q1 or Q2 differ, if before the separation of John and Holly, the sheriff had served a notice of seizure on the bank? Would it matter whether or not the bank had paid the sheriff before the separation? Would your answers differ if the seizure or bank's payment took place at the respective times described in Q 2?

4 John and Holly lived in a house which had been registered solely in John's name. They separated just after Jacky's execution was filed. Can Jacky execute against the house? What are Holly's rights? Would it matter whether or not any of the actions described in Q2 had been taken by Holly? Would your answer be different if John and Holly had separated before Jacky's execution was filed? Would your answer to any of these questions be different if the house had originally been registered in Holly's name alone?

The Family Law Reform Act, 1978, S.O. 1978, c 2

2. (10) Where an order made under this Act affects real property, the order does not affect the acquisition of an interest in the real property by a person in good faith without notice of the order, unless the order is registered in the proper land registry office.

3. In this Part ...

(*b*) 'family assets' means a matrimonial home as determined under Part III and property owned by one spouse or both spouses and ordinarily used or enjoyed by both spouses or one or more of their children while the spouses are residing together for shelter or transportation or for household, educational, recreational, social or aesthetic purposes, and includes,

    (i) money in an account with a chartered bank, savings office, credit union or trust company where the account is ordinarily used for shelter or transportation or for household, educational, recreational, social or aesthetic purposes,

    (ii) where property owned by a corporation, partnership or trustee would, if it were owned by a spouse, be a family asset, shares in the corporation or an interest in the partnership or trust owned by the spouse having a market value equal to the value of the benefit the spouse has in respect of the property,

    (iii) property over which a spouse has, either alone or in conjunction with another person, a power of appointment exercisable in favour of himself or herself, if the property would be a family asset if it were owned by the spouse, and

    (iv) property disposed of by a spouse but over which the spouse has, either alone or in conjunction with another person, a power to revoke the disposition or a power to consume, invoke or dispose of the property, if the property would be a family asset if it were owned by the spouse,

but does not include property that the spouses have agreed by a domestic contract is not to be included in the family assets ...

4. (1) Subject to subsection 4, where a decree *nisi* of divorce is pronounced or a marriage is declared a nullity or where the spouses are separated and there is no reasonable prospect of the resumption of cohabitation, each spouse is entitled to have the family assets divided in equal shares notwithstanding the ownership of the assets by the spouses as determinable for other purposes and notwithstanding any order under section 7.

(2) The court may, upon the application of a person who is the spouse of another, determine any matter respecting the division of family assets between them.

(3) The rights under subsection 1 are personal as between the spouses but any application commenced under subsection 2 before the death of a spouse may be continued by or against the estate of the deceased spouse.

(4) The court may make a division of family assets resulting in shares that are not equal where the court is of the opinion that a division of the family assets in equal shares would be inequitable, having regard to,

(*a*) any agreement other than a domestic contract;

(*b*) the duration of the period of cohabitation under the marriage;

(*c*) the duration of the period during which the spouses have lived separate and apart;

(*d*) the date when the property was acquired;

(*e*) the extent to which property was acquired by one spouse by inheritance or by gift; or

(*f*) any other circumstance relating to the acquisition, disposition, preservation, maintenance, improvement or use of property rendering it inequitable for the division of family assets to be in equal shares.

(5) The purpose of this section is to recognize that child care, household management and financial provision are the joint responsibilities of the spouses and that inherent in the marital relationship there is joint contribution, whether financial or otherwise, by the spouses to the assumption of these responsibilities, entitling each spouse to an equal division of the family assets, subject to the equitable considerations set out in subsections 4 and 6.

(6) The court shall make a division of any property that is not a family asset where,

(*a*) a spouse has unreasonably impoverished the family assets; or (*b*) the result of a division of the family assets would be inequitable in all the circumstances, having regard to,

      (i) the considerations set out in clauses *a* to *f* of subsection 4, and

      (ii) the effect of the assumption by one spouse of any of the responsibilities set out in subsection 5 on the ability of the other spouse to acquire, manage, maintain, operate or improve property that is not a family asset.

6. In an application under section 4, the court may order,

(*a*) that the title to any specified property directed to a spouse in the division be transferred to or in trust for or vested in the spouse whether absolutely, for life or for a term of years;

(*b*) the partition or sale of any property;

(*c*) that payment be made out of the proceeds of sale to one or both spouses, and the amount thereof;

(*d*) that any property forming part of the share of either or both spouses be transferred to or in trust for or vested in a child to whom a spouse owes an obligation to provide support;

(*e*) that either or both spouses give security for the performance of any obligation imposed by the order, including a charge on property; and

(*f*) that either spouse pay to the other such sum as is set out in the order for the purpose of adjusting the division,

and may make such other orders or directions as are ancillary thereto ...

9. In or pending an application under section 4, 7 or 8, the court may make such interim order as it considers necessary for restraining the dissipation of the property and for the possession, delivering up, safekeeping and preservation of the property ...

11. (1) The rule of law applying a presumption of advancement in questions of the ownership of property as between husband and wife is abolished and in place thereof the rule of law applying a presumption of a resulting trust shall be applied in the same manner as if they were not married, except that,

(*a*) the fact that property is placed or taken in the name of spouses as joint tenants is *prima facie* proof that each spouse is intended to have on a severance of the joint tenancy a one-half beneficial interest in the property; and

(*b*) money on deposit in a chartered bank, savings office, credit union or trust company in the name of both spouses shall be deemed to be in the name of the spouses as joint tenants for the purposes of clause *a*.

(2) Subsection 1 applies notwithstanding that the event giving rise to the presumption occurred before this section comes into force ...

39. (1) Property in which a person has an interest and that is or has been occupied by the person and his or her spouse as their family residence is their matrimonial home.

(2) Subsection 1 applies notwithstanding that its application results in more than one matrimonial home ...

40. (1) A spouse is equally entitled to any right of possession of the other spouse in a matrimonial home ...

42. (1) No spouse shall dispose of or encumber any interest in a matrimonial home unless,

(*a*) the other spouse joins in the instrument or consents to the transaction;

(*b*) the other spouse has released all rights under this Part by a separation agreement;

(*c*) the transaction is authorized by court order or an order has been made releasing the property as a matrimonial home; or

(*d*) the property is not designated as a matrimonial home under section 41 and an instrument designating another property as a matrimonial home of the spouses is registered under section 41 and not cancelled.

(4) This section does not apply to the acquisition of an interest in property by operation of law or of a lien under section 18 of *The Legal Aid Act.*

43. (1) Where a person is proceeding to realize upon a lien, encumbrance or execution or exercises a forfeiture against property that is a matrimonial home, the spouse who has a right of possession by virtue of section 40 has the same right of redemption or relief against forfeiture as the other spouse has and is entitled to any notice respecting the claim and its enforcement or realization to which the other spouse is entitled.

(2) Any notice to which a spouse is entitled by virtue of subsection 1 shall be deemed to be sufficiently given if served or given personally or by registered mail addressed to the person to whom notice is to be given at his or her usual or last known address or, where none, the address of the matrimonial home, and, where notice is served or given by mail, the service shall be deemed to have been made on the fifth day after the day of mailing ...

(3) Where a spouse makes any payment by way of or on account of redemption or relief against forfeiture under the right conferred by subsection 1, the payment shall be applied in satisfaction of the claim giving rise to the lien, encumbrance, execution or forfeiture.

(4) Notwithstanding any other Act, where a person who commences a proceeding to realize upon a lien, encumbrance or execution or to exercise a forfeiture does not have sufficient particulars of a spouse entitled under subsection 1 for the purposes of the proceeding, and a notice given under subsection 2 is not responded to, the proceeding may continue in the absence of the spouse and without regard to the interest of the spouse and any final order in the proceeding terminates the rights of the spouse under this section.

45. (1) Notwithstanding the ownership of a matrimonial home and its contents, and notwithstanding section 40, the court on application may by order,

(a) direct that one spouse be given exclusive possession of a matrimonial home or part thereof for life or for such lesser period as the court directs and release any other property that is a matrimonial home from the application of this Part;

(e) authorize the disposition or encumbrance of the interest of a spouse in a matrimonial home subject to the right to exclusive possession of the other spouse as ordered; and

(3) An order under subsection 1 for exclusive possession may be made only if, in the opinion of the court, other provision for shelter is not adequate in the circumstances or it is in the best interests of a child to do so.

x Partnership Interests: Rule 551 prevents execution against the interest of one partner in a partnership. Instead a special procedure for making such an interest answerable for the partner's debt is provided. An order may be made charging the interest of the debtor in the partnership, and a receiver appointed to collect 'the partner's share of profits whether already declared or accruing and ... any money that may be coming to him in respect of the partnership.'

Sandham v *Sandham Bros.*, [1933] 3 D.L.R. 292 (Ont. C.A.)

MIDDLETON, J.A.: Motion by plaintiff for judgment in an undefended action, said to be made in pursuance of R. 63, which provides that, 'in default of appearance when the plaintiff's claim is for an account, the plaintiff may apply for a judgment for the taking of the account claimed, with all directions usual in similar cases.'

The circumstances giving rise to this action are unusual. Dorothy Sandham, the plaintiff, brought an action in this Court against Charles C. Sandham, her husband, and such proceedings were had in that action that an order was made by Raney, J., on March 24, 1933, directing payment of the sum of $120 on account of interim alimony and $100 for interim disbursements and also directing further payments by way of interim alimony. I am told, but it is not shown, that an execution was issued and placed in the hands of the sheriff.

Charles C. Sandham is said to be a member of the firm of Sandham Bros. and an order was made on April 7, 1933, by Jeffrey, J., supposedly under the authority of R. 556 which authorizes the making of an order charging the partner's interest in the partnership property and profits with the payment of the amount of executions in the sheriff's hands and further provides that, 'by the same or a subsequent order a receiver may be appointed of the partner's share of profits whether already declared or accruing and of any other money which may be coming to him (the execution debtor) in respect of the partnership, and the Court may direct all accounts and inquiries and give all such other directions as might be directed or given if the charge had been given by the partner.'

Instead of following the provisions of this Rule the order makes no reference to the execution but charges the share of Sandham 'with the payment of all moneys from time to time owing by the said Sandham to the plaintiff by virtue of the order made by the Honourable Mr. Justice Raney on March 24, 1933' and the plaintiff is by a subsequent clause appointed receiver without remuneration and without security to collect, get in and receive all moneys coming to Sandham in respect of his share of the profits of the partnership business whether already declared or accruing due and all other moneys which may be coming to him in respect of the partnership to the extent of the moneys payable under the earlier order and the costs of this order. This last clause which ignores the provisions of the Creditors Relief Act. R.S.O. 1927. c 113, is a device by which this particular creditor will be given a preference over any others who may have executions or who may desire to come in under the provisions of the Creditors Relief Act and share in the proceeds of any execution. It will be observed that for some reason this order stopped short at the making of the charging order and the appointment of the receiver and did not go farther and direct the taking of any account to ascertain the position of affairs as between the execution debtor and the partnership.

Before the passing of s 23 of the English Partnership Act, 1890 (Imp.). c 39, and here before the passing of R. 556 which follows in substance the same lines, the method of enforcing a judgment against the interest of a partner in the assets of a firm was exceedingly complicated and cumbrous. This section, according to the statement of Sir Frederick Pollock, was drafted by Lindley, L.J., for the purpose of clarifying and simplifying the situation and we are fortunate in having an explanation of the situation and of the section by Lindley, L.J., in the case of *Brown, Janson & Co. v Hutchinson & Co.*, [1895] 1 Q.B. 737, at pp 738–9. The procedure under the old practice is thus described: 'When a creditor obtained a judgment against one partner and he wanted to obtain the benefit of that judgment against the share of that partner in the firm, the first thing was to issue a fi. fa., and the sheriff went down to the partnership place of business, seized everything, stopped the business, drove the solvent partners wild, and caused the execution creditor to bring an action in Chancery in order to get an injunction to take an account and pay over that which was due by the execution debtor.'

The new statute 'puts a stop at once to all such proceedings' and a new and intelligible procedure is provided by which the Judge is empowered to make an order charging the party's interest with payment of the amount of the debt that has no immediate effect upon the co-partners at all. 'It simply amounts to this – that the interest of their co-partner in the business is charged just as if he had given an equitable charge over his interest. It does not harass or affect the other partners in the least. Then, in order to give effect to that charge, provision is made for the appointment of a receiver of that partner's share and profits. The effect of that is that the appointment of a receiver operates as an injunction against the execution debtor receiving anything from his co-partners, and if his co-partners pay over to him anything with knowledge of the appointment of the receiver they may get into trouble. But then that does not produce money, except money which the co-partners may hand over, or could hand over to the judgment debtor partner if it were not for the receiver. In order to get the full benefit of the charge, the second proceeds ... [as in our Rule] ... That means this – that an order may be made to take an account of what is due from the co-partners to the judgment debtor partner, and there is a clause (s 33, sub-s 2) which enables the solvent partners to treat that as a dissolution. There is a clause which enables the solvent partners to proceed, if they think fit, to get rid of the judgment debtor. That is the machinery provided' (pp 730–40) ...

As the practice under this Rule appears to be rather unsettled, I thought it desirable to investigate the matter at some little length and to emphasize the following points:

First. The only substantial difference between the English statute and ours is that an application may be made in England by a judgment creditor. Here the application can only be made by an execution creditor. This is for the purpose of making it plain that the benefit of proceedings will enure to the benefit of all execution creditors entitled to share under the Creditors Relief Act.

Second. The only proceedings that can, be taken are those authorized by the Rule and there is no authority for the bringing of an independent action by the receiver.

Third. Although the Court has discretion to direct the taking of an account such discretion ought not to be exercised so long as the partnership is still existing. It is hard to see what kind of an accounting the plaintiff can expect. What is to be done in ascertaining the outstanding liabilities of the firm? Are creditors' rights in any way to be affected? Are assets to be sold? As long as the partnership continues the rights of the debtor partner, it appears to me, cannot be ascertained. He can receive nothing. The situation will probably provoke a dissolution at the instance of the continuing partners but until it does nothing can be done.

Fifth. The material on this motion is entirely inadequate. The motion purports to be made under R. 63 but it is not shown that the writ was ever served, nor is it shown that there is any default in entering appearance. Strange to say a draft judgment entirely destructive of the partnership and in effect directing its dissolution and directing the partnership to pay the costs of this action is produced said to be approved by counsel on behalf of the defendants. If this is a correct result, it is an exceedingly serious thing when an action for alimony is brought or a divorce is sought against an individual member of a firm. The Divorce Act (Ontario), 1930 (Can.), c 14, dissolving the matrimonial partnership does not purport to interfere with a business partnership.

The general principle that future earnings cannot be reached by receivership is applicable. *Holmes* v *Millage*, [1893] 1 Q.B. 551: *Central Bank of Canada* v *Ellis* (1893), 20 A.R. (Ont.) 384. It is only the debtor's 'share of the profits whether already declared or accruing' and 'money which may be coming to' the debtor 'in respect of the partnership' that is taken. The motion should be turned into a motion for judgment and the action is dismissed without costs.

Action dismissed.

xi Company Shares

NOTE The owners of shares of joint stock companies possess 'rights' against their company (to dividends, to a percentage of the assets on dissolution, etc.). The owners of shares are usually given share certificates as evidence of the ownership of shares, and are registered in the corporation's register as owners. Standard clauses in corporate documents state that the company is entitled to treat the person registered as owner on the corporate register as owner of the shares, whatever may be the true state of beneficial ownership. Thus changes in the ownership of shares must be registered in the corporate register to be effective as against the company. Only then is the company required to treat the transferee as owner of the shares entitled to vote and receive dividends in respect of them.

Section 92 of The Business Corporations Act, R.S.O. 1970, c 53, requires the corporation to register the transfer if there is no notice of an adverse claim and if the transfer is not contrary to restrictions on transfer of shares.

If a transfer has not been registered but the shares have nevertheless been transferred, they cannot be seized in execution against the transferor: *Re Montgomery and Wrights Ltd.* (1917), 38 O.L.R. 335 (S.C.). However there is no reason why they should not be exigible in the hands of the transferee (s 14(1)).

If the debtor's shares are in a private company, the sheriff must first offer them for sale to the shareholders before selling them to the public (The Execution Act, s 15). However, problems arise if the shares themselves are subject to restrictions on transfer. Such restrictions are common in private (non-offering) companies and are permitted by s 189(1)(m) of The Business Corporations Act, and s 168(1) of the Canada Business Corporations Act. The same section of the federal Act provides that even a public corporation may by special resolution amend its articles to constrain transfer of its shares for any reason. Such a special resolution concerning restriction might require that any transferee be approved by the board of directors which may be authorized to withhold its consent for *any* reason or without giving reasons. Are such shares exigible, non-exigible, or exigible only upon condition that the restriction is met (e.g. that the board approves the sheriff's purchaser as transferee)?

This question was raised in *Re Phillips and La Paloma Sweets* (1921), 51 O.L.R. 125, (Ont. C.A.). Middleton, J held that the phrase 'transferable shares' in The Execution Act (then s 12, now s 14) applied only to 'freely transferable' shares and did not include shares subject to restriction on transfer. Thus, at least in earlier times, restricted transfer shares were not subject to execution.

On the other hand, in the more recent case of *Associates Finance Co. Ltd.* v *Webber et al.* (1972), 28 D.L.R. (3d) 673 (B.C.S.C.), infra, the Court, considering sections 17–23 of the British Columbia Execution Act, held that the right of the sheriff to seize and sell shares in a private corporation could not be defeated by provisions in the articles of association restricting the transfer of shares.

Associates Finance Co. Ltd. v *Webber et al.* (1972), 28 D.L.R. (3d) 673 (B.C.S.C.)

ANDERSON, J.: This is an *ex parte* application for the following relief:

A A Charging Order that all of the stock of the Defendant, Roy Webber in Grenada Lands Ltd., and Webber Realty Ltd., stand charged with the payment of the Plaintiff's Judgment herein, until payment, and costs;

B That Grenada Lands Ltd., and Webber Realty Ltd., be restrained from permitting a transfer of such stock until further Order of this Honourable Court.

C That unless the Defendant shall within fourteen days of the service of the Order sought herein on him show to this Honourable Court cause to the contrary, then upon proof of service of the Order, the Order sought shall be made absolute.

The facts are as follows:

1 The plaintiff obtained judgment on November 10, 1971, for the sum of $5,297.07.

2 The defendant Webber was examined in aid of execution on December 20, 1971.

3 The said defendant is a director of Grenada Lands Ltd. and owns 49 common shares in that company (49% of issued shares).

4 The said defendant is a director of Webber Realty Ltd. and owns 50 common shares in that company (50% of issued shares).

5 The articles of association of both companies are identical and restrict the transfer of shares as follows:

[The provisions of the articles of association are omitted.]

Counsel for the plaintiff frankly admits that there are judgments of the Supreme Court of British Columbia which indicate that charging orders will not be granted in respect of shares held by a judgment debtor in a private company because execution proceedings are available to the judgment creditor under the *Execution Act*, R.S.B.C. 1960, c 135. He submits that the language used in the judgments is *Obiter dicta* and that, therefore, I am not bound to follow the said judgments. Counsel for the plaintiff asks, in addition, that if I find that a charging order cannot be granted that I spell out clearly the rights of a judgment creditor under execution proceedings taken pursuant to ss 17 to 22 of the *Execution Act*.

This is an important matter because it requires the determination of the following issues:

1 Does the fact that the articles of association contain restrictions against the transfer of shares prohibit execution proceedings against those shares?

2 If execution proceedings are available, in the above circumstances, can the sale and registration of the sale be compelled?

3 If execution proceedings are available can a charging order be granted?

The relevant provisions of the *Execution Act* are as follows:

17. All corporations established for the purpose of trade or profit, or for the construction of any work, or for the acquisition of gain, shall be deemed incorporated companies for the purpose of sections 18 to 23, inclusive, although they are not called companies in the Act or charter incorporating them, or in their memorandum or articles of association.

18. All stock, shares, and dividends of shareholders in an incorporated company in the Province, having transferable joint stock or shares, shall be held to be personal property, and are liable to bona fide creditors for debts, and may be attached, seized, and sold under writs of execution in like manner as other personal property.

19. (1) The Sheriff to whom a writ of execution is addressed, on being informed on behalf of the plaintiff that the defendant has such stock or shares, and on being required to seize the same, shall forthwith serve a copy of the writ of execution on the incorporated company with a notice that all the stock or shares which the defendant has in the capital stock of the company are seized accordingly.

(2) From the time of service no transfer of the stock or shares by the defendant shall be valid, unless the seizure has been discharged.

(3) Every seizure and sale made under the same shall include all dividends, premiums, bonuses, or other pecuniary profits upon the stock or shares seized, and the same shall not, after notice as aforesaid, be paid by the company to anyone except the person to whom the stock or shares have been sold by the Sheriff, unless the seizure is discharged, on pain of paying the same twice.

20. If the incorporated company has more than one place where service of process may be made upon it, and there is some place where transfers of stock or shares may be notified to and entered by the company so as to be valid as regards the company, or where dividends or profits as aforesaid on the stock or shares may be paid other than the place where service of such notice has been made, the notice does not affect any transfer or payment of dividends or profits duly made and entered at any such other place, so as to subject the company to pay twice, or to affect the rights of any bona fide purchaser, until after the expiration of a period from the time of service sufficient for the transmission of notice of service by post from the place where it has been made to such other place, which notice it is the duty of the company to transmit by post.

21. The stock or shares in the said capital stock shall be held to be personal property, found by the Sheriff in the place where notice of the seizure thereof is served as aforesaid.

22. Where any such stock or share is sold under a writ of execution, the Sheriff by whom the writ has been executed shall, within ten days after sale, serve upon the incorporated company, at some place where service of process may be made, an attested copy of the writ of execution, with his certificate endorsed thereon, certifying the name of the purchaser, who is thereafter the holder of the stock or share, and has the same rights and is under the same obligations as if he had duly purchased the stock or share from the proprietor thereof; and the proper officer of the company shall enter such sale as a transfer in the manner by law provided.

23. Nothing in this Act shall be construed to impair the remedy which the plaintiff might, without this Act, have had against any stock or shares in such capital stock as aforesaid, by charging order, attachment, or otherwise, and sections 19 to 20, inclusive, apply to such remedy in so far as they can be applied thereto.

In the case of *Annett* v *Randall* (unreported), on June 30, 1952, Macfarlane, J., refused to make a charging order on the ground, *inter alia*, that execution could be taken against shares in private companies. At p 2 of his judgment he said in part:

The *Execution Act*, R.S.B.C. 1948, c 114, ss 17 to 23, declares that all shares in any incorporated company in the Province, having transferable joint stock or shares ... may be attached, seized and sold under writs of execution in like manner as other personal property. It then establishes a procedure for seizure and sale of shares and for the completion of sale and transfer. If these shares were still in the name of the judgment debtor unencumbered or if he had the legal estate in these shares, then the process indicated by these sections must be followed: *vide, Spiers* v *The Queen* (1896), 4 B.C.R. 388 at p 395, where Davie, C.J., says:
'The Execution Act confers a new right upon a judgment creditor and points out the manner in which such right is to be executed, and according to well recognized legal principles where a right is conferred by a statute, and the method of enforcing that right is enacted by the said statute, that is the method you can adopt, and no other, see *Ross* v *Rugge-Price*, 1 Ex. Div. 269; and also Maxwell on Statutes, 3rd Ed. p 521 ...'

At p. 6 of his judgment he said:

If the provisions of s 16 are to be interpreted as applicable to shares it would seem to me that the equity in the shares of any judgment debtor would be liable to seizure and sale under writs of execution and such remedy would be available under the provisions of our *Execution Act*. In such an event, there would be no need for a charging order. There would be no need likewise for proceeding by way of equitable execution. If such is the case, the order would not be available because of the provisions of the *Execution Act* for the reasons which I have indicated earlier *vide Spiers* v *The Queen, supra.*

At p 8 of his judgment he said: 'I think that the sections in our *Execution Act* do permit the issuance of execution on the judgment against the interest of the judgment debtor in these shares.' ...

The judgments in the above cases, while dealing with the refusal by a company to transfer shares seized by the Sheriff, do not make it clear that there was a restriction in the articles with respect to the transfer of shares. In the Australian case of *Ex p. Trevascus* (1879), 5 V.L.R. 195 (Supreme Court at Law), this issue was faced squarely by the Court. In that case, the shares had to be first offered to existing shareholders before a stranger could purchase them, and in argument counsel for the company contended as follows at p. 198:

As to the other condition, that shares are to be first offered to the company, that is a condition to prevent undesirable members being thrust into the company. The shareholder becomes such upon the condition (among others), that there shall be no transfer of the share until it has first been offered to the company, and he must abide by it. As to the effect of the sale by the bailiff, of course, property cannot be shut out from the general operation of law; but the question is, whether a purchaser can, by operation of law, be thrust into a partnership in this way. Sec. 81 of the '*County Court Statute* 1869' expressly enacts that the transfer by the bailiff shall be a valid transfer to all intents and purposes as *if such transfer had been made by the holder*, that is, subject to the same conditions; and that is all we contend for. No legislation makes shares in a company transferable by the mere will of the holder. This transfer may be fully operative as against the former holder, and give a right, as against him, to all profits arising from the share, without compelling the other shareholders to accept the transferee as one of themselves – to do something which they have agreed shall not be done – something contrary to the constitution of the corporation.

The judgment of Stawell, C.J., at p. 199 reads as follows:

I think this application should be granted. The power of the company to decline to register a transfer, can apply only to a voluntary transfer, not to a transfer *in invitum*. The conditions must not be construed so as to defeat the common law rights of a judgment creditor, unless the words of the Act leave no alternative. The condition allowing the company to decline to register a transfer by a shareholder indebted to it, applies only to an indebtedness *qua* member. The whole purview of the Act is confined to matters among the members *inter se*. It was never intended to give the company, as to debts outside the constitution of the company, a preferential claim above all other creditors.

In the Ontario case, *Re Phillips and La Paloma Sweets Ltd.* (1921), 66 D.L.R. 577, 51 O.L.R. 125, it was held by Middleton, J., that the directors of a private company will not be forced by mandatory order to record the transfer of shares in the company seized by the Sheriff under an execution and subsequently sold to a third party. At pp 578–9 D.L.R., pp 126–8 O.R. his judgment reads as follows:

Under the statute (the Ontario Companies Act, R.S.O. 1914, ch. 178) a 'private company' is one in which, *inter alia*, 'the right to transfer its shares is restricted,' sec. 2(*c*) (i); and by sec. 56(1), shares are to be transferable 'in such manner and subject to such conditions and restrictions as by this Act ... (or) the letters patent ... may be prescribed.'

The provision in the charter is, therefore, valid.

It is elementary law that an execution creditor, apart from some statutory provision, has no greater right than the execution debtor, and that the sheriff's sale can only give to the purchaser the right and title of the debtor; so here the applicant has no greater or other right than the execution debtor unless he can point to some statute assisting him.

The case law is collected and discussed in Lindley on the Law of Companies, 6th ed., vol. 1, p 647, and it is there stated as the result that when by the constitution of the company the consent of the directors is required, 'the power of assenting or dissenting to a transfer is reposed in them as trustees, and they must exercise that power accordingly, and not capriciously. At the same time, if their consent to a transfer is necessary, and, in giving or refusing their consent to a transfer, they act *bona fide*, with a view to the protection of the interests of the company, the exercise of their discretion will not be interfered with ... If the directors refuse their consent to a transfer they are not bound to state their reasons for refusal ...; if their conduct is questioned the onus of proving that they have acted improperly is on the person complaining of their conduct.'

In the case of a private company the situation is not essentially different from a partnership, and it is almost impossible to imagine any case in which the Court would interfere unless some flagrantly improper motive could be shewn, e.g., an attempt by the directors to force a sale to themselves at a gross undervaluation. No suggestion of *mala fides* is here made.

Reliance is placed upon the provisions of the Execution Act, R.S.O. 1914, ch. 80, sec. 12 *et seq.* That statute provides only for the seizure and sale of 'transferable shares.' That, I think, does not include shares which can be transferred only with the consent of the directors, but applies only to shares which the debtor can freely transfer. The provision found in the Companies Act, sec. 60, must be regarded as subordinate to the wider provision in sec. 56(1), and cannot be intended to conflict with the power which it gives to restrict the right to transfer.

It is said that this will leave an execution creditor of a shareholder in such a company without remedy. I do not think that that is so, as a receiver may be appointed to receive all dividends payable. Apart from the statute, this was the only remedy of the creditor of one member of partnership.

I am not prepared to follow the judgment of Middleton, J., for the following reasons:

1 While Macfarlane, J., did not refer to *Re Phillips and La Paloma Sweets, Ltd., supra*, in either of his judgments, I am convinced that as Macfarlane, J., was a most careful Judge that he would not have overlooked that case.

2 The reasoning in *Ex p. Trevascus, supra*, appeals to me.

3 The word 'transferable' should not bear the restricted interpretation placed upon it by Middleton, J. As Lush, L.J., said giving judgment in *Gathercole v Smith* (1881), 17 Ch.D. 1 at p 9: 'The word "transferable," I agree with Lord Justice James, is a word of the widest import, and includes every means by which the property may be passed from one person to another.'

4 There are no restrictions in the *Execution Act*, which would have the effect of limiting the plain meaning of s 22 of the said Act, which clearly requires 'the proper officer of the company to enter such sale [by the Sheriff] as a transfer in the manner by law provided.'

[An analysis of the historical background is omitted.]

6 'Execution' does not mean 'seizure' but 'seizure and sale'. The present practice of the Sheriff seizing shares in private companies and holding them in his custody is not correct. His duty is to seize and sell, in accordance with the articles of association (save those articles which absolutely prohibit transfers at the discretion of the directors) by which he is not bound.

7 The *Execution Act* was intended to overcome the obstacles confronting creditors resulting from the cumbersome procedures required to be followed in respect of charging orders granted pursuant to the *Judgments Act*, 1838 (U.K.), c 110. Section 23 of the *Execution Act* is not a limiting section and, therefore, ss 17 to 22 inclusive of the said Act must have been intended to give additional remedies to a judgment creditor.

I am not unaware that there is considerable force behind the contention that the freedom of the shareholders of a private company to remain a closed group would be jeopardized by following *Ex p. Trevascus, supra.* As against this contention, is the judgment creditor to be deprived of his right to have his judgment satisfied because of the existence of an alleged doctrine that shareholders may remain a 'closed' group regardless of all other factors?

It seems to me that the historical background of this matter indicates that it must have been the intention of the Legislature to infringe on the alleged right to remain a 'closed' group. The 'closed' group does, after all, have the first right to purchase in accordance with the articles of association.

If I am wrong in my opinion that the *Execution Act* compels the transfer of shares to a stranger (if the 'closed' group does not buy) great prejudice would accrue to the judgment debtor. In accordance with the judgments of Macfarlane, J., in *Annett* v *Randall, supra,* and *Gould, Thorpe and Easton et al.* v *Ablitt* (1958), 26 W.W.R. 274, the shares of the judgment debtor could be seized and sold but the purchaser could not obtain registration of his shares. In these circumstances the purchaser could obtain an order directing how the shares could be voted and no dividends could be paid out to the judgment debtor. It follows that for practical purposes the judgment debtor would be deprived of most of his rights as a shareholder but for practical reasons, the 'bid' price for the shares would be much lower than if the shares could be transferred on the books of the company to the purchaser.

I have read the article by C.R.B. Dunlop, entitled 'Some Aspects of the Charging Order as a Remedy for Unsecured Creditors', *U.B.C. Law Review* (1967), vol. 3, p. 83, where this matter is thoroughly reviewed. I have also examined Fraser & Stewart, *Canadian Company Law,* 5th ed. (1960), pp 266 to 268, and Lindley, *Law of Companies,* 6th ed. (1902), vol. 1, at p 647. The said article and the passages referred to in the texts have not caused me to change my opinion.

In conclusion, I would add that, in my view, the modern trend of our jurisprudence is to, where possible, prevent the use of restrictive corporate devices which have the effect of defeating the rights of creditors. The right to remain a 'closed' corporation is a privilege granted by the Legislature, subject to a condition imposed by the same Legislature that the shares held by a judgment debtor may be seized and sold in execution proceedings and that the purchaser of the shares has the right to become a registered shareholder.

A perusal of the transcript of the examination of the judgment debtor in aid of execution, indicates that the two corporations, in which the said debtor is a '50%' shareholder, have substantial assets. In my opinion, the judgment debtor should not be entitled to evade his creditors by merely stating: 'As a director of Grenada Lands Ltd., I decline to permit the transfer of my shares to the person who purchased them from the Sheriff.'

In the result, the application for a charging order is refused. The plaintiff has his remedy pursuant to ss 17 to 22 of the *Execution Act,* which, as I have already stated, oblige the Sheriff to

seize and sell the shares in accordance with the articles of association. The company cannot refuse to register the transfer merely because the articles provide that the directors may decline to accept any transfer.
Application dismissed.

For a comment on this case: see Slutsky, 'Note on *Associates Finance* v *Webber*' (1972), 30 *The Advocate* 240.

QUESTIONS
1 Section 15 of Ontario's *Execution Act* was enacted after the decision in *La Paloma Sweets* (s.o. 1929, c 35, s 4). Does it effectively nullify a restriction on share transfers and permit unrestrained execution by the sheriff? What does 'private company' mean? There is no definition of this term in the The Execution Act. Should the definition provided in The Securities Act, R.S.O. 1970, c 426, s 1(1)14 be applied? (It should also be noted that the term 'private company' is no longer strictly applicable under The Business Corporations Act, R.S.O. 1970, c 53. Companies are now classified as 'offering' or 'non-offering' depending upon whether or not shares are sold to the public.)
2 Can the sheriff seize restricted shares in federal or extra-provincial companies?

NOTE In situations where execution against corporate shares is impossible, difficult or unwieldly, a creditor may be able to use a form of equitable execution (a charging order on the shares themselves, or a receiver in respect of dividend payments): see Chapter 11, below.

d / Purchasers of Goods from the Sheriff

i Introductory Note: Consider the position of a purchaser of goods from the Sheriff at an execution sale. The goods purchased may have been subject to prior rights at the time of seizure by the Sheriff, such as those arising out of a chattel mortgage or conditional sales contract. What is the relationship between holders of those prior rights and the rights of the purchaser? Can the prior rights be enforced against the purchaser or against others who subsequently buy from the purchaser?

In the absence of legislation to the contrary, the general rule is that a purchaser from the Sheriff can acquire only such legal and equitable right, title and interest as the debtor possessed at the time of sale (or perhaps at the time of the goods being 'bound' by the execution, if the debtor had larger rights which he had not validly passed on to a 'protected purchaser'): *Continental Trust Co.* v *Mineral Products Co.* (1904), 3 N.B. Eq. 28, aff'd (1905), 37 N.B. 140, aff'd (1906), 37 S.C.R. 517; *Jones Bros. (Holloway) Ltd.* v *Woodhouse*, [1923] 2 K.B. 117.

Before 1976, the principal Ontario statutes bearing on the question of the priority of antecedent security interests were The Bills of Sale and Chattel Mortgages Act, R.S.O. 1970, c 45, and The Conditional Sales Act, R.S.O. 1970, c 76 (both repealed by proclamation effective April 1, 1976). Under both statutes, a properly registered security interest – whether that of a chattel mortgagee or conditional seller – took priority over a purchaser at an execution sale. This order of priority seems fair enough;

an execution purchaser ought to be treated no better than an ordinary purchaser from the debtor, who would take title subject to validly created and registered security interests.

However, where the security interest was not properly registered, the title obtained by an execution purchaser without notice of the security interest depended on the nature of the interest. Where the interest arose under a chattel mortgage, the execution purchaser took priority over the secured party: see The Bills of Sale and Chattel Mortgages Act, ss 1(b), 8. But where the interest arose under a conditional sales contract, the secured party took priority: see The Conditional Sales Act, s 2; *Commercial Credit Corp.* v *Niagara Finance Co.*, [1940] 3 D.L.R. 1 (S.C.C.). There seemed little basis for distinguishing in this way between the two types of interests, and in fact, the conditional sales legislation of most other provinces protects an execution creditor against the interest of an unregistered conditional seller.

ii The Personal Property Security Act, R.S.O. 1970, c 344, as amended: The validity and priority of all consensual security interests in personal property (with limited exceptions) are now governed by The Personal Property Security Act, (proclaimed in force effective April 1, 1976). The relevant provisions of the Act follow:

2. Subject to subsection 1 of section 3, this Act applies
(*a*) to every transaction without regard to its form and without regard to the person who has title to the collateral that in substance creates a security interest, including, without limiting the foregoing.
   (i) a chattel mortgage, conditional sale, equipment trust, floating charge, pledge, trust deed or trust receipt, and
   (ii) an assignment, lease or consignment intended as security; and
(*b*) to every assignment of book debts not intended as security, but not to an assignment for the general benefit of creditors to which *The Assignments and Preferences Act* applies.
12. (1) A security interest attaches when,
(*a*) the parties intend it to attach;
(*b*) value is given; and
(*c*) the debtor has rights in the collateral.
21. A security interest is perfected when,
(*a*) it has attached; and
(*b*) all steps required for perfection under any provision of this Act have been completed, regardless of the order of occurrence.
22. (1) Except as provided in subsection 3, an unperfected security interest is subordinate to,
(*a*) the interest of a person,
   (i) who is entitled to a priority under this or any other Act, or
   (ii) who, without knowledge of the security interest and before it is perfected, assumes control of the collateral through legal process, or
   (iii) who represents the creditors of the debtor as assignee for the benefit of creditors, trustee in bankruptcy or receiver; and
(*b*) the interest of a transferee who is not a secured party to the extent that he gives value without knowledge of the security interest and before it is perfected,

  (i) of chattel paper, documents of title, securities, instruments or goods in bulk or otherwise, not in the ordinary course of the business of the transferor and where the transferee receives delivery of the collateral, or

  (ii) of intangibles.

(2) The rights of a person under subclause iii of clause *a* of subsection 1 in respect of the collateral are referable to the date from which his status has effect and arise without regard to the personal knowledge of the representative if any represented creditor was, on the relevant date, without knowledge of the unperfected security interest.

(3) A purchase-money security interest that is registered before or within ten days after the debtor's possession of the collateral commences has priority over,

 (*a*) an interest set out in subclause ii or iii of clause *a* of subsection 1; and

 (*b*) transfers in bulk or otherwise, not in the ordinary course of business, occurring between the security interest's attaching and its being registered.

24. Except as provided in section 26, possession of the collateral by the secured party, or on his behalf by a person other than the debtor or the debtor's agent, perfects a security interest in,

 (*a*) chattel paper;

 (*b*) goods;

 (*c*) instruments;

 (*d*) securities;

 (*e*) letters of credit and advices of credit; or

 (*f*) negotiable documents of title,

but, subject to section 23, only during its actual holding as collateral.

25. (1) Subject to section 21, registration perfects a security interest in,

 (*a*) chattel paper;

 (*b*) goods;

 (*c*) intangibles; or

 (*d*) documents of title.

(2) A security interest is not perfected until it is registered except in the case of a security interest,

 (*a*) in collateral in possession of the secured party under section 24; or

 (*b*) temporarily perfected in instruments, securities or negotiable documents of title under section 26.

64. (1) Except as otherwise provided herein, this Act applies only to a security agreement made on or after the day on which this section comes into force, and does not apply to a security agreement made before such day.

(2) Subject to section 65, a security agreement made before the day on which this section comes into force that required a registration in order to comply with *The Assignment of Book Debts Act, The Bills of Sale and Chattel Mortgages Act* or *The Conditional Sales Act* continues to have such force and effect as if those Acts had not been repealed if a financing statement is registered pursuant to this Act within ninety days after the execution of the security agreement, and section 63 applies, *mutatis mutandis*, in respect to any extension of such time.

65. (1) Where a security interest was covered by an unexpired filing or registration under *The Assignment of Book Debts Act, The Bills of Sale and Chattel Mortgages Act* or *The Conditional Sales Act* and in respect of which a financing statement was filed before section 18 of the Statutes of Ontario, 1973, chapter 102, comes into force,

 (*a*) the financing statement and any filed financing change statement relating thereto shall be deemed to be registered; and (*b*) the security interest to which the financing statement relates shall be deemed to be perfected,

under this Act and subject to this Act, the effect of the prior filing or registration is continued for the unexpired portion of the filing or registration period.

(2) Upon the request of any person and upon payment of the prescribed fee, any chattel mortgage registered under *The Bills of Sale and Chattel Mortgages Act*, any contract registered under *The Conditional Sales Act* or any assignment of book debts registered under *The Assignment of Book Debts Act* shall, subject to section 67, be provided for inspection.

The concept of perfection is central to the operation of the Act. By s 21, a security interest is perfected when it has attached and when all steps required for perfection have been completed; where goods seized by the sheriff are concerned, perfection will normally occur on registration of the interest (s 25). By s 22(1)(a)(ii), an unperfected security interest is subordinate to the interest of a person who without knowledge of the security interest assumes control of the collateral through legal process. 'Legal process' includes the process of execution and sale, and this means, in essence, that where the prior interest is registered, it will prevail over the interest of an execution purchaser, but where no registration has taken place, an execution purchaser will take priority.

Until the section has been authoritatively construed, however, its precise meaning will remain in doubt. In order to succeed against the holder of a prior security interest, the purchaser must 'assume control' before the interest is perfected. Does this involve taking actual possession of the collateral after the sale? or will the sale itself suffice? Or perhaps just the Sheriff's seizure or the issue of a writ of execution? Should the answer depend on the nature of the collateral? For commentary on s 22 and the remainder of the Act, see Catzman et al., *Personal Property Security Law in Ontario* (1976).

It should be noted that under the transitional provisions of the Act, the priority of certain security interests may still fall to be determined by The Bills of Sale and Chattel Mortgages Act and The Conditional Sales Act: see ss 64, 65.

iii The Problem of Renewals: Under The Bills of Sale and Chattel Mortgages Act, priorities problems arose when renewals of chattel mortgages were not filed or were filed late. The Act provided that unless a renewal was filed within a prescribed period, a registered mortgage ceased to be valid after one year as against creditors of the mortgagor and as against subsequent purchasers and mortgagees in good faith for valuable consideration (s 25(1)), though a late renewal could be filed with the permission of a judge (s 25(11)). The consequences of a late renewal varied. It preserved the priority of the mortgagee where no further credit was advanced to the mortgagor in the interval between expiry and renewal: *Re Dainty Confections Ltd.* (1936), 18 C.B.R. 67 (Ont. C.A.). However, where the mortgagor made an assignment in bankruptcy in that interval, the mortgage was valid as against the trustee in bankruptcy but not as against creditors who had advanced credit during that time: *Re Durocher* (1957), 36 C.B.R. 122 (S.C.O.).

Under The Personal Property Security Act, the question of when credit is advanced is no longer relevant. The applicable provisions of the Act, in addition to those set out supra, are the following:

52. Where a security interest has been perfected by registration, the registration may be renewed,

(*a*) before the expiration of the registration period, by the registration of a financing change statement in the prescribed form; or

(*b*) notwithstanding subsection 3 of section 47, after the expiration of the registration period, by the registration of a financing statement in the prescribed form.

53. (1) Where the collateral is other than instruments, securities, letters of credit, advices of credit or negotiable documents of title, registration under this Act of,

(*a*) a financing statement constitutes,

(i) notice of the security interest to which it relates to all persons claiming any interest such collateral, and

(ii) subject to section 21, perfection of the security interest,

during the period of three years following such registration;

(*b*) a financing change statement under clause *a* of section 52 extends the effect of the registration of the financing statement to which it relates during the period of three years following the registration of the financing change statement;

(*c*) a financing statement under clause *b* of section 52 extends the effect of the registration of the original financing statement during the period of three years following the registration of the financing statement under clause *b* of section 52, but when such registration has prejudiced the rights that any person acquired by an act or thing done by him during the period that the security interest was unperfected, the registration shall be presumed not to have occurred for the purpose of obtaining such rights ...

(2) For the purposes of this section, the period of three years in respect of the registration of a financing statement or a financing change statement is a period of time commencing with the time assigned to the registration of the statement by the registrar or branch registrar and ending with the expiry of the third anniversary of the date of the registration.

The effect of these sections is that after the three year registration period, the security interest is no longer perfected unless a statement has been filed in accordance with s 52(a). Late renewals are permitted by s 52(b), and these ordinarily reach back to cure the unperfected period: s 53(1)(c). But because of the proviso in s 53(1)(c), a security interest renewed late will be subordinate to the interest of an execution purchaser within s 22(1)(a)(ii) or a trustee in bankruptcy within s 22(1)(a)(iii) where the purchaser assumed control of the collateral or the estate became bankrupt in the period between expiration and renewal.

iv Interpleader: The sheriff can incur liability by seizing property which does not belong to the debtor. In a case where title is contested, the sheriff's safest course is to interplead. He is expressly permitted to do so (R. 632).

In interpleader proceedings, the Court decides which of competing claims has the highest entitlement. If the sheriff receives a third party claim to assets seized, he will notify the executing creditor. If the creditor admits the claim, the property will be returned to the claimant, and the sheriff is free from any liability in respect of the seizure (R. 644). The Rules do not stipulate that the sheriff is free from liability if the matter goes on to trial. However, the sheriff may be protected under the provisions of The Public Authorities Protection Act (infra, p 276).

In practice, the sheriff is usually very careful. He will not seize goods without an express direction from the creditor and many sheriffs will only seize after an indemnity agreement has been signed by the creditor's lawyer personally, agreeing to save the sheriff harmless in respect of any liability which the sheriff might incur as a result of the directed seizure. There seems to be no authority for the sheriff's exaction of such indemnity agreements. However, a limited right to demand a bond is given by s 20 of The Execution Act when seizure of property in the possession of a third party is requested. Should the sheriff be entitled to such bonds?

In England the sheriff may apply to a judge or master for an order 'protecting him from any action in respect to the said seizure and possession of said goods' (R.S.C., Ord. 57, r 16A). This immunity, however, is not absolute. Orders will only be given when damage caused by the sheriff is minor: *Cave* v *Capel*, [1954] 1 All E.R. 428 (C.A.).

Is this a better idea?

Ontario Supreme Court, Rules of Practice, R.R.O. 1970, Reg. 545.

INTERPLEADER

Rule 632

Relief by way of interpleader may be granted.
- (*a*) where the person seeking relief (hereinafter called the applicant) is under liability for any debt, money, goods or chattels, for or in respect of which he is, or expects to be, sued by two or more persons (hereinafter called the claimants) making adverse claim thereto; or
- (*b*) where the applicant is a sheriff and claim is made to any money, goods or chattels, lands or tenements, taken or intended to be taken in execution under a writ of execution, or to the proceeds or value thereof, by any person other than the person against whom the process issued.

Rule 633

The applicant shall satisfy the court by affidavit or otherwise,
- (*a*) that he claims no interest in the subject-matter in dispute, other than in respect of a lien or for charges or costs;
- (*b*) that he does not collude with any of the claimants; and
- (*c*) that he is willing to pay or transfer the subject-matter into court, or to dispose of it as the court directs.

Rule 636

The applicant may make a motion calling on the claimants to appear and state the nature and particulars of their claims, and either to maintain or relinquish them.

Rule 612

Where a sheriff applies for relief by interpleader and any execution creditor declines to join in contesting the claim of the adverse claimant, the court may direct that such creditor be excluded from any benefit that may be derived from the contestation of the claim.

Rule 644

When a sheriff finds property in the possession of a debtor against whose property he has a writ or other process in his hands, and claim is set up to such property by or on behalf of a third person who is out of possession or is in joint possession with the debtor, the claim of such third person shall be made in writing, and upon receipt thereof the sheriff shall forthwith give notice thereof to the execution creditor, and the execution creditor shall, within seven days thereafter, give notice to the sheriff that he admits or disputes the claim, and, if the execution creditor admits the title of the claimant and gives notice as directed by this rule, he is only liable to the sheriff for fees and expenses incurred before the receipt of the notice admitting the claim, and no action shall be brought against the sheriff in respect of the seizure of the property.

Rule 645

Where the execution creditor does not in due time admit or dispute the title of the claimant to the property and the claimant does not withdraw his claim thereto by notice in writing to the sheriff, the sheriff may apply for relief by interpleader.

Rule 647

Where there is an execution from the Supreme Court, the application for interpleader shall be made in the Supreme Court notwithstanding that other executions in the sheriff's hands have issued from county or small claims courts. [Amended o. Reg. 761/73, s 1.]

Rule 648

(1) Where an issue is directed to be tried, the costs of the sheriff incurred in consequence of the adverse claim are a first lien or charge upon the moneys or goods that may be found in the issue to be applicable upon the execution.

(2) The sheriff may also tax such costs, and serve a copy of the certificate of taxation upon each of the parties to the issue, and the successful party upon the issue shall tax such costs as part of his costs of the cause, and upon receipt of the costs shall pay them over to the sheriff.

(3) Where after the service of the certificate the party succeeding upon the issue neglects or refuses to tax such costs, the sheriff may obtain an order that the successful party pay them.

(4) Where the proceedings are compromised between the parties thereto, the costs of the sheriff shall be paid by the party by whom the execution was issued.

Rule 649

Where, after the seizure, an issue is directed, and the property seized remains, pending the trial of the issue, in the custody of the sheriff who seized the property, the court may make an order for the payment to the sheriff of a reasonable sum for his trouble in and about the custody of the property, and the sheriff has a lien upon the property for payment of the same in the event that the property is held to be exigible against the claimant.

Rule 650

The court may make all such orders respecting the satisfaction or payment of any lien or charges of the applicant as are just and reasonable.

Rule 653

Where the amount claimed under or by virtue of writs of execution in the sheriff's hands does not exceed the sum of $1200, exclusive of interest and sheriff's costs, or when the goods seized are not, in the opinion of the judge or other person making the order, of the value of more than $400, the issue may be directed to be tried in a county court, and in such case all subsequent proceedings shall be had and taken in the county court.

Rule 654
Where the amount of the execution or the value of the goods does not exceed $200, the issue may be directed to be tried in a small claims court, and thereafter all proceedings shall be carried on in such court.

Rule 655
Where money has been paid into court and an issue has been directed to be tried in the county or small claims court, the money shall be paid out upon the order of the county or small claims court.

The Public Authorities Protection Act, R.S.O. 1970, c 374, as amended.

11. (1) No action, prosecution or other proceeding lies or shall be instituted against any person for an act done in pursuance or execution or intended execution of any statutory or other public duty or authority, or in respect of any alleged neglect or default in the execution of any such duty or authority, unless it is commenced within six months next after the cause of action arose, or, in case of continuance of injury or damage, within six months after the ceasing thereof.

(2) Subsection 1 does not apply to an action, prosecution or proceeding against,

(*a*) a sheriff for an act, neglect or default in certifying as to a writ of execution that binds land

...

16. A sheriff or his officer acting under a writ of execution or other process shall be deemed to be a person acting in the discharge of a public duty or authority within the meaning of this Act.

NOTE By s 2 of S.O. 1976, c 19, s 11(2) of The Public Authorities Protection Act 'applies in respect of causes of action arising before or after [the legislation adding s 11(2)] comes into force'.

The Execution Act, R.S.O. 1970, c 152

20. (1) A sheriff is not, without written instructions and a bond as hereinafter mentioned, obliged to seize property in the possession of a third person claiming it and not in the possession of the debtor against whose property the execution was issued.

(2) The instructions shall specify the property in such a way as to enable the sheriff to identify it.

(3) The bond shall be a bond of indemnity to the sheriff and his assigns, with two sufficient sureties who shall justify in double the value of the property, and the value shall be stated in an affidavit by the creditor or his solicitor or agent attached to the bond.

(4) The bond shall be assignable to the claimant, and shall be conditioned that the persons executing it shall be liable for the damages, costs and expenses that the sheriff or the claimant may be put to by the seizure and subsequent proceedings, including interpleader proceedings, if any, and which he does not recover from other persons who ought to pay them.

(5) If the sheriff is not satisfied with the bond offered, the matter in difference shall be determined by a judge of the county or district court of the county or district.

(6) Nothing in this section limits the rights of the sheriff to apply for relief by interpleader.

e / Functions and Responsibilities of the Sheriff

i Relationship With the Execution Creditor: When a writ of *fi.fa.* is lodged with the sheriff, the sheriff will usually attend on the debtor, see what assets appear to be available for execution, and report back to the execution creditor. Seizure will usually only be made on the express direction of the creditor or his lawyers (see excerpts from sheriff's file below at pp 466–96). As mentioned above, some sheriffs will require a personal bond from the creditor's lawyer, agreeing to indemnify the sheriff in respect of any liability which he may incur as a result of seizing as directed by the creditor. There is no statutory authority for such bonds. Why would a lawyer sign one?

Morris v *Salberg* (1899), 22 Q.B.D. 614 (C.A.)

LORD ESHER, M.R.: In this case the sheriff was directed by a writ of fieri facias to seize the goods of the judgment debtor, but he has seized the goods of the wrong person. The question is whether the execution creditor is liable in respect of such wrongful seizure. The writ directed the sheriff to seize the goods of G.M. Morris. The execution creditor's solicitor indorsed on the back of the writ a description, which, I apprehend, is no part of the writ, in the following terms: 'The defendant is a gentleman who resides at Sarnau Park, Llandyssil, Cardigan, South Wales.' The residence so given was not that of the execution debtor but that of his father. The question is whether that indorsement on the writ was a direction to the sheriff or not.

The question in any case whether it does amount to a direction to seize the particular goods seized appears to be a question of fact for the jury or other tribunal which has to decide the facts. Therefore we have in this case something indorsed on the writ by the defendant's solicitor, by whose action in making such indorsement the defendant is bound; and, even if it was not meant to be a direction to seize the goods seized, yet I think if it was in such a form as to mislead the sheriff into thinking that it was, the result would be the same: for, if a person makes a statement that may well mislead, and does in fact mislead, the sheriff into thinking that he was directed to seize the goods seized, it seems to me that such a statement renders the maker of it liable as if he had intended to give such a direction. The learned judge at the trial left to the jury the question whether the sheriff seized the goods of the plaintiff instead of the execution debtor's goods because he was misled by the direction which he received from the execution creditor's solicitor. The jury would, in order to answer this question, have to consider whether the direction was intended to point to the particular goods seized or was a direction given in such a form as was likely to mislead the sheriff into seizing those goods. The jury answered the question in the affirmative. The learned judge afterwards came to the conclusion that the result of the decided cases was that nothing indorsed on the writ, whether by the execution creditor or his solicitor, could amount to a direction to the sheriff so as to affect the question of liability for the seizure of the goods. It is difficult to reconcile that conclusion with the case to which I have before referred, in which such a direction was held to be evidence of a direction to the sheriff to levy on the goods seized. Another authority to which reference must be made on the subject is *Jarmain* v *Hooper*. ... in which it seems to me that the conclusion at which they arrived really amounts to a decision that such an indorsement on the writ may be equivalent to a direction to the sheriff, and may constitute the sheriff the bailiff of the execution creditor, and that, though it be given, not by the execution creditor himself, but by his attorney, the execution creditor will be liable. ... In the present case there is an indorsement on the writ which was evidence for the jury upon the question which was put to them, and they answered that question in the affirmative. I think that their finding brings this case within *Jarmain* v *Hooper* and that the learned judge ought to have given judgment accordingly. The appeal must, therefore, be allowed and judgment entered for the plaintiff for the damages found by the jury.

FRY L.J.: ... The question, therefore, is, whether such a direction was given by the defendant in the present case as made the sheriff his servant for the purpose of seizing these goods. The indorsement on the writ was relied on for the plaintiff as amounting to such a direction. It was argued for the defendant that the indorsement cannot be regarded as such a direction to the sheriff: and in support of that argument our attention was directed to the case of *Childers* v *Wooler*. ... But whether this case is looked at with reference to the decision in *Jarmain* v *Hooper*, or with reference to that in *Childers* v *Wooler*, the result seems to be the same. If *Jarmain* v *Hooper* be correct, then the indorsement on the writ was a sufficient direction to the sheriff to make the execution creditor liable for his act in seizing the goods, and the case will be governed by that decision. If on the other hand *Childers* v *Wooler* be right, it follows that subsequent circumstances shewing a ratification would be admissible to fix the defendant with liability, and it is admitted that, if there can be a ratification, there was one in this case. The true view appears to me to be that the previous direction of the execution creditor may make the sheriff his servant for the purpose of seizing the goods, and an indorsement on the writ may amount to such a direction, and it is a question of fact whether in the particular case it does so. In the present case the jury have in substance found that the indorsement on the writ did amount to such a direction. No objection has been taken to such finding, and I can see none. I think the judgment ought to have followed the finding of the jury. For these reasons I think this appeal should be allowed.

LOPES, L.J., concurred.
Appeal allowed.

Graves v *Sprague* (1920), 48 N.B.R. 36 (S.C.)

[In seeking to execute against the assets of one Mrs. Graves, the execution creditor, Sprague, personally instructed the sheriff to seize and sell hay which did not belong to the execution debtor. At trial, the creditor was found liable for trespass and conversion.]

SIR J.D. HAZEN, C.J.: The sole question raised by the appellant on his appeal is as to whether or not there was in fact or in law conversion by the defendant William A. Sprague of the hay belonging to the Robinson plaintiffs. The question as to whether there was a trespass to plaintiff's real estate or not is not raised by the appellant, no doubt because admittedly the defendant Sprague had gone upon the plaintiff's land with the constable, showed him the hay which was seized and sold, and further went there on the day of the sale. With respect to conversion, the point involved is this, – did the defendant Sprague personally take part in the seizure and sale of this hay under the execution? The authorities are clear that if a party or his attorney in any way intervenes, directs or takes part in the acts of an officer under an execution, then the party so intervening, directing or taking part constitutes the officer his agent for the purposes of that act, and is responsible for all matters ensuing as a result of the action of the officer. ...

   Now in this case it appears from the evidence of the constable, Gough, that William Sprague and Squire Cannon employed him to seize some hay, and told him to go and levy on the hay that

William Sprague put up, and sell it; that William Sprague went with him, told him what barn to go to, came down with him to the barn – 'and Sprague went down and attended to the barn and said to levy on the hay in there.' The defendant Sprague says he did not tell Gough to go and take the hay; that he told him that that was the hay that Mrs. Graves said was hers that he cut, and that she gave him her obligation to pay; that he was with Gough and went down and showed him the hay but he did not know the barn or the hay he cut from anybody else's. It appears therefore that the defendant after delivering the execution to the constable took him down upon the land owned by the Robinson plaintiffs, showed him the hay owned by the Robinson plaintiffs, and said that that was the property of Mrs. Graves, and in my opinion this constitutes a case of interference on the part of the defendant, and the defendant is answerable for the consequence of what the constable did in obeying his instructions. Reading all the evidence, I think it is clear that in levying on the hay that was the property of the Robinson children, the constable was acting under instructions received from the defendant Sprague. The learned trial judge regarded Sprague's evidence as being unsatisfactory, and evidently attached little or no credence to it.

As stated before, the trial judge did not specifically find as a fact that Sprague interfered with and directed the constable, but having found the defendant Sprague liable for the conversion, the Appellate Court will assume that he found the facts in favour of the respondent, and that judgment will not be disturbed if there is evidence to justify such finding. See *Johnson* v *Jack* (1901) 35 N.B.R. 492. It is open to the court in any event to draw inferences that might have been drawn by the trial judge, and it is impossible to read the evidence in the case without coming to the conclusion that Sprague interfered in such a manner as to render himself liable for the action of the constable in improperly seizing the hay of the Robinson plaintiffs under an execution in a suit to which they were not parties, and there is ample evidence to support the judge's finding as I understand it to have been, and it ought not, I think, to be disturbed.
[The appeal was dismissed.]

ii The Mechanics of Seizure: The following cases illustrate three problems faced by a sheriff attempting to seize goods on the premises of an execution debtor:
1 What constitutes seizure? Must the sheriff actually take the goods away from the premises or may he leave them in the possession of the debtor? If he does leave them in the possession of the debtor what steps must be taken to ensure that the goods remain seized in law?
2 How much may/must the sheriff seize? As we shall see (Chapter 13 infra) the sheriff is seizing on behalf of all creditors and is authorized to seize enough to satisfy all of their debts. On the other hand if he seizes goods of a value greater than sufficient to pay all judgment debts, he may be liable to the debtor for excessive seizure.
3 Where is the sale to take place? Under what circumstances, if any, may a sale take place on the debtor's premises?

Watson v *Murray & Co.*, [1955] 1 All E.R. 350 (Q.B.D.)

[In execution of writs of *fi.fa.* defendant Sheriff's Officers entered the plaintiff's (debtor's) dress shop to seize the shop contents. The Officers left the goods in plaintiff's hands after she had agreed not to remove anything from the shop. The value of the goods purportedly seized was in excess of the amount required to satisfy plaintiff's indebtedness. Some months later, the Sheriff decided to hold the sale on the premises of the plaintiff. The Sheriff's officers prepared lots for

sale and closed the shop for one week, excluding the plaintiff. By the time the shop was
re-opened for the sale the plaintiff had satisfied the judgment so that no sale was necessary. The
plaintiff sued the defendants for excessive seizure, trespass to goods and land, and in detinue or
conversion for the value of two garments lost during the time of the defendants' trespass.]

HILBERY, J.: The first question to be considered is whether what took place when Mr. May went
to the premises on Jan. 7, armed with the writ of fi. fa., amounted in law to a seizure of the
plaintiff's goods. Mr. May is now dead, but his report on his visit is in evidence. He states that on
calling he informed the plaintiff of the nature of his visit and was told by her that there was a bill
of sale on all the stock and fittings in the shop in favour of Mr. Mitchener; she stated that her
solicitor had tried evidently unsuccessfully to arrange for payment of the debt by instalments
and that she was not in a position to pay anything on account that day. Mr. May reported that it
was a very good class shop and fairly well stocked with ladies' dresses, suits, gloves, stockings,
etc. The plaintiff's evidence was that Mr. May came at about 10.30 a.m. on Monday, Jan. 7,
handed the plaintiff the defendants' card showing that they were sheriff's officers and he was
their representative, and said that he must take charge of everything in the shop; that she said
she did not want him in the shop and asked what right he had to stay there, that Mr. May then
produced a printed form and said that if she signed it and guaranteed to pay him the money which
she took, except whatever was required for staff wages, he need not stay all the time. Thereupon
the plaintiff signed the printed form which the defendants regularly use and which is known as a
'walking possession' agreement. It is in the following terms:

Dated (blank) To the Sheriff of the County of Surrey and to Messrs. Murray & Co., his officers.
(Blank) v (Blank). In consideration of your not keeping the man in charge of the goods seized
herein in close possession, and allowing him to leave each night and attend each day (or as may
be arranged) I hereby authorise and empower you and your representative to re-enter my house
and premises, No. (blank) [address] at any time you may think proper, under a writ of fi. fa. in
the above action dated (blank) and if necessary to use force for that purpose, and I also
undertake not to remove, or allow to be removed, any of the goods in the meantime, and to pay
the possession money day by day.

It was argued for the defendants – these being the facts, and I think the plaintiff's evidence
here is substantially accurate – that there was no seizure: that all that Mr. May did and said only
amounted to an explanation by him of what the legal situation would be if the plaintiff did not
either satisfy the judgment debt or sign the walking possession agreement and that as the
plaintiff thereupon signed the agreement no seizure was made and the defendants contented
themselves with the notional possession which resulted from the agreement. I am unable to
accept this contention.

On the subject of what is sufficient to constitute a levy or seizure by the sheriff in execution of
a writ of fi. fa. there is fortunately some authority. In *Bissicks v Bath Colliery Co., Ltd.* [(1877), 2
Ex.D. 459 46 L.J. Ex. 611, affd. (1878), 3 Ex.D. 174, 47 L.J.Q.B. 408 (C.A.)], where the sheriff's
officer went to the plaintiff's premises and told them he had a warrant to execute a writ of fi. fa.
for £28 7s. 2d. and that he required immediate payment, otherwise further proceedings would be
taken and the man must remain in possession, the plaintiff paid the sums demanded, including
poundage and levy fees, the court held that the sheriff was entitled to both these items.
COCKBURN, C.J., said (2 Ex.D. at p 462): 'We must look to see if the writ has been virtually

executed', and CLEASBY, B., said (ibid.): '… I think in this case there was in substance an actual levy …' On appeal from that decision BRAMWELL, L.J., said (3 Ex.D. at p 175):

The question is whether, upon the facts, there was a seizure … upon the whole I think there was a seizure, for the officer did threaten to leave a man in possession.

BRETT, L.J., said (ibid.):

I agree that there must be a seizure; but upon the facts I think there was a seizure. The sheriff's officer went to the plaintiff's house with a man, he obtained entry into the house, and whilst he was there the plaintiff's goods were under his control; he spoke as if he had made a seizure, and he treated what he was doing as if it was a seizure …

In addition it has been expressly stated by BRETT, L.J., in *Mortimore* v *Cragg* [(1878) 3 C.P.D. 216, 47 L.J.Q.B. 348] (3 C.P.D. at p 219) that

… Where an execution issues the transaction may be divided into four parts: 1. The delivery of the writ to the sheriff: 2. Seizure: 3. The possible payment of money after seizure: 4. If no payment, sale.

There can be no doubt that Mr. May went on each occasion armed with a warrant for the purpose of executing a writ of fi. fa. When he says in his report that he informed the plaintiff of the nature of his visit, and the plaintiff, as I believe, asked what right he had to stay there and expressed her objection to his staying, and when I find that he took an agreement in the form in which he did take it, I am satisfied that there was what amounted to a seizure. The opening words of the agreement are 'in consideration of your not keeping the man in charge of the goods seized herein in close possession'. Those are words chosen and put forward by the defendants themselves. They are only consistent with the fact that goods have been seized. Furthermore, by the concluding words of the agreement the plaintiff undertook 'not to remove, or allow to be removed, any of the goods in the meantime, and to pay possession money day by day'. Again, those words are only consistent with there having been a seizure. In *Gladstone* v *Padwick* [(1871), L.R. 6 Exch. 203, 40 L.J. Ex. 154], one of the questions was whether what was done by the sheriff's officer on a certain date amounted to an actual seizure, and BRAMWELL, B., said in the course of his judgment (L.R. 6 Exch. at p 212):

It is admitted, and it is clear, that it is not necessary for the sheriff to lay his hand on a single article … I am of opinion that, where property is all one holding, as it were here, if the sheriff goes and makes known … that he is come to seize, and does, so far as words and intention can go, seize all the goods on that holding, he has done enough …

Those words are applicable to what took place on each of the occasions in January, March, May and June when Mr. May called at the plaintiff's shop and premises to execute the several writs of fi. fa. which figure in this case.

It was urged for the defendants that the position of the sheriff which resulted from what was done and said on each of the occasions when Mr. May called on the plaintiff, and entered her premises for the purpose of executing the writ, was not that the defendants as sheriff's officers had seized, but that they had obtained contractual rights under the several walking possession agreements which the plaintiff signed the result of which was to give them a notional possession. It is true that in *Lumsden* v *Burnett* [[1898] 2 Q.B. 177, 67 L.J.Q.B. 661], A. L. SMITH, L.J., spoke of such an agreement as giving only a constructive possession and CHITTY, L.J., spoke of it as giving a possession merely constructive or notional. In that case, the court held that the existence of such an agreement was strong evidence to show that the officer leaving the premises in the terms of such an agreement was not abandoning possession. In that case, as in this, after leaving the premises having obtained the walking possession agreement, the officer paid a subsequent visit or visits to the premises to see that the goods were not being removed. I think it is right to say that after seizure the sheriff may continue in possession either actually by leaving a man in the premises or notionally under such a walking possession agreement as was obtained on each occasion from the plaintiff in this case.

Since therefore in my view there was on each occasion a seizure, it becomes necessary to consider whether in January and March or in May and June the seizures were excessive so as to give rise to an action on the case against the sheriff. That an excessive seizure gives such a cause of action was decided in *Gawler* v *Chaplin* [(1848) 2 Exch. 503, 18 L.J. Ex. 42]. In that case the first alleged breach of duty on the part of the sheriffs was that they had wrongfully seized goods of the plaintiff of greater value than sufficient to pay the debt, interest, poundage and expenses, although they well knew part would be sufficient. On motion in arrest of judgment after verdict the question was whether that alleged breach was good in law. It was held that it was. In giving the judgment of the court PARKE, B., said (2 Exch. at p 507).

... in the first instance, the duty of the sheriff is confined to seizing goods that would be reasonably sufficient, if sold, to pay the sum endorsed on the writ – that is, the debt, interest upon the debt, poundage, and expenses; and if the sheriff seizes more, prima facie he is a wrongdoer ...

There can be no doubt on the evidence that the stock in the plaintiff's shop was far more extensive than it was necessary to seize to satisfy the judgment debt in respect of which either of the writs of fi. fa. in hand in January and February was issued even including the other charges enumerated by PARKE, B.

There was therefore in my judgment a seizure on each occasion which was excessive; but it resulted in no damage to the plaintiff. She was allowed to carry on her business as before and did so until the sheriff was paid ...

The questions which have to be decided in connection with these happenings in June and July are first, did the defendants trespass by preparing for this sale on the premises and by using the premises for their preparations for the sale and by posting the bills announcing the sale on the plaintiff's premises without her permission and in spite of her objection of which they knew, and second, did the defendants on this occasion make an excessive seizure in taking for sale what appears in the catalogue.

On the second question there was much evidence on both sides. The plaintiff's contention that the seizure was excessive is mainly based on evidence that at such a sale you might ordinarily expect to realise a certain fraction or percentage of the retail prices of the articles and on the fact that at a later date the fixtures which were included in the catalogue sold for a comparatively large sum and the other articles realised, when sold by tender, about twenty-five per cent. of their retail price. On the other hand the defendants' evidence and contention was that it is in the highest degree uncertain what such goods will fetch under hammer, much depending on whether there is a good or a poor attendance at the sale: that a sale such as this will be likely to realise less if held in the country than if held in a London auction room; that such a sale largely depends on the weather and on the trade buyers attending, and that the sheriff must always allow a margin as he has a duty to the execution creditors to execute the writ so as to make of the goods sufficient to satisfy the executions.

I am satisfied that the defendants, in lotting and cataloguing what they did, acted in good faith, and I am not satisfied, having regard to the hazards attending such a sale, that there was an excessive seizure. It must be remembered that most of the goods in question were seasonal and fashion goods. Moreover, it by no means follows that anything like all the lots would necessarily have got a bid at all.

The serious question which remains is the question whether the defendants had any right in law to insist on using the plaintiff's premises as they did for the purposes connected with holding this sale there. It is clear that the writ of fi. fa. does not require or authorise the sheriff to seize the land or premises of a debtor. It requires him to make of the goods of the debtor sufficient to satisfy the execution creditor's judgment debt. It gives the sheriff a right to remain on the debtor's premises for a reasonable time and no longer (see *Ash* v *Dawnay* [(1852), 8 Exch. 237, 22 L.J. Ex. 59)], and it empowers him to sell sufficient of the debtor's goods to satisfy the debt in respect of which the writ was issued. *Reed* v *Harrison* [(1778), 2 Wm. Bl. 1218, 96 E.R. 717] is authority for saying, as the headnote to that case expresses it, that on attachment of goods, the officer cannot legally continue in possession of the defendant's house, or keep the goods therein for a long and unreasonable time, but must remove them to a place of safe custody: else he is a trespasser ab initio.

At common law the sheriff's duty is to remove the goods to some place where they can be safely kept until they are sold, but I cannot find any English authority which decides that he can, if he chooses, use the debtor's premises for the purpose of holding a sale there. It does not appear to me that in this case it is established that it was impossible to hold the sale anywhere else than on the plaintiff's premises. It was no doubt extremely difficult in the particular circumstances to arrange for it elsewhere, and no doubt the defendants decided that it was expedient to hold the sale at the plaintiff's shop, but the plaintiff objected and they knew that she objected. They must in those circumstances, it seems to me, show that they had a legal right to do what they did notwithstanding the plaintiff's objection.

In Mather on Sheriff and Execution Law (3rd Edn. at p 126) there is reference to an Irish case in which, it is said, it was held that a sale should as a rule take place on the execution debtor's premises (*Re Purcell* [(1884), 13 L.R. Ir. 489)], but the learned editor immediately goes on to say:

It would certainly be better that the sheriff should obtain the debtor's licence to hold the sale upon his premises, as there appears to be some doubt as to his authority to use the premises for the purpose of a sale.

In my view an examination of the facts and the judgment in the Irish case shows that the statement that it was there held that a sale should as a rule take place on the execution debtor's premises is an over-statement. That opinion was expressed passim by MILLER, J., when he said (13 L.R. Ir. at p 496):

... he (the sheriff) does not allege that he made any attempt whatever to make any sale of the goods upon the premises of the execution debtor, which was his primary duty: ...

This statement was made in a part of his judgment when the learned judge was commenting on the sheriff's claim to his expenses in removing and returning goods of the debtor to the debtor's premises, but after he had already decided that the sheriff could recover only the fees and expenses which were provided for him by the Act 6 Anne c 26, s 16 and s 23, and by the Act 43 Geo. 3 c 46, s 5, and that these expenses of removal and of return of the goods were not provided for the sheriff by those statutes. The case is not, therefore, in my view a direct authority for the proposition that it is the duty of the sheriff to sell the debtor's goods on the debtor's premises. Counsel before me in this case have not found (nor have I been able to find) any authority which decides that such is the duty of the sheriff acting under a writ of fi. fa. The defendants' evidence in this case shows that the practice is to remove and sell in an auction room such goods as were here seized. It may be that if the sheriff can show that it was not possible to sell the goods except on the debtor's premises, it would be lawful for him so to do. Part of his duty is to sell the goods so as to make of them sufficient to satisfy the debt which is the subject of the writ of fi. fa. which he has to execute and the law will not require of him that which is impossible. But the defendants in this case have not established that it was impossible to remove and sell the goods away from the plaintiff's premises. They have shown that by the concessions they had made to the plaintiff it had become extremely difficult for them so to do before an act of bankruptcy by the plaintiff was committed, but their evidence does not amount to more than this.

There were, therefore, in my view trespasses on the plaintiff's property committed by them when they did those acts which were solely done for the purposes of and incidental to the holding of the sale on the plaintiff's premises. The acts which in my view were such trespasses were the locking of the plaintiff's premises so as to exclude her therefrom when they had lotted the goods; the opening of the plaintiff's premises to the public for the viewing of the goods catalogued and the admission by them to the plaintiff's premises of all who chose to come in for the ostensible purpose of viewing the goods; and the posting of their posters on the plaintiff's premises.

What damage the plaintiff suffered in consequence it is difficult to say, but the poster certainly was in terms which would convey to anyone reading it that the plaintiff's stock and the fixtures in her shop were being sold, and anyone reading it might reasonably have concluded that the business life of the shop was ended. The result was said to have been that the plaintiff's takings thereafter were so prejudicially affected that she was obliged finally to sell up and close down. That her takings afterwards were trifling compared with what they formerly had been was shown by the accounts of the business, but to what extent this would inevitably have been the case owing to her grave financial difficulties it is not possible to decide. But I do not think it can be doubted that the posting on the premises of such bills as were put there must have been damaging to her chances of making a business recovery. Moreover the fact that the bills were there on the viewing day and on the morning of the day of the intended sale in spite of her protests and in spite of the fact that she had once before then abated the trespass by removing the poster bills amounted to conduct which aggravated the damage and which may properly be taken into consideration. I assess the damages for these trespasses, therefore, as more than nominal and award £300.
Judgment for the plaintiff.

Re Bishop and Traders Finance Corporation Ltd. et al, (1966) 56 D.L.R. (2d) 685 (Ont. C.A.)

The judgment of the Court was delivered by Kelly, J.A.: ...
Traders, after recovering judgment against DeBruyne in the amount of $4,158 and $450 for costs, on December 5, 1962, delivered to the Sheriff a writ of *fi. fa*. The Sheriff alleged that in

pursuance of the writ he made two seizures of the tobacco crops of DeBruyne, the first on April 16, 1963, and the second on February 5, 1964; in the light of the dates of the alleged seizures it is apparent that the Sheriff acted with respect to a harvested, not to a growing crop. On April 16, 1963, the Sheriff delivered to the Board a document entitled 'Tobacco Crop Seizure' reading as follows:

Sheriff's Office
County of Oxford
In the Supreme Court of Ontario

BETWEEN:

Traders Finance Corporation Limited

Plaintiff

—and—
Refin DeBruyne

Defendant

This is to advise you that on the 5th day of December, 1962 the Plaintiff recovered Judgment in the Supreme Court of Ontario for $4,158.00 for debt and costs of $450.00 plus interest to date of payment together with Sheriff's costs, poundage and incidental expenses.

Subsequently, namely, pursuant to the Writ of Fi Fa taken out by the Plaintiff, the tobacco crop belonging to the said defendant Refin DeBruyne is seized by me under the said Writ to satisfy the amount of the aforesaid mentioned Judgment and costs. We understand that this tobacco is to be delivered to and sold by the Ontario Flue-Cured Tobacco Growers' Marketing Board and this is to advise you that all cheques issued by your Board for this tobacco crop up to the value of $4,158.00 for debt and costs of $450.00 plus interest to date of payment, together with Sheriff's fees, poundage and incidental expenses, should have the name of the Sheriff, County of Oxford, included as one of the payees.

DATED at Woodstock, Ontario, this 16th day of April, 1963.

'J. B. Martin'
DEPUTY SHERIFF, COUNTY OF OXFORD

On February 5, 1964, the Sheriff delivered to the Board a further document entitled 'Tobacco Crop Seizure' which save as to date, was identical with the one delivered on April 16, 1963. The record does not disclose whether the Sheriff made an actual seizure of the tobacco crop or whether the delivery to the Board of the said 'Notice of Seizure' itself constituted what he alleged was a seizure. For the purposes of this judgment, I am assuming that an actual seizure was made by the Sheriff prior to the delivery of the tobacco crop to the Board.

In dealing with the alleged seizure and its effect, it will be helpful to review briefly the rights and obligations of a Sheriff with whom is lodged a writ of *fi. fa.*

The *Execution Act*, R.S.O. 1960, c 126 s 9(1) [am. 1960–61, c 25, s 1], provides that a writ of execution binds the goods and lands against which it is issued, *i.e.*, the judgment debtor's goods and lands in the Sheriff's bailiwick, from the time of delivery thereof to the Sheriff for execution. The apparent effect of this section is modified by the interpretation which has been placed on the word 'binds'. As here used with respect to goods, 'binds' means that the Sheriff acquires a legal right to seize such goods: 16 Hals., 3rd ed., p 43, para. 64. The ownership of goods as distinguished from land, by the execution debtor and his ability to pass the property therein to others is not affected by the presence in the Sheriff's hands of a writ of *fi. fa.* upon which the Sheriff has not made a seizure.

When a Sheriff actually seizes goods he acquires a special property in them which enables him to retain possession and control over them and in due course to sell so much of the goods as may be necessary to realize the amount due on the writ. When a Sheriff effects a sale he can convey to the purchaser the judgment debtor's title to the goods: and he is entitled to retain the purchase price till it becomes distributable under the provisions of the *Creditors' Relief Act*.

To bring into existence the Sheriff's special property in the goods, it is essential that he make a seizure, and to keep alive the special property it is essential that until sale he retain possession of the goods seized. While it is not requisite that the Sheriff remove the goods into a place where they are in his actual and sole possession and control, nevertheless he must in some manner assert his possessory right. This is commonly done by keeping a bailiff in possession in the premises where the goods are found when seized. Another acceptable and more common procedure is for the Sheriff, after making a formal seizure and taking an inventory of the goods to take from the debtor a written undertaking not to remove the goods nor to permit their removal by anyone else. This relieves the debtor of the annoyance and expense of the constant attendance of the Sheriff or his officer on the premises. This is referred to as 'walking possession' and is a clear demonstration that the Sheriff is continuing to assert his property in these goods.

If, however, the Sheriff holding no such undertaking from the judgment debtor discontinues his actual possession of the goods seized, and does not continue to assert that the right to possession is his alone, the goods cease to be under seizure and the Sheriff's special property ceases to exist: *Blades* v *Arundale* (1813), 1 M. & S. 711, 105 E.R. 265; *Ackland* v *Paynter* (1820), 8 Price 95, 146 E.R. 1142; *Young* v *Dencher; Bank of Toronto* v *Adames, Sheriff of Acadia*, [1923] 1 D.L.R. 432 at p 436, 18 A.L.R. 496, [1923] 1 W.W.R. 136. It has been held in some cases that a temporary absence of the Sheriff's bailiff, *e.g.*, for the purpose of getting a meal, will not necessarily break the continuity of the possession but under these circumstances it is incumbent for the Sheriff to show that the absence of the bailiff was caused by some urgent necessity and was consistent with an evident intention of non-abandonment.

The record does not set out the actual steps taken by the Sheriff with respect to the tobacco crops of DeBruyne with the particularity which one would have wished; but from a careful reading of the 'Notice of Seizure' received by the Board from the Sheriff there can be no conclusion other than that, even if an actual seizure had been made, the Sheriff permitted DeBruyne himself to deliver the tobacco crops to the Board and that the only claim or title to the tobacco crops asserted by the Sheriff was to have his name included as one of the payees on any cheque to be issued by the Board for the proceeds of the sale of the tobacco crops.

Had the Sheriff actually seized the crop, delivered it to the Board for sale by the Board as his agent and in so delivering it insisted that the proceeds of the sale up to the amount necessary to satisfy the writs in his hands be paid to him in priority to all other persons claiming from DeBruyne any part of the purchase price of DeBruyne's crop, it might have indicated that the Sheriff continued in possession of the tobacco crop by his agent, the Board; or if the Sheriff had actually seized the crop and taken from DeBruyne a written undertaking that the goods would not be removed by DeBruyne or any other person, had directed DeBruyne to deposit the tobacco crop in the Board warehouse, that might have indicated that the Sheriff was continuing in possession through the agency of the Board. If the Sheriff had asserted the same right to the proceeds of the sale by the Board as he would have asserted with respect to the proceeds of a sale conducted by him, he might have contended that the Board was only used by him as a means of conducting the sale he was entitled to hold, no other means being available by reason of the Regulation of the Board.

But a fair reading of the 'Notice of Seizure' convinces me that the Sheriff did not remain in possession and that his direction that his name be included as one of the payees is quite inconsistent with the position which he would be required by his office to maintain, *i.e.*, that he was entitled to receive the proceeds to be dealt with by him as he was required by law to deal with them.

In my view any seizure made by the Sheriff, if there was one, was not followed by his continuous possession down to the time of sale and that, therefore, the tobacco crops ceased to be subject to seizure and the Sheriff ceased to have in them the special property above referred to, prior to the time the crops were sold by the Board.

Regina v *Vroom*, [1975] 4 W.W.R. 113 (Alta. S.C. A.D.)

[The sheriff came to the dwelling house of the execution debtor to effect seizure of certain goods listed in the seizure documents. The sheriff neither saw nor laid his hands on the goods to be seized. Instead he told the debtor that the goods were being seized and had him sign an undertaking to hold the goods as bailee for the sheriff. When the execution debtor was served a demand for delivery up of possession he refused to comply and was charged with theft contrary to s 285 of the Criminal Code, R.S.C. 1970, c C-34, which provides:

[e]very one who is a bailee of anything that is under lawful seizure by a peace officer or public officer in the execution of the duties of his office, and who is obliged by law or agreement to produce and deliver it to that officer or to another person entitled thereto at a certain time and place, or upon demand, steals it if he does not produce and deliver it in accordance with his obligation, but he does not steal it if his failure to produce and deliver it is not the result of a wilful act or omission by him.

The debtor was acquitted on the ground that the evidence did not establish that the goods had been lawfully seized. The Crown appealed.]

PROWSE J.A.: In my view the Crown failed to establish beyond a reasonable doubt that the goods in question, which it alleges were the subject of a lawful seizure, were on the accused's premises when the purported seizure was made.

In this respect the learned trial Judge said:

I also have some serious doubt as to whether or not a lawful seizure was made for the reasons given by Mr. Clark in his remarks. It is clear on the evidence that the sheriff's bailiff never did see and identify the goods which he purported to seize and also that some or all of the goods were not on the premises at that time.

The authorities make it clear that the jurisdiction of the sheriff at Calgary is the judicial district of Calgary and with respect to a seizure Lamont J. in *Dodd* v *Vail* (1913), 6 Sask. L.R. 22, 3 W.W.R. 796 at 798, 23 W.L.R. 62, 9 D.L.R. 534, affirmed 4 W.W.R. 291, 23 W.L.R. 903, 10 D.L.R. 694 (C.A.), stated: 'To make a valid seizure he must be upon the premises where the goods are'. This case was referred to by McLaurin J. (as he then was) in *Rex* v *Jacobson*, [1944] 1 W.W.R. 97 at 99, 81 C.C.C. 104 (Alta.):

In that case it is observed that a sheriff cannot sit in his office and by a purely intellectual operation make a seizure of goods miles away, but to make a valid seizure he must be upon the premises where the goods are, or so close thereto that if his authority to seize is disputed by one in actual possession he is in a position to lay hands on the goods.

The question in the present case is whether the Crown has established that any of the goods in question were upon the accused's premises when the purported seizure was made.

The evidence of the sheriff's bailiff is that in making the purported seizure he did not follow his usual procedure which was 'to see the goods or to be assured that the goods are there'. He also stated that at the time of making the seizure he understood that some or all of the goods were in fact in Holland.

In my view this evidence establishes that a lawful seizure was not made. The sheriff's bailiff did not ascertain if any of the goods he was purporting to seize were on the premises and he not only gave no reason for believing they were but stated that he was under the impression that 'some, if not all of the goods' were not.

With respect to the bailee's undertaking signed by the accused I would refer to s 16 of The Seizures Act, R.S.A. 1970, c 338, which reads as follows:

16.   The sheriff at any time after making a seizure of any goods under a writ of execution or by virtue of a power of distress may appoint the debtor or some other person as his agent to hold and keep the goods so seized for and on behalf of the sheriff, upon the debtor or such other person signing an undertaking to hold the goods seized as bailee for the sheriff and to deliver up the possession thereof to the sheriff on demand.

And it follows that this is a document that is to be completed at 'any time after making a seizure'.

Whatever its effect may be in civil proceeding, I need not consider; but I am of the view that the accused's signature on the undertaking by itself cannot be treated as an admission by the accused that the goods were lawfully seized if they were not in fact on the premises at the time of the purported seizure.

I have also considered whether, in the light of the circumstances disclosed in the evidence, the accused's signature can be treated as an admission that the items listed were on the premises. I think not. The bailiff gave no evidence that suggested that the accused read the document before signing it. Further, he gave no particulars of any conversations with the accused that supported the conclusion that the goods were on the premises but rather he stated he formed the impression that they were not and this evidence detracts from any inference that might other-wise be drawn. Still further, the only word in the document that assists the Crown is the word 'possession' which is equivocal as 'possession' does not require physical presence for 'My power of using a thing is not destroyed by my voluntary absence from it, for I can go to it when I will' (Salmond on Jurisprudence, 9th ed., p 387, in dealing with the 'Relation of the Possessor To The Thing Possessed'), whereas the presence of the goods on the premises was required to constitute a valid seizure. In this regard it will be noted that the space left blank in the undertaking was not filled in by the bailiff, that is, he did not designate the premises in which the goods were to be held, which supports the conclusion that he did not know where they were.

In conclusion I would dismiss the appeal on the ground that the doubt expressed by the trial Judge was justified as the evidence does not establish that the goods were lawfully seized.

CLEMENT, J.A. (dissenting): ... The broad scope of the inquiry at common law into the legality of a seizure is made apparent in *Brook* v *Booker* (1909), 41 S.C.R. 331, 6 E.L.R. 435, where there was in question the validity of a purported seizure of the hull of a steamer sunk in a canal. The bailiff had stood on the bank of the canal, some 500 yards distant from the hull, when he professed to make the seizure, but he was not seen doing so by the owner or anyone on his behalf. Apparently he gave no notice to the owner of the purported seizure. Fitzpatrick c.j.c., speaking for the Court, adopted at p 335 the answer to the question 'What is a seizure?' that had been given by Taschereau j. in the Court of King's Bench: the sense of which, as I understand it, is that it is a material act, that is to say, an act of appreciable significance for the purpose, to bring the seized chattel within the custody of the law. If on the one hand it is not necessary for the bailiff actually to touch the chattel to be seized, on the other hand something more is necessary than a purely intellectual or imaginary operation.

It was upon the foregoing premise that Lamont j. in *Dodd* v *Vail* (1913), 6 Sask. L.R. 22, 3 w.w.r. 796 at 798, 23 w.l.r. 62, 9 d.l.r. 534, affirmed 4 w.w.r. 291, 23 w.l.r. 903, 10 d.l.r. 694 (c.a.), observed:

To make a valid seizure he must be upon the premises where the goods are, or so close thereto, that if his authority to seize is disputed by one in actual possession he is in a position to lay hands on the goods.

Earlier in his judgment he had said (pp 797–98):

An entry upon premises on which goods are situated, together with an intimation of an intention to seize the goods, will constitute a valid seizure, Halsbury, Vol. 14, p 54; *Swann* v *Earl of Falmouth* (1828), 8 b. & c. 456, 108 e.r. 1112.

The passage in Halsbury on which he relied in part, now 16 Hals. (3d) 55, para. 84, fully supports this view. That passage itself is based on earlier authorities and it will be helpful to the direction of the inquiry to observe what acts various courts have considered to be material.

[Clement ja then referred to the cases discussed in *Watson* v *Murray*, supra, and continued:] I must now turn to s 25(1) of The Seizures Act. In my opinion, properly construed, it does not abrogate the requirements of the common law for a legal seizure. Rather, it states explicitly and in detail, as a duty of the sheriff on making a seizure, matters which at common law would be taken into account in determining the legality of a seizure. By it, having regard to the prescribed Form a, the execution debtor is informed that a seizure has been made, and on what goods the seizure is levied. It does not, in my view, determine exclusively what constitutes a legal seizure; but the performance of that duty must be strong prima facie evidence that a legal seizure has been made. When the performance is pursuant to para. (*b*) I would think it might well be difficult to refute the prima facie case.

Save for one circumstance, it is plain that the evidence of the bailiff presented a prima facie case of seizure within the cases I have referred to, sufficient to put Vroom on his defence. But it is objected that the bailiff was unable to say that the goods listed in the notice of seizure were in the residence of Vroom in Calgary and that, indeed, he was under the impression at the time that some of them were in fact in Holland. He did not get this impression from Vroom, so far as the record discloses, and Vroom did not give evidence. The cases to which I have referred make it clear to me that it is not necessary for a bailiff to identify personally each article he seizes. The salient requirements are that he make it clear to the execution debtor that his purpose is to effect a seizure, and that he notify the execution debtor of the goods he is seizing. This is what happened here. Vroom made no objection that the goods, or any of them, listed on the notice then served on him were not in his possession. So far from doing so, he treated it as a seizure of the whole list by signing the bailee's undertaking in respect of the whole, in which there is his specific acknowledgment of the seizure thereof. By this also he was put on his defence to establish, if he could, that there was no bailment because the goods purporting thereby to be bailed were not there to be held and kept by him. Further than that, it is of some evidentiary value that a part of the goods were found in the residence in Kinnard to which he had apparently moved afterwards. In this view, the Crown made out a prima facie case of legal seizure of the goods under the law of Alberta, which was not controverted in any way by evidence. I adapt to these circumstances the principle stated by Duff J. (later C.J.C.) in *Rex v Picariello and Lassandro*, [1923] 1 W.W.R. 1489, 39 C.C.C. 229, [1923] 2 D.L.R. 706 at 713 (Can.), namely, that where a prima facie case is established which without explanation constitutes the offence charged, the accused cannot properly be acquitted upon some imaginary state of facts, the existence of which finds no proof in the evidence. It is urged that the evidence elicited from the bailiff, above noted, that it was his impression that at least some, if not all, of the goods were in Holland at the relevant time, gives rise to a reasonable doubt that the goods were there to seize, with the corollary that if they were in Holland they would be beyond the jurisdiction of the bailiff to seize. I do not accept this argument. An impression, gained from some unspecified source, is not proof of a fact but merely some evidence of a state of mind of the bailiff. I do not consider that to be relevant. What is to be examined is what took place as a matter of fact. Contemporaneous with the seizure Vroom by his bailee's undertaking acknowledged the seizure of the whole, and undertook to keep them at the specified address in Calgary. Subsequently some of the goods were found in his new residence in British Columbia. In such circumstances it was for Vroom to adduce evidence affording a foundation for the defences put forward.

See: *Pacific Finance Acceptance Co. Ltd.* v *Corbett*, [1977] 2 W.W.R. 280 (Alta. D. Ct.), in which a sheriff's bailiff attended upon the respondent at her place of business and served her with a notice of seizure. At that time the subject-matter of the seizure, the respondent's car, was undergoing repairs at a gas station. The sheriff's bailiff did not know where the care was, and therefore was unable to lay hands on the goods or exercise any control over them. Feehan DCJ held that such service was ineffective to constitute a valid seizure, even though the debtor signed the bailee's undertaking. The improper service could not be cured since the seizure itself was a condition precedent of any such appointment:

It is clear that the sheriff cannot appoint the debtor until after making a seizure. He therefore cannot say that the debtor's acceptance of that appointment cures improper service so as to create a lawful seizure. The debtor cannot accept an appointment which cannot be made.

iii The Use of Force: There is no statute expressly regulating the methods which may be used by the sheriff to effect forceable seizure of exigible items in the possession of the debtor. The common law has filled the void to some extent. While the sheriff may not use force to break open the outer door of a *dwelling house* to execute a writ of *fi. fa.* (*Hudson* v *Fletcher* (1909), 12 W.L.R. 15, below at p 292), he may enter if the door is not locked. If, however, the occupant of the house seeks to bar entry to the sheriff, the sheriff may not enter by forceable means: *Vaughan* v *McKenzie*, [1968] 1 All E.R. 1154 (below at p 294). (See also *Semayne's Case* (1604), 5 Coke 91a, 77 Eng. Rep. 194). If a window is open the sheriff may enter through it; if however, the window is closed, he may not open it to gain entry, even though it is not locked. Once the sheriff has gained entry, he may then break open doors, cupboards and enclosures within the house. Finally, while the sheriff may be criminally and tortiously liable for an illegal entry, the validity of the seizure and sale of the property is probably not affected thereby. (Generally, see *Halsbury's Laws of England* (3rd ed) vol. 34, pp 686–7, for authorities supporting the above propositions.) ·

In Canada, the Criminal Code, R.S.C. 1970, c C-34, gives protection to the sheriff (who is deemed a 'peace officer') against criminal prosecution for acts committed in the execution of his duties. To what extent do these provisions and the provisions of The Public Authorities Protection Act, R.S.O. 1970, c 374, outlined below, change the apparent common law position with respect to the civil liability of sheriffs for forceable entry of a dwelling house?

The Criminal Code, R.S.C. 1970, c C-34

2.

...

'peace officer' includes

    (*a*) a mayor, warden, reeve, sheriff, deputy sheriff, sheriff's officer and justice of the peace,

    ...

    (*c*) a police officer, police constable, bailiff, constable, or other person employed for the preservation and maintenance of the public peace or for the service or execution of civil process ...

PROTECTION OF PERSONS ACTING UNDER AUTHORITY – Idem – When not protected – When protected.

    25. (1) Every one who is required or authorized by law to do anything in the administration or enforcement of the law

    (*a*) as a private person,

    (*b*) as a peace officer or public officer,

    (*c*) in aid of a peace officer or public officer, or

    (*d*) by virtue of his office,

is, if he acts on reasonable and probable grounds, justified in doing what he is required or authorized to do and in using as much force as is necessary for that purpose.

    (2) Where a person is required or authorized by law to execute a process or to carry out a sentence, he or any person who assists him is, if he acts in good faith, justified in executing the process or in carrying out the sentence notwithstanding that the process or sentence is defective or that it was issued or imposed without jurisdiction or in excess of jurisdiction.

    (3) Subject to subsection (4), a person is not justified for the purposes of subsection (1) in using force that is intended or is likely to cause death or grievous bodily harm unless he believes on reasonable and probable grounds that it is necessary for the purpose of preserving himself or any one under his protection from death or grievous bodily harm.

EXCESSIVE FORCE.

    26. Every one who is authorized by law to use force is criminally responsible for any excess thereof according to the nature and quality of the act that constitutes the excess. 1953–54, c 51, s 26.

MISCONDUCT OF OFFICERS EXECUTING PROCESS.

    117. Every peace officer or coroner who, being entrusted with the execution of a process, wilfully (*a*) misconducts himself in the execution of the process, or

(*b*) makes a false return to the process,

is guilty of an indictable offence and is liable to imprisonment for two years.

OFFENCES RELATING TO PUBLIC OR PEACE OFFICER.

118. Every one who

(*a*) resists or wilfully obstructs a public officer or peace officer in the execution of his duty or any person lawfully acting in aid of such an officer ...

(*c*) resists or wilfully obstructs any person in the lawful execution of a process against lands or goods or in making a lawful distress or seizure,

is guilty of

(*d*) an indictable offence and is liable to imprisonment for two years, or

(*e*) an offence punishable on summary conviction.

The Public Authorities Protection Act, R.S.O. 1970, c 374, ss 11, 12, 13, 16, as amended.

11. (1) No action, prosecution or other proceeding lies or shall be instituted against any person for an act done in pursuance or execution or intended execution of any statutory or other public duty or authority, or in respect of any alleged neglect or default in the execution of any such duty or authority, unless it is commenced within six months next after the cause of action arose, or, in case of continuance of injury or damage, within six months after the ceasing thereof.

12. No action or other proceedings shall be commenced or prosecuted against any person for or by reason of anything done in obedience to a *mandamus* or mandatory order.

13. No action shall be brought against a judge, justice of the peace of officer for anything done by him under the supposed authority of a statute of Ontario or of Canada that was beyond the legislative jurisdiction of the Legislature or of the Parliament of Canada, as the case may be, if the action would not lie against him had the statute been within the legislative jurisdiction of the Legislature or Parliament that assumed to enact it ...

16. A sheriff or his officer acting under a writ of execution or other process shall be deemed to be a person acting in the discharge of a public duty or authority within the meaning of this Act.

NOTE In the course of his judgment in *Eccles* v *Bourque* (1974), 19 C.C.C. (2d) 129, at p 132 (S.C.C.) Dickson J commented on the distinctions between the civil process and the criminal process, regarding entry into a dwelling against the will of the householder:

In the case of civil process the rule is that if a Sheriff's officer enters the house of A to execute process against the goods of B or to arrest B he enters at his peril and if the goods or B, as the case may be, are not present, he is guilty of trespass. It is said the entry can be justified only by the event: *Johnson* v *Leigh* (1815), 6 Taunt. 246, 128 E.R. 1029; *Morrish* v *Murrey* (1844), 13 M. & W. 52, 153 E.R. 22; *Southam* v *Smout*, [1964] 1 Q.B. 308. But in the execution of criminal process the test is whether there are reasonable and probable grounds for acting. If so, the entry does not become unlawful if the fugitive is not found on the premises. The entry of the police is legal or illegal from the moment of entry and does not change character from the result.

Hudson v *Fletcher* (1909), 12 W.L.R. 15 (Sask. K.B.)

[The plaintiff, one Hudson, was the president of a corporation against which a writ of execution had been issued. The sheriff seized goods contained in the company's store by breaking open the doors. The plaintiff lived above the store. He claimed that the seizure was illegal on two grounds. First, the goods seized had been assigned by the company to the plaintiff prior to the issuing of execution. The Court rejected this argument. Secondly, he argued that the sheriff was liable for trespass on the grounds that the sheriff had illegally forced entry by breaking the outer door of the dwelling house. The Court accepted this second submission.]

WETMORE, C.J.: ... The plaintiff Hudson lived above this store. It was his dwelling. He had practically, I think lived there before the alleged assignments to him, that is, he sometimes stayed there and sometimes at his farm. However, be that as it may, on 29th May, when the bailiff entered the premises, he was living over the store. The building was all under one roof. There were 3 entrances to the store, 2 in front and one in the rear. All these entrances were fastened. The bailiff went upstairs and interviewed Hudson and told him he had the executions, and requested him to open the store, and he refused to do so. The bailiff then forced open one of the outer doors of the store with a pry. It was fastened with some sort of a catch over the door, but he forced this open and entered. I hold that to be a breaking open of the store.

It is contended, in the first place, against the defendants Fletcher and Grant, that this entry was unlawful; that the dwelling house being over the store rendered the breaking of this outer door a breaking of the outer door of the dwelling house.

There was no communication in any way between the apartments upstairs, which Hudson occupied as a dwelling-house, and the store. This upstairs portion was reached by stairs which were outside the building altogether, through a door on the upstairs flat. The question therefore arises, was this a breaking of the outer door of the dwelling-house? Because, if it was, the sheriff and his bailiff were guilty of an unlawful entry, and would be responsible in damages.

Were I to decide this question upon my own unaided judgment, I think I should have little difficulty in reaching the conclusion that the sheriff's bailiff was justified in entering this building in the way he did. In *Lee* v *Gansel*, 1 Cowp., Lord Mansfield, C.J., in delivering the judgment of the Court, states at p 6 the reason for the law that the outer door of a man's dwelling-house may not be broken open to execute process. He says: 'This has been long and well understood. The ground of it is this: that otherwise the consequences would be fatal, for it would leave the family within naked and exposed to thieves and robbers.' It seems to me that in a building situated as the one in question, the family, living upstairs, would be no more exposed to thieves and robbers by one of the doors of the store being forced open than they were before such breaking, because the thieves and robbers could not get into the dwelling part of the building from the store. I am satisfied that, as the law now stands, by virtue of recent enactments both here and in England, the breaking and entry of a store situated as this one, would not constitute burglary. But, assuming that I can not be aided in this matter by the consideration whether this store was a dwelling-house so as to make it the subject of a burglary under the statutes, I must be governed by the common law and not the statute law. *Hodder* v *Williams*, [1895] 2 Q.B. 663, is the latest case I can find dealing with the question of what building may be broken into through the outer door to execute process. In that case the sheriff's bailiff broke open the outer door of a building occupied as a workshop and for storage of goods, no one living in it, and it not being connected with the dwelling-house; the Court held that the breaking was justifiable. The authorities bearing on the question, from Semayne's Case, 5 Rep. 91a, 1 Sm. L.C., 9th ed., p 99, down, were discussed, and, while the Court held, as I have stated, that the breaking of the outer door of that building was justifiable, the several Judges very clearly laid down that they so held because the rule did not include buildings not connected with the dwelling-house. Lord Esher, M.R., at p 666, says: 'It seems clear that "house" in that maxim means "dwelling-house," and does not include other buildings, such as barns or outhouses not connected with a dwelling-house.' And Lopes, L.J., at p 667, says: 'It has frequently been stated as the law that this privilege only extends to the dwelling-house and not to a barn or other building not connected with or within the curtilage of the dwelling-house ... The doctrine relied upon has never been supposed to apply to anything but a dwelling-house, and has never operated to prevent a sheriff from breaking open the door of any building not being a dwelling-house or connected with a dwelling-house.' And Kay, L.J., at p 667, says: 'A barn or outhouse not connected with the dwelling-house may be broken open in order to levy execution.' It will be observed that all the Judges lay it down, it seems to me by clear implication, that, in order to justify the breaking of an outer door, the building must not be connected with the dwelling-house or within its curtilage. I am therefore reluctantly forced to the conclusion that the breaking open of the door of this store was unlawful.

Regina v *Higgs*, 2 C. & K. 332, was the strongest case brought under my notice for the plaintiff. In that case the prisoner was indicted for burglary. He broke into a dairy of the prosecutor. This dairy adjoined a kiln, one of the walls of which supported one end of the dairy, and the kiln adjoined the dwelling-house, one end of it being supported by one of the walls of such dwelling-house. There was no internal communication from the dwelling-house to the dairy. To get from the dwelling-house to the dairy, a person had to go from the dwelling-house by a door into the yard and from the yard by another door into the dairy. It was held that the dairy was not a part of the dwelling-house, but it will be observed that in that case neither the kiln nor the dairy was under the same roof as the dwelling-house, and that the roofs of the kiln and the dairy were lower than that of the dwelling-house ...

I am of opinion that the damages by reason of the wrongful entry should not in this case by very heavy; in fact I think that they should be not much more than nominal. Technically, under the law, the outer door of the dwelling-house was broken open. In good practical common sense the outer door of the dwelling-house was not broken open at all. The plaintiff's occupation of the dwelling portion of the building was not interfered with in the slightest degree. I will therefore only award $20 as damages.

Vaughan v *McKenzie*, (C.A.) [1968] 1 All E.R. 1154

LORD PARKER, C.J.: On May 5, 1967, a warrant of execution against the goods of the respondent was issued by the Leeds county court for some £91 in respect of costs. The appellant, who is a bailiff of the Leeds county court, went with another bailiff on May 22 to the house where the respondent lived. When they got there, the house was closed, the respondent being away. The bailiffs waited, and later the respondent returned with her child. Outside the front door, the appellant and the other bailiff told the respondent that they were bailiffs, and had come to levy execution on her goods. It is true that no warrant was produced to her, but it is quite clear that she knew full well who they were, and what they had come about, because she immediately told them that she had written to the county court and the Lord Chancellor regarding these costs, and she said that she would not admit them to the house.

What happened then, was that she and the child entered the house and immediately attempted to shut the door, but the other bailiff, Mr. Richmond, got his foot in the door and pushed against it, the respondent on her side pushing to keep him out. The appellant came to the assistance of Mr. Richmond, and both of them forced the door open with the object of gaining entry to the house, whereupon the respondent finding a milk bottle handy, picked it up and struck the appellant on the head with the bottle of milk, whereby he sustained a one inch long cut requiring three stitches. Those are the short facts of this case. The magistrate stated his opinion in this form:

(a) That the appellant and Richmond were not justified in law for the purpose of gaining entry to execute a civil warrant, in attempting to push open the door which the respondent was endeavouring to close against them and that they were accordingly trespassers; (b) that, in any event, the appellant and Richmond, not having shown or read the warrant to the respondent, were not acting in the execution of their duty.

So far as that latter reason is concerned, I am quite satisfied that the magistrate was wrong. This was a case where she plainly knew that they were bailiffs, and plainly knew the object with which they had come, and the fact that the warrant was not produced was not, in the circumstances, fatal to these proceedings.

The real question here is whether the bailiffs were justified in attempting to push open the door by force against the will of the respondent. I confess that in the course of the argument my own feeling was that the magistrate had come to a right conclusion, and it is to be observed that in *Southam v Smout* [[1962] 3 All E.R. 104], which was dealing with the mode of entry which is lawful there is a passage in the judgment of LORD DENNING, M.R., where, after referring to *Nash v Lucas* [(1867), L.R. 2 Q.B. 590] he said [[1963] 3 All E.R. at p 108]:

SIR ALEXANDER COCKBURN, C.J., said that the later authorities say you may open a door which is only fastened by a latch. He thought that was going a very long way, further than the American courts had done, but the authorities were limited to the case where the door is shut but can be opened without violence.

I find it difficult to see what the real difference is, for present purposes, between a door which is momentarily opened but which is sought to be closed and can only be opened fully by violence, and a door which is shut and which can only be opened by violence.

However, in the course of the proceedings WINN, L.J., with his usual industry, found the case of *Broughton v Wilkerson* [(1880), 44 J.P. 781]. The facts of that case were almost identical with the present; there the bailiff went to the respondent's house, he knocked at the outer front door, which was locked; the respondent came to the door, opened it and held it until they had an altercation; the appellant then took hold of the door, put his foot between it and the doorpost and shoved his shoulder against it to obtain entry; he did not produce the warrant or tell the respondent what his business was, but the respondent knew him well and said: 'You, you shan't come in' and shoved him out. SIR ALEXANDER COCKBURN, C.J. said [(1880), 44 J.P. at 781]:

The justices seem to give a wrong reason for their decision, but the decision was right. The officer had no right to force his way into the respondent's house, which was the respondent's castle. Whether the officer was known or not this was illegal, and therefore he was not in the execution of his duty at all when he was assaulted. He seems to have provoked the assault. I think as he was clearly not in the execution of his duty, our judgment must be for the respondent.

LUSH, J., said [(1880), 44 J.P. at 781]:

Every man's house is his castle. That has been settled long ago, and a bailiff cannot force his way inside to lay execution for a debt. It is impossible to read this case and say that the bailiff was in execution of his duty.

Further industry, this time on the part of counsel for the appellant, has found that that case has been approved in *Rossiter* v *Conway* [(1893), 58 J.P. 350]. That case differed in certain immaterial respects; it was a constable executing a warrant of distress; that does not affect the matter, and instead of a foot between the door and the door post it was an arm. The court in that case held that the constable was not acting in the execution of his duty, and relied on and approved the earlier case of *Broughton* v *Wilkerson* (5). Both those cases are binding on this court, and I have no doubt in those circumstances that this appeal must be dismissed.

WINN, L.J.: I agree. The essential criterion in any such situation as there was in the present case is whether the householder has left a means of entrance available for the bailiff without the employment of any degree of force. As LORD PARKER, C.J., has said, this is a case where a foot was interposed between the door post and the door itself. In the other two cases arms were thrust in, but it is perfectly clear that whilst in those cases some force was used, in neither of them was entrance being sought vi et armis.
[The appeal was dismissed.]

Globe and Mail, August 5, 1975

Brampton bailiff says he's powerless
DESPITE ORDERS, JAILING OF DEBTORS IS IGNORED

BRAMPTON Orders against debtors issued in Brampton small claims court are being ignored with full blessing of the Attorney-General's Department.

James McCracken, a bailiff whose job it is to execute the orders, say he has about 150 of them issued in the past five years lying around his office unexecuted. He said most of them are orders to commit someone to jail for contempt of the Brampton small claims court but that he is powerless to serve them.

A court source says that written on most orders is a notation: 'Please note – the bailiff is in the habit of ignoring court orders. For any questions, contact the bailiff.'

An example is a recent committal order against a Bolton barn builder who was sued by Michael Neville, 30, of Bolton for unpaid salary just before Christmas last year.

Peter O'Hara of Port-A-Stall, who declared personal bankruptcy in May, did not show up in court until a judgment was issued in his absence ordering him to pay Mr. Neville $400 plus costs. On June 5 a committal order was issued.

Mr. McCracken still has the order and says since the company is padlocked and he cannot break in, all he can do is to go to Bolton, take a look at the padlock and return.

Mr. McCracken says that over the past five years he received an average of between 25 and 35 orders a year and he brought in only two people. He said the two were allowed to go after they apologized.

The court handled 2,000 claims last year. The maximum claim it can handle is $400. [Now $1000: see The Small Claims Courts Act, R.S.O. 1970, c 439, s 54, as amended S.O. 1977, c 52, s 4.] Of these, 90 per cent are paid up without problems. Orders against people and companies are issued on the remaining 10 per cent.

Mr. McCracken says he cannot do anything about the orders. He says he is a peace officer and not a policeman, so he cannot force entry to execute an order. He can only call the policy to help if his life is in jeopardy.

'Besides, I get mileage only for the first trip. Not if I go back again. This (policy) is left over from the horse and buggy days.'

Mr. Neville said he wanted the satisfaction of seeing Mr. O'Hara jailed after he knew that despite the judgment there was no way he could get his money. He said it took him from January to May, $50 in court costs and $100 in four half days of lost wages, to get the worthless judgment.

Ron Sherman of the Attorney General's office says Mr. Neville cannot get that satisfaction because the law isn't vindictive. 'We don't really put people in jail for debts. It is simply a policy not to enforce them (orders) from small claims court.'

He said the order may be for contempt of court, but one is still dealing with a debt.

He said that under the Bailiff's Act even if the bailiff knows there is someone inside who is not opening the door, he cannot break open the door without being charged with breaking and entering.

Asked whether ignoring such court orders – especially for contempt of court – doesn't undermine the court's respect, he said the small claims court was a people's court, where both parties were friends and just wanted questions answered.

He said some of the claims were for 50 cents and one could not jail a person for that. 'All we can hope for is that judges use their discretion and make proper orders,' he said.

As for Mr. McCracken, he says: 'Ours is a hard life. I travel 35,000 miles a year. The previous bailiff was found dead in his car. His body was found in the car on a cold night ...'

QUESTIONS

1 The sheriff receives a writ of *fi. fa.* procured by a creditor. He attends at the debtor's residence and a man answers the door. The sheriff asks for the debtor and is informed that the debtor no longer resides there. The sheriff asks if he can look around the house and permission is refused. As the door begins to be closed by the occupant, the sheriff blocks it with his foot, and looking in, sees what appears to be a valuable painting. The sheriff pushes at the door knocking over the occupant and breaking his arm. The sheriff seizes the painting and leaves (after calling for an ambulance). The man in the house is later identified as the debtor and the painting was his. The painting is sold at the sheriff's sale.

   What liability, if any, has the sheriff incurred? Is the sale valid? What would your answers be if the man in the house were *not* the debtor?

2 Should the sheriff be given greater powers in effecting seizures? Or does he have too many already? What kind of considerations are relevant to your answers?

3 A obtained judgment against B on a debt secured by a land mortgage, and filed a *fi. fa.* A later foreclosed on the mortgage and sold the property to C. The legal effect of foreclosure and sale is to bar any creditor's action on the debt originally secured by the mortgage. B insists that A remove the execution from the sheriff's office and A, honestly believing the judgment not to have been fully satisfied (the sale price obtained on the sale to C was less than the amount of the mortgage debt then due), refuses. What can B do?

   See *Price* v *Letros* (1974), 2 O.R. (2d) 292 (C.A.).

4 X obtained judgment and issued execution against Y, the debtor. X instructed his

solicitor, z, to take action to satisfy the judgment. Then y paid x, who forgot to inform z. z instructed the sheriff to levy on y's goods. After the seizure, y sues x and z. What result?

See: *Clissold* v *Cratchley*, [1910] 2 k.b. 244.

iv The Duty to Obtain a Fair Price: When the sheriff sells exigible assets of the execution debtor he has a duty to obtain a reasonable price. While it may not be possible to obtain fair market value for property sold in a sheriff's sale (given the disadvantageous nature of such sales) the sheriff nevertheless must make a very reasonable attempt to obtain a fair price in the circumstances: *Smith* v *Colles*, [1871] 2 v.r. 195 (infra). Where the sheriff makes a return that he has property on hand for want of buyers, the execution creditor may instruct him to sell the property for 'the best price that can be obtained'. (Ontario Supreme Court, Rules of Practice, r.r.o. 1970, Reg. 545, r. 559). Where there are prospective buyers but no offer is made which reasonably approaches the value of the property, the sheriff should not sell the property to them, but should postpone the auction to another date or should make a return that the property remains in his hands for want of buyers: *Pease* v *Tudge* (1915), 19 d.l.r. 158 (below at p 299).

Smith v *Colles*, [1871] 2 v.r. 195 (s.c.).

Barry, a.c.j.: Rule *nisi* to set aside a verdict for Defendant and enter a verdict for Plaintiff, with damages £164 7s.

It appears that a writ was sent to the Sheriff, without note or comment. The Sheriff was therefore required to do his duty according to the exigency of the writ. What was his duty? His duty was to levy without delay, and make the money required with all reasonable despatch. What is reasonable despatch was put beyond all doubt by the evidence as to the manner in which the goods levied on were offered for sale and sold. They were seized on Friday, were advertised for sale in two newspapers published the next morning. The advertisement announced that they were to be sold on the afternoon of the same day – Saturday. What occasion was there for this unusual despatch. The Sheriff appears to have been affected not so much by the stimulus of discreet diligence, as by the influence of panic. He listened complacently to rumours which turned out to be absolutely without foundation. He was told that there were claims against the property, and he apprehended that these, which turned out to be altogether imaginary and without foundation, would assume a tangible form and substance, and that some person might intercept him before he could complete the sale. Thus what is called merely activity to anticipate other existing claims, was in fact most disastrous speed, which led to the sacrifice of valuable property. This property was sold by the Sheriff for £10, and within three weeks it was resold by the purchaser for £240. There must be some reason to account for this great disparity in price. A sale by the Sheriff, or by a landlord under a distress for rent, or by a mortgagee, or by any compulsory process, is usually one at which a full and fair value for the goods can hardly be expected. It is a sale under coercion and for cash, and buyers must be prepared to complete their purchases on the spot. Such sales are advantageous to purchasers, and disadvantageous to the person whose goods are sold. Some allowance must consequently be made for the smallness of the prices obtained at such sales. Nevertheless there is not a sufficient reason for the great disparity in the prices obtained at the two sales. Although there is no direct evidence on the point, there is none that the second sale was not for cash. Evidence was given that the property might have fetched £400 if not disposed of under the disadvantageous circumstances which usually attend a sheriff's sale; and it seems to be conceded that it was unaltered in any particular. There was nothing to show that the title was in any respect better than when sold by the Sheriff. The cause for the disparity must, therefore, be the undue celerity with which the goods were forced on to a premature sale, and the improved price obtained on the second sale may therefore be attributed in a great degree, if not altogether, to the purchaser having satisfied himself by such inquiries and investigations as should have been made by the Sheriff.

In several of the cases cited, which are of undoubted authority, the charge of negligence on the part of the Sheriff was preferred by the owner of the goods levied on for a wasteful sacrifice of his property. This is a case of a creditor complaining that property adquate to pay his debt was sold with great indifference to the ordinary necessary precautions which it was his duty to take in order to insure a sale at a fair price; that he only received £4 of his claim of £167. The principle which governs each is the same, whoever may be the complainant. Whatever may be our inclination to support such public officers, either by protecting them against the consequences of their delay, by issuing a writ of *venditioni exponas*, in which instance they must in obedience to the order sell the goods for whatever they may bring, or by directing that contesting claimants shall interplead, we do not think this is a case in which the Defendant is entitled to hold his verdict. The rule will be made absolute.

Rule absolute to enter a verdict for the Plaintiff for £164 7s.

Pease v *Tudge* (1915), 19 D.L.R. 158 (Sask. s.c.)

LAMONT, J.: This is an application to confirm a sale made by the sheriff of a mortgage seized under execution. The facts are as follows: The plaintiff, having obtained a judgment against L.T. Tudge, and Sarah Tudge, his wife, issued execution thereon on January 5th, 1911, for $92.25. The execution was duly filed in the land titles office. At that time Sarah Tudge was the owner of a mortgage for $2,265 on the north-west quarter of 13-15-1, w. 2nd, made by Albert Schwalm to her. She had sold the quarter section to Schwalm, and had received the mortgage back. The mortgage was subject to a prior mortgage of $1,800. The value of the land covered by the mortgage I find to be $6,500. In May, 1913, the sheriff made seizure of the mortgage belonging to Sarah Tudge. He advertised the mortgage for sale by posting a notice of sale in his own office and in the office of the local registrar and six other places in Moosomin. On June 21 he offered the mortgage for sale. There were no bidders present. On June 28 he again offered it, with a similar result. On July 5 he again offered it, on which occasion he received an offer of $100 from A.T. Procter, and sold the mortgage to him for that sum. On the application to confirm the sale, counsel for Mrs. Tudge offered to pay the amount of the execution, interest, and all costs to date. This was refused. The affidavit of Mrs. Tudge shows that since January, 1911, she has been living in British Columbia, and that the first information she received that the mortgage had been seized was the notice of motion to confirm the sale. It also shews that at the time the mortgage was seized there was due to Mrs. Tudge from the mortgagor far more than enough to satisfy the execution and costs. I am of opinion the application must be refused. The duty of a sheriff in selling property seized under execution is laid down in Hals. Laws of England, vol. 14, p 56, as follows:

It is the duty of the sheriff within a reasonable time after seizure, to sell the goods for a *reasonable* price.

And he cites as authority for that proposition the case of *Keightley* v *Birch* (1814), 3 Campbell 521, the headnote of which in part reads:

The sheriff, having taken goods in execution under a *fi. fa.*, is not justified in selling them to the highest bidder, but if he cannot obtain a reasonable price should return that they remain in his hands for want of buyers.

In giving judgment in that case, Lord Ellenborough said:

If the goods taken in execution were really worth £300 or £400, I think the sheriffs are liable for selling them at £72 15s. 10d. The return ought to have been that they had taken goods which remained in their hands from want of buyers. If a chattel worth a thousand pounds is put up for sale and only five pounds bid for it, the sheriff ought not to part with it for that sum, and he may fairly say that it remains in his hands for want of a buyer. He ought to wait for a *venditioni exponas*, the meaning of which is, 'Sell for the best price you can obtain.'

A return by a sheriff that goods and chattels seized remain in his hands unsold for want of buyers is applicable not only to a case where no bids have been made for the goods, but also where no offer is made of a sum reasonably approaching their value 14 Hals. 58 & 59. I am, therefore, of opinion that the sheriff should not have sold a mortgage worth $2,200 for $100, but that he should have made a return that the mortgage remained on his hands for want of buyers. If, then, the execution creditor desired, I am of opinion that, following the English practice, he should have made an application for an order directing the sheriff to sell for the best price he could obtain. This order would be obtained upon personal notice to Mrs. Tudge, and if upon such notice being given and the order being made, Mrs. Tudge did not pay off the execution or find someone to purchase the mortgage at a reasonable figure, she could not complain if a reasonable price was not obtained for the mortgage.

As pointed out by Lord Ellenborough in *Keightley* v *Birch, supra*, sheriffs may often find themselves in difficult positions in which they must act at their peril. Cases may arise in which a sheriff may be honestly in doubt as to whether the price offered is a reasonable one or not. In such cases I take it that, if there was any reasonable evidence on which a Court could hold that a reasonable man would have reached the same conclusion as the sheriff, the course followed by the sheriff would be upheld. In the present case no one can say that $100 is a reasonable price for a mortgage which is a security for over $2,200 on property worth $6,500, on which there is only a prior incumbrance of $1,800. Furthermore, having seized the mortgage, and there being more than enough due from the mortgagor to satisfy the execution and costs, I cannot see why the sheriff could not have collected from him sufficient to pay off the judgment.

The application will, therefore, be refused.

Application refused.

NOTE Many cases have found the sheriff in breach of his obligation to obtain a fair price. In *Fair & Co. et al.* v *Wardstrom* (1919), 47 D.L.R. 16 (Alta. C.A.) a bailiff on the suggestion of a prospective bidder, sold goods in one block rather than by separate parcels. As a result substantially less money was received than represented the fair value of the goods. The judgment creditor succeeded in an action against the sheriff to recover the deficiency. In performing his functions the sheriff must exercise 'the judgment and discretion which a reasonably careful businessman would exercise under the circumstances' (at p 18, per Simmons J). See also *Owen* v *Daly*, [1955] V.L.R. 442, (which held that statutory provisions prescribing the procedure to be used by the Sheriff in connection with the sale did not abolish the common law duty to obtain a fair price); *Mullet* v *Challis* (1851), 16 Q.B. 239; *Lockley* v *Pye* (1841), 10 L.J. Ex. 305; *Wright* v *Child* (1866), L.R. 1 Ex. 358; *Edge* v *Kavanagh* (1888), 24 L.R. Ir. 1; *Watson* v *McDonnell* (1843), 6 O.S. 450.

In *Keystone Shingles and Lumber Ltd.* v *Royal Plate Glass & General Ins. Co.* (1957), 9 D.L.R. (2d) 337, the Supreme Court of Canada agreed with the execution debtor's contention that the sheriff had failed to discharge his duty to obtain a fair price in neglecting to make a proper inventory and appraisal of the goods. The plaintiff's action failed, however, on the technical ground that he had not adduced evidence of the price that should have been obtained by the sheriff at a forced sale. Even though breach of duty is proved, the plaintiff must show that he suffered damage thereby.

While the existence of the duty of care is well established, it may be difficult to determine in any particular cases whether or not the sheriff was in breach of that duty: see *Maple Leaf Lumber Co.* v *Caldbrick & Pierce* (1917), 40 O.L.R. 512 (C.A.).

Where the creditor gives instructions to the sheriff not to sell the property for under a certain price and the sheriff is not able to obtain a bid of that amount, the creditor may be deemed to have made an offer to purchase the property, and the sheriff, in withdrawing the property from further sale, may be regarded as having accepted the offer. In these circumstances, the debtor may be entitled to a credit of such 'contract price' on account of the judgment debt: *Corsbie* v *Case Threshing Machine Co.* (1914), 14 D.L.R. 55 (Sask. S.C.).

Trebilcock & Shulman – 'The Pathology of Credit Breakdown' (1976), 22 *McGill L.J.* 415, at 441–2, 445.

The excerpt reproduced below reports some of the results of interviews of a random sample of Montreal debtors who had had personal effects seized or wages garnished within the six months preceding the summer of 1972. Footnotes are omitted.

Of the debtors in the Debtor Survey who had had goods seized under execution, 50% said that the bailiff effecting the service had demanded payment at the time of seizure and 50% said he had not.

At the time of seizure, 61.6% of the debtors seized had no knowledge of their rights, 10.2% knew they had the right to withdraw $1,000 of goods or necessities, 2.5% knew they had the right to choose the exempt goods, 2.5% knew they had a right to appoint a solvent guardian to guarantee production of the goods on the date of sale, and 23% were aware of more than one of these rights. In 93% of all seizure cases, the bailiff provided the debtor with no information as to his rights. In 56.5% of cases, debtors claimed that the bailiff seized goods belonging to someone else. One reason why this figure is so high (apart from secured creditors' claims) is that 45.5% of the married debtors in the Debtor Survey claimed to have marriage contracts. In 95% of cases the bailiff chose the $1,000 worth of goods to be exempt from seizure. In 93% of cases the debtor made no attempt to appoint a solvent guardian and in 7% of the cases an attempt was made but one could not be found. In 44% of the cases, the seized goods were removed from the home, in 51% the goods were left in the home, and in 5% some seized goods were removed and some left. In 22% of cases, seizure papers were left and were signed by the debtor. In 44% of cases seizure papers were left but the debtor refused to sign them and in 34% of cases debtors claimed that the bailiff left no seizure papers (although he is required to do so).

From our impression of bailiffs' sales notices and the observations of the member of the research team who worked with a bailiff for part of the summer, most sales of non-business debtors are held at their place of residence. This avoids both moving the goods and, by virtue of the potential humiliation, increases the pressure on the debtor to settle. In the seizures that had reached a determination at the time of interview, 79% resulted in the debtor settling the claim to avoid sale. Only in the remaining 21% of cases did seizure proceed to sale. We believe even these figures probably over-state the percentage of seizures that generally proceed to sale. A member of the research team telephoned bailiffs' offices on the morning of 36 separate advertised sales and not one sale was proceeding. There appear to be several explanations for this. Seizure is used as a form of pressure on the debtor and appears to prove highly effective in this respect. Oppositions to seizure, either by the debtor or by a third party, prevent many sales, perhaps as many as 50%, according to the Court File Survey. Thirdly, the uncertain timing and dispersed locations of most of the sales hopelessly undermine the efficiency of the procedure as a form of liquidating unpaid debt claims. This latter inference was supported by our observations of a number of bailiffs' sales. There were rarely more than six people present and often only two or three. Often the bailiff would 'knock down' goods to members of his own staff. The other buyers were almost invariably second-hand dealers. Because the effectiveness of a seizure lies primarily in the threat it represents, in a sense the more 'value destruction' it causes the more effective it is as a collection weapon. We reproduce below the minutes of sale from an actual sale:

Debt: $1,438.54
Creditor: national credit card company
Debtor: Doctor
Number of Buyers at Sale: 1

1 1 complete rosewood wall hanging unit, consisting of liquor bar, custom cabinet for stereo and records, six drawer cabinet and serving tray, further cabinet with drop-down desk, 8 rosewood scatter shelves, size of unit 15′ long, floor to ceiling, (new, still in crates) Estimated value $3,000	Sold:	$100.00
2 4 seater leather chesterfield and matching leather armchair (new) Estimated value $4,000	Sold:	$275.00
3 2 rosewood end tables with glass tops (new) Estimated value $600	Sold:	$ 10.00
4 2 leather pouffes Estimated value $200	Sold:	$ 2.00
5 1 1974 Smith Corona portable typewriter and carrying case	Sold:	$ 15.00
6 1 decor lamp for wall unit (chrome, glass and rose-wood) Estimated value $285	Sold:	$ 10.00
7 1 20″ Black and White Admiral portable T.V. (year old) (1974)	Sold:	$ 26.00

Of the debtors seized, 64.5% had never been seized before, 11% had been seized once before, 9% had been seized twice before, and 15.5% had been seized three or more times previously. The Court File Survey shows that 9% of debtors were seized twice successively for the same debt. Thus for a significant portion of the debtors seized (35%), seizure had become almost a way of life.

It must be noted that while bailiffs are court officers in the sense that they effect service of court documents and execute orders of the court, in fact, in Montreal they operate in firms as independent entrepreneurs who charge creditors on a piecework basis, in accordance with court tariffs. They are normally required to be members of the Bailiffs Corporation of Montreal, which has self-regulating powers over admission and discipline. In 1972, there were about 75 member-bailiffs in the corporation. The corporation does not exercise rigorous disciplinary action. The Pointe St Charles study reports that as of 1972, a bailiff was last suspended for misconduct in 1952. Fines do not seem to enjoy much greater popularity. The Pointe St Charles study reports that in one case where a bailiff attempted to conduct a seizure, he was refused entry by the wife of the debtor who told him he could only make the seizure over her dead body. He replied that 'this can easily be arranged.' For this, the corporation fined him $300.

Other abuses clearly abound: failure to advise debtors of their statutory rights, contrived mileage charges on service, 'sewer' service, conflict of interest on sales and routine overseizure. An extreme example of the latter involved a seizure, against an elderly unemployed janitor on welfare, of an $880 stereo set for non-payment of the $17 balance of a $32 doctor's bill. In order to retrieve the set, the $17 plus $92 in various legal costs had to be paid, together with an additional $24 for retransportation charges.

NOTE The Sheriff for the Judicial District of York rarely seizes chattels and even more rarely sells them. If a sale is to take place, the sheriff advises the creditor to appear and bid at the sale. Why would he do so? What liability might ensue should the creditor be the only bidder and should the property be knocked down to him at a low price?

QUESTIONS Would you approve of a rule which required that before sale, qualified appraisers assess the value of the property to be sold, and that a sheriff's sale only be valid if a price of (say) seventy-five per cent of the assessed value was obtained? What are the ramifications of such a rule?

Should execution sales be allowed at all? If so, what procedural changes should be made?

Should the creditor (or sheriff) have a greater responsibility to assure that a fair price is obtained?

The suggestion has been made that a debtor ought to be compelled to sell non-exigible assets himself and turn over the proceeds to satisfy judgment debts. He would be required to state, on oath, that all items were sold and that all exigible assets had been disclosed. Failure to make honest attempts to sell, or concealment of assets would be punishable by imprisonment of the debtor. What do you think of such a suggestion?

Do you think it would be a good idea to have a 'respite time' after judgment and before execution is allowed? Consider this suggestion: after judgment a debtor would be required to remit the non-exempt part of his salary to a trustee for his creditors. So long as the debtor voluntarily complied with this requirement, no execution process could issue against the debtor. This system would apply only to debtors with net assets of (say) less than $10,000.

10
Garnishment

a / Note

The materials in this chapter consider procedural and substantive problems involved in attempts to satisfy judgments by means of garnishment of debts 'owing to' the judgment debtor. As you will recall, 'to garnish a debt' does not mean to put vegetables around it. Garnishment is the procedure whereby debts 'owing to' the judgment debtor are diverted away and are ordered to be paid to someone else for the benefit of creditors of the debtor. A garnishee (the debtor's debtor) who fails to obey a garnishment order and pays the debt to the debtor, may find that he is obliged to pay the debt a second time, to creditors.

In the context of consumer debt in Ontario, garnishment is a very widely used mode of execution. In fact, the seizure and sale procedures under writs of *fi.fa.* will ordinarily only be undertaken as a very last resort, after every attempt to divert debts owing to the debtor has failed. The creditor's reasons for using garnishment as the main tool are easy to find. Execution by way of garnishment produces 'real value'; that is, a one dollar debt diverted from being paid to the debtor and directed to the creditor instead, satisfies one dollar of the debt owing to the creditor. A three thousand dollar automobile diverted from the debtor and sold at an execution sale may produce only one thousand dollars for the creditor, thus severely injuring the debtor without producing the real value of the property in satisfaction of the debt. (Recall the discussion by Leff, supra at p 36). As well, seizure proceedings are viewed as bad public relations by creditors, and are deprecated by sheriffs and bailiffs as being very unpleasant. Nor will most debtors own sufficient assets clear of security interests to take them above exemption limits. Seizure and sale are also more time-consuming and costly to a creditor; after you have read the materials in this chapter, compare the costs involved in garnishing the debtor's wages with those involved in selling his interest in real property (see the sheriff's file, infra, pp 466–96).

However, garnishment presents serious problems of its own. Is it fair that the garnishee, totally isolated from the debtor-creditor relationship which produced the judgment debt, should be forced to bear the costs of determining the validity of garnishment orders or making payments to persons other than its debtor, on pain of being forced to pay a second time if wrong? What about the hidden transaction costs involved in garnishment of wages, the debt most frequently diverted? What kind of protection should be extended to garnishees or debtors to try to minimize these risks and costs?

b / Supreme Court of Ontario Rules of Practice, R.R.O. 1970, Reg. 545

Rule 597

(1) The court, upon the ex parte application of the judgment creditor, upon affidavit stating that the judgment is unsatisfied and,

(*a*) that some person within Ontario is indebted to the judgment debtor; or

(*b*) that some person not within Ontario is indebted to the judgment debtor and that the debt to be attached is one for which such person might be sued in Ontario by the judgment debtor,

may order that all debts owing or accruing from such third person (hereinafter called the garnishee) to the judgment debtor, shall be attached to answer the judgment debt and that the garnishee do at a time named show cause why he should not pay the judgment creditor or so much thereof as is sufficient to satisfy the judgment debt and the claims of any other execution creditors. Notice of the application to pay over shall, unless dispensed with, be given to the judgment debtor (Form 78).

(2) Where the garnishee is not within Ontario and is neither a British subject nor in British dominions, notice of the order and not the order itself shall be served (Form 79).

(3) Where a debt owing from a firm carrying on business within Ontario, but having members out of Ontario, is attached, service may be effected upon any person having control or management of the partnership business or any member of the firm within Ontario.

Rule 598

The garnishee shall be deemed to be indebted, although any debt sought to be attached has been assigned, charged or encumbered by the judgment debtor, if the assignment, charge or encumbrance is fraudulent as against creditors or is otherwise impeachable by them.

Rule 599

The order from the time of service binds the debts attached.

Rule 600

If the garnishee admits his liability, he may pay the amount admitted into court, less $3 for his costs of paying in, and give notice of such payment to the judgment creditor.

Rule 601

(1) If the garnishee does not pay into court the amount due from him to the judgment debtor and does not dispute the debt due or claimed to be due from him to the judgment debtor, or, if he does not appear upon notice to him, then the court may order payment into court of the debt (Form 80).

(2) If the debt is not payable at the time of the attachment, an order may be made for the payment thereof when it becomes payable.

Rule 602

If the garnishee disputes his liability, the court may determine the dispute in a summary way or may order that an issue be tried in such manner as is directed.

Rule 603

1 Where a garnishee has notice of an assignment of the debt or a claim thereto or charge

thereon, he shall give notice thereof, and the court may order the assigneee or the claimant to appear and state the nature and particulars of his claim

2 After hearing the allegations of such third person and of any other person who by the same or a subsequent order may be ordered to appear, or in the case of such third person not appearing when ordered, the court may order payment of the amount due from the garnishee, or may order an issue to be tried, or may bar the claim of the third person, or may make such other order as seems just.

Rule 604

Where the debt claimed to be due or accruing from a garnishee is of an amount recoverable in a county court, the order to show cause shall require the garnishee to appear before the judge of the county court of the county within which the garnishee resides, on a day and at a place within his county to be appointed by such judge, and the garnishee shall be served with notice of the day and place appointed and all subsequent proceedings shall then be taken and carried on before such judge.

Rule 605

(1) Where the debt claimed to be due or accruing from a garnishee is of an amount recoverable in a small claims court, the order to show cause shall require the garnishee to appear before the judge of the small claims court within whose jurisdiction the garnishee resides, on a day to be appointed in writing by such judge, and the garnishee shall be served with notice of the day appointed.

(2) The proceedings shall thereafter be carried on before the judge as though the garnishment summons had been issued out of the small claims court, and all proceedings may thereafter be carried on in the small claims court, and execution may be issued in the division court to enforce any order or judgment made.

Rule 606

Payment into court or under an order by the garnishee is a valid discharge to him as against the judgment debtor or any assignee or claimant of whose claim he has given notice and who has been called upon to show cause under the preceding rules.

c / The Small Claims Courts Act, R.S.O. 1970, c 439

130. ...

(3) Where a person has a judgment in the Supreme Court or in a county or district court and he desires to garnish the wages of the judgment debtor, he may file a certified copy of the judgment in the small claims court having jurisdiction to issue a direction to garnish the wages of the judgment debtor, and thereupon the clerk of that court shall enter the judgment in the same manner as a transcript of judgment from another small claims court, and thereafter directions to garnish the wages of the judgment debtor may issue and subsequent proceedings thereon be taken as though the direction to garnish had been issued under a small claims court judgment.

(4) Where directions to garnish are issued under subsection 3 and judgment is given against the garnishee, the judgment shall not be for an amount exceeding the jurisdiction of the court in a personal action.

141. For the purposes of garnishment proceedings under this Act,

(*a*) money that is earned or owing, although not yet due or payable, shall be deemed to be "owing or accruing"; and

(*b*) a reference to the amount of the judgment creditor's judgment or the plaintiff's claim, or words of like import, shall be deemed to include the amount of costs that have been incurred.

142. (1) After judgment has been recovered, the clerk of the court in which the judgment was recovered or the clerk of the court to which the judgment has been transcripted shall, upon the filing of an affidavit as required by subsection 2, issue a direction to garnish directing that all debts owing or accruing to the judgment debtor be attached to satisfy the judgment.

(2) Upon the making of the application, there shall be filed with the clerk an affidavit stating,

(*a*) the date and amount of the judgment and the amount remaining unsatisfied;

(*b*) that the deponent has reason to believe that the person sought to be named as garnishee,

   (i) resides or carries on business in the county where the court is located, and

   (ii) is indebted to the judgment debtor;

(*c*) where the judgment creditor intends to effect service of the direction by registered mail, the address where the judgment debtor and garnishee reside or carry on business; and

(*d*) where the judgment creditor seeks to obtain a direction to garnish in respect of wages and without exemption, that the debt was incurred for board or lodging or that the judgment debtor is an unmarried person having no one dependent upon him for support.

(3) The direction to garnish, which shall be in the prescribed form, and the affidavit used upon the application therefor shall be prepared,

(*a*) where the judgment creditor has a solicitor or agent, by the solicitor or agent; and

(*b*) where the judgment creditor has no solicitor or agent, by the judgment creditor or, if he so requests, by the clerk of the court.

143. The following notices shall appear upon every direction to garnish:

A / NOTICE TO GARNISHEE

Within ten days after the mailing to you or personal service upon you of this direction you are required to either,

(*a*) pay to the clerk of the court the amount owing or accruing from you to the judgment debtor or sufficient thereof to satisfy the judgment of the judgment creditor including costs; or

(*b*) file with the clerk of the court a statement signed by you stating,

   (i) that at the time of the receipt by you of this direction to garnish there was no money owing or accruing from you to the judgment debtor, and

   (ii) where you rely upon a statutory or other defence or set-off, the particulars thereof.

Where an amount less than the amount of the judgment debt is paid to the clerk of the court, you are required to file with the clerk a statement signed by you in explanation thereof.

Upon your default in complying with the requirement above set out, the judgment creditor may apply to the court for judgment against you, the garnishee, for an amount equal to the unpaid portion of his judgment against the judgment debtor and for his costs.

Where the amount sought to be garnished is wages, this notice shall be read subject to *The Wages Act.*

B / NOTICE TO JUDGMENT DEBTOR

At any time within ten days after the mailing to or personal service upon you of this direction you may dispute this direction to garnish or any of the statements therein contained by filing with the clerk of the court a notice setting out the particulars of your dispute.

C / NOTICE TO ALL PARTIES TO THIS PROCEEDING
Any of the parties to this proceeding, that is to say, any judgment creditor, judgment debtor or garnishee, may in writing request the clerk of the court to place it upon the trial list in order that the rights of any such party may be determined.

144. (1) The direction to garnish shall be served upon both the judgment debtor and the garnishee as soon as is convenient, and, in any event, not more than fifteen days after its issue.

(2) Service may be effected,

(*a*)   by personal service; or

(*b*)   by registered mail addressed to each or either of them at the address set out in the affidavit referred to in section 142.

145. Service upon the garnishee of the direction to garnish has the effect, subject to the rights of other persons, of attaching and binding in his hands all debts then owing or accruing from him to the judgment debtor, and payment by the garnishee into court of the debt so attached to the extent to which the judgment is unsatisfied is to that extent a discharge of the debt.

146. Subject to any request for a hearing by a judge, money paid into court by a garnishee pursuant to a direction to garnish shall, upon the filing with the clerk of an affidavit proving service upon the judgment debtor of the direction to garnish, be paid out to the judgment creditor, but no such payment to the judgment creditor shall be made until fifteen days after the date of such service.

147. Payment by the garnishee after service on him of the direction to garnish, otherwise than into court, except by leave of the judge, is, to the extent of the judgment creditor's claim and costs, void, and the garnishee is liable to again make payment to the extent of the judgment creditor's claim, unless the judge otherwise orders.

148. (1) Where a party requests the clerk in writing to place the proceeding upon the trial list, the clerk shall place it upon the list for the first court day in respect of which notice as herein required may be given, and at least ten days before such day shall mail notice thereof by registered mail to each of the parties to the proceeding.

(2) Upon the hearing, the judge shall determine the matter in a summary manner and make such order as he considers fit, and, where the garnishee has defaulted under the notice lettered A set out in section 143, he may give judgment in favour of the judgment creditor against the garnishee.

(3) Upon a hearing, in determining any question of liability as between the judgment debtor and the garnishee, the judge shall have regard to any statutory or other defence or set-off that has been set up by the garnishee.

149. Where a person other than the judgment creditor or judgment debtor claims to be entitled to the debt owing or accruing from the garnishee or any part thereof by assignment or otherwise, the judge, after notice to all persons interested, may inquire into and decide upon the claim, and, where there is more than one claim, decide upon the priority in which the respective claims are entitled to rank on the debt as the justice of the case requires.

150. Where a direction to garnish has been issued and no moneys are realized thereon, the costs thereof shall not be costs against the judgment debtor, unless the judge, who may give his direction upon an *ex parte* application, otherwise directs.

155. Where a person other than the plaintiff or defendant, claims to be entitled to the debt owing or accruing from the garnishee or any part thereof by assignment or otherwise, the judge, after notice to all persons interested, may inquire into and decide upon the claim, and, where there is more than one claim, decide upon the priority in which the respective claims are entitled to rank on the debt as the justice of the case requires.

d / The Apportionment Act, R.S.O. 1970, c 23

[The following provisions can be of assistance in determining whether or not particular accounts are subject to garnishment.]

1. In this Act,
   (*a*) 'annuities' includes salaries and pensions;
   (*b*) 'dividends' includes all payments made by the name of dividend, bonus or otherwise out of revenues of trading or other public companies divisible between all or any of the members, whether such payments are usually made or declared at any fixed times or otherwise, but does not include payments in the nature of a return or reimbursement of capital ...

2. Dividends shall, for the purposes of this Act, be deemed to have accrued by equal daily increment during and within the period for or in respect of which the payment of the dividends is declared or expressed to be made.

3. All rents, annuities, dividends, and other periodical payments in the nature of income, whether reserved or made payable under an instrument in writing or otherwise, shall, like interest on money lent, be considered as accruing from day to day, and are apportionable in respect of time accordingly.

e / The Creditors' Relief Act, R.S.O. 1970, c 97

4. (1) A creditor who attaches a debt shall be deemed to do so for the benefit of all creditors of his debtor as well as for himself.

(2) Payment of such debt shall be made to the sheriff of the county in which the garnishee resides, or, if there are more garnishees than one in respect of the same debt, then to the sheriff of the county in which any one of them resides.

(3) This section does not apply to debts attached by proceedings in a small claims court unless before the amount recovered by the garnishment proceedings is actually received by the creditor an execution against the property of the debtor is placed in the hands of the sheriff of such county.

(4) Where money is paid to a sheriff in whose hands there is no execution against the property of the debtor and there is in the hands of the sheriff of another county an execution against the property of the debtor, the court or a judge on the application of the last-mentioned sheriff or of a creditor or of the debtor may direct, on such terms as to costs and otherwise as seem just, that such money be paid over to the last-mentioned sheriff to be distributed by him as if such money had then been paid to him by the garnishee, and the court or judge shall fix the compensation to be paid to the sheriff by whom the money was received from the garnishee for his services.

(5) Where money that a sheriff is entitled to receive under this section is paid into a small claims court, the sheriff is entitled to demand and receive it from the clerk of the court for the purpose of distributing it under this Act.

(6) An attaching creditor is entitled to share in respect of his claim against the debtor in any

distribution made under this Act, but his share shall not exceed the amount recovered by his garnishment proceedings unless he has in due time placed an execution or a certificate given under this Act in the sheriff's hands.

(7) The sheriff is entitled to poundage upon money received and distributed by him under this section at the rate of 1¼ per cent and no more.

(8) If an attached debt that the sheriff is entitled to receive or any part of it is received by the attaching creditor, the sheriff may recover it from him; but a clerk of a small claims court is not liable for making payment to the creditor unless at the time of payment he has notice that there is an execution against the property of the debtor in the sheriff's hands.

f / Note

Rule 597 requires that the garnishee be inside Ontario or that the debt be one in respect of which an action could be brought in Ontario by the judgment debtor. The Rule has been considered in a few cases.

In *McMulkin* v *Traders Bank* (1912), 6 D.L.R. 184 (Ont. C.A.) the bank transferred the debtor's account to an Alberta branch from an Ontario branch before receiving the garnishee order. It was held that the debtor could still have sued on the account in Ontario and that the garnishee order was therefore properly made.

In *Century Indemnity Co.* v *Rogers*, [1932] 2 D.L.R. 582 (S.C.C.), an American resident incurred liability in respect of an automobile accident in Ontario. A garnishee order was served on her United States 'resident' insurer at its Ontario office. The existence of the Ontario office made the insurer 'a person within Ontario' and the order was therefore authorized by Rule 597.

g / Note: Special Creditors

As well as the powers of garnishment created by the Rules of Practice and The Small Claims Courts Act, many similar powers are given to 'special creditors'. For instance, powers akin to rights of garnishment are included in the Income Tax Act (R.S.C. 1952, c 148 as amended, s 224); The Employment Standards Act (S.O. 1974, c 112, s 52); The Workmen's Compensation Act (R.S.O. 1970, c 505, ss 112, 116); The Corporations Tax Act, 1972 (S.O. 1972, c 143, s 168); The Retail Sales Tax Act (R.S.O. 1970, c 415, s 31) and The Business Corporations Act, (R.S.O. 1970, c 53, s 231), *inter alia*. For a more complete list of relevant statutes and discussion of the privileged position granted by them to certain creditors, see Chapter 14, infra.

2 EFFECT OF SERVICE OF THE GARNISHMENT ORDER: PRIORITIES PROBLEMS BETWEEN GARNISHOR AND PRIOR ASSIGNEES OF THE DEBT

a / Introductory Note

The general rule that the execution creditor stands in the shoes of the debtor and can obtain no greater property interest in the exigible assets of the debtor than the debtor himself has, is as applicable to garnishment as it is to other forms of execution. When the debtor has legally assigned the whole of his interest in a particular debt owed to him prior to the service of a garnishee order, no debt remains 'owing to' the judgment debtor which can be attached by the garnishor. If, however, the debtor gives an assignment of present and future book debts, or creates a floating charge on his book debts, the priorities situation is less clear. The presence of the floating charge makes it difficult to determine the exact nature of the interest retained by the judgment debtor.

A floating charge is a security instrument creating an equitable charge on all assets of the debtor, present or future. The floating charge does not, however, attach to any particular asset immediately, but rather 'hovers' over all assets within its scope until some later event – known as 'crystallization' – causes it to attach to whatever specific assets within its scope the debtor then owns. The very nature of a floating charge implies that the chargor may carry on business and deal with assets covered by it in the ordinary course of business until crystallization. This power to transact business in the ordinary course is sometimes expressly given to the chargor in the charge itself. After crystallization, however, the charge holder has a mortgage on the assets still owned by the chargor, and has the right to seize and sell those assets as a mortgagee of specific property. The event triggering crystallization is usually defined in the floating charge, but in any event includes the appointment of a receiver, or the commencement of an action to enforce the security.

Suppose crystallization occurs in the interval between the service of the first garnishee order and payment out under the final order (R. 597). As between the holder of a prior floating charge and the garnishor, who has the highest right to payment of the debt ordered garnished?

Rule 599 of the Ontario Rules of Practice provides that from the time of service the order 'binds the debts attached.' Similarly, s 145 of The Small Claims Courts Act provides that service of the direction to garnish 'has the effect, subject to the rights of other persons, of attaching and binding in his hands all debts then owing and accruing ...'

What is the effect of the order's 'binding' of a debt? The cases are difficult to reconcile on this fundamental point, and have supported three different meanings for the term 'binds'.

The first holds that when a debt is 'bound', the property in the debt is absolutely transferred from the judgment debtor to the garnishor. Thus, if a floating charge is crystallized after the service of the garnishee order, but before payment out, the floating charge cannot attach the debt, as the property in the debt is no longer in the judgment debtor: *Kare* v *North-West Packers Ltd. and McGuckin*, [1955] 2 D.L.R. 407 (Man. C.A.) (infra, p 313).

A second view holds that the 'binding' of a debt upon service of the garnishee order does not pass the property in the debt to the garnishor, but rather, creates an 'equitable charge' or 'security' in the debt in his favour. On this view, the prior equitable interest of a floating charge holder takes priority over the subsequent equitable interest of the garnishor, where crystallization occurs at any time prior to payment out: *Imperial Oil Ltd.* v *Abilene Contracting Co. Ltd.* (1966), 57 D.L.R. (2d) 572 (B.C.C.A.).

The third view holds that the 'binding' of a debt merely operates to prevent the judgment debtor from further dealing with the debt to the prejudice of the garnishor: *Harrison* v *Aiton* (1880), 20 N.B.R. 371. The debt remains the property of the judgment debtor, and the rights of the garnishor remain subject to the equities existing at the time of service of the order. The result is similar to that which occurs under the second definition of 'binds' – the equitable interest of a holder of a prior floating charge which crystallizes before payment out takes priority over the interest of the garnishor.

Which definition of 'the binding effect' do you think is correct? Do the cases reach their definitions through mechanical jurisprudence or do policy considerations determine the choice? What policy considerations are relevant to the choice?

With the proclamation effective April 1, 1976 of The Personal Property Security Act, R.S.O. 1970, c 344 as amended (the relevant portions of which are reproduced supra at pp 270–3), another element has been added to the problem of the relative priority of a garnishment order and a floating charge. The Act is specifically expressed to apply to floating charges: see s 2. It should however be noted that corporate securities whose registration is provided for in The Corporation Securities Registration Act, R.S.O. 1970, c 88, are excluded from the application of the PPSA by s 3.

On the surface, there appears to be a conflict between the nature of a floating charge and that of the perfection which is necessary under the Act to preserve the priority of a secured party vis à vis an executing creditor. As mentioned above, a floating charge does not attach to any particular asset of the debtor until crystallization; yet under The Personal Property Security Act, there can be no perfection of a security interest until it has attached: s 21. This seems to indicate that a floating charge must remain unperfected until crystallization. Accordingly, if a garnishing creditor 'without knowledge of the security interest ... assumes control of the collateral through legal process' before crystallization (s 22(1) (a) (ii)), the security interest will be defeated.

If this is the correct view of the way in which the Act affects the floating charge, then the important question is the meaning of the phrase 'assumes control of the collateral'. Where the collateral is a debt, does the garnishing creditor assume control upon the service of the garnishee order? Or not until payment out? Until the Act is construed, the answer remains uncertain, but a court's attitude toward the question would not likely differ significantly from the way in which it approaches the question of the effect of a debt being 'bound'.

By focussing on the intention of the parties to a floating charge as to the time of attachment, a different interpretation of the Act is possible. Under s 12(1), a security interest attaches, (once value is given and the debtor has rights in the collateral), when the parties intend it to attach. If the parties can be said to intend that the interest attach when the other two requirements of s 12(1) are met, (subject only to the right of the debtor to deal with the collateral), then the floating charge will be perfected by registration of the security agreement and will take priority over the interest of any garnishing creditor. Those who drafted the Act proceeded on this view: see Catzman et al, *Personal Property Security Law in Ontario* (1976) at pp 62–7.

The problem of what is bound by a garnishment order presents itself in another aspect. Suppose that the garnishee owes the debtor an amount greater than the judgment debt pursuant to which the garnishment order was obtained. It has been held that the judgment debtor may assign his interest in the debt to the extent of the excess of the debt over the amount of the judgment debt in respect of which the garnishment order was obtained. A garnishee who pays the amount of the assigned excess into Court pursuant to a second garnishment order made after the assignment, will be liable to the assignee: *Yates* v *Terry*, [1902] 1 K.B. 527 (C.A.) (infra p 322). How much should the garnishee pay into court under the first order? The full amount owing to the judgment debtor? Or only enough to pay the judgment of the garnishing creditor? Consider the effects of Rules 597 and 606, and section 4(1) of The Creditors' Relief Act, supra.

i *Kare* v *North West Packers Ltd. et al*, [1955] 2 D.L.R. 407 (Man. C.A.)

The judgment appealed from is as follows:

FREEDMAN J.: This is a contest for priority between the plaintiff in his capacity as a garnishing creditor, and one Lovell Gough Stevens in his capacity as a receiver and manager appointed by debenture holders under certain debentures issued by the defendant company.

The debentures in question were issued by the company on July 18, 1946, and were duly registered on August 2, 1946, in accordance with the requirements of s 465 of the *Companies Act*, R.S.M. 1940, c 36. By their terms a first floating charge was created on the company's undertaking and all its property and assets, present and future. The debentures also provided that the principal monies thereby secured should immediately become payable if the company made default for a period of 60 days in the payment of interest. The company was so in default on March 31, 1954, when a meeting of debenture holders was called for April 9, 1954. At such meeting the debenture holders, acting under the powers contained in the debentures, appointed the said Stevens as receiver and manager, with power among other things 'to take possession of, collect and get in the property and assets charged by the debentures'.

It is common ground that the action of the debenture holders was precipitated by the plaintiff, who, on March 29, 1954, had sued the defendant company for $12,314.64. On the same date the plaintiff obtained a garnishing order in which seven named creditors of the company were the garnishees. As a result of the service of the garnishing order the sum of $154 has already been paid into Court ...

I may add that on April 19, 1954, the plaintiff entered judgment by default against the company for the amount of his claim and costs.

The plaintiff stresses the somewhat unusual circumstance that the debenture holders, instead of being strangers and third parties in the strict sense, are themselves almost all shareholders of the company. (Two of them, I note, are garnishees as well.) The plaintiff argues that since the debenture holders are internally connected with the company as shareholders, their position equitably is not as strong as that of the plaintiff, who admittedly is an ordinary trade creditor having no financial interest as an investor in the company.

I confess that I am not able to see the force of this submission. A person may surely occupy more than one capacity. A shareholder of a company may also be one of its creditors, secured or unsecured. I am not aware of any doctrine of equity, nor has any been cited to me, by which the rights of a creditor of a company are to be impaired or diminished simply because he happens also to be one of its shareholders. This so-called 'equitable' argument does not derive from equity at all. It is simply an attempt to obtain for the plaintiff, an unsecured creditor, preferential treatment over the debenture holders, secured creditors, on the ground that the latter are within and the former is outside the company.

One may, perhaps understand the plaintiff's sense of grievance in finding that individuals who were active in the internal management of the company when the debt to him was incurred should now emerge as contestants for priority with him in their capacity as debenture holders. But the short answer is that the debentures were duly registered according to law, and their terms were available to all actual or potential creditors of the company, including the plaintiff. Accordingly I must weigh the rights deriving from the debentures and the rights under the garnishing order according to recognized principles of law, disregarding the argument based on what is here miscalled 'equity'.

Because the time element is of some importance in this case, I refer once again to certain vital dates. On March 29, 1954, the plaintiff obtained his garnishing order. On April 9th, Stevens was appointed receiver and manager. On April 19th, the plaintiff obtained default judgment against the company. The determination of priority between the contestants herein involves a consideration of the nature of a floating charge and just how and when the same becomes crystallized or fixed as a specific charge.

The plaintiff suggests that the debentures are defective in form in that they contain no provision for the floating charge ever to become crystallized. It is true that debentures often provide that 'the security hereby constituted shall become enforceable in each and every of the events following'. But useful as words of this character may be they are not indispensable to the crystallizing of a floating charge.

... The vital thing is that by the debentures the company should charge its undertaking and all its property and assets, present and future, by way of a floating charge. This the company has done. Moreover other terms of the debentures set forth the circumstances in which the principal monies secured by the debentures shall immediately become payable, and the rights accruing to the holders thereupon, including the right to crystallize the floating charge. I find, therefore, that the attack upon the debentures as inadequate in form, must fail.

What is a floating charge? Out of the multitude of cases on the subject I refer to two, which simply and clearly set forth the nature of such a security.

Lord Macnaghten in *Governments Stock and Other Securities Inv. Co. v Manila R. Co.*, [1897] A.C. 81 at p 86, speaks thus: 'A floating security is an equitable charge on the assets for the time being of a going concern. It attaches to the subject charged in the varying condition in which it happens to be from time to time. It is of the essence of such a charge that it remains dormant until the undertaking charged ceases to be a going concern, or until the person in whose favour the charge is created intervenes. His right to intervene may of course be suspended by agreement. But if there is no agreement for suspension, he may exercise his right whenever he pleases after default.'

Again, in *Evans v Rival Granite Quarries Ltd.*, [1910] 2 K.B. at pp 999–1000, the following appears, *per* Buckley L.J.: 'A floating security ... is a floating mortgage applying to every item comprised in the security, but not specifically affecting any item until some event occurs or some act on the part of the mortgagee is done which causes it to crystallize into a fixed security ... it is a mortgage presently affecting all the items expressed to be included in it, but not specifically affecting any item till the happening of the event which causes the security to crystallize as regards all the items. This crystallization may be brought about in various ways. A receiver may be appointed, or the company may go into liquidation and a liquidator be appointed, or any event may happen which is defined as bringing to an end the licence to the company to carry on business.'

The points of significance which I take to be relevant to the present enquiry are that a floating charge remains dormant until it is crystallized by the intervention of the person in whose favour it is created; and that such intervention may occur by the appointment of a receiver.

Since Stevens was appointed as such receiver by the debenture holders on April 9, 1954, that is the date on which the floating security became crystallized, and the date with reference to which the issue of priority must be decided.

The garnishing order was issued on March 29th. It was issued on the same day as the statement of claim by which the plaintiff commenced his action. At that time the debenture holders had only a floating charge. But on April 9th, while the plaintiff's action was still pending, and before the plaintiff became entitled to payment of any monies that may have been attached by his garnishing order, the floating charge had become crystallized or fixed. In such circumstances the authorities make it plain that the debenture holders take precedence over the garnishing creditor.

The precise point is dealt with by Kerr on Receivers, 12th ed., thus (p 192): 'But the title of the receiver prevails over that of execution creditors who have not completed their execution ... and therefore is good against a person who has obtained a garnishee order *nisi* (citing *Norton* v *Yates*, [1906] 1 K.B. 112), or even absolute, if the charge crystallises before actual payment (citing *Cairney* v *Back*, [1906] 2 K.B. 746).'

The terms 'garnishing order *nisi*' and 'garnishing order absolute' are not in use under the Manitoba practice. The garnishing order under Q.B. R. 526 attaches debts due or accruing due from the garnishee to the debtor, and calls upon the garnishee to notify the garnisher within 7 days as to the existence of such debts and why the garnishee should not pay the same into Court. While it differs from both the order *nisi* and order absolute (*vide*, Encyclopaedia of Court Forms and Precedents, vol. 9, p 222; also Holmested & Langton, Forms & Precedents, 3rd ed., Forms 1068 and 1070), it is much closer in character to the former than to the latter. A garnishing order under our R. 526 must be considered according to principles analogous to those which would be applied to a garnishing order *nisi*, in those jurisdictions where such exist, rather than to a garnishing order absolute. The cases agree without variance, and counsel for the plaintiff concedes, that a garnishing order *nisi* will not take priority over a floating charge. (*Vide, Industrial Dev. Bk* v *Valley Dairy Ltd.*, [1953]. 1 D.L.R. 788, O.R. 70.) In the meantime, on April 9th, the floating charge became a fixed charge, thereby securing priority to the debenture holders.

Were it necessary for me to make a finding on the matter, I would hold that the same result would follow even in the case of a so-called garnishing order absolute, before payment has been properly made thereunder to the garnisher. That appears to be the effect of the decision in *Cairney* v *Back, supra*. The *Cairney* case is not referred to, and may not have been cited to the Court, in the *Industrial Dev. Bk, case, supra*.

My conclusion, therefore, is that the receiver is entitled to priority as against the plaintiff ...

ADAMSON, J.A. (for the Court of Appeal): There are two questions: The first is: What is the effect of the garnishing order? The second is: To what is a receiver for debenture-holders who have a floating charge on the assets of the company entitled?

Queen's Bench Rules 524–533 provide for the Attachment of Debts. If a plaintiff has judgment or has launched an action for a liquidated claim 'the court may order that all debts, obligations, and liabilities owing, payable, or accruing due from such person (hereinafter called ''the garnishee'') to the debtor shall be attached': Q.B. R. 526.

Rule 527 provides, in part, that 'A garnishing order ... from the time of service, shall bind the debts, obligations, and liabilities attached' ...

The effect of the garnishing order is that 'from the time of service' upon the garnishee it bound 'the debts, obligations, and liabilities attached', and an order for payment over to the garnisher goes if, first, the plaintiff gets judgment against the defendant, if he had not already obtained it; second, that the garnishee was in fact indebted to the defendant when the order was served: *Donohoe* v *Hall Bros. & Co.* (1895), 24 S.C.R. 683, *per* Sedgewick J at p 688; *Vater* v *Styles*, [1930] 3 D.L.R. 509, 42 B.C.R. 463, *Re General Horticultural Co.* (1886), 32 Ch.D. 512; *Anantapadmanabhaswami* v *Official Receiver of Secunderabad*, [1933] A.C. 394 at p 400; *Galbraith* v *Grimshaw*, [1910] A.C. 508.

The question is then: Did the defendant own the monies due it by the garnishees, and were they in a position to deal with them in the ordinary course of business or had they effectively transferred such monies to the debenture-holders? The security of the debenture-holders was 'floating' or 'dormant' or still in abeyance until the receiver was appointed. When the receiver was appointed, the plaintiff already had an effective equitable charge binding the sums owing by the various garnishees to the extent of the defendant's indebtedness to the plaintiff, and the receiver took subject to that charge: *Emanuel v Bridger* (1874), L.R. 9 Q.B. 286. What the receiver seeks to do here is to have his rights made effective *nunc pro tunc*. This is not in accordance with the meaning of a floating charge as stated in the various cases such as *Evans v Rival Granite Quarries Ltd.*, [1910] 2 K.B. 979.

The position and rights of debenture-holders who have a floating charge is stated with clarity in *Governments Stock etc. Investment Co. v Manila R. Co.*, [1897] A.C. 81 at p 86, and *Evans v Rival Granite Quarries Ltd.*, *supra*, and numerous other cases. The debenture-holders cannot take the position that they will allow the company to continue to carry on business and reserve the right, while still permitting it to go on obtaining credit, or preventing anyone who deals with it from obtaining payment. Until the debenture-holders appoint a receiver or take legal proceedings to enforce their security, that security does not attach to any specific asset of the company ...

The contention of the respondent (receiver) is that, while the defendant could have assigned the monies or given a mortgage in the course of its business, those same assets are not subject to the processes of the law. It seems to me that the inevitable conclusion from the meaning and effect of a floating charge and what was said in the *Rival Granite Quarries Ltd.* case is that the receiver for debenture-holders take subject to the equities which the ordinary course of business has brought about: *Gt. Lakes Petroleum Co. v Border Cities Oil Ltd.*, [1934], 2 D.L.R. 743, O.R. 244; *Robson v Smith*, [1895] 2 Ch. 118. On April 9, 1954, when the receiver was appointed and the floating charge crystallized, these monies had already been taken in execution. The receiver, in equity and by authority, takes subject to the garnishing order ...

There are additional reasons for allowing the appeal.

All the equities are with the plaintiff. The debenture-holders and the shareholders are largely the same persons. The company in effect had no capital. The capital stock which was issued was for services in organizing the company and as a bonus to those who purchased debentures. The debentures were issued when the company was organized in January, 1946. Interest was payable annually on April 1st. No interest was ever paid. The debentures have been in default for years and no action was taken by the debenture-holders until after garnishment in this action. The debenture-holders permitted the company to continue to do business and obtain credit and, when these creditors attempt to collect, the shareholders step in as debenture-holders and claim the only assets of the company. Moreover, to a large extent the difficulties of this company arose through giving credit to its own directors, officers and shareholders who are also debenture-holders. If the receiver's submission is right, any profits must go to the share-debenture-holders; if there was a loss, the creditors who had trusted them suffered the loss. It is all very well to say that the plaintiff should have searched and informed himself of the general set-up of the company and refused to give credit: we all know that a large percentage of business is done on mutual trust; a person who gives credit is justified in proceeding on the assumption that those who get credit intend to pay their honest debts – they are not required to anticipate that there is a deliberate scheme to avoid doing so. Those debenture-holders who did not join in the course which has been followed are to be commended. The words of Buckley L.J. in *Re Newdigate*

Colliery Ltd., [1912] 1 Ch. 468, 'Ought not the Court to act as an honourable man would', deserve a much wider application than in the circumstances of that particular case. Ought not the Court to see to it that those who ask its assistance 'act as an honourable man would'? 'He who seeks equity must do equity.' In the circumstances of this case a Court of equity should not use its powers to defeat the plaintiff's claim.

I would allow the appeal with costs here and in the Queen's Bench.
Appeal allowed.

QUESTIONS
1 Do you prefer the trial judgment of Freedman J or the judgment of Adamson JA (for the Court of Appeal) in *Kare*? Why?
2 How much weight ought to be attached to the fact of the virtual identity of the debentureholders, shareholders and directors?

ii *Industrial Development Bank* v *Valley Dairy Ltd.*, [1953] 1 D.L.R. 788 (Ont. H.C.J.)

Application to establish the priorities of various claimants as to funds in the hands of a Sheriff.
JUDSON, J.: The Industrial Development Bank is the holder of a chattel mortgage from the defendant company. The chattel mortgage also contains a floating charge on all the assets and undertaking of the company, both present and future. The floating charge is in much the usual form and contains express power enabling the company, in the ordinary course of business, to deal with its property until the security becomes enforceable.

On December 28 and 30, 1949, certain execution creditors obtained garnishee orders nisi against debtors of the defendant company. On January 7, 1950, the plaintiff issued a writ to enforce its security. The writ was served on January 9th. On January 11th and 12th the execution creditors had their garnishee orders made absolute. On January 14th the Sheriff of the County of Carleton was appointed receiver to get in and administer the assets of the defendant company. The Sheriff has in his hands three sums of money, $548.19, the proceeds of a seizure made under a writ of execution issued by one James Henry; $1,518.01 as a result of the garnishee orders; $375.70 collected by him in his capacity as receiver. The plaintiff claims the proceeds of these garnishee orders as property to which the floating charge attaches ... The execution creditors resist both these claims ...

The next question that I have to decide is when the floating charge crystallized. There is no doubt that the appointment of a receiver crystallizes a floating charge: *Re Florence Land & Public Works Co.* (1878), 10 Ch.D. 530 at p 541; *Evans* v *Rival Granite Quarries Ltd.*, [1910] 2 K.B. 979 at p 1001. There is doubt whether the issue of a writ in a debenture-holder's action will have the same effect. In one case it was held that the issue of a writ did not crystallize the floating charge so as to prevent the company from issuing further debentures of the same series: *Re Hubbard & Co.* (1898), 68 L.J. Ch. 54. However, Vaughan Williams, L.J., in *Evans* v *Rival Granite Quarries*, [1910] 2 K.B. at p 986, thought that the bringing of an action was sufficient. This is a leading case on the nature of a floating charge. It was followed in *Great Lakes Petroleum Co.* v *Border Cities Oil Co.*, [1943] 2 D.L.R. 743, O.R. 244. The opinion of Vaughan Williams, L.J., was part of the ratio decidendi and I follow it and hold that the floating charge in question here crystallized on January 7, 1950 the date of the issue of the writ. Therefore as to the second fund of $1,518.01 held by the Sheriff by reason of the garnishee orders, the bank has priority over the execution creditors, for at the time when the floating charge crystallized the garnishee orders had not been made absolute. An execution creditor who completes his execution by obtaining a garnishee order absolute while a charge remains a floating one, obtains priority over the charge. A garnishee order nisi will not give him this priority: *Norton* v *Yates*, [1906] 1 K.B. 112; *Evans* v *Rival Granite Quarries, supra.* The bank has no claim against the first fund of $548.19, this execution having been completed before the issue of the writ. This fund is, however, subject to the two statutory charges. They were in existence at the time of the seizure ...

As to costs, one counsel, appointed by the Court, appeared on behalf of all the execution creditors. He should have his costs out of the funds in the hands of the Sheriff. I think that this is a case where I should make the same order for all parties represented on the motion.

For a recent case applying *Industrial Development Bank* v *Valley Dairy Ltd.*, see *Ontario Development Corp.* v *I.C. Suatac Construction Ltd.* (1975), 20 C.B.R. (N.S.) 174 (S.C.O.); varied (1976), 22 C.B.R. (N.S.) 42 (Ont. C.A.)

NOTE The view accepted by the Court of Appeal in *Kare* has been expressly rejected in other cases in favour of the theory that the garnishee order merely prevents the debtor from dealing with the debt to the prejudice of the garnishing creditor. See, for example: *Imperial Oil Ltd.* v *Abilene Contracting Co. Ltd.* (1966), 57 D.L.R. (2d) 572 (B.C.C.A.); *Stacey Lumber Co.* v *Cazier* (1914), 17 D.L.R. 823 (Alta. S.C.); *Gandy & Allison Ltd.* v *Erectors & Constructors Ltd.* (1963), 43 D.L.R. (2d) 461 (N.B. Co. Ct.).

For a case distinguishing *Kare* on the grounds that the equities were with the first encumbrancers, and not with the defendant who had loaned money to the debtor company with knowledge that the plaintiff's earlier debenture was in default, see *Elrae Estates* v *P. J. Industries* (1973), 38 D.L.R. (3d) 94 (B.C.S.C.).

In Manitoba, however, until recently, the Courts have consistently followed *Kare*: see e.g. *Re McCurdy Supply Co. Ltd.* v *Doyle* (1957), 21 W.W.R. (N.S.) 288. But in *General Brake & Clutch Service Ltd.* v *W. A. Scott & Sons Ltd.* (1975), 59 D.L.R. (3d) 741 (Man. C.A.), Freedman C.J.M., the trial judge in *Kare*, mustered a majority of the Court of Appeal to reject the authority of the case:

iii *General Brake & Clutch Service Ltd.* v *W. A. Scott & Sons Ltd.* (1975), 59 D.L.R. (3d) 741 (Man. C.A.)

FREEDMAN, C.J.M.: We deal on this appeal with competing claims to certain moneys in Court that were paid in pursuant to two garnishing orders. The contestants are the plaintiff company, which asserts priority in its role as garnishor, and a Court-appointed receiver of the defendant company's property and assets, who claims the moneys are subject to the charging provisions of a duly registered debenture. A contest of this kind between a garnishing creditor and a receiver for a debenture-holder is precisely what this Court encountered in *Kare* v *North West Packers Ltd.* ...

There the Court, reversing the judgment of the Court of Queen's Bench ... held in favour of the garnishing creditor. This Court's judgment in *Kare* has been the subject of question and doubt in later judicial pronouncements. Its authority accordingly merits consideration and review. The present case affords opportunity for such a review. ...

[His Lordship set out the facts. A debenture had been crystallized by the appointment of a receiver one day after a post-judgment garnishment order had been served on the debtor's debtor, but before payment into court by the garnishee or payment out by the court. Freedman, CJM continued:]

We have then a situation in which the garnishing creditor served its garnishing orders before the crystallization of the charge contained in the debenture. But that crystallization occurred very soon after, indeed before payment into Court and of course before payment out, the latter event not yet having taken place. The plaintiff as garnishing creditor contends that it has priority, arguing that the service of the garnishing order operated as an absolute transfer from the judgment debtor to the judgment creditor of the property in the debt attached. The receiver on the other hand claims priority on the view that the debt attached represented an asset of the defendant company that was subject to the floating charge, and that, the floating charge having become a fixed charge before the garnishment was completed by payment out, the moneys in Court are properly payable to the receiver.

The plaintiff's position is supported by the judgment of this Court in *Kare v North West Packers Ltd.*, *supra*. An analysis of that judgment is accordingly required. It seems to me that in arriving at his conclusion, Adamson, J.A. (later C.J.M.), rested heavily on a comment made by James, L.J., in the case of *Ex p. Joselyne, Re Watt* (1878), 8 Ch. D. 327, 47 L.J. Bk. 91. I quote from Adamson, J.A., as follows [at p 413 D.L.R., pp. 253–4 W.W.R.]:

The question of a garnisher's rights is discussed in *Ex p. Joselyne, Re Watt* (1878), 8 Ch.D. 327. In that case James L.J., said, at pp 330–1: 'The moment the order of attachment was served upon the garnishee the property in the debt due from him was absolutely transferred from the judgment debtor to the judgment creditor. The garnishee could then only pay his debt to the judgment creditor of his original debtor. The property in the debt was transferred, and there was a complete and perfect security the moment the order of attachment was served.'

With respect, the observation of James, L.J., was inaccurate when he made it and it has continued so to this day. It was recognized as inaccurate by Brett, L.J., in the case of *Chatterton v Watney* (1881), 17 Ch.D. 259 ...

The inaccuracy of James, L.J.'s observation has also been recognized in various judicial pronouncements in Canada. Thus Williams, C.J.Q.B., in the case of *Re Doyle (a Bankrupt); McCurdy Supply Co. Ltd.* (1957), 22 W.W.R. 651 at p 656 ... [affd 23 W.W.R. 661], referring to this very language of James, L.J., said:

The first sentence in the quoted portion of the judgment is *dictum* and was never accepted by the English courts. It was almost at once explained and qualified. Mr. Bowles cited many of these cases to me. They are: *Chatterton v Watney* (1881), 17 Ch. D. 259, 50 L.J. Ch. 535 (C.A.), affirming Bacon, V.C. (1881), 16 Ch. D. 378, 50 L.J. Ch. 227. (Brett, L.J. said James, L.J., in using the word 'transfer' must be taken to have said it colloquially, and see per Cotton, L.J., a member of the court which decided *Ex parte Joselyne; In re Watts, supra*, and Jessel, M.R., 'the garnishee rules do not operate to transfer the debt attached'); *Re Combined Weighing & Advertising Machine Co.* (1889), 43 Ch. D. 99, 59 L.J. Ch. 26 (C.A.); *Geisse v Taylor*, [1905] 2 K.B. 658, 74 L.J.K.B. 912 (Alverstone, C.J.); *Norton v Yates*, [1906] 1 K.B. 112, 75 L.J.K.B. 250 (Warrington, J.); *Cairney v Back*, [1906] 2 K.B. 746, 75 L.J.K.B. 1015 (Walton, J.).

By treating the service of the garnishing order as having the effect of transferring the property in the debt from the judgment debtor to the judgment creditor, Adamson, J.A., concluded that the attached debt had thereby gone beyond the reach of the receiver claiming under the debenture. The garnishing creditor was accordingly declared to have priority over the receiver. But, with respect, James, L.J., was wrong in his assessment of the effect of service of a garnishing order, and Adamson, J.A., was similarly wrong in applying that erroneous assessment in the *Kare* case.

In the present matter Dewar, C.J.Q.B., referred to *Kare* as a 'binding authority in Manitoba'. It does, of course, bind the other Courts of this province. It does not, however, bind any Courts of other provinces. And it is surely relevant to point out that *Kare* has there been the subject of question and adverse comment.

Thus a similar matter faced Ruttan, J., in the British Columbia case of *Re Mardee's Ready-to-Wear Ltd.* (1957), 9 D.L.R. (2d) 745, 22 W.W.R. 515, 36 C.B.R. 149, the contest there, however, being between a garnishing creditor and a trustee in bankruptcy. In that case counsel for the garnishing creditor relied upon the already-quoted language of James, L.J., as authority for the principle that mere service of a garnishing order upon the garnishee transferred the property in the debt from the judgment debtor to the judgment creditor, and thereby constituted a complete and perfect security. Counsel pointed out that the principle there set forth had been followed in Manitoba in *Kare* v *North West Packers, supra*. But Ruttan, J., declared that counsel had not read far enough in his English authorities. He pointed out that the decision in *Ex p. Joselyne, Re Watt, supra*, had been considered in the later case of *Chatterton* v *Watney, supra*. He then quoted the language of Brett, L.J., to which I have already referred. Not following *Kare*, Ruttan, J., concluded that the garnishing creditor did not have priority over the trustee in bankruptcy.

A similar contest between a garnishing creditor and a trustee in bankruptcy came before the Supreme Court of Canada in *Canadian Credit Men's Trust Ass'n Ltd.* v *Beaver Trucking Ltd., et al.* (1959), 17 D.L.R. (2d) 161, [1959] S.C.R. 311, 38 C.B.R. 1. Counsel for the judgment creditor, relying on the *Kare* case, argued that the service of a garnishing order upon a garnishee was enough to make the garnishor a secured creditor, with resultant priority over the trustee in bankruptcy. Judson, J., for the majority of the Court, first of all distinguished *Kare* as not having been a case in bankruptcy. But he then went on to use these words (at p 168 D.L.R., pp 320–1 S.C.R.):

In litigation concerned solely with the position of the garnisheeing creditor under s 41(1) of the *Bankruptcy Act* it is unnecessary to enquire further into the authority of *Kare* v *North West Packers Ltd. & McGuckin* as a determination of rights between such a creditor and the holder of a floating charge seeking to enforce his security, and although I express no opinion on this matter, these reasons should not be taken as an indirect affirmation of the principle of that decision.

I read that language as raising a question about the reliability and authority of the *Kare* decision.

In the British Columbia case of *B.C. Millwork Products Ltd.* v *Overhead Door Sales (Vancouver) Ltd.* (1961), 26 D.L.R. (2d) 753, 34 W.W.R. 86, Collins, J., made reference to this very language of Judson, J. Partly because of what Judson, J., had said as well as on principle, Collins, J., came to the conclusion that the *Kare* case should not be followed.

The Court of Appeal of British Columbia took a similar view of *Kare* in *Imperial Oil Ltd.* v *Abilene Contracting Co. Ltd.* (1966), 57 D.L.R. (2d) 572, 56 W.W.R. 757. Davey, J.A. (later C.J.B.C.), delivering the judgment of the Court, said at p 575 D.L.R., p 760 W.W.R.:

I can see no substantial distinction for these purposes between a garnishee order *nisi* and the seizure of goods subject to a floating charge under a writ of *fi. fa.* If the floating charge crystallizes at any time after seizure, at least up to the time of sale, the resulting specific charge takes priority over the seizure ... The reasoning rests upon the principle that an execution creditor has no greater rights in the property of his debtor than the debtor himself, and that the debtor's property is subject to the debenture-holder's rights under the floating charge, which entitles him to a specific charge upon the seized property if and when the floating charge crystallizes before execution is completed.

Dealing specifically with the *Kare* case, Davey, J.A., said that in his opinion it was wrongly decided and that the reasoning of the Judge of first instance in *Kare* was to be preferred.

Finally, on this point, I refer to the judgment of Tritschler, C.J.Q.B., in *Armstrong Contracting Canada Ltd.* v *Public Cold Storage Brandon Ltd.* (1969), 6 D.L.R. (3d) 622. That case involved a contest between a garnishing creditor and a receiver on behalf of the Manitoba Development Fund, a debenture holder. In that case the learned Judge concluded that the floating charge under the debenture had crystallized even before the plaintiff issued its garnishing order. Counsel for the receiver submitted that, even if the fund's floating charge had not crystallized before service of the garnishing order, it had become fixed before payment into Court by the garnishee and certainly before payment out of Court. Counsel for the receiver invited the learned Chief Justice of the Court of Queen's Bench not to follow *Kare* because of the doubt cast on that case in various judicial pronouncements. Tritschler, C.J.Q.B., said that it was not necessary to deal with that submission. Had it been necessary, he would have said that *Kare* was still binding on the Court of Queen's Bench for Manitoba. But then he added these significant words [at p 625]: 'The authority of *Kare* requires consideration but that cannot be given here.'

It can, however, in my view be given in this Court.

The law on the question facing us here has been summed up by *Kerr on Receivers*, 14th ed. (1972), p 159, thus:

But the title of the receiver prevails over that of execution creditors who have not completed their execution ... and therefore is good against a person who has obtained a garnishing order nisi, or even absolute, if the charge crystallises before actual payment.

On the basis of the authorities set out above, I have reached the conclusion that *Kare* was wrongly decided and that it should no longer be followed.

In the result I hold that the claim of the receiver has priority over that of the garnishing creditor. I would direct that the moneys in Court be paid to the receiver accordingly.

I would allow the appeal. This is not a case for costs.

[Guy JA dissented on the ground that this case was distinguishable from *Kare*, because in the earlier case the floating charge crystallized after the garnishing order had been served upon the garnishee, but before the garnishor had obtained judgment. In *General Brake*, however, judgment was obtained by the plaintiff respondent against the defendant appellant before the garnishing order was issued and served. The garnishees had been ordered to pay the money into Court, and that money could only be credited to the judgment creditor, since the claim of the appellant was not a prior claim.]

For an analysis of the nature of the floating charge and priority problems related thereto, see J.H. Farrar, 'Floating Charges and Priorities' (1974), 38 *The Conveyancer* (N.S.) 315 and R.R. Pennington, 'The Genesis of the Floating Charge' (1960), 23 *Mod. L. Rev.* 630.

b / Rights of Garnishors, Garnishees and Assignees

NOTE Several cases have held that a judgment creditor will not gain priority over a prior assignee of the debt by serving the garnishee summons before the assignee gives notice of the assignment: *Imperial Bank of Canada* v *Western Supply & Equipment Co.* (1918), 39 D.L.R. 803 (Alta. S.C.); *O'Neil & Co.* v *Galbraith & Sons* (1914), 7 W.W.R. 155 (B.C.S.C.); *Turner* v *Waterloo Manufacturing Co.*, [1926] 2 D.L.R. 706 (Man. C.A.); *Lettner* v *Pioneer Truck Equipment Ltd.* (1964), 47 W.W.R. 343 (Man. C.A.). Why not?

Consider the position of the party served with a garnishee order. What difficulties might he face?

Yates v *Terry*, [1902] I K.B. 527 (C.A.)

COLLINS M.R.: This is an appeal by the plaintiff against the result of proceedings which were commenced by him in the county court. He obtained judgment, but on appeal to the Divisional Court the decision in his favour was reversed and judgment given for the defendant. He sued as the assignee of a debt due from the defendant to one Henderson, and he gave notice of the assignment to the defendant. Prior to the giving of that notice a garnishee order had been served on the defendant attaching all debts due from him to Henderson, to answer the judgment that had been obtained in the county court against Henderson. After the assignment and notice a second garnishee order was served on the defendant, in respect of another judgment obtained against Henderson in the same county court. Under these circumstances, what the defendant did, with regard to the fund in his hand, was to appropriate a sufficient sum to meet the judgment on which the first garnishee order was founded, and this sum he paid into court. He appropriated the balance in his hands towards satisfaction of the judgment on which the second garnishee order was founded, and he paid it into court in the action in which that judgment was obtained. That was an appropriation which entirely ignored the intervening rights of the plaintiff as assignee. The county court judge held, on another ground than that argued before us, that the plaintiff was entitled to recover; and it certainly seems to me that he was. It was contended in answer to the plaintiff's claim that the effect of the first garnishee summons was to attach in the defendant's hands the whole of the debt due from him to Henderson, and not merely so much as was sufficient to satisfy the judgment debt, and it was said that while the attachment subsisted it would have been wrong to appropriate any part of the fund to any other purpose, and that therefore the assignment could not take effect. This argument is not applicable to the facts of this case, for the defendant freed himself, so far as the balance of the money was concerned, from liability under the first attachment by the payment into court. He was affected with notice of the assignment to the plaintiff, and held the balance of the money for the assignee, and, as that exhausted the fund in his hands, he was under no liability under the second garnishee order. He remained under liability to pay the money to the plaintiff, and cannot raise the defence that he has paid it away elsewhere, because he did not pay it under any exigency but of his own motion.

I am therefore of opinion that the appeal should be allowed, and the judgment of the county court judge in favour of the plaintiff restored.

ROMER L.J.: I agree. Where a debtor has been served with a garnishee order covering an amount less than the amount in his hands, no doubt he cannot be compelled to make any payment out of the money in his hands to any one else so long as the attachment is in force. At the same time, it must be remembered that garnishee proceedings are for the purpose of enabling a judgment creditor of the person to whom the debt which is garnished is due to realize his judgment. The person in whose hands the debt is garnished holds it subject to the right of the judgment creditor, and has himself no right to the balance after satisfaction of the judgment. That right to the balance still remains in the person who originally had the right to the whole, and it is capable of assignment. Such a right was assigned in this case, and the assignment completed by notice; so that everything was done to make the assignment effective as to the debt in the hands of the defendant, subject to the right of the judgment creditor under the first garnishee order. In the result there was a balance left in the hands of the defendant bound by the assignment, and it was his duty not to let the subsequent garnishee order pass without notice that the fund was not really that of the judgment debtor, so that it could be attached, but that of an assignee. By breach of that obligation the assignee has lost his money, and according to well-known principles the defendant is liable for that loss.
[The appeal was allowed.]

NOTE See Rule 603 of the Ontario Supreme Court Rules of Practice, supra p 305, prescribing the procedure to be followed when a garnishee has notice of an assignment.

Will a garnishee always be protected by the provisions of Rules 603 and 606? Consider the following facts: a floating charge contains a provision by which the charge crystallizes immediately upon the chargor's (debtor's) suffering any judgment to be signed against him; a creditor obtains judgment against the chargor and serves a garnishee order nisi (R. 597) on a debtor of the judgment debtor (the garnishee); the garnishee is unaware of the existence of the floating charge or of its terms providing for 'automatic crystallization'; the garnishee admits liability and pays the debt into court pursuant to Rule 600; will the garnishee be protected by Rule 606 in a subsequent action by the floating chargeholder against him? For a somewhat similar fact situation, see *Armstrong Contracting* v *Public Cold Storage Brandon Ltd.* (1969), 6 D.L.R. (3d) 622 (Man. Q.B.), where, however, the issue presented by this question did not arise.

3 DEBTS SUBJECT TO GARNISHMENT

a / Introductory Note
Both Rule 597 of the Supreme Court Rules of Practice, and s 142 of The Small Claims Courts Act provide that only 'debts owing or accruing ... to the judgment debtor' may be garnished. Garnishment has occasionally been made extremely difficult because of the interpretation given to these words. After you have read the material in this Chapter, consider whether the extended definition in s 141 of The Small Claims Courts Act means that the interpretation of the phrase 'owing or accruing due' should be

different in Small Claims Court garnishment than in cases of garnishment in the higher Courts. The Small Claims Court garnishment procedure is often used by holders of County or Supreme Court judgments. Why?

The manner in which the phrase is interpreted will determine when a garnishment order must be made (or served), and the number of debts which the order will bind.

A threshold problem involves the question of whether a debt exists at all at the relevant time. Although this matter was raised generally in Chapter 1, it merits special attention in the context of garnishment.

The issue has sometimes been confused by 'the entire contracts rule.' In the *Law of Contract*, (4th Ed.), Treitel defines the rule as follows:

A contract is said to be 'entire' where it provides for *complete* performance by one party before the other is to pay or render such other counterperformance as may be agreed. At common law a party who fails to complete performance of an entire contract cannot recover anything. (at p 678)

Thus, in *Sumpter* v *Hedges*, [1898] 1 Q.B. 673, a contractor had agreed to build a house for a lump sum. He ran out of money and was unable to complete the work. He could not recover *any* money for the partial completion of the contract. Similarly, in *Cutter* v *Powell* (1795), 6 T.R. 320, a sailor's contract provided for the payment of a lump sum upon the completion of a voyage. The sailor died before the ship arrived at its destination. The contract was held to be an 'entire contract' and the administrator of his estate was unable to recover any compensation in respect of the time the sailor had served on board the ship before his death.

Citing *Button* v *Thompson* (1869), L.R. 4 C.P. 330, Treitel points out (at p 682) that 'the question whether a particular obligation is entire or severable is one of construction; and where a party agrees to do work under a contract, the Courts are reluctant to construe the contract as to require complete performance before payment is due.'

Where a contract is entire, and has not been completely performed, no debt can exist in respect of the part performance, and thus garnishment before complete performance is impossible. Consider the application of the entire contracts rule to the case of *Quercetti* v *Tranquilli* (infra p 325). What does its application do to the holding in that case? Of course, the fact that a contract is entire does not change the fact that once the entire performance is rendered, a debt may exist though the time for payment has not yet arrived (*Garner* v *Strickland* (infra p 326)).

Some of the problems created by the entire contracts rule for the timing of garnishment proceedings may be solved by provisions of The Apportionment Act, considered in *Lee* v *MacDonald*, infra p 328. If (for instance), a salary can be regarded as having been 'earned' from day to day, a creditor can garnish it at any time before payment, although the garnishee need only pay in response to the garnishment order at such time as he would be required to pay the judgment debtor had no garnishment intervened.

The smooth operation of The Apportionment Act to produce results similar to that reached in *Lee* v *MacDonald* may be frustrated if dicta suggest that The Apportionment Act cannot be used by a party in breach of his obligations. For instance, suppose rent is payable to a landlord at the completion of one month's occupancy by a tenant. Can a creditor of the landlord garnish the rent half way through the month? Apparently so, if The Apportionment Act applies, for half of the rent would be deemed earned thereunder, mid-way in the month. But can the landlord rely on the Act to claim half a month's rent if he wrongfully turns the tenant out on the 16th day of the month? And if he cannot, can the creditor rely on The Apportionment Act as of the 15th of the month, if no one knows until the end of the month whether or not the landlord can use The Apportionment Act? See the dicta in *Clapham* v *Draper* (1885), Cab. E1. 484, and *Moriarty* v *Regents' Garage Co.*, [1921] 1 K.B. 423 at 434 where the view is expressed that The Apportionment Act cannot be used by a party in breach. Surely these views ought not to be accepted. Should an employee who has an entire contract for six months' work and who is properly dismissed for cause two days from the end not be allowed to recover anything? Such a view would negate the policy supporting The Apportionment Act. Dicta against the view may be found in the judgment of McCardie J in the *Moriarty* case (at 448–9). The failure to consider this problem at all in *Lee* v *MacDonald* may mean that the 'better' view of McCardie J will prevail in Canada.

Problems of whether a debt exists at all may be raised when the obligation to pay is somehow conditional. These problems are discussed infra, p 340ff.

Canadian Bank of Commerce v *Dabrowski et al.* (infra p 336), raises a second 'timing question' involved in garnishment proceedings. Does the garnishment order attach debts in existence at the time the order is made, or at the time of service?

Although we have already considered what types of debt may be exempt from garnishment generally, certain particular debts may become exempt depending on the definition given to the word 'debt'. The problem is illustrated by *Moir* v *Franciotta* (infra p 339).

b / Debts Owing or Accruing Due

i *Quercetti* v *Tranquilli*, [1941] 4 D.L.R. 63 (B.C.C.A.)

The judgment of the Court was delivered by
McDONALD J.A.: This is an appeal from an order made by His Honour Judge Lennox dismissing an application by the judgment debtor to set aside a garnishing order, dated December 5, 1940, and served on the garnishee at 4 o'clock on that day. The garnishee and judgment debtor filed affidavits to the effect that the salary of the judgment debtor (who was employed by the garnishee as a floor-worker), for the week ending at midnight Thursday, December 5, 1940, was not payable to him until Friday, December 6, 1940, and that the said judgment debtor was not entitled to payment of his said salary until said Friday, December 6, 1940, and that the said arrangements for payment were a part of the terms of his employment.

Under the *Attachment of Debts Act* [R.S.B.C. 1936, c 17, s 3(1)] all debts owing, payable, or accruing due from the garnishee to the judgment debtor may be attached. The point for decision is whether or not the salary of the judgment debtor under the circumstances above mentioned was effectually attached by the order which was served. On the authorities I think the question must be answered in the negative. The words 'or accruing due' are to be found originally in the *Common Law Procedure Act*. They were carried into the Ontario *Common Law Procedure Act* and later into other Ontario statutes. These words were the subject of many decisions in Ontario, the result of such decisions I think being that the test to be applied is whether or not the judgment debtor himself could have brought action against the garnishee for the money in question at the moment when the attaching order was served. Applying that test to the present case I think it is clear on the evidence which was before the learned Judge below and which appears in the appeal book that no such action could have been successfully brought. In *Shanly v Moore* (1863), 3 P.R. (Ont.) 223 it was held that a salary payable to the physician of a municipal corporation who held his appointment at the will of the corporation at an annual salary of $400, payable quarterly, was neither a debt due nor accruing due within the meaning of the *Common Law Procedure Act* and therefore could not be attached. In *McCraney* v *McLeod* (1885), 10 P.R. (Ont.) 539 a contractor had contracted to erect a house for the price of $1,225, of which $600 was paid during the progress of construction and the remainder was payable on completion and it was held by the Master in Chambers, whose judgment was affirmed by Rose J., that at the time of the serving of the attaching order on March 15, 1884, the house not having been finished, no debt existed according to the terms of the contract, and though the owner had actually taken possession on April 1, no promise to pay had arisen by implication and therefore there was nothing upon which the attaching order could operate. So also in *Central Bk. of Canada* v *Ellis* (1893), 20 O.A.R. 364 it was held by the Court of Appeal that the salary of a judgment debtor not actually due or accruing due at the time of service of the attaching order, but which might thereafter become due, could not be attached to answer the judgment debt, and it was so held even although it was argued that *Consolidated Rule* 935, then in force, had very much extended the powers of attachment of debts.

Several other technical objections were taken to the form of the affidavit and of the order but as the above in my opinion disposes of the case it is not necessary to deal with these matters.

I would allow the appeal with costs here and below.

Appeal allowed.

NOTE If wages are paid in advance they are not garnishable, for there is no debt due at any relevant time: *Wilson* v *Fleming* (1901), 1 O.L.R. 599 (Div. Ct.); *Fallis* v *Wilson* (1907), 13 O.L.R. 595. In the latter case, Cartwright, Master in Chambers said (at p 597): 'There is no law which forbids an employer to pay his servant's wages in advance ... If any one, to save himself annoyance, deliberately pays in advance, the creditor is helpless ...'

QUESTION Would it matter that the 'advance payment scheme' was first used by the debtor and his debtor after the former had suffered judgment to be entered against him, and as a deliberate means of making garnishment impossible?

ii *Garner* v *Strickland and Western Forest Industries Ltd.*, [1955] 4 D.L.R. 329 (B.C.C.A.)

The judgment of the Court was delivered by
SIDNEY SMITH J.A.: This case raises the neat point whether wages earned but not payable at the time a garnishing order is served on the employer are well attached. Counsel for the garnishee told us his client in contesting the present attachment was not acting capriciously but simply sought clarification of the principle for its future guidance. This is quite understandable.

The defendant is a logger employed by the garnishee. The plaintiff having a judgment against the defendant served a garnishing order on May 18th last and an issue was directed on the garnishee's liability. The order directing the issue did not specify the exact amount of time to which the question of liability was directed. His Honour Judge Hanna giving his decision on the issue states that 'the question to be decided by me is whether or not at the time of service of the garnishing order there was an attachable debt'.

This language follows the usual wording of an issue and the case was argued throughout on the basis that liability at the time of service was the bone of contention. On this point reference may be made to an interesting article by Mr. D.M. Gordon, Q.C., in the Canadian Bar Review of last December, *viz.*, 32 C.B.R. 1141.

The defendant logger was employed upon a daily basis. He was actually paid twice monthly, and it was a term of his employment that his payments were only to be made up to a date a week earlier than the pay day. He was paid on the 8th of each month for his earnings up to the end of the previous month and on the 23rd for his earnings up to the 15th. The garnishing order here was served, as we have said, on the 18th.

The learned Judge who tried the issue decided that the order attached nothing, saying: 'I am holding that the time of payment is part of the contract of employment, that the employee in this case could not have enforced payment at an earlier time and following the decision in *Quercetti* v *Tranquilli* I hold that the garnishing order was ineffective.'

The garnishing order, as is usual, attached 'all debts, obligations and liabilities owing, payable or accruing due'. The respondent before us followed the reasoning of the learned Judge and his factum puts his case thus: 'At the time the garnishing order was served the wages of the judgment debtor would only be "accruing due" if at that moment of time he could have brought action for such wages against his employer'.

[His Lordship referred to the decision in *Quercetti* and continued:]

We have no criticism to make of the decision in *Quercetti* v *Tranquilli* which was perfectly sound, but, with deference, we consider that the above principle is far too broadly stated as the basis of liability under all garnishing orders. In *Quercetti* v *Tranquilli* the order held to be ineffective was served half an hour before the wages sought to be attached were fully earned. Where it is a question whether money has been earned or not then the test proposed by McDonald J.A. [in *Quercetti*] is perfectly sound and it was the right test in the case before him. But the present case is essentially different. There can be debts already owing but not yet recoverable by action because the parties have postponed the date of payment. The debt is a present debt, the payment is to be a future payment. There are many cases in which such debts have been held garnishable; we doubt if this proposition has ever been disputed.

We think a striking example of this principle may be found in *Tapp* v *Jones* (1875), L.R. 10 Q.B. 591. There the debtor had agreed to pay the garnishee a sum of money by monthly instalments over a period and it was held that even the future instalments could be attached, though the order absolute against the garnishee could only direct him to pay over the money as it became payable. It would appear that the fact that a garnisheed debt cannot be sued for until a later maturity date has been reached has nothing to do with the matter except so far as it affects the form of the order absolute to be made against a garnishee.

There is an obvious distinction between an obligation to pay which is only conditional on the effluxion of time and an obligation which is merely inchoate until the other party has fully rendered services which are a condition precedent to the completion of the obligation. In the language of Lamont J.A. in *Barsi* v *Farcas*, [1924] 1 D.L.R. 1154, 18 S.L.R. 158, the distinction is made between a 'perfected debt' and a 'conditional one'. He illustrates the difference aptly by comparing the money payable under a mortgage with that payable under an agreement for sale which is affected by questions of title, etc. In the *Quercetti* case if the employee had failed to perform the work which he had been employed to do in the last half-hour of his employment he would not have been entitled to any wages. So his wages were not accruing due.

How different to that is the present case! Here the wages were earned from day to day and there was no question of the employer's obligation to pay being inchoate or conditional. Nothing but the effluxion of time was needed to make it absolute. The wages were therefore attachable.

Respondent's counsel said that if the defendant had quit his job on the 18th the money then earned would have been payable to him. However, counsel added 'but he did not quit'. The significance of this circumstance was not apparent. We think it had none. Even if while the defendant was employed he had later done some act that gave the employer a claim against him, it would not have meant anything. The authorities show that a counterclaim or even a set-off arising after the order is served does not cut down the amount attached. Still less could the bare possibility that the counterclaim might arise mean anything of any consequence here. It is not even suggested that any cross-claim ever did arise.

The remarks of McDonald J.A. were *obiter* and were directed to facts entirely different from those here; therefore we do not feel in any way bound by them. We think that that learned Judge would have been the first to concede that they were not meant to apply to a case like the present.

Counsel for the respondent argued in the alternative that the addition of the definition of debt or moneys accruing due and of s-s (3) to s 3 of the *Attachment of Debts Act*, R.S.B.C. 1936, c 17, by 1944, c 1, ss 2 and 3, following the decision in *Quercetti* v *Tranquilli, supra*, was intended to restrict the right to attach salary or wages to those which had accrued due or become payable or which would accrue due or become payable within 4 days after swearing the necessary affidavit. Neither the history nor the language supports that construction. Whatever additional rights of attachment may be conferred by the subsection, salary and wages remain attachable whenever the circumstances meet the requirements of s 3(1) of the Act.

We accordingly would allow the appeal.

Appeal allowed.

QUESTION Assuming that the exact facts of *Garner* occur in Ontario and that garnishment proceedings are undertaken under the Rules, what order will be made on the 'show cause proceeding'?

iii *Lee* v *MacDonald* (1970), 12 D.L.R. (3d) 404 (N.S. Co. Ct.)

O'HEARN, CO.CT.J.: This is an application under Supreme Court Rules O. XLIII for the attachment of the defendant's wages or salary. On the application, counsel for the defendant made three objections and these were supported by counsel for the garnishee ...

The third objection is based on the affidavit of David Steele, deputy city clerk of the City of Dartmouth, and proposes that the order *nisi* was served on April 8, 1970, that at that time there were no debts owing or accruing due from the Board of School Commissioners for the City of Dartmouth to the judgment debtor, and:

4. That under a Group Professional Agreement between the Board of School Commissioners of the City of Dartmouth and The Nova Scotia Teachers' Union Article IV, section D states 'During the months of September, October, November, December, January, February, March, April, May and June, every teacher on a full-time basis shall be paid by cheque twice each month – that is, on the 15th and on the last teaching day of the aforementioned months.'

The defendant and the garnishee rely on the decision of McLellan, Co.Ct.J., in *G.A.C. International Finance Corp. Ltd.* v *Toomey et al.* (1967), 64 D.L.R. (2d) 559. They are relying on *Hall et al.* v *Pritchett* (1877), 3 Q.B.D. 215, in which it was decided that a salary, payable periodically, cannot be attached before it is payable. They also referred to *Holmes* v *Millage*, [1893] 1 Q.B. 551 (C.A.), where the Court of Appeal decided that there was no jurisdiction to enforce satisfaction of a judgment debt by appointing the receiver of the future earnings of the judgment debtor. In that case, the plaintiff had applied for a garnishee order but, as no weekly payments were in arrear, no order was made, according to Lindley, L.J. ...

There is, of course, a multitude of cases on garnishee orders against salaries, but these cases seem to represent the sources of the opinion that a salary cannot be garnished before it is payable, and this is curious because it is not a necessary conclusion from the facts of any particular case, and in all these cases the *Apportionment Act,* 1870 (U.K.), c 35, and its predecessor statutes have been ignored.

This, of course, is understandable in the case of the statutes before the *Apportionment Act, 1870: i.e.,* 1738, 11 Geo. II, c 19, s 15; 1834 (U.K.), c 22; 1836 (U.K.), c 71; 1851 (U.K.), c 25; and 1860 (U.K.), c 154. Under these Acts, the chief cause of transmission of interest is death, although other causes are taken into account, so that it would not readily occur to Bench and Bar that attachments were included within the meaning of these enactments. In the *Apportionment Act, 1870,* however, the wording of s 2, providing for apportionment from day to day, is quite general. This does not appear to be affected by any other provisions of the enactment.

Our *Apportionment Act,* R.S.N.S. 1967, c 10, is in substantially the same words as the *Apportionment Act, 1870* (with some modernization of format), and I would read it to mean the following: Except where it is expressly stipulated that no apportionment shall take place (and except also, the case of annual sums made payable in policies of assurance of any description), all rents, annuities (including salaries and pensions – s 1(a)), dividends and other periodical payments in the nature of income, shall, like interest on money lent, be considered as accruing from day to day during the period for which the payment is to be made and are apportionable in respect to time accordingly. Despite the apportionment, the end of the income period is retained, that is, the payment date, by s 3 of the Act.

Now, if this means anything, it means that, subject to any agreement to the contrary, the person who earns a salary acquires a claim to it from day to day and the person who has to pay it acquires an obligation to pay it from day to day, as earned. These are existing rights and obligations to be discharged in the future so that if a person on salary dies or is prevented from continuing to earn during a part of a payment period, he or his estate becomes entitled to the portion of the salary that he has earned which will, however, be payable only at the end of the pay period. This reasoning would surely be applied in favour of the salary earner and it should also be applied in favour of his creditor unless there is good reason to the contrary. While the judgment creditor is not entitled to recover any more than the judgment debtor could recover against the garnishee, there seems to be no good reason why the judgment creditor should not be allowed a remedy against the real rights of the judgment debtor, to the extent that the statute law seems to allow. In this regard, one cannot avoid the suspicion that the Courts have been very rigid about the right of garnishee because of the drastic nature of that remedy. However, in this province, it is now possible to make proper provision for the maintenance of the debtor and his wife and family in a garnishee order absolute and the remedy is now, here at least, a much more civilized one than some measures possible under the *Collection Act,* R.S.N.S. 1967, c 39, such as imprisonment for debt. I therefore propose to approach the present problem on the basis that salaries accrue from day to day and become existing obligations of the employer in that way, although they are payable only on the payment dates.

In the instant case, there is an affidavit submitted on behalf of the garnishee and, while it denies that anything was due to the judgment debtor on the date that the garnishee received the

order, it seems to rely on the payment provisions of the general contract governing the teachers' union. It does not, of course make it clear that the accrual provisions of the *Apportionment Act* have been bypassed or excluded. The practice followed in some of the cases, where there was this type of uncertainty, was to direct an issue and, accordingly, if the parties wish it, I am prepared to hear evidence on the contract or any collateral matters so that it can be determined whether the garnishee order *nisi* did, in fact, attach any present obligation of the garnishee to the judgment debtor.
Order accordingly.

See also *Main Brothers* v *McInnes* (1901), 4 Terr. L.R. 517; *Town of Morse* v *Lyone*, [1917] 3 W.W.R. 351 (Sask. S.C.); *Stump* v *Batzold*, [1931] 2 W.W.R. 784 (B.C.S.C.); and *G.A.C. International Finance Corp. Ltd.* v *Toomey et al.* (1967), 64 D.L.R. (2d) 559 (N.S. Co. Ct.), in which the Court came to a conclusion opposite to that reached in *Lee* v *MacDonald* (though without reference to the Apportionment Act).

iv *Sandy* v *Yukon Construction Co. Ltd. and Rush and Tompkins Construction Ltd.* (1961), 26 D.L.R. (2d) 254 (Alta. S.C.)

The judgment of the Court was delivered by
JOHNSON, J.A.: This is an appeal from an order of Greschuk, J., declaring that moneys paid into Court by the garnishee were not garnishable and ordering payment out of these moneys to the defendant.

The garnishee is a construction contractor and the defendant is a sub-contractor whose tender for a part of the work was accepted. The subcontractor's price was $19,600 and the acceptance of the tender was made subject to 'the terms and conditions overleaf'. Two of these conditions, particularly, were relied on by the respondent as showing that no moneys were attachable at the date of the service of the garnishee:

(3) The amount certified by the Architect to be due in respect of the sub-contract work and any authorized variation thereof shall not become payable until fourteen days after the receipt by the Contractor of the appropriate Architects Certificate and remittance from the Employer.

(9) If the Sub-Contractor at any time refuses or neglects to supply a sufficient amount of labour or materials of proper quality, or fails in any way to perform the Work according to schedule, or cause stoppage or delay of or interference with the Work of the General Contractor or of other Sub-Contractors or fails in performance of any agreements herein, or becomes insolvent, the General Contractor shall be free after three days' written notice to the Sub-Contractor, to provide through others such labour and materials and deduct costs of same from any money due or thereafter to be due the Sub-Contractor under this Contract. The General Contractor also be free to terminate their services of the Sub-Contractor for said Work and to take possession for purpose of completing Work in this Contract of all materials, tools, and equipment, and to employ others to finish the work and to provide materials therefore. Upon termination no further payment shall be made to the Sub-Contractor until the said Work shall be wholly finished, at which time, if the unpaid balance of the amount to be paid under this Contract shall exceed the expense incurred by the General Contractor, such excess shall be paid to the Sub-Contractor; but if such expense shall exceed such unpaid balance, then the Sub-Contractor shall pay the difference to the General Contractor. The expense incurred by the General

Contractor shall include costs of materials, finishing Work and damage resulting from Sub-Contractor's fault.

The contract was entered into on September 22, 1958, and in January 1959, the architect had issued a certificate and $2,700 was paid to the subcontractor. On August 31, 1959, the defendant, claiming it had completed its work, rendered an account for $15,580. The garnishee was issued September 24th and to it the garnishee filed the following reply:

September 25, 1959

Clerk of the Supreme Court
   of Northern Alberta,
100 St. & 102A Avenue,
Edmonton, Alberta.
Dear Sir: *Re: Garnishee Summons #20292*

With reference to the above mentioned Garnishee Summons, our letter of September 24th and your telephone conversation of today with the writer.

The Defendant holds a subcontract agreement with this company to perform certain works at one or our contracts located at Fort Smith, N.W.T.

At this time, we are unable to state definitely the amount of our indebtedness to the defendant as the contract performance is not yet complete, holdbacks on progress payments are not yet due for settlement as the contract as a whole is incomplete and the release of holdback by our employing authority has not yet been received.

Under the terms and conditions of our agreement with Yukon Construction, any monies are not due for payment until a specified lapse of time after receipt of monies from the owner.

Should there be no unforseen circumstances affecting the value of the works and services done, we believe our indebtedness may be approximately $20,000.00.

We trust this is the information you require at this time.

Yours truly,
RUSH & TOMPKINS CONSTRUCTION LTD.
Per: '*R. S. Everett per JB*'
R. S. Everett

The amount of $20,000 mentioned must have been an error for the whole contract was only $19,600 and a part of this, as I have mentioned, had been paid. On December 29th, the garnishee paid into Court $16,445.15. It was not until May 5, 1960, that the defendant made this application.

Our garnishee Rules, 550 *et seq.*, use similar language to that used in the *Common Law Procedure Act* of 1854 (17 & 18 Vict., see c 125, ss 61 to 67) which permitted the attachment of debts owed by third parties to execution debtors. These sections now appear as O. 45, rr. 1 to 10 of the English Rules. As far as this application is concerned, the pertinent words of the English Rule are 'all debts owing or accruing from such third person', describing what might be attached. In our Rules, Rule 551 uses 'debts, if any, due or accruing due from the garnishee'.

The learned Chamber Judge gave no written reasons for declaring that the garnishee did not attach any moneys under this contract. The respondent has advanced several arguments in support of this order. One of the principal arguments was that, because at the time the garnishee was issued the defendant could not have sued for these monies, they could not be garnisheed, and a quotation from *Faas et al.* v *McManus*, [1930] 1 D.L.R. 302 at p 304, 24 A.L.R. 317, was relied upon. Hyndman, J.A., giving judgment for the Court, quoted a paragraph from the judgment of Sedgewick, J., in *Donohoe* v *Hull Bros. & Co.* (1895), 24 S.C.R. 683 at p 688:

Now one elementary principle runs through all these cases, viz., to enable a judgment creditor to obtain an order compelling a third person (the garnishee) to pay to him a debt which he would otherwise have to pay the judgment debtor, the debtor must be in a position to maintain an action for it against the garnishee, and the debt must be of such a character that it would vest in the debtor's assignee or trustee in backruptcy if he became insolvent. [p 305]

While there can be no question of the correctness of *Faas et al.* v *McManus*, the test which has been quoted cannot be said to be strictly correct. To insist that the defendant 'must be in a position to maintain an action for it against the garnishee' is to ignore the words 'accruing due' in Rule 551. Debts have been held to be attachable when they could not be sued for because they had not yet become due, *Tapp* v *Jones* (1875), L.R. 10 Q.B. 591, and *Garner* v *Strickland & Western Forest Industries Ltd.*, [1955] 4 D.L.R. 329.

The principal argument was that because the architect was required to give his certificate before any moneys became payable, no debt came into existence until the certificate was given. This can only be so if the giving of the certificate is a condition precedent to any debt coming into existence and not merely a condition precedent to there being any right to receive the debt. I do not think that this is so. *O'Driscoll* v *Manchester Ins. Committee*, [1915] 3 K.B. 499, while not a building contract, was one where the decision of an insurance committee had to be given before doctors, who were a part of the national insurance scheme, could receive their fees. The fees the doctor would receive were dependent both on the amount paid into the pool by the insured and the aggregate amount of all of the doctors' bills submitted, and the Court held that the garnishee was valid even though it had been served before the committee had settled the amount which would ultimately come to the judgment debtor. Bankes, L.J., at pp 516–7 says:

It is well established that 'debts owing or accruing' include debts debita in praesenti solvenda in futuro. The matter is well put in the Annual Practice, 1915, p 808: 'But the distinction must be borne in mind between the case where there is an existing debt, payment whereof is deferred, and the case where both the debt and its payment rest in the future. In the former case there is an attachable debt, in the latter case there is not.' If, for instance, a sum of money is payable on the happening of a contingency, there is no debt owing or accruing. But the mere fact that the amount is not ascertained does not show that there is no debt. In the present case there was on April 9, 1914, a debt debitum in praesenti but solvendum in futuro. It is not necessary to say exactly at what moment of time the debt was created.

Swinfen Eady, L.J., at pp 512–3 says:

Here there is a debt, uncertain in amount, which will become certain when the accounts are finally dealt with by the Insurance Committee. Therefore there was a 'debt' at the material date, though it was not presently payable and the amount was not ascertained. It is not like a case where there is a mere probability of a debt, as, for instance, where a person has to serve for a fixed period before being entitled to any salary, and he has served part of that period at the time the garnishee order nisi is served. In such a case there is no 'debt' until he has served the whole period.

It is suggested that this contract is an entire contract and no debt arises until the whole work is done. An examination of the agreement does not bear this out. It provides for interim payments as the work progresses with only the final payment retained until the work has been completed and accepted. Nor do I think that certification of the amount by the architect is a condition precedent to there being any indebtedness at all. It is, as condition (3) says, a certificate of the amount 'to be due'. There is nothing to suggest in the granting or refusing of a certificate that there is 'the happening of any contingency' (mentioned by Bankes, L.J., in the *O'Driscoll* case, *supra*) preventing the establishment of a debt as the work is done, although, of course, the absence of the certificate in most cases will prevent the contractor from being able to sue. I say in most cases, for there are cases where the Courts have permitted recovery even where no certificate has been given.
[His Lordship cited two cases in which the Court allowed suits where the architect had failed to certify, and continued:]
It is inherent, I think, in both of these judgments that a prior debt existed before the certificate came into existence and that the certificate requirement merely postponed the payment until the certificate had been given. If the indebtedness was conditional upon the certificate, it would have been impossible for the Courts to have given the judgments they did in these cases.

The effect of condition (9) (quoted above) remains to be considered. Are the rights given to the general contractor – *i.e.*, to complete the work if the subcontractor fails to do so or if the contractor elects to terminate the contract, and to charge the cost of completing the project against the value of the work done – inconsistent with the existence of a debt before a certificate is granted? On the contrary, it acknowledges, tacitly at least, that a debt is created as the work is completed and it is this debt that is to be charged with the cost of completing the contract if the contractor invokes this condition. If the contractor took over under this condition before half of the work had been completed, the value of the uncompleted work would, of course, exceed the value of the work done and there would be no debt to garnishee (see *Webster* v *Webster* (1862), 31 Beav. 393, 54 E.R. 1191). If more than half of the work had been done before the contractor stepped in, there would remain an attachable debt, the amount of which could not be determined until the cost of completing the contract had been determined. It is the facts as they exist when the garnishee is served which must determine the existence of a debt. I would gather from the examination of Mr. Ross upon his affidavit that the subcontractor had considered that it had completed its contract and had submitted its final bill before the garnishee was issued. If this work was in fact completed, then the amount subsequently paid into Court is properly attachable by the garnishee. If there is any doubt about this an issue should be directed to determine the amount of the indebtedness when the garnishee was served.

I have dealt in some detail with the effect of the architect's certificate because of a recent decision of the Court of Queen's Bench in England, a case which was not referred to in argument. In *Dunlop & Ranken Ltd.* v *Hendall Steel Structures Ltd.*, [1957] 3 All E.R. 344, the Court, consisting of Lord Goddard, C.J., Donovan and Havers, J.J., held that until the architect's certificate was obtained under an R.I.B.A. form of building contract, there was no debt which could be attached. Lord Goddard, C.J., adopts a statement which appears in the Annual Practice of 1957 under O. 45, r 1 (I have mentioned the similarity to our garnishee Rules 550 and 551) (p 347):

In the case, for example, of a building contract in the R.I.B.A. form, where the builder is paid on the certificate of the architect, it is plain that money in the hands of the building owner cannot be attached until a certificate is issued, and then only for the amount mentioned in that certificate.

The Annual Practice, 1956 gives the authority for this statement as an article headed 'Building Contracts and Garnishee Orders' (1941), 191 L.T.Jo. 180. The article concludes with the following:

In a case which recently came before a Master of the King's Bench Division, a summons was issued to make absolute a garnishee order nisi which had been made in respect of monies in the hands of a building owner. There was evidence to the effect that a considerable amount of work had been done by the builder for which he would be entitled to payment on certificate, but there was no certificate. The judgment creditor pressed for an order absolute, relying on *O'Driscoll's* case (1915), 115 L.T. Rep. 683). He argued that, inasmuch as work had been done under the contract, there must be money 'due' from the building owner to become payable on the issue of the architect's certificate. The Master refused to make the order absolute, holding that nothing could be said to be 'due' under the building contract until the issue of a certificate. He pointed out that the architect might never issue a certificate at all and that until he did so the building owner was not liable.

Observe the subtle distinction between this case and that of *O'Driscoll*. There it was admitted that something was actually due from the garnishee – the only question was how much. In a building case, however much work may have been done, payment for it is not due until the architect certifies, and only money 'owing and accruing' can be garnished.

The subtle distinction escapes me. The nature of building contracts, unless, of course, they are contracts under which nothing is payable until completion, does not warrant changing the plain wording of o. 45, r 1, from 'debts owing *or* accruing due' to 'debts owing *and* accruing due'. The mere fact that the value of the work done may be charged with various amounts which may be owed by the subcontractor to the contractor, does not, unless the amount of these charges exceeds the value of the work done, prevent there being an indebtedness. The R.I.B.A. contract mentioned in the above case, is not reproduced in full and it may be that it does contain clauses which prevent any indebtedness arising unless the contract is completed. There is nothing in the present contract having that effect. I would allow the appeal and set aside the order appealed from and direct the defendant pay back into Court the amount paid in by the garnishee. Upon this being done, the respondent will be entitled to apply to a Judge of the Trial Division to direct an issue to determine the amount of the garnishee's indebtedness on the date of the service of the garnishee, if it so desires.

The appellant is entitled to his costs here and in the Court below.
Appeal allowed.

QUESTION Do you agree?

v *Webb* v *Stenton* (1883), 11 Q.B.D. 518 (C.A.)

BRETT, M.R.: In this case the judgment creditor sought to attach certain moneys in the hands of the trustees of the judgment debtor, alleged to be debts, or accruing debts, from the trustees to the judgment debtor.

Now the relation between the trustees and the judgment debtor was this – the judgment debtor was entitled, as cestui que trust, to a share of the proceeds of certain property, which would, if it came at all into the hands of the trustees, come half yearly. It seems to me that there was nothing else which could be called a debt, and that at the time when the order was applied for there was no money, the proceeds of this property, in the hands of the trustees. It is true that if everything went on well, at the next half year there would come into the hands of the trustees money from the proceeds of this property, and a share of that would be payable from the trustees to the judgment debtor, the cestui que trust.

The question is, whether, under these circumstances the judgment creditor can obtain the garnishee order sought for. The Divisional Court refused to make the order on the ground that there was not debt due, or accruing debt, at the time when the order was applied for which could be attached under Order XLV., rule 2, of the Judicature Act, and I am of opinion that the decision of the Divisional Court was right.

It is necessary to look at the words of Order XLV., rule 2. [His Lordship here read that rule.]

It seems to me upon the plain reading of rule 2 of Order XLV, that no order can be made unless some person at the time the order is made is indebted to the judgment debtor. If there be a person so indebted, then the order will be that all debts owing or accruing from such person to the judgment debtor shall be attached. If there is a debt due payable in presenti, of course an order may be made to attach that debt. If there is not a debt payable in presenti, but there is a debt in existence, debitum in presenti, but payable in futuro, it seems to me that such an order could be made with regard to that debt although it be the only debt and there is no debt payable in presenti, because such third person is indebted to the judgment debtor, and that would satisfy the words of the rule.

In the present case the statement of the special case shews there is no debt payable in presenti, and therefore the question comes to be whether that which is sought to be attached is an accruing debt within Order XLV., rule 2, and that casts upon us the duty of saying what is the meaning of 'accruing debt' in this rule 2.

Now can it mean any debt which may at any future time arise between the judgment debtor and the person sought to be made a garnishee, there being no contract at that time between the judgment debtor and such person, or anything which can make any relation of any kind, legal or equitable, between them? To state the proposition is to shew its absurdity. Then can it be this, that it may be a debt which there is some probability may in future arise? Who can say where there is nothing out of which a debt can be said in law to arise, that it is probable that a debt may arise, as for instance a probability that the parties will make a contract. If it is not a debt it will not do. It must be something which the law recognises as a debt. In the former statute, viz., The Common Law Procedure Act, 1854, as well as in this rule, it is called an accruing debt, and in 1858, in the case of *Jones* v *Thompson* (27 L.J. (Q.B.) 234), the judges of the Queen's Bench thus construed the words 'a debt owing or accruing' in s 61 of the Common Law Procedure Act, 1854 (17 & 18 Vict. c 125), Crompton, J., said: 'I myself at chambers have always acted on the supposition that the garnishee clauses apply only to cases in which there is an existing debt, though it may be only accruing. On that principle I have refused to make orders attaching rent before it became due, and instalments of an annuity not yet due, because they were not yet debts.' Wightman, J., said, 'Mr. Prentice relies on the words "or accruing," but I think that these words are intended to apply to those cases in which there is debitum in presenti, solvendum in futuro. I think that, to bring the case within the statute, there must be a debt, though it need not be yet due.' Again, Crompton, J., there said: 'There must, under this Act, be a debt as much as in bankruptcy. I do not agree that the use of the word "accruing" makes a distinction on this point; there must be a debt, though it may be not yet due. I have always acted on the principle that it is not enough to shew that it is very probable that there soon will be a debt, but that it must be shewn that there is a debt, though it need not be yet due.' I cannot conceive anything more clear and decisive than that, and if we are to construe 'accruing debt' in this case in any other sense than that, it is obvious that we must overrule that decision and say that it was wrong. ...

Therefore, for the reasons I have given, I put the interpretation I have mentioned on 'accruing debt' in this rule 2, and then the only question is whether that which is attempted to be attached here is an accruing debt according to such interpretation. It is obvious it is not. There is a sum of money which is to be payable out of the proceeds of property when it comes to the hands of the trustees. Nobody can say that until then it is in any legal or equitable sense a debt which is debitum in presenti. The money may never come to these trustees without any fault of their own, for they may die or cease to be trustees before anything can become due. Therefore there are contingencies upon which no debt may ever arise, and all that can be said of it is, that it is probable that at the end of half-a-year money will come into the hands of the trustees, but until it does come into their hands, there is no debt existing between them and their cestui que trust. There may probably be other remedies by which the creditor of the judgment debtor can get relief, but in my opinion he cannot, in the case now before us, get relief under Order xlv., rule 2.

Therefore I am of opinion that the judgment of the Divisional Court was right, and that this appeal must be dismissed.

LINDLEY, L.J.: I quite concur in the last observation Lord Justice Fry has made.
Appeal dismissed.

QUESTION Should the answer depend upon the nature of the trust property?

NOTE In *Brandt* v *Burrows* (1966), 56 D.L.R. (2d) 576 (Sask. Q.B.) the garnishee had been authorized by the executor of an estate to make a proper distribution of moneys to which the judgment debtor was entitled under a will. Tucker J held that the moneys in the control of the garnishee were attachable:

Presumably until receiving autorization from the executor to pay money to which the defendant might have been entitled under the will in question, the garnishee could not have been sued by the defendant for such money as they would have been accountable for such money to the executor of the estate. However, when authorized by the executor to pay any money to which the defendant was entitled under the will to the defendant, the garnishee was holding money to which the defendant was entitled and she was entitled to demand and enforce by suit payment of same as against the garnishee. (at p 577).

See also: *Canadian Acceptance Corporation* v *Desrochers and Benoit*, [1975] 5 W.W.R. 185 (Man. Q.B.).

vi *Canadian Bank of Commerce* v *Dabrowski and Dabrowski and Hunt* (1954), 13 W.W.R. 442 (B.C.S.C.)

COADY, J.: In this action a garnishee order was issued on March 3, 1954. Pursuant to that order the garnishee paid into court $1,261.86 on March 16, 1954, with notice that the said money was claimed by the Bank of Montreal and by one Plakoln.

[Meanwhile] the Bank of Montreal had issued a writ on March 9 against the defendants herein and had also on the same date issued a garnishee order which was served on the garnishee herein before payment into court of the above moneys.

A chamber summons was then issued by the plaintiff herein dated April 13, 1954, and returnable on May 3, 1954, calling upon the Bank of Montreal and Plakoln to appear and state the nature and particulars of their claim to the said moneys. On the hearing of the chamber summons before me counsel appeared representing the Bank of Montreal but Plakoln did not appear nor was she represented by counsel. The garnishee was also represented by counsel before me since it was claimed by the plaintiff that the moneys paid into court by the garnishee did not represent all of the moneys due, payable or accruing due from the garnishee to the defendants.

Particulars of the claim of the Bank of Montreal were filed pursuant to a direction given by the Chief Justice. The claim of the Bank of Montreal to the moneys is based upon the submission that security was held by the bank pursuant to secs 88 and 89 of the *Bank Act*, R.S.C. 1952, ch. 12, on the livestock, farm machinery and equipment, the property of the defendants, which were sold by the garnishee as auctioneer for and at the request of the defendants. The garnishee order was directed to the attachment of the moneys received by the auctioneer.

Counsel for the Bank of Montreal further submits that the plaintiff's garnishee order is invalid and should be set aside on the ground that at the time the said garnishee order was issued there were no debts, obligations or liabilities owing, payable or accruing due from the garnishee to the defendants.

The auction sale was held on March 3, 1954, commencing at about 11:30 a.m. The garnishee order was issued at or about 10 a.m. on the same day.

The garnishee paid the moneys into court on the assumption that the garnishee order was a valid order.

It seems clear upon the authorities that when the garnishee order was issued herein there were no debts or obligations owing, payable or accruing due from the garnishee to the defendants. It is true moneys did become due and payable at a later time on the same day after the auction sale was held and apparently prior to the service of the garnishee order, but that does not help the plaintiff since the essential time is the time when the garnishee order was issued, not the time it was served. The plaintiff's garnishee order therefore must be set aside: *Vater v Styles*; *Metropolitan Life Insur. Co. (Garnishee)*, [1930] 2 W.W.R. 241, 42 B.C.R. 463. A number of other cases are noted in *Power's Index-Digest of Western Practice Cases* on this point.

The claim of the Bank of Montreal to payment of the moneys paid into court cannot, it seems to me, be decided upon this application. The judgment debtors may have some claim to advance in that connection in respect of their indebtedness to the bank, or, if indebted, to the bank's claim to the money in court, or it may be that the garnishee order issued by the Bank of Montreal in its action of March 9, 1954, may not be a valid order. That issue is one between the parties to that other action, it seems to me, and must be decided in that action. It is unnecessary in view of my finding on the plaintiff's garnishee order to make any finding on the validity of the security claimed by the Bank of Montreal on the livestock and machinery sold, which matter was argued before me at some length. The disposition of the moneys now in court may be spoken to.

vii D.M. Gordon, Case and Comment (1954), 32 *Can. Bar. Rev.* 1141, at pp 1144–6.

Let us consider some of the anomalies that will result if the *Dabrowski* ruling prevails. Take the case where the garnishee is a bank and when the garnishing order issues the defendant has an account of $1.00, but when it is served has an account of $1,000. According to the *Dabrowski* ruling, the order is only operative as to $1.00. But how can such a result be justified? The order cannot be set aside on the basis that no money was owing at the date of the order (even if that were a good basis); it cannot be set aside on the basis that the affidavit leading the order was untrue, for it was not.

The only theory on which limitation of the attachment to $1.00 could be argued would be this: the registrar's order is what attaches the debt, and he must be regarded as attaching only debts that exist when he makes his order. That view however is negatived by authority. In *Re Stanhope Silkstone Collieries Co.* it was held that a creditor of a company, who obtained a garnishing order but did not serve it until after a winding-up order was made against the company, was not a secured creditor at the beginning of the winding-up. Bramwell L.J. said at page 163 that the order

does not purport to attach the debts, but orders 'that they be attached', that is, upon something further being done. It is like the order for the attachment of a person for contempt. He is not attached upon the writ issuing, but he is attached under it.

This seems to make sense, and rationalizes the assumption that obviously prevails in England, namely, that the date of service of a garnishing order is the sole test as to what it catches. The very term 'garnishing' seems to support Bramwell L.J.; for the literal meaning of 'garnish', which has rather been forgotten, is 'warn'. Obviously a registrar cannot 'warn' a garnishee by merely making an order; he only enables the plaintiff to warn the garnishee by service.

If the plaintiff must run the risk that the obligation to the defendant may be lessened between the time of the order and the time of the service, why should the risks be all one way? Why should he not equally have the benefit of any interim increase in the garnishee's obligation?

Where nothing is owing by the garnishee when the order is made but a substantial sum is owing when it is served, no doubt the order ought not to stand if the plaintiff made his affidavit of the garnishee's indebtedness knowing it to be false. But the plaintiff only swears that he is informed of the indebtedness and believes it exists, and if this is literally true, there is no deception even if the information proves untrue. In the *Dabrowski* case the order was set aside, not because the affidavit was proved untrue, but because there was in fact nothing owing at the date of the order. But if there had been $1.00 owing at the time, that objection would have been unfounded. It is hard to see how the order could then have been held not to operate, even to the extent of many thousand dollars, if these were due when the order was served. It is certainly hard to see why a debt of $1.00 when the order was made should make all this difference.

Apparently, according to English views, it would make no difference. In *Vinall v DePass*, for instance, the House of Lords refused to hold a garnishing order bad because the only debt suggested in the affidavit to lead it was not really due; it was enough that the garnishee owed something.

The *Dabrowski* ruling could create great practical difficulties, even intolerable hardship, particularly where the garnishee is a bank, as it is in perhaps most cases. Hitherto, when a garnishee disputed liability for the whole or part of the sum named in the order, the garnishee filed a dispute note stating that at the time of service of the order he was not indebted, or only indebted in a named sum, which he paid into court. The *Dabrowski* ruling requires him to say that neither when the order was made nor when it was served was he indebted, and he can safely pay in only the least sum owing by him at either of these times. But, particularly in the case of a garnishee bank, that course may be quite impossible to follow. Cheques may be paid or received by a bank at any moment during banking hours. This does not matter too much if service of the order alone counts. But if the bank can only pay into court the amount due when an order was made, which may have been days before the bank knows of it, then its position becomes hopeless. How can the bank possibly tell whether a sum received or paid out on the same day as a garnishing order was signed was received or paid before or after the moment when the order was signed? Registrars do not keep records of the moments when they sign orders, nor do banks keep records of the moments when they receive or pay cheques.

These considerations alone show that the *Dabrowski* ruling makes the position of banks impossible. And other garnishees could be almost equally embarrassed. The hardships that such a ruling must in time produce would prove intolerable. The very fact that it would do so throws the strongest doubt on its soundness.

QUESTIONS Assume that the practical difficulties raised by Gordon are as serious as he suggests they are. How should this 'fact' of practical difficulty affect the court's decision the next time that a case similar to *Dabrowski* is presented to it? What could you, as counsel, for the bank, do to assist the court in reversing *Dabrowski*?

NOTE See also *Imperial Oil Ltd.* v *Moore* (1964), 49 W.W.R. 694 (Alta. D. Ct.) which held that although the existence of a debt due or accruing due by a garnishee to a defendant was to be determined by reference to the date of issue of the garnishee summons, it was the amount due on the date of service that determined the amount attached.

In *McCready Products Ltd.* v *United Building Supplies* (1962), 33 D.L.R. (2d) 313 (B.C.C.A.), the garnishee gave the defendant a cheque for a debt which was owing to her. The defendant endorsed her cheque to the bank, and the amount was credited to her account. Later on the same day, the garnishee was served with a garnishing order. On being served, the garnishee stopped payment on the cheque, and paid the amount owing into court. The Court held that no debt was owing to the debtor at the time of service of the garnishing order, and that the money paid into court was not subject to attachment. The debt due to the defendant was paid prior to the service of the garnishing order and therefore was not attached. The defendant was not in a position to maintain an action for the debt against the garnishee, and *Quercetti* v *Tranquilli* had established that as being the test of whether a debt was attachable. Accordingly, the garnishing order was ineffective, and the garnishee was entitled to the monies which it had paid into court.

viii *Moir* v *Franciotta* (1931), 40 O.W.N. 485 (Co. Ct.).

The defendant Celeste Franciotta obtained judgment against the plaintiffs for her costs of an action taxed at $53. On the 9th April, 1931, the Forest Hill Contracting Company was declared bankrupt, and A.E. Brocklesby was appointed trustee. The plaintiff John W. Moir filed a claim with the trustee for wages, and the trustee admitted that Moir was entitled to a dividend thereon of $39.60. Celeste Franciotta sought to attach this dividend.

WIDDIFIELD, JUN. CO. C.J., in a written judgment, said that as 70 per cent of the dividend was exempt under the Wages Act, the amount in dispute was very small; but, in view of the numerous applications for attaching orders, the contention raised by the garnishee was important.

The garnishee and judgment debtor contend that a dividend in bankruptcy proceedings is not attachable. If *Prout* v *Gregory* (1889), 24 Q.B.D. 281, is good law, this contention must prevail. There it was sought to attach a dividend payable under an administration in bankruptcy and it was held that the dividend was not attachable.

In *In re Cowans' Estate* (1880), 14 Ch.D. 638, Hall, V.-C., held that moneys in the hands of a receiver are liable to garnishment. This was followed in our courts in *Leaming* v *Woon* (1882), 7 A.R. 42, but in *Stuart* v *Grough* (1888), 15 A.R. 299, it was held that *Leaming* v *Woon* was not to be followed, being founded on *In re Cowans' Estate*, which is now overruled by *Webb* v *Stenton* (1883), 11 Q.B.D. 518, 530.

As far back as 1869 it was held in *Boyd* v *Haynes*, 5 P.R. 15, that to found attachment proceedings there must be a legal debt due by a legal debtor to a legal creditor. The test is, could the judgment debtor have sued the garnishee? *Webster* v *Webster* (1862), 6 L.T.R. 11. Here it is plain that the judgment debtor could not have sued the garnishee: *Hunter* v *Greensill* (1872), 8 L.R.C.P. 24. See sec. 74(4) of the Bankruptcy Act.

The application will be dismissed – no costs.

NOTE Other cases reaching the same result as that arrived at in *Moir* include: *Firestone Tire & Rubber Co.* v *Douglas*, [1940] O.W.N. 143 and *Monarch Lumber Co. Ltd.* v *Klotz and Scherr*, [1947] 1 W.W.R. 543.

Section 74(4) was substantially similar to the present s 119(3) of The Bankruptcy Act, in providing that 'no action for a dividend lies against the trustee but if the trustee refused or fails to pay any dividend after having been directed to do so by the inspectors the Court may, on the application of any creditor, order him to pay it and also to pay personally interest thereon for the time that it is withheld and the costs of the application.' Can you refute Judge Widdifield's reasoning in *Moir*?

c / Conditional or Contingent Debts

i Insurance Proceeds

Vater v *Styles*, [1930] 3 D.L.R. 509 (B.C.C.A.).

MACDONALD, J.A.: The plaintiff recovered judgment against the defendant for $189.65, for groceries supplied and obtained from the registrar an order attaching monies alleged to be due and payable to defendant by the Metropolitan Life Ins. Co. The order was served on the garnishee on August 7, 1929, in respect to a sum of $214 which would be due and payable to the defendant under certain conditions on November 3, 1929. The garnishee waited until after November 3 and as it would then, in the ordinary course, be obliged to pay defendant $214.20, it paid into Court under the garnishee order the sum of $189.65, forwarding the balance to the defendant. The defendant applied successfully to the Judge of the County Court to vacate the attaching order on the ground that when served no monies were 'owing, payable or accruing due' by the Insurance Company to him within the meaning of s 3 of the Attachments of Debts Act, R.S.B. 1924, c 17. From that order plaintiff appeals.

The defendant's employer carried with the Metropolitan Life Ins. Co. a group policy of insurance for the benefit of employees, including defendant. It provided for total and permanent disability benefits. In 1928 the defendant became totally disabled and unfit for employment and because of this disability was entitled to receive from the Insurance Company five yearly instalments of $214 each; the instalment in question being due, as stated, on November 3, 1929. This sum would only be payable to the defendant, however, if he was (1) still disabled, and (2) alive. If he died before that date, by the terms of the policy it would be payable to his wife as beneficiary. If his physical disability disappeared before November 3, he would not receive it. To quote from the policy, 'such instalment payments will be made only during the continuance of such disability.' If the Act contemplates monies that must inevitably accrue due on that date the plaintiff cannot hold this order. Appellant submitted that the possibility of future occurrence that might provide a defence against the recovery of the instalment – a condition which might not arise at all – was no ground for refusing to attach the amount, and he referred to *Sparks* v *Younge* (1858), 8 Ir. C.L.R. 251. I do not think, however, that a sum of money, which on November 3 might be legally due and owing to defendant's wife or through recovery from disability might not be payable at all, is 'owing payable and accruing due to the defendant.' True upon his disability, the obligation was created but upon his recovery if that occurred within the time referred to it would disappear. It is a conditional obligation and as such not attachable. An accruing debt is one not yet payable but still an existing obligation. That cannot be said where conditions may arise which would either prevent payment or vest the amount in another: *Barsi* v *Farcas*, [1924] 1 D.L.R. 1154, 18 S.L.R. 158. It is dependent upon conditions which may not be fulfilled: *Lake of the Woods Milling Co.* v *Collin*, 13 Man. L.R. 154.

I would dismiss the appeal.

Appeal dismissed.

NOTE The status of the proceeds of insurance policies after the event insured against has occurred has long been a subject of controversy.

In England, insurance proceeds may not be attachable. In the leading case of *Israelson* v *Dawson (Port of Manchester Insurance Co*, garnishees), [1933] 1 K.B. 301 (C.A.), the defendant had injured the plaintiff in a motor accident. Defendant's insurer had promised to indemnify him in respect of all sums for which he might become liable as a result of motor accidents. Greer LJ found that the insurer owed no attachable debt to the defendant. He said:

Have the insurance Company promised by this policy to pay the defendant in the action the 150 pounds for which judgment has been given? After full consideration I have come to the conclusion that they have not so promised, but that what they have promised is to indemnify him against such payment as he may have to make, and they may do that, not by paying him anything, but by paying to some other persons the amount the insured has to pay them. That is not a promise to pay him anything; it is one of the risks they undertake – namely, to indemnify him against legal liability incurred by him when driving a motor car ....

I also agree in thinking that many difficulties will arise when it becomes necessary to define the liability of the Insurance Company under their policy; so many that in the exercise of my discretion I should not consider this a proper case for a garnishee order at all ....

This case was followed in *Fouad Bishara Jabbour* v *Custodian of Absentee's Property of State of Israel*, [1954] 1 All E.R. 145 (Eng. Q.B.). Pearson J distinguished debts from claims for unliquidated damages. Where a sum certain is owed, there is a debt. However, if it is not a sum certain, it is a claim for unliquidated damages. Insurance proceeds were held to belong in the latter category – they were not fit subjects for garnishee orders.

The law in Canada has developed differently. Where the entitlement to insurance is conditional only, there is no attachable debt. Thus in *Vater* v *Styles*, supra, proceeds on a disability policy were not attachable because the insured might recover before the date of payment of the proceeds (an annually payable pension). In *Ryan* v *Eatock*, [1943] O.W.N. 590 (S.C.) however, proceeds of life insurance policies on the life of the defendant's late husband not yet paid out were held subject to garnishment, for the amount of money owing was a sum certain.

In 1932, the Supreme Court of Canada considered the problem in *Century Indemnity Co.* v *Rogers*, [1932] 2 D.L.R. 582. This case involved the same situation as *Israelson* v *Dawson*, supra. The plaintiff was injured by the defendant in a motor accident, and received judgment against her. He immediately moved to attach the insurance proceeds payable to the defendant. The insurance policy limited recovery to situations where the amount of loss or expense had been fixed by judgment or settlement. This led to the following analysis by Lamont J:

Whether apart from this clause the claim of the insured under the policy would have been a claim for unliquidated damages, it is unnecessary to inquire. By this clause the appellants [insurance company] impliedly agreed that the insured would be entitled to recover on the policy when the legal liability against which she had been insured was determined as to amount by a judgment against her after trial. This, in our opinion, is the meaning which the parties intended the clause to bear. The amount of her loss in this case having been determined by judgment, the right of the insured to recover that amount under the policy could no longer be disputed by the appellants. They were, therefore, under obligation to pay a fixed and definite sum to the insured at the time the attaching order was made.

Consider also the English view that insurance proceeds, while not attachable debts, are nevertheless choses in action. Section 19 of The Execution Act allows choses in action to be seized and actions undertaken by the sheriff in his own name to recover them. Is it more convenient to garnishee or to seize entitlement to insurance proceeds?

In Ontario, see now The Insurance Act, R.S.O. 1970, c 224, s 225 which provides:

225. (1) Any person who has a claim against an insured for which indemnity is provided by a contract evidenced by a motor vehicle liability policy, notwithstanding that such person is not a party to the contract, may, upon recovering a judgment therefor in any province or territory of Canada against the insured, have the insurance money payable under the contract applied in or towards satisfaction of his judgment and of any other judgments or claims against the insured covered by the contract and may, on behalf of himself and all persons having such judgments or claims, maintain an action against the insurer to have the insurance money so applied.

(2) No action shall be brought against an insurer under subsection 1 after the expiration of one year from the final determination of the action against the insured, including appeals if any.

(3) A creditor of the insured is not entitled to share in the insurance money payable under any contract unless his claim is one for which indemnity is provided for by that contract.

(4) The right of a person who is entitled under subsection 1 to have insurance money applied upon his judgment or claim is not prejudiced by,

    (*a*) An assignment, waiver, surrender, cancellation or discharge of the contract, or of any interest therein or of the proceeds thereof, made by the insured after the happening of the event giving rise to a claim under the contract;

(*b*) any act or default of the insured before or after that event in contravention of this Part or of the terms of the contract; or

(*c*) any contravention of the *Criminal Code* (Canada) or a statute of any province or territory of Canada or of any state or the District of Columbia of the United States of America by the owner or driver of the automobile,

and nothing mentioned in clause *a, b* or *c* is available to the insurer as a defence in an action brought under subsection 1.

(5) It is not a defence to an action under this section that an instrument issued as a motor vehicle liability policy by a person engaged in the business of an insurer and alleged by a party to the action to be such a policy is not a motor vehicle liability policy, and this section applies *mutatis mutandis* to the instrument....

[Section 225 is an extremely long section: it continues to specify procedures, insurer's rights etc. in an action brought under s 225(1)].

ii Trust Funds: See *Webb* v *Stenton* and the note following it at pp 334, supra.

iii Note: Conditional Debts: Many cases have held so-called 'conditional debts' to be not attachable. In *Rat Portage Lumber Co.* v *Harty* (1917), 40 O.L.R. 322 (C.A.), the judgment debtor assigned to his bank, as security for all his existing and future indebtedness to the bank, 'all moneys due or that might become due to him' under contracts he had with a railway company. The bank was obligated to account to the judgment debtor in excess of his indebtedness to the bank. The judgment debtor completed his obligations under the contract. Prior to receiving payment from the railway company pursuant to the assignment, the bank was served with the garnishee order which demanded that the bank pay out the excess of moneys to be paid by the railway company to the bank over the judgment debtor's indebtedness to the bank. The bank resisted the garnishee order on the ground that at the date of service of the garnishee order, the judgment debtor was indebted to the bank for an amount in excess of the amount of money received at that time from the railway company. As such, the bank maintained that no debts were owing or accruing due to the judgment debtor at the date of service of the order. The majority of the Court of Appeal agreed with the bank's position:

Now the case before us seems to be much more like the trustee cases ... than like the *O'Driscoll* case: see *Webb* v *Stenton* ... The state of affairs when the attaching order was served was that, if Harty had earned from the railway company more than the amount of the bank's claim against him, and if the railway company did pay the bank, the bank would become indebted to Harty; but the receipt by the bank of the money and the consequent liability of the bank to Harty were, it seems to me, contingencies ... and not a certainty ... (*per* Rose J at p 331)

In a strong dissenting judgment, Meredith CJCP was of the opinion that at the time of service of the garnishee order, the bank owed to the judgment debtor a debt which was attachable. He said:

At all times after the assignment was taken by the respondents, they were under a legal obligation to get in the money and pay, to the judgment debtor, the balance of it. When the garnishee orders were served, the money was payable to them, and they had already received a little more than $1,000 of it; there was no uncertainty regarding it or indeed the amount of it: it was money coming to the judgment debtor, and none the less accruing to him because it had to pass through the respondents' hands before he should receive it. I can perceive no good reason why money thus coming to a judgment debtor, and money which the garnishee is under a legal obligation to him to get in, and put into a special account subject to his order, and to pay over to him, may not be attached in garnishee proceedings, though of course no order for payment over can be made until the money has come to the hands of the garnishee: and the cases seem to me to quite warrant that conclusion ...

And need I add that this case is not one in which the garnishees were under no obligation to the judgment debtor; that, by reason of the assignment, they were not in the position of one who becomes answerable on the money count for money received for the use of another only when the money has been so received? The respondents were at all times liable to account to the judgment debtor and to pay over the surplus of the moneys received as soon as it was ascertained on such an accounting: and, before the order in question was made – on the 2nd April, 1917 – the respondents had received all the moneys due and payable to them under the assignment; and there was apparently a surplus of such moneys in their hands after payment of all their claims against the judgment debtor, their customer, of over $1,300, according to the testimony of their manager at Fort Frances. If this money of the judgment debtor, so in the hands of these garnishees – subject to any prior charges upon it, if any – cannot be reached by the judgment creditors in these proceedings, garnishee proceedings, instead of being made effectual by the rulings of the Courts, will be reduced to something like a farce ...

In these circumstances, if it be the law that the appellants can have no relief in this Court in these proceedings, if it be the law that a judgment debtor can defeat garnishee proceedings by merely appointing an agent to receive for him the moneys coming to him, and by making an assignment of them to such agent, some one else must say no. I can say only that, if that be the law, there is some good reason for some of the harshest things that have been said against it. (at pp 335–7)

Which opinion do you prefer? Why? *Rat Portage* was subsequently considered and approved by the Ontario Court of Appeal in *P. Lyall & Sons Construction Co. Ltd.* v *Baker*, [1933] O.R. 286.

Several cases have held that a judgment creditor may not attach by way of garnishment the balance of purchase money payable to a judgment debtor vendor under an agreement for the sale of land where payment is conditional upon the vendor's conveying good title: *Barsi* v *Farcas*, [1924] 1 D.L.R. 1154 (Sask. C.A.): *Reed* v *Renton*, [1924] 2 W.W.R. 223 (Alta. S.C.); *Faas* v *McManus*, [1930] 1 D.L.R. 302 (Alta. C.A.); *Lampman & Laidlaw Ltd.* v *Levine* (1960), 22 D.L.R. (2d) 605 (B.C.C.A.).

Similarly, in *Beneficial Finance Co. of Can.* v *Meech et al.* (1963), 39 D.L.R. (2d) 422, the Saskatchewan Court of Appeal held that a 'retirement allowance', which provided for the payment of $100 per month to the former employee if she survived a certain period, was not attachable because it was not an absolute debt, but only a conditional debt: '[t]he garnishee's liability to pay, and Miss Meech's right to collect, the monthly payment of $100 only arises at the expiration of each month if she is alive at that time; that is, there is neither an obligation to pay, nor a right to collect, until these two conditions are fulfilled.' (per Culliton CJS at p 425). Would this case be decided the same way in Ontario?

In *Brown* v *Garrison et al.* (1968), 63 W.W.R. (N.S.) 248, the British Columbia Court of Appeal rejected the garnishor's submission that 'the service of the garnishing order created an equitable charge on a debt not then due, and that, although it did not "catch" the debt so that it had to be paid into Court, equitable rights maintainable in the future were generated subject to prior rights of the ... garnishee against the judgment debtor'. The Court was of the opinion that '[i]t is unthinkable that a garnishing order which is ineffectual because no debt exists or is accruing within the meaning of the statute, should be considered to remain in existence to form a charge on a debt which on certain conditions being fulfilled may arise in the future.' (per Bull JA at p 252).

See also *Pe Ben Industries* v *Chinook Construction*, [1977] 3 W.W.R. 481 (B.C.C.A.), where the Court decided that unliquidated damages, whether arising in contract or in tort, could not be the subject matter of garnishee proceeding.

d / Bank Accounts

One obvious place to find a debt owing to the judgment debtor is in his bank. However, before any attachment of a bank account credit balance can be made, the creditor will have to know specific information. The Bank Act, R.S.C. 1970, c B-1, provides that:

96. (4) A writ or process originating a legal proceeding or issued therein or in pursuance thereof or an order or injunction made by a court affects and binds only property in the possession of the bank belonging to or moneys to the credit of, a person at the branch where such writ, process, order or injunction or notice thereof is served.

Is s 96(4) constitutional?

i Deposit Accounts

Bel-Fran Investments Ltd. v *Pantuity Holdings Limited and Bank of Montreal (Garnishee)*, [1975] 6 W.W.R. 374 (B.C.S.C. in chambers)

ANDERSON J.: This is a motion to set aside a garnishing order on the following grounds:

'That the Garnishing Order before Judgment issued herein on the 19th day of February, 1975 and directed to the Bank of Montreal as Garnishee be set aside on the following grounds: [The first three grounds are omitted.]

D That the funds paid into Court by the Garnishee are not legally attachable since they are not debts, obligations or obligations owing, payable or accruing due from the Garnishee to the Defendant.'

[His Lordship rejected the applicant's first three submissions and continued:]

The defendant had deposited in the Bank of Montreal the sum of $725,000 subject to the terms of a 'term deposit receipt' dated 10th January 1975, and maturing on 9th April 1975. As of the date of the service of the garnishing order the deposit had not matured. The 'term deposit receipt' was not transferable and reads as follows:

'TERM DEPOSIT RECEIPT – NOT TRANSFERABLE

'... Subject to the terms and conditions herein set forth. The said sum may be withdrawn in whole or in part before the maturity date. Partial withdrawal shall be subject to the maintenance of a minimum deposit as may be determined by the Bank from time to time. Withdrawal in whole or in part is subject to the Bank's right to require seven (7) days prior notice thereof. If part or all of the said sum is withdrawn before the maturity date interest thereon will be paid in such cases at the rate indicated in the interest Rate Schedule shown hereon pertaining to the elapsed period of the Deposit and the amount of any overpayment of interest will be deducted from the Deposit and any balance of accrued interest payable. No interest will be paid beyond the maturity date.

'If the term of this Receipt is for less than one year, interest will be paid at its maturity date or date of withdrawal. If the term of this receipt is for one year or more, interest will be paid half-yearly on the last day of April and October. Payment of principal and any accrued and unpaid interest, at maturity or prior to withdrawal of principal, will be made only to the registered holder upon surrender of this Receipt at the issuing branch and completion of the receipt provided for this purpose.'

It is submitted that the deposit was not a 'debt or obligation due or accruing due' from the Bank of Montreal to the judgment debtor as of the date the affidavit in support of the garnishing order was sworn.

The Attachment of Debts Act, R.S.B.C. 1960, c 20, s 3(7) [en. 1968, c 12, s 26; am. 1971, c 6, s 2], reads as follows:

7 In this section, the expressions 'debt due' and 'debts due' include debts, obligations, and liabilities owing, payable, or accruing due and wages that would in the ordinary course of employment become owing, payable, or due within seven days after the date on which an affidavit has been sworn under subsection (1) or subsection (2).

The defendant relies on the judgment of the Court of Appeal in *Bagley* v *Winsome* (*National Provincial Bank, Garnishee*), [1952] 2 Q.B. 236, [1952] 1 All E.R. 637. The headnote in that case reads as follows:

A judgment debtor had a sum of money in a deposit account with a bank, the contract between the bank and the debtor being subject to the conditions (*a*) that fourteen days' notice should be given of a withdrawal, and (*b*) that money could be withdrawn only on a personal application by the debtor at the Bank and on production of the deposit book. On Jan. 11, 1952, a notice of withdrawal given by the debtor expired, and, on the same day, the judgment creditor issued a garnishee summons against the bank. The debtor did not apply, personally or at all, for repayment of the money and it was still with the bank.

HELD: as the judgment debtor had failed to comply with all the terms of the contract of deposit, he could not obtain payment from the bank of the money in his deposit account, and the judgment creditor could not be in a better position than the debtor; therefore, the sum standing to the credit of the debtor's deposit account was not a debt 'owing or accruing' to him from the bank, within the meaning of R.S.C., Ord. 45, r 1, and the County Court Rules, Ord. 27, r 1, and it was not a proper subject of garnishee proceedings.

The terms of the contract in the *Bagley* case, supra, are similar to the case at bar as follows:

Bagley

1. Type of account: deposit account.	3. Personal application must be made.
2. All withdrawals are subject to 14 days' notice.	4. Deposit book must be produced at bank when any money is withdrawn.

Case at bar

1. Type of account: term deposit.
2. Withdrawal in whole or in part subject to the bank's right to require seven days' prior notice thereof.
3. Payment will be made only to registered holder.
4. Payment will be made only upon surrender of term deposit receipt at the issuing branch and completion of receipt provided for this purpose.

In *Bagley* the requirement of notice was fulfilled but the requirement of personally presenting the deposit book was obviously not compiled with. In the case at bar the bank has not been given notice. It should be noted, however, that the terms of the term deposit agreement are that the withdrawal is subject to the bank's right to require notice. The logical implication of these words is that no notice is required unless the bank exercises this right.

While there are many similarities between the *Bagley* case and the case at bar there are, in my opinion, several features which serve to illustrate the distinction between the *Bagley* 'deposit account' and the term deposit in the case at bar.

Sir Raymond Evershed M.R. in giving judgment in the *Bagley* case made reference to *Joachimson* v *Swiss Bank Corpn.*, [1921] 3 K.B. 110, where it was held that the service of a garnishing order was equivalent to a demand made by the judgment debtor. While accepting the judgment in the *Joachimson* case as being good law he refused to extend the principle enunciated in that case to the facts in the *Bagley* case. At pp 639–40 he said:

I turn to a consideration of the present case. It has for a long time been well established that this form of execution is available in the case of a current account with a banker. Until 1921 it was not apprehended that there was any problem involved, having regard to the contract between banker and customer, in such circumstances, but in that year there came to be decided, again in this court, *Joachimson* v *Swiss Bank Corpn.* The problem of the true nature of garnishee proceedings in relation to current accounts was indirectly raised, for the question was whether the plaintiffs, Joachimson (a firm), could say that a cause of action had accrued against the defendant bank in regard to the repayment of an account in the absence of a demand made by the customer, and the Court of Appeal held that in the case of a current account a cause of action did not arise until the demand had been made. In the course of the argument the attention of the court was drawn to the question how, if that were so, were the well established garnishee proceedings in relation to current accounts to be justified, since, at any rate, in nine cases out of ten, no demand for payment would have been made at the time when the garnishee proceedings occurred. It was, I think, a serious problem, but the three members of the court (BANKES, WARRINGTON and ATKIN, L.JJ.), were undaunted by that consideration in the conclusion at which they arrived in the particular case, and said in effect: 'The service of the garnishee summons should be taken as operating as a demand, and that will avoid the difficulty.' Although it was not strictly necessary for them to decide the point, I think they clearly indicated that the answer to the point was as I have stated it, and, as counsel for the judgment creditor in his reply indicated, I think that the later decision of this court in *Rekstin* v *Severo Sibirsko Gosudarstvennoe Akcionernoe Obschestvo Komseverputj & Bank for Russian Trade*, [1933] 1 K.B. 47, shows that such a view must now be taken as accepted: see, e.g., the judgment of SLESSER, L.J., in *Rekstin's* case.

Counsel for the judgment creditor in the present case contends that, if the service of a garnishee summons can operate as a demand by the judgment debtor, there is no logical reason why it should not be taken as operating as satisfaction of any other conditions such as those which apply in the case of a deposit account. I cannot accept that argument. It seems to me that the two conditions with which we are concerned in this contract – the notice, on the one hand, and the personal application with the production of the deposit book, on the other hand – are of a somewhat different character. The deposit book is the document of title to the deposit account. As other cases have illustrated, delivery of it to a third person may operate as an effective donatio mortis causa. At the same time I think it is an unnatural and wrong use of language to suggest that where, as here, a notice of withdrawal has been given, there remains only a contingent debt. If the service of the notice of withdrawal can be regarded as a demand for payment, still the bank is entitled to rely and insist on the contract which only obliges it to pay on satisfaction of the other condition. That condition may or may not be satisfied at some indefinite future time, and in the meantime the judgment creditor cannot, as it seems to me, be in a better position than the party to the contract with the bank, namely, the judgment debtor. I am not, therefore, satisfied that in such a case as the present, on the facts that I have stated, the deposit account can and should be treated, in consequence of the decision in *Joachimson* v *Swiss Bank Corpn.* [supra], as a debt 'owing or accruing' within the meaning of the relevant rules.

It will be noted that Sir Raymond Evershed M.R., in giving judgment, stated that the deposit book was a document of title to the deposit account and could be delivered to a third person and operate as an effective donatio mortis causa. I do not think that the term deposit receipt, being clearly non-transferable, could constitute a valid donatio mortis causa upon delivery to a third person. Accordingly in the case at bar if the service of the garnishing order is treated as amounting to the delivery up to the term deposit receipt, the rights of third parties would not and could not be affected. In England, apparently, the recipient of the deposit book may have obtained some right to the account itself.

I have already noted that in the *Bagley* case 'withdrawals were subject to fourteen days' notice', whereas in the case at bar the bank merely reserves the right to require seven days' prior notice of withdrawal.

My view is that all the conditions of the term deposit receipt in the case at bar concern only the bank and are mere matters of procedure and administration, and are all satisfied by the service of the garnishing order. The bank would be protected by the Court upon any protest by the defendant that payment had been made without personal delivery of the term deposit receipt. While a third party might hold the term deposit receipt as security for a loan, I do not think that in the face of the clear terms of the deposit receipt (that it is a personal document and not assignable) a third party could obtain any rights against the bank ...
[The motion to set aside the garnishing order was dismissed.]

See also *Olinyk* v *Olinyk*, [1975] W.W.D. 129 (Alta. S.C.), which held that a certificate of deposit was attachable, even though it was a condition of the deposit that the certificate must be surrendered to receive payment, and the judgment debtor refused to surrender the certificate to the garnishee bank. McDonald J held that the debt was 'due' although it was not payable until the maturity date. The term that payment would not be made unless the certificates were surrendered did not make the debt a conditional one so that a garnishee summons would not attach.

In *McGregor* v *Bamerical International Financial Corp. Ltd.*, [1977] 1 W.W.R. 653 (B.C.S.C.), the defendant Bamerical had obtained a certificate of deposit, in the amount of $43,500, from the garnishee bank. The certificate was to mature in six years, but there was a provision for withdrawal before maturity on 24 hours' notice. Bamerical then guaranteed the indebtedness of a company, and hypothecated all of its securities, including the certificate of deposit, to the bank. The company was indebted and in default to the bank at the time a garnishing order against Bamerical was served on the bank. The bank redeemed the certificate of deposit, and credited the $43,500 against the company's indebtedness.

The Court held that the application of proceeds by the bank was proper. The service of the garnishing order had the effect of demanding payment, and therefore payment by the bank had to be made within 24 hours subject to any other accounting between the defendant debtor. Since Bamerical had clearly assigned the certificate of deposit to the bank, the bank properly applied the proceeds against the company's indebtedness.

For a case applying *Bagley* v *Winsome*, see *Re Australia and New Zealand Savings Bank Ltd.*, [1972] v.r. 690 (s.c.). On an attempt to execute against a savings bank account belonging to the judgment debtor the Court held that the credit balance was not an attachable debt, because the presentation of the passbook and signed withdrawal form were prerequisites of withdrawal from the account. The provision in the passbook was classified as a condition precedent to any obligation on the part of the bank to repay moneys deposited to the credit of the accounts, and as this condition had not been complied with at the date of the garnishing order, there was no debt owing or accruing from the bank to the judgment debtor. *Re Australia and New Zealand Savings Bank* was followed in *Bank of New South Wales Savings Bank Ltd.* v *Fremantle Auto Centre Pty. Ltd.*, [1973] w.a.r. 161 (s.c.).

ii Joint Accounts: Difficulties have arisen in the course of attempts to garnish joint bank accounts. The central question is whether or not a joint bank account involves a debt payable to the debtor. If it does, it can be garnished; on the other hand, if it is payable to the debtor and another person, it may not be attachable. The cases which follow illustrate some of the difficulties the Courts have encountered in handling the problem.

Re Davis, Nash and Davis v *Royal Bank of Canada* (1958), 13 D.L.R. (2d) 411 (B.C.S.C.).

LORD, J.: The Royal Bank of Canada, pursuant to a garnishing order duly obtained by the plaintiff, brought into Court the sum of $1,048.28, but set out in its Answer of Garnishee that it was indebted, under obligation and liable in that amount to the defendant C.W. Nash and his wife Aileen H. Nash in respect of a joint account with the defendant, from which account either the defendant or his said wife might withdraw all or any moneys therein, and asked that no order be made without the determination of the Court as to whether the said account and moneys therein are available in garnishee proceedings.

The moneys were paid in prior to judgment and the plaintiff, having succeeded at the trial and in the Court of Appeal now applies for payment out.

The printed bank form constituting this joint account, and which was signed by both Nash and his wife, reads as follows:

In order effectually to constitute the account mentioned on the reverse of this card a joint account, each of the undersigned hereby assigns and transfers to all the undersigned jointly and to the survivor or survivors of them all moneys heretofore or hereafter credited to said account and all interest thereon to be the joint property of the undersigned and the property of the survivor or survivors of them. For valuable consideration received, the undersigned hereby agree jointly and each with the other(s) of them and also with The Royal Bank of Canada that all moneys heretofore or hereafter credited to said account and all interest thereon shall be and continue the joint property of the undersigned with right of survivorship and that said bank may accept as a sufficient discharge for any sums withdrawn from said account any order or receipt signed by any one or more of the undersigned without any signature or consent of the other(s) and that the death of one or more of the undersigned shall not affect the right of the survivors or any one of them or the sole survivor to withdraw said moneys and interest and to give a valid discharge therefor, subject, however, to the requirements of any Succession Duty Act in respect of such moneys and interest.

Further, said bank is hereby authorized to credit such account with all moneys and the proceeds of all promises or orders to pay money, bonds, debentures, securities and coupons signed by or the property of, or received by said bank for the credit or account of or payable to, the undersigned or any of them, and to endorse any thereof on their behalf.

The garnishing order herein ordered that 'all debts, obligations and liabilities owing, payable, or accruing due' from the garnishee to the defendant be attached up to the amount named therein, and paid into Court. The neat point for decision is, can this order attach moneys in a joint bank account which is to the credit of the judgment debtor and another.

Counsel were able to find only one Canadian case directly in point: *Empire Fertilizers Ltd.* v *Cioci*, [1934] 4 D.L.R. 804, O.W.N. 535. The judgment is only partly reported, but it would appear that the defendant Cioci was a judgment debtor who had a joint account with his wife in a branch of the Royal Bank of Canada in Toronto. It was sought to attach the moneys in this account under a judgment recovered against the defendant husband alone. The learned County Court Judge in holding the moneys were attachable had this to say at p 805: 'If the judgment debtor, B. N. Cioci, had given to the judgment creditor a cheque signed by B. N. Cioci alone on the Royal Bank, Jane and Annette Branch, Toronto, for the amount owing by Cioci on the judgment, the bank, on presentment of such cheque for payment, would have had to pay it, on the penalty of an action for damages by B. N. Cioci, against the bank if such cheque had been dishonoured. I see no reason why this judgment creditor of B. N. Cioci should not have recourse to these proceedings to compel such appropriation of these funds as was within the power of Cioci himself at the time of the issue and service of the garnishee summons on the bank and as is still within his power, to the extent of $134.50, which by the bank manager's letter of April 13, 1934, is admittedly held by the bank pending the judgment in this action. *Stadder* v *Can. Bk. Commerce*, [1929] 3 D.L.R. 651, 64 O.L.R. 69.'

The report of the case merely states that the Ontario Court of Appeal 'without calling on counsel for respondent dismissed the appeal from the judgment of Field, Co.Ct.J., *infra*'. Presumably that Court adopted the reasoning of the learned trial Judge.

In England, the Court of Appeal, under very similar circumstances came to a different conclusion in *Hirschhorn* v *Evans*, [1938] 3 All E.R. 491. That was also a case in which a judgment debtor and his wife had a joint account with the bank upon which account either of them could draw, and a garnishee order was issued against the bank in respect of a debt owned by the judgment debtor. The County Court Judge, from whom the appeal was taken, evidently found that the moneys were attachable on the ground that the account was the husband's account as the whole of the moneys therein had been provided by him. The Court of Appeal found that there was no evidence to support this finding of fact, and Greer L.J. would allow the appeal on that ground. He differed, however, from Slesser and MacKinnon L.JJ. who held to quote the headnote, that 'A joint account with a bank, even if owned by a husband and wife, cannot be attached under a garnishee order in respect of a debt owed by one of the joint owners.'

Slesser L.J. at pp 494–5 said: 'In my view, the right construction to put upon the opening of the account on Feb. 8, 1935, notwithstanding the fact that both the judgment debtor and his wife were thereby authorised to sign cheques, is that that account was a joint account. I entertain no doubt that, if the bank had failed to meet its obligations, the rights under this account could only have been exercised by both the persons, the husband and the wife, joining in whatever claim might be appropriate under the account.'

The learned Judge then went on to quote Fry L.J. in *Macdonald v Tacquah Gold Mine Co.* (1884), 13 Q.B.D. 535 at p 539: ' "I adhere to what was said by this court in *Webb v Stenton* as to the word 'indebted' in that rule. Then can it be said that the defendant company was indebted to the judgment debtor when they were indebted to him and another person jointly only? It seems clearly it cannot, and that the words of the rule are not applicable to such a case. If they were, the result would be to enable a judgment creditor to attach a debt due to two persons in order to answer for the debt due to him from the judgment debtor alone, which would be altogether contrary to justice." '

He then continued at pp 495–6: 'What is said here is that, in so far as each of these persons has the right to demand payment of the money in the account under the specific authorisation to accept the signature of either of them, this account is in its nature several as well as joint. I am unable to accept that view. It seems to me that it amounts to no more than that the bank are under an obligation at any time to meet the demand of either the husband or the wife, and to that extent, when that demand is dishonoured, the bank would be responsible for failure to meet that payment. If the argument here for the judgment creditor be well-maintained, it would follow that the bank would be in this dilemma; the whole account being sterilised owing to the operation of this order, they would be unable to meet the demands of the wife which she is entitled, under the contract with the bank, to make, because that would be prevented by an order which, on the face of it, applies to the husband only. I cannot think that any such position arises merely because each party may, as regards a specific cheque, create a specific debt in relation to that matter.

'I think that one has to look at the account as a whole, and, looking at the account as a whole, I think that it is in the nature of a joint account on which the bank are liable to both parties jointly, and, consequently, the garnishee order is misconceived in stating that the bank are indebted to the said judgment debtor in the sum there stated whereas, in reality, they are indebted to the judgment debtor and to his wife jointly.'

MacKinnon L.J. said at p 497: 'It is true that there was an authority on the bank to honour cheques upon that joint account if the cheques were signed by one or other of them. That simply means: "Either of us has authority on behalf of, and as agent for, both of us to sign cheques." It would amount to no more than an added authorisation to the bank. "Upon this our joint account you are authorised to honour cheques drawn by our clerk or agent, John Smith," notwithstanding that it was, and at all times remains, a joint account.'

And further on the same page he says: 'As the account was in the joint names, and not in the name of the judgment debtor, the bank took the view that the summons did not attach any part of their debt on the joint account, and they could not dishonour cheques drawn on the joint account. I think that they were right in that view.

'If authority be needed, it can be supplied by part of a single sentence in the judgment of Pollock B., in *Beasley v Roney*, [1891] 1 Q.B. 509 at p 512: "the debt owing by a garnishee to a judgment debtor which can be attached to answer the judgment debt must be a debt due to the judgment debtor alone, and that where it is only due to him jointly with another it cannot be attached."''

There is no evidence before me to show whether the moneys in the account may have been contributed only by the husband or wife or both, so that no question arises in equity as to whether either of them may be considered as being on the account merely as trustee.

The nature of this type of bank account is described in *Niles* v *Lake*, [1947], 2 D.L.R. 248, S.C.R. 291, where a form similar in language to the one above set out was involved. Rand J. said at pp 260–1 D.L.R., pp 307–8 S.C.R.: 'A careful examination of its language makes it perfectly clear to me that what was intended by all parties was the creation of a relationship to the bank in such terms as would preclude any challenge to the irrevocable authority of either of the depositors to deal with the account in unqualified fashions ... that an estoppel should be raised that would remove the possibility of controversy between the depositors or persons representing them involving the bank ... These are all constituent elements of a conclusive relation to the bank; whatever the interest in the money of the depositors *inter se*, these were the terms interposed between them and the bank.'

There can be no doubt that the bank is liable to both parties jointly. It is indebted to two persons, and as Slesser L.J. pointed out in *Hirschhorn* v *Evans, supra*, 'the garnishee order is misconceived in stating that the bank are indebted to the said judgment debtor in the sum there stated, whereas, in reality, they are indebted to the judgment debtor and to his wife jointly'.

The reasoning of Slesser and MacKinnon L.JJ. in the above case and the statement of Fry L.J. that to enable a judgment creditor to attach a debt due to two persons in order to answer for the debt due to him from the judgment debtor alone would be altogether contrary to justice, convinces me that the attachment here cannot stand, and although the decision in *Empire Fertilizers Ltd.* v *Cioci, supra*, may not be in accord with this decision, I do not feel that I can follow it.

The application, insofar as it involves a balance remaining in Court and paid in by the Imperial Bank of Canada on a different garnishing order is granted. This account was in the name of the defendant Nash alone, and this part of the application was not opposed. So far as the application concerns moneys paid in by the Royal Bank of Canada it must fail with costs against the plaintiff.

In *Royal Bank of Canada* v *Tompkins*, [1976] W.W.D. 174 (B.C.S.C.), a garnishing order was served on the garnishee to attach the defendant's interest in money held in trust by the garnishee and payable jointly to the defendant and his wife on the completion of the sale of land held by them in joint tenancy. Spencer LJSC held that as the garnishee owed two persons jointly, it could not be said that the debt was due to either of them; accordingly, the garnishee was not liable to pay the money out. The joint tenancy could not be severed because the defendant's interest in the land would have been exigible under The Execution Act. The wife would be deprived of her right of survivorship if each of the parties was declared a beneficial owner of one-half of the fund.

One approach that can be taken is to look at the contribution record of the joint account owners to determine the extent to which the account may be garnished:

Re Adler, [1951] O.W.N. 681 (H.C.J.)

A motion for a declaration that the trustee in bankruptcy had good title to $779.15 paid to him by the clerk of a Division Court.

URQUHART J. [after stating the nature of the motion]: Mr. and Mrs. Adler had a joint bank account, and on Mr. Adler paying a creditor therefrom, other creditors garnished the account, whereupon the bank (a trust company) paid the amount into the Division Court at St. Thomas. On the debtor's going into bankruptcy, the trustee claimed from the Court and got possession of the proceeds, less some costs.

Mrs. Adler says that in November 1950 she, having sold a business and settled up, found herself with $1,320 in her hands. She opened a joint bank account, signing a very meagre form, in the name of her husband and herself. Her idea was to enable her husband, who was then a commercial traveller, to issue small cheques when he needed money for expenses on the road, he being paid on a commission basis.

Only two cheques were drawn: one on the day of deposit for $373.90 to meet the wife's liabilities, and one for $105.48 to a creditor of the husband, both signed by the husband with permission of the wife. Why the husband should have signed to meet the wife's expenses is unexplained. The garnishee immediately followed the latter cheque.

Breaking the case down it is apparent that:

(1) It was all the wife's money; the debtor acquired no ownership. He could only sign by his wife's permission and for certain definite purposes.

(2) The moneys were deposited 'to be held on a joint tenancy'. The usual long form adopted by banks was not used. The document gives the husband no property; it merely permits the trust company to honour cheques signed by him.

(3) The 'strings' attached were not communicated to the bank, but this does not give a creditor the right to seize moneys which belong to a third party.

The trustee relies upon the case of *Empire Fertilizers Ltd.* v *Cioci*, [1934] O.W.N. 535, [1934] 4 D.L.R. 804, but to my mind that case does not help in that the money may have been deposited by either or both, and the wording of the direction was much more elaborate.

I have examined the numerous cases cited by the claimant, but need not discuss them.

On the evidence, the moneys were, at all times, the property of the wife, and under her direction. Creditors would have no recourse to them and therefore the trustee must return to her what he received.

Judgment that the trustee pay to Mrs. Adler $779.15. Since Mrs. Adler created the situation, no costs will be awarded to her; costs of the trustee out of the estate.

Order accordingly.

In *Harrods Ltd.* v *Tester*, [1937] 2 All E.R. 236, (C.A.) the judgment creditor sought to garnishee funds in a bank account in the name of the judgment debtor. It was established that the judgment debtor had not made any contribution to the account – the money having been deposited solely by her husband. The Court held that the husband had rebutted the presumption of advancement, and that in the absence of evidence of a fraudulent scheme to prevent execution, the bank account was not attachable.

'Note' (1957), 71 *Harv. L. Rev.* 557. Garnishment – property subject to garnishment – joint account depositor has burden of proving his ownership of funds to prevent their garnishment for debts of other depositor. – *Leaf* v *McGowan* (Ill. App. 1957).

A creditor instituted a garnishment action against a savings bank to satisfy a judgment from money held in a joint bank account. The debtor's codepositor intervened and moved to dismiss on the grounds that a joint account is not garnishable and that he owned the funds in the joint account. The trial court denied the codepositor's motion to dismiss. On appeal, *held*, affirmed. A joint account is garnishable and the burden of proving how much of the account should be exempt from garnishment is on the nondebtor depositor. *Leaf* v *McGowan*, 13 Ill. App. 2d 58, 141 N.E. 2d 67 (1957).

Joint accounts are peculiarly difficult to categorize in common-law terminology. Although they contain a survivorship feature, making them analogous to a joint tenancy, this analogy is weakened by the 'joint and several' ownership feature – the right of each depositor, as against the bank, to withdraw all the funds. It is not surprising, therefore, that the problem of the extent to which joint accounts are garnishable for the debts of one depositor has given rise to a wide variety of solutions. At one extreme, the English courts hold that a joint account is immune from garnishment because, under English law, payment under compulsion to the attaching creditor will not protect the garnishee bank in a suit by the nondebtor. At the other extreme, it has been held that the entire account is subject to garnishment on the theory that the creditor is 'subrogated' to the power exercisable by the debtor-depositor to withdraw all the money. Both views can be logically supported, and they have the advantage of simplicity in that they avoid the necessity of proving the actual ownership of the deposits. However, they ignore the fact that the power of either depositor to withdraw all the funds simply protects the bank and is in no way determinative of the depositors' rights inter se.

A third view is that the joint account should be garnishable only in proportion to the debtor's ownership of the funds, as to which parol evidence is admissible to show the respective contributions of each depositor, as well as any intent of one to make a gift to the other. This approach enables courts to distinguish between two essentially different types of accounts: (1) the 'convenience' account, usually involving a husband and a wife, which will often 'sacrifice precision to convenience and becloud the respective rights of the depositors'; and (2) the savings account used as a device for making testamentary gift. The 'convenience' account, with the exception of the case in which one depositor is merely an agent of the other to make deposits and withdrawals, may present an evidentiary problem due to the fact that the parties may not have kept careful records and may not have adverted to the issue of their rights in the joint fund. In the second type of account, although the donee has the power as against the bank to withdraw the funds, there is an informal understanding between the depositors that the gift is not to take effect until the donor's death. Under the view that parol evidence is admissible to show ownership in a garnishment proceeding, a joint savings account would be garnishable for the donee's debts only to the extent that a presently effective gift was intended.

Once it is decided to admit parol evidence on the issue of ownership, the decision as to who is to bear the burden of proof may be conclusive since the records will often be nonexistent and the parties' intent impossible to ascertain. Prior to the present case, the law of Illinois placed on the garnisher the burden of proving that the debtor owned any of the funds in the joint account. An alternative solution is to create an arbitrary presumption that each depositor owns half the funds, and to place the burden of proof on the party attempting to rebut this presumption. This is the solution normally reached in those jurisdictions in which there are statutes providing for joint-tenancy treatment of joint accounts which by implication adopt the common-law presumption of equal ownership in controversies between depositors.

The court in the present case rejected both solutions and held that the evidence that the debtor had an interest in the joint account is prima facie proof of his ownership of the whole account; thus the burden was placed on the nondebtor to prove how much of the account should be exempted. The court reasoned that, since the depositors' use of a joint account gives them the power to obscure their respective rights in the fund, it is more equitable to place the burden of proof on the non-debtor depositor than on the garnisher. This resolution seems desirable because the facts of actual ownership are peculiarly within the knowledge of the depositors. The court also rejected the reasoning of a Minnesota court, which would punish the depositors for having chosen a 'loose system of dealing with money' by holding the entire account garnishable and not permitting an inquiry into the issue of ownership. The court's approach in the present case treats each case on its merits and permits actual ownership to prevail in cases in which accurate records have been kept. It thus reaches a solution which would appear to effect the fairest compromise between the rights of creditors and those of joint-account depositors.

NOTE For analyses of the law relating to property interests in joint bank accounts, see: D.M.W. Waters, 'The Doctrine of Resulting Trusts in Common Law Canada' (1970–71), 16 *McGill Law Journal* 187, at pp 217–34; M.C. Cullity, 'Joint Bank Accounts with volunteers' (1969), 85 L.Q.R. 530; W.M.H. Grover, Note (1959), 17 *U. of T. Fac. L. Rev.* 159.

QUESTIONS
1 Consider again questions 1, 2 and 3 at p 257, and assume that Jacky attempted to execute by garnishment, rather than by seizing. What would the rights of the parties be on interpleader proceedings initiated by the bank?
2 What would the rights of the parties be if the bank were to allege that it held a promissory note signed by John and payable on demand, and an authorization by John to recoup the indebtedness from John's account without further notice to John? Would it matter what steps the bank had taken before issue or service of the garnishment?

e / Debts to a Partnership
Problems similar to those encountered in garnisheeing a joint bank account also arise when the judgment debtor has an interest in a partnership, another type of joint .interest.

Hoon v Maloff et al. (Jarvis Constn. Co. Ltd. et al., garnishees) (1964), 42 D.L.R. (2d) 770 (B.C.S.C.)

AIKINS, J.: On June 1, 1962, the plaintiff procured a garnishing order before judgment directed to Jarvis Construction Co. Ltd., Frank Kutchen, L. or Lyman Jones, and Canadian Imperial Bank of Commerce as garnishees. On September 20, 1962, the garnishee Jarvis Construction Co. Ltd. paid the sum of $2761.76 into Court and filed an answer to the garnishing order. The material part of the answer reads as follows:

The Garnishee brings into Court the sum of $2761.76 and says at the time of the service of the Garnishee Order herein upon it, it was indebted, under obligation and liable in the sum of $2761.76 to Frank Kutchen, Lyman Jones and Frank Maloff, carrying on business under the firm name and style of 'Maloff, Jones and Kutchen', and the said Maloff, Jones and Kutchen in respect of a contract with the Garnishee. The Garnishee asks that no order be made without the determination of this Honourable Court as to whether the said monies herein paid into Court are available in garnishee proceedings. The Garnishee, if indebted whatsoever to the Defendant, Frank Maloff, if at all in respect of the said monies, is not indebted to him in any other respect whatsoever.

Application is made for payment out to Maloff, Jones and Kutchen. The ground of the application is that Jarvis Construction Co. Ltd. was not indebted to the defendant Frank Maloff but was indebted to a partnership consisting of Maloff, Jones and Kutchen. It is not in dispute that the Maloff who is a defendant in this action is the Maloff who is a partner in the firm Maloff, Jones and Kutchen.

I am satisfied on the material that the garnishee, Jarvis Construction Co. Ltd., was not indebted to either the defendant Maloff Construction Co. Ltd. or the defendant Maloff and that the indebtedness of the Jarvis Construction Co. Ltd. was to the partnership consisting of the defendant Maloff and Jones and Kutchen.

The ground upon which the applicants rely is simply that the garnishee was not indebted to the defendant Maloff. It is submitted that in order for money owing by a garnishee to a defendant to be attachable the debt must be owing to the defendant alone and not to a partnership of which the defendant is a member, or to the defendant jointly with another or others. I think this argument is sound. I was not referred to any case involving attachment of a debt owing to a partnership, but the principle to be applied is clearly stated in *Re Davis, Nash and Davis* v *Royal Bank of Canada* (1958), 13 D.L.R. (2d) 411, 25 W.W.R. 630. In this case Lord, J. (now J.A.), considered the effect of a garnishing order on money on deposit in a joint bank account to the credit of a judgment debtor and another and held, relying upon *Hirschhorn* v *Evans*, [1938] 2 K.B. 801, 107 L.J.K.B. 756, and declining to follow *Empire Fertilizers Ltd.* v *Cioci*, [1934] 4 D.L.R. 804, [1934] O.W.N. 535 (to which I was referred), that the money on deposit in the joint account could not be attached to pay a judgment debt of one co-depositor, notwithstanding that under the agreement between the bank and the co-depositors either one of the co-depositors had authority to withdraw money on deposit in the joint account. It was argued for the plaintiff that any one of the three partners of the firm of Maloff, Jones and Kutchen could have received the money owing from the garnishee to the firm and could have given a receipt therefor. This however is not the case because the debt is treated as owing to one partner alone, but because a partner receiving a debt and giving a receipt is regarded as an agent of the firm and his other partners for the purposes of the partnership business. (See s 8 of the *Partnership Act*, R.S.B.C. 1960, c 277.) The point is analogous to that which arose in the *Hirschhorn* case in which the money in a joint bank account could be withdrawn by either of the co-depositors. I take a quotation from the judgment of MacKinnon, L.J., in the *Hirschhorn* case used by Lord, J., in *Re Daris*, at p 414 D.L.R., p 634 W.W.R. (the quotation is from p 762 of the Law Journal report (*supra*) of *Hirschhorn* v *Evans*):

It is true that there was an authority on the bank to honour cheques upon that joint account if the cheques were signed by one or other of them. That simply means: 'Either of us has authority on behalf of and as agent for both of us to sign cheques.'

Re Davis, Nash and Davis v *Royal Bank* and the authorities therein referred to make it clear that a debt due from a garnishee to a defendant and another jointly cannot be attached by a plaintiff to satisfy money owing by the defendant to the plaintiff.

For these reasons, in my view, the money owing from Jarvis Construction Co. Ltd. to the partnership of Maloff, Jones and Kutchen was not attachable to meet the debt of one partner, the defendant Maloff, alone ...

NOTE The exigibility of the interest of a partner in the partnership was considered, supra, at pp 260–2.

f / Other Debts Subject to Garnishment

No comprehensive list of all the various types of debt subject to garnishment can be formulated. The general rules, however, are clear: if a debt is owing or accruing due to the judgment debtor it is garnishable, unless somehow exempted from garnishment on the grounds of public policy or by statute (see Chapter 8, ante). Examples of some 'unusual' debts held garnishable include: moneys due on a mortgage of land (*Royal Bank* v *Lee*, [1929] 4 D.L.R. 975 (Alta. C.A.); *MacPherson Fruit Co.* v *Hayden* (1905), 2 W.L.R. 427 (N.W.T.)); moneys due on a chattel mortgage (*Stimson* v *Hamilton* (1905), 1 W.L.R. 20 (N.W.T.); moneys due on a promissory note (*Roblee* v *Rankin* (1884), 11 S.C.R. 137) or on a demand note (*Royal Bank* v *Hogg*, [1930] 2 D.L.R. 488 (Ont. C.A.)); rent (*Vigars-Shears Lumber Co.* v *Port Arthur Curling etc. Co.* (1921), 20 O.W.N. 224 (C.A.)); *Elliot* v *Forrester*, [1918] 2 W.W.R. 220 (Man. K.B.)).

For a particularly unusual fact situation, see: *Hershfield* v *Amos et al. (Dept. of Mines and Natural Resources of Manitoba, garnishee)* (1971), 21 D.L.R. (3d) 597 (Man. C.A.), in which the Provincial government department paid money into Court following service of a garnishment order on it. The payment in deprived the government of the option of not paying money to the debtor which it had under legislation designed to give discretionary relief to commercial fishermen injured by mercury pollution. The payment in meant the department had agreed to pay; there was a debt, and it was garnishable.

4 PROTECTION OF WAGES

Exemptions from garnishment were discussed generally in Chapter 8. However, because the debt most often garnished is the debtor's wages, this section focuses specific attention on the legislation affecting their exigibility.

a / The Wages Act, R.S.O. 1970, c 486 as amended

7. (1) Seventy per cent of any debt due or accruing due to any mechanic, workman, labourer, servant, clerk or employee for or in respect of his wages is exempt from seizure or attachment, provided that if a creditor of any such mechanic, workman, labourer, servant, clerk or employee, who has initiated proceedings by way of seizure or attachment of the wages of any such mechanic, workman, labourer, servant, clerk or employee, desires to contend that having regard to the nature of the debt and the circumstances of the debtor, it is unreasonable that as much as 70 per cent of such debtor's wages should be exempt, the judge may in any particular case, upon a hearing of the matter, reduce such percentage of exemption.

(3) If the debtor desires to contend that in the circumstances of any particular case, having regard to the size of his family, the wages he is earning and any other matter or thing that the judge may consider proper to take into account, the exemption allowed by this section should be increased, the judge has power to increase and to make an order providing for an increase of exemption that he may consider just and reasonable under all the circumstances.

(4) Where the creditor intends to apply for a reduction in the amount of the exemption, he shall give notice of the intention to the employer at the time of the service of the notice or other process garnishing or attaching the wages, and if he fails to give the notice, the employer may pay into court so much only of the wages of the debtor as would not be exempt under subsection 1 and may pay the balance of the wages to the debtor.

(5) Subject to subsection 4, the debtor or creditor without waiting for the regular sittings of the court may apply to the judge upon at least five days' notice in writing to the other party or his solicitor for an order fixing the amount of the debtor's exemption, and upon the making of the order, if the employer has paid the whole or any part of the wages into court and the amount so paid in equals or exceeds the amount allowed by way of exemption, such sum shall be forthwith paid out to the debtor, and in case the amount paid in is less than the amount so allowed, the whole amount paid in shall be paid out to the debtor.

(6) Subject to subsection 7, an assignment of wages or any portion thereof to secure payment of a debt whether heretofore or hereafter given is invalid.

(7) A debtor may assign to a credit union to which *The Credit Unions Act* applies such portion of his wages as does not exceed the portion thereof that is liable to attachment or seizure under this section.

b / Note: The English Position

In England, wages were not attachable for civil debts until 1971, except in satisfaction of maintenance orders. The Payne Committee on the Enforcement of Judgment Debts, 1969, recommended that they be attachable. Its reasons for the recommendation were simplicity, orderliness, and efficiency. The Report states:

It is not possible, since men have human failings, to prevent some of them from running into debt and the law must provide adequate machinery for debt collection.

It should be noted that the Committee saw wage garnishment as a more humane alternative than imprisonment for debt.

The report resulted in the passage of the Attachment of Earnings Act 1971 (U.K.) of which the relevant provisions are as follows:

3. (3) For an attachment of earnings order to be made on the application of any person other than the debtor it must appear to the court that the debtor has failed to make one or more payments required by the relevant adjudication.

6. (5) The order shall specify

(*a*) The normal deduction rate, that is to say, the rate (expressed as a sum of money per week, month, or other period) at which the court thinks it is reasonable for the debtor's earnings to be applied to meeting his liability under the relevant adjudication; and

(*b*) the protected earnings rate, that is to say the rate (so expressed) below which, having regard to the debtor's resources and needs, the court thinks it reasonable that the earnings actually paid to him should not be reduced.

c / Note: Protection of the Debtor-Employee from Dismissal

Employers dislike garnishment proceedings. The employer may incur additional administrative costs in calculating the amount to be paid in answer to the order; in paying the response to the order; and in paying the exempt portion of the wage to the debtor. As well, some employers feel affronted when they find that 'well-paid' employees are unable to pay their debts. The employer may begin to feel the employee is an irresponsible person if he is unable to pay his debts before garnishment is necessary. However, the employer is forbidden from dismissing his employee on this basis:

The Employment Standards Act, 1974, s.o. 1974, c 112 as amended

9. No employer shall dismiss or suspend an employee on the ground that garnishment proceedings are or may be taken against the employee or that an attachment order under section 30 of The Family Law Reform Act, 1978, has been or may be made against the employee.

[Section 30 of The Family Law Reform Act, 1978 is reproduced infra, p 361.]

However, debtors frequently complain that garnishment proceedings have resulted in their being fired. An employer who decides that his worker is undesirable can usually manage to find some reasonably tenable excuse to fire the employee without revealing the true (and illegal), reason. The hidden transaction costs of wage garnishment are thus extremely high, and the threat of it often suffices to bring an errant debtor into line.

Some jurisdictions have attempted to give the debtor more job security in the face of wage garnishment:

Quebec Code of Civil Procedure

650. No employer shall, on pain of all damages, dismiss or suspend an employee merely because his salary or wages have been seized by garnishment.

When an employee is dismissed or suspended while his salary or wages are seized by garnishment, there shall be a presumption that he has been dismissed or suspended because of such seizure by garnishment, and it shall be incumbent upon the employer to prove that the employee has been dismissed or suspended for another fair and sufficient reason.

The damages payable by the employer for wrongful dismissal under this section are 'all damages' ('tous dommages-intérêts'), and therefore include damages payable to both the employee and his creditor. Is the debtor better off under the Quebec legislation? Can any statute adequately protect the employee-debtor? Should wage garnishment be allowed at all? Should there be a precondition that the debtor fail to pay voluntarily the garnishable portion of his salary for each pay period?

5 PROPOSALS FOR REFORM

Many jurisdictions have enacted debtor-protective schemes. A sampling of techniques now operative is presented below. As you read and evaluate these solutions, consider the reallocation of transaction costs and the consequences of the reallocation that would accompany adoption of any of the schemes.

a / Pre-trial Garnishment and the Requirement of a Bond

New Mexico has sought to minimize the harm caused by *pre-trial* garnishment with the enactment of legislation permitting such garnishment only if the plaintiff-creditor files a bond in the amount of twice the value of the claim: N.M. Stat. Ann. s 36-14-1(A) (Supp. 1969). The defendant, if he wishes, may dissolve the garnishment upon the filing of a bond in the same amount: N.M. Stat. Ann. s 36-14-11. Is this a satisfactory resolution of the problem? Are the interests of a low income debtor who has defaulted in making payments on a conditional sales contract because of defects in product quality protected by this proposal? Should pre-trial garnishment be allowed at all?

b / Execution Against Property First

Because of the hardship accompanying the process of wage garnishment, some jurisdictions have provided that execution against property must be attempted before a wage debt may be garnished. For example, the Tennessee Code provides that the sheriff may not garnishee a wage unless he has an unsatisfied writ of execution in his hands (Tenn. C.A. ss 26-501) and has not been able to find *personal property* of the debtor in his county sufficient to satisfy the execution (Tenn. C.A. s 26-502). See also *General Truck Sales Inc.* v *Simmons*, (1961) 343 S.W. 2d 884 (Tenn.)

These proposals assume that garnishment is in fact a harsher remedy than execution. Is this assumption necessarily correct? Should the legislation differentiate between garnishment of wage debts and garnishment of all other debts? Should the prior execution requirement be applicable to both real and personal property or should it be limited to either alone? (Sheriffs frequently allege that they find execution against goods and chattels of the debtor difficult and unrewarding and therefore do not make much use of such execution.) How effective would this proposal really be in minimizing the harshness of the present system of wage garnishment?

c / The Continuing Garnishee Order

As we have already noted, a garnishee order only attaches debts presently due or accruing due. Future debts which are merely contingent are not within the scope of a garnishee order, no matter how probable it is that the debt will soon become due. Thus, where wages are to be garnished, the creditor must procure a garnishee order for each and every pay cheque. Evaluate the administrative, social and economic costs to the debtor, the creditor and the garnishee-employer which accompany this cumbersome procedure. In order to overcome these costs (or perhaps to reallocate them along the parties) some jurisdictions have fashioned a 'once and for all' garnishment procedure, the scope of which extends to both present and future debts: N.Y. C.P.L.R. 5231 (1963); Ill. Ann. Stat., ch 62, s 73 (Smith-Hurd Supp. 1969); La. Rev. Stat., tit. 13, s 3923 (1964); Ga. Code Ann. s 46-208 (1965).

Ontario has recently adopted a continuing garnishment order scheme in respect of the enforcement of orders for support and maintenance:

The Family Law Reform Act, 1978, s.o. 1978, c 2

30. (1) Where the court considers it appropriate in a proceeding under section 28 [which prescribes some remedies for a creditor whose debtor has defaulted upon an order for support or maintenance], the court may make an attachment order directing the employer of the debtor to deduct from any remuneration of the debtor due at the time the order is served on the employer or thereafter due or accruing due such amount as is named in the order and to pay the amounts deducted into court, and section 7 of *The Wages Act* [which normally exempts seventy per cent of the wages of a debtor from execution] does not apply.

d / The Instalment Payment Order

The instalment payment order has often been suggested as a reasonable alternative to wage garnishment. Like wage garnishment, it provides for the satisfaction of the judgment debt by means of periodic payments over time; unlike garnishment, the employer is not directly involved in the enforcement process. In Ontario its use is somewhat limited to: The Small Claims Courts Act, R.S.O. 1970, c 439, s 131(8) (supra, at p 153); The Wages Act, R.S.O. 1970, c 486, s 8 (supra at p 169).

Instalment payments are more widely sanctioned in other jurisdictions: Attachment of Debts Act, R.S.B.C. 1960, c 20, as amended by S.B.C. 1971, c 6, s 3B and S.B.C. 1975, c 4, s 2; The Garnishment Act, R.S.M. 1970, c G20, s 10(1); Conn. Gen. Stat. Ann. s 52-361 (Supp. 1972); Mass. Gen. Laws Ann. ch 224, s 16 (1958); R.I. Gen. Laws Ann. ss 9-28-5, 9-28-6 (1970); N.Y. C.P.L.R. 5226 (1963).

The New York provisions are wider in scope than those of Canadian jurisdictions: N.Y. C.P.L.R. 5226 (1963)

... [W]here it is shown that the judgment debtor is receiving or will receive money from any source, or is attempting to impede the judgment creditor by rendering services without adequate compensation, the court shall order that the judgment debtor make specified instalment payments to the judgment creditor. In fixing the amount of payments the court shall take into consideration the reasonable requirements of the debtor and his dependants, any payments required to be made by him or deducted from the money he would otherwise receive in satisfaction of other judgments and wage assignments, the amount due on the judgment, and the amount being or to be received, or if the judgment debtor is attempting to impede the judgment creditor by rendering services without adequate compensation, the reasonable value of the services rendered.

Even more comprehensive is Maine's fairly recent instalment payment scheme. (Me. Rev. Stat. Ann. tit. 14, s 3121 ff Supp. 1972). See also Note, 'Post-judgment Procedures for the Collection of Small Debts: The Maine Solution' (1973), 25 *Maine L. Rev.* 43. The first step in the process is the initiation by the creditor of a 'debtor disclosure hearing' wherein the debtor is examined as to the nature of his assets and his financial position (s 3125). If the hearing discloses exigible assets the court may order that the property be turned over directly to the creditor (s 3131) or may impose a lien on the property until the judgment debt is discharged (s 3132).

Where it is shown in the disclosure hearing that the judgment debtor is receiving money or earnings from a source which is not otherwise exempt from attachment, the court may make an order for the payment of the judgment by instalments out of that income (s 3127). The power to make an instalment payment order may be exercised either in addition to, or in substitution for any other type of order allowed by the statute (s 3133). However, only if the debtor defaults on three consecutive payments *and* fails to show good cause for such default may the court order the employer to pay the creditor directly (s 3137).

Similar to the Maine scheme is the proposal of the Report of the Joint Working Party on the Enforcement of Judgments, Orders & Decrees of the Courts of Northern Ireland (the Anderson Report), p 48, para. 138, which suggests that garnishment be prohibited unless there is default in an order for the payment of instalments *and* the enforcement officer is satisfied that the debtor does in fact have the means to pay, taking into consideration his personal requirements and family commitments.

In New York State, the 'income execution' has replaced the old garnishment procedure (N.Y. C.P.L.R. S 5231 (1963)). Where a person is receiving or will receive wages of not more than $85 per week, the sheriff may serve an income execution on the debtor ordering him to pay by instalments not more than 10% of his income as it is received. Only when the debtor fails to pay the required instalments may the Sheriff serve the execution on the employer ordering the employer to pay the instalments in satisfaction of the debt.

Is the instalment payment order (backed up by the court's power to jail for contempt of such an order) an adequate alternative to garnishment? What do you think of the suggestion that it cannot work, because default in the payment of the original debt is frequently caused by the debtor's lack of discipline and inability to manage his financial affairs?

e / The Ohio Trusteeship Plan Prior to Garnishment

Ohio has sought to ameliorate the position of the debtor wage-earner by the introduction of a debtor trusteeship plan which is in many aspects similar to the US Federal wage-earner plan under Chapter XIII of the Bankruptcy Act, 11 U.S.C. ss 1001–1086 (1964) and Arrangements for the Consumer Debtor, the Bankruptcy Bill, ss 63–94, (discussed at pp 719–35, infra). The Ohio legislation is unique insofar as it provides that the judgment debtor must be given notice of any proposed garnishment within five to thirty days *before* it is to be sought (s 1911.40). During this period the debtor may, if he wishes, apply for trusteeship without having to be subjected to wage garnishment. Another feature of the legislation is that the judge to whom an application for the appointment of a trustee has been made has no discretion to refuse the request; the debtor may take advantage of the plan *as of right*.

2329. (70) Appointment of a trustee.

Any person upon whom a demand has been made in accordance with section 1911.40 of the Revised Code may apply to any judge of a county court or judge of a municipal court within this state, in whose jurisdiction he resides, or, if he is not a resident of Ohio, in whose jurisdiction his place of employment is located, for the appointment of a trustee to receive that portion of the personal earnings of the debtor not exempt from execution, attachment, or proceedings in aid of execution, and such additional sums as the debtor voluntarily pays or assigns to said trustee. Such person shall file with said application a full, accurate, and complete statement, under oath, of the names of his secured and unsecured creditors with liquidated claims, their addresses, and amount due to each. Upon such application and filing, such judge shall appoint a trustee to distribute such funds to said creditors of the debtor at the time of said application and filing.

If a debtor fails, through mistake or otherwise, to list a creditor, said creditor or debtor may apply to the court, with notice to the other party, to list such creditors in the trusteeship. Any person who becomes a creditor after the appointment of a trustee, may be listed in such trusteeship and such creditor shall share in any distribution made by the trustee after the next ensuing distribution.

No proceedings in attachment, in aid of execution, or other action to subject the personal earnings of the debtor to the payment of claims shall be brought or maintained by any creditor so long as at least the amount of the personal earnings of such debtor not exempt from execution, attachment, or proceedings in aid of execution are paid to the trustee at regular intervals as fixed by the county court or the municipal court judge. This section does not prohibit creditors from recovering judgment against such debtor or prohibit levy, under a writ of attachment or execution, upon any other property which is not exempt from execution.

The maintaining of a proceedings in attachment, in aid of execution, or otherwise in violation of this section shall be void and may be prevented by writ of prohibition in addition to all other remedies provided by law. Such judge shall provide by rule or otherwise for notice to creditors, the authentication and proof of claims, and time and manner of payment of the debtor, the distribution of funds, the bond of the trustee if required, and for all other matters necessary or proper to carry into effect the jurisdiction conferred by this section.

The personal earnings of the debtor exempted by law shall not be liable to the plaintiff for the costs of any proceedings brought to recover a judgment for debt, damage, fine, or amercement, nor for any proceedings in attachment or aid of execution to satisfy such judgment; provided such debtor has listed said creditor as to name, amount of claim, and the amount due as provided in section 1911.40 of the Revised Code, and makes payment as provided for in this section.

Upon such application for a trustee the judge in the court in which such application is made shall designate the clerk of such court to act as trustee and said clerk shall serve without additional compensation and his official bond shall be construed as conditioned upon the fulfillment of the trust, and no additional bond shall be required.

The trusteeship shall terminate upon the failure of the debtor to make the payments required by this section and in accordance with the rules established by the county court or municipal judge, and all privileges in this section exempt from attachment, garnishment, proceedings in aid of execution, or any other action to subject personal earnings of such debtor to payment of claims or judgments shall terminate upon such neglect.

If a trusteeship is dismissed for nonpayment, as provided by this section, the trusteeship shall not be reinstated and the debtor shall not be permitted to file a new trusteeship for a period of six months from date of dismissal of the trusteeship, unless upon motion supported by affidavit, he proves to the satisfaction of the court that failure to maintain the trusteeship agreement was not due to willful neglect.

2329. (71) Participation by secured creditor in trusteeship.

Any creditor who holds a chattel mortgage or any other lien or encumbrance on the property of any applicant for trusteeship under section 2329.70 of the Revised Code may participate in a trusteeship.

The holder of a chattel mortgage or other encumbrance may elect to participate in a trusteeship, subject to the terms of a written agreement with the debtor, filed with and approved by the court in which the application for trusteeship is filed. If the holder of a chattel mortgage elects to participate in the trusteeship, he shall be estopped to assert his lien or other encumbrance so long as the debtor complies with the terms of such agreement and with section 2329.70 of the Revised Code. Upon the failure of the debtor to maintain such agreement, the creditor may be released from the trusteeship, upon written request to the court, to pursue his chattel property or other remedies as provided by law, which are not in violation of section 2329.70 of the Revised Code.

Upon the receipt of a notice of the filing of an application for trusteeship as provided in section 2329.70 of the Revised Code, a secured creditor shall file with the court, in writing, his election to participate and his agreement with the debtor, if such has been created, or his objection to being included. Failure of a secured creditor to answer such notice as provided in section 2329.70 of the Revised Code within ten days after receiving such notice, shall be held by the court as an election to participate in the trusteeship, and such creditor shall be estopped to assert his lien for so long as the debtor maintains his trusteeship agreement, as provided by section 2329.70 of the Revised Code.

Is the treatment of more recent creditors satisfactory? Should the legislation aim to discourage the already overcommitted debtor from obtaining further credit? How? Should the obtaining of further credit be a criminal offence? Should it bring the trusteeship to an end? Should new creditors be enjoined from enforcing their claims until the trusteeship has terminated?

How should secured creditors be affected by the trusteeship? Should they be required to participate in the plan and forego their ordinary remedy of repossession while the plan is in effect?

During the existence of the trusteeship should the creditors only be prevented from garnishing the debtor's wages (as in the Ohio plan) or should they also be prevented from exercising other means of enforcement?

What considerations might lead the debtor to choose the trusteeship plan over outright bankruptcy?

f / Dismissal From Employment

In Ontario, it is illegal to dismiss an employee because of a garnishment of wages (or apprehended garnishment of wages): The Employment Standards Act, s 9, supra at p 359. The offence is punishable by a fine of not more than $1,000 (s 43). Is this sanction strong enough to be effective? Does it give a civil cause of action for wrongful dismissal? (In the United States, it has been held that the employee dismissal provisions of the Consumer Credit Protection Act, 1968 – which are substantially the same as the Ontario provisions – do not give the employee a civil cause of action for their breach: *Oldham* v *Oldham* (1972), 337 Fed. Supp. 1039 (Iowa). In New York, the dismissed employee may sue for up to six weeks' wages and may be ordered reinstated: N.Y. C.P.L.R. S 5252. (See also s 5.202(6) of the Uniform Consumer Credit Code.) Article 650 of the Quebec Code of Civil Procedure, 13–14 Eliz. II, 1965 c 80, Vol. II provides that 'no employer shall, on pain of all damages, dismiss or suspend an employee merely because his salary or wages have been seized by garnishment'. Does this provision also give the creditor-garnishor a civil cause of action?

Even with a civil cause of action, the problem of enforcement of a rule prohibiting discharge on account of garnishment proceedings remains. How is an employee to prove that he was dismissed *solely* on account of the garnishment? Should the onus be shifted onto the employer to prove that the employee was not fired for an improper purpose?

Who should bear the employer's administrative costs of garnishment? In Wisconsin, the creditor-garnishor must pay the employer $3.00 for this purpose: Wis. Stat. s 267.06 (1971). In Ontario, the garnishee may deduct $3.00 from the amount paid into Court to cover his costs: Supreme Court of Ontario, Rules of Practice, R.R.O. 1970, Reg. 545, Rule 600. Is this sufficient?

Finally, is it desirable that creditors or their agents be prevented from contacting the debtor's employer prior to judgment? (Recall the letter reproduced supra on page 111.) Some jurisdictions have proscribed such communications, except for the purpose of verifying the status of the employee: Debt Collection Act, S.B.C. 1973, c 26, s 14(1)(b); the Wisconsin Consumer Act, Wis. Stat. s 427.104(1)(d) (1971). Can this prohibition be enforced effectively? Does it go far enough? Too far?

g / Abolition of Wage Garnishment

Wage garnishment has been abolished in a few jurisdictions. It is not available in Pennsylvania (Pa. Stat. Ann. Tit. 42, s 886 (1966)) or Texas (Tex. Rev. Civ. Stat. Art. 4099 (1965)). In Florida it has been abolished in respect of the head of the household (Fla. Stat. s 222.11 (1961)), and in Minnesota it is not allowed for the first 6 months after the debtor has been on welfare (Minn. Stat. Ann. s 550.37 (Supp. 1969)). In Canada, New Brunswick has been the only province to abolish wage garnishment completely (S.N.B. 1971, c 36).

Should wage garnishment be abolished here? In order to answer this question it will be necessary to weigh the economic benefits derived from wage garnishment (for example, will the abolition or restriction of wage garnishment significantly affect the extent to which credit is extended?) against the social costs alleged to accompany the use of the remedy (e.g. bankruptcy, relations with the employer, etc.). In this connection see Anderson, 'Coercive Collection and Exempt Property in Texas' (1975), 13 *Houston L. Rev.* 84, attributing 'dramatic increases in debtor harassment' to the abolition of wage garnishment. There has however been significant support for abolition: see Brunn, 'Wage Garnishment in California; A Study and Recommendations' (1965), 53 *Calif. L. Rev.* 1214; Sweeney, 'Abolition of Wage Garnishment' (1969), 38 *Ford L. Rev.* 197; Kerr, 'Wage Garnishment Should Be Prohibited' (1969), 2 *J.L. Reform (Prospectus)* 371; Saffer, 'Argument for the Abolition of Wage Garnishment' (1964), 52 *Ill. B.J.* 1026; Note, 'Wage Garnishment: Remedy or Revenge' (1974), 5 *Loyola U. L.J.* (Chicago) 140.

11
Residual Methods of Execution

I INTRODUCTION

This chapter describes several of the infrequently employed modes of levying execution. It considers the circumstances in which these unusual means of executing might be helpful and the property exigible through each of these means.

a / C.R.B. Dunlop, 'Execution Against Personal Property in England and British Columbia' (1972), 7 *U.B.C.L. Rev.* 171, 177–93. (Footnotes omitted.)

EQUITABLE EXECUTION IN ENGLAND

The courts of equity became involved in the problem of creditors' remedies in two ways. First, Chancery itself frequently made decrees ordering the defendant to pay a sum of money to the plaintiff, and it became necessary to develop an adequate system for enforcing such decrees. Secondly, creditors who had gone to judgment at common law but had failed, because of the narrowness of fi. fa. and elegit, to collect their claims, began at an early stage to ask for equity's assistance to reach the full range of the debtor's assets. At first, the courts of equity enforced their own decrees and aided the judgment creditor at common law by putting pressure directly on the person of the recalcitrant debtor. However the threat of imprisonment for contempt proved to be costly and inefficient in some cases and excessively coercive in others, and equity timidly began to move away from its exclusive reliance on a remedy in personam towards a variety of processes designed to reach the property of the debtor. Equity developed three major remedies, two of which remain significant today; they are, in order of their creation, sequestration, receivership, and the charging order as an exercise of equitable execution.

Sequestration
The writ of sequestration was an order directed to four or more persons, nominated as commissioners, giving them authority to seize the personal property, and the rents and profits of the real property of the judgment debtor. It was used whether the contempt was in failing to appear and answer the bill or in failing to obey the decree. Originally property seized by the sequestrators was simply detained until he complied with the order in question. By 1750, however, equity was permitting sequestrators on final process (i.e. where sequestration had issued to enforce a decree) to sell sequestered property and to use the proceeds to pay the judgment creditor's claim. Originally the only property available to sequestration was property involved in the suit, but the remedy was later extended to any property of the person in contempt, subject to certain limitations discussed below.

Sequestration was potentially a powerful and all-inclusive creditor's remedy capable of curing the defects of fi. fa. and elegit. Yet, by the end of the nineteenth century, sequestration had not realized its promise. It was used, sometimes successfully, but it had become somewhat of a rarity, a trend which continues today.

The reasons for the failure of sequestration to become an important remedy are complex and not altogether clear. One reason is that the remedy was clumsy, involving the creditor in a complex and expensive procedure. After the Judicature Acts, the courts acted to simplify the rules governing the writ by eliminating the requirement of a prior execution at law, and other procedural steps. Still it is not surprising that sequestration fell into disuse as equity and the legislature provided simpler and more effective remedies.

A more fundamental reason for the failure of sequestration lay in its historical tie to the Lord Chancellor's power to commit for contempt. Sequestration was held to be available only where the person against whom it was issued was in contempt for disobedience of the Court. Towards the end of the nineteenth century, some courts drew from this rule the corollary that sequestration could be obtained only where the judgment in question ordered the judgment debtor to pay a sum of money to the judgment creditor or into court by a certain date. As a result, sequestration was seen as unavailable for most common law judgments which simply establish and quantify the liability of the defendant to the plaintiff. The late nineteenth century cases narrow the scope of sequestration and reverse the current of earlier authority which permitted it to be used by creditors with common law money judgments to reach non-exigible assets. The result has been that sequestration has become a rarity in England today, principally used in cases resulting from non-payment of maintenance according to a time schedule set out in the court order or separation agreement.

Receivership

Receivership as a form of equitable execution seems to have developed later than sequestration, but it quickly became the more important remedy. The Lords Chancellor of the eighteenth and nineteenth centuries would order the appointment of a receiver in a variety of circumstances to enforce the rights of secured creditors, or to preserve property pending litigation or where there was danger of the property being damaged or dissipated. We are concerned here only with receivership as a remedy extended to a creditor who is unable to enforce his equitable decree or his common law judgment by other means.

The receiver is appointed by the court to receive the rents and profits of real estate, or to get in and collect personal estate. Where the appointment of a receiver is an exercise of equitable execution, he will be empowered to sell the personalty and to distribute the proceeds, and rents and profits of real estate to the judgment creditors. A peculiar advantage of receivership over sequestration and over the common law writs is that receivers can be appointed before judgment, sometimes on an ex parte motion, in cases where property might be dissipated before judgment. Receivers have been appointed where the plaintiff received a declaration of his right to receive damages but before the amount was ascertained. On the other hand, where the plaintiff had a judgment for costs which were untaxed, he was refused a receiver on the ground that he was not entitled to issue legal execution and therefore could not issue equitable execution.

Before the Judicature Acts, the procedure to obtain a receiver was complex, and it was usually necessary to issue legal execution as a condition precedent, even where it was known that fi. fa. or elegit would realize nothing. Following the Acts, the procedure for obtaining a receiving order was simplified and the requirement of a futile prior legal execution was abandoned. Where there was property which could be seized at law, it was often said to be essential that the legal means of execution should be exhausted before obtaining a receiver, but there were cases going the other way. Like sequestration, the granting of a receiver was discretionary, and the discretion would not be exercised unless it could be shown that the property in question was of sufficient value to merit the expense.

The most important limitation on the remedy of receivership, that is, the kinds of property which can be reached by the remedy, will be discussed later.

The Charging Order as a Form of Equitable Execution
We have noted earlier that the Judgments Act of 1838 as well as extending the writ of fi. fa. to cover money, created the charging order remedy against government stock, funds, and annuities, and shares in public companies. Strictly viewed, the Judgments Act did not enable a judgment creditor to reach debts due to the judgment debtor, or funds or assets in court or in the hands of a court officer and owing to the judgment debtor. The Common Law Procedure Acts enabled the creditor to attach debts, but funds and assets *in custodia legis* remained exempt. This anomalous exception was removed not by the legislature but by the courts, through the creation of the charging order as an exercise of equitable execution.

The first step in this process was taken by Lord Truro in *Watts* v *Jefferyes* [(1851) 42 E.R. 324 (L.C.)]. In that case, the petitioner recovered judgment against the debtor and issued a writ of fi. fa. The petitioner then presented a petition in Chancery which stated that the Attorney-General was about to draw a cheque for £500 payable to the judgment debtor, pursuant to an order in another Chancery suit. The petitioner prayed that the court should order the Attorney-General to deliver the cheque, not to the judgment debtor, but to the sheriff. An interim order was obtained, the order expired, and the cheque was delivered to an agent for the judgment debtor. The agent subsequently returned the cheque to the Attorney-General.

The Lord Chancellor granted the petition. The problem before him was that while the cheque could be regarded as the property of the judgment debtor, it was not in his possession but in the possession of an officer of the court. Thus it could not be reached by fi. fa., even as amplified by the Judgments Act. On the other hand, the aim of the Judgments Act was clearly to extend the remedies of creditors, and the court 'would not be astute in finding out technical objections to deprive the creditor of the remedy which it was manifestly the object of the Legislature to confer on him.'

Watts v *Jefferyes* was explained, and an analogy to the charging order was drawn, in the decision of the Court of Appeal in *Brereton* v *Edwards* [(1888) 21 Q.B.D. 488 (C.A.)]. The judgment debtor in that case had a share in a fund being held in the Chancery Division in an administration action. An order had been made that the fund be paid to the judgment debtor but the sum was still in court when the judgment creditors in the present action obtained a charging order nisi against it. The guardians of the fund in the administration now sought to challenge the charging order.

The Court of Appeal upheld the charging order. The trial judge had apparently granted it on the assumption that he had power so to do under the Judgments Act, but the Court of Appeal chose instead to uphold the order on the basis of *Watts* v *Jefferyes*, Lindley L.J. explained the *Watts* case as follows:

That case goes a very long way, for it shews that, when there was property of a judgment debtor which could be seized under a fi. fa., that property could be reached by the judgment creditor, although it was in the custody of the Court of Chancery. After consulting our colleagues in the other division of this Court, we think that there is no reason in principle why cash standing to the credit of a judgment debtor in the Chancery Division should not be handed over to his judgment creditor, there being no authority or practice to the contrary.

The argument that monies in court should only be obtained by appointment of a receiver was quickly rejected. '[Appointing a receiver] would be the merest formality, when such an appointment would be useless or worse than useless. What could be the use of appointing a receiver of money which was already in the hands of the Court? In my opinion a charging order is quite sufficient, without the appointment of a receiver.'

Since *Brereton* v *Edwards*, charging orders have been used to charge monies held in trust for the judgment debtor in court, in the hands of an official receiver, or in the hands of a receiver appointed by the court. Such monies will not be charged when the judgment debtor's interest in the money has been assigned before the date of the charging order. It is apparently not necessary for a judgment creditor to issue legal execution first before applying for a charging order, although this is not clear.

The most recent decision on the charging order as an exercise of equitable execution suggests a reluctance on the part of the courts to expand the remedy. In *L.C.C.* v *Monks*, [(1959) Ch. 239] the court refused to permit a fund in the Chancery Division of the High Court to be charged with an order obtained from a County Court. The decision in part turns on the legislation governing the County Court, but Danckwerts J. buttresses his conclusion by a restrictive interpretation of the cases.

The real basis of [*Brereton* v *Edwards* and *In re Prior*] seems to me to be that, where the court has the fund under its own control, as in the case of a fund standing to the credit of some account of the Paymaster-General, the Paymaster-General being the officer of the High Court and all the judges of any Division of the High Court being judges of that court, the judges will enforce a High Court judgment by directing their officer to pay out the money or by making a charging order on the fund in question, so that the judgment creditor shall not be defeated with regard to satisfaction of the judgment.

The implication is that the charging order is of no value where the fund is not in the control of the court which is asked to grant the charging order.

Kinds of Property Available to Equitable Execution
We come now to the central and difficult problem of the kinds of property subject to equitable execution. The law is difficult to state because of the vacillation of the equity judges as to the proper rules to lay down, a vacillation which has continued into the twentieth century and which permeates the cases on equitable execution today.

Equity's uncertainty flowed from two opposing pressures on the judges. On the one hand, they were urged to aid the judgment creditor who was unable to satisfy his judgment at law because of the inadequacies of fi. fa. and elegit. On the other hand, they felt keenly the pressure of the maxim, 'Equity follows the law,' a maxim which, strictly interpreted, would have made any resort to equity a useless venture. Caught between these pressures, the equity judges tried to work out a viable and an intellectually acceptable compromise. As we study the cases, we can see different solutions being tried out, some more liberal than others, and we can see later judges seeking to rewrite the earlier cases to fit a new theory. An objective analysis of the cases reveals no clear pattern but much room for discretion on the part of a judge today. One must conclude that the rules governing equitable execution are still very much in the making.

The equity judges were faced with two issues. The less important question was whether equitable execution was available against an asset which could be seized by some form of legal execution. The second, more important problem was to decide what kinds of property which were *not* exigible at common law could be taken in equity. The judges reached unanimity on some classes of assets, but were not able to establish firm general principles applicable to all kinds of personal property.

As to one class of assets, the courts of equity developed a clear rule. They would permit execution against equitable interests in personal property, or in the rents and profits of real property, where the legal title was held by someone other than the debtor and where the property, if owned entirely by the debtor, would have been exigible by fi. fa. or elegit. Indeed the common law's refusal to permit equitable interests to be reached by fi. fa. presumed equity's willingness to aid the creditor to reach such interests. ...

The Judicature Acts simplified the procedure for executing against equitable interests, for example, by eliminating the requirement of prior fi. fa. or elegit, but otherwise the law remained as it did before the Acts. Indeed the courts made it clear in several cases that the Judicature Acts did not abolish by implication remedies existing before the Acts.

Another class of asset which the courts consistently held to be available to equitable execution was that of monies in court payable to the judgment debtor. We have already discussed the use of the charging order as a device to reach funds in court, but sequestration and receivership were also used to accomplish the same result. Some form of equitable execution has been granted against a deposit paid on presentation of a notice of appeal, monies taken on an earlier sequestration and monies payable to the judgment debtor from an estate being administered in court. ...

It was equally certain that some kinds of assets would never be available to equitable execution. We have already noted the refusal of the courts to permit execution where the assets sought to be attached is of slight value or is dependent on the exercise of discretion by a third person. The other class of assets which could not be obtained by equitable execution were those choses in action which were unassignable because of statutory or contractual provisions or because of public policy. Certain kinds of pensions or half-pay for military personnel which involved a possible liability for future services were regarded as unassignable, either because of public policy or because of statutory prohibitions. On the other hand, pensions which did not involve the possibility of future services could be the subject of equitable execution, unless assignment was prohibited by statute.

In the case of assignable pensions payable by the Crown, the courts would not give orders directed to the Crown, but would order the judgment debtor to turn over all pension payments to the sequestrators or the receivers, who were further empowered to receive the payments directly from the Crown. By this somewhat devious stratagem, the courts created an imperfect but an apparently effective way around the immunity of the Crown to the normal process of enforcement of judgments.

The other great category of unassignable choses in action were the rights of deserted or divorced spouses to alimony or maintenance. With some exceptions, monies so payable could not be the subject of equitable execution.

As far as we have gone, the law is clear enough. But when we move outside the categories of assets described above, the picture becomes confused and murky. At times, the courts appear to have taken a very liberal view of the scope of equitable execution, extending it to debts and choses in action. But, particularly towards the end of the nineteenth century, the courts sought to restrict and shrink equitable execution by surrounding it with limiting conditions. The extent of change in the rules about exigibility of property in equity can best be seen by discussing the cases chronologically.

The cases before 1838 reveal graphically the uncertainty of the judges as to the proper limits to be placed on equitable execution. There are early decisions in which creditors successfully sought the aid of equity to reach equitable interests in choses in action, especially stock, but in other contemporaneous decisions there are strong statements that where assets may not be seized at common law, those assets, or equitable interests in them, may not be taken in equity. The latter group of cases advance various reasons for this restrictive position: other remedies are available, such as imprisonment or outlawry, furthermore, equity should follow the law, which implies that equity should follow law's restrictive limits placed on fi. fa. and elegit.

A more fundamental explanation for the restrictive position lay in the rudimentary nature of equitable execution in the eighteenth century. The judges had not yet worked out forms of equitable execution which would permit the creditor, in effect, to seize and sell equitable interests. Instead the judges saw themselves as able only to remove impediments which lay in the way of creditors seizing the property at common law. Where a debtor had conveyed his land to trustees, equity would intervene to set aside the conveyance, if fraudulent, or to permit the judgment creditor to redeem the mortgage, thus permitting him to proceed at law under his writ of elegit. If an asset was not exigible at common law, then there was no point to equity removing impediments created by transfers or mortgages.

This restrictive analysis is unanswerable, given the state of equitable execution in the eighteenth and early nineteenth centuries. But with the development of sequestration, receiver-ship, and the charging order, equitable execution ceased to be simply a supplement to legal execution, and began to look like and to function as a parallel system of execution operating directly against the assets of the debtor. Given this development, together with a growing sentiment against imprisonment for debt, we would expect to find an increased willingness on the part of the courts of equity to permit execution against assets not exigible at common law.

This willingness is expressed clearly by Lord Loughborough at the end of the eighteenth century in *Simmonds* v *Lord Kinnaird*. [(1799) 31 E.R. 380 (L.C.)] The case was decided on a pleading point, but counsel argued at length whether or not choses in action could be reached in equity. The Lord Chancellor was clearly sympathetic to the view that they could:

I wish the process could go the extent you desire. When one considers the immense mass of property, that may be possessed in this kingdom, answerable for nothing. Suppose, a great landed estate was converted into an annuity upon the consolidated fund: no process can reach it, unless this Court can get at it. On the other hand I am not aware of all the consequences of either impounding the money in the hands of the bankers or making them pay the money.

The nineteenth century saw a great development in the classes of assets which could be reached by equitable execution, although there was much dispute as to how far equity could or should go. Moved by the policy enunciated by Lord Loughborough, the courts began to say that equitable execution would reach choses in action, and they permitted creditors to use equity to reach pensions, bank accounts, monies held by a stakeholder, dividends on stock held by trustees, the income for life from a post-nuptial settlement or a revisionary interest of a debtor under a will, the arrears of income owing to a wife under a marriage settlement with a restraint on anticipation, an amount awarded to the debtor by an arbitrator, and even the debtor's legal interest in property subject to an equitable mortgage.

During this period, the courts were prepared to go very far to enable creditors to reach assets through equitable execution. On the one hand, creditors were permitted to take property which could have been executed against at common law. On the other hand, it was suggested that if a money obligation fell short of being a debt garnishable under the Common Law Procedure Acts, such obligation could nonetheless be reached by appointment of a receiver. Much of the discussion in the cases asumes the exigibility in equity of choses in action, and concentrates on the procedures necessary to protect third parties and the means by which they can be forced to pay over to the sequestrators or receiver rather than the judgment debtor.

If we were to stop at this point, a reader might conclude that equitable execution in the nineteenth century had expanded to reach most kinds of property which escaped execution at common law, even as modified by legislation. However, in the last twenty years of the century, the development of equitable execution underwent a dramatic reversal. A series of decisions of the Court of Appeal placed significant limitations on the remedies of sequestration and receivership, and effectively reversed some of the decisions we have discussed earlier.

The first important limitation placed on equitable execution by the late nineteenth century cases was that the remedy was not available against assets which might be reached at common law. The new rule is stated clearly by Fry L.J. in *In re Shephard*:

The idea that a receivership order is a form of execution is in my opinion erroneous. A receiver was appointed by the Court of Chancery in aid of a judgment at law when the plaintiff shewed that he had sued out the proper writ of execution, and was met by certain difficulties arising from the nature of the property which prevented his obtaining possession at law, and in these circumstances only did the Court of Chancery interfere in aid of a legal judgment for a legal debt. Relief by the appointment of a receiver went on the ground that execution could not be had, and therefore it was not execution. Moreover, the appointment of a receiver was an act requiring the exercise of judicial power on the part of the Court; the circumstances to which I have referred had to be proved before the Court would make the order. All these considerations tend to show that the appointment of a receiver was not execution, but was equitable relief granted under circumstances which made it right that legal difficulties should be removed out of the creditor's way. It has often been spoken of by judges as 'equitable execution,' but I am afraid that this concise expression has led to the erroneous idea that the appointment of a receiver is a form of execution which can be obtained without shewing to the Court the existence of the circumstances creating the equity on which alone the jurisdiction arises. [(1890) 43 Ch. D. 131, 138 (C..)]

The theory enunciated by Fry L.J. in this passage sounds remarkably like the analysis of equitable execution developed by the eighteenth and early nineteenth century judges in cases like *Dundas* v *Dutens* [(1790) 30 E.R. 298 (L.C.)] and *Grogan* v *Cooke* [(1812) 2 Ball & B 230 (Ir.) (L.C.)]. But in the intervening period, equitable execution had developed into a system which operated directly against the assets of the judgment debtor and, to that extent, the limitations on the remedy enunciated by Fry L.J. were historically false. Yet, historically false or not, the theory, enunciated in terms of impediments to legal execution, became the orthodox test for deciding whether to grant equitable execution. The courts would now refuse in most cases to grant the equitable remedies where legal execution was available.

A couple of cases indicate the way in which the courts applied the theory to restrict equitable execution. In *Harris* v *Beauchamp Brothers* [[1894] 1 Q.B. 801 (C.A.)], the plaintiff obtained judgment against a firm of two partners, one of whom was an infant. There was evidence that the adult partner had assigned to the infant partner certain of the partnership assets, which included book debts, monies, and the proceeds of fire insurance policies. The Court of Appeal reversed a receiving order on the ground that the assets of the judgment debtors could be reached by fi. fa. or garnishment.

An even more dramatic case is *Morgan* v *Hart* [[1914] 2 K.B. 183 (C.A.)]. The judgment debtor in that case had removed all his furniture to a large furniture repository at Southend. The owner of the repository refused to identify which furniture belonged to the judgment debtor with the result that the judgment creditor was unable to seize. An application for a receiver was refused. The Court of Appeal said that the judgment creditor might apply for an examination in aid of execution and then seize.

In all of these cases, the courts were pressed with the argument that section 25(8) of the Judicature Act of 1873 had empowered the courts to grant receivers where such an order appeared to the court to be just or convenient. The history of the interpretation of section 25(8) parallels the history of equitable execution generally. For a decade or so, section 25(8) was interpreted expansively, but the decisions in the last twenty years of the century read the section much more restrictively. These cases decided that the section did not broaden the jurisdiction to grant equitable execution. Courts were still bound by the rules as they had existed before the Judicature Act except that some of the cumbersome procedure existing before fusion had been eliminated.

To this generally restrictive interpretation, the courts attached one caveat. Cases might arise where 'special circumstances' demanded the grant of a receiver, even though legal execution was or would be available. Such a case was *Goldschmidt* v *Oberrheinische Metallwerke*, decided in 1906 [[1906] 1 K.B. 373 (C.A.)]. In that case, the judgment debtors were a company incorporated and carrying on business in Germany, and having no property within the jurisdiction. It appeared that several customers of the judgment debtors were, or would shortly become, indebted to them, although the judgment creditor had no precise information about the debts. It further appeared that the judgment debtors were attempting to collect the debts and thus avoid garnishment. On these facts, the Court of Appeal was prepared to grant a receiver. While the *Goldschmidt* case would appear to be a clear case for a receiver, one is hard pressed to distinguish it in substance from the later case of *Morgan* v *Hart* where there was what appeared to be a similar attempt to evade execution. It is obvious that the court in the later case was not anxious to expand the category of 'special circumstances'.

The second great limitation which the late nineteenth century cases placed on equitable execution was the rule that where an asset had not been exigible at law or in equity before the Judicature Acts, such asset could not be reached afterwards. Applying this rule, the courts refused to grant equitable execution against the future profits of a business, the future earnings of a judgment debtor, and a patent which was as yet undeveloped [[1909] 2 K.B. 903 (C.A.)]. *Edwards and Co.* v *Picard*, the case of the patent, is particularly interesting as an extreme example of the restrictive attitude now taken.

In that case the judgment debtor lived in Paris, and had no exigible property within the jurisdiction. He was the owner of three English patents, but there was no evidence that he was in receipt of any profits or royalties therefrom. A majority of the Court of Appeal dismissed an appeal from the refusal of a trial judge to appoint a receiver. Vaughan Williams L.J. described a patent as follows:

It is chose in action, created by the exercise of the Royal prerogative, and entirely distinct from the right of property in a chattel created under it; and the patentee's right under the patent, being a chose in action, cannot be taken under a fi. fa., or levari facias, since it has no locality, and therefore cannot be found upon the premises. ... I do not think that there is any property of the patentee for the receiver to receive, and I do not know to whom he could give notice.

A patent cannot be seized at common law nor is there any authority before the Judicature Acts to permit equitable execution. Thus the asset escapes the judgment creditor entirely.

The judgment of Buckley L.J. gives us further insight into the extent of the restrictions placed on equitable execution in this period. He began by observing that the rights which a patent gives are legal rights, created at common law. The conclusion he drew is interesting.

This right is a legal right. There is no question of equity in the matter. This right must either be amenable to execution at law, or not at all. Equitable execution is relief given on the ground that there is no remedy by execution at law; it operates by removing a hindrance which prevents execution at law. There is here no hindrance for equity to remove. It is not a case in which the debtor has an equitable interest only in property which could have been reached at law if he had had the legal interest in it. The property is property in which he has the legal interest.

If this view of equitable execution is followed through logically, it would mean that equitable execution is available in only one case, *i.e.*, where there is an asset in which the judgment debtor has an equitable interest and which would be exigible if the legal title was restored to the judgment debtor. But, as we have seen, this was only one of many cases in which the nineteenth century courts permitted equitable execution. Debts, stock, bank accounts and many choses in action had been taken by sequestration and receivership despite the fact that the rights in these assets enjoyed by the judgment debtor were not equitable but legal, in the sense that they were rights enforceable at common law. The quoted statement is much narrower than the cases justify. If it is accepted literally, the remedy virtually disappears.

Even as the Court of Appeal was trying to narrow down and limit equitable execution, decisions were being made which continued the more liberal and expansive tradition of the earlier cases. During the same period as *Edwards and Co.* v *Picard* and *Morgan* v *Hart*, courts were holding that equitable execution could be used to reach goods subject to a possessory lien, a wife's share in an estate, an equitable reversionary interest in personalty, and the rental income from leased furniture. There have not been many recent cases of equitable execution but what cases there are suggest that the English judges are still prepared to use receivership in the expansive spirit of the mid-nineteenth century cases when they feel it just to do so.

It is beyond the scope of this paper to do more than speculate on the reasons for the courts' abrupt change of judicial policy toward the end of the nineteenth century. It may be that the late nineteenth century judges, under the influence of academics like Maitland, were moved to cut down areas of equitable discretion in which the rules were not clear and equity did not follow the law in any intelligible sense. A more obvious explanation for the judges' *volte-face* was the increasing amount of legislation which dealt with creditors' remedies and thus pre-empted the reforming efforts of the courts. Whatever the reasons, the cases remain as fascinating proof of the courts' capacity to make (and unmake) law while denying their power to do so.

2 EQUITABLE EXECUTION BY WAY OF APPOINTMENT OF A RECEIVER

a / The Judicature Act, R.S.O. 1970, c 228

19. (1) A mandamus or an injunction may be granted or a receiver appointed by an interlocutory order of the court in all cases in which it appears to the court to be just or convenient that the order should be made, and any such order may be made either unconditionally or upon such terms and conditions as the court considers just ...

b / The Creditors' Relief Act, R.S.O. 1970, c 97

24. Where a judgment creditor obtains the appointment of a receiver by way of equitable execution of property of his debtor, the receiver shall pay into court the money received by him by virtue of his receivership, and it is subject to section 23, but the creditor is entitled to be paid thereout the costs of and incidental to the receivership order and the proceedings thereon in priority to the claims of all other creditors.

c / Some Judicial Precedents

i *Re Karch* (1922), 53 O.L.R. 112 (S.C.)

ORDE, J.: The applicant, Magdalena Karch, is the wife of Charles Frederick Karch. On the 19th June, 1912, Magdalena Karch recovered a judgment for alimony against her husband, under which there is now a large amount of money owing to her, and there are also certain orders in another action under which she is entitled to be paid certain moneys by her husband. Henry William Karch, a brother of Charles Frederick Karch, died on the 15th December, 1919, leaving a will containing certain provisions in favour of Charles Frederick Karch, and on the 13th March, 1920, an order was made at the instance of Magdalena Karch appointing her a receiver to get in the moneys of the estate coming to her husband to the extent of her judgments.

The Canada Trust Company, which is now the trustee of the estate, takes the position that under the terms of the will it cannot pay over the moneys in question to the receiver, and this motion is now made by the receiver for the interpretation of the will.

After the usual direction for the payment of debts, etc., the will gives the whole estate to the executors and trustees upon trust, (A) to pay a sister $1,000, (B) to pay to a brother and two sisters each one-fifth of the residuary estate. Then follow certain trusts as to another one-fifth, which are the subject of this motion, namely: – '(c) To hold in trust for my brother Charles Frederick Karch one-fifth of my said residuary estate and to pay during the lifetime of my brother Charles Frederick Karch in the discretion however of my trustees, the income, rents and profits arising from the share of my said brother Charles Frederick Karch to my brother Charles Frederick Karch. I direct that in case the wife of my said brother Charles Frederick Karch makes any application for an increased allowance of alimony on account of this devise, that thereupon my trustees shall withhold from my brother Charles Frederick Karch any rents, profits or income arising from his share of my estate, and that such income, rents and profits shall (in the discretion of my trustees) be withheld from my brother (Charles Frederick Karch during the lifetime of my brother Charles Frederick Karch and allowed to accumulate as long as his wife survives him, but in case she predeceases him, then such income, rents and profits may thereupon be paid over to my said brother by said trustees.

'(D) After the death of my brother Charles Frederick Karch I direct that his share in my estate shall be held upon the same trusts and conditions and be administered in the same manner as my brother the said Charles Frederick Karch is devising and bequeathing his property by his will and my said trustees are in every way to administer the trust hereby created after the death of my brother Charles Frederick Karch as if his share of my estate was a portion of the estate of the said Charles Frederick Karch dealt with by his will.'

There is here an absolute gift of the corpus of the one fifth share to Charles Frederick Karch, followed by a direction to pay the income to him for life, with power in certain events to the trustees to withhold the income, but not so that it is given in such event to any other person; it is merely to accumulate for Karch's benefit. Then at Karch's death the share and accumulated income are to form part of his estate.

There can be no question that this gift is an absolute immediate gift of the corpus of the one-fifth share to Charles Frederick Karch. He is of full age, and, there being no person interested in the trust-fund but himself, the elaborate provisions as to the payment or accumulation of interest during his lifetime are of no effect whatever, and he can therefore put an end to the trust at any time and demand the payment of the corpus.

This being the case, is a judgment creditor entitled, by way of equitable execution, through the medium of a receivership order, to exercise the same right to compel the trustee to pay over so much of the moneys to which Karch is entitled as will satisfy the judgments? Where moneys are payable to a judgment debtor in the absolute discretion of some other person they cannot be reached by way of equitable execution: *Regina* v *Judge of the County Court of Lincolnshire* (1887), 20 Q.B.D. 167. But here the moneys are really under Karch's control: he can assign them or incumber them. They will form part of his estate at his death, and would undoubtedly form part of his estate on his bankruptcy. He cannot, by merely refraining from exercising his right to put an end to the trust, evade the payment of his judgment debts.

I must hold, therefore, that the applicant as receiver is entitled to be paid forthwith by the trustee so much of the moneys payable to Karch as will satisfy the amounts due under the judgment and orders in question, for principal, interest, and costs. Her costs of this application are also to be paid out of the trust-moneys.

ii *Garry Finance Corporation Limited* v *Heizman*, [1939] 1 W.W.R. 541 (Man. Co. Ct.)

STACPOOLE, C.C.J.: This was an action commenced by the plaintiff against the defendant to which W. E. Smith, the third party, was added by order of the Court and judgment in favour of the defendant against the third party has been recovered.

The facts seem to be that the defendant Dr. Heizman purchased from Smith, the third party, a second-hand automobile, trading in one of his own as part payment and paying a certain sum in cash, Smith having guaranteed that the automobile so sold to Dr. Heizman was free of encumbrance. This it appears was not the fact and the automobile was subsequently repossessed from Dr. Heizman under a lien held by another party upon the machine.

The defendant Dr. Heizman issued execution against the goods of Smith which was returned *nulla bona* by the bailiff. Dr. Heizman thereupon launched a motion asking for a receiver to be appointed by way of equitable relief to assist him in recovering the amount of his judgment from Smith ...

After hearing argument of counsel for both parties, it appears to me that the law is quite clear that equitable relief would only be granted in such case as the Court of Chancery would have granted it before the merging of chancery matters and common law matters in one Court.

I am of the opinion that this application might well come within the reasoning of the case of *Goldschmidt* v *Oberrheinische Metallwerke* [1906] 1 K.B. 373, in which an application was made to appoint a receiver by way of an equitable execution in order to realize the plaintiff's judgment, and Vaughan Williams, L.J., at p 375, says:

'I think that the special circumstances of this case are sufficient to entitle the plaintiff to the remedy for which he applies, and to entitle himself to which he must show that the circumstances are such as to render it practically very difficult, if not impossible, to obtain any fruit of his judgment, unless what has been called equitable execution be granted to him. In the case of *Manchester and Liverpool District Banking Co.* v *Parkinson* (1889) 22 Q.B.D. 173, 58 L.J.Q.B. 262, Fry, L.J. said in giving judgment, in reference to the *Judicature Act, 1873*, s. 25: "I do not say that there would have been no jurisdiction to appoint a receiver under that section, if there had been special circumstances in the case rendering it just or convenient to make such an order. It may be, for instance, that an order could be made for appointment of a receiver to hold property liable to execution, to prevent someone making away with it, or to get in debts, where under particular circumstances it was a more convenient mode of procuring satisfaction of the judgment than the usual process of attachment." In my judgment this case falls within those words.'

It seems to me that in this instance, while there is a legal remedy given Heizman by way of execution against the goods and chattels of Smith, it is merely a remedy of theory and practically is of no value whatever. The facts are in this instance, as shown by the affidavit of the applicant filed in support of the motion, that there are a large number of secondhand automobiles in the possession of Smith, each of which is encumbered by a chattel mortgage registered in the Winnipeg County Court office, and if the goods were to be put up for sale under a bailiff's seizure it is quite easy to see that under the hammer they would be knocked down, if they realized anything, for so small a sum that it would be useless to pursue this remedy, but, each automobile being the subject of a chattel mortgage, it is fair to presume, and I think the Court might almost take judicial notice of it as a fact, that mortgagees do not advance the full value of the article mortgaged and there is, in the course of such dealings with a mortgage, the equity left in the mortgagor but if such equity were to be put to auction it is problematical, in fact, most unlikely, that it would produce enough to pay for the costs of sale.

I am, therefore, of the opinion that this is one of those cases in which taking the ordinary legal remedy to realize would be fruitless. Heizman would recover nothing on his judgment, Smith possibly would lose any equity he had for a mere bagatelle in the way of money, and, in fact, from all points of view, it would be better to grant the order asked for, for if an auction sale took place Smith possibly would be ruined, and Dr. Heizman would get nothing, whereas, if a receiver is appointed, Smith's business is not interfered with. If there are moneys coming to Smith over and above the mortgages – which the affidavits would lead one to believe – then these moneys can be obtained and Dr. Heizman's judgment against Smith reduced by such sums as are obtained to the benefit of Dr. Heizman and also avoiding the detriment to Smith which might ensue from sale ...

QUESTIONS Will a receiver be appointed where other methods are available that will succeed in recovering the property? Should this remedy be a last resort or a remedy of convenience?

iii *McCart* v *McCart and Adams*, [1947] O.W.N. 48 (H.C.J.)

BARLOW, J.: An application by the defendant McCart for an order for leave to appeal from an order of Wilson J., dated the 24th June 1946, providing 'that the Sheriff of the County of York be and he is hereby appointed receiver without security to collect, get in and receive the debts due and owing to the said defendant, Howard W. D. McCart, at the date hereof, to the extent of the amount due to the plaintiff'.

By virtue of The Judicature Act, R.S.O. 1937, c 100, s 16, a receiver may be appointed 'by an interlocutory order of the Court, in all cases in which it appears to the Court to be just or convenient that such order should be made'.

The plaintiff has a judgment against the defendant McCart for alimony.

The defendant applicant is a doctor, and the intention of the order appointing the sheriff as receiver is to enable him to collect the many small accounts of the said defendant, outstanding.

The examination of the defendant applicant as a judgment debtor shows some 225 or more small accounts owing to him, ranging from $3 to $158, and averaging less than $20 each.

Counsel for the defendant applicant contends that a receiver should never be appointed if any other method of execution is available. He contends that since the accounts could be reached by garnishee proceedings, the receiving order ought not to have been made.

If an attempt were made to realize by way of garnishee proceedings, it would result in over 200 garnishee orders being obtained from the Master in the one action, with all the attendant expense, which would exceed, in practically all the accounts, the individual amount owing to the defendant applicant. It is clear to me that garnishee proceedings would be entirely impracticable and inadequate, and would involve unnecessary expense, without, in many instances, producing any result. Counsel for the defendant applicant cites in support of his contention *Re Asselin and Cleghorn* (1903), 6 O.L.R. 170; *Millar et al.* v *Thompson* (1900), 19 P.R. 294; *Harris* v *Beauchamp Brothers*, [1894] 1 Q.B. 801 at 810, and *The Manchester and Liverpool District Banking Company, Limited* v *Parkinson* (1888), 22 Q.B.D. 173.

After a careful perusal of these cases, it is clear to me that they do not conflict with the order as made. The governing words in s 16 of The Judicature Act, quoted above, are 'just and convenient'. The above-cited cases show that if special circumstances are shown so that the ordinary procedure by way of garnishment or writ of *fi. fa.* is practically useless by reason of being cumbersome and expensive, a receiver may be appointed. It is a matter of discretion to be exercised by the judge making the order. Unless I find that the judge has proceeded on a wrong principle, I should not grant leave to appeal. I cannot so find ...
[His Lordship referred to a number of cases and continued:]

After a careful perusal of the law, I cannot find that there is any conflict in the decisions. Furthermore, I am satisfied that the learned judge properly exercised his discretion in making the order on the facts disclosed, and that his order is right.

The application for leave to appeal will be dismissed with costs.
Motion dismissed with costs.

QUESTIONS Is the convenience of the creditor more important than the right to privacy and personal integrity of the debtor? Should a receiving order have been made in *McCart?*

iv *Collins* v *Hall*, [1938] O.W.N. 477 (H.C.J.)

GODFREY J., in a written judgment, said that the plaintiffs had an unsatisfied judgment against the defendants. The defendants are a firm of practising solicitors. This motion is made for the appointment of a receiver.

(1) in respect of the book debts and assets of the former firm of Hall and Hall;

(2) in respect of the firm of Hall, Hall and Stevenson;

(3) in respect of the income of the present firm of Hall and Hall;

(4) in respect of rents from premises owned by the Stevenson estate, part of which is rented by the defendants.

In support of the motion there was filed an affidavit of J.D. Collins, one of the plaintiffs. This affidavit, after setting out the facts regarding the judgment and that a return of nulla bona had been made to the writs of execution and that the judgment is unsatisfied, stated that the defendant B.D. Hall was examined viva voce under oath as a judgment debtor on the 26th June, 1936, and his examination did not reveal any exigible assets of the defendant or of his co-defendant; that the defendant E.H.D. Hall was examined viva voce under oath as a judgment debtor on the 22nd of June, 1936, and on the 10th of July, 1936, and that his examination did not reveal any exigible assets of the defendants or either of them; that J.W. Stevenson, a former partner in the firm of Hall, Hall and Stevenson, who is now dead, had been examined prior to his death under oath, and his examination did not reveal any exigible assets of the defendants or either of them.

The affidavit further stated that he, the deponent, had been advised by his solicitors, and verily believed, that the building occupied by the defendants is held in the name of the wife of said Stevenson as trustee for the use and benefit of the partnership or partnerships in which the defendants are members; that as the said building is located on leasehold property it is not exigible under the execution against the defendants in this action.

He further states that, as a result of numerous searches and inquiries made by his solicitors, there are no exigible assets of the defendants or either of them, which could be realized upon under the plaintiffs' executions in this action.

The defendant B.D. Hall in an affidavit states that his entire income is from the earnings of the firm of Hall, Hall and Stevenson; that since the death of his partner he has been unable to draw any income from the said firm since that date as the total receipts exceeded the total expenditures for wages and office expenses by only about $30.00; that he has no assets whatever out of which he derives an income.

The defendant E.H.D. Hall is 88 years of age. He states in his affidavit that his total income is $140 a month, which he is allowed by the other members of his firm and received from the Peterborough Utilities Commission; that there is no agreement for continuation of such payment and the same might be discontinued at any time; that he has no other means of earning; that he is blind and there is no prospect of earning more.

The general law as to the appointment of a receiver has been stated by Meredith J. in *Re Asselin and Cleghorn* (1903), 6 O.L.R. 170:

The applicant's claim is by no means a modest one; it is, in effect, that he be appointed a sort of general assignee, for his own benefit only, of, substantially, all his debtor's property and earnings, and that the debtor be obliged to carry on business so that the applicant may have the earnings, until his debt is satisfied.

Such a mode of enforcing execution might be convenient for a creditor, but hardly so for a debtor and his family, and it certainly would not be just, or in the public interests.

It is strange that the introduction of the words 'a receiver' may be 'appointed ... in all cases in which it shall appear to the Court to be just or convenient that such order should be made,' should have given such exaggerated notions to some creditors of new means of enforcement of their claims as seem to have prevailed among them; means by which they might acquire not only the property of the debtor usually seized under execution, but also every sort of property, right, or interest, no matter how remote or contingent, that he might have, as well as all that he might acquire until the debt was fully paid, including all sorts of rights of action.

There was no good excuse for such notions; they were but the offspring of rapacity. The law is reasonable in regard to enforcement of payment of debts; it does not permit of enslaving ... of honest debtors ...

It is not in the public interests, nor indeed really in a creditor's interest, that the debtor should be denuded of all that he possesses; all interests require that an honest debtor should not be deprived of the means of earning a livelihood and of all means of acquiring money to pay his debts. Too great rapacity in creditors may defeat rather than further their object.

It would be a reversal of the whole trend of modern legislation if the enactment before mentioned had any such wide-spread effect. The words quoted give no sort of real encouragement to the notion.

In *Bedell* v *Gefaell*, [1938] O.W.N. 437, Middleton J.A. said: 'It is also well settled law in this Province that by no process of the Court, receivership or garnishment, can future earnings be taken in execution.'

'A receiver will not be appointed by way of equitable execution for untaxed costs': Halsbury's Laws of England, 2nd Ed., vol. 14 at page 142.

'The Court will not appoint a receiver where the effect may be merely the loss of the property of right; nor will a receiver be appointed unless it is reasonably clear that benefit will be derived from the appointment.' See *Re Asselin and Cleghorn* (supra) per Meredith J.. at page 173.

It is clear from the evidence filed, both by the plaintiffs and defendants, that no benefit will result to the plaintiffs from the appointment of a receiver. The learned Justice said that he was not satisfied on the material filed that the defendants have any interest in the building owned by the Stevenson estate.

Plaintiff's counsel relied on Rule 556, but this Rule is applicable to profits and not to personal earnings.

Mr. Pickup in his argument suggested that there might be some uncollected book debts of the firm of Hall, Hall and Stevenson, and stated that he was willing to give an undertaking by the defendants that any sum due the defendants from that source would be paid the plaintiffs. Upon this undertaking being given the motion is dismissed with costs to the defendants fixed at $75.00 to be set off pro tanto against the plaintiffs' judgment.

Order accordingly.

v *Dowell* v *Aikenhead*, [1961] O.W.N. 174 (H.C.J.)

[This was an application by the plaintiff as judgment creditor for the appointment of a receiver by way of equitable execution.

The judgment debtor was a beneficiary of the estate of his father. Under his father's will the defendant was entitled to a share in the residue after the death of his mother if he should survive his mother or if he should predecease his mother leaving issue or a wife him surviving.]

MOORHOUSE, J.: The widow being alive at this time it appears that the judgment debtor's interest is a contingent interest only. I believe it to be the policy of the Court to refuse to appoint a receiver by way of equitable execution in respect of monies payable only on a contingency: *Manufacturers Lbr. Co.* v *Pigeon* (1911), 24 O.L.R. 354, *Strang* v *Beal* (1922), 52 O.L.R. 208. I believe it to be reasonably clear also that a receiver should not be appointed unless it is reasonably clear that benefit will be derived from the appointment.

If the appointment of a receiver would or is intended to interfere with the action of the executors, it should not be made. If it does not interfere, it is nugatory and perhaps embarrassing: *Re McInnes* v *McGaw* (1898), 30 O.R. 38. The applicant was unable to refer me to any authority where a receiver had been appointed in respect of a contingent interest, and I therefore think that the application should be dismissed.

The respondent is entitled to its costs of the application but I think, in all the circumstances, it is only fair that they may be set off against the costs which the defendant is liable to pay. Application dismissed.

NOTE For examples of cases where execution by way of *fi.fa.* or garnishment was impossible but where it might have been appropriate to appoint a receiver see *Re Phillips and La Paloma Sweets* (1921), 51 O.L.R. 125 (supra at p 263) (receipt of stock dividends); *Webb* v *Stenton* (1883), 11 Q.B.D. 518 (supra at p 334) (contingent interest of a *cestui que trust*); and *Rat Portage Lumber Co.* v *Harty* (1917), 40 O.L.R. 322 (C.A.) (supra at p 343) (money expected to come into hands of third party shortly, but not yet received and thus not garnishable.

Suppose that an employer has the practice of paying his employee in advance before the wages are either due or earned. May the employee's wages ever be garnished? May a receiver be appointed to collect the payments from the employer? See *Fallis* v *Wilson* (1907), 13 O.L.R. 595.

d / Partnership Assets

i Ontario Supreme Court, Rules of Practice, R.R.O. 1970, Reg. 545

Rule 551

(1) Under an execution against one partner, partnership assets shall not be taken in execution, but an order may be made charging the partner's interest in the partnership property and profits with the payment of the amount of the executions in the sheriff's hands, and by the same or a subsequent order a receiver may be appointed of the partner's share of profits whether already declared or accruing and of any other money that may be coming to him in respect of the partnership, and the court may direct all accounts and inquiries and give all such other directions as might be directed or given as if the charge had been given by the partner.

(2) The other partners may redeem the interest charged, or, in the event of a sale, may purchase the same.

ii The Partnerships Act, R.S.O. 1970, c 339

31. (1) An assignment by a partner of his share in the partnership, either absolute or by way of mortgage or redeemable charge, does not, as against the other partners, entitle the assignee, during the continuance of the partnership, to interfere in the management or administration of the partnership business or affairs, or to require any accounts of the partnership transactions, or to inspect the partnership books, but entitles the assignee only to receive the share of profits to which the assigning partner would otherwise be entitled, and the assignee must accept the account of profits agreed to by the partners.

(2) A partnership may, at the option of the other partners, be dissolved if any partner suffers his share of the partnership property to be charged under this Act for his separate debt.

The following works may be referred to for a more detailed analysis of the varied circumstances in which a receiver may be appointed: Kerr, *On the Law and Practice as to Receivers*, Raymond Walton, ed. (15th ed.), 1978; Cababe, *Attachment of Debts and Receivers by Way of Equitable Execution* (2d ed.), 1888; Clark, *A Treatise on the*

Law and Practice of Receivers (3rd ed.), 1959; and Holmstead and Gale, *Ontario Judicature Act and Rules of Practice*, 1968, vol. 1, pp 119–20, 125–33.

3 CHARGING ORDERS

a / The Judicature Act, R.S.O. 1970, c 228

CHARGING ORDERS ON STOCKS, ETC.

143. (1) If a person against whom a judgment has been entered in any of Her Majesty's courts in Ontario has any government stock, funds or annuities, or any stock or shares of or in a public company in Ontario, whether incorporated or not, standing in his name in his own right, or in the name of any person in trust for him, a judge of the Supreme Court, on the application of any judgment creditor, may order that the stock, funds, annuities, or shares of such of them or such part thereof as he thinks fit shall stand charged with the payment of the amount for which judgment has been so recovered, and interest thereon, and the order entitles the judgment creditor to all such remedies as he would have been entitled to if the charge had been made in his favour by the judgment debtor; but no proceedings shall be taken to have the benefit of the charge until after the expiration of six months from the date of the order.

(2) Every such order shall be made in the first instance *ex parte* and without any notice to the judgment debtor and is an order to show cause only, and the order, if any government stock, funds or annuities standing in the name of the judgment debtor in his own right or in the name of any person in trust for him are to be affected, restrains any transfer thereof being made in the meantime and until the order has been made absolute or discharged; and if any stock or shares of or in any public company standing in the name of the judgment debtor in his own right or in the name of any person in trust for him are to be affected by the order, in like manner restrains such public company from permitting a transfer thereof.

(3) If, after notice of such order to the person to be restrained thereby, or, in the case of a corporation, to any authorized agent of the corporation, and before the order is discharged or made absolute, the corporation or person permits any such transfer to be made, the corporation or person so permitting the transfer is liable to the judgment creditor for the value or amount of the property so charged and so transferred, or such part thereof as is sufficient to satisfy his judgment, and no disposition of the judgment debtor in the meantime is valid or effectual as against the judgment creditor.

(4) Unless the judgment debtor, within a time to be mentioned in such order, shows to a judge sufficient cause to the contrary, the order shall, after proof of notice thereof to the judgment debtor, his solicitor or agent, be made absolute.

(5) A judge, upon the application of the judgment debtor or any person interested, may discharge or vary such order.

(6) This section extends to the interest of a judgment debtor, whether in possession, remainder, or reversion, and whether vested or contingent as well in any such stock, funds, annuities or shares, as also in the dividends, interest or annual produce of any such stock, funds, annuities or shares.

(7) Where such a judgment debtor has an estate, right, title or interest, vested or contingent, in possession, remainder, or reversion in or to stock, funds, annuities or shares standing in the name of The Accountant of the Supreme Court or in or to the dividends, interest or annual produce thereof, the judge may make any order as to the stock, funds, annuities or shares, or the

interest, dividends or annual produce thereof, in the same way as if the same had been standing in the name of a trustee of the judgment debtor.

(8) No such order as to any stock, funds, annuities or shares standing in the name of the Accountant, or as to the interest, dividends or annual produce thereof, prevents any incorporated bank or any public company from permitting a transfer of the stock, funds, annuities or shares, or payment of the interest, dividends or annual produce thereof, in such manner as the Supreme Court directs, or has any greater effect than if the judgment debtor had charged the stock, funds, annuities or shares, or the interest, dividends or annual produce thereof, in favour of the judgment creditor with the amount of the sum mentioned in the order.

b / Ontario Supreme Court, Rules of Practice, R.R.O. 1970, Reg. 545, Rules 696, 730

Rule 696

(1) Where a solicitor has been employed to prosecute or defend any cause or matter, the court may, upon a summary application, declare such solicitor, or his personal representatives, to be entitled to a charge upon the property recovered or preserved through the instrumentality of such solicitor, for his costs, charges and expenses of or in reference to such cause, matter or proceeding, and all conveyances and acts done to defeat, or which may operate to defeat, such charge or right are, unless made to a bona fide purchaser for value without notice, absolutely void and of no effect as against such charge.

(2) The court may make an order for taxation of such costs, charges and expenses and for the raising and payment of the same out of the property.

Rule 730

Any person claiming to be interested in, or to have a lien or charge upon, or an assignment of, any money or securities in court, or invested in the name of the Accountant, or any portion thereof, or claiming to have the same applied towards the satisfaction of any judgment or execution against the person to whose credit such moneys or securities stand, or for whose benefit the same are held by the Accountant may, upon an affidavit verifying his claim, apply ex parte for an order directing that such money or securities shall not be paid out or dealt with except upon notice to him (Form 73).

c / S.R. Ellis, 'The Charging Order – A Neglected Means of Enforcement?' (1962), 20 *U. of T. Faculty of Law Rev.* 35, at pp 40–4 (Footnotes omitted)

Before proceeding to consider other possible applications of the statutory charging order, the writer proposes first to examine what advantage, if any, the use of the charging order has over other forms of execution ...
One obvious advantage, of course, is that there are situations where the use of a charging order will be the only method of realizing on assets open to the creditor. These situations, however, will arise only rarely and will be dealt with later. It is proposed at the moment to examine the case where the lawyer has a choice, as in the case of the fund in court noted above, between the charging order on the one hand and one of the usual methods of execution on the other. Is there anything to be gained by choosing the charging order? The answer would appear to be that there probably is. There seem to be excellent grounds for believing that a charging order gives its holder priority over other execution creditors in proceedings under The Creditors' Relief Act, and in addition, there is at least a possibility that it puts him in the position of a secured creditor

under the Bankruptcy Act. These are obviously substantial benefits which by the terms of The Creditors' Relief Act and the Bankruptcy Act are not normally available under the usual forms of execution, and, in view of the apparently infrequent use of the charging order in Ontario, the writer puts them forward rather hesitantly. However, there does appear to be considerable support for both propositions.

Assuming for the moment that what is said above with respect to The Creditors' Relief Act and the Bankruptcy Act may be true, there is a preliminary difficulty which must be met before it can be said that any practical advantage arises therefrom. The question is, will an Ontario court make a charging order in circumstances where other forms of execution are readily available? Will the courts accede to the policy of The Creditors' Relief Act or the Bankruptcy Act being circumvented by resort to a charging order, where the order is in substance merely an alternative form of execution? In the 1958 decision of *Gould* v *Ablitt* the British Columbia Supreme Court, in considering an application for a charging order against shares, recognized that the Judgments Act, 1838 was part of the law of British Columbia 'insofar as it is applicable and insofar as it has not been altered by our Execution Act.' However, it held that 'in respect of shares ... if they are not subject to execution under the *Execution Act*, a charging order may be made. If the shares are subject to execution under the *Execution Act*, there is no need for a charging order and in fact ... the English Act is [not] applicable.' Would an Ontario Court adopt the same view? There seem to be reasonable grounds for thinking that it would not. It may, first of all, be noted that in the *Ablitt* case the British Columbia court was being asked to prefer an English-made statute over a domestic statute. In Ontario, where the charging order provisions have been incorporated into The Judicature Act, the charging order would at least initially have a standing in the eyes of the court equal to other statutory methods of execution. Secondly, having regard to the facts in the *Ablitt* case, the court's statement was obiter dictum, and standing opposed to that statement is another dictum of more persuasive authority emanating from the Manitoba Court of Appeal in *Goodbun* v *Mitchell*. There, where the possibility of applying the charging order in the circumstances under consideration was examined, Trueman J.A. made the following statement:

Section 14 and its related sections [the sections of the Manitoba Execution Act applying to execution against shares] were enacted to give to a judgment creditor a more direct and simpler method of reaching shares of a bank or company owned by the judgment debtor than that provided by the Judgments Act, 1838. The Act is not repealed or superseded in all its parts by section 14, and may be resorted to independently or in aid of the section.

Finally, in The Execution Act of Ontario, immediately following the provision for execution against shares of a company, it is enacted that:

Nothing in this Act affects any remedy that the execution creditor might, without this Act, have had against any such shares or the dividends, premiums, bonuses or other pecuniary profits in respect thereof, and subsections 1 to 4 apply to such remedy insofar as they can be applied thereto.

This provision would prima facie seem to preclude a court from taking the view adopted in the *Ablitt* case and, while there is a similar provision in the British Columbia Execution Act, from what appears in the opinion the court seems to have failed to consider it.

It is, therefore, the writer's submission that an Ontario Court would have little basis for rejecting an application for a charging order on the grounds of the existence of an alternative form of execution, and that there is at least a reasonable possibility that no objection to such an application would be taken.

Assuming then that a charging order can be obtained, is there any substance to the above-noted suggestions that the charging order may not come within the provisions of The Creditors' Relief Act and that the holder of a charging order may possibly be a secured creditor within the provisions of the Bankruptcy Act? Considering first The Creditors' Relief Act, it may be noted at once that the words 'charging order' do not appear in any of its provisions. The Act, however, speaks of 'creditors by execution', defining 'execution' as *including* a writ of fieri facias, and of 'attaching' creditors, and contains a broad general statement of purpose, all of which might be thought capable of a sufficiently broad interpretation as to include charging orders. The question is, will the Act be interpreted broadly so as to encompass the charging order or narrowly so as to exclude it?

There seems to be considerable judicial support for the view that the latter approach will prevail. A case in point is the decision of an Ontario Court in *McLean* v *Allen*. Here the issue was whether, in view of the provisions of The Creditors' Relief Act, an appointment of a receiver by way of equitable execution ought to have been declared to be for the benefit of all the creditors of the defendant. Street J. said:

The decisions upon this subject are conflicting, and for the present I think I should follow those of the learned Chief Justices of the Queen's Bench Division and of the Common Pleas Division, in which my brother Falconbridge has concurred, and hold that the provisions of The Creditors' Relief Act form an exception to the general rule, and are not to be extended to cases not actually provided for in that Act.

Another case to the same effect is the recent British Columbia Supreme Court decision in *Hale* v *Ross*. The issue there was whether a creditor, who had obtained an attaching order before any writ, or warrant of execution, or certificate under The Creditors' Relief Act was placed in the hands of the sheriff by the other execution creditors, was required to share the debtor's assets with those creditors. The court said:

Notwithstanding that The Creditors' Relief Act ... is intituled 'An Act To Prevent Priority Amongst Execution Creditors', and that section 3 thereof provides:
> Subject to the provisions hereinafter contained, there shall be no priority among creditors by execution from the Supreme Court or County Courts,

it is clear ... that the judgment creditor is under no legal obligation to share with them [the other creditors] the fruits of her prior successful attachment proceedings. The fact that payment of the attached money ... was made after warrants of execution on behalf of the other claimants were delivered to the sheriff does not affect the matter, because service of the attaching order before judgment created a charge upon the moneys attached ... and no interest of the sheriff could arise therein unless at that time there were executions in his hands. To this extent, as learned judges have held heretofore, does the law reward the first attaching creditor for her diligence.

What was said there with respect to attaching orders would appear to apply equally to charging orders.

Another case indicative of the narrow technical interpretation which courts are prone to apply in this area of the law and which also supports the general proposition that the due application of the charging order provisions will not be inhibited by a result contrary to a clear expression of legislative intent in a correlative statute, is *Prat* v *Hitchcock*, a decision of the British Columbia Court of Appeal. This case involved a charging order against a fund in court. The issue was whether the debtor could rely on the exemption provisions in the Execution Act to protect a portion of that fund from the effect of the charging order. The section of the Execution Act in question reads as follows:

The following personal property shall be exempt from forced seizure or sale by any process at law or in equity ...

within the technical meaning the law has ascribed to those words. It may be noted that the charging order here was an order by way of equitable execution only and did not have the legislative backing of a statutory order.

Before leaving The Creditors' Relief Act, it might be noted that there is no reason to suppose that the holder of a charging order would not be entitled to the benefit of s 32 (11) of that Act.

While there is nothing in any of the above to justify a firm conclusion as to whether an Ontario court would apply the provisions of The Creditors' Relief Act to the charging order, there is sufficient evidence, it is submitted, to establish a reasonable probability that those provisions would not be applied and that the priority of a holder of a charging order over other execution creditors in proceedings under The Creditors' Relief Act would be recognized.

It was conceded that, if the section applied, a portion of the fund in court would be exempt. Despite the very general nature of the words, 'by *any* process at law or in equity', which constituted an open invitation to the court to bring to bear against the charging order the obvious legislative policy behind the section, the majority of the court held that the section did not apply. The charging order procedure could not be described as a 'forced seizure or sale'

Do you agree that by the use of a charging order a creditor can gain a priority he would not otherwise have? *Should* such a creditor obtain a special priority?

Note that s 24 of The Creditors' Relief Act (supra, p 375) was enacted subsequent to *McLean* v *Allen* (1890), 14 P.R. 291 (Ont. Q.B.D.), mentioned in Ellis' article. What effect, if any, does this have on the conclusion he draws?

d / For a case applying Rule 696, supra p 383, see *Doyle* v *Doyle*, (1974), 4 O.R. (2d) 111 (H.C.J.), holding that a judgment for costs obtained by a solicitor for his client was 'property recovered or preserved through the instrumentality of such solicitor'; accordingly, the solicitor was entitled to a charging order against the costs.

e / Note

The principal obstacle to the making of a charging order is the general rule that equitable execution is not possible if the property is exigible at law (i.e. by *fi. fa.* under The Execution Act or by way of garnishment). Thus in *Associates Finance Co. Ltd.* v *Webber* (1972), 4 W.W.R. 31 (B.C.S.C.) (supra at p 263) Anderson J. of the British Columbia Supreme Court suggested that because company shares are now exigible at law, a charging order should not be made.

QUESTIONS
Is the charging order authorized by s 143 of The Judicature Act a form of equitable execution? Does the limitation on equitable execution (that 'execution at law be impossible') apply to orders authorized by the legislation?

4 ATTACHMENT, COMMITTAL AND SEQUESTRATION

a / Ontario Supreme Court, Rules of Practice, R.R.O. 1970, Reg. 545

Rule 569
A judgment requiring any person to do an act, other than the payment of money, or to abstain for doing anything, may be enforced by attachment or by committal.

Rule 570
A writ of attachment shall not be issued without the leave of the court or a judge, on notice to the person against whom the attachment is to be issued.

Rule 571
Where a person is taken or detained in custody under a writ of attachment, without obeying the judgment, then, upon the sheriff's return that the person has been so taken or detained, the party prosecuting the judgment is entitled upon motion to a writ of sequestration against the estate and effects of the disobedient person.

Rule 572
If an attachment cannot be executed against the person refusing or neglecting to obey the judgment by reason of his being out of the jurisdiction of the court or of his having absconded or that with due diligence he cannot be found or if in any other case the court thinks proper to dispense with a writ of attachment, an order may be granted for a writ of sequestration against the estate and effects of the disobedient person, and it is not necessary for that purpose to issue an attachment.

Rule 573
If a person who is ordered to pay money neglects to obey the judgment, the court may, upon the application of the party prosecuting the judgment, at the expiration of the time limited for performance, make an order for a writ of sequestration (Form 126).

Rule 574
A writ of sequestration shall be directed to the sheriff, unless otherwise ordered.

Rule 575
Where a person has been committed to jail for contempt of court, there to be detained and imprisoned until he has purged his contempt, if it be made to appear that he is in actual custody under such committal, the court may modify the order and limit the term of imprisonment or grant such other relief as in the nature and circumstances of the case seems just, but any relief that may be granted to any such person does not relieve him from any civil liability.

Rule 576

Any judgment against a corporation wilfully disobeyed may be enforced by sequestration against the corporation or by attachment against the directors or other officers of the corporation.

Rule 577

Any corporation or individual disobeying a judgment or guilty of any other contempt of court may be fined and such fine may be in lieu of or addition to punishment by attachment, committal or sequestration.

Rule 578

Any person not a party against whom obedience to a judgment may be enforced is liable to the same process and punishment as if he were a party.

Rule 579

If a mandamus granted in an action or otherwise, or a mandatory order, injunction or judgment for specific performance of a contract, is not complied with, the court, besides or instead of proceeding against the disobedient party for contempt, may direct that the act required to be done may be done so far as practicable by the party by whom the judgment has been obtained, or some other person appointed by the court, at the cost of the disobedient party, and, upon the act being done, the expenses incurred may be ascertained in such manner as the court directs, and execution may issue for the amount so ascertained and for costs.

b / The Small Claims Courts Act, R.S.O. 1970, c 439

135. (1) Where a judge has ordered a judgment debtor to be committed to a correctional institution, the order shall be enforced by the bailiff, unless the judge directs that the judgment debtor appear before him at a named time and place to explain his contempt, in which case notice thereof shall be sent to the judgment debtor by mail or served personally as directed by the judge.

(2) Where the judgment debtor appears to explain his contempt,

(*a*) if the judge is of opinion that the default was wilful, he shall order the bailiff to enforce the warrant of commitment; or

(*b*) if the judge is of opinion that the default was not wilful, he shall order the judgment debtor to attend for examination at the next sittings of the court to be held for the hearing of judgment summonses and, in the event that the judgment debtor does not so attend, the judge presiding at the sittings may order that he be forthwith committed to a correctional institution.

(3) Where the judgment debtor does not appear at the time and place named in the notice, the judge may direct that the warrant of commitment be enforced. s 134(3).

137. (1) Where an order of commitment has been made, the clerk shall issue, under the seal of the court, a warrant of commitment directed to the bailiff of any court in the county and the bailiff may, by virtue of the warrant, take the party and deliver him to the superintendent of the correctional institution in which he has been directed to be imprisoned. R.S.O. 1960.

(2) All constables and other peace officers within their respective jurisdictions shall aid in the execution of the warrant, and the superintendent of the correctional institution shall receive and keep the party therein until discharged under this Act, or otherwise, in due course of law.

138. A party shall be discharged out of custody,

(*a*) by order of the judge; or

(*b*) at the expiration of the time prescribed in the warrant of commitment.

139. (1) The judge may rescind or alter the order for payment made upon a judgment summons or show cause summons and make any further or other order for the payment of the debt or damages recovered and costs forthwith, or by instalments, or in any other manner that he thinks reasonable.

(2) The judge may rescind or alter or stay the operation of any order of commitment made by him, whether or not it has been acted on.

187. (1) Every person who interferes with a bailiff or officer or his deputy or assistant while in the execution of his duty, or makes or attempts to rescue any property seized or attached under process of the court, is guilty of an offence and liable to a penalty of not more than $20, to be recovered by order of the court or on summary conviction before a provincial judge, and is also liable to be imprisoned, by order of the court or provincial judge, for any term of not more than three months.

NOTE Other instances in which a recalcitrant debtor may be committed have been discussed elsewhere: see The Absconding Debtors Act, R.S.O. 1970, c 2, ss 2–7 (supra at p 129) and The Fraudulent Debtors Arrest Act, R.S.O. 1970, c 183, ss 2–4 (supra at p 132).

Note also ss 28, 29 and 37 of The Family Law Reform Act, 1978, S.O. 1978, c 2 reproduced at p 444–5 below.

c / *Leaseconcept Ltd.* v *French* (1976), 1 C.P.C. 160 (S.C.O.)

REID J.: This is an application for an order pursuant to R. 527 to correct what is said to be an accidental slip or omission in an order that has been issued or, alternatively, under R. 529 for an order to carry that order into operation.

First, a brief history. On 31st January 1975, Holland J., at trial, gave judgment for Leaseconcept against French for $12,000 with interest or, alternatively, requiring French to deliver possession of a library to Leaseconcept against payment of a sum. No appeal was taken from that judgment.

French did not pay the $12,000 and interest. Leaseconcept obtained a writ of delivery from this Court and attended on French with the writ and a certified cheque for the sum to be paid, but French refused to accept the cheque and to deliver possession of the library, claiming that he was judgment-proof.

Leaseconcept applied to this Court for an order that French be attached or in the alternative, committed, for contempt in refusing to obey the judgment or, in the further alternative, for sequestration of twice the value of the property in question. This motion came before me and was heard with a motion by French to set aside the judgment of Holland J. The motions were argued at length. Extensive material was filed. After reserving, I dismissed French's motion and granted Leaseconcept's.

Leaseconcept took out an order dated 24th February 1975. I set out its substance:

'Between:

LEASECONCEPT LTD.
Plaintiff
and
STEPHEN CHARLES FRENCH
Defendant

'UPON MOTION made on 17th, 19th and 20th February 1975, unto this Court on behalf of the plaintiff the said application having been adjourned from Chambers, for an order that the defendant, Stephen Charles French be attached and that he be taken into custody and forthwith detained at the common goal or in the alternative, that the said Stephen Charles French be committed to jail for contempt of court and either be detained until he has purged the contempt or in the further alternative, directing that the Sheriff take goods and chattels of the judgment debtor, Stephen Charles French of double the value of the property in question, to be kept until the further order of the court to enforce obedience to the judgment, and an order for costs, and upon reading the affidavits of Lawrence Dale Pringle and Stephen Charles French, filed, and upon hearing counsel for the plaintiff and the defendant, this Court was pleased to direct this motion to stand over the judgment, and the same coming on this day for judgment:

'I. THIS COURT DOTH ORDER that the motion will be granted, but its operation shall be stayed for a period of seven days, during which time, the subject property shall be preserved pursuant to R. 372, and shall not be moved or dealt with in any way whatsoever.

'2. AND IT IS ORDERED that the said Stephen Charles French do pay the costs of this motion.'

French appealed my decisions to the Court of Appeal. The Court dismissed the appeal with costs.

Leaseconcept then attempted to enforce its order but was unable to induce the Sheriff to act upon it, apparently because it contained no positive direction to him to take French into custody and that the relief asked being in the alternative, he was uncertain how to proceed.

On the motion that led to the order of 24th February, no argument was addressed to the alternative nature of the relief required; I did not address myself to it in my reasons. I can understand the Sheriff's reluctance to act on the order Leaseconcept took out. I do not think it should have been taken out in that form, but no objection to its form was apparently made by French. The problem posed by the order as drafted was patent yet no application was made to me to settle it pursuant to R. 537. That would have been the preferable way to deal with it.

I must however deal with it now because I did not adjudicate on the sequence in which the relief requested should be effected. Being alternative, it could not all be effected at once.

The entire tenor of our law is to make committal and attachment of the person a last resort for the enforcement of judgments. Committal or attachment should only be granted where reasonable attempts to obtain satisfaction by alternative methods have failed. We were recently reminded of this by Denning M.R. in *Danchevsky v Danchevsky*, [1974] 3 All E.R. 934 at 937:

'Whenever there is a reasonable alternative available instead of committal to prison, that alternative must be taken.'

Sequestration, which effects the property but not the person of a defaulter, should therefore be attempted first.

Accordingly, the proceeding by way of sequestration may proceed forthwith. An order shall go pursuant to R. 573. There is no question here of awaiting the expiry of a time limited for performance; the judgment of Holland J. was effective upon its pronouncement. In conformance with R. 574 a writ of sequestration in Form 126 shall issue, directed to the Sheriff.

If, by this means, the judgment is not satisfied within a reasonable time Leaseconcept may renew this motion and its request for attachment or committal on seven days' notice which may be served personally on French or by ordinary mail addressed to French at 18 Robinwood Avenue, Toronto, and if service is made in either of these ways, it shall not be a defence that notice was not actually received.

Because I am of the view that this problem should have been avoided before the order in question was issued, there shall be no costs of this motion.
Order accordingly.

For further discussion of the circumstances in which attachment or committal is appropriate, see *Link* v *Thompson* (1917), 40 O.L.R. 222.

NOTE If the 'library' involved in *Leaseconcept* was comprised of law books, one can easily understand why the defendant might have defaulted on his lease payments. Stephen Charles French, Q.C. was disbarred by the Law Society of Upper Canada for professional misconduct, following its discovery of violations of Law Society trust fund rules. French was exceedingly litigious in the battle preceding his disbarment. Details of the proceedings can be gleaned from the reports of some of the litigation: see *Law Society of Upper Canada* v *French* (1975), 49 D.L.R. (3d) 1 (S.C.C.); *Re French and Law Society of Upper Canada (No. 2)* (1976), 57 D.L.R. (3d) 481 (Ont. C.A.); and *Re French and Law Society of Upper Canada (No. 3)* (1976), 57 D.L.R. (3d) 490 (Ont. Div. Ct.) for representative samples.

12
Rights of the Debtor after Judgment

INTRODUCTION

The materials in earlier chapters suggested that enforcement proceedings may operate or may be perceived to operate very harshly upon some debtors. Frequently debtors allege that their financial troubles are merely temporary; that if left to continue at work or in business without the inconvenience, embarrassment or harassment of judgment collection procedures, they will be able to satisfy all outstanding claims.

The general rule is that such debtors must seek the forbearance of their creditors. Normally, creditors are free to pursue most enforcement devices shortly after judgment is rendered. This chapter surveys some of the techniques available to debtors who wish to postpone execution otherwise than by the grace of their creditors. It considers procedures available through appealing judgments or through being permitted to make periodic instalment payments. It will be apparent that relief from immediate execution is available in very few cases. Some proposals to make this relief available more generally were considered in Chapter 10 above. Proposals with similar purposes but which involve substantial reform of the execution process itself are considered in Chapter 15, below.

I DELAYING EXECUTION

a / Stay of Execution Pending Appeal

i Supreme Court of Ontario Rules of Practice, R.R.O. 1970, Reg. 545

Rule 505
The judge at the trial may stay the entry of judgment or the issue of execution, for a period not exceeding thirty days, but this does not prevent the settlement of the judgment.

Rule 506
(1) If the judgment appealed from awards a mandamus, or an injunction, or alimony or maintenance for a spouse or children, execution thereof shall not be stayed upon an appeal being set down, unless it shall be otherwise ordered by the judge appealed from or by a judge of the appellate court. In all other cases unless otherwise ordered by a judge of the appellate court, upon an appeal being set down, execution of the judgment appealed from shall be stayed pending the disposition of the appeal.

(2) Where leave to appeal from an interlocutory order is granted, the judge hearing the application may give directions as to staying proceedings.

Rule 507
Where an execution has been issued and is thereafter stayed upon an appeal, the appellant is entitled to obtain a certificate from the Registrar that the execution has been stayed pending the appeal, and, upon the certificate being lodged with the sheriff, the execution shall be superseded, but the execution debtor shall pay the sheriff's fees and the sum so paid shall be allowed to him as part of the costs of the appeal.

Rule 508
Where the execution of a judgment is stayed pending an appeal, all further proceedings in the action, other than the issue of the judgment and the taxation of costs thereunder, shall be stayed unless otherwise ordered by a judge of the Appellate Court.

ii Supreme Court Act, R.S.C. 1970, c S-19

70. (1) Upon filing and serving the notice of appeal and depositing security as required by section 66, execution shall be stayed in the original cause, except that

(*a*) where the judgment appealed from directs an assignment or delivery of documents or personal property, the execution of the judgment shall not be stayed until the things directed to be assigned or delivered have been brought into court, or placed in the custody of such officer or receiver as the court appoints, nor until security has been given to the satisfaction of the court appealed from, or of a judge thereof, in such sum as the court or judge directs, that the appellant will obey the order or judgment of the Supreme Court;

(*b*) where the judgment appealed from directs the execution of a conveyance or any other instrument, the execution of the judgment shall not be stayed until the instrument has been executed and deposited with the proper officer of the court appealed from, to abide the order or judgment of the Supreme Court;

(*c*) where the judgment appealed from directs the sale or delivery of possession of real property, chattels real or immovables, the execution of the judgment shall not be stayed until security has been entered into to the satisfaction of the court appealed from, or a judge thereof, and in such amount as the last mentioned court or judge directs, that during the possession of the property by the appellant he will not commit, or suffer to be committed, any waste on the property, and that if the judgment is affirmed, he will pay the value of the use and occupation of the property from the time the appeal is brought until delivery of possession thereof, and also, if the judgment is for the sale of property and the payment of a deficiency arising upon the sale, that the appellant will pay the deficiency; and

(*d*) where the judgment appealed from directs the payment of money, either as a debt or for damages or costs, the execution of the judgment shall not be stayed until the appellant has given security to the satisfaction of the court appealed from, or of a judge thereof, that if the judgment or any part thereof is affirmed, the appellant will pay the amount thereby directed to be paid, or the part thereof as to which the judgment is affirmed, if it is affirmed only as to part, and all damages awarded against the appellant on such appeal.

(2) Where the court appealed from is a court of appeal, and the assignment or conveyance, document, instrument, property or thing as aforesaid, has been deposited in the custody of the proper officer of the court in which the cause originated, the consent of the party desiring to appeal to the Supreme Court, that it shall so remain to abide the judgment of the Supreme Court, is binding on him and shall be deemed a compliance with the requirements in that behalf of this section.

(3) In any case in which execution may be stayed on the giving of security under this section, the security may be given by the same instrument whereby the security prescribed in section 66 is given.

See: *Foundation Co. of Canada* v *Prince Albert Pulp Co. Ltd.* (1974), 46 D.L.R. (3d) 629 (Sask. C.A.), varied (1976), 68 D.L.R. (3d) 283 (S.C.C.), which held that s 70(1)(d) of the Supreme Court Act did not apply to a judgment in a mechanic's lien action which required a non-contracting owner to pay certain sums into court, and on failure to pay, permitted an application to set the terms of sale of the property. Consequently, execution was stayed automatically upon the filing of the owner's appeal.

iii The County Courts Act, R.S.O. 1970, c 94

24. Subject to *The Judicature Act* and to the rules of court, the practice and procedure of the Supreme Court apply to the county and district courts.

35. Subject to section 36, the judge of the county or district court appealed from may, upon application to him, stay proceedings in the action to enable the appeal to be brought, upon such terms and for such time as he considers just.

iv The Small Claims Courts Act, R.S.O. 1970, c 439

102. (1) The judge may order the times and the proportions in which a sum and costs recovered by judgment shall be paid, having regard to section 117.

(2) Unless otherwise ordered, execution shall not issue within fifteen days after the entry of judgment, but the judge may order the amount of the judgment or any instalment thereof to be paid into court.

112. (1) The appeal shall be made in the time and manner prescribed by the rules of court.

(2) After the appeal has been set down to be heard, the execution of the judgment appealed from shall be stayed pending the appeal, unless otherwise ordered by a judge of the Supreme Court.

117. Except where a new trial is granted, the issue of execution shall not be postponed for more than fifty days from the service of the summons, without the consent of the party entitled thereto, but, if it is proved to the satisfaction of the judge that a party is unable from sickness or other cause to pay the debt or damages recovered against him, or any instalment thereof ordered to be paid, or that for any other reason the issue of execution should be further postponed, the judge may stay the judgment, order or execution for such time and on such terms as he thinks fit, and so from time to time until it is proved that the cause of disability has ceased.

139. (1) The judge may rescind or alter the order for payment made upon a judgment summons or show cause summons and make any further or other order for the payment of the debt or damages recovered and costs forthwith, or by instalments, or in any other manner that he thinks reasonable.

(2) The judge may rescind or alter or stay the operation of any order of commitment made by him, whether or not it has been acted on.

v *Schipper* v *Linkon Co. Ltd.*, [1957] O.W.N. 481 (H.C.J.)

FERGUSON J.: The defendant Linkon Company Limited commenced an action against Louis
Raxlen, the plaintiff in this action Marcus Schipper, and others to set aside conveyances and
mortgages affecting a hotel property in Schreiber, Ontario. One of the mortgages sought to be
set aside was held by Marcus Schipper for $52,000. Schipper resisted this claim and in a separate
action endeavoured to foreclose the said mortgage. In the result the action for foreclosure was
dismissed and the mortgage was set aside. The trial Judge, however, held that Schipper had a
lien against the hotel property at $25,526.84, less such sums as Marcus Schipper had received
through that mortgage: [1955] O.W.N. 434. On appeal to the Court of Appeal the lien, which was
to be subject to such deductions, was increased to $26,283.52: [1957] O.W.N. 82. Linkon
Company Limited was awarded costs against Schipper which were duly taxed on 6th May 1957,
at $7,859.59. Some communication between solicitors with respect to the payment of costs
followed the taxation but was completely barren of results. So the solicitor for the Linkon
Company issued a writ of *fieri facias* on 23rd August 1957, and the Sheriff in due course attended
on Mr. Schipper to collect. Thereupon Mr. Schipper's solicitor commenced this action and
obtained the *ex parte* injunction I have referred to which he now seeks to continue until trial.

Counsel for Marcus Schipper argues that it is highly unjust that the Linkon Company should
compel Schipper to pay $7,859.59 to them when the Linkon Company owes Schipper
$26,283.52. Therefore Schipper seeks to set such costs off against his lien. Under Rule 538 every
judgment creditor shall be entitled immediately to issue one or more writ or writs of *fieri facias*.
Under Rule 499 the Judge at trial may 'stay the entry of judgment or the issue of execution for a
period not exceeding thirty days ...' The Rules provide that a stay may be granted in certain
other circumstances which are not material to this case. Sections 126 and 127 of The Judicature
Act deal with the setting off of mutual debts between the plaintiff and the defendant in an action.
Section 15(f) of The Judicature Act, R.S.O. 1950, c 190 provides that:

No cause or proceedings shall be restrained by prohibition or injunction; but every matter of
equity on which an injunction against the prosecution of any such cause or proceeding might
have been obtained, prior to The Ontario Judicature Act, 1881, either unconditionally or on any
terms or conditions, may be relied on by way of defence thereto; but nothing in this Act shall
disable the court from directing a stay of proceedings in any cause or matter pending before it;
and any person ... who would have been entitled, prior to The Ontario Judicature Act, 1881, to
apply to any court to restrain the prosecution thereof, or who may be entitled to enforce, by
attachment or otherwise, any judgment, or order, contrary to which all or any part of the
proceedings in such cause or matter may have been taken, may apply to the court by motion in a
summary way, for a stay of proceedings ...

In the first place I may say that it appears from the section which I have just quoted that in
Ontario once there is a formal judgment in a cause the Court has no power, except in instances
not material here, to impose any restriction upon the unqualified right of a judgment creditor
given by Rule 538 to enforce the judgment by execution except the qualified right conferred by
Rule 499 to stay the entry of judgment or the issue of execution for a period not exceeding thirty
days. In this connection reference should be made to the case of *Leonard* v *Wharton* (1921), 50
O.L.R. 609.

Holmsted's Judicature Act, 5th edition, p 63 has the statement that execution by a sheriff is a proceeding within the meaning of The Judicature Act and consequently cannot be restrained by injunction.

This is clear, of course, from s 15(f) which I have cited above. However, it is not sought to restrain the sheriff in this case but only the party and it is argued that I have the power to stay the proceedings on the execution. The answer is, I think, clearly set forth in the case of *Emberson, et al.* v *Fisher, et al.*, [1944] O.W.N. 375, [1944] 2 D.L.R. 572. In that case at the trial the plaintiffs were awarded costs of the action to be paid by the defendant forthwith. A reference was ordered, costs of the reference were reserved until after the Master had made his report. The defendants applied for an order staying the issuing of execution or other proceedings 'until after the Master shall have made his report.' Laidlaw J.A. stated at p 376:

... I am of the opinion that there is no jurisdiction in the Court to restrain the plaintiffs from exercising their right to immediate payment of costs of the action.

It was argued that the power to stay is found in s 15(f) of The Judicature Act, *supra*, whenever the Court might, before the Judicature Act, grant a stay. That argument was rejected by Laidlaw J.A. in the following unqualified language:

The defendants were not entitled, prior to the Judicature Act 1881, to apply to the Court to stay the issue of execution after final judgment. No such right is given by s 15(f) of the present Act.

So that I think that execution cannot be restrained by injunction or stayed under the Judicature Act or Rules.

I have listened intently to counsel for the plaintiff and have examined the cases cited including *Grills* v *Farah* (1910), 21 O.L.R. 457. With respect, I think he would have the Court apply in this motion the same rights of set-off as would be available to him in an action involving mutual debts between an execution creditor and his execution debtor, notwithstanding that the execution debtor has brought a fresh action in which he asks for that stay.

The motion must be dismissed and the injunction be dissolved with costs to the defendant. Motion dismissed.

NOTE As *Schipper* v *Linkon* indicates, the courts generally have no jurisdiction to prohibit the judgment creditor from exercising his rights of execution. However, the courts probably do have inherent jurisdiction to restrain execution in order to prevent an abuse of process. As well, the debtor can get relief in a case where the judgment debt is in fact satisfied but the creditor refuses to withdraw the writ of execution filed with the sheriff. See: *Price* v *Letros* (1974), 2 O.R. (2d) 292 (C.A.).

vi The Highway Traffic Act, R.S.O. 1970, c 202

138. (1) The driver's licence of every person who fails to satisfy a judgment rendered against him by any court in Ontario that has become final by affirmation on appeal or by expiry without appeal of the time allowed for appeal, for damages on account of injury to or the death of any person, or on account of damage to property, occasioned by a motor vehicle, within fifteen days from the date upon which such judgment became final shall be suspended by the Registrar upon receiving a certificate of such final judgment from the court in which the same is rendered and after fifteen days notice has been sent to such person of intention to suspend his licence unless such judgment is satisfied within such period, and shall remain so suspended and shall not at any time thereafter be renewed, nor shall any new driver's licence be thereafter issued to such person, until such judgment is satisfied or discharged, otherwise than by a discharge in bankruptcy, to the extent of the minimum limits of liability required by *The Insurance Act* in respect of motor vehicle liability policies.

(2) Notwithstanding subsection 1, the Registrar shall not suspend under subsection 1 the driver's licence of any person who is indebted to the Motor Vehicle Accident Claims Fund.

(3) A judgment debtor may, on due notice to the judgment creditor, apply to the court in which the trial judgment was obtained for the privilege of paying the judgment in instalments, and the court may, in its discretion, so order, fixing the amounts and times of payment of the instalments, and while the judgment debtor is not in default in payment of such instalments, he shall be deemed not in default in payment of the judgment, and the Minister may restore the driver's licence of the judgment debtor, but such driver's licence shall again be suspended and remain suspended, as provided in subsection 1, if the Registrar is satisfied of default made by the judgment debtor in compliance with the terms of the court order.

(4) The Lieutenant Governor in Council, upon the report of the Minister that a province or state has enacted legislation similar in effect to subsection 1 and that such legislation extends and applies to judgments rendered and become final against residents of that province or state by any court of competent jurisdiction in Ontario, may declare that the provisions of subsection 1 shall extend and apply to judgments rendered and become final against residents of Ontario by any court of competent jurisdiction in such province or state.

NOTE Orders have been made under s 138(4) declaring that the provisions of subsection 1 extend and apply to judgments rendered against residents of Ontario by the courts of all states of the United States of America, all Canadian provinces, and the Northwest and Yukon Territories.

2 CONSOLIDATION ORDERS

a / The Small Claims Court Act, R.S.O. 1970, c 439

156. (1) A judgment debtor against whom more than two small claims court judgments remain unsatisfied in whole or in part may apply to the judge of the court of the division in which he resides for a consolidation order.

(2) Upon the application, the judgment debtor shall file his own affidavit setting forth,

(*a*) the names and addresses of the creditors who have obtained judgment against him in a small claims court, the date, amount and other particulars of each judgment, and the amount that he owes to each such judgment creditor;

(*b*) the amount of his income from all sources, naming them;

(*c*) his business or occupation, and the address of his employer;

(*d*) a statement of his family or like obligations and of any other relevant facts.

(3) Notice of the time and place of the hearing of the application shall be given by the

judgment debtor to the creditors mentioned in clause a of subsection 2 by registered mail or personal service at least eight days before the day fixed for the hearing, and, upon the hearing, the judgment debtor shall file an affidavit setting forth that such creditors have been given such notice.

(4) Upon the application, the judge may make a consolidation order or dismiss the application.

(5) Before making a consolidation order the judge shall determine the average weekly income of the judgment debtor for the three-month period immediately before the making of the application, making all proper allowances where the occupation is of a seasonal nature, and shall order the following amounts, calculated to the nearest dollar, to be paid into court under the consolidation order, subject always to any variation that, because of extenuating or other special circumstances, the judge considers proper:

1 15 per cent of the average weekly income, where the average weekly income does not exceed $30.

2 20 per cent of the average weekly income, where the average weekly income exceeds $30 and does not exceed $40.

3 25 per cent of the average weekly income, where the average weekly income exceeds $40 and does not exceed $50.

4 30 per cent of the average weekly income, where the average weekly income exceeds $50.

(6) Where the amounts ordered to be paid under subsection 5 have been varied because of extenuating or other special circumstances such amounts shall not be less than 10 per cent of the average weekly income of the judgment debtor.

(7) A consolidation order shall set out,

(a) a list of the small claims court judgments outstanding against the judgment debtor, indicating in each case the date, court and amount and the amount still outstanding;

(b) the amounts to be paid into court by the judgment debtor under the consolidation order; and

(c) the times of such payments.

157. (1) The original consolidation order shall be filed with the clerk of the court in which it was made and a copy thereof, certified by such clerk, may be filed by the judgment debtor in any other small claims court.

(2) Upon the filing of the original consolidation order, the clerk shall open a consolidation account in the name of the judgment debtor and shall credit thereto all payments made under the consolidation order.

158. (1) Where a judgment creditor objects to the amount directed to be paid or to any other judgment creditor being included in the consolidation order, he may apply to the judge for an appointment to determine the matter.

(2) Notice of the appointment shall be sent by registered mail to such persons as the judge directs, and, upon the appointment, the judge shall deal with the matter in a summary manner, and his determination is final.

159. (1) Where a judgment is obtained against the judgment debtor after the date of the consolidation order for a debt incurred before the date of the consolidation order, the judgment creditor may deliver to the clerk of the court in charge of the consolidation order a notice of his judgment, and his name shall forthwith be added to the consolidation order and he shall thereafter share in the distribution under the consolidation order.

(2) Where a judgment is obtained against the judgment debtor after the date of the consolidation order for a debt incurred after the date of the consolidation order, the consolidation order thereupon terminates.

(3) Where the judgment debtor applies for a further consolidation order, the judge shall examine the nature of the further debt or debts incurred and may make such order.

160. A judgment debtor in respect of whom a consolidation order has been made may, either before default has occurred or not later than the tenth day after default has occurred, apply to the judge for a stay of proceedings, and, upon notice of the hearing being sent by registered mail to all judgment creditors, or such of them as the judge directs, the judge shall hear the application and may by order grant such stay of proceedings as he considers fit or he may dismiss the application.

161. (1) Subject to subsection 2, no garnishment summons and no proceedings subsequent to judgment, except an execution against lands, shall be taken or continued against the judgment debtor named therein in a small claims court in which a consolidation order or a certified copy thereof is filed.

(2) Where a judgment debtor is in default for a period of twenty days under a consolidation order, the consolidation order is thereupon terminated, subject to any order under section 160 that may have been made before such date, and any judgment creditor named in the consolidation order may obtain from the clerk of the court in which the consolidation order was made a certificate of termination for the purpose of filing it in any court in which a copy of the consolidation order is filed.

(3) Where a consolidation order has been terminated under subsection 2, the clerk of the court shall notify, by mail, the judgment creditors named in the order of its termination.

(4) Where a consolidation order has terminated under subsection 2, no further consolidation order shall be made in respect of such judgment debtor for a period of one year from the date of such termination.

162. Notwithstanding subsection 1 of section 161, where a judgment is transferred under subsection 3 of section 130 and a consolidation order has been made against the judgment debtor, the clerk of the court shall add the judgment to the consolidation order but only to the extent of $400 where the court is in a county and $800 where the court is in a provisional judicial district.

163. (1) All moneys paid into a consolidation account belong to the judgment creditors named in the consolidation order who shall share *pro rata* in the distribution of the moneys.

(2) The clerk shall distribute the moneys paid into the consolidation account on account of the judgments at least once every six months, and at the time of distribution shall prepare a distribution sheet showing the total amount paid and the distribution thereof.

(3) The distribution shall be on a *pro rata* basis according to the amount of each of the judgments filed with the clerk, or as nearly so as is practicable to the nearest dollar.

(4) The clerk is entitled to a fee of 10 per cent of the amount paid in of which amount 5 per cent shall be charged to the judgment creditors and 5 per cent to the judgment debtor.

(5) The amount of the postage paid shall be deducted from the amounts paid to the judgment creditors.

b / *Re Landry* (1974), 1 O.R. (2d) 107 (Dist. Ct.)

VANNINI, DIST.CT.J.: This is an application for a consolidation order pursuant to s 156(1) of the *Small Claims Courts Act*, R.S.O. 1970, c 439, which provides:

156. (1) A judgment debtor against whom more than two small claims court judgments remain unsatisfied in whole or in part may apply to the judge of the court of the division in which he resides for a consolidation order.

There is only one unsatisfied Small Claims Court judgment against the applicant and three against him in the District Court which are filed in this Small Claims Court pursuant to s 130(3) of the Act ...

Counsel for [the only judgment creditor to appear] opposed the making of a consolidation order on the ground of want of jurisdiction as the judgment debtor had only one unsatisfied judgment in a Small Claims Court whereas the section in question was only applicable when there were 'more than two small claims court judgments' against him.

Counsel for the judgment debtor submits that the three District Court judgments which are filed in this Small Claims Court pursuant to s 130(3) of the Act are by virtue thereof Small Claims Court judgments within the meaning and scope of s 156(1) and that by reason thereof the judgment debtor is entitled to apply for a consolidation order in respect of all of the judgments filed against him in this Small Claims Court.

After a careful consideration of all of the relevant provisions of the *Small Claims Courts Act* bearing upon this jurisdictional issue I have concluded and do hold that a judgment in the Supreme Court or in a County or District Court which is filed in a Small Claims Court pursuant to s 130(3) of the Act is not a Small Claims Court judgment within the meaning and for the purpose of s 156 of the Act.

The Act does not make a Supreme or a County or District Court judgment a Small Claims Court judgment. Each such judgment remains a judgment of the Court in which it was made. Indeed, no action may be taken in a Small Claims Court upon a judgment or order of the Supreme Court or a County Court where execution may issue upon or in respect thereof: s 53(*e*) of the Act.

Of s 53(e), McKeown in *Division Court Handbook*, 2nd ed. (1966), p 38, states:

The purpose of this section is to prevent the extraordinary methods of collection available in Division Courts to be extended to cases where higher court procedure had proven unsatisfactory. The legislature did not intend that any but Division Court judgments should be enforced by judgment summons proceedings.

See, also, Bicknell and Seager, *Division Court Manual*, 5th ed. (1939), pp 72–3, to the same effect.

Section 130(3) of the Act permits the filing of a superior Court judgment in a Small Claims Court so that 'thereafter directions to garnish the wages of the judgment debtor may issue and subsequent proceedings therein be taken as though the direction to the garnish had been issued under a small claims court judgment', in which case any judgment against a garnishee is limited to the amount of the jurisdiction of the Small Claims Court in a personal action.

In short, s 130(3) only makes applicable the simpler and less expensive proceedings of the *Small Claims Courts Act* for the realization of judgments obtained in the superior Courts and it does not make applicable thereto the execution and judgment summons proceedings of that Act. By filing his Superior Court judgment in a Small Claims Court the creditor may avail himself only of the garnishment proceedings of the Small Claims Court and of no other of the proceedings that are otherwise available therein which are available only in respect of a judgment obtained in a Small Claims Court.

However, when a consolidation order is made against a judgment debtor in a Small Claims Court judgment the clerk of that Court is required to add the superior Court judgments filed pursuant to s 130(3) to the consolidation order but only to the extent of the monetary jurisdiction of the particular Small Claims Court.

It is clear, therefore, that a superior Court judgment is not by s 130(3) assimilated thereunder for all purposes of enforcement with a Small Claims Court judgment ...

That s 156(1) is limited to Small Claims Court judgments only is further substantiated by s-s (2) thereof, which provides that upon an application for a consolidation order:

156. (2) ... the judgment debtor shall file his own affidavit setting forth,

(*a*) the names and addresses of the creditors who have obtained judgment against him in a small claims court, the date, amount and other particulars of each judgment, and the amount that he owes to each such judgment creditor.

and by s-s (7), which provides:

(7) A consolidation order shall set out,

(*a*) a list of the small claims court judgments outstanding against the judgment debtor, indicating in each case the date, court and amount and the amount still outstanding;

As with the language of s 156(1) it is equally clear from these requirements that the application for, and the consolidation order itself are not only applicable but restricted to Small Claims Court judgments in excess of two and in whatever and however many such Courts they may have been obtained.

Once a consolidation order is made in respect of such Small Claims Court judgments it is required to be filed with the Clerk of the Court in which it was made and a certified copy thereof may be filed by the judgment debtor in any other Small Claims Court; s 157(1), whereupon 'no garnishment summons and no proceedings subsequent to judgment, except an execution against lands, shall be taken or continued against the judgment debtor named therein *in a small claims court* in which a consolidation order or a certified copy thereof is filed': s 161(1). The emphasis is mine.

Notwithstanding s 161(1), upon the making of a consolidation order against a judgment debtor in a Small Claims Court all superior Court judgments filed pursuant to s 130(3) are required to be added by the Clerk to the consolidation order but only to the extent of the monetary jurisdiction of the particular Small Claims Court in which such judgments are filed: s 162.

All payments made under a consolidation order are paid into the consolidation account opened pursuant to s 157(2) and all moneys so paid therein belong to the judgment creditors named in the consolidation order, including those superior Court judgments which are added thereto pursuant to s 162, and all such judgment creditors are entitled to share *pro rata* in the distribution of these moneys: s 163(1).

A consolidation order may therefore include the following judgments:

1 the Small Claims Court judgments set out on the making of the original consolidation order: s 156(7);
2 the Small Claims Court judgments obtained after the date of the consolidation order for a debt incurred before the date of the consolidation order: s 159(1), and
3 the superior Court judgments filed pursuant to s 130(3): s 162.

...

Notwithstanding this, the full effect of s 161(1) of the Act is to stay in Small Claims Court in which a consolidation order or a certified copy thereof is filed and is outstanding all garnishment summonses and all other proceedings subsequent to judgment, except an execution against lands, against the judgment debtor named in the judgment whether it be a Small Claims Court judgment or a superior Court judgment which is filed pursuant to s 130(3) ...

By the interpretation section of the *Judicature Act*, R.S.O. 1970, c 228, ' "judgment" includes an order' and by s 31 of the *Interpretation Act*, R.S.O. 1970, c 225, the interpretation section of the *Judicature Act* is made to extend 'to all Acts relating to legal matters'. It follows, therefore, that 'judgment' in ss 130(3) and 161(1) relating to consolidation orders includes any order made in the superior Courts for the payment of money ...

In respect of such superior Court judgments and orders ... all proceedings in a Small Claims Court are stayed as long as there is an outstanding consolidation order therein and any proceeding for their enforcement can only be taken in the Courts in which the judgment was obtained or the order was made in the manner provided by law for their enforcement in such Courts ...

In the result, there being only one Small Claims Court judgment against the applicant, this Court is without jurisdiction to make a consolidation order and for this reason the application is dismissed.

Application dismissed.

NOTE Under s 156(4) the granting of a consolidation order is discretionary. For an indication of the circumstances in which that discretion will be exercised against the granting of an order, see *Re Young*, (1974), 4 O.R. (2d) 390 (Small Claims Court). One of the creditors of the applicant for an order was his divorced wife, who had obtained a judgment in the Supreme Court for maintenance of the children of the marriage and had filed it in Small Claims Court. She resisted the consolidation order on the ground that it would enable the debtor to reduce the maintenance payments to a negligible amount. The debtor argued that as the wife had elected to file her judgment in the Small Claims Court, she should be treated like any other creditor in that Court. Gould Co. Ct. J refused the consolidation order in view of the public interest in the maintenance of the children and the complexity of determining the amount due at any particular time under an order for continuing maintenance.

QUESTIONS

1 Do you agree with the interpretation Vannini, Dist. Ct. J. gave to The Small Claims Courts Act in *Re Landry*? Can you reach (and justify), a different interpretation?

2 Should the jurisdictional requirement of 'more than two small claims court judgments ... unsatisfied' be abolished? Why (not)?

3 Should a 'consolidation order' be permitted in respect of one or more judgments of County or Supreme Courts?

4 Suppose that a judgment summons has been served on the debtor, pursuant to s 131 of The Small Claims Court Act, supra. An examination is held in open Court, and at the conclusion of the examination the Judge makes an order 'pursuant to s 131(8) of the said Act,' for the payment by the debtor to the creditor of fifty dollars per month. Can the creditor use information he has gained at the examination and garnish the debtor's bank account? Can he issue execution? Would it make any difference if the debtor was paying at the times specified in the judgment summons order?

NOTE The practice of the small claims courts of the Judicial District of York in such situations is interesting. The courts will permit the creditor to issue an execution against land owned by a judgment debtor (The Small Claims Courts Act, s 126, supra, p 222), but will not permit any steps to be taken under it and will not permit any other method of attempting to satisfy the judgment to be used by the creditor so long as an order made on a judgment summons examination is outstanding.

Is this practice authorized by the Act?

13
Priorities among Creditors

The Creditors' Relief Act provides a scheme for the distribution of money recovered through execution procedures. These funds are shared by the creditor responsible for directing the successful execution, with other eligible creditors of the debtor.

The priorities established by the Act are subject to the extraordinary priorities accorded to 'special creditors', considered in Chapter 14, below.

2 THE LEGISLATION

a / The Execution Act, R.S.O. 1970, c 152

19. (5) Subject to *The Creditor's Relief Act*, the sheriff shall pay over to the party who sued out the execution the money so paid or recovered, or a sufficient sum to discharge the amount directed to be levied, and if, after satisfaction thereof and of the fees, poundage and expenses of the sheriff, a surplus remains, it shall be paid to the party against whom the execution issued.

b / The Creditors' Relief Act, R.S.O. 1970, c 97

3. Subject to this Act, there is no priority among creditors by execution from the Supreme Court or from a county court.

4. (1) A creditor who attaches a debt shall be deemed to do so for the benefit of all creditors of his debtor as well as for himself.

(2) Payment of such debt shall be made to the sheriff of the county in which the garnishee resides, or, if there are more garnishees than one in respect of the same debt, then to the sheriff of the county in which any one of them resides.

(3) This section does not apply to debts attached by proceedings in a small claims court unless before the amount recovered by the garnishment proceedings is actually received by the creditor an execution against the property of the debtor is placed in the hands of the sheriff of such county.

(4) Where money is paid to a sheriff in whose hands there is no execution against the property of the debtor and there is in the hands of the sheriff of another county an execution against the property of the debtor, the court or a judge on the application of the last-mentioned sheriff or of a creditor or of the debtor may direct, on such terms as to costs and otherwise as seem just, that such money be paid over to the last-mentioned sheriff to be distributed by him as if such money had then been paid to him by the garnishee, and the court or judge shall fix the compensation to

be paid to the sheriff by whom the money was received from the garnishee for his services.

(5) Where money that a sheriff is entitled to receive under this section is paid into a small claims court, the sheriff is entitled to demand and receive it from the clerk of the court for the purpose of distributing it under this Act.

(6) An attaching creditor is entitled to share in respect of his claim against the debtor in any distribution made under this Act, but his share shall not exceed the amount recovered by his garnishment proceedings unless he has in due time placed an execution or a certificate given under this Act in the sheriff's hands.

(7) The sheriff is entitled to poundage upon money received and distributed by him under this section at the rate of $1\frac{1}{4}$ per cent and no more.

(8) If an attached debt that the sheriff is entitled to receive or any part of it is received by the attaching creditor, the sheriff may recover it from him; but a clerk of a small claims court is not liable for making payment to the creditor unless at the time of payment he has notice that there is an execution against the property of the debtor in the sheriff's hands.

(9) This section does not apply to an attachment made under section 30 of The Family Law Reform Act, 1978.

5. (1) Where a sheriff levies money under an execution against the property of a debtor or receives money in respect of a debt that has been attached or sold under section 15 of *The Absconding Debtors Act*, he shall forthwith make an entry in Form 1 in a book to be kept in his office, and such book shall be open to the public for inspection without charge.

(2) The money shall thereafter be distributed rateably among all execution creditors and other creditors whose executions or certificates given under this Act were in the sheriff's hands at the time of the levy or receipt of the money or who deliver their executions or certificates to the sheriff within one month from the entry, subject to the provisions hereinafter contained as to the retention of dividends in the case of contested claims, and to the payment of the costs of the creditor under whose execution the amount was made, and subject also to subsection 6 of section 4, and, as respects money recovered by garnishment proceedings, subject to the payment thereout to the creditor who obtained the attaching order of his costs of such proceedings.

(3) Subsection 2 does not apply to money received by a sheriff as the proceeds of a sale of property by him under an interpleader order; but upon the determination of the interpleader proceeding in favour of the creditors the money, whether in the sheriff's hands or in court pending such determination, shall, subject to subsection 4, be distributed by the sheriff among the creditors contesting the adverse claim.

(4) Where proceedings are taken by a sheriff for relief under any provisions relating to interpleader, those creditors only who are parties thereto and who agree to contribute *pro rata* in proportion to the amount of their executions or certificates to the expense of contesting any adverse claim are entitled to share in any benefit that may be derived from the contestation of such claim so far as is necessary to satisfy their executions or certificates.

(5) The judge making the interpleader order may direct that one creditor has the carriage of the interpleader proceedings on behalf of all creditors interested, and the costs thereof, as between solicitor and client, are a first charge upon the money or goods that may be found by the proceedings to be applicable upon the executions or certificates.

(6) Upon an interpleader application the judge may allow to other creditors who desire to take part in the contest a reasonable time in which to place their executions or certificates in the sheriff's hands upon such terms as to costs and otherwise as are considered just.

(7) Where the sheriff, subsequent to the entry but within the month, levies a further amount from the property of a debtor or receives money in respect of a debt that has been attached or sold, it shall be dealt with as if it had been levied or received before the entry.

(8) If, after the month, a further amount is so levied or received, a new notice shall be entered and the distribution to be made of the amount so levied or received and of any further amount levied or received within a month of the entry of the last-mentioned entry shall be governed by the entry thereof in accordance with the foregoing provisions of this section and so from time to time as further amounts are so levied or received.

(9) Where a creditor has shared in a previous distribution, he is entitled to share in a subsequent one only in respect of the amount remaining due to him after crediting what he has received in a previous distribution.

(10) In distributing money under this section creditors who have executions against goods or lands only or against goods and lands are entitled to share rateably with all others and money realized under execution against either goods or lands or against both, or under an attaching order.

(11) Subject to subsection 6 of section 4, a creditor is not entitled to share in the distribution unless by the delivery of an execution or otherwise under this Act he has established a claim against the debtor either alone or jointly with some other person.

(12) Where money in the hands of the sheriff for distribution is the proceeds of the property of an absconding debtor against whom an order of attachment has been issued under *The Absconding Debtors Act*, the period mentioned in subsection 2 is two months, and subsection 8 shall be read as if the words 'the month' in the first line were 'the two months'.

6. (1) If a debtor permits an execution issued against him under which any of his goods or chattels are seized by a sheriff to remain unsatisfied in the sheriff's hands until within two days of the time fixed by the sheriff for the sale thereof, or for twenty days after the seizure, or allows an execution against his lands to remain unsatisfied for nine months after it has been placed in the sheriff's hands, the proceedings hereinafter authorized may be taken by other creditors or claimants in respect of debts that are overdue.

(2) When a sale has taken place under an execution, the proceedings hereinafter authorized may be taken by any creditor of the execution debtor even though his claim is not then due.

7. (1) An affidavit in Form 2 of the debt and the particulars thereof may be made in duplicate by the creditor, or by one of the creditors in case of a joint debt, or by a person cognizant of the facts.

(2) Before or simultaneously with the filing with the clerk of the county court of the affidavit, there shall be filed with him a certificate of the sheriff, or an affidavit, showing that such proceedings have been had against the debtor as entitle the creditor to proceed under this Act.

(3) The claimant shall serve on the debtor one of the duplicates and a notice in Form 3.

(4) Where the affidavit and notice are to be served out of Ontario, the judge shall by order fix the time after which the next step may be taken by the claimant as hereinafter provided.

9. (1) Where the claim is not contested in the manner hereinafter mentioned, after ten days from the day of service, or after the time mentioned in the order provided for by subsection 4 of section 7, as the case may be, on the application of the claimant and his filing proof of due service of the affidavit and notice, or, where the claim is contested, upon the determination of a dispute in favour of the claimant, either in whole or in part, the clerk of the county court shall deliver to the creditor a certificate in Form 5 and, where the claim is disputed as to a part only, the claimant may elect, by a writing filed with the clerk, to abandon such part and is entitled to a certificate as to the residue.

(2) Upon delivery of the certificate to the sheriff the claimant shall be deemed to be an execution creditor within the meaning of this Act, and is entitled to share in any distribution as if he had delivered an execution to the sheriff, and the certificate binds the lands and goods of the debtor in the same manner as an execution, subject, however, to the debt being afterwards disputed by a creditor as hereinafter provided.

(3) For the purpose of interpleader proceedings the certificate shall be deemed to be an execution.

(4) If the certificate is obtained by a solicitor, his name and address shall be endorsed thereon, and, if obtained by the claimant in person, there shall be endorsed thereon a statement of some place in or within three miles of the county town of the county in which the proceedings are being taken at which service may be made upon him, and, in default thereof, service of any notice, paper or document may be made upon the claimant by sending it by registered mail addressed to him at the county town.

(5) On receiving the certificate the sheriff shall make a further seizure of the property of the debtor to the amount of the debt so claimed and the sheriff's fees, and so from time to time in case further certificates are received.

(6) A certificate remains in force for three years from the date thereof, but may from time to time be renewed in the same manner as an execution.

(7) Notwithstanding the expiry of an execution or certificate before the termination of the month during which a notice of money having been levied or received is required to be entered, the execution or certificate, as to any money levied or received during such month, shall be deemed to be in full force and effect.

10. (1) The claim may be contested by the debtor or by a creditor of the debtor.

12. (1) Where a claim is contested by a creditor after a certificate has been placed in the sheriff's hands, the sheriff, unless the judge otherwise orders, shall levy as if the contestation had not been made, and shall, until the determination of the contestation, retain in the bank the amount that would be apportionable to the claim if valid, and shall, as soon after the expiry of the month as is practicable, distribute the residue of the money made among those entitled thereto.

(2) The claimant whose claim is contested may apply to the judge for an order allowing his claim and determining the amount, and, if he does not make such application within eight days after receiving notice of the contestation or within such further time, if any, as the judge allows, he shall be taken to have abandoned his claim.

(3) Where the contestant is a creditor and there is reason to believe that the contestation is not being carried on in good faith, any other creditor may apply for an order permitting him to intervene in the contestation.

13. (1) The judge may determine any question in dispute in a summary manner or may direct an action to be brought or an issue to be tried with or without a jury in any court and in any county for the determination thereof, and may make such order as to the costs of the proceedings as he considers just.

15. (1) The clerk of the county court shall keep a book in which, before giving a certificate or issuing an execution for a claim, he shall enter the following particulars with reference to every claim in respect of which he gives a certificate or issues an execution:

1 The names of the claimant and the debtor.

2 The date of the entry.

3 The amount of the debt, exclusive of costs.

4 The amount of costs.

5 If the proceedings have been set aside, that fact, and shortly the reason therefor.

(2) The entry has, subject to this act, the effect of and is a final judgment of the court for the debt and costs.

16. A creditor who has recovered a judgment in a small claims court against the debtor may deliver to the sheriff a certificate, under the hand of the clerk and the seal of the small claims court, of the amount of his judgment and of the costs to which he is entitled, and the certificate so delivered shall have the same effect, for the purposes of this Act, as if the creditor had delivered to the sheriff an execution from a county court.

17. Where a creditor has taken in one county the prescribed proceedings in respect of his claim and desires to establish his claim for the purposes of this Act in another county, he may do so by obtaining from the clerk of the county court of the county first mentioned another certificate in Form 5, and delivering it to the sheriff of such other county, and the delivery of the certificate to the sheriff has the same effect in such other county from the time of the delivery thereof as if the certificate had been issued by the clerk of the county court of such other county upon the proceedings therein.

18. A creditor entitled to obtain a certificate from the clerk of a county court may also sue out an execution into any county in the same manner as on an ordinary judgment; but this does not prejudice the right of any other creditor to contest the claim of the first-mentioned creditor under this Act.

19. (1) Where a claim is contested in one county, the decision thereon shall, as between the parties to the contestation, determine the amount of the claim for the purposes of this Act and in all other counties in which the claim is filed, and the certificate of the clerk of the county court of the county in which the contestation has taken place as to the result thereof is sufficient evidence of the decision.

21. (1) Where proceedings have been taken against a debtor under *The Absconding Debtors Act* and his property has been attached under an order of attachment before an execution has been placed in the hands of the sheriff and the money levied is the proceeds of such property or a part thereof, the cost of the order of attachment, or, if there are more than one, the one first placed in the sheriff's hands and the proceedings thereon have priority over the claim of all other creditors.

(2) Where an attaching creditor is entitled to priority under subsection 1, the priority provided for by subsection 2 of section 5 shall not be given to the execution creditor. s 21.

23. Where there is in a court a fund belonging to an execution debtor or to which he is entitled, it or a sufficient part thereof to meet the executions and certificates in the sheriff's hands may, on the application of the sheriff or any person interested, be paid over to the sheriff, and it shall be deemed to be money levied under execution within the meaning of this Act.

24. Where a judgment creditor obtains the appointment of a receiver by way of equitable execution of property of his debtor, the receiver shall pay into court the money received by him by virtue of his receivership, and it is subject to section 23, but the creditor is entitled to be paid thereout the costs of and incidental to the receivership order and the proceedings thereon in priority to the claims of all other creditors.

25. (1) If the sheriff does not find property of a debtor leviable under the executions and certificates in his hands sufficient to pay the same in full, but finds property or the proceeds thereof in the hands of the bailiff of a small claims court under an execution or attachment against the debtor, the sheriff shall demand and obtain them from the bailiff, who shall forthwith deliver them to the sheriff with a copy of every execution and attachment in his hands against the debtor and a memorandum showing the amount to be levied under the execution, including the bailiff's fees, and the date upon which each execution or attachment was received by him.

(2) If the bailiff fails to deliver any of such property or the proceeds thereof, he shall pay

double the value of that which is retained, which may be recovered by the sheriff from him with costs of suit, and shall be accounted for by the sheriff as part of the estate of the debtor.

(3) The costs and disbursements of the bailiff are a first charge upon such property or the proceeds thereof and shall be paid by the sheriff to the bailiff upon demand after being taxed by the small claims court clerk.

(4) The sheriff shall distribute the proceeds among the creditors entitled to share in the distribution, and the small claims court execution creditors are entitled without further proof to stand in the same position as creditors whose executions are in the sheriff's hands.

26. Where the amount levied by the sheriff is not sufficient to pay the executions and certificates with costs in full, the money shall be applied to the payment rateably of such debts and costs of the creditors, after retaining the sheriff's fees including poundage, and after payment in full of the taxed costs and the costs of the execution to the creditor at whose instance and under whose execution the seizure and levy were made where he is entitled to priority therefor under this Act.

29. (1) Where money is made under an execution, it shall be taken to have been made under all the executions and certificates entitled to the benefit thereof, and, upon payment being made to the person entitled under any such execution or certificate, the sheriff shall endorse thereon a memorandum of the amount so paid, but he shall not, except on the request of the party who issued the execution, or by direction of the court out of which the same issued, or of a judge thereof, return the execution until it has been fully satisfied or has expired, in which latter case the sheriff shall make a formal return of the amount made thereunder.

(2) The like proceedings may be taken to compel payment by the sheriff of money payable in respect to a certificate as can now be had to compel the return by the sheriff of an execution.

30. Pending the distribution, the sheriff shall keep, in the book mentioned in section 5, a statement in Form 6 showing,

(a) the amounts levied or received and the dates of levy or receipt;

(b) each execution, certificate or order in his hands at the time of making the entry in Form 1, or subsequently received during the month, the amount thereof, for debt and costs, and the date of receipt, and such statement shall be amended from time to time as additional amounts are levied or received or further executions, certificates or orders are received.

31. The sheriff shall at all times without fee answer any reasonable question that he is asked orally respecting the property of the debtor by a creditor or any one acting on the creditor's behalf, and shall facilitate the obtaining by him of full information respecting the property and the probable dividend to be realized therefrom in his county, or any other information in connection with the property that the creditor may reasonably desire to obtain.

32. (1) Where at the time for distribution the money is insufficient to pay all claims in full, the sheriff shall first prepare for examination by the debtor and his creditors a list of the creditors entitled to share in the distribution, with the amount due to each for principal, interest and costs.

(2) The list shall be so arranged as to show the amount payable to each creditor and the total amount to be distributed, and the sheriff shall deliver or send by registered mail a copy of the list to each creditor or his solicitor.

(3) If within eight days after all the copies have been delivered or posted, or within such further time as the judge may allow, no objection is made as provided by this Act, the sheriff shall make distribution forthwith pursuant to such list.

(4) If objection is made, the sheriff shall forthwith distribute rateably so much of the money made, and among such persons, as will not interfere with the effect of the objection in case it should be allowed.

(5) Any person affected by the proposed scheme of distribution may contest it by giving

within the time mentioned in subsection 3, a notice in writing to the sheriff stating his objection to the scheme and the grounds thereof.

(6) The contestant shall within eight days thereafter apply to the judge for an order adjudicating upon the matter in dispute, otherwise the contestation shall be taken to be abandoned.

(7) The contestant shall, within the time mentioned in subsection 6, obtain from the judge an appointment for hearing and determining the matter in dispute.

(8) A copy of the appointment and a notice in writing in Form 7 of the objections stating the grounds thereof shall be served by the contestant upon the debtor, unless he is the contestant, and upon the creditors or such of them as the judge may direct.

(9) The judge may determine any question in dispute in a summary manner, or may direct an action to be brought or an issue to be tried with or without a jury in any court and in any county for the determination thereof, and may make such order as to the costs of the proceedings as he considers just, subsections 2 and 3 of section 13 apply.

(10) Where a claimant is held to be not entitled or to be entitled to part only of his claim, the money retained pending the contestation or the portion as to which the claimant has failed shall be distributed among the creditors who would have been entitled to it as it would have been distributed had the claim in respect thereof not been made.

(11) Where a debtor has executed a mortgage or other charge, otherwise valid, upon his property or a part thereof after the receipt of an execution by the sheriff and before distribution, such mortgage or charge shall not prevent the sheriff from selling the property under an execution or certificate placed in his hands before distribution as if such mortgage or charge had not been given, nor prevent creditors whose executions or certificates are subsequent thereto from sharing in the distribution; but, in distributing the money realized from the sale of such property, the sheriff shall deduct and pay to the person entitled thereto the amount of such mortgage or charge from the amount that would otherwise be payable out of the proceeds of such property to such subsequent creditors.

(12) In the case provided for in subsection 11, the sheriff shall prepare a separate scheme of distribution of the proceeds of the encumbered property without reference to the mortgage or charge, and from the dividends payable according to such scheme to subsequent creditors there shall be deducted the amount of the mortgage or charge, and the amount so deducted shall be paid to the encumbrancer.

37. Where there are in the sheriff's hands several executions and certificates and there does not appear to be sufficient property to pay all and his own fees, he may apply for an order attaching any debt owing to the execution debtor by any person resident in the county of the sheriff, whether the debt is owing by such person alone or jointly with another person resident or not resident in the county, and to procure an order and to obtain and enforce payment of the debt the sheriff may take the same proceedings as a creditor, and in such case an execution may be directed to him in the same manner as if the attachment were by a creditor, and the proceeds of the debt attached shall be dealt with and distributed in the same manner as if he had realized the proceeds under execution.

NOTE

i In a distribution among creditors, the sheriff ought to include all creditors who have filed writs of execution. A court order for distribution obtained by a receiver to 'subsisting writ holders' was held to include all creditors whose writs identified the debtor with reasonable accuracy, in *Giguere* v *Pilon* (1976), 66 D.L.R. (3d) 693 (Alta. s.c.) Where one creditor had been overpaid through neglect of the sheriff to include other creditors in a distribution under a receivership, the court had the power to order a subsequent distribution to be adjusted accordingly.

ii Section 3 of The Creditor's Relief Act states that it alone establishes priorities amongst creditors. However, Section 3 of The Wages Act, R.S.O. 1970, c 486 provides:

3. All persons who, at the time of the seizure by the sheriff or who within one month prior thereto, were in the employment of the execution debtor, and who become entitled to share in the distribution of money levied out of the property of a debtor within the meaning of *The Creditors' Relief Act* are entitled to be paid out of such money the wages due to them by the execution debtor, not exceeding three months' wages, in priority to the claims of the other creditors of the execution debtor, and are entitled to share *pro rata* with such other creditors as to the residue, if any, of their claims.

Section 14 of The Employment Standards Act, S.O. 1974, c 112 provides:

14. Notwithstanding the provisions of any other Act and except upon a distribution made by a trustee under the *Bankruptcy Act* (Canada), wages shall have priority to the claims or rights and be paid in priority to the claims or rights, including the claims or rights of the Crown, of all preferred, ordinary or general creditors of the employer to the extent of $2,000 for each employee.

Which statute is to be believed? See the discussion of this problem in Chapter 14, infra pp 460–4.

iii Recall (or re-read) Rules 600–606 (pp 305–6 supra). The garnishee is directed by the Rules to pay debts owed to the judgment debtor into court. However s 4 of The Creditors' Relief Act requires all attached debts to be paid to the sheriff of the county in which the garnishee resides (except in the case of money paid into the small claims court). The garnishee order form (below), directs payment into court. What is the garnishee to do? If the Act takes priority, does the Rule discharging the debt as between garnishee and debtor protect the garnishee who has paid to the sheriff rather than into court (R.606)?

In *Imperial Bank of Canada* v *Boyd* (1918), 14 O.W.N. 230 (S.C.), the Act was held to determine what procedure the garnishee ought to follow. Relevant statutory provisions today include:

The Judicature Act, R.S.O. 1970, c 228

114. (10) Subject to the approval of the Lieutenant Governor in Council, the Rules Committee may at any time amend or repeal any of the rules and may make any further or additional rules for carrying this Act into effect, and in particular for, ...

    (*g*) regulating generally any matters relating to the practice and procedure of the courts or to the duties of the officers thereof, or to the costs of proceedings therein, and every other matter deemed expedient for better attaining the ends of justice, advancing the remedies of suitors and carrying into effect this Act and all other Acts respecting the courts ...

    (11) Where provisions in respect of practice or procedure are contained in any statute, rules

may be made modifying such provisions to any extent that is considered necessary for adapting them to the general practice and usage of the court, unless that power is expressly excluded.

(12) Any provisions relating to the payment, transfer or deposit into, or in, or out of any court of any money or property, or to the dealing therewith, shall, for the purposes of this section, be deemed to be provisions relating to practice and procedure.

Supreme Court of Ontario, Rules of Practice, R.R.O. 1970, Reg. 545.

Rule 817

(1) The forms contained in the Appendix hereto shall be used with such variations or modifications as circumstances may require, and any variance therefrom, not being in matter of substance does not affect their regularity.

(2) The provisions contained in the form prescribed shall be deemed to be authorized by these rules.

Form 78

A.B., Judgment Creditor

and

C.D., Judgment Debtor

and

E.F., Garnishee

Upon the application of ...., and upon reading the affidavit of ...., filed, and upon hearing the solicitor [*or* counsel] for ....;

1. It is ordered that all debts owing or accruing due from the above-named garnishee to the above-named judgment debtor be attached.

2. And it is further ordered that the said garnishee attend before the .... in chambers (*or as the case may be*) on .... day, the .... day of ...., 19............, at .... o'clock in the .... noon, to show cause why the debt due from him to the said judgment debtor should not be paid into court to the credit of this matter.

[*Amended*, O.Reg. 520/71, s 9.]

Form 80

Garnishment Order—Final

(Rule 601)

Upon the application of .... and upon reading the affidavit of ...., filed, and the order herein dated the .... day of ...., 19............, whereby it was ordered that all debts owing or accruing due from the above-named garnishee to the above-named judgment debtor should be attached, and upon hearing the solicitor [*or* counsel] for ....

1. It is ordered that the said garnishee do forthwith pay the debt due from him to the said judgment debtor into Court to the credit of this matter.

2. And it is further ordered that the costs of the judgment creditor of this application be first paid from the said money and that the balance be then paid to the sheriff of the .... of .... to be dealt with under *The Creditors' Relief Act*.

[*Amended*, O.Reg. 520/71, s 11.]

iv Subsections (11) and (12) of s 32 present another problem. By s 10 of The Execution Act, lands are bound from the time of delivery of the *fi.fa* to the sheriff. A mortgage on the land given by the debtor after receipt of one writ of execution does not prejudice the rights of the execution creditor. However the debtor can mortgage such interest as he has subject to the rights of the creditor. What happens when an execution is filed, a mortgage is given, a sale takes place under the execution, and then another creditor is entitled to share in the distribution of the proceeds of the execution sale, by virtue of s 5(2) of The Creditor's Relief Act? Assume that an execution authorizing the making of $10,000 is filed. Then a mortgage securing a loan of $6,000 is given by the debtor. Executions for $5,000 and $5,000 are then filed. One of the latter executions is with respect to a claim for wages of $5,000. The sheriff's sale of the land yields $15,000. How should the sheriff divide the money on hand?

3 SOME CASES

a / *Union Bank of Canada* v *Taylor* (1915), 33 O.L.R. 255 (S.C.)

BOYD, C.: The moneys to be distributed in this case were made available for the satisfaction of creditors and incumbrancers by the intervention of the Court in a suit to have a transfer of the property (land) declared void as to creditors. The land was sold subject to the claims of prior mortgagees – prior, that is, to the date of the first execution. The proceeds of the sale are to be distributed among those entitled according to their priorities. Those entitled may be classified thus: first in time, execution creditors having charges on the land; second, the claim of La Banque Nationale under a subsequent mortgage; thirdly, a group of creditors whose executions are later in date than this mortgage; fourthly, another later mortgage to one Douglas and another to one Bickell; fifthly, another group, still later in date, of execution creditors; then, a fourth subsequent mortgage to the Traders Bank; and lastly, another group of creditors whose executions are in the hands of the Sheriff. The amount realised by the sale is enough to pay in full the first group of executions, also the bank mortgage, and probably the next group of execution creditors. The Master has in this way settled the priorities and the manner of payment. It is objected on the appeal that the Master should have followed the directions given to Sheriffs in the Creditors Relief Act, R.S.O. 1914, ch. 81, sec. 33, sub-secs. 11 and 12. The meaning imputed to that statute is that the groups of execution creditors should be gathered in one scheme of distribution (irrespective of the different mortgages) and the proceeds of the sale divided ratably among all as on an equal footing. The result would thus probably be that the bank mortgage would be paid in full, and the execution creditors prior to this mortgage would receive a fraction of their charges. One obvious answer to this is, that the first execution creditors are prior to that mortgage, and the second execution creditors are subsequent to that mortgage, and so have their charge on a different estate in the land, lessened in value by the amount of the mortgage.

The Act does not appear to contemplate such a state of things as here exists: a succession of mortgages registered at different dates with groups of executions in the intervals between the different mortgages. The effect of the Act appears to be to pay a subsequent mortgage in full by reducing the amount of a prior execution, and this gives to a subsequent mortgage a better status as against a prior execution charged on the lands than existed when the mortgage transaction was effected between the owner and the mortgagee. If this is the meaning and result of the Act, I do not feel disposed to extend its methods to the distribution of assets in this Court.

I do not think the analogy of the statute should be imported into these equitable proceedings. If the bank mortgage had been enforced by suit, the subsequent executions would have been wiped out if the creditors had not redeemed; and, if foreclosure ensued, that would leave the prior executions in full force. When the mortgage was made, it was subject to the existing executions, and there was no equity to have that mortgage paid out of the land in priority to the prior charges. The course of the Court is well settled and is carefully expounded in the cases cited and followed by the Master of *Roach* v *McLachlan* (1892), 19 A.R. 496, and *Breithaupt* v *Marr* (1893), 20 A.R. 689.

The appeal is dismissed with costs.

b / *Benjamin Moore & Co. Ltd.* v *Finnie*, [1954] O.W.N. 772 (Co. Ct.)

LANG CO. CT. J.: This is a contestation by Benjamin Moore & Co. Limited of a schedule of distribution under The Creditors' Relief Act, R.S.O. 1950, c 78, prepared by the Sheriff of the County of Waterloo under date of 1st June 1954.

On 13th January 1954 the contestant filed in the sheriff's office a writ of execution in the above case in the sum of $4,263.66 and $61.75 costs. Between that date and 20th January 1954 a notice of seizure of moneys in the hands of Mr. A.W.A. White allegedly owing to the defendant was served on him, and on 7th May 1954 Mr. White paid to the sheriff the sum of $3,628.64 pursuant to the notice. On the same date the sheriff made an entry in his book in accordance with the provisions of s 5(1) of The Creditors' Relief Act. In the meantime ten other creditors had obtained judgment against the above-named defendant and had deposited executions in the sheriff's hands, ranging from 24th March to 22nd April 1954. The sheriff in his statement of distribution, after deducting his own fees and expenses and giving priority to the costs of the contestant, who was the first execution creditor, proposed to divide the balance *pro rata* among all the execution creditors.

The plaintiff served notice contesting the proposed scheme of distribution on the ground that the contestant was entitled to all the moneys by virtue of the provisions of s 5(2) of The Creditors' Relief Act. Subsections 1 and 2 of s 5 read as follows:

(1) Where a sheriff levies money under an execution against the property of a debtor, or receives money in respect of a debt which has been attached or sold under section 15 of *The Absconding Debtors Act*, he shall forthwith make an entry (Form 1) in a book to be kept in his office, and such book shall be open to the public for inspection without charge.

(2) The money shall thereafter be distributed rateably among all execution creditors and other creditors whose executions or certificates given under this Act were in the sheriff's hands at the time of the levy or receipt of the money, or who deliver their executions or certificates to the sheriff within one month from the entry ...

Counsel for the contestant based his contention entirely on the meaning of the word 'levy'. He argued that the words 'seizure' and 'levy' were synonymous, and that the levy took place and was complete on the date of the seizure, that is, on or before 20th January 1954, and that since no other executions were in the hands of the sheriff within one month from 20th January the plaintiff was therefore entitled to the entire moneys in the sheriff's hands.

The judgment in *Trust and Loan Company* v *Cook* (1910), 3 Sask. L.R. 210, 14 W.L.R. 727, is authority for the proposition that money paid to the sheriff by a mortgagee in order to secure the discharge and release of an execution is not money levied, and that there can be no levy without a seizure. There are many cases that are of assistance in determining what is a levy. In *Badiuk* v *Moore*, [1929] 3 W.W.R. 115, [1930] 1 D.L.R. 47, there was a seizure, a sale was advertised for 15th June and moneys were paid by the debtor to the sheriff on 12th June. It was contended that 'levy' included both seizure and sale and that if there was no sale there was no levy. Ford J. said at pp. 116–7:

This argument is unsound in my opinion. The money was not paid to the sheriff because of the order for sale but by the compulsion of the seizure and the means taken to realize. The money was therefore 'levied' within the meaning of *The Creditors' Relief Act* and there being another execution in the sheriff's hands against the property of the debtor the sheriff must act under that statute by the plain terms of which all priority among creditors by execution is abolished. If authority were needed reference may be made to *Mortimore* v *Cragg* (1878), 3 C.P.D. 216, 47 L.J.Q.B. 348. In that case Brett L.J. said:

'A levy in its legal meaning seems to me to be where goods are seized and money is obtained by the compulsion of the seizure, and does not necessarily comprise "sale" at all,' and again this learned Judge says:

'There is a "levy" when anything is obtained by the compulsion of seizure, although there is no sale.'

There is nothing in either *Trust and Loan Co.* v *Cook*, [*supra*] nor in *Terminal Grain Co.* v *Soderberg*, [1925] 1 W.W.R. 9, differing from this view.

Stroud's Judicial Dictionary, 2nd ed. 1903, at p 1088 (vol. 2), cites numerous cases on the meaning of the word 'levy', all of which indicate that to levy means to collect or exact or obtain moneys as a result of a seizure. It therefore follows that the sheriff in this case did not complete the levy until 7th May, the date on which he received the money as a result of the seizure made on or about 20th January. He made an entry in the book pursuant to The Creditors' Relief Act on 7th May. All creditors who had executions filed in his hands within one month after 7th May are entitled to receive their *pro rata* share on distribution.

I find that the sheriff's statement of distribution is properly prepared in accordance with the provisions of The Creditors' Relief Act.

It is interesting also to look at Form 1 under the Act, which form is referred to in s 5(1). That subsection provides that where a sheriff levies moneys 'he shall forthwith make an entry (Form 1) in a book to be kept in his office'. It would be impossible for the sheriff to complete this form until he had received moneys, because the first two lines of the form read as follows: 'I have on this day in may hands for distribution under The Creditors' Relief Act among the creditors of C.D. the sum of $............' It could not be done on the date of the seizure unless the moneys were also received on the same date. The Act is based on the assumption that the levy is complete on the date of the receipt of the moneys and not before.

The contestation will therefore be dismissed, and the schedule of distribution as prepared by the sheriff is confirmed. All parties will pay their own costs of the contestation.
Contestation dismissed.

c / *Re Sudbury Daily Star Ltd.* v *Moxon's Furniture Ltd. et al.*, [1955] 5 D.L.R. 590 (Ont. Dist. Ct.)

ST. AUBIN D.C.J.: In this application the plaintiff contests the proposed scheme of distribution dated July 6, 1955, prepared by the Sheriff for the District of Sudbury and delivered to the creditors of Thomas Moxon, all of which pursuant to s 32 of the *Creditors' Relief Act*, R.S.O. 1950, c 78, and the said plaintiff submits that it should be included and shown as sharing in the said scheme for the amount of its judgment and costs.

The grounds alleged in the notice of contestation are that an order under the *Absconding Debtors Act*, R.S.O. 1950, c 1, having been made against the said Thomas Moxon and filed with the Sheriff on July 12, 1955, in the action of *Journal Printing Co.* v *Moxon*, the money in the hands of the said Sheriff should be distributed ratably among all execution creditors who delivered their executions to him within 2 months from the entry mentioned in s 5(1) of the *Creditors' Relief Act*.

The said notice of contestation, with the appointment, returnable on July 26, 1955, was duly served upon all execution creditors and various parties were represented by counsel upon the hearing which took place before me on August 2, 1955, when I reserved my decision.

The facts in chronological order are as follows:

April 12, 1955: Seizure by Sheriff of stock-in-trade of Thomas Moxon, at 12½ Elgin St. N., Sudbury, under an execution against the judgment debtor's property in the action of *Robert Syme* v *Moxon, et al*.

May 30, 1955: Sale of the said stock-in-trade by the Sheriff.

June 3, 1955: Proceeds of sale received by the Sheriff and entry made pursuant to s 5(1) of the *Creditors' Relief Act*.

July 4, 1955: Last day allowed by Sheriff for the filing of executions, certificates or orders as the one-month period provided by s 5(1) fell on a Sunday, July 3, 1955.

July 5, 1955: Default judgment obtained by the present applicant against the above-named defendants for $7,086.20 and costs, $98, and certificate filed with the Sheriff.

July 6, 1955: Proposed scheme of distribution with reference to creditors entitled to share as of and including July 4, 1955.

July 12, 1955: Order made by His Honour Judge J.M. Cooper under the *Absconding Debtors Act* against Thomas Moxon and filed with the Sheriff in the said action of *Journal Printing Co.* v *Moxon* to 'attach the furniture possessed to the use and benefit of the said Thomas Moxon now stored with Provincial Police Constable George Foster at the Village of Warren, in the District of Sudbury ... to satisfy the plaintiff a certain debt amounting to $200.00 with costs of suit, and to satisfy the debts and demands of such other creditors of the said Thomas Moxon as shall duly place their orders of attachment in the hands of the said Sheriff or otherwise lawfully notify him of their claims and duly prosecute the same'.

July 14, 1955: Notice of contestation filed and served by the Sudbury Daily Star Ltd.

It is argued by counsel for the said contestant that as a result of the order made against Thomas Moxon under the *Absconding Debtors Act* that s-s (12) of s 5 of the *Creditors' Relief Act* applies and the period of time within which the executions or certificates must be placed in the Sheriff's hands is extended to two months instead of one month.

Mr. Valin on behalf of his clients (other counsel for creditors included in the scheme of distribution concurring) argues that the said subsection (12) does not apply because Moxon was not an absconding debtor when the Sheriff made the seizure and the levy from which he realized the moneys now available for distribution: that the execution creditors who filed their claims with the Sheriff prior to and including July 4th alone have the right to share in the said distribution; the rights of these execution creditors had 'crystallized or vested' and they were entitled to receive their distributive share on July 5th and those rights could not in any way be defeated by the order made only on July 12th.

Counsel have not been able to cite any decision in point and I have been unable to find any reported cases in which s 5(12) has been interpreted by the Courts. However, Mr. Valin did cite the following cases: *Union Bank* v *Taylor* (1915), 23 D.L.R. 679, 33 O.L.R. 255; *Benjamin Moore & Co.* v *Finnie*, [1955] 1 D.L.R. 557, [1954] O.W.N. 772, and *Maxwell* v *Scharfe* (1889), 18 O.R.

529, the latter two cases being of some assistance. These are authorities for the proposition that the levy under an execution takes place when the property of the debtor is sold. Upon such levy it is the duty of the Sheriff forthwith to make the entry under s 5(1) and subsequently to make distribution as provided by and in strict compliance with the *Creditors' Relief Act*. Armour c.j. at p 531 of the last-mentioned case says: 'The sale of the goods changed the property in the goods from the execution debtor to the purchaser, and discharged the execution debtor *pro tanto*, and the sale was complete when the execution debtor lost his property in the goods which became bested in those by whom they were bought, and the sheriff thereupon became responsible to the execution creditor for their price.'

In the matter before me the Sheriff became responsible to the execution creditors for the moneys received on June 3, 1955, and only the creditors whose executions or certificates were in the Sheriff's hands on or before July 4th were entitled to distribution on July 5th. In my opinion the order of July 12th, made under the *Absconding Debtors Act*, could not, and did not, effect any change in the period of time provided for by s 5(2) of the *Creditors' Relief Act*. A careful consideration of s 5(2) in the light of the provisions of the *Absconding Debtors Act* leads me to the conclusion that only the real or personal property of which the absconding debtor is possessed at the time of the making of the order may be seized and taken under an order of attachment under that Act for the satisfying of his debts, and when the order was made on July 12th the property of which the Sheriff still had the proceeds was no longer possessed by the debtor and had not been so possessed since at least the sale on May 30th, when the property became that of the purchaser.

It seems to me that the period of 2 months provided for by s 5(12) applies only to moneys that are proceeds of the property of an absconding debtor seized and taken under an order of attachment for the satisfying of his debts under the *Absconding Debtors Act*, and does not apply to a levy under executions such as in the present proceedings.

It is also of some importance to note that the property attached by the order of July 12th, that is, the furniture stored at Warren which was to be seized and taken, was indeed not the property which was sold and levied upon by the Sheriff on May 30th.

The contestation of the Sudbury Daily Star Ltd., must therefore fail and the distribution shall be made according to the scheme prepared by the Sheriff and forming part of ex. 2 filed.

The point in issue being a new one, and no costs having been demanded by any of the parties, none will be allowed.

Contestation rejected.

4 PROPOSALS FOR REFORM

QUESTIONS Should all unsecured creditors be treated equally, without regard to the time at which they advanced the credit or to the nature of the investigation which they conducted at that time into the debtors' ability to repay the debt? What other criteria can you suggest as possible bases for allocating priorities among creditors of an over-committed debtor? Some criteria, and priority reform proposals constructed upon them are presented below.

NOTE

i The 'Order of Delivery' and 'Order of Levy' Rules: In a substantial number of American jurisdictions, priority depends upon the order in which the judgment is delivered to the sheriff for enforcement: See, e.g., 12 Pa. Stat. § 2291, Pa. Rules of Court 3137. In many other states, priority is determined by the order in which a levy (i.e. a seizure) is made by the sheriff pursuant to the writ of execution: see, e.g., Cal. Code Civ. Proc. § 688. Is either of these rules a fair means of determining priority? In the context of the modern consumer credit market – where it is not unusual for several lenders to extend credit to the same person (who is often already overcommitted) – are 'first come, first served' rules sound policy choices?

ii The 'Order of Extending Credit' Rule: Others have argued that the present Ontario system of priorities (based upon equality between creditors) and the two systems outlined above do nothing to encourage creditors to exercise more restraint in granting credit. They propose a system of priority based upon the order in which credit is extended. They argue that to the extent that the creditor is in a better position to predict the value of the risk and the chances of repayment – based upon the creditor having accurate information of the debtor's credit position at the time credit is extended – the more responsible will he be in extending credit to the proposed borrower.

For example, Karl E. Wenk, Jr. and Professor John E. Moye (in 'Debtor-Creditor Remedies: A new Proposal' (1969), 54 *Corn. L. Rev.* 249) have suggested that all unsecured credit transactions contain a 'financing statement' which would be filed in a central registry office. The act of filing would perfect the unsecured debt. Priority would be based upon the order in which the debt was perfected. Transactions involving sums below a set minimum amount would not have to be filed, but would be deemed perfected from the date of the transaction. Wenk and Moye argue that this system would have three significant advantages over all others. First, it discourages the debtor from giving a voluntary preference to one creditor over the others. Secondly, under such a system, discharges in bankruptcy could be prohibited in most cases. Finally, and perhaps most importantly, they argue that the system discourages a creditor down the line who is seeking a too high rate of return from extending credit to his marginal point and thereby forcing other creditors getting a lower rate of return beyond their marginal points. For if the last creditor causes default (because of the exorbitant rate of interest he is charging), he must wait until all previous debts are paid before he may enforce his debt.

Another suggestion for a system of priority based upon the order of extending credit has been proposed by Professor W.A. Sturges in 'A Proposed State Collection Act' (1934), 43 *Yale L.J.* 1055. His proposal calls for a system of 'underfiling' similar to that of the Ontario Creditors' Relief Act, except that creditors who had filed under the main action would not share equally in the distribution, but rather would share in accordance with the order in which credit was extended. (They would, of course, gain priority over prior creditors who had not properly underfiled.)

How would you evaluate the desirability of such proposals?

14
Special Creditors

The enforcement procedures described in earlier chapters are available to all unsecured creditors. The materials in this chapter consider special enforcement rights available to some types of creditor. Unusually effective procedures are provided to some of these creditors as a matter of conscious policy choice. Some special rights exist as vestiges of historic preferences of certain classes of creditor; their continued availability raises complex problems and sometimes conflicts with more contemporary decisions to prefer other types of creditors. As you read the materials, in this chapter consider the appropriateness of the overall patterns of preference of the 'special creditors'.

I THE RIGHT OF THE CROWN TO PRIORITY OF PAYMENT

a / Crown Prerogative

By the early common law, the Crown had an absolute right to priority of execution. If a subject and the Crown were each owed a judgment debt by a debtor, the subject (creditor) was not entitled to sue out any writ of execution until the Crown's debt had been satisfied in full. Although the Crown's right to priority of *execution* was later abolished, the courts held that the Crown still retained a prerogative right to priority of payment of Crown debts: *R. v Hamilton* (1962), 39 W.W.R. (N.S.) 545 (infra p 424). If the rights of the Crown come into conflict with the rights of a subject in respect of the payment of debts of equal degree (e.g. judgment debts), the Crown, by such prerogative right, takes priority over the general (subject) creditor. Thus if four creditors have judgments of $1,000 each while the Crown has a judgment (or its equivalent, see infra) for $4,000, the Crown will have its claim paid in full while the general creditors get nothing. The harshness of the operation of the Crown privilege against the subject may be illustrated if one assumes that the subject creditors are suppliers of materials which the debtor has used to manufacture a product which he has sold to produce the estate of $4,000, while the Crown's claim is in respect of income tax unpaid by the debtor some years ago.

Historically, the existence of the Crown's priority can be explained on the basis that writs of execution are issued out of the Queen's courts of justice. Insofar as the courts will cause a writ to be issued at all in favour of one of the Crown's subjects, it is only at the sufferance of the Crown. In another context, the rationale behind the doctrine seems to be that public policy requires that the integrity of the public treasury remain intact.

The 'persons' who are 'the Crown', and thus possessors of the privileged right to payment, include the Crown in the right of the Dominion and provinces, and those boards and administrative agencies which by virtue of their position as agents of the Crown or by statute are clothed with the Crown's privileges. The Courts have looked at two factors to determine if a body is an agent of the Crown. First, are the *functions* of the body similar to those of the Crown? Secondly, to what extent does the Crown *control* the operations of the body? See *Tamlin* v *Hannaford*, [1950] 1 K.B. 18 (C.A.); *R. v Ontario Labour Relations Board* (1971), 19 D.L.R. (3d) 47 (S.C.O.); and *Kawneer Co. of Canada Ltd.* v *Bank of Canada* (1975), 9 O.R. (2d) 468 (H.C.J.)

As you read the materials in this chapter, consider whether the Crown's priority can be justified as a general rule. Can it be justified in particular instances?

By virtue of its prerogative, the Crown may sue out a 'writ of extent' against the property of the debtor: *Emerson* v *Simpson* (1962), 32 D.L.R. (2d) 603. An 'extent in chief' may issue against the Crown's debtor under which the sheriff may seize the assets of the debtor to be sold for the benefit of the Crown. In addition, an inquisition may be held to determine if any debts are owed to the Crown's debtor, in which case a writ of extent in the second degree may issue against those so indebted. The writ of extent is a very powerful form of execution. As noted above, the Crown's claim has priority over other claims of equal degree, subject to legislation restricting its priority. A writ of extent may be issued *before* judgment, thus enabling the sheriff to take possession of the debtor's property (to be held until judgment) to the disadvantage of all other judgment creditors who could otherwise have proceeded to complete their executions and convert the property of their debtor into a fund available for the satisfaction of their claims.

b / Statutory Liens, Priorities, and Special Forms of Execution
In addition to the general royal prerogative, many statutes create liens and give priority to claims of the Crown and other government agencies. Examples of such Ontario legislation are reproduced below:

i Provincial Statutes Giving a First Lien and Charge or Creating a 'Crown Debt'
  1 The Corporations Tax Act, S.O. 1972, c 143, s 167
  2 The Fire Marshals Act, R.S.O. 1970, c 172, s 19(15)
  3 The Gift Tax Act, S.O. 1972, c 12, ss 43–7
  4 The Income Tax Act, R.S.O. 1970, c 217, s 28–30
  5 The Land Speculation Tax Act, S.O. 1974, c 17, s 5
  6 The Mining Tax Act, R.S.O. 1970, c 275, s 26
  7 The Motor Vehicle Fuel Tax Act, R.S.O. 1970, c 282, s 17
  8 The Municipal Affairs Act, R.S.O. 1970, c 118, s 47
  9 The Power Corporation Act, R.S.O. 1970, c 354, as amended by S.O. 1973, c 57
 10 The Provincial Land Tax Act, R.S.O. 1970, c 370, s 26
 11 The Public Utilities Act, R.S.O. 1970, c 390, s 30
 12 The Retail Sales Tax Act, R.S.O. 1970, c 415, s 18
 13 The Succession Duty Act, R.S.O. 1970, c 449, s 21
 14 The Tobacco Tax Act, R.S.O. 1970, c 463, s 8
 15 The Workmen's Compensation Act, R.S.O. 1970, c 505, ss 112, 113.
Every province has a similar plethora of statutes granting special status to Crown debts.

NOTE By s 116(3) of The Workmen's Compensation Act, R.S.O. 1970, c 505, unpaid assessments certified under s 112 of the Act as owing by an employer constitute 'a first lien upon all the property ... of the Employer used in ... the industry with respect to which the employer is assessed, subject only to municipal taxes ...' In *Crown Trust Co.* v *Workmen's Compensation Board* (1975), 7 O.R. (2d) 466 (H.C.J.) the plaintiffs were secured creditors of an employer holding a mortgage and a floating charge that had crystallized. Subsequently a lien under The Workmen's Compensation Act came into existence. Houlden J held that the lien under the Act only attached the employer's interest in the property and not the property itself. Consequently, the earlier securities took priority over the statutory lien.

Other statutes specify with greater precision the nature of the Crown priority, see, for example, s 167 (2) of The Corporations Tax Act, S.O. 1972, c 143 as amended, creating a special lien 'in priority to every claim, privilege, lien or encumbrance, whenever created'.

ii Miscellaneous Provincial Statutes
1 The Assessment Act, R.S.O. 1970, c 32, s 7(4). (Business assessment tax is not a charge upon land.)
2 The Health Insurance Act, S.O. 1972, c 91, ss 47, 48. (Directors may be liable for failing to remit insurance premiums.)
3 The Legal Aid Act, R.S.O. 1970, c 239, s 18 (Debt owed to Law Society for legal aid plan constitutes lien on land.)
4 The Municipal Act, R.S.O. 1970, c 284, s 511 (Debt for taxes are a special lien on land, in priority to every other claim except Crown debt.)

iii Federal Statutes Giving a First Lien and Charge or Creating 'Crown Debts'
1 Canada Pension Plan, R.S.C. 1970, c C-5, s 24
2 Customs Act, R.S.C. 1970, c C-40, s 102
3 Excise Tax Act, R.S.C. 1970, c E-13, s 16(4)
4 Income Tax Act, S.C. 1970–71–72 c 63, ss 222, 223
5 Unemployment Insurance Act, S.C. 1970, 71, 72, c 48, ss 49, 71

iv Statutes Creating a Special Right to Garnishment
In addition to giving the Crown a first lien and priority various Federal and Provincial statutes create a special right to garnish a debt belonging to the Crown's debtor. The Income Tax Act, S.C. 1970–71–72, c 63, s 224 is a typical example:

GARNISHMENT
224. (1) When the Minister has knowledge or suspects that a person is or is about to become indebted or liable to make any payment to a person liable to make a payment under this Act, he may, by registered letter or by a letter served personally, require him to pay the moneys otherwise payable to that person in whole or in part to the Receiver General of Canada on account of the liability under this Act.

IDEM
(2) The receipt of the Minister for moneys paid as required under this section is a good and sufficient discharge of the original liability to the extent of the payment.

IDEM

(3) Where the Minister has, under this section, required an employer to pay to the Receiver General of Canada on account of an employee's liability under this Act moneys otherwise payable by the employer to the employee as remuneration, the requirement is applicable to all future payments by the employer to the employee in respect of remuneration until the liability under this Act is satisfied and operates to require payments to the Receiver General out of each payment of remuneration of such amount as may be stipulated by the Minister in the registered letter.

IDEM

(4) Every person who has discharged any liability to a person liable to make a payment under this Act without complying with a requirement under this section is liable to pay to Her Majesty an amount equal to the liability discharged or the amount which he was required under this section to pay to the Receiver General of Canada, whichever is the lesser.

v Statutes Creating Special Rights to Distress: Most of the statutes mentioned above also give the Crown special rights to seize chattels for non-payment of debt. For example, section 225 of the Income Tax Act, provides:

SEIZURE OF CHATTELS

225. (1) Where a person has failed to make a payment as required by this Act, the Minister, on giving 30 days' notice by registered mail addressed to his last known place of residence, may, whether or not there is an objection to or appeal in respect of the assessment not disposed of, issue a certificate of the failure and direct that the goods and chattels of the person in default be seized.

IDEM

(2) Property seized under this section shall be kept for 10 days at the cost and charges of the owner and, if he does not pay the amount due together with the costs and charges within the 10 days, the property seized shall be sold by public auction.

IDEM

(3) Except in the case of perishable goods, notice of the sale setting forth the time and place thereof, together with a general description of the property to be sold shall, a reasonable time before the goods are sold, be published at least once in one or more newspapers of general local circulation.

IDEM

(4) Any surplus resulting from the sale after deduction of the amount owing and all costs and charges shall be paid or returned to the owner of the property seized.

IDEM

(5) Such goods and chattels of any person in default as would be exempt from seizure under a writ of execution issued out of a superior court of the province in which the seizure is made are exempt from seizure under this section.

Examples of statutes having similar provisions include:
1 The Corporation Tax Act, S.O. 1972, c 143, s 168

2 The Income Tax Act, R.S.O. 1970, c 217, s 31
3 The Land Speculation Tax Act, S.O. 1974, c 17, s 14
4 The Retail Sales Tax Act, R.S.O. 1970, c 415, s 3.
Corresponding statutes exist in most provinces. Other federal examples of such legislation include the Unemployment Insurance Act, S.C. 1970–71–72, c 48 s 80.

In general, the Crown's claim is effective from the time when the 'demand on third parties' is served on the debtor's debtor: *Bank of Montreal* v *Union Gas Co. of Can. Ltd.* (1969), 7 D.L.R. (3d) 25 (Ont. C.A.) (infra p 427).

c / Attempts to Limit the Crown's Priority
The Crown's priority can often work substantial hardship on general creditors. In recognition of this problem the priority of the Crown has been attenuated in several respects both by the common law and by legislative action:

i The only assets to which the Crown's priority attaches are those assets owned by the debtor upon crystallization of the Crown's claim. If the debtor legally transfers his property or creates equities and encumbrances on it prior to the 'crystallization' of the Crown's claim, the prior interests are not defeated by the Crown's prerogative: *Sandberg* v *Meurer & M.N.R.*, [1949] 1 D.L.R. 422 (Man. C.A.) (infra p 430).

ii The Crown may be unable to assert a prerogative right to priority of payment in respect of a debt arising out of a strictly commercial transaction between a private individual and the Crown. These debts may not be 'Crown debts', within the meaning of the prerogative right, and may be treated differently from debts arising (e.g.) from non-payment of taxes due to the Crown: *R.* v *Workmen's Compensation Board and the City of Edmonton* (1962), 36 D.L.R. (2d) 166 (Alta. D.C.) (infra p 431).

iii If the Crown wishes to gain a priority, its claim must be asserted in the proper manner. The mere obtaining of a judgment may not be enough; to perfect its priority, some further action on the Crown's part may be required. For example, in *Tudor Holdings Ltd.* v *Robertson et al.* (1973), 43 D.L.R. (3d) 752 (B.C.S.C.) (infra p 434) the Crown was denied priority because it had not availed itself of the proper procedures under The Creditors' Relief Act.

iv Various statutes have also cut down the Crown's priority. For example, section 107(1) of the Bankruptcy Act, R.S.C. 1970, c B-3 postpones the Crown's claims in favour of those claims specified in the legislation. Section 14 of The Employment Standards Act, S.O. 1974, c 112 gives priority to claims for unpaid wages up to $2,000 over claims of all other creditors, including the claims of the Crown in right of the Province.

d / Priority As Between The Dominion And Provincial Governments
Where claims are made both by the Crown in the right of the Dominion and the Crown in the right of a province against the estate of a debtor, the claims rank *pari passu*, in the absence of legislation to the contrary. However, because of the paramountcy of its legislation, the Dominion Parliament may modify or abrogate completely the priority of the Crown in the right of a province. Unless Parliament expressly states an intention to modify the position of a 'provincial Crown claim' in this manner it is presumed that

all Crown debts rank *pari passu*: *In Re Silver Bros. Ltd.*, [1932] 2 D.L.R. 673 (P.C.) (infra p 436). Provincial legislation can neither bind nor affect the prerogative rights of the Crown in the right of the Dominion: *Re Adams Shoe Co.*, [1923] 4 D.L.R. 927.

e / Some Cases

i *Regina* v *Hamilton* (1962), 39 W.W.R. (N.S.) 545 (Man. Q.B.)

[The Crown in the right of the Dominion, having obtained judgments against the judgment debtor in respect of money advanced by the Canadian Wheat Board, filed certificates of judgment against the judgment debtor's lands (pursuant to the Judgments Act, R.S.M. 1954, c 129). Writs of *fieri facias* were issued by the Crown and other judgment creditors, some of whom had filed certificates of judgment prior in time to those of the Crown. No actual seizure had been made under these writs when the Crown sought an order that the interest of the judgment debtor in the lands be sold.]

FERGUSON, J.: ... The applicant claims that the crown, by virtue of its prerogatives affecting the situation involved in this case, is entitled to payment of its said judgments in priority to those of Hydraulic and the bank as well as those of the two subsequent judgment creditors. The main issue before the court would appear to be aptly stated by Mr. Grimble, counsel for the bank, in his written argument, as follows:

To sum up it is submitted that the 'lien and charge' of the Bank having been created prior to that of the Crown it is not a case of equal rights but of a prior and subsequent charge on land, nor is it a case of lien and charge that is in progress to completion but a complete lien and charge which is enforceable but not yet enforced, and the claim of the Crown for priority should not be allowed.

[His Lordship referred to section 3 of the Judgments Act, supra which provides that upon the registration of a certificate of judgment in a land titles office 'the judgment shall ... bind and form a lien and charge all lands of the judgment debtor ...', and continued:]
The crown's prerogatives are numerous and varied and have always been esteemed an express part of the common law of England, and, except where they have been obliterated or altered by competent legislation, remain as part of our law existing today.
One of the leading cases dealing with the crown's prerogatives in respect of the collection of its debts is that of *Rex* v *Wells and Allnutt* (1807), 16 East 278, 104 ER 1094. I quote from the judgment of Macdonald, L.C.B. at p 1096:

By the common law the Crown was entitled to prior execution for its debts. This does not mean preference as between two executions sued out, the one by the Crown, the other by the subject; but the Crown was to be first satisfied its debt, before the subject could take out any execution at all. The Crown protected its debtor against all executions by the subject, till the Crown's debt was paid.

Then came the statute of 33 Henry VIII, ch. 39, sec. 74, and the learned judge, dealing with this statute, said, at p 1096:

... the language of 33 Hen. 8 is that the King's suit and process shall be preferred before the suit of any person, and that he shall have first execution. It is not, that his execution shall be preferred, but that he shall have first execution; that is, he shall have execution before the subject shall be permitted to have his execution, which seems to have a pretty plain reference to this prerogative which went to restrain the subject from taking any execution at all, till the Crown's debt was satisfied ...

The learned lord chief baron makes a further pronouncement at p 1097, which I consider of importance in the instant case, namely:

The property is so far bound by delivery of the writ, that as between subject and subject, the question of priority is determined: but as against the Crown it is not bound at all. But I take it *the property* is in no sense and to no purpose in the world altered either by delivery of the writ or by the actual taking possession of the goods. [The italics are mine.]
...
An effect of the rule which I wish to emphasize is well stated in *Broom's Legal Maxims*, 9th ed., at p 49, as follows:

Again, the rule is that, where the sheriff seizes under a *fi. fa.*, and, after seizure, but before sale under such writ, a writ of extent is sued out and delivered to the sheriff, the Crown is entitled to priority, and the sheriff must sell under the extent, and satisfy the Crown's debt, before he sells under the *fi. fa.* ... The same principle applies where goods in the hands of the sheriff under a *fi. fa.*, and before sale, are seized by officers of the customs under a warrant to levy a penalty incurred by the defendant for an offence against the revenue laws; and where the Crown levies a distress upon goods after a subject has distrained upon them, but before he has completed his distress by sale.

Among the cases cited for the above proposition are *Giles* v *Grover and Pollard* (1832), 9 Bing 128, at 191, 131 ER 563 (H.L.). This is a lengthy decision of the House of Lords and is most informative ...

The learned judge [Alderson, B.] makes a pronouncement (at p 574) which I also regard as of importance in the instant case, viz.:

If, however, the right of the subject be complete and perfect before that of the king commences, it is manifest that the rule does not apply, for there is no point of time at which the two rights are in conflict; nor can there be a question which of the two ought to prevail in a case where one, that of the subject, has prevailed already. But if whilst the right of the subject is still in progress towards completion, the right of the crown arises, it seems to me that the two rights do come into conflict together at one and the same time, and that the consequence in that case is that the right of the crown ought to prevail. Lord Mansfield expresses this proposition in shorter language when he says, 'No inception of an execution can bar the crown:' *Cooper* v *Chitty* (1756) 1 Burr 20, 97 ER 166.

Now, if we proceed to apply these principles to the determination of the present case, it will appear that the material facts are these: J.S. has obtained judgment against a crown debtor, has issued a *fieri facias* upon that judgment, and has delivered the writ to the sheriff, and the sheriff, in execution thereof, has seized the goods of the crown debtor; the question then is this, Is the right of the subject perfect at the time when the goods are seized by the sheriff, or is *there any further act to be done in order to make that right consummate?*

The most simple criterion of this seems to be, whether, without any thing further being done, the execution creditor is entitled to call upon the sheriff for the possession of the goods or to pay him the debt. Now, I do not believe that it was ever contended, that the execution creditor is entitled to the possession of the goods themselves, unless under some contract made between the sheriff and him, which would be equivalent to a sale under the writ. Nor can he call upon the sheriff, even after a return of goods seized *ad valentiam*, to pay to him the debt for which the levy is made ...

From these premises, two propositions seem to me to follow: first, that *at no period of time at all does the execution creditor obtain any property whatsoever in the goods themselves*: and, secondly, that *the general property in the goods seized remains, until the sale, in the debtor, and is not changed by the seizure: Milton* v *Eldrington* (1554) 1 Dyer 98b, 73 ER 215. After sale the case is very different; for, by the sale, the property is wholly changed from the debtor to the vendee of the sheriff, and the money, the produce of the goods, then becomes the property of the creditor; for which he may maintain an action for money had and received, and for which the sheriff is responsible to him, the original debtor being then wholly and finally discharged: *Perkinson* v *Gilford* (1639) Cro Car 539, 79 ER 1064. The rule is thus expressly laid down by Mr. Baron Garrow in delivering the opinion of the Court, after full consideration in the case of *Higgins* v *M'Adam* (1829) 3 Y & J 1, 148 ER 1068. 'The rule is, that when execution is executed, the property is changed; and execution is said to be executed when a sale has taken place.' *It is not, therefore, till after the sale, that the right of the execution creditor becomes consummate.* And it would follow, from thence, that *it is not till after the sale that the right of the creditor ceases to concur with the right of the crown.* If, therefore, the right of the crown arises at any period prior to the sale, it seems to me, that on the principles above laid down, it ought to have the preference. [The italics are mine.] ...

I find that in proceedings under sec. 3 of *The Judgments Act* and Q.B.R. 511 of this province, that there is one fundamental right involved, and only one, this being the same right existing at common law and in all other common-law jurisdictions, and that is the right of a judgment creditor to sell the exigible lands of his judgment debtor in order to satisfy his judgment and costs. The procedure required to complete this right is merely complementary or assistive to it and it differs in other provinces and jurisdictions, but the right itself is singular and undivided. Whatever these different procedural steps may be, whether they be by way of registering an execution or a certificate of judgment against land in the appropriate land titles office, or whether a sale is made by a sheriff or some other official, or whether a sale is completed by a conveyance or a vesting order, they are all directed toward the fulfilment of this same common right, and the result is the same in each case, namely, a sale of the land concerned. The registration of an execution or a certificate of judgment therefore merely constitutes the first procedural step along the road to complete execution of the right which is consummated by a sale and payment.

In the meantime the judgment creditor acquires no property right in the subject-matter of the sale as such remains in the judgment debtor until the sale of the property is perfected and fully completed.

I find that *The Judgments Act* does not refer to the crown in the right of Canada and does not bind or purport to bind Her Majesty in the right of Canada.

I further find that the rights of the said subject judgment creditors, Hydraulic Engineering & Mfg. Co. Ltd., Canadian Imperial Bank of Commerce, Clive H. Haig, and Henry S. Leveton Estate, are not complete or perfect but merely in progress towards completion.

I further find that the rights of the said subjects in respect of their said judgments are of equal degree as those of Her Majesty the Queen as a judgment creditor, and that they subsist at the same time as, and concur, conflict, and compete with the rights of Her Majesty in respect of her said judgments, and accordingly the claim of the crown must prevail ...'

Other cases in which the Crown's claim was given priority over general creditors include: *Liquidators of Maritime Bank* v *Receiver General of N.B.*, [1892] A.C. 437 (P.C.); *R.* v *Bank of Nova Scotia* (1885), 11 S.C.R. 1; *Crowther* v *A.-G. of Can.* (1959), 17 D.L.R. (2d) 437 (N.S.C.A.); *Re West & Co.* (1922), 62 D.L.R. 207, (1921), 50 O.L.R. 631.

NOTE In *Gandy & Allison Ltd.* v *Erectors & Constructors Ltd.* (1963), 43 D.L.R. (2d) 461, an ordinary creditor of the debtor argued that the Crown statutory notices or garnishments deprived him of property rights without affording him an opportunity to be heard either before or after the issuing of the statutory garnishment, and as such was contrary to the Bill of Rights. The Court rejected this argument: the Bill of Rights did not purport to repeal or alter the prerogative right of the Crown to preference of payment.

For a modern example of the use of the writ of extent see *Emerson* v *Simpson* (1962), 32 D.L.R. (2d) 603 (B.C.S.C.) where the Crown registered on title a writ of extent, thereby taking priority over a prior judgment registered pursuant to the B.C. Land Registry Act. For an historically interesting analysis of the writ of extent see Joseph Chitty, *A Treatise on the Law of the Prerogatives of the Crown*, Joseph Butterworth and Son (1820), pp 243–338.

ii *Bank of Montreal* v *Union Gas Co. of Canada Ltd.* (1969), 7 D.L.R. (3d) 25 (Ont. C.A.)

The judgment of the court was delivered by
JESSUP, J.A.: This is an appeal from the judgment of Hartt, J., dismissing the action with costs.

William S. Salmon Limited (hereinafter called the contractor) is a company carrying on business in the London area as a contractor. On May 15, 1959, the contractor executed a general assignment of book debts in the following form in favour of the plaintiff and the assignment was duly registered ...

The assignment was given to secure advances by the plaintiff to the contractor. No notice was given to any of the debtors of the contractor until on or about March 25, 1966. Until then all payments by the debtors of the contractor were made to it.

The contractor had undertaken work for the defendant and by March 14, 1966, the work had been completed so that as of that date the defendant owed a sum of money in excess of $10,000 to the contractor. On March 14, 1966, pursuant to s 120 of the *Income Tax Act*, R.S.C. 1952, c 148, a demand in writing was made by the Department of National Revenue, Taxation Division, on the defendant for the sum of $8,570.60 plus accrued interest from moneys otherwise payable to the contractor ...

On March 24, 1966, the defendant paid, pursuant to the statutory demand, the sum of $2,887.52 to the Receiver-General of Canada. On or about March 26, 1966, the defendant then received from the plaintiff a letter advising the defendant of the general assignment of book debts executed by the contractor on May 15, 1959, and requiring all amounts now owing or becoming due by the defendant to the contractor to be paid to the plaintiff. On March 29, 1966, the defendant acknowledged receipt of the notice from the plaintiff and advised it would make payment to the plaintiff directly for any amounts owing to the contractor. On or about April 13, 1966, the defendant received from the Department of National Revenue a further statutory demand requiring the defendant to deduct from moneys payable to the contractor the remaining balance claimed by the Department of $5,750.58. On April 14, 1966, the defendant paid this balance to the Department. Subsequently the defendant paid to the plaintiff the balance it owed the contractor after deducting the said sums of $2,887.52 and $5,750.58.

The plaintiff's claim in this action was for $5,750.58 the amount of the payment made by the defendant to the Department on April 14, 1966 ...

The principles on which the plaintiff founds it case are stated in Halsbury's Laws of England, 3rd ed., vol. 4, p 498:

1026 *Notice not necessary as between assignor and assignee.* As between the assignor and the assignee, an equitable assignment, whether voluntary or for value, is absolute and complete without notice having been given to the debtor or fundholder, for notice does not render the title perfect, and formerly was not even a step in the title. Moreover, notice is not necessary as against third persons who stand in the same position as the assignor, such as persons claiming under a subsequent assignment as volunteers, or a creditor who has obtained a charging order, or an order appointing a receiver, or a garnishee order, even though in the last case the judgment creditor gives notice to the trustee before the assignee, or the trustee in bankruptcy of the assignor. [As amended by 1968 Cumulative Supplement.]

Thus it is argued the Crown is in the position of a garnisheeing creditor and can have no higher claim to the moneys in the hands of the defendant than the assignor-contractor under the assignment. But while the priority mentioned in Halsbury of an assignee who has not given notice can be asserted in derogation of the rights of a subsequent garnisheeing creditor while the fund in question is in being as, for instance, upon payment into Court by the fundholder, or perhaps in an action against the garnisheeing creditor, the law is clear that a debtor who has not received notice of an assignment can pay the assignor with immunity and will not be liable to pay over again to the assignee: *cf.* 4 Hals., 3rd ed., p 498: J.C. Vaines, *Personal Property*, 4th ed., p 259; W.R. Warren, *Choses in Action*, 1899, p 87; J. Williams, *Principles of the Law of Personal Property*, 18th ed., p 38. It follows as a matter of principle and elementary justice that neither will he be liable to the prior assignee where he pays, in the absence of notice, according to the order of a Court issued at the instance of a garnisheeing creditor or under the compulsion of a statutory duty as imposed by s 120(1). Thus the plaintiff could not assert a claim to the sum of $2,887.52 paid by the defendant to the Department on March 14, 1966, and before the plaintiff had given notice of the assignment which it held although counsel for the plaintiff took the position that it was a matter of grace no such claim was made in the present action. In my opinion s 120(1) is intended to preserve and continue such immunity of a fundholder or debtor even after he has received notice of a prior assignment. It creates a charge not on moneys owing or accruing due as in the case of an attaching or garnishee order but on 'moneys otherwise payable' *at the time of delivery of the demand.* It seems to me the construction I adopt is necessary to give effect to the plain words of the statute. The charge created by the section, in my view, is a continuing charge crystallized by the state of affairs at the time of delivery of the statutory demand, and accordingly it is not affected by the subsequent knowledge of a debtor upon whom a demand under the statute has been made that the funds so charged have previously been assigned away to a third party.

Alternatively the plaintiff relied on the fact that notice of its assignment had been given to the defendant before the second statutory demand was delivered and it is argued the force of the first statutory demand was spent or nullified by the second. I cannot accept that argument. While neither of the statutory demands in an exhibit there is no suggestion in the evidence that the second demand purported by any words to vitiate the force of the first and there is no authority in the statute by which it could have such a purported effect. In my opinion, s 120(1) of the statute, from the time of delivery of the first demand, imposed a continuing duty which was not discharged until the amount mentioned in such demand, including the interest mentioned, was paid to the Crown. The second demand can be regarded as having been delivered *ex abundanti cautela*.

Moreover, I conclude there is an alternate ground which defeats the plaintiff's claim. In my view s 120(1) creates a charge in favour of the Crown, upon delivery of a demand under the section, which is an equitable charge. I take this to be also the view of Munroe, J., expressed in *A.-G. Can.* v *Workmen's Compensation Board of British Columbia* (1968), 67 D.L.R. (2d) 16 at pp 19–20. *Quoad* the fund of debt in question here the plaintiff's assignment is of a debt to become due in the future and the assignment is therefore an equitable one: *Tailby* v *Official Receiver* (1888), 13 App. Cas. 523. As between two claims founded in equity and on the basis of the principle in *Dearle* v *Hall* (1828), 3 Russ. 1, 38 E.R. 475, in my opinion, priority must go to he who first gives notice. *Dearle* v *Hall*, it is true, was a contest between competing equitable assignments and Lord Macnaghten in *Ward* v *Duncombe*, [1893] A.C. 369, was of the view that the rule in *Dearle* v *Hall* ought not to be extended to a new case. But as Lord Reid observed in *B.S. Lyle Ltd.* v *Rosher*, [1959] 1 W.L.R. 8 at p 196, '... that must, I think, mean a case where there is a significant distinction from the position in *Dearle* v *Hall*'. In my view there is no such significant distinction in the facts of this case and they are embraced in the principles which provide the *ratio* in *Dearle* v *Hall*.

NOTE Where notice of a general assignment of books debts and a third party demand under s 224(1) (formerly s 120(1)) of the Income Tax Act are received simultaneously, or in circumstances in which it is impossible to ascertain which was received first, the Crown's claim takes priority by virtue of its prerogative: *Bank of Montreal* v *Attorney-General of Canada* (1970), 14 D.L.R. (3d) 619 (B.C.S.C.).

Bank of Montreal v *Union Gas Co.*, supra, has not been followed in Alberta. In *Attorney General of Canada* v *Royal Bank of Canada*, [1979] 1 W.W.R. 479, affirming [1977] 6 W.W.R. 170, the Alberta Appellate Division held that a prior equitable assignment takes priority over a s 224(1) demand, even though notice of the assignment is not given until after the demand is served. The Court specifically disagreed with the 'alternate ground' for decision in *Union Gas*; s 224(1), it concluded, does not create an equitable interest in favour of the Crown on the delivery of a third party demand.

Where a bank receives a s 224(1) demand it is obliged by law to pay the specified amount notwithstanding the customer's instructions to the contrary: *Bank of Montreal* v *Boudreau* (1975), 49 D.L.R. (3d) 249 (N.B.S.C., A.D.).

QUESTIONS

1 Who should pay the administrative costs involved in complying with third party demand notices?
2 *Boudreau* raised (but found it unnecessary to answer) the question of what happens when a notice is defective. What would have been the result in the *Union Gas* case if

the notice had been defectively signed? Would a small individual debtor of the Government's debtor know if a demand were regular or not? Who ought to pay if a notice is defective but the third party pays the Government Ministry?

3 Many statutes authorize third party demands before the Crown has obtained any judgment. Should the Crown be able to collect its debts this way? You might also consider the huge costs involved in Governmental collection when the Department is authorized to make extensive searches on the premises of third parties, and retain documents owned by such third parties. (See for example section 231 of the Income Tax Act, s.c. 1970–71–72, c 63.) Should the Government be allowed to externalize these costs?

iii / *Sandberg* v *Meurer and Minister of National Revenue*, [1949] 1 D.L.R. 422 (Man. C.A.)

ADAMSON J.A.: The defendant Sigurdson contracted to build or repair buildings on the defendant Meurer's land. In carrying out such contract, he employed the plaintiffs Sandberg and Topping. These two plaintiffs filed mechanics' liens under which the learned Referee has adjudged them to be entitled to $1,413.02. The defendant Meurer (the owner) has paid into Court the sum of $1,266, being the amount required to be retained by the owner under the provisions of the *Mechanics' Lien Act*, though as a matter of fact he only held back $680.

The Minister of National Revenue (claimant), appellant, who has a judgment against the defendant Sigurdson in the sum of $413 and costs for deductions made by him as an employer from his employees under the *Income War Tax Act*, claims a first charge on the monies paid into Court by the owner, Meurer, as being an asset of Sigurdson's under s 92(7A) of the *Income War Tax Act*, which reads as follows: 'Every person who deducts or withholds an amount under this section is liable to pay to His Majesty on the day fixed by or pursuant to subsection two of this section an amount equal to the amount so deducted or withheld and such liability shall constitute a first charge on the assets of such person and shall, notwithstanding the *Bank Act*, the *Bankruptcy Act* or any other statute or law, rank for payment in priority to all other claims, either of His Majesty in right of a province of Canada or any other person, of whatsoever kind heretofore or hereafter arising, save and except only the judicial costs, fees and lawful expenses of an assignee or other public officer charged with the administration or distribution of such assets.'

The question, therefore is whether or not these monies were assets of the defendant Sigurdson within the meaning of this section. It should be noted that the appellant's judgment is not for monies deducted by him on this particular contract. So far as is shown, they were never in a special account as provided for in s 92(7) of the above-mentioned Act. It should be observed, too, that under the *Mechanics' Lien Act*, a special lien for payment of wages and materials is created. When the monies were paid into Court under this Act, they became subject to the lienholder's claims. As assets they are in the same legal position as property which has been mortgaged or hypothecated as security.

What are 'assets' within the meaning of this section, 92(7A), and similar statutes has been adjudicated upon in a number of cases.

In *R.* v *Hyde*, [1928] 2 W.W.R. 253 Kilgour J, in dealing with a similar provision under the *Special War Revenue Act* of 1915, which gave the Crown a first charge on the assets of a person indebted for sales tax, held that the word 'assets' was not intended to include any other assets than such as were the property of the debtor at the time his assets were sought to be administered. In that case the learned Judge adopted the view of Rose J. in *Goodman* v *Bk. of Toronto*, [1925] 1 D.L.R. 1184, 56 O.L.R. 318 [affd [1925] 3 D.L.R. 99, 57 O.L.R. 109].

In *R.* v *Jack Pine Lbr. Co.*, [1928] 4 D.L.R. 976, Ford J. held that the Crown could not claim a sales tax debt from a chattel mortgagee who has seized and sold goods which were the property of the debtor while s 17 of the *Special War Revenue Amendment Act*, 1922, was in force ...

The most recent case is *Re Rosenberg*, [1948] 4 D.L.R. 205, O.W.N. 637, which judgment was given by Urquhart J. in the Supreme Court of Ontario. He held that [p 206]: 'The trustee is entitled to distribute only *assets* of the estate among the unsecured creditors, and the assets are determined after the encumbrances, such as a chattel mortgage, or a lien under s 88 of the *Bank Act*, 1944–45 (Can.), c 39, are paid.' He goes on to say [p. 207]: 'It is well settled that "assets" include only what is left after such claims have been taken care of.'

It must, therefore, be held that assets include only such properties of the debtor as are available for payment of his debts, and the claim of the appellant to the monies in Court under the *Mechanics' Lien Act* is subject to the payment of such liens as have been found by the Master to be payable. As there are not sufficient monies to satisfy those liens, the application of the claimant should be dismissed with costs.

The rights of the Crown have been so clearly and frequently settled under the above and similar provisions that one cannot but wonder why the parties were put to the expense of these proceedings.

Appeal dismissed.

See *Bartlet* v *Osterhout*, [1931] 3 D.L.R. 609 which held that in the circumstances, the Crown's claim against the judgment debtor did not take priority over the earlier claim of the judgment debtor's mortgagee.

NOTE Under a writ of extent, the Crown can only take property owned by the debtor at the time of the issuance of the writ; the Crown cannot take property previously transferred, assigned, or encumbered *R.* v *'The City of Windsor'* (1896), 5 Ex. C.R. 223 and *Clarkson* v *A.-G. of Canada* (1889), 16 O.A.R. 202 (C.A.)

QUESTION Can the *Union Gas* and *Sandberg* cases be reconciled? Is either decision preferable?

iv *The Queen* v *Workmen's Compensation Board And City of Edmonton* (1962), 36 D.L.R. (2d) 166, (Alta D.C.)

BUCHANAN, C.J.D.C.: This action is brought, pursuant to an interpleader order, to determine priorities among the three parties hereto, in the distribution by the Sheriff of the Edmonton Judicial District of the approximate sum of $1,160, presently held by him. This sum resulted from debt collection activities of the three parties directed against Hubtop Construction Company Ltd. of Edmonton, debtor to all three.

On September 9, 1959, the Workmen's Compensation Board (for convenience styled 'the Board') filed with the Sheriff its distress warrant dated September 3, 1959, authorizing seizure for recovery of unpaid assessments totalling $2,505.35, but suggesting that a preliminary letter be sent by the Sheriff to the debtor before seizure. On September 11, 1959, there was filed with the Sheriff on behalf of the Provincial Treasurer of the Province of Alberta (hereinafter called 'the Treasurer') a distress warrant, based on two chattel mortgages, granted by the debtor to the

Treasurer, to secure advances made to the debtor, whereby seizure of certain chattels described therein, for recovery of the sum of $87,902.30, interest and costs was authorized. Seizure was affected September 15, 1959. On October 28, 1959, the City of Edmonton (for convenience, styled 'the City') filed with the Sheriff its distress warrant based on a claim for unpaid business tax of $457 owing by the debtor. On January 19, 1961, the Board instructed sale of the chattels seized under the Treasurer's warrant, resulting in the receipt by the Sheriff of the net sum of $1,160. Successively the Board, the City and the Treasurer claimed priority in the disbursement of that fund. This action resulted.

The treasurer bases his claim on the royal prerogative and if successful takes the entire sum in the Sheriff's hands ...

In *Re H.J. Webb & Co.*, [1922] 2 Ch. 369, when heard by the Appeal Court, the issue being the right of the Crown to priority for payment of its debt under a voluntary winding-up, Lord Sterndale, M.R., at p 377 stated:

In this case the debt was in respect of money received by the company for a quantity of frozen rabbits imported by the Food Controller and sold by the Company as his agents. *It is difficult to conceive anything more different from the Crown debts in contemplation at the time when the Royal Prerogative took its rise.* The case must however be resolved on the ordinary principles applying to the prerogative.

Prima facie, such a debt is admitted to be a debt due to the Crown and so payable in priority to other debts in any circumstances. (Italics added)

It should be noted that in this case the Appeal Court held that the prerogative right of the Crown to priority had been negatived by the provisions of the *Companies (Consolidation) Act*, 1908 (U.K.), c 69. When the decision of the Appeal Court came to be heard on appeal, before the House of Lords, *sub nom. Food Controller et al.* v *Cork*, [1923] A.C. 647, much more vigorous comments were made by their Lordships of that House as to the changed nature of alleged Crown debts subsequent to 'the time when the Royal Prerogative took its rise', though as in the Court of Appeal, their Lordships' decision was based upon legislation applicable to the Crown ...

Lord Shaw was ... outspoken in his strictures upon what he deemed the unjustified widening of the interpretation placed upon 'Crown debts', thus, at p 665:

It might be sufficient to leave the matter there: but in case the treatment of this appeal should ever be attempted as a precedent for recognition on a wide scale of what are Crown debts, I desire to make the following observations. I think, with the Master of the Rolls, that the expression 'Crown debts' and 'debts due to the Crown' are unfortunate expressions. *They do suggest that, under the name of prerogative, something is being claimed higher than that justice which is distributed among subjects of the Crown, and this even under ordinary contracts, the construction of which among such subjects would not permit of the operation of preference.* (Italics added) ...

My Lords, I venture to interpose much doubt as to the application or extension of the expression used by Macdonald C.B., 'that where the King's and the subject's title concur the King's shall be preferred,' and the modernization of it given by Lord Macnaghten, to cases of ordinary commercial or industrial contracts entered into by a Government department in the course of the business or enterprise which it carries on. If a special statute confers upon such departments priorities, preferences, excuses for misfeasance or exemptions from liability, then of course the statute controls the situation. *But if the proposition above cited should ever be used to justify or widen the royal prerogative by the inclusion of ordinary contracts into the range of privilege, then it is, I think, very important to realize that this dictum of Lord Macnaghten's occurred in a case in which the nature of the debts, as Crown debts, and that in a very strict sense, was clear beyond all question.* (Italics mine.)

After describing the nature of the debt in the case then at bar, the noble Lord went on [pp 667–8]:

How is this a Crown debt? It springs out of no power vested in the Crown by way of the imposition of a duty or a tax. It is not in the ordinary enumeration of debts incurred for the service of the country. It is an instance simply of a debt arising under ordinary transactions of principal and agent. A Government department, in the course of realizing Government property, appointed an agent to conduct a transaction. That agent defaulted to the extent of nearly 10,000*l.* and then became bankrupt. The debt arises purely in commercio.
It is unnecessary in this case to commit oneself to the proposition that when Departments of Government enter into the commercial or industrial sphere they do so with such an enormous leverage against all competitors or subjects of the Crown. (Italics added)
As at present advised, I can imagine nothing more damaging to the royal prerogative. As time proceeds, the Government does no doubt increasingly enter into the commercial or industrial sphere; but if the argument suggested be sound, it would further appear as a consequence that as spheres of Government action widen, the prerogative of the Crown grows larger and larger and the escape from obligations or the use of preference over the rights of the ordinary citizens would in a greater and greater measure extend. These questions are enormously important; they will have, unless Parliament itself interposes to clarify the situation, to be decided some day ...

Counsel have not referred me to any recent judgments of Canadian Courts nor I have I found any containing decisions or opinions as to the extent of the royal prerogative in respect of that species of debt variously described as 'Crown debts in a changed age', or 'cases of ordinary commercial or industrial contracts entered into by a Government Department in the course of the business or enterprise which it carries on' ... [His Lordship referred briefly to seven Canadian decisions, and continued:] In all, the claim of the Crown was awarded priority. In five of the seven cases the Crown's claim was in respect of income tax; in none was the Crown's claim in respect of a debt arising, as in the case at bar, out of an ordinary business transaction between the Crown, actively engaged in business, and another commercial conern.
I therefore adopt, with respect, the views, though *obiter dicta*, so vigorously expressed by the Lord Chancellor, Lord Atkinson and Lord Shaw in the *Food Controller* case, *supra*, and hold that the claim of the Treasurer herein, based on two chattel mortgages granted as security for a loan made by the Treasury Branch to the debtor in the course of the financial or banking business carried on by the Treasurer is not of the kind or nature held from earliest times to be included in or covered by the royal prerogative, and that therefore it must – as to the claim of the Board, by reason of the wide terms of s-ss (4) and (5) of s 77 and s-ss (1) and (10) of s 79 of the *Workmen's Compensation Act*, and as to the claim of the City, by reason of ss 482 and 567 of the *City Act*, all cited *supra* – rank as of inferior status. I have already held that the privilege accorded the Crown when its claims concur with those of the City, as set out in the final words of s 567 of the *City Act*, quoted above, relates and is confined to that variety of 'Crown debts' traditionally held to be covered by royal prerogative and not to the commercial category ...

The Court of Appeal upheld the trial judgment on this point. See (1963), 40 D.L.R. (2d) 243.
See also *Re Cardston District U.F.A. Co.-Op. Assn.*, [1925] 4 D.L.R. 897, and *Alberta Government Telephones v Selk*, [1974] 4 W.W.R. 205 (Alta. D.C.).

v *Tudor Holdings Ltd.* v *Robertson et al.* (1973), 43 D.L.R. (3d) 752 (B.C.S.C.)

ANDERSON, J.: This is a motion brought by the defendant, the Bank of Montreal, for payment out of moneys paid into Court, pursuant to the provisions of the *Creditor's Relief Act*, R.S.B.C. 1960, c 85, as follows:

To the defendant, Bank of Montreal $10.292.42
To the defendant, Bank of British Columbia $1,493.24
To Her Majesty the Queen in right of Canada $4,368.68

There is no contest between the defendant banks and the issue here is whether the Crown is entitled to take all the moneys paid into Court on the basis that it obtained a judgment against Robertson on February 13, 1973, in the sum of $90,692.38. It is admitted that the Crown is entitled to payment of $4,368.68, pursuant to a judgment obtained on March 16, 1972.

The sequence of events is as follows:

July 6, 1972, Bank of Montreal registration of judgment $22,304.57
Sept. 11, 1972, Federal Crown charging order $4,368.68
Oct. 10, 1972, Federal Crown registration of charging order $4,368.68
Feb. 2, 1973, Bank of British Columbia registration of judgment $3,236.63
May 14, 1973, Federal Crown charging order $90,692.38
June 1, 1973, Federal Crown registration of charging order $90,692.38

Foreclosure proceedings were commenced by the plaintiff on February 23, 1973.

On May 10, 1973, Mackoff, Co.Ct.J (L.J.S.C.) (as he then was), made an order for sale in the foreclosure proceedings and the Attorney-General for Canada was given conduct of the sale.

On July 24, 1973, Hutcheon, Co.Ct.J. (L.J.S.C.), approved a sale of the mortgaged premises and ordered, *inter alia*, that the sum of $16,154.33 be paid into Court, pending the determination of the dispute between the defendant banks and the federal Crown.

The charging order for $90,692.38 made by Sheppard, J., reads in part as follows:

IT IS ORDERED THAT THE FOLLOWING LAND or interest in land of the Defendant, under the name of Gordon Waldron Robertson, Namely:
An undivided half interest as tenant in common with Mary Jane Robertson of an estate in fee simple in:
All and singular that certain parcel or tract of land and premises situate lying and being in the City of Vancouver in the Province of British Columbia more particularly known and described as:

>Lot 31
>Block 896
>District Lot 526
>Group 1, New Westminster District
>Plan 10198

according to the records of the Land Registry Office at Vancouver in the Province of British Columbia: *subject to encumbrances as appear by the said Affidavit*, STAND CHARGED with the payment to the Receiver General of Canada on behalf of Her Majesty the Queen of $90,692.38 with interest at the rate of 6% per annum on the sum of $75,285.49 from the 16th day of December, 1972, to date of payment, together with costs of the Interim Order and of this Order, the said costs to be taxed and added to the judgment debt.

AND IT IS FURTHER ORDERED that the interim charge heretofore imposed by the ORDER IMPOSING CHARGE ON LAND; ORDER TO SHOW CAUSE pronounced herein the 29th day of March, 1973, aforementioned, be wholly incorporated in and merged into the charge absolute imposed hereby, so that the charge created by registration of this Order may be endorsed upon the records of a Land Registry Office with priority as from registration of the said interim charge heretofore imposed.

(Emphasis mine.)

The affidavit referred to in the charging order had exhibited to it a certificate of encumbrances which indicates that the judgments obtained by the defendant banks were registered 'encumbrances' and the said charging order was, therefore, made subject to the said judgments ...

While it appears that the prerogative rights of the Crown are very wide, I think the Crown, in order to succeed, must avail itself of those rights. Here the Crown has made application under a federal statute and obtained an absolute charging order vesting the Crown with an interest in land, subject to the judgments obtained by the defendant banks. No application has been made to amend the order obtained. No other proceedings have been taken by the Crown under the *Creditor's Relief Act* or otherwise. There have been no proceedings to withdraw the charging order from the Land Registry Office.

In my view, in so far as the 'lands' of Robertson and the proceeds of the sale thereof are concerned, the status of the Crown became crystallized and that status is not subject to change now. I am also of the opinion that I should not make an order which would obviously be in conflict with the order made by the learned Federal Court Judge.

Even if I am wrong in holding that the Crown cannot seek an alternative remedy at this time, I would hold that the Crown cannot merely by reason of the fact that it holds a judgment against the judgment debtor, seek to claim against the funds in Court. The funds in Court are now the property of those who have properly availed themselves of their rights under the *Creditor's Relief Act*.

I reject the argument that the charging order obtained by the Crown is similar in nature to the registration of a judgment, as was the case in *Re Young* (1968), 70 D.L.R. (2d) 594, 66 W.W.R. 193, where it was held that the mere registration of a judgment did not sever a joint tenancy. The absolute charge here amounts to far more than the registration of a judgment and in fact, creates an interest in the Crown similar to a mortgage payable on demand.

For the above reasons, I refuse the application of the Crown and order that the moneys paid into Court be divided between the defendant banks and the Crown as follows:

To the defendant, Bank of Montreal $10,292.42

To the defendant, Bank of British Columbia $1,493.24

To Her Majesty the Queen in right of Canada $4,368.68

Judgment accordingly.

See also *Re Excelsior Elec. Dairy Mach. Ltd.*, [1923] 3 D.L.R. 1176 (S.C.O.) which held that 'the priorities ... which may accrue to the Crown by virtue of its prerogative right to proceed by way of [writ of] extent ... are dependant upon the issue of the writ itself, and if the right to issue the writ has gone no prerogative rights which depend for their existence upon the fact that the writ had issued can be deemed to exist merely because the Crown might have issued a writ of extent.' (at p 1178, per Orde, J)

QUESTION In *Tudor* (supra), why was the Crown permitted to have its claim under the charging order of September 11, 1972, satisfied in full?

vi *In Re Silver Bros. Ltd.*, [1932] 2 D.L.R. 673 (P.C.)

VISCOUNT DUNEDIN: This is an appeal from a judgment of the Supreme Court of Canada pronounced on September 26, 1929 allowing an appeal from a judgment of the Court of King's Bench (Appeal Side) for the Province of Quebec ...

On December 31, 1923, an order of the Superior Court of the Province of Quebec was made, declaring Messrs. Silver Brothers, Ltd., bankrupt.

The Government of the Dominion of Canada duly filed with the trustee in bankruptcy a claim in the sum of $3,707.07 for sales tax imposed in virtue of the Special War Revenue Act, 1915 (Can.), c 8, the said tax having become due subsequent to June 28, 1922, the date on which a certain amendment to the Special War Revenue Act, 1915, namely 1922 (Can.), c 47, came into force.

The Government of the Province of Quebec also duly filed with the trustee a claim in the sum of $527.42 for taxes due by the debtor for the years 1921, 1922 and 1923 under the provisions of arts. 1345 *et seq.* of R.S.Q. 1909, imposing a tax on commercial corporations.

The moneys realized from the sale of the assets of the insolvent estate, after the payment of costs and expenses of the trustee, amounted to $2,353.51, a sum insufficient to pay the two claims aforesaid.

The trustee in his final dividend sheet treated the claim of the Dominion as privileged, according to it the sum of $2,353.51 aforesaid in priority to the claim of the Province, and paid over to the Dominion $2,000 out of this sum.

The Attorney-General of Quebec filed in the Superior Court a petition disputing the dividend sheet and claiming that the debt due to the Province was privileged as a result of art. 1357 of R.S.Q. 1909, and that the claim of the Dominion was not privileged and that s 17 of the Special Revenue Act as enacted by 1922 (Can.), c 47, was *ultra vires*, or that if the said section was *intra vires* that the claims of the respective Governments were equally privileged and should be paid concurrently.

Section 17 of the Special War Revenue Act aforesaid provides as follows:—

Notwithstanding the provisions of *The Bank Act* and *The Bankruptcy Act*, or any other statute or law, the liability to the Crown of any person, firm or corporation for the payment of the excise taxes specified in *The Special War Revenue Act, 1915*, and amendments thereto, shall constitute a first charge on the assets of such person, firm or corporation, and shall rank for payment in priority to all other claims of whatsoever kind heretofore or hereafter arising save and except only the judicial costs, fees and lawful expenses of an assignee or other public officer charged with the administration or distribution of such assets.

This provision came into force on June 28, 1922, and remained in force until July 1, 1925, when it was repealed by 1925 (Can.), c 26, s 9.

Article 1357 of R.S.Q. aforesaid provides as follows: 'All sums due to the Crown in virtue of this section shall constitute a privileged debt, ranking immediately after law costs;' and came into force in 1906 (c 10) ...

The appeal before their Lordships was argued upon two grounds. The first, and it is this which bulks almost exclusively in the judgments of the Courts below, was that on the proper construction of the well-known ss 91 and 92 of the B.N.A. Act, 1867, c 3, the Dominion had no power to enact s 17 above quoted so as to prejudice the rights of the Government of the Province of Quebec. As to this question their Lordships have no hesitation in preferring the views of the majority of the Judges of the Supreme Court. It would be of no service to go over again the familiar ground of what may be called the competing claims of the two sections and to restate what has been so often stated. As lately as 1929 in the case of *Re Fisheries Act, 1914; A.-G. Can. v A.-G. B.C.*, [1930] 1 D.L.R. 194, Lord Tomlin, delivering the judgment of the Board, laid down at p 197 four propositions regarding the conflict of Dominion and provincial jurisdiction in terms which need not here at length be repeated. Now, looking at s 17 and the way it speaks of the preference, it would not be difficult to hold that it was a rule only applicable in bankruptcy. If that is so, then the matter is ended for bankruptcy is head 21 of s 91. But let it be assumed that it is rather a natural concomitant of taxation, then the case falls clearly under the fourth head laid down by Lord Tomlin. It runs thus:

There can be a domain in which provincial and Dominion legislation may overlap in which case neither legislation will be *ultra vires* if the field is clear, but if the field is not clear and the two legislations meet the Dominion legislation must prevail.

As a matter of fact, this is the textual reproduction of what had been said by Lord Dunedin as long ago as 1907, in the case of *G.T.R. v A.-G. Can.*, [1907] A.C. 65. Now, here so far as taxation itself is concerned, the field is clear. The two taxations, Dominion and provincial, can stand side by side without interfering with each other, but as soon as you come to the concomitant privileges of absolute priority they cannot stand side by side and must clash; consequently the Dominion must prevail.

There was, however, another ground of appeal clearly raised by the reasons of appeal and strenuously insisted upon before their Lordships, and that is based on the effect of s 16 of the Interpretation Act, R.S.C. 1906, c 1, a Dominion Act. This section reads as follows:

16. No provision or enactment in any Act shall affect, in any manner whatsoever, the rights of His Majesty, his heirs or successors, unless it is expressly stated therein that His Majesty shall be bound thereby.

Relying on that section, counsel for the Province says: Here is a debt due to His Majesty in Quebec. That debt is an asset of His Majesty, to be applied in Quebec for the purposes of Quebec according to the advice of the Quebec ministers. If the claim of the Dominion is upheld the money to satisfy this debt is swept away into the coffers of the Dominion. Therefore by this statute His Majesty is being bound to the detriment of one of his rights and there is no express statement in the statute that His Majesty is to be so bound ...

His first point had been stated by the learned Chief Justice. Inasmuch as the section says that it is to apply notwithstanding the provisions of the Bank Act and the Bankruptcy Act or 'any other statute or law,' he says it escapes the provision of the Interpretation Act. Now, first of all, the Interpretation Act is a general Act meant to apply to all future as well as to all present legislation, and their Lordships doubt whether it could be excluded except by special reference.

But, apart from that, the Bank Act and the Bankruptcy Act both deal with preferences, and that is the reason why they are particularly mentioned; and it follows that 'any other statute or law' must be *ejusdem generis*; that is to say, dealing with preferences. Their Lordships have accordingly no difficulty in rejecting this contention. It is perhaps right here to mention the method in which the learned trial Judge got rid of the effect of s 16, though it was not adopted by any of the Judges who formed the majority in the Supreme Court. He says that s 17 is in a later statute than s 16, and, therefore, in view of the maxim *posteriora prioribus derogant*, s 16 must give way. But this entirely misses the point that the maxim only applies when the two statutes cannot live together. There is no difficulty in the statute that enacts s 17 living with the Interpretation Act. The clause of the Interpretation Act is, so to speak, written into every statute. Thus the later statute gives perfectly good priority against all and sundry, but says that this priority does not affect the Crown right in the province ...

The next point made was that the provisions of s 16 do not apply when what is being done is not to affect the Crown prejudicially, but to give a benefit to the Crown, and along with this it is urged that there is only one Crown and reference is made to the case of *A.-G. Que.* v *Nipissing Central Ry. Co.*, [1926] 3 D.L.R. 545, 32 C.R.C. 96. It is quite true that the section refers to cases where the Crown would be 'bound,' *i.e.*, subjected to liability, and not to those where the Crown is benefited. But the fallacy lies in the application of this truth to the case in question. *Quoad* the Crown in the Dominion of Canada the Special War Revenue Act confers a benefit, but *quoad* the Crown in the Province of Quebec it proposes to bind the Crown to its disadvantage. It is true that there is only one Crown, but as regards Crown revenues and Crown property by legislation assented to by the Crown there is a distinction made between the revenues and property in the Province and the revenues and property in the Dominion. There are two separate statutory purses. In each the ingathering and expending authority is different. The *Nipissing* case *supra*, is quite on all fours with this doctrine. What was decided there was that when a statute *ex hypothesi intra vires* had said that a railway with consent of the Governor-General could take on paying compensation Crown lands, that meant Crown lands in the Province as well as in the Dominion. It will be at once observed that the point raised here could not be raised there. There was no doubt as to the mention of the Crown, and the only question was one of interpretation. Did the term 'Crown lands' mean Crown lands everywhere or only in the Dominion? There was no reason for limiting the interpretation. Crown lands in the Province were just as much Crown lands as Crown lands in the Dominion. The Crown in the Province was not prejudiced. The compensation money would be paid to the provincial exchequer except in the cases where there was a special purpose or trust under which the lands were vested in the Crown, and in that case there was a special direction under s-s 4.

Upon the whole matter, therefore, their Lordships think that the plea of the appellant is good. The effect of s 16, is so to speak, to add to the words of s 17, 'but this priority shall not operate against any right in the Crown in a Province, where such right would be diminished by the priority being asserted against it.' Whether the strict result of this view should be to give to the Province an overriding priority need not be discussed. Counsel for the Province did not ask for such relief; he was content that the two debts should rank *pari passu*.

NOTE See generally, *Re Nivalla Ice Cream Co.*, [1934] 4 D.L.R. 741 (Ont. H.C.J.), *Re Mendelsohn* (1960), 25 D.L.R. (2d) 778 (Ont. H.C.), and *Calgary* v *Walter's Trucking Services Ltd.* (1965), 51 W.W.R. (N.S.) 407 (Alta. C.A.).

For cases rejecting provincial statutes which purport to affect the priority of the Crown in the right of the Dominion see *R.* v *Lithwick* (1921), 57 D.L.R. 1 (Ex. Ct.), *Re Adams Shoe Co.*, [1923] 4 D.L.R. 927, *Toronto and Toronto Electric Commissioners* v

Wade, [1932] 3 D.L.R. 509 (Ont. C.A.); *Sternschein* v *The Queen* (1965), 50 D.L.R. (2d) 762 (Man. Q.B.)

For cases accepting the proposition that the Dominion has power to abrogate the priority of the Crown in the right of the provinces see *Industrial Development Bank* v *Valley Dairy Ltd.*, [1953] O.R. 70 (H.C.J.); *Re Clemenshaw* (1962), 33 D.L.R. (2d) 524 (B.C.S.C.); and *Re Pacific Western Airlines and the Queen in Right of Alberta* (1976), 66 D.L.R. (3d) 507 (F.C.A.), reversed on other grounds (1977), 14 N.R. 21 (S.C.C.).

f / Note: Tassé Committee

The Study Committee on Bankruptcy and Insolvency Legislation (Tassé Committee) undertook an extensive study into the law of bankruptcy in Canada, and produced its report in June of 1970 recommending changes in the legislation and practice. Although the question of priorities in bankruptcy is considered below, the views of the Committee about the Crown's privileged position as against general creditors in a bankruptcy may be aptly applied to the Crown's privileged position as against general unsecured creditors in situations outside of bankruptcy. The Committee stated (at 122–4) [some footnotes have been omitted]:

3.2.075 *Crown Priority*: The last priority, but the priority under which the largest amounts are paid, is that of the Crown. The history of the Crown priority goes back a long time. In *Magna Carta*, it was said that: 'The King's debtor dying, the King shall be first paid'. At common law, the Crown had a prerogative right to be paid first. The Crown continued to assert its prerogative after the enactment of the first Bankruptcy Acts, on the ground that a statute could not bind the Crown. Eventually, the application of the *Bankruptcy Act* was extended to the Crown, but it continued to assert the necessity of a priority in its favour, on the ground that the Crown was invariably, certainly in respect of taxes, an unwilling creditor and could not choose its debtor. For these reasons, it was in the public interest and necessary for the protection of the public treasury that it be paid first.

3.2.076 It is, we believe, important to re-examine the public policy in respect of the Crown priority. It must be determined whether such a priority is justified in a modern society. Certainly, it is not necessary for the financial stability of the government. [To measure the loss of revenue to the government due to the abolition of the Crown priority in a given year, it would be necessary to ascertain the total dividends paid to the government in that year and then deduct from this the sum it would have received as an ordinary creditor. One would, however, have to take into account the fact that due to a smaller loss, the other creditors would have to pay a higher income tax. Lastly, one must consider the possibility that the elimination of the priority would improve bankruptcy administration by increasing the chances of a better dividend for the ordinary creditors and by encouraging them to better look after their own interests.] The argument that the Crown cannot choose its own debtor has some relevance in claims for taxes, but none, as regards contractual claims. In this respect, it should be pointed out that individuals claiming damages do not choose their debtors either; and yet, they do not benefit by a priority of rank. One wonders whether, in our economy of easy credit, the businessman has always the economic freedom to choose his debtor or whether he is not bound, to a certain point, to give credit to the same extent as do his closest competitors. It could even be argued that the government should rank after ordinary creditors, as the public treasury is, in fact, in a better position than anyone to bear the inevitable losses. The government can, in effect, divide the burden of tax left unpaid by the bankrupt among all the tax paying public. It would be more logical for the government to do this, than to take advantage of the bankruptcy of an insolvent taxpayer to reimburse itself, at the expense of the creditors who have already suffered losses. Certainly, there can be no rational explanation for the government to attempt to obtain payment of the tax due by a bankrupt from his creditors. Such a proposition offends one's sense of natural justice.

3.2.077 Whatever the logic or lack of logic there is in the priority of the Crown, the cumulative impact of the priority has substantially increased since the Second World War. Crown priorities have grown in three dimensions: (1) the rates of existing or old taxes have been increased; (2) there have been many new kinds of taxes; and (3) the Crown has become extensively engaged in business, particularly through the use of Crown corporations to which the Crown priority has been held, in many cases, to apply. [*In re Spartan Air Services Limited* (1960), 1 C.B.R.(N.S.) 33 (Ont. Registrar).] The apathy of creditors to take part in the administration of an estate in bankruptcy can very well be explained by reason of the Crown priority. Very often, for the creditors to involve themselves in the administration of estates is equivalent to their volunteering as agents of the public treasury.

3.2.078 Professor J.A. MacLachlan, in his usual forthright manner and perhaps with some exaggeration, very harshly criticized the priority of the Government of the United States under its *Bankruptcy Act*, in these words:

The unprecedented multiplicity and magnitude of tax claims is greatly aggravated by their priority ... They strike the commercial community where it is weak by further impairing the financial condition of creditors who have had the misfortune of extending credit to a bankrupt. Unless governments can stop proliferating taxes to lavish largesse on politically favoured groups and to give public credit to those unworthy of private credit, bankruptcy may become just another device for paying official salaries. Dividends of priority creditors and to general creditors in bankruptcy have been less than 5¢ per capita per annum in relation to the national population, so that revenue at stake is chicken feed, but the commerical repercussions of accentuating bankruptcy frustrations may be disproportionate.

3.2.079 In our opinion, the priority of the Crown in our modern society cannot be justified and we recommend that it be abolished.

See also: W.T. Plumb, 'Tax Recommendations of the Commission on Bankruptcy Laws – Priority and Dischargeability of Tax Claims' (1974), 59 *Cornell L. Rev.* 991; and for support of the view that governments should enjoy priorities see Shanker, 'The Worthier Creditors', 1 *Can. Bus. L.J.* 342 (1976).

2 ENFORCING FAMILY SUPPORT OBLIGATIONS

a / Introduction
This section is divided into two parts: Parts (b) and (c) consider the rights of 'family members' to support and to the protection of property rights in proceedings other than divorce proceedings. Part (d) considers the rights of spouses and children upon divorce.

b / Family Support Generally
In Ontario, until very recently, only spouses, children and parents could obtain rights to support from another spouse, parent, or child. Relief was available to wives through

their common law rights to alimony, or under the provisions of The Deserted Wives' and Children's Maintenance Act, R.S.O. 1970, c 128, in cases in which the wife had been abandoned by her husband. (Such a wife also had the right to pledge her husband's credit for purchases in many cases). Children had rights to maintenance under the common law, by virtue of The Infants Act, R.S.O. 1970, c 222, The Children's Maintance Act, R.S.O. 1970, c 67 and under The Deserted Wives' and Children's Maintenance Act (supra). Judgments ordering support in these cases were usually enforceable through process of the provincial courts (family division), either directly, or following registration there of the judgment of another court. (See, for instance, The Provincial Courts' Act, R.S.O. 1970, c 369, s 25(1) which permits registration and enforcement in the provincial court of (inter alia) orders to pay alimony.) Note also the exceptional remedy provided by Rule 383 of the Supreme Court of Ontario Rules of Practice, R.R.O. 1970, which provides for the striking out of pleadings of a party who is able but refuses to pay interim alimony or disbursement charges after having been ordered to do so, and as well permits postponement of the trial in such circumstances.

Parents were entitled to maintenance in some cases, under The Parents' Maintenance Act, R.S.O. 1970, c 336. Orders made against children for the support of parents were enforceable as if they had been convictions in summary proceedings (The Parents' Maintenance Act, ss 6 and 7).

As well, additional 'enforcement' rights were available by virtue of s 197 of the Criminal Code, R.S.C. 1970, c C-34, which creates the offence of failing to provide necessaries to persons to whom a duty is owed. The offence may be treated as a summary conviction matter, or may be prosecuted as an indictable offence, in which case the convict is liable to imprisonment for two years.

Much of this family support system has now been abolished in Ontario (apart from transitional provisions) and has been replaced with the scheme established by The Family Law Reform Act, 1978, S.O. 1978, c 2. The Act provides for the sharing of 'family assets' between 'spouses' (the term is defined to include other than validly legally married persons) upon the breakdown of the relationship. It provides for support obligations among spouses (even more broadly defined than the definition adopted for family assets sharing purposes), and children. It contains further provisions guaranteeing to spouses equal rights to possession of the matrimonial home.

Rights to alimony, to orders under The Deserted Wives' and Children's Maintenance Act, to pledge credit, and to support as a child, or parent under the statutes and common law previously in force are all abolished in favour of the obligations created, and enforcement procedures provided under The Family Law Reform Act.

It is beyond the scope of this book to consider in any detail the substantive rights granted to family members. The rights are described in the statutory excerpts reproduced below only to the extent necessary to make comprehensible the special enforcement procedures created by the legislation.

c / The Family Law Reform Act, 1978, S.O. 1978, c 2.

2. (10) Where an order made under this Act affects real property, the order does not affect the acquisition of an interest in the real property by a person in good faith without notice of the order, unless the order is registered in the proper land registry office.

[Section 4 of the Act provides for the sharing of family assets on breakdown of the relationship.]
   6. In an application under section 4, the court may order,
   (*a*) that the title to any specified property directed to a spouse in the division be transferred to or in trust for or vested in the spouse whether absolutely, for life or for a term of years;
   (*b*) to partition or sale of any property;
   (*c*) that payment be made out of the proceeds of sale to one or both spouses, and the amount thereof;
   (*d*) that any property forming part of the share of either or both spouses be transferred to or in trust for or vested in a child to whom a spouse owes an obligation to provide support;
   (*e*) that either or both spouses give security for the performance of any obligation imposed by the order, including a charge on property, and
   (*f*) that either spouse pay to the other such sum as is set out in the order for the purpose of adjusting the division,
and may make such other orders or directions as are ancillary thereto.
   7. Any person may apply to the court for the determination of any question between that person and his or her spouse or former spouse as to the ownership or right to possession of any particular property, except where an application or an order has been made respecting the property under section 4 or 6, and the court may,
   (*a*) declare the ownership or right to possession;
   (*b*) where the property has been disposed of, order payment in compensation for the interest of either party;
   (*c*) order that the property be partitioned or sold for the purpose of realizing the interests therein; and
   (*d*) order that either or both spouses give security for the performance of any obligation imposed by the order, including a charge on property,
and may make such other orders or directions as are ancillary thereto.
[Section 8 permits the court to order an award to a spouse who has contributed to the acquisition of property.]
   9. In or pending an application under section 4, 7 or 8, the court may make such interim order as it considers necessary for restraining the dissipation of the property and for the possession, delivering up, safekeeping and preservation of the property.
   10. Where a court orders security for the performance of any obligation under this Part or charges a property therewith, the court may, upon application and notice to all persons having an interest in the property, direct its sale for the purpose of realizing the security or charge.
[Sections 14–17 create family support obligations.]
   18. (1) A court may, upon application, order a person to provide support for his or her dependants and determine the amount thereof.
   (2) An application for an order for the support of a dependant may be made by the dependant or a parent of the dependant or under subsection 3.
   (3) An application for an order for the support of a dependant who is a spouse or a dependant child of the spouse may be made by,
   (*a*) the Ministry of Community and Social Services in the name of the Minister; or
   (*b*) a municipal corporation, including a metropolitan, district or regional municipality, but not including an area municipality thereof,
if the Ministry or municipality is providing a benefit under *The Family Benefits Act* or assistance under *The General Welfare Assistance Act* in respect of the support of the dependent.
   (4) The court may set aside a provision for support in a domestic contract or paternity

agreement and may determine and order support in an application under subsection 1 notwithstanding that the contract or agreement contains an express provision excluding the application of this section.

(a) where the provision for support or the waiver of the right to support results in circumstances that are unconscionable;

(b) where the provision for support is to a spouse who qualifies for an allowance for support out of public money; or

(c) where there has been default in the payment of support under the contract or agreement.

(5) In determining the amount, if any, of support in relation to need the court shall consider all the circumstances of the parties, including,

(a) the assets and means of the dependant and of the respondent and any benefit or loss of benefit under a pension plan or annuity;

(b) the capacity of the dependant to provide for his or her own support;

(c) the capacity of the respondent to provide support;

(d) the age and the physical and mental health of the dependant and of the respondent;

(e) the length of time the dependant and respondent cohabited;

(f) the needs of the dependant, in determining which the court may have regard to the accustomed standard of living while the parties resided together;

(g) the measures available for the dependant to become financially independent and the length of time and cost involved to enable the dependant to take such measures;

(h) the legal obligation of the respondent to provide support for any other person;

(i) the desirability of the dependant or respondent remaining at home to care for a child;

(j) a contribution by the dependant to the realization of the career potential of the respondent;

(k) where the dependant is a child, his or her aptitude for and reasonable prospects of obtaining an education;

(l) where the dependant is a spouse, the effect on his or her earning capacity of the responsibilities assumed during cohabitation;

(m) where the dependant is a spouse, whether the dependant has undertaken the care of a child who is of the age of eighteen years or over and unable by reason of illness, disability or other cause to withdraw from the charge or his or her parents;

(n) where the dependant is a spouse, whether the dependant has undertaken to assist in the continuation of a program of education for a child who is of the age of eighteen years or over and unable for that reason to withdraw from the charge of his or her parents;

(o) where the dependant is a spouse, any housekeeping, child care or other domestic service performed by the spouse for the family, in the same way as if the spouse were devoting the time spent in performing that service in remunerative employment and were contributing the earnings therefrom to the support of the family; and

(p) any other legal right of the dependant to support other than out of public money.

(6) The obligation to provide support for a spouse exists without regard to the conduct of either spouse, but the court may in determining the amount of support have regard to a course of conduct that is so unconscionable as to constitute an obvious and gross repudiation of the relationship.

21. (1) Where an order for support has been made or confirmed and where the court is satisfied that there has been a material change in the circumstances of the dependant or the respondent or evidence has become available that was not available on the previous hearing, the court may, upon the application of any person named in the order or referred to in subsection 3

of section 18, discharge, vary or suspend any term of the order, prospectively or retroactively, relieve the respondent from the payment of part or all of the arrears or any interest due thereon and make such other order under section 19 as the court considers appropriate in the circumstances referred to in section 18.

(2) An application under subsection 1 shall be made to the court that made the order or to a co-ordinate court in another part of Ontario.

(3) No application under subsection 1 shall be made within six months after the making of the order for support or the disposition of any other application under subsection 1 in respect of the same order, except by leave of the court.

(4) This section applies to orders for maintenance of alimony made before this section comes into force or in a proceeding commenced before this section comes into force.

22. In or pending an application under section 18 or appearance to a notice under section 28, or where an order for support has been made, the court may make such interim or final order as it considers necessary for restraining the disposition or wasting of assets that would impair or defeat the claim or order for the payment of support.

24. Where an application is made under section 18 or a notice is issued under section 28 and a judge of the court is satisfied that the respondent or debtor is about to leave Ontario, the judge may issue a warrant in the form prescribed by the rules of the court for the arrest of the respondent or debtor.

26. (1) Where it appears to a court that,

(a) for the purpose of bringing an application under this Part; or

(b) for the purpose of the enforcement of an order for support, custody or access,
the proposed applicant or person in whose favour the order is made has need to learn or confirm the whereabouts of the proposed respondent or person against whom the order is made, the court may order any person or public agency to provide the court with such particulars of the address as are contained in the records in its custody and the person or agency shall provide to the court such particulars as it is able to provide.

(2) This section binds the Crown in right of Ontario.

27. (1) The clerk of the Unified Family Court or of a provincial court (family division), upon the request of a person entitled to support under an order for support or maintenance enforceable in Ontario or other persons or agency mentioned in subsection 3 of section 18 and upon the filing of such material as is prescribed by the rules of the court may enforce the order.

(2) For the purposes of enforcing an order filed under subsection 1, a provincial court (family division) has the power to issue execution and garnishment in accordance with the rules of the court and section 145 of *The Small Claims Courts Act* and subsection 3 of section 4 of *The Creditors' Relief Act* apply to a garnishment issued by the provincial court (family division).

(3) Notwithstanding section 25 of *The Proceedings Against the Crown Act*, an attachment under subsection 1 of section 30 and any other execution, garnishment or attachment or process in the nature thereof for the payment of an amount owing or accruing under an order for support or maintenance, may be issued against the Crown.

28. (1) Where there is default in payment under an order for support or maintenance, a clerk of the Unified Family Court or a provincial court (family division) may require the debtor, upon notice,

(a) to file a statement of financial information referred to in section 23;

(b) submit to an examination as to assets and means; and

(c) appear before the court to explain the default.

(2) If the debtor fails to appear as required after being served with a notice, or if the court is satisfied that the debtor cannot be served or intends to leave Ontario without appearing as required after being served, the court giving the notice may issue a warrant for the arrest of the debtor for the purpose of compelling attendance.

29. (1) Where the debtor fails to satisfy the court that the default is owing to his or her inability to pay and where the court is satisfied that all other practicable means that are available under this Act for enforcing payment have been considered, the court may,

(*a*) order imprisonment for a term of not more than ninety days to be served intermittently or as ordered by the court; or

(*b*) make such other order as may be made upon summary conviction for an offence that is punishable by imprisonment.

(2) The order for imprisonment under subsection 1 may be made conditional upon default in the performance of a condition set out in the order, including the performance of a community service order.

30. (1) Where the court considers it appropriate in a proceeding under section 28, the court may make an attachment order directing the employer of the debtor to deduct from any remuneration of the debtor due at the time the order is served on the employer or thereafter due or accruing due such amount as is named in the order and to pay the amounts deducted into court, and section 7 of *The Wages Act* does not apply.

(2) Where an application is made under section 21, the court may discharge, vary or suspend any term of an order made under subsection 1.

(3) An order under subsection 1 has priority over any other seizure or attachment of wages arising before or after the service of the order.

31. Where the court considers it appropriate in a proceeding under section 28, the court may order the debtor to give security for the payment of support or may charge any property of the debtor with payment of an amount for the provision of necessaries or preventing the dependant from becoming a public charge.

32. Where a court orders security for the payment of support under this Part or charges property therewith, the court may, upon application and notice to all persons having an interest in the property, direct its sale for the purpose of realizing the security or charge.

...

37. (1) In addition to its powers in respect of contempt, every provincial court (family division) may punish by fine or imprisonment, or by both, any wilful contempt of or resistance to its process, rules or orders under this Act, but the fine shall not in any case exceed $1,000 nor shall the imprisonment exceed ninety days.

(2) An order for imprisonment under subsection 1 may be made conditional upon default in the performance of a condition set out in the order and may provide for the imprisonment to be served intermittently.

[Sections 38–41 create rights in respect of the matrimonial home.]

42. (1) No spouse shall dispose of or encumber any interest in a matrimonial home unless,

(*a*) the other spouse joins in the instrument or consents to the transaction;

(*b*) the other spouse has released all rights under this Part by a separation agreement;

(*c*) the transaction is authorized by court order or an order has been made releasing the property as a matrimonial home; or

(*d*) the property is not designated as a matrimonial home under section 41 and an instrument designating another property as a matrimonial home of the spouses is registered under section 41 and not cancelled.

44. The court may, on the application of a spouse or person having an interest in property, by order,

(*d*) direct the setting aside of any transaction disposing of or encumbering an interest in the matrimonial home contrary to subsection 1 of section 42 and the revesting of the interest or any part of the interest upon such terms and subject to such conditions as the court considers appropriate.

d / Maintenance Upon Divorce

Divorce Act, R.S.C. 1970, c D-8
[Sections 10 and 11(1) provide for the granting of interim and final maintenance upon the granting of a divorce decree.]

11. (2) An order made pursuant to this section may be varied from time to time or rescinded by the court that made the order if it thinks it fit and just to do so having regard to the conduct of the parties since the making of the order or any change in the condition, means or other circumstances of either of them.

...

15. An order made under section 10 or 11 by any court may be registered in any other superior court in Canada and may be enforced in like manner as an order of that superior court or in such other manner as is provided for by any rules of court or regulations made under section 19.

The Family Law Reform Act, 1978, S.O. 1978, c 2

18. (5) In determining the amount, if any, of support in relation to need, the court shall consider all the circumstances of the parties, including,

(*p*) any other legal right of the dependant to support other than out of public money.

19. (3) Where an application is made under section 18, the court may make such interim order as the court considers appropriate.

(4) An order for support is assignable to an agency referred to in subsection 3 of section 18.

(5) Unless an order to provide support otherwise provides, it terminates upon the death of the person having the obligation to provide support, and the liability for amounts under the order coming due and unpaid in the preceding twelve months is a debt of his or her estate.

20. (1) Where an action for divorce is commenced under the *Divorce Act* (Canada), any application for support or custody under this Part that has not been determined is stayed except by leave of the court.

(2) Where a marriage is terminated by a decree absolute of divorce or declared a nullity and the question of support was not judicially determined in the divorce or nullity proceedings, an order for support made under this Part continues in force according to its terms.

21. (1) Where an order for support has been made or confirmed and where the court is satisfied that there has been a material change in the circumstances of the dependant or the respondent or evidence has become available that was not available on the previous hearing, the court may, upon the application of any person named in the order or referred to in subsection 3 of section 18, discharge, vary or suspend any term of the order, prospectively or retroactively, relieve the respondent from the payment of part or all of the arrears or any interest due thereon and make such other order under section 19 as the court considers appropriate in the circumstances referred to in section 18.

e / The Problem of Arrears

NOTE Suppose a husband has not made support payments over a period of several years. Does the court have jurisdiction to grant a discharge of the 'debt'?

In the case of arrears of alimony payments, the authorities are divided. The courts of most jurisdictions in Canada have adopted the English position that the amount of arrears recoverable is in the discretion of the court but that ordinarily, a wife will not be allowed to recover more than one year's arrears: *McMillan* v *McMillan and Weisgarber*, [1949] 2 D.L.R. 762 (Sask. C.A.); *Murray* v *Murray* (1952), 5 W.W.R. 704 (B.C.S.C.). In Ontario, however, the Courts took the position that they have no jurisdiction to alter a previous order for payments of alimony: *Knox* v *Knox*, [1942] O.W.N. 462 (S.C.); *M.* v *M.*, [1947] 3 D.L.R. 74 (Ont. H.C.J.); *Lear* v *Lear* (1974), 5 O.R. (2d) 572 (C.A.).

The policy underlying the one-year rule is that the purpose of providing alimony is to allow the wife to sustain herself. If she allows the arrears to accumulate over a period of time, 'obviously' she does not require the payments to sustain herself, and therefore should not be allowed to recover the arrears.

The technical problems which the courts saw as preventing their retrospective varying of or discharging of support payment orders seem to have been obviated by the provisions of s 21 (supra). Should the courts now adopt a 'one year rule'?

The one year rule is applicable, if at all, only to arrears accumulated after an order of the court. The rule is not applicable in an action for the arrears owing under a separation agreement: *Hill* v *Hill* (1963), 46 W.W.R. 158 (B.C.C.A.); *Eveleigh* v *Eveleigh*, [1969] 2 O.R. 644 (H.C.J.).

With respect to maintenance pursuant to an order under The Deserted Wives' and Children's Maintenance Act, the statutory language was held to authorize the Court to discharge payments in arrear: *The Queen* v *MacDonald* (1976), 74 D.L.R. (3d) 57 (Ont. H.C.J.). Courts administering equivalent legislation in other provinces have come to the same conclusion: see, for instance, *Lamontagne* v *Lamontagne* (1964), 47 W.W.R. 321 (Man. C.A.); *MacKenzie* v *MacKenzie* (1973), 12 R.F.L. 192 (Sask. Q.B.).

Similarly, after an initial holding to the contrary (*Ormandy* v *Ormandy* (1974), 6 O.R. (2d) 241 (H.C.J.)), Ontario courts have held that they are authorized by s 11(2) of the Divorce Act, supra, to revoke a previous maintenance order or to alter retroactively the amount of arrears owing under an order for maintenance made in divorce proceedings: *Englar* v *Englar* (1978), 19 O.R. (2d) 561 (C.A.).

Assume that Husband is in arrears in respect of 15 months' payments of maintenance (ordered to be paid under the Divorce Act). What would Wife have to do in order to garnish debts owing to Husband? Now assume that Wife is indebted to Creditor who has sued her, obtained judgment and filed a *fi. fa.* with the sheriff. Can Creditor require the sheriff to attach Wife's maintenance benefits? Can Creditor institute garnishment proceedings in respect of them? Equitable execution?

3 THE TAXATION OF A SOLICITOR'S BILL

The Solicitors Act, R.S.O. 1970, c 441

3. Where the retainer of the solicitor is not disputed and there are no special circumstances,

an order may be obtained on *praecipe* from the proper officer in the county in which the solicitor resides,

  (*a*) by the client, for the delivery and taxation of the solicitor's bill;

  (*b*) by the client, for the taxation of a bill already delivered, within one month from its delivery;

  (*c*) by the solicitor, for the taxation of a bill already delivered, at any time after the expiration of one month from its delivery, if no order for its taxation has been previously made.

  4. (1) No such reference shall be directed upon an application made by the party chargeable with such bill after a verdict or judgement has been obtained, or after twelve months from the time such bill was delivered, sent or left as aforesaid, except under special circumstances to be proved to the satisfaction of the court or judge to whom the application for the reference is made.

  13. Every application to refer a bill for taxation, or for the delivery of a bill, or for the delivering up of deeds, documents and papers, shall be made *In the matter of* (*the solicitor*), and upon the taxation of the bill the report of the officer by whom the bill is taxed, unless set aside or varied, is final and conclusive as to the amount thereof, and payment of the amount found to be due and directed to be paid may be enforced according to the practice of the court in which the reference was made.

Can you justify the preferred position of the lawyer-creditor?

4 UTILITY SHUT-OFFS

Utility companies have what amounts to a special right of prejudgment execution: they can simply cut off service. This has considerably more effect than do refusals to continue dealing in other commerical contexts: the monopolistic character of most utilities makes it difficult to find alternative sources of supply and the continuous use of and need for supply of the utility product or service means that a shut-off has serious immediate consequences.

These consequences are especially grave in the winter season. There are reported cases of deaths resulting from shutting off utilities: In January 19, 1972, the Montreal Star reported the death (by exposure) of a 67-year-old women after her electricity supply was cut off for non-payment of electricity bills.

The practice of cutting off supply is legally authorized in Ontario. The Public Utilities Act, R.S.O. 1970, c 390, governs water, artificial and natural gas, electricity, steam, and hot water. Section 27(3) allows municipal corporations operating utilities to shut them off where default in payment has occurred, and allows suit for the arrears. Similarly, section 59 allows private companies to stop supply on forty-eight hours' notice: they can sue for the debt as well. In the case of telephones under provincial jurisdiction, the notice period is seven days, and the notice must be in writing (The Telephone Act, R.S.O. 1970, c 457, s 89(3)). Are such preferred collection tactics justifiable?

This question was considered recently by the Supreme Court of the United States. In *Memphis Light, Gas and Water Division* v *Craft* (1978), 98 S.Ct. 1554, the Court held (Burger CJ and Stevens and Rehnquist JJ dissenting), that the power company did not have authority to cut off service to customers who were alleging defences to the charges claimed by the power company. The company was subject to due process requirements obliging it:

1 to notify customers of the course of action proposed (i.e. termination of service);

2 to apprise customers of their rights to challenge accounts claimed by the company;

and

3 to provide some mechanism whereby differences (in respect of the accounts) between the company and its customers could be considered.

Only after satisfaction of such procedural prerequisites could service be terminated. As the company's due process obligations had not been fulfilled, the customers were entitled to relief.

Utility companies often protect themselves against default by demanding deposits for commencement of service. These are also authorized by The Public Utilities Act, R.S.O. 1970, c 390. Section 50(4) provides:

Any corporation before supplying any public utility to any person or to any building or premises, or as a condition of continuing to supply the utility, may require any consumer to give reasonable security for the payment of the proper charges therefore or for carrying the public utility into the building or premises.

In British Columbia, where no such provision protects the utility companies, a recent case held that the practice of charging deposits to poor people was improper and enjoined it: *Chastain* v *B.C. Hydro Authority*, [1973] 2 W.W.R. 481 (B.C.S.C.). See, however, *Nelson* v *Hilliard*, [1976] 6 W.W.R. 761 (B.C.C.A.), holding valid a by-law requiring a security deposit for a city-operated electrical utility, the amount of which varied according to the applicant's credit-worthiness and according to whether he was a property-owner: the power to differentiate was 'in respect of conditions of supply'.

Members of the Community Legal Services Clinic at Pointe St. Charles in Montreal wrote a Report in January of 1972 concerning the practices of Gaz Metropolitan in their area. It was their feeling that where damage occurs there may be grounds for a conviction for criminal negligence. The test for that offence is enunciated in the English case of *R.* v *Bateman* (1925), 94 L.J.K.B. 791, [1925] All E.R. 45, and the crime is committed if

in the opinion of the jury, the negligence of the accused ... showed such disregard for the life and safety of others as to amount to a crime against the state and conduct deserving punishment.

In light of the Ontario legislative provisions, do you think that such an argument is open here? How could you make use of this opinion in a case of a threatened utility shut-off?

In Toronto, there is partial relief against shut-offs for the poor. Families with children may be able to have their arrears paid by the Children's Aid Society so that the health of children will not be impaired.

5 COMPENSATION FOR LOSS OF PROPERTY AS A RESULT OF A CRIMINAL ACT

Criminal Code, R.S.C. 1970, c C-34.

653. (1) A court that convicts an accused of an indictable offence may, upon the application of a person aggrieved, at the time sentence is imposed, order the accused to pay to that person an amount by way of satisfaction or compensation for loss of or damage to property suffered by the applicant as a result of the commission of the offence of which the accused is convicted.

(2) Where an amount that is ordered to be paid under subsection 1 is not paid forthwith the applicant may, by filing the order, enter as a judgment, in the superior court of the province in which the trial was held, the amount ordered to be paid, and that judgment is enforceable against the accused in the same manner as if it were a judgment rendered against the accused in that court in civil proceedings.

(3) All or any part of an amount that is ordered to be paid under subsection 1 may, if the court making the order is satisfied that ownership of or right to possession of those moneys is not disputed by claimants other than the accused and the court so directs, be taken out of moneys found in the possession of the accused at the time of his arrest.

NOTE In *R.* v *Zelensky* (1978), 86 D.L.R. (3d) 179 the Supreme Court of Canada upheld the constitutionality of s 653 (reversing the decision of the Manitoba Court of Appeal which had declared it to be *ultra vires* the Parliament of Canada ((1976), 73 D.L.R. (3d) 596.))

6 THE WAGE EARNER AS CREDITOR

a / Extended Liability For Wages Beyond the Immediate Employer

i The Business Corporations Act, R.S.O. 1970, c 53

139. (1) The directors of a corporation are jointly and severally liable to the employees of the corporation to whom *The Master and Servant Act* applies for all debts that become due while they are directors for services performed for the corporation, not exceeding six months wages, and for the vacation pay accrued for not more than twelve months under *The Employment Standards Act*, and the regulations thereunder or under any collective agreement made by the corporation.

(2) A director is liable under subsection 1,

(*a*) only if,

   (i) the corporation has been sued for the debt within six months after it has become due and execution against the corporation has been returned unsatisfied in whole or in part, or

   (ii) the corporation has within that period gone into liquidation or has been ordered to be wound up or has made an authorized assignment under the *Bankruptcy Act* (Canada), or a receiving order under the *Bankruptcy Act* (Canada) has been made against it and, in any such case, the claim for the debt has been proved; and

(*b*) he is sued for the debt while he is a director or within two years after he ceases to be a director.

(3) After execution has been so returned against the corporation, the amount recoverable against the director is the amount remaining unsatisfied on the execution.

(4) If the claim for the debt has been proved in liquidation or winding-up proceedings or under the *Bankruptcy Act* (Canada), a director who pays the debt is entitled to any preference that the creditor paid would have been entitled to or, if a judgment has been recovered for the debt, the director is entitled to an assignment of the judgment.

ii Canada Business Corporations Act, S.C. 1974–5, c 33, s 114

114. (1) Liability of directors for wages – Directors of a corporation are jointly and severally liable to employees of the corporation for all debts not exceeding six months' wages payable to each such employee for services performed for the corporation while they are such directors respectively.

(2) Conditions precedent to liability – A director is not liable under subsection 1 unless

(*a*) the corporation has been sued for the debt within six months after it has become due and execution has been returned unsatisfied in whole or in part;

(*b*) the corporation has commenced liquidation and dissolution proceedings or has been dissolved and a claim for the debt has been proved within six months after the earlier of the date of commencement of the liquidation and dissolution proceedings and the date of dissolution; or

(*c*) the corporation has made an assignment or a receiving order has been made against it under the *Bankruptcy Act* and a claim for the debt has been proved within six months after the date of the assignment or receiving order.

(3) Limitation – A director is not liable under this section unless he is sued for a debt referred to in subsection (1) while he is a director or within two years after he has ceased to be a director.

(4) Amount due after execution – Where execution referred to in paragraph 2 (*a*) has issued, the amount recoverable from a director is the amount remaining unsatisfied after execution.

(5) Subrogation of director – Where a director pays a debt referred to in subsection 1 that is proved in liquidation and dissolution or bankruptcy proceedings, he is entitled to any preference that the employee would have been entitled to, and where a judgment has been obtained he is entitled to an assignment of the judgment.

(6) Contribution – A director who has satisfied a claim under this section is entitled to contribution from the other directors who were liable for the claim.

QUESTION Each of these statutes makes directors liable to 'employees' for 'services performed'. Can you think of situations where this choice of words could cause difficulties?

For an example of a court's attempt to construe a similar statute broadly, see *Zavitz v Brock* (1974), 3 O.R. (2d) 583 (C.A.) (decided under the precedent Ontario Act creating liability to 'clerks, labourers, servants, apprentices and other wage earners' for all debts 'for services performed for the company, not exceeding six months' wages'.)

iii The Employment Standards Act, S.O. 1974, c 112

12. (1) Where before or after this Act comes into force associated or related activities, businesses, trades or undertakings are or were carried on by or through more than one corporation, individual, firm, syndicate or association, or any combination thereof, under common control or direction, and a person is or was an employee of such corporations, individuals, firms, syndicates or associations, or any combination thereof, an employment standards officer may treat the corporations, individuals, firms, syndicates or associations as one employer for the purposes of this Act.

(2) The corporations, individuals, firms, syndicates or associations treated as one employer shall be individually liable for any contravention of this Act and the regulations.

13. (1) In this section,

(*a*) 'business' includes an activity, trade or undertaking, or a part or parts thereof;

(*b*) 'sells' includes leases, transfers or any other manner of disposition and 'sale' has a corresponding meaning.

(2) Where an employer sells his business to a purchaser who employs an employee of the

employer, the employment of the employee shall not be terminated by the sale, and the period of employment of the employee with the employer shall be deemed to have been employment with the purchaser for the purposes of Parts VII, VIII, XI and XII.

(3) Where an employer sells his business to a purchaser who does not employ an employee of the employer, the employer shall comply with part XII.

15. Every employer shall be deemed to hold vacation pay accruing due to an employee in trust for the employee whether or not the amount therefor has in fact been kept separate and apart by the employer and the vacation pay becomes a lien and charge upon the assets of the employer that in the ordinary course of business would be entered in books of account whether so entered or not.

b / Summary Means of Enforcing a Wage Debt

i The Employment Standards Act, S.O. 1974, c 112

6. No civil remedy of an employee against an employer is suspended or affected by this Act.

47. (1) Where an employment standards officer finds that an employee is entitled to any wages from an employer, he may,

(*a*) arrange with the employer that the employer pay directly to the employee the wages to which the employee is entitled;

(*b*) receive from the employer on behalf of the employee any wages to be paid to the employee as the result of a compromise or settlement; or

(*c*) issue an order in writing to the employer to pay forthwith to the Director in trust any wages to which an employee is entitled and such order shall provide in addition for payment by the employer to the Director of a penalty of 10 per cent of the wages or the sum of $25, whichever is the greater, provided that the order shall not order the employer to pay a sum exceeding $4,000 for an employee.

(2) Where an employment standards officer issues an order under subsection 1, the order shall contain or have attached thereto information indicating the nature of the amount to be paid to an employee.

(3) An order issued under subsection 1 may order an employer to pay wages to one or more than one employee to which one or more than one employee is entitled for one or more than one failure to comply with a contract or more than one contract of employment or with this Act and the regulations.

(4) An order issued under subsection 1 shall be delivered to the employer by registered mail addressed to the employer at his or its last known place of business or served personally in the case of an individual and if the employer is a corporation upon the president, vice-president, secretary, treasurer, director, manager or person in charge of any branch of the corporation.

(5) A certificate of the Director certifying that the order was served upon or sent by registered mail to the employer and accompanied by a true copy of the order is admissible as evidence of the issue, service, mailing and receipt of the order.

(6) Every employer to whom an order is issued under subsection 1 shall comply with it in accordance with its terms.

52. (1) Where the Director has knowledge or suspects that a person is or is about to become indebted or liable to make any payment to an employer who is liable to make any payment under this Act, he may, by registered letter or by a letter served personally, demand that the person pay the moneys otherwise payable to the employer in whole or in part to the Director in trust on account of the liability under this Act.

(2) The receipt of the Director for moneys paid as required under this section is a good and sufficient discharge of the original liability to the extent of the payment.

(3) Every person who has discharged any liability to an employer who is liable to make a payment under this Act without complying with a demand under this section is liable to pay an amount equal to the liability discharged or the amount that he was required under this section to pay, whichever is the lesser.

59. (1) Every person who contravenes any provision of this Act or the regulations or a decision, requirement or order made under this Act is guilty of an offence and on summary conviction is liable to a fine of not more than $10,000 or to imprisonment for a term of not more than six months, or to both.

...

63. (1) No proceeding or prosecution under this Act shall be commenced more than two years after the facts upon which the proceeding or prosecution is based first came to the knowledge of the Director.

(2) In a proceeding or prosecution under this Act, no employee shall be entitled to recover any moneys due to him more than two years before the facts upon which the proceeding or prosecution is based first came to the knowledge of the Director.

(3) A statement as to the time when the facts upon which the proceeding or prosecution is based first came to the knowledge of the Director purporting to be certified by the Director, is, without proof of the office or signature of the Director, evidence of the facts stated therein.

[The sections reproduced above present only the broadest outline of the apparatus established by the legislation.]

What advantages are there in using the enforcement methods provided by this Act to collect employment benefits?

ii The Master and Servant Act, R.S.O. 1970, c 263

4. (1) Upon the complaint on oath of a servant or labourer against his master or employer concerning any non-payment of wages a justice of the peace may summon the master or employer to appear before him at a reasonable time to be stated in the summons, and he or some other justice upon proof on oath of the personal service of the summons, or of its service as hereinafter authorized, shall examine into the matter of the complaint, whether or not the master or employer appears, and upon due proof of the cause of complaint the justice may discharge the servant or labourer from the service or employment of the master or employer, and may direct the payment to him of any wages found to be due, not exceeding the sum of $500 and the justice shall make such order as to him seems just and reasonable for the payment of such wages, with costs, and in case of the non-payment of the same, together with the costs, for the space of eight days after the order has been made the justice shall issue his warrant of distress for the levying of the wages, together with the costs of the order and of the distress.

(2) Where the justice of the peace before whom a complaint is laid under this section is satisfied that the master or employer is about to quit the territorial jurisdiction of the justice of the peace, the justice of the peace may issue a warrant in Form 1 for the arrest of the master or employer.

(3) A complaint may be prosecuted and determined in any county or district in which the person complained against is found, or in any county or district in which the person complained against carries on business.

(4) Proceedings may be taken under this Act within six months after the engagement or

employment has ceased, or within six months after the last instalment of wages under the agreement of hiring has become due, whichever last happens.

(5) Proceedings may be had for non-payment of wages in respect of service or labour performed in Ontario upon a verbal or written agreement or bargain made out of Ontario.

(6) Where the master or employer claims a set-off or makes a claim for unliquidated damages, the justice of the peace shall investigate the same and give judgment for the balance of wages, if any, due to the claimant after deducting the set-off or claim.

(7) The justice of the peace does not have jurisdiction to adjudicate upon a set-off or claim exceeding the claim for wages except to the extent of the wages.

5. Where the proceedings are taken before a provincial judge, and payment of wages is ordered by him to be made by the master or employer to the servant or labourer, and the same are not paid within the time limited by the order, the same proceedings may be taken by the person claiming the benefit of the order as may be taken by a party having an unsatisfied judgment or order in a small claims court for the payment of any debt, damages or costs, as respects the examination of the judgment debtor touching his estate and effects, the means he has of discharging his liability, and the disposal he has made of any property, and the provincial judge has the like power and authority to enforce payment of the debt as are possessed by a judge of a small claims court in like cases, and the practice and proceedings thereon shall be the same as nearly as may be and have the same effect as provided in *The Small Claims Courts Act*, with respect to judgment debtors.

6. Subject to section 8, the provincial judge may name in the order for payment of wages such time, not exceeding twenty-one days, as to him may seem just and reasonable for the payment of the same and costs, and in case of non-payment within such time the complainant is entitled to take forthwith the proceedings for enforcing payment herein provided.

7. Where an order is made under this Act by a provincial judge for the payment of money such order may be proceeded upon and enforced in the manner provided by section 694 of the *Criminal Code* (Canada) and it applies as if it were set out and enacted herein.

8. (1) In the case of wages due to any mechanic, labourer or other person in respect of work of the character mentioned in section 5 of *The Mechanics' Lien Act* the jurisdiction of a provincial judge in a city under this Act extends to wages for thirty days, or for a balance equal to the wages for thirty days, though the same or the balance thereof exceed the sum of $400.

(2) Where no specific rate of wages has been expressly agreed to between the parties, the provincial judge in a city may order payment of the wages, reckoning the amount thereof according to the current rate of wages in the city in like cases, or according to what may appear to be a just and reasonable allowance.

(3) The order shall direct payment of the wages to be made forthwith, and a warrant of distress shall be issued accordingly, unless the master or employer makes oath, and the provincial judge believes, that the master or employer is unable to make the payment forthwith, and expects to be able to pay and intends to pay the same within the time given, and unless also the provincial judge considers the proposed delay to be under the circumstances reasonable, and the provincial judge, if he sees fit, may order security to be given as a condition of delay.

(4) In case of an adjournment at the instance of the master or employer the same shall be on payment for the claimant's time in attending the court, the amount to be fixed by the provincial judge, and such payment shall be made forthwith unless the provincial judge sees reason for dispensing with immediate payment.

(5) The order for payment may be filed in the small claims court that would be the proper court for bringing an action for the wages, and on such filing the order becomes a judgment of such small claims court and may be enforced as a judgment of that court.

The question of whether or not an 'employee' is within the class entitled to use this Act, is one to be determined on the facts of each case.

Winkler v *High-Test Electrical Manufacturing Ltd.*, [1965] 1 O.R. 386 (H.C.J.)

HAINES, J.: This is an appeal by way of stated case from the order of Magistrate R.B. Dnieper, dismissing a complaint laid by the appellant under the provisions of the *Master and Servant Act* against High-Test Electrical Manufacturing Limited (hereinafter referred to as 'High-Test').

On August 20, 1964, the appellant Winkler made a complaint on oath before a Justice of the Peace that High-Test, on July 17, 1964, unlawfully did not pay to the complainant the sum of $500, being the amount of wages due and owing, contrary to s 4 of the *Master and Servant Act*, R.S.O. 1960, c 230, as amended by 1961–62, c 77, s 1.

From the stated case, it appears that Winkler was employed by High-Test to carry on the duties of its general manager, for which he was paid a salary of $250 a week. He also held shares in High-Test and was its vice-president.

On July 7, 1964, the president of the company 'temporarily suspended' him, and this complaint was subsequently made in respect of salary alleged to be owing but unpaid for the first two weeks after his suspension. At the conclusion of the evidence, the learned Magistrate ruled that the *Master and Servant Act* was never intended to be used by a person in a managerial position, but was designed for the protection and assistance of labourers. He therefore dismissed the complaint. Winkler now appeals to this Court on the ground that the learned Magistrate's decision was erroneous in point of law.

[His Lordship set out s 4(1) of The Master and Servant Act and continued:]

Various sections of the Act refer to 'workman', 'servant', 'master', 'labourer', and 'mechanic', but these terms are not defined in the statute. In the absence of any guidance from the Legislature, it must be presumed that they were meant to bear their ordinary meaning at common law. The argument on this appeal was not directed to the question whether Winkler was a 'labourer', but rather to the correctness of the learned Magistrate's ruling that he was not a 'servant' within the meaning of s 4(1).

The learned Magistrate was of the opinion that the Act did not apply to Winkler, because he was vice-president and a shareholder of his corporate employer, and was charged with carrying on the duties of its general manager. In my view, the mere fact that a complainant is a shareholder or officer of the company from which he seeks to recover wages is not fatal to the Court's jurisdiction to hear his application. The real question is whether he is a 'servant' or 'labourer'. Winkler is not precluded from being a servant of High-Test simply because he is a shareholder and vice-president of the company. Further, the designation of a person as 'General Manager' is not in itself sufficient reason to prevent him from invoking the provisions of the Act. In recent years, it has become common for employers to dignify menial positions with imposing titles, and it would be anomalous to hold that an inventive employer could, by astute choice of job designations, place his employees beyond the purview of the Act.

Counsel for the respondent indicated by reference to the history of the legislation that its original purpose was to prohibit slavery in Upper Canada. (See C.S.U.C. 1859, c 75, ss 1 and 2.) From this, he argued that the Act must be restricted in its present day application to members of the labouring class. When read as a whole, however, the Act cannot sustain this narrow construction. For example, s 12 [am. 1961–62, s 2], which declares that agreements purporting to oust the application of the statute are null and void, expressly does not apply 'to any manager, officer or superintendent'. The inference is plain that, although these persons are excepted from the provisions of that section, the Legislature has considered them to fall within the ambit of the Act in other respects.

The question that must be determined on every application of this nature is whether the relationship of master and servant has been established between the person summoned and the complainant. The existence of this relationship is a question of fact in each case. Traditionally, the essential characteristic of the master-servant relation is the employer's power not only to direct what work the servant is to do, but also the manner in which the work is to be done. (See Batt, *Law of Master and Servant*, 4th ed., pp 5 to 6). Although this is the primary test, regard must also be had to a number of other considerations, including the master's power of selection of his servant; the terms of the engagement; the method and frequency of remuneration; and the master's right to suspend or dismiss. See 25 Hals., 3rd ed., p 448, para. 872, and the cases therein cited.

The *Master and Servant Act* affords to a limited class of persons, namely, servants and labourers, a summary and inexpensive method of recovering outstanding wages. In my view, the obligation rests upon a complainant who invokes the Act to satisfy the Court that he is one of those persons entitled to take advantage of the extraordinary procedure which it affords. If he fails to discharge this obligation, the Court may not entertain his application, leaving him free to assert his claim in conventional proceedings.

From what appears in the stated case, it is clear that the appellant failed to satisfy this onus. The learned Magistrate's order was therefore correct in law, and the appeal is dismissed with costs.

Appeal dismissed.

See also *Cooke* v *C.K.O.Y.*, [1963] 2 O.R. 257, where the Court held that a consultant to a radio station who had complete freedom to determine the scope of his own duties; to hire and fire employees, and to determine important aspects of the radio station's programming policy, could not claim the benefit of The Master and Servant Act.

iii The Apprenticeship and Tradesmen's Qualification Act, R.S.O. 1970, c 24

17. (2) In addition to any fine that may be imposed on an employer for his failure to pay an apprentice the wages due an apprentice, the provincial judge may order the employer to pay to the Director in trust for the apprentice an amount equal to the arrears of wages to which the apprentice is entitled, and, when the order becomes final, a copy of it, certified as a true copy by the provincial judge who made it, may be filed by the Director with the clerk of the county or district court of a county or district in which the employer carries on business or, where the amount of arrears does not exceed $400, with the clerk of a like small claims court, and, when so filed and upon payment of the fees of the clerk of the court, such order becomes an order of the court in which it is filed and may be enforced as a judgment of the court against the employer for the amount mentioned in the order and the fees so paid.

iv The Industrial Standards Act, R.S.O. 1970, c 221, s 19(1), (2)

19. (1) Every employer who contravenes a schedule that is applicable to him or who permits or condones work in contravention thereof is guilty of an offence and on summary conviction is liable, for a first offence, to a fine of not less than $50 and not more than $200 and, in default of payment, to imprisonment for a term of not more than two months, and, for any subsequent offence, to a fine of not less than $100 and not more than $1,000 and, in default of payment, to imprisonment for a term of not more than six months, and, where the conviction is for failing to pay the minimum rate of wages prescribed by the schedule, shall be ordered to pay to the Director, as an additional penalty, the full amount of the wages found to be unpaid to any employee under the schedule, and the Director, in his discretion, may direct that the whole or a part of such wages be either forfeited to the Crown or paid to the employee or employees entitled thereto.

(2) A copy of an order for payment of wages made under subsection 1 that has become final, certified as a true copy by the provincial judge who made it, may be filed by the Director with the clerk of the county or district court of a county or district in which the employer carries on business or, where the amount ordered to be paid does not exceed $400, with the clerk of a like small claims court, and, when so filed the clerk of a like small claims court, and, when so filed and upon payment of the fees of the clerk of the court, such order becomes an order of the court in which it is filed and may be enforced as a judgment of the court against the employer for the amount mentioned in the order and the fees so paid.

v The Ministry of Transportation and Communications Creditors Payment Act, s.o. 1975, c 44

2. (1) Where a contractor does not pay a creditor in accordance with his obligation to do so under the contract, the creditor may, not later than 120 days after the last day on which the labour, materials or services were provided, send to the appropriate office of the Ministry by registered mail a notice setting out the nature and amount of his claim.

(2) The Minister may, after notice in writing to the contractor and surety, if any, pay the claimant the amount settled upon and deduct the amount so paid from any moneys due or that may become due to the contractor on any account or from the moneys or securities, if any, deposited by the contractor with the Ministry, and, if there are insufficient moneys due or to become due to the contractor to permit of such deduction, the surety, if any, shall pay to the Ministry upon demand an amount sufficient to make up the deficiency.

(3) In paying a claim under subsection 2, the Minister may act upon any evidence that he considers sufficient and may compromise any disputed liability, and such payment is not open to dispute or question by the contractor or the surety, if any, but is final and binding upon them.

This statute was proclaimed on 1 January 1976. It incorporates the provisions of The Public Works Creditors Payment Act, R.S.O. 1970, c 394 which was repealed by s.o. 1975, c 45 (proclaimed 1 January 1976). However, the Act is applicable only to contracts with the Ministry of Transportation and Communications. The remaining Ministries have been brought within the ambit of The Mechanics Lien Act by s.o. 1975, c 43 (proclaimed 1 January 1976). The Public Works Creditors Payment Act is still applicable to work done under contracts entered into before its repeal.

vi The Government Contracts Hours and Wages Act, R.S.O. 1970, c 194: This statute does not give the wage earner a summary method of enforcing payment of wages. Rather it contains provisions regulating the payment of a fair wage and the creation of acceptable working conditions for persons employed by contractors doing construction work for the provincial government. Section 4 makes it an offence to contravene the Act. The penalty is a fine of not less than $50 and not more than $500.

vii Possessory Liens for Some Workers: Where a person expends energy or expense in improving an article left with him for that purpose, the worker may be entitled to a possessory lien on the article improved, to secure payment of the sum owing in respect of the improvements. This common law right ultimately authorizes the worker to sell the article and to deduct the amounts owing to him before remitting the balance of the proceeds to the article's former owner. However, matters rarely get this far, and the threat to detain the article normally induces the owner to pay for the services of the worker.

This sort of possessory lien has been described as follows:

The Common-law principle seems to be clear that, if a person has an article delivered or entrusted to him on which he does some work or bestows trouble or expense, he has a right to retain it until his charge is paid for that particular work or expense. *But* he must assert his right and maintain his possession, otherwise he loses his right and thereafter cannot assert it upon the article even though it subsequently comes properly into his possession ...

[Per Edwards DCJ in *Compass Mapping Corpn.* v *Maw* (1954), 1 W.W.R. (N.S.) 108 (Alta. Dist. Ct.) at p 111.]

The principle can assist such diverse workers as shoemakers, cleaners, accountants and lawyers (who can retain files and documents until paid), auctioneers, carriers and bankers. For a partial list, see p. 609, infra.

c / Priority of Wage Claimants

i The Wages Act, R.S.O. 1970, c 486

1. In this Act, 'wages' means wages or salary whether the employment in respect of which the same is payable is by time or by the job or piece or otherwise.

2. Where an assignment of any real or personal property is made for the general benefit of creditors, the assignee shall pay, in priority to the claims of the ordinary or general creditors of the assignor, the wages of all persons in the employment of the assignor at the time of the making of the assignment or within one month before the making thereof, not exceeding three months' wages, and such persons rank as ordinary or general creditors for the residue, if any, of their claims.

3. All persons who, at the time of the seizure by the sheriff or who within one month prior thereto, were in the employment of the execution debtor, and who become entitled to share in the distribution of money levied out of the property of a debtor within the meaning of *The Creditors' Relief Act* are entitled to be paid out of such money the wages due to them by the execution debtor, not exceeding three months' wages, in priority to the claims of the other creditors of the execution debtor, and are entitled to share *pro rata* with such other creditors as to the residue, if any, of their claims.

4. All persons in the employment of an absconding debtor at the time of a seizure by the sheriff under *The Absconding Debtors Act*, or within one month prior thereto, are entitled to be paid by the sheriff, out of any moneys realized out of the property of the debtor, the wages due to them by the debtor, not exceeding three months' wages, in priority to the claims of the other creditors of the debtor, and are entitled to share *pro rata* with such other creditors as to the residue, if any, of their claims.

5. In the administration of the estate of any person dying on or after the 13th day of April, 1897, any person in the employment of the deceased at the time of his death, or within one month prior thereto, who is entitled to share in the distribution of the estate, is entitled to his wages, not exceeding three months' wages, in priority to the claims of the ordinary or general creditors of the deceased, and such person is entitled to rank as an ordinary or general creditor of the deceased for the residue, if any, of his claim.

ii The Employment Standards Act, s.o. 1974, c 112

14. Notwithstanding the provisions of any other Act and except upon a distribution made by a trustee under the *Bankruptcy Act* (Canada), wages shall have priority to the claims or rights and be paid in priority to the claims or rights, including the claims or rights of the Crown, of all preferred, ordinary or general creditors of the employer to the extent of $2,000 for each employee.

15. Every employer shall be deemed to hold vacation pay accruing due to an employee in trust for the employee whether or not the amount therefor has in fact been kept separate and apart by the employer and the vacation pay becomes a lien and charge upon the assets of the employer that in the ordinary course of business would be entered in books of account whether so entered or not.

See *Re Dairy Maid Chocolates Ltd.* (1973), 31 D.L.R. (3d) 699 (s.c.o.) which held that s 8(2) of The Employment Standards Act (the predecessor to s 15) was *intra vires* the province, and effectively excluded vacation pay held in trust from the assets available to the trustee in bankruptcy. The Court in *MacMillan et al.* v *Frizell Plumbing and Heating Ltd. et al.* (1975), 56 D.L.R. (3d) 415 (N.s.s.C.) agreed with the reasoning of *Re Dairy Maid Chocolates Ltd.* in considering s 34 of the Nova Scotia Labour Standards Code, s.N.s. 1972, c 10 (a provision substantially similar to Ontario's s 15).

See also *Canadian Imperial Bank of Commerce* v *Brooker Trade Bindery Ltd.* (1975), 20 C.B.R. (N.s.) 280 (Ont.) which followed *Dairy Maid*. This was a contest between unpaid employees and secured creditors; the Master held that unpaid vacation pay arising prior in time to the creation of a debenture given by the employer constituted a valid trust fund to be paid before any payment to the debenture holder.

iii Bankruptcy Act: Under the Bankruptcy Bill (s-14), wage creditors are included in the class of preferred creditors to the extent of $2,000, and thus have priority to that amount over most other unsecured creditors. See p 839, infra.

iv The Mechanics' Lien Act, R.s.o. 1970, c 267, s 15

15. (1) Every workman whose lien is for wages has priority to the extent of thirty days' wages over all other liens derived through the same contractor or subcontractor to the extent of and on the 15 per cent directed to be retained by section 11 to which the contractor or subcontractor through whom the lien is derived is entitled, and all such workmen rank thereon *pari passu*.

(2) Every workman is entitled to enforce a lien in respect of any contract or subcontract that has not been completed and, notwithstanding anything to the contrary in this Act, may serve a notice of motion on the proper persons, returnable in four days after service thereof before the

judge or officer having jurisdiction to try an action under this Act, that the applicant will on the return of the motion ask for judgement on his claim for lien, registered particulars of which shall accompany the notice of motion duly verified by affidavit.

(3) If the contract has not been completed when the lien is claimed by a workman, the percentage shall be calculated on the value of the work done or materials placed or furnished by the contractor or subcontractor by whom the workman is employed, having regard to the contract price, if any.

(4) Every device by an owner, contractor or subcontractor to defeat the priority given to a workman for his wages and every payment made for the purpose of defeating or impairing a lien are void.

v The Woodmen's Lien for Wages Act, R.S.O. 1970, c 504

5. (1) A person performing labour has a lien upon the logs or timber in connection with which the labour is performed for the amount due for such labour, and the lien has precedence over all other claims or liens thereon, except a claim or lien of the Crown for any dues or charges or that a timber slide company or any owner of a slide or boom may have thereon for tolls.

(2) A contractor who has entered into any agreement under the terms of which he himself or by others in his employ has cut, removed, taken out or driven logs or timber, shall be deemed to be a person performing labour upon logs or timber within the meaning of this section, and such cutting, removal, taking out and driving shall be deemed to be the performance of labour within the meaning of this section.

d / Priorities Problems

The inconsistencies among the wage priorities prescribed by s 14 of The Employment Standards Act, and s 3 of The Wages Act, and the mode of distribution of funds prescribed by The Creditors' Relief Act (supra), have created difficult problems. Consider the following cases:

i *Re Campeau Corporation and Provincial Bank of Canada et al.* (1975), 7 O.R. (2d) 73 (Div. Ct.)

HOULDEN, J.: This is an appeal from an order of the Local Master at Ottawa dated April 9, 1974, in which the Local Master determined the priorities with respect to a fund paid into Court by Campeau Corporation (Campeau) pursuant to an interpleader order of March 5, 1974.

On December 8, 1972, Cafco Building Cleaning Limited (Cafco) executed a general assignment of book debts in favour of the Provincial Bank of Canada (the Bank). The assignment was registered pursuant to the *Assignment of Book Debts Act*, R.S.O. 1970, c 33, on December 11, 1972, in the office of the Clerk of the Judicial District of Ottawa-Carleton as No. 289624.

During the months of October and November, 1973, Cafco became indebted to its employees in the amount of $32,768.50 for wages. In these proceedings, Lucien Aubin and Gary Pelletier, two of the employees, are acting on behalf of all employees of Cafco with claims for unpaid wages. During the month of November, 1973, Cafco generally ceased to honour its obligations to its creditors.

Campeau is the owner of a building in the City of Ottawa known as 'Place de Ville'. A contract was entered into between Cafco and Campeau whereby Cafco performed the cleaning services in this building. On November 26, 1973, the contract was terminated. At the date of termination, the sum of $23,418.77 was due and owing by Campeau to Cafco.

On December 13, 1973, the Bank notified Campeau of its assignment and requested Campeau to pay all moneys due and owing to Cafco to the Bank. At that date, Cafco was indebted to the Bank in the amount of $16,657.50.

Pursuant to the interpleader order of March 5, 1974, Campeau paid $18,851.67 into Court, having withheld the balance for payment of a claim of the Workmen's Compensation Board of Ontario.

The competing claimants to the fund paid into Court were (a) the Bank, which claimed to be entitled to the money as a secured creditor under its general assignment of book debts, (b) the employees of Cafco with claims for unpaid wages, who claimed the money pursuant to s 8(1) of the *Employment Standards Act*, R.S.O. 1970, c 147, (c) the Receiver-General of Canada, and (d) Robert Lee Simpson, an execution creditor. The Local Master found that the employees had priority over the other claimants. As the unpaid claims of the employees were in excess of the amount in the fund, the Local Master did not have to establish a scheme of priorities. Robert Lee Simpson and the Receiver-General of Canada have not appealed from the Local Master's order; their claims are therefore not in issue in this appeal ...

Turning then to the merits of the appeal, the Local Master held that the employees were entitled to the fund by virtue of the provisions of s 8(1) of the *Employment Standards Act*, which reads as follows:

8(1) Notwithstanding the provisions of any other Act, a person to whom unpaid wages is due and owing by an employer shall have first priority over the claims or rights, including the claims or rights of the Crown, of all preferred, ordinary or general creditors of the employer to the extent of $2,000.

Counsel for the employees argued first that 'preferred creditors' in s 8(1) should be read as including secured creditors. Accordingly, even if the Bank were found to be a secured creditor, the wage-earners would have priority over the Bank. The *Employment Standards Act* does not define 'preferred creditors'. But to my mind, the words are clearly not intended to include secured creditors. I believe that 'preferred creditors' only refers to unsecured creditors who by common law or statute are given priority over other unsecured creditors. If the statute intended to give priority to unpaid claims of wage-earners over secured creditors, I think it would have done so in clear and specific terms as is done, for instance, in s 88(5) of the *Bank Act*, R.S.C. 1970, C B-1.

Counsel for the employees contended next that the wage-earners were given a statutory lien by s 8(1) and thus, the wage-earners were secured creditors. A statutory charge or lien against property must be created in clear and precise terms: *Dinning* v *Workmen's Compensation Board*, [1932] 1 D.L.R. 373, 13 C.B.R. 256, [1932] 1 W.W.R. 136. For an example of the type of wording which can be used to create a charge or lien, reference can be made to the wording of the British Columbia *Workmen's Compensation Act* as set out in *Re Clemenshaw; Workmen's Compensation Board* v *Canadian Credit Men's Trust Ass'n Ltd.* (1962), 36 D.L.R. (2d) 245 at pp 246–7, 4 C.B.R. (N.S.) 238 at p 240, 40 W.W.R. 199. On the plain reading of s 8(1), it does not, in my opinion, create a charge or lien on the property of the employer for unpaid wages; rather, it merely provides for priority of payment of such claims over certain classes of creditors and those classes of creditors do not, in my view, include secured creditors.

[The Court rejected the claim that the Bank's general assignment of book debts was a floating charge which did not become crystallized until after the employees' claims for wages arose.] On November 26, 1973, when Campeau owed Cafco $23,418.77, the Bank by virtue of its assignment had an equitable charge on the money that was due and owing. The Bank was not a preferred, ordinary or general creditor of Cafco; it was a secured creditor. By reason of its assignment, the Bank, to use the words of Bankes, L.J., in *Re Lind*, had 'an enforceable security as against the property assigned'.

In any event, if the Bank only received a floating charge, counsel for the employees conceeded that if the Court found that preferred creditors in s 8(1) did not include secured creditors, the wage-earners would only have priority if they received a statutory lien by the terms of s 8(1) of the *Employment Standards Act*; and as I have pointed out, it is my opinion they did not. Therefore, even if the Bank only had a floating charge, by virtue of its assignment of book debts, it would still have priority over the claims of wage-earners by reason of the notice that it gave to Campeau on December 13, 1973.

In statutes such as the *Bankruptcy Act*, R.S.C. 1970, c B-3, s 107(1) (*d*), and the *Winding-up Act*, R.S.C. 1970, c W-10, s 72, the Legislature has attempted to give priority to unpaid claims of wage-earners over ordinary creditors in the case of bankruptcy or winding-up. While this is commendable, it is also important that persons advancing money on the strength of security should have their rights protected. This principle has been recognized in s 49 of the *Bankruptcy Act*, and in s 79 of the *Winding-up Act*. As I have endeavoured to point out, I believe it was the intention of the Legislature in s 8(1) of the *Employment Standards Act* to give priority to unpaid wage-earners over the claims of other unsecured creditors (this, of course, would have no application to the *Bankruptcy Act* or *Winding-up Act*: *Re Lewis's Department Store Ltd.* (1972), 17 C.B.R. (N.S.) 113). But I do not believe the Legislature had any intention of interfering with the rights of secured creditors by the enactment of s 8(1). And I think it would be wrong to extend the provisions of s 8(1) by implication to include secured creditors: Craies, *Statute Law*, 7th ed., at p 71.

See also *Re The Queen and Board of Industrial Relations* (1976), 64 D.L.R. (3d) 294 (Alta. S.C.), in which the Court, construing equivalent Alberta legislation, came to a similar conclusion: wage claims were entitled to priority over the claims of all other unsecured creditors, but were subordinate to the claim of a secured creditor.

ii *Roach v McLachlan* (1892), 19 O.A.R. 496 (C.A.)

OSLER, J.A.: This is an appeal from the judgment of the Judge of the County Court of the county of Elgin, confirming the sheriff's scheme of distribution under the Creditor's Relief Act, of moneys levied by him under certain writs of *fieri facias* against the goods of one John McLachlan.

The contest, as presented to the learned Judge below, and as it comes before us on this appeal, is between the execution creditors Roach & Miller and a chattel mortgagee John A. Robinson on the one hand, and certain other execution creditors, N. McLachlan, Wm. Porter, W.B. Whitesides, and J. McLandres, whose executions were delivered to the sheriff subsequent to Robinson's chattel mortgage, on the other.

These last mentioned execution creditors, whose judgments were recovered for wages due to them by the execution debtor, have been held entitled to priority over the first execution creditor in the distribution of the proceeds of the sale, and the whole of such proceeds, after deducting the costs and sheriff's fees, etc., have been accordingly divided between them to the exclusion of the first execution creditor and of the mortgagee. The reason assigned for this decision is, that the Wage Earners' Act, R.S.O. ch. 127, sec. 3, gives the wages creditors priority in the sheriff's scheme of distribution over all other creditors of the execution debtor, and that being thus placed in a position of priority to the first execution creditors, they necessarily also become prior to the mortgagee to whom those creditors are paramount. This is the only point involved in the appeal.

I observe that the mortgagee Robinson was one of the claimants in the alleged interpleader proceedings, but no order was made barring his claim or directing an issue in respect of it, or otherwise disposing of it. He appears here, as he appeared before the sheriff and on the appeal to the learned Judge below, as a person claiming to share in the proceeds of the sale and to be placed on the distribution or dividend sheet, and he seems to have thought that he had gained some right of that kind because, as it is said, he had agreed to contribute *pro rata* to the expense of contesting the adverse claims which were barred (having been abandoned), as the result of the interpleader proceedings. But that is an entire misapprehension of his position. He is not an execution creditor but a person claiming adversely, or subject, to execution creditors. The Creditors' Relief Act, sec. 4, sub-sec. 3, gives him no right to join with such execution creditors in contesting other claims, or to share in the distribution of the proceeds of the sale under an execution, and he could not, under any circumstances, be placed upon the sheriff's dividend sheet. He had, therefore, no *locus standi* in any of these proceedings, and has none in this appeal. If his claim be disputed it must be so in the ordinary way, viz., in an interpleader proceeding at the instance of the sheriff. His mortgage, however, is in fact disputed by nobody, and it appears to be a security taken in good faith to secure money actually advanced by him to the execution debtor.

The contest is therefore one between the first execution creditors and those who came in afterwards subsequent to the mortgage.

I have read, with attention, the very careful judgement delivered by the learned junior Judge, and, with all respect, find myself unable to agree that the subsequent execution creditors are entitled to priority. I think, on the contrary, that as the proceeds of the sale are not sufficient to pay the first execution and the mortgage in full, the effect of the latter is to cut them out altogether.

The ground on which I so hold was not, I think, presented to the learned Judge's attention.

We must be careful not to extend the Creditors' Relief Act, or the Act respecting wages, to cases which they do not expressly provide for. They are Acts of an exceptional and incomplete character, and necessarily so, being, as it were, even if *intra vires*, but crippled substitutes for insolvent legislation.

Those, therefore, who attempt to take advantage of these provisions must shew that they are clearly within them.

Section 3 of the Wages' Act, R.S.O. ch. 127, enacts that all persons in the employment of an execution debtor at the time of the entry of the notice mentioned in section 4 of the Creditors' Relief Act, or within one month before such entry, who shall become entitled to share in the distribution of money levied out of the property of a debtor within the meaning of such Act, shall be entitled to be paid out of such money the wages or salary due to them by the execution debtor not exceeding three months' wages or salary, in priority to the claims of the other creditors of the execution debtor and *pro rata* with such other creditors as to the residue of their claims.

This Act and the Creditors' Relief Act profess to deal only with the levy of money upon an execution against the property of *the debtor*. They do not interfere with the rights of mortgagees or the rights of creditors, as they may be affected or altered by a mortgage or sale of such property after the issue of an execution.

Notwithstanding the execution the property remains the debtor's property to sell or mortgage it as he pleases. If he does so, it ceases to be his property and becomes the property of the purchaser or the mortgagee subject to the execution. If it is then sold under the execution it is sold, not as the property of the debtor but as that of the purchaser or mortgagee, and executions which come in subsequent to the mortgage cannot be entitled to share in the proceeds of the sale, for the first execution being a charge on the property to the full amount of it, the creditor is entitled to enforce it so long as anything remains due thereon; and therefore whether the property has been sold, or merely mortgaged, if subsequent execution creditors are entitled to share *pari passu* in the proceeds of the sale under the first execution, it becomes necessary in order to satisfy it to sell more than would have been required for that purpose had there been no other executions. Every dollar which is applied upon such other executions is so much taken from the purchaser or mortgagee, and where the property is, say, of sufficient value to meet the first execution and the mortgage, it is easy to see that by this process the subsequent executions are being placed in the same position as the first execution creditor, and gain a priority over the purchaser or the mortgagee which they never had, and which the Acts referred to do not give them. They have no interest in anything but the equity of redemption, and if they wish to reach that they must pay off the first execution and the mortgage, or confine their claim to so much of the proceeds of the sale under the first execution as may represent it.

I cannot see that the fact of the goods having been sold makes any difference in the rights of the parties, or that the first execution creditor or the mortgagee are thereby placed in any worse or different position than they would have been in if the mortgagee had chosen to pay off the execution: *Gray* v *Coughlin*, 18 S.C.R. 553.

I entirely agree with the judgment of my brother Rose in *Davies Brewing and Malting Co.* v *Smith*, 10 P.R. 627, the principle of which applies to and covers the case before us.

I am therefore of the opinion that the appeal should be allowed: that the sheriff's scheme of distribution should be set aside, and that it should be declared that the whole of the proceeds of the sale are applicable upon the first execution.

The respondents must pay the costs of the appeal.

QUESTIONS AND NOTES Is this scheme of distribution appropriate?

Sections 32(11) and 32(12) of The Creditors' Relief Act, R.S.O. 1970, c 97 (supra at p 410) were first enacted in 1899 by 62 Vict. c 11, s 13. How would they affect the result reached in *Roach* v *McLachlan*, if that case were to arise today?

This problem has been considered on several occasions. The Ontario Court of Appeal significantly narrowed the scope of *Roach* in *Re Harrison* (1915), 25 O.L.R. 45. In 1921, the authority of the case was rejected completely, the court finding that section 35(11) 'completely overrides the scheme of distribution under earlier enactments as interpreted by *Roach* v *McLachlan*, and *Re Harrison*': *Re Huff and Vary* (1921), 20 O.W.N. 28. The Supreme Court of Ontario (in bankruptcy) has also held that where one creditor files an execution before the debtor executes a mortgage, and subsequent creditors are able to 'shelter under the prior execution', that all execution creditors *and* the mortgage creditor share pari passu in the proceeds of execution: *In re Riggs* (1938), 19 C.B.R. 222.

15
The Operation of the Execution System and Proposals for Reform

This chapter begins by presenting some of the documents contained in a judgment enforcement file of the sheriff of the Judicial District of York. The documents are designed to provide some insight into the practical workings of the law relating to the execution process which we have just discussed. The file begins with a writ of *fi. fa.* commanding the Sheriff to collect on a judgment of $28,299.49 and costs, and continues through to the sale of the debtor's interest in land and satisfaction in full of the judgment debt.

The latter part of this Chapter considers proposals for substantial reform of the institutional framework in which the enforcement of judgment debts takes place.

File begins on p 466.

Dye & Durham Co Limited
FORM NO. 663

FORM 1
WRIT OF FIERI FACIAS

REGISTRAR'S
FILE NO. 6064/74/MLA

In the Supreme Court of Ontario

IN THE MATTER OF THE MECHANICS' LIEN ACT R.S.O. 1970, Chapter 267

Between

B.J.R. SUPPLIES LIMITED

PLAINTIFF(S)

AND

J.B.L. CONSTRUCTION LIMITED, NOSMO KING, carrying on business under the firm name and style NOSMO CONSTRUCTION, and KING CONSTRUCTION CO. LTD.

DEFENDANT(S)

Elizabeth the Second, by the Grace of God of the United Kingdom, Canada and Her other Realms and Territories QUEEN, Head of the Commonwealth, Defender of the Faith.

To the Sheriff of THE JUDICIAL DISTRICT OF YORK ———— **Greeting.**

We Command You that of the goods and chattels and lands and tenements in your bailiwick of NOSMO KING you cause to be made the sum of $28,299.49 and also of the goods and chattels and lands and tenements in your bailiwick of J.B.L. CONSTRUCTION LIMITED you cause to be made the sum of $17,000

E.J.C. ~~you cause to be made the sum of~~ XXXXXXXXXXXXXXXXX

and also interest thereon from Jan. 23 1976, { *day of the judgment or order, or day on which the money is directed to be paid, or day from which interest is directed by the order to run, as the case may be* which sum of money and interest were by a judgment and report———————— in this action bearing the ~~dates of~~ dates of January 13 1975, and January 23rd, 1976, respectively———

adjudged to be paid by the said Defendants as aforesaid

to the Plaintiff ,

E.J.C. ~~and also the further sum of~~ XX ,

~~for the taxed costs of this writ~~

~~mentioned in the judgment, together~~ with interest at the rate of 5% per annum thereon ~~from~~ xx ~~19xxxxxxxxxxxxxxxxxxxxxxx~~

And We Further Command You that so much thereof as you shall have made from the said goods and chattels and lands and tenements be paid out according to law and if required so to do, make appear to our Justices of the Supreme Court of Ontario in what manner you shall have executed this our writ.

In Witness Whereof this writ is signed for the Supreme Court of Ontario by EDWARD FITZGERALD CONOVER Registrar

of the said Court at Toronto , this 25 day of May , 1976.

Conover
Registrar S.C.O.

THE FOLLOWING ENDORSEMENT MUST BE COM-
PLETED BY THE PERSON FILING THIS WRIT AT OR
BEFORE THE TIME OF FILING.

MR. SHERIFF:

Levy the sum of NOSMO KING $ 28,299.49
J.B.L. CONST. $17,000,00

with interest at 5% per annum from Jan. 23 19 76 ,

~~XXXXXXXX~~ $ ~~XXXXXX~~,

with interest at 5% per annum ~~from~~ 19X

and for this writ $

together with your own fees, poundage and incidental expenses.

• MESSRS. BLACK & WHITE
signature of person filing writ

P.O. BOX 7754, TOR., ONT.
address

*when such person is in the employ of a solicitor, the
name and address of the solicitor shall be inserted here.

REC'D MAY 27/76
48834

S. C. O.

WRIT DATED MAY 25/76

B.J.R. SUPPLIES LIMITED

vs.

J.B.L. CONSTRUCTION LIMITED,
NOSMO KING, c.o.b. as
NOSMO CONSTRUCTION & KING
CONSTRUCTION

Writ of Fieri Facias

This writ was issued by:

MESSRS. BLACK & WHITE

of the City of Toronto

in the Municipality of Metropolitan Toronto

solicitor(s) for the said
PLAINTIFF

who reside(s) at

444 BACKWATER LANE, TORONTO

THE FOLLOWING ENDORSEMENT MUST BE COM-
PLETED BY THE OFFICER AT THE OFFICE WHEREIN
THIS WRIT WAS ISSUED OR RENEWED (*as the case may be*).

The

is entitled to receive for this and other writs and renewals of the same, the following sums:

For	$	Signature of Officer
This writ		
1st ren'l		
2nd ren'l		
3rd ren'l		

WHEN APPLICABLE, THE FOLLOWING ENDORSE-
MENT MUST BE COMPLETED BY THE SHERIFF WITH
WHOM THIS WRIT IS FILED OR, IF IT IS NOT FILED
WITH A SHERIFF, BY THE REGISTRAR AT THE OFFICE
WHEREIN THE WRIT WAS ISSUED.

RENEWAL OF WRIT

This writ has been renewed for a further period of
six years from the date indicated hereunder:

Date	Signature of Officer

INITIAL (GENERAL) DIRECTION BY CREDITOR'S LAWYERS TO SHERIFF

BLACK & WHITE
Barristers and Solicitors

                                                    May 13, 1976

Office of the Sheriff
361 University Avenue
Toronto, Ontario

Dear Sirs:

                    Re: B.J.R. Supplies vs. Nosmo King
                          No. MLA 6064/74

     We are the solicitors for the Plaintiff, B.J.R. Supplies Limited
who did file with your office a Writ of Fieri Facias recently against
the Defendant, Nosmo King. Would you be good enough to attend at
the residence of Mr. King, below mentioned, and attempt to satisfy
our Writ of Execution.

          Nosmo King
          27 Baltic Ave.
          Toronto, Ontario

                                        Yours very truly,

                                        BLACK & WHITE

                                        Per: J.T. Black

LETTER FROM CREDITOR'S LAWYERS TO SHERIFF DIRECTING SEIZURE OF A MORTGAGE

BLACK & WHITE
Barristers & Solicitors   May 25, 1976

Office of the Sheriff
361 University Avenue
Toronto, Ontario

                    Re: Action No. MLA 6064/74
                          B.J.R. Supplies v. King et al.

     We are the solicitors for the Plaintiff in this matter and did
file with your office a Writ of Fieri Facias.

     Our investigation indicates that the Defendant Nosmo King is
the holder, as mortgagee, of the below mentioned Charge registered
the 2nd day of December, 1975 in the amount of $4,900.00 as Instru-
ment No. A-54767 mortgagor - Mildred Fudge; mortgagee - Nosmo King.

     Would you be good enough to effect a seizure of the proceeds of
this mortgage. For your information, we enclose herewith copy of
the said Charge which is registered at the Office of Land Titles
at Toronto.

                                        Yours very truly,

                                        BLACK & WHITE

                                        Per: J.T. Black

[The standard form charge enclosed with this letter is omitted from these materials.].

DIRECTION TO SHERIFF TO SEIZE SPECIFIC DEBTS

BLACK & WHITE
Barristers & Solicitors   June 2, 1976

Office of the Sheriff
361 University Avenue
Toronto, Ontario

                    Re: Action No. MLA 6064/74
                          BJR Supplies Limited v.
                          King and J.B.L. Construction

     We are the solicitors for the Plaintiff in this matter and would
be pleased if you would be kind enough to make the following seizures
in order to satisfy the Writ of Fieri Facias which was filed with
your office in May of 1976. These seizures are with reference to
the Defendant, Nosmo King, carrying on business under the firm name
and style of Nosmo Construction and not with reference to the other
defendant.

     (a) Canadian Imperial Bank of Commerce,
          1011 Wilson Ave. Branch
          Downsview, Ontario

          Seize Bank Account

     (b) Stream Holdings Limited and Rivulet Holdings Limited
          per: W. Stanley
          120 Landover Avenue
          Downsview, Ontario

          Seize Proceeds of contract between Nosmo King
          c.o.b. Nosmo Construction

     We would be pleased to pay your fee for the requisite seizures
thereon.

                              Yours very truly,

                              BLACK & WHITE

                              Per J.T. Black

LETTER FROM SHERIFF'S OFFICER TO CREDITOR'S LAWYERS REQUESTING FURTHER
PARTICULARS

June 3rd, 1976

Messrs. Black & White
Barristers & Solicitors   Our File #48834

Attention: Mr. J.T. Black

Dear Sir

                    Re: B.J.R. Supplies Limited
                                   v.
                         Nosmo King & J.B.L. Construction Limited

    We acknowledge receipt of your letter under date of May 25th,
1976, requesting we seize the proceeds of this Mortgage.

    However we note you have not given us enough information, and
we are enclosing herewith attached, form to completed with the
information required. We also require the address of the Mortgagor.

    In the meantime we shall levy as requested on Nosmo King at
the address given.

                              Yours truly,

                              For Sheriff, Judicial
                              District of York

To the Registrar of LAND TITLES FOR TORONTO AND YORK

By Virtue of an Execution issued out of the   Supreme Court of Ontario

whereby I am commanded to levy of the goods and chattels of   NOSMO KING

$28,299.49   for debt and $ nil   for costs lately adjudged to be paid by

the said   NOSMO KING

to B.J.R. SUPPLIES LIMITED

besides the costs of Execution I have this day seized and taken in Execution all the estate, right, title and

interest of the said   NOSMO KING

in a mortgage made by   MILDRED FUDGE

to the said   NOSMO KING

bearing date the   28th   day of   November   A.D. 19 75

and registered in the Registry Office for

on the   2nd   day of   November   A.D. 1975

as Number A-54767   ~~but~~ Parcel 5-1   Plan M-505

~~Township~~   Toronto, Ontario

and in the monies secured thereby, and this notice is given for the purpose of binding the interest of the

said   NOSMO KING

under Sections 21 to 25 of the Execution Act.

DATED this   8th   day of June, 1976.

A.D. 19

Sheriff of the Judicial District
of York.
Court House,
University Avenue,
Toronto 1.

OUR FILE #48834

FORM F1-586

B.H. LTD.

NOTICE OF SEIZURE OF BANK ACCOUNT BALANCE

In the SUPREME COURT OF ONTARIO

Between B.J.R. SUPPLIES LIMITED

PLAINTIFF,

AND

J.B.L. CONSTRUCTION LIMITED, NOSMO KING, c.o.b.
under the firm name and style NOSMO CONSTRUCTION
and KING CONSTRUCTION

DEFENDANT,S

Take Notice that pursuant to Writ(s) of Fieri Facias, issued in

~~this cause a copy of which is hereto attached~~

these causes, in my hands (3 executions) } all deposits, credits, book debts,

accounts receivable, choses in action, and all cheques, bills of exchange, promissory notes,

bonds, mortgages, specialties or other securities, and equities therein belonging

to NOSMO KING

up to the amount of $33,302.94

are hereby seized according to the tenor of the said Writ(s), and I demand payment of same

forthwith.

PLEASE MAKE CHEQUE PAYABLE TO SHERIFF, JUDICIAL DISTRICT OF YORK

OR ALTERNATIVELY REPLY TO THIS NOTICE FORTHWITH.

DATED this 10th day of June

A.D. 19 76 .

For

P.J. Ambrose

Sheriff of the Judicial District of York
Room 108, Court House,
University Avenue, Toronto, Ontario.
965-7405

To : CANADIAN IMPERIAL BANK OF
COMMERCE
1011 Wilson Avenue.
Downsview, Ontario

OUR FILE NO. 48834

FORM F1-194

NOTICE OF SEIZURE OF A SPECIFIC DEBT

In the SUPREME COURT OF ONTARIO

Between B.J.R. SUPPLIES LIMITED

PLAINTIFF,

AND

J.B.L. CONSTRUCTION LIMITED, NOSMO KING, c.o.b. under
the firm name and style NOSMO CONSTRUCTION, and
KING CONSTRUCTION CO. LTD.

DEFENDANT,S

Take Notice that pursuant to Writ(s) of Fieri Facias, issued in

~~this causes a copy of which is hereto attached~~ } all deposits, credits, book debts,

these causes, in my hands (3 executions) }

accounts receivable, choses in action, and all cheques, bills of exchange, promissory notes,

bonds, mortgages, specialties or other securities, and equities therein belonging

NOSMO KING
to____

up to the amount of $ 33,302.94 _______________________________

are hereby seized according to the tenor of the said Writ(s), and I demand payment of same

forthwith. (SEIZE PROCEEDS OF CONTRACT OF NOSMO KING, c.o.b. NOSMO
CONSTRUCTION)

PLEASE MAKE CHEQUE PAYABLE TO SHERIFF, JUDICIAL DISTRICT OF YORK
OR ALTERNATIVELY REPLY TO THIS NOTICE FORTHWITH

DATED this 10th **day of** June

A.D. 19 76 .

For

To STREAM HOLDINGS LIMITED
c/o W. STANLEY
120 LANDOVER AVENUE
DOWNSVIEW, ONT.

Sheriff of the Judicial District of York.
Room 108, Court House,
University Avenue, Toronto, Ontario.

OUR FILE NO. 48834
FORM F1-194

LETTER FROM RECIPIENT OF A NOTICE OF SEIZURE OF DEBTS

CANADIAN IMPERIAL
BANK OF COMMERCE
1011 Wilson Ave. Branch

June 11, 1976

Sheriff of the Judicial District of York
Room 108, Court House
University Avenue
Toronto, Ontario
Dear Sir:

> Re: File No. 48834
>   B.J.R. Supplies Limited
>
>   and
>
>   J.B.L. Construction Limited,
>   Nosmo King, c.o.d. under the
>   firm name and style Nosmo
>   Construction and King Construct-
>   ion Co. Ltd.

At the time of receipt by us, June 10, 1976 of this Writ of Fieri Facias there was no money owing or accruing from us to the above mentioned judgment debtor or any one of them.

Yours truly,

[signature: Beetle]

C. Beetle
Manager

LETTER FROM SHERIFF'S OFFICER TO CREDITOR'S LAWYER ADVISING OF MORTGAGE
SEIZURE

June 14th, 1976

Our File #48834

Messrs. Black & White
Barristers & Solicitors
Toronto, Ontario

ATTENTION: MR. J.T. BLACK

Dear Sir:

Re: B.J.R. Supplies Limited v. Nosmo King

As per your direction under date of June 8th, 1976, we have
registered the Mortgage in Land Titles as of today's date and also
sent notice to Mildred Fudge by Registered letter. We are enclosing
notices for your information, and will advise as to the results.

Yours truly,

For, Sheriff, Judicial
District of York

Encl.

LETTER FROM RECIPIENT OF A NOTICE OF SEIZURE OF DEBTS

120 Landover Ave.
Downsview, Ontario

June 15, 1976

Sheriff of the Judicial District of York
Room 108, Court House
University Avenue
Toronto, Ontario

Dear Sir:

>   Re: Nosmo King
>   Nosmo Construction
>   File No. 48834

Please be advised that the above-mentioned Nosmo King (Nosmo Construction) does not work for our firm and we are not indebted to him for any monies.

>   Yours truly,
>
>   STREAM HOLDINGS LIMITED
>
>
>
>   Per: W. Stanley

Encl. - 1

LETTER FROM RECIPIENT OF A NOTICE OF SEIZURE OF DEBTS

120 Landover Ave.
Downsview, Ontario

June 15, 1976

Sheriff of the Judicial District of York
Room 108, Court House
University Avenue
Toronto, Ontario

Dear Sir:

> Re: Nosmo King
>   Nosmo Construction
>   File: 48834

    Please be advised that RIVULET HOLDINGS LIMITED is not my
company.

Yours truly,

Per: W. Stanley

Encl. - 1

NOTICE OF SEIZURE OF MORTGAGE PAYMENTS

IN THE SUPREME COURT OF ONTARIO

B E T W E E N:

                B.J.R. SUPPLIES LIMITED
                                              PLAINTIFF

                        and

                NOSMO KING
                                              DEFENDANT

        TAKE NOTICE that pursuant to a Writ of Fieri Facias issued
in this cause, all payments on MORTGAGE bearing date the 28th
day of November, 1975 and registered in the Office of Land Titles
for Toronto on the 2nd day of December, 1975, as NUMBER A-54767.
PARCEL 5-1, PLAN M-505, Toronto, Ontario owing to NOSMO KING ,
Defendant, are hereby seized and I DEMAND THAT PAYMENTS OF THE
SAID MORTGAGE BE MADE DIRECT TO THIS OFFICE.

        Cheques payable to the order "Sheriff, Judicial District of
York."

        Dated at Toronto this 2nd day of July, 1976.

MORTGAGE NUMBER AMENDED JULY 2nd, 1976.

                                For, Sheriff, Judicial District
                                of York,

                                Room 108, Court House
                                361 University Ave.
                                Toronto, Ontario

TO: MILDRED FUDGE,
      27 BALTIC AVE.   OUR FILE #48834
      TORONTO, ONTARIO
                             R E G I S T E R E D

LETTER FROM SHERIFF TO CREDITOR'S LAWYER ADVISING OF DISTRIBUTION

August 23, 1976

Our file #48834

Messrs. Black & White
Barristers and Solicitors
Toronto, Ontario

Dear Sirs:

        Re: B.J.R. Supplies Limited
                v.
          Nosmo King, c.o.b. as
          Nosmo Construction and
          King Construction Co. Ltd.

I enclose herewith a cheque for $24.50, payable to the plaintiff, being proceeds of a mortgage payment.

Yours very truly,

Sheriff, Judicial
District of York

Encl.

DIRECTION TO SHERIFF TO SEIZE SPECIFIC DEBTS

BLACK & WHITE
Barristers & Solicitors

                                        June 1, 1977

Office of the Sheriff
Executions Department
New Court House
Toronto, Ontario

Dear Sirs:

                Re: B.J.R. Supplies Limited v. King et al.
                     S.C.O. Action No. MLA 6064/78

     We are solicitors for B.J.R. Supplies Limited and obtained
judgment against Nosmo King in the sum of $28,299.49. To date
there has been no payment by King, in satisfaction of this
judgment.

     We filed with your office a Writ of Fieri Facias on May 25th,
1976.

     Would you be kind enough to issue a Notice of Seizure on the
below mentioned, as we are advised that they will be making a payment
to King under a building contract. Our information suggests that a
Notice of Seizure will be most effective if it is served upon the
below mentioned on Wednesday, June 9th, 1977. We would be most
grateful if you could accommodate us in this regard.

          LUMBER PEOPLE LIMITED
          14 GRIT DRIVE
          WESTON, ONTARIO

          ATTENTION: MR. JERRY KNOT

     We shall be pleased to pay your fee for the requisite service
herein.

                         Yours very truly,

                         BLACK & WHITE

                         Per: J.T. Black

NOTICE OF SEIZURE OF DEBT AND ALLEGED DEBTOR'S RESPONSE

In the SUPREME COURT OF ONTARIO

Between B.J.R. SUPPLIES LIMITED

PLAINTIFF,

AND

J.B.L. CONSTRUCTION LIMITED, NOSMO KING, c.o.b.
under the firm name and style NOSMO CONSTRUCTION,
and KING CONSTRUCTION CO. LTD.

DEFENDANTS

Take Notice that pursuant to Writ(s) of Fieri Facias, issued in

~~this cause a copy of which is hereto attached,~~

these causes, in my hands 3 executions } all deposits, credits, book debts,

accounts receivable, choses in action, and all cheques, bills of exchange, promissory notes,

bonds, mortgages, specialties or other securities, and equities therein belonging

to NOSMO KING ____

up to the amount of $ 34,892.72 ____

are hereby seized according to the tenor of the said Writ(s), and I demand payment of same

forthwith.

PLEASE MAKE CHEQUE PAYABLE TO SHERIFF, JUDICIAL DISTRICT OF YORK

OR ALTERNATIVELY REPLY TO THIS NOTICE FORTHWITH

DATED this   3rd   **day of**   June

A.D. 19 77 .   4:15 p.m.

For

P.J. Ambrose

To Lumber People Limited
14 Grit Avenue
Weston, Ontario

Attention: Mr. Jerry Knot

Sheriff of the Judicial District of York
Room 108, Court House,
University Avenue, Toronto, Ontario.

*We do not owe any
money to the above:
Signed: Jerry Knot
PRESIDENT*

OUR FILE NO. 48834

FORM F1-194

LETTER FROM CREDITOR'S LAWYER TO SHERIFF

BLACK & WHITE
Barristers & Solicitors

September 9, 1977

Sheriff's Office
Court House
361 University Avenue
Toronto, Ontario
M5G 1T5

Dear Sirs:

> Re: Your File No. 48834
>   B.J.R. Supplies v. King et al.

We acknowledge receipt of your letter dated June 14th, 1977 in connection with the above captioned matter. The aforementioned letter advised that a seizure was conducted on June 3rd, 1977 and requested our information and comments with respect to the said seizure. Attached to the letter was a copy of a reply received by your office by Mr. Jerry Knot, an officer of Lumber People Limited.

If the seizure was conducted on June 3rd, 1977, then it is our position that the reply made by Lumber People Limited is false and that the said Lumber People Limited has willfully disobeyed the seizure notice. I enclose herewith two cheques each drawn by Lumber People Limited, the first being No. 1211 dated June 3rd, 1977 and the second being No. 1227 dated June 17th, 1977 each payable to N.K. Construction and each in the amount of $2,000.00.

It is our position that Lumber People Limited delivered the aforementioned two cheques to Nosmo King who is carrying on business under the name of N.K. Construction, knowing full well this to be the case. As you will note from the back of the cheques, there appears to be initials which we submit are those of Nosmo King. We enclose herewith copies of the aforementioned cheques and also a letter dated May 31st, 1977 on the letterhead of the company and also signed by Nosmo King, under which the words N.K. Construction are written. Thus, it is perfectly clear that Lumber People Limited through its corporate officer Jerry Knot knew full well that Nosmo King was the recipient of the aforementioned two cheques.

Would you kindly advise the writer if you are able to take any proceedings against Mr. Jerry Knot or the signatory to the return to your Notice of Seizure, for making a false return to same.

Yours very truly,

BLACK & WHITE

Per: J.T. Black

LETTER FROM SHERIFF'S OFFICER TO CREDITOR'S LAWYERS

September 13th, 1977

Our File #48834

Messrs. Black & White
Barristers and Solicitors
Toronto, Ontario

ATTENTION: J.T. BLACK

Dear Sir:

> Re: B.J.R. Supplies Limited v.
>   Nosmo King, c.o.b. as Nosmo Construction,
>   King Construction Ltd.

We acknowledge your writing of September 9th, 1977 in reference to the above file and contents noted.

Regretfully, we advise that it is not the policy of the office to pursue the validity of individual returns in attachment. For reasons, the least of which is staff complements, this office can only support the solicitor by way of affidavit on any application he would make in the Courts.

Should you wish to discuss the matter further with Sheriff's Counsel, we would direct you to Robert Kay at 965-0120.

Yours truly,

SHERIFF,
JUDICICAL DISTRICT OF YORK

Per:

LETTER FROM CREDITOR'S LAWYERS TO SHERIFF REQUESTING SALE OF DEBTOR'S
INTEREST IN LAND

BLACK & WHITE
Barristers & Solicitors

                                    October 21, 1977

Sheriff
361 University Avenue
Toronto, Ontario

Dear Sir:

                Re: B.J.R. Supplies Limited v. Nosmo King
                      Your File No. 48834

     We are the solicitors for the plaintiff in this matter and have
filed with your office a Writ of Execution in June 1976. We would
request that you be kind enough to sell the interest of Nosmo King
in the following property.

   (a)   Legal Description of Property

   That certain parcel of land situate in the City of Toronto,
   in the Municipality of Metropolitan Toronto (formerly the
   County of York) and Province of Ontario, and being composed
   of Lot Five (5) as shown on Plan M-505 filed in the Office
   of Land Titles at Toronto.

   (b)   Ownership of Property

   Mildred Fudge and Nosmo King as joint tenants and not as
   tenants in common.

   (c)   Municipal and Physical Description of Property

   27 Baltic Avenue, Toronto, Ontario on which is situated
   a three storey semi-detached brick and imitation brick
   structure. It is situated on a lot of 19 feet more or
   less by a depth of 100 feet on the east side of Baltic
   Avenue. It consists of seven rooms with an enclosed
   veranda. A public lane at the rear provides access to
   the property. There is no garage.

                                         .../2

2

(d) <u>Encumbrances Against the Property</u>

<u>First Mortgage</u> - Mortgage dated August 4th, 1972 in favour
of John Horn; present principal amount of $16,000.00.

<u>Second Mortgage</u> - Mortgage dated March 20th, 1974 in favour
of David Peters present value is $9,000.00.

Yours very truly,

BLACK AND WHITE

Per: *J.T. Black*

LETTER FROM SHERIFF'S OFFICER TO CREDITOR'S LAWYERS

November 18th, 1977

Our File 48834

Messrs. Black & White
Barristers and Solicitors
Toronto, Ontario

ATTENTION: J.T. BLACK

Dear Sir:

Re: B.J.R. Supplies Limited v. Nosmo King et al.

My officers, F. Saltes and R. Moore attended at 27 Baltic Ave. on November 2nd, 1977 and could get no answer and left their calling card instructing the defendant to contact the Sheriff's office in reference to this matter.

Subsequently Mr. Moore spoke to the defendant on November 16th and advised him that the Sheriff's office has instructions to sell his residence if the judgment is not satisfied. The defendant stated he will contact Mr. Black as soon as possible to arrange settlement.

The premises attended is semi-detached, frame asphalt siding, brick front, front only aluminum storms and aluminum front door not attached, closed in verandah, back lane, cement and entrance to back yard. The premises appears to contain 7 rooms, 1 bath, oil heating and mutual side lane.

My officers could find no goods or chattels on which to levy, therefore my return to your Writ is nulla bona.

Yours truly,

SHERIFF,
JUDICIAL DISTRICT OF YORK

Per:

LETTER FROM CREDITOR'S LAWYERS TO SHERIFF DIRECTING SALE OF DEBTOR'S INTEREST IN LAND

```
BLACK & WHITE
Barristers & Solicitors

                                   November 24, 1977



Sheriff's Office
Judicial District of York
Court House
361 University Avenue
Toronto, Ontario
M5G 1T5

Dear Sirs:

          Re:  B.J.R. Supplies v. King et al.
               Your File No. 48834
          ________________________________________


     We have and thank you for your letter of November 18th, 1977.
Mr. King did not pay up our Judgment and accordingly we would request
that you be kind enough to continue with your sale of Mr. King's
interest in the premises.

                         Yours very truly,

                         BLACK & WHITE

                         Per: J.T. Black
```

LETTER OF ADVICE FROM SHERIFF'S OFFICER TO CREDITOR'S LAWYERS

November 29th, 1977

Our File #48834

Messrs. Black & White
Barristers, Solicitors
Toronto, Ontario

ATTENTION: Mr. J.T. BLACK

Dear Sir:

Re: B.J.R. Supplies Limited
v. Nosmo King et al.

We are enclosing herewith Notice of Sheriff's Sale to take place on Friday, January 20th, 1978.

A Display Ad will appear in the Ontario Gazette on Saturday, December 10th, 1977 and Display Ads will appear in the Toronto Sun on the following days -

Thursday, January 5th, 1978
Thursday, January 12th, 1978

Notices have been sent to the above named Defendant by Registered and Regular Mail as of todays date.

Yours truly,

SHERIFF, JUDICIAL DISTRICT OF YORK

SHERIFF'S NOTICE OF SALE OF LAND UNDER EXECUTION

<u>SHERIFF'S SALE OF LANDS</u>

BY VIRTUE of a writ of Fieri Facias issued out of the Supreme Court of Ontario, against the lands and tenements of NOSMO KING carrying on business under the firm name and style of NOSMO CONSTRUCTION, Defendants at the suit of B.J.R. SUPPLIES LIMITED, Plaintiff, I have seized and taken in execution all the right, title, interest and <u>EQUITY OF REDEMPTION</u> of <u>NOSMO KING</u>, one of the Defendants, in and to:

ALL AND SINGULAR that certain parcel or tract of land and premises situate, lying and being in the City of Toronto, in the Municipality of Metropolitan Toronto (formerly the County of York) and Province of Ontario, and being composed of Lot Five (5) as shown on Plan M-505, filed on the Office of Land Titles at Toronto.

ON THE PREMISES is said to be erected a three storey semi-detached brick and imitation brick structure. It is situated on a lot of 19 feet more or less by a depth of 100 feet on the east side of Baltic Avenue. It consists of seven rooms with an enclosed veranda. A public lane at the rear provides access to the property. Ther is no garage.

MUNICIPALLY known as <u>27 BALTIC AVENUE, TORONTO, ONTARIO.</u>

ALL OF WHICH SAID right, title, interest and <u>EQUITY OF REDEMPTION</u>

of <u>NOSMO KING</u>, one of the Defendants, in the said lands and tenements,

I shall offer for sale by Public Auction in my Office, Room 108,

Court House, 361 University Ave., Toronto, Ontario, on <u>FRIDAY, JANUARY</u>

<u>20th, 1978 at 2:00 O''CLOCK IN THE AFTERNOON.</u>

Dated at Toronto this 29th day of November, 1977.

        TERMS: CASH
              DEPOSIT 10% OF BID PRICE AT TIME OF
              SALE (MINIMUM $300.00)
              TEN DAYS TO ARRANGE FINANCING
              DELIVERY ONLY ON PAYMENT IN FULL

THIS SALE IS SUBJECT TO CANCELLATION UP TO TIME OF SALE WITHOUT ANY FURTHER NOTICE.

                  Philip J. Ambrose, Sheriff,
                  Judicial District of York

                  965-7405

OUR FILE #43348

LETTER FROM SHERIFF'S OFFICER TO NEWSPAPER

December 28th, 1977

Our File #48834

The Toronto Sun
333 King St. E.
Toronto, Ontario

Attention: Mr. Tuttle
            Display Advertising

Dear Sir:

                    Re: Land Sale
                         Nosmo King - Def.
                         27 Baltic Ave.
                         Toronto, Ontario

    Please insert the enclosed advertisement as a Display Ad in
the Toronto Sun Issues of -

            THURSDAY, JANUARY 5th, 1978
            THURSDAY, JANUARY 12th, 1978

    When remitting your statement, in triplicate, kindly give
the DEFENDANT'S NAME, OUR FILE NUMBER and Affidavit that Ads
appeared in the Toronto Sun. Thanking you.

                    Yours truly,

                    Sheriff, Judicial District of York

[The invoice from the *Toronto Sun* in the amount of $194.40, together with a copy of
the advertisement and affidavit of publication, are omitted.]

AGREEMENT OF PURCHASE AND SALE BETWEEN SHERIFF AND PURCHASER AT SHERIFF'S SALE OF LAND

AGREEMENT OF PURCHASE

OUR FILE # 48834

IN THE   SUPREME COURT OF ONTARIO

B E T W E E N :

B.J.R. SUPPLIES LIMITED

PLAINTIFF

and

NOSMO KING, carrying on business under the
firm name and style KING CONSTRUCTION CO.
LTD.

DEFENDANT

I HEREBY AGREE to and do purchase from the SHERIFF FOR THE
JUDICIAL DISTRICT OF YORK under the above execution:

ALL OF WHICH SAID RIGHT, TITLE, INTEREST AND EQUITY OF REDEMPTION OF NOSMO KING,
ONE OF THE DEFENDANTS IN THE SAID LANDS AND TENEMENTS MUNICIPALLY KNOWN AS
27 BALTIC AVENUE, TORONTO, ONTARIO.

For the Price and Sum of $ 6,600.00 .... Payable as Follows

$ 660 .... herewith as a deposit and I agree to pay the balance of $ 5,940.00 ....

within 10 days of the day of sale and if not paid then my deposit is forfeited as damages.

Dated at Toronto this   20th   day of   January   A.D. 1978

____
Signature of Purchaser

____
Address of Purchaser

CONDITIONS OF SALE

The highest bidder shall be the purchaser, and if any dispute arises as to the last or highest bid, the articles shall again
be put up for sale at a date to be announced.

No person shall retract his bid.

The purchaser shall at the time of sale sign the above Agreement of Purchase, and the terms are CASH at time of sale
or a deposit of at least 10% OF BID PRICE (MINIMUM $300.00) with the balance within 10 DAYS or deposit forfeited.

DEPOSIT AT TIME OF SALE NOT REFUNDABLE UNDER ANY CONDITION.

Delivery only on payment of full bid price.

FORM F1-573

LETTER FROM SHERIFF'S OFFICER TO MINISTRY OF REVENUE

February 7th, 1978

Our File #48834

Ministry of Revenue
77 Bloor St. W.
7th Floor
Toronto, Ontario

Attention: Mr. A. Jackson

Dear Sir:

      Re: SHERRIFF'S SALE OF LANDS
          Nosmo King - Def.

    Enclosed please find copies of Notice of Sale and Agreement
to purchase property which was exposed for Public Auction.

    In accordance with Land Speculation Tax Act and the new policy
established, we would request your Department issue a Lien Clearance
Certificate for the above capitoned property.

    Thank you for the attention you will have shown.

Yours truly,

Sheriff, Judicial District
of York

Per:

[The Ministry responded in due course, enclosing a lien clearance
 certificate.]

LETTER FROM SHERIFF'S OFFICER TO CREDITOR ADVISING OF DISTRIBUTION

March 14th, 1978

Our file #48834

Messrs. Black & White
Barristers & Solicitors
Toronto, Ontario

Dear Sirs:

Re: B.J.R. Supplies Limited
v.
Nosmo King

I enclose herewith cheque for $6,335.10, payable to the plaintiff, being proceeds of sale of property, less sheriffs fees and expenses amounting to $264.90.

Yours very truly,

Sheriff, Judical District of York

LETTER TO SHERIFF FROM CREDITOR'S LAWYERS

BLACK & WHITE
BARRISTERS & SOLICITORS

                              March 17, 1978

Office of the Sheriff
361 University Avenue
Toronto, Ontario

Dear Sir:

                    Re: Your file No. 48834
                         B.J.R. Supplies v. King

     We are the solicitors for the plaintiff in this matter. You
may recall that we did on June 14th, 1976 instruct you to seize
the monies owing on a Charge between Nosmo King as Chargee and
Mildred Fudge as Chargor. Pursuant to our instructions, you
registered on the abstract of title at the Office of Land Titles
at Toronto, a Notice of Seizure as Instrument No. A-555931.

     In as much as the interest of Nosmo King has now been sold
pursuant to an auction sale held at your office, and the monies
owing under the aforementioned charge would no longer be applicable,
we are advised by the Master of Land Titles that it is necessary that
the aforesaid Notice of Seizure be deleted from the title. Accordingly,
would you be kind enough to register the appropriate documentation
on title to affect the discharge of this Notice of Seizure.

     Thanking you for hour co-operation.

                              Yours very truly,

                              BLACK & WHITE

                              Per: J.T. Black

BLACK & WHITE
BARRISTERS AND SOLICITORS

June 1, 1978

Office of the Sheriff
Judicial District of York
361 University Avenue
Toronto, Ontario

Dear Sirs:

                    Re: B.J.R. Supplies Limited v. Nosmo King
                         File No. 43348

        We are solicitors for the plaintiff and did file with your
office a Writ of Execution on May 27th, 1976. The judgment has
now been paid and we would request that you return to this office
the Writ of Execution.

                              Yours very truly,

                              BLACK & WHITE

                              Per: J.T. Black

3 PROPOSALS FOR REFORM

a / The Enforcement Office

i Report of the Committee on the Enforcement of Judgment Debts (The Payne Report) (1969) pp 86–9.

A NEW ENFORCEMENT SYSTEM

314. The ground covered in this section should throw into perspective the requirements of a new enforcement system and enable acceptable principles of enforcement to be determined. Bearing in mind the defects suggested in paragraph 293 it may be useful to state the principles in summary form as follows:

(*a*) There should be an integrated system for the enforcement of the judgment debts of all civil courts subject to specified exceptions.

(*b*) The process for the enforcement of judgment debts should be capable of reaching out to all the income, assets and property of the judgment debtor subject to specified exceptions.

(*c*) The modes of enforcement should be capable of being employed concurrently or consecutively in one continuous process.

(*d*) Full information about the means, property, assets and circumstances of the debtor should be ascertained before enforcement is pursued and the onus of disclosing the information should be placed upon the debtor.

(*e*) The proceeds recovered in the course of the enforcement of judgment debts should be fairly distributed amongst the judgment creditors subject to specified priorities between them.

(*f*) The procedure should provide for the fair treatment of the judgment debtor.

(*g*) The system should contain methods for the control of credit of judgment debtors.

(*h*) The system should be operated by machinery which should be efficient, effective, expeditious and fair.

315. With those principles before us we have endeavoured to design a new system containing features which will meet the complaints made against the present methods of enforcement and solve the problems which have arisen in the past.

A NEW ENFORCEMENT OFFICE

316. The first and vital step is to replace the present miscellany of enforcement courts and processes by a new office in which an integrated system of enforcement of judgment debts can be operated. We have already dealt with some substantial improvements, which will facilitate integration, in the changes of jurisdiction and transfer of the bulk of civil debt recovery to the county court, recommended in Part II.

317. In section 2 of this Part we describe the constitution, establishment and functions of a new Enforcement Office to be attached in each district to the existing county court office. It will be under the control of the registrar acting as the Enforcement Officer and will be staffed by the county court clerks and bailiffs.

318. Into that office will pass for enforcement all money judgments against a debtor who resides or carries on business within the jurisdiction of the office, wherever the judgments themselves may have been entered. In that way the Enforcement Office will from the start of enforcement be in a position to ensure the ordered control of the debtor's affairs which is fundamental to a proper system of enforcement. It will be able to ascertain and compare the claims and rights of the creditors, both against the debtor and as between themselves, to supervise the orderly liquidation of the judgment debts, to assist the creditor in obtaining from the debtor as much as he can properly afford, and to liquidate the debts as expeditiously as possible; to determine priorities between the creditors, disputes between the creditors and the debtor or third parties, and finally to protect the debtor against undue hardship or harassment.

KNOWLEDGE OF THE MEANS, ASSETS AND CIRCUMSTANCES OF THE DEBTOR

319. In sections 2 and 3 of this Part we seek to remove the past complaints relating to the ascertainment of the means, assets and relevant circumstances of the debtor. It is proposed that the duty be placed upon the debtor to make a full disclosure of his affairs immediately after an application to enforce a money judgment has been lodged against him, that he should be required to complete a questionnaire in a standard form, which will be filed and kept at the Enforcement Office, and that whenever necessary he may be compelled to attend for examination as to his means and circumstances and to produce any relevant documents. A file for each debtor will be kept in the Enforcement Office so that the whole picture and state of his indebtedness to all his creditors can at any time be ascertained by examination of his file.

THE PROPERTY OF THE DEBTOR AVAILABLE FOR ENFORCEMENT

320. Once the relevant information about the debtor and his affairs has been recorded, the decision as to the appropriate mode of enforcement can be made, and it is at that stage that, as we think, further major improvements on the present system can be introduced:

(*a*) The whole of the debtor's property and assets and his wages, salary or other income will become available for attachment by the appropriate modes of enforcement.

(*b*) The Enforcement Officer, on the application of the creditor or creditors, will be able to exercise his discretion and order such one or more modes of enforcement as may be requisite for the satisfaction, forthwith or by instalments, of the judgment or judgments before him. They may be used separately, consecutively or concurrently as the circumstances may demand.

(*c*) The Enforcement Office will be empowered to consider the position of the debtor and his family and to avoid any unjust or excessive order.

(*d*) The overlapping of modes of enforcement will be prevented because the Enforcement Officer, whether he is enforcing one judgment or a number of judgments, will sanction the use of one or more modes of enforcement for the benefit of all the judgment creditors who are enforcing judgments at any given time. There will be no free-for-all amongst the creditors. One will not be able to steal a march on another, if that other has come to the Enforcement Office for enforcement.

It should be noted that while the recommendations of the Payne Report have been generally well received in England (see, for example, (1969), 119 *New L.J.* 164, 181, 229) the major recommendation for the establishment of an Enforcement Office has not been accepted by Parliament. However, the Administration of Justice Act, 1970 did accept some of the Committee's recommendations for the limitation of the remedy of imprisonment for debt; for outlawing of the harassment of debtors; and for extension of wage garnishment. For criticism of this piece-meal approach to debtor-creditor reform see Harper, 'Administration of Justice Act, 1970: Enforcement of Debt Provisions' (1971), 34 *Mod. L. Rev.* 61.

ii The Northern Ireland Enforcement of Judgments Office: Unlike England, Northern Ireland has enacted legislation creating an Enforcement of Judgments Office, based upon the *Report of the Joint Working Party on the Enforcement of Judgments, Orders and Decrees of the Courts of Northern Ireland*, 1965 (*The Anderson Committee Report*).

Judgments (Enforcement) Act (Northern Ireland), 1969, c 30

PART I: ENFORCEMENT OF JUDGMENTS

1. (1) Every judgment to which this Act applies shall be enforceable in accordance with the provisions of this Act; and save as provided by Schedule 5 the functions of under-sheriffs in relation to the enforcement of judgments and to other matters provided for by this Act are hereby abolished.

(2) Subject to section 2, the judgments to which this Act applies are

(*a*) money judgments;

(*b*) judgments under which a person is entitled to possession of any land, including a writ of restitution made upon a conviction for forcible entry or detainer and a warrant issued under section 1 (2) of the Summary Jurisdiction (Miscellaneous Provisions) Act (Northern Ireland) 1946;

(*c*) judgments under which a person is entitled to the delivery of any goods;

(*d*) judgments requiring any person to pay any money into court or to do any act within a limited time, so far as sections 92 to 94 (and so much of Part XI as is applicable to those sections) relate to such judgments;

(*e*) other judgments to which this Act may be applied by any statutory provision; and

(*f*) money judgments given outside Northern Ireland and enforceable in Northern Ireland under any statutory provision.

[Section 3 creates the 'Enforcement of Judgments Office.]

PART III JURISDICTION OF ENFORCEMENT OF JUDGMENTS OFFICE

8. Subject to the provisions of this Act, the jurisdiction relating to the enforcement of judgments which immediately before the commencement of this Act was exercised by any court shall be vested in the Office.

9. Nothing in this Act shall enable the Office

(*a*) to make or enforce any order of sequestration or any order of committal; or

(*b*) to perform any functions relating to the enforcement of judgments which were, immediately before the commencement of this Act, performed by the Admiralty Marshal.

10. (1) Without prejudice to the generality of section 8 and to any powers conferred by this Act but subject to section 9, the Office may

(*a*) make enforcement orders;

(*b*) issue custody warrants;

(*c*) subject to sections 22 and 25, issue processes for the attendance and examination

(i) of debtors as to their means; and

(ii) of any other persons appearing to the Office to be in possession of any information relevant to the means of such debtors;

(*d*) conduct the examinations referred to in paragraph (*c*);

(*e*) receive moneys in respect of payments of the whole or parts of amounts recoverable on foot of judgments;

(*f*) subject to any other statutory provision, stay enforcement of any judgment, whether before or after an application for enforcement has been made under section 18 or section 19 (1) and either absolutely or on such terms and conditions as it may consider proper;

(*g*) set aside, discharge or vary, either upon the application of a party to the proceedings or of its own motion

  (i) any enforcement order; or

  (ii) any custody warrant issued by it or any seizure made pursuant to an authorisation given under section 44; or

  (iii) any certificate of unenforceability; or

  (iv) any notice or direction issued or given by it; and

(*h*) issue notices of unenforceability and grant certificates of unenforceability.

(2) The power conferred by paragraph F of subsection 1 shall include power to stay enforcement on the ground that, having regard to the liabilities of the debtor (in addition to the amount recoverable on foot of the judgment) the property of the debtor ought in the opinion of the Office to be administered for the benefit of all his creditors.

11. Any order of the Office shall have the like force and effect as an order of the High Court.

12. The records of the Office shall be deemed to be court records.

13. (1) Subject to the provisions of this Act, the Office may enforce a judgment by all or any of the following methods

(*a*) an instalment order under section 31;

(*b*) an order of seizure under section 32 or an authorisation given under section 44;

(*c*) an order charging land under section 46;

(*d*) an order for delivery of possession of land under section 53;

(*e*) an order for the delivery of goods under section 57;

(*f*) a charging order on funds, stock or shares under section 58;

(*g*) an order for the sale of funds, stock or shares under section 60;

(*h*) a debenture order under section 61;

(*i*) a stop order under section 62;

(*j*) a restraining order under section 66;

(*k*) a partnership order under section 67;

(*l*) an order appointing a receiver under section 68;

(*m*) an attachment of debts order under section 69;

(*n*) an attachment of earnings order under section 73.

(2) The method of enforcement of a money judgment shall be in the discretion of the Office and an applicant for enforcement may not require the use of any particular method.

(3) Without prejudice to any liability for the payment of stamp duty on any document executed to give effect to any such order as is specified in subsection 1, stamp duty shall not be payable on any such order.

14. (1) An application under section 18 or section 19 shall not be accepted by the Office

(*a*) in respect of a judgment

  (i) which may be enforced only by leave of a court, without leave of that court;

  (ii) which has been stayed or postponed, so long as such stay or postponement remains in force;

(*b*) without the leave of a designated officer, after the expiration of six years from the date on which the judgment became enforceable; or (*c*) after the expiration of twelve years from the date on which the judgment became enforceable; or

(*d*) in such other circumstances as may be prescribed by rules.

(2) An application under section 18 shall not be proceeded with where it is withdrawn by the creditor.

(3) Subject to subsection (1), the creditor may notwithstanding such withdrawal, make a fresh application under section 18 if he thinks fit so to do.

15. Where it appears to the Office that a money judgment cannot be enforced either wholly or partly within a reasonable time by any enforcement order, it shall issue to the creditor and to the debtor a notice of unenforceability.

16. Where the Office has issued a notice of unenforceability it shall give the debtor and the creditor to whom the notice has been issued an opportunity of being heard as to why a certificate of unenforceability should not be granted; and if, after giving the debtor and the creditor such an opportunity, the Office is satisfied that the money judgment in respect of which the notice of unenforceability has been issued cannot within a reasonable time be enforced either wholly or partly, it shall forthwith

(*a*) grant a certificate of unenforceability in respect of that judgment; and

(*b*) publish notice of the grant of that certificate in such manner as may be prescribed by rules; but if not so satisfied shall refuse to grant a certificate.

17. (1) A certificate of unenforceability shall remain in operation for a period of six months from the date on which it is granted.

(2) Where a certificate of unenforceability is in operation an enforcement order shall not be made on the application for the enforcement of the money judgment in respect of which the certificate was granted or on any such application bearing a later serial number in accordance with the provisions of section 20.

PART IV COMMENCEMENT OF ENFORCEMENT

18. Subject to section 14(1), any person entitled to enforce a judgment may on payment of the enforcement fee fixed by regulations apply to the Office in accordance with rules for enforcement of that judgment.

19. (1) Where the outstanding balance of all moneys due and payable under the judgment exceeds five hundred pounds or such other amount as may be fixed by regulations, the creditor may, in the first instance, upon payment of the preliminary enforcement fee so fixed apply to the Office for the issue of a custody warrant and a report as to the means of the debtor pursuant to section 21 (3) or upon an examination pursuant to section 22.

(2) If the creditor to whom the report referred to in subsection 1 is delivered fails to apply for enforcement of the judgment in accordance with the provisions of section 18 within ten days or such longer period as the Office may allow after such delivery, the Office shall forthwith discharge the custody warrant, and thereupon the application under subsection 1 shall cease to have effect.

20. (1) The Office shall, on receipt of an application under section 18 or section 19 (1), assign to that application a serial number, so however, that, where a creditor who has made an application under section 19 (1) makes, in accordance with section 19 (2), an application under section 18 for the enforcement of the same judgment, the last-mentioned application shall be assigned the same serial number as the application under section 19 (1).

(2) Where applications are made in respect of more than one money judgment against the

same debtor, the enforcement of such judgments shall, except as otherwise provided by any statutory provision, be effected so that a pending application bearing an earlier serial number shall be dealt with in priority to any such application bearing a later serial number.

21. (1) A custody warrant shall be issued by the Office forthwith after an application has been duly made

    (*a*) under section 18, where no custody warrant is in force under section 19 in respect of the same judgment against the same debtor;

    (*b*) under section 19 (1);

and the Office shall cause such warrant to be served on the debtor.

    (2) On the service of a custody warrant, all goods

    (*a*) upon all premises occupied by the debtor;

    (*b*) in any other place, being goods under the sole control of the debtor or under the joint control of the debtor and any of his dependants;

shall, as from the service of the warrant (save such as may be specified therein or exempted by rules), be deemed to be in the custody and possession of the Office.

    (3) The debtor or, where the debtor is a company, any director, officer or servant of the company shall after service of a custody warrant give to the enforcement officer such information as to the means of the debtor or, as the case may be, the assets and liabilities of the debtor company, as that officer may require.

    (4) Upon payment by or on behalf of the debtor of the amount recoverable on foot of the judgment or on discharge of the custody warrant, the custody and possession of the goods of the debtor by the Office pursuant to such warrant shall terminate.

Examination as to means

22. Where any debtor other than a company

    (*a*) is liable to pay an amount exceeding fifty pounds (or such greater amount as may be fixed by regulations) due on foot of a judgment; or

    (*b*) resides or carries on business within any petty sessions district specified in Schedule 1 and has failed or refused to answer or to answer satisfactorily any questions as to his means put to him by an enforcement officer under section 21 (3);

that debtor may be summoned by the Office to appear before a designated officer to be examined as to his means and to produce all books, documents and things in his possession or under his control relevant thereto.

23. If without just excuse a debtor fails to attend in pursuance of a summons served on him under section 22, the Office may make an attendance order directing him to appear before a designated officer and to produce all books, documents and things relating to his means.

24. If it appears to the Office that a debtor

    (*a*) is wilfully evading service of a summons issued under section 22 or an attendance order made under section 23; or

    (*b*) without just excuse has failed to attend before a designated officer in pursuance of such an attendance order;

the Office may on application by or on behalf of the creditor in writing and substantiated on oath issue a warrant for the arrest of the debtor.

25. Where

    (*a*) a summons has been issued pursuant to section 22 (*a*); or

    (*b*) the debtor is a company;

the Office may issue a summons requiring the attendance before a designated officer of any person appearing to the Office to be able to give information as to the means of the debtor or, as the case may be, the assets and liabilities of the debtor company, and sections 23 and 24 shall apply to such person as if he were a debtor to whom section 22 applies.

26. (1) Where any debtor other than a company is liable to pay an amount not exceeding fifty pounds (or such greater amount as may be fixed by regulations) due on foot of a judgment and does not reside or carry on business in any of the petty sessions districts specified in Schedule 1 and has failed or refused to answer or to answer satisfactorily any questions put to him by an enforcement officer under section 21 (3), that debtor may be summoned on complaint made by or on behalf of the creditor under Part IX of the Magistrates' Courts Act (Northern Ireland) 1964 to appear before a court of summary jurisdiction and be examined as to his means and to produce all books, documents and things in his possession or under his control relevant thereto.

(2) If

(*a*) a debtor without just excuse fails to attend, pursuant to a summons issued under subsection 1, before a court of summary jurisdiction; or

(*b*) it appears to such a court that a debtor is wilfully evading service of such a summons; that court on hearing such evidence as it considers necessary, or a justice of the peace on complaint in writing and substantiated on oath, may issue a warrant for the arrest of the debtor.

PART V ENFORCEMENT ORDERS

Payment by instalments

31. Where it appears that a debtor has or will have the means to satisfy by instalments within a reasonable time the whole or any part of the amount recoverable on foot of a judgment, the Office may, in accordance with rules, make an instalment order for the payment by the debtor of the whole or part of such amount.

[Sections 33–9 prescribe the types of property interests that may be seized and the methods that may be used to effect seizure.]

40. (1) Any goods seized under an order of seizure shall be sold under the direction of the Office and in accordance with regulations.

(2) Save as otherwise fixed by regulations, the Office shall appoint a valuer or broker to value any goods liable to seizure and to sell in accordance with regulations any goods so seized.

(3) There shall be paid to any valuer or broker appointed under subsection (2) fees in accordance with a schedule of fees fixed by regulations and approved by the Ministry of Finance.

41. A purchaser of any goods seized under an order of seizure and sold to him under the direction of the Office shall receive a good title to such goods.

42. The proceeds of the sale of any goods sold pursuant to section 40 shall in any event be retained by the Office for twenty-one days from the date of sale.

43. (1) Where property of a debtor has been taken into custody under a custody warrant or is subject to an order of seizure or has been sold under section 40 or otherwise realised, any person claiming to have an interest therein may apply to the Office in accordance with rules to have his interest determined.

(2) If it appears on the hearing of an application under subsection (1) that the claimant has a sole interest in the whole or a severable part of such property, then

(*a*) if the property has not been sold or otherwise realised an order may be made for the delivery to the claimant of the property or the part so claimed;

(*b*) if the property has been sold or otherwise realised and the proceeds thereof are held by the Office, an order may be made that there be paid to the claimant the proceeds of sale or realisation of the property or of the part so claimed.

(3) If it appears on the hearing of an application under subsection 1 that the claimant has any interest other than that specified in subsection 2 in any such property, then

(*a*) if the property has not been sold or otherwise realised, an order may be made that

    (i) that property be delivered to the claimant upon payment by him to the Office of such amount representing the value of the debtor's interest in that property as may be specified in the order; or

    (ii) if the claimant does not seek possession of such property or does not make payment pursuant to an order under sub-paragraph (i), that property be sold or otherwise realised and out of the proceeds thereof there be paid to the claimant such amount representing the value of the claimant's interest in that property as may be specified in the order;

(*b*) if the property has been sold or otherwise realised, an order may be made that out of the proceeds of the sale or realisation there be paid to the claimant such amount representing the value of the claimant's interest in that property as may be specified in the order.

(4) On the hearing of any application under this section an order may be made

(*a*) referring the claim for hearing and determination by a judge of the High Court or by the county court; or

(*b*) directing that the proceeds of the sale of the property be lodged either in the High Court or the county court.

[Sections 45–72 make special provision for enforcement against land, the delivery of goods, enforcement against debentures, funds in court, shares in private companies and partnerships, the appointment of a receiver and the attachment of debts.]

Attachment of earnings

73. (1) Subject to subsections (2) and (3) and to any other statutory provision, the Office may, if on the application of a creditor it appears that a debtor against whom an instalment order has been made under section 31 is a person to whom earnings fall to be paid, make an attachment of earnings order requiring the person to whom it is directed (being a person appearing to be the employer by whom those earnings are wholly or partly paid) to make out of those earnings or part thereof such payments as may be specified in the order.

(2) An attachment of earnings order shall not be made if it appears that the debt is due to the debtor's employer or, where the employer is a company, to any other company which is the holding company or a subsidary company (within the meaning of section 148 of the Companies Act (Northern Ireland) 1960) of the company which is the debtor's employer.

(3) An attachment of earnings order may be made if, and only if, the Office is satisfied that the debtor

(*a*) has without just cause refused or failed to comply with an instalment order made under section 31; and

(*b*) has or will have the means (after due allowance has been made for all his reasonable subsisting personal and family obligations) to satisfy within a reasonable time by instalments deducted from his earnings the whole or any part of the amount recoverable on foot of the judgment.

(4) An attachment of earnings order shall contain such matter as may be prescribed by rules.

PART VI ENFORCEMENT IN RELATION TO INSOLVENCY AND WINDING-UP

78. The grant of a certificate of unenforceability under section 16 shall, in relation to the debtor in respect of whom it is issued, be deemed to be an act of bankruptcy or, where the debtor is a company, a circumstance in which the company is unable to pay its debts; and accordingly the Bankruptcy (Ireland) Amendment Act 1872 and the Companies Act (Northern Ireland) 1960 shall have effect subject to the provisions of the Second Schedule.

PART IX REGISTRATION OF JUDGMENTS AND PENDING ACTIONS

97. (1) A register of judgments shall be kept by the Office and may, in accordance with regulations, be inspected by any member of the public.

(2) There shall be entered in the register of judgments such particulars as may be fixed by regulations of

(*a*) all judgments in respect of which an application has been made under section 18 or section 19 (1);

(*b*) all judgments in respect of which a stay of enforcement has been made by a court on the ground of the debtor's inability to pay forthwith the amount due thereunder;

(*c*) all attachment of earnings orders made by a court;

(*d*) all orders made under section 88; and

(*e*) other matters relating to the enforcement of such judgments as are specified in paragraphs (*a*) and (*b*).

(3) Where a court makes an attachment of earnings order or an order under section 88 or stays enforcement on the ground of the debtor's inability to pay, the proper officer of that court shall, upon the making of the order, transmit a copy thereof to the Office.

[Recently, a report of the New South Wales Law Reform Commission has recommended the creation of a system of enforcement of judgments based upon the Northern Ireland model: see New South Wales Law Reform Commission, *Draft Proposal Relating to the Enforcement of Money Judgments*, 1975.] A similar scheme was proposed by the Attorney General's department in New Brunswick and is currently under detailed study.

QUESTIONS

1 Does the Northern Ireland model make the present system more efficient? More just? If so, how?

2 Should the Enforcement Office be given any additional powers or duties? Should any of the proposed powers or duties be withheld from the Enforcement Office?

3 To what extent ought the creditor be involved in the selection of the *mode* of enforcement? The Payne Report recommended that the initiative to take any particular mode of enforcement should be left to the creditor; the Enforcement Office should always have the authority of the creditor or creditors for any particular step taken (para. 381). While the creditor(s) would be able to give the Enforcement Office the general authority to take all necessary steps to have the judgment(s) satisfied, every judgment creditor would be entitled to apply for a particular mode of enforcement to be employed or not to be employed against the debtor. The Enforcement Office, however, would have the final discretion whether or not to make an order in the terms asked for (para. 403–6).

Upon what basis should the costs of enforcement be assessed and allocated? The Payne Report (para. 422) recommended that only one fee be payable at the time of the application for enforcement, regardless of the number of subsequent applications and the types of specific modes of enforcement employed. It suggested that the fee should be related to the amount of the unsatisfied judgment and should be added to the total amount payable by the judgment debtor.

4 As a matter of policy, is it appropriate that the same fee be paid for the issuing of one garnishee order as that paid for the issuing of four garnishee orders in order to satisfy a debt of the same amount? Who should bear the cost of the fee: the debtor? the creditor? the state?

5 In conjunction with the Enforcement Office, would it be useful to establish a central register of judgment debts? When should the judgment be registered: as soon as the judgment is entered? upon the application for enforcement? when the judgment debt has remained unsatisfied for a period of one month?

6 To what extent should the Enforcement Office have the power to vary, discharge or set aside an enforcement order?

7 Given the comprehensive nature of the Enforcement Office procedure, should there be a limitation period for the enforcement of a judgment? If so, how long should be allowed?

8 As a matter of policy, should the Enforcement Office also regulate the collection of debts prior to judgment? If so, can you devise monitoring and enforcement mechanisms that would make this administratively feasible?

4 THE REFORM OF CREDITOR'S REMEDIES AND THE CREDIT MARKET: HEREIN OF NEWTON'S THIRD LAW

Any reformer of the present enforcement system must evaluate his own revised system in the context of the credit market as a whole. Will the proposed expansion or restriction of creditors' remedies result in a beneficial or detrimental change in the way credit will be extended in the future? Will certain classes of persons be excluded from access to, or be included in the credit market when they ought not to be? While it is often quite simple for the academic to suggest reform (or indeed revolution) of the present system on the basis of visceral feelings – this is the 'right' or 'decent' manner in which to allocate the transaction costs accompanying debt collection – he or she must always remember that Newton's Third Law may be as relevant to the study of creditors' remedies as it is to physics.

Professors Cayne and Trebilcock suggested that severe exclusionary and degenerative consequences would accompany the adoption of proposals for radical restrictions on creditors' remedies. (See Cayne & Trebilcock, 'Market Considerations in the Formulation of Consumer Protection Policy', supra at p 61.) Are their assumptions correct? And even if they are, what policy choices are dictated by their conclusions? In this context consider the following article:

Wallace, 'The Logic of Consumer Credit Reform' (1973), 82 *Yale L.J.* 461 (footnotes omitted).

A consumer credit reform movement has been mobilizing to restrict or abolish remedies such as the cognovit note, balloon clause, deficiency judgment, wage garnishment, holder in due course status, and repossession without hearing. Momentum has been added by recent judicial decisions such as *Fuentes* v *Shevin*, in which replevin without notice in most circumstances was declared unconstitutional. But some commentators have objected that the ultimate effect of such reform may be to limit the amount of credit available to low-income consumers. Critics contend that limiting the creditor's ability to coerce repayment will increase creditor cost, thereby increasing the price or reducing the volume of credit available, with the most severe effects falling on low-income borrowers. Three assumptions underlie much of the past criticism of consumer credit reform: First, that restrictions on creditor remedies, such as those noted above, will increase the price or reduce the volume of credit: second, that such tampering with consumer sovereignty will result in allocative inefficiency in the credit market; and third, that this increase in price or reduction in volume of credit will disproportionately affect low-income consumers and thus offend our sense of distributive justice. This article will question the accuracy of the first assumption, and suggest that gains in allocative efficiency and increases in distributive justice may result even if reform increases the price or reduces the volume of credit.

I CONSUMER CREDIT REFORM AND THE PRICE AND VOLUME OF CREDIT

The assumption that consumer credit reform will increase the price or reduce the volume of credit rests upon two minor premises: First that significant reform will be costly to the creditor: and second, that he will respond by either raising the price or reducing the volume of credit offered. While there is some empirical evidence supporting these premises, there is also some to the contrary, and their validity is at best uncertain.

A The Probability that Reform will be Costly to the Creditor
Significant reform need not increase creditor costs. Additional costs will result only if reform leads to a higher rate of default, greater quantities of uncollectible debts, or more costly collection procedures.

1 Will reform increase the rate of default? Those who contend that a significant reduction in coercive creditor remedies will increase the rate of default find in the present legal system elements of moral suasion, deterrence, and coercion which prompt the debtor to meet his obligations. They appear to reason that if creditor remedies are restricted, the legal system will no longer support the principle that debts must be repaid, deter default through fear, or coerce repayment through direct sanctions. As a result, the rate of default will increase.

Yet it seems just as reasonable to assume that the debtor's own morality and sense of obligation, and those of his community, are equally determinative of whether or not he repays. There appears to be a clear consensus among almost all segments of society regardless of the efficacy of official sanctions, that obligations must be fulfilled. Professor Caplovitz found a strong willingness among debtors to meet their obligations, even in the face of adversity, despite an absence of effective legal sanctions against nonpayment. The moral and deterrent impact of creditor remedies may depend less on their severity than on their efficacy in reinforcing ethical motivation and social disapproval, and their certainty of enforcement. For example, there is evidence that debtors find the mere service of process to be a powerful impetus to repayment.

Finally, it seems likely that significant non-legal sanctions would operate through credit-rating systems even in the absence of legal coercion. A restriction of creditor remedies should encourage the development of more accurate credit bureaus, providing information that should permit the identification of high-risk debtors, particularly those with a history of delinquency. In this way, if legal regulation subsides, informal regulation through the market should continue to provide a substantial deterrent to defaults. Thus, without empirical support it is simply not clear that restrictions on coercive creditor remedies will dilute either the moral suasion or deterrent effect on defaultors.

2 Will reform increase uncollectible defaulted debts? The contention that restriction of creditor coercion will necessarily increase the number of uncollectible debts is equally challenge-

able. A debt becomes uncollectible primarily due to the recalcitrance of the debtor and the encumbrance of his assets. Reducing coercive remedies may not, in fact, significantly alter either of these factors.

Legal coercion applied after default seems even less likely to reduce debtor recalcitrance than when it is applied before. First, the motivation to repay after default may be considerably lower, because the debtor has already endured whatever sense of shame or failure accompanies default. Moreover, debtors who have defaulted have usually done so because they are already under considerable financial pressure; repaying after default would mean even greater hardship.

A reformed system of consumer credit, however, might still arouse fear and psychological pressure sufficient to induce potential defaulters to continue repayment at the same or nearly the same rate as under more coercive remedies. Of particular importance is the fact that once they have defaulted, debtors still know that they will be 'apprehended' and be under some further legal obligation.

It is doubtful, moreover, that creditors now gain very much from coercive remedies which allow them to reach debtors' assets directly. Coercive remedies may themselves encumber remaining assets and thus make repayment all the more difficult. This is particularly true where the debtor's major source of funds is future income. Coercive remedies tend to eliminate this asset when, for example, employers annoyed with having to garnish wages could respond by firing the debtor, or when garnished employees lose their incentive to continue working. Repossession or execution are also often inefficient remedies because the creditor rarely receives full repayment. Indeed, the expense of some coercive measures may even exceed their return. The only satisfaction a creditor realizes in such situations, as Professor Leff has shown, is spite.

3 Will reform mean more costly collection procedures? While restriction of creditor coercion might well cause short-term increases in collection costs, other consumer credit reforms, geared less to the elimination of harsh remedies and more toward positive creditor or debtor services, may actually produce savings which would more than offset these increases. More efficient information systems could reduce default rates by providing creditors with more complete data on potential borrowers: therapeutic counseling might reduce the number of debtors who repeatedly find themselves in credit difficulty, by advising potential borrowers and by helping defaulted debtors deal with their debts. While such reforms would obviously not be cost free, in the absence of clear empirical evidence, one cannot conclude that reforms of this type would inevitably have a noticeable effect on the price or availability of credit.

B The Probability that the Creditor will Respond to Increased Costs by Raising the Price or Reducing the Volume of Credit
Any actual increase in costs to the creditor that does result from restricting coercion will produce price increases or volume reductions only if the creditor's cost structure forces such a response. Several studies suggest a direct relationship between the overall price of credit and the size of the creditor's provisions for bad debts. But such provisions may not be directly related to the cost of dealing with high-risk debtors. At least one study has found no significant relationship between the level of debtor risk and the price of the credit offered. Thus, provisions for bad debts may merely signal creditors' lack of efficiency or vigor in collecting, shaped in part by the fact that creditors often operate under imperfect competition and are rarely under strong pressure to keep their expenses as low as possible. Faced with increased collection or default costs and an elastic demand for credit, creditors may well respond by streamlining their presently inefficient collection efforts rather than by raising prices or curtailing loans: and, as

has already been suggested, more efficient collection procedures need not mean harsher collection tactics.

None of this is meant to suggest that an increase in the price or a reduction in the volume of credit offered after the elimination of creditor coercion is impossible. It is only to note that they are not *necessary* and *direct* consequences, given the present state of empirical research. A thorough appraisal of any specific reform should consider the probabilities of such results but then move on to a second and perhaps more important question: What would be the impact of reform on the efficient use of all resources?

II CONSUMER CREDIT REFORM AND ALLOCATIVE EFFICIENCY

One basis for evaluating consumer credit reform must be its effect on the allocative efficiency of the credit market. Allocative efficiency is achieved when the quantity of credit purchased maximizes social gains from credit resources relative to potential gains from all other resources. Thus, under perfect allocative efficiency, debtors would purchase credit up to and not beyond that point where the last dollar spent on credit produces more net benefits to society than if it were spent elsewhere. This perfectly allocated condition could obtain if all the social costs and benefits generated by a credit transaction were reflected in the credit contract and if all imperfections were eliminated from the credit market. Although the fulfillment of these conditions may be difficult, entailing huge administrative costs, the consumer credit market could be made *more* allocatively efficient than it now is, by taking measures to minimize market imperfections and bring as many credit-generated costs and benefits as possible to bear on the credit contract. Another way to make the credit market more allocatively efficient would be to impose direct controls after deciding on an optimal amount of credit by careful analysis of all relevant costs and benefits and then allocating credit accordingly.

Of course any tampering with the present credit market would involve probabilities and uncertainties. The risk that debtors, creditors, or the market will behave in unforeseen ways would have to be reflected in the decision to initiate a specific reform. Moreover, such calculations must also account for the expense of adopting and administering a reformed system. The administrative costs of imposing a perfectly allocated system may, in reality, be prohibitive.

Opponents of reform may argue that any tampering with consumer sovereignty would result in less allocative efficiency: Reforms which eliminate coercive remedies or supply services such as screening or therapy should not be imposed (so the argument might run) because if debtors or creditors wanted such reform they would purchase it. But if prospective debtors wish to purchase cheaper credit along with the chance of default and coercive creditor tactics, they should be allowed to do so. The opponents of reform may ask: Why run the high risk of misallocation by *imposing* reform when we already know what creditors and debtors want because we see them bargain for it in the marketplace?

But such arguments may fail to see the serious imperfections in the credit market which prevent the freely bargained supply of credit from being allocatively efficient. Such imperfections may lead to an oversupply or undersupply of credit regardless of the bargain between creditors and debtors. At times the effects may cancel each other out, but such a fortuitous result would be purely accidental.

A Possible Imperfections in the Current Credit Market

1 Imperfections Leading to Undersupply: Several imperfections exist in the credit market which may result in too little credit being purchased. These include:

Concentration in the credit industry. Instead of a highly competitive credit market in which creditors bid against each other to attract debtors, the credit market exhibits a large number of monopolistic characteristics, at least at the local level. Typically, a small number of creditors serve low-income areas and many low-income buyers do not have the transportation or information necessary to shop intelligently. Depending on the degree of monopoly and elasticity of demand for credit, creditors may raise prices to maximize their own profits, causing debtors to purchase a smaller quantity of credit than they would if the price reflected its real cost. Reform aimed at this imperfection might include an increase in debtor information, subsidies to debtor mobility, price ceilings on credit sales, or the elimination of artificial barriers to competition arising from present licensing laws.

Unavailable debtor services. Another imperfection contributing to undersupply is the lack of certain services for debtors which, if supplied, would make credit far more attractive. If, for example, at the time of entering the credit transaction debtors could purchase an insurance policy entitling them to assistance in the event of default, and if such assistance reduced the cost of future anguish by a greater amount than it increased costs, rational debtors would purchase more credit. Of course, if the service caused creditor costs to increase by an amount equal to or greater than the debtor's net gain (perhaps because debtors who no longer feared future anguish would not feel as great an incentive to repay) the competitive price of credit would increase to wipe out any debtor gain, and there would be no overall increase in the amount of credit purchased.

The free market has probably not exploited such potential increases in allocative efficiency and supplied such debtor services due to debtor short-sightedness and a lack of creditor ability to exploit economies of scale. To encourage debtors to demand such reforms, they could be supplied with information about the likelihood of future hardship and the advantages of the debtor service. Reform might also subsidize creditors until economies of scale were reached.

Unavailable creditor services. A third imperfection in the credit market occurs to the extent that creditors do not differentiate between high-risk and low-risk debtors. Misallocations result when low-risk debtors purchase too little credit because credit is offered at too high a price relative to the risk that they will default, and high-risk debtors are purchasing too much credit at too low a price. If better information were available, creditors could price discriminate between such debtors. Better discrimination would enable them to reduce uncollectible debts and costly collection practices and, in a competitive market, offer a greater quantity of credit at lower prices. The reason that such services are not now available may have to do with legal difficulties blocking creditor cooperation or problems in achieving economies of scale. To the extent that the cost of such services when fully developed would be less than the cost savings they produced, reform which subsidizes or develops such services should increase allocative efficiency.

Macro-economic benefits. A final imperfection causing an undersupply of credit occurs to the extent that credit produces benefits other than those accruing to the purchaser. If such external benefits of credit were included in the credit transaction, more credit would be purchased. For example, consumer credit may well promote economic growth by permitting the anticipation of purchases and shifting demand toward durable goods industries which have greater potential for expansion. Of course, consumers must repay their loans with interest, thereby reducing later expenditures by a proportionate amount. But insofar as credit adds to the normal growth in demand, capital accumulation and technical innovation occur earlier, resulting in a more advanced economy with higher productivity.

Economic stability may be another macro-economic benefit of credit. It is often assumed that credit spurs the economy at the beginning of an upswing by allowing consumers to anticipate spending power. It is said to moderate downturns by providing consumers with the means of maintaining prior levels of consumption, thereby dampening the cyclical plunge. Unfortunately, studies to date fail to substantiate the assertion that the consumer credit system has such a favorable impact on growth and stability. If credit is now undersupplied to high-risk, low-income debtors, there is little evidence that such an undersupply significantly affects overall demand. Thus, these possible external benefits to the economy generated by credit would not seem significant enough to warrant the risks and costs of reform.

2 Imperfections Leading to Oversupply: Market imperfections causing excessive use of credit occur to the extent that credit use generates costs which are greater than its actual price. If such external costs could be brought to bear on the credit transaction, the price of credit would be higher and less would be purchased. The most important of these costs include:

Public subsidization of the regulatory system. Society as a whole now finances the apparatus which regulates the credit market – the judges, administrators, legal service lawyers, enforcement officials, and clerical employees. The payment of such expenses is a clear subsidization of the credit market.

Lost productivity. Another external cost to society consists of work time lost by debtors due to court appearances, meetings with creditors, and general psychological stress. Many debtors may be forced to take jobs not commensurate with their skills or hazardous to their health in order to cope with economic crisis. Others may lose their jobs and spend days or months finding another. Entire families may be affected: For example, the debtors' children may terminate their education in order to take low-skill jobs, thereby missing vocational opportunities and reducing the economy's productivity.

Loss of respect for government. Those who are subjected to coercive collection tactics employed by the present system, as some empirical studies show, may emerge from the process with much less respect for the courts and legal system. Such attitudes may make it more difficult to maintain an ordered society, particularly when all the entire debtor's family is affected.

Hardship for debtor and family. In addition to these costs to society in general, substantial burdens accrue to the debtors themselves – burdens which are not reflected in the price of credit. The debtor must endure the hardship of repaying debts when, as a result, his personal standard of living is reduced and his financial flexibility limited. The debtor may suffer the frustration of being unable to obtain a remedy for faulty goods because the credit contract does not permit him to withhold the balance of the purchase price from the creditor-assignee of the seller. He may also suffer from psychological pressure inherent in devices such as repossession, deficiency judgments, garnishment, and other execution processes. Simultaneously, he may face the social censure and personal guilt associated with the failure to meet his obligations. A number of recent studies substantiate the magnitude of anguish, shame, and suffering associated with default and the present coercive remedies. Nearly forty-five per cent of Caplovitz's study reported physical ailments assertedly related to the pressures of default. Other defaulters have reported increased marital difficulty, reduced expenditures on food and other living expenses, and substantial worry over loss of employment. Many of these costs may undergo a kind of multiplier effect as the debtor's suffering affects his entire family.

The current system cannot allocate credit efficiently if debtors who enter the credit transaction fail to appreciate the probability of default occurring and the consequences following for themselves and their families. If the debtor underestimates either the probability of default or the amount of hardship resulting therefrom he will demand more credit than his informed preferences would dictate. If most debtors underestimate these risks, the demand for credit will be inflated.

3 Reform Techniques for Reducing Oversupply: Reform could aim at eliminating such external costs, *e.g.*, by prohibiting the coercive creditor practices which cause them, or at bringing the costs to bear in the credit transaction. Prohibition risks eliminating benefits that may, in some cases, exceed the costs which are eliminated. Further, some of these costs are so difficult to quantify or so remote that an error in estimating them may wipe out any prospective gain. Those costs for which the risk of such error is substantial should therefore *not be internalized*. It would seem that reform could most easily aim at internalizing the costs falling upon the debtor and his family.

Reform could respond to the external costs falling upon the debtor and his family in three distinct ways: By so improving debtor foresight of the risks and consequences of default that these consequences would no longer be 'external' to the credit bargain: by prohibiting the causes of the costs; and by internalizing the costs through a kind of corrective tax levy.

A DEBTOR EDUCATION Debtors might be forced to recognize the probability of default occurring and the consequences following default through a program of education and counseling. If the debtor could be compelled to feel the depth of hardship associated with default, his demand for credit would reflect more accurately his true preferences. His demand for credit would be further enlightened if he could estimate more accurately his particular level of risk. If debtor demand for credit then fell, the competitive creditor would have a choice: either maintain coercive remedies and sell credit at the new lower price, or eliminate coercion and sell at a higher price reflecting the increased creditor costs resulting from such elimination. If the cost to the creditor of eliminating remedies is higher than the cost to the informed debtor of having them employed, the creditor will be content to sell credit with coercion at the lower price; if not, the creditor will eliminate the devices. The creditor's choice would be, in any case, an allocatively efficient one.

Of course, an education program sufficiently graphic to alter consumer behavior probably would be extraordinarily difficult to construct. Counseling in this area has rarely proven effective because of the strong consumer biases in favor of immediate gratification and an unwillingness to take full account of future hardship and risk. For such an education program to be successful, it would have to affect the deepest of character traits: even if that were possible, the costs of doing so would probably exceed any concomitant gains in allocative efficiency.

B PROHIBITION OF CERTAIN CREDITOR REMEDIES If coercive creditor techniques were simply abolished there would obviously be no need to internalize their harmful effects. But any such elimination of creditor remedies would fail to produce allocative efficiency if creditor costs were thereby increased more than the harm to debtors was decreased. If this occurred, the competitive price of credit would rise above the price sufficient to internalize the hardships of coercive remedies. Such a situation should be unlikely, however, as the value of coercive remedies to creditors is generally low while the costs to debtors are high. Moreover, creditors deprived of coercive remedies would have more incentive to improve their own information systems, thus increasing their capacity to assess the riskiness of individual debtors and reducing another market imperfection. They would also have more incentive to control the sales practices and quality of items bought with credit. Instead of insisting on payment from debtors who indicate strong dissatisfaction with purchased items, creditors would be more likely to throw the credit contract back to the seller under a repurchase agreement.

It should be noted, however, that abolition of creditor remedies may have costly side effects. The concomitant price increase might trigger, for example, an underworld loan shark market which employed genuinely abusive, self-help remedies. And abolition may not ameliorate entirely the anguish, shame and loss of self-respect which commonly result from default. In order to eliminate such guilt, reform might have to alter the definition of default, *e.g.*, by making liable only those whose failure to pay resulted from negligence or bad faith. One might also consider programs designed to aid the debtor and his family – to teach them to marshal their assets and bargain with their creditors, while at the same time adjusting them to the idea that they were overcommitted. Such a program, perhaps financed by the creditors much as is their fire insurance, could combine, as in Great Britain, legal and social aid in one agency. Creditor financing would of course have allocative effects of its own.

C INTERNALIZATION THROUGH SPECIFIC LEVIES Government might intervene to internalize the costs of creditor remedies by imposing a direct charge, equal to the estimated external costs, on their use. The charge might be imposed on any credit contract which provided for coercive remedies, or it might be imposed upon the actual use of such remedies. It would promote allocative efficiency to the extent that it compelled creditors to avoid the use of coercive remedies whenever the social cost of using them exceeded the benefits. Thus, the competitive price of credit would reflect either the social cost of the coercive remedy or the cost to the creditor of foresaking it, whichever was lower.

Two objections can be raised against such a proposal. It might be contended first that the external costs would be impossible for the government to quantify and translate into selective charges. In response, it may be argued that the calculation would be possible within a certain acceptable margin of error.

Secondly, one might object that it seems unjust and irrational for debtors to end up paying for charges which reflect the likely hardships they will endure from coercive remedies. That is, while the user charge may produce allocative efficiency, its distributive impact would be regressive. This objection might be met if the proceeds of the charges were used to subsidize debtors who incurred the hardships of default. While such subsidies might have a detrimental impact on allocative efficiency to the extent debtors relied on them, the risk seems rather small in light of the distributive equities involved.

B Will Reform Increase Administrative Costs? The impact of reform on governmental expenditures would vary tremendously with the reform package chosen. A package that reduced the risk of underestimating or overestimating the externalities of the present system might entail huge administrative expenditures, while a package that more or less ignored the risk of misallocations might actually involve less administrative expense than the present system. For example, attempts to achieve the optimal allocation of credit resources through economic analysis and to limit by government regulation credit resources to that prescribed allocation, might be less costly than an attempt to achieve that allocation by rebuilding the market. Although the costs of such analysis and direct regulation would undoubtedly be large, the costs of rebuilding the market could be even larger. Yet, that market, once rebuilt, might be capable of automatically producing a better allocation of resources than one imposed by the government.

If there is a trade-off between risk of misallocation and administrative expense, one goal of reform should be to find the best mix between the two. It might be, for example, that if defaulting debtors were liable only for negligent default, creditors would be less likely to use the court system, and judicial expenses would thereby decrease. For the trade-off to work, however, this decrease would have to offset the additional expense of the new means of handling non-negligent defaults.

Of course, even if the costs of administering reform were substantial, those costs might well produce further savings elsewhere in the credit system. For example, if the government were to provide the service of 'skip-tracing' interstate debtors, its administrative cost might be less than the cost of an analogous service carried on by creditors.

In light of these uncertainties and risks, reform in consumer credit should be instituted wherever possible as an experiment to be adjusted periodically, rather than a permanent panacea. Experimenting through the legislative process may, of course, be difficult, as a government benefit once conferred is often difficult politically to retract. But the prospect of achieving substantial credit reform without major administrative expense appears to justify some experimentation. Reforms involving even substantial regulatory cost might also be attempted, if the potential gains in allocative efficiency appeared great enough to support the risk. Still, there are likely to be some technical difficulties in measuring external costs, and political problems in convincing legislatures to terminate unsuccessful reform experiments.

III CONSUMER CREDIT REFORM AND WEALTH DISTRIBUTION

Another basis for evaluating consumer credit reform would be its effect on the distribution of wealth. Such a concern is obviously relevant to credit reform; indeed the ostensible motive behind many reform proposals is to reduce the suffering and injustice visited on those who cannot pay their exorbitant debts. Moreover, there are few who would vent their disapproval of the present system by denying high-risk borrowers the opportunity to borrow. Thus, the question inevitably arises: If reform ends the credit of the poor, high-risk debtor, is he really helped?

The argument that consumer credit reform will deny low-income consumers credit and thereby worsen their plight begins with the assertion, discussed above, that reform will increase creditor costs, producing a credit price increase or volume reduction. But even if such events occur, it may not follow that this loss of credit would markedly affect the distribution of wealth.

Such a loss will not affect individual purchasing power. Although credit does enable the low-income consumer to purchase goods and services without recourse to savings or current income, thereby creating a semblance of increased purchasing power in the short run, his net purchasing power in the long run will be *less* than that of a consumer who does not borrow: The credit consumer must eventually pay for his credit, and these interest payments will reduce his subsequent purchasing power.

Short-term increases in purchasing power may, however, produce advantages which the low-income consumer would otherwise be denied. First, the credit purchase of certain durable goods may provide the consumer with long-term economies (for example, the use of a private washing machine instead of public laundry). Second, credit purchase before sufficient savings have been accumulated could provide the consumer with a hedge against inflation which might otherwise sap the value of such savings. Third, credit may provide the consumer lacking discipline to save for durables with an attractive forced-savings device. Fourth, it may give consumers the psychic benefit of being able to consume above their normal income level. Fifth, it may prove a means for withstanding temporary economic adversities such as job loss or illness. Finally, and perhaps most importantly, credit purchases made before the accumulation of savings often allow younger people to enjoy goods they will ultimately be able to afford, by allowing them to redistribute their lifetime earnings to best fit their needs.

Simultaneously, a denial of credit may cause specific hardships. The very process of being refused credit may produce embarrassment and humiliation. The stigma of having been judged unworthy of credit is similar to the defaulter's sense of guilt, though the poor credit risk will probably cease seeking and accept his no-credit status. However, such acceptance may take the form of turning to criminal sources for credit. As noted above, in such a situation both the real and hidden external costs of credit may increase to rather gruesome proportions. Of course, the risk and high prices associated with such borrowing should discourage most debtors from pursuing this alternative under normal conditions. And even if debtors did desire such loans, a simple way of urging them back into the legitimate market would be to eliminate usury ceilings and allow prices to increase dramatically with risk.

In sum, credit may provide flexibility, ease, and economy – advantages which bear a direct relationship to the willingness of debtors to pay the price of credit. Thus, denying credit to high-risk debtors may cause them some frustration, although they may gain both by not paying interest charges and by avoiding the hardships associated with default. These latter gains may, in fact, outweigh the disadvantages from the absence of credit. Indeed, reform may be viewed as providing a benefit to everyone who uses credit by reducing the risk of serious hardship associated with default. In this way, price increases or volume reductions caused by reform may be seen as 'payments' for compulsory insurance against misfortune.

How well these increases or reductions match the risk depends, of course, on how broadly the risk category is defined. If, in order to guard against losses in a reformed system, creditors respond by charging all their customers the same higher price or reducing the amount of credit available to all regardless of risk, the low-risk (and more wealthy) borrowers will be subsidizing the insurance of the high-risk (and poorer) ones. There will thus be a wealth transfer from rich to poor. But if, on the other hand, creditors discriminate according to risk, there will be less of this transfer effect. Of course, the actual distribution is likely to be far more complicated. If the credit market is segmented between low-risk, wealthy debtors borrowing from banks, and higher-risk, poor debtors borrowing from loan companies, the banks may not respond to reforms at all, while the loan companies would probably increase their prices substantially. If this happened, wealth would be redistributed to some degree from low-income borrowers who repaid their debts to those who did not. Meanwhile, the highest risk debtors would probably be denied loans altogether. In any case, regardless of how segmented the credit market, poor debtors would not *necessarily* find themselves worse off; some, in fact, might be better off.

To the extent that reform did not increase creditor expenses, it would have very little wealth transfer impact on creditors. Even if it does raise operating costs, creditors might pass a part of the costs on to debtors unless, as suggested above, demand for credit is highly elastic and at the same time creditors already enjoy monopoly profits. Yet, even under these conditions, little wealth transfer is likely to result because creditors would, in the long term, withdraw their investments from credit markets and reinvest in other sectors of the economy. Thus the only possible transfer of wealth away from the creditor would occur if the profit margin in the credit industry were substantially higher than in other investment opportunities. Yet studies indicate the contrary.

There is thus no certainty whatever that the wealth distribution impact of consumer credit reform would be regressive. If a given consumer credit reform did not increase creditor expenses, little or no redistribution would occur, though debtors as a group might be better off than they were before reform. If, instead, reform did increase creditor costs and the demand for credit were relatively inelastic, creditors would be likely to pass the increased costs along to the debtors; a wealth transfer might then occur from lower-risk debtors to higher-risk debtors who pay the same price for credit. If reform increased creditor costs and the demand for credit were relatively elastic, creditors might lose some wealth in reducing the volume of credit offered and converting their investments to other sectors of the economy; debtors who under these circumstances refrained from paying the higher price of credit might also lose certain advantages associated with credit, but would gain by avoiding the risk of default.

IV VALUE CHOICES

An evaluation of various consumer credit reforms can go only so far. There will be some critics who insist that any benefits from reform are not as significant as the moral effrontery of allowing defaulting debtors to avoid their just deserts. Other critics will claim that debtors should be free to choose the high-risk of future suffering if that is what they want. Still others may argue that if we are interested in increasing allocative efficiency or redistributing wealth, there are far easier and more efficient ways of doing so than by becoming embroiled in the consumer credit market.

To admit the validity of such criticisms is merely to acknowledge that value choices underlie all policy decisions, and that argument must, after a certain point, give way to the most basic value differences. Yet it should be noted that some reforms may challenge basic values less than others. Reforms which are not likely to increase creditor costs present few difficulties for critics who are concerned about freedom of choice or the means of redistributing wealth, since such reform may be relatively inexpensive. The abolition of holder-in-due-course devices, restriction of wage garnishment, and the removal of the 'blanket' clauses which give the creditor an interest in virtually all the debtor's household goods appear to fall in this class.

Other proposals which seem likely to increase creditor costs and thus affect the price or volume of credit include the restriction of coercive tactics available to creditors after default, abolition of deficiency and default judgments, and article nine repossession. When high-risk debtors are forced to forego credit because of such reforms, critics worried about freedom of choice are likely to argue that high-risk debtors should at least have the option of purchasing credit at a lower price and at a higher risk of misfortune. These critics may well reject reformers' repeated warnings that consumers have a shortsighted bias in favor of immediate gratification, lack bargaining strength, and are likely to fall victim to advertising. When the cost of reform is not internalized within the credit transaction but subsidized by the government instead, critics concerned with efficiency are likely to claim that there are cheaper ways of maximizing social welfare and redistributing wealth; and critics concerned with redistribution are likely to argue that general taxpayers should not pay for the faults of a few culpable debtors. These critics are in effect refusing to accept debtor difficulty as a general misfortune falling upon various income groups at various times, similar to job loss or temporary illness as an appropriate concern of government.

Thus, we can only indicate the appropriate questions that need to be asked, highlighting those areas where more empirical work is needed. Proposals for consumer credit reform abound. What is most needed now is a willingness to evaluate them rationally, confining disagreement to ultimate differences in values.

See also Kripke, 'Consumer Credit Regulation: A Creditor-Oriented Viewpoint' (1968), 68 *Col. L. Rev.* 445; Kripke, 'Gesture and Reality in Consumer Credit Reform' (1969), 44 *N.Y. U.L. Rev.* 1; The Wisconsin Consumer Act, 1971 (perhaps the most extensive consumer credit legislation in existence); Davis, 'Legislative Restriction of Creditor Powers and Remedies; A Case Study of the Negotiation and Drafting of the Wisconsin Consumer Act' (1973), 72 *Mich. L. Rev.* 1.

16
Mechanics' Liens

a / Mechanics' Liens: A Pyramid of Special Creditors
Mechanics' lien legislation in Canada has created a self-contained statutory scheme of rights protecting contractors, subcontractors, material suppliers, renters of equipment (in some provinces), and other creditors involved in construction projects. The aim of the legislation is to give these persons special rights not enjoyed at common law in addition to their remedies as ordinary creditors. The policy underlying the legislation emphasizes that to the extent these protected persons confer lasting benefits on land, an 'owner' of the land (as defined by the statute) ought not to enjoy the increase in value without paying for it.

The legislation attempts to accomplish its purpose by means of three main tools: giving those improving land a lien against ownership interests in the land benefitted; requiring a 'holdback' of instalment payments made during construction – a reserve of funds to which claimants can look for satisfaction of their claims –; and creating a trust in favour of construction creditors of money paid on account. It is vital to remember that each right is separate from and independent of any other; a person may retain one right although others have been lost.

The rights cannot be understood without considering the nature of the difficulties they are designed to alleviate. The typical building project involves a pyramid of individuals in various legal relationships. A property owner will usually hire a general contractor whose job is to assure that the work is carried out in accordance with the contract specifications. The contract between the owner and the contractor is called the 'head', 'prime' or 'main' contract. This head, or general contractor will usually employ sub-contractors to construct particular aspects of the project (electrical, mechanical, plumbing, carpentry, etc.) Subcontractors may in turn employ sub-subcontractors to perform a portion of their responsibilities. The head contractor and each of the subcontractors will have contractual relationships with employees, persons supplying materials and equipment, as well as banks lending money to them, usually by way of overdraught. The diagram on p 518 may be of assistance in sorting out the relationships.

The process is complicated still further by the progress payment method of remuneration ordinarily used in the construction industry. When the general contractor has completed a part of the project (usually having borrowed money from his bank to pay his employees, suppliers, and so on during construction of that stage) he will apply to the owner for an agreed upon percentage of the total contract price. When the owner's architect (or perhaps the architect of the bank financing the owner) has made an on-site inspection and found the project completed to the stage specified by the agreement

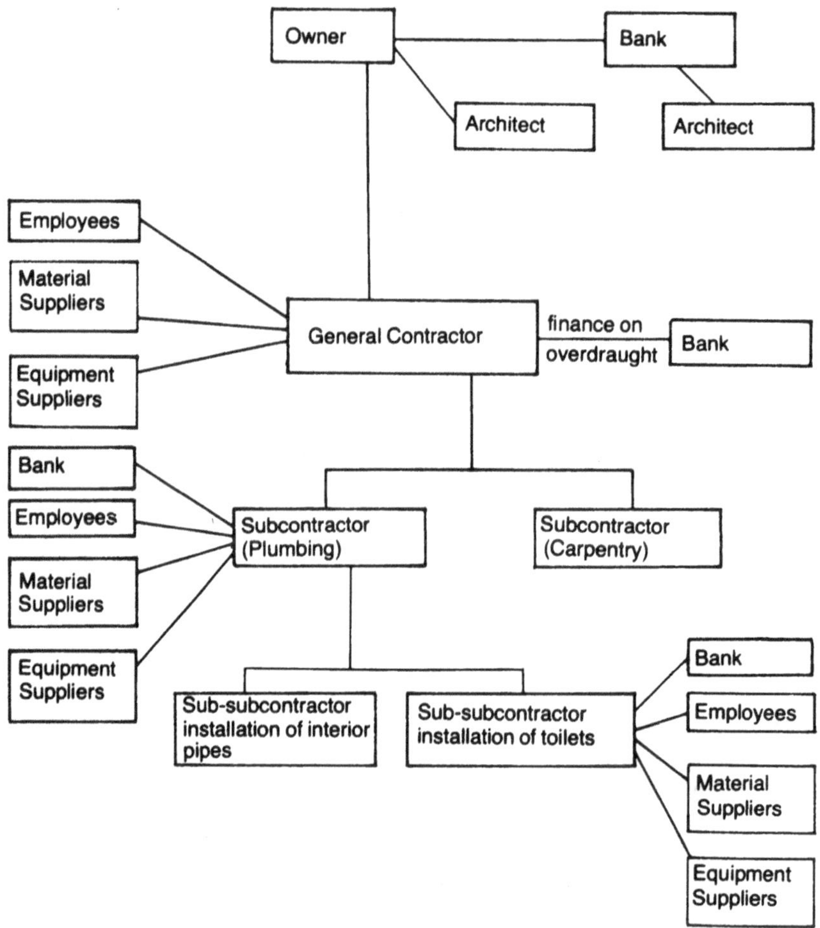

between the owner and head contractor, the bank will advance funds to the owner, who will then pay the specified amount to the general contractor. The general contractor will deposit the funds in his bank and will pay his subcontractors, who will pay their sub-subcontractors, and so on down the line. Because of the time lag inherent in the use of periodic progress payments, every individual down the line must have or obtain sufficient funding to allow him to pay his debts which fall due before he receives his progress payment.

Bankruptcies are not uncommon in the construction industry. In 1965, approximately 13% of all Canadian commercial failures occurred in this field (Krawec, Memo on The Mechanics' Lien Act, Ministry of the Attorney General, 1974). Such a bankruptcy causes great hardship to employees, subcontractors and material suppliers of the bankrupt. Because of the pyramid of interrelationships and the time lag in payments, a bankruptcy of an individual at one point along the line has a 'domino' effect on all participants in the project 'down the line' from him. Such persons have very little chance of recovering much in the bankruptcy, and absent mechanics' lien rights, would have no right of action in rem against the land, and no right of action in personam against anyone with whom they have no contractual relationship.

b / Excerpts from a Construction Contract
Canadian Construction Association, Standard Form of Stipulated Price Construction Contract

ARTICLE A-4 PAYMENT

(a) Subject to applicable legislation and, where such legislation does not exist or apply, in accordance with such prescribed regulations or industry practice respecting holdback percentages and in accordance with the provisions of the General Conditions of the Contract, the Owner shall:

    (1) make monthly payments to the Contractor on account of the Contract Price. The amounts of such payments shall be as certified by the Engineer; and

    (2) upon Substantial Performance of the Work as certified by the Engineer pay to the Contractor any unpaid balance of holdback monies then due; and

    (3) upon Total Performance of the Work as certified by the Engineer pay to the Contractor any unpaid balance of the Contract Price then due.

(b) If the Owner fails to make payments to the Contractor as they become due under the terms of this Contract or in any award by arbitration or court, interest at the rate of 1 per cent per month of such unpaid amounts including earned interest, shall also become due and payable until payment. Such interest shall be calculated and added to any unpaid amounts monthly.

GC 16 SETTLEMENT OF DISPUTES

16.1 In the case of any dispute arising between the Owner and the Contractor as to their respective rights and obligations under the Contract, either party hereto shall be entitled to give to the other notice of such dispute. In the event that the parties have agreed to submit such disputes to arbitration pursuant to a Supplementary General Condition to the Contract, or by subsequent agreement, either party may thereupon request arbitration pursuant to such provisions. In the event that no provision or agreement is made for arbitration, then either party may seek recourse in such judicial tribunal as the circumstances may require.

16.2 Arbitration proceedings or legal proceedings shall not take place until after the performance or alleged performance of the disputed work except:

    (a) when the dispute concerns a certificate for payment,

    (b) where either party can show that the matter in dispute requires immediate consideration while evidence is available,

    (c) in the case of legal proceedings, where the action may become prescribed by reason of delay.

GC 22 APPLICATION FOR PAYMENT

22.1 Applications for payment on account as provided for in Article A-4 may be made monthly as the Work progresses.

22.2 Applications for payment shall be dated the last day of the agreed monthly payment period and the amount claimed shall be for the value, proportionate to the amount of the Contract, of work performed and products delivered to the site at that date.

22.3 The Contractor shall submit to the Engineer before the first application for payment, a schedule of values of the various parts of the Work, aggregating the total amount of the Contract Price and divided so as to facilitate evaluation of applications for payment.

22.4 This schedule shall be made out in such form, and supported by such evidence as to its correctness, as the Engineer may reasonably direct, and when approved by the Engineer shall be used as the basis for application for payment, unless it be found to be in error.

22.5 When making application for payment, the Contractor shall submit a statement based upon this schedule. Claims for products delivered to the site but not yet incorporated into the Work shall be supported by such evidence as the Engineer may reasonably require to establish the value and delivery of the products.

22.6 Applications for release of holdback monies following the Substantial Performance of the Work and the application for final payment shall be made at the time and in the manner set forth in GC 23 – Certificates and Payments.

GC 23 CERTIFICATES AND PAYMENTS

23.1 The Engineer shall, within ten (10) days of receipt of an application for payment from the Contractor submitted in accordance with GC 22 – Application for Payment, issue a certificate for payment in the amount applied for or such other amount as he shall determine to be properly due. If the Engineer amends the application, he shall promptly notify the Contractor in writing giving his reasons for the amendment.

23.2 The Owner shall within five (5) days of the issuance of a certificate for payment by the Engineer, make payment to the Contractor on account in accordance with the provisions of Article A-4 of the Agreement.

23.3 Notwithstanding any other provisions of this Contract:
(a) If on account of climatic or other conditions reasonably beyond the control of the Contractor there are items of work that cannot be performed, the payment in full for work which has been performed as certified by the Engineer shall not be withheld or delayed by the Owner on account thereof, but the Owner may withhold from the Contract Price until the remaining work is finished only such monies as the Engineer shall determine are sufficient and reasonable to cover the cost of performing such remaining work and to adequately protect the Owner from claims;
(b) Where legislation permits and where, upon application by the Contractor, the Engineer has certified that a Subcontract has been totally performed to his satisfaction prior to the Substantial Performance of this Contract, the Owner shall pay the Contractor the holdback retained for such Subcontractor on the day following the expiration of the Statutory Limitation Period stipulated in the Mechanics' Lien Act applicable to the place of building.

23.4 Notwithstanding the provisions of 23.3 (b) and notwithstanding the wording of such certificates the Contractor shall ensure that such work is protected pending the Total Performance of the Contract and be responsible for the correction of any defects in it regardless of whether or not they were apparent when such certificates were issued.

23.5 The Engineer shall, within ten (10) days of receipt of an application from the Contractor for a certificate of Substantial Performance, make an inspection and assessment of the Work to verify the validity of the application. The Engineer shall within seven (7) days of his inspection notify the Contractor of his approval or disapproval of the application. When the Engineer finds the Work to be substantially performed he shall issue such a certificate. The date of this certificate shall be the date of Substantial Performance of the Contract. Immediately following the issuance of the Certificate of Substantial Performance, the Engineer, in consultation with the Contractor shall establish a reasonable date for the Total Performance of the Contract.

23.6 Following the issuance of the Certificate of Substantial Performance and upon receipt from the Contractor of all documentation called for in the Contract Documents the Engineer shall issue a certificate for payment of holdback monies. The release of holdback monies authorized by this certificate shall become due and payable on the day following the expiration of the Statutory Limitation Period stipulated in the Mechanics' Lien Act applicable to the place of building, or where such legislation does not exist or apply in accordance with such other legislation, regulations governing privileges, industry practice or such other provisions which may be agreed to between the parties, providing that no lien or privilege claims against the Work exist and the Contractor has submitted to the Owner a sworn statement that all accounts for labour, subcontract, products, construction machinery and equipment and any other indebtedness which may have been incurred by the Contractor in the Substantial Performance of the Work and for which the Owner might in any way be held responsible have been paid in full except holdback monies properly retained.

23.7 The Engineer shall within ten (10) days of receipt of an application from the Contractor for payment upon Total Performance of the Contract, make an inspection and assessment of the work to verify the validity of the application. The Engineer shall within seven (7) days of his inspection notify the Contractor of his approval or disapproval of the application. When the Engineer finds the Work to be totally performed to his satisfaction, he shall issue a Certificate of Total Performance and certify for payment the remaining monies due to the Contractor under the Contract less any holdback monies which are required to be retained. The date of this certificate shall be the date of Total Performance of the Contract. The Owner shall, within five (5) days of issuance of such certificate, make payment to the Contractor in accordance with the provisions of Article A-4 of the Agreement.

23.8 The release of any remaining holdback monies shall become due and payable on the day following the expiration of the Statutory Limitation Period stipulated in the Mechanics' Lien Act applicable to the place of building, or where such legislation does not exist or apply in accordance with such other legislation, regulations governing privileges, industry practice or such other provisions which may be agreed to between the parties, provided that no claims against the Work exist and the Contractor has submitted to the Owner a sworn statement that all accounts for labour, subcontracts, products, construction machinery and equipment and any other indebtedness which may have been incurred by the Contractor in the Total Performance of the Work and for which the Owner might in any way be held responsible have been paid in full except holdback monies properly retained.

23.9 No certificate for payment, or any payment made thereunder, nor any partial or entire use of occupancy of the Work by the Owner shall constitute an acceptance of any work or products not in accordance with the Contract Documents.

23.10 The issuance of the Certificate of Total Performance shall constitute a waiver of all claims by the Owner against the Contractor except those previously made in writing and still unsettled, if any, and those arising from the provisions of GC 33 – Warranty.
The acceptance of the Certificate of Total Performance or of the payment due thereunder shall constitute a waiver of all claims by the Contractor against the Owner except those made in writing prior to his application for payment upon Total Performance of the Contract and still unsettled, if any.

2 THE LEGISLATION

a / The Mechanics' Lien Act, R.S.O. 1970, c 267, as amended

1. (1) In this Act,
  (*a*) 'completion of the contract' means substantial performance, not necessarily total performance, of the contract;
  (*b*) 'contractor' means a person contracting with or employed directly by the owner or his

agent for the doing of work or the placing or furnishing of materials for any of the purposes mentioned in this Act;

(*ba*) 'Crown' includes Crown agencies to which *The Crown Agency Act* applies;

(*bb*) 'estate or interest in land' includes a statutory right given or reserved to the Crown to enter any lands or premises of any person or public authority for the purpose of doing any work, construction, repair or maintenance in, upon, through, over or under any such lands or premises;

(*c*) 'materials' includes every kind of movable property;

(*d*) 'owner' includes any person and corporation, including the Crown, a municipal corporation and a railway company, having any estate or interest in the land upon which or in respect of which work is done or materials are placed or furnished, at whose request, and

    (i) upon whose credit, or

    (ii) on whose behalf, or

    (iii) with whose privity or consent, or

    (iv) for whose direct benefit,

work is done or materials are placed or furnished and all persons claiming under him or it whose rights are acquired after the work in respect of which the lien is claimed is commenced or the materials placed or furnished have been commenced to be placed or furnished;

(*da*) 'public work' means the property of the Crown and includes land in which the Crown has an estate or interest, and also includes all works and properties acquired, constructed, extended, enlarged, repaired, equipped or improved at the expense of the Crown, or for the acquisition, construction, repairing, equipping, extending, enlarging or improving of which any public money is appropriated by the Legislature, but not any work for which money is appropriated as a subsidy only;

(*e*) 'registrar' includes a master of titles;

(*f*) 'registry office' includes a land titles office;

(*g*) 'subcontractor' means a person not contracting with or employed directly by the owner or his agent for any of the purposes mentioned in this Act, but contracting with or employed by a contractor or, under him, by another subcontractor;

(*h*) 'wages' means the money earned by a workman for work done by time or as piece work, and includes all monetary supplementary benefits, whether by statute, contract or collective bargaining agreement;

(*i*) 'workman' means a person employed for wages in any kind of labour, whether employed under a contract of service or not.

(2) In this Act, the expression 'the doing of work' includes the performance of a service, and corresponding expressions have corresponding meanings.

(3) For the purposes of this Act, a contract shall be deemed to be substantially performed,

(*a*) when the work or a substantial part thereof is ready for use or is being used for the purpose intended; and

(*b*) when the work to be done under the contract is capable of completion or correction at a cost of not more than,

    (i) 3 per cent of the first $250,000 of the contract price,

    (ii) 2 per cent of the next $250,000 of the contract price, and

    (iii) 1 per cent of the balance of the contract price.

(4) For the purpose of this Act, where the work or a substantial part thereof is ready for use or is being used for the purpose intended and where the work cannot be completed expeditiously

for reasons beyond the control of the contractor, the value of the work to be completed shall be deducted from the contract price in determining substantial performance.

1a. (1) Subject to subsection 2 of section 5, this Act binds the Crown but does not apply in respect of work under a contract as defined in *The Ministry of Transportation and Communications Creditors Payment Act, 1975* and to which that Act applies.

(2) Section 7 of *The Proceedings Against the Crown Act* does not apply in respect of proceedings against the Crown under this Act.

GENERAL

2. (1) All sums received by a builder, contractor or subcontractor on account of the contract price constitute a trust fund in his hands for the benefit of the owner, builder, contractor, subcontractor, Workmen's Compensation Board, workmen, and persons who have supplied materials on account of the contract or who have rented equipment to be used on the contract site, and the builder, contractor or subcontractor, as the case may be, is the trustee of all such sums so received by him and he shall not appropriate or convert any part thereof to his own use or to any use not authorized by the trust until all workmen and all persons who have supplied materials on the contract or who have rented equipment to be used on the contract site and all subcontractors are paid for work done or materials supplied on the contract and the Workmen's Compensation Board is paid any assessment with respect thereto.

(2) Notwithstanding subsection 1, where a builder, contractor or subcontractor has paid in whole or in part for any materials supplied on account of the contract or for any rented equipment or has paid any workman who has performed any work or any subcontractor who has placed or furnished any materials in respect of the contract, the retention by such builder, contractor or subcontractor of a sum equal to the sum so paid by him shall be deemed not to be an appropriation or conversion thereof to his own use or to any use not authorized by the trust.

(3) Where a sum becomes payable under a contract to a contractor by an owner on the certificate of a person authorized under the contract to make such a certificate, an amount equal to the sum so certified that is in the owner's hands or received by him at any time thereafter shall, until paid to the contractor, constitute a trust fund in the owner's hands for the benefit of the contractor, subcontractor, Workmen's Compensation Board, workmen, and persons who have supplied materials on account of the contract or who have rented equipment to be used on the contract site, and the owner shall not appropriate or convert any part thereof to his own use or to any use not authorized by the trust until all workmen and all persons who have supplied materials on the contract or who have rented equipment to be used on the contract site and all contractors and subcontractors are paid for work done or materials supplied on the contract and the Workmen's Compensation Board is paid any assessment with respect thereto.

(4) All sums received by an owner, other than the Crown, a municipality as defined in The Department of Municipal Affairs Act or a metropolitan or regional municipality or a local board thereof, which are to be used in the financing, including the purchase price of the land and the payment of prior encumbrances, of a building, structure or work, constitute, subject to the payment of the purchase price of the land and prior encumbrances, a trust fund in the hands of the owner for the benefit of the persons mentioned in subsection 1, and, until the claims of all such persons have been paid, the owner shall not appropriate or convert any part thereof to his own use or to any use not authorized by the trust.

(5) Notwithstanding subsection 4, where an owner has himself paid in whole or in part for any work done, for any materials placed or furnished or for any rented equipment, the retention by him from any moneys received from the lender under subsection 4 of a sum equal to the sum so

paid by him shall be deemed not to be an appropriation or conversion thereof to his own use or to any use not authorized by the trust.

(6) Notwithstanding anything in this section, where money is lent to a person upon whom a trust is imposed by this section and is used by him to pay in whole or in part for any work done, for any materials placed or furnished or for any rented equipment, trust moneys may be applied to discharge the loan to the extent that the lender's money was so used by the trustee, and any sum so applied shall be deemed not to be an appropriation or conversion to the trustee's own use or to any use not authorized by the trust.

(7) Every person upon whom a trust is imposed by this section who knowingly appropriates or converts any part of any trust moneys referred to in subsection 1,3 or 4 to his own use or to any use not authorized by the trust is guilty of an offence and on summary conviction is liable to a fine of not more than $5,000 or to imprisonment for a term of not more than two years, or to both, and every director or officer of a corporation who knowingly assents to or acquiesces in any such offence by the corporation is guilty of such offence, in addition to the corporation, and on summary conviction is liable to a fine of not more $5,000 or to imprisonment for a term of not more than two years, or to both.

3. No action to assert any claim to trust moneys referred to in section 2 shall be commenced against a lender of money to a person upon whom a trust is imposed by that section except,

    (*a*) in the case of a claim by a contractor or subcontractor in cases not provided for in clauses *b*, *c* and *d*, within nine months after the completion or abandonment of the contract or subcontract;

    (*b*) in the case of a claim for materials, within nine months after the placing or furnishing of the last material;

    (*c*) in the case of a claim for services, within nine months after the completion of the service; or

    (*d*) in the case of a claim for wages, within nine months after the last work was done for which the claim is made.

4. (1) Every agreement, oral or written, express or implied, on the part of any workman that this Act does not apply to him or that the remedies provided by it are not available for his benefit is void.

(2) Subsection 1 does not apply,

    (*a*) to a manager, officer or foreman; or

    (*b*) to any person whose wages are more than $50 a day.

(3) No agreement deprives any person otherwise entitled to a lien under this Act, who is not a party to the agreement, of the benefit of the lien, but it attaches, notwithstanding such agreement.

CREATION OF LIENS

5. (1) Unless he signs an express agreement to the contrary and in that case subject to section 4, any person who does any work upon or in respect of, or places or furnishes any materials to be used in, the making, constructing, erecting, fitting, altering, improving or repairing of any land, building, structure or works or the appurtenances to any of them for any owner, contractor or subcontractor by virtue thereof has a lien for the price of the work or materials upon the estate or interest of the owner in the land, building, structure or works and appurtenances and the land occupied thereby or enjoyed therewith, or upon or in respect of which the work is done, or upon which the materials are placed or furnished to be used, limited, however, in amount to the sum justly due to the person entitled to the lien and to the sum justly owing, except as herein provided, by the owner, and the placing or furnishing of the materials to be used upon the land or such other place in the immediate vicinity of the land designated by the owner or his agent is good and sufficient delivery for the purpose of this Act, but delivery on the designated land does not make such land subject to a lien.

(2) Where the land or premises upon or in respect of which any work is done or materials are placed or furnished is,

(*a*) a public street or highway owned by a municipality; or

(*b*) a public work,

the lien given by subsection 1 does not in any event attach to such land or premises but shall instead constitute a charge on amounts directed to be retained by section 11, and the provisions of this Act shall be construed, *mutatis mutandis*, to have effect without requiring the registration or enforcement of a lien or a claim for lien against such land or premises.

(3) The lien given by subsection 1 attaches as therein set out where the materials delivered to be used are incorporated into the land, building, structure or works, notwithstanding that the materials may not have been delivered in strict accordance with subsection 1.

(4) In subsection 1, 'agent' includes the contractor or subcontractor for whom the materials are placed or furnished, unless the person placing or furnishing the materials has had actual notice from the owner to the contrary.

(5) A person who rents equipment to an owner, contractor or subcontractor for use on a contract site shall be deemed for the purposes of this Act to have performed a service for which he has a lien for the price of the rental of the equipment used on the contract site, limited, however, in amount to the sum justly owed and due to the person entitled to the lien from the owner, builder, contractor of subcontractor in respect of the rental of the equipment.

6. Where work is done or materials are placed or furnished to be used upon or in respect of the land of a married woman, or in which she has an interest or an inchoate right of dower, with the privity or consent of her husband, he shall be presumed conclusively to be acting as her agent as well as for himself for the purposes of this Act unless before doing the work or placing or furnishing the materials the person doing the work or placing or furnishing the materials has had actual notice to the contrary.

7. (1) Where the estate or interest upon which the lien attaches is leasehold, the fee simple is also subject to the lien if the person doing the work or placing or furnishing the materials gives notice in writing, by personal service, to the owner in fee simple or his agent of the work to be done or materials to be placed or furnished unless the owner in fee simple or his agent within fifteen days thereafter gives notice in writing, by personal service, to such person that he will not be responsible therefor.

(2) No forfeiture or attempted forfeiture of the lease on the part of the landlord, or cancellation or attempted cancellation of the lease except for non-payment of rent, deprives any person otherwise entitled to a lien of the benefit of the lien, but the person entitled to the lien may pay any rent accruing after he becomes so entitled, and the amount so paid may be added to his claim.

(3) Where the land and premises upon or in respect of which any work is done or materials are placed or furnished are encumbered by a mortgage or other charge that was registered in the proper registry office before any lien under this Act arose, the mortgage or other charge has priority over all liens under this Act to the extent of the actual value of the land and premises at the time the first lien arose, such value to be ascertained by the judge or officer having jurisdiction to try an action under this Act.

(4) The time at which the first lien arose shall be deemed to be the time at which the first work

was done or the first materials placed or furnished, irrespective of whether a claim for lien in respect thereof is registered or enforced and whether or not such lien is before the court.

(5) Any mortgage existing as a valid security, notwithstanding that it is a prior mortgage within the meaning of subsection 3, may also secure future advances, subject to subsection 1 of section 14.

(6) A registered agreement for the sale and purchase of land and any moneys *bona fide* secured or payable thereunder has the same priority over a lien as is provided for a mortgage and mortgage moneys in subsections 3 and 5, and for the purposes of this Act the seller shall be deemed to be a mortgagee, and any moneys *bona fide* secured and payable under such agreement shall be deemed to be mortgage moneys *bona fide* secured or advanced.

8. Where any of the property upon which a lien attaches is wholly or partly destroyed by fire, any money received by reason of any insurance thereon by an owner or prior mortgagee or chargee shall take the place of the property so destroyed and is, after satisfying any prior mortgage or charge in the manner and to the extent set out in subsection 3 of section 7, subject to the claims of all persons for liens to the same extent as if the money had been realized by a sale of the property in an action to enforce the lien.

9. Save as herein otherwise provided, the lien does not attach so as to make the owner liable for a greater sum than the sum payable by the owner to the contractor.

10. Save as herein otherwise provided, where the lien is claimed by any person other than the contractor, the amount that may be claimed in respect thereof is limited to the amount owing to the contractor or subcontractor or other person for whom the work has been done or the materials were placed or furnished.

11. (1) In all cases, the person primarily liable upon a contract under or by virtue of which a lien may arise shall, as the work is done or the materials are furnished under the contract, retain for a period of thirty-seven days after the completion or abandonment of the work done or to be done under the contract 15 per cent of the value of the work and materials actually done, placed or furnished, as mentioned in section 5, irrespective of whether the contract or subcontract provides for partial payments or payment on completion of the work, and the value shall be calculated upon evidence given in that regard on the basis of the contract price or, if there is no specific contract price, on the basis of the actual value of the work or materials.

(2) Where a contract is under the supervision of an architect, engineer or other person upon whose certificate payments are to be made and thirty-seven days have elapsed after a certificate issued by that architect, engineer or other person to the effect that the subcontract has been completed to his satisfaction has been given to the person primarily liable upon that contract and to the person who became a subcontractor by a subcontract made directly under that contract, the amount to be retained by the person primarily liable upon that contract shall be reduced by 15 per cent of the subcontract price or, if there is no specific subcontract price, by 15 per cent of the actual value of the work done or materials placed or furnished under that subcontract, but this subsection does not operate if and so long as any lien derived under that subcontract is preserved by anything done under this Act.

(3) Where a certificate issued by an architect, engineer or other person to the effect that a subcontract by which a subcontractor became a subcontractor has been completed to the satisfaction of that architect, engineer or other person has been given to that subcontractor, then, for the purposes of subsections 1, 2 and 3 of section 21, section 23 and section 23*a* that subcontract and any materials placed or furnished or to be placed or furnished thereunder and any work done or to be done thereunder shall, so far as concerns any lien thereunder of that subcontractor, be deemed to have been completed or placed or furnished not later than the time at which the certificate was so given.

(4) Where an architect, engineer or other person neglects or refuses to issue and deliver a certificate upon which payments are to be made under a contract or subcontract, the judge or officer having jurisdiction to try an action under this Act, upon application and upon being satisfied that the certificate should have been issued and delivered may, upon such terms and conditions as to costs and otherwise as he deems just, make an order that the work or materials to which the certificate would have related has been done or placed or furnished, as the case may be, and any such order has the same force and effect as if the certificate had been issued and delivered by the architect, engineer or other person.

(5) The lien is a charge upon the amount directed to be retained by this section in favour of lien claimants whose liens are derived under persons to whom the moneys so required to be retained are respectively payable.

(5a) Where the lien does not attach to the land by virtue of subsection 2 of section 5, and a person claiming a lien gives to the owner, or a contractor or subcontractor notice in writing of the lien, the owner, contractor or subcontractor so notified shall retain out of amounts payable to the contractor or subcontractor under whom the lien is derived an amount equal to the amount claimed in the notice.

(6) All payments up to 85 per cent as fixed by subsection 1 and payments permitted as a result of the operation of subsections 2 and 3 made in good faith by an owner to a contractor, or by a contractor to a subcontractor, or by one subcontractor to another subcontractor, before notice in writing of the lien given by the person claiming the lien to the owner, contractor or subcontractor, as the case may be, operate as a discharge *pro tanto* of the lien.

(7) Payment of the percentage required to be retained under this section may be validly made so as to discharge all claims in respect of such percentage after the expiration of the period of thirty-seven days mentioned in subsection 1 unless in the meantime the appropriate steps have been taken to preserve the lien as provided by sections 22 and 23, or 22a and 23a, as the case may be, in which case the owner may pay the percentage into court in the proceedings, and such payment constitutes valid payment in discharge of the owner to the amount thereof.

(8) Every contract shall be deemed to be amended in so far as is necessary to be in conformity with this section.

(9) Where the contractor or subcontractor makes default in completing his contract, the percentage required to be retained shall not, as against any lien claimant who by virtue of subsection 5 has a charge thereupon, be applied by the owner, contractor or subcontractor to the completion of the contract or for any other purpose nor to the payment of damages for the non-completion of the contract by the contractor or subcontractor nor in payment or satisfaction of any claim against the contractor or subcontractor.

12. If an owner, contractor or subcontractor makes a payment to any person entitled to a lien under section 5 for or on account of any debt, justly due to him for work done or for materials placed or furnished to be used as therein mentioned, for which he is not primarily liable, and within three days afterwards gives written notice of the payment to the person primarily liable, or his agent, the payment shall be deemed to be a payment on his contract generally to the contractor or subcontractor primarily liable but not so as to affect the percentage to be retained by the owner as provided by section 11.

13. Every subcontractor is entitled to enforce his lien notwithstanding the non-completion or abandonment of the contract by any contractor or subcontractor under whom he claims.

14. (1) The lien has priority over all judgments, executions, assignments, attachments, garnishments and receiving orders recovered, issued or made after the lien arises, and over all payments or advances made on account of any conveyance or mortgage after notice in writing of the lien has been given to the person making such payments or after registration of a claim for the

lien as hereinafter provided, and, in the absence of such notice in writing or the registration of a claim for lien, all such payments or advances have priority over any such lien.

(2) Except where it is otherwise provided by this Act, no person entitled to a lien on any property or money is entitled to any priority or preference over another person of the same class entitled to a lien on such property or money, and each class of lienholders ranks *pari passu* for their several amounts, and the proceeds of any sale shall be distributed among them *pro rata* according to their several classes and rights.

(3) Any conveyance, mortgage or charge of or on land given to any person entitled to a lien thereon under this Act in payment of or as security for any such claim, whether given before or after such lien claim has arisen, shall, as against other parties entitled to liens under this Act, on any such land be deemed to be fraudulent and void.

PRIORITY OF WAGES

15. (1) Every workman whose lien is for wages has priority to the extent of thirty days wages over all other liens derived through the same contractor or subcontractor to the extent of and on the 15 per cent directed to be retained by section 11 to which the contractor or subcontractor through whom the lien is derived is entitled, and all such workmen rank thereon *pari passu*.

(2) Every workman is entitled to enforce a lien in respect of any contract or subcontract that has not been completed and, notwithstanding anything to the contrary in this Act, may serve a notice of motion on the proper persons, returnable in four days after service thereof before the judge or officer having jurisdiction to try an action under this Act, that the applicant will on the return of the motion ask for judgment on his claim for lien, registered particulars of which shall accompany the notice of motion duly verified by affidavit.

(3) If the contract has not been completed when the lien is claimed by a workman, the percentage shall be calculated on the value of the work done or materials placed or furnished by the contractor or subcontractor by whom the workman is employed, having regard to the contract price, if any.

(4) Every device by an owner, contractor or subcontractor to defeat the priority given to a workman for his wages and every payment made for the purpose of defeating or impairing a lien are void.

REGISTRATION

16. (1) A claim for a lien may be registered in the proper registry office and shall set out,

(*a*) the name and an address for service of the person claiming the lien and of the owner or of the person whom the person claiming the lien, or his agent, believes to be the owner of the land, and of the person for whom the work was or is to be done, or the materials were or are to be placed or furnished, and the time within which the same was or was to be done or placed or furnished;

(*b*) a short description of the work done or to be done, or the materials placed or furnished or to be placed or furnished;

(*c*) the sum claimed as due or to become due;

(*d*) a description of the land as required by *The Land Titles Act* or *The Registry Act* and the regulations thereunder, as the case may be; and

(*e*) the date of expiry of the period of credit if credit has been given.

(12) The claim shall be verified in duplicate by the affidavit of the person claiming the lien, or of his agent or assignee who has a personal knowledge of the matters required to be verified, and the affidavit of the agent or assignee shall state that he has such knowledge.

(3) When it is desired to register a claim for lien against a railway, it is sufficient description of the land of the railway company to describe it as the land of the railway company, and every such claim shall be registered in the general register in the office for the registry division within which the lien is claimed to have arisen.

17. (1) A claim for lien may include claims against any number of properties, and any number of persons claiming liens upon the same property may unite therein, but, where more than one lien is included in one claim, each claim for lien shall be verified by affidavit as provided in section 16.

(2) The judge or officer trying the action has jurisdiction equitably to apportion against the respective properties the amounts included in any claim or claims under subsection 1.

18. (1) Substantial compliance with sections 16, 17, 21*a* and 29 is sufficient and no claim for lien is invalidated by reason of failure to comply with any of the requirements of such sections unless, in the opinion of the judge or officer trying the action, the owner, contractor or sub-contractor, mortgagee or other person is prejudiced thereby, and then only to the extent to which he is thereby prejudiced.

(2) Nothing in this section dispenses with the requirement of registration of the claim for lien.

19. A duplicate of the claim for lien, bearing the registrar's certificate of registration, shall be filed on or before the trial of the action, where the action is to be tried in the Judicial District of York, in the office of the master of the Supreme Court, or, where the action is to be tried elsewhere, in the office of the clerk of the county or district court of the county or district in which the action is to be tried.

20. Where a claim is so registered, the person entitled to a lien shall be deemed to be a purchaser *pro tanto* and a purchaser within the provisions of *The Registry Act* and *The Land Titles Act*, but, except as herein otherwise provided, those Acts do not apply to any lien arising under this Act.

21. (1) A claim for lien by a contractor or subcontractor in cases not otherwise provided for may be registered before or during the performance of the contract or of the subcontract or within thirty-seven days after the completion or abandonment of the contract or of the sub-contract, as the case may be.

(2) A claim for lien for materials may be registered before or during the placing or furnishing thereof, or within thirty-seven days after the placing or furnishing of the last material so placed or furnished.

(3) A claim for lien for services may be registered at any time during the performance of the service or within thirty-seven days after the completion of the service.

(4) A claim for lien for wages may be registered at any time during the doing of the work for which the wages are claimed or within thirty-seven days after the last work was done for which the lien is claimed.

21*a*. (1) Without limiting the generality of subsection 2 of section 5, where the lien does not attach to the land by virtue of subsection 2 of section 5, sections 16, 17, 19 and 20 do not apply.

(2) Where the lien does not attach to the land by virtue of subsection 2 of section 5, any person who is claiming a lien shall give notice thereof in writing to the owner in the manner hereafter provided.

(3) Where the claim is in respect of a public street or highway owned by a municipality, the notice required to be given to the owner by subsection 2 shall be given to the clerk of the municipality.

(4) Where the claim is in respect of a public work, the notice required by subsection 2 to be given to the owner shall be given to the Ministry or Crown agency for whom the work is done or the materials are placed or furnished, or to such office as is prescribed by the regulations.

(5) The notice required by subsection 2 shall be given within the time allowed for registration under section 21.

(6) The notice required by subsection 2 may be served personally, or it may be sent by registered mail, in which case the date of mailing shall be deemed to be the date on which the notice was given.

(7) The notice required shall set out,

(*a*) the name and address of the person making the claim and of the person for whom the work was done or the materials were placed or furnished, and the time within which the same was done or placed or furnished;

(*b*) a short description of the work done or the materials placed or furnished;

(*c*) the sum claimed as due;

(*d*) the address or a description of the location of the land;

(*e*) the date of expiry of the period of credit if credit has been given.

(8) The matters set out in the notice shall be verified by the affidavit of the person claiming the lien, or his agent or assignee who has a personal knowledge of the matters, and the affidavit of the agent or assignee shall state that he has such knowledge.

EXPIRY AND DISCHARGE

22. (1) Every lien for which a claim is not registered ceases to exist on the expiration of the time limited in section 21 for the registration thereof.

(2) Upon an action under this Act being commenced, a certificate thereof shall be registered in the registry office in which the claim for lien is registered.

(3) Where a certificate of action has been registered for two years or more in the registry office and no appointment has been taken out for the trial of the action, the judge or, in the Judicial District of York, the master, may, upon the application *ex parte* of any interested person, make an order vacating the certificate of action and discharging all liens depending thereon.

(4) This section does not apply to liens which, by virtue of subsection 2 of section 5, do not attach to the land.

22a. Where the lien does not attach to the land by virtue of subsection 2 of section 5, every lien for which notice has not been given as required by section 21*a* ceases to exist at the expiration of the time limited in section 21*a* for giving notice of claim thereof.

23. Every lien for which a claim is registered ceases to exist on the expiration of ninety days after the work has been completed or the materials have been placed or furnished, or after the expiry of the period of credit, where such period is mentioned in the registered claim for lien, unless in the meantime an action is commenced to realize the claim or in which a subsisting claim may be realized, and a certificate is registered as provided by section 22.

23a. Every lien which by virtue of subsection 2 of section 5 does not attach to the land ceases to exist on the expiration of ninety days after,

(*a*) the work has been completed or abandoned;

(*b*) the materials have been placed or furnished; or

(*c*) the expiry of the period of credit, where such period is mentioned in the notice referred to in section 21*a*,

unless in the meantime an action under this Act is commenced to realize the claim or in which a subsisting claim may be realized.

24. The rights of a lien claimant may be assigned by an instrument in writing and, if not assigned, upon his death pass to his personal representative.

25. (1) A claim for lien may be discharged by the registration of a receipt acknowledging payment, (*a*) where made by a lien claimant that is not a corporation, signed by the lien claimant or his agent duly authorized in writing and verified by affidavit; or

(*b*) where made by a lien claimant that is a corporation sealed with its corporate seal.

(2) Upon application, the judge or, in the Judicial District of York, the master, may, at any time,

(*a*) allow security for or payment into court of the amount of the claim of the lien claimant and the amount of the claims of any other subsisting lien claimants together with such costs as he may fix, and thereupon order that the registration of the claim for lien or liens and the registration of the certificate of action, if any, be vacated;

(*b*) upon any other proper ground, order that the registration of the claim for lien or liens and the registration of the certificate of action, if any, be vacated; or

(*c*) upon proper grounds, dismiss the action.

(3) Notwithstanding sections 22, and 23, where an order to vacate the registration of a lien is made under clause *a* or *b* of subsection 2, the lien does not cease to exist for the reason that no certificate of action is registered.

(4) Any money so paid into court, or any bond or other security for securing the like amount and satisfactory to the judge or officer, takes the place of the property discharged and is subject to the claims of every person who has at the time of the application a subsisting claim for lien or given notice of the claim under subsection 6 of section 11 or section 14 to the same extent as if the money, bond or other security was realized by a sale of the property in an action to enforce the lien, but such amount as the judge or officer finds to be owing to the person whose lien has been so vacated is a first charge upon the money, bond or other security.

(5) Where the certificate required by section 22 or 23 has not been registered within the prescribed time and an application is made to vacate the registration of a claim for lien after the time for registration of the certificate, the order vacating the lien may be made *ex parte* upon production of a certificate of search under *The Land Titles Act* or of a registrar's abstract under *The Registry Act*, as the case may be, together with a certified copy of the registered claim for lien.

(6) Where money has been paid into court or a bond deposited in court pursuant to an order under subsection 2, the judge or, in the Judicial District of York, the master, may, upon such notice to the parties as he may require, order the money to be paid out to the persons entitled thereto or the delivery up of the bond for cancellation, as the case may be.

(7) An order discharging a claim for lien or vacating a certificate of action shall be registered by registering the order or a certificate thereof, under the seal of the court, that includes a description of the land as required by *The Land Titles Act* or *The Registry Act* and the regulations thereunder, as the case may be, and a reference to the registration number of every registered claim for lien and certificate of action affected thereby.

EFFECT OF TAKING SECURITY OR EXTENDING TIME

26. 1 The taking of any security for, or the acceptance of any promissory note or bill of exchange for, or the taking of any acknowledgment of the claim, or the giving of time for the payment thereof, or the taking of any proceedings for the recovery, or the recovery of a personal judgment for the claim, does not merge, waive, pay, satisfy, prejudice or destroy the lien unless the lien claimant agrees in writing that it has that effect.

(2) Where any such promissory note or bill of exchange has been negotiated, the lien claimant does not thereby lose his right to claim for lien if, at the time of bringing his action to enforce it or where an action is brought by another lien claimant, he is, at the time of proving his claim in the action, the holder of such promissory note or bill of exchange.

(3) Nothing in subsection 2 extends the time limited by this Act for bringing an action to enforce a claim for lien.

(4) A person who has extended the time for payment of a claim for which he has a claim for lien in order to obtain the benefit of this section shall commence an action to enforce the claim within the time prescribed by this Act and shall register a certificate as required by sections 22 and 23, but no further proceedings shall be taken in the action until the expiration of such extension of time.

27. Where the period of credit in respect of a claim has not expired or there has been an extension of time for payment of the claim, the lien claimant may nevertheless, if an action is commenced by any other person to enforce a claim for lien against the same property, prove and obtain payment of his claim in the action as if the period of credit or the extended time had expired.

LIEN CLAIMANT'S RIGHTS TO INFORMATION

28. (1) Any lien claimant may in writing at any time demand of the owner or his agent the production, for inspection, of the contract or agreement with the contractor for or in respect of which the work was or is to be done or the materials were or are to be placed or furnished, if the contract or agreement is in writing or, if not in writing, the terms of the contract or agreement and the state of the accounts between the owner and the contractor, and, if the owner or his agent does not, at the time of the demand or within a reasonable time thereafter, produce the contract or agreement if in writing or, if not in writing, does not inform the person making the demand of the terms of the contract or agreement and the amount due and unpaid upon the contract or agreement or if he knowingly falsely states the terms of the contract or agreement or the amount due or unpaid thereon and if the person claiming the lien sustains loss by reason of the refusal or neglect or false statement, the owner is liable to him for the amount of the loss in an action therefor or in any action for the enforcement of a lien under this Act, and subsection 4 of section 38 applies.

(2) Any lien claimant may in writing at any time demand of a mortgagee or unpaid vendor or his agent the terms of any mortgage on the land or of any agreement for the purchase of the land in respect of which the work was or is to be done or the materials were or are to be placed or furnished and a statement showing the amount advanced on the mortgage or the amount owing on the agreement, as the case may be, and, if the mortgagee or vendor or his agent fails to inform the lien claimant at the time of the demand or within a reasonable time thereafter of the terms of the mortgage or agreement and the amount advanced or owing thereon or if he knowingly falsely states the terms of the mortgage or agreement and the amount owing thereon and the lien claimant sustains loss by the refusal or neglect or misstatement, the mortgagee or vendor is liable to him for the amount of the loss in an action therefor or in any action for the enforcement of a lien under this Act, and subsection 4 of section 38 applies.

(3) The judge or, in the Judicial District of York, the master, may, on a summary application at any time before or after an action is commenced for the enforcement of the claim for lien, make an order requiring the owner or his agent or the mortgagee or his agent or the unpaid vendor or his agent or the contractor or his agent or the subcontractor or his agent, as the case may be, to produce and permit any lien claimant to inspect any such contract or agreement or mortgage or agreement for sale or the accounts or any other relevant document upon such terms as to costs as the judge or master considers just.

ACTIONS

29. (1) A claim for lien is enforceable in an action in the Supreme Court.

(2) An action under this section shall be commenced by filing a statement of claim in the office of the local registrar of the Supreme Court in the county or district in which the land or part thereof is situate.

(3) The statement of claim shall be served within thirty days after it is filed, but the judge having jurisdiction to try the action or, in the Judicial District of York, the master, may extend the time for service.

(4) The time for delivering the statement of defence in the action shall be the same as for entering an appearance in an action in the Supreme Court.

(5) It is not necessary to make any lien claimants parties defendant to the action, but all lien claimants served with the notice of trial shall for all purposes be deemed to be parties to the action.

(6) After the commencement of the action, any lien claimant or other person interested may apply to the judge having jurisdiction to try the action or, in the Judicial District of York, a judge of the Supreme Court, to speed the trial of the action.

30. Any number of lien claimants claiming liens on the same land may join in an action, and an action brought by a lien claimant shall be deemed to be brought on behalf of himself and all other lien claimants.

31. (1) Except in the Judicial District of York, the action shall be tried by the local judge of the Supreme Court in the county or district in which the action was commenced, but, upon the application of any party or other interested person made according to the practice of the Supreme Court and upon notice, the court may direct that the action be tried by a judge of the Supreme Court at the regular sittings of the court for the trial of actions in the county or district in which the action was commenced.

(2) In the Judicial District of York, the action shall be tried by a judge of the Supreme Court, but,

(*a*) on motion after defence or defence to counterclaim, if any, has been delivered or the time for such delivery has expired, a judge of the Supreme Court may refer the whole action to the master for trial pursuant to section 72 of *The Judicature Act*; or

(*b*) at the trial, a judge of the Supreme Court may direct a reference to the master pursuant to section 71 or 72 of *The Judicature Act*.

(3) Where on motion the whole action is referred to the master for trial, any person brought into the proceedings subsequent thereto and served with a notice of trial may apply to a judge of the Supreme Court to set aside the judgment directing the reference within seven days after service of notice of trial and, if such person fails to make such application, he is bound by such judgment as if he were originally a party thereto.

(4) Where the action is referred to the master for trial, he may grant leave to amend any pleading.

32. The local judges of the Supreme Court and the master to whom a reference for trial has been directed, in addition to their ordinary powers, have all the jurisdiction, powers and authority of the Supreme Court to try and completely dispose of the action and questions arising therein and all questions of set-off and counterclaim arising under the building contract or out of the work done or materials furnished to the property in question.

33. Where an owner enters into an entire contract for the supply of materials to be used in several buildings, the person supplying the materials may ask to have his lien follow the form of the contract and that it be for an entire sum upon all the buildings, but, in case the owner has sold one or more of the buildings, the judge or officer trying the action has jurisdiction equitably to apportion against the respective buildings the amount included in the claim for lien under the entire contract.

34. (1) At any time after the delivery of the statement of claim, the judge having jurisdiction to try the action or, in the Judicial District of York, a judge of the Supreme Court, may, on the application of any lien claimant, mortgagee or other person interested, appoint a receiver of the rents and profits of the property against which the claim for lien is registered upon such terms and upon the giving of such security or without security as the judge considers just.

(2) Any lien claimant, mortgagee or other person interested may make an application to the judge having jurisdiction to try the action or, in the Judicial District of York, a judge of the Supreme Court, at any time before or after judgment, who may hear *viva voce* or affidavit evidence or both and appoint, upon such terms and upon the giving of such security or without security as the judge considers just, a trustee or trustees with power to manage, mortgage, lease and sell, or manage, mortgage, lease or sell, the property against which the claim for lien is registered, and the exericise of such powers shall be under the supervision and direction of the court, and with power, when so directed by the court, to complete or partially complete the property, and, in the event that mortgage moneys are advanced to the trustee or trustees as the result of any of the powers conferred upon him or them under this subsection, such moneys take priority over every claim of lien existing as of the date of the appointment.

(3) Any property directed to be sold under subsection 2 may be offered for sale subject to any mortgage or other charge or encumbrance if the judge so directs.

(4) The proceeds of any sale made by a trustee or trustees under subsection 2 shall be paid into court and are subject to the claims of all lien claimants, mortgages or other persons interested in the property so sold as their respective rights are determined, and, in so far as applicable, section 39 applies.

(5) The judge shall make all necessary orders for the completion of any mortgage, lease or sale authorized to be made under subsection 2.

(6) Any vesting order made of property sold by a trustee or trustees appointed under subsection 2 vests the title of the property free from all claims for liens, encumbrances and interests of any kind including dower, except in cases where sale is made subject to any mortgage, charge, encumbrance or interest as hereinbefore provided, but nothing in this section or elsewhere in this Act shall be deemed to extinguish the right to dower, if any, of any married woman or the right to have the value of her dower ascertained and deducted from the proceeds of the sale so paid into court.

35. At any time after delivery of the statement of claim and before judgment, or after judgment and pending the hearing and determination of any appeal, any lien claimant, mortgagee or other interested person may make an application to the judge having jurisdiction to try the action or who tried the action, as the case may be, or, in the Judicial District of York, a judge of the Supreme Court, who may hear *viva voce* or affidavit evidence or both and make an order for the preservation of any property pending the determination of the action and any appeal.

36. Where more actions than one are brought to realize liens in respect of the same land, the judge or officer having jurisdiction to try the action may, on the application of any party to any one of the actions or on the application of any other person interested, consolidate all such actions into one action and award the conduct of the consolidated action to any plaintiff as the judge or officer considers just.

37. Any lien claimant entitled to the benefit of an action may at any time apply to the judge or officer having jurisdiction to try the action for the carriage of the proceedings, and the judge or officer may make an order awarding such lien claimant the carriage of the proceedings.

38. (1) After the delivery of the statement of defence where the plaintiff's claim is disputed, or after the time for delivery of defence in all other cases, either party may apply *ex parte* to a judge or officer having jurisdiction to try the action to fix a day for the trial thereof, and the judge or officer shall appoint the time and place of trial, and the order, signed by the judge or officer, shall form part of the record of the proceedings.

(2) The party obtaining an appointment for the trial shall, at least ten clear days before the day appointed, serve notice of trial upon the solicitors for the defendants who appear by solicitors and upon the defendants who appear in person, and upon all the lienholders who have registered their claims as required by this Act or of whose claims he has notice, and upon all other persons having any charge, encumbrance or claim on the land subsequent in priority to the lien, who are not parties, and such service shall be personal unless otherwise directed by the judge or officer who may direct in what manner the notice of trial is to be served.

(3) Where any person interested in the land has been served with a statement of claim and makes default in delivering a statement of defence, he shall nevertheless be served with notice of trial and is entitled to defend on such terms as to costs and otherwise as the judge or officer having jurisdiction to try the action considers just.

(4) The judge, or where a reference for trial is directed, the master,

(*a*) shall try the action, including any set-off and counter-claim, and all questions that arise therein or that are necessary to be tried in order to completely dispose of the action and to adjust the rights and liabilities of the persons appearing before him or upon whom notice of trial has been served;

(*b*) shall take all accounts, make all inquiries, give all directions and do all other things necessary to finally dispose of the action and of all matters, questions and accounts arising therein or at the trial, and to adjust the rights and liabilities of and give all necessary relief to all parties to the action and all persons who have been served with the notice of trial; and

(*c*) shall embody the results of the trial,

(i) in the case of a judge, in a judgment, and

(ii) in the case of a master, in a report,

which judgment or report may direct payment forthwith by the person or persons primarily liable to pay the amount of the claims and costs as ascertained by the judgment or report, and execution may be issued therefor forthwith in the case of a judgment and after confirmation thereof, in the case of a report.

(5) The form of the judgment or report may be varied by the judge or officer in order to meet the circumstances of the case so as to afford to any party to the proceedings any right or remedy in the judgment or report to which he may be entitled.

(6) The judge or officer may order that the estate or interest charged with the lien be sold, and may direct the sale to take place at any time after judgment or confirmation of the report, allowing, however, a reasonable time for advertising the sale.

(7) A lien claimant who did not prove his claim at the trial, on application to the judge or officer before whom the action or reference was tried, may be let in to prove his claim, on such terms as to costs and otherwise as are deemed just, at any time before the amount realized in the action for the satisfaction of liens has been distributed, and, where his claim is allowed, the judgment or report shall be amended so as to include his claim.

(8) Any lien claimant for an amount not exceeding $200 may be represented by an agent who is not a barrister and solicitor.

(9) An action or reference under this Act may be tried by any judge or officer having jurisdiction to try the action or reference notwithstanding that the time and place for the trial or reference thereof were appointed and fixed by another judge or officer.

(10) Any party to an action under this Act or any other interested person may at any time and

from time to time apply to the judge having jurisdiction to try the action or, in the Judicial District of York, the master, for directions as to pleadings, discovery, production or any other matter relating to the action or reference, including the cross-examination of a lien claimant or his agent or assignee on his affidavit verifying the claim.

39. (1) Where a sale is had, the moneys arising therefrom shall be paid into court to the credit of the action, and the judge or officer before whom the action was tried shall direct to whom the moneys in court shall be paid and may add to the claim of the person conducting the action his fees and actual disbursements incurred in connection with the sale, and, where sufficient to satisfy the judgment and costs is not realized from the sale, he shall certify the amount of the deficiency and the names of the persons who are entitled to recover the same, showing the amount that each is entitled to recover and the persons adjudged to pay the same, giving credit for payments made, if any, under subsection 4 of section 38, and the persons so entitled may enforce payment of the amounts so found to be due by execution or otherwise.

(2) The judge or officer before whom the action was tried may make all necessary orders for the completion of the sale and for vesting the property in the purchaser.

40. Where a lien claimant fails to establish a lien, he may nevertheless recover a personal judgment against any party to the action for such sum as may appear to be due to him and which he might recover in an action against such party.

41. Where property subject to a lien is sold in an action to enforce a lien, every lienholder is entitled to share in the proceeds of the sale in respect of the amount then owing to him, although the same or part thereof was not payable at the time of the commencement of the action or is not then presently payable.

STATED CASE

42. (1) If in the course of proceedings to enforce a lien a question of law arises, the judge or officer trying the case may, at the request of any party, state the question in the form of a stated case for the opinion of the Court of Appeal, and the stated case shall thereupon be set down to be heard before the Court of Appeal and notice of hearing shall be served by the party setting down upon all parties concerned.

(2) The stated case shall set forth the facts material for the determination of the question raised, and all papers necessary for the hearing of the stated case by the Court of Appeal shall be transmitted to the registrar of the Supreme Court.

APPEAL

43. (1) Except where the amount of a judgment or report made on a reference for trial in respect of a claim or counterclaim is $200 or less, an appeal lies from any judgment or report under this Act to the Court of Appeal.

(2) Where a question is referred to the master for inquiry and report under subsection 2 of section 31, an appeal lies in the manner prescribed by the rules of court.

(3) Where an action is referred to the master for trial under subsection 2 of section 31, the report shall be filed and shall be deemed to be confirmed at the expiration of fifteen days from the date of service of notice of filing the same, unless notice of appeal is served within that time.

(4) An appeal from a judgment or report made on a reference for trial lies in like manner and to the same extent as from the decision of a judge trying an action in the Supreme Court without a jury.

(5) The costs of an appeal shall not be governed by subsections 2 and 3 of section 45 but, subject to any order of the Court of Appeal, shall be upon the scale of costs allowed in county

court appeals where the amount involved is within the proper competence of the county court, and, where it exceeds that amount, upon the Supreme Court scale.

FEES AND COSTS

44. The fee payable by every plaintiff, every plaintiff by counterclaim and every lien claimant, including every person recovering a personal judgment, in any action to realize a lien under this Act is,

(a) $5 on a claim or counterclaim not exceeding $500;

(b) $10 on a claim or counterclaim exceeding $500 but not exceeding $1,000;

(c) $10 on a claim or counterclaim exceeding $1,000 plus $1 for every $1,000 or fraction thereof in excess of $1,000,

but no fee is payable on a claim for wages only, and in no case shall the fee on a claim exceed $75 or on a counterclaim exceed $25.

45. (1) Subject to subsections 2, 3, 4 and 5, any order as to costs in an action under this Act is in the discretion of the judge or officer who tries the action.

(2) The costs of the action, exclusive of actual disbursements, awarded to the plaintiffs and successful lienholders, shall not exceed in the aggregate 25 per cent of the total amount found to have been actually due on the liens at the time of the registration thereof, and shall be apportioned and borne in such proportion as the judge or officer who tries the action may direct, but in making the apportionment he shall have regard to the actual services rendered by or on behalf of the parties respectively, provided that, where a counterclaim is set up by a defendant, the amount and apportionment of the costs in respect thereof are in the discretion of the judge or officer who tries the action.

(3) Where costs are awarded against the plaintiff or other persons claiming liens, they shall not exceed, except in the case of a counterclaim, 25 per cent of the claim of the plaintiff and the other claimants, besides actual disbursements, and shall be apportioned and borne as the judge or officer who tries the action may direct.

(4) Where the least expensive course is not taken by a plaintiff, the costs allowed to him shall in no case exceed what would have been incurred if the least expensive course had been taken.

(5) Where a lien is discharged or vacated under section 25 or where judgment is given in favour of or against a claim for a lien, in addition to the costs of the action, the judge or officer who tries the action may allow a reasonable amount for the costs of drawing and registering the claim for lien or of vacating the registration thereof, but this does not apply where the claimant fails to establish a valid lien.

RULES OF PRACTICE

46. (1) The object of this Act being to enforce liens at the least expense, the procedure shall be as far as possible of a summary character, having regard to the amount and nature of the liens in question.

(2) Except where otherwise provided by this Act, no interlocutory proceedings shall be permitted without the consent of the judge having jurisdiction to try the action or, in the Judicial District of York, the master, and then only upon proper proof that such proceedings are necessary.

(3) The judge or officer having jurisdiction to try the action may obtain the assistance of any merchant, accountant, actuary, building contractor, architect, engineer or person in such way as he deems fit, the better to enable him to determine any matter of fact in question, and may fix the remuneration of any such person and direct payment thereof by any of the parties.

(4) Unless otherwise provided in this Act, the Rules of Practice and Procedure of the Supreme Court apply to proceedings under this Act.

SERVICE OF DOCUMENTS

47. Except where otherwise directed by the judge having jurisdiction to try the action or, in the Judicial District of York, the master, all documents relating to an action under this Act, other than statements of claim and notices of trial, are sufficiently served upon the intended recipient if sent by registered mail addressed to the intended recipient at his address for service.

LIENS ON CHATTELS

48. (1) Every person who has bestowed money, skill or materials upon any chattel or thing in the alteration of improvement of its properties or for the purpose of imparting an additional value to it, so as thereby to be entitled to a lien upon the chattel or thing for the amount or value of the money or skill and material bestowed, has, while the lien exists but not afterwards, in case the amount to which he is entitled remains unpaid for three months after it ought to have been paid, the right, in addition to any other remedy to which he may be entitled, to sell by auction the chattel or thing on giving one week's notice by advertisement in a newspaper having general circulation in the municipality in which the work was done, setting forth the name of the person indebted, the amount of the debt, a description of the chattel or thing to be sold, the time and place of sale, and the name of the auctioneer, and leaving a like notice in writing at the last known place of residence, if any, of the owner, if he is a resident of the municipality.

(2) Such person shall apply the proceeds of the sale in payment of the amount due to him and the costs of advertising and sale and shall upon application pay over any surplus to the person entitled thereto.

49. The Lieutenant Governor in Council may make regulations.

(*a*) prescribing forms and providing for their use;

(*b*) providing for and requiring the posting of notices on building sites;

(*c*) prescribing the appropriate offices of the Crown to which notice of a claim for lien must be sent.

b / Mechanics' Lien Legislation in Other Provinces
Alberta: The Builders' Liens Act, R.S.A. 1970, c 35, as amended.
British Columbia: Mechanics' Lien Act, R.S.B.C. 1960, c 238, as amended.
Manitoba: The Builders and Workers Act, C.C.S.M., c B90; The Mechanics' Liens Act, C.C.S.M., c M80
New Brunswick: Mechanics' Lien Act, R.S.N.B. 1973, c M-6.
Newfoundland: The Mechanics' Lien Act, R.S. Nfld. 1970, c 229, as amended.
Nova Scotia: Mechanics' Lien Act, R.S.N.S. 1967, c 178.
Prince Edward Island: Mechanics' Lien Act, R.S.P.E.I. 1974, c M-7.
Quebec: Civil Code art. 2013, as amended.
Saskatchewan: The Mechanics' Lien Act, 1973, S.S. 1973, c 62, as amended.

c / Note: Completion of the Contract
The determination of the time at which the contract is 'complete' is often of critical importance to a person seeking to assert rights under mechanics' lien legislation.
1 In Ontario, a claim for lien may only be registered within thirty-seven (37) days of the 'completion or abandonment of the contract' (s 21(1)). Failure to register in time renders the lien unenforceable (s 22(1)).

2 Even if the lien is registered, it ceases to exist 90 days after the 'work has been completed' unless an action is commenced and a certificate of action duly registered (s 23(1)) within that time.

3 A contractor or subcontractor may initiate an action to assert a claim to trust moneys against a lender of money to a person upon whom a trust is imposed only within 9 months of the completion of the contract (s 3(a)).

4 Fifteen percent of the value of work done or of materials supplied must be held back for thirty-seven (37) days after 'completion or abandonment of the work done under the contract' (s 11(1)).

In Ontario, prior to the recent amendments (s.o. 1968–9, c 65), the Act contained no definition of 'completion of the contract'. As a result, courts were left to work out their own definition of 'completion'. Seeking to defeat the lien claims of contractors who would return several months after the parties thought the work was completed to make minor repairs or adjustments, thus extending the time periods contemplated by the Act for assertion of the various statutory rights, owners sought to rely on the common law doctrine of 'substantial performance'.

This doctrine is really a rule of construction employed to obviate the harshness of the entire contract rule. (Recall the discussion of entire contracts supra at pp 324–5.) The doctrine was forcefully enunciated by Pickford LJ in *Dakin & Co. Ltd.* v *Lee*, [1916] 1 K.B. 566 (C.A.):

Certainly I have not the slightest wish to differ from the view that if a man agrees to do a certain amount of work for a lump sum and only does part of it he cannot sue for the lump sum; but I cannot accept the proposition that if a man agrees to do a certain amount of work for a lump sum every breach which he makes of that contract by doing his work badly, or by omitting some small portion of it, is an abandonment of his contract, or is only a performance of part of his contract, so that he cannot be paid his lump sum. It seems to me that there would be a performance of the contract although some part of it was done badly, and that seems to me to be the position here ...

There is nothing in all this that seems to me to amount to doing only a part of the work contracted for and abandoning the rest. What the plaintiffs have done is to perform the work which they had contracted to do, but they have done some part of it insufficiently and badly; and that does not disentitle them to be paid, but it does entitle the defendant to deduct such an amount as is sufficient to put that insufficiently done work into the condition in which it ought to have been according to the contract. (at p 580 and p 581)

The courts, however, generally rejected the suggestion that the doctrine of substantial performance could be used to determine the time of completion and to start the running of limitation periods. It did not matter that the work that remained to be completed was trivial, so long as it was done in good faith to complete the contract. The test remained '... [had] there been such performance of the contract as to entitle the contractor to maintain an action for the whole amount due thereunder?': *County of Lambton* v *Canadian Comstock Co. Ltd. et al.* (1960), 21 D.L.R. (2d) 689 (S.C.C.) *per* Judson J at p 695. See also *Russell* v *Ontario Foundation & Engineering Co.*, [1926] 1 D.L.R. 760 (Ont. C.A.); *Foster* v *Brocklebank* (1915), 22 D.L.R. 38 (Alta. S.C.); *Carr & Son* v *Dempsey*, [1931] 1 D.L.R. 984 (B.C. Co. Ct.); *Modern Construction Co. Ltd.* v *Maritime Rock Products Ltd.*, [1963] S.C.R. 347, 39 D.L.R. (2d) 539; *Day* v *Crown Grain Co.* (1907), 39 S.C.R. 258, affirmed [1908] A.C. 504. For an example of 'bad faith' see *Ocean Steel & Construction Ltd.* v *Kenny Construction Co. Ltd. et al.* (1973), 31 D.L.R. (3d) 441 (N.S.S.C.A.D.) where the lien claimant returned eight months after the work had been performed to put in a bolt, and such performance was superfluous to the due completion of the contract.

It has been held, however, that while the doctrine of substantial performance was not applicable to mechanics' lien actions so as to start the time period for registration running, it could be applied to determine if persons claiming the lien could recover the contract price in their lien action: *Fred Pierce Ltd. et al.* v *Troke* (1957), 8 D.L.R. (2d) 5 (N.S.S.C.). See, for example, *Adams* v *McGreevy* (1907), 17 Man. R. 115 where the Court denied the claim for a lien on the ground that the action was commenced more than the prescribed time after the completion of the contract, but allowed a personal action on the contract on the grounds that there had been substantial performance.

Two further points should be noted. Although both parties believe the contract to be completed, if it is in fact not completed, the times for registration will not run: *B.A. Robinson Plumbing & Heating Ltd.* v *Stewart et al.* (1961), 28 D.L.R. (2d) 167 (Ont. C.A.), where a claimant was called back to supply an essential part of an exhaust fan that had been omitted by mistake.

As well, parties may themselves define when the contract is to be considered completed. Thus where the parties stipulate that the work is to be completed to the satisfaction of an architect, the time for registration cannot begin to run until such time as the architect in good faith so signifies even though the work is otherwise complete: *The Vokes Hardware Co.* v *Grand Trunk Railway Co. and S.F. Whitham* (1906), 12 O.L.R. 344 (C.A.); *Metal Studios Ltd.* v *City of Kitchener* (1925), 29 O.W.N. 216 (C.A.)

Note, however, that where a supervisor of a building contract gives a certificate to a subcontractor to the effect that the subcontract has been substantially completed at the date of the certificate, time begins to run against the subcontractor for the purpose of filing a lien as of that date. This is so even though more remains to be done under the subcontract, and is done at a later date: *Western Realty Projects Ltd.* v *Superior Grout and Gunite Ltd. et al.*, [1975] 6 W.W.R. 366 (Alta. S.C., Master).

See also *Dobbelsteyn Elec. Ltd. et al.*, v *Whittaker Textiles (Marysville)* (1976), 14 N.B.R. (2d) 584, where the plaintiff was employed to do the electrical work involved in renovating and construction industrial buildings. Part of the work was done pursuant to a formal written contract and the rest by virtue of a series of ad hoc arrangements. The defendant objected to the lien, claiming that it was filed outside of the statutory period for substantial completion of the written contract. Stevenson J held that the lien was valid, because where there was a continuing arrangement, the contractor was not required, in order to preserve his lien rights, to file a lien claim after completing each piece of work.

An amendment introduced in S.O. 1968–9, c 65 ought to alleviate some of the difficulties (and unfairness) resulting from the Courts' refusal to apply the doctrine of substantial performance in the mechanics' lien context. 'Completion of the contract' is now specifically defined: 'substantial performance, not necessarily total performance of the contract' (s 1(1) (a)). Subsections 1(3) and 1(4) describe in even greater detail when a contract has been 'completed'. Every common law province, with the exception of Manitoba and Nova Scotia, defines 'completion' in a similar manner: Alberta s 2(1)(a); British Columbia s 2; New Brunswick s 1(a); Newfoundland s 2(1)(a); Prince Edward Island s 1(a); and Saskatchewan s 1(2). However only Alberta (s 2(2)),

Newfoundland (s 2(2)) and Saskatchewan (s 1(2)) have provisions defining deemed substantial performance in terms similar to those of subsections 1(3) and 1(4).

Note that the doctrine of substantial performance introduced by s.o. 1968–9, c 65, s 1(3), applies to sub-contractors as well as contractors: *Union Electric Supply Co. Ltd.* v *Joice-Sweanor Electric Ltd.* et al. (1975), 7 O.R. (2d) 227 (C.A.). See also *Crestile Ltd.* v *New Generation Properties* (1976), 13 O.R. (2d) 670 (Master), where it was held that 'contract price' in s (13)(b) includes the price of work done pursuant to the original contract as augmented by extras.

QUESTIONS

1 Note that what the Act defines is 'completion of the contract'. Is the new definition applicable to section 23(1) which speaks of the time when work has been 'completed'? If not, what result would follow? See Bristow, 'Substantial Completion of Contracts Under the Mechanics' Lien Act, 1968–69, Ontario' (1972), 20 *Chitty's L.J.* 124, and *Hasler Brothers Ltd.* v *Phillips et al.* (1962), 40 W.W.R. (N.S.) 445 (B.C. C.A.).

2 On May 2, 1974, O, the owner of an apartment building, entered into a contract with C for the purchase of windows and doors at a total cost of $5,000. The materials were to be installed by O herself, but the contract provided for C to make the final adjustment to the windows and doors once they had been installed. All of the materials were delivered on May, 1974, but O did not install them until October 12, 1974. On October 24, 1974 C performed the 'final adjustment' of the doors and windows. This adjustment included the installation of a small amount of weather-stripping. The cost of this service represented only $14 of the total contract price $5,000. C sought to register a lien claim on October 25, 1975. Would he have succeeded on the basis of the old legislation? Will he succeed after the amendment of the statute? Would the result be different if the contract did not provide for C to make adjustments, but rather was a contract solely for the supply of materials? (See *Glenway Supply (Alta.) Ltd.* v *Knobloch et al.*, [1972] 6 W.W.R. 513 (Alta. C.A.); *Mor Light Ltd.* v *Rikki's Investments Ltd.*, [1975] W.W.D. 156 (B.C. Co. Ct.)).

3 Evaluate the position of the lien claimant both before and after the amended definition of 'completion of the contract', in the following situations:

    i O, a homeowner, enters into a contract with C to completely renovate O's old air conditioning system. The total contract price is $3,000. On February 1, 1975, C informs O that the work is complete. By April 3, 1975, C, still unpaid, wishes to register a lien claim against O's land. His lawyer advises him that since it is now more than thirty-seven days after completion of the contract, his lien rights have ceased to exist. C is determined to assert his lien rights and turns up at O's residence to make a 'pre-summer-inspection' of the system. Much to his delight, C finds that he had neglected to put in a switch worth $90.75. In all other respects, the system was ready for use. What result?

    ii Suppose the system had been completely installed but C was required to return three months later to make repairs pursuant to a one year warranty. Can C still claim a lien? (See *J.R. Stephenson Ltd.* v *Woodward Stores (Edmonton) Ltd. et al.* (1959), 27 W.W.R. 695, 18 D.L.R. (2d) 212 (Alta. S.C.).

    iii Suppose the contract had specifically called for the installation of an 'Ace Motor'. Because such a motor was not available at the time, an 'Apex Motor' having the same capacity was installed. Three months later, c returns to install the 'Ace Motor'. Can he claim the lien? (See *Deeves* v *Coulson Construction Co. Ltd. et al.*, [1941] 3 W.W.R. 858 (Alta. S.C.)).

iv Suppose the contract had specifically provided for the installation of a system having a 10,000 B.T.U. capacity. The system installed had only a 5,000 B.T.U. capacity. O discovers this one week after the installation but asks c not to make the specific alterations until after the summer is over. The alterations are made 9 months after the work is otherwise complete. Can C now claim a lien? (See *Whimster* v *Crow's Nest Pass Coal Co.* (1910), 13 W.L.R. 621 (B.C. Co. Ct.)

3 RIGHTS OF LIEN CLAIMANTS

a / Note: Creation of the Lien

The lien right is created by section 5 of the Ontario Act. It arises in favour of 'any person who does work upon or in respect of, or places any materials to be used in, the making, constructing, erecting, fitting, altering, improving or repairing of any land, building, structure or works ...' (s 5(1)). [Lien rights are given in similar terms in each of the other provinces: in Alberta, see ss 4(1), 7(1); in British Columbia, s 5; in Manitoba, ss 4(1), 5(1); in New Brunswick, s 4; in Newfoundland, s 7(1); in Nova Scotia, s 5; in Prince Edward Island, s 2; and in Saskatchewan, s 12.]

The lien permits a claimant to recover the value of his contribution from the 'owner' of the benefitted lands. It is a right to obtain personal judgment against the owner, even though the claimant is in no direct contractual relationship with him. As well, it is a right, under certain circumstances, to sell the interest of the owner of the land in satisfaction of that judgment. The lien claimant thus becomes a secured creditor. The lien right means that a claimant has priority advantages he would not have as an ordinary execution creditor, for the lien 'binds the land' from the time it arises, rather than the time execution is obtained and filed with the sheriff. It is important to distinguish between the *creation* of the lien and its *enforceability*. The lien arises immediately upon the commencement of the work on the land or the delivery of the first materials: in Ontario, see s 7(4); *Swanson* v *Mollison* (1907), 6 W.L.R. 678 (Alta.); *O'Brien* v *McCoig* (1928), 63 O.L.R. 351, [1929] 1 D.L.R. 906 (C.A.); *McCauley* v *Powell* (1908), 7 W.L.R. 443 (Alta.). Creation of the lien is in no way dependent on registration; however, the lien rights may be lost through failure to register in the time required by statute. As we shall see (infra, at p 590ff) the determination of the exact time at which the lien arises has important implications in priority disputes between lien claimants and other persons having a claim against the land.

There are two major limitations on the monetary amount of the lien right. First, the lien claim is limited to the amount 'justly due' to the lien claimant himself. Second, it is limited to the amount justly owing by the owner on the contract, unless the owner has not observed the holdback requirements of the Act.

Since lien rights exist in derogation of the common law, courts have interpreted the statute strictly when the question raised is whether or not any particular lien claimant is a person given a lien by the Act. See, for example, *Clarkson Co. and Young Ltd. et al.* v *Ace Lumber Ltd.*, [1963] S.C.R. 110, 36 D.L.R. (2d) 554, where the Supreme Court of Canada held that a person who merely rented equipment to a subcontractor to be used on a construction site was not a 'person who performs any service' on the land, and therefore was not entitled to a lien. Contrast *Clarkson* v *Ace Lumber* with *Cigas*

Products Ltd v Tamarisk Devs. Ltd., [1976] 6 W.W.R. 733 (B.C. Co. Ct.). In *Cigas* the plaintiff lien claimant rented propane tanks and heaters to a general contractor for use in construction. The claimant installed the tanks and heaters and supplied the fuel. The Court held that the claimant was entitled to a lien for the cost of installation and the fuel used, but not the rental price.

See also *Inter Property Investment* v *Trpchich* (1975), 11 O.R. (2d) 568 (S.C.), where a lien claim by a company for work performed by its president in his personal capacity was held not to be valid. Note, as well, *E.E. McCoy Co. Ltd. et.* v *Venus Elec. Ltd.* (1977), 19 N.B.R. (2d) 299 (Q.B.), where a welder was held not entitled to a lien for the cost of his vapour barrier because it did not constitute an improvement to the land; and *Dobblesteyn Elec. Ltd.* v *Whittaker Textiles Ltd.* (1976), 14 N.B.R. (2d) 584 (Q.B.), where a similar decision was reached in respect of a claim by a supplier of hardware used to install heavy machinery in a textile plant.

A wide class of persons has, however, been held entitled to lien rights:

1 Contractors.

2 Subcontractors. See *Re Terra Cotta Contracting Co. Ltd.*, [1964] 1 O.R. 661 (S.C.); but cf. *Cam Cement Contractors Ltd.* v *Royal Bank of Canada* (1973), 38 D.L.R. (3d) 427 (B.C.C.A.)

3 Wage earners. See *Davis et al.* v *The Crown Point Mining Co.* (1901), 3 O.L.R. 69 (C.A.), holding that a cook working at a mining camp was not entitled to a lien for wages but that a blacksmith who sharpened tools used in the mine was so entitled. Cf. *Hutchinson* v *Berridge et al.*, [1922] 2 W.W.R. 710 (Alta. C.A.), where a mining cook was held entitled to a lien.

4 Persons supplying material with the intention that the material be used for the special purposes enumerated in the Act. See *Giroday Sawmills Ltd.* v *Roberts*, [1935] 2 D.L.R. 737 (B.C.C.A.); *Brooks-Sandford Co.* v *Theodore Telier Construction Co.* (1910), 22 O.L.R. (C.A.); *Lumberland Inc.* v *Nineteen Hundred Tower Ltd.* (1975), 10 N.R. 393 (S.C.C.), where it was held that the plaintiff was entitled to a lien for the price of lumber used in the construction of a building, even though it was not incorporated in the building, but used for concrete forms.

5 Persons who have leased equipment to be used in construction. This class of creditor is specifically covered only by the Ontario (s 5(5)), Newfoundland (s 8), Alberta (s 4(4)) and Saskatchewan (s 2(1)(m)) statutes. In most other provinces, persons who merely lease equipment are not entitled to lien rights unless they also supply their employees as operators of the equipment: *Re Bodner Rd. Construction Ltd.* (1963), 43 W.W.R. 641 (Man. Q.B.); *Northcoast Forest Products Ltd.* v *Eakins Construction Ltd.* (1960), 35 W.W.R. 233 (B.C.S.C.); *Crowell Brothers* v *Maritime Minerals Ltd.*, [1940] 2 D.L.R. 472 (N.S.C.A.).

6 Architects. Whether an architect who prepares the plans but does not also supervise the construction is entitled to a lien depends on how the particular statute is construed. In *P.R. Collings and Assoc. Ltd.* v *Jolin Holdings Ltd.*, [1978] 3 W.W.R. 602, the Saskatchewan District Court held that architectural services per se do not found a lien. Such an architect was denied a lien under the British Columbia Act (*Scott et al.* v *Lindstrom et al.* (1964), 50 W.W.R. 573, 48 D.L.R. (2d) 286) but was found entitled to lien rights under Alberta's Act (*Inglewood Plumbing & Gas fitting Ltd.* v *Northgate Development Ltd.* (1965), 54 W.W.R. 225, 54 D.L.R. (2d) 509).

7 Vendors of goods under conditional sales contracts. Such a vendor, however, must have elected to proceed under The Mechanics' Lien Act instead of the relevant

conditional sales legislation: *Primeau Argo Block Co.* v *Ludor Construction Ltd.*, [1966] 1 o.r. 245 (Co. Ct.); *Hill* v *Storey* (1915), 34 o.l.r. 489, 25 d.l.r. 247 (c.a.); *U.S. Construction Co.* v *Rat Portage Lumber Co.* (1915), 9 w.w.r. 657, 25 d.l.r. 162 (Man. c.a.).

8 Other miscellaneous claimants who come within the provisions of s 5; e.g. engineers with approved engineering plans which would improve the value of the land: *Jenkins* v *Wilin Const. Ltd.* (1978), 25 n.s.r. (2d) 19 (Co. Ct.); *Rasmussens' Ltd. et al.,* v *Melville Country Club et al.,* [1977] 4 w.w.r. 382 (Sask. d. Ct.); *Armbro Materials Construction Ltd.* v *230056 Invts. Ltd. et al.* (1975), 9 o.r. (2d) 226 (s.c.)

Comprehensive cataloguing of the circumstances in which particular claims may be asserted is beyond the scope of these materials: see, further, Macklem and Bristow, *Mechanics' Liens in Canada* 59–115 (4th ed. 1978).

b / Note: The Owner

Mechanics' liens may be asserted only against the interest of 'owners' (as defined in s 1(1)(d) of the Act) of land benefitted by a claimant's contribution (s 5(1)). The lien is an entirely statute-given right and therefore cannot affect the interest of any person who does not come within the statutory definition of 'owner'. (See, for example, *Beaver Lumber Co.* v *Saskatchewan General Trusts Co.; Re Soloman Estates* (1922), 70 d.l.r. 690). A purchaser at a sale under the lien rights acquires only the interest of the 'owner' being sold. Thus, if the owner has the fee simple, the purchaser will acquire absolute ownership of the land (subject of course to any prior encumbrances); if however, the owner has merely a life estate, the purchaser acquires that interest only.

In asserting a lien, the claimant must show: (1) that the person against whom the assertion is made has an 'estate or interest in the land'; (2) that the work was done or the materials furnished in such a manner as to give rise to a lien within the meaning of section 5; (3) that this was done at the owner's request and upon his credit, or on his behalf, or with his privity or consent, or for his direct benefit.

i 'Estate or Interest': The Courts have construed the words 'any person … having any estate or interest' liberally. Included is not only the interest of the owner in fee simple, but also, in proper circumstances, the interest of a landlord (*Orr* v *Robertson* (1915), 34 o.l.r. 147 (c.a.)); the interest of a tenant (*High River Trading Co.* v *Anderson* (1909), 10 w.l.r. 126 (Alta.); *Prentice* v *Brown* (1914), 17 d.l.r. 36 (Alta. c.a.); *Roy* v *Couturier Construction Ltd.* (1965), 51 m.p.r. 360 (n.b.c.a.)); the interest of a purchaser of land (*John C. Love Lumber Co. Ltd.* v *Moore,* [1963] 1 o.r. 245 (c.a.); *Kahn* v *Wacket,* [1957] o.w.n. 557, 11 d.l.r. (2d) 414 (c.a.); *Trustee of Watt Milling Co.* v *Jackson,* [1951] o.w.n. 841; *Clarke* v *Williams et al.* [1939] 3 w.w.r. 481 (B.C. Co. Ct.)); and the interests of equitable interest holders (*Blight* v *Ray* (1893), 23 o.r. 415.) Note, however, that individual members of a co-operative association are not 'owners' against whose individual estates or interests a lien may attach for work performed for the association itself unless they themselves have contracted or dealt directly with the claimant: *Henuset Ranches & Construction Ltd.* v *East Central Gas Co-op Ltd.* (1977), 87 d.l.r. (3d) 298 (Alta. a.d.).

The limited circumstances in which a mortgagee may be considered an 'owner' are discussed in *Andre Knight Ltd.* v *Presement,* [1967] 2 o.r. 289 (c.a.) (infra p 552) and *Northern Electric Co. Ltd.* v *Manufacturers Ins. Co.* (1976), 79 d.l.r. (3d) 336 (infra p 556).

Despite the tendency of courts to give great latitude to the variety of interests that may be subjected to a lien, not all property interests are included. The principal limitation is that the lien may attach only to rights in real property and not personalty: *Pankka* v *Butchart*, [1956] O.R. 837, 4 D.L.R. (2d) 345 (C.A.). Thus, in *Cunningham* v *Sigfusson*, [1928] 1 D.L.R. 726, the Saskatchewan Court of Appeal held that a person who was in possession of land on the understanding that he would be given a right of first refusal upon sale of the property, was not an 'owner'. In *Kelly* v *Progressive Builders Ltd.* (1971), 1 Nfld. & P.E.I. R. 1 (Nfld. S.C.), the Court held that a lien claim registered subsequent to a sale to a bona fide purchaser for value without notice did not attach to the proceeds of sale in the hands of the vendor.

In most provinces, another major limitation on the types of lienable interests is the general principle that the Crown is not subject to the provisions of any statute unless expressly mentioned therein. (See, for example, the Interpretation Act, R.S.N.S. 1967, c 151, s 13; R.S.B.C. 1960, c 199, s 35.) Thus, the Crown's interest in land is generally exempt from mechanics' liens. However, recent amendments to the Ontario Act have rendered every interest in land of the provincial Crown subject to mechanics' liens (s 1a) except with respect to public streets or highways owned by a municipality or public works (s 5(2)).

While the types of interest in land that may be subjected to mechanics' liens are varied, the limited circumstances in which a person having a lienable interest may be considered an 'owner' for the purposes of the Act have circumscribed the application of the Act.

ii 'Request': A lien claimant must always establish a 'request' for his work or material by the owner as well as one of the other requirements of s 1(d), before the owner's interest is lienable. The cases have held that the requisite request of an owner may be either express or implied. Nor need it have been made directly by the owner to the lien claimant. These principles were enunciated in *Orr* v *Robertson* (1915), 23 D.L.R. 17 (Ont. C.A.) by Riddell J at p 18:

While to render the interest of the owner liable, the building ... must have been at his request, express or implied, there is no need that this request be made or expressed to the contractor – if the owner request to another to build ... and the other proceeds to build, by himself or by an independent contractor or in whatever manner, the building being in pursuance of the request, the statue is satisfied.

Request is most easily implied when the owner grants an interest in the land to another person on condition that the latter build on the land in a prescribed manner. Thus, in *Orr* v *Robertson*, supra, the 'owner' was a lessee of land who sublet his interest on the condition that the sublessee build according to plans approved by the sublessor. A 'request' also has been implied by the courts in other cases: *B.C. Mills Co.* v *Horrobin* (1906), 5 W.L.R. 275 (B.C.C.A.); *Stead Lumber Co. Ltd.* v *Lewis* (1957), 13 D.L.R. (2d) 34 (Nfld.); *B.C. Granitoid Co.* v *Dominion Shipbuilding Co.*, [1918] 2 W.W.R. 919 (B.C.C.A.); *Naftolin* v *Skene*, [1932] 1 D.L.R. 412 (Ont. C.A.); *Wasdell* v *White* (1906), 4 W.L.R. 562 (Man.); *Fulton Hardware Co.* v *Mitchell*, [1923] 4 D.L.R. 1205 (Ont.).

On the other hand, mere knowledge of, and consent to the construction is not sufficient to permit the implication of 'request'; more active conduct is required. For example, see *Beaver Lumber Co.* v *Korotky*, [1927] 1 W.W.R. 945 (Sask.), where although a landlady had knowledge of her 'boarder's' building activities, on the facts, she had not impliedly consented to them; *MacDonald-Rowe Woodworking Co.* v *MacDonald* (1963), 39 D.L.R. (2d) 63 (P.E.I. C.A.), where the court held that the fact that the person ordering the construction was the brother of the owner of the land alone is not sufficient to imply a request.

Before an owner will be liable under The Mechanics' Lien Act for materials supplied, the supplier must prove that the materials were furnished at the request, express or implied, of the owner. See *Kent & Co.* v *Legere* (1975), 65 D.L.R. (3d) 144 (N.B.S.C.A.D.), for a case holding an owner not liable where the evidence established that the materials were ordered fraudulently by an unnamed person pretending to call on behalf of the owner. However, note the dissent of Hughes CJNB, who would have granted a lien to the supplier if the fraudulent order had been placed by a contractor unable to obtain credit in his own name; a contractor would have implied authority in such a situation to order the material in the owner's name.

QUESTION As a matter of policy, is it proper that a lien cannot attach to the interest of a person who has knowledge of, has consented to, and has benefited from the construction, but has not requested it?

Note that in two provinces the Court can, in some circumstances, impute 'ownership' notwithstanding the absence of actual request. The British Columbia Mechanics' Lien Act, R.S.B.C. 1960, c 238, s 14 provides that

all improvements done with the knowledge, but not at the request of the owner ... shall be held to have been done at the instance and request of the owner ...; but this does not apply to any improvements done after there has been posted, on at least two conspicuous places upon the land, or upon the improvements thereon ... a notice in writing that he will not be responsible for such improvements, or after actual notice in writing to the above effect has reached the person claiming a lien ...

See *Baker* v *Williams* (1916), 23 B.C.R. 124 (C.A.); *Isitt* v *Merritt Collieries, Ltd.*, [1920] 1 W.W.R. 879 (B.C.). Alberta's Act used to contain a similar provision, but it was repealed. However, decisions under that Act may be useful in construing the British Columbia legislation: *Johnson & Johnson, Ltd.* v *Butler* (1914), 7 W.W.R. 385 (Alta.); *Rogers Lumber Yards Ltd.* v *Jacobs*, [1924] 2 W.W.R. 1128, [1924] 3 D.L.R. 814 (Alta. C.A.); *Hutchinson et al.* v *Berridge et al.* (1922), 66 D.L.R. 753 (Alta. C.A.). Alberta's Act (s 4(2)) now provides that a lien may attach to mineral interests (but not to a fee simple interest) despite the absence of an express request, where work is done in connection with the recovery of a mineral.

iii 'Privity and/or Consent': Section 1(d)(iii) includes within the statutory definition of 'owner' persons who have requested performance and with whose 'privity or consent work is done or materials furnished.' The Ontario statute formerly read 'privity and consent', but when the Act underwent a major revision in 1968, it was changed to its present wording. Similar language is found only in the British Columbia and Manitoba legislation; all other provinces use 'privity and consent'.

The classic definition of 'privity and consent' is that provided by Anglin J in *Marshall Brick Co* v *York Farmers Colonization Co.* (1917), 54 S.C.R. 569, at 581:

While it is difficult if not impossible to assign to each of the three words 'request', 'privity' and 'consent' a meaning which will not to some extent overlap that of either of the others ... I accept as settled law the view enunciated in *Graham* v *Williams*, 8 O.R. 478, 9 O.R. 458, and approved in *Gearing* v *Robinson*, 27 A.R.(Ont.) 364, at 371, that 'privity and consent' involves 'something in the nature of a direct dealing between the contractor and the persons whose interest is sought to be charged ... Mere knowledge of, or mere consent to, the work being done is not sufficient.

It is, of course, a question of fact in each case whether there has been such 'direct dealing' between the alleged 'owner' and the lien claimant as will permit a finding of 'privity and consent'. While it may be difficult in any particular case to predict whether or not a court will make a finding of 'direct dealing', it is safe to say that something just short of a strictly contractual relationship is required for 'privity and consent' to be found. Thus in *Marshall Brick Co.* supra, a vendor of land stipulated in its agreement of sale that the purchaser build four houses in accordance with certain plans. The agreement also provided for the advancing to the purchaser of funds sufficient to pay for the cost of the buildings, and for the forfeiture of these sums and all improvements made on the lands upon default by the purchaser. Before completion, the purchaser became insolvent and the vendor took possession of the lands. The Court held that despite the fact that the owner had requested the work, there was no direct dealing between the vendor and the lien claimants sufficient to give rise to 'privity and consent'. Other cases have made the same finding in similar circumstances: *Eddy Co.* v *Chamberlain* (1917), 37 D.L.R. 711 (N.B.C.A.); *Michaelis* v *Ryan Motors*, [1923] 1 W.W.R. 401, [1923] 1 D.L.R. 1186 (Sask. K.B.); *Thoreson* v *Zumwalt*, [1922] 1 W.W.R. 959, 63 D.L.R. 713 (Sask. K.B.); *Partridge* v *Dunham*, [1932] 1 W.W.R. 99, [1932] 1 D.L.R. 600 (Man. C.A.); *Nuspel* v *Lem Foo*, [1949] O.W.N. 476; *Kosobuski* v *Extension Mining Co. Ltd.*, [1929] 3 D.L.R. 379 (Ont. C.A.); *Scott* v *Cusack*, [1941] 1 D.L.R. 116 (Alta. C.A.); *Stuart & Sinclair Ltd.* v *Biltmore Park Estates Ltd.*, [1931] O.R. 315, [1931] 3 D.L.R. 345 (C.A.); *Cut-rate Plate Glass Co.* v *Solodinski* (1915), 25 D.L.R. 533 (Ont. C.A.); *Morgan* v *Sunray Petroleum Corporation*, [1941] 2 W.W.R. 517 (Alta.); *Swalm* v *Fairway Finance Ltd.* (1965), 52 W.W.R. 626 (Alta.); *Northern Electric Co. Ltd.* v *Frank Warkentin Electric Ltd. et al.* (1972), 27 D.L.R. (3d) 519 (Man. C.A.); *Sandon Construction Ltd.* v *Cafik*, [1973] 2 O.R. 553, 34 D.L.R. (3d) 609 (C.A.).

Where a person having an interest in the land takes an active part in the actual financing of the project and has direct contact with the contractor, 'privity and consent' may be found: *Rogers Lumber Co.* v *Gray and Hosmer* (1913), 4 W.W.R. 294, 10 D.L.R. 698 (Sask. C.A.); *Hazel* v *Lund* (1915), 9 W.W.R. 749, 25 D.L.R. 204 (B.C.C.A.). See also *Noranda Exploration Co. Ltd.* v *Sigurdson* (1975), 53 D.L.R. (3d) 641 (S.C.C.).

The position of a subcontractor asserting a lien on the basis of privity and consent was recently considered by the Supreme Court of Canada in *Northern Electric Co. Ltd.* v *Manufacturers Insurance Co.* (1976), 79 D.L.R. (3d) 336, where Martland J said at pp 350–1 that

in order for a subcontractor to claim a lien on the basis that the person against whom the lien is claimed was privy to and consented to the work being done, it is necessary to show a direct dealing between that person and the contractor who carried out the work, through whom the subcontractor claims. If there is such direct dealing, the Act does not contemplate that there must be a direct dealing between that person and the various subcontractors in order to enable them to file valid liens.

QUESTIONS Is the change in the wording of the Ontario statute in 1968 legally significant? Suppose that a lessor requires his tenant to make certain repairs. The tenant's contractor contacts the lessor to establish that such repairs are authorized. In all other respects the contractor deals solely with the tenant. Is the lessor an 'owner' within the meaning of the Act?

Many courts seem to concentrate solely on the 'privity and consent' problem without going on to examine the other factors upon which 'ownership' within the meaning of the Act may be established. Upon finding that there has been no 'direct dealing', the courts often do not consider whether there has nevertheless been 'direct benefit'. Consider the approaches taken in the following two cases.

iv *Dalgleish* v *The Prescott Arena Company Limited and Woodward*, [1951] O.R. 121 (C.A.)

HENDERSON J.A.: An appeal by the plaintiff from the judgment of His Honour Judge Lewis, Local Judge at Brockville, of the 17th May 1950, whereby the plaintiff recovered judgment against the defendant Reginald Woodward in the sum of $2,594.49, and the action against the defendant The Prescott Arena Company Limited was dismissed. The defendant Woodward does not appeal.

The plaintiff claims to be entitled to a lien against the property of the defendant The Prescott Area Company Limited under The Mechanics' Lien Act, R.S.O. 1937, c 200, s 1(c).

The Prescott Arena Company Limited is a community enterprise in the town of Prescott, and leases from the Dominion Government an area building in that town. The present lease is for a term of 10 years from 6th December 1949 at a nominal rental of $1 per year. The defendant Woodward is a resident of Cornwall, with some experience in the promotion of sports and recreational activities, and had been the manager of the Calumet Hockey Club in Cornwall.

In the first week of November 1948, following a preliminary discussion between Woodward and an officer of The Prescott Arena Company Limited, Woodward got in touch with the plaintiff, who is a contractor, and asked him to go to Prescott for the purpose of seeing the arena and deciding what repair work might be necessary to have done to it. The plaintiff and Woodward went to Prescott and first went to the arena and looked it over, to determine what renovations were necessary. These two then had a discussion with three members of the board of The Prescott Arena Company Limited with a view to the defendant Woodward obtaining a lease (or sublease) from the Arena Company. As a result of the discussion, it was agreed that a lease would be granted to Woodward if he, on his part, would agree to make certain extensive renovations to the arena building. The plaintiff was present at this conversation and says he was not much interested in that aspect of the matter.

The renovations agreed upon were subsequently embodied in the lease from the Arena Company to Woodward, which is ex. 6. The lease also provided that Woodward would provide public skating in the arena at least two nights a week, and would also allow certain clubs the use of the rink on Saturday mornings, and afternoons during the term of the lease.

Following these discussions, the plaintiff proceeded to do certain work as a general contractor, pursuant to a verbal contract arrived at between him and Woodward. This work was finished in the middle of December 1948, and on 18th December 1948 the plaintiff sent his bill to the defendant Woodward. Besides the bill for the work done on the Prescott arena, the invoice included an item for the transportation of the Calumet Hockey Club of Cornwall.

The plaintiff returned in January or February to adjust the locks on some doors that did not fit right, but did no further work of any kind with regard to the repairs originally stipulated for in the lease.

In April 1949 Woodward decided to try having some flooring installed in the arena, so that he could carry on some summer activities such as a boxing show and dancing.

The part taken by the plaintiff in the work which Woodward then decided to carry on involved a total of $12.77, for which he rendered an account to Woodward. This work was done on 13th and 18th April 1949, and an account for that amount was sent on 25th April 1949, addressed to the Calumet Hockey Rink, Cornwall.

On 13th May 1949, the plaintiff filed a mechanics' lien in the amount of $2,214.54, and in this action he took the position that the lien was a lien not only on the leasehold interest of Woodward in the premises but also upon the leasehold interest of The Prescott Arena Company Limited.

We are indebted to counsel for a very full and interesting discussion of the cases involved, of which I append a list, but do not require to discuss them in detail.

The Mechanics' Lien Act is now R.S.O. 1950, c 227, but the sections involved are in the same language as those of the former Act.

'Owner' is defined in s 1(c), and the answer of the respondent to the appeal is first that the respondent is not an 'owner' within the meaning of the Act. While the Arena Company had imposed upon Woodward an obligation to make certain repairs, and while the Arena Company knew that the plaintiff was the contractor hired by Woodward to do these repairs, there were no direct dealings between the Arena Company and the plaintiff contractor, and at no time did there exist any contractual relation between them. Admittedly no instructions were at any time given by the Arena Company to the plaintiff with respect to the doing of any of the work, and mere knowledge that the work is being done is not enough to fix the owner with liability. I agree with the conclusion of the learned trial judge in this respect. I am of opinion, however, that the plaintiff's lien was not filed until after the expiration of the time required for the filing of a lien, and in this respect I do not agree with the conclusion of the learned trial judge.

For these reasons I am of opinion that the appeal fails and should be dismissed with costs.

v *City of Hamilton* v *Cipriani* (1976), 67 D.L.R. (3d) 1 (S.C.C.)

LASKIN, C.J.C.: This appeal is brought here by the City of Hamilton to challenge the findings and conclusions in the Courts below that certain land, registered in the name of the city and upon which a secondary sewage treatment plant for the city was built, was subject to claims of lien arising out of a contract between the Ontario Water Resources Commission and a general contractor, W.A. McDougall Limited, now insolvent, which provided for the construction of the plant. The lien claims were made and properly filed by subcontractors of McDougall's excavation subcontractor which had abandoned its contract owing to financial difficulties.

The city had proposed to deal directly with McDougall and, indeed, a contract between them had been prepared under which construction was to proceed. Because of limitations upon the city as to the financing of the project, involved in Ontario Municipal Board approval, it could not obligate itself directly to McDougall, and it sought the assistance of the Ontario Water Resources Commission which had an interest in the matter under its statutory authority and responsibilities. In the result, the city entered into an agreement with the Commission under which the latter undertook to have the plant built, to pay the contractor and to accept repayment from the city over a 40-year period. Instead of the Commission becoming owner of the plant and charging the city for its use (the Commission's standard arrangement), the agreement provided for ultimate ownership by the city, but that in the meantime the city would, at the Commission's request, transfer to it land upon which the plant would be built, which would be reconveyed when full payment was made. No land was in fact conveyed under this agreement and, at the material time, so far as these proceedings are concerned, the city remained the legal and beneficial owner of the land upon which construction took place.

The Commission adopted the contract which the city had proposed to execute with McDougall, there being merely a substitution of its name for that of the city as the party liable for the construction. There was, in addition, a provision included that the *Public Works Creditors Payment Act*, 1962–63 (Ont.) c 121 [now R.S.O. 1970, c 394], would apply. This Act was recently repealed but, having been in force when the mechanics' lien proceedings were taken, an argument was founded on it to which I will refer later in these reasons [see 1975, c 45, s 1; proclaimed in force January 1, 1976].

The Ontario Court of Appeal, in reasons delivered by Schroeder, J.A., summarized the material findings of fact made by the trial Judge, and I reproduce that Court's summary as follows [39 D.L.R. (3d) 641 at pp 643–4, 1 O.R. (2d) 169]:

A The purpose of the City in its dealings with the Commission was to obtain financial assistance in construction of sewage works for the City and the City accomplished that purpose by contracting with the Commission to have the work done, for which work the City would pay the Commission.

B The City was at all relevant times the registered owner of the lands upon which and in respect of which the work was done.

C As at the date of trial the City had neither transferred nor become obligated to transfer any land to the Commission and as a result had a lienable estate or interest in the lands at the relevant time.

D Even if the Commission became entitled to a transfer of land, since the purpose was to obtain security for the City's obligations under the agreement the City would still have an estate or interest therein, as would an owner of an equity of redemption, and the *Mechanics' Lien Act*, R.S.O. 1970, c 267, would apply to such interest.

E The work was done at the City's request and for its direct benefit so as to constitute the City 'owner' within the meaning of the *Mechanics' Lien Act*. The secondary plant was designed and built so as to be operated with the primary plant as one complete unit for a common purpose and, as a result, the primary plant and the lands upon which it is built are enjoyed with the secondary plant and the lands on which it is built pursuant to s. 5(1) of the *Mechanics' Lien Act*.

The main contentions of the appellant city were, first, that if there was an owner within the meaning of the *Mechanics' Lien Act*, 1968–69 (Ont.), c 65 [now R.S.O. 1970, c 267], it was the Commission which, being an agent of the Crown, was not subject to the Act as it stood at the time of the proceedings herein; second, even if the city had an estate or interest in the affected land it did not come within the definition of 'owner' in s 1 (d) because, there being no direct dealing between it and McDougall, it could not be said that the construction was being done at its request; third, this was a case where no right or duty existed to maintain a holdback pursuant to s 11 because the holdback requirement had to be based on the contract between the city and the Commission, and not only was this a contract to which (by reason of Crown immunity) the Act did not apply but it was not a contract under or by virtue of which a lien could arise, within the meaning of s 11; and, fourth, the city risked having to pay twice under the judgments below, both to the lien claimants and to the Commission, and this introduced a conflict with s 9 of the Act which provides that:

9. Save as herein otherwise provided, the lien does not attach so as to make the owner liable for a greater sum than the sum payable by the owner to the contractor.

Schroeder, J.A., in the Ontario Court of Appeal, looking to the substance of the transactions between the city, the Commission and McDougall, construed the interrelationship as one where the Commission became the general contractor for the city and, as such, proceeded to carry out its contract through another general contractor. In my opinion, this is a proper analysis, recognizing the fact that the Commission was being the city's banker. The city was and remained the 'owner' within s 1 (*d*) so as to make its land lienable under s 5 and it is idle formalism to contend that the work was not done at its request. I do not regard *Marshall Brick Co.* v *York Farmers Colonization Co.* (1917), 36 D.L.R. 420, 54 S.C.R. 569, as standing in the way of this conclusion. That case turned largely on the words 'privity and consent' which were then conjunctive under the statute and they are now disjunctive. If the submission is that direct dealing is required before a request can be found, I am unable to accept such a limitation under the present *Mechanics' Lien Act*.

The Commission's status as an agent of the Crown is irrelevant to the present proceedings; it is not involved as an 'owner', and I do not think that the city can find any comfort in the *Public Works Creditors Payment Act* which does not oblige a creditor to resort to the Act (with its discretionary power to the Crown as to whether it will pay or not). Admittedly, a creditor can look elsewhere for his recovery, and I see nothing in the contention of alleged prejudice to the Crown when a creditor invokes the *Mechanics' Lien Act*. The prejudice alleged appears to be based on the view that the Crown's property or funds may be affected adversely if the city is allowed to recoup from the Commission any payments made to discharge the liens. This is an unworthy proposition, suggesting that the Crown might be able to settle for less than what is owing the unpaid creditors. At the same time, the contention rings strange with the assertion of the city that it may have to pay twice, that is both to the lien claimants and to the Commission. Schroeder, J.A., was of opinion that the city would reduce its obligation to the Commission to the extent of its payments, but whether this is so or not, it is not an issue that calls for decision in the present proceedings. The argument on s 9 of the Act, in so far as it is posited on the likelihood of double payment by the city, is also without merit in the circumstances herein and is not an answer to the valid liens.

It remains only to refer to s 11, the holdback provision. Counsel for the appellant contending, as already noted, that there was no right or duty to maintain a holdback in this case, submitted in effect that this precluded enforcement of the lien. Counsel for the respondent contended that in the present case it was the city that was 'the person primarily liable upon a contract ... by virtue of which a lien may arise' within s 11, and that the obligation thereunder to maintain a holdback does not depend on a fund being available out of which the holdback must be reserved. Whether this contention is correct or not on the facts of this case, I do not think that a valid claim of lien against an owner under s 5 can be defeated by showing that the owner is not a 'person primarily liable' under s 11 and hence not obliged to maintain a holdback. The right to resort to the owner's interest in the affected land is the principal remedy; s 11 provides merely an ancillary resort for realizing the lien claim.

I would dismiss the appeal with costs.

Appeal dismissed.

c / The Mortgagee as Owner

i *Andre Knight Ltd.* v *Presement*, [1967] 2 O.R. 289 (C.A.)

[Lipton and Presement (as Lipton's nominee) assembled land which they wished to develop as a shopping centre. In order to finance the project, Allstate Life Assurance Co. loaned them $224,000, taking back first and second mortgages in the amounts of $200,000 and $24,000 respectively. The mortgages required that buildings be constructed according to plans and specifications approved by Allstate. At a later date, Lipton and Presement conveyed to Allstate an undivided one-half interest in the equity of redemption in consideration of $1,000. At the time Allstate acquired this latter interest, it had knowledge that construction work was in progress.

After money had been advanced on the mortgages and the mortgages and deed of conveyance to Allstate were registered, mechanics' lien claims were registered against the land. Allstate argued that being a mortgagee who had made advances prior to the registration of the mechanics' lien claims, it took priority over such claims. The lien claimants argued that because of Allstate's involvement in the whole project it was an 'owner' within the meaning of section 1(c) of The Mechanics' Lien Act, R.S.O. 1960, c 233.]

LASKIN, J.A.: ... The trial Judge made five findings of fact which underlie his conclusion that the two Allstate companies were 'owners' under s 1(c) of the *Mechanics' Lien Act*, and that hence, notwithstanding their prior registered mortgages, their interests were subject to the plaintiff's lien. He held, first, that on the evidence, mainly that of Walsh, the borrowing arrangements between Lipton and the Allstate companies had been concluded in the latter part of April, 1964, and amounted to a contract between them; second, this contract preceded the consummation of the construction contract between the plaintiff and Lipton (through Presement) which took place on May 7, 1964: third, the construction contract was concluded on the strength of the commitments of the Allstate companies made in April; fourth, the Allstate companies were undisclosed principals of Lipton as of May 7, 1964, but they were not liable on the construction contract since they remained undisclosed at the time it was made, did not ratify it later by conduct or otherwise, and the plaintiff, having elected to sue Lipton on the contract (as a person who did make himself a party thereto), could not also sue his principals; and fifth, since the Allstate companies had an interest in the subject land prior to May 7, 1964, which was before construction began, and since Lipton was their agent (if indeed they were not also, as vendor and purchasers, engaged in a joint venture), it must be found that there was an implied request by them to have the construction work done, and it was done on their credit and with their privity and consent so as to make them 'owners' within s 1(c).

With the greatest respect to the trial Judge's course of reasoning, it proceeds on a mistaken view of the evidence of Walsh. The telephone call and telegram, which I have referred to above and which the trial Judge also mentioned in his reasons, were not made in April but on May 19, 1964. Moreover, it can no more be said that a contract was made on that date between Lipton and the Allstate companies than it can be said that the construction contract was made on receipt of the plaintiff's letter of May 7, 1964. In both cases, and certainly in that of the Allstate negotiations, offers were being made. The trial Judge is also in error in finding that the construction contract was concluded on May 7th, and it was hence wrong to say both that there was a contract with the Allstate companies before the construction contract was made and that the latter contract was made on the strength of the former.

I have no doubt that Lipton entered into the construction contract in the expectation that he would work out a deal with the Allstate companies. He did say on discovery that he had arranged to sell a half interest to Allstate *prior to the commencement of construction*. On the whole of the evidence, this could be after the construction contract was made. The *viva voce* evidence at trial given by Lipton, Walsh and Resnick (which I have already summarized) shows that the first mortgage and the equity arrangements were made at different times. and that the advances under them depended on completion of the building and execution of the intended lease. As Lipton put it, 'I was to deliver the finished product and they were to be equal partners.' There is in the record a letter of September 14, 1964, from Lipton to Allstate Insurance Co., attention of Walsh, advising that the building was nearing completion and that negotiations were on foot for the lease to Oshawa Wholesale Ltd. It went on as follows:

We shall notify you immediately after the building is completed and would appreciate prompt action in this matter because the writer can certainly use the financial portion of this transaction as soon as the building is fully completed to the satisfaction of the lessees and you may rest assured that we will lose no time in advising you accordingly and produce the necessary documents in accordance with our negotiations.

It must be remembered too that Lipton was able to secure interim financing from other sources. In these circumstances, I do not see how it can be held that Lipton was an agent for the Allstate companies as undisclosed principals. There was no appeal by the plaintiff from the holding that the Allstate companies were not liable on the construction contract, but the important question that remains is whether, there being no agency, there is any basis for holding either or both of the Allstate companies to be 'owners' within the *Mechanics' Lien Act*.
[His Lordship then referred to section 1(c) of the Act and continued:]
On the facts hereinbefore recited, the relevant inquiry is whether it can be said that (1) after the Allstate companies had acquired an estate or interest in the Collingwood property, construction work was done (a) at their request, and (b) with their privity and consent, or for their direct benefit (s-cls (i) and (ii) aforesaid are not germane); or (2) the Allstate companies are caught as 'owners' because they are persons claiming under Lipton, having acquired their rights after commencement of the construction work.
I shall deal first with the second inquiry because it involves an issue which does not appear to have been confronted directly in any previous judgment of this Court. In brief, my conclusion is that the Allstate companies do not, either in respect of their mortgage interests or the half interest in the equity, claim 'under' Lipton-Presement but rather 'through' them. The phrase 'claiming under' has reference to such interests as those of lessees; and I would hold that if a lien claim is good against the fee simple owner who authorized the construction out of which it arose it is good against any holder under him of subordinate tenurial rights in the land acquired after the work for which the lien is claimed has begun. I shall now elaborate on this conclusion.
The phrase 'claiming under' has been in the *Mechanics' Lien Act* without other qualification or embellishment since 1874, when the word 'owner' was defined by s 1 of 1873 (Ont.), c 20, being the first amendment of the original *Mechanics' Lien Act*, 1873 (Ont.), c 27. Since a person 'claiming under' an 'owner' (as now defined in the first part of s 1 (c)), and who acquires his rights after the work for which a lien is claimed has begun, is also an 'owner' for the purposes of the Act, it would follow that, unless the Act otherwise provided, the registration of his interest prior to the registration of the claim of lien would not avail him to preserve his acquired interest from the grasp of the lien. There is nothing in the Act that gives any priority to a 'claiming under'

owner through prior registration, and hence it becomes of prime importance to decide what is meant by 'claiming under' within the present s 1 (c).

I take, for purposes of illustration, the ordinary case of a fee simple owner who enters into a construction contract and during its currency sells or mortgages his fee simple in all or part of the land on which construction is proceeding. The purchaser or mortgagee is not party to the construction contract nor in any way involved with directing or supervising its performance. Unless the purchaser or mortgagee is a person 'claiming under', he is not otherwise caught by the Act save as ss 7 and 13 may be applicable.

Section 7 (3) limits the priority of a mortgage, already existing before the lienable work has begun, to the actual value of the land at the time such work is begun: see *O'Brien* v *McCoig*, 63 O.L.R. 351, [1929] 1 D.L.R. 906. Future advances under such a prior mortgage may also be secured but subject to s 13 (1) which is the general provision of the Act dealing with the priority of a mechanic's lien. It is in the following terms:

13. (1) The lien has priority over all judgments, executions, assignments, attachments, garnishments, and receiving orders recovered, issued or made after the lien arises, and over all payments or advances made on account of any conveyance or mortgage after notice in writing of the lien has been given at the address endorsed on such conveyance or mortgage pursuant to section 45 of *The Registry Act* to the person making such payments or after registration of a claim for the lien as hereinafter provided, and in the absence of such notice in writing or the registration of a claim for lien all such payments or advances have priority over any such lien.

The first part of s 13(1) is not relevant to the issue under discussion. The second part, respecting priority of the lien 'over all payments or advances made on account of any conveyance or mortgage', depends on whether previous notice in writing has been given of the lien or on whether there has been previous registration of the lien. It seems to me to be implicit, if not explicit, as a deduction from s 13(1), that if payments have been made under a conveyance or mortgage before any notice of lien or registration of lien has been given or effected, they result in priority of the conveyance or mortgage accordingly. It would be odd, in my opinion, to widen the scope of s 13(1) by an extended interpretation of the words 'claiming under'. Certainly where, as here, all the mortgage and equity money has been paid over and the respective deeds registered before written notice of lien or registration of lien has been effected, there can be no right to any priority in the lien claimant under s 13(1) in respect of the interests acquired under the deeds.

The necessary reconciliation of s 13(1) with the 'claiming under' provisions of s 1 (c) lies in reading the latter in the way I have indicated above, namely, as covering subordinate tenurial interests, and not as including a grantee or mortgagee in fee simple. I am strengthened in this view by such cases as *Sterling Lumber Co.* v *Jones* (1916), 36 O.L.R. 153, 29 D.L.R. 288; *Charters* v *McCracken* (1916), 36 O.L.R. 260, 29 D.L.R. 756; and *Cut-Rate Plate Glass Co.* v *Solodinski* (1915), 34 O.L.R. 604, 25 D.L.R. 533, because on their facts they raise the question under discussion and yet in none of them was the lien claimant, as a subsequent registrant, successful as against prior registered purchasers of unfinished buildings; see also *Warwick* v *Sheppard* (1917), 39 O.L.R. 99, 35 D.L.R. 98 ...

Turning to the first inquiry, I do not think it necessary to deal separately with the positions of the two Allstate companies. There are, of course, formal differences. Counsel for the plaintiff respondent is recorded in the transcript of evidence as alleging a partnership arrangement only between Lipton and Allstate Insurance Co. which also became second mortgagee; the involvement of Allstate Life Insurance Co. was only as first mortgagee. However, this does not matter in my view of the case. It seems to me that the position of Allstate Insurance Co., as purchaser of an interest in the land, is governed initially by s 7(6) of the *Mechanics' Lien Act*, reading as follows:

7. (6) Where there is an agreement for the purchase of land and the purchase money or a part thereof is unpaid and no conveyance has been made to the purchaser, he shall for the purposes of this Act be deemed a mortgagor and the seller a mortgagee.

This provision recognizes the security interest of an unpaid seller as being equivalent to that of a mortgagee, but beyond this the mortgage relationship has no built-in magic, and does not itself answer the question whether the mortgage is a prior one in respect of the lien (as to which see s 7(3)) or whether, if it is, future advances thereunder may also have priority as against a lien (as to which see ss 7(5) and 13(1)). Moreover, it does not preclude a finding, if there is evidence to support it, that the purchaser-mortgagor is an 'owner'.

In this latter respect, Allstate Insurance Co. is in the unique position that, as a second mortgagee as well as owner of one-half of the equity, it is both mortgagor and mortgagee for the purposes of the Act. In both capacities it would have an estate or interest in the land; and we are driven back to determine in the case of both Allstate companies whether, if they were not 'owners' when the construction contract was let, they became 'owners' later so as to subject their interests to a lien claim in respect of work thereafter performed. As already noted, they would have priority as mortgagees only when they registered their mortgages without notice or knowledge of any existing lien claim: *see Charters* v *McCracken, supra*, at p 266 O.L.R., p 760 D.L.R. Such priority would be effective in respect of the full amounts of the mortgages which had been advanced before the lien claim came to their notice.

There is some analogy between the present case and *Cut-Rate Plate Glass Co.* v *Solodinski, supra*, a judgment of the Appellate Division. There B agreed to buy from S certain land upon which S was building three houses; possession was to be given on May 1st when the houses would be finished. Prior to that time a conveyance to B was registered. Very little remained to be done by that date, and B took possession in that month. One of the contractors completed its contract with S by about June 13th, and indeed, did some additional work later, but did not register its lien claim until August 6th. B visited the property once or twice between the date of possession and the beginning of August but had no communication, direct or indirect, with the contractor. It was held that B did not become liable as an 'owner'. So here, there is nothing to indicate any involvement of the Allstate companies with the plaintiff when they acquired their interests or even when they contracted for them. Mere specification that the plans for the building should have their approval (in fact, they did not) is not enough to bring the Allstate companies within the definition of 'owner', especially when it was not a term of the mortgage arrangements that Lipton must build. Although on a view taken (but not unanimously) in *Marshall Brick Co.* v *York Farmers Colonization Co.* (1917), 54 S.C.R. 569, 36 D.L.R. 420, the Allstate companies would not be caught even if their mortgage arrangements had imposed an obligation on Lipton to build, this phase of the matter need not be pursued. Of course, there would have been no consummation of the mortgage arrangements if the building as contemplated had not been erected; but this is different from a transaction under which an obligation to build or to complete a building is imposed.

It is trite law that the mere fact that the Allstate companies knew that building was going on and were aware that their money, when advanced, would be (so to speak) put into the venture, does not make them subject to the liabilities of an 'owner': see *Gearing v Robinson* (1900), 27 O.A.R. 364; and *cf. Stuart & Sinclair Ltd.* v *Biltmore Park Estates Ltd.*, [1931] O.R. 315, [1931] 3 D.L.R. 345. This, in my view, crystallizes the position of the Allstate companies. It is quite different from the situation that arose in *Freedman v Guaranty Trust Co. of Canada*, 64 O.L.R. 200, [1929] 4 D.L.R. 32. In short, the facts in this case, as I view them, do not bring the Allstate companies within the definition of 'owner' in s 1 (c). An expanded definition, such as that considered in *Earl F. Wakefield Co.* v *Oil City Petroleums (Leduc) Ltd. et al.*, [1958] S.C.R. 361, 14 D.L.R. (2d) 609 [affid *sub nom. Ponoka-Calmar Oils Ltd. et al.* v *Earl F. Wakefield Co. et al.*, 21 D.L.R. (2d) 577, 29 W.W.R. 638, [1960] A.C. 18], would be necessary to embrace them.

The present case comes down to this. On the facts, the mortgage transactions and the sale of half of the equity were concluded and the money involved all paid over before the registration of the claim of lien. The deeds conveying the mortgage and equity interests were registered before registration of the claim of lien. There is no evidence of any such intervention in the building operations by the Allstate companies as to constitute them, by virtue thereof, 'owners' within the definition in the *Mechanics' Lien Act*, even as to work remaining to be done at any particular time. The Allstate companies, for reasons already developed, are not 'owners' in the character of persons claiming under Lipton-Presement because they claim *through* the latter rather than *under* them. In the result, I would allow the appeals of the Allstate companies and of the trustee, set aside the judgement below in so far as it upheld the plaintiff's claim of lien against these appellants, and dismiss such claim. They are entitled to their costs here and at the trial. The appellants Lipton, Presement and M.H. Lipton Real Estate Ltd. (which was added as a defendant at the trial) are entitled to their costs of their successful appeal against the award of general damages against them.

Appeal allowed in part.

ii *Northern Electric Co. Ltd.* v *Manufacturers Insurance Co.* (1976), 79 D.L.R. (3d) 336 (S.C.C.)

[A real estate developer, Metropolitan, entered into an agreement with the respondent, a mortgage lender, to finance the construction of an apartment building. The developer conveyed a parcel of land to the respondent, which granted an 80 year lease back to the developer. The developer then borrowed $1,236,000 from the respondent, secured by a mortgage on the developer's leasehold interest in the land. The agreement provided for construction in accordance with plans and specifications approved by the respondent. During construction of the building, the developer became insolvent and bankruptcy proceedings ensued. The appellant commenced a lien action against the developer and the respondent, and was unsuccessful in the Nova Scotia courts against both: against the developer, because leave of the bankruptcy court for the action had not been sought, and against the respondent, because in the view of the Nova Scotia Appeal Division, it was not an owner within the meaning of the Mechanics' Lien Act, R.S.N.S. 1967, c 178, since the work had not been done at its request. The Appeal Division held that the relationship between the developer and the respondent was not one of joint venturers but rather one of borrower and lender.]

LASKIN C.J.C.:... The result of the arrangement between Metropolitan and the respondent was to give the latter title to the land and building, full possession on the termination of the 80-year lease, and in the meantime the right to share in the profits from the apartment building as well as to receive monthly rent payments during the leasehold period. This was no mere mortgage investment by the respondent requiring it to reconvey the property on repayment of its loan but, rather, the financing, for its own benefit as owner, of a property development to be carried out for it by another who brought into it the land on which the development was to take place and who would stand to gain (apart from being paid for the land) from the revenues of the development over the period of its leasehold. In the events that happened, Metropolitan lost its leasehold interest when a second mortgagee thereof foreclosed and Metropolitan's rights were sold.

It is my brother Martland's conclusion that on the facts herein the respondent is an 'owner' as that term is defined in s 1(d) of the Act which reads as follows:

1. In this Act ...
(d) 'owner' extends to any person, body corporate or politic, including a municipal corporation and a railway company, having any estate or interest in the land upon or in respect of which the work or service is done, or materials are placed or furnished, at whose request and
   (i) upon whose credit; or
   (ii) on whose behalf; or
   (iii) with whose privity and consent; or
   (iv) for whose direct benefit;
   work, or service is performed or materials are placed or furnished, and all persons claiming under him or them whose rights are acquired after the work or service in respect of which the lien is claimed is commenced or the materials furnished have been commenced to be furnished;

That conclusion is based on the view that under the arrangement with Metropolitan, by which the respondent obtained an estate or interest in the land upon which the apartment building was constructed, the work of construction was done at its request and with its privity and consent. I agree with this assessment so far as it goes. In coming to the conclusion that the respondent was an 'owner' as aforesaid, Justice Martland examined the *Warkentin* case and was satisfied that on its facts it differed from the present case. At the same time, he rejected the contention of the appellant that the work was done either upon the respondent's credit, within s 1(d)(i), or on its behalf, within s 1(d)(ii).

Coffin, J.A., who spoke for the Nova Scotia Court of Appeal [53 D.L.R. (3d) 303, 10 N.S.R. (2d) 97], had also concluded that there was 'privity and consent' on the respondent's part and (to quote him [at p 311]):

That being so, my doubts, in view of my [adverse] conclusion as to joint venture, as to whether it can in any way be said that the work was done on behalf of or for the direct benefit of [the respondent] under subcls. (ii) and (iv) of s 1(d), are perhaps not important.

Coffin, J.A., refused, however, to find that the work was done at the respondent's request, either expressly or impliedly, and I agree with my brother Martland that Coffin, J.A., was wrong in failing to make that finding.

I would go further than the Nova Scotia Court of Appeal and further than my brother Martland in assessing whether the respondent is an 'owner' under s 1(d). In my opinion, the work herein can properly be said to have been done also on the respondent's behalf, if not also for its direct benefit. It may be said that it was also done on behalf of Metropolitan and for its direct benefit, but, if so, this does not preclude a similar finding in respect of the respondent, having regard to the arrangement between it and Metropolitan. The outright purchase by the respondent of the land on which the apartment building was to be built, the fact that title to the building would belong to the respondent no less than the title to the land, without any revestment right in Metropolitan, and the fact that, to the knowledge of the respondent, Metropolitan was to act as contractor on the project which was to proceed according to plans and specifications approved by the respondent and under the latter's financial control, are significant indications to me that the work was being done and the materials furnished more on behalf of the respondent than on behalf of Metropolitan, and more for its direct benefit than for the direct benefit of Metropolitan. ...

Section 5, so far as relevant, declares that a lien arises when a person performs work upon or furnishes material to be used in the construction of a building 'for any owner, contractor or subcontractor'. It seems plain to me that once it is determined that the respondent is an owner within s 1(d), as being a person at whose request and on whose behalf work is done or materials are furnished in respect of land in which that person has an estate or interest, it is also 'any owner' under s 5, as a person for whom the work is done or the materials are furnished in respect of the construction project. It is unnecessary, therefore, for me to decide whether the respondent is also within s 5 as an 'owner' by reason of work being done or materials being furnished at its request and with its privity and consent. I incline to the view that it is also within s 5 on that basis, especially when Metropolitan, the developer, was also the general contractor for the construction project carried out under the letters of commitment between it and the respondent. [Martland J, who delivered a dissenting judgment, also held the respondent to be an owner. The basis of his dissent was that the respondent was not required to maintain a holdback because the developer was not a contractor.]

QUESTION D is the owner in fee simple of land. On July 5, 1975 she enters into an agreement with s. Company whereby the latter agrees to build a house on the property. In another agreement signed on the same date, D agrees to convey her land to s. Company for $1.00 and s. Company agrees to provide funds for building the house by mortgaging the property. s. Company further agrees to sell the land back to D for $70,000 upon the completion of construction. No part of the cost of construction is due or payable by D until completion. On July 6, 1975, D conveys the land to s. Company. The deed is registered on July 11, 1975. On July 16 s. Company mortgages the property to x as security for a loan of $50,000. The mortgage is registered on July 18, 1975. s. Company completes only part of the work before abandoning the project and absconding with the funds. P, a subcontractor hired by s. Company to work on the site, seeks to assert a lien claim against D to the extent of $30,000. Is D an 'owner' within the meaning of the Act? If so, how should the lien claim be resolved? See *Freedman* v *Guaranty Trust Co.*, [1929] 4 D.L.R. 32 (Ont. C.A.).

d / Note: Enforcing the Lien
The lien arises when the work is done or the materials are furnished. No further action is required to perfect it. However, lien rights may be lost unless proper enforcement steps are taken. In practice, as long as debtors are paying timeously lien creditors will not take enforcement procedures although they can do so earlier. But, when debtors begin to default enforcement steps will frequently be taken by many of the lien creditors.

Three basic steps are required to preserve a mechanics' lien. First, the claimant must register a claim for lien in the land registry office for the land registry division in which the land to be charged is situate (s 16). This may be done before or during performance of the contract, or within 37 days after the completion or abandonment of the contract, or within 37 days of furnishing the last materials (s 21)). If the lien claim is not registered within the time prescribed by section 21, the lien ceases to exist and cannot be revived thereafter (s 22(1)). This 'final termination' of the lien is a marked change from the law as it existed prior to the 1968–9 amendments. The former law recognized the 'sheltering' or 'umbrella' principle, whereby a lien claim which had ceased to exist could be revived if another lien claimant commenced an action and registered a certificate of action within the proper time. (See The Mechanics' Lien Act, R.S.O. 1960, c 233, ss 21(5), 22(1).) Only Nova Scotia (s 24) and Saskatchewan (s 37) still retain the 'umbrella' principle. All other provinces have provisions substantially similar to Ontario's s 22(1).

The second step in the enforcement procedure is the giving of notice to those higher up in the contractual pyramid (e.g. the owner, the contractor, and mortgagees). Until the lien claimant gives such notice, those higher up may safely pay the contractor and discharge lien claims pro tanto (subject, of course, to the holdback provisions: see ss 11(6) and 14(1)).

Finally, the claimant must commence an action in the Supreme Court of Ontario and file a certificate of action in the appropriate registry office, both within ninety days from the completion of the work (*not* from the filing of the lien claim); otherwise the lien will be extinguished (ss 22(2), 23(1)).

Lien enforcement proceedings, however, are class actions, and an action brought by any one claimant is deemed to be brought on behalf of all others (s 30). Therefore a lien claimant who does not himself commence an action within the ninety day period may still 'shelter' behind the action of any other lien claimant, so long as it is properly commenced within ninety days of the completion of the former's work. In *Brousseau* v *Muircrest Investments Ltd.* (1977), 75 D.L.R. (3d) 161, the Ontario Court of Appeal held that the words 'in the meantime' in s 23(1) establish only an expiry date and not a commencement date as well. Accordingly, a claimant was able to shelter behind a certificate of action filed by another claimant eight months before the registration of the lien claim sought to be preserved. In *Brousseau*, the sheltering claimant's lien had come into existence when the other claimant's certificate was filed; the Court left open the question whether a certificate can protect a claim for lien where the lien is not yet in existence at the time the certificate is filed.

After trial, the successful lien claimant will be given personal judgment against the person with whom he was in direct contractual relation. The judgment will also provide that the owner's interest in the property be sold if the indebtedness is not satisfied within a set time period.

If the owner fails to pay into court the amount required to satisfy the claims, the lien claimant may then take the required steps to have the owner's interest sold. The lien claimant may proceed to apply to the judge or officer trying the case for an ex parte order for sale. The judge or officer will grant the order upon the production of a certificate of non-payment obtained from the accountant of the Supreme Court of Ontario and an affidavit of non-payment prepared by the lien claimant. Prior to the sale the lien claimant will obtain an appointment to finalize arrangements of the manner of sale. This must be served on the mortgagees, execution creditors and all other lien claimants. The Act itself does not specifically provide for the method of sale.

Therefore the sale is usually conducted in a manner similar to sale under execution pursuant to the Rules of Practice of the Supreme Court of Ontario: see The Mechanics' Lien Act, supra, s 46(4). If the sale does not realize funds sufficient to discharge the lien, the lien claimant will have personal judgment against the owner, and thereafter may take every other legal means to enforce his judgment.

Even if a lien claimant fails to establish his lien, he may still be given personal judgment against any party to the action (s 40). However, the scope of s 40 is limited. No personal judgment in respect of negligence or even or intentional torts can be based upon it; and in the absence of a direct contractual relationship judgment cannot be given under s 40. Only lien rights transcend privity: see *Northern Electric Co. Ltd.* v *Frank Warkentin Electric Ltd. et al.* (1972), 27 D.L.R. (3d) 519 (Man. C.A.), below at p 591 esp. p 595; *Alros Products Ltd.* v *Dalecore Construction Ltd.* (1973), 2 O.R. (2d) 312, 42 D.L.R. (3d) 656 (C.A.); and *Western Caissons (Man.) Ltd. et al.* v *Trident Construction Ltd. et al.* (1975), 54 D.L.R. (3d) 289 (Man. Co. Ct.). See, however, *A.J. (Archie) Goodale Ltd.* v *Risidore Brothers Ltd.* (1975), 8 O.R. (2d) 427, 58 D.L.R. (3d) 203 (C.A.), which held that s 40 is not limited to a situation where the lien claimant had established that he would have had a valid lien if he had taken the proper steps and followed the required procedure. The section is wide enough to include an action where the claim is one which is not legally the subject of a lien under the Act.

In *Standard Industries Ltd.* v *E-F Wood Specialties Inc.* (1977), 78 D.L.R. (3d) 280 (Ont. H.C.J.), it was held that s 40 does not preclude a separate personal action; providing there is no prejudice to the defendant which cannot be compensated by costs, a common law action and a mechanics' lien action may proceed simultaneously.

4 THE HOLDBACK

a / Note

It is probably clear to you by now that the procedural difficulties involved in assertion of lien rights mean that if the lien were the only right given to construction industry creditors, many small creditors would find the process overly cumbersome and lengthy. Some further protection is required which will provide a fund available for the satisfaction of lien claimants' demands.

Such protection is provided by the 'holdback' provisions included in all mechanics' lien legislation. Funds of money are reserved to which claimants can look for satisfaction of their claims. Creation of holdback funds is a procedure separate from, and in addition to creation of the several trust funds (s 2). While trust funds are created for the benefit of persons immediately below each trustee, holdback rights accrue to the benefit of those 'two rungs down the ladder'. For example, the owner holds trust funds for the benefit of his contractor but holds the holdback funds for the benefit of subcontractors.

In Ontario, s 11 creates the holdback scheme. Any person primarily liable on a contract under which a mechanics' lien may arise is obliged to retain 15 percent of the value of the work done or materials supplied for 37 days after completion or abandonment of the contract. It is important to note that the holdback provisions are applicable to all persons primarily liable on a contract: the owner holds back 15 percent from the head contractor; the head contractor holds back 15 percent from his subcontractors and so on down the line. [The holdback provisions in each province vary: in Alberta (s

15(2)), 15% is held back for 35 days; in British Columbia (s 21(1)), 15% for 40 days; in Manitoba (s 9(1) (2)), 20% for 30 days or 15% if the value of the work is greater than $15,000; in New Brunswick (s 15(1)(3)), 20% for 60 days, or 15% if the value of the work is greater than $15,000; in Newfoundland (s 13(1)), 10% for 30 days, or 20% for 45 days if the value of the work is greater than $15,000; in Nova Scotia (s 12(1)), 20% for 45 days; in Prince Edward Island (s 15(1)(3)), 20% for 60 days, or 15% if the value of the work is greater than $15,000; and in Saskatchewan (s 19(1)(3)), 20% for 37 days or 15% if the value of the work is greater than $25,000.]

During the holdback period, claimants may file their claims in the proper registry office. If none are filed within the statutory period, the holdback money may safely be paid to contractual creditors, and any potential lien liability is thereby discharged (s 11(7)). If the lien claimants have taken steps to enforce their liens (ss 22 and 23) the owner may pay the money into court, thereby discharging his obligations and his interest in the land from lien claims.

What happens to the remaining 85% of the contract price? Section 11(6) provides that payments up to 85% of the value of work done or materials furnished made in good faith prior to notice in writing of the lien, discharge the lien to the extent of such payments. The Act is not explicit about what happens if payment is made notwithstanding notice of the lien. It has been held that by necessary inference, payment after written notice does not operate as to discharge lien liability: see for example, *Canadian Comstock Co.* v *Toronto Transit Commission et al.*, [1970] S.C.R. 205, 8 D.L.R. (3d) 582; *S.I. Guttman Ltd.* v *James D. Mokry Ltd.*, [1969] 1 O.R. 7, 1 D.L.R. (3d) 253. Note that registration of the lien claim is not notice for the purpose of section 11(6); notice *in writing* must be given to the person making the payments. Nevertheless, when making final payment of the 15 percent holdback pursuant to section 11(7), the lien claimant must search his title to ensure that lien enforcement proceedings have not been commenced.

One important question which often arises in holdback disputes concerns the precise effect of the state of accounts between the owner and his head contractor on the duties of the owner with respect to the holdback funds. The resolution of this issue challenges the efficacy of the holdback provisions.

Section 9 limits the amount of the owner's liability to a sum not greater than the amount owing to the contractor 'save as herein otherwise provided'. Similarly, section 10 limits the amount of the lien of persons other than the contractor, to the amount owing to the contractor, again unless otherwise provided in the Act. Ordinarily, a computation of the amount owing would take account of a set-off. For instance, if a bankrupt head contractor is owed $250,000 on the final instalment of the contract, but his abandonment has resulted in damages to the owner of $150,000, the 'amount owing' is only $100,000. Unless a specific section of the Act provides otherwise, the operation of section 9 would enable the owner to set-off the $150,000 in derogation of the rights of lien claimants.

Do any other sections of the Act 'provide otherwise'? Section 11(1) requires the owner to hold back 15 percent of the value of the work. Section 11(6) provides that upon the default of the contractor or subcontractor the 15 percent holdback ('statutory holdback') may not be used to complete the contract or as a fund against which the set-off moneys owed to the owner. Therefore it is clear that together sections 11(1) and 11(6) do 'provide otherwise'; the 15 percent statutory holdback must be paid by the owner no matter what the state of accounts between the owner and his head contractor may be.

Suppose that a lien claimant has given written notice of his lien before the owner has paid the head contractor the full eight-five percent of the value of the work done and materials furnished, so that payments made thereafter would not discharge mechanics' liens pro tanto (s 11(6)). The owner in such a case retains the fifteen percent statutory holdback, and, as well an additional amount, the 'notice holdback'. Suppose that the head contractor abandons the job, leaving the owner with a claim for damages as great as the amount of the 'notice holdback'. May the owner set-off the amount of the 'notice holdback' against his claim for damages against the head contractor, or does he hold *that* holdback, as well as the 'statutory holdback', solely for the benefit of holdback fund beneficiaries? Subcontractors have argued that section 13 'provides otherwise' to prevent the owner from setting-off the amount in excess of the statutory holdback. Section 13 provides that 'every subcontractor is entitled to enforce his lien notwithstanding the non-completion or abandonment of the contract by any contractor or subcontractor under whom he claims.'

In *Vaillancourt Lumber Co. Ltd.* v *Trustees of Separate School Section No. 2, Township of Balfour* (1964), 42 D.L.R. (2d) 610 (Ont. C.A.) (below), the contractor paid over the full 85 percent despite intervening notice of lien claims, and was required by the Court to pay the amount of the lien claims not '*pro tanto* discharged' (s 11(6)) in addition to the 15 percent statutory holdback. Referring to the present section 13 the Court held that '[t]he effect of this subsection is to preclude the owner under any circumstances from setting up as against subcontractors who claim liens a penalty for non-completion' (per McGillivray JA at p 421).

Since *Vaillancourt*, the Court of Appeal has retreated from this seemingly blanket refusal to allow set-offs against holdback funds. In *Guttman* v *James Mokry Ltd.* [1969] 1 O.R. 7 (C.A.) (infra, p 566), the Court allowed the owner to set-off his damages against the 'notice holdback', thereby defeating part of the subcontractor's lien claims. The Court distinguished the case from *Vaillancourt* on the basis that the owner in *Guttman* did not make any payments to the defaulting contractor after receiving notice of lien claims. The *Guttman* reasoning has been approved by the Supreme Court of Canada in *Canadian Comstock Co. Ltd.* v *Toronto Transit Commission et al.*, [1970] S.C.R. 205, 8 D.L.R. (3d) 582, and *Noranda Exploration Co. Ltd. et al.* v *Sigurdson* (1975), 53 D.L.R. (3d) 641. It has also recently been followed in *Scarborough Painting Ltd.* v *Buckley et al.* (1975), 4 O.R. 253 (Master).

QUESTIONS Can the distinction taken in *Guttman* from the reasons of the Court of Appeal in *Vaillancourt* be supported? Whatever you may think of such a distinction, what advice would you give an owner who has received written notice of a lien claim?

b / *Vaillancourt Lumber Co. Ltd.* v *Trustees of Separate School Section No. 2, Township of Balfour* (1964), 42 D.L.R. (2d) 610 (Ont. C.A.)

The judgment of the Court was delivered by
McGILLIVRAY, J.A.: This is an appeal by the defendant, the trustees of the Separate School Section No. 2 in the Township of Balfour, hereinafter referred to as the 'owner', from the judgment of His Honour Judge Cooper whereby the plaintiff and other lienholders were found

entitled to liens which together with costs amounted to $9,850.93; and whereby the appellant as owner was ordered to pay into Court the sum of $3,712.55 which was in addition to the statutory hold back of $6,138.38 previously paid into Court.

There is no dispute as to the facts. The contract in question was made by the appellant with its co-defendant Rio Construction Company for construction of a school building at a contract price of $56,012.40. At a date unspecified the contractor abandoned the work at which time the work completed was valued at $40,922.54. At the time of abandonment the appellant had paid to the contractor a total sum of $34,784.16. He then paid into Court the hold back of $6,318.38, making a total payment in all of $40,922.54.

On May 12, 1962, and some time prior to the work being abandoned the respondent filed a mechanics' lien for $4,551.78 the proper amount of which was agreed at trial to be $4,130.95 and by notices in writing of April 13, 1962, and May 3, 1962, gave notice of the lien to the appellant.

Subsequent to these notices the appellant made payments to the contractor of $12,822.41 on May 18, 1962, and of $3,923.60 on June 27, 1962. As both of these payments were made upon progress certificates by the architect it must be assumed that abandonment by the contractor occurred subsequent to the last payment on June 27th. The appellant completed construction of the school and paid out for this purpose the sum of $23,322.23.

The trial Judge found as follows:

A The appellant was required to retain for the benefit of lienholders in addition to the statutory hold back of $6,138.38 the sum of $4,130.95 being the amount of the respondent's lien of which notice had been given, a total in all of $10,269.33.

B That the total of all liens and costs amounted to $9,850.93 for which amount the appellant was responsible. The appellant was accordingly directed to pay into Court the additional sum of $3,712.55 which together with the amount of the hold back already paid in would comprise a fund sufficient to satisfy the liens.

C The appellant should have judgment against the contractor for an amount computed as follows:

Amount by which cost to complete exceeded contract price	$ 8,232.37
Additional amount to be paid into Court on account of liens	3,712.55
	$11,944.92

An appeal is taken against this finding upon the ground that, even had $4,130.95 been retained, after notice of the lien, by the owner, lien claimants would have been entitled to none of it because the owner had a claim against the contractor for non-completion amounting to more than that sum; and such being the base there should be no judgment for, or payment to the lien claimants of more than the statutory hold back of $6,138.38.

The point now raised was dealt with by this Court in *Len Ariss & Co.* v *Peloso*, 14 D.L.R. (2d) 178, [1958] O.R. 643, but the appellant submits that the point was not argued to the Court at that time and so should be further considered. I do not recall if the exact point was raised in argument in that case but having written the judgment of the majority I am in a position to say that the matter was considered and I believe the judgment makes this clear. I shall, however, deal with the present submission.

The appellant accepts as law the fact that where an owner receives notice in writing of a lien he must retain the sum therein set out in addition to the statutory hold back till such time as the lien is paid or discharged: *Craig* v *Cromwell* (1900), 27 O.A.R. 585; *Piggot* v *Drake*, [1933] O.W.N. 197; *Ariss* v *Peloso, supra*. It submits, however, that, while lien claimants have a statutory charge against the hold back (15% in this case) by reason of s 11(5) of the *Mechanics' Lien Act*,

R.S.O. 1960, c 233, moneys held back pursuant to notice are not similarly charged with payment of the lien or liens and, as a consequence, where the contractor has abandoned the work as in this case the owner is entitled to set off cost of completion against any moneys otherwise owing under the contract. The effect of this in the present instance would result in no funds above the statutory hold back being available for lien claimants.

In support of this argument reference is made to the following sections of the Act:

10. Save as herein otherwise provided, where the lien is claimed by any person other than the contractor, the amount that may be claimed in respect thereof is limited to the amount owing to the contractor or subcontractor or other person for whom the work or service has been done or the materials placed or furnished.

11. (1) In all cases, the person primarily liable upon any contract under or by virtue of which a lien may arise shall, as the work is done or materials are furnished under the contract, retain for a period of thirty-seven days after the completion or abandonment of the work done or to be done under the contract 20 per cent of the value of the work, service and materials actually done, placed or furnished, as mentioned in section 5, irrespective of whether the contract or subcontract provides for partial payments or payment on completion of the work and the value shall be calculated upon evidence given in that regard on the basis of the contract price or, if there is no specific contract price, on the basis of the actual value of the work, service or materials.

(2) Where the contract price or actual value exceeds $25,000, the amount to be retained is 15 per cent instead of 20 per cent.

(5) The lien is a charge upon the amount directed to be retained by this section in favour of lienholders whose liens are derived under persons to whom the moneys so required to be retained are respectively payable.

(6) All payments up to 80 per cent as fixed by subsection 1 or up to 85 per cent as fixed by subsection 2 and payments permitted as a result of the operation of subsections 3 and 4 made in good faith by an owner to a contractor, or by a contractor to a subcontractor, or by one subcontractor to another subcontractor, before notice in writing of the lien given by the person claiming the lien to the owner, contractor or subcontractor, as the case may be, operate as a discharge *pro tanto* of the lien.

It is by reason of s 11(6) that the Court requires the owner to retain (if the lien is not paid off or discharged) the sum set out in the notice of lien and it is upon the wording of the subsection that the appellant relies in submitting, as it does, that the lien is not made a charge against the moneys held back. The point taken is an interesting one but not one to which a specific answer need be given in the circumstances here present for once it is decided that the subsection in question requires the said money to be held back it becomes a part of the contract price in the owner's hands awaiting the disposition of the Court. The Court in turn, where the contractor has abandoned the contract as in this instance (and in the *Ariss* v *Peloso* case), is governed not by s 11(6) but by s 12(2) which reads:

12. (2) Every subcontractor is entitled to enforce his lien notwithstanding the non-completion or abandonment of the contract by any contractor or subcontractor under whom he claims.

The effect of this subsection is to preclude the owner under any circumstances from setting up as against subcontractors who claim liens a claim for a penalty for non-completion. I can best refer to the judgment of Masten, J.A., speaking for the majority of the Court in *Freedman v Guaranty Trust Co.*, [1929] 4 D.L.R. 32, 64 O.L.R. 200, where a predecessor section identical in form to the present was under consideration. I quote from pp 35–7 D.L.R., pp 203–5 O.L.R. of that judgment:

This enactment appears to me to carry with it two implications: first, that the subcontractor has a lien by virtue of doing his work or supplying materials; and, second, that non-completion and abandonment as obstacles in the way of enforcement of the subcontractor's lien are abolished, and with them necessarily disappear as against the subcontractor's lien the subsidiary concomitants and incidents of non-completion, one of which is that nothing had become due from the owner to the principal contractor. Hence the result of the new statutory provision is that the subcontractor is no longer prevented from enforcing his lien by the circumstance that there is nothing owing by the owner to the principal contractor. In other words, he is by this clause of the statute placed in the same position with regard to enforcement of his lien as though the work as it stood at the date of abandonment was *pro tanto* a legal fulfilment of the contract and as if the principal contractor was entitled to recover against the owner on a *quantum meruit* for the value of the work so far as completed. ...

The limitations prescribed by ss 5, 9, and 10 of the Act are expressly made *subject to the specific provisions elsewhere found in the Act.*

By s 5 any person, whether contractor or subcontractor, who performs any work or furnishes any materials shall by virtue thereof have a lien upon the estate or interest of the owner in the property on which the work was done or to which the materials were supplied. He does not acquire a lien on a fund but a lien on the physical property, and this lien arises by the doing of the work or the furnishing of the material.

While a lien exists as soon as the work is done or the materials supplied, the amount for which it can be enforced is, by s 5 subject to two limitations: (*a*) it is limited to the sum justly due to the person entitled to the lien; (*b*) it is limited to the sum 'justly owing, *except as herein provided*, by the owner.'

These two limitations are repeated and amplified by ss 9 and 10 of the Act, which read as follows:

9. Save as herein otherwise provided the lien shall not attach so as to make the owner liable for a greater sum than the sum payable by the owner to the contractor.

10. Save as herein otherwise provided where the lien is claimed by any person other than the contractor the amount which may be claimed in respect thereof shall be limited to the amount owing to the contractor or subcontractor or other person for whom the work or service has been done or the materials placed or furnished.

But it is to be observed that each of the above sections begins with the words 'save as herein otherwise provided,' and, by s 12(2), it is otherwise provided, as it seems to me.

Again it is important in this connection to observe the state of the law prior to the passing of s 12(2). As I understand the law to have existed, it is that if at the time when the contractor abandoned the work there was an amount due to him by the owner, the lien of the subcontractor would, without the aid of s-s (2), be enforceable to the extent of the balance so due from the owner to the contractor.

If the amendment in question is to be interpreted as applying only to cases where there is a balance actually payable by the owner to the contractor at the date of the abandonment, it is entirely nugatory and was unnecessary and valueless, for without s-s (2) the subcontractor's lien was an effective charge on whatever amount had become due and owing from the owner to the contractor at the moment of abandonment. It is reasonable to assume that the legislature meant to accomplish some purpose when it added s-s (2) to the Act. But, if any effect is to be given to the amendment, it can only be by making the subcontractor's lien enforceable notwithstanding the fact that nothing is payable by the owner to the contractor in consequence of the contract being abandoned.

To apply the above decision to the present case, had the owner retained in its hands the additional amount specified in the notice there would have been more than enough together with the statutory holdback to settle all the lien claims of subcontractors and against such there could not be set off any amount for non-competition. For this reason there is found to be no merit in the present appeal.

The hardship imposed upon an owner called upon to pay twice for the same work was pointed out to the Court but no hardship need occur if the owner proceeds in a proper fashion. He can and would I should think in the usual practice, upon receiving notice and before paying further moneys, either demand that the contractor pay the lien forthwith or pay it himself as provided by s 12(1). In the present instance the owner did neither and by paying the contractor some $16,744 after receipt of notice of the lien it enabled the contractor to deprive lien claimants of money to which they were entitled. Someone under these circumstances must suffer the loss and the owner at least could cause it to be avoided had it not proceeded at its peril to make the payments mentioned.

I would dismiss this appeal with costs.

Appeal dismissed.

QUESTION What does the Court mean by 'part of the contract price' when it says (at p 564): '... [O]nce it is decided that the subsection in question requires the said money to be held back it becomes a part of the contract price in the owner's hands awaiting the disposition of the Court'?

c / *S.I. Guttman Ltd.* v *James D. Mokry Ltd.*, [1969] 1 O.R. 7 (C.A.)

SCHROEDER, J.A.: The Board of Education for the Borough of Scarborough (hereinafter referred to as the 'Board') appeals from the findings of D.D. MacRae, Master, in a report made on March 18, 1968, pursuant to a judgment of reference under the *Mechanics' Lien Act*, R.S.O. 1960, c 233.

On March 14, 1967, the Board entered into a contract with its co-defendant for the construction of a school building to be erected for the price or sum of $1,073,000, later reduced by an amending agreement to $1,066,197.02. When the work was still in its early stages the contractor abandoned the undertaking and went into bankruptcy on September 29, 1967. The material facts are not in dispute and may be stated summarily as follows:

A At the time of abandonment the value of the work as it stood was $144,200.

B The amount of the statutory holdback pursuant to s 11(2) of the Act was $21,630, being 15% of $144,200.

C The Board had paid the principal contractor the sum of $99,960 prior to the work stoppage and therefore had on hand the sum of $44,240.

D On September 21, 1967, the respondent wrote a letter to the appellant advising that it had on that date registered a claim for lien against the school property without specifying the amount of its claim. It should be noted that the claim for lien thus registered was for the sum of

$193,684.82, although the amount then owing to it and subsequently proved was $27,619.23.
E After deducting from $44,240 in the Board's hands the amount of the statutory holdback,
$21,630, there remained a balance of $22,610 which all parties agreed was less than sufficient
to enable the Board to complete the building on the basis of the contract price.

The appellant had paid into Court the sum of $21,630 retained by it as required by s 11(2). The
learned Master held that the appellant was liable to the lienholders in the further sum of $22,610,
the amount in its hands after payment into Court of the statutory holdback, and in so doing he
purported to follow and apply the principles deduced by him from the judgments of this Court in
Freedman v Guaranty Trust Co. of Canada, 64 O.L.R. 200 [1929] 4 D.L.R. 32; *Len Ariss & Co.
Ltd. v Peloso*, [1958] O.R. 643, 14 D.L.R. (2d) 178, and in *Vaillancourt Lumber Co. Ltd. v
Trustees S.S. Section 2, Balfour Tp.*, [1964] 1 O.R. 418, 42 D.L.R. (2d) 610.

The sole issue raised in the present appeal is whether the appellant has satisfied its obligations
under the statute by paying into Court the sum of $21,630. It is contended that on a proper
construction of the authorities relied upon by the Master it was entitled to apply the amount of
$22,610 in diminution of its loss or damage in respect of the non-completion of the project and
that the amount justly owing to the contractor for the value of the unfinished work is $44,240 less
the said sum of $22,610, or $21,630, the latter amount representing the statutory retention
calculated as prescribed by the Act.

With deference to the opinion of the learned Master I take the view that he has misconstrued
the relevant provisions of the Act as a result of his misapprehension of the true effect of the
judgments which he purported to follow. As a general rule there is no privity of contract between
an owner and a subcontractor, and there is no such relationship here. To the extent that the Act
provides for a limited claim in favour of a subcontractor against an owner or other person
primarily liable on the contract despite such want of privity, that right being a creature of statute
and derogating, as it does, from the owner's rights at common law or in equity, must be strictly
construed and not extended beyond the meaning of the plain words of the statute.

Section 5(1) which creates the lien expressly limits it 'to the sum justly due to the person
entitled to the lien and to the sum justly owing, except as herein provided, by the owner'. The
same concept is carried into the provisions of ss 9 and 10. The saving terms of the Act which
make other provision and establish a restricted artificial privity between the owner and subcontractor are to be found in s 11(1) and (2) which impose upon the person primarily liable upon
any contract, which would necessarily include the owner, the obligation of retaining a fund
calculated as therein prescribed for the protection of subcontractors entitled to a lien who, by
virtue of s 11(5), acquire a charge on the amount so directed to be retained. Section 11(8)
provides that 'Every contract is amended in so far as is necessary to be in conformity with this
section.' Section 11(6), (7) and (9) and s 12(1) and (2) have given rise to much discussion in
mechanics' lien cases and it is principally upon the provisions of those sections that counsel for
the respondent relies in his submissions advanced in support of the Master's adjudication ...

It was urged by respondent's counsel that s 12(2) is plainly in conflict with the provisions of ss
5(1), 9 and 10 and creates an exception thereto in so far as any claim may be made by an owner
that loss or damage resulting from non-completion or abandonment of a contract by the principal
contractor must be taken into account in determining what amount is justly due, owing or
payable by him to the head contractor. Such a broad interpretation would render nugatory the
restrictive provisions of ss 5(1), 9 and 10 hereinbefore mentioned. The predecessor of s 12(2)
was contained in an amendment to the Act made in 1923. It was made plain in the judgment of
Masten, J.A., in *Freedman v Guaranty Trust Co. of Canada, supra*, that the purpose of the
amendment was to abrogate the legal obstacle created by the principle enunciated in *Appleby* v

Myers (1867), L.R. 2 C.P. 651, where it was held that where a contractor engaged to do work or supply materials for a specific sum to be paid on completion of the whole, he was not entitled to recover anything until the whole work was completed unless he was prevented from doing so by the default of the owner. See also *H. Dakin & Co., Ltd.* v *Lee*, [1916] 1 K.B. 566, as to the rights of a contractor who undertakes to supply work and labour under the terms of a lump sum contract but abandons the work and leaves it unfinished. The learned jurist sums up his views as to the effect of the amendment at p 203 O.L.R. p 35 D.L.R., in the words following:

This enactment appears to me to carry with it two implications: first, that the subcontractor has a lien by virtue of doing his work or supplying materials; and, second, that non-completion and abandonment as obstacles in the way of enforcement of the subcontractor's lien are abolished, and with them necessarily disappear as against the subcontractor's lien the subsidiary concomitants and incidents of non-completion, one of which is that nothing had become due from the owner to the principal contractor. Hence the result of the new statutory provision is that the subcontractor is no longer prevented from enforcing his lien by the circumstance that there is nothing owing by the owner to the principal contractor. In other words, he is by this clause of the statute placed in the same position with regard to enforcement of his lien as though the work as it stood at the date of abandonment was *pro tanto* a legal fulfilment of the contract and as if the principal contractor was entitled to recover against the owner on a *quantum meruit* for the value of the work so far as completed.

In the *Freedman* case the value of the uncompleted building was not determined by an expert's appraisal. It was arrived at by deducting from the contract price of $7,070 the cost of completion which was estimated at $3,800. Thus the cost of the work at the time of abandonment was held to be $3,270. It is not apparent, therefore, that the owners sustained any loss or damage by reason of the completed cost of the abandoned work exceeding the contract price. The owners contended that their claim for cost of completion should be increased but the Court of Appeal refused to interfere with the findings below on that issue. The balance due to the contractor and the corresponding sum available for the subcontractors was therefore not subject to deduction for loss or damage under that head.

At p 206 O.L.R., p. 36 D.L.R., Masten, J.A., quoted with approval the principle stated in *Rockel on Mechanics' Liens* (an American textbook) that a subcontractor is entitled to 'a lien for the reasonable value of his materials and work *after deducting any claims or damages for non-performance of the contract by the principal contractor*'. (The italics are mine.) He then proceeded to direct that an allowance be made to the owners for damage and loss sustained by them in consequence of their being prevented and delayed from occupying the completed house pursuant to the contract, to be determined on a reference if the owners so desired. The Court was concerned only with the amount of the fund as claimed by the lienholders and the opposing claims of the owners and it is plain that the latter allowance would be deductible from that fund, the principal contractor having absconded. If such a claim was deductible from any balance due to the principal contractor before determining the amount divisible among subcontractors then, *a fortiori*, loss or damage represented by a provable excess in the cost of completion of the building above the contract price could scarcely be treated differently. This view is fortified by the learned jurist's observation on p 205 O.L.R., p 37 D.L.R., that 'the general purpose of our Mechanics' Lien Act being to protect the claims of those who supply work and materials so long as the owner is not prejudiced'. In my experience the principle which I have deduced from the *Freedman* case has been observed in practice since the date of that judgment and if that is not the correct view to be taken the Courts of this Province have committed a long succession of errors since 1929.

The authority of the judgment in *Freedman* v *Guaranty Trust Co. of Canada, supra,* has never been questioned so far as I am aware. Nor do I think that the later decisions of this Court in *Len Ariss & Co. Ltd.* v *Peloso,* [1958] O.R. 643, 14 D.L.R. (2d) 178, and in *Vaillancourt Lumber Co. Ltd.* v *Trustees S.S. Section 2, Balfour Tp.,* [1964] 1 O.R. 418, 42 D.L.R. (2d) 610, derogate from its authority. The issue in the latter two cases was not as clearcut as it was in the *Freedman* case or in the present case. Rather, it was complicated by the fact that one or more of the lien claimants had served notice of their claims as contemplated by s 11(6), and that in both cases the owners had continued to make further payments to the principal contractor without requiring him either to pay those claims or to make payment thereof themselves as authorized by s 12(1). In *Len Ariss & Co. Ltd.* v *Peloso,* McGillivray, J.A., referred to a passage of the judgment of Osler, J.A., in *Craig* v *Cromwell* (1900), 27 O.A.R. 585, where that learned jurist, declaring the object of such notices, stated at p 587:

I am of opinion that the notice was sufficient. The object of the notice is to warn the owner that he cannot safely make payments on account of the contract price, even within the 80 per cent. margin, because of the existence of liens of which he was not otherwise bound to inform himself or to look for. The notice does not compel him to pay the lien. It does not prove the existence of the lien. Its sole purpose is to stay the hand of the paymaster until he shall be satisfied – either by the direction of the debtor or of the Court, in case proceedings to realize the lien are taken – that there is a lien, and that some amount is really due and owing to the lienholder.

The present case is clearly distinguishable from the *Len Ariss* and *Vaillancourt* cases by reason of the fact that the Board made no payment whatsoever to the defaulting contractor after receipt of the respondent's notice of claim for lien. It therefore did nothing in violation of the provisions of the statute and hence incurred no liability to pay the subcontractor anything beyond the statutory retention. A perusal of the reasons for judgment of McGillivray, J.A., in both of the above-mentioned cases makes it abundantly clear that not only did he not intend to depart from the principles laid down by Masten, J.A., in *Freedman* v *Guaranty Trust Co. of Canada,* 64 O.L.R. 200, [1929] 4 D.L.R. 32, but he reiterated those principles and declared them to be binding upon the Court.

I should like to add that s 11(9) in providing that no part of the statutory holdback shall be applied by the owner to the completion of the contract or for any other purpose, nor to the payment of damages for non-completion of the contract by the contractor nor in payment or satisfaction of any claim against the contractor, if not quite a statutory recognition of the principle of the *Freedman* case is not, at least, out of harmony with it. I re-emphasize the view expressed earlier that the provisions of s 12(2) on the one hand and those of ss 5(1), 9 and 10 are not in conflict and can easily be reconciled by adopting and applying the construction placed upon the predecessor of s 12(2) by this Court in the *Freedman* case.

I would allow the appeal with costs and direct that the Master's report be varied to accord with the foregoing reasons for judgment.

EVANS, J.A., agrees with SCHROEDER, J.A.

LASKIN, J.A. (dissenting): The appeal herein raises a difficult question which has not, apparently, been laid to rest by the three Ontario Court of Appeal judgments cited in argument and considered by my brother Schroeder whose reasons I have had the advantage of reading. I do not subscribe to his conclusion because I take a different view than he does of *Freedman* v *Guaranty Trust Co. of Canada*, 64 O.L.R. 200, [1929] 4 D.L.R. 32; and having regard to the comfort which opposing counsel have found for their respective positions in *Len Ariss & Co. Ltd.* v *Peloso*, [1958] O.R. 643, 14 D.L.R. (2d) 178, and in *Vaillancourt Lumber Co. Ltd.* v *Trustees S.S. Section 2, Balfour Tp.*, [1964] 1 O.R. 418, 42 D.L.R. (2d) 610, I see some advantage in a fresh look at the issue which confronts us.

[His Lordship was of the opinion that the Mechanics' Lien Act was enacted for the purpose of overcoming the inadequacies of the common law, and as such, it ought not to be given a narrow construction. He then continued:]

What I have said has special relevance for the significance of s 12(2) of the Act, first enacted by 1923 (Ont.), c 30, s 13. This provision is in favour of a subcontractor only; and it suggests that the lien claim of such a person was no longer to be affected by the state of reciprocal rights and liabilities between the contractor and the owner arising out of such a fundamental breach of contract by the contractor as the non-completion or abandonment of the work undertaken for the owner.

Of course, the merit of this suggestion must be tested in relation to other relevant provisions of the Act, and this, in my view, is the nub of the present case.

The common law on this matter, as between contractor and owner, was apparently felt to be declared in such cases as *Appleby* v *Myers* (1867), L.R. 2 C.P. 651, and *Sumpter* v *Hedges*, [1898] 1 Q.B. 673, reflecting the 'entire contract' doctrine; and this common law, reinforced by other contract doctrines under which an innocent party was entitled to refuse to go on in case of fundamental breach and to sue for damages, was read into the *Mechanics' Lien Act* to affect the position of the subcontractor, although the issue of breach or abandonment and consequent cross-claims for damages were between the owner and the contractor. This much at least clearly emerges from *Freedman* v *Guaranty Trust Co. of Canada, supra*.

Section 12(2) was intended, according to Masten, J.A., in the *Freedman* case, to relieve the subcontractor from the fatal consequences to his lien resulting from the main contractor's abandonment of an entire contract. It therefore modified the meaning of the words 'the sum justly owing to the owner', then as now found in s 5 of the *Mechanics' Lien Act*. These were the words which put a limit upon the right to lien; and the abandonment of an entire contract by the contractor had previously meant that no sum was justly owing by the owner. The position contended for by the appellant in the present case would require the Court to consider the contractor's abandonment as still a relevant factor bearing on the subcontractor's right of lien if on the evidence or by an admission (which was the case here) the owner's costs of completion would exceed the difference between the contract price and the sum already paid to the contractor plus the statutory holdback so as to eat up the sum left in hand as representing the remaining value of the abandoned work.

It is this position which causes the perplexity here. In short, is the issue of abandonment and all its consequences as between contractor and owner to be ruled out in considering the subcontractor's right to lien, or is abandonment to have a qualified operation (and in practice a still fatal effect) upon the subcontractor's lien rights?

I wish to refer, in my approach to this question, to other aspects of Masten, J.A.'s views in the *Freedman* case. It is clearly stated in s 5 that the limitation of the right of lien to the sum justly owing to the owner is 'except as herein provided'; and similar words of exception modify ss 9 and 10 of the Act. To what extent then is it otherwise provided by s 12(2)? On this point there is the further observation by Masten, J.A. (at p 204 O.L.R., p 36 D.L.R.), that under the law prior to the enactment of s 12(2) 'if at the time when the contractor abandoned the work there was an amount due to him by the owner, the lien of the subcontractor would, without the aid of subsec. 2, be enforceable to the extent of the balance so due from the owner to the contractor'. And he continues [pp 204–5 O.L.R., pp 36–7 D.L.R.]:

If the amendment in question is to be interpreted as applying only to cases where there is a balance actually payable by the owner to the contractor at the date of the abandonment, it is entirely nugatory and was unnecessary and valueless, for without subsec. 2 the subcontractor's lien was an effective charge on whatever amount had become due and owing from the owner to the contractor at the moment of abandonment. It is reasonable to assume that the Legislature meant to accomplish some purpose when it added subsec. 2 to the Act. But, if any effect is to be given to the amendment, it can only be by making the subcontractor's lien enforceable not-withstanding the fact that nothing is payable by the owner to the contractor in consequence of the contract being abandoned.

It is manifest that Masten, J.A., was dealing with two classes of contracts; one the entire contract, and, second, a contract calling for intermediate payments at various stages of the work or upon progress certificates; and as to the latter the 'all or nothing' rule did not apply, before the enactment of s 12(2), to frustrate a subcontractor's lien claim merely because the main contractor had later abandoned the work.

... I think it important to say a further word about the consequences of abandonment of a contract. The rule in *Appleby* v *Myers* and in *Sumpter* v *Hedges* looks at abandonment only from the standpoint of a contractor seeking to recover for work alone, or for work and materials supplied, up to the time of abandonment. Those cases do not (because they did not have to) deal with the remedies open to the owner as a result of the abandonment. The common law gave him the right, in the case of an entire contract, not only to resist any claim for payment made by the abandoning contractor but also the right to sue for damages even if the abandonment amounted to a material breach of contract by which he was himself excused from further obligation. I would read s 12(2) as embracing in its language ('every subcontractor is entitled to enforce his lien notwithstanding the non-completion or abandonment of the contract by the contractor ...') all the consequences of abandonment, as between contractor and owner, and as making them irrelevant to a consideration of a subcontractor's lien claim. Otherwise it becomes impossible to say that he may enforce his lien notwithstanding abandonment. Certainly, he cannot on the submission made by the appellant herein; and yet there has been an abandonment.

On p 205 O.L.R., p 37 D.L.R., of his reasons, Masten, J.A., considered certain mathematical calculations by the trial Judge to arrive at the value of the work done by the abandoning contractor. One of the sums taken into account was that necessary to complete the building. But it is important to note that it was used not to measure any claim of the owner for damages but to determine the value of the work done; it was subtracted from the contract price for this purpose and left a gain in the owner's hands which it was obliged to disgorge in favour of the liens of subcontractors. Whether value would have been determined in this way if the cost of completion exceeded the contract price is something I cannot answer; but it should be remembered that an entire contract was involved in the *Freedman* case under which nothing was payable (and nothing was in fact paid) until completion. The present case is different in this respect ...

Two other features of the Act must be considered for the decision of the present case. There is, first, the requirement of a statutory holdback for a prescribed period; and, on the principle contended for by the appellant owner herein, this sum will be both the minimum and the maximum to which a subcontractor can resort in realization of his lien where there has been abandonment with the consequences to the owner conceded in this case. There is, second, the obligation imposed upon a subcontractor lien claimant under s 11(6) to give notice to the owner to prevent payments (apart from the statutory holdback), from operating as a discharge *pro tanto* of the lien if made in good faith to the contractor.

The provision for a statutory holdback was already in the *Mechanics' Lien Act* when what is now s 12(2) was first introduced. It should be noted that by s 11(5) the lien of a subcontractor is a charge upon the holdback fund, and thus is minimally secured even if its effect under s 5 as a lien upon land is found to be illusory. (It is arguable that the amount directed to be retained under s 11(5) includes not only the statutory holdback but also the additional money in hand that is intercepted by a notice given under s 11(6), but I shall return to this later.) What strikes me as relevant to the issue in dispute here is the fact that the enactment of what is now s 12(2) must have been with a view to protection of the subcontractor beyond the statutory holdback to which he already had a right to resort.

In this respect, the sanctity or immunity of the holdback fund is fortified by s 11(9) against any attempt of the owner to apply it against the costs of completion or against damages for non-completion arising from the default of the contractor. I suppose it can be argued that a similar express provision should be found to fortify the alleged effect of s 12(2), but I draw attention again to the fact that it is a special provision to protect subcontractors only and, assessed against the background of the pre-existing law, its provisions speak plainly enough to me.

Turning to the notice obligation upon a subcontractor under s 11(6) (an obligation which was met in this case in relation to the $22,610 which is the sum of money involved in this litigation), I do not think that any distinction can be drawn in respect of the owner's obligation to a subcontractor according to whether the owner bowed to the notice or not. The purpose of the notice is not to protect the owner but rather to engage his obligation to a subcontractor lien claimant in respect of money on hand payable to a contractor. If, despite the notice, the owner pays money to the contractor but is still in a position of advantage against him by reason of his abandonment of the contract, I do not see that disregard of the notice makes any difference if the true principle is that asserted by the present appellant. On the other hand, if the owner stays further payments and is found to be in the position of advantage just mentioned, again the subcontractor loses on the principle just adverted to.

As I view the matter, the notice provided for by s 11(6) does not answer the central question in this case; it means merely that the subcontractor lien claimant will lose an advantage he might otherwise have if he fails to give the notice. What that advantage is, with respect to payments up to 80% or 85% of the value of the work done, is not determined under s 11(6).

The matter comes down to this: Does the subcontractor who is entitled to a lien and who has given notice under s 11(6) have a claim upon the money, representing the remaining value of the abandoned work, which ranks ahead of the cross-claim of the owner under which that money would otherwise be absorbed? There are statements in *Vaillancourt Lumber Co. Ltd.* v *Trustees S.S. Section 2, Balfour Tp.*, [1964] 1 O.R. 418, 42 D.L.R. (2d) 610, that require an affirmative answer to this question; for example, McGillivray, J.A., said, at p 421 O.R., p 613 D.L.R., referring to s 12(2), that 'The effect of this subsection is to preclude the owner under any circumstances from setting up as against subcontractors who claim liens a claim for a penalty for non-completion.' This is explicit, and I do not see that anything in it turns on the fact that the owner had disregarded a notice given under s 11(6); and it gives the subcontractor lien claimants rights beyond the statutory holdback. Indeed, as McGillivray, J.A., put it in the *Vaillancourt* case (also at p 421 O.R., p 613 D.L.R.), 'once it is decided that [s 11(6)] requires the said money [*i.e.*, funds above the statutory holdback] to be held back it becomes a part of the contract price in the owner's hands awaiting the disposition of the Court'; and he continues that the Court in turn, where the contractor has abandoned the work is governed by s 12(2) in dealing with the money, and not by s 11(6).

A similar view, under similar enactments, has been taken by the Alberta Appellate Division in *Horwitz* v *Blankert & Anderson (Brick Contractors) Ltd.* (1960), 24 D.L.R. (2d) 684, 32 W.W.R. 540. The Court made it clear that subcontractor lienholders are not limited to the statutory holdback where the value of the work done at the time of abandonment of the main contract exceeds the amount of the holdback and is caught by notice of lien or has been paid over prior thereto but not in good faith. Reliance for this conclusion is placed on the reasons of Masten, J.A., in *Freedman* v *Guaranty Trust Co. of Canada*, 64 O.L.R. 200, [1929] 4 D.L.R. 32, and there is no suggestion that any cross-claim of the owner against the defaulting contractor is to be taken into account in measuring the innocent subcontractors' lien rights. It may be that the cost of completion would not exceed the difference between the contract price and the value of the work up to time of abandonment, going beyond the statutory holdback, but nothing is said on this score in the reasons for judgment.

I would add only that Smith, J.A. (now C.J.A.), speaking for the Court in the *Horwitz* case stated that were it not for s 20 of the Alberta Act, similar to s 12(2) of our Act, there might well be doubt whether anything could be recovered by the subcontractor lien claimant in view of the terms of s 15, which is in terms similar to ss 9 and 10 of our Act.

I summarize my views as follows. Sections 5, 9 and 10 of the *Mechanics' Lien Act*, limiting an owner's liability in respect of a lien to 'the sum justly owing by the owner', and to 'the sum payable by the owner to the contractor', and to 'the sum owing to the contractor', are all qualified by 'save as otherwise provided' clauses. The statutory holdback provisions are, of course, within the exception but so are s 12(2) and s 11(6). It is my view that so far as an innocent subcontractor lien claimant is concerned, the relations of the owner and the contractor *inter se* are *res inter alios acta*. The owner is, of course, also innocent in the circumstances of an abandonment of the work by the contractor, but his choice of a contractor should not be a risk assumed by a subcontractor whose right to a lien is original under the Act and not derivative. It is one thing to say that nothing is owing to the contractor by the owner as a result of the abandonment; it is another thing to say that the value of the work done for the owner should be offset against a subcontractor by the owner's cross-claim against the contractor.

If, instead of going bankrupt as here, the contractor had simply disappeared, should the subcontractor be denied relief merely because the owner would have a cross-claim sufficient to eat up any surplus value in the work done up to abandonment? I suppose a Court could stay the matter or put the owner under a burden of proving that he could not realize his cross-claim without appropriating the surplus value in the work done (beyond payments properly made and excepting the statutory holdback); and, in any event, it may be thought imprudent to speculate on facts not before us. But it is important to project a situation which is within the scope of the issue presented for decision. In the present case there was an admission of the size of the cross-claim; in other cases there may be no such admission, and evidence will have to be led to burden a proceeding with the resolution of tertiary interests. I do not wish to court accusation of begging the question in making this statement. But it falls within the compass of my concern that an innocent subcontractor, who may even have contributed most of the value to work that is abandoned by the contractor, should be denied relief because of a situation which he cannot control and for which the statute puts primary responsibility upon the owner.

I would dismiss the appeal with costs.

Appeal allowed; Master's report varied.

d / Note

In *Noranda Exploration Co. Ltd.* v *Sigurdson* (1975), 53 D.L.R. (3d) 641 the Supreme
Court of Canada had to consider s 19(2) of the British Columbia Mechanics' Lien Act,
R.S.B.C. 1960, c 238 which provides:

As to all liens, except that of the contractor, the whole contract price is payable in money, and
shall not be diminished by any prior or subsequent indebtedness, set-off, or counterclaim in
favour of the owner against the contractor.

There is no similar provision in the Ontario Act considered in *Guttman*, supra and
Canadian Comstock, supra. The Court was of the opinion that the owner could set off
the cost of completion against the notice holdback fund:

A type of statutory provision similar to s 19(2) of the British Columbia *Mechanics' Lien Act* has
been considered in two cases in the Supreme Court of California: *Hampton et al.* v *Christensen
et al.* (1906), 84 P. 200, and *Builders' Supply Depot et al.* v *O'Connor et al.* (1907), 88 P. 982. In
both of those cases, the learned Judges came to the conclusion that the statutory provision was
intended to prevent the owner making deductions for items not arising under the terms of the
contract but outside the terms of the contract and did not apply when the owner was obliged to
furnish material and labour to complete a contract abandoned by the head contractor. It is this
interpretation of s 19(2) which is advanced by the appellant in the present case. I am of the
opinion that such an interpretation of s 19(2) is the only method by which that section can be
reconciled with the general principle stated in s 6 of the British Columbia Act: that the owner's
liability is limited to 'the sum payable by the owner to the contractor'.
To give s 19(2) of the British Columbia *Mechanics' Lien Act* the broader interpretation resulting
from the decision of the Court of Appeal for British Columbia in the present appeal is to render s
21(6) of that statute redundant. [Section 21(6) is the British Columbia equivalent of Ontario's
section 11(9)]. If a lien covers all amounts unpaid by the owner to the head contractor at the date
of the abandonment of the contract by the latter then there would be no need to make a special
provision preventing the application of the percentage required to be retained by the owner
under the provisions of s 21(1) by that owner or contractor for the completion of the contract or
any other purpose. On the other hand, the narrower interpretation of s 19(2) of the *Mechanics
Lien Act* does leave a field in which that provision may operate efficiently.
There may be other accounts as between the owner and the head contractor which would be
affected by such a provision as s 19(2) of the British Columbia Act: the owner might be entitled to
set-off or part of the contract price might have been payable by the owner to the head contractor
by means of conveyance of other property to the head contractor. Such a provision would be
nullified by the words of s 19(2) requiring 'that the whole contract price is payable in money.'
The owner might well be in the business of manufacturing material which material, under the
contract, he might supply to the head contractor at a stated price. Again, the words of s 19(2)
would prevent such a transaction affecting subcontractors' liens. Contractors ordinarily enter
into many building contracts and frequently enter into more than one building contract with the
same owner. There is always the possibility, and, in fact, probability, under those circumstances of counter-accounts and adjustments coming up between such owners and such
head contractors. The effect of s 19(2) is to eliminate all such adjusting items except those
concerned with the very contract in question.

Therefore, the narrow construction of s 19(2) is not such a one as to render the provision useless. It is to be noted that s 19(2), by its words, creates no new cause of action in favour of lien claimants and that such cause of action was created only by s 21. (per Spence, J at pp 647–8).

For an interpretation of the relevant provisions of the Alberta Act see *Horwitz* v *Rigaux Building Enterprises Ltd.* (1960), 32 W.W.R. 540, 24 D.L.R. (2d) 684 (C.A.). (The set-off problem did not arise in that case.) The Saskatchewan Court of Appeal decision in *Western Tractor and Equipment Co. Ltd.* v *Milestone School Unit No. 12* (1960), 33 W.W.R. 249, 25 D.L.R. (2d) 493, is consistent with *Guttman*. The owner in that case was allowed to deduct the cost of completion from the excess of the holdback moneys in its hands. See also: *Otis Elevator Co. Ltd. et al.* v *Commonwealth Holiday Inns of Canada Ltd. et al.*, [1972] 2 O.R. 536, 26 D.L.R. (3d) 140 (Co. Ct.).

QUESTIONS

1 An owner of land (o), contracts with a general contractor (G) to build a building on the land of o, at a cost of $1,000,000. The contract provides that progress payments will be made at various stages of construction. o's architect will certify that those stages have been reached. G commences construction, and is paid a total of $70,000 pursuant to certificates issued by the architect. Later, a workman (w), claims a mechanics' lien on the property, registers his lien in the appropriate registry office, and sends a letter to o notifying him of his claim to lien, in the amount of $150,000. G shortly thereafter abandons the project. At the time of abandonment, the value of the work done, is ascertained to be $100,000. o has held back $15,000, being the 15% holdback requirement of section 11(1) of The Mechanics' Lien Act. At this point o has paid to G $70,000, but has paid none of that amount after the receipt of the letter from w. o thus has on hand $30,000, being:
A $15,000 (statutory holdback)
B $15,000 (owing to G)
Evidence is given to show that it will cost $1,050,000 to complete the project, in other words o will have to pay $50,000 over the contract price with G to complete. w asserts a lien against the $15,000 statutory holdback, and against the $15,000 owing by o to G. o tries to set off his $50,000 damages (against G) against the $150,000 owing to G, and against the $15,000 statutory holdback. Can he do so?
2 May the owner deduct from the holdback a Workmen's Compensation Board assessment for which The Workmen's Compensation Act renders him and a subcontractor jointly liable to pay, but for which the Act entitles him to claim against the subcontractor for the amount he is required to pay? See *Union Electric Co. Ltd.* v *Gillin Engineering & Construction Ltd. et al.*, [1971] 3 O.R. 125 (H.C.J.); *Shoquist Construction Co.* v *Norfolk and Retailers Trust and Savings Co. Ltd. et al.*, [1974] 5 W.W.R. 513 (Sask. Q.B. Master). See also *Rasmussens Ltd. et al.* v *Melville Country Club et al.*, [1977] 4 W.W.R. 382 (Sask. D. Ct.), for a case discussing whether or not the Department of National Revenue could attach the holdback.
3 A contractor did building work for an owner. The work was completed and all amounts owed in respect of it were properly paid by the owner. Later, the contractor was called upon to do some repair work under a five-year guarantee clause contained in the original contract. The contractor hired a subcontractor to perform

the work. Is the owner under a duty to retain a holdback fund? Is the interest of the owner lienable? See *Canadian Cutting and Coring (Toronto) Ltd.* v *Howson et al.,* [1968] 2 O.R. 449.

4 C contracts with O to build an apartment building on O's land. The work is completed on August 4, 1975. O pays C the full contract price on August 10, 1975, neglecting to hold back the 15 percent of the value of the work done and materials furnished, as required by The Mechanics' Lien Act. S, C's subcontractor, does not register a lien claim until December 10, 1975. Can S assert any rights against O in respect of O's failure to retain the necessary holdback? See *Doig* v *Stehn,* [1924] 1 W.W.R. 1169, [1924] 2 D.L.R. 627 (Sask. C.A.); *M.L. Plumbing and Heating Ltd.* v *Smithson* (1977), 73 D.L.R. (3d) 481 (Sask. C.A.).

5 As a matter of policy, what consequences should flow from an owner's failure to retain required holdback funds?

5 THE TRUST FUND

a / Note

The third independent special right given to construction industry creditors involves the creation of trusts of certain funds of money in the hands of their debtors. This procedure is intended to assure that when money is paid over to any party on the 'construction pyramid' (in satisfaction or partial satisfaction of the contract price, or by way of advances of financing) such funds remain 'within the construction group', safe from outside creditors of persons higher up the pyramid, until those lower down have been paid.

One such trust fund is created by section 2(1). Under it, all funds received by a builder, contractor or subcontractor on account of the contract price constitute a trust fund for the named beneficiaries (generally, persons in direct contractual relationships with them). The trustee cannot convert any part of the trust funds to his own use until beneficiaries are paid. Thus, when a contractor receives a progress payment, he may not keep it and attribute it to his share of the profits until he has first paid project creditors. There are two major exceptions to this rule. Subsection 2(2) allows a contractor who has paid out money on account of the contract price himself, to retain that amount for his own use. Similarly, subsection 2 (6) allows the contractor to reimburse out of contract payments, a bank that has lent him money where the loan has been used to pay for work done. (This right is really an extrapolation from the right conferred by subsection 2(2), allowing the contractor to retain contract moneys to the extent that he has paid his workers or subcontractors out of his own pocket.)

A second trust fund is created by subsection 2(4). All sums received by an owner (other than the Crown and municipalities) intended to finance the construction project may not be converted to the owner's purposes except in the situations allowed by subsections 2(2) and 2(6).

Finally, subsection 2(3) creates a deemed trust of all sums already in the owner's hands (or received afterwards) payable by the owner upon certification by a person (generally an architect) authorized under the contract to make such a certificate. These funds remain subject to this deemed trust until they are paid to the contractor or other persons entitled under the certificate.

The duty of an owner under s 2(3) of the Act as a trustee paying out moneys on the certificate of a duly authorized person is to act as a reasonable trustee. The beneficiaries of the trust fund are both the contractor and the subcontractor. In *Bre-Aar Excavating Ltd.* v *D'Angela Const. Ltd.* (1975), 8 O.R. (2d) 598, 58 D.L.R. (3d) 654 (S.C.), the owner was advised by the architect, on whose certificate he was to act, that the contractor owed subcontractors approximately the amount that he owed to the contractor. It paid out the money to the contractor. The Court held that it had not been acting as a reasonable trustee, and should have stayed its hand as paymaster.

In addition, subsection 2(7) makes it an offence for anyone knowingly to appropriate trust funds for any unauthorized purpose. Section 3 limits the time for asserting claims to trust moneys.

Not all provinces provide for the creation of these special trusts. The legislation of Manitoba (The Builders and Workers Act, C.C.S.M. 1970, c B90, s 3), British Columbia (s 3) and New Brunswick (s 2A) provides only for the trust of sums received on account of the contract price. (The Ontario s 2(2) exception is found only in the British Columbia and New Brunswick legislation.) Note that under the British Columbia legislation, a person who dealt with funds which came within s 3 in a manner inconsistent with that section was in breach of the section, even if it was done innocently: *Horsman Brothers Holdings* v *Panton*, [1976] 3 W.W.R. 745 (B.C.S.C.).

Saskatchewan's legislation (s 3) is substantially similar to Ontario's, but does not include the exception in s 2(5) of the Ontario Act. Saskatchewan has, however, made important additions to the Ontario model. First, where any part of the consideration of the contract between the owner and his contractor does not consist of money, the value of that part of the consideration is deemed to be money held on trust for the beneficiaries (s 3(5)). Second, insurance moneys received or receivable as a result of damage to improvements on the land are also made trust funds (s 4). Third, the lien is made specially applicable to trust funds. As well, the lien is given priority over all general and special assignments and judgments, attachments, garnishments, receiving orders or rights of set-off (s 5(1)). Finally, subject to two exceptions (s 3(2) and s 4), the legislation provides for the distribution of trust funds among the beneficiaries on a pro rata basis (s 5(2)).

In some instances, courts have been willing to find a trust relationship in situations not precisely covered by the governing statute, on the basis of the 'intent and purpose' or 'spirit and intention' of the legislation. Thus in *Anden Vinyl Products Ltd.* v *Gauss* (1976), 77 D.L.R. (3d) 694 (Ont. Co. Ct.), the court held that where an owner had notice of subcontractors' claims, money in the hands of the owner and owing to the contractor was impressed with a trust, even though no architect's certificate was contemplated by the contract (as required by s 2(3) of the Ontario Act) and no money was borrowed to finance the project (as required by s 2(4)).

Trust fund beneficiaries have several advantages. The trust funds are not available to general creditors of the 'trustee'. Nor do such funds go into the hands of a trustee in bankruptcy on failure of the trustee. Finally, trust rights can be enforceable in circumstances where lien rights are not. For instance, a right to trust money may be asserted although a lien has ceased to exist because of a claimant's failure to register or to commence an action within the proper time. As well, the trusts may be enforced by beneficiaries involved in construction on Crown lands, even when such lands are not subject to mechanics' liens: *Canadian Bank of Commerce* v *T. McAvity & Sons Ltd.*, [1959] S.C.R. 478, 17 D.L.R. (2d) 529; *Crane Canada Ltd.* v *McBeath Plumbing & Heating Ltd.* (1965), 54 W.W.R. 119 (B.C.S.C.); *Wells H. Morton & Co.* v *Can. Credit Men's Trust Association Ltd.* (1965), 53 W.W.R. 178, 52 D.L.R. (2d) 625 (Man. C.A.); *Bank of Nova Scotia* v *O. & O. Contractors Ltd.* (1965), 55 W.W.R. 103, 56 D.L.R. (2d) 90 (B.C.C.A.); *Cronkhite Supply Ltd.* v *Workers' Compensation Board* (1976), 1 B.C.L.R. 142.

The operation of the trust provisions is not wholly free from doubt. In *Royal Trust Co.* v *Trustee of the Estate of Universal Sheet Metals Ltd.* (1970), 8 D.L.R. (3d) 432, the Ontario Court of Appeal held that a debt owed by the trust beneficiary to the trustee could be set-off against trust funds. The Saskatchewan legislation (s 5(1) noted supra) prevents 'any set-off' whatsoever.

Questions have been raised concerning the manner in which trust funds are to be distributed. Generally speaking, the trustee is under no obligation to make a pro rata distribution amongst beneficiaries; all payments to beneficiaries are pro tanto discharges of the trust obligation, however such funds are split amongst deserving beneficiaries: *Minneapolis-Honeywell Regulator Co.* v *Empire Brass Manufacturing Co.*, [1955] S.C.R. 694, [1955] 3 D.L.R. 561; *Crane Canada Ltd.* v *McBeath Plumbing & Heating Ltd.* (1965), 54 W.W.R. 119 (B.C.S.C.). Thus, a contractor may elect to pay his own workers or any one of his subcontractors to the exclusion of all other beneficiaries. The trustee's discretion, however, has been limited in cases of bankruptcy and insolvency, in which cases equity requires him to make a pro rata distribution: *In Re Putherborough Construction Co.* (1958), 37 C.B.R. 6 (S.C.O.); *Guaranty Trust Co. of Canada* v *Beamont*, [1967] 1 O.R. 479. The Saskatchewan legislation provides specifically for pro rata distribution in all cases. Is such an approach preferable?

A third type of problem arises when trust money is in the hands of a third party, either by virtue of an assignment or through a bank's attempt to reduce an overdraught by appropriating trust funds deposited in the trustee's account. The peculiar problems faced by banks in these circumstances are canvassed in *John M.M. Troup Ltd.* v *Royal Bank of Canada* (1962), 34 D.L.R. (2d) 556 (below) and *Clarkson Co. Ltd.* v *Canadian Bank of Commerce* (1966), 57 D.L.R. (2d) 193 (infra, p 582). Note that section 2(6) was added to the Act in 1970 for the ostensible purpose of protecting banks. How well does it accomplish that objective?

b / *John M.M. Troup Ltd. et al.* v *Royal Bank of Canada* (1962), 34 D.L.R. (2d) 556 (S.C.C.) (footnotes omitted).

JUDSON, J.: The appellants claim against the respondent bank under s 3(1) of *The Mechanics' Lien Act*, R.S.O. 1950, c 227, as amended by 1952, c 54, s 1. Their claim was rejected at the trial and on appeal (Morden J.A. dissenting) ...

The appellants were sub-contractors of Town & Country Construction Limited, which company held the main contract from the County of Lambton for the construction of a public building. Their accounts remained unpaid but they omitted to file claims for liens against the building. On March 2, 1956, the contractor deposited a cheque for $77,000 in its current account with the respondent bank. This cheque was drawn by the County of Lambton in favour of the contractor and represented the greater part of the holdback on this contract required under *The*

Mechanics' Lien Act. The appellants say that they are beneficiaries of the trust created by s 3(1) of *The Mechanics' Lien Act* and that the bank must pay them because it received their money, appropriated it to its own use and therefore participated in a breach of trust.

The facts are fully stated in the judgments of the learned trial judge and the Court of Appeal. I will summarize them briefly. The contractor's head office was in the Town of Brampton and its account was carried in the branch of the respondent bank in that town. The contractor was engaged on several important contracts at one time in widely separated parts of the province. It did not open a separate account for each contract. All its receipts went into one current account and its disbursements were paid from the same account. As far as I can see from the evidence, all its receipts were from owners for whom it was building and its disbursements were to sub-contractors, material men and wage-earners and for the other ordinary expenses of a firm of contractors. Its volume of business was large and its account was very active as is shown in the statement for the period December 15, 1955, to April 8, 1957, contained in the reasons of Porter C.J.O. On December 15, 1955, the overdraft was approximately $70,000. It reached almost $109,000 immediately before the payment in question in this action. The $77,000 deposit reduced the overdraft to $36,000. There was a credit balance in the account on March 13, 1956, because of the sale on instructions of the customer of $50,000 Dominion of Canada bonds held as security. After this date there was a credit balance in the account except for the period April 12 to April 20, 1956, when the overdraft was approximately $7,000. The account remained active until September 1956.

As security for the overdraft the bank held Government of Canada bonds of the face amount of $95,000, a general assignment of book debts, a guarantee of another company, a personal guarantee from the principal shareholder of the customer, and an assignment of a life insurance policy on that shareholder's life. After the sale of the $50,000 Dominion of Canada bonds on the customer's instructions and the establishment of a credit balance in the current account, the customer asked for and received the return of the remaining $45,000 Dominion of Canada bonds held as security. Both the trial judge and the Court of Appeal reviewed in detail the dealings between bank and customer and came to the conclusion that the $77,000 deposit of March 2, 1956, was made and received in the ordinary course of business. These are concurrent findings of fact and should not be disturbed.

What was the extent of the bank's knowledge when the customer made the deposit? It knew that the cheque for $77,000 had been received by the customer as part of the contract price on the construction project in the County of Lambton. It knew that this cheque represented a substantial part of the holdback. Payment by the county was therefore very strong evidence that the officials of the county thought that there were no enforceable mechanics' liens except those that had been provided for in the rest of the holdback. The bank had no knowledge of any unpaid accounts of the plaintiffs or of any other sub-contractors. The bank was in a fully secured position and had no knowledge of any financial difficulties of the customer and had no reason to suspect that the deposit in the current account of the customer was an appropriation or conversion of any part of the contract price to any use not authorized by the trust created by s 3 of *The Mechanics' Lien Act*.

On these facts, with an amply secured overdraft and no reason to press for payment, a bank does not participate in a breach of trust merely because it received payment by a cheque drawn by a third party in favour of the customer and deposited in the customer's current account. It seems to me that in the circumstances, the bank cannot be chargeable with notice of breach of trust. The strongest evidence of good faith is that the cheque was taken for value in the ordinary course of business and that as a result of the reduction in the overdraft and the sale of the securities to liquidate the remaining overdraft, the bank surrendered the balance of its security. It did not matter to the bank whether it was paid in the ordinary course or by a realization of security and the absence of benefit to the bank from the deposit is cogent evidence, on which the trial judge was entitled to act, of non-participation in a breach of trust.

The only knowledge that the bank had of a possibility that the contractor was a trustee was imputed knowledge of the provisions of s 3(1) of *The Mechanics' Lien Act* and I make the same assumption as the Court of Appeal in this respect and take it that the branch manager knew of this provision of *The Mechanics' Lien Act*. But in the circumstances of this case, he did not know and had no reason to inquire into the possibility of a breach of trust and he is not chargeable with notice of a breach of trust. I agree with the judgment in the Court of Appeal and at trial in distinguishing this case from *Fonthill Lumber Ltd. et al.* v *Bank of Montreal* [19 D.L.R. (2d) 618, [1959] O.R. 451], which is based on proof of knowledge of the existence of the trust under s 3(1) and knowledge of the commission of a breach of trust.

The appellants also argued that they were entitled to succeed on the authority of *Minneapolis-Honeywell Regulator Co. Ltd.* v *Empire Brass Mfg. Co. Ltd.* [[1955] 3 D.L.R. 561, [1955] S.C.R. 694] and *Canadian Bank of Commerce* v *McAvity* 17 D.L.R. (2d) 529, [1959] S.C.R. 478]. The basis of this argument is that the bank held an assignment of book debts from the customer and that this document provided that all moneys received by the customer (*i.e.*, the contractor) from the collection of the debts under assignment should be received in trust for the bank, and that if the bank's trustee or agent received these moneys in trust for the bank, they were already subject to the prior statutory trust created by s 3(1) in favour of the appellants.

The fallacy in this argument is that the contractor did not receive this cheque under the assignment of book debts as trustee for the bank. The bank made no use of this assignment and served no notice on the County of Lambton under it. The assignment of book debts, it is true, was registered but until notice was given, it could have no effect on a payment made in the ordinary course of business by the County of Lambton to the contractor. Both judgments in the courts below properly distinguish a claim by the bank as assignee from the present one. There was no stakeholder against whom competing claims were being made by the bank as assignee of book debts and by s 3(1) claimants as beneficiaries of a trust. The appellants' claims on this ground were properly rejected.

The respondent bank also submitted that this legislation was unconstitutional. While it is true that the rights given by s 3(1) do not depend on the right to a lien, it is competent provincial legislation in relation to the obligations of a building contractor, which is clearly within s 92(13) of the *British North America Act*. If there is any force in the submission, it must be because competent provincial legislation comes into conflict with and to that extent is overborne or rendered inapplicable by valid federal legislation. It is suggested that the legislation is in conflict with federal legislation on banking and bankruptcy but in my opinion the conflict does not exist in either field. The bank is in the same position with this trust as with any other trust and the ordinary principles must apply. The fact that it may make it difficult for the bank to deal with one particular class of customer does not raise question of conflict. Nor does difficulty of dealing bring the legislation within the principles stated in *Reference re Alberta Statutes*. [[1938] 2 D.L.R. 81, [1938] S.C.R. 100, [1938] 4 D.L.R. 433, [1939] A.C. 117.]

As to bankruptcy, the creation of the trust by s 3(1) does affect the amount of property divisible among the creditors but so does any other trust validly created.

I would dismiss the appeal with costs.

LOCKE, J. (dissenting): [His Lordship's statement of the facts is omitted] … Had the County of Lambton paid to the contractor the sum of $77,000 in currency instead of by cheque, the money would have been, in its hands, impressed with a trust in favour of, *inter alia*, the sub-contractors and, until they were paid, the contractor would have been prohibited from converting it to its own use. When the money was so received by the contractor it would have been held by it, by virtue of s 5 of *The Assignment of Book Debts Act*, in trust for the bank, subject to what is, in effect, a statutory lien. Would any one seriously suggest in these circumstances that, had the currency then been paid over by the contractor to its *cestui que trust*, the bank, as would have been its duty by reason of – and only by reason of – the assignment, it would be freed of this lien or charge? The right of the subcontractors is not 'an equitable right' as has been suggested. It is a statutory right conferred by s 3.

How then is the situation altered when the county paid the $77,000 by cheque? That cheque and the moneys realized from it were subject to the same charge and, unless the bank should attempt to support its claim on the ground that it became holder in due course of the cheque – and no such insupportable claim has been advanced on its behalf – the situation would, of necessity, be exactly the same as if the amount had been paid in currency. It is perhaps unnecessary to point out that, but for the assignment of book debts, the contractor, after satisfying the claims of the sub-contractors, could have used the moneys for its own purposes and deposited it elsewhere. But as between the contractor and the bank the latter was the *cestui que trust*, the former merely holding the cheque on its behalf. Since as between the contractor and the bank the cause of action in respect of which the cheque was given was the property of the bank, the latter could not attain the position of the holder in due course of the cheque as defined by s 56 of the *Bills of Exchange Act*, R.S.C. 1952, c 15, for obvious reasons.

While the facts in the *Minneapolis-Honeywell* case differed from those in the present matter, the statement of Rand J. to which I have above referred is, in my opinion, directly applicable.

The decisive point in the case is that as between the contractor and the bank the cheque and the moneys realized from it, subject to the statutory trust created by s 3 of *The Mechanics' Lien Act* for the benefit of workmen, supply men and sub-contractors, were the property of the bank, and the endorsement and delivery of the cheque merely passed the legal title to it.

The fallacy of the proposition that by failing to notify the County of Lambton of the assignment and requiring it to pay the moneys directly to the bank, or by failing to expressly require the contractor to endorse the cheque to it under the assignment, the sub-contractors may be deprived of their statutory rights appears to me to be demonstrated by stating it.
[Cartwright, J. and Martland, J. concurred with the majority judgment. Their judgments are omitted.]

QUESTION As noted above, Saskatchewan's Act (s 5(1)) specifically imposes a lien on the trust fund in favour of the trustee's beneficiaries. Had Ontario's Act contained a similar provision how would *Troup* have been decided?

c / Note
Banks have been found liable for similar reasons in other cases: *Minneapolis-Honeywell Regulator Co.* v *Empire Brass Mfg. Co.*, [1955] S.C.R. 694; *Fonthill Lumber Co.* v *Bank of Montreal*, [1959] O.R. 451 (C.A.); *Aetna Roofing (1965) Ltd.* v *Robinson*, [1971] 4 W.W.R. 191 (Man. Q.B.); and more recently in *Groves-Raffin Construction Ltd.* v *Bank of N.S.* (1975), 51 D.L.R. (3d) 380 (B.C.S.C.); varied (1975), 64 D.L.R. (3d) 78 (B.C.C.A.). The bank in this case had knowledge that there were outstanding accounts payable by the builder in connection with his project, and that the builder was in financial difficulties. In addition, the bank was not in a fully secured position. The construction company had violated its trust under the Mechanics' Lien

Act when it paid off the bank, and the bank was a party to that breach when it accepted those diverted trust funds for its own benefit. On the other hand, where the bank receives a deposit of trust funds, and in good faith, and in the ordinary course of business, without knowledge that the money is part of a trust fund, appropriates it, the bank will not be held to be party to a breach of trust: *Standard Electric Co.* v *Royal Bank of Canada*, [1960] O.W.N. 367, 24 D.L.R. (2d) 467 (S.C.): *Canadian Pittsburgh Industries Ltd.* v *Bank of Nova Scotia* (1962), 5 C.B.R. (N.S.) 266, 37 D.L.R. (2d) 120 (B.C.S.C.); *Pilkington Glass Ltd.* v *Canadian Imperial Bank of Commerce* (1964), 46 W.W.R. 345 42 D.L.R. (2d) 504 (B.C.S.C.); *Ross* v *Royal Bank of Canada*, [1966] 1 O.R. 90, 52 D.L.R. (2d) 578 (H.C.J.); *George W. Crothers Ltd.* v *Bank of Nova Scotia*, [1967] 1 O.R. 424, 61 D.L.R. (2d) 113 (C.A.). Do you agree?

d / *Clarkson Company Limited* v *Canadian Imperial Bank of Commerce*, (1966), 57 D.L.R. (2d) 193 (S.C.C.)

CARTWRIGHT J.: This is an appeal from a judgment of the Court of Appeal for Ontario allowing an appeal from a judgment of Gale J., as he then was, and dismissing the action with costs payable to the respondent the Canadian Bank of Commerce. The judgment of Gale J. declared that a sum of $31,999.01 received by the defendant Gels General Contractors Limited and deposited to the credit of its account in the defendant bank, or so much thereof as the plaintiff and all others on whose behalf it sues should be found entitled to, constituted a trust fund under s 3 of *The Mechanics' Lien Act*, directed a reference and judgment against the bank for the amount found due on the reference with interest and costs. The judgment provided that the declaration as to the trust fund should be binding on the defendant Gels General Contractors Limited but that otherwise the action as against it should be dismissed without costs.

The defendant Gels General Contractors Limited, hereinafter sometimes referred to as 'Gels', entered into a contract with the Board of Education for the City of Toronto for the construction of a school. The contract in question is dated November 9, 1959. The contract price was approximately $833,000. Gels entered into subcontracts with various subcontractors for part of the work and material including a subcontract with the plaintiff company covering the plumbing and heating. Work on the main contract commenced about December 1, 1959. As the job progressed part of the work was done by Gels through its own employees and part by the subcontractors through their employees. Some of the materials were obtained by Gels from suppliers with whom it dealt and some were supplied by the subcontractors. Gels paid the wages of its employees when the wages were earned and paid its suppliers as the materials were invoiced without waiting for any progress certificate from the architects. About once a month the subcontractors billed Gels for the value of the work estimated by them to have been done to date and Gels in turn prepared and submitted to the Board through the architects a requisition for payment on account of the contract price, the amount of the payment being calculated by reference to the total value of the work done and material supplied to date and to the total contract price and giving credit for any payments previously made on account. The total value of the work done to the date of the requisition included work done and material supplied by Gels through its employees and suppliers. The requisition was checked by the architects and the amount as approved by them, less the statutory holdback of 15 per cent, was paid by the Board to Gels and deposited by Gels in its bank account with the defendant bank. Gels would then issue cheques to the subcontractors for amounts owing by it to them. During the intervals between the submitting of the requisition and the receipt of payment from the Board work on the job continued so that by the time the subcontractors received payment there was an additional amount owing to them by Gels and an additional amount owing to Gels by the Board.

The sum of $31,999.01 in question in this action was paid by the Board on October 27 pursuant to a progress certificate issued by the architects to Gels dated October 13, 1960, following a requisition by Gels dated September 30, 1960. The amount actually approved by the architects was $31,899.01 but by error the cheque was issued for the larger amount. Gels deposited the cheque in its account with the respondent Bank on October 27.

On October 28 Gels issued cheques to the subcontractors including one to the plaintiff for $14,450 but these cheques were dishonoured because the bank applied the whole of the $31,999.01 on an overdraft in the Gels account thereby reducing the overdraft to $6,419.70.

At the date of entering into the contract with the Board Gels had its bank account in the Avenue Road and Dunblaine Branch of the respondent bank in the City of Toronto and it continued to do all its banking there during all relevant times. From November, 1959, to the end of the year 1960, Gels was engaged chiefly on its contract with the Board but it was also engaged on some other building projects. All its receipts from whatever source were deposited in its bank account with the respondent bank and all disbursements were made by cheques drawn on that account including disbursements unconnected with the contract with the Board.

At the time of commencing work on the contract Gels had arranged with the bank for a credit of $45,000. By October, 1960, the bank had decided that it was unwilling to continue to extend credit to Gels and viewed with some alarm the state of its account. To the knowledge of the branch manager of the bank Gels was being pressed for payment by the subcontractors and mechanics' liens had been filed on July 25 and October 7. In these circumstances the branch manager decided to appropriate the next payment received by Gels from the Board in reduction of Gels' overdraft and not to extend further credit; he did not so advise Livingstone who was the general manager and virtual owner of Gels.

On ample evidence the learned trial judge has found that, at the time it appropriated the $31,999.01 in reduction of the overdraft, the bank, through its branch manager, knew that it was a sum received by Gels on account of the contract price under its contract with the Board and that a number of subcontractors had not been paid for work done and materials supplied on that contract. The contract was finally completed but the plaintiff and other subcontractors have not been paid in full.

The learned trial judge found that on the evidence it was reasonably clear that in the month of October, 1960, between the date of the requisition for payment and the receipt of the $31,999.01 Gels had paid out to its own employees and suppliers amounts totalling more than sum.

On these findings of fact, the question to be determined was as to the effect of s 3 of *The Mechanics' Lien Act* which reads as follows:

3. (1) All sums received by a builder or contractor or a subcontractor on account of the contract price are and constitute a trust fund in the hands of the builder or contractor, or of the subcontractor, as the case may be, for the benefit of the proprietor, builder or contractor, subcontractors, Workmen's Compensation Board, workmen and persons who have supplied material on account of the contract, and the builder or contractor or the subcontractor, as the case may be, is the trustee of all such sums so received by him, and until all workmen and all persons who have supplied material on the contract and all subcontractors are paid for work done or material supplied on the contract and the Workmen's Compensation Board is paid any assessment with respect thereto, may not appropriate or convert any part thereof to his own use or to any use not authorized by the trust.

(2) Every builder, contractor or subcontractor who appropriates or converts any part of the contract price referred to in subsection (1) to his own use or to any use not authorized by the trust is guilty of an offence and on summary conviction is liable to a fine of not more than $5,000.00 or to imprisonment for a term of not more than two years or both, and every director or officer of a corporation who knowingly assents to or acquiesces in any such offence by the corporation is guilty of such offence in addition to the corporation.

(3) Notwithstanding the other provisions of this section, where a builder, contractor or subcontractor has paid in whole or part for any materials supplied on account of the contract, or any workman or subcontractor who has performed any work or services or placed or furnished any material in respect of such contract, the retention by such builder, contractor or subcontractor of any amount so paid by him shall not be deemed an appropriation or conversion thereof to his own use or to any use not authorized by the trust.

The reasons of the learned trial judge make it clear that, had he regarded the question as being *res integra*, he would have construed subs. (3) as modifying the effect of subs. (1) so as to constitute the contractor not only a trustee of all sums received by him on account of the contract price but also a beneficiary under the trust created by the subsection to the extent that he had paid out of his own funds for work done and materials supplied in performance of the contract. The learned judge was however of opinion that he was bound to hold otherwise by the judgment of the Court of Appeal delivered by Schroeder J.A. in *Fonthill Lumber Ltd.* v *Bank of Montreal* [19 D.L.R. (2d) 618 at 633, [1959] O.R. 451] and particularly the following passage at p 470:

It was urged that the bank manager might have believed that the contractor had paid out of his own money for the materials supplied on account of the contracts in question or for work performed thereon with the result, that in using the moneys on deposit to pay his indebtedness to the bank he was not to be deemed to be appropriating or converting these moneys by virtue of s 3(3). Obviously, the fallacy of this argument lies in the fact that he was thereby divesting himself of the money, and s 3(3) only prevents the retention thereof by the builder from operating as a wrongful appropriation or conversion within the meaning of that section.

The Court of Appeal regarded the passage just quoted as *obiter dictum* and disagreed with it. Roach J.A. who delivered the unanimous judgment of the Court said in part:

By virtue of s 3(1) the sums which are the subject of the trust thereby created are any sums 'received by a builder or contractor or a subcontractor on account of the contract price'. When, as in this case, an owner makes an interim payment to a general contractor pursuant to a progress certificate it is made on account of the whole contract price. The certificate on the strength of which the Board paid the $31,999.01 states in terms that Gels 'is entitled to a payment of $31,899.01 being tenth: Payment on the contract'.

Who are the beneficiaries of that trust? It is plain from subs. (1) that they are and were thereby intended to be all those persons who contributed to the totality of the work and material up to the date of payment. Included among them, in the instant case, was Gels which had contributed to that totality through its own workmen and material men.

Gels was therefore both a trustee of the $31,999.01 received by it and one of the beneficiaries of that trust. Subsection (1) standing by itself prohibited Gels from appropriating or converting any part of that trust fund to its own use or to any use not authorized by the trust until, among others, all subcontractors had been paid. By reason of that prohibition a subcontractor would have a preferential right to payment out of the trust fund to compensate him not only for any moneys expended by him but also for his earned profit before Gels, as the general contractor, could have recourse to the fund to compensate itself even for moneys expended by it for labour or material that had gone into the building.

In 1952 the Legislature amended s 3 by adding thereto subss (2) and (3). In my opinion on the plain wording of subs (3) Gels as the contractor was entitled to retain out of the trust fund sufficient to recoup itself for moneys that it had paid to its employees, workmen, material men or subcontractors. The word 'retention' as used in subsection (3) cannot mean retention as part of the trust fund. The 'retention' thereby authorized is a retention which, were it not for subs. (3), would amount to a prohibited appropriation or conversion by the contractor to his own use and a retention in the trust fund obviously would not amount to such an appropriation or conversion. The contractor is still not put on an equal footing with the subcontractor. The former has only the right to recoup itself out of the trust fund for moneys actually expended out of its own pocket for labour or material or in payments to subcontractors; the latter's beneficial interest in the trust fund includes not only any amount expended out of its pocket for that purpose but also its earned profit.

There is nothing in the whole of s 3 amounting to a direction as to the manner in which the trust fund created by subs. (1) is to be apportioned among those entitled and in the absence of such a direction it has been held by Rand. J. in *Minneapolis-Honeywell Regulator Co. Limited* v *Empire Brass Manufacturing Co. Limited* [1955] S.C.R. 694 at 697 that the trustee has a discretionary power and his obligation is satisfied when the trust moneys are paid out to persons entitled whatever the division. Certainly so long as the trust fund was used for a trust purpose the position of the bank would not be affected whether or not Gels unduly preferred itself in retaining out of the trust fund sufficient to recoup itself to the detriment of other beneficiaries.

This passage, in my opinion, correctly interprets s 3. It appears to have been the view which the learned trial judge would have adopted had he felt free to do so.

After discussing the *Fonthill* case Roach J.A. concluded his reasons as follows:

When the $31,999.01 came into the hands of Gels it did constitute a trust fund but for the reasons stated Gels was entitled to retain it for its own use by way of recoupment for moneys expended out of its own pocket for labour and material that had gone into the job and for payments made to subcontractors without thereby committing a breach of the trust. This it did by putting that money within the reach of the bank which, as it was entitled to do, applied it on Gels' indebtedness. That indebtedness had been incurred in the first place when the bank advanced moneys to Gels so that Gels could thus expend it.

The appeal should be allowed with costs and the action dismissed with costs.

With respect, it appears to me that in the first sentence of this passage Roach J.A. overlooked an aspect of the matter to which the learned trial judge had called attention. After considering the argument of counsel for the bank that there had been no breach of trust on the part of Gels because it had expended out of its own funds in fulfilment of the contract during the month of October more than $31,999.01. Gale J. continued:

Had the argument on behalf of the Bank on this point succeeded, it would not have meant necessarily that the action would be dismissed. I say that for this reason: the trust could only be discharged to the extent that all payments made by Gels out of its own funds exceeded any monies retained by it from draws. In other words, to make subsection (3) effective, it would have to be shown that the total of all monies paid out by Gels on the contract prior to October 27 was at least $31,999.01 greater than the total of draws received by it prior to that date, and the fact that Gels expended more in October than it received in that month would not automatically give it the right to keep the whole of the $31,999.01.

I also venture to add that had I been obliged to consider this last point, I would have been inclined to the view, having regard to *Pleet* v *Canadian Northern Quebec R.W. Co.*, 50 O.L.R. 223, affirmed [1923] 4 D.L.R. 1112, that the onus of establishing that the whole or any part of the $31,999.01 was released from the trust would rest upon the Bank.

I am in agreement with the first paragraph of this passage. It will be necessary to consider the second paragraph later.

In answer to questions from the bench counsel for the appellant and for the respondent stated that it is not possible to determine from the evidence in the record whether, as of October 27, 1960, the total of all payments made by Gels out of its own funds in fulfilment of the contract exceeded the total moneys retained by it out of sums received by it on account of the contract price.

In this state of affairs it would at first appear that judgment must go against the party on whom lay the onus of proving the matters of fact referred to in the preceding paragraph. For the appellant it was contended that the onus lay upon the bank not only for the reason indicated by the learned trial judge in the second paragraph of the passage last quoted above but also because it was established that the bank had appropriated in discharge of Gels' personal liability to it moneys which it knew that Gels had received in trust. The appellant argues that the fact that under certain circumstances Gels might also turn out to be a beneficiary of the trust was not sufficient to place on the plaintiff the onus of proving that Gels was not beneficially entitled to the trust fund.

For the respondent bank it is argued that the plaintiff having alleged a breach of trust the onus of shewing that Gels was not entitled as beneficiary lay upon the plaintiff because until that was shewn there was no proof that a breach of trust had been committed.

I have reached the conclusion that in the circumstances of this case the onus lay upon the respondent bank to shew that Gels was entitled as beneficiary to all or part of the $31,999.01, and that it has not discharged that onus.

In determining what result flows from this it is necessary to consider the course of the proceedings at the trial. Before any evidence was called an agreement as to certain facts was filed. It concludes with the following paragraph:

8 Should it be held that the sum of $31,999.01 is subject to a trust and there was any breach of trust with respect thereto to which the bank was a party and a reference is directed, the parties shall be free to adduce such evidence as they see fit as to the amount of the payment of $31,999.01 discharged from the trust and the amounts of the claims of the plaintiff and other subcontractors on whose behalf this action has been brought thereagainst.

It does not appear to me that the wording of this paragraph relieved either party from the necessity of leading such evidence as was necessary to prove or disprove that (i) the sum of $31,999.01 or part thereof, was subject to a trust, (ii) that there was a breach of that trust, and (iii) that the bank was a party to the breach. Unless each of these three matters were found the action would fail and there would be no occasion for a reference.

On the evidence in the record and the findings of the learned trial judge it is established that Gels received the $31,999.01 impressed with the trust created by s 3 of *The Mechanics' Lien Act*, that the claims of several beneficiaries under that trust remained unpaid and that the bank with knowledge of these facts applied the sum in question in reduction of the personal liability of Gels to it. If the matter rested there it would appear that the appeal should be allowed and the judgment at trial restored. It does however appear from the record that Gels paid substantial sums to subcontractors out of its own funds. As already pointed out, there is no way of determining from the record as it stands whether or not the total of the sums so paid by Gels for work done and materials supplied in performance of the contract exceeded the total of all payments received by it on account of the contract price. The judgment at the trial directs a reference in the following terms:

4 AND THIS COURT DOTH FURTHER DIRECT a reference to the Master of the Supreme Court of Ontario to ascertain which of the plaintiff and all others on whose behalf it sues under Section 3 of the *Mechanics' Lien Act*, are to participate in the said fund, and their respective degrees of participation, the parties to be free to adduce upon such reference such evidence as they see fit as to the amount of the said sum of $31,999.01, subsequently discharged from the trust and the amount of the claims of the plaintiff and all others on whose behalf it sued thereagainst.

It would not appear that on the reference so directed the bank could give evidence to shew that Gels was beneficially entitled to all or part of the sum of $31,999.01; the judgment decides the contrary. While the judgment was founded primarily on the view of the law propounded in the passage from the judgment in the *Fonthill* case, quoted above, which has now been rejected, the learned trial judge also indicated his inclination to the view that the onus of proving that Gels was beneficially entitled to all or any part of the sum in question lay upon the bank and had not been discharged. I have already expressed my agreement with this view.

In the circumstances it appears to me that the proper course is to allow the appeal and restore the judgment at the trial.

I wish, however, to rest my judgment also on another ground put forward by counsel for the appellant. Assuming, for the purposes of this branch of the matter, that in fact when Gels deposited the cheque for $31,999.01 the total of all payments made by it out of its own funds in fulfilment of the contract exceeded by that amount the total of all payments received by it on account of the contract price, the result would not be that the $31,999.01 was not subject to the statutory trust created by s 3; it would be, as pointed out by Roach J.A., that Gels was trustee of the fund and also one of the beneficiaries of the trust. In *Minneapolis-Honeywell Regulator Co. Ltd.* v *Empire Brass Manufacturing Co. Ltd.* [[1955] 3 D.L.R. 561], Rand J. was speaking for the majority of the Court when he held that s 19 of the *Mechanics' Lien Act* of British Columbia, which is indistinguishable from s 3(1) of the Ontario Act, did not require the statutory trustee (in that case a subcontractor) to make a *pro rata* distribution among the beneficiaries. His actual words at p 697 were:

Section 19 does not, however, require that they be distributed on a *pro rata* basis. The subcontractor has, in this respect, a discretionary power, and his obligation is satisfied when the trust moneys are paid out to persons entitled, whatever the division. This, of course, might be affected by rights of unpaid trust creditors under other provisions of law.

This pronouncement appears to treat the trust created by the statute as an exception to the general rule that a trustee must hold an even hand between the beneficiaries and not benefit one at the expense of the others but, accepting it as stating the rule applicable to this trust, the situation is as follows. When Gels received the $31,999.01 it did so as trustee but had a discretionary power to pay it to one or more of the beneficiaries to the exclusion of the others. It had therefore, in the assumed situation, a discretion to retain it all for itself. Gels acted throughout by its general manager Livingstone and it appears to me that the only reasonable inference to be drawn from the relevant evidence is that Livingstone decided not to retain the money for Gels but to pay it out to the plaintiff and the others on whose behalf the plaintiff sues. It is elementary that a trustee cannot delegate the exercise of a discretion committed to him by the instrument creating the trust and *a fortiori* he cannot be compelled by a creditor who is a stranger to the trust to exercise his discretion in a particular manner which will benefit that stranger to the detriment of the beneficiaries.

We are not here concerned with any question which would arise if the bank without knowledge of the existence of the trust had acquired legal title to the trust fund. The findings that the branch manager was fully aware of the existence of the trust and of the intention of Gels to distribute the fund among the beneficiaries other than itself cannot be successfully challenged.

For these reasons I have reached the conclusion that even if the state of the accounts, which was not proved, was such that Gels had the right to retain the $31,999.01 this circumstance would not assist the respondent; Gels did not elect to exercise the right of retention. Gels' relationship to the bank was that of a debtor to its creditor; its relationship to the plaintiff and those on whose behalf it sues was a dual one, that of a debtor to its creditors and that of a trustee to the beneficiaries of the trust. It chose to exercise its discretion in favour of the beneficiaries; the bank had no standing to require it to alter that choice. On this view it does not matter whether the state of the accounts in connection with the contract was such that Gels would have had the right to retain the fund in question for its own use had it seen fit to do so.

With respect, I think that Roach J.A. was in error when he said, at the conclusion of his reasons in the passage quoted above, that Gels by putting the money within the reach of the bank was evidencing an intention to retain it for its own use. The evidence is to the contrary. Livingstone's intention, which in the circumstances was the intention of Gels, was to follow an established practice of depositing the trust moneys in Gel's only bank account and paying it out forthwith to its subcontractors who were beneficiaries of the trust; that this was his intention was well known to the branch manager of the bank.

To summarize, it is my opinion that the appeal succeeds on two grounds. Firstly, it having been established that the $31,999.01 came into the possession of Gels impressed with the trust created by subs (1) of s 3 of *The Mechanics' Lien Act* and that there were unpaid subcontractors who were *prima facie* entitled to the trust fund, the onus of proving the facts, if they existed, which would bring the case within the exception created by subs (3) lay upon the bank and that onus was not satisfied. Secondly, even if the state of the accounts at that date when the $31,999.01 was received by Gels was such that it was entitled under subs (3) to retain that sum for its own use, its decision whether or not to do so involved the exercise of a discretion vested in it as trustee and the only inference that can reasonably be drawn from the evidence is that it decided to exercise that discretion in favour of the plaintiff and those on whose behalf it sues and not in its own favour.

I would allow the appeal, set aside the judgment of the Court of Appeal and restore the judgment of the learned trial judge. The appellant will recover from the respondent bank its costs in the Court of Appeal and in this Court.

JUDSON J. (*dissenting*): This action was brought by the Clarkson Company Limited as trustee for certain lien claimants against the Canadian Bank of Commerce and Gels General Contractors Limited for breach of trust. The contractor was alleged to have received a certain cheque for $31,999.01 as trustee under s 3(1) of *The Mechanics' Lien Act* and to have misapplied it by enabling the bank to pay off an overdraft out of the proceeds of this cheque. The Court of Appeal held that the case fell within s 3(3) of *The Mechanics' Lien Act* and that there was no breach of trust. In so finding they disapproved of the dictum in *Fonthill Lumber Limited* v *Bank of Montreal*. That dictum had said that the right given by s 3(3) was merely a right of retention. The Court of Appeal held that it did not mean retention as part of the trust fund but enabled the contractor, where the conditions of subs (3) were met, to use the money for the discharge of his own obligations.

I agree with this interpretation of subs (3). It is clear that the learned trial judge would himself have placed the same interpretation on the subsection had he not considered himself bound by the decision in *Fonthill*. It has to be remembered that the *ratio* of the trial decision in this case was that there was a breach of trust because subs (3) did not authorize more than a retention.

Now the argument is submitted to us that there was a breach of trust unless the third party, the bank that received the money, can show by going through every draw on the contract (and it should be noted that this was the tenth draw) that the job owed the construction company at least $31,999.01 more than the total of the draws. Each side on the appeal admitted that the case had not been presented in such a way as to make this possible. The appellant says that the onus was on the bank to do this. With this I do not agree. The plaintiff, in instituting this action, undertook the burden when he sued a third party of proving a trust and proving knowing participation in the breach of trust, and I think that the Court of Appeal was right in finding on a review of the facts of the case that s-s (3) applied, that there was no breach of trust, that the construction company was entitled to apply the cheque in payment of its overdraft, and that the bank was entitled to receive this payment.

The facts are set out in great detail in the reasons at trial and summarized in the reasons of the Court of Appeal. All that I need to say is that they show that the construction company was borrowing from the bank from month to month for the purpose of paying accounts for the job, that when the time approached for another draw it was heavily in debt to the bank, that whenever it deposited a cheque for the draw it cleared off the existing indebtedness as far as the cheque would go and then began to borrow again to pay off more debts. It was always behind because the owner never did or could pay everything owing up to the date of the cheque. For example, the cheque for $31,999.01 in question in this action was dated October 27, 1960 and was issued pursuant to a progress certificate from the architects dated October 13, 1960, which, in turn, was based upon a requisition issued by the construction company dated September 30, 1960.

I have no doubt that when the construction company deposited this cheque it expected to go on as before. It issued cheques on October 28 payable to subcontractors. These were dishonoured because the bank appropriated the whole of the cheque, which reduced the overdraft to $6,417.70, and then refused to honour further cheques. It is clear that the bank had given no undertaking that it would continue to honour cheques for which there were no funds and that the construction company when it made the deposit had not attempted to impose any conditions that further cheques would be honoured.

In these circumstances and with the rejection of the interpretation given to subs (3) in the *Fonthill* case, I am in full agreement with the reasons of Roach j.a. in the Court of Appeal that there was no breach of trust in the deposit of this cheque into an overdrawn account and that the bank was entitled to apply it on the overdraft.

I would dismiss the appeal with costs.

Appeal allowed with costs, JUDSON J. dissenting.

QUESTIONS
1 Where should the onus of proof in such circumstances be placed?
2 Is it sensible to require specific appropriation by the contractor (to himself)?
3 What is the effect of s 2(6)? If banks are permitted to apply trust funds to existing construction-created indebtedness, should they be able, as well, to force a specific appropriation upon 'the trustee'?

6 PRIORITIES

a / Introductory Note

The policy objectives of mechanics' lien legislation could not be achieved unless mechanics' lien claimants were given some form of preference over other persons having claims against the owner of the land. Thus, mechanics' liens have priority over judgments, executions, garnishments, receiving orders, assignments and attachments created *after the lien arises* (s 14(1)). In such situations, the 'equality among execution creditors' provisions of The Creditors' Relief Act, supra p 404, cannot affect the special priority of mechanics' lien claimants. Where executions are created before a mechanics' lien arises, how does the lien claimant go about sharing equally with the holders of those executions?

b / The Position of Mortgagees and Purchasers

i NOTE A mortgage registered before any lien arises receives priority over subsequent liens to the extent of the actual value of the land at the time the first lien arose (s 7(3)). While most provinces have provisions similar to Ontario's s 7(3), some differ in important matters of detail. For example, in the Alberta (s 9(2)) and British Columbia (s 7(1)) legislation, the prior mortgage has priority for money secured or advanced prior to the *registration* of the lien. In Nova Scotia, the earlier mortgage has priority except to the increased selling value of the land attributable to the work or service performed or materials supplied where the mortgagee has consented to the work (s 7(3)).

Where payments and advances are made on account of mortgages or registered agreements of purchase and sale (which by s 7(6) are deemed to be mortgages) the mortgage (or agreement) has priority to the extent of such payments unless the payments are made after notice in writing or registration of the lien, even though the payments were made after the lien arose (s 14(1)): *Northern Electric Co. Ltd.* v *Frank Warkentin Electric Ltd. et al.* (1972), 27 D.L.R. (3d) 519 (Man. C.A.) (infra, p 591). It has been clearly established that in order to gain priority against competing mortgagees or purchasers, a lien claimant must give the notice required by the statute, i.e. notice in writing or registration of the lien claim; mere knowledge that building is taking place on the land, or that a claim for lien might arise, is not sufficient to disentitle the mortagee (or purchaser) from priority: *D. Porter & Son* v *MacLeod* (1951), 29 M.P.R. 83 (N.S. Co. Ct.); *Security Lumber Co* v *Acme Plumbing Shop Ltd.*, [1930] 2 W.W.R. 663, [1930] 4 D.L.R. 454 (Sask. C.A.); *Sterling Lumber Co.* v *Jones* (1916), 29 D.L.R. 288 (Ont. C.A.); *Andre Knight Ltd.* v *Presement et al.*, [1967] 2 O.R. 289, 63 D.L.R. (2d) 314 (C.A.) (supra p 552). The legislation in force in Manitoba (s 11(1)), New Brunswick (s

9(2)), Newfoundland (s 16(1)), Nova Scotia (s 14(1)) and Saskatchewan (s 26(1)) also requires either written notice or registration. Alberta (s 9(2)) and British Columbia (s 7(1)), and Prince Edward Island (s 9(2)) require registration of the lien alone.

See *Bank of Montreal* v *Ehattesaht Co-operative Enterprises Ass'n* (1976), 71 D.L.R. (3d) 757 (B.C.S.C.), where a mortgage registered under an existing debenture, one day after a mechanics' lien claim was filed, was held to be subsequent in priority to the lien claim.

Problems sometimes arise in determining what are 'advances' made on account of a mortgage and what is the precise time at which they are made. In *Canadian Comstock Co. Ltd.* v *186 King St. (Lond.) Ltd.*, [1964] 2 O.R. 439 (C.A.), money deposited by the mortgagee in a special account to be withdrawn by the mortgagor only for payment of construction costs and only with the mortgagee's consent was held to constitute an advance within the meaning of the Act. Interest on principal sums advanced was accorded the same priority given the principal in *Sullivan & Son Ltd.* v *Rideau Carleton Raceway Holdings Ltd.* (1971), 12 D.L.R. (3d) 662 (S.C.C.), where Judson J observed at p 664 that the

right to interest is an essential, inseparable, constituent part of the advance made on account of the mortgage. Without such a right no building loans would ever be made in a commercial way. The registration of a claim for lien or notice in writing of such a claim cannot stop the running of interest or affect the mortgagee's priority for continuing interest in advances validly made under s 13(1) [now s 14(1)] of the *Mechanics' Lien Act* [of Ontario].

On the other hand, a bonus stipulated for in a mortgage (i.e. the mortgagor agreed to repay a sum greater than the amount of principal actually advanced to it) was held not to be a protected advance in *Godden Lumber Co.* v *Morrow*, [1962] O.W.N. 17 (Co. Ct.)

ii *Northern Electric Co. Ltd.* v *Frank Warkentin Electric Ltd.* (1972), 27 D.L.R. (3d) 519 (Man. C.A.)

DICKSON, J.A.: This is an appeal from a judgment of Solomon, Co.Ct.J., as he then was, in a mechanics' lien action respecting an apartment block, the Victoria Arms, located at 700 Setter St. in the City of St. James-Assiniboia. The block contains 277 suites, a parkade capable of holding 330 cars and a partially completed swimming pool.

The moving spirit behind the apartment block developed was Mr. Frank Quiring, a contractor, who owned or controlled all of the issued shares in two companies, Victoria Park Development Ltd., (Victoria Park) and Quiring Construction Ltd., (Quiring Construction). In respect of the development Victoria Park appeared as 'owner' and Quiring Construction as general contractor. The 'bridge' of short-term financing was provided by Crosstown Credit Union Society Limited (Crosstown) and the mortgage, or long-term financing by Canada Life Assurance Company (Canada Life).

The transaction was effected in a manner which has become common in recent years, by way of leaseback and mortgage of the leasehold. The land upon which the apartment block, parkade and pool were to be built, Parcels B and C, was owned by Victoria Park and sold by it to Canada Life for $350,000. Canada Life as lessor entered into a 99-year lease with Victoria Park as lessee. The leasehold estate thus created was then mortgaged by Victoria Park to Canada Life for

$2,300,000. The leasehold estate is also subject to an encumbrance in favour of Crosstown for $500,000.

Through inadvertence during the course of construction the parkade and swimming pool were in part built not on Parcels B and C but on land adjoining, referred to as Parcel A, owned by Victoria Park but subject to an encumbrance for $500,000 to Crosstown. The encroachment did not extend on to all of Parcel A, only a small part; the parkade encroached seven feet, with a somewhat greater encroachment by the swimming pool.

A new plan was prepared to reflect the encroachments. This plan encompassed the encroachments and land for a set-back required by the municipal zoning regulation, within two relatively small parcels, designated Parcels 1 and 2 on the plan.

In summary, the title situation therefore is this: The fee simple to Parcels B and C is owned by Canada Life, subject to a 99-year lease to Victoria Park, mortgaged to Canada Life and encumbered to Crosstown. The fee simple to Parcel A (covering Parcel 1, Parcel 2 and other land) is Victoria Park, subject to an encumbrance to Crosstown. All parcels are also subject, I would add, to many mechanics' liens which will be later referred to in some detail.

Priorities

The Judge found, and the evidence supports that finding, that Canada Life had advanced under its mortgage the sum of $1,400,000 before it had notice of any mechanics' lien. In respect of those advances the Judge gave Canada Life *first priority* against Parcels B and C. In addition to those advances Canada Life disbursed $20,969.67 in the payment of Manitoba Hydro accounts and the Judge held Canada Life entitled to first priority in respect of such payments.

Section 11(1) of the *Mechanics' Liens Act*, R.S.M. 1970, c M80, gives the lien created by the Act priority over all mortgage advances made after notice in writing of the lien or after registration of lien. Mortgage advances made before notice of lien or registration of lien therefore take priority. The priority accorded the advances of $1,400,000 would therefore appear to be consistent with the statute.

An argument was, however, advanced against it. It runs in this manner. Before the improvements were made, the leasehold estate had *nil* value; the only value presently in the leasehold is that created by the improvements affected by the lienholders; s 4(2) of the *Mechanics' Liens Act* provides that a lien arises from the date of commencement of the work; Northern Electric Company Limited (Northern Electric) filed its lien in January, 1970, in respect of work done in September, 1968; the Canada Life mortgage was executed and registered in August, 1968; s 5(3) provides, in effect, that if the land upon which the work is done is encumbered by a mortgage created *before* the commencement of the work (*i.e.*, the Canada Life mortgage), that mortgage has priority over a lien *only* (*Dure* v *Roed* (1917), 34 D.L.R. 38, [1917] 1 W.W.R. 1395; 27 Man. R. 417) to the extent of the actual value of the land at the time the improvements were commenced; the mortgage therefore had priority to the extent of zero. I do not agree.

Let us accept, *arguendo*, that 'land' and 'leasehold' are synonymous for present purposes, that the leasehold interest of Victoria Arms was of no value at the time it was mortgaged to Canada Life, and that the Canada Life mortgage was a 'prior' mortgage. None of these circumstances serves to negate s 11(1) of the Act, the effect of which is to permit a mortgage, whether 'prior' (one which exists in fact before the first lien arises) or 'subsequent' (all mortgages which are not prior mortgages) securing future advances to gain priority over mechanics' liens prior to notice, or registration, of lien: *Mechanics' Liens in Canada* (1962), by Macklem and Bristow, p 115. See also the recent judgment of this Court in *Winnipeg Supply &*

Fuel Co. Ltd. v *Genevieve Mortgage Corp. Ltd. et al.* (1971), 23 D.L.R. (3d) 160, [1972] 1 W.W.R. 651.

The result may be, as the learned authors of *Mechanics' Liens in Canada* point out, at p 115, that 'a mortgage which is advanced in a lump sum prior to the time at which the first lien arises may not be in as favourable a position as to the amount of its priority as a building mortgage which is advanced from time to time as the work progresses'.

In *Genevieve Mortgage* this Court was called upon to consider priorities in respect of both a 'prior' mortgage and a 'subsequent' mortgage and stated [at pp 174–5]:

Section 5(3) of the *Mechanics' Liens Act* is of limited application. It would come into play in the normal course in the case of a lump sum mortgage fully advanced before commencement of work on the land. Absent this section, the mortgage would have priority for the full amount secured, which could be unlimited. This might work a hardship upon those who later did work or placed materials on the land. Hence s 5(3), which limits the mortgagee's priority to the value of the land at the time the improvements were commenced. A mortgage of this nature is referred to in some of the cases as 'prior' mortgage. The $300,000 mortgage in favour of Genevieve is such a mortgage. The mortgage was placed on the land and mortgage monies disbursed before the work began. There were no mortgage advances, as that phrase is generally understood, under that mortgage. The second mortgage is different. It does not, in our view, fall under s 5(3). It was not registered until December 16, 1968, more than two months after the improvements were commenced. There were progressive advances under this mortgage from February, 1969 to February, 1970. The sum of $664,671.82 was advanced prior to December 11, 1970, the date of registration of the first lien and $107,746.13 thereafter. In our opinion s 11(1) of the *Mechanics' Liens Act* is intended to have application in the case of a subsequent mortgage upon which progress payments have been made without notice in writing of any lien and prior to registration of a lien. The object is to permit a mortgagee to make advances to an owner for the purpose of paying workmen and materialmen. So long as no one gives notice of a lien claim or registers a lien the mortgagee is safe in the assumption that workmen and materialmen are being paid as the work progresses. When this turns out not to be the case the mortgagee thereafter makes advances at his peril.

The Court was concerned, in the *Genevieve Mortgage* case, with the application of s 11(1) to a subsequent mortgage and gave priority to mortgage advances made without notice of and prior to registration of a lien. The same principle applies with respect to mortgage advances under a prior mortgage. Section 11(1) applies to the Canada Life mortgage and not s 5(3).

One of the appellants has challenged the attribution of first priority to the payments made by Canada Life to Manitoba Hydro. The payments were made for heating and lighting accounts and in order to preserve, not only for Canada Life but for all concerned, the apartment building and tenancies. The wisdom of the payments cannot be debated; no attempt was made to challenge the amounts; the sole question was whether it was within the powers of the Judge under the Act to ascribe first priority to such payments. In my view the requisite authority is to be found in s 39(1) which requires the Judge, on the trial of the action, to 'adjust the rights and liabilities of, and give all necessary relief to', the persons appearing before him. These words are quite obviously broad in meaning and in effect; their amplitude is in no way diminished when read with s 39(2) which requires the Judge to 'dispose finally and completely of the action and of all matters, questions, and accounts, arising therein or at the trial'.

Section 11(1) must, of course, be considered. It affords, to any lien created by the Act, priority over payments or advances made on account of any mortgage after notice of lien. The Hydro payments were mortgage payments in the narrow sense that they were secured under the terms of the mortgage, but they differ from normal mortgage advances in that they were not made to the mortgagor or his order, but to a third party for sole purpose of preserving of the asset. For that reason, in my view, they do not fall within s 11(1).

Another question was raised, with regard to the authority of Canada Life to make the mortgage advances with it in fact made. It was submitted that monies were paid by Canada Life without being authorized by 'orders to pay' or 'directions to pay' executed by Victoria Park. There are two answers to this submission: first, Victoria Park is the only party which could properly raise this claim but in fact did not do so; second, although at the trial the only order to pay produced was one authorizing payment of $500,000, additional orders to pay, which had been mislaid but were located after trial, were produced during the hearing of the appeal. Following such production, counsel who had challenged the orders to pay was invited to examine the further orders and pursue the matter further if he wished. The absence of further argument would suggest he was satisfied with the sufficiency of the further orders.

The Judge gave *second priority* to mechanics' lien claims totalling $66,247.62, including costs, registered by those who had not signed conditional waivers of lien in favour of Canada Life, and *third priority* to advances of $321,548.46, plus costs, made by Canada Life after receiving written notice of the lien of Northern Electric. The figure of $321,548.46 appears to be in error; I would think it should read $317,548.46.

Canada Life appeals the loss of first priority of two construction advances, each in the amount of $150,000, made May 1, 1970, and May 15, 1970. The facts briefly are these. During the first four months of 1970, ten different companies filed claims for lien. Following a meeting in March, 1970, all these liens were paid out and settled with the exception of three: Northern Electric, B.A. Robinson Co. Ltd. (Robinson), and Amesco (1967) Ltd. (Amesco). The amount claimed in respect of these three liens was paid into Court pursuant to s 25(2) of the Act, which provides that 'Upon application, a judge may receive security or payment in Court in lieu of the amount of the claim, and may thereupon vacate the registration of the lien'. By order of the Judge these three liens were vacated from the leasehold title on April 28, 1970. Canada Life submits that the construction advances in May, 1970, were made without notice of any liens, except (a) Northern Electric, Robinson and Amesco liens, registration of which had been vacated because of the payment into Court, and (b) the other liens referred to above which had either been discharged before the advances, or were discharged out of the money advanced or the pool of funds set up in March, 1970, by Victoria Park. That statement was not disputed by counsel for any of the other parties. According to the certificates of search filed in the proceedings the mechanics' lien of earliest registration, appearing on the certificates of title is that of R. Litz & Sons Company Limited, registered June 18, 1970. This claim for lien was registered more than a month after the May, 1970 construction advances. Of earlier date, however, is a *lis pendens* filed by Northern Electric on March 10, 1970, and still on the titles. This raises a question as to the effect of s 25(2), and the interrelation of that section with s 11(1).

The purpose of s 25(2) is obviously to clear the title of lien claims, by permitting an applicant to pay money into Court to secure the claims. The money then stands in place of the property: *Bank of Montreal* v *Township of Sidney*, [1955] 4 D.L.R. 87, [1955] O.W.N. 581. Registration of the liens is vacated, but the lien claims must still be established: *Pedlar People Ltd.* v *McMahon Plastering Co. Ltd.* (1960), 33 W.W.R. 47.

It would seem consistent with the spirit of the Act and, in particular, the obvious intent of s

25(2), that if a mortgagee or owner clears title by (a) paying the claims of some lien claimants, and (b) paying into Court an amount sufficient to meet all other registered claims for lien, then, such mortgagee, in the absence of notice in writing of any unregistered lien claim, is free to make mortgage advances to the mortgagor or his order, secure in the knowledge that lien claimants who have neither registered nor given notice up to that date will not later gain priority over the advances.

The Act does not, in my view, give lienholders the right to claim in priority back to the date of filing of a lien which was discharged or vacated from the title prior to registration of the lien in respect of which priority is claimed. Any other interpretation would make s 25(2) meaningless. What about the *lis pendens*? It was registered by Northern Electric prior to the application to pay into Court. It is still against the title because the action commenced by Northern Electric to establish its claim is still continuing. If lien claimants cannot obtain priority over mortgage advances by attempting to relate to mechanics' liens, registration of which was vacated, they cannot achieve the same result by trying to relate to a *lis pendens*; there is simply nothing to relate to. Northern Electric does not have any claim against the lands in question here. Suppliers who filed liens which were later discharged do not have any claim against these lands. If none of these has a claim, *a fortiori* no one claiming through or under or in association with or by virtue of, them has a claim. I would accordingly allow the appeal of Canada Life in respect to the priority to be given to the construction advances made on May 1, 1970, and May 15, 1970. Such advances are entitled to *first priority*.

Non-construction advances of Canada Life, consisting of an inspection fee of $10,000 charged September 18, 1970, and legal fees of $7,548.46 charged May 20, 1971, both dates being subsequent to later lien registrations, will continue to have *third priority*.

The Judge gave *fourth priority* to lien claimants who signed conditional waivers, postponing their rights to those of Canada Life. Subject to what is said below regarding the position of several of these claimants, I would confirm the placing of the conditional waiver claimants in a position of *fourth priority*.

[His Lordship rejected the arguments that Canada Life, Victoria Park, and Quiring Construction were partners in a joint venture and that Canada Life was an 'owner' within the meaning of the Act. He also refused to pierce the corporate veil and treat Victoria Park (the owner) and Quiring Construction (the general contractor) as one entity. The personal judgements granted by the trial judge in favour of some lien holders against Victoria Park were quashed]:
Unless it can be established, on the evidence, that the two corporations are but *alter egos* for Mr. Quiring, or that by reason of mutual covenants, conspiracy, fraud, agency, one of the corporations is liable for the obligations of the other, no legal ground exists for interblending the bodies corporate. The evidence does not support any such findings. A general contractor is liable to subcontractors with whom it entered into contractual arrangements; in the normal course, an owner is not. None of the lien claimants alleged or attempted to prove that it was dealing with Victoria Park. The written contracts were with Quiring Construction.
That part of his judgment in which he gave personal judgment against Victoria Park to those claimants set out in Schedule 5 of the judgment must accordingly be reversed, for the reasons given and also for another reason. Section 43 of the *Mechanics' Lien Act* specifically restricts the power to give personal judgment where the claim for lien fails:

43. Where any claimant fails for any reason to establish a valid lien, he may nevertheless recover in the action a personal judgment against the parties to the action for such sum as may appear to be due to him and which he might recover in an action in contract against the parties.

This section at once creates and limits the right to give personal judgment to those actions which sound in contract only. Nothing in what is here said is intended to foreclose the right of any party, if he has proper grounds, to show that monies standing to the credit of Victoria Park are in fact beneficially the property of Quiring Construction.
[Freedman, C.J.M. and Hall, J.A. concurred with Dickson J.A., Monnin, J.A. dissented in part. Guy, J.A. concurred with Monnin, J.A.]

iii NOTE The decision in *Warkentin* is consistent with a long line of cases which have considered priority disputes between mortgagees and lien claimants who did not give the required statutory notice prior to the advancing of money under mortgages: *Kievell* v *Murray* (1884), 2 Man. R. 209 (C.A.); *McVean* v *Tiffin* (1885), 13 O.A.R. 1 (C.A.); *Reinhart* v *Shutt* (1888), 15 O.R. 325 (Chanc. Div.); *Cook* v *Belshaw* (1893), 23 O.R. 545 (Chanc. Div.); *McDonald* v *Consolidated Gold Lake Co.* (1902), 40 N.S.R. 363 (C.A.); *McRae* v *Planta*, [1924] 2 W.W.R. 323, [1924] 2 D.L.R. 408 (B.C.C.A.); *O'Brien* v *McCoig*, [1929] 1 D.L.R. 906 (Ont. C.A.); *D. Porter & Son* v *MacLeod* (1951), 29 M.P.R. 83 (N.S. Co. Ct.); *C.M.H.C.* v *Wood* (1967), 53 M.P.R. 294, 64 D.L.R. (2d) 706 (Nfld. S.C.); *Muttart Builder's Supplies Ltd.* v *Hutton Construction (Brantford) Ltd.*, [1973] 2 O.R. 238, 33 D.L.R. (3d) 410 (Co. Ct.); *Whitehead* v *Trustee of Estate of Lach General Contractors Ltd. et al.* (1974), 46 D.L.R. (3d) 500, 3 O.R. (2d) 680 (C.A.); *Northern Electric Co. Ltd.* v *Manufacturers Life Insurance Co. and Metropolitan Projects Ltd.* (1974), 10 N.S.R. (2d) 97, (1975), 53 D.L.R. (3d) 303 (C.A.), reversed on other grounds (1976), 79 D.L.R. (3d) 336 (S.C.C.).

c / The Position of Vendors and Purchasers

NOTE Priority disputes between lien claimants and vendors of property are resolved in the same fashion as those involving claimants and mortgagees. The combined effect of section 7(6) and section 14(1) is to put the registered interest of a vendor of land in the same position as a mortgagee.

The effect of registration of a mechanics' lien claim is that the claimant is deemed to be a purchaser pro tanto and a purchaser within the meaning of The Registry Act, R.S.O. 1970, c 409 and The Land Titles Act, R.S.O. 1970, c 234. Where a mechanics' lien claim is registered prior to registration of an agreement of purchase and sale the lien has priority over the interest of the purchaser by virtue of section 70 of The Registry Act, supra, which establishes the general rule that priority of registration prevails unless there has been actual notice of a subsequently registered instrument: *Dutton-Wall Lumber Co.* v *Freemanson and Wilhelm*, [1923] 3 W.W.R. 1317, [1923] 4 D.L.R. 940 (Sask. C.A.); *Harrell* v *Mosier*, [1956] O.R. 152, 1 D.L.R. (2d) 671 (C.A.). Conversely, a bona fide purchaser for value without actual notice of the lien has priority over a lien which is subsequently registered. Mere knowledge that building is taking place on the land and that mechanics' lien may arise does not constitute actual notice. See: *Whitehead* v *Trustee of Estate of Lach General Contractors Ltd. et al.* (1974), 3 O.R. (2d) 680, 46 D.L.R. (3d) 500 (C.A.); *Hager* v *United Sheet Metal Ltd.*, [1954] S.C.R. 384, [1954] 3 D.L.R. 145; *Morton* v *Grant* (1956), 3 D.L.R. (2d) 478 (Ont. C.A.); *George Taylor Hardware Ltd.* v *Balzer*, [1967] 2 O.R. 306 (C.A.); *Sterling Lumber Co.* v *Jones* (1916), 36 O.L.R. 153, 29 D.L.R. 688 (C.A.); *Stinson* v *McKendrick*, [1924] 2 D.L.R. 1000 (Ont. C.A.).

The position in British Columbia may be different. In *Carr & Son and Carr Plumbing & Heating Ltd.* v *Rayward and Bell* (1955), 17 W.W.R. 399, Archibald, Co. Ct. J held that under the British Columbia legislation a mechanics' lien claimant had priority over a bona fide purchaser without notice even though the claim was registered after the issuance to the purchaser of a certificate of title.

QUESTIONS

1 As a matter of policy, should the interest of a bona fide purchaser be subject to mechanics' liens arising prior to purchase? If so, to what extent?
2 M agreed to purchase land from L in a speculative venture. M paid most of the purchase price, but $1,300 was still owed to L on that account. The agreement of purchase and sale was registered on January 1, 1975. Construction began on January 8. X agreed to lend M $1,500 to help finance the development and M granted X a mortgage (registered on January 10, 1975) as security for advances to be made. M's financial position deteriorated, and being unable to pay L the balance owing under the agreement of purchase and sale, he conveyed back to L all his interest in the land, in consideration of the forgiveness of the debt of $1,300 due to L, and of L's assuming the mortgage to X at its full face amount of $1,500. L registered his deed on February 5, 1975. Claims for mechanics' liens in the amount of $3,500 were registered on February 7. At the date of registration of the lien claims, only $750 of the mortgage assumed by L had been advanced by X. The evidence shows that at all times L knew that construction was taking place on the land; he had not received, however, any notice in writing of the lien claims. Settle the priorities of the parties to funds realized on a sale in the lien proceedings. Cf. *Charters* v *McCracken* (1916), 29 D.L.R. 756 (Ont. C.A.).

d / Note: The Position of Execution Creditors: Problems arise in reconciling the priority provisions of The Mechanics' Lien Act with those of The Creditor's Relief Act (supra, p 404). In *Beaver Lumber Co.* v *Quebec Bank* (1918), 42 D.L.R. 779 (Sask. C.A.) the abstract of title of the owner's lands showed the following encumbrances in chronological order: (1) a mechanics' lien in favour of Beaver Lumber; (2) executions in favour of the Quebec Bank; (3) a second mechanics' lien in favour of Hart; (4) several executions in favour of other persons. At trial, the mechanics' lien in favour of Hart was held invalid. The Judge ordered the property to be sold. The proceeds were to be applied first to satisfy the mechanics' lien. Any surplus would then be distributed amongst all of the remaining execution creditors. The Court of Appeal rejected the bank's argument that with respect to any surplus, its claim ought to take priority over the claims of subsequent execution creditors because of the intervening (though admittedly invalid) mechanics' lien. The Court of Appeal held that 'the moneys resulting from the sale of the property belonged to the execution creditors after the plaintiff's [lien] claim was satisfied, those executions being the only remaining encumbrances against the land' (per Lamont JA at p 780). Lamont JA went on to say, however, that

[i]t is, I think, clear that only those execution creditors who executions attached to the land while it was the property of the execution debtor are entitled to share in the proceeds of that land. An execution against goods only of the debtor, or an execution against his lands filed after

the land had been sold, would have no claim upon the land, and could not share in the distribution. (at p 781)

QUESTION Consider the following fact situation. A mechanics' lien action was instituted on behalf of lien claimants A, B and C, claiming $5,000, $1,000 and $1,000 respectively. Prior to the action, X had filed a writ of *fi. fa.* The Court found that A was entitled to a mechanics' lien but that the lien claims of B and C were invalid. Pursuant to s 40 of *The Mechanics' Lien Act*, however, the Court allowed B and C to have personal judgment against the owner for the sums due to them. The lands was subsequently sold for $6,000. Prior to the distribution of the funds, B and C filed writs of *fi. fa.* with the Sheriff. How should the funds be distributed? Would your answer be different if B and C had filed their writs with the Sheriff immediately after the judgment but prior to the sale of the property? See *S. McCord & Co. Ltd.* v *Chatfield et al.*, [1946] O.W.N. 1.

e / Priority Among Lien Claimants

i NOTE In general, there is no priority between lienholders of *the same class*; each *class* ranks pari passu and members are paid on a pro rate basis out of the proceeds of sale (s 14(2)). The major exception is the special priority of workers whose lien is for wages (s 15(1)). This priority is given only in respect of payment out of the 15% statutory holdback on the payments otherwise owing to the workers' employer. In other respects, wage earners rank equally with all other lien claimants: see *Cole* v *Pearson* (1908), 17 O.L.R. 46 (C.A.). Who are 'lienholders of the same class'? In *McPherson et al.* v *Gedge* (1883), 4 O.R. 246, at p 261, Osler, JA defined the phrase as including all persons who have 'contracted directly with or were employed by the same contractor'. Some of the problems in determining which lien claimants are of the same class are discussed in *Rideau Aluminum & Steels Ltd.* v *McKechnie*, [1964] 1 O.R. 523, (C.A.), *infra*.

ii *Rideau Aluminum & Steels Ltd.* v *McKechnie*, [1964] 1 O.R. 523 (C.A.)

McGILLIVRAY, J. A.: This is an appeal from His Honour Judge Macdonald pronounced on June 4, 1962. The action brought by lienholders arose in connection with construction of a home for the aged known as 'Carleton Lodge' erected pursuant to an agreement between the Corporation of the County of Carleton, hereinafter referred to as the 'owner' and Boreal Construction Company Limited represented in this action by D.F. McKechnie, its Trustee in Bankruptcy. For convenience this company will be referred to as the 'contractor'.

The appeal as to the manner in which funds in Court were directed to be distributed between the different classes of lienholders.

The facts are as follows: The contract price including extras was found at trial to be $728,555.26 of which amount there remained owing $202,464.26. $200,000 of the latter amount was paid into Court. The contractor proved a lien for $202,464.26. Subcontractors proved liens for $158,381.51 and sub-subcontractors claiming through Hawkesbury Plumbing & Heating Co. Ltd. (hereinafter referred to as 'Hawkesbury') proved liens for $47,809.92. The judgment provided that, from the moneys in Court, the subcontractors be paid $158,383.51 and costs, the sub-contractors $26,811.74 and costs and the balance, 3,954.75, be paid to the trustee of the contractor.

From this judgment the trustee of the contractor appeals upon the following grounds:

1 That the moneys in Court should be shared between the contractor and those claiming through him in proportion to the amount for which their liens were proved.

...

I find no merit in the first ground of appeal. The method of distribution sought, if given effect, would be in conflict with the whole scheme and purpose of the *Mechanics' Lien Act*, R.S.O. 1960, c 233 and could only be done if that section of the Act which specifies that lienholders are to rank *pari passu* within their own classes, were to be disregarded.

The submission made, using round figures, is as follows: the contractor has proved a lien for $202,464.26. Other lien claimants have ranked against moneys in Court for $196,000. The moneys in Court should accordingly be distributed between the contractor and the subcontractors on a basis of approximately 50% to the latter and 50% to the contractor. The resulting effect would be that subcontractors whom the contractor has not paid and who, as a consequence, have had to file liens would be deprived of their right to recover in full from the moneys in Court and be forced to share the sums otherwise payable to them with the contractor. They would then be required to claim for their deficiencies against the contractor and share whatever sum might be available in its hands with other claimants including those who had failed to file or prove liens. This proposition need only be stated to furnish its own answer. It would be quite inconsistent with the scheme of the Act, the purpose of which, as has been oft-times stated, is to protect those who furnish work and services against an owner acquiring improvements to his land for which, by reason of the contract agreement, he need not pay, and is also to protect them against an impecunious or unscrupulous contractor. To acquire this protection subcontractors must file and prove liens in accordance with the Act. Once they have done this I have no hesitancy in finding, following the principles which underlie the Act that they establish a claim against the money in the hands of the owner to the exclusion of those who have not proved liens and in preference to any lien that can be asserted by the contractor.

Turning now to the Act itself s 13(2) makes it apparent that the contractor cannot share on an equal basis with those claiming through him. It reads:

13. (2) Except where it is otherwise provided by this Act, no person entitled to a lien or any property or money is entitled to any priority or preference over another person of the same class entitled to a lien on such property or money, and each class of lien-holders ranks *pari passu* for their several amounts, and the proceeds of any sale shall be distributed among them *pro rata* according to their several classes and rights.

1 There are to be different classes of lienholders.
2 Within a class there is to be no priority between lienholders.
3 Different classes are to be ranked step by step and moneys are to be distributed among them according to their several classes and rights.

To summarize, a distinction is to be made between classes; and only *within* a class are parties to rank without priority for distribution. The right of claimant to rank, or not, or for how much, against the sum in the owner's hands accordingly depends upon the class to which he belongs. In *McPherson et al.* v *Gedge* (1884), 4 O.R. 246, it was said that lienholders of the same class are those who have contracted directly with or were employed by the same person. It need hardly be pointed out that the contractor is not of the same class as the subcontractors in this action and that its claim to share on an equal basis with such subcontractors is excluded by the subsection above quoted. The trial Judge was empowered by s 35(4) (*b*) to take accounts and give all necessary relief to all parties to the action. He has taken such accounts and has assessed the amounts payable and directed payment to the lienholders according to their class, the contractor, in the lowest class, receiving only the balance after other lien payments have been made. In this he was correct for liens once filed took precedence over any claim by the contractor against the owner and, to the extent to which the liens were allowed, the contractor never had money owing to him by the owner after such filing. As a consequence, the bankruptcy of the contractor having occurred at it did after filing of the liens, no greater interest became vested in the trustee from the contract mentioned than a right to payment of the sum still owing under the contract after payment of liens as directed by the Court. The appeal on this ground fails. I should add the judgment in these lien actions should indicate clearly that the omnibus lien of the contractor has been satisfied, where such is the case, to the extent that moneys have been distributed to those claiming liens through him.

[Consideration of the second ground of appeal is omitted]

[The concurring judgment of Mackay, JA is omitted. McLennan, JA agreed with Mackay, JA] The appeal is dismissed.

[The judgment was affirmed without reasons in the Supreme Court of Canada: (1965), 48 D.L.R. (2d) 659.]

f / Note: Miscellaneous Priorities Problems

In *Her Majesty the Queen* v *C.J. Moulton Ltd.*, (1975) C.T.C. 98, the Federal Court, Trial Division considered the question of whether or not the trust created under section 2(1) of The Mechanics' Lien Act of Ontario is prior to a claim by the Crown for income tax pursuant to a demand issued under section 224 of the Income Tax Act (supra, p 421).

In the case, payments were made by the defendant company to a subcontractor, M, after the defendant had received a notice to pay amounts to the Tax Department on account of M's tax liability. In its defence, the defendant alleged that the payments to M had priority because they were subject to a trust under The Mechanics' Lien Act. It was found as a fact that the payment to M was made prior to payments to the defendant by the owner on account of the contract price and accordingly it could not be said that the payments made to M were out of a trust fund as contemplated by The Mechanics' Lien Act. After making this finding, the Court went on, however, to consider whether or not the defendant would have been entitled to make the payments to M assuming that the trust had in fact been created. After reviewing the authorities, Mr. Justice Cattanach held that it would not have been a defence, i.e., that in fact the claim of the Crown under the Income Tax Act had priority. More precisely, he held that the obligation to the Crown, created at the time the demand was served on the defendant, created a debt due to the Crown by the defendant and that it was appropriate for the defendant to set off against his liability to M the debt due by the defendant to the Crown by reason of the demand. The judgment was reversed on procedural grounds: [1975] C.T.C. 631 (F.C.C.A.).

Cf. *H. & H. Trucking Ltd.* v *Midas Aggregates Ltd. et al.* (1974), 46 D.L.R. (3d) 637 (B.C. Co. Ct.) where mechanics' liens were filed after a s 224 demand was served on the owner. MacKinnon, Co. Ct. J. held that notwithstanding the fact that no trust was created in the hands of the owner, at the time the demand was served, the time had not yet expired for the subcontractors and workmen to file their lien claims:

[T]he intention of the *Mechanics' Lien Act* is to give protection to [those] ... who perform services and supply materials for contracts of this nature. To allow outside creditors, including the Government, to have any priority to these funds defeat this intention. (at p 639)

See also *Anden Vinyl Products Ltd.* v *Gauss* (1976), 77 D.L.R. (3d) 694 (Ont. Co. Ct.), where the Court proceeded on the basis of a concession by the parties, including the Ministry of National Revenue, that a valid trust would take priority over a third party tax demand.

In *Coast Lighting Ltd.* v *Trend Buildings Ltd.* (1970), 11 D.L.R. (3d) 735 (B.C. Co. Ct.) D Ltd. was served with a pre-trial garnishee order on January 7, 1970. On January 13, D informed the registrar of the court that it was holding $998.55 pursuant to the holdback provisions of the Mechanics' Lien Act, R.S.B.C. 1960, C. 238. On January 19 the plaintiff obtained judgment and immediately issued execution against the defendant. On January 21 the sheriff executed the writ of *fi. fa.*, but only realized a small part of the $1,532.62 judgment. On January 28, pursuant to the garnishee order, D paid into court the $998.55 holdback because the mechanics' lien had been withdrawn. Soon afterward, the sheriff received other writs of execution against the property of the defendant. The Court considered the validity of the attachment. If the garnishment was not a nullity, could it take priority over the claims of other execution creditors upon the removal of the prior mechanics' lien charge? Tyrwhitt-Drake Co. Ct. J resolved the problem in the following manner (at p 737):

In my opinion, moneys subject to a charge under the *Mechanics' Lien Act* are liable to be attached under the *Attachment of Debts Act*, R.S.B.C. 1960, c 20; but the attachment is subject to the charge. Should the moneys be dealt with in the ordinary course of procedure under the *Mechanics' Lien Act*, it might well be that the attachment would in fact be abortive, as those moneys would have been properly paid to a person with a prior right to that of the attaching creditor.
There mere existence of a charge under the *Mechanics' Lien Act* does not, in my view, in itself vitiate attachment proceedings what is charged and make a garnishing order a mullity. The effect of the charge is simply that the operation of such an order is suspended so long as the charge remains in force.
In this case the charge ceased to exist while the moneys were still in the hands of the garnishee and subject to it. The contingent right of the plaintiff accordingly became vested.
It follows that the plaintiff is entitled to the money in Court, which is to be paid out to it, and to its costs of the motion.

For an interesting priorities problem arising between a mechanics' lien claim and a subsequent receiving order see *College Housing Co-Operative Ltd. et al.* v *Baxter Student Housing Ltd. et al.* (1975), 57 D.L.R. (3d) 1 (S.C.C.), reversing (1975), 50 D.L.R. 122 (Man. C.A.). The Supreme Court of Canada had to consider whether there was jurisdiction in the lower Court to appoint a receiver to receive the balance of first mortgage proceeds. The trial judge, who had been affirmed on appeal, ordered that any money paid by the mortgagee was to have priority over any registered or unregistered charges or encumbrances. At the time the order was made a mechanics' lien had been filed and litigation was in progress over responsibility for doing remedial work on the building. The owner of the property had sought the order so repairs could be made and the building used. The Supreme Court of Canada allowed the appeal, and dismissed the application for the order, as the priority given to the mortgagee was contrary to s 11(1) of the Manitoba Act, which made a registered lien a paramount legal charge not subject to being defeated or eroded in any manner.

7 LIENS AGAINST CHATTELS

a / Repairers' Liens

i The Present Law in Ontario: Ontario Law Reform Commission, *Report on the Non-Possessory Repairman's Lien* 7–12 (1972) (footnotes omitted)

A consideration of the law in Ontario governing the lien acquired by a person who works on the chattels of another will form the basis of the first chapter of this report. Four areas will be examined: the creation and extent of the lien, persons entitled to the lien, the rights of the lienholder as against third parties, and deficiencies in the present law.

I CREATION AND EXTENT OF THE LIEN

When a workman bestows skill, labour or money upon personal property with the express or implied authority of the owner, a particular lien attaches to such property at common law and continues in existence so long as the property remains in the lien claimant's possession. There can be no lien upon any property unless it is in the possession of the person claiming the lien, and the lien gives the workman the right to retain possession of the property until the reasonable charges for his services have been paid or satisfied, unless the lien is inconsistent with the terms of the contract of repair. The lien extends only to the goods in the repairman's possession upon which the work was performed, but not to other goods previously released. The lien usually arises by implication of law, as an incident of the contract to repair, and is rooted in possession; it is lost if possession is given up, and remains lost even though possession is later regained. An exception to this, however, occurs when there is a conditional surrender of possession by the person claiming the lien, on the understanding that the lien will continue notwithstanding the surrender of possession. Such a lien would appear to be based directly on contract, and indeed it has been held that a lien may arise by contract. Finally, the lien applies, apart from agreement, express or implied, only to the sum actually due to the repairman for materials and labour expended by him and does not extend to warehousing charges; a person who has a lien upon a chattel and keeps the chattel in order to enforce his lien (that is, for his benefit) cannot make a claim for so keeping it.

In the absence of agreement, the lienholder has no right at common law to sell the chattel upon which he has performed the repairs, but in 1878 the predecessor to what is now section 48 of *The Mechanics' Lien Act* first appeared in Ontario, and gave the lienholder, in addition to any other remedy to which he may be entitled, the right of selling, upon compliance with the conditions set out in the section, the personal property to which the lien attached. Section 48 reads as follows:

48. (1) Every person who has bestowed money, skill or materials upon any chattel or thing in the alteration or improvement of its properties or for the purpose of imparting an additional value to it, so as thereby to be entitled to a lien upon the chattel or thing for the amount or value of the money or skill and material bestowed, has, while the lien exists but not afterwards, in case the amount to which he is entitled remains unpaid for three months after it ought to have been paid, the right, in addition to any other remedy to which he may be entitled, to sell by auction the chattel or thing on giving one week's notice by advertisement in a newspaper having general circulation in the municipality in which the work was done, setting forth the name of the person indebted, the amount of the debt, a description of the chattel or thing to be sold, the time and place of sale, and the name of the auctioneer, and leaving a like notice in writing at the last known place of residence, if any, of the owner, if he is a resident of the municipality.

(2) Such person shall apply the proceeds of the sale in payment of the amount due to him and the costs of advertising and sale and shall upon application pay over any surplus to the person entitled thereto.

It may be noted that section 48 does not attempt to create or confer a lien but merely recognizes the common law possessory lien, and confers an additional remedy on the lienholder, namely the power of sale. Such a power of sale extends to every person who is entitled to a lien by virtue of altering or improving personal property by the bestowing of money, skill or materials upon such property, does not arise until the lienholder has remained unpaid for three months, and is subject to certain requirements as to notice. Since the section does not itself create the lien, the common law rules as to the creation of the lien are still applicable; the right to sell exists only while the lien exists and, as was indicated earlier, the lien essentially is a possessory one.

2 PERSONS ENTITLED TO THE LIEN

As we have seen, the right to a lien is not restricted to the repairman of one particular type of chattel, but extends to anyone who for reward alters or improves a chattel for another, and the reported cases deal with liens arising in a wide variety of trades. In addition, the power of sale conferred by section 48 of *The Mechanics' Lien Act* extends to all persons who are entitled to claim a lien.

3 RIGHTS OF THE LIENHOLDER AS AGAINST THIRD PARTIES

The question arises as to the rights of the lien claimant where the chattels upon which he has performed his services are subject to a prior security interest such as a chattel mortgage or a conditional sale agreement. The case law in Ontario is clear that when an artisan has repaired, added to or improved an article in the legal possession of a purchaser under a conditional sale contract or of a chattel mortgagor, the purchaser or mortgagor in possession of the article has the implied authority of the owner to authorize the work and thereby subject the article to the lien of the artisan. This would appear to be so even though the security agreement contains a stipulation that the conditional purchaser or mortgagor will keep the chattel free of the liens and encumbrances, the reason being that the artisan's lien is an incident of the contract to repair and arises by operation of law and thus is different from a security interest such as a chattel mortgage that arises through deliberate action by the person in possession. This result would appear to us to be a sensible one, as it would seem to be onerous to require a repairman, who may often be running a very small business, to carry out a search for, and ascertain the terms of, any security interest affecting chattels before he starts to work on those chattels. This point will be examined in greater detail later.

Reference must also be made to *The Personal Property Security Act*, which will shortly govern most security interests in Ontario; while the Act does not apply in general to liens given by statute or rule of law, it does have something to say with respect to priorities between liens on the one hand and interests secured under *The Personal Property Security Act* on the other. Section 32 reads as follows:

32. Where a person in the ordinary course of business furnishes materials or services with respect to goods in his possession that are subject to a security interest, any lien that he has in respect to such materials or services has priority over a perfected security interest unless the lien is given by an Act that does not provide that the lien has such priority.

Two comments may be made with regard to this section of *The Personal Property Security Act*. In the first place, it refers to goods in the possession of the lien claimant, so it is arguable (but not entirely clear) that it applies only to the possessory lien and would not apply to a non-possessory lien if legislation providing for such a lien were enacted. Secondly, with regard to liens created by statute, section 32 seems to vary somewhat the presumption set out in Article 9 of the Uniform Commercial Code, which was the model upon which *The Personal Property Security Act* was based. Article 9 states that a lien has priority over a perfected security interest unless the lien is statutory and the statute provides that the lien has no such priority, whereas section 32 states that a lien has priority unless the lien is created by a statute that does not provide for such priority. In other words, if the statute creating the lien is silent as to priorities, the lien takes priority over a perfected security interest under Article 9, whereas under section 32 the lien ranks behind the perfected security interest. However, if the proposition stated earlier is accepted, namely that the possessory lien in Ontario is created by the common law and not by statute, then the priority of the possessory lien is preserved over all perfected security interests.

4 DEFICIENCIES IN THE PRESENT LAW

Our main concern in this report is with the deficiencies in the present law flowing from the fact that the lien is possessory, although we shall also make some recommendations concerning the power of sale at present given to the possessory lienholder by section 48 of *The Mechanics' Lien Act*. The fact that the lien is lost if possession of the chattel is surrendered results in a situation that is often unsatisfactory both from the point of view of the repairman and of the owner of the chattel. If the repairman, for one reason or another, is unwilling or unable to extend credit to the person whose chattel he has repaired, (a not unusual situation where he is running a small business), he is compelled to hold on to the chattel if he wishes to preserve his lien, with the following results:

i Storage costs are incurred on the part of the repairman, especially in the case of large chattels such as motor vehicles; such costs cannot be included as part of his claim for a lien, on the theory that the retention of the chattel is for the benefit of the repairman and not the owner of the chattel. Nevertheless, the repairman is put to some disadvantage where space is at a premium and the chattel to be stored is large, and in some cases repairmen such as garagemen surrender possession of the chattel in the hope of being paid eventually, but, upon remaining unpaid, are often not able to give up the time required to enforce their claim through the courts.

ii The owner of the chattel may be inconvenienced as he is deprived of the possession and use of the chattel so long as it is in the repairman's hands. Where the chattel is used for the purpose of earning a living, such as may be the case, for example, with a motor vehicle or a farm vehicle, the inconvenience to the owner may amount to severe hardship, which is compounded if the chattel must be used to earn the money needed to pay the repairman and cannot be so used because the repairman wishes to preserve his lien.

Thus the present law, with its emphasis on possession, often results in great inconvenience both to the repairman and to the owner of the chattel. The unsatisfactory results of the present law are emphasized all the more when it is realized that in many cases, especially in the case of expensive chattels, the amount of the debts secured by the lien is low in relation to the value of the chattel, or, to put the matter another way, the security is disproportionate to the debt. There are clearly situations where it is desirable, in the view of the Commission, that the repairman be allowed to preserve his lien while delivering up possession of the chattel.

In some instances, attempts are made by repairmen such as automobile repairmen to preserve their lien by contract; the vehicle is surrendered and a memorandum is placed upon a cheque given in payment for the repairs, to the effect that in consideration of the surrender of possession of the vehicle, the garage retains its right to repossess the vehicle should the cheque not be honoured by the bank. Such a contract is not registerable, however, and the position of the repairman would appear to be most precarious as against, for example, a person to whom the owner of the chattel gives a chattel mortgage immediately after having the repairs carried out, as far as the question of priorities is concerned. Such a situation is far from satisfactory and we are of the view that it should be clarified through the provision of a non-possessory lien as part of a legislative framework establishing a clear system of priorities between the lien claimant and other persons claiming an interest in the same chattel. The deficiencies of the possessory lien are not of equal magnitude in respect to all chattels, however, and the question as to what types of chattels should be made subject to the non-possessory lien will be examined in a later chapter, although we note at this point that in 1955 a Select Committee of the Ontario Legislature recommended that a garageman should be able to release a vehicle from his possession and retain his lien, subject to his fulfilling certain conditions.

ii *Royal A. Vaillancourt Co. Ltd.* v *Trans Canada Credit Corp. Ltd.* (1963), 37 D.L.R. (2d) 450 (Ont. C.A.)

KELLY, J.A.: The plaintiff appeals from the judgment of Walsh, J., dated September 6, 1962, delivered after a trial at North Bay, whereby the learned trial Judge held that the plaintiff at the time the defendant allegedly repossessed the tractor referred to in the pleadings, *i.e.*, October, 1958, was entitled to a lien upon such tractor to the extent of $1,500 for the value of its equipment and for an additional sum of $3,523.45 for work performed; the judgment also directed a reference to the Local Master at North Bay to enquire and report, (a) whether the sum of $2,473 received by the defendant on the sale of the tractor was fair and reasonable and, if not, what would be a fair and reasonable sum, and (b) to divide the sum found to be the reasonable sale price between the plaintiff and the defendant in the proportion of the amounts owed to them respectively by one John Boisvenue on account of the said tractor, namely, $5,029 to the plaintiff and $5,726 to the defendant. The defendant cross-appeals alleging (1) that the plaintiff had not established the existence of any valid lien, and (2) that the plaintiff at the time of the alleged repossession in October, 1958, by reason of interruption of continuous and exclusive possession, had lost any lien which might have existed theretofore.

The relevant facts giving rise to the controversy between the parties appear to be as follows:

On January 10, 1958, one Boisvenue executed a chattel mortgage in favour of the defendant, one of the items upon which it was secured being an International T.D. 9 wide-gauge crawler tractor; neither before nor immediately after January 10, 1958, did the defendant have possession of the tractor; it was left in the possession of Boisvenue and was used by him in logging operations in which he was engaged; default in the payments under the chattel mortgage having occurred in the middle of March, 1958, the defendant delivered to Boisvenue a 'notice of repossession and intention to sell' with respect to the articles secured by the chattel mortgage other than the tractor; eventually the defendant took physical possession and resold these particular articles. The tractor was, in March, 1958, on the property of the Staniforth Lumber Company for whom Boisvenue was doing some work and apparently remained there until removed by Boisvenue; in August the tractor was taken by Boisvenue to the plaintiff's repair garage and extensive repairs to it were ordered by Boisvenue, the cost of which amounted to some $3,500; when the repairs were substantially completed, the tractor was taken, for the purpose of testing and making final adjustments, to a hunting camp owned by the president of the plaintiff, which camp was about 12 miles distant from the plaintiff's garage; for the purpose of carrying out these tests, the plaintiff attached to the bulldozer certain equipment of its own, a blade and other attachments, the value of which was, according to the uncontradicted evidence tendered by the plaintiff, $1,750; the tests were carried out on two or more successive weekends and entailed pushing rocks and trees aside on a trail which had been previously opened in the camp or near it; adjustments shown by the tests to have been necessary, were made by mechanics who were in the employ of the plaintiff; on or about October 24, 1958, the defendant, wishing to repossess the tractor, through its employee Bradley made enquiries of the plaintiff's president as to where the tractor was; he was told it was in the bush for testing but was not informed as to its exact location; he was also informed at that time that the plaintiff claimed a lien on the tractor for the repairs it had executed; without the consent or in fact the knowledge of the plaintiff, the employees of the defendant, 2 or 3 days later, went to the hunting camp late in the afternoon and worked 12 hours with a crew of men getting the bulldozer out of the bush; a 'notice of repossession and intention to sell' dated October 28, 1958 (ex. 13), similar in form to ex. 14, was sent to Boisvenue, this latter notice advising Boisvenue that the defendant had repossessed the tractor on October 28th and that in default of payment of $5,726 on or before November 5th, the tractor would be sold; eventually the defendant sold the tractor to one Courchesne for $2,473.

This action was brought by the plaintiff to enforce its lien for repairs and for damages for the conversion of the blade and other attachments belonging to the plaintiff which had been attached to the tractor on October 28th when the tractor had been removed by the defendant from the hunting camp. At common law, when a workman bestowed skill, labour or money upon personal property with the express or implied authority of the owner, a particular lien attached to such personal property and continued in existence so long as such personal property remained in the lien-claimant's possession: *Bevan* v *Waters* (1828), Mood. & M. 235, 173 E.R. 1143; (1828), 3 Car. & P. 520, 172 E.R. 529.

It has been consistently held that when an artisan has repaired, added to, or improved an article in the legal possession of a purchaser under a conditional sales contract or of a chattel mortgagor, the purchaser or mortgagor in possession of the article has the implied authority of the owner to authorize the work and thereby subject the article to the lien of the artisan: *Commercial Finance Corp. Ltd.* v *Stratford* (1920), 47 O.L.R. 892; *Bank of Montreal* v *Guaranty Silk Dyeing & Finishing Co.*, [1935] 4 D.L.R. 483 at p 488, 16 C.B.R. 363, [1935] O.R. 493 at p 505.

The existence of such a right to lien in favour of the artisan is recognized by s 48 of the *Mechanics' Lien Act*, R.S.O. 1960, c 233. This section, although it does not attempt to create or confer a lien on personal property, does give to the lienholder, in addition to any other remedy to which he may be entitled, the right of selling, upon compliance with the conditions set out in the section, the personal property to which the lien attaches.

In the present case, counsel for the defendant concedes that from January 10, 1958, to March 18, 1958, Boisvenue, despite the existence of the chattel mortgage in favour of the defendant, had the implied authority of the defendant to authorize repairs to the tractor which would have given rise to a lien to which the title of the defendant would have been subject.

The defendant puts forth two grounds of defence: First, that the defendant in March, 1958, had taken technical possession of the tractor and that therefore Boisvenue, when he delivered the tractor to the plaintiff for the purpose of having repairs executed upon it, was not in legal possession of it and had no authority, express or implied, to order repairs to be made; and second, even if it be assumed that a valid lien had come into existence by virtue of the repairs done by the plaintiff, the plaintiff in employing the tractor for the personal uses of its own in opening roads on or about the hunting camp belonging to its president had thereby given up the possession, the continuance of which was necessary in order to keep the lien alive.

During the course of the argument, counsel for the plaintiff withdrew any attack upon the resale of the tractor as being improvident and stated that he would limit his claim as a lienholder to the proceeds of the sale, namely, $2,473, and his claim for the conversion of plaintiff's attachments to the sum of $1,750.

When the defendant permitted Boisvenue to continue in possession of the tractor after the execution of the chattel mortgage in its favour, it accorded to Boisvenue such a possession of the tractor that any repairs executed on it at Boisvenue's request would have given rise to a lien on it which would have taken priority to the claim of the defendant as chattel mortgagee. The onus is on the defendant to prove that the possession which it had accorded Boisvenue had been effectively terminated by a retaking of possession by the defendant. It is inherent in the finding of the trial Judge that he came to the conclusion that this onus had not been discharged; I consider that there is ample evidence to justify the trial Judge's finding in this respect. The absence from the notice of March 10, 1958, of any reference to the tractor and the inclusion in the notice of October 28, 1958, of reference to the tractor, together with the complete inactivity of the defendant in transforming its title under the chattel mortgage into possession until the latter part of October, 1958, can lead to no other conclusion than that, for reasons best known to the defendant, in March, 1958, the defendant elected not to repossess the tractor and deferred action to that end until October, 1958, at which time the plaintiff had obtained priority over the defendant to the extent of its lien for repairs.

Turning to the second contention of the defendant, *i.e.*, that the plaintiff's lien had been lost by virtue of the surrender of possession by the lienholder when it permitted the tractor to be made use of for the personal uses of its president, there is no evidence to contradict the statements of the plaintiff's witnesses that the sole purpose of taking the tractor to the hunting camp was for testing and that the sole reason for doing what work was done there, alleged to be opening roads for the benefit of the president of the plaintiff, was in the course of reasonably necessary tests. Here again the defendant has failed to show that the plaintiff has lost its right to a lien on the tractor by reason of having interrupted its possession of it prior to the time when the tractor was taken by the defendant forcibly and without the plaintiff's consent and by means of a trespass upon the property of the plaintiff company's president which property the president had made available to the plaintiff for the purpose of testing the tractor.

In view of the fact that counsel for the plaintiff has agreed to limit the quantum of his lien to the amount recovered on the resale of the tractor, the plaintiff's claim should be allowed as follows:

Lien for repairs $2473.00
Damages for conversion of plaintiff's equipment $1750.00

The appeal will be allowed with costs, the judgment below will be varied and as varied will provide that the plaintiff recover from the defendant the sum of $4,223 and costs.
Appeal allowed.

iii NOTE: THE LAW IN OTHER PROVINCES The legislation of four provinces provides for the preservation of the lien against motor vehicles in certain cases where the lien-holder no longer has possession of the chattel: Alberta – The Garagemen's Lien Act, R.S.A. 1970, c 155, as amended; British Columbia – Mechanics' Lien Act, R.S.B.C. 1960, c 238, as amended; Manitoba – The Garage Keepers' Act, C.C.S.M., c G10; Saskatchewan – The Garage Keepers' Act, 1970, S.S. 1970, c 25.

Generally speaking this legislation provides that where a garageman, before surrendering possession of a motor vehicle or aircraft, obtains an acknowledgment of indebtedness, his lien is not lost by the surrender of possession of the chattel if he files an affidavit or claim for lien at a specified place, within a specified time. The lien continues for a further specified period. It will cease to exist after that time unless the chattel has been seized in accordance with the provisions of the legislation. Note that the non-possessory lien in Manitoba's statute does not extend to aircraft but does extend to farm vehicles.

The Alberta, British Columbia and Manitoba legislation generally provides that once the lienholder surrenders possession of the chattel, in a priority contest with a subsequently created charge or claim on the vehicle, priority of registration prevails. The Saskatchewan legislation, however, provides that the lien has priority over the interest of a conditional seller or chattel mortgagee whether or not such interest was created before or after the creation of the garage keeper's lien. Note that this provision is not applicable to defeat the interest of a bona fide purchaser, for value, without notice of the lien, where such interest arose when the vehicle was out of the garage keeper's possession and before the filing of a lien claim.

In light of the legislative framework found in these provinces, the Ontario Law Reform Commission has recommended that Ontario enact similar legislation creating a non-possessory lien covering the repair of automobiles, trucks, farm tractors, snowmobiles, other types of motor vehicles and aircraft. (*Report*, supra, at p 27). The non-possessory lien would cease unless a lien claim is registered within twenty-one days after the surrender of the vehicle. The claim would have to be registered with the registrar of personal property security pursuant to The Personal Property Security Act, R.S.O. 1970, c 344. The Commission also makes four recommendations regarding priorities between the garageman's non-possessory lien and other interests in the same vehicle:

i where a garageman has registered a claim of lien, the lien should take priority over a security interest under *The Personal Property Security Act* which arose and was perfected before the services giving rise to the non-possessory lien were performed,
ii where a garageman has registered a claim of lien, the lien should be subject to a security interest under *The Personal Property Security Act* which was created and registered in good faith without express notice of the lien after the surrender of possession of the vehicle and before

the claim of lien was registered, but the lien should be clearly stated to have priority over the security interest in all other circumstances,
iii a person who purchases a vehicle in good faith, without express notice of the lien, after possession of the vehicle has been surrendered by the garageman and before the latter has registered his claim of lien, should take the vehicle free of the claim of the garageman,
iv where two or more garagemen claim a non-possessory lien upon the same vehicle, the order of registration should determine priorities among them (at p 44 of the Report).

QUESTIONS What do you think of the Law Reform Commission's recommendations? Should the non-possessory lien be extended to all chattels? Why or why not?

b / Note: Miscellaneous Liens
At common law or by statute, a wide variety of persons are entitled to liens for labour or expenditure on chattels entrusted to them. They include the following:
1 accountants, on books of account: *Compass Mapping Corp. of Canada Ltd.* v *Maw, Devonshire & Co.* (1954), 11 W.W.R. (N.S.) 108 (Alta. S.C.)
2 artists, on portraits painted: *Dempsey* v *Carson* (1862), 11 U.C.C.P. 462
3 cab drivers, on baggage transported: *McQuarrie* v *Duggan* (1910), 44 N.S.R. 185 (C.A.)
4 innkeepers, on guests' personal effects: *United Typewriter Co.* v *King Edward Hotel Co.* (1914), 32 O.L.R. 126 (C.A.); *The Innkeepers Act*, R.S.O. 1970, c 223, s 2(1)
5 solicitors, on clients' documents: *Re Andrew Motherwell Ltd.* (1921), 21 O.W.N. 108
6 veterinarians, on animals treated: *McBride* v *Bailey* (1857), 6 U.C.C.P. 523
7 warehousemen, on property stored: *The Warehousemen's Lien Act*, R.S.O. 1970, c 488.

17
Impeachable Transactions

I INTRODUCTION

The problems to which the law of impeachable transactions is addressed are not of recent origin. As noted in Loisseaux, *Cases on Creditors Remedies* 249 (1966),

[T]he dishonest person in debt, or facing a large prospective debt, has for at least the past four centuries tended to react in the same manner. The debtor will attempt to conceal some or all of his property. If he is a little more sophisticated he will frequently try to convey it to a relative or a friend, who will make an express promise to return the property after the financial trouble has passed. In more desperate straits, such a debtor may simply transfer his assets to friends and relatives for little or no consideration, just to keep the assets from his creditors.

A second problem faces creditors of a debtor with multiple creditors. The debtor will frequently make a transfer of his property which benefits some but prejudices others of his creditors. Freely permitting such transfers would subvert the priorities among creditors otherwise established by law (e.g. by The Creditors Relief Act).

The present law of fraudulent conveyances, as the first type of transfers referred to are termed, is derived from the Statute of Elizabeth, 13 Eliz., c 5 (1570). The statute imposed criminal penalties on the guilty debtors, with jurisdiction in the Star Chamber, and also declared the transfers to be void. The nature of the transactions struck at by the statute is apparent from its first paragraph:

AN ACT AGAINST FRAUDULENT DEEDS, ALIENATIONS, ETC.
For the avoiding and abolishing of feigned, covinous and fraudulent feoffments, gifts, grants, alienations, conveyances, bonds, suits, judgments and executions, as well of lands and tenements as of goods and chattels, more commonly used and practised in these days than hath been seen or heard heretofore: which feoffments, gifts, grants, alienations, conveyances, bonds, suits, judgments and executions, have been and are devised and contrived of malice, fraud, covin, collusion or guile, to the end, purpose and intent, to delay, hinder or defraud creditors and others of their just and lawful actions, suits, debts, accounts, damages, penalties, forfeitures, heriots, mortuaries and reliefs, not only to the let or hindrance of the due course and execution of law and justice, but also to the overthrow of all true and plain dealing, bargaining and chevisance between man and man, without which no commonwealth or civil society can be maintained or continued.

The most celebrated early application of the statute occurred in *Twyne's Case* (1601), 3 Co. Rep. 806, 76 E.R. 809 (Star Chamber). In 1600, Pierce sold sheep to

Twyne, who did not drive them away, as ordinarily he should have done. After some time had elapsed, and Pierce had shorn the sheep and marked them as his own, a judgment creditor of Pierce attempted to have the sheep seized in execution. Twyne then appeared to block the seizure, asserting that the sheep were his.

The Court held that the conveyance had the signs and marks of fraud. The donor continued in possession, and used the sheep as his own; he traded with others on these terms, with the result that he defrauded and deceived them. The transfer was made in secret, and it was made pending the writ; there was a trust between the parties, and trust is the cover of fraud.

The report of the case concludes:

and therefore, reader, when any gift shall be to you in satisfaction of a debt, by one who is indebted to others also; 1st, Let it be made in a public manner, and before the neighbours, and not in private, for secrecy is a mark of fraud. 2nd, Let the goods and chattels be appraised by good people to the very value, and take a gift in particular in satisfaction of your debt. 3rd, Immediately after the gift, take the possession of them; for continuance of the possession in the donor, is a sign of trust ... And by the judgment of the whole Court Twyne was convicted of fraud, and he and all the others of a riot

Fraudulent preferences, as the second type of transfers are called, were forbidden neither at common law nor under the Statute of Elizabeth; a debtor could pay his debts in any order he pleased. It is only under modern statutes that these transactions may be set aside.

In some provinces, a single statute now governs both conveyances and preferences; others have separate statutes for each. In addition, the Statute of Elizabeth is still in force in several provinces as part of their received law, either instead of or along side of fraudulent conveyances legislation.

The relevant legislation is as follows: in Alberta, The Fraudulent Preferences Act, R.S.A. 1970, c 148; in British Columbia, Fraudulent Conveyances Act, R.S.B.C. 1960, c 155, and Fraudulent Preferences Act, R.S.B.C. 1960, c 156; in Manitoba, The Assignments Act, C.C.S.M., c A150, and The Fraudulent Conveyances Act, C.C.S.M., c F160; in New Brunswick, Assignments and Preferences Act, R.S.N.B. 1972, c A-16; in Newfoundland, The Fraudulent Conveyances Act. S.N. 1974, c 29; in Nova Scotia, Assignments and Preferences Act, R.S.N.S. 1967, c 16; in Ontario, The Assignments and Preferences Act, R.S.O. 1970, c 34, and The Fraudulent Conveyances Act, R.S.O. 1970, c 182; in Prince Edward Island, Frauds on Creditors Act, R.S.P.E.I. 1974, c F-13; in Quebec, Civil Code, arts. 1032–40; and in Saskatchewan, The Fraudulent Preferences Act, R.S.S. 1965, c 397.

Where the debtor is a bankrupt, fraudulent conveyances and preferences may be set aside by the trustee in bankruptcy. Under the Bankruptcy Act, R.S.C. 1970, c B-3, s 50(6), the trustee is expressly authorized to use remedies provided by provincial law for this purpose, in addition to those set out in the Act itself. In the Bankruptcy Bill (s-14), section 10(3) prohibits the trustee from resorting to provincial fraudulent transactions legislation. For a discussion of the constitutional issues arising out of the co-existence of provincial legislation with the Bankruptcy Act, see pp 643–5, 708–18, infra; pp 806–32 concerning the power of the trustee to set aside and review antecedent transactions of the bankrupt.

2 FRAUDULENT CONVEYANCES

a / The Legislation

i The Fraudulent Conveyances Act, R.S.O. 1970, c 182

1. In this Act,
   (*a*) 'conveyance' includes gift, grant, alienation, bargain, charge, encumbrance, limitation of use or uses of, in, to or out of real property or personal property by writing or otherwise;
   (*b*) 'personal property' includes goods, chattels, effects, bills, bonds, notes and securities, and shares, dividends, premiums and bonuses in a bank, company or corporation, and any interest therein;
   (*c*) 'real property' includes lands, tenements, hereditaments and any estate or interest therein.

2. Every conveyance of real property or personal property and every bond, suit, judgment and execution heretofore or hereafter made with intent to defeat, hinder, delay or defraud creditors or others of their just and lawful actions, suits, debts, accounts, damages, penalties or forfeitures are void as against such persons and their assigns.

3. Section 2 does not apply to an estate or interest in real property or personal property conveyed upon good consideration and *bona fide* to a person not having at the time of the conveyance to him notice or knowledge of the intent set forth in that section.

4. Section 2 applies to every conveyance executed with the intent set forth in that section notwithstanding that it was executed upon a valuable consideration and with the intention, as between the parties to it, of actually transferring to and for the benefit of the transferee the interest expressed to be thereby transferred, unless it is protected under section 3 by reason of *bona fides* and want of notice or knowledge on the part of the purchaser.

5. Every conveyance of real property heretofore or hereafter made with intent to defraud and deceive the purchaser shall be deemed to be void only as against that person and his assigns and all persons lawfully claiming under him or them who have purchased or hereafter purchased for money or other good consideration the same real property or a part thereof.

ii Supreme Court of Ontario, Rules of Practice, R.R.O. 1970, Reg. 545

Rule 589
The court may order any clerk or employee or former clerk or employee of the judgment debtor, or any person or the officer or officers of any corporation to whom the debtor has made a transfer of his property or effects, exigible under execution, since the date when the liability or debt that was the subject of the action in which judgment was obtained was incurred, or, where the judgment is for costs only, since the commencement of the cause or matter, to submit to being examined upon oath as to the estate and effects of the debtor, and as to the property and means he had when the debt or liability aforesaid was incurred, or, in the case of a judgment for costs only, at the date of the commencement of the cause or matter, and as to the property or means he still has of discharging the judgment, and as to the disposal he has made of any property since contracting the debt or incurring the liability, and as to any and what debts are owing to him.

Rule 590
Where the court is satisfied that there is reasonable ground for supposing that a person or corporation is in possession of any property of the judgment debtor exigible under execution, it

may order such person or any officer of the corporation to attend and submit to examination touching the property and means of the judgment debtor.

b / Introductory Note

The conveyances which may be set aside under The Fraudulent Conveyances Act are those entered into 'with intent to defeat, hinder, delay or defraud creditors or others'. The nature of the requisite intent varies according to whether the transfer is made voluntarily (i.e. without consideration) or for good consideration. As Armour CJ explained in *Oliver* v *McLaughlin* (1893), 24 O.R. 41 (C.A.)

> where a conveyance is made upon good consideration ... it is necessary under the statute in order to set it aside to shew the fraudulent intent of both parties to it. But where a conveyance is voluntary, it is only necessary to shew the fraudulent intent of the maker of it.

The burden of proving intention is also less onerous in the latter situation than in the former. Where the conveyance is voluntary and has the effect of hindering creditors, it may be that intention will be inferred: *Freeman* v *Pope* (1870), L.R. 5 Ch. App. 538, infra; but cf. *Ex parte Mercer* (1886), 17 Q.B.D. 290 (C.A.), infra p 615; *Mandryk* v *Merko* (1972), 19 D.L.R. (3d) 238 (Man. C.A.), infra p 617. However, where the transfer is made for valuable consideration, those seeking to set it aside must show an actual fraudulent intent shared by both parties to the transfer, and this is so even when the transferee is aware of the insolvent circumstances of the debtor: *Hickerson* v *Parrington* (1891), 18 O.A.R. 635. Meeting this burden will be easier if the creditor can point to certain 'badges of fraud' marking the transaction; these are discussed in *Solomon* v *Solomon* (1977), 79 D.L.R. (3d) 264 (Ont. H.C.J.), infra p 631.

Where the transfer is between close relatives, the burden of upholding the transaction may shift to the parties to it: *Koop* v *Smith* (1915), 25 D.L.R. 355 (S.C.C.), infra p 637. One final circumstance which may give rise to an inference of fraudulent intent is the transfer of property by a debtor on the eve of entering a hazardous business: *Mackay* v *Douglas* (1892), L.R. 14 Eq. 106, infra p 624.

Note that it is only a transfer of exigible property which may be attacked as a fraudulent conveyance: *Lodor* v *Creighton* (1860), 9 U.C.C.P. 295.

In *Robert Reiser & Co.* v *Nadore Food Processing Equipment Ltd.* (1977), 81 D.L.R. (3d) 278 (Ont. H.C.J.), Steele J held that an interlocutory injunction may be granted in an action to set aside a conveyance, provided the court is satisfied that there is a strong indication that the conveyance may have been fraudulent.

c / Voluntary Conveyances

i The Requirement of Intent

Freeman v *Pope* (1870), L.R. 5 Ch. App. 538

LORD HATHERLEY, L.C.: The principle on which the statute of 13 Eliz. c 5 proceeds is this, that persons must be just before they are generous, and that debts must be paid before gifts can be made.

The difficulty the Vice-Chancellor seems to have felt in this case was, that if he, as a special juryman, had been asked whether there was actually any intention on the part of the settlor in this case to defeat, hinder, or delay his creditors, he should have come to the conclusion that he had no such intention. With great deference to the view of the Vice-Chancellor, and with all the respect which I most unfeignedly entertain for his judgment, it appears to me that this does not put the question exactly on the right ground; for it would never be left to a special jury to find, *simpliciter*, whether the settlor intended to defeat, hinder, or delay his creditors, without a direction from the Judge that if the necessary effect of the instrument was to defeat, hinder, or delay the creditors, that necessary effect was to be considered as evidencing an intention to do so. A jury would undoubtedly be so directed, lest they should fall into the error of speculating as to what was actually passing in the mind of the settlor, which can hardly ever be satisfactorily ascertained, instead of judging of his intention by the necessary consequences of his act, which consequences can always be estimated from the facts of the case. Of course there may be cases – of which *Spirett* v *Willows* (1) 3 *D.J. KS.* 293 is an instance – in which there is direct and positive evidence of an intention to defraud, independently of the consequences which may have followed, or which might have been expected to follow from the act. In *Spirett* v *Willows* the settlor, being solvent at the time, but having contracted a considerable debt, which would fall due in the course of a few weeks, made a voluntary settlement by which he withdrew a large portion of his property from the payment of debts, after which he collected the rest of his assets and (apparently in the most reckless and profligate manner) spent them, thus depriving the expectant creditor of the means of being paid. In that case there was clear and plain evidence of an actual intention to defeat creditors. But it is established by the authorities that in the absence of any such direct proof of intention, if a person owing debts makes a settlement which subtracts from the property which is the proper fund for the payment of those debts, an amount without which the debts cannot be paid, then, since it is the necessary consequence of the settlement (supposing it effectual) that some creditors must remain unpaid, it would be the duty of the Judge to direct the jury that they must infer the intent of the settlor to have been to defeat or delay his creditors, and that the case is within the statute.

The circumstances of the present case are these: The settlor was pressed by his creditors on the 3rd of March, 1863. He was a clergyman with a very good income, but a life income only. He has a life-annuity of between £180 and £190 a year, and besides that he had an income from his benefice – his income from the two sources amounting to about £1000 a year. But at the same time his creditors were pressing him, and he had to borrow from Mrs. *Walpole*, who lived with him as his housekeeper, a sum of £350 wherewith to pay the pressing creditors. That accordingly was done, and he handed over to her as security the only property he had in the world beyond his life income and the policy which is now in question, namely, his furniture, and a copyhold of trifling value. It is said, however, that the value of the furniture exceeded (and I will take it to be so) by about £200 the value of the debt which was secured to Mrs. *Walpole*. That debt may be put out of consideration, not only on that account, but because Mrs. *Walpole*, being herself a trustee of the settlement which is impeached, cannot be heard to complain of that settlement. But he also owed at the time of this pressure a debt of £339 to his bankers at *Norwich*, and he required, for the purpose of clearing the pressing demands upon him, not only the sum which he borrowed from Mrs. *Walpole*, but an additional sum of £150, which sum the bankers agreed to furnish, making their debt altogether, at the date of the execution of this settlement, a debt of £489. They made with him an arrangement (which probably was intended, in a great measure, as a friendly act towards a gentleman who was seventy-three years of age, and the duration of whose life, therefore, could not be expected to be very long), that they would for the present (for it cannot be held to be more than a present arrangement) suspend the proceedings, which, it appears, they were contemplating, upon his allowing his solicitor to receive part of his income, pay £100 a year towards liquidating the £489 (which was to be carried to what is called a 'dead account'), and pay the residue into their branch bank at *Aylsham*, to an account upon which the settlor might draw. That arrangement was made, but there was no bargain on the part of the bankers that they would not sue at any time they thought fit; and, on the other hand, they had nothing in the shape of security for the payment of their debt, for they had not taken out sequestration, and there could be nothing in the shape of a charge upon the living except through the medium of a sequestration. When the settlor had made the voluntary assignment of the policy, he stood in this position, that he had literally nothing wherewithal to pay or to give security for the debt of £489, except the surplus value of the furniture, which must be taken to be worth about £200, and he was clearly and completely insolvent the moment he had executed the settlement, even if we assume that some portion of his tithes and of the annuity was due to him. It appears that a payment of the tithes was made in January, and we cannot suppose that there was more owing to him than the £200 which was paid in May, two months after the date of the deed; and if we add to that £200 as the surplus value of the furniture, and add something for an apportioned part of the annuity, the whole put together would not meet the £489. He, in truth, was at that time insolvent; and there I put it more favourably than I ought to put it, because he could not at once put his hands upon that sum, so as to apply it towards satisfying the debt, at any time between March and May. The case, therefore, is one of those where an intention to delay creditors is to be assumed from the act ...

It seems to me that the difficulty felt by the Vice-Chancellor arose from his thinking that it was necessary to prove an actual intention to delay creditors, where the facts are such as to shew that the necessary consequence of what was done was to delay them. If we had to decide the question of actual intention, probably we might conclude that the settlor, when he made the settlement, was not thinking about his creditors at all, but was only thinking of the lady whom he wished to benefit; and that his whole mind being given up to considerations of generosity and kindness towards her, he forgot that his creditors had higher claims upon him, and he provided for her without providing for them. It makes no difference that Messrs. *Gurney*, the bankers, seem to have been willing to forego the immediate payment of their debt; the question is, whether they could not within a month or less after the execution of the settlement, if they had been so minded, have called in the debt and overturned the settlement? Beyond all doubt they could, on the ground that it did not leave sufficient property to pay their debt; and this being so, we are not to speculate about what was actually passing in his mind. I am quite willing to believe that he had no deliberate intention of depriving his creditors of a fund to which they were entitled, but he did an act which, in point of fact, withdrew that fund from them, and dealt with it by way of bounty. That being so, I come to the conclusion that the decree of the learned Vice-Chancellor is right. [The concurring judgment of Sir G.M. Giffard LJ is omitted.]

Freeman v Pope was followed in the context of intercorporate dealings in *Atlantic Acceptance Corp. v Distributors Acceptance Corp.* (1963), 38 D.L.R. (2d) 307 (Ont. H.C.J.).

Ex parte Mercer (1886), 17 Q.B.D. 290 (C.A.)

LORD ESHER, M.R.: I think the decision of the Divisional Court was right.

The argument was first put in this way – it is necessary to prove that the bankrupt, at the date of the voluntary settlement, intended to defeat and delay a creditor or his creditors generally; the necessary consequence of what he did was to defeat and delay his creditors; and, therefore, as a proposition of law, the tribunal which had to consider whether he did intend to defeat and delay his creditors was bound to find that he did. In support of that proposition dicta of great and eminent judges were cited. I will venture to say as strongly as I can that to my mind that proposition is monstrous. It is said that it is a necessary inference that a man intends the natural and necessary result of his acts. If you want to find out the intention in a man's mind, of course you cannot look into his mind, but, if circumstances are proved from which you believe that he had a particular intention, you infer as a matter of fact that he had that intention. No doubt, in coming to a particular conclusion as to the intention in a man's mind, you should take into account the necessary result of the acts which he has done. I do not use the words 'necessary result' metaphysically, but in their ordinary business sense, and of course, if there was nothing to the contrary, you would come to the conclusion that the man did intend the necessary result of his acts. But, if other circumstances make you believe that the man did not intend to do that which you are asked to find that he did intend, to say that, because that was the necessary result of what he did, you must find, contrary to the other evidence, that he did actually intend to do it, is to ask one to find that to be a fact which one really believes to be untrue in fact. Whether the fact that the necessary effect of a voluntary deed is to defeat or delay the creditors of the grantor will make the deed void under the statute of Elizabeth, although there was no such intent in his mind at the time when he executed it, is a question which we are not now called upon to decide. But that is a question wholly independent of the question of intention. That may be the law; the Courts may have put that construction on the statute. But that is a different proposition from that which was put forward in argument, and I will not undertake to decide it now. It must be recollected that the statute of Elizabeth applies, and may make a deed void, even though the grantor never becomes a bankrupt. But this case was at first argued, not upon that footing, but upon the assumption that, if the natural or necessary effect of what the settlor did was to defeat or delay his creditors, the Court must find that he actually had that intent. That proposition or doctrine I entirely abjure.

We must look at all the facts of this case. The bankrupt was a captain of a merchant ship, and there is no evidence whether his employment ceased at the end of every voyage, or whether it was a constant employment. He had promised to marry Miss Vyse. Then he went to Hong Kong, and there he married another lady, and so laid himself open to an action for breach of promise of marriage by Miss Vyse. That action having been brought, might, so far as any one could foretell, have resulted in a verdict either for 1s. or for 500*l.* damages; no one could tell what the result would be. Well, he married the lady in Hong Kong in May, and in October there came out to him, by the same post from England, the information that he had become entitled to a legacy of 500*l.*, and also the information that Miss Vyse had brought an action against him for breach of promise of marriage. This was the first time that he had had any intimation of the fact that he had any realized fortune, and he immediately settled the 500*l.* upon his wife and children.

Now, what was his position at that time? According to his evidence, which is not disputed, (for he has not been cross-examined on his affidavit), he did not owe a shilling in the world. There is no evidence that he had not money owing to him for wages, and in all probability he had, because, if his voyage did not terminate at Hong Kong (and there is no evidence that it did), if he had got to take his ship home to England, in all probability his wages were not payable until the end of the voyage. If so, he would have means to that extent, and he did not owe a shilling.

Now with regard to the action, how could any one – how could his legal adviser – have told him what the amount of the verdict was likely to be? If the verdict had been for 50*l.*, and he had had 50*l.* coming to him at the end of his voyage, he would have been able to pay it, and on another occasion he would have been able to pay the costs. It was entirely a matter of speculation what the amount of the verdict would be. Therefore he was not insolvent; it was not the necessary consequence of what he did to defeat or delay the plaintiff in the action, for, if the verdict had been for a small amount, she would not necessarily have been delayed for a week.

In order to make this deed void under the Statute of Elizabeth (however far that statute may be stretched), we are bound in the present case to find that there was an actual intent in the bankrupt's mind to defeat or delay his creditors, and there is no evidence of such an intent. He has sworn that he was not thinking of his creditors. The only creditor, that it is suggested he had to think about, was Miss Vyse, and no one could tell what the verdict in her action would be. But what happened afterwards? It is obvious that, when the action came on for trial, evidence must have been given about this 500*l*. legacy to which the defendant was entitled, and the jury took the vindictive view of the plaintiff, and gave her as damages the whole of the defendant's realized property. It was a startling verdict, which I certainly should not have anticipated, and I do not see why he was bound to anticipate it. When you have got those facts, and you are asked to conclude that the bankrupt actually intended to defeat Miss Vyse's claim, it seems to me that the Divisional Court were perfectly justified in declining to find that he had any such intent. Upon the facts, I cannot find that there was such an intent.

The appeal must be dismissed.

[The concurring judgments of Lindley and Lopes ᴌᴊᴊ are omitted.]

Mandryk v *Merko* (1972), 19 D.L.R. (3d) 238 (Man. C.A.)

The judgment of the Court was delivered by

Fʀᴇᴇᴅᴍᴀɴ, ᴊ.ᴀ.: The action giving rise to this appeal was one to set aside certain conveyances of land made by the defendant Nicholas Merko on the ground that they were made with intent to defeat, hinder, delay or defraud his creditors. It is claimed that these conveyances were null and void as against the plaintiff by virtue of the provisions of s 3 of the *Fraudulent Conveyances Act*, ʀ.s.ᴍ. 1954, c 91, which reads as follows:

3. Every conveyance of real property or personal property and every bond, suit, judgment and execution at any time had or made or at any time hereafter to be had or made with intent to defeat, hinder, delay or defraud creditors or others of their just and lawful actions, suits, debts, accounts, damages, penalties or forfeitures shall be null and void as against such persons and their assigns.

The learned trial Judge, Hung, ᴊ., reached the conclusion that there was no fraudulent intent in the conveyances. He expressly found the defendants to be truthful witnesses. Accordingly he accepted their testimony, which specifically denied any such fraudulent intent. On the basis of his findings of fact and of credibility he concluded that the plaintiff's action was not maintainable. This is an appeal against its dismissal.

[Freedman ᴊᴀ found that there was no fraud involved in the conveyance of the first two parcels. He continued:]

This leaves the third parcel of land, consisting of three lots in Gilbert Plains. These, too, were transferred on July 8, 1965, by Nicholas Merko to his wife. Nicholas asserts that the reason for the transfer was that in the spring of 1965 he became ill, with symptoms of heart trouble. Because of this illness he thought it desirable to transfer the Dauphin farm and the Gilbert Plains lots to his wife. That was the reason for the course of action taken by Nicholas. It was in no way motivated by any intent to defeat, hinder, delay or defraud the plaintiff. Once again it must be pointed out that on this issue the learned trial Judge expressly found in favour of the defendants. There is substantial evidence in the record to support that finding, and an appellate Court should be slow to overrule it. On the facts of this case we do not feel warranted in doing so here.

It may incidentally be pointed out that on the Gilbert Plains lots there was a house which had originally been on the Dauphin quarter-section above referred to. To the extent that the transfer of the Gilbert Plains lots related to this house, the defendants contended that this was merely a reconveyance to the wife of what actually belonged to her. The learned trial Judge's findings support the defendant on this point as well, thereby furnishing another ground on which the judgment may rest. But it is enough to say that the conveyance of the Gilbert Plains lots was not made with any intent to defeat or hinder the plaintiff.

One further factual circumstance needs to be noted. At the time when the transfers were made by the defendant, the plaintiff was not yet a creditor possessed of an existing debt. He was at most a person with a potential debt arising from a claim for damages. These damages were based on an alleged assault committed upon the plaintiff by the defendant, Nicholas Merko. At the time when the transfers in question were made the plaintiff's damage action had been commenced and the statement of claim had been served, but the matter was still a long way from judgment. Indeed, the judgment was not obtained until December 5, 1967. The length of time between suit and judgment clearly suggests that the plaintiff's claim was not admitted but was the subject of a dispute that necessitated a trial.

The present appeal accordingly concerns a case in which the plaintiff sought and failed to establish that the impugned conveyances were null and void under s 3 of the *Fraudulent Conveyances Act*. To the extent that the judgment rests upon issues of fact, it is plain that these were decided against the plaintiff and in favour of the defendants. But Mr. O'Sullivan, counsel for the plaintiff (who was not counsel at the trial before Hung, J.), contends that, regardless of what occurred in the area of fact, the learned trial Judge made an error in law. His position is that the learned trial Judge failed to consider and apply the principle enunciated in the case of *Freeman* v *Pope* (1870), L.R. 5 Ch. App. 538. In that case Lord Hatherley, L.C., stated at p 540, that the principle on which the statute, 'An Act against fraudulent Deeds, Alienations, etc.', 1570, Eliz. 1, c 5 (the source of the *Fraudulent Conveyances Act* of Manitoba), is based, is 'that persons must be just before they are generous, and that debts must be paid before gifts can be made'. Accordingly, if the necessary effect of a conveyance was to defeat, hinder or delay the creditors, that necessary effect was to be considered as evidencing an intention to do so. In such a case it would be the duty of the Judge to direct the jury that they must infer the intent of the settlor to have been to defeat or delay his creditors. If in fact the transfer was not made with that intent, that would make no difference. According to *Freeman* v *Pope*, the law presumes such an intent, and that absolutely.

There is no doubt that the language of *Freeman* v *Pope*, *supra*, appears to be comprehensive enough to warrant such a construction. But the question at once arises whether the general language used in *Freeman* v *Pope* was intended to apply to every case, or whether it was to be limited to factual situations similar to the one with which it dealt. There is authority indicating that, if a grantor with debts makes a transfer the effect of which is to render him unable to meet his then existing liabilities, that circumstance furnishes very strong evidence of an intent to defraud his creditors, *but such evidence is not conclusive*. Halsbury puts the matter in just that way: *vide*, 17 Hals., 3rd ed., p 658, para. 1270, as follows:

1270 *Indebtedness not conclusive evidence*. The fact that the grantor was at the time of the alienation indebted to a considerable extent, though not amounting to insolvency, especially if by the alienation he rendered himself unable to meet his then existing liabilities, furnishes very strong evidence of an intent to defraud his creditors, but such evidence is not conclusive.

For the statement that such an alienation by a transferor 'furnishes very strong evidence of an intent to defraud his creditors' Halsbury cites, among other cases, *Freeman* v *Pope, supra*. In support of the qualification, 'but such evidence is not conclusive', Halsbury cites, among other cases, *Ex p. Mercer; Re Wise* (1886), 17 Q.B.D. 290, to which reference must now be made.

There are certain parallels between the case of *Ex p. Mercer* and the present one. In both, the defendant had made a voluntary transfer of property. In both, the transferor later became bankrupt. In both, the effect of the transfer was to render the defendant unable to pay his debts. In both, the plaintiff, at the time of the transfer, was not yet a creditor for an ascertained debt but rather was no more than a claimant for damages in a matter whose outcome was uncertain. Finally, in both, there was specific evidence that the transfers were made for reasons other than to defeat, delay or defraud creditors.

Freeman v *Pope, supra*, was considered by the Court in the *Mercer* case. In the Divisional Court, Grantham, J., referring to *Freeman* v *Pope* and similar cases, made this comment [at p 295]:

When learned judges have said that, if the necessary result of a settlement is to hinder creditors, it must be taken to have been executed with that intent, this observation must be taken as applied to the character of the particular case in which it was made.

In the Court of Appeal, Lord Esher, M.R., used the following language [at pp 298–9]:

But, if other circumstances make you believe that the man did not intend to do that which you are asked to find that he did intend, to say that, because that was the necessary result of what he did, you must find, contrary to the other evidence, that he did actually intend to do it, is to ask one to find that to be a fact which one really believes to be untrue in fact.

In the present case we have actual evidence, accepted by the learned trial Judge, that the transfers were not made with any fraudulent intent. That evidence cannot be ignored and has to be placed in the scale for consideration along with the *Freeman* v *Pope* presumption. However strong the presumption may be that if the necessary effect of a voluntary transfer is to delay or defeat creditors an intention to do so should be inferred, it is not conclusive. In an appropriate case the presumption may have to yield in favour of cogent and affirmative evidence establishing an honest purpose in the making of the transfer, a purpose in no way designed to prejudice creditors. The present is such a case.
Appeal dismissed.

ii The Need for Actual Creditors

Clinton v *Sellars* (1908), 1 Alta. L.R. 135 (S.C.)

STUART, J.: ... There are possibly two views which may be taken as to the nature of this action; or rather it is possible, perhaps, to discover two grounds of action as being suggested in the statement of claim. First we may view it as an action to set aside a fraudulent gift of property from George Sellars to his wife; and secondly, it may be, perhaps, contended that the plaintiff in his claim is alleging alternatively that there never was any real gift at all, even as between the parties, but that the property was the property of the judgment debtor even as between him and his wife, that it stood in her name merely as a trustee for him, and the relief prayed is a declaration that she is such a trustee.

With reference to the first ground, I am bound to say that I have found it rather difficult, though perhaps it is not impossible to discover even in the statement of claim itself any allegations of facts that would constitute fraud. The rule is that there must either be a debt in existence at the date of the alleged fraudulent conveyance, or, if there is not, then there must be a fraudulent scheme entered into for the direct purpose of defrauding creditors whose claim might afterwards arise. Now there was no evidence at all that there was a single unpaid debt of George Sellars in existence prior to the 2nd of February, 1908, at which date I suppose the commission was earned by which judgment was obtained against him. That being so, the question is, was there any gift of property from George Sellars to the defendant subsequent to the date. I think that question must be answered in the negative. The facts are that the property, at least one portion of the real estate, stood in the defendant's name on the 22nd of January, 1906, the date of one of the certificates of title, and as to another portion, it stood in her name as long ago as October the 12th, 1903. Of course the property was apparently only gradually paid for, and no doubt the proceeds of the business which the plaintiff alleges really belonged originally to George Sellars, were from time to time applied in making payments on the property, and in reducing encumbrances. These payments, it may be suggested, constituted gifts by George Sellars to his wife; but it does not appear that any such payment was made on or subsequent to the 2nd of February, 1906. It may be said, of course, as to the chattel property in the hotel, this was never registered at any time in the wife's name, but it was not shown that the husband made any gift of this to his wife subsequent to the 2nd of February, 1906. It may be suggested, too, that the taking of the mortgage from the purchasers in the wife's name constituted a gift from the husband to the wife; but I do not see how this contention could be supported.

As to the real estate, the property already stood in her name, and it was surely a natural thing to do to take the mortgage therefor in her name as well. It simply amounted to a change in the form from real estate to personalty, or from real estate to a charge upon real estate. That certainly could not of itself constitute a gift from the husband to the wife. As to the chattel property in the hotel, which was no doubt included in the sale for $14,000, I cannot see in respect to this either, that the taking of the mortgage in the wife's name for the balance of the total purchase money constituted a gift of that chattel property, or of the proceeds of it, by the husband to the wife. It appears that $2,000 was paid in cash, and a bill of sale of the chattel property was put in evidence, which shows a consideration of $2,000.

For all that appears in the evidence George Sellars may have got that $2,000 in cash and put it in his pocket and may have it still. The burden of proving a gift was on the plaintiff, and I do not think that he has adduced any evidence to show that there was a gift of this chattel property or of the proceeds of it from the husband to the wife subsequent to the 2nd of February, 1906.

It is true also that the liquor license stood in the name of George Sellars; and this, I have no doubt, was transferred by him to the purchasers subsequent to the 2nd of February, 1906. This license was to go with the property and was covered by the total purchase price. It would have yet a few months to run after the 17th of March, 1906, the date of the mortgage. In itself it is not an asset available to a creditor under a writ of execution. Considered by itself, and as dissociated from the property, and in view of the short term it had yet to run, and of the possibility of the purchasers securing a license independently for themselves, I do not see that any particular tangible value can be placed upon it; at any rate, no attempt was made to prove that it possessed a pecuniary value, or what the amount of that value would be even upon a reference. If one were made to inquire as to its value, it seems to me the evidence would necessarily be so much a pure matter of guess work and opinion that it is impossible for me now to consider any portion of the purchase price or of the mortgage security as being referable to it. I think it quite unlikely that the parties ever entertained any thought of placing any separate value upon it.

It seems to me that it was incumbent upon the plaintiff to show with respect to both the chattel property and the license that the value of these was included in the mortgage. If he had shown this clearly, and had also shown clearly the preliminary fact that, as to the chattel property this was the property of George Sellars up to the date of the mortgage, he might possibly have made out a case in this direction. The existence of even one debt unpaid is no doubt sufficient, if it is shown that the debtor gave away all of his property subsequent to the incurring of the debt and before it was paid, but for the reasons I have given I do not think the plaintiff has made out his case on this ground.

Nor do I think it is possible for me to find as a fact the existence of a fraudulent scheme or conspiracy entered into by the husband and wife for the purpose of defeating creditors whose debts might subsequently arise. It is only upon this ground, if at all, that the plaintiff's statement of claim can be said not to be demurrable. It certainly presents a peculiar state of facts as fraudulent, Paragraph 4 of the claim is particularly a strange one. In such a case as this we usually find it alleged that the wife has been carrying on business in her own name with the connivance of the husband; but in this paragraph, oddly enough, it is alleged that the business was carried on in the husband's name and that it was his business. So far there would, I should hope, be nothing fraudulent. Otherwise, most business men are fraudulent, for that is exactly what they do. Of course it is stated that 'the defendant had the property registered in her own name.'

But I have certainly yet to learn that it is fraudulent for a hotel keeper to carry on a licensed hotel business without having the property registered in his name; otherwise, every hotel keeper who rents his premises would be fraudulent. If it is fraudulent for a wife to own the property in which her husband carries on business in his own name, or if such a condition of affairs is to suggest a fraudulent scheme or conspiracy, then I must reverse my opinion as to what a wife and husband may properly do. And what other facts are there besides this to indicate a fraudulent purpose? It is said that the husband carried on a hotel business in his own name for a number of years. It is not shown that he ever failed to pay a single honest debt during that time, or that there is a single business creditor who is sorry on his account, and yet we are asked to believe that the fact, that as far back as 1903 part of the property, who's ever it was, was registered in the name of the wife, indicated the existence of a fraudulent scheme to defeat future creditors, and that too, when the only creditor who ever turns up is a man whose claim is for a commission on the sale of the property. This is surely not a debt which the parties can be held to have been looking forward to so many years ahead and to have entered into a scheme to avoid. Where such a scheme is entered into the debts anticipated must surely be debts which will probably arise out of the conduct of the business itself, and not one which arises after all business debts have been paid, when the parties are going out of business, and only incidentally in connection with the sale of the property. In the absence of a single other circumstance which would suggest the existence of a fraudulent scheme, it seems to me impossible for me to find on these facts that any such scheme was ever thought of by the defendant or her husband. So far, therefore, as this may be considered an action to set aside a fraudulent conveyance, I think the plaintiff must fail. ...

Gauthier v *Woollatt*, [1940] 1 D.L.R. 275 (Ont. H.C.J.)

ROACH J.: In an action in this Court in 1934 the late C. Harold Gauthier obtained judgment against the defendant William R. Woollatt, his father, and two brothers for $25,000 and interest and costs upon a promissory note made by them in his favour dated January 22, 1926, and which became due on January 25, 1929. There remains unpaid on the judgment approximately $23,000. The said note was collaterally secured by,

First – an assignment by way of mortgage from William R. Woollatt to Gauthier of the former's two-fifths interest in certain lands in the City of Windsor referred to during the trial as the Zakoor property.

Second – A first mortgage from Woollatt's father covering the latter's home in the Town of Walkerville.

Third – an assignment of the father's interest in certain lands in the Town of Amherstburg.

In 1927 the defendant William R. Woollatt had purchased or agreed to purchase certain farm lands in the Township of Anderdon in the County of Essex. Those lands consisted of two parcels. The vendor of one was a man named Janisse and the purchase-price was $6,850. The vendor of the other was a man named Scarfe and the purchase-price was $13,000. By December, 1928, the purchase-price of both parcels had been paid in full and by deed dated December 10, 1928, Janisse, on the instructions of Woollatt, conveyed the one parcel to the latter's wife, the defendant Mabel Alice Woollatt, and by deed dated December 21, 1928, Scarfe on similar instructions conveyed the other parcel to the defendant Mabel Alice Woollatt.

In this action the plaintiff asks a declaration that the defendant Mabel Alice Woollatt held the said lands in trust for her husband on the ground that he caused the title thereof to be placed in her name to defeat, hinder or delay his creditors.

In 1924 the Molsons Bank recovered judgment in an action in the Court against the defendant W.R. Woollatt and others in the sum of $46,193.63. A writ of *fieri facias* was filed with the Sheriff of the County of Essex against all the judgment debtors on January 16, 1924, was withdrawn on December 31, 1925, was refiled on the same day, was subsequently renewed and was finally withdrawn on February 18, 1929.

The defendants deny the allegation of fraud and plead that the said lands were conveyed to the wife as a gift from her husband. The defendant wife had no funds of her own and the full purchase-price of these lands were paid by the husband.

The husband was examined as a judgment debtor on January 13, 1936, and the following are some of the questions and answers from that examination:

'Q. You have given us all the real estate? A. I can't remember anything else at all. The farm out here is Mrs. Woollatt's because it was bought while that judgment was on. Q. Where is that farm? A. Out on the Huron line ... Q. How many acres in the farm? A. One hundred. That is the farm I bought in '27. Q. You paid the purchase-price for it did you? A. Yes. Q. How much? A. $20,000. Q. You took it in Mrs. Woollatt's name? A. Yes.'

The plaintiff did not call any witness to prove the amount, if any, remaining unpaid on the judgment in favour of the Molsons Bank at the date of the conveyances in question. Counsel for the defendants cited *Dancey* v *Brown* (1914), 19 D.L.R. 862, 31 O.L.R. 152. At p 866 Mulock C.J.Ex. (as he then was) states: 'The recovery of judgment, and the evidence of the Clerk of the Division Court that a writ of execution had been placed in the bailiff's hands, does not, as against a person not a party to that action, prove that the debt is still unpaid.' That was a case in which the plaintiff was a creditor whose claim arose subsequent to the making of a voluntary conveyance and he was relying upon prior claims alleged still to be in existence and unpaid. I suppose, in so far as proving any balance owing, there is no distinction between the probative value of an execution in the hands of a bailiff and one in the sheriff's hands. It is the amount due on the execution in the sheriff's hands which is a lien on the lands of the execution debtor.

Paraphrased, Woollatt's answer on his examination was: 'I put that property in my wife's name to prevent the execution in favour of the Molsons Bank attaching to it.' That statement would be evidence against the husband only; but where the conveyance is voluntary it is only necessary to show fraudulent intent on the part of the donor. *Oliver* v *McLaughlin* (1893), 24 O.R. 41.

The defendants called one Loveridge as a witness. He and Woollatt owned as tenants in common a real estate sub-division near the City of Windsor. They were selling lots in this sub-division. He says: 'The bank (i.e. the Molsons Bank) held us up in giving deeds in our sub-division. In January, 1927, I took over Woollatt's one-third interest in the sub-division and gave the bank my note for approximately $20,000 which I paid off in monthly payments over a two year period. In 1929 Woollatt redeemed his one-third interest by paying me approximately $20,000.' From other evidence it is clear that this money came from the sale in January, 1929, of the assets and undertaking of a company in which Woollatt was a substantial shareholder. This explains the withdrawal of the execution on February 18, 1929.

In my view the proof which was lacking in *Dancey* v *Brown, supra*, exists in the case at bar.

Counsel for the defendants next argued that the plaintiff is not a creditor entitled to avail himself of the statute (the *Fraudulent Conveyances Act*, R.S.O. 1937, c 149) because at the times of the settlements he held security. In my opinion much depends on the selling value of the security at the date of the settlement.

I find as a fact on the evidence that as of the dates of the conveyances in question the then selling value of the security was greater than the debt. Due to shrinkage in values of real estate this is no longer the case. In fact the debtor subsequently released to the creditor all his interest in one of the securities, *viz.* the Zakoor property, on account of the debt, and the selling value of the remaining security is only about one-third of the balance owing on the debt ...

There is no evidence that as of the date of the institution of this action there remained unpaid any debts which were owing at the date of the last conveyance in question, except the debt owing to Gauthier. That debt was not then due and at that time was amply secured. Because of the sufficiency of his security this plaintiff at that time could not have impeached the conveyances in question because he was not then damnified. In this respect the present case differs from the case of *Sun Life Ass'ce Co.* v *Elliott, supra*, and *Smith* v *Robertson, supra*. The plaintiff was not then such a creditor as the statute was designed to protect. By reason of shrinkage in value of real estate he has since become a creditor within the meaning and purpose of the statute. In this respect he is a subsequent creditor.

As I read the cases a subsequent creditor may in certain circumstances successfully impeach a fraudulent conveyance. Those cases, speaking generally, fall into two classes:

First – Those in which a subsequent creditor impeaches the conveyance while there still remains unpaid a creditor whose claim existed at the date of the conveyance in question.

Second – Those in which the purpose of the settlor was, by such conveyances, to put his assets beyond the chances and uncertainties of the business in which he was then engaged or into which he then contemplated venturing, that is the settlor's purpose was to defraud or hinder creditors generally. In these cases it is not necessary that, at the date of the commencement of the action, there should remain unpaid a debt which was owing at the date of the impeached conveyance.

Cases falling within the second class include *Mackay* v *Douglas* (1872), L.R. 14 Eq. 106, and in our own Courts *Ferguson* v *Kenny* (1889), 16 O.A.R. 276, and *Ottawa Wine Vaults Co.* v *McGuire* (1912), 8 D.L.R. 229, 27 O.L.R. 319 (affd 13 D.L.R. 81).

The present case does not come within either of the foregoing classes.

May on Fraudulent and Voluntary Conveyances, 3rd ed., p 43, speaks of a third class as follows: 'If the conveyance has been made with the actual intention of delaying, hindering or defrauding the grantor's existing creditors and although subsequent creditors do not appear to have been in his contemplation at the time it seems that the conveyance will be void as against subsequent creditors who are delayed, hindered or defrauded as a necessary result of the conveyance even though, in the meantime, the claims of existing creditors have been satisfied.'

I have not found any reported case the decision in which rested on this proposition ...

In the absence of decided authority to the contrary, it would seem to me that a settlor who, in embarrassed financial circumstances, makes a settlement admittedly for the purpose of protecting the property thereby settled against the claims of existing creditors, purges his fraud by paying those creditors, provided, of course, that, in paying them, he does not substitute new creditors for the old ones. Even though his earlier generosity had been at the expense of his justice toward his creditors, having paid those creditors and thereby discharged his legal and moral obligation to them and having none others in contemplation, is the conveyance to be forever regarded as contaminated? In my opinion this is not so. By a turn in the wheel of fortune the settlor, instead of wincing under the pinch of financial distress, may become fabulously wealthy. He still desires that the beneficiary of his earlier generosity should enjoy the gift. If it is tainted what could or should the settlor do to purify it? Is he to cause it to be reconveyed to himself and then, simply because he is now in a position to make the gift without any suggestion of fraudulent intent being imputed to him, make a new conveyance thereof to the beneficiary? These would be idle motions and, because they are lacking, is the gift in the hands of the beneficiary to be subject to attack by a subsequent creditor in the event that evil days again overtake the settlor? I do not think that was the purpose or intent of the statute.

In my view of the evidence those are the circumstances in this case. The settlor acquired a large amount of cash shortly after the date of the impeached conveyances and paid off the Molsons Bank debt and there is no suggestion that there were any other debts. From January 10, 1929, to May 10, 1929, Woollatt received over $100,000 in cash out of the realization of other assets.

The note held by Gauthier matured on January 25, 1929. Gauthier did not demand payment. Instead he and Woollatt together on February 13, 1929, embarked on a new venture, the purchase of what was referred to in evidence as the Thompson property, involving a very substantial cash investment by each of them.

I do not attribute any bad faith to Mrs. Woollatt. I think she understood her husband was making a gift of this property to her and she accepted it as such.

For the reasons stated the plaintiff's action fails and is dismissed with costs.
Action dismissed.

iii Entering a Hazardous Course of Business

Mackay v *Douglas* (1872), L.R. 14 Eq. 106

Sir R. Malins, v.c.: This case raises as important a question, probably, on this branch of the law as has ever been brought before the Court.

The circumstances are very simple. Mr. *Douglas* had been for some years a clerk in various mercantile houses, and in the autumn of 1863 was a clerk to a firm carrying on business in *London*, *Liverpool*, and *Calcutta*, under the names of *William Grant & Co.*, *James Smith & Co.*, and *Grant, Smith, & Co.* His salary, which was for some time £200 a year, had latterly been raised to £500.

In the latter part of the year 1863 his employers were engaged on a very large scale in speculations in jute, which is an article subject to very considerable variations in price. These speculations, which I think were of a reckless and unjustifiable character, were to some extent carried on by the aid of Mr. *Douglas*, and it is not attempted to be denied that he was to some extent interested in the result of them. The Plaintiffs say that he was interested jointly as a partner, and certainly there is a passage in Mr. *Smith's* evidence which seems to sustain that view.

But, though I do not intend to rest my conclusion on any such grounds, it is not unimportant to observe that for several months before the settlement in question was made he was certainly, either on his own account or on account of the firm whose servant he was, engaged in these reckless speculations in jute. In this state of things the firm were carrying on business in *London* and *Liverpool*, and in connection with some other persons in *India*. Of the English partners it is only necessary to refer to Mr. *Smith* and Mr. *Grant*. Proposals had been made for the retirement of Mr. *Grant*, and this business was to be carried on by Mr. *Smith* alone, or with such persons as he should think proper to take into partnership with him. It is perfectly plain, for it is shewn under the hand of Mr. *Douglas* himself, that he entertained the expectation of going into partnership with Mr. *Smith*, his employer, if Mr. *Grant* retired. That is very distinctly shewn in a letter so early as the 11th of September, 1863, written by Mr. *Douglas* to Mr. *James Smith*. It gives the particulars of some purchases of jute and so forth, and then he says:

[His Honour then read the passage in the letter above set out, and continued:]

So matters went on, and in October, the very next month, Mr. *Douglas*, who in the course of his clerkship had amassed a sum of money which he says amounted to about £3000 or £4000, but which I cannot make out amounted to so much, entered into this transaction. He was a married man, having at the time no child, but in the progress of this business the first child of the marriage was born, and on the 8th of October, 1863, while it appears that he certainly had it in his mind as a probable event that he would go into partnership with his employer Mr. *Smith*, he entered into a contract to purchase a leasehold house, which is the subject of this suit. The contract was on the 30th of October, and the purchase was completed by an assignment to himself on the 2nd of November. All was right so far, and nobody can complain of that part of the transaction. But while he was carrying on the negotiation for the partnership, on the 19th of January, he saw his solicitor, and talked of making, but did not give him positive instructions to make, a settlement of the leasehold house, which was worth from £1500 to £1800. On the 12th of February, 1864, he gave final instructions to his solicitor to prepare a voluntary settlement of that property, and in pursuance of the instructions the settlement was prepared and duly executed on the 24th of February, 1864.

Now the trusts of that settlement were for Mrs. *Douglas* for her life to her separate use in the usual way, with remainder to himself if he should survive her for life, or until he should become bankrupt or insolvent. Then there were the usual trusts for children, and in default of children, to himself absolutely. On the 8th of April following (forty-four days, I think, is the precise time, but it may be called six weeks afterwards,) he entered into partnership with Mr. *Smith*. The partnership, in point of profits, was to commence from the 1st of May, that is, Mr. *Grant's* contract was to go out on the 30th of April, and the arrangement between *Smith* and *Douglas* was, that he should succeed on the next day. Accordingly the business begins actively on the 1st of May, 1864, that is, rather more than two months from the time when the voluntary settlement was executed; but it must, for the purpose for which I look at it, be considered as commencing when the articles of partnership were signed.

Mr. *Douglas* went to *India*, and his partner, Mr. *Smith*, remained at home, and whether with the connivance, or approbation, or knowledge of *Douglas*, it seems somewhat uncertain, but it is certain that the business was so conducted that the firm was in difficulties so early as the month of November in the same year. They were borrowing and were embarrassed; the embarrassments so much increased that in the following month of March they failed for the sum of £347,000, and up to this time their dividend has been fourpence in the pound, and I am told that there is a possibility that there may be another penny, so that probably they will not pay sixpence in the pound.

Now to all these proceedings, however innocent Mr. *Douglas* may have been while in *India*, I must regard him as a party, because one partner is liable for the misfeasance of another. One of the most fruitful sources of ruin to men of the world is the recklessness or want of principle of partners, and it is one of the perils to which every man exposes himself who enters into partnership with another.

Now this question seems to me to raise a most important point. Can a man who contemplates trade, or who, in point of fact, whether he contemplates it at the time or very shortly afterwards, enters into trade, and thereby incurs liabilities which end in a disastrous state of affairs, make a voluntary settlement which shall be good against the creditors who become so in the course of his trade? I am not aware of any case upon the exact point, and none was cited, although almost all the cases which have occurred upon the subject were mentioned. But is the Statute of *Elizabeth* so very short in its effect that it will not cover a case where a man on the very eve of entering into trade takes the bulk of his property and puts it into a voluntary settlement and becomes insolvent a few months afterwards? Is it to be said that such a settlement cannot be reached by any principle of law? I think not ... Mr. *Douglas*, having become bankrupt or insolvent within seven months after the execution of the settlement, has the burden cast upon him of shewing, not merely that he was solvent, but that he was in a situation which justified him in making a voluntary settlement of the great bulk of his property ...
I am satisfied from the evidence that Mr. *Douglas* contemplated a partnership, and that the probability of such a partnership was the inducement to him to make the settlement. He had very likely never heard of the Statute of *Elizabeth*; but taking a common business-like view of the matter, and considering the rather reckless nature of the business into which he was entering, he wished to make a provision out of the leasehold house which he had bought for his wife and any children he might have. I cannot hesitate to come to the conclusion that the inducement to him to make this settlement on the very eve, as I consider it, of his going into business was to protect this property from any risk ...
The statute speaks of cases where the creditors 'are, shall, or might be in any wise disturbed, hindered, delayed, or defrauded,' and it is not necessary to shew an intention to do that, because if the settlement must have that effect the Court presumes the intention and will attribute it to the settlor. That is distinctly laid down by the present Lord Chancellor, on appeal from Vice-Chancellor *James*, in *Freeman* v *Pope* [(1870) L.R. 5 Ch. App. 538] ... So I dare say that Mr. *Douglas* had no fraudulent intention, according to his view, in making the settlement, and that he thought it a prudent thing to protect his wife and children. But in doing that he has, within the

meaning of this statute, committed a fraudulent act, because, going into trade, he was taking away the only property which would be available for his creditors.

This happens to be a small amount of property with reference to the debts incurred, and with reference to the position of Mr. *Douglas* when the settlement was executed. But if I were now to decide against the Plaintiffs my decision would be applicable to any case. Suppose then the case of a man with a large fortune, and having a fancy (and I have known such cases) for going into trade. He says: 'I am going into trade; I believe I may make a great deal of money by it, but nobody knows what may happen. Therefore, I will make this large fortune safe by settling it on my wife and children absolutely.' The law is perfectly settled that if a man is solvent at the time and after the time of taking away the property which is put into the settlement he remains solvent, and does not at the time contemplate doing anything which could lead to insolvency, that settlement will be good ... So, in the present case, if Mr. *Douglas* had neither gone into nor contemplated going into trade at the time, but some years afterwards, by a totally new arrangement, made up his mind to do so, I should have had no hesitation in coming to the conclusion that his subsequent insolvency could have had no effect in producing invalidity of the settlement which he had made upon his wife and family.

The only rule I have found laid down on the subject that commends itself to my judgment, as I think it must commend itself to the judgment of all right-thinking men, is laid down in a very few words by Lord *Hardwicke* in *Stileman* v *Ashdown* [2 Atk. 477]. 'It is not necessary that a man should actually be indebted at the time he enters into a voluntary settlement to make it fraudulent; for if a man does it with a view to his being indebted at a future time it is equally fraudulent.' ... [I]f a man does it with a view of being indebted at a future time, that is, with a view to a state of things in which he may become indebted, that makes it fraudulent, just as if he were indebted at the time. In the present case Mr. *Douglas* made the settlement, as I am perfectly satisfied, with the view that he was going into partnership in which he might become bankrupt or insolvent and utterly ruined; and therefore he did it with the view that he might be indebted, and the settlement in my opinion was fraudulent and void against creditors. The conclusion which I arrive at proceeds upon the broad ground that a man who contemplates going into trade cannot on the eve of doing so take the bulk of his property out of the reach of those who may become his creditors in his trading operations.

[His Honour then referred to some of the correspondence as shewing that it was treated in January, 1864, as almost a settled thing that he was to go into the business, and continued:]

I therefore hold that the settlement of the 24th of February, 1864, was absolutely null and void against the creditors within the meaning of the Statute of *Elizabeth*, and consequently that when Mr. *Douglas* executed the deed by which he vested all his property either at law or in equity in the inspectors or trustees, this property vested in them as being his, just as much as if the settlement of the 24th of February had never been executed.

McGuire v *Ottawa Wine Vaults Co.* (1913), 48 S.C.R. 44

DAVIES J. (dissenting): This is an appeal from a judgment of the Court of Appeal for Ontario reversing the judgment of the Divisional Court (Chief Justice Falconbridge dissenting), and restoring the judgment of the trial judge, Chief Justice Mulock, setting aside a conveyance made by the appellant John L. McGuire to his wife of the former's equity in a hotel property in the Village of Madoc, on the ground that such conveyance was fraudulent and void as against the grantor's creditors under the statute 13 Elizabeth.

The debts due the creditors of McGuire at the time of the execution of the impeached conveyance, outside of the mortgage debt secured upon the property conveyed, were contracted some time subsequent to the conveyance. Only two creditors gave evidence respecting the debts due them and it shewed that their debts were contracted long after the impeached settlement was made. There was no evidence that any of McGuire's debts which were due at the date of the settlement remained unpaid at the date of the insolvents' assignment.

The mortgage debt was one secured upon property much more than sufficient to pay it and may, therefore, for the purposes of this action, be disregarded. *Jenkyn* v *Vaughan* (1856), 3 Drew 419, at p 426.

It may be conceded as established by the cases that the statute extends to subsequent creditors. They have the same right to set aside an alienation made with intent to delay, hinder or defraud them, as creditors whose debts were due at the date of the alienation, but they have a more difficult task in proving a fraudulent intent on the part of the grantor in the case of a voluntary settlement. In such case they must prove either an express intent to delay, hinder or defraud creditors or that after the settlement the grantor had not sufficient means or reasonable expectation of being able to pay his then existing debts. 15 Halsbury's Laws of England, page 88 par. 180. The cases there cited I think support that proposition.

The courts below have all found that the impeached settlement was a voluntary one and I shall deal with the case on that finding, though I am bound to say I should have some difficulty in reaching it on the evidence.

There is no pretence for saying that any fraudulent intent under the statute was proved and the single question left was whether the grantor after the settlement was left without sufficient means or reasonable expectations of being able to pay his then existing debts and so that a fraudulent intent might be inferred.

As to the financial condition of McGuire at the time he made the settlement, I think the statement embodied by Riddell J. in his judgment a fair and proper one. It omits the Madoc property, the settlement of which is in question, and the mortgage upon it, and subject to which the property was conveyed to Mrs. McGuire, and aside from that shews McGuire to have been left with assets of the value of $14,180 and liabilities amounting to $3,947.

Amongst the assets was included $8,500 which he had paid for the Ottawa business and chattels, including the 'good will'. I agree that looking at McGuire's financial position from a business stand point there is no reason in the world why its value should not be taken into consideration. But when you are considering that financial position with respect to a settlement made by the man upon his wife of part of his property, and determining the 'intent' with which it was made, to omit the value of such good will from your consideration would be, to my mind, most unfair ...

I have already stated why I accept Mr. Justice Riddell's statement of McGuire's financial position at the time he made the settlement as correct. It shewed McGuire to have had a very handsome surplus of assets over debts and quite justified the settlement he made upon his wife. His business in Ottawa had continued prosperous from the time he bought it and remained so for six or eight months afterwards. The firm's obligations seem to have been met with reasonable promptness as they matured and to McGuire the outlook was promising. There was no indication or anticipation by either defendant that the venture was likely to prove a failure. My conclusion is that McGuire was clearly solvent when he made the settlement. He made that settlement in consequence of a promise given by him to his wife when at his solicitation she joined with him in the conveyance of some property he owned in Toronto. He and she both thought she had a dower interest in that property. They may have been wrong in their belief, but from their evidence both husband and wife believed she had. She thought she had a moral claim at any rate to the Madoc property as she had done as much if not more to build it up and make it what it was as her husband had done. He admitted that to be so. She was apparently living in Toronto with her two invalid daughters and the settlement seems to have been made when their home there was broken up and a very short time after she signed away whatever rights she had in the Toronto property. It was made at a time when, if the statement of his financial condition I accept is correct, he was undoubtedly entitled to make it. Even if the onus of proving that is cast upon him on the assumption of the settlement being a voluntary one, I think he has discharged it.

What, then, if this story is true, brought about the insolvency? A perusal of the evidence satisfies me that it was brought about by causes which could not have been foreseen or anticipated when he made the impeached settlement.

In the summer of 1909, McGuire Bros. were compelled by the License Commissioners to move their bar from the corner of Bank and Sparks Streets, a great thoroughfare, to the upper side of Bank Street. This change necessitated extensive alterations being made claimed to have cost about $4,000. This, of course, was not, and could not have been, anticipated in November, 1908. To make these necessary changes good paying tenants of theirs were dispossessed and their rentals lost. In the early part of 1910 the fire took place causing further damage to their business and much loss. McGuire states in his evidence that the direct loss in the receipts of the bar from the change compelled by the License Commissioners was 25%. The rentals of the tenants they had to dispossess so as to make room for the new bar amounted to $110 per month, and McGuire says they were not able to get a tenant for the corner they vacated. Then the municipality brought into effect a by-law to reduce the number of licenses in the city and that made it impossible for them to sell out. Reverses began about June, 1909. They struggled from that date under the adverse circumstances I have above stated from the evidence, to meet their obligations until December. Then followed the plaintiffs' suit and the assignment followed by the landlord's distress for three months' advance rent and the sale under the distress with its usual pitiful returns.

In all of these facts as stated in evidence, I see nothing to justify the conclusion that the insolvency could have possibly been foreseen in November, 1908. The proper inference is that it was brought about by causes which could not have been reasonably foreseen at that time or for many months afterwards, and so forms an exception to the general rule respecting voluntary conveyances preceding insolvency.

It was said that this case was governed by that of *Mackay* v *Douglas* (1872), L.R. 14 Eq. 106. I do not think so. The broad ground upon which that case was decided is stated by the Vice-Chancellor at page 122 to be that a man who contemplates going into trade cannot on the eve of doing so take the bulk of his property out of the reach of those who may become his creditors in his trading operations. The facts of the two cases are not analogous. McGuire was not like a man 'going into trade' for the first time when or immediately after he made the settlement. He appears to have been for the greater part of his life in the hotel business, and he did not, as I have shewn, take the bulk of his property out of the reach of his creditors. I think it is a case forming an exception to the principle laid down in *Mackay* v *Douglas* ...

The settlement impeached did not embrace 'all of his property' or indeed the larger part of it. It embraced practically that part of the property which the wife had herself in great part built up. It was made by a man who was not insolvent at the time he made it, but became so afterwards from accidents and causes which he neither did nor could have anticipated. It does seem to me to be rather the refinement of irony when the two chief creditors, the Wine Vault Company and the Capital Brewing Company, in order to defeat the claim of the wife and children to a portion of the property which the life's labours of the former largely created, unite to proclaim a business a 'hazardous' one which they themselves exist upon and supply with the 'sinews of war' to keep alive and on a commercial basis.

I am of opinion that the appeal should be allowed and the judgment of the Divisional Court restored ...

DUFF J.: I think there is not sufficient ground for impeaching the finding of the learned trial judge that the conveyance was voluntary; but I do not agree that the circumstances justify the conclusion that the necessary effect of the conveyance was to defeat or delay existing creditors. The burden was consequently upon the plaintiffs at the outset to shew that the conveyance was made by the debtor with a view to protecting himself or his family against the consequences of failure in the business into which he had a short time before entered. I think the fact that a collapse did come within a few months after the execution of the conveyance was sufficient to shift the burden to the appellants of shewing that such was not the intent of the transaction. I do not think that burden has been discharged.

[Anglin and Idington JJ wrote separate concurring judgments.]

NOTE AND QUESTIONS In *Fleming* v *Edwards* (1896), 23 O.A.R. 718, it was held that the *Mackay* v *Douglas* rule does not apply where the debtor is entering a business which does not appear risky, for example a business in which he has had experience and success in the past.

1 Is this position sustainable after *McGuire* v *Ottawa Wine Vaults Co.*? Should *Mackay* v *Douglas* apply in all business situations?
2 Suppose that instead of conveying his property to his wife, McGuire had incorporated a company to carry on the hotel business. Is there any functional difference between the two situations? Can you justify the different legal consequences?

Compare with *Mackay* v *Douglas* the Australian case of *Williams* v *Lloyd* (1933), 50 C.L.R. 341 (H.C.). There a wealthy man had transferred his property to his wife and daughter in 1926 while financially solvent. In 1929, after serious financial difficulties, he transferred his remaining property, and also falsified a mortgage he took in 1928 so it appeared his daughter had done so. There was evidence he had continued to deal with all the transferred property as if it were his.

The Court agreed that the 1929 transfers were impeachable but overruled a trial decision impeaching the 1926 transfers. He was in good financial shape in 1926, and subsequent events should not form a basis for attacking the transfer. With respect to the *Mackay* v *Douglas* question this case raised, Dixon J. said the transfer was not impeachable:

The persuasions of his wife to make over the property appear to have been directed not to protecting it against future creditors but to withdrawing the capital from the danger of what she thought imprudent or at least hazardous investment ...
A real intent to defeat or delay creditors must exist, and the question always is whether, upon all the circumstances of the transaction, the transfer or other disposition was in fact made with that intent.

Does *Williams* v *Lloyd* represent the law in Canada or in England? If not, which approach do you prefer?

631 Impeachable Transactions

d / Conveyances for Valuable Consideration

i The Requirement of Intent

Owen Sound General and Marine Hospital v *Mann*, [1953] 3 D.L.R. 417 (Ont. H.C.J.)

ANGER J.: ... Adequacy of consideration is not necessary to uphold a transaction under the
Fraudulent Conveyances Act: Reaume v *Guichard* (1856), 6 U.C.C.P. 170; *Carradice* v *Currie*
(1872), 19 Gr. 108; although in some cases the inadequacy may be some evidence of guilty
knowledge: *Carradice* v *Currie, supra; Buckland* v *Rose* (1859), 7 Gr. 440 at pp 447–8; *Black* v
Fountain (1876), 23 Gr. 174. Also the fact that the result of a conveyance is to defeat creditors is
not necessarily proof that the intent of the grantor was fraudulent: *Godfrey* v *Poole* (1888), 13
App. Cas. 497; *Carr* v *Corfield* (1890), 20 O.R. 218; *Oliver* v *McLaughlin* (1893), 24 O.R. 41;
Crombie v *Young* (1894), 26 O.R. 194; *Montgomery* v *Corbit* (1895), 24 O.A.R. 311; *Elgin Loan &
Savings Co.* v *Orchard* (1904), 7 O.L.R. 695. Where a deed is not voluntary but is for value, there
is no presumption of fraudulent intent from the fact that creditors are defeated by it, the intent
must be deduced from the whole evidence as a fact and, although the fact that creditors have
been defeated may be considered as an aid, that fact has not the conclusive effect which the
Courts have attached to the fact in the case of voluntary settlements: *Beavis* v *Maguire* (1882), 7
O.A.R. 704 at p 707. The burden of proving fraudulent intent by the parties to a conveyance is
ordinarily upon the plaintiff, but nevertheless where there is a conveyance between near
relatives which has the effect of defeating or delaying creditors, although there is no absolute
rule that the burden of proof is upon the defendants, the principle of *res ipsa loquitur* may
properly be applied to a transaction between near relatives in suspicious circumstances, so as to
place upon the defendants the burden of establishing by corroborative evidence, other than the
testimony of interested parties, the *bona fides* of the transaction: see the comment of Duff J. as
he then was, in *Koop* v *Smith* 25 D.L.R. at p 359, 51 S.C.R. at p 559, followed in *Kemp* v *Reaume*
(1931), 40 O.W.N. 482. Undue haste by the parties to a conveyance to assure a priority over
creditors of the vendor, the fact that there is no immediate or early change of possession
following the conveyance, and the relationship between the parties, are all factors relevant to
show an intent to defeat or defraud creditors: *Ferguson* v *Lastewka*, [1946] 4 D.L.R. 531, O.R.
577, in which Le Bel J. reviewed the authorities.

Solomon v *Solomon* (1977), 79 D.L.R. (3d) 264 (Ont. H.C.J.)

KREVER J: ... The plaintiff and the defendant Solomon had been married to each other until
December 14, 1970, when the marriage was dissolved by a decree absolute granted at trial by
Mr. Justice Henderson who, at the same time, also ordered that the defendant Solomon pay the
plaintiff maintenance for her and the two children of the marriage in the weekly sum of $65, of
which $25 was in respect of her own maintenance. The defendant Solomon has failed to make
any payments of maintenance since the beginning of April, 1971. During the subsistence of their
marriage the plaintiff and the defendant Solomon had become the owners as joint tenants of the
matrimonial home at 534 Scofield Ave., in the City of Windsor, the property in question in this
action. After the commencement of partition proceedings, the plaintiff, on April 1, 1971,
conveyed her interest in the property to the defendant Solomon and received from him upon
doing so the sum of $11,310.59. This figure included the value of one-half of the parties' equity in
the property. The plaintiff and the defendant Solomon had agreed on a valuation of the property,

as of the date of closing, in the amount of $26,500, and there is no suggestion that this amount did not truly reflect the fair market value at that time. In addition to her share of the equity in the property the plaintiff also received upon closing $1,000 as 'Part Payment of Arrears of Interim and permanent maintenance,' as well as the taxed costs of the divorce action and the costs of the partition proceedings. The funds from which the plaintiff received this money were obtained by the defendant Solomon by means of a loan of $11,500 from the defendant Krawec which was secured by a mortgage in that amount from the defendant Solomon to the defendant Krawec and registered on April 5, 1971. The defendant Krawec was aware that the purpose of the proceeds of the mortgage was 'to pay her [the plaintiff's] share of the money and whatever else was owed'. At the time the proceeds were advanced to the defendant Solomon the defendant Krawec knew he had been divorced and there was an understanding, but no formal agreement, between the defendants that the defendant Krawec would purchase the property from the defendant Solomon.

In June 1970, the defendant Krawec had submitted to the plaintiff and the defendant Solomon a standard-form written offer to purchase the property for the sum of $26,500 of which $18,500 was to be cash and the balance of approximately $8,000 was to be by way of the assumption of the existing mortgage in that amount. That offer was accepted in writing by the defendant Solomon but, as it was not accepted by the plaintiff, the sale did not take place. On April 21, 1971, the defendant Solomon was in arrears in respect of his obligation to pay maintenance to the plaintiff, an order dated December 14, 1970, possibly the decree absolute of divorce although this is far from clear, was on title, having been registered against the property on April 2, 1971, and a writ of *fieri facias* against the defendant Solomon, in which the plaintiff was the execution creditor, had been lodged with the Sheriff of the County of Essex. On the same date the defendant Solomon was also indebted to other creditors.

April 21, 1971, was the date on which the defendant Solomon conveyed the subject property to the defendant Krawec. The deed was dated, executed, and registered on that date ... [The solicitor] was not instructed to, and did not in fact, search the title or search executions before the deed was registered. Had the title been searched it would have revealed that an order made in a matter between the plaintiff and the defendant Solomon and dated December 14, 1970, had been registered against the property on April 2, 1971. Had a search of executions in the Sheriff's office been made before the registration of the deed on April 21, 1971, it would have revealed the plaintiff's writ of *fieri facias* which had been filed with the Sheriff on January 20, 1971 ...

In the transaction between the defendants the purchase price of $27,500 was shown in the land transfer tax affidavit as consisting of securities transferred to the value of $11,975 (of which, I find, $11,500 was represented by the previously mentioned mortgage which merged with the deed), balances of existing encumbrances with interest at the date of transfer in the sum of $7,500 and 'monies secured by mortgage under this transaction,' in the sum of $8,025. A mortgage for $8,025 from the defendant Krawec to the defendant Solomon was dated, executed, and registered on April 21, 1971. That mortgage was discharged within less than two months by a discharge of mortgage from the defendant Solomon to the defendant Krawec dated June 8, 1971, and registered June 10, 1971. The evidence led by the plaintiff in respect of this discharge is that the discharge, filed as ex. 2 at trial, is in the usual form, recites that the defendant Krawec had satisfied all money due on the mortgage and that, although no money passed through the hands of the defendant Krawec's solicitor who prepared the discharge and saw to its execution, the defendant Krawec satisfied the money due under the mortgage by the payment of cash to the defendant Solomon. On the basis of this uncontradicted evidence, I find as a fact that the money due under the mortgage was actually paid. The money secured under the mortgage had been payable in equal monthly instalments of $120, including interest at 6% per annum until the whole of the principle sum was fully paid.

The defendant Solomon suffered a disabling injury in November, 1970, and has been unable to work since that time. In 1971, he owned a car which he had purchased new in 1969 or 1970, and had financed through his bank. In 1970, while he was in the Workmen's Compensation Hospital in Toronto, he became unable to keep up his payment to the bank in respect of the loan obtained to acquire the car. He thereupon sold the car to the defendant Krawec for $300 cash and the assumption by her of the outstanding indebtedness. He also sold to her his damaged aluminum boat and his tools. I infer from the evidence that the tools referred to were not the tools which he had used when he worked as a plumber, but rather the usual tools associated with home ownership. The defendant Krawec therefore became the owner, for value, of the assets of the defendant Solomon who, for all practical purposes, being without assets and employment, is judgment proof.

The defendant Krawec moved into the subject property upon the completion of the transaction between her and the defendant Solomon by which she became the owner. The defendant Solomon, however, did not thereupon vacate the premises, but remained in them as a roomer for as long as the defendant Krawec remained the owner. By a deed dated September 23, 1973, and registered November 14, 1973, the defendant Krawec conveyed the subject property to two *bona fide* purchasers for value, without notice, who are not parties to this action. At the time of the delivery of possession to these purchasers, the defendant Solomon was in hospital but when he was released he moved into the defendant Krawec's new home, again as a roomer. The evidence indicates that, with respect to the subject property and the defendant Krawec's new home, the relationship between the defendant Krawec and the defendant Solomon was that of landlady and roomer respectively ...

Having found that the conveyance from the defendant Solomon to the defendant Krawec was for valuable consideration and was not a voluntary conveyance, I must be concerned with the determination of the question whether the defendant Krawec shared or knew of the defendant Solomon's intent to defeat, hinder, delay or defraud his creditors at the time he conveyed the property. For the purposes of this determination, I am prepared to assume, as against the defendant Krawec, that, despite the minimal weight of the evidence on the point, the defendant Solomon, himself, had that intention. In the circumstances of this case, the burden of proving the necessary state of mind on the part of the defendant Krawec is on the plaintiff. I accept, as a sound starting point, the proposition put by Middleton, J.A., in *Shephard* v *Shephard* (1925), 56 O.L.R. 555 at p 558, [1925] 2 D.L.R. 897 at pp 899–900:

The learned trial Judge has, I think, rightly adopted the principle ... that where once the Court is convinced of the actuality of the transaction, and that valuable consideration has been given, the plaintiff cannot succeed without actually proving an intention to defraud creditors of the grantor; and this, it appears to me, must be based upon something far beyond mere suspicion. Suspicion will not shift the onus in a case of this kind. ...

There is, as I have indicated, no direct evidence that the defendant Krawec was privy to the defendant Solomon's intent to defraud the plaintiff. Any finding to that effect that is to be made must rest, therefore, on circumstantial evidence. Circumstances that are merely suspicious are not sufficient. But all the circumstances surrounding the conveyance of the property must be examined to determine if there are among them some which have been termed 'badges of fraud'.

In *Bank of Montreal* v *Vandine et al.*, [1953] 1 D.L.R. 456, 33 M.P.R. 368, the Appeal Division of the Supreme Court of New Brunswick affirmed the judgment of Harrison, J., who listed the following features of transactions alleged to be made with fraudulent intent as badges of fraud:

1 Secrecy
2 Generality of Conveyances, by which is meant the inclusion of all or substantially all of the debtor's assets
3 Continuance in possession by debtor
4 Some benefit retained under the settlement to the settlor.

He included as minor badges of fraud:

5 Gross excess of value of property over price paid and
6 Cash taken in payment instead of a cheque.

In *Ferguson* v *Lastewka et al.*, [1946] O.R. 577, [1946] 4 D.L.R. 531, LeBel, J., looked upon the following circumstances as supporting an inference of fraud on the part of the grantee:

1 Knowledge of the likelihood of a successful action by the plaintiff against the grantor
2 Unusual haste in closing
3 No immediate or early change of possession following the conveyance, adding that 'joint possession raised a presumption of fraud,''
4 The relationship between the parties to the conveyance.

In *Royal Bank of Canada* v *Sullivan and Herr*, [1957] O.W.N. 68 at p 72, 6 D.L.R. (2d) 559 at p 567 [affirmed [1957] O.W.N. 520, 10 D.L.R. (2d) 494], Thompson, J., held to be badges of fraud secrecy in the transaction and feverish haste to register the mortgage, the conveyance sought to be set aside, on the eve of the plaintiff's judgment. In an earlier case, *Kvasnedsky* v *Birnbaum* (1923), 25 O.W.N. 29, Orde, J., held that knowledge on the part of the grantee of the grantor's insolvent circumstances, though by itself insufficient to impute to the grantee knowledge of the grantor's intent to defraud his creditors, was an important circumstance if there were other grounds for suspicion. On the facts of the case before him, he found other grounds in the grantor's remaining in possession, which tended to delay the discovery of the sale, and the absence of any certificate as to title, or as to arrears of taxes or as to executions in the Sheriff's hands.

It is apparent from a survey of the decisions that each case must turn on its own special facts. The special facts of this case, when examined carefully, do not, in my opinion, lead one to the conclusion that the defendant Krawec had knowledge, at the material time, of the defendant Solomon's intent in conveying the property. Neither secrecy nor undue haste has been shown. The speed with which the mortgage given back on closing was discharged has given rise to some suspicion in my mind but I am unable to put it any higher than that. The property was sold at what must, on any reasonable view, be considered its fair market value, and the continued residence of the defendant Solomon in the premises as a *bona fide* roomer has been satisfactorily proved. The transfer by the defendant Solomon of his assets – his damaged boat, his car and his household tools – to the defendant Krawec seems to me to have no significance. On the evidence, the transfer of these items of personal property, and, indeed, the impugned transaction itself, seem to me to be equally consistent with an expectation on the part of the defendant Krawec that the receipt by the defendant Solomon of the proceeds would enable him to discharge his obligations as with any other conclusion. As I have shown, the evidence adduced by the plaintiff was that the defendant Krawec believed that the purpose of the proceeds of the mortgage given before the sale in question was to enable the defendant Solomon to pay the plaintiff 'her share of the money and whatever else was owed'. There was no evidence that the defendant Krawec knew that the plaintiff had a judgment against the defendant Solomon for maintenance. Even if the defendant Krawec had that knowledge, it would not support a conclusion that she therefore knew of the defendant Solomon's intent. The following language of Orde, J., in *Kvasnedsky* v *Birnbaum, supra*, seems to me to be apposite [p 30]:

It does not necessarily follow, however, that knowledge on the part of the intending purchaser of the vendor's insolvency imputes to the purchaser knowledge of the vendor's intent to defraud his creditors, and it is incumbent upon the plaintiff to bring home to the purchaser knowledge of that intent in order to impeach, under the statute of Elizabeth, a conveyance made upon a valuable consideration: *Hickerson* v *Parrington* (1891), 18 A.R., 635. There is no law to prevent one who is insolvent from disposing of his property. He may be doing so in good faith and for the purpose of realising the moneys with which to pay his creditors. So that a purchaser for value is not, merely because of his knowledge of the vendor's insolvency, to be presumed to have knowledge of a fraudulent intent which may not in fact exist.

Since knowledge of a grantor's insolvency or indebtedness does not cause a grantee to cease to be an innocent purchaser for value without notice of the grantor's fraudulent intent, I am unable to find significant the defendant Krawec's failure to instruct her solicitor to search the title to the property or to search executions in the Sheriff's office. At most those searches would have revealed, as previously indicated, that an order, the nature of which is not shown by the evidence, in a matter between the plaintiff and the defendant Solomon, dated December 14, 1970, had been registered April 2, 1971, and that a writ of *fieri facias* had been filed with the Sheriff on January 20, 1971, or, more simply, that the plaintiff was an execution creditor of the defendant Solomon. Knowledge of that kind does not invest the defendant Krawec with knowledge of the defendant Solomon's intent.

To sum up, after a consideration of all the circumstances surrounding the transaction between the two defendants, I am unable to conclude that the plaintiff has proved that the defendant Krawec was privy to the defendant Solomon's intent to defeat, hinder, delay or defraud the plaintiff. I am, of course, suspicious, but I am obliged to act on the evidence and, again, suspicion is not enough ...

Action dismissed.

Re Panfab Corp., [1971] 2 O.R. 202 (H.C.J.)

HOULDEN, J.: This is an appeal from the report of the Registrar dated June 12, 1970, made after the trial of an issue. The facts have been carefully detailed by the Registrar in his reasons which accompanied the report. The appeal is only as to the findings of the Registrar that certain debentures dated February 11, 1966, given by the bankrupt company in favour of Elsie Last in the amount of $26,100 and Victor Last in the amount of $4,000 were fraudulent and void under ss 64 and 64A [enacted 1966–67, c 32, s 11] of the *Bankruptcy Act*, R.S.C. 1952, c 14.

Victor Last advanced money to the bankrupt on or about August 31, 1965. Elsie Last advanced her funds in October, 1965. At the time the advances were made, there were no arrangements for the parties to receive debentures as security for their loans. In the case of Victor Last, he was to receive a note. With reference to Elsie Last, she had put a mortgage on her home to raise the money, and the debtor company was to make the payments on the mortgage as they fell due.

When the moneys were received in October, the company was in dire need of working capital, and, although the funds gave a temporary respite, by January, 1966, the company urgently needed further financing. This was arranged through Samuel Hogg and Lillian Casselton, two of the directors and officers of the company. To protect these new advances, debentures were given under the *Corporation Securities Registration Act*, R.S.O. 1960, c 70, and debentures were also issued to Elsie Last and Victor Last in respect of their loans. The effective date of the debentures is February 11, 1966. The petition in bankruptcy was filed on February 9, 1967.

The learned Registrar found, and there has been no attack on these findings, that the company was insolvent at the date the debentures were given and that the receipt of the debentures had the effect of giving Victor Last and Elsie Last a preference over other creditors. He further found that the giving of the securities came within ss 64 and 64A of the *Bankruptcy Act*, and that Elsie Last and Victor Last were persons related to the bankrupt company within the meaning of s 2B(2) (*b*) [enacted 1966–67, c 32, s 1] of the *Bankruptcy Act* ...

The last issue is whether or not the debentures fall within the provisions of the *Fraudulent Conveyances Act*. Counsel for the creditors points out the following badges of fraud: (a) the debentures were given for a past-due debt; (b) the debentures were given to relatives of Eugene Last who had *de facto* control of Panfab; (c) the company was insolvent at the time the debentures were given; (d) in effect, the debentures took away all the assets of the company which should have been available to creditors.

Even if all these matters are accepted, it does not make the giving of the debentures void. The problem was dealt with by the Supreme Court of Canada in *Mulcahy et al.* v *Archibald* (1898), 28 s.c.r. 523. Sedgewick, J., who delivered the judgment of the Court, stated the relevant principles at p 529:

> The statute of Elizabeth, while making void transfers, the object of which is to defeat or delay creditors, does not make void but expressly protects them in the interest of transferees who have given valuable consideration therefor, and it has been decided over and over again that knowledge on the part of such a transferee of the motive or design of the transferor is not conclusive of bad faith or will not preclude him from obtaining the benefit of his security. So long as there is an existing debt and the transfer to him is made for the purpose of securing that debt and he does not either directly or indirectly make himself an instrument for the purpose of subsequently benefiting the transferor, he is protected and the transaction cannot be held void.

In the *Mulcahy* case at p 529, Sedgewick, J., quoted the words of Jessel, M.R., in *Middleton* v *Pollock* (1876), 2 Ch.D. 104 at p 108:

> 'It has been decided, if decision were wanted, that a payment is *bona fide* within the meaning of the statute of Elizabeth, although the man who made the payment was insolvent at the time to his own knowledge, and even although the creditors who accepted the money knew it ... The meaning of the statute is that the debtor must not retain a benefit for himself.'

See also *P.E.I. Mutual Fire Ins. Co. et al.* v *Best* (1933), 7 M.P.R. 107.

On the basis of this authority, 'bona fide' in s 3 of the *Fraudulent Conveyances Act* means that the debtor must not have retained a benefit to himself and in this case no such benefit was retained by Panfab. The transfer was made to give security to Victor Last and Eugene Last for an existing debt, and, even if Panfab knew it was insolvent and Victor Last and Elsie Last knew of the insolvency, this is not sufficient to void the transaction where there was no intention of subsequently directly or indirectly benefiting Panfab.

With reluctance, therefore, the appeal must be allowed ...

ii Transfers Between Relatives

Koop v *Smith* (1915), 25 D.L.R. 355 (S.C.C.)

DUFF, J.: I think this appeal should be allowed and the judgment of the Chief Justice, who tried the action, restored. The majority of the Court of Appeal appear, if I may say so with respect, to have fallen into the error of treating the relationship of the parties to the impeached transaction as possessing no very material significance. The trial Judge, on the other hand, treated the relationship as decisive in this sense that it determined the point of view from which the evidence was to be considered and the all important question of the onus of proof. The trial Judge indeed appears to have laid it down as a proposition of law that a transaction of this kind between two near relatives, carried out in circumstances in themselves sufficient to excite suspicion, can only be supported (in an action brought to impeach it by creditors) if the reality or the *bona fides* of it are established by evidence other than the testimony of the interested parties; and there is a series of authorities in the Ontario Courts which has been supposed to decide that, and it may be that it is the settled law of Ontario to-day.

I do not think the proposition put thus absolutely is part of the English law or of the law of British Columbia; but I think it is a maxim of prudence based upon experience that in such cases a tribunal of fact may properly act upon that when suspicion touching the reality or the *bona fides* of a transaction between near relatives arises from the circumstances in which the transaction took place then the fact of relationship itself is sufficient to put the burden of explanation upon the parties interested and that, in such a case, the testimony of the parties must be scrutinized with care and suspicion; and it is very seldom that such evidence can safely be acted upon as in itself sufficient. In other words, I think the weight of the fact of relationship and the question of necessity of corroboration are primarily questions for the discretion of the trial Judge subject, of course, to review; and that any trial Judge will in such cases have regard to the course of common experience as indicated by the pronouncements and practice of very able and experienced judges such as Armour, C.J., and Mowat, V.C., and will depart from the practice only in very exceptional circumstances.

I may add that I think it doubtful whether the Ontario decisions when properly read really do lay it down as a rule of law that the fact of relationship is sufficient in itself to shift the burden of establishing the burden of proof in the strict sense. It may be that the proper construction of these cases is that the burden of giving evidence and not the burden of the issue is shifted. (As to this distinction see the admirable chapter IX, in Professor Thayer's 'Law of Evidence.') In my own view as indicated above, even this would be putting the matter just a little too high; I think the true rule is that suspicious circumstances coupled with relationship make a case of *res ipsa loquitar* which the tribunal of fact may and will generally treat as a sufficient *primâ facie* case, but that it is not strictly in law bound to do so; and that the question of the necessity of corroboration is strictly a question of fact. Having examined the evidence carefully I am satisfied that the trial Judge was entitled to take the course he did take and not only that the evidence, as I read it in the record, casts the burden of explanation upon the respondent, but that the testimony given by her brother ought not in the circumstances to be accepted as establishing either the actual existence of the debt or of the *bona fides* of the transaction.

[Davies, Idington, Anglin and Brodeur JJ also gave reasons for allowing the appeal.]

NOTE A recent Ontario case which applied *Koop* v *Smith* was *Gallop* v *Hamlin* (1973), 1 O.R. (2d) 156 (C.A.). A transfer of funds had been made to a relative allegedly to repay a debt which had existed for 25 years. There was no written acknowledgment of either the debt or the repayment. The Court held that the transaction could be upheld only if bona fides were established by evidence of other than the interested parties. Cf. *Toronto-Dominion Bank* v *Michael*, [1973] 1 W.W.R. 656 (Alta. S.C., A.D.), holding that there is no rule of law requiring independent corroboration.

The principles governing conveyances between close relatives also apply to transfers between individuals and companies which they control (*Burton* v *R. & M. Insurance Ltd.* (1977), 81 D.L.R. (3d) 455 (Alta. S.C.); *Re Martineau* (1969), 5 D.L.R. (3d) 165 (B.C.S.C.)) and to transfers between unmarried parties living together as husband and wife (*Lee* v *Lee* (1978), 82 D.L.R. (3d) 429 (Nfld. D.C.)).

iii Conveyances to Avoid Prospective Civil Liability

Ferguson v *Lastewka*, [1946] 4 D.L.R. 531 (Ont. H.C.J.)

LEBEL J.: The plaintiff is an execution creditor of the defendant Michael Lastewka for $12,075 and costs. She seeks to set aside, as fraudulent and void against her and other creditors, a conveyance dated July 3, 1944, made by the said defendant to his daughter and her husband, the other defendants. The plaintiff's judgment, on which execution remained wholly unsatisfied at the time of the trial, was recovered in an action instituted on November 21, 1944, for damages sustained in a motor car accident as a result of which the plaintiff was seriously injured and her husband was killed. The motor accident occurred on April 3, 1944.

The circumstances under which the defendant Lastewka acquired the lands described in the impeached conveyance, and later conveyed them to his co-defendants, are these:

In the early summer of 1943, all the defendants resided in Montreal. With a view to purchasing a farm in the Niagara district, Lastewka sold his home in Montreal. He was then indebted to the defendant Andrew Ewaschuk in the sum of $1,500 but he arranged with Ewaschuk that the latter should accept his promissory note for the amount of the debt, without interest, maturing July 1, 1944. On August 14, 1943, Lastewka purchased 15 acres in Lincoln County, being part of a fruit farm owned by one James A. Johnson. He paid $2,000 in cash and gave Mr. Johnson a mortgage for $2,200, the balance of the purchase-price. In erecting a house and barn on the property, and in commencing his farm operations, he said, he used up all his available cash. In November, 1943, he borrowed $500 from a bank, and he swore that he secured loans from a sister amounting in all to $300 and incurred other debts. On July 3, 1944, the date of the disputed conveyance, besides the mortgage indebtedness and the Ewaschuk note, he said on his examination for discovery, which was read in as part of the plaintiff's case, that he owed in the neighbourhood of

$1,350 to the bank and the others. Soon after Lastewka's purchase of the fruit farm the Ewaschuks visited him there and they became interested in acquiring property in the vicinity for themselves. That such might be their decision was suggested in a letter the defendant Milly Ewaschuk wrote to her mother as early as August 1, 1943. In another letter, dated February 8, 1944, Milly Ewaschuk told her mother that she and her husband had a prospective buyer for their Montreal house, and that they were interested in the farm adjoining the Lastewkas', *i.e.* Mr. Johnson's. She also said they would like to obtain payment of the promissory note or at least $1,000 on account. The Ewaschuks completed the sale of their Montreal house, Milly Ewaschuk swore, a few days before they heard of the motor car accident. On May 1 and 2, 1944, their furniture was moved from Montreal to the Lastewka farm. The Ewaschuks followed in the same month. Andrew Ewaschuk interviewed Mr. Johnson with a view to buying his farm but the price was apparently too high. Ewaschuk also looked at some other farms in the vicinity before returning to Montreal to secure a National Selective Service release from his employment in a war plant there. He testified that up to the time that he returned to Montreal for this purpose he had no intention of purchasing his father-in-law's farm. After securing the release mentioned, Ewaschuk returned to the Lastewkas' farm, but in the meantime, on June 21, 1944, Lastewka had been convicted of an offence related to the operation of his motor vehicle involved in the accident, and he was now serving a three months' sentence in the Ontario Reformatory at Guelph. Ewaschuk swore that his mother-in-law then informed him that her husband had decided to sell the farm and would give him the first chance to buy. On his examination for discovery (Question 166, also read in as part of the plaintiff's case) Ewaschuk swore that his mother-in-law had said that the price was $5,400. Ewaschuk then sought the advice of Thomas R. BeGora, a solicitor of this Court in St. Catharines, and a few days later instructed him to draw a deed from Lastewka to himself and his wife as joint tenants, in consideration of the amount mentioned. Mr. BeGora prepared the deed but did not fill out the land transfer tax affidavit because he did not know all necessary details. The deed as drawn, however, included a covenant for the assumption of the Johnson mortgage. On July 3, 1944, Mr. BeGora, Andrew Ewaschuk, and a man named Baraniuk, drove to Guelph and interviewed Lastewka in the reformatory. Lastewka testified that at this interview he told Ewaschuk that if he paid him $2,000, the equivalent of the amount he himself had paid down on the purchase of the farm, assumed the balance owing on the Johnson mortgage, *viz.*, $1,900, and returned his promissory note for $1,500, that he could have the farm. These amounts total the consideration said to have been mentioned by Mrs. Lastewka. Mr. BeGora then filled in the land transfer tax affidavit and Lastewka executed the deed and handed it back to Mr. BeGora. The document was signed later by the Ewaschuks and by Mrs. Lastewka. Ewaschuk returned the promissory note to Mrs. Lastewka, and, as directed by her husband, gave her his cheque for $2,000 some days later. Out of the proceeds of this cheque, it was said, the bank and all Lastewka's existing creditors were paid off, and Lastewka's wife swore that she afterwards deposited the balance in her own bank account.

The plaintiff alleges that the impeached conveyance was executed and delivered in pursuance of a fraudulent scheme 'for the purpose of defeating, defrauding and delaying the plaintiff and other creditors,' and Mr. Lancaster argued that the Court should find that the consideration set up by the defendants in support of the transaction was illusory and inadequate, and in any event that there was an intention on the part of the defendants to defraud the plaintiff and Lastewka's other creditors. Mr. Schreiber contended that the sale to the Ewaschuks was for valuable consideration, and argued that these defendants were as much entitled to take advantage of

Lastewka's financial embarrassment, and the predicament he found himself in, as a result of the accident, as a stranger would be entitled to do; in effect, that the purchase of the farm by the Ewaschuks was for valuable consideration and was *bona fide.*

I am unable to accede to the plaintiff's contention that the consideration paid by the Ewaschuks was illusory or inadequate. I find as a fact that Lastewka owed Andrew Ewaschuk the sum of $1,500, that Ewaschuk assumed the balance owing on the Johnson mortgage, and that he paid Mrs. Lastewka on her husband's instructions the balance of the purchase-price, *viz.,* $2,000. As a result, I find that the impeached conveyance was given for valuable and adequate consideration, and I conclude, as counsel for the plaintiff conceded at the close of his argument, that to succeed the plaintiff must establish an actual and express intent to defraud creditors on the part of Lastewka, and that the Ewaschuks were privy to such intent: see *Hickerson* v *Parrington* (1891), 18 O.A.R. 635 at pp 640–41; May on Fraudulent and Voluntary Conveyances, 3rd ed., p 62; and *Cadogan* v *Kennett* (1776), 2 Cowp. 432 at p 434, 98 E.R. 1171 ...

The circumstances so far related show that it was within the knowledge of all the defendants that while the damage action was not commenced for some seven months following the date of the impeached conveyance – due to the nature of the plaintiff's injuries and her long hospitalization – the accident occurred four months earlier; also, that just prior to the date of the disputed instrument, Lastewka was convicted of an offence in connection with the accident, and was in custody as a result.

The plaintiff's counsel relied upon these factors, as well as on others to be mentioned, as proof of actual fraud, and urged that the conveyance was delivered *pendente lite*, in effect, if not in fact, as a mere scheme or trick to defeat creditors and the plaintiff in particular.

In *Cadogan* v *Kennett*, 2 Cowp. at p 434, Lord Mansfield C.J. said: 'So, if a man knows of a judgment and execution, and, with a view to defeat it, purchases the debtor's goods, it is void: because, the purpose is iniquitous. It is assisting one man to cheat another, which the law will never allow.'

I am satisfied that the principle enunciated by Lord Mansfield is equally applicable in cases where a creditor has not recovered judgment at the date of the impeached conveyance, but the purchaser, knowing of the creditor's pending or likely action, purchases the debtor's property with a view to defeating the expected execution: see *Gurofski* v *Harris* (1896), 27 O.R. 201; *Hopkinson* v *Westerman* (1919), 48 D.L.R. 597, 45 O.L.R. 208; May on Fraudulent and Voluntary Conveyances, 3rd ed., p 102; *McMullen* v *Dr. Barnardo's Homes*, 26 O.W.N. 168; *Goyan* v *Kinash*, [1945] 2 D.L.R. 749; *Barling* v *Bishopp* (1860), 29 Beav. 417, 54 E.R. 689; and *Edmunds* v *Edmunds*, [1904] P. 362.

A careful consideration of the evidence and the exhibits, in the light of the principles mentioned, has satisfied me that Lastewka conveyed his farm intending to defraud his creditors, and the plaintiff in particular, and that Andrew Ewaschuk and Milly Ewaschuk, on a lesser scale, were parties to the fraud. I am satisfied that the plaintiff has discharged the onus upon her in this regard ...

I should not conclude my reasons without adding that I am satisfied that Mr. BeGora was in no way privy to the fraud of the defendants. The advice he gave Ewaschuk was sound, and he was not present during the conversation between Lastewka and Ewaschuk which preceded execution of the conveyance by the former, and which Baraniuk overheard in part at least. The whole incident, however, is illustrative of the fact that solicitors, in circumstances suggestive of possible fraud, must be extremely watchful of their own position in the matter. It should be mentioned, too, that the solicitor for the Ewaschuks waived any question of privilege in so far as Mr. BeGora's evidence was concerned, and none was claimed by Lastewka.

The plaintiff's action succeeds and there will be judgment declaring that the conveyance from the defendant Michael Lastewka to his co-defendants (20535 for the Township of Grantham) is null and void against the plaintiff and other creditors of Michael Lastewka. The plaintiff is entitled to her costs.
Judgment for plaintiff.

Compare with *Ferguson* v *Lastewka* the cases of *Ex parte Mercer,* supra p 615, and *Mandryk* v *Merko*, supra p 617. Note that spouses seeking maintenance have been held to be 'others' within the phrase 'creditors or others' in s 2 of the Act, and may therefore seek to have conveyances set aside: *Shephard* v *Shephard* (1925), 56 O.L.R. 555 (C.A.); *Murdoch* v *Murdoch* (1976), 1 Alta. L.R. (2d) 135 (S.C.).

3 FRAUDULENT PREFERENCES

a / The Assignments and Preferences Act, R.S.O. 1970, c 34

3. Every confession of judgment, *cognovit actionem* or warrant of attorney to confess judgment given by a person, being at the time in insolvent circumstances or unable to pay his debts in full or knowing himself to be on the eve of insolvency, voluntarily or by collusion with a creditor with intent thereby to defeat, hinder, delay or prejudice his creditors wholly or in part, or to give one or more of his creditors a preference over his other creditors or over any one or more of them, is void as against the creditors of the person giving the same and is ineffectual to support any judgment or execution.

4. (1) Subject to section 5, every gift, conveyance, assignment or transfer, delivery over or payment of goods, chattels or effects, or of bills, bonds, notes or securities, or of shares, dividends, premiums or bonus in any bank, company or corporation, or of any other property, real or personal, made by a person at a time when he is in insolvent circumstances or is unable to pay his debts in full, or knows that he is on the eve of insolvency, with intent to defeat, hinder, delay or prejudice his creditors, or any one or more of them, is void as against the creditor or creditors injured, delayed or prejudiced.

(2) Subject to section 5, every such gift, conveyance, assignment or transfer, delivery over or payment made by a person being at the time in insolvent circumstances, or unable to pay his debts in full, or knowing himself to be on the eve of insolvency, to or for a creditor with the intent to give such creditor an unjust preference over his other creditors or over any one or more of them is void as against the creditor or creditors injured, delayed, prejudiced or postponed.

(3) Subject to section 5, if such a transaction with or for a creditor has the effect of giving that creditor a preference over the other creditors of the debtor or over any one or more of them, it shall, in and with respect to any action or proceeding that, within sixty days thereafter, is brought, had or taken to impeach or set aside such transaction, be presumed *prima facie* to have been made with the intent mentioned in subsection 2, and to be an unjust preference within the meaning of this Act whether it be made voluntarily or under pressure.

(4) Subject to section 5, if such a transaction with or for a creditor has the effect of giving that creditor a preference over the other creditors of the debtor or over any one or more of them, it shall, if the debtor within sixty days after the transaction makes an assignment for the benefit of his creditors, be presumed *prima facie* to have been made with the intent mentioned in subsection 2, and to be an unjust preference within the meaning of this Act whether it be made voluntarily or under pressure.

(5) The word 'creditor' in the fifth line of subsection 2, in the second line of subsection 3, and in the second line of subsection 4, includes any surety and the endorser of any promissory note or bill of exchange who would upon payment by him of the debt, promissory note or bill of exchange, in respect of which such suretyship was entered into or such endorsement was given, become a creditor of the person giving the preference within the meaning of those subsections.

5. (1) Nothing in section 4 applies to an assignment made to the sheriff of the county or district in which the debtor resides or carries on business or, with the consent of a majority of his creditors having claims of $100 and upwards computed according to section 24, to another assignee resident in Ontario, for the purpose of paying rateably and proportionately and without preference or priority all the creditors of the debtor their just debts, nor to any *bona fide* sale or payment made in the ordinary course of trade or calling to an innocent purchaser or person, nor to any payment of money to a creditor, nor to any *bona fide* conveyance, assignment, transfer or delivery over of any goods or property of any kind, that is made in consideration of a present actual *bona fide* payment in money, or by way of security for a present actual *bona fide* advance of money, or that is made in consideration of a present actual *bona fide* sale or delivery of goods or other property where the money paid or the goods or other property sold or delivered bear a fair and reasonable relative value to the consideration therefor.

(2) In the case of a valid sale of goods or other property and payment or transfer of the consideration or part thereof by the purchaser to a creditor of the vendor under circumstances that would render void such a payment or transfer by the debtor personally and directly, the payment or transfer, even though valid as respects the purchaser, is void as respects the creditor to whom it is made.

(3) Every assignment for the general benefit of creditors that is not void under section 4, but is not made to the sheriff nor to any other person with the prescribed consent of creditors, is void as against a subsequent assignment that is in conformity with this Act, and is subject in other respects to the provisions thereof until and unless a subsequent assignment is executed in accordance therewith.

(4) Where a payment has been made that is void under this Act and any valuable security was given up in consideration of the payment, the creditor is entitled to have the security restored or its value made good to him before, or as a condition of, the return of the payment.

(5) Nothing in this Act.

(*a*) affects *The Wages Act* or prevents a debtor providing for payment of wages due by him in accordance with that Act;

(*b*) affects any payment of money to a creditor where the creditor, by reason or on account of the payment, has lost or been deprived of, or has in good faith given up, any valid security that he held for the payment of the debt so paid unless the security is restored or its value made good to the creditor;

(*c*) applies to the substitution in good faith of one security for another security for the same debt so far as the debtor's estate is not thereby lessened in value to the other creditors; or

(*d*) invalidates a security given to a creditor for a pre-existing debt where, by reason or on account of the giving of the security, an advance in money is made to the debtor by the creditor in the *bona fide* belief that the advance will enable the debtor to continue his trade or business and to pay his debts in full.

12. (1) In the case of a gift, conveyance, assignment or transfer of any property, real or personal, that is invalid against creditors, if the person to whom the gift, conveyance, assignment or transfer was made has sold or disposed of, realized or collected the property or any part thereof, the money or other proceeds may be seized or recovered in an action by a person who would be entitled to seize and recover the property if it had remained in the possession or control of the debtor or of the person to whom the gift, conveyance, transfer, delivery or payment was made, and such right to seize and recover belongs not only to an assignee for the general benefit of the creditors of the debtor but, where there is no such assignment, to all creditors of the debtor.

(2) Where there is no assignment for the benefit of creditors and the proceeds are of such a character as to be seizable under execution, they may be seized under the execution of any creditor and are subject to *The Creditors' Relief Act.*

(3) Where there is no assignment for the benefit of creditors and whether the proceeds are or are not of such a character as to be seizable under execution, an action may be brought therefor by a creditor, whether an execution creditor or not, on behalf of himself and all other creditors, or such other proceedings may be taken as are necessary to render the proceeds available for the general benefit of the creditors.

(4) This section does not apply as against innocent purchasers of the property.

b / Introductory Note

The reach of The Assignments and Preferences Act is limited both by what it requires and what it excepts from its coverage. For a transaction to be set aside by a creditor as a fraudulent preference, s 4(2) requires that the creditor establish both insolvency and intent, and both knowledge of the insolvency and the intent to prefer must be shared by both parties to the transfer: *Benallack v Bank of British North America* (1905), 36 S.C.R. 120. Where the transaction is attacked within sixty days, the presumption set up by s 4(3), (4) may assist the creditor in proving intent; however, shared knowledge of the insolvency must first be shown before the presumption can arise: *Caulfield, Burns & Gibson Ltd. v Kitchen*, [1956] O.W.N. 697 (H.C.J.), infra p 646. Where the transaction is attacked beyond the sixty day period, a showing by the debtor that the transfer was made as the result of pressure by the transferee will rebut any suggestion of intention to prefer: see infra, p 659.

Section 5 of the Act protects a wide class of transactions from being set aside as preferential. Perhaps the most significant exception is contained in s 5(1), under which s 4 is inapplicable to 'any payment of money to a creditor'; the Act therefore applies only to transfers of other kinds of property, and to the giving of security interests which may prefer certain creditors by enlarging their rights.

Where a transfer of property is invalid against creditors and the transferee has sold or disposed of it to a third party, s 12 of the Act authorizes the impeaching creditor to recover the proceeds of the disposition from the original transferee. Although there is no similar provision in The Fraudulent Conveyances Act, it was recently held by the Ontario Court of Appeal, overruling authority to the contrary, that the words of the section were broad enough to encompass transactions invalid under that statute as well: *Westinghouse Canada Ltd. v Buchar* (1975), 59 D.L.R. (3d) 641. The Manitoba Court of Appeal had earlier come to the same conclusion under that province's Assignments Act: *John Deere Ltd. v Paddock* (1972), 32 D.L.R. (3d) 773. A creditor using s 12 should bring a class action on behalf of all other creditors, and any proceeds recovered are subject to disposition under The Creditors' Relief Act: *Westinghouse Canada Ltd. v Buchar*, supra.

c / Note: The Constitutional Issue

Because the operation of provincial fraudulent preferences legislation is premised on insolvency, doubts have been raised concerning its constitutionality in the face of s 91(21) of the British North America Act, which assigns to the federal Parliament exclusive jurisdiction in relation to matters of 'bankruptcy and insolvency'. Even assuming the legislation's validity, it has also been argued that federal treatment of preferences in the Bankruptcy Act renders the provincial statutes inoperative by virtue of the doctrine of paramountcy. With the exception of Quebec, the provinces first enacted their preferences legislation during the period 1880 to 1919, when there was no federal bankruptcy statute.

These questions have arisen primarily in the context of attempts by trustees in bankruptcy to overcome the limitation periods set out in the Bankruptcy Act by resort to remedies provided under provincial law. The British Columbia preferences statute was held inoperative in *Hoffar Ltd.* v *Canadian Credit Men's Trust Ass'n*, [1929] 2 D.L.R. 73 (B.C.C.A.), leave to appeal refused [1929] S.C.R. 180; similar decisions were reached in respect of the Ontario statute in *Re Trenwith*, [1934] O.R. 326 (C.A.), and *Re Bozanich*, [1942] S.C.R. 130. In *Re McIntosh-Marshall Equipment Ltd.* (1964), 48 D.L.R. (2d) 619 (Alta. S.C., A.D.), affirming 48 W.W.R. 420, the trial judge's holding that the Alberta legislation was ultra vires was modified to a holding that it was either ultra vires or inoperative.

The federal response to the earlier of these cases was the enactment in 1949 of s 50(6) of the Bankruptcy Act, R.S.C. 1970, c B-3, as follows:

50. (6) The provisions of this Act shall not be deemed to abrogate or supersede the substantive provisions of any other law or statute relating to property and civil rights that are not in conflict with this Act, and the trustee is entitled to avail himself of all rights and remedies provided by such law or statute as supplementary to and in addition to the rights and remedies provided by this Act.

The constitutional questions again came before the Supreme Court of Canada in *Robinson* v *Countrywide Factors Ltd.* (1977), 72 D.L.R. (3d) 500. The Court held in a 5 to 4 decision both that the Saskatchewan Fraudulent Preferences Act was valid provincial legislation and that it could be used by a trustee in bankruptcy to attack a transaction made outside the limitation period prescribed by the Bankruptcy Act. According to Spence J, with whom Judson, Ritchie and Pigeon JJ concurred,

the better view is to confine the effect of what is now s 73 of the Bankruptcy Act to providing for the invalidity of transactions within its exact scope. To that extent, the Parliament of Canada, by valid legislation upon 'bankruptcy' and 'insolvency', has covered the field but has refrained from completely covering the whole field of transactions avoided by provincial legislation. I am of the opinion that the enactment in 1949 of the provisions now found in s 50(6) of the Bankruptcy Act was a plain indication that Parliament recognized that provisions in provincial statutes dealing with preferential transactions were still valid provincial enactments in reference to 'property' and 'civil rights' and were valuable aids to trustees in bankruptcy in attacking the validity of such transactions and should be available to the said trustees in bankruptcy.

The opinion of Beetz J was that [t]he power to repress fraud by avoiding fraudulent conveyances and preferences is an indisputable part of provincial jurisdiction over property and civil rights. The risk of fraud is increased when a debtor finds himself in a situation of impending or actual insolvency and, in my view, provincial laws can, without undergoing a change in nature, focus upon that situation as upon a proper occasion to attain their object. Given their purpose, they do not cease to be laws in relation to property and civil rights simply because they are timely and effective or because Parliament could enact similar laws in relation to bankruptcy and insolvency.

In a dissenting judgment with which Martland, Dickson and de Grandpré JJ concurred, Laskin CJC said:

It is plain to me that if provincial legislation avowedly directed to insolvency, and to transactions between debtor and creditor consummated in a situation of insolvency, can be sustained as validly enacted, unless overborne by competent federal legislation, there is a serious breach of the principle of exclusiveness which embraces insolvency under s 91(21) ...

[Section 50(6)] does not provide for the effacement of federal legislation to allow provincial legislation to operate but relates to provincial provisions which satisfy two conditions: first, they must be provisions which are independently valid; and second, they must be provisions which do not conflict with the application and operation of federal provisions. I do not see how provincial legislation whose operation is predicated on insolvency can be anything but insolvency legislation, nor do I see how a provincial statute can validly provide that what a federal statute says is not impeachable can nonetheless be impeached. There is no difference, in my view, between the situation where a province seeks to narrow the period of impeachability of a transaction and the situation where it seeks to enlarge it, especially when in either case it is doing this from the standpoint of insolvency as the triggering factor. This is a different thing from legislation dealing only with fraudulent preferences apart from or unrelated to insolvency. Here, although such legislation may be valid in the absence of federal legislation, there may nonetheless be operative incompatibility in particular cases but no general supersession or preclusion.

d / The Requirement of Insolvency

i *Clarke* v *Sutherland*, [1917] 3 W.W.R. 624 (Alta. S.C., A.D.)

HARVEY C.J.: The plaintiff is an execution creditor of the defendant Sutherland and the action is to set aside a conveyance to the co-defendant as a preference.

Shortly the facts are that Sutherland transferred a quarter section of land to one Storer receiving other land in exchange. It was found that there were executions registered against the lands conveyed to Storer and he could not get the title as agreed. An agreement was entered into whereby Storer, in consideration of a promise by the defendant and his wife to convey to him an unspecified quarter section within four months, transferred the land first transferred to him to the defendant trust company which holds it in trust for two banks who have taken it in satisfaction of executions which they had registered against the defendant Sutherland. It is this conveyance to the trust company that is attacked.

It is apparent at once that there is room for doubt whether the plaintiff has been deprived of any right or in any way prejudiced by the transaction. Other difficulties also suggest themselves. However, Mr. Justice Hyndman, the trial Judge, dismissed the action upon the ground that the plaintiff had failed to prove that his debtor was insolvent and in my opinion he was right in that conclusion. The action is rested upon sec. 41 of *The Assignments Act* (ch. 6 of 1907). That applies only in the case of a transfer 'by a person at any time when he is in insolvent circumstances, or is unable to pay his debts in full, or knows that he is on the eve of insolvency.' Without considering the particular meaning of insolvency it is clear that, speaking generally, it means inability to pay one's liabilities. That condition, therefore, depends on both assets and liabilities. That one does not pay one's debts is by no means proof that one cannot. The only evidence of insolvency in the present case makes no reference whatever to the defendant's assets. He was not a witness himself and the only evidence on the point was to the effect that there were debts against him unsatisfied some of which were execution debts upon which the sheriff, in whose hands they were, was unable to realize.

There is no evidence that he had no assets in any other sheriff's district or in any other province, but there is in one of the letters filed as an exhibit a threat to commence an action in Manitoba which would apparently be for the purpose of reaching assets there.

It is suggested that because the plaintiff swore that he had tried in every way that he could to realize on the judgment and when asked what he had done said that 'he had seized the stuff on the farm and had the defendant up for examination' on three different occasions, without giving any indication of what he learned, he had satisfied the burden in this respect.

The burden of proving insolvency is on the plaintiff as part of his case, but since the facts to establish this are not generally within the plaintiff's knowledge but are within the knowledge of the debtor whose act is sought to be annulled, the same strictness ought naturally not be required that would be demanded under other conditions. However, such facts must be proved as will suffice to warrant a reasonable inference of insolvency and the facts in the present case are as consistent with the defendant's unwillingness as with his inability to pay his debts, leaving aside the question of whether temporary inability, based, not on an insufficiency of assets but on market or other conditions, is insolvency within the meaning of the Act. I agree therefore with the trial Judge that the plaintiff has not satisfied the onus of proof in this respect and I would therefore, without considering any of the other difficulties, dismiss the appeal with costs. Appeal dismissed with costs.

ii *Caulfield, Burns & Gibson Ltd.* v *Kitchen*, [1956] O.W.N. 697 (H.C.J.)

LEBEL J.: This is an attack upon a chattel mortgage dated 26th July 1955, given by the defendant Kitchen to the defendant Leta M. Brooks. The transaction was disputed within 60 days of the date mentioned and counsel for the plaintiffs relies on the *prima facie* presumption of an unjust preference contained in s 4(3) of The Assignments and Preferences Act, R.S.O. 1950, c 26. He also contends that the transaction is void under The Fraudulent Conveyances Act, R.S.O. 1950, c 148.

On 29th November 1952 the defendant Brooks sold her haberdashery business in the town of Delhi to Kitchen for $20,000 under an agreement. By its terms Kitchen agreed to pay the balance of the purchase-price, namely, $14,900 (with interest at 4 per cent from 1st January 1953, payable yearly on the 1st day of January in each year) in monthly instalments of $150 each, commencing on 15th August 1953.

Kitchen did not make his interests payments in 1954 and 1955 but he made his principal payments fairly promptly.

The haberdashery business, though owned by the defendant Leta M. Brooks, was managed by her husband. She was inactive in the business and in the events leading up to this suit. Therefore, where I use the name 'Brooks' I shall be understood to refer to the husband.

Mr. John C. Hanselman, a solicitor practising in Delhi, drew both documents but he said he was not acting for Kitchen at the time of the disputed chattel mortgage.

This latter document was given to secure the sum of $12,560, being the balance owing under the agreement, including the interest in arrear. The monthly principal payments and the rate of interest remained the same except that the principal payments were made payable on the 1st of the month instead of the 15th as formerly.

Kitchen made default under the chattel mortgage and on 13th August 1955 Brooks forced an entry to the store premises, seized the cash receipts and started selling merchandise. He was stopped by an injunction and the parties settled their differences shortly afterwards. Kitchen received his costs and $710, said to have been the value of merchandise sold by Brooks.

The present action was commenced on 23rd September 1955. The claims of the plaintiffs and those they represent against Kitchen amount to $6,874.15. By agreement the merchandise in the store has been sold and the proceeds, amounting to $5,547.37, are held in trust awaiting the outcome of this suit.

Before the plaintiffs can succeed under subs 1 or subs 2 of s 4 of The Assignments and Preferences Act they must show that Kitchen was 'in insolvent circumstances or [was] unable to pay his debts in full or [knew] that he was on the eve of insolvency', and even where the transaction is attacked within 60 days they must prove this state of affairs before they can rely on the *prima facie* presumption of an unjust preference under subs 3.

Furthermore, on the authority of *Benallack et al.* v *The Bank of British North America et al.* (1905), 36 S.C.R. 120: 'In order to render such an assignment void there must be knowledge of the insolvency on the part of both parties and concurrence of intention to obtain an unlawful preference over the other creditors: *Molsons Bank* v *Halter* (18 Can. S.C.R. 88); *Stephens* v *McArthur* (19 Can. S.C.R. 446); and *Gibbons* v *McDonald* (20 Can. S.C.R. 587) referred to.' (The above excerpt is from the headnote, which is borne out by the text.)

The question that first arises, therefore, is: Was Kitchen insolvent or on the eve of insolvency on 26th July 1955, and if he was, did Brooks know that he was in that condition? While the circumstances are suspicious, I am unable to give an affirmative answer to this question upon the evidence.

Brooks must have known that Kitchen lacked sufficient working capital from the beginning, because while a chattel mortgage had been discussed at the time he sold the business he said the idea had been dismissed for the reason that he wanted Kitchen 'to get on his feet' before he considered a chattel mortgage, and he must have known that to get on his feet Kitchen would have to be able to buy merchandise on terms that would not be available to him if the business was subject to a chattel mortgage.

Brooks said that he heard rumours about Kitchen 'not being in very good shape', but only after the delivery of the chattel mortgage. One wonders why in this small town of some 3,000 population he had not heard these rumours before.

Brooks knew that Kitchen was not paying the interest under his agreement and knew, as early as August 1954, that he was giving post-dated cheques in payment of certain past-due accounts for merchandise, and he also knew then, if not earlier, that Kitchen lacked industry and was careless to the point of slovenliness about his accounts generally – all real harbingers of financial trouble.

He also must be held to know, because his solicitor Mr. Hanselman knew, that Kitchen had been sued in May or June 1955 by one Duval. But whether he knew that Kitchen had to refinance his car to settle that debt is not clear.

Mr. Livermore for Brooks argues that proof of financial embarrassment is not proof of insolvency, on the authority of *Re Webb* (1921), 51 O.L.R. 5, 64 D.L.R. 633, 2 C.B.R. 16, and I agree, but embarrassment is a factor to be considered – an important factor. One hears of financially-embarrassed persons who were not insolvent but rarely, if ever, of persons in business who were insolvent and were not embarrassed financially. However, at the trial Kitchen was a witness for the plaintiffs and he appeared unfriendly to Brooks, no doubt because of the trouble commencing on 13th August, but even so he did not say that he was insolvent or on the eve of insolvency on 26th July 1955. From what he said his indebtedness amounted to about $20,000, that is, the equivalent, approximately, of the consideration he had agreed to pay Brooks for the business, but what the physical assets were worth then, and whether goodwill was included in the purchase-price, he did not say. He did not state the value of his assets at the time he gave the chattel mortgage, or what amount he might have expected to realize from their fair liquidation. No statement of his affairs at any time was put in in evidence. In these circumstances, including the circumstance that there is now only $5,547.37 held in trust awaiting the outcome of this suit, it is impossible to find that Kitchen was insolvent or on the eve of insolvency at the material time. And while I have real suspicion about Kitchen's solvency, as I have said, it follows that Brooks did not know that Kitchen was in the financial condition mentioned in s 4 of the Act.

The argument based upon The Fraudulent Conveyances Act can be dealt with very briefly. The plaintiffs do not have to establish insolvency on this branch of the case, but in commercial cases the attack is made, almost universally, from that point of vantage. Here there is no ground on which it could be held that this conveyance was 'made with the intent to defeat, hinder, delay or defraud creditors or others' within the meaning of s 2 of this statute. Unlike The Assignments and Preferences Act, it, like the statute 13 Eliz. 5, does not prohit preferring one creditor to another: *McMaster* v *Clare* (1859), 7 Gr. 550; *Ashley* v *Brown* (1890), 17 O.A.R. 500 at 503; *Perkins Electric Co. Limited* v *Orpen* (1921), 21 O.W.N. 135, afirmed (1922), 70 D.L.R. 397, following *Hopkinson* v *Westerman* (1919), 45 O.L.R. 208, 48 D.L.R. 597. The question of a preference does not arise under this branch of the case.

The action is accordingly dismissed, but, in view of the suspicious circumstances, without costs.
Action dismissed without costs.

e / The Requirement of Intent

i Transactions Attacked Within Sixty Days

NOTE Whether a transfer which merely has the effect of giving a preference may be set aside if attacked within sixty days has been a matter of some dispute. *Hazell* v *Cullen* (1914), 20 B.C.R. 603 (S.C.), and *Empire Sash & Door Co.* v *Maranda* (1911), 21 Man. R. 605 (K.B.), both hold that the mere existence of a preference is sufficient if the transfer is impeached within this period, and that no intent need be proven.

The Ontario view, however, appears to be that s 4(3) and (4) do not eliminate the need to show intent, and that the presumption of intent raised by the circumstance of preferential effect may be rebutted by evidence showing that intent was absent: *Dana* v *McLean* (1901), 2 O.L.R. 466 (C.A.). This is in accord with the words of the section, which states that intent is to 'be presumed prima facie.'

Other problems under this section include the dating of the sixty-day period. See, for example, *Breese* v *Knox* (1896), 24 O.A.R. 203 (date of agreement v date of execution of documents); *Curry* v *Kirkpatrick* (1910), 8 E.L.R. 455 (N.S.) (auction within 60 days before general assignment); *Ferguson* v *Bryans* (1904), 15 Man. L.R. 170 (amendment to statement of claim after 60 days); *Desjardine* v *Callison*, [1928] 1 w.w.r. 526, [1928] 2 d.l.r. 35 (Alta.) (service of documents v issue of writ); *Hodge* v *McLean*, [1919] 3 w.w.r. 1108, 50 d.l.r. 123 (Sask. c.a.) (conveyance v agreement); *Totem Radio Supply Co.* v *Stone* (1959), 38 c.b.r. 112, 29 w.w.r. 552 (b.c.) (registration v agreement).

ii Transactions Not Attacked Within Sixty Days

Brocklesby v *Freedman-Ellis Co.*, [1932] o.r. 439 (c.a.), reversing [1932] o.r. 56 (h.c.j.)
The judgment appealed from was as follows:

RANEY, J.: The plaintiff is trustee in the bankruptcy of Adrian T. Pommier, who, until his assignment for the benefit of creditors on the 14th March, 1928, was a retail jeweller at Timmins; and the defendant company is a wholesale dealer in diamonds in Toronto, and was a creditor of Pommier.

The issue directed by Mr. Justice Fisher on the 3rd May, 1928, is whether the return of a quantity of diamonds by Pommier to the defendant company, some months prior to his assignment for the benefit of creditors, was a fraudulent preference as against the trustee in bankruptcy.

In February and March, 1927, Pommier purchased from the defendant company unmounted diamonds to the invoice value of $4,206.40. In June following he had a fire in his store. The damages from the fire were mostly to his show-cases, which had been purchased a few months earlier from the National Show Case Company, under a lien contract which required him to keep them insured for its benefit. The insurance on the show-cases was $4,000, and that was all the insurance carried by Pommier at the time of the fire.

The defendant company had sold the diamonds to Pommier on easy terms – $100 a month for the first five months, beginning with March, 1927; after that, more substantial payments.

On the happening of the fire, Pommier notified the defendant company and some of his other principal creditors by wire, and within two or three days Mr. Ellis of the defendant company went to Timmins, and for the two following months the defendant company was active in assisting Pommier in the adjustment of his affairs, which were not in good order before the fire, and were further complicated by that event.

The financial statement which Pommier had furnished to his banker in January, 1927, shewed a surplus of upwards of $37,000, which the banker cut down to $17,000. In May, 1927, a man named Rajotte, who was employed by Pommier as a clerk and bookkeeper in his store, made up a statement shewing a surplus of $36,000, and gave Pommier a certificate stating that he had gone fully into his affairs and found him to be on a good footing. The statement and certificate did not disclose Rajotte's connection with Pommier, but gave his address as 457 Mount Pleasant-avenue, Westmount, Montreal, and 'any one requiring information' was invited to correspond with him. Copies of this statement and certificate were sent by Pommier to his creditors, who, apparently, were left to draw their own inferences as to the identity of Rajotte.

In his evidence Pommier said that the actual damages from the fire to his show-cases was about $500. The insurance company paid, however, as for a total loss, that is to say, $4,000. In his evidence in these proceedings, Pommier reckoned that, making an allowance of $1,500 for damages to his stock-in-trade, he had made a profit from the fire of about $2,000, against which was his loss from business whilst his store was closed for repairs and renovation, and the rental of other premises.

At the time of the assignment, Pommier's trade liabilities were $19,000. The assignee realised better than $5,000 from the sale of his stock-in-trade, which was, I find, sold to the best advantage. His other assets, which were pledged to the bank, did not realise enough to pay the bank's claim.

In one of Ellis' interviews with Pommier's banker whilst Ellis was in Timmins, the return of some of the unmounted diamonds was suggested in order to relieve Pommier to that extent of his liabilities. This suggestion was also discussed at that time between Ellis and Pommier. Before Ellis left Timmins he collaborated with Pommier in drafting a re-assuring circular letter to Pommier's creditors.

After Ellis' return to Toronto, he wrote to Pommier on the 23rd June, advising him with reference to a claim of about $500 which was being pressed by one of his creditors, and asking Pommier to let him have as quickly as possible the entire list of his creditors, so that he might get in touch with them. Then on the 7th July, Ellis wrote again to Pommier referring to the large amount of his paper which the defendant company had on discount, and saying how important it was that the payments which he had promised to make should be made. In this letter he also complained that Pommier had paid one of his creditors in full, saying: 'I have just learned that you have paid Harry Fogler in full. Now, Pommier, if you are going to take care of everybody who is a little difficult, then those who are friends of yours are going to suffer through their not receiving their proportion of moneys you take in.' Two days later, on the 9th July, Ellis wrote to Pommier again. After mentioning another matter, he proceeded: 'I did mention to Mr. Grasett that we would be willing to take back some of the goods we sold you in order to assist you,' and he proceeded to indicate by numbers the stones which he was willing to take back. The total amounted to $1,935.65. On the 15th July, Pommier sent back stones to the invoice value of $2,712.35.

The Mr. Grasett mentioned by Mr. Ellis in his letter was the manager of the bank which carried Pommier's account. He was a witness at the trial, and I was not impressed either by the accuracy of his recollection of the events as to which he gave evidence, or as to the precautions that had been taken by him in the matter of the line of credit that was given by him to Pommier.

At the time of the fire, Pommier's fourth note for $100, which had matured on the 4th June, was unpaid. This note was paid by Pommier to Ellis before the return of the latter to Toronto. The fifth note for $100 matured on the 4th July, and in his letter to Pommier of the 7th July Ellis said: 'I do hope that you have not permitted your note of $100 which matured on the 4th to be returned. You remember, I spoke to you of the large amount of your paper which we have under discount and how important it was to see that small amounts which you assured us would be paid are paid. If this, through any reason, should come back, please let us have cheque by return.'

As a matter of fact, the evidence shews that this note had been paid by Pommier on the 1st July, without waiting for the expiry of the days of grace.

On the 15th July, when the diamonds were returned, Pommier's liability to the defendant company represented by promissory notes, was as follows:

	Promissory note maturing	
	September 4th	500.00
	October 4th	1,500.00
	November 4th	484.20
	November 4th	922.20
	Total	$3,706.40

Credit for the returned diamonds was passed by the defendant company in its books, not to the notes, that would mature in August and September, but to those that would mature in October and November.

After the signing of the extension agreement of the 6th August, Pommier paid to the defendant company $252.50 to cover Ellis' expenses to Timmins after the fire, and to cover depreciation in the value of the returned diamonds, and by way of refund of the Dominion sales tax which the defendant company had paid at the time of the sale of the diamonds to Pommier in February.

A fortnight or so after the return of the diamonds, Pommier was in Toronto to confer with his creditors, and Mr. Freedman, in the absence of Mr. Ellis, sent him to Montreal to see his creditors there. On Pommier's return to Toronto early in August, Ellis and Freedman formulated an extension agreement for signature by Pommier's Montreal and Toronto creditors. A term of the extension agreement was that Pommier would make monthly payments to Meyers & Company of Montreal, who, after the return of the diamonds to the defendant company, was his principal creditor, and who was to act as trustee for the creditors.

The creditors, including the show-case company, which held the lien on his show-cases and an assignment of the insurance, having signed the extension agreement, the insurance moneys were divided between the bank and the Montreal trustee, and during the following months Pommier made certain payments to Meyers & Company for distribution among his creditors.

When Pommier visited Montreal he told Mr. Meyers, of Meyers & Company, with whom he was on personally friendly terms, about the return of the diamonds to the defendant company, and the account which that company later sent to Meyers & Company, as trustee for creditors, shewed a credit of $2,712.35 for returned merchandise.

Representatives of two of the Toronto creditors knew, when they consented to the extension agreement, of the return of the diamonds. Mr. Levy, of Saunders, Lorie & Co., having heard of the return of the diamonds, raised the question before he signed the extension agreement, and was assured that the diamonds had been sent to Pommier on approval. Mr. Levy is one of the inspectors of the estate. Mr. MacNamara of P.W. Ellis & Co., another creditor, also knew of the return of the stones and sympathised with the indignation of Mr. Levy, but nevertheless signed the extension agreement. Representatives of other creditors, called as witnesses, testified that they knew nothing about the return of the stones until after the assignment in bankruptcy in March, 1928. Not only so, but at least one of the creditors was assured, at a meeting at the office of the defendant company when the extension agreement was signed, that Pommier's stock-in-trade was still intact.

Thus, not only was there no voluntary communication either by Pommier or by Ellis, as to the return of the diamonds, to any creditor, except to Meyers & Company, before the extension agreement was signed, but there was a misrepresentation as to the facts.

It is not against the law for a creditor to seek payment of his debt from an insolvent debtor, and there is no prohibition in law against a preference by the debtor of one of his creditors, except as found in the Bankruptcy Act, R.S.C. 1927, ch. 11, sec. 64, and in the Assignments and Preferences Act, R.S.O. 1927, ch. 134, sec. 5. Clearly the Bankruptcy Act has no application to cases where, as here, the act of preference was not within the three months' limitation. For a similar reason, subsecs. 3 and 4 of sec. 5 of the Assignments and Preferences Act have no application.

To succeed in this action the plaintiff must bring himself within subsec. 2 of sec. 5 of that Act, which provides that every transfer of goods 'made by a person being at the time in insolvent circumstances, or unable to pay his debts in full, or knowing himself to be on the eve of insolvency,' to a creditor, 'with the intent to give such creditor an unjust preference over his other creditors,' shall be null and void.

On the language of this subsection, and without the assistance of judicial interpretation, it is clear that three conditions must concur to enable the plaintiff, in such an action as this, to succeed: (1) The debtor must have been in insolvent circumstances, or unable to pay his debts in full, or must have known himself to be on the eve of insolvency; (2) the intention of the debtor must have been to give to the favoured creditor an unjust preference; and (3) the effect of the transaction must have been to give a favoured creditor such a preference. But in the course of the years judicial glosses have added to the plaintiff's burden, and in the present state of the authorities he must also prove: (4) that the creditor knew that the debtor's financial situation was that described in the section; (5) that there was an intention on the part of the favoured creditor to get a preference; and (6) that the preference was not only an unjust, but a fraudulent preference. And then, if a plaintiff succeeds in proving all these things, he is still liable to be met with the defence that the transaction was not the voluntary act of the debtor, but the result of pressure from the creditor, or of some other extraneous influence.

Firstly, then, was Pommier in insolvent circumstances, or unable to pay his debts in full, or did he know himself to be on the eve of insolvency, when he returned the diamonds? A debtor is legally insolvent when he has not sufficient property to pay all his debts, and he is commercially insolvent when he is unable to meet his obligations as they become due in the ordinary course of business. (*Rae* v *Macdonald (1886)*, 13 O.R. 353, per Rose, J., at pp 357, 360.) My conclusion is that Pommier was insolvent in both senses when he purchased the diamonds from the defendant company in February, 1927, and that this was so at all times between that time and the time of his assignment in March, 1928.

Secondly, what was Pommier's intention when he returned the stones? The suggestion of a return of some of the diamonds undoubtedly came from the defendant company. Pommier was, I judge from the evidence, more or less passive in the matter. Without the assistance of the defendant company he saw bankruptcy immediately in front of him, and he was willing to adopt whatever course the company might suggest that seemed to give a promise of postponing the evil day.

Thirdly, the effect of the transaction was undoubtedly to give the defendant company a preference over the other creditors.

Fourthly, was the defendant company aware, when the stones were returned, that Pommier was in insolvent circumstances, or unable to pay his debts in full, or that he was on the eve of insolvency? There is no doubt that, at the time of the preparation of the extension agreement early in August, the defendant company knew that Pommier was insolvent. But did the defendant company know this at the time it received the diamonds back from Pommier? This question can be conveniently considered along with the fifth and sixth questions – Was it the intention of the defendant company, in accepting the return of the diamonds, to get a preference over the other creditors? And was the preference which the defendant company secured not only an unjust preference, but a fraudulent preference? (*Davidson* v *Ross* (1876), 24 Gr. 22, per Moss, J.A., at p 81.) These questions are not easily answered, and I have reached a conclusion as to them with a good deal of difficulty.

Mr. Ellis was an experienced jeweller, and, I judge from his appearance and evidence, a shrewd and capable business man. He went to Timmins to protect his company's interest. It was important to that interest that he should know just what Pommier's financial position was. He saw Pommier's stock-in-trade, and conferred with Pommier's banker, and assisted Pommier in drafting a re-assuring letter to creditors whose paper had matured or was maturing. Then, after his return to Toronto, and within a week, he was urging Pommier to hasten to let him have an entire list of creditors, with the amounts owing – because 'I want to get in touch with them from this end.' And he added, 'If there are any who have placed their accounts for collection, please let me know.'

When Ellis returned from Timmins he was, I have no doubt, throughly well satisfied of the instability of Pommier's financial position. He knew that Pommier was not then paying his commercial obligations as they became due in the ordinary course of business.

In coming to a decision on the evidence as to the knowledge to be imputed to the defendant company of Pommier's insolvency when they accepted the return of the diamonds, and of the intention of Pommier to give and of the defendant company to get a preference over the other creditors, I am not unmindful of what was so well expressed by Mr. Justice Moss in *Davidson* v *Ross*, *supra*, at p 89, where the learned Judge emphasises the onus that is cast upon the plaintiff of proving with satisfactory clearness every essential constituent of a charge of fraud:

He has to meet the general presumption of law in favour of innocence and honesty. It is a matter of every day experience that courts declare an impeached transaction to be surrounded with circumstances of grave suspicion; but that the evidence not having carried the case beyond the region of suspicion, and fraud being a thing to be definitely proved, and not be be presumed, the transaction cannot be set aside. Facts must be proved which can lead the judicial mind to no other conclusion than that of fraud. If the evidence in such a case leaves the matter in doubt, the complainant must fail. If the case proved is consistent with honesty, the defendant must succeed.

If the evidence in this case had stopped with the return of the diamonds. I think probably I should have come to a conclusion similar to that reached by Mr. Justice Orde in *Re Webb* (1921), 51 O.L.R. 5 – that the evidence, whilst establishing knowledge on the part of the defendant company of Pommier's financial embarrassment in June, 1927, fell short of establishing its knowledge at that time that he was in insolvent circumstances, or unable to pay his debts in full, or knew himself to be on the eve of insolvency. But the evidence did not stop there.

When it came to the extension agreement, if the defendant company had declined to assist Pommier until the other creditors had been told the facts about the return of the diamonds, it would have been doing what it ought to have done. Some of the creditors, if they had known the facts, would have refused to sign. Insolvency would then, no doubt, have immediately super-vened, and the assignee would, in all likelihood, have attacked the transaction, as he does now, but with the difference that the presumption would then have been in his favour.

The failure of the defendant company and of Pommier to disclose to the creditors generally, whom they were asking to sign the extension agreement, the fact of the subtraction from Pommier's assets of so large a proportion of his stock-in-trade – and of that part of his stock-in-trade which was at once the most stable and the most liquid – for the benefit of the defendant company, was not fair dealing with the creditors who were not informed. But it was more than that. It was evidence that both Pommier and the defendant company knew at that time, and were concealing the fact, that there had been an unjust preference – in other words, a voluntary, and therefore a fraudulent, preference of the defendant company. Secrecy is one of the badges of fraud.

Finally, the case is not within the doctrine of pressure. On the 15th July, 1928, when the stones were returned, Pommier owed the defendant company $3,706.40, but no part of the indebtedness was then presently demandable. The last $100 note which had fallen due on the 4th July had been paid, and the $300 note would not mature until the 4th of August. The defendant company was not, therefore, in a position to issue a writ, and the return of the stones was a purely voluntary and friendly act on the part of Pommier. In this respect the case is within the law as stated in *Strachan* v *Barton* (1856), 11 Ex. 647, and *Meriden Silver Co.* v *Lee & Chillas* (1882), 2 O.R. 451.

There will be a declaration that the transaction was an unjust preference within subsec. 2 of sec. 5 of the Assignments and Preferences Act, and a reference to the Master to ascertain the value of the returned diamonds as of the date of their return, and judgment for the amount found by the Master, with interest from the 15th July, 1927, and the costs of the issue and the action, including the reference.

In the Court of Appeal:

RIDDELL, J.A.: One Pommier of the Town of Timmins, having made an authorized assignment in bankruptcy to the plaintiff, the trustee claimed that a certain transaction, the subject of these proceedings, was an unjust preference. The matter coming before the Judge in Chambers in Bankruptcy. Fisher, J.A., that learned Judge directed the trial of an issue in which the trusteee should be plaintiff, and the defendant, defendant, 'and the question to be tried ... be whether the return of diamonds by the said ... Pommier to Freedman-Ellis, Ltd. (i.e., the defendant) on or about June 20th, 1927, is a fraudulent preference against the said trustee (i.e., the plaintiff), and the other creditors of the above-named debtor.'

The opinion of the Court being taken on two points of law, it was declared (*Re Pommier* (1930), 65 O.L.R. 415), that the plaintiff was entitled to invoke the provisions of the Assignments and Preferences Act, R.S.O. 1927, c. 162; and, also, that the said Act is not abrogated by the Bankruptcy Act, and any provision thereof, not in conflict with the Bankruptcy Act, is valid, and the trustee can invoke the aid of the Court to set aside as preferential, a transaction between a bankrupt and a creditor which took place more than three months before the assignment. We, of course, accept the law, as so laid down.

After certain vicissitudes, unnecessary to mention, the case came on for trial before Raney, J., without a jury at Toronto, when that learned Judge found in favour of the trustee; the defendant now appeals.

I have read and reread the evidence and have had the advantage of a full and careful argument on both sides; and I am unable to see in the transaction complained of anything but the honest desire of an honest trader to assist an embarrassed customer to avoid bankruptcy by reducing his liability to the former, taking back goods which the debtor found himself unable to dispose of. This is a not unusual practice, and if followed with an honest intention, not the intention thereby to obtain a preference over the other creditors, it is not objectionable or to be avoided as fraudulent against the other creditors or the assignee, who represents them.

It is unnecessary to go through the transaction: it is sufficiently described in the reasons for the judgment complained of. No doubt, the dealings of the defendant with the debtor will bear the construction put upon them by the plaintiff, which has been accepted by the learned trial Judge; but everything is equally consistent with honesty of intention and purpose; and the usual presumptions of honesty should prevail.

I would allow the appeal with costs, here and below.

Appeal allowed.

Codville v *Fraser* (1902), 14 Man. R. 12 (C.A.)

KILLAM, C.J.: Two main questions arise in the present case. That which is naturally the first is whether a mortgage to the defendant of the stock in trade of a retail merchant to secure his indebtedness to the defendant was made with intent to give the defendant a preference over the other creditors or had such effect.

Under the decision of the Supreme Court of Canada in *Stephens* v *McArthur*, 19 S.C.R. 446, a transaction is not to be considered as having the effect of giving a preference unless the debtor has the intent to prefer.

Mr. Justice Bain found that in this case there was the intent and his decision upon that point is challenged on this appeal.

The received doctrine now in England appears to be that, in order to avoid a transaction as entered into 'with a view of giving' a creditor a preference under the Bankruptcy Acts, it should appear that the 'dominant' motive of the debtor was to give a preference ...

If the debtor's account is to be taken as correct, it appears to me that there could not properly be any other inference than that his dominant motive was to make an arrangement for continuing the business. As we can see the case now, this was practically hopeless; but parties in his position do not usually recognize this so clearly as it appears afterwards to others. I do not think that we are warranted in assuming that all this is mere subterfuge. It is true that the amending Act declares that a *prima facie* presumption is to arise from the effect of a transaction. But I do not think that this would justify us in looking only to the effect and in refusing to attach any weight to the debtor's account of the circumstances upon an assumption that his account has not been accepted by the trial Judge.

It is quite true that the alleged arrangement between the debtor and the defendant was not a definite, enforceable agreement. But for the purpose of estimating intent, this does not seem to be necessary: *In re Wilkinson*, 22 Ch. D. 788; *Webster* v. *Crickmore, supra*.

Nor does it appear to me important to determine whether the defendant's agent was acting *bona fide* or anticipated that the other creditors could be arranged with and the business continue, it being only the debtor's mental attitude that we are considering ...

The transaction was not attacked as a fraud upon the debtor himself; and, while the statement of claim alleged that the mortgage was given with intent to defeat, delay and prejudice the creditors, there was no attempt to uphold the judgment upon such a ground.

With considerable regret I have come to the conclusion that we cannot affirm the judgment. Having formed this opinion upon the first ground of appeal, it is unnecessary to express any opinion upon the second. Such an expression is the less called for at present, as there seems a probability that the Legislature will shortly substitute other provisions for those upon which the difficulty arises.

I would allow the appeal with costs and dismiss the action with costs.

RICHARDS, J. (dissenting): I concur in the views of the Chief Justice that the dominant motive in the debtor's mind was the hope that by giving the conveyance he would be enabled to carry on business, and that it is not necessary that the promises on which the transfer was got should be legally binding on the defendant.

But, with deference, I am unable to agree that the question of good faith on the part of defendant's agent, in making those promises, is not material.

On a careful consideration of the evidence I am led to the conclusion that there was not in this case an intention at any time to carry out the promises made to the debtor. If so, then I think that a good consideration to uphold the transaction as against the plaintiffs has not been shown by proving merely what was in the mind of the debtor.

It is strongly arguable from the absence of reference in the cases to the transferee's good or bad faith that the question is immaterial. But, in that absence, I feel at liberty, though with much hesitation, to hold that the question is material. A debtor facing the question of business failure will usually grasp at anything that may be held out to him as a means of tiding over. To hold that an undue advantage given by him when in that condition of mind, on the strength of promises merely made to procure that advantage and without intention to fulfil them, can be maintained and enjoyed by the party making such promises, seems to me to put a premium on fraud.

It is argued that, even if the debtor could set aside such a transfer, a creditor attacking it can not, as there was no privity of contract between him and the creditor who got the advantage. The best opinion I can form as to that is that it is the intention of the Act to allow the attacking creditor to set aside what the debtor could, and for that purpose the Act should, I think, be liberally, and not strictly, construed.

As my brother judges are in favor of allowing the appeal, and as new legislative enactments are about to be made on the questions in dispute in this action, it is unnecessary for me to go into the other points raised, further than to say that I think the judgment appealed from should be upheld and a liberal construction in favor of attacking creditors given to the sections of the statute in question. Without such they would be of little practical value.

I think the appeal should be dismissed with costs.

DUBUC, J., concurred with KILLAM, C.J.
Appeal allowed with costs and action dismissed with costs.

Royal Bank of Canada v *Sullivan* (1956), 6 D.L.R. (2d) 559 (Ont. H.C.J.)

THOMPSON J.: This is an action brought by the plaintiff bank, a judgment creditor of the defendant Sullivan, on behalf of itself and all others of his creditors, to set aside a certain mortgage dated March 2, 1954, (ex. 8), made by the defendant Sullivan (his wife Annabel joining to bar her dower) in favour of the defendant Herr, for securing repayment of the sum of $4,690.72 and interest upon the security of certain lands in the Village of Hastings, Ontario, referred to in the evidence as 'the garage property'.

The plaintiff seeks to avoid the impeached instrument as a fraudulent conveyance under the provisions of the *Fraudulent Conveyances Act*, R.S.O. 1950, c 148, and also as constituting a fraudulent or unjust preference within the meaning of the *Assignments and Preferences Act*, R.S.O. 1950, c 26.

The defendant Sullivan purchased the garage property in the year 1946 and thereupon erected a building and established himself a general garage business. For some few years he enjoyed an apparent measure of business success. By the year 1951 he had established a line of credit with the plaintiff bank and from then on and from time to time it made him advances, until in the month of November, 1953, we find him indebted to the bank in the sum of approximately $19,000. For this the plaintiff held three demand promissory notes and the personal guarantee of his wife, but little or no other security.

After urging reduction or liquidation of the loan without success, the bank finally on November 27, 1953, instituted action against Sullivan and his wife to recover the monies owing. He was served with the Writ of Summons on December 4, 1953. These proceedings culminated in a judgment against him, upon an opposed motion for judgment under R. 57, on March 2, 1954, (ex. 5).

A writ of *fieri facias* (ex. 7) issued to the Sheriff of the United Counties of Northumberland and Durham and was filed with him on March 29, 1954. Some abortive attempt was made by the Sheriff to execute the writ; nothing was realized; and the whole of the judgment and costs remains unpaid. Although no return of the writ was made, it appears apparent that Sullivan had not then nor has he now any exigible assets.

At the time the bank commenced action to recover its loans Sullivan was still the owner of the garage business and property and in addition held and owned several parcels of real property. His equity in these assets, he himself values at $15,000. At the same time, upon his own admission, his liabilities then overdue, and which he says he was unable to meet, amounted to approximately $30,600. He was hopelessly insolvent and remains so. As he himself puts it upon his examination for discovery, which was read into the evidence at trial, he was 'bankrupt'. He was admittedly angry at the bank's action, and after having avowedly expressed his intention of hindering and defeating the bank's recovery, he on November 12, 1953, commenced a process of denudation and proceeded to strip himself of his assets. Between that date and the date the bank recovered its judgment, he had transferred, handed over or conveyed, including the garage undertaking, all of his assets, with the exception of the garage real property, to his employee son Bernard Joseph Sullivan, who in turn mortgaged a substantial portion of them to some of his father's creditors and to secure his father's obligations. On the date the bank recovered judgment he mortgaged his only remaining asset, the garage real property, to his co-defendant in this action, by way of the instrument which is now under attack.

The defendant Herr is a drover and rancher with some 25 years experience as such. He resides at the Township of Percy, some four miles from Sullivan's place of business. He is a man of reputed financial substance and an experienced lender of money. He has known Sullivan for some 15 years and of late years has been a frequent visitor at his garage at Hastings, a village of some 950 inhabitants. He posed in the witness-box as an ignorant, illiterate and inexperienced man of business. I am not at all convinced that that is his true role. He impressed me as a man of inherent and native shrewdness and while perhaps uneducated, in the academic sense of the word, as one who, through the hard school of experience, had gleaned a reasonably acute knowledge of business affairs. Nor am I satisfied that his relationship and association with Sullivan has been of that casual nature in which they would both have me believe.

The mortgage in question was admittedly given to secure an antecedent or pre-existing debt owing by Sullivan to Herr. It is said that Herr advanced or loaned to Sullivan in January of 1950 the sum of $1,000, in February of 1950 the sum of $1,135 and in December of 1951 the sum of $2,000. On March 2, 1954, the amount owing on these loans together with interest was stated to be $4,135.72, the expressed consideration for the mortgage. None of these monies have been repaid.

The son Bernard Joseph, as the voluntary transferee of his father's business and business personal assets is still carrying on business in the mortgaged premises, with no overt change of name or ostensible change of business conditions.

There can be no question that the result of this conveyance by way of mortgage has been in fact to hinder, delay and defeat the plaintiff and others of Sullivan's creditors in the recovery of their just claims as against him.

This result, however, is not in itself, sufficient to establish fraudulent intent in such a case as this. Once good or valuable consideration to support the transaction has been shown, proof of an actual intention to defraud creditors of the grantor must exist and there must be a concurrence of such intention on the part of the grantor and the grantee before the conveyance can be avoided under the *Fraudulent Conveyances Act: Hickerson* v *Parrington* (1891), 18 O.A.R. 635; *Ferguson* v *Lastewka*, [1946], 4 D.L.R. 531, O.R. 577.

An existing debt is sufficient consideration to support the transfer, in the absence of actual fraud on the part of the grantee: *Mulcahy* v *Archibald* (1898), 28 S.C.R. 523.

Under the *Assignments and Preferences Act*, in the absence of attack upon the transaction within 60 days after its consummation, the presumptions provided for by s 4 thereof do not arise, and the plaintiff is driven to establish a concurrence of fraudulent intent upon the part of the debtor and the creditor to create an unjust preference: *Connerty* v *Cross* (1922), 22 O.W.N. 467; *Johnson* v *Hope* (1890), 17 O.A.R. 10; *Ashley* v *Brown* (1890), 17 O.A.R. 500.

But where the natural consequence of the alienation is to delay, hinder or defraud creditors, or the circumstances under which the alienation is made, bear one or more of the badges or *indicia* of fraud, the onus of upholding the alienation is imposed upon the defendants, even in cases where there has been an actual, present advance of money: *Struthers* v *Chamandy* (1917), 42 O.L.R. 508 at p 520.

In all cases, a dominating fraudulent intention on the part of the transferor to which the transferee is privy will override all enquiry into the consideration: *McMullen* v *Dr. Barnardo's Homes Nat'l Inc. Ass'n*, (1924), 26 O.W.N. 168; *Ferguson* v *Lastewka, supra; Munro* v *Standard Bank* (1913), 16 D.L.R. 293, 30 O.L.R. 12. As in many cases of this nature, where avertments and denials of fraud and unjust dealing pertain, the evidence here is in large measure conflicting and highly controversial ...

The question of intent to defraud creditors is one of fact which the Court must determine on the merits of each particular case, after taking into account all the circumstances surrounding the making of the conveyance: *Ferguson* v *Lastewka*, [1946] 4 D.L.R. at p 535.

The circumstances in this case are, to my mind, consistent with but one conclusion, namely; that the transaction between the defendants was a fraudulent scheme upon the part of both parties to defeat, hinder and delay the plaintiff and other creditors of Sullivan and made with the predominant intention on the one hand to give and on the other to receive an unjust preference.

The defendants resort to the doctrine of pressure in an effort to uphold the impeached transaction. I am not convinced that there was in fact pressure in the sense that the term is employed in s 4 of the *Assignments and Preferences Act*. Moreover, as the dominating intention of both defendants was to secure an unjust preference over the plaintiff bank, and avowedly so, the evidence tendered as to pressure, even if accepted, would not be sufficient to protect the transaction: See *Clemmow* v *Converse* (1869), 16 Gr. 547 at p 549; *Munro* v *Standard Bank*, 16 D.L.R. 293; *Ex p. Hall, Re Cooper* (1882), L.R. 19 Ch. 580 at p 585.

As bearing upon the question of intent, there are readily discernible in the evidence, badges of fraud other than those already specifically dealt with; for example, the secrecy of the transfer of Sullivan's business undertaking to his son and the feverish haste to complete and register the mortgage instrument on the eve of the bank's judgment.

In the result the plaintiff's action succeeds and there will be judgment declaring that the mortgage from the defendant John Alphonsus Sullivan (his wife Annabel joining to bar her dower) to his co-defendant James Patrick Herr, bearing date March 2, 1954, and registered as No. 2836 for the Village of Hastings is null and void as against the plaintiff and other creditors of John Alphonsus Sullivan. The mortgage as against such creditors will be set aside.

The plaintiff will have its costs of action against both defendants.

Judgment for plaintiff.

[The judgment of Thompson J was affirmed on appeal (1957), 10 D.L.R. (2d) 494 (Ont. C.A.)].

iii The Doctrine of Pressure

NOTE If a transfer is made as the result of pressure on the part of a creditor, it will not be set aside as a fraudulent preference. The doctrine of pressure was explained as follows by Strong J in *Stephens* v *McArthur* (1891), 19 S.C.R. 446:

the doctrine had its origin as far back as the time of Lord Mansfield (see *Harman* v *Fishar*, Cowp. 117, and *Thompson* v *Freeman*, 1 T.R. 155) and the books are full of cases down to recent times all recognizing the doctrine and treating it as one necessarily arising from the primary and natural import of the word 'preference' as meaning a voluntary act on the part of the debtor and therefore as a term which is not applicable to an act brought about by the active interference of the creditor.

Courts have not been unanimous concerning the amount of pressure necessary to validate what would otherwise be a preference. In *Stephens* v *McArthur*, supra, Strong J continued in this vein: '[t]hen as to what acts are sufficient to constitute pressure the decided cases are equally explicit ... [A] mere demand by the creditor without even a threat of, much less a resort to, legal proceedings is sufficient pressure to rebut the presumption of preference.'

For other cases holding to this view, see *Slater* v *Oliver* (1884), 7 O.R. 158 (C.A.); *Beattie* v *Wenger* (1897), 24 O.A.R. 72.

There are judges who have felt that a greater degree of pressure is required for the doctrine to come into effect. See, for example, *Re Carson*, [1924] 4 D.L.R. 492 (Ont. C.A.), where Orde JA stated that 'pressure must involve the threat or the belief that legal proceedings are about to be taken. Pressure must be something from without, which induces the debtor to satisfy the pressing creditor.'

The doctrine of pressure is not applicable within the sixty day period: s 4(3), (4).

QUESTIONS
1 Does the doctrine of pressure reward obnoxious or harassing creditors? Is it consistent with contemporary views as to the proper scope of extra-judicial collection?
2 Does it make sense to require intent by the creditor to defraud? Should debtors be able to choose which of their creditors to repay?
3 Evaluate the following proposal recently made by the Law Reform Commission of British Columbia (see *Working Paper No. 21, The Creditors' Relief Act* 94–6 (1976)):

The *Creditor's Relief Act* should be amended to provide that any payments made, or property transferred, to a creditor in total or partial satisfaction of a debt after the creditor has begun judicial proceedings to enforce his claim against the debtor, or made after the recipient creditor becomes aware of enforcement measures taken by other creditors to which the *Creditors' Relief Act* applies, are deemed to be proceeds of an enforcement measure initiated by the recipient creditor which must be remitted to the sheriff for distribution under the *Creditors' Relief Act*, and any money not so remitted may be recovered by the sheriff in an action against the recipient creditor.

Would such an amendment be preferable to the present preferences legislation? Should it be available as a supplement?

18
Introduction to Bankruptcy

INTRODUCTION

Bankruptcy is often the end-point in the collection process for both creditors and debtors.

This chapter describes the historical origins of bankruptcy law and traces its evolution from a largely penal body of legal principles to a largely civil regime today. Attention is focussed on the several social objectives of the present law including on the one hand providing for the equitable enforcement of creditors' claims and on the other, facilitating the financial rehabilitation of the over-committed debtor. The materials go on to consider the appropriate objectives for a modern bankruptcy regime and how well our existing law meets those objectives. A comparative summary of the present and proposed Bankruptcy Act is provided.

The chapter concludes with a brief consideration of the issue of jurisdiction in the Canadian federal system.

I THE HISTORY OF BANKRUPTCY AND BANKRUPTCY LEGISLATION

Report of the Study Committee on Bankruptcy and Insolvency Legislation, *1970*, pp 7–18; 24–5 (hereinafter referred to as the Tassé Report)

1.1.01 *An Expanding Concept*: The long history of bankruptcy has been one of an expanding concept. From the harsh and merciless treatment of debtors, the law, through many stages, has come to recognize that, while there may be fraudulent debtors from whom society must be protected, an honest bankrupt is not a contradiction of terms. Upon this cornerstone has been built the modern law of bankruptcy.

1.1.02 In primitive societies, the debtor's lot was hard. There was no exception to the rule that he must pay his debts in full. If he could not pay with his property, he paid with his person.

1.1.03 *The Code of Hammurabi*: Written more than 4000 years ago, the Code of Hammurabi, King of Babylon, contained several sections concerning the relations between debtors and creditors. According to this Code, the creditor was entitled to levy a 'distress' or 'pledge', called a *nipûtum*, if the debt was not paid when it became due. It was not necessary for the creditor to first obtain judgment, but he was penalized if he wrongfully levied a distress. While oxen of the plough and grain were exempted from seizure, the debtor's wife, a child or a slave could be brought as *nipûtum* to the creditor's house. There they were put to work until the debt was satisfied. In addition to the *nipûtum*, the Code considered the case where the debtor voluntarily surrendered a dependant into bondage by selling him, with or without a right of redemption, to a merchant or to the creditor himself. The position of the dependant in the house of his new master seems to be similar to that of the *nipûtum*, but, in the case of a wife or child, the servitude came to an end after three years service. Finally, if the debt of the creditor was not satisfied one way or another, there seems little doubt that the debtor could be adjudicated to him as a bond-servant. [G.R. Driver and John C. Miles, *The Babylonian Laws*, Oxford, The Clarendon Press, 1952, vol. 1, pp 208–221.]

1.1.04 *The Law of Ancient Greece*: By the end of the 7th Century, B.C., in Athens, the new class of mercantile capitalists virtually owned the entire peasant class with mortgages on nearly every small holding in Attica. The peasants could not resist foreclosures on their lands and on their persons, which often were included in their pledges. The poor were in a state of bondage to the rich, both themselves, their wives, and their children. The political situation was critical. In order to avert a revolution, Solon cancelled all existing mortgages and debts, released debtors from bondage and made illegal those contracts in which a person's liberty was pledged. [G. Glotz, *La Cité Grecque*, Paris, La Renaissance du Livre, 1928, p 140; W. Seagle, *Men of Law*, New York, The MacMillan Company, 1947, p 38; M.I. Rostovtzeff, *A History of the Ancient World*, 2nd ed., vol. 1, The Orient and Greece, Oxford, The Clarendon Press, 1945, c.15.]

1.1.05 *The Roman Law*: When, in the middle of the 5th Century, B.C., Rome decided to codify its laws, it sent three commissioners to Greece to study the laws of Solon. The code that resulted is known as the *Law of the Twelve Tables*. Contrary to the spirit of the reform of Solon, the Roman jurists maintained the execution against the person. After the fulfilment of certain formalities, the unpaid creditor had the power to seize the debtor himself. This seizure, called *manus injectio*, gave the creditor authority to bring the debtor to his home and keep him in chains for sixty days. During this period, the debtor, still the owner of his property and a Roman citizen, could try to settle his debts with his creditor. To allow for the possibility of a ransom being paid, the creditor was required to take him three times to the market place giving notice of the amount of the debt each time. Finally, if at the end of sixty days, the creditor was not fully paid, he could, it would seem, put the debtor to death or sell him into foreign slavery. According to certain modern writers, the creditors could even divide between them the body of the debtor. If this was so, there is no proof that such an inhuman treatment was ever applied. It must also be noted that the *paterfamilias* could, as was the case under the *Hammurabi Code*, in order to avoid his slavery, raise money by leasing out the services of the members of his family. In Roman law, this is known as *mancipium* [Raymond Monier, *Manuel Elementaire de Droit Romain*, 6th ed., Paris, Editions Domat-Montchrestien, 1947, Tome 1, pp 31–32, 146–150 and 224; W.W. Buckland, *A Text Book of Roman Law from Augustus to Justinian*, 3rd ed., Cambridge, The University Press, 1963, pp 618–623.] During the centuries that followed the promulgation of the *Law of the Twelve Tables*, the severity of the *manus injectio* was progressively reduced. By the end of the Republic, the unpaid creditor could still imprison the debtor or make the debtor work for him in satisfaction of the debt but he could no longer put him to death or sell him into slavery.

1.1.06 As Ihéring pointed out, early Roman law only recognized execution against the person:

Ce qu'un individu a acquis au prix de son corps et de sa vie, ou à la sueur de son front, semble devenir une partie de lui-même. Quiconque entame cette propriété doit payer; s'il ne peut restituer, son propre corps répond de ce qu'il a enlevé. [R. Ihéring, *L'Esprit du Droit Romain*, Meulenaere's translation, 3rd ed., Paris, vol. 1, 1886, p 136.]

This was the rule under Roman law until the end of the Republic, when the *Edict of the Praetor* alleviated the harshness of the old quiritarian law. About that time, one praetor developed a method of execution against property known as *venditio bonorum*. This fundamental reform, for the first time, established a link between the assets and the liabilities of a person. Moreover, this was in the nature of a procedure for the collective execution against the property of an insolvent or recalcitrant debtor. To quote W.W. Buckland, 'It is in effect the Roman equivalent of bankruptcy proceedings.' [Raymond Monier, *op. cit.*, pp 171–174; W.W. Buckland, *op. cit.*, p 644.]

1.1.07 Thus, by the end of the Republic, Roman law recognized two methods of execution, one against the person and the other against property. The debtor could, however, by the time of Augustus, avoid execution against his person by making a *cessio bonorum*, that is to say, by surrendering to his creditors everything he owned. About three centuries later, the *cessio bonorum* was not available to debtors who had squandered their property or concealed it from their creditors. According to an imperial ordinance of the year 379, this procedure was only allowed when the insolvency of the debtor was due to an act of God. Under Justinian, the use of the *cessio bonorum* had become so widespread that the *Corpus Juris* scarcely mentions imprisonment for debt. [Raymond Monier, *op. cit.*, pp 149, 171 and 202, W.W. Buckland, *op. cit.*, p 645. Fritz Schulz, *Classical Roman Law*, Oxford, The Clarendon Press, 1951, p 214.]

1.1.08 *The Italian Cities*: As trade and the use of credit developed, the ordinary law of debtor and creditor became inadequate to cope with the problem of the insolvent trader. Towards the end of the Mediaeval Ages, the Italian cities attempted to deal with this problem and new concepts, such as the 'act of bankruptcy' [Israel Treiman, *Acts of Bankruptcy: A Mediaeval Concept in Modern Bankruptcy Law*, (1938), 52 Harv. L.R., p 189.] were developed by legal writers of the time. It is from the Italian *bancarupta* that the word 'bankrupt' is derived. It may be literally translated as 'bank broken' or 'bench broken'. The allusion is said to be the custom of breaking the table of a defaulting tradesman.

1.1.09 *The French Law*: In France, and elsewhere in Europe, the Roman law, in its ultimate stages, became the basis of the law merchant. The French *Ordinance of 1673* is celebrated as being the first great codification of the law merchant in France. This Ordinance and the *Code de Commerce de 1807* had great influence in most civil law jurisdictions of the world.

1.1.10 *The English Law*: In England, one of the first insolvency statutes was enacted in 1351. [25 Edw. III, U.K.S. 1351-2, C 23.] In an attempt to promote commercial integrity, it provided that, if any merchant of the Company of Lombard Merchants acknowledged himself bound in a debt, the Company should answer for it. Apparently, this was by reason of the fact that some of these merchants had, in the past, left the country without paying their debts.

1.1.11 At Common Law, a creditor has to resort to a very expensive, lengthy and cumbersome procedure to obtain an attachment of his debtor's property. Execution cannot be obtained against a debtor's entire estate but only against the property described in the writ. If there was a plurality of creditors, they took the property of the debtor in the order of their attachments. The race was to the swift. The rule was 'first come, first served'. [W.S. Holdsworth, *History of English Law*, Vol. VIII, London, p 232.]

1.1.12 The first Bankruptcy Statutes provided a summary method for the collective execution of all of the debtor's property, both movable and immovable. They stressed the rights of creditors. The only concern shown in respect of the debtor was that he should surrender all of his property and that no fraud on his part should go undetected and unpunished. Under the first of these statutes, the property was liquidated and distributed 'to every of the said creditors a portion, rate and rate alike, according to the quantity of their debts.' [34 & 35 Hen. VIII, U.K.S.,

1542, C. 4.] The preamble of this statute stated: 'where divers and sundry persons craftily obtaining into their own hands great substance of other Mens (sic) Goods, do suddenly flee to Parts unknown, or keep their Houses not minding to pay or restore to any (sic) their Creditors, their Debts and Duties, but at their own Wills and Pleasures Consume the Substance obtained by credit of other Men for their own Pleasure and delicate Living against all Reason, Equity and good Conscience.'

1.1.13 Although the English *Bankruptcy Act* of 1542 was directed against any debtor who attempted to defeat his creditors by fraudulent means, the Act of 1571 [13 Eliz. 1, U.K.S., 1571, C.7] restricted bankruptcy to those who were engaged in trade. This distinction was to be maintained for almost 300 years. A debtor who was not in trade and who could not pay his debts was imprisoned until some person paid them for him.

1.1.14 The first English Act showing concern for the rehabilitation of the debtor was enacted in 1705 in the reign of Anne. [4 & 5 Anne, U.K.S., 1705, C. 17.] A debtor who was a merchant could get a discharge of all his debts owing at the time of his bankruptcy provided he surrendered all of his property and conformed to the other provisions of the statute. However, the legislator remained very much aware of the continuing problem of the fraudulent debtor. So, while being given new privileges, the debtor had to be free from fraud and submit himself to the control of the Court. Evidence of the concern of the legislator that debtors might abuse the privileges given to them was the severity of the penalty for a debtor who did not strictly comply with the law. The penalty, in the past, had been to stand in the pillory or have an ear cut off. The new penalty was hanging. This penalty applied, for example, if the bankrupt failed to surrender himself to the court, committed perjury on his examination or fraudulently concealed his assets. ['The punishment of death for not surrendering, or submitting to be examined, for concealing property, was first introduced by the 4 and 5 Anne, continued by the 5 Geo. 1, and afterwards by the 5 Geo. 2, C. 30; and it was not until the reign of his present majesty that the penalty was changed to the milder one of transportation.' *Eden on Bankruptcy Laws*, 382. The last reference to the statute of 'his present majesty' is 1 Geo. IV, U.K.S., 1821, C. 115.]

1.1.15 In the middle of the 18th Century, Sir William Blackstone, commenting on the Law of England, had this to say about bankruptcy:

The Laws of England, more widely, have steered in the middle between both extremes: providing at once against the inhumanity of the creditor, who is not suffered to confine an honest bankrupt after his effects are delivered up; and at the same time taking care that all his just debts shall be paid; so far as the effects will extend. But still they are cautious of encouraging prodigality and extravagance by this indulgence to debtors; and therefore they allow the benefit of the laws of bankruptcy to none but actual traders; since that set of men are, generally speaking, the only persons liable to accidental losses, and to an inability of paying their debts, without any fault of their own. If persons in other situations of life run in debt without the power of payment, they must take the consequences of their own indiscretion, even though they may meet with sudden accidents that may reduce their fortunes: for the law holds it to be an unjustifiable practice, for any person but a tradesman to encumber himself with debts of any considerable value. If a gentleman, or one in a liberal profession, at a time of contracting his debts, has a sufficient fund to pay them, the delay of payment is a species of dishonesty, and a temporary injustice to his creditor: and if, at such time, he has no sufficient fund, the dishonesty and the injustice is the greater. He cannot therefore, murmur, if he suffers the punishment which he has voluntarily drawn upon himself. But in mercantile transactions, the case is far otherwise. Trade cannot be carried on without mutual credit on both sides: the contracting of debts is therefore here not only justifiable, but necessary. And if by accidental calamities, as by the loss of a ship in a tempest, the failure of brother traders, or by the non-payment of persons out of trade, a merchant or tradesman becomes incapable of discharging his own debts, it is his misfortune and not his fault. To the misfortunes, therefore, of debtors, the law had given a compassionate remedy, but denied it to their faults: since at the same time that it provides for the security of commerce, by enacting that every considerable trader may be declared a bankrupt, for the benefit of his creditors as well as himself, it has also to discourage extravagance, declared that no one shall be capable of being made a bankrupt, but only a trader, nor capable of receiving the full benefit of the statutes, but only an industrious trader. [W. Blackstone, *Commentaries on the Laws of England*, Book II, Oxford, the Clarendon Press, 1766, pp 473–4.]

...

1.1.17 In the early part of the 19th Century, a number of statutes were passed for the relief of insolvent debtors who were not engaged in trade and therefore could not be made bankrupt. Originally, the insolvency acts provided only for the release from imprisonment of the debtor. He was not released of his debts and remained liable for their repayment. Later legislation provided for the discharge of persons who were imprisoned for their debts if they surrendered all of their goods for the benefit of their creditors. In 1812 [52 Geo. III, U.K.S., 1812, C. 165], the laws relating to insolvency were administered by a court of record known as the Court for the Relief of Insolvent Debtors. By the *Bankruptcy Act* of 1861 [24 & 25 Vic. U.K.S., 1861, C. 135], which made persons other than traders subject to bankruptcy law, this Court was abolished and its jurisdiction transferred to the Court of Bankruptcy. In 1869, by the *Bankruptcy Repeal and Insolvent Court Act* [32 & 33 Vic. U.K.S., 1869, C. 83], all insolvency statutes theretofore existing were extinguished. Imprisonment for debt was abolished altogether, except in the case of a dishonest person who could pay his debts but refused to do so. The legal distinction between bankruptcy and insolvency was thus all but eliminated.

1.1.18 In the history of bankruptcy, there is much experimentation concerning who should liquidate and supervise an estate. In 1831, for example, the English legislation provided for the joint administration by official assignees and assignees chosen by the creditors. In 1869, the system of administration, at the insistence of the trading community, reverted to a system of creditor liquidation. The creditors chose the trustee who was supervised by a committee of inspectors also chosen by the creditors. Abuses soon arose, however, particularly in regard to the solicitation of proxies, which often permitted a minority of creditors to control and manipulate the administration of an estate in their interests to the prejudice of the majority of creditors.

1.1.19 It was recognized in England that the system of creditor control over the administration of a bankruptcy estate, as provided by the 1869 Act, had failed. The English *Bankruptcy Act of 1883* devised a new system of joint official and creditor control. Although minor amendments have been made to this Act, the system of administration, that it created, has not changed in any material respect. When Joseph Chamberlain, the then President of the Board of Trade, spoke on the second reading of the Bill for the 1883 Act, he explained the philosophy of his new legislation as follows:

He, (Joseph Chamberlain), asked the House to keep in mind two main, and, at the same time, distinct objects of any good Bankruptcy Law. Those were, firstly, in the honest administration of bankrupt estates, with a view to the fair and speedy distribution of the assets among the creditors, whose property they were; and, in the second place their object should be, following the idea that prevention was better than cure, to do something to improve the general tone of commercial morality, to promote honest trading, and to lessen the number of failures. In other words, Parliament had to endeavour, as far as possible, to protect the salvage, and also to diminish the number of wrecks.

His next point was that, with regard to those two most important objects, there was only one way by which they could be secured and that was by securing an independent and impartial examination into the circumstances of each case; and that was the cardinal principle of this Bill ... What happened when a bankruptcy took place which might easily cause misery to thousands of people and bring ruin on many homes? It was treated as if it were entirely a matter of private concern, and allowed to become a scramble between the debtor and his advisers – who were often his confederates – on the one hand, and the creditors on the other. Meanwhile, the great public interests at stake in all these questions were entirely and absolutely ignored, as there was nobody to represent them, and the practice which was followed in the case of other calamities was, in this case, entirely absent. In the case of accidents by sea and by land – railway accidents, for instance – it was incumbent upon a Government Department to institute an inquiry. There were inquiries in the case of accidents in mines, and of boiler explosions, and sad as those disasters were, they did not, in the majority of cases, cause so much misery as a bad bankruptcy, which brought ruin to many families by carrying off the fruits of their labour and industry ... Now, it would be seen that the provision which he had described (a description of duties and responsibilities of the official receiver, the office of which was first created by this Bill) constituted a system which he thought they might fairly call a system of official inquiry, and which went on all fours with a similar system in the matters of accident to which he had referred. He did not think that without some such limited officialism as this any satisfactory inquiry was even possible. No investigation could be worth anything unless it was conducted by an independent and impartial officer ... [J. Chamberlain, *Hansard's Parliament Debates* (England), 3rd series, Vol. CCLXXVII, p 817, March 19, 1883.]

1.1.20 *Conclusion*: In this chapter we have examined how the insolvent debtor was treated under the laws of several of the civilizations of the ancient world and, in particular, under the law of Rome. Among the modern bankruptcy systems, the only one here studied in any detail was the English system, as it was upon it that the Canadian legislation was modelled.

1.1.21 Over the years, the principles underlying the English Insolvency and Bankruptcy Law changed considerably. While, at the outset, the legislation was of a purely criminal nature, this character has been progressively attenuated as the legal treatment given to debtors became more and more humane. The former 'creditors acts', very strict with debtors, eventually recognized the necessity to give the honest and unfortunate debtor a chance to rehabilitate himself. This chance was given to insolvent traders as early as 1705 and, about one century later, extended to all debtors. Finally, after a great deal of experimentation in the field of bankruptcy administration, England opted for a compromise between official and creditor control. As will be seen in the next chapter, the element of officialism in the English system is much greater than in its Canadian counterpart.

THE CANADIAN LEGISLATION SINCE CONFEDERATION

1.2.01 *Principal Milestones*: In the hundred years since Confederation, the following Statutes constitute the important milestones of bankruptcy and insolvency legislation:

1869: *The Insolvent Act of 1869*	32–33 Vic., Can. S. 1869, C. 16
1875: *The Insolvent Act of 1875*	38 Vic., Can. S. 1875, C. 16
1880: *An Act to repeal the Acts Respecting Insolvency now in force in Canada*	43 Vic., Can. S. 1880, C. 1
1882: *An Act respecting Insolvent Banks, Insurance Companies, Loan Companies, Building Societies and Trading Corporations*, later renamed the *Winding-Up Act* (for insolvent companies)	45 Vic., Can. S. 1882, C. 23
1889: *The Winding Up Amendment Act, 1889* (extended to solvent companies)	52 Vic., Can. S. 1889, C. 32
1919: *The Bankruptcy Act*	9–10 Geo. V, Can. S. 1919, C. 36
1923: *The Bankruptcy Act Amendment Act, 1923* (companies prohibited from making proposals without previously being adjudged bankrupt; office of custodian created; office of official receivers created)	13–14 Geo. V, Can. S. 1923, C. 31
1932: *The Bankruptcy Act Amendment Act, 1932* (office of Superintendent created)	22–23 Geo. V, Can. S. 1932, C. 39
1933: *The Companies' Creditors Arrangement Act, 1933*	23–24 Geo. V, Can. S. 1932–33, C. 36
1934: *The Farmers' Creditors Arrangement Act, 1934*	24–25 Geo. V, Can. S. 1934, C. 53
1943: *The Farmers' Creditors Arrangement Act, 1943*	7 Geo. VI, Can. S. 1943, C. 26
1949: *Bankruptcy Act, 1949*	13 Geo. VI, Can. S. 1949 (2nd Session) C. 7
1953: *An Act to Amend the Companies' Creditors Arrangement Act, 1933* (act restricted to arrangement including an arrangement between a company and its bondholders).	1–2 El. II, Can. S. 1952–53, C. 3
1966: *An Act to Amend the Bankruptcy Act*	14–15 El. II, Can. S. 1966–67, C. 32

1.2.02 *The First Insolvency Legislation After Confederation*: The Acts of 1869 and 1875 applied only to insolvent traders. From 1874 to 1878 there was a serious depression in Canada resulting in many commercial failures. This caused much public resentment particularly in the rural areas of the country which led to the enactment of *The Insolvency Acts Repeal Act* in 1880. The following quotations from the debates in the House of Commons indicate something of the public opinion of the time and the reasons for the repeal. The anger directed at those who appeared to be acting fraudulently still has a timeliness:

Mr. Colby: Whatever may have been the necessity of the law when it was passed, I think that now it is unquestionably a fact that it has outlived its usefulness and that public opinion is

definitely settled and has declared itself in a way that is unmistakeable, in favour of an immediate
and summary repeal of the Act ... (the law) became rather a means of escape for the dishonest
and designing debtor than a mere means of relief for the honest and unfortunate debtor ...
experience has also shown in this country, and in other countries I believe, that the rapacity of
assignees, the dishonesty of debtors, the greed of some creditors, the inattention of others, have
thwarted the beneficient intentions of the law; and instead of there being an economical and
honest administration of assets, the practical operation of the law has been characterized by a
wasteful extravagance, and too often by a dishonest administration. I think it is unmistakeably
the case in this country where the law has been a long time on the Statute-Book, that it has
tended to the demoralisation of trade, and to lower the standard of commercial morality. It has
tended to recklessness in trading and in living to extravagance. It has tempted many persons,
wholly unsuited for business, to risk their fortune in business enterprises that were little
understood by them. The whole effect of the law in recent years has been unfortunate and
disastrous. I think, sir, that it is the sentiment of the people of this country, generally, that it has
tended, in some considerable degree, if not to create, at all events to aggravate, the commercial
distress which has unhappily prevailed in this country. [Canada, *House of Commons Debates*,
1880, 2nd Session, 4th Parliament, Vol. 1, pp 102 and 103.]
Mr. Sproule: ... Public opinion has been too strong against the continuance of these laws, which
apply to one class of the community only, to prevent their continuance upon the Statutes of our
country. They have only held out inducements for parties so disposed to shape their affairs in
such a way, even to change from one line to another, so as to enable them to take advantage of
the Act, and pay their debts with twenty, thirty or forty cents on the dollar. I believe it is
generally recognized that there is not more than one honest trader out of every three or four who
have taken the benefit of that act since it was placed on the Statute-Book. It seems strange that if
the law was so beneficial, it should have been made applicable only to commercial people, and
that all professional men, labourers and mechanics, and all the agricultural classes of the
community should be entirely left out from the benefits supposed to accrue from that law ...
[*Ibid*, p 107.]

1.2.03 By a coincidence that appears not to be accidental, the *Bill to Repeal the Insolvency Acts*
was read for the third time on March 4, 1880, while on March 5, 1880, assent was given, in
Ontario, to 'An *Act to Abolish Priorities of and Amongst Execution Creditors.*' [43 Vic., Ont. S.
1880, c. 10. This Act is now known as the *Creditors' Relief Act.*] In the discussion in the House
of Commons, it was said that the Ontario Bill, which was similar to the law prevailing in Quebec,
would provide for just and equitable distribution of estates and the hope was expressed that
other provinces would enact similar legislation.
1.2.04 *The Winding-Up Act*: It was soon found that, without an *Insolvency Act*, there was no
convenient way to wind up insolvent companies. Boards of Trade, in most of the large cities,
passed resolutions requesting new legislation. In 1882, the *Insolvent Banks, Insurance Companies and Trading Corporations Act*, later to be known as the *Winding-Up Act*, was enacted.
1.2.05 In some countries, such as England and Australia, the *Bankruptcy Act* applies only to
individuals and there is other legislation for the liquidation of insolvent companies. With the
existence of the *Winding-Up Act*, this dichotomy could have developed in Canada. However,
when the *Bankruptcy Act* of 1919 was enacted, it applied to both individuals and corporations.
From 1919 until 1966, there were, in effect, two separate Acts in competition with each other
relating to the insolvency of limited liability companies. These two Acts differ in substance and
technique. In bankruptcy, for example, the property of the bankrupt vests in the trustee; under

the *Winding-Up Act*, title to the property of the company remains in the company, but its control and management are taken from the directors and placed in the liquidator. The *Bankruptcy Act* binds the Crown, while the *Winding-Up Act* does not. Under the *Bankruptcy Act*, an act of bankruptcy must be proved to obtain a receiving order, while, under the *Winding-Up Act*, a winding-up order may be obtained if the debtor is insolvent or deemed to be insolvent. Neither banks, insurance companies nor railway companies may be liquidated under the *Bankruptcy Act*, but they may be wound up under the *Winding-Up Act*. The *Bankruptcy Act* is characterized by an administration, for the most part, controlled by creditors, while, under the *Winding-Up Act*, the administration is controlled by the court. This duality is restricted by the amendments to the *Bankruptcy Act* in 1966, which provide in effect that the *Bankruptcy Act* should take precedence over the *Winding-Up Act*. Thus, now, where a petition for a receiving order or an assignment is filed under the *Bankruptcy Act*, in respect of a corporation, the *Winding-Up Act* does not extend or apply to that corporation. [*An Act to amend the Bankruptcy Act*, 14–15 Eliz. II, Can. s. 1966, c. 32, s 169A.]

1.2.06 *The Period from 1880 to 1919*: During the thirty-nine years when there was no federal bankruptcy or insolvency legislation relating to individuals, the only relief available to insolvent individuals was through provincial legislation. There were, in Quebec, articles 763–780 of *The Code of Civil Procedure* and, in the other provinces, the Assignment and Preferences Acts. The first of these Acts was an *Act Respecting Assignments for the Benefit of Creditors* passed by the Ontario Legislature in 1885, some five years after enacting what is now *The Creditors' Relief Act*.

1.2.07 Under provincial legislation, an insolvent debtor makes an assignment of his property to an authorized trustee licensed by the province. The authorized trustee is then required to liquidate the estate under the supervision of inspectors. For this, he is paid a fee from the debtor's estate. What characterizes provincial legislation, and since 1919, distinguishes it from the *Bankruptcy Act* is that a creditor cannot force a debtor to make an assignment; once an assignment is made, there is no provision in the legislation permitting a debtor to make a composition with his creditors and a debtor does not receive a release of his debts or a discharge.

1.2.08 *The 1919 Bankruptcy Act*: By 1917, there was considerable agitation across the country in support of the enactment of a national *Bankruptcy Act*. A committee of the Canadian Bar Association was created to draft such an act. This, in turn, disturbed some businessmen and authorized trustees licensed by the provinces. They felt that an act drafted by lawyers would provide for some form of court controlled administration instead of the provincial system of creditor control whereby estates were liquidated by the authorized trustees under the supervision of inspectors. One of the largest firms of authorized trustees, the Canadian Credit Men's Trust Association, retained Mr. H.P. Grundy, K.C. of Winnipeg, and instructed him to draft a Bill based upon creditor control and retaining the essential features of the provincial Assignments and Preferences Acts.

1.2.09 The Bill, based upon Mr. Grundy's draft, was first introduced in the House of Commons on March 27, 1918 as a war measure. On the motion for first reading, it was said:

Mr. Jacobs ... I think that I can claim for this Bill that it is essentially a war measure at this particular time. We must be prepared when the war comes to a close, to be able to handle the situation which is bound to arise in this country as a result of the long continued struggle and of the readjustments which must be made ... By this measure it is proposed that the courts shall carefully scrutinize the business dealings and the business relations of traders, and shall make a distinction – shall separate the sheep from the goats. When the court is of the opinion that a debtor has been obliged to assign through misfortune, he shall be given the necessary relief. If, on the other hand, it should be found in scrutinizing his affairs, that he wrecked his own business wilfully, then, of course, he should receive no relief whatever. [Canada, *House of Commons Debates*, 1918, 1st Session, 13th Parliament, Vol. 1, p 206.]

The Bill, later referred to a special committee and then reintroduced in the House of Commons during the following session, [*Ibid*, p 563] was enacted in 1919.

1.2.10 *The Office of the Custodian Created in 1923*: It had been hoped that the system of administration established by the 1919 Act and based upon the practice prevailing under the provincial Assignments Acts would prevent the occurring of the abuses that had helped to discredit the old Insolvency Acts. It was soon found, however, that most of the business under the new Act was not going to the experienced organizations of trustees that had efficiently handled most of the business under the provincial Assignments Acts. The work of a trustee attracted many unqualified and inexperienced persons, and, as there was then not enough business, this resulted in many trustees openly soliciting business and often lead to collusive and inefficient administration of estates.

1.2.11 In an attempt to rectify the abuses surrounding the appointment of trustees, particularly in voluntary assignments where the debtor was nominating his own trustee, the office of custodian was created in 1923. In many respects, the custodian fulfilled several of the functions of the official receiver in England until the first meeting of the creditors. The custodian was in effect the first trustee in every estate. He had to take possession of the property of the debtor and was responsible for its safekeeping until the appointment of the trustee at the first meeting of creditors. In practice, it soon developed that the custodian was invariably appointed trustee. As a result, the office of the custodian served no useful purpose and was ultimately abolished in 1949.

1.2.12 *The Office of Superintendent of Bankruptcy created in 1932*: The lack of safeguards surrounding the appointment of trustees encouraged the activities of dishonest trustees. There were scandals involving inefficient and collusive liquidations by incompetent and untrustworthy trustees. The supervision of trustees by creditors was ineffectual and the demand grew for some form of government supervision. [Canadian Credit Men's Trust Association Ltd., Minutes of the 17th Annual Meeting, p 143.]

1.2.13 At the Annual Meeting of the Canadian Credit Men's Trust Association Ltd., in 1927, attention was called to the office of 'Accountant of Court' created under the *Bankruptcy Act* of Scotland. The Accountant, who was appointed by the court on the recommendation of the Crown, had the responsibility to examine the charges and conduct of trustees and inspectors in every proceeding.

1.2.14 In 1929, the late Lewis Duncan, Q.C., an acknowledged bankruptcy specialist, after comparing the English, French and United States systems, suggested that there was a need in Canada for an adequately staffed bankruptcy department with offices at strategic centres. [In a letter to Robert H. Thayer, an investigator working on the report known as the *Donovan Report*. This letter can be found at p 59 of the appendix to the *Report, Bankruptcy Administration in Canada*, which can be found at p 237 of the said *Donovan Report*, whose full title is: The Joint Committee of the Association of the Bar of the City of New York, the New York County Lawyers' Association and the Bronx County Bar Association, *Report submitted to the Hon. Thomas D. Thacher, Judge of the United States District Court for the Southern District of New York*, on March 22, 1930, by William J. Donovan, Counsel to the Petitioners.]

1.2.15 In 1932, the office of the Superintendent was created. It was contemplated that the Superintendent would provide an independent, impartial and official supervision of trustees administering estates under the *Bankruptcy Act*. Except for the increased investigatory powers

given to it in 1966, the office of the Superintendent has remained unaltered and compares with
that of the Inspector General in Bankruptcy established in England in 1883.

1.2.16 *The 1949 Bankruptcy Act*: The present Canadian *Bankruptcy Act* was enacted in 1949.
The intention of the new Act was said to be 'to clarify and simplify the legislation'. The following
extract from Hansard, when the Bill was first introduced in the Senate, explains the history of
the Bill and the principal changes:

Hon. J. Gordon Fogo: Honourable senators, it has sometimes been said that legislation in
Canada is passed hastily and that those interested and the public in general are not given an
opportunity to study its provisions. I do not think that can be said of this Bill F, which appears to
have had a rather checkered career. This, I believe, is the fourth time that the bill has been
introduced in this honourable House. It was first brought down in the year 1946, in a somewhat
different form from the present measure, and was laid over for study for a period during which
representations concerning it were made. Subsequently, in 1948, it came up again in a revised
form. And, as most honourable senators will remember, it was introduced for a third time at the
first session of this year, but unfortunately, owing to early dissolution, consideration of it was
not completed. The present bill, I am informed, with very few exceptions, is practically identical
with the bill that was before the Senate last session ... The bill provides a more orderly
arrangement of subjects and the language in many sections of the Act has been simplified. One or
two of the more notable changes should be mentioned. The bill reinstates a provision which was
in the *Bankruptcy Act* of 1919. During the period from 1919 to 1923 the Act contained a provision
whereby an insolvent person could make a proposal to his creditors without making an assignment or having a receiving order made against him, and thereby suffering the stigma of
bankruptcy. The bill now provides that an insolvent person may make such a proposal without
going through the procedure of bankruptcy.
A further change which has been generally accepted as an improvement is a code for the
administration of small estates in an economical and inexpensive manner. This section of the bill
covers estates with assets of $500 or less, and provides a simplified procedure for their
administration.
One other notable innovation of this bill is found in sections 127 to 129, which deal with the
discharge of bankrupts. Under the existing legislation it has been necessary for a bankrupt, after
the administration was completed, to apply to get his discharge. For various reasons, whether
because the debtor did not know he was entitled to do this, or for other reasons, it was not
customary for bankrupts to apply to their discharge. Following legislation in other countries – I
think in the United States, and perhaps in Australia – this bill incorporates what might be
regarded as an automatic application for discharge, because the occurring of the bankruptcy
through assignment or receiving order in the first instance is also treated as an application for
discharge. The debtor of course has to satisfy the court that he qualifies before he gets his
discharge, and the conditions are laid down.
To move on quickly and in a very summary way: there are other miscellaneous provisions which
might be mentioned. The new bill vests a greater measure of control in the creditors and
inspectors. The powers of the superintendent have been made more explicit ... The remuneration of trustees has been increased; that is, the maximum remuneration has been enlarged from 5
to 7½ per cent ... The office of the custodian is eliminated ... [Canada, *Debates of the Senate*,
1949, 2nd Session, 21st Parliament, p 97.]

1.2.17 *The 1966 Amendment*: During the fifties and early sixties, there was an increasing
number of complaints about fraudulent bankruptcies. The complaint was also made that the

investigatory machinery was not adequate to cope with the problem. As a result, the *Bankruptcy Act* was amended in 1966 so as to give the Superintendent wider powers of investigation. He may now investigate offences under any Act of Parliament, whether they have occurred before or after bankruptcy.

1.2.18 Many other significant amendments were made in 1966. One relates to non-arms' length transactions, and enables trustees better to deal with the transactions entered into by a debtor to the prejudice of his creditors. Part x of the *Bankruptcy Act* was also enacted. It provides for a system of orderly payment of debts under the supervision of the courts, but it is effective only in provinces where the Lieutenant Governor in Council has requested the Governor in Council to proclaim it in force.

...

1.2.35 *Conclusion*: At the end of this brief description of how the bankruptcy and insolvency system developed in Canada, there are a number of comments that come to mind.

1.2.36 Although, at the outset, the legislation was almost entirely borrowed from England, in the course of time, amendments were made to the original legislation to better adapt it to Canadian conditions and special statutes were passed to meet particular problems. Little attempt was made, however, to integrate new legislation with the existing legislation or to make a single comprehensive Act. The result has been a multiplicity of statutes and systems which often lead to inequity and inefficiency.

1.2.37 With the multiplicity of systems, the debtor and the creditor sometimes have the choice of the system under which to proceed and, under certain circumstances, they can fare better under one system than another. A creditor, for example, may be better protected or may have a higher priority for a dividend under one system than another. Similarly, the penalty provisions applicable to debtors may vary.

1.2.38 Many corporations may be liquidated under either the *Winding-Up Act* or the *Bankruptcy Act*. There are transactions that may be set aside as fraudulent preferences under one of these Acts, which could not be set aside, as such, under the other. However, since the 1966 amendments to the *Bankruptcy Act*, the *Winding-Up Act* does not apply to a corporation, where a petition is filed under the *Bankruptcy Act*. While the opportunity of a debtor or creditor to elect to take proceedings under the *Winding-Up Act*, and thus forestall proceedings under the *Bankruptcy Act*, has been reduced, inequities are still possible. The majority of creditors, for example, may wish to take proceedings under the *Winding-Up Act* to reach a creditor who has received a preference that may be set aside as fraudulent under the *Winding-Up Act*, but not under the *Bankruptcy Act*. The creditor who is alleged to have obtained a fraudulent preference, or a creditor friendly to him, may effectively block the proceedings under the *Winding-Up Act* by making a petition under the *Bankruptcy Act*.

1.2.39 There are situations, however, where no choice is given to the debtor or the creditors as to which statute may be used. A number of statutes apply in whole or in part, for example, to particular debtors, such as banks, insurance companies and railways. This situation may also lead to inequity as both debtors and creditors, under the particular statutes, may, without good reason, fare differently than those who come within the provisions of other statutes.

1.2.40 Moreover, in spite of the multiplicity of systems and statutes, there are a number of debtors whose affairs cannot be liquidated under existing federal legislation. The non-trading corporations, for example, would be in that category. It is not clear, either, whether any of this legislation applies to the winding-up, by reason of their insolvency, of some corporations, such as provincial trust companies and certain building societies.

1.2.41 Finally, the existing legislation may also be criticized for being, to a considerable degree, either rudimentary or out-dated. Much of it was designed when social and commercial conditions were very much different than what they are today. In other cases, legislation designed to meet a particular emergency survived long after the emergency had passed and the conditions changed. The procedure for the liquidation of insolvent railways is a good example of rudimentary legislation. Under present conditions, as a practical matter, special legislation would probably be required to effectively liquidate a railway company by reason of its insolvency, as existing legislation is silent in respect to many matters of importance. The *Farmers' Creditors Arrangement Act* is an example of special legislation inspired by a national emergency that has been long out of date, but which has never been repealed, brought up to date or incorporated into the principal statute.

NOTE The present Canadian Bankruptcy Act was enacted in 1949 and, largely because of fundamental changes in the role of credit in our society since World War II, was widely thought to have become outdated. In 1966 a Study Committee headed by Roger Tassé was established to review the bankruptcy and insolvency legislation in Canada. The recommendations of the Committee were first embodied in Bill C-60, which received first reading in the House of Commons in 1975. The Bill underwent substantial revision, was reintroduced as Bill s-11, which received first reading in March, 1978, and was further revised, being reintroduced as Bill s-14, which received first reading on 27th February 1979. Unless otherwise indicated, statutory references hereinafter are to the provisions of s-14.

2 THE OBJECTIVES OF BANKRUPTCY LEGISLATION

Tassé Report, pp 51–88

2:1:01 *Bankruptcy and the Legal Order*: No law can be examined in isolation from the society it serves. Law has been described as a scheme of social ends that involves the continuous balancing of conflicting interests. Although 'the end of law is peace, the life of law is a struggle = a struggle of nations, of the state power, of classes of individuals.' [Rudolph von Ihéring, *Der Kamps Ums Recht* (The Struggle for Law) 1872, quoted in W. Seagle, *Men of Law*, New York: The MacMillan Co., 1947, p 38.] Roscoe Pound described 'the legal order as a regime of adjusting relations and ordering conduct through the systematic and orderly application of the force of a politically organized society, in order to prevent friction in the human use and the enjoyment of the goods of existence and eliminate waste of them.' [R. Pound, *Introduction to American Law* in Vanderbilt, *Studying Law*, p 379.]

2:1:02 Bankruptcy legislation is an attempt, on the one hand, to identify and relieve the insolvent debtor who cannot meet his obligations; and, on the other hand, to ensure that his creditors will be treated fairly and equitably. In accomplishing this, it is essential that we endeavour to balance our social needs and beliefs with the requirements of our credit oriented economy.

2:1:03 Although there has been a steady evolution in the Canadian bankruptcy legislation, the fact that it has remained substantially the same for so long without any major revision seems to indicate that it has, for some time, achieved reasonable success in identifying and relieving the honest but unfortunate debtor without sacrificing the needs of creditors for fair and equitable treatment. The general satisfaction that may have, however, existed previously with the legislation no longer prevails.

2:1:04 We live in an affluent society. It is characterized by mass production, mass consumption, built-in obsolescence, television, the electric appliance industry, the industries catering to the boating, camera and sporting enthusiast, the two and three car family, the new ease and convenience of travel and the urbanization of the population. Accompanying this new affluence have been changing concepts of the morality of work and debt, new methods of doing business and financing, increased taxation, tax avoidance schemes, the proliferation of limited liability corporations, the advent of the credit card economy, with the 'I can get it wholesale', 'buy now, pay later' and expense account living, inroads by organized crime and the increasing incidence of white collar crime. The question must be asked whether any *Bankruptcy Act* framed before all this came into existence or attained widespread proportions is well adapted to the needs of our present society. It would be surprising if the underlying premises of our present Act were still relevant. New principles, however, cannot be formulated and no attempt can be made to arrive at a new balance between competing interests until the existing areas of friction are identified and fundamental problems are discussed.

2.1.05 *Methods of Production and Marketing*: Modern methods of production and marketing have contributed to a very great extent to making the bankruptcy and insolvency legislation out-of-date. From the Roman times until the last century, a plough, for example, had an economic value that scarcely depreciated when it changed hands. Goods were then in short supply and consumers did not place the same premium, as they do today, on a new article as compared to a used one. For this reason, from the time of the *cessio bonorum*, the assets of a debtor did not substantially depreciate when they passed from the hands of a debtor to those of his creditors. This factor contributed to make it profitable for the creditors to put into operation the bankruptcy process. As goods retained their value, the proceeds from the realization of the bankrupt estate were more likely to exceed the cost of administration.

2.1.06 Today, the overwhelming goal of the modern industrial system is to achieve the greatest possible rate of corporate growth as measured in sales. J.K. Galbraith, in *The New Industrial State*, writes: 'The individual serves the industrial system not by supplying it with savings and the resulting capital. He serves it by consuming its products ... a family's standard of living becomes an index of its achievement. It helps insure that the production and *pari passu* the consumption of goods will be the prime measure of social accomplishment.' [J.K. Galbraith, *The New Industrial State*; Boston, Houghton Mifflin Co.; 1967; p 49.] Under these circumstances, used goods in the hands of a trustee in bankruptcy have only a fraction of the value they had while in the hands of the debtor. This is particularly true in the case of consumer bankruptcies. But even in a business bankruptcy, inventories of completely manufactured goods are very often sold by trustees much below their cost. This is, frequently, by reason of the fact that customary manufacturers' warranties cannot be given or honoured. Even where goods have been converted into accounts receivable, the amount a trustee is expected to recover is usually much less than their value, although the debtor, if he had not become bankrupt, would normally have counted upon collecting the full amount with only a small allowance for bad debts. Seasonable goods lose much of their value if sold in the off-season. Inventory, in the course of manufacture, often has no more than scrap value. Many assets depreciate very quickly. Newly produced motor vehicles may depreciate as much as forty per cent for the first year. Basically, the problem is that a trustee must liquidate the goods of a debtor outside of the normal marketing channels. This contributes to the diminishing dividends paid to unsecured creditors.

2.1.07 *The Credit System*: Another important factor that has put the bankruptcy system out of balance is the explosive use of credit, particularly consumer credit, since the second world war. New and burgeoning consumer oriented industries have expanded through complex methods of mass production. This has been made possible only because of the emergence of mass markets which, in the case of durable consumer goods, such as expensive appliances and motor cars, require readily available financing provided for by the instalment payment plan.

2.1.08 One would expect that most credit transactions are entered into by credit grantors only after a careful consideration of the capacity of the borrower or purchaser to fulfill his obligation. This is often not the case. Some producers may choose to operate closer to full capacity in order to lower their costs and, to dispose of the production, may deliberately extend credit to the marginal or sub-marginal risks. The same may be true of wholesalers, retailers and finance institutions who may attempt to increase their volume of business in relation to their overhead. Finally, it is relevant to recall that bad debts are anticipated by those in business. A reserve or allowance is made for bad debts as a cost of doing business. This reduces the income tax payable by the credit grantor and has the effect of distributing his losses over all of the tax-paying public.

2.1.09 The principles underlying the *Bankruptcy Act* developed when there was much less credit and when the credit that was granted was only extended after careful consideration. Today, 'the endless stream of persuasion via television, radio, magazines, newspapers, billboards and in the mail has become a predominant part of our environment.' [Canada, *Report on Consumer Credit* of the Special Joint Committee of the Senate and the House of Commons on Consumer Credit and Cost of Living, Ottawa, Queen's Printer, 1967.] The businessman and the consumer are exhorted to buy now and pay later; in short, to become indebted.

2.1.10 As far as consumers are concerned, one of the main reasons for their discontent is often the ambivalent attitude on the part of their creditors. Too often, a debtor is persuaded to buy something against his own interest by a high pressure salesman. If the debtor later finds that he is unable to pay and withholds payment, his wages are garnished. If this triggers a bankruptcy, he is told that he is responsible for his misfortune.

2.1.11 Not only creditors, but also debtors, may abuse the credit system. Opportunity for gain at the expense of others has always presented great temptations. During the centuries preceding the development of our credit economy, the sanctions against insolvent debtors have been progressively alleviated. As the law is now more humane and lenient, some debtors, with loose moral standards or not personally affected by the stigma that, in the minds of some, attaches to bankruptcy, may abuse the credit facilities.

2.1.12 The legislation should curb the abuses of credit by both creditors and debtors. The legal consequences of granting or receiving credit must be readjusted to meet changed conditions. As there are good and bad debtors, so are there good and bad creditors. As all debtors are not treated the same, neither should all creditors. The traditional concept that 'equality is equity' and its corollary that creditors, as a rule, should be paid *pari passu* needs re-examination.

2.1.13 *Consumer Bankruptcies:* The plight of the consumer or wage-earner debtor is one of the most important problems that must be faced in the field of bankruptcy in Canada. To a certain extent, this group of debtors represent the social and economic casualties of our industrial and credit system and must be so regarded.

2.1.14 It must not be forgotten that in our society the producer and marketing organizations make vast investments in sales promotion and advertising aimed at creating a demand to buy more. To facilitate this, the greater use of consumer credit is encouraged. It has become the normal pattern of urban life in Canada. Too often those who should most strongly resist this pressure are those who are the least educationally, intellectually and culturally prepared to withstand the pressure.

2.1.15 The size of the problem may also be seen in a statistic provided by the Division Court Referee, County of York, in Toronto. This position was created to assist the County Court

Judge in Chambers to make orders for payment of debts that are fair to all parties concerned. In 1968, the Referee in Toronto interviewed a total of approximately 7,500 persons who declared debts amounting to over $20,000,000. [Taken from the records of the Division Court Referee for the County of York.]

2.1.16 Many of those who resort to consumer credit find that they are in a trap from which they cannot escape. Through bad fortune, with one financial emergency following another and often from mismanagement, this group of debtors become deeper and more hopelessly in debt. Interest piles up on interest, and as payments are not sufficient to cover the interest, the principal of the debt is very often increased instead of being reduced.

2.1.17 There is much personal tragedy for those who become hopelessly in debt. Each case involves a person who has failed, a person who has been defeated. The failure and defeat not only affect the debtor, but his wife, family, friends and acquaintances. Many children, to escape a harsh, bleak and degrading environment, marry young and become themselves members of the chronic poor.

2.1.18 The facilities that society provides to relieve the consumer debtor, too often, are not effective or are illusory. In a great majority of cases, bankruptcy is financially beyond the reach of those who most need it. Similarly, there is no adequate, simple and inexpensive procedure permitting a small debtor to make an arrangement with all of his creditors either inside or outside the *Bankruptcy Act*. Moreover, the remedies available to creditors often result in debtors being disproportionately punished for their defaults.

2.1.19 It is frequently said that the *Bankruptcy Act* functions so as to rehabilitate the small debtor. The general uncertainty and confusion over what is meant by rehabilitation is well described by the Honourable Joe Lee, Referee in Bankruptcy for the Eastern District of Kentucky, who wrote recently:–

A review of the literature reveals that there is disagreement as to what is actually meant by rehabilitation. There is no generally accepted definition, certainly none that spells out goals in such a way as to identify the nature and degree of change expected. Does the *Bankruptcy Act* assume that those people charged with its implementation will educate debtors who come seeking help? If so, to what extent, and is this the sole area in which the court might be expected to operate in restoring the debtor to economic health or is the intent or expectation that efforts will also be made to change attitudes and values? If rehabilitation is taken in its narrowest sense to mean restoration of the petitioner to a former debt-free status, then the court need only lead him through each step of bankruptcy or Chapter XIII proceedings [Chapter XIII of the *United States Act* provides a procedure for the consolidation of debts of wage-earners] and it has finished its job. However, if the Act commissioned the court to administer the system in such a way that the debtor is restored to a 'healthy *working* state', Webster's third definition of the word, then it is the debtor's behaviour and not his state of being that the court must affect. This is not simply a matter of semantics. Rendering an individual debt-free *could* be accepted as a rehabilitative procedure. This would, at the same time, obviate the need for further research or even discussion. However, if there has been little research, there has been much discussion. Whether pro or con (Chapter XIII) and whatever the understanding of the meaning of rehabilitation, authorities addressing themselves to this subject clearly endorse the broader definition; and if the court is charged with influencing behaviour, economic behaviour after bankruptcy must be considered in any evaluative study of the system. Since there is ample evidence from the social sciences that attitudes and values have a significant effect on any complex behaviour pattern, it follows that an enlightened court can also justify adopting procedures calculated to influence debtors' economic attitudes and values, and research must, in turn, focus on changes in attitudes and values. [J. Lee, *What Shall We Do For The Consumer Bankrupt?* in 44 *Journal of the National Conference of Referees in Bankruptcy*, January, 1970, p 13, f.n. 12. The italics are those of the author.]

2.1.20 *The Stigma of Bankruptcy:* An underlying assumption of the *Bankruptcy Act* is that there is an economic and social stigma attached to bankruptcy. Until recently, most people took pride in paying their debts and it was a matter of shame for them and their families when they could not. This attitude towards work and debt often had a religious sanctification. In Genesis, for example, it is written 'In the sweat of thy face shalt thou eat bred …' [*The Bible*, Authorized King James Version, 3 Genesis 19, Toronto, Oxford University Press, 1941] and Emerson's maxim was 'wilt thou seal up the avenues of ill? Pay every debt as if God wrote the bill.' [Emerson, *Suum Cuique*, cited in Hoyt's *New Cyclopedia of Practical Quotations*, Funk and Wagnall's Co., 1927, p 181.] In the case of those for whom the stigma was real, there was an acceptance of responsibility for one's conduct and the results of it. The disgrace of bankruptcy, more than any legal sanction, effectively removed the bankrupt from business and thereby protected both the business community and the public from the incompetent or dishonest businessman.

2.1.21 In our modern society, there are increasingly fewer people who regard work either as a means of serving God or as an end in itself. Work is more often regarded as a necessary evil or as means to securing economic well-being. At the same time, there is a tendency to give more weight to those factors that encourage the diminution of the responsibility of the individual. It is also becoming apparent that there is an increasing number of persons who more readily accept bankruptcy as a solution to their financial problems. To many, what is legally right is morally right and individual bankruptcy is not a disgrace but just smart business tactics. [G.A. Brunner, *Personal Bankruptcy: Trends and Characteristics*, Columbus, The Ohio State University, 1965, p 4.]

2.1.22 The changing attitude of society towards bankruptcy is probably the principal reason for the failure of the present system of the conditional discharge of bankrupts to function effectively. Many choose to remain bankrupt rather than to meet the conditions that may have been imposed. They are more interested in living on a week to week basis than in accumulating assets that could vest in the trustee.

2.1.23 *The Secured Creditor:* When the first Canadian *Bankruptcy Act* was enacted, most creditors were unsecured and the amount owed to secured creditors was often only a small part of the total debt. This may be one of the reasons why the bankruptcy and insolvency legislation interferes so little with the rights of secured creditors and that they, to all intents and purposes liquidate their security free from the strict control and supervision imposed by the *Bankruptcy Act* and the *Winding-Up Act*.

2.1.24 Over the years, new methods of financing have increased the secured debts of almost all commercial debtors. Much financing is now done through security given under section 88 of the *Bank Act* and through new methods of factoring whereby loans are given by the factor to a vendor on the security of a continuing lien on his inventory and accounts receivable. It is expected that legislation similar to article 9 of the United States *Uniform Commercial Code* [*Uniform Commercial Code*, art. 9 (1968) (U.S.A.)] will soon be enacted in most provinces. This has already been done in Ontario by the enactment of the *Personal Property Security Act*. Under this type of legislation, it is anticipated that most debtors will have a single major supplier of credit who will usually have a security interest in all of the debtor's inventory and accounts receivable.

2.1.25 The growth of secured financing and the pressure for a uniform system for the single filing of personal property securities may be regarded as a reaction of the business community to the weakening of credit protection. A supplier of unsecured credit needs to know whether the proposed debtor is, in fact, the owner of all what he appears to own. With a multiple system of filing liens, this is often difficult, if not impossible, to ascertain with certainty. The same supplier of credit will also want to be assured that, if his debtor should fail, the bankruptcy system will intervene at the earliest point of time to protect the remaining property of the debtor for his benefit and that of the other creditors. The small dividend, [See *infra* in 2.2.06] which, on the average, is paid to unsecured creditors, indicates that the *Bankruptcy Act* does little, under modern conditions, to protect unsecured credit. The unsatisfactory system of quickly ascertaining whether a proposed debtor does, in fact, own what he appears to own, and the failure of the bankruptcy system to ensure a reasonable dividend to the unsecured supplier of credit, on the failure of the debtor, have greatly increased the risk of the unsecured credit grantor. Where the risk of extending unsecured credit appears too great, secured financing becomes much more attractive.

2.1.26 For all estates closed during 1969, $89,105,473 was paid to secured creditors, while only $31,919,837 was available for the payment of the costs of administration and unsecured debts. These figures do not include the amounts liquidated by secured creditors outside of bankruptcy such as through receiverships and foreclosure. [From the records of the Office of the Superintendent of Bankruptcy.]

2.1.27 It would not be surprising if the dollar value of property liquidated annually through receiverships were substantially greater than that liquidated through commercial bankruptcies. *Atlantic Acceptance Corporation Limited* is a case in point. It is the largest single financial failure in Canada with losses in excess of sixty-four million dollars. It is being liquidated by a receiver outside of the provisions of the *Bankruptcy Act*.

2.1.28 It may well be that, if secured financing continues to increase, almost all liquidations of the property of an insolvent commercial debtor, in the not too distant future, will be done outside of the *Bankruptcy Act*. This should cause concern, because, in such type of liquidation, there are not the controls and protection that are available under the *Bankruptcy Act*. In these circumstances, the senior secured creditor may, for example, liquidate the security for an amount sufficient only to pay himself in full, with no regard to the position of the other creditors.

2.1.29 To a great extent, what has been said regarding commercial debtors is equally applicable to consumer debtors. More of their indebtedness is secured resulting in repossessions and liquidations outside of the bankruptcy process. Motor cars, furniture and the larger household appliances are sold under conditional sale agreements whereby the title is reserved in the vendor until the full price is paid. The property owned outright by a consumer is very often taken as security, when, hard pressed to keep up payments, he seeks to re-finance his obligations. When the consumer can no longer meet these obligations, the conditional vendor or chattel mortgagee repossesses the property and liquidates it according to his rights. Very often, too, the extent of his secured indebtedness prevents or makes it difficult for the consumer to make an arrangement to pay his creditors over a period of time, as the secured creditors cannot be bound by the arrangement unless they consent.

2.1.30 *The Limited Liability Corporation:* A corporation is a legal entity separate and distinct from its shareholders. As a rule, it is only the corporation that is bound by the action done in its name or on its behalf, and not its shareholders, directors or officers. The abuse of this rule has posed serious problems in bankruptcy administration.

2.1.31 The *Bankruptcy Act* treats corporations in almost all respects as if they were individuals. There are only a very few sections of the Act that deal with the special circumstances of corporations. Section 118, for example, specifies who must perform the duties of a bankrupt, where the bankrupt is a corporation, and section 162 imposes a penal liability upon officers of a corporation and others who authorize, condone or participate in the commission of an offence. [See also s 46 of the *Bankruptcy Act* regarding contributory shareholders; R.S.C. 1952, C 14, as amended by 14–15 Eliz. II; Can. s., 1966–67, C 25 and 32.] Special rules have also been devised to reach the individuals who control corporations, where dividends have been paid, or shares redeemed, while the corporation was insolvent. [Section 67B of the *Bankruptcy Act*.] Under company legislation, liability is also usually imposed upon directors for the payment of arrears of wages to employees. [See, for example, *Canada Corporations Act*, R.S.C., 1952, C 53, S. 97.]

2.1.32 In many respects, the *Bankruptcy Act* is ineffective in the case of limited liability corporations. Sanctions against undischarged bankrupts, for example, are meaningless, where the debtor is a corporation. The device of the limited liability corporation is often used to make a mockery of the provisions of the *Bankruptcy Act* designed to keep out of business the dishonest or incompetent businessman. To use the words of Senator David A. Croll, 'more and more businesses have clothed themselves in corporate garments which have neither bodies to be kicked nor souls to be damned.' [Canada, *Debates of the Senate*, 1962–63, 1st Session, 25th Parliament, p 111.]

2.1.33 In actual practice, there is little apparent difference between an individual in business, in his own right, and an individual who does business through a limited liability company of which he is the beneficial owner of all of its shares. There is, however, a very real difference when a bankruptcy occurs. In the one case, the individual is required to surrender all of his property that is not exempt from seizure. He may also be refused a discharge or have a discharge granted subject to conditions. This may effectively keep him out of business for some time. In the other case, the individual, on the bankruptcy of his company, may keep all of his own personal property. The company, alone, is required to surrender its property and it is, as a rule, immaterial to the individual whether or not the company is given a discharge. The inconvenience caused to this individual often lasts no longer than it takes to incorporate a new company. The use of a limited company in such a manner can often put the law in disrepute.

2.1.34 The corporate veil has been frequently pierced in company, combines and taxing statutes. Sometimes, this has not been easy to accomplish, but one should not be discouraged, as an English judge once said: 'the legislature can forge a sledge-hammer capable of cracking open the corporate shell.' [*Bank Voor Handel en Scheepvaart* v *Slatford* (1953) 1 Q.B. 248 at 278 (C.A.) per Devlin J. (See generally on this question L.C.B. Gower, *The Principles of Modern Company Law*, 3rd ed., London, Stevens & Sons, 1969, p 189).] A principle that commends itself was contained, some years ago, in the following dictum in the reasons for judgment of a case tried in the United States: 'When the notion of legal entity is used to defeat public convenience, justify wrong, protect fraud or defend crime, the law will regard the corporation as an association of persons.' [*U.S.* v *Milwaukee Refrigerator Transit Co.*, 142 Fed. 247 at 255 (1905).]

2.1.35 *Fraud*: More than three hundred years ago, Lord Coke said: '... fraud and deceit abound in these days more than in former times.' [*Twyne's Case*, 3 Co. Rep. 806; 76 Eng. Rep. 809 at 815 (Star Chamber 1601).] The problem of fraud in bankruptcy administration is still with us. But fraud is not a matter peculiar to bankruptcy. It is, for example, the opinion of J.K. Galbraith that: 'As more goods are produced and owned, the greater are the opportunities for fraud and the more property that must be protected. If the provision of public law enforcement services does not keep pace, the counterpart of increased well-being will, we may be certain, be increased crime.' [J.K. Galbraith, *The Affluent Society*, Boston, Houghton Mifflin Co., 1958, p. 256.] Fraud is the crime that characterizes the affluent society. In recent decades, there has been an increasing number of deceptive and fraudulent marketing practices involving merchandise swindles, security frauds, frauds against the consumer and frauds against the government. Immoral and sharp business practices are often increasingly, deliberately and cynically practised.

2.1.36 The temptation to gain at the expense of others is a part of human nature. Thus, the debtor may hide some of his assets on the eve of his bankruptcy. This might take the form of a fraudulent and surreptitious transfer of assets to his wife or his relatives. It can, also, be a concealment of assets or an out and out theft.

2.1.37 Arson used to be a favourite device to wind up an unsuccessful business, permitting the debtor to retire on the proceeds of the fire insurance. Due to the efficiency of public and private investigators, the hazard, to the arsonist, that he will be detected has substantially increased. Sophisticated merchandise swindles have not, however, always attracted the same vigilance of law enforcement agencies. Until recently, criminals could engage in this type of crime without the same risk of detection, arrest and conviction. This has led to the planned bankruptcy.

2.1.38 In the United States, planned bankruptcies have recently been referred to as 'the newest and fastest growing business fraud.' The scheme has been described as follows:

In essence, the planned bankruptcy is a merchandising swindle based on the abuse of credit, either legitimately or fraudulently established. The scheme consists of (1) overpurchasing of inventory on credit, (2) sales or other disposition of the merchandise thus obtained, (3) concealment of the proceeds, (4) non-payment of creditors, and finally (5) the filing of an involuntary petition in bankruptcy, by creditors. We refer to this as a planned bankruptcy since, at the very inception of the scheme, the operators make elaborate plans for hiring attorneys and formulate various explanations to be used to describe why assets are not on hand when creditors file the involuntary bankruptcy petition ... There are indications that upwards of 200 planned bankruptcies a year are inspired, directed and controlled by organized criminal groups (The 'Outfit', 'Cosa Nostra' or 'mafia'). [N.E. Kossack and S. Davidson, *Bankruptcy: Legal Problems and Fraud Schemes* in *Credit and Financial Management*, May 1966, pp. 30–31. Mr. Kossack was the former Chief of the Fraud Section and First Assistant in the Criminal Division of the United States Department of Justice. Mr. Davidson was an attorney in the Fraud Section of the Criminal Division of the Department of Justice.]

2.1.39 There are 'planned bankruptcies' in Canada. [See, for example, the recent judgment of *La Reine* v *Tanguay*, no: 3078/69, Cour des Sessions de la Paix, P. Québec, District de Montréal, 30 janvier 1970.] The available evidence does not permit us, however, to make an estimate of the frequency with which they occur in this country. We must, nonetheless, be prepared to cope with the planned bankruptcy in Canada and, if the weapons at our disposal are not effective, new ones should be designed.

2.1.40 The planned bankruptcy and the other types of fraud so far described have been fraud on the part of the debtor. There also have been instances of fraud on the part of the trustee, creditors and others in connection with the administration of estates in bankruptcy. Property that is not adequately protected and power without adequate supervision are always an invitation to fraud. 'Fraud thrives on bad organization, poor administration, unclear responsibility and loose lines of authority.' [*Problems of Bankruptcy*, Report and Research Proposal of the Brookings Institution, December, 1964, p 43 (not published); See also G.J. Fonzi, *Bankruptcy for Fun and Profit* in *Greater Philadelphia Magazine*, May, 1964, p 29; N.E. Kossack and S. Davidson, *Bankruptcy Fraud: The Unholy Alliance Moves In* in *Credit and Financial Management*, April 1966, p 20; N.E. Kossack and S. Davidson, *Bankruptcy: Legal Problems and Fraud Schemes* in *Credit and Financial Management*, May, 1966, p 28; N.E. Kossack and S. Davidson, *Bankruptcy Fraud*, Sept. 8, 1966, Federal Bar Association Annual Convention; N.E. Kossack and S. Davidson, *Bankruptcy Fraud, Alliance for Enforcement* in *Journal of the National Association of Referees in Bankruptcy*, Jan. 1966, p 12; N.E. Kossack, '*Scam*' = *The Planned Bankruptcy Racket* in *The New York Certified Public Accountant*, June, 1965, p 417; E.T. Silverstein, *How to Prevent Credit Frauds* in *Credit and Financial Management*, Oct., 1967, p 30.]

2.1.41 *International Bankruptcies*: The elements of any bankruptcy are the debtor, his creditors and the property of the debtor. When these are all located in one country, the law of bankruptcy is complex. When the elements involve more than one country, the law is highly complex. The world of today is marked by an intense economic intercourse that is more and more engaged on an international scale. One result of this has been more bankruptcies with international complications, with all the special difficulties associated with them.

2.1.42 In all cases involving matters that, either wholly or in part, arise abroad or involving persons or property situated in a foreign country, a critical question for the Court is to determine whether it has jurisdiction. Once the decision is made that it has jurisdiction, it must then be determined whether it is the duty of that Court to apply domestic or foreign law in the circumstances. Some examples will illustrate the extent of the problem of competence regarding the legal effects of bankruptcy:

A what is the legal effect of a bankruptcy in one country upon the status and assets of a debtor in another country?

B what is the effect of an arrangement made in one country upon the creditors in another?

C what is the position of foreign and domestic creditors in the case where conflicting priorities are given to creditors of the same debtor in bankruptcies in different countries?

D what is the international effect of a discharge?

2.1.43 The problems arising out of the conflict of laws, as they relate to bankruptcy, have attracted legal scholars for centuries. Two schools of thought have developed. The one advocates 'unity' or 'universality', so as to permit a bankruptcy to embrace property outside of the country of the bankruptcy. The opposing school of thought advocates 'territoriality' or 'multiplicity', with the result that assets of a debtor in a country other than the country of the bankruptcy are not affected by the bankruptcy and may be freely disposed of by the debtor, but conversely, are subject to attachment by the creditors of the debtor in the country in which the assets are located.

2.1.44 In theory, the 'unity' or 'universality' doctrine is more just to creditors, as all of the assets of a debtor in every country are available to all of the creditors. The disadvantage of the application of the universality doctrine is that the creditors of a foreign bankrupt cannot attach the assets of the debtor in their own country and have to prove their claims in the foreign bankruptcy. On the other hand, the application of the territorial principle can give creditors, in one country, the opportunity to gain an advantage over creditors in other countries. This can result, for example, when the country with local assets has the 'race is to the swift' system for attachments, which gives the first attaching creditor a higher right than subsequent attaching creditors. The inconveniences of territoriality, however, may be considerably reduced between countries that have relatively the same bankruptcy systems with the same judicial and economic effects. Certainly, the basic aim of equal distribution of all assets among all creditors can be better achieved, when all claims are admitted in all administrations and when the dividends paid in one administration are taken into account in others.

2.1.45 The injustice and inconvenience so often found in international bankruptcies could be reduced through the greater use of bankruptcy treaties. There is no lack of international studies relating to, and precedents for, this type of treaty. France has had a series of conventions with a number of its neighbours, which include the *Franco-Swiss Convention* of June 15, 1869, the *Franco-Belgium Convention* of July 8, 1899, the *Franco-Italian Convention* of June 3, 1930, the *French-Saar Conventions* of March 3, 1950 and of May 20, 1953, and the *Franco-German* treaty on the Saar of October 27, 1956. A convention involving a number of American states, based upon universality, resulted from a conference in Havana in 1921. A treaty between the Nether-lands and Belgium concerning territorial jurisdiction in bankruptcy and the execution of judg-ments was entered into in 1925. Fifteen Latin-American countries, Bolivia, Brazil, Chile, Costa Rica, Cuba, The Dominican Republic, Ecuador, El Salvador, Guatemala, Haiti, Honduras, Nicaragua, Panama, Peru and Venezuela adhered to the *Bustamante* Code of Private Interna-tional Law, adopted by the Sixth Pan-American Conference in Havana in 1928. This Code contains conflict rules relating to bankruptcy. For example, where an insolvent has only one domicile, there can be only one bankruptcy comprising all the assets and liabilities in the contracting states. In 1933, Denmark, Finland, Iceland, Norway and Sweden concluded a convention on bankruptcy, based upon the principle of universality. The convention secured the extra-territorial effect in all these countries to a bankruptcy declared by the courts of the debtor domiciled in one of them and provided that all of the assets, wherever located, are at the disposal of the trustee. More recently, the Scandinavian countries have been meeting in an attempt to write a common Bankruptcy Act. A similar attempt, to at least reconcile the different Bankruptcy Acts of its member countries, is being made by the Common Market countries.

2.1.46 It is important, for a trading nation such as Canada, to promote trade and protect its traders. Any uncertainty concerning the nature or application of foreign laws, as they relate to international commercial transactions, may have the effect of restraining trade. One method adopted by Canada to minimize the risk of a Canadian exporter from such unavoidable risks as the insolvency of a foreign buyer was the creation, in 1944, of the *Export Credits Insurance Corporation*, [*Export Credits Insurance Act*, R.S.C., 1952, c. 105.] now the *Export Development Corporation* [*Export Development Act*, 17-18 Eliz. II, Can. s. 1968-1969, c. 39.]. As the corporation is subrogated to any losses, it can have, and indirectly the Government of Canada as well, a direct financial interest in the bankruptcies of the debtors of the insured exporters.

2.1.47 In 1905, Mr. Justice Nesbitt of the Supreme Court of Canada, when addressing the Universal Congress of Lawyers and Jurists in St. Louis said: 'I think that it is a very great pity that there should not be some legislation immediately regulating many questions of International law, at any rate, between Canada and the United States. The growing interchange of business, owing to geographical continuity, makes it very important that there should be well-defined rules applicable to both countries upon many questions which are constantly arising. Take, for instance, bankruptcies, receiverships, administrations.' [In a discussion of *To what extent should Judicial Action by Courts of a Foreign Nation be recognized?* in *Universal Congress of Lawyers and Jurists*, St. Louis, U.S.A., 1905, p 226.]

2.1.48 *World Wide Concern in Bankruptcy and Insolvency Law Reform*: Before concluding this chapter, it should be pointed out that Canada is not alone in its concern about the operation of its bankruptcy and insolvency legislation. In the last few years, France has substantially modified its bankruptcy legislation. Australia appointed a committee in 1956 to review its *Bankruptcy Act*. A report was made in 1962. A new Bankruptcy Act, as recommended by the committee, was enacted in 1966 and came into force in 1968. In 1955, a Bankruptcy Law Amendment Committee was appointed in England. Its report was made in 1957 and has not, as yet, been acted upon. In the United States, the Brookings Institution has been conducting a study of Bankruptcy Problems since 1964. For a number of years the Advisory Committee to the United States Supreme Court on Bankruptcy Rules, which was appointed by Chief Justice Warren in 1960, has been holding regular meetings and its report is not expected before a year or more. Recently, a resolution to create a commission to study the bankruptcy laws of the United States was passed by the United States Congress. [United States, *Senate Joint Resolution 88*, 1st Session, 91st Congress.] Bankruptcy studies have also been made or are still being conducted in Scotland, Eire, Japan and the Scandinavian and the Common Market countries.

2.1.49 *Conclusion*: The many changes that have occurred both in Canada and elsewhere in recent decades, have influenced our way of life, have overburdened the bankruptcy and insolvency system and rendered much of it out of date. Because of the inadequacy of our bankruptcy system and its inability to efficiently and fairly adjust relations between debtors and creditors, justice has suffered. A new bankruptcy system must take into account the new realities ...

3.0.01 In this Part, proposals for reforms are made. Before this is done, it is essential to shortly refer to what we believe must be the aims and objectives of a comprehensive bankruptcy and insolvency system for Canada.

3.0.02 *The System must Promote Equity*: In the first place, it is always important to keep in mind that bankruptcy is a system whereby the creditors are compelled to adjust and reorganize their relations with the debtor and each other in regard to the property of the debtor. [See Max Radin, *The Nature of Bankruptcy*, (1940), 89 Pen. L.R. 1 at 9.] From time to time, the bankruptcy process is extended or modified, so as to better serve economic and social ends. This cannot be done, however, without a price being paid. For every person or group who receives more or fares better, another person or group may receive less or fare not so well. Almost one hundred years ago, Chief Justice Waite of the Supreme Court of the United States said that bankruptcy is an example in which the general welfare of the community is achieved by mutual sacrifices of various groups in it. [*Canada Southern R.R.* v *Gebbard* (1883) 109 U.S. 527 at 536.] It is important, therefore, that above all else, the bankruptcy system should be fair and equitable in the demands it makes and the settlements it imposes.

3.0.03 In every province, means are provided for the execution of judgements. These vary from province to province and, to the extent that specific statutory provisions are made to adjust the rights of competing creditors of an insolvent debtor, they may well be *ultra vires*. A bankruptcy act should provide a procedure for the collective execution against the assets of an insolvent debtor, which should be uniform, as a general rule, in every province, and be equally available to all creditors, without regard to the province in which they reside or in which the assets are situated.

3.0.04 The property of the debtor, under the collective execution process provided by a bankruptcy system, must be seized, preserved and distributed among all of the creditors. In achieving this, equity must be done among and for all creditors and their debtor. Creditors must be protected from over-reaching and grasping creditors as well as from fraudulent debtors. Assets that a debtor has given away or in any other way disposed of, with the effect of giving some creditors an unjustifiable preference over the others or, in any way, defeating the creditors generally, must be pursued and recovered. Moreover, the economic impact of bankruptcy should be diffused by spreading the losses fairly over as wide a group as possible; and no priorities in the order of distribution should be allowed, unless they are justified on solid grounds.

3.0.05 *The Over-riding Public Interest*: There is an over-riding public interest in the bankruptcy system. It is expressed on the levels of social and economic concern. In the first place, it is recognized that, of all the resources the country possesses, its human resources are the most valuable. In the second place, it is recognized that the growth of the country's economic productivity and institutions depends, to a large measure, on the successful resolution of conflicts stemming from the financial difficulties of its citizens. In addition, once it has been accepted that it is in the interest of the country to establish a fair and equitable system for the adjustment of the conflicts between a debtor and his creditors and to relieve and rehabilitate the over-burdened debtor, there is a public interest that the system be not abused.

3.0.06 *The System must be Extended to all Debtors*: In our society, where credit is so freely available, the bankruptcy process should be equally available, as a last resort solution to financial disaster, to all debtors whether in business or not. By the same token, no class of debtors should be immune from bankruptcy if they fail to make an arrangement with their creditors. This is not to say, however, that all debtors should always be treated the same. For example, in the case of the failure of a bank or railway, the national interest may require that a special opportunity be given to assist or reorganize the enterprise or that a different method of liquidation be used so as to minimize the impact of the failure upon the country.

3.0.07 *The Social Dimension of Bankruptcy:* From the social point of view, the fact that a citizen is over-burdened with debts or harassed by his creditors may be the source of much evil. Through his inability to solve his financial problems and support himself and his family, much hardship and unhappiness may result to him, his family and the country at large. 'The tensions built up in harassed individuals and families frequently contribute to family breakdown, mental illness, crime and economic dependency.' [Canada, *Report on Consumer Credit* of the Special Joint Committee of the Senate and the House of Commons on Consumer Credit and Cost of Living, Ottawa, Queen's Printer, 1967, p 58, quoting from a brief presented on behalf of the *Family Bureau of Greater Winnipeg*.]

3.0.08 Bankruptcy is, today, the 'escape door' to the harassed or over-burdened debtor. In the past, it has taken many other forms. We have seen, for example, how, in ancient times, a debtor would pledge and, perhaps later, sell his wife and children to escape the barbaric punishment that was the fate of those who could not pay their debts in full. In the Middle Ages, it was a common practice for such a debtor to escape his creditors by becoming an outlaw or by fleeing the country. Whenever the right to bankruptcy as an 'escape door' is restricted, or when it is too difficult to become bankrupt, there is a great danger that debtors will resort to crime and desert their families they can no longer support and their responsibilities they can no longer face.

3.0.09 There is also a great social waste in having a large class of harassed or over-burdened debtors and of undischarged bankrupts. One of the principal objectives of the new act should be to minimize this waste and to make the most of the human resources represented by this group of debtors. Speedy and effective measures to promote their social and economic rehabilitation are imperative. A debtor should be able, and should be encouraged, to make an arrangement with his creditors, when he has the ability to pay his debts in whole or in part. When the burden of debt becomes too great, a debtor should not be prevented from entering bankruptcy. Once in bankruptcy, a debtor should be encouraged, subject to appropriate safeguards, to become, as quickly as possible, a self-supporting and productive member of his community. Measures must also be designed to protect the discharged debtor from the pressure of creditors endeavouring to persuade him to undertake to pay his discharged debts, thereby defeating one of the primary purposes of the Act.

3.0.10 *The System must Facilitate the Rehabilitation of the Debtor*: Indeed, we believe that, in respect of the individual debtor, the principal objective of the bankruptcy system should be to rehabilitate him and give him an opportunity to make a fresh economic start in life. Whether the debtor is good or bad should not affect his right in this regard. All debtors should be encouraged to become self-supporting as quickly as possible and be protected from the harassment of their creditors. There should be no bar to a debtor seeking employment, retaining what he earns and providing for the care and security of himself and his dependents. Equity would, however, demand that, where a large amount of property is retained by a bankrupt by reason of the appropriate exemption statutes, his right to be released of his debts should not be absolute. Equity would also demand that, if a debtor, within a certain period of time after his bankruptcy, acquires great wealth, he should be called upon to share it with his creditors.

3.0.11 This approach would emphasize, as we think it should, the civil, as opposed to the quasi-criminal, character of the bankruptcy process. The fact that the debtor has committed an offence for which he would have an answer under relevant statutes should not deprive him of the opportunity to make a fresh economic start in life.

3.0.12 *The Credit and Economic System must be Protected*: On the economic level, it is important to preserve public confidence in the credit system of the country. 'From the vantage point of borrowers and lenders, an important goal is continuity of credit facilities on reasonable terms for reasonably good risks.' [*Problems of Bankruptcy*, Report and Research Proposal of the Brookings Institution, Washington D.C., December, 1964, p 13 (not published).] Without the means of protecting both debtors from harassment by their creditors and the credit extended by creditors, a loss of public confidence in the system could easily develop.

3.0.13 There is also a strong public interest in the economic recovery of an enterprise that has failed or is in danger of failing. Such an enterprise, provided it is economically viable, should be given all reasonable opportunities to be reorganized.

3.0.14 *The System must Promote Commercial Morality*: It is important, too, that commercial morality be encouraged and the public be protected by preventing the dishonest or incompetent bankrupt from a too early return to business. Those who have abused the confidence formerly entrusted to them or have been dishonest or reckless, or who have otherwise disregarded or flouted accepted standards of commercial morality, should be prevented from doing business on their own for some period of time. The bankruptcy system should make it as difficult as possible for those who have failed in business to renew the methods they formerly adopted to the detriment of the community. Nothing, however, should prevent the honest and competent debtor from re-entering the business community.

3.0.15 On the failure of a corporation, new elements must be considered. The corporate technique has undoubtedly contributed a great deal to the development of the modern industrial state. Though essential in our economic system, this technique should not be permitted to be used as a means of defeating the aims and objectives of a modern bankruptcy system. For example, a man who has been inexcusably imprudent, dishonest or guilty of a serious infraction to the accepted standards of commercial morality should be subject to the same sanctions and disabilities, whether he is acting in his personal capacity or as the officer or agent of a corporation.

3.0.16 *Caveat*: In the following chapters, we discuss how these aims and objectives could be achieved. Reference will be made only to the important mechanisms and procedures that, we believe, are required in order to have a bankruptcy and insolvency system adapted to the need of Canadians. Many minor amendments and additions to the present law will be contained in the Bill that we are currently drafting.

3 A COMPARISON OF THE PRESENT BANKRUPTCY REGIME AND THE PROPOSED BILL ON BANKRUPTCY

Background Papers for the Bankruptcy and Insolvency Bill (1978): Consumer and Corporate Affairs, Canada, pp 8–28

[Note: the following material compares Bill s-11 with the present Bankruptcy Act. Bill s-11 has been superseded by Bill s-14, and the material should be read in that light; few major points of comparison are affected. Section number references have been changed where necessary to refer to Bill s-14.]

Part 1 Interpretation and Application

Present Law (ss 2–4)

Because it touches on all aspects of the law, the bankruptcy law includes within its scope a great many concepts and necessarily employs an extensive, specialized vocabulary. Although the present Bankruptcy Act contains some twenty-five definitions and a number of rules concerning related persons, because of a lack of precision in the language used, many of its substantive provisions remain unclear.

Proposed Law (ss 2–10)

Part 1 of the Bill sets out roughly twice as many defined terms as the present Act with a view to reconciling a number of related civil law and common law concepts, clarifying a number of ambiguities that exist under present law, and condensing considerably the text of the Bill. The Bill also attempts to simplify and clarify the complicated rules defining related persons that are contained in the present Act.

Although a conscious effort was made not to embody substantive rules in defined terms, for the sake of drafting brevity – and to minimize ambiguity – it was found necessary to describe expressly in Part 1 a number of concepts. An important example is the refinement of the concepts 'insolvent', and 'ceased to pay his debts generally as they become due', which have been cast to make clear that it is a debtor's state of insolvency alone that makes the bankruptcy law applicable. Thus there will be no need, as under present law, to prove in addition to insolvency an 'act of bankruptcy', an archaism in the law carried over from the time when application of the bankruptcy law connoted punishment for a specified breach of commercial morality. To underline both their complexity and their importance throughout the Bill these concepts are set out in distinct sections.

The Bill also includes a definition of the concept of 'security interest', which in effect abrogates the title or lien theories that still exist in a number of Canadian jurisdictions, and substitutes instead a functional test, similar to that of the Ontario *Personal Property Security Act*, which, to determine a creditor's rights in property of a debtor, requires a court to scrutinize the real nature of the transaction between the debtor and secured creditor irrespective of any reservation of ownership in the creditor. The generic concept of a security interest will render it impossible for creditors to escape the application of the bankruptcy law simply by characterizing their transactions with the debtor as leases or conditional sales.

Compared to Bill C-60, the Bill includes a number of new definitions required by the introduction of concepts that were not envisaged by Bill C-60. For example, the words 'consumer bankrupt' and 'consumer debtor' are new defined words, required because the Bill includes a number of simplified rules applicable only in the case of consumers, such as consumer debtor arrangements (Part III) and consumer bankruptcies (Part V, section 163). Similarly, the word 'registrar' is a new defined word; the registrar is, under the Bill, the taxation officer (instead of the administrator as under Bill C-60) in addition to being the court official responsible for many judicial or quasi-judicial matters in bankruptcy proceedings. Other definitions or concepts have been added to this Part of the Bill, such as the words 'claim' and 'receiver' and the concept of 'amounts of debts of consumer debtor'. Other definitions and concepts such as the definitions of 'arrangement by way of composition', 'arrangement by way of extension of time', 'preventive arrangement', 'proposal' and the declaration of what constitutes a 'conflict of interest' have been deleted from the earlier version of the Bill.

The Bill also clarifies that an arrangement may not be made or a petition filed in respect of agents of governments, such as municipalities or Crown corporations. Finally, the Bill includes a statement to the effect that its provisions prevail over any other law but is not deemed to abrogate the substantive provisions of other laws relating to property and civil rights that are not in conflict with the Bill.

Part II Administration

GENERAL

The specific objectives of the federal bankruptcy law are quite straightforward: to provide an effective means to collect and liquidate a debtor's assets; to ensure equitable distribution of the proceeds realized from those assets among the creditors of the debtor; and, where feasible, to rehabilitate the debtor as a useful member of the community. In short, the bankruptcy law aims to maintain a reasonable balance of interests among debtors, creditors and the public generally. But in order to achieve these objectives the bankruptcy law may affect legal institutions that exist in both the civil and common law systems and modify them to a certain extent.

The bankruptcy law is therefore inherently complicated. It sets out a large number of substantive rules concerning the respective property and contractual rights of creditors among themselves and in relation to the debtor. These rules are, however, only ancillary to the central purpose of the bankruptcy law, which is to set up a uniform, effective administrative system to deal with the affairs of insolvent debtors. It is for this reason that the administrative structure embodied in the bankruptcy law is correctly characterized as the foundation of the bankruptcy system.

The five principal elements of this administrative structure are the Superintendent of Bankruptcy, the official receiver (called the 'Administrator' in the Bill), the courts, the trustees, and the creditors.

Present Law (ss 5–23)

SUPERINTENDENT OF BANKRUPTCY

At the centre of the administrative structure is the Superintendent of Bankruptcy who is
responsible to make recommendations with respect to the licensing of trustees, to direct audits
and to evaluate the performance of trustees, to maintain surveillance over estates, to detect any
improper or unlawful acts, to investigate suspected offences against the Bankruptcy Act or any
other federal statute, and to administer the small debtor program that was begun in 1972. Since
1966 the Department of Consumer and Corporate Affairs has set up regional and local bankruptcy offices in major centres across Canada through which the Superintendent carries out
most of his estate surveillance, detection, investigation and small debtor administration functions.

OFFICIAL RECEIVER

Although an insolvent debtor may initially seek advice from a trustee or a lawyer, his first formal
contact with the administrative process is with the official receiver. Official receivers are
appointed by the Governor-in-Council for each bankruptcy division (province) and are officers
of the court. The duties of the official receiver are to accept the debtor's assignment, to appoint
the trustee in the estate and to set an estate bond to be filed by the trustee, to chair the first
meeting of creditors in bankrupt estates and to examine the debtor in respect of his affairs.

COURTS

In addition to the judicial function of resolving conflicts in adversary proceedings, the Act
imposes responsibility on the Court to distinguish between the unfortunate debtor and the
conniving one, and accordingly to exercise its power to release or discharge the debtor from his
debts and from his status of bankrupt. The Court is also required to tax the accounts of trustees
and solicitors acting for the estate and, upon application, to give directions with respect to estate
administration. Generally, the registrar of the Court conducts most of the non-contentious
business.

TRUSTEE

The Bankruptcy Act requires that the property of each bankrupt estate be vested in and
administered by a licensed trustee, a legal structure that is analogous to the common law system
for the administration of the estate of a deceased person. To qualify as a licensed trustee, a
candidate must demonstrate a thorough knowledge of bankruptcy law and its application, have
substantial business experience, and have satisfactory financial and other resources available to
administer estates under the Bankruptcy Act.

The statutory responsibility of the trustee is to administer the affairs of the bankrupt estate.
This administration includes the preparation of an inventory, gathering in and realizing assets,
liquidating assets, distributing the proceeds in accordance with the Bankruptcy Act, and
rendering a final account of the administration to the creditors and the court.

CREDITORS

Finally, the Act envisages an important role for creditors who, at the first meeting, normally nominate a board of inspectors. Like the directors of a corporation, these inspectors are required to maintain policy control over the administrative decisions of the trustee. With the exception of the larger estates, it generally is found that creditors tend to ignore the first meeting of creditors and so impose upon the trustee nominated by the official receiver the duty to administer the estate without the benefit of effective creditor direction.

Proposed Law (ss 11–62)

GENERAL

Part II introduces a number of policies that are reflected repeatedly throughout the Bill. It sets out an administrative structure that better reflects the real exercise of functions and permits greater administrative efficiency, particularly by dealing with specific issues on an exceptions basis wherever possible; e.g., by requiring the bankrupt to apply formally for discharge only where a caveat is filed. Part II also facilitates a broad delegation of authority from the Superintendent to local Administrators to ensure closer contact with the interested parties and greater sensitivity to local conditions.

One of the important changes in the present Bill compared to *Bill C-60* is the possibility of delegation to a province of the administration of consumer debtor arrangements and bankruptcies. This change will permit better use of existing provincial personnel and facilities and should furnish better service at the local level.

Part II sets out rules concerning conflicts of interest and the bonding of trustees. The conflict rules in effect constitute a conflict of interest code to govern the qualification and conduct of trustees, inspectors, solicitors and others involved in the administration of an estate. Certain persons are rendered ineligible to be appointed or to act as trustees. Generally these persons include those who were closely related to the debtor during the two years immediately preceding the bankruptcy or arrangement, e.g., partners, officers, employers and employees of the debtor; those related to an officer of the debtor where the debtor is a corporation; auditors, accountants and solicitors of the debtor; and persons acting as trustees or related to a trustee acting under a trust indenture.

Under *Bill C-60* the court's permission was required to allow a trustee having a conflict of interest to act in the administration of an estate where it was in the best interest of creditors. This is changed under the Bill to require a trustee to make full disclosure to the creditors in any event of the potential conflict of interest. In addition, a trustee may act for a secured creditor while he is the trustee of an estate only if he meets two conditions: 1) he must obtain an opinion of a solicitor who does not act for the secured creditor as to the validity of the security interest as against the estate; and 2) he must make full disclosure of his involvement to the creditors or the inspectors.

At present a trustee is required to put up three kinds of security to ensure that he faithfully performs his duties as trustee. First, upon receiving a licence, a trustee is always required to deposit with the Superintendent of Bankruptcy a fidelity bond issued by an insurance company. In addition, the trustee is required to deposit with the Superintendent government or government guaranteed bonds in an amount that is fixed by policy and that varies according to the number and size of the estates the trustee administers.

Finally, the official receiver also requires a trustee to furnish a fidelity bond in respect of each estate he administers. This bonding system has proved to be expensive. Moreover, the Superintendent has experienced difficulties when attempting to recover under the fidelity bonds where a trustee is found to be in breach of his fiduciary duty.

To overcome these difficulties an Indemnity Account is proposed, which would be financed by fees paid by trustees and moneys recovered in satisfaction of any claim paid out of the Indemnity Account. Any person who obtains a judgment against a trustee on grounds of a breach of fiduciary duty will be entitled to be indemnified out of the Account.

SUPERINTENDENT

The present functions of the Superintendent continue substantially unchanged. He will, however, have more direct and broader responsibilities in a number of areas. Instead of making licensing recommendations to the Minister, the Superintendent is empowered to decide issues concerning the licensing of trustees, subject only to judicial review of the particular administrative action under the *Federal Court Act*. Consonant with the general policy of administration on an exceptions basis, under the *Bill* trustees will be issued permanent licences instead of annual licences, subject to the payment of an annual fee and to cancellation of licence for cause.

The Superintendent's powers of detection and investigation are expanded to encompass arrangements as well as bankruptcies and may be exercised as soon as a proceeding under the Bill has been filed.

BANKRUPTCY ADMINISTRATOR (FORMER OFFICIAL RECEIVER)

The local bankruptcy official is called the 'Administrator' in the Bill; first because that name is more descriptive of his functions, and second because the phrase 'official receiver' wrongly connoted that property vested in the bankruptcy official. In fact, the property of a bankrupt's estate vests only in a trustee.

The bankruptcy Administrator continues under the Bill to be responsible to carry out what were the functions of the official receiver, particularly those administrative functions such as accepting copies of and recording petitions, examining debtors, and chairing first meetings of creditors. In addition, under the Bill, the bankruptcy Administrator has a duty, where he is of the opinion that a debtor caused his bankruptcy by rash or hazardous speculation, reckless business conduct or other abuses of the credit system, to file a caveat within six months after the date of bankruptcy and so block the discharge of the debtor.

The bankruptcy Administrator will also be empowered to prepare and administer small debtor arrangements. Also, he will be required to administer consumer bankruptcies where no private trustee is willing to act and may administer a commercial bankruptcy where no private sector trustee will undertake administration of the particular estate and there are allegations of facts that may require further investigation.

COURTS

The present Bill departs substantially from *Bill C-60* in formally reintroducing the position of registrar of the court. The main responsibilities of the registrar will be in the passing of estate accounts submitted by solicitors and accountants; he will continue, as under the present Act, to exercise important judicial or quasi-judicial functions under the authority of the court.

Consistent with the general administration policy of the Bill, a bankrupt will be automatically discharged six months after the date of bankruptcy except where a bankruptcy Administrator on his own or at the request of the trustee or a creditor files a caveat to block such discharge. The bankrupt may apply to court to have the caveat set aside or removed on the ground that he has rehabilitated himself. Thus the court considers discharges only in exceptional cases.

TRUSTEE

Although the Bankruptcy Committee Report had recommended substituting public sector trustees for private trustees, after considering comments on the Report, the Government concluded that the Bill should continue to assign responsibility for the administration of commercial bankruptcies to private sector trustees because private sector trustees are better equipped to adjust to a variable work load and to react to emergency situations. There are a number of provisions in the *Bill* that are intended to clarify the rights, duties, liabilities and powers of trustees, but in general their functions and responsibilities under the *Bill* are the same as under the present law.

Also, continuing present policy, public sector trustees, i.e., 'federal trustees' will be restricted to handling small debtor estates, consumer bankruptcies and if there are facts that may require investigation, commercial estates that no private sector trustee will undertake to administer.

CREDITORS

Because ordinary unsecured creditors actually realize, on average, only a small percentage of their claims against bankrupt estates, they are reluctant to commit further resources directly to administer those estates. As a result, the administration is left almost entirely to the trustee, subject only to the surveillance of the Superintendent. Although the *Bill* cuts down the number of claims of preferred creditors, ordinary unsecured creditors will continue to be reluctant to participate. Nevertheless by making the functions of creditors and inspectors clearer and by rendering administration more efficient, the *Bill* thus further attempts to induce the unsecured creditors to play a more active role.

Part III Arrangements for the Consumer Debtor

Present Law (ss 188–213)

The commonplace use of revolving accounts, credit cards and institutional consumer lending services made available during the past twenty years has made virtually every Canadian a user of credit and, as a corollary, has led to an enormous growth in the aggregate amount of consumer debt outstanding, that is from about $0.8 billion in 1947 to $8 billion in 1967 and to more than $29 billion in 1977. Given the aggressive efforts of lenders to promote their credit services, it is not surprising that an increasingly large number of householders become seriously overburdened by debts they cannot repay, particularly where the household is affected by some unforeseen catastrophe.

Under the present *Bankruptcy Act* an insolvent consumer or wage earner debtor may resort to bankruptcy for relief from his debts, but until mid-1972, this remedy was often illusory, since in many cases he did not have sufficient funds (approximately $500) to secure the services of a licensed private trustee to administer the estate as required by the Bankruptcy Act. In 1972 the government, by a decision of Cabinet, introduced the Small Debtor Program to assist wage earner debtors with low income and little property who are unable to obtain the services of a private trustee. Under this program, a public servant administers the estate for a nominal fee or even, in specific cases of hardship, without receiving any fee.

An insolvent consumer or wage earner debtor who wishes to avoid the social stigma of bankruptcy may choose to make a proposal to his creditors under Part III of the present Act in the same way as a commercial debtor. This remedy, again, is largely illusory because most consumers who are in financial difficulty cannot afford the services of a private trustee. Furthermore, the mandatory procedures of the present *Act*, which were designed for insolvent businesses, are too cumbersome to permit efficient administration of arrangements for consumer debtors.

A third remedy available to the insolvent consumer debtor is debt consolidation under Part X of the present Act. That Part was enacted in 1966 as a result of a decision of the Supreme Court of Canada that similar legislation enacted by Alberta in 1956 was not valid because it was primarily bankruptcy and insolvency legislation and therefore exclusively a federal matter. Part X provides for a simple and inexpensive procedure whereby specified insolvent debtors may apply to the clerk of the Court for a consolidation order. The debtor undertakes to pay fixed amounts to the Court for distribution among creditors until all his debts are paid in full. In sum, this Part legitimates only an extension of time to repay, not a composition that effects a rateable reduction of creditors' claims. Moreover, Part X is only in force in those Provinces which request it. Only six Provinces, not including Ontario and Quebec, have implemented Part X. Thus a large number of Canadiens are denied access even to this limited form of relief.

Proposed Law (ss 63–97)

ARRANGEMENTS

Although the main objective of Part III remains unchanged by providing overburdened debtors with an alternative remedy to their financial difficulties, the present *Bill* differs substantially from *Bill C-60*.

SCOPE OF PART

Only individuals, whether in business or not, whose liabilities do not exceed $20,000, or such greater amount as may be prescribed, may avail themselves of the arrangement provisions of Part III. In the computation of this amount no account is taken of debts secured by real property, where such property is the principal residence of the debtor. The maximum duration of a consumer arrangement remains 3 years, but in special circumstances the term may be extended by one year. No debtor can be compelled to choose an arrangement instead of seeking complete discharge through bankruptcy proceedings.

STAY OF PROCEEDINGS

Unlike *Bill C-60*, the filing by a debtor of a request to formulate a proposed arrangement does not bar any creditor, whether secured or unsecured, from exercising a remedy against the debtor or his property. The stay of proceedings begins only after a proposed arrangement has been formulated. If there are compelling reasons requiring a stay of proceedings prior to the formulation of the proposed arrangement, the debtor may, before filing a request, file a notice of intention stating his intention to file a request; the filing of such notice grants to the debtor a ten-day stay of proceedings to allow him to formulate a feasible arrangement free from the pressure of proceedings taken against him. In order to prevent abuses, the stay of proceedings would not apply where a notice is filed within six months of the filing of any previous notice of intention.

ADMINISTRATION

In order to streamline the administrative process and to facilitate the administration of consumer debtor arrangements, the *Bill* no longer distinguishes between extension arrangements and composition arrangements. Whether the debtor proposes to pay his debts in full or in part during an extended period of time, the systems and procedures to be followed are identical. The proposed arrangement is sent to the creditors to be affected by the arrangement and unless 50% in value of those creditors request a meeting, no meeting will be held and the arrangement, as formulated, is deemed to be approved. If a meeting of creditors is requested, the administrator will call a meeting where the creditors may accept, reject or amend (with the concurrence of the debtor and administrator) the proposed arrangement. Unless rejected or amended by a majority of the creditors entitled to vote, whether or not they are present or represented at the meeting, the proposed arrangement is deemed to be approved as formulated. The same procedure would apply where variations to the arrangement are proposed during the term of the arrangement.

This streamlined and simplified procedure should facilitate the administration of consumer debtor arrangements by the administrator. A conscious effort was also made to integrate in Part III all sections required to administer consumer debtor arrangements; under *Bill* C-60 this was done by reference to sections scattered throughout the Bill, especially in Part VI. Now Part III is essentially a stand alone part. This integration is especially important since the Bill contemplated the delegation of the administration of these arrangements to provincial administrators who might not be involved in the administration of any other parts of the Bill.

Another feature of the *Bill* that should facilitate the administration of consumer arrangements is the introduction of what is commonly referred to as a 'basket' proposed arrangement. Under this approach the debtor would offer to pay a stated amount of money out of his future income without specifying the portion of each debt that would be paid.

SECURED CREDITORS

With the exception of creditors whose claims are secured by real property, all secured creditors are bound by a consumer arrangement. However, a creditor who has a security interest in personal property, if more than one-third of the original purchase price is outstanding, may elect within 20 days after a notice has been sent to him by the bankruptcy Administrator not to participate in the arrangement. If he does elect not to participate, his rights are confined to his security interest and his claim against the debtor or his estate for any deficiency balance is barred. It must also be noted that with respect to a collateral security interest in real property, a claim may be admissible and therefore subject to the arrangement if the value of the property subject to the security interest is less than the amount of the debt. In those circumstances the secured creditor may be required to assess the value of the real property subject to his security interest and to relinquish the amount of his security interest that exceeds the value of the pertinent property.

Finally, the *Bill* provides that the administrator may request from the secured creditor the filing of a proof of security interest; in addition, the court may postpone the right of a secured creditor to realize the property subject to his security interest if such postponement does not materially adversely affect the secured creditor.

REHABILITATION OF THE DEBTOR

The *Bill*, by creating a strong incentive to enter into an arrangement instead of bankruptcy, emphasizes debtor rehabilitation through better financial planning. In any case, the *Bill* requires the Administrator to exercise such supervision and give such advice to the debtor as will assist him to rehabilitate himself financially and carry out his financial obligations. The Adminstrator may refer the debtor to guidance and counselling agencies in the community. As one of the rehabilitative measures, he may also permit the debtor, after an arrangement has been in effect for at least 6 months, to make payments directly to the creditors if the Administrator is satisfied that the debtor is able to manage his financial affairs.

CONSEQUENCES OF DEFAULT

Where a debtor fails to comply with the terms of an arrangement the Court may annul it. If he defaults in his payments in an amount equal to the total of three months payments, or if the debtor does not make his payment within ten days after a payment becomes payable where such payments are due on longer basis than a monthly basis, the arrangement is deemed to have been set aside and all the rights of creditors revive, including any right to repossess or seize in execution the assets of the debtor. There is no automatic bankruptcy, but of course a defaulting debtor may petition himself into bankruptcy. In addition, the Bill introduces a short form petition granting to any creditor or creditors having claims of $1,000 or more the right to file a petition in bankruptcy with the Administrator as an alternative to filing it with the court according to the usual procedure. After a debtor defaults under an arrangement, he is not entitled, without leave of the Court, to make another proposal for an arrangement unless all debts which were part of the previous arrangement are paid.

If an arrangement is not a satisfactory solution, any debtor has a right to go into voluntary bankruptcy. The Administrator will continue to assist those debtors who elect bankruptcy but cannot afford the services of a private trustee.

Part IV Commercial Arrangements

Present Law (ss 32–46)

Bankruptcy and insolvency laws have long recognized that a firm may get into short term financial difficulties because of a general economic crisis or a sudden change of market conditions that is clearly beyond the control of the firm. If a firm cannot survive the rigours of competition in the long run, then the bankruptcy law should make it possible to liquidate and dissolve that firm with a minimum of formality and cost, freeing its capital to be used by another enterprise. But where a firm is viable, if bankruptcy were the only solution to short term difficulties, then the bankruptcy law itself would tend to be forcing a less than optimal use of economic resources. The present federal laws therefore facilitate and even encourage proposals for commercial arrangements.

Proposals, more properly called proposals for an arrangement, may be made at present under one or more of several federal statutes. Most proposals relating to unregulated business corporations are made under Part III of the present *Bankruptcy Act*, but such corporations may also make a proposal under the *Winding-Up Act* or the *Companies Creditors' Arrangement Act*. The *Bankruptcy Act* does not apply to banks and other financial intermediaries, which can therefore make proposals only under the *Winding-up Act* or the *Companies Creditors' Arrangement Act*. Railway companies may make an arrangement only under certain vestigial provisions of the *Exchequer Court Act*.

A proposal under the present *Bankruptcy Act* may be filed by a debtor before or after he is bankrupt. When a debtor files a proposal, no creditor affected by it may institute or continue any action or proceeding to enforce a claim. However, secured creditors are not affected by the proposal, and creditors whose debts are not dischargeable, such as suppliers of necessaries, are not bound by it. Furthermore, the proposal must provide for payment in full of the claims of creditors having a priority under the Act and for the payment of the trustee's fees and disbursements. In order to bind unsecured creditors, the proposal must be accepted by a majority of them representing three-fourths in value of claims and must also be approved by the Court. In sum, under the present *Act*, a proponent of a proposal must overcome a number of formidable obstacles.

One of the great merits of a proposal is that the debtor continues to manage his business unless the proposal states otherwise or the creditors, with the consent of the debtor, impose conditions. Unlike bankruptcy, the debtor's property does not automatically vest in the trustee.

If a proposal is rejected by the creditors or by the Court, or if after it has been accepted and approved it is annulled by the Court for default or for other reasons, the debtor is deemed to be bankrupt. To ensure that debtors do not abuse the privilege of making proposals and thus stall inevitable bankruptcy, the *Bankruptcy Act* was amended in 1966 to make the automatic bankruptcy retroactive to the date of filing a proposal (except where the proposal is annulled by the Court). The aim of this retroactive provision is to enable the trustee to recover fraudulent dispositions, including preferential transfers, made by the debtor within the prescribed delay periods which are calculated retrospectively from the filing date.

Proposals under the *Companies Creditors' Arrangement Act* are generally made with respect to creditors who hold debentures issued under a trust indenture. The now obsolete *Farmers Creditors' Arrangement Act* authorized the Court to formulate a proposal for a farmer. In contrast, under the *Bankruptcy Act* no person other than the debtor can make a proposal.

The *Bankruptcy Act* requires the trustee with whom the proposal is lodged to make an appraisal and investigation of the affairs and property of the debtor, in order to enable the trustee to estimate with reasonable accuracy the financial situation of the debtor and the cause of his financial difficulties or insolvency, and to report the result of his enquiry to the meeting of creditors. The debtor must also submit a copy of the trustee's report to the Court when he seeks the required court approval of the proposal. But the present *Act* does not require the debtor to disclose details of payments made or promised to be made by him to the trustee for future services or to other parties outside of the terms of the proposal itself.

Proposed Law (ss 98–133)

The primary object of Part IV of the *Bill* is to provide a new, integrated and flexible procedure to facilitate a wide variety of arrangements. However, banks and other financial intermediaries such as trust companies and credit unions are not permitted to take advantage of this Part. This prohibition reflects the policy conclusion that if a financial intermediary is in such serious trouble that it must resort to an arrangement with creditors it should not, in the public interest, be permitted to continue in business. The *Bill* has been modified, however, to allow an insurance company to make an arrangement under Part IV, subject to the prior approval of the Superintendent of Insurance.

NOTICE OF INTENTION

The *Bill* recognizes that it is in the interest of creditors that the debtor have reasonable time to prepare a carefully considered and workable proposal for an arrangement, free from pressure or harassment. It therefore allows the debtor to file a Notice of Intention with the Administrator stating that he proposes to file a proposed arrangement with a view to preventing bankruptcy. If the debtor files this Notice, all legal proceedings against him by creditors, including secured creditors, are automatically stayed for a period of 10 days or for such longer period as the court may determine. However, on the filing of a Notice, an interim receiver is automatically appointed in order to protect the interests of creditors.

To obtain further immunity from legal proceedings, the debtor must file a proposed arrangement within the stipulated time. If he fails to do so within ten days after the Notice is filed or within such longer period of time as the court may determine, the Notice is deemed withdrawn and the proceedings on any petition filed for a bankruptcy order may continue or a bankruptcy order is automatically made against the debtor, unless the court otherwise orders.

PERSONS ENTITLED TO MAKE A PROPOSED ARRANGEMENT

In addition to the debtor himself, where a bankruptcy order has been made against a debtor or where a corporation is being dissolved, the *Bill* permits the bankruptcy trustee or the liquidator of the corporation, as the case may be, to make a proposed arrangement in respect of the debtor. Furthermore, any creditor, a trustee appointed under a trust indenture, or a receiver of a corporation is entitled to make a proposed arrangement for a debtor who is bankrupt.

REQUIRED PROVISIONS OF A PROPOSED ARRANGEMENT

The Bill makes it mandatory for the debtor to disclose all payments made or promised to be made by him to the trustee and others in connection with the proposed arrangement, including payments to be made outside of the proposed arrangement. The debtor must also clearly set out the amount and terms of payment, including the grant of any security interest to secure payment that he proposes to make. If the proposed arrangement is to be guaranteed, it must also set out the terms of the guarantee.

POSSIBLE ADDITIONAL PROVISIONS OF A PROPOSED ARRANGEMENT

Any provision that is reasonable in the circumstances may be included in a proposed arrangement. The present *Bill* specifically provides that a proposed arrangement may alter the order of payment of claims and that the arrangement provisions supersede the order of priority determined under section 261 of the *Bill*; in addition, a debtor is granted the right to terminate partly performed contracts, subject to the control of the court to prevent abuses. The Bill also impliedly gives the proponent of an arrangement broad powers to define classes. And he may also apply to a court to determine if a creditor affected by the arrangement has been properly

placed in a class of creditors. This application may be made even before the first meeting of
creditors, enabling the proponent to minimize technical problems at the meeting of creditors,
particularly by constraining the need for exercise of the chairman's discretion to designate
classes, which is a decision that may be reviewed by a court and therefore may engender
substantial delays.

DUTIES OF THE TRUSTEE

The *Bill* places additional duties on a trustee who agrees to carry out a proposed arrangement.
His investigation into the debtor's affairs must be adequate to enable him to arrive at an opinion
and to report to the creditors that the debtor has dealt fairly with them and that the debtor has not
entered into transactions or disposed of property in fraud of his creditors. In sum, the trustee
must exercise the same vigilance in respect of preferential and reviewable transactions as he
would if a bankruptcy order had been made against the debtor and bring any such facts to the
notice of the creditors.

FORMULATION OF ARRANGEMENTS BY COURT

The *Bill* also permits Court formulated arrangement, adopting a feature of the *Farmers Creditors' Arrangement Act*. Recognizing that a firm may be the life blood of a community, the *Bill*
empowers the Court to formulate a proposed arrangement in respect of a debtor whose debts
exceed one million dollars, if the Court is of the opinion that in the public interest all efforts
should be made to continue the firm in business rather than dissolve it through the bankruptcy
process. The Court, may, however, decline to formulate an arrangement where the proposed
arrangement would not be just and equitable to the creditors.

Part v Bankruptcy

Present Law (ss 24–31; 49–79; 139–52)

The law applicable to insolvent debtors is now set out in several federal statutes. The *Bankruptcy Act* applies to all individual and corporate debtors other than financial intermediaries and
railway companies, which are subject to specific insolvency provisions set out in the respective
regulatory acts that apply to them. The *Winding-Up Act* applies mainly to the liquidation and
dissolution of solvent business corporations but can also apply to any insolvent corporation,
whether incorporated federally or provincially. An insolvent corporation, however, can be
compelled to be wound up under the *Bankruptcy Act*. These repetitive and frequently overlapping insolvency laws engender much uncertainty and confusion.

COMMENCEMENT OF BANKRUPTCY PROCEEDINGS

The present *Bankruptcy Act* does not give any practical relief to a small debtor whose total
liabilities are relatively small. Nor does it permit anyone who is not a creditor to initiate any
action when he becomes aware that a debtor is in financial difficulties. This exclusive reliance on
creditors often defeats the purposes of bankruptcy law, especially where, on the one hand,
creditors are unaware that the debtor is attempting to save himself from utter ruin or, on the

other hand, to preserve for himself, at their expense, as many of the unencumbered assets as possible. As a result, it does not adequately protect the public interest.

STAY OF PROCEEDINGS

To prevent a scramble among creditors, the *Bankruptcy Act*, upon the bankruptcy of a debtor, automatically stays any legal proceedings against a bankrupt except where a Court expressly permits such proceedings to be initiated or continued. But this automatic stay generally does not affect secured creditors whose rights may be postponed only by an order of the Court and then only for a period not exceeding six months. A secured creditor may often realize his security interest by prompt repossession and disposal of the debtor's property even before being restrained by Court order, thus leaving little or nothing for other creditors. In contrast, the *Winding-Up Act* stays all legal proceedings by creditors to enable the liquidator to obtain a complete overview of the debtor's affairs.

DISCHARGE OF THE BANKRUPT

The filing of an assignment by and the making of a receiving order against an individual automatically operates as an application for his discharge from his status as a bankrupt, but in order that debts and liabilities may be released, the Court must make a formal order of discharge. Upon hearing an application for discharge, a Court has power to suspend a discharge or to impose conditions on the bankrupt. The practice of granting discharges varies widely across the country. Debtors often fail to obtain an unqualified discharge, and as a result they continue to have the status of bankrupt and to be subject to a bankrupt's civil disabilities, particularly the bar against carrying on business on credit. Corporate bankrupts must apply formally for discharge which is granted only if creditors' claims are paid in full, a case that rarely occurs.

The status of bankrupt to which a corporation is subject, however, does not affect the human agents = the directors and officers = who control it; they are free to embark on new ventures almost unblemished by the status of the corporation they managed. The only exception is the report, introduced by the 1966 amendments, that is prepared by the trustee and filed with the Superintendent of Bankruptcy and with the official receiver, which may impute blame for the bankruptcy to named directors and officers.

Although the report is available to the public, it is seldom effective to restrain the activities of persons who were responsible for the bankruptcy of a corporation, and it is grossly inadequate to cope with the problem of 'planned bankruptcies'.

AVOIDANCE AND REVIEW OF TRANSACTIONS

Both the *Bankruptcy Act* and the *Winding-Up Act* contain provisions designed to enable the Court to set aside gifts, settlements and fraudulent preferences occurring within certain time periods before a bankruptcy or corporate dissolution.

Proposed Law (ss 134–234)

The *Bill* sets out a comprehensive bankruptcy and insolvency system, integrating in one statute the usual insolvency provisions, which will now apply not only to ordinary business firms but also to insolvent financial intermediaries, stockbrokers, and railway companies, thus obviating the repetitive and overlapping provisions that now exist in the federal laws. In addition, the *Bill* introduces a number of important innovations relating to bankruptcies that are designed to render the proposed law clearer, fairer, and easier to administer.

COMMENCEMENT OF BANKRUPTCY PROCEEDINGS

Any person or corporation, without limitation as to the nature of his occupation or the amount of debt, may apply for a bankruptcy order in respect of himself. One or more unsecured creditors having aggregate claims in excess of $1,000 may also petition a debtor other than a farmer or fisherman into bankruptcy. A corporation found to be insolvent when it is being wound up under any other legislation, for example, a corporation law, must be brought within the framework of the bankruptcy statute. Specific rules apply to partnerships, stockbrokers and insurance companies.

Also, where a department or agency of the federal or a provincial government exercises regulatory or supervisory authority over the financial affairs of a debtor, it may initiate bankruptcy proceedings in respect of the debtor through the appropriate Attorney General where necessary for the protection of the public interest.

STAY OF PROCEEDINGS

The present Bill modifies substantially the provisions regarding stay of proceedings. With respect to claims of unsecured creditors, the stay is absolutely binding on the creditor as of the date of filing of a petition for a bankruptcy order, unless the creditor is expressly excepted by Court order. With respect to a secured creditor's claim, many innovations are set out in the Bill to enable the trustee better to evaluate the overall condition of the debtor's affairs and to plan his administration accordingly without unduly interfering with the rights of a secured creditor. First, where a petition is filed, the stay does not apply against a secured creditor unless the court expressly states otherwise. Second, where a bankruptcy order is made, a secured creditor's rights to deal with property of the debtor are, subject to certain exceptions, stayed until ten days after the date of the first meeting of creditors or after the filing of a proof of security interest, whichever is the later. This limited stay should give the trustee time to elect whether he should redeem or require the property to be realized or surrender it to the creditor. Specific rules govern the conduct of the trustee, depending upon the election he makes. Where a trustee needs more time to determine the course of action he should take in the best interest of the estate, he may apply to a court for a further stay where this can be done without materially adversely affecting the secured creditor.

Whenever a stay applies with respect to a secured creditor, the Bill provides that he may nevertheless exercise a number of remedies of a protective nature, such as disposing of property that is perishable or likely to depreciate rapidly in value. On the other hand, the Bill imposes certain duties on the secured creditor where he realizes property subject to a security interest; the secured creditor must act honestly and in good faith, realize property in a timely and commercially reasonable manner, and make full disclosure to the trustee of any action taken in respect of the property.

Government creditors, whether the Crown in right of Canada or a province or a subordinate agency, are in nearly all circumstances treated like all other creditors. If a government creditor makes a claim as a secured creditor it must file a proof of security interest showing that it has perfected its security interest in the same manner – by registration or otherwise – as any other secured creditor is required to perfect his security interest.

EXEMPT PROPERTY

Continuing the policy of the present Act, property held in trust, property that is exempt from seizure under a provincial law, disablement benefits, and amounts payable under a retirement savings plan registered under the *Income Tax Act* do not vest in the trustee. Also, as a general rule, wages and property acquired by a bankrupt before he is discharged do not automatically vest in the trustee; but where the bankrupt earns an income in excess of $500 per month or acquires by gift or otherwise property in excess of his reasonable requirements the trustee may apply to the Court for an order vesting the excess in him for distribution among the creditors.

CONSUMER BANKRUPTCIES

Another feature of the Bill is to provide simplified procedures in the case of consumer bankruptcies. For the purpose of the Bill, a consumer is defined to include any individual whose debts do not exceed twenty thousand dollars, excluding debts secured by the principal residence of the debtor. Some of the simplified procedures include the following: income tax refunds resulting from the over-deduction of taxes at source do not vest in the trustee; no meeting of creditors will be held unless the majority of creditors request one, and a proof of claim need not be filed where no dividend is expected to be paid. These simplified procedures should accelerate the proceedings and cut down on costs without depriving the creditors of their right to control the administration of these estates.

DISCHARGE OF THE BANKRUPT

When a bankruptcy order is made in respect of a debtor, the debtor is released from all his debts except a fine, an obligation in respect of a bail bond or recognizance, an obligation to pay family maintenance, or any debt arising out of fraud where the debtor has been convicted of such fraud under the *Criminal Code*. Also, he is not released from a debt he failed to disclose to the trustee, but his continuing liability is limited to the amount the creditor would have received had the trustee known about the claim.

Consonant with the administration by exception policy of the Bill, a debtor is not required to apply to a Court for a discharge. A corporate bankrupt can be discharged only if it pays all its debts in full. An individual bankrupt is automatically discharged six months after the date of the bankruptcy order affecting him unless an Administrator files, within that six-month period, a caveat stating he has reason to believe that the bankrupt substantially aggravated his insolvency by reckless business conduct, gross incompetence, carelessness or similar means, or that he has committed specified bankruptcy offences. The trustee of the estate as well as any creditor of the bankrupt may apply to the Court for an order directing the Administrator to file a caveat. The Court may also set aside a caveat that has been filed. If not set aside the caveat has effect for 5 years or such shorter period of time as may be ordered by the Court, thus hindering the bankrupt from obtaining credit to carry on business and continuing his liability to the estate for wages or after-acquired property in excess of his reasonable needs.

The procedure described above also applies to an 'agent' or 'former agent' of a bankrupt. A caveat may be filed within one year of the bankruptcy of a corporation against an agent or former agent by the Administrator or on an application to a court by the trustee of the estate or a creditor of the bankrupt. With a view to promoting the integrity of the credit system, the Bill empowers the Court to revive all debts from which a bankrupt has been released within 5 years of his current bankruptcy, if the Court is of the opinion that the bankrupt has abused the bankruptcy process to the detriment of his creditors.

DIRECTORS AND OFFICERS OF CORPORATIONS – LIABILITY AND DISCHARGE

The Bill introduces several new provisions concerning the status and personal liability of directors and officers of corporations. First, the Bill prohibits a bankrupt from continuing to act or from being elected or appointed as a director of a corporation. Second, the Bill imposes personal liability on directors and officers and former directors and officers (within 2 years before the bankruptcy) for debts of the corporation that remain outstanding as claims against the estate, where the director or officer has in his own interest – and hence in breach of his fiduciary duty to the corporation – continued to carry on a business that was not in the interest of the corporation, continued to carry on business by resorting to sales below cost or similar improper means, conducted business with a view to delaying or defrauding creditors, or committed specified bankruptcy offences. Third, a director or officer is also personally liable for outstanding corporate debts if he fails to keep accounts that enable the trustee to distinguish between the corporation's property and the property of the director or officer. Finally, where bankruptcy order is made in respect of a corporation, the directors and former directors of the corporation are jointly and severally liable to employees of the corporation for unpaid wages not exceeding $2,500 for each employee.

AVOIDANCE AND REVIEW OF TRANSACTIONS

The Bill sets out a comprehensive code in respect of fraudulent transfers and preferential payments in respect of both arm's length and non-arm's length transactions. The purpose of the code is to include, as far as possible, those transactions that have the effect of defeating the legitimate expectations of honest creditors. It attempts to achieve this purpose by extending the provisions in the present Bankruptcy Act and by bringing the law more into conformity with prevailing business practices.

The proposed Bill includes a specific section designed to render inoperative provincial laws on fraudulent preferences and conveyances in the case of insolvency because of the decision of the Supreme Court of Canada in the case of *Robinson* v *Countrywide Factors Ltd.* [1977] 23 C.B.R. (n.s.) 97. In that case the Supreme Court, by a majority decision, decided that the Saskatchewan *Fraudulent Preferences Act* is not ultra vires and that sections 3 and 4 of that *Act* are not specifically in conflict with the fraudulent preference provisions of the *Bankruptcy Act*. As implied by the Chief Justice, who wrote the minority judgment, there is in fact an overall conflict between the two systems: the bias of the *Act* is to encourage creditors to keep a debtor alive, for example, by supplying inventory without great risk until bankruptcy is imminent; the bias of some provincial laws is to favour the mass of the creditors at the expense of the creditor who took the risk of continuing to supply inventory while the debtor was in financial trouble. Because there is a clear and sharp conflict between policy objectives, the *Bill* expressly provides for federal occupation of the preferences field where a bankruptcy order is made.

With respect to gifts, a court may set aside any transfer of a gratuitous nature or with a merely nominal consideration where the interest of the donor does not pass irrevocably at least six months before the filing of a bankruptcy petition; this time period is extended to one year where the gift is made between related persons. In addition, the court may set aside a gift where, at the time the interest of the donor passes irrevocably, the donor is insolvent or unable to pay his debts without the aid of the property comprised in the gift. These rules are based on the basic principle that before being generous with his property a debtor must provide for the payment of his debts.

With respect to transfers that have the effect of giving a preference to a creditor, the Bill distinguishes between a transfer made by persons who deal with each other in an accepted business manner and a transfer made by persons who do not so deal with each other. In the first case, which is known as a preference at arm's length, the court may set aside the transfer only if the trustee can prove that it was made less than six months before the filing of the petition and with the intent of the insolvent debtor to give a preference. In the case of a non-arm's length preference, the burden of proof that the transfer was not a preference is normally on the creditor. The Bill deals specifically with preferences granted by a debtor to a person who had previously guaranteed his debts.

The proposed Bill reintroduces the common law intent to prefer test. However, it clarifies that proof of the intent of a debtor to give a preference is normally sufficient and declares that evidence that a transfer was made under pressure is not receivable to substantiate such transfer.

In addition to the above provisions, the Bill deals specifically with the problems created when a debtor makes a lump sum payment of premium on an insurance policy, assigns accounts receivable due to him, or substitutes other property previously released or returned by a creditor. It also sets out the powers of the Court where a transfer is set aside and deals specifically with the recovering of property or its value where such property has been reconveyed to another person.

As a general defence, the Bill provides that a Court may not set aside a transfer if the creditor proves that at any time after the transfer was made the debtor was solvent. In any case, proceedings to avoid transfers caught by the code must be brought by the trustee within 3 years of the date of bankruptcy.

LEASES OF REAL PROPERTY

To deal with a frequent and particularly intractable problem the Bill sets out a number of provisions to specify the respective rights, duties and powers of a lessor, lessee and the trustee where a lessee becomes bankrupt. In particular, the Bill makes clear the trustee's right to occupy the leased property and to retain or disclaim the lease and also the lessor's right to receive rent. In addition, the Bill contains provisions to clarify the rights of a sub-lessee and of a mortgagee of the leasehold.

Part VI Arrangements and Bankruptcy

Present Law (ss 80–128)

Part v of the present *Bankruptcy Act* sets out the substantive rules that govern the most important aspects of estate administration, including rules relating to filing proofs of claim, staying of creditor proceedings, priorities among creditors and the resulting scheme of distribution, creditors and inspectors meetings, and the powers of boards of inspectors. These rules also apply, in most circumstances, to a proposal made by a debtor under Part III.

CLAIMS AGAINST AN ESTATE

Any creditor, whether secured or unsecured, may file a claim with the trustee if his claim arose before the date of bankruptcy. Where a claim is merely contingent or is for an unliquidated amount, the trustee has to apply to the Court for directions. The Court may value the claim or, where damages have to be assessed, direct that the issue be tried.

The *Act* empowers the trustee to reject or reduce any claim that a creditor cannot prove, but he cannot reject or reduce it on the ground that the underlying transaction was harsh or unconscionable or that the cost of borrowing was excessive. In Provinces having legislation against unconscionable transactions, the trustee must apply to a Court to rule on the validity of the claim under the applicable law.

RELEASE OF DEBTS

When a bankrupt obtains his discharge from the Court, he is released from all debts and liabilities except those within a small category, such as a fine or penalty, debts incurred fraudulently, family maintenance, and debts for necessaries. Despite this release from his debts, it is possible for a creditor to take advantage of the discharged debtor's financial plight and induce him to pay the released debt. Whether a subsequent promise to pay a released debt is valid is not clear under existing law, but if a creditor gives further credit to the debtor on condition that the debtor also repays the released debt, it appears that the obligation in effect revives, unless it can be repudiated as an unlawful penalty or unconscionable under provincial law.

SCHEME OF DISTRIBUTION

Although not immediately clear from the text of the present Act, the law in fact divides creditors into four classes: secured, preferred, ordinary unsecured, and deferred creditors. Except as mentioned above, the secured creditor remains essentially outside of the statutory scheme of distribution, free to exercise his rights against the debtor's property unless the trustee intervenes. And even then the secured creditor has absolute priority to the extent of his security interest. Preferred creditors are creditors to whom parliament has given special priority to ensure the administration of the estate or to achieve greater equity among claimants. These preferred claims include funeral expenses, costs of administration, the Superintendent's levy, arrears of wages, arrears of municipal taxes, three months' rent arrears, U.I.C. and Workmen's Compensation withholdings and so on. After these preferred claims are paid in full, the ordinary unsecured creditors share any balance rateably. If, after unsecured creditors are paid, a further balance remains it is paid rateably to the deferred creditors. Any remaining surplus is paid to the debtor. All creditors in a specific category are paid rateably. But the order of priority is strict: no payment is made to a lower priority creditor until all higher priority creditors are paid in full.

MEETINGS OF CREDITORS

The present Act requires the trustee to call the first meeting of creditors of an estate within 5 days of his appointment and hold it within 15 days after the notices have been mailed. It sets out the procedure at meetings, including quorum, voting and proxies. The purpose of the meeting is to inform the creditors of the financial affairs of the bankrupt, to appoint inspectors, to affirm the trustee's appointment or to substitute another trustee, and to obtain directions from the creditors. Because under the present *Act* the secured and preferred creditors claims rarely leave any residue to satisfy the claims of ordinary unsecured creditors, a recurring problem in recent years has been the difficulty of obtaining a quorum at the first meeting of creditors in almost all but large estates. This is especially true of summary administration cases (individual bankrupt having less than $500.00 assets after deducting secured creditors claims). As a result, the administration of an estate during the first, and often critical, weeks is delayed and the checks on the powers of the trustee that the meeting is designed to provide are generally ineffective.

Proposed Law (ss 235–317)

Part VI of the Bill introduces a number of significant changes to the present law. It applies to commercial arrangements under Part IV and to all bankruptcies including consumer bankruptcies unless expressly stated otherwise.

CLAIMS AGAINST THE ESTATE

The Bill empowers the trustee summarily to set aside or reduce any claim, priority or security interest on property. His decision may be appealed to the Court. The Bill also requires the trustee to value contingent and unliquidated claims filed with him. Again, his valuation may be appealed to the Court.

RELEASE OF DEBTS

A bankruptcy order has the effect of releasing the debtor from all debts and liabilities except (a) a fine or penalty imposed by a Court, (b) a debt arising out of a recognizance or bail bond, (c) a liability to maintain a spouse or child for a period subsequent to an arrangement or bankruptcy and (d) a debt arising out of fraud where the debtor has been convicted of such fraud under the *Criminal Code*. A debt thus released cannot be revived by agreement even if the creditor furnishes new consideration.

SCHEME OF DISTRIBUTION

The Bill sets out an order of priority that reduces considerably the classes of preferred creditors (certain administrative costs, wage arrears, lessor's claim for three months arrears of rent, and Crown claims for moneys deemed held in trust up to a maximum of the cash on hand or on deposit), clarifies the position of ordinary unsecured creditors, and particularizes the rights of deferred creditors. Although long, the order of priorities provisions of the Bill, which are necessarily the nucleus of a bankruptcy law, attempt to clear up what is an unnecessarily arcane and complicated area of the law.

MEETINGS OF CREDITORS

Although it varies time periods slightly, the Bill essentially continues the basic policies of the present law: the trustee is required to call the first meeting of creditors, which must be held within 30 days of the date of the bankruptcy order; and the trustee may call any subsequent meeting of creditors and is required to do so when directed by the Court, the board of inspectors, or a specified number of creditors.

One of the policies of the Bill is to encourage creditors to participate more actively in estate administration, therefore the Bill sets out a fairly detailed code of procedures to govern meetings of creditors, the election of inspectors, and the rights and duties of inspectors. To make possible improved representation for minority creditors the Bill permits a creditor to cumulate his votes and cast all of them for one inspector.

Because creditors have little interest in estates with few assets, they frequently neglect to attend meetings, even to elect a board of inspectors. The Bill therefore empowers the Superintendent to appoint inspectors where the creditors fail to do so and to appoint an inspector where the Crown is a creditor.

INTERNATIONAL INSOLVENCIES

The Bill sets out flexible international insolvency provisions that will give a court broad discretion to permit coordination of insolvency proceedings in Canada with concurrent bankruptcy proceedings in another jurisdiction.

NOTE Discussion of parts VII and VIII, dealing with bankruptcy of securities firms and insurance companies, has been omitted.

Part IX Receiverships

Present Law (ss 28–30)

The appointment of a sequestrator or receiver is an ancient legal institution designed to empower a creditor, acting through the receiver as an independent third party, to take possession of the debtor's property in which the creditor has a security interest with a view to preserving the property, collecting rents, or even liquidating the property to realize his claim. In all jurisdictions in Canada other than Quebec a receiver may be appointed either by the court, in which case he is an officer of the court, or by the creditor in accordance with the express terms of a mortgage or trust indenture, in which case he is usually characterized as an agent of the debtor and not of the creditor. In Quebec the same ends may be achieved by the judicial appointment of a sequestrator to manage property pending resolution of a dispute or the extra-judicial appointment of an agent for a creditor in possession pursuant to the terms of a trust indenture. For convenience the *Bill* subsumes both a receiver and an agent of a creditor in the definition 'receiver'.

A receiver may be appointed by a court or extra-judicially by a creditor because the debtor is in default in respect of one of a great many possible conditions stipulated in the agreement creating the security interest; for example, failure to insure, failure to pay property taxes, improper sale of inventory covered by a floating charge, improper assignment of accounts receivable, improper conversion of the proceeds arising from the sale of secured assets, and so on. More frequently, however, a receiver is appointed because the debtor is insolvent or becomes bankrupt.

Under the present *Bankruptcy Act*, because the bankruptcy administration is generally subject to the prior rights of secured creditors, a receiver may be appointed before or after the date of bankruptcy to take possession of all the assets of the estate, leaving few if any assets to be administered by a trustee in bankruptcy. This is particularly true where the creditor has a very comprehensive security interest under a trust indenture. Such a security interest can include a specific charge on identifiable assets, and also a floating charge on present and future-acquired revolving assets, such as inventories and accounts receivable, which floating charge crystallizes as a fixed charge at the moment of bankruptcy or even before bankruptcy upon the appointment of a receiver.

That is not to say, however, that a trustee in bankruptcy should always be involved in the administration of assets of a debtor subject to a secured creditor's security interest, for frequently the assets can be realized more effectively by a receiver. Under present law, however, there is no mechanism to permit either the unsecured creditors or the Superintendent of Bankruptcy to maintain any surveillance over the receiver's conduct to ensure that the receiver acts fairly, keeping in mind the residual claims of all subordinate creditors.

Proposed Law (ss 354–59)

Recognizing that the appointment of a receiver is an effective remedy to protect legitimate creditor interests, the *Bill* does not attempt to displace receivers in all cases where a bankruptcy occurs. But a court may, upon the application of an interested person, impose additional duties upon a receiver, terminate the appointment of a receiver and appoint another person in his place or make some ancillary order, where it appears that there might be a surplus left after the secured creditor realizes his security, unless the receiver proves to the satisfaction of the court that a court order would materially adversely affect the creditor or that any surplus is improbable.

Thus instead of setting out rules to govern the conduct of a receiver in case of insolvency, the *Bill* empowers a court, where it decides to intervene, to give directions to the receiver or his successor with respect to all dealings with the debtor's property. And in any case the receiver is required, upon demand, to furnish specified information about the receivership to a bankruptcy administration or a trustee in bankruptcy. In sum, these procedures ensure, on an exceptions basis, that the interested parties will have the right to know by what authority a receiver acts and what he is doing and also to apply to have a court intervene where it appears there might be a surplus available for distribution among the subordinate secured creditors, the persons having claims against the debtor's estate, and the debtor, particularly where there are grounds for believing a receiver is not acting honestly or in good faith or is not dealing with the property of the debtor under his control in a commercially reasonable manner.

The *Bill* largely continues the substance of Part IX of the predecessor bill (C-60). The one major exception is the addition of express, statutory standards relating to a receiver's duty to act in good faith and duty of care. Although probably only declaratory of present law, the good faith standard serves as a constant reminder to a receiver that he is, like a corporate director or officer, a fiduciary and therefore must not only act honestly but must also avoid any material conflict of interest or duty that might prejudice the debtor. The standard of care, which requires that a receiver deal with a debtor's property in a commercially reasonable manner, is probably also largely declaratory of existing law, but it makes clear that a receiver, when realizing property of a debtor, has a statutory duty to use reasonable care or, in other words a duty not to sacrifice negligently the interests of the debtor to the interests of the creditor for whom the receiver acts. Like the corporation law provisions relating to the fiduciary duty and duty of care of directors and officers, these duty provisions do not attempt to establish any static rules or even specific standards of conduct, reflecting the reality that both the fiduciary duty and duty of care concepts are relativistic by nature and therefore depend largely on the circumstances or factors of each case. Nevertheless, this statutory provision should dispel any doubts about a receiver's duty in relation to an insolvent debtor, irrespective of whether the receiver is appointed by a court or under a contract or whether he is characterized as an agent of the debtor or of the secured creditor.

Part x Offences

Present Law (ss 169–79)

The principal purposes of the penal provisions set out in the present Bankruptcy Act are to promote commercial honesty and to ensure that the estate of a bankrupt is lawfully administered. These offences complement the offences set out in the *Criminal Code* and can be invoked as a basis for prosecution only after a bankruptcy actually occurs. Some provisions, however, reach back to cover offences – e.g., fraudulent transfer or receiving of property – that occurred before the date of bankruptcy.

In general, these penal provisions promote commercial morality by making it an offence for a debtor alone or acting in concert with one or more of his creditors to conceal or misappropriate property that should have fallen into the debtor's estate. And these penal provisions ensure honest administration by making it an offence for any unqualified person to act as trustee, for a creditor to make a false claim, for an inspector to accept an unlawful fee, or for a trustee to commit a breach of specified statutory duties.

The various offences set out in the present *Act*, depending upon their relative seriousness, are punishable on indictment or on summary conviction. Prosecution of an indictable offence must be commenced within 5 years and prosecution of a summary conviction offence must be commenced within 3 years of the commission of the offence. In most cases the applicable penalty is mandatory imprisonment.

The 1966 amendments to the present Act increased considerably the Superintendent's powers to undertake or to direct the detection and investigation of suspected bankruptcy offences, enabling him to initiate investigations instead of simply urging the appropriate provincial Attorney General to act. Also in 1966 the Superintendent established detection and investigation divisions in regional offices across Canada, staffed by auditors and trained investigators who are better able to detect and investigate local cases. Contemporaneously, the R.C.M.P. established special bankruptcy squads in major centres to assist the Superintendent in his investigations.

In sum, therefore, a person suspected of a bankruptcy offence may be investigated and charged under the *Bankruptcy Act*, and, if the misconduct is also a general crime, may also be investigated and charged under the *Criminal Code*.

Proposed Law (ss 360–80)

The proposed law essentially continues the substantive offences and the investigative procedures of the present *Act*. The Bill does, however, add several modifications: its scope is extended to include arrangements as well as bankruptcies; it authorizes an investigation to begin at once upon the commencement of insolvency proceedings; it removes the time limit on prosecuting indictable offences and reduces the time limit on summary conviction offences to 2 years; it extends the bribery rules to include all persons involved in a bankruptcy administration

– a bankruptcy administrator, trustee, inspector, solicitor or auctioneer; and it adds a new offence concerning the failure of a director of a corporation who becomes bankrupt to resign as director. The Bill also introduces new sentencing provisions, giving the Court greater discretion to impose a fine instead of imprisonment or to impose fine and imprisonment, rather than impose mandatory imprisonment, which is now the general rule.

Part XI Courts and Evidence

Present Law (ss 153–58)

The present *Bankruptcy Act*, in contrast to the pre 1949 statute, does not create a separate bankruptcy court. Instead, in line with the general policy of Parliament not to establish a duality of Courts, it vests original jurisdiction with respect to bankruptcy matters in the Superior Court of each province. Generally, however, the Chief Justice of the province specifically assigns one or more judges to exercise judicial powers conferred by the *Act* and appoints or designates the registrar, clerks and other officers to transact the business of the court. Proceedings before the court are instituted and conducted in accordance with the *General Rules* enacted pursuant to the *Act*, or, in cases where the *Act* or the *Rules* make no provision, in accordance with the ordinary rules of procedure of the Court that apply to civil matters. In addition, in respect of bankruptcy matters, the *Act* requires the court to have a seal, makes each court auxiliary to each other court, and makes an order of one court enforceable by another court anywhere in Canada.

Proposed Law (ss 381–409)

Part XI of the Bill proposes to continue the basic structure and authority of the court; but in addition it provides for the transfer to the court of any proceedings taken in any court if they affect the rights and interests of a bankrupt or his estate with a view to eliminating jurisdictional conflicts.

Under the Bill, estate accounts would continue to be passed by the registrar, subject to appeal to the court. A court still hears applications for discharge from bankruptcy, but in contrast to the present *Act*, instead of discharge of a bankrupt by court order in all cases, the bankrupt is automatically discharged 6 months after the date of the bankruptcy order unless a caveat is filed within that period to block the discharge, shifting the onus to the debtor to apply to the court to have the caveat removed. Thus the court hears discharge applications only in exceptional cases.

Two other important innovations are included in this Part of the Bill. First, wherever the words 'upon application' are used throughout the Bill, these words mean, under subsection 385(1), that any interested person has the right to apply to a court, unless the Bill otherwise states expressly who may apply. Second, a court is granted the power to shorten or extend the period of time during which a proceeding must be taken or an act or thing done under Bill, either before or after the expiration of the prescribed time.

Part XI of the Bill also deals with rules of evidence in bankruptcy proceedings. It includes provisions clarifying in what circumstances and under what conditions a document made in the course of a proceeding or the evidence of any person examined pursuant to the Act is admissible. The bill also simplifies the rules that apply where property of a debtor is seized and held as evidence of an offence under the *Bankruptcy Act* or the *Criminal Code* by providing that a sample or proper description of the seized property is receivable as evidence in the prosecution of the offence without the necessity of retaining under seizure or producing at the trial the seized property in its entirety, as it presently the case.

Part XII General and Transitional

Present Law

The four statutes proposed to be repealed or in effect abrogated by the Bill – the *Bankruptcy Act*, the *Winding-up Act*, the *Companies' Creditors Arrangement Act*, and the *Farmers' Creditors Arrangement Act* – contain a number of miscellaneous provisions of general application and also relatively broad rule making powers to prescribe regulations governing administration, court practice and procedure, and tariffs of fees.

Proposed Law (ss 410–20)

The Bill, in Part XII, attempts to consolidate these general rules in one Part. These general rules are designed to resolve on a Canada-wide basis specific problems that recur frequently: e.g., rules concerning the estate of a deceased bankrupt, the continuance of a statutory limitation or prescription period while a proceeding is stayed under the Bill, and the status of a married woman.

This Part also consolidates all the pertinent regulation making powers which under the present *Winding-Up Act* are vested in the courts and under the *Bankruptcy Act* are vested in the Governor-in-Council but supplemented by rules of court. Under the Bill all regulation making powers vest in the Governor-in-Council. These include power to make regulations authorized or required to be 'prescribed', to determine the form and time of notice, to establish fees for specific services, and to establish the amount the Superintendent may levy against each estate to recover his administrative costs.

Consistent with the overall concern of the Bill to adhere to exacting administrative law standards – for example, administration by exception to minimize unnecessary paper work, express licensing criteria to guide judicial review of licensing decisions, express right of appeal to a court in respect of the taxation of accounts, and judicial control over many investigative powers – the Bill subjects the regulation making powers exercised under it to close public scrutiny, particularly by requiring pre-publication of proposed rules and forms.

The Bill sets out a number of transitional provisions to make clear that existing proceedings will continue under the former law, and also to ensure that a cross reference in the statutes or corporate constitutions to a predecessor Act such as the *Winding-Up Act* is deemed to be reference to the new act. Finally the Bill provides that, unless the court has issued a conditional discharge, each individual who became bankrupt under the present *Act* is automatically released from his debts within five years from the date of his bankruptcy, a transition policy that is consonant with the automatic discharge provisions of the proposed law.

4 THE QUESTION OF JURISDICTION

Tassé Report, pp 35–45

1.4.01 Before recommending any legislative changes, it is necessary to describe the constitutional grant of power in Canada with respect to bankruptcy and insolvency. In doing so, we shall not discuss whether this grant of power is appropriate or not, as this is beyond our terms of reference. Our aim is simply to ascertain the limits of the respective legislative powers of the federal and provincial governments. As the Canadian Constitutional Law is complicated and

difficult to summarize, we shall do no more than review some of the most important constitutional cases. We think it appropriate, however, to begin our study by referring briefly to the
constitution of some other federal states.

1.4.02 *Comparative Constitutional Law*: Of the various countries visited by the Committee,
three have a federal constitution: Switzerland, Australia and the United States. In all these
countries, the federal legislature has legislative authority over bankruptcy and insolvency.

1.4.03 In the case of Switzerland, article 4 of the Constitution gives the federal Parliament
legislative authority over bankruptcy and execution of money judgments. However, at the time
when the constitution went into effect, the Cantons retained the power to legislate on these
matters until they were dealt with by federal legislation. Today, it is generally agreed that the
federal legislature has made full use of its power and that, consequently, there are no more
unfilled gaps within which the Cantons can still legislate [Amos, J. Peaslee, *Constitutions of
Nations*, rev. 3rd ed., The Hague, Martinus Nijhoff, 1968, vol. 3, p 64; Jean-François Aubert,
Traité de Droit constitutionnel suisse, Dalloz, 1967, vol. 1, pp 261 to 263.]

1.4.04 In Australia, the federal Parliament, according to the interpretation given to the Constitution by the courts, does not have general legislative authority over the incorporation of
companies. [It should be noted that the *Australian Capital Territory* has authority to create,
regulate and liquidate companies within its territory. It is in the exercise of this authority that the
A.C.T. has adopted *The Companies Ordinance 1962–1963*.] For the same reasons, it is doubtful
that it possesses such authority over the winding-up of solvent companies. However, in article
51, the Constitution expressly grants to the federal Parliament legislative power over bankruptcy and insolvency. The federal Parliament has passed legislation in the exercise of this
power, but section 7 of the *Bankruptcy Act, 1966* makes it impossible for corporations to go into
voluntary or forced bankruptcy. The result of this is that only natural persons can be adjudged
bankrupt and that companies, even if they are insolvent, can only be wound up under the law of
the States. It seems, nonetheless, that the Australian Parliament would have authority to extend
the scope of the law on bankruptcy to include insolvent corporations [B. H. McPherson, *The
Law of Company Liquidation*, Sydney, The Law Book Company Limited, 1968, pp 24 and 25.]
As for the possibility of applying the law of the States in the field of bankruptcy, the matter is
discussed as follows in a recent treatise:

The provisions of the various Bankruptcy Acts or Insolvency Acts in existence in the States or
Territories prior to 1st August, 1928 (the date when the first Commonwealth Bankruptcy Act
1924–1927 commenced) can sometimes be important by virtue of s 9 of the Commonwealth Act.
This section provides that the Act does not affect any State or Territory laws providing for
'matters not dealt with expressly or by necessary implication in this Act.'
Obviously a State Parliament is not empowered by s 9 to provide for an alternative set of
proceedings and merely by giving them a different name, to establish a jurisdiction covering the
same ground. If the Commonwealth Act provides any way by which a matter may be adjudicated or makes any rules for proceedings in the particular circumstances, it prevails over any
State legislation on the subject. Thus it is only a court exercising jurisdiction under the
Commonwealth Act that is entitled to decide whether a deed of arrangement between a debtor
and his creditors is valid. But if there is no provision in the Commonwealth Act that governs the
matter and a State Act governing another branch of law has such a provision the latter is
applicable.
There is indeed a wide range of subjects in which State legislation touches incidentally upon
bankruptcy, or in which bankruptcy proceedings affect rights acquired under a State Act. In

many such cases the Commonwealth Act does not make any provision. The most common example of such incidental matters occurs when a State Act provides for a specified result to occur upon the bankruptcy of a party to a transaction. In such a case, the State law is valid unless the Bankruptcy Act expressly or by necessary implication overrides the State provision. [Dennis J. Rose, *Laws' Australian Bankruptcy Law*, 5th ed., Sydney, The Law Book Co. Ltd., 1967, p 5.]

1.4.05 The American Constitution grants to Congress the legislative authority to pass 'uniform laws on the subject of bankruptcies throughout the United States.' Thus it is apparent from the very wording of the Constitution that Congress could not, in its legislation, adopt different terms and conditions for the various States, for, in order to be constitutional, every provision must apply to all the States. Moreover, the legislative power of Congress not being exclusive, the States can legislate in the absence of federal legislation. As Congress has passed a Bankruptcy Act and this Act is still in force, it may be asked whether there is still room for the States to also enact bankruptcy legislation. This question is discussed as follows by a writer:

The enactment of a national bankrupt law does not operate to annul State laws on the same subject, but simply to suspend their operation so long as the national regulations are in force. Upon the repeal of the Federal law the State laws at once revive, and do not need reenactment. So also a State law passed while a Federal bankruptcy law is in force goes at once into force with the repeal of the Federal statute.

The precise effect of the enactment of a Federal bankruptcy law in suspending the operation of existing State laws is not definitely determinable from the decisions of either the State or Federal courts. That a State law covering the same ground as the national act, even though its provisions be not inconsistent therewith, is suspended is generally, though not uniformly, admitted. If, then, it be conceded that the intention of Congress was, by the enactment of a bankrupt law, to cover the entire subject, all State laws relating to bankruptcy are suspended while the national law remains in force.

Even if the view be accepted that by the act of 1898 the general subject of bankruptcy is fully covered there still remains, in many cases, the difficulty of determining when State laws relating to general assignments for the benefit of creditors, receivership of corporations, etc., may be held to be in the nature of bankruptcy laws and as such rendered inoperative during the existence of the Federal law. [W.W. Willoughby, *The Constitutional Law of the United States*, 2nd ed., vol. II, New York, Baker, Voorhis & Co., 1929, S. 644, pp 1099 and 1100.]

1.4.06 The word 'bankruptcies' used in the American constitution has been given a very broad meaning by the courts. According to the Supreme Court,

The subject of bankruptcies is incapable of final definition. The concept changes. It has been recognized that it is not limited to the connotation of the phrase in England or the United States at the time of the formulation of the constitution. An adjudication in bankruptcy is not essential to the jurisdiction.

The subject of bankruptcies is nothing less than the subject of the relation between an insolvent or non-paying debtor and his creditors extending to his and their relief. [*Wright* v *Union Central Insurance Co.* (1938), 304 U.S. 502 at 513.]

As a result of this position taken by the American courts,

The subject of bankruptcies embraces the entire field of debtor-creditor relationships for the purpose of the equitable distribution of a debtor's estate, rehabilitation of the debtor, and the protection of the credit structure against anything materially contributing toward its impairment. [*Collier on Bankruptcy*, edited by J.W. Moore, 14th ed., New York, Matthew Bender, 1969, vol. 1, p 6.]

1.4.07 *Basis for Federal Legislative Authority*: In Canada, as in Switzerland, Australia and the United States, the federal Parliament has legislative authority over insolvency and bankruptcy. What is the justification for giving this power to the federal authorities? As regards the Canadian Constitution, Judge Wurtele, of the Superior Court of the Province of Quebec, supplied the following explanation in his reasons for a judgment delivered in 1888:

The Dominion is formed of different provinces, and there is, of course, more or less diversity in their laws regulating the collection of debts and the settlement of the estates of insolvents; and the power of the provincial courts to execute provincial laws does not extend beyond the territory of the province to which they belong. It is therefore in the interest of the trade and commerce of the whole Dominion that there should be one uniform law for all the provinces, regulating proceedings in the case of insolvent debtors, unrestricted in its operation by provincial boundaries, that it should be possible to obtain a national execution, and not merely a limited provincial one, against the estate of an insolvent debtor, who might hold property in several provinces, or transfer it from his own province into another. [*Dupont et vir* v *La Cie de Moulin à Bardeau Chanfréné*, (1888) II *The Legal News*, p 225 at p 227.]

1.4.08 In its introductory words, section 91 of the *British North America Act, 1867*, gives to the Parliament of Canada the authority 'to make Laws for the Peace, Order and good Government of Canada, in relation to all Matters not coming with the Classes of Subjects by this Act assigned exclusively to the Legislatures of the Provinces'. 'For greater Certainty,' it enumerates certain classes of subjects, after having granted to the Parliament of Canada the exclusive legislative authority over all matters coming within them. As 'Bankruptcy and Insolvency' are enumerated under head 21, all matters coming within these classes of subjects would be beyond the legislative competence of the provincial legislatures, even if the Parliament of Canada had enacted no legislation in relation thereto. [*Union Colliery Co.* v *Bryden*, (*1899*), *A.C. 580 at 588*; *A.-G. Can* v *A.-G. Ont.* (1898) A.C. 700 (Fisheries Case); *A.G. for Can.* v *Attorney-General for Ont., Que.* and *N.S.*, (1898) A.C. 700 at 715; *Reference re Debt Adjustment Act*, 1937, 1943 A.C. 356; *Reference re The Orderly Payment of Debts Act*, 1959 (Alberta), (1960) 1 C.B.R. (n.s.) at p 207 and p 222.]

1.4.09 Section 91 also contains in its enumeration certain classes of subjects connected with bankruptcy, namely, the regulation of trade and commerce under head 2, interest under head 19 and the criminal law under head 27. As the exclusive legislative authority of the Parliament of Canada extends to all matters coming within these classes of subjects, it is, from a constitutional point of view, purely academic to consider, for instance, whether a legislative provision is, in pith and substance, bankruptcy legislation or criminal law legislation.

1.4.10 In the legal terminology, the federal legislation is bisected into that which is *per se* federal and that which is merely ancillary to a class of subject under the exclusive legislative authority of the Parliament of Canada. According to Mr. Justice Laskin, this is a distinction without a difference:

(The) use (of the 'trenching' doctrine) to explain a privileged encroachment on provincal legislative authority is purely gratuitous because once a court is satisfied that impugned legislation carried a federal 'aspect,' no invasion of provincial legislative authority exists ... To say that the Dominion in legislating in relation to a matter coming within an enumerated class of subject in section 91 can also enact provisions which are necessarily incidental to effective legislation under the enumerated class is a tortuous method of explaining the 'aspect' doctrine ... Legislation, as the Judicial Committee has itself said from time to time, must be considered as a whole and its aspect ascertained in the light of all its provisions. To make what can only be an artificial distinction between those provisions of a federal enactment which are strictly in a federal aspect and those necessarily incidental to the effective operation of the legislation, is to trifle with legislative objectives and with the draftsman's efforts to realize them. [Bora Laskin, *Peace, Order and Good Government Re-examined* (1947) 25 Can. Bar Rev. 1954, at pp 1060 and 1061.]

1.4.11 In 1894, at a time when no federal legislation on bankruptcy and insolvency was in force in Canada, an *obiter dictum* from Lord Herschell, of the Judicial Committee of the Privy Council, explained the 'ancillary' doctrine in its application to bankruptcy and insolvency as follows:

(Their Lordships) would observe that a system of bankruptcy legislation may frequently require various ancillary provisions for the purpose of preventing the scheme of the Act from being defeated. It may be necessary for this purpose to deal with the effect of executions and other matters which would otherwise be within the legislative competence of the provincial legislature. Their Lordships do not doubt that it would be open to the Dominion Parliament to deal with such matters as part of a bankruptcy law, and the provincial legislature would doubtless be then precluded from interfering with this legislation inasmuch as such interference would affect the bankruptcy law of the Dominion Parliament [*A.-G. Ont.* v *A.-G. Can.* (1894) A.C. 189, p 200.]

This *obiter dictum* was in line with a previous pronouncement of the Judicial Committee in a case where it had to decide whether, in enacting *The Insolvency Act* in 1875, the Parliament of Canada could limit appeals:

It would be impossible to advance a step in the constitution of a scheme for the administration of insolvent estates without interfering with and modifying the ordinary rights of property, and other civil rights, nor without providing some mode of special procedure for the vesting, realization and distribution of the estate, and the settlement of liabilities of the insolvent. Procedure must necessarily form an essential part of any law dealing with insolvency. It is therefore, to be presumed, indeed it is a necessary implication, that the Imperial Statute, in assigning to the Dominion Parliament the subjects of bankruptcy and insolvency, intended to confer on it legislative power to interfere with property, civil rights and procedure within the provinces, so far as a general law relating to these subjects might affect them. Their Lordships, therefore, think that the Parliament of Canada would not infringe the exclusive powers given to the provincial legislature by enacting that the judgment of the Court of Queen's Bench in matters of insolvency should be final. ... [*Cushing* v *Dupuy*, (1880) 5 A.C. 409, p 415.]

1.4.12 *Provincial Legislation on Bankruptcy and Insolvency:* The provincial legislatures do not possess legislative authority over bankruptcy and insolvency and could not pass valid laws in this field, even in the absence of federal legislation. This result follows logically from the fact that sections 91 and 92 grant to the Parliament of Canada and to the provincial legislatures exclusive legislative power in their respective fields. As it was stated by the Judicial Committee of the Privy Council,

the abstinence of the Dominion Parliament from legislating to the full limit of its powers could not have the effect of transferring to any provincial legislature and legislative power which had been assigned to the Dominion by s 91 ... *Union Colliery Co.* v *Bryden*, (1899) A.C. 580, at p 588; see also *A. G. Can.* v *A. G. Ont.* (1898) A.C. 700.

1.4.13 It should not be inferred from the foregoing that the Provincial legislatures cannot pass legislation having effect in the field of bankruptcy and insolvency. However, such legislation is only *intra vires* insofar as it deals with matters outside this field and included in the classes of subjects enumerated in section 92. Thus, in 1894, a decision of the Judicial Committee of the Privy Council recognized the legislative authority of Ontario to pass legislation regarding assignments of property. In explaining the decision, Lord Herschell emphasized the fact that the assignment of property was not subject to the insolvency of the debtor:

Moreover, the operation of an assignment for the benefit of creditors was precisely the same, whether the assignor was or was not in fact insolvent. It was open to any debtor who might deem his solvency doubtful, and who desired in that case that his creditors should be equitably dealt with, to make an assignment for their benefit. The validity of the assignment and its effect would in no way depend on the insolvency of the assignor, and their Lordships think it clear that the 9th section would equally apply whether the assignor was or was not insolvent ... [*A.-G. Ont.* v *A.G. Can.*, (1894) A.C. 189, at p 199. This decision was commented on as follows by Kerwin C.J.C. (Taschereau, Fauteux, Abbot, Judson and Ritchie concurring) in the *Reference re The Orderly Payment of Debts Act, 1959 (Alberta)* (1960) 1 C.B.R. (n.s.) 212: '... it is doubtful whether, in view of later pronouncements of the Judicial Committee it would at this date be decided in the same sense, even in the absence of Dominion legislation upon the subject of bankruptcy and insolvency.']

1.4.14 As, in legislating on a matter within its legislative authority, a Provincial legislature can affect matters relating to bankruptcy and insolvency, that is to say, modify the rights and obligations of an insolvent person and of his creditors, the possibility of a conflict between a provincial act and federal legislation exists. In such a case, the latter would prevail.
1.4.15 On a reference to the Supreme Court of Canada, Mr. Justice Cartwright summed up as follows the conditions under which a provincial act can, without being *ultra vires*, modify the rights and obligations of an insolvent person and of his creditors:

In every decision of the Judicial Committee or of this Court in which provincial legislation, impugned on the ground that it affected the rights and obligations of an insolvent entity and its creditors and thereby trenched on the subject matter comprised in head 21 of s 91, has been upheld it appears that in the view of the Court, two conditions were found to exist:
i that the impugned legislation was not in pith and substance primarily in relation to bankruptcy and insolvency but rather in relation to one or more of the matters enumerated in s 92; and

ii that insofar as it affected the rights and obligations of an insolvent and its creditors, it did not conflict with existing valid legislation of Parliament enacted in exercise of the power contained in head 21 of s 91: [*Reference re: The Orderly Payment of Debts Act, 1959, (Alberta)*, (1960–61) 1 c.b.r. (n.s.) 207 at pp 226 and 227.]

1.4.16 *Provincial Legislation Concerning Transactions of Debtors in Fraud of Creditors:* There is both federal and provincial legislation designed to protect creditors from the fraudulent transactions of their debtors.

1.4.17 In Quebec, the legislation is contained in articles 1032 *et seq.* of the *Civil Code*, which authorize creditors to bring an 'action paulienne'. One of the most common examples where such an action may be brought is where an insolvent debtor makes a preferential payment to a creditor who has knowledge of the insolvency of the debtor. As the articles of the *Civil Code* giving rise to 'L'action paulienne' were enacted in 1866, there can be no doubt as to their initial constitutional validity on the advent of Confederation in the following year. Section 129 of the *British North America Act* provides that all existing legislation would continue in force after Confederation 'subject nevertheless ... to be repealed, abolished or altered by the Parliament of Canada, or by the legislature of the respective Province, according to the authority of the Parliament or that Legislature under this Act.'

1.4.18 Whether it is the Parliament of Canada or the Legislature of the Province of Quebec that has the authority to alter the provisions of the *Civil Code* relating to 'l'action paulienne' depends upon the view one takes as to the nature of this legislation. If it is considered to be in pith and substance a matter of insolvency, it comes within the legislative authority of the federal Parliament. If, on the other hand, it is considered to be a matter primarily relating to 'Property and Civil Rights', it comes under the legislative authority of the Province of Quebec. However, in either hypothesis, it is important to determine whether or not the legislation is in conflict with valid federal legislation, such as the *Bankruptcy Act*, for in the case of the first hypothesis there would be an implicit abrogation, and, in the context of the second, the legislation would be considered to be inoperative due to the paramountcy of the federal legislation. On this last point, the observation should be made that the Quebec Courts have invariably interpreted 'l'action paulienne' as not repugnant, but as supplemental, to the law of bankruptcy.

1.4.19 In the common law provinces, the situation is different. Instead of a pre-confederation statute followed by the federal *Bankruptcy Act*, as in the case of Quebec, there was provincial legislation [See for British Columbia: *The Fraudulent Conveyances Act* (1960) r.s.b.c. c. 155 and *The Fraudulent Preferences act* (1960) r.s.b.c. c. 156; for Alberta: *The Fraudulent Preferences Act* (1955) r.s.a. c. 120; for Saskatchewan: *The Fraudulent Preferences Act* (1965) r.s.s. c. 397; for Manitoba: *The Fraudulent Conveyances Act* (1954) r.s.m. c. 91 and *The Assignments Act* (1954) r.s.m. c. 11; for Ontario: *The Assignments and Preferences Act* (1914) r.s.o. c. 194 and (1960) r.s.o. c. 25 and *The Fraudulent Conveyances Act* (1960) r.s.o. c. 154; for New Brunswick: *The Assignments and Preferences Act* (1952) r.s.n.b. c. 13, and, finally, for Nova Scotia: *The Assignments and Preferences Act* (1967), r.s.n.s., c. 16.] after Confederation in the form of Fraudulent Conveyances Acts and Fraudulent Preferences Acts. The latter, as their names indicate, are concerned with preferential payments. They permit certain preferences to be set aside, indpendently of bankruptcy, as is also permitted by article 1036 of the Quebec *Civil Code*. The necessity for this provincial legislation in the Common Law provinces is due to the fact that there was no federal bankruptcy legislation from 1880 to 1919.

1.4.20. The courts have considered the constitutionality of *The Fraudulent Preferences Act* of Alberta, *The Fraudulent Preferences Act* of British Columbia and the *Assignments and Prefer-*

ences act of Ontario. The Supreme Court of Alberta found the Alberta statute unconstitutional. According to Mr. Justice Milvain:

Its pith and substance is directly and only that of dealing with matters hinged on insolvency. [Re *McIntosh – Marshall Equipment Ltd.: Nash* v *Guelph Engineering Co.* (1964) 48 W.W.R. 420; (1965) 7 C.B.R. (n.s.) 84 at p 88.]

This judgment was upheld by the Court of Appeal, but it was only prepared to hold that the Act was either *ultra vires* or inoperative.

1.4.21 Both *The Fraudulent Preferences Act* of British Columbia [*Hoffar Ltd.* v *Canadian Credit Men's Trust Association Ltd.* (1929) S.C.R. 180.] and *The Assignments and Preferences Act* of Ontario were held to be inoperative. The majority of the Ontario Court of Appeal, in *In re Trenwith* adopted the view expressed by Mr. Justice Masten at the trial:

It seems to me that the common field of the legislation respecting the distribution of the estates of insolvents having now become occupied by the Dominion Bankruptcy Act, the provisions of the Assignments and Preferences Act respecting the preference of one creditor over another have been thereby superseded and have ceased to have any operation. [*Re Trenwith* (1933–34) 15 C.B.R. 372, at p 376.]

In the *Bozanich Case* Chief Justice Duff expressed the same opinion:

I may add that, in my opinion, the provisions R.S.O. 1926 c 26 in relation to preference are superseded by section 64, and that the authority of the Ontario Leglislature to enact such legislation is, in consequence of the enactment of section 64, suspended in virtue of the concluding paragraph of section 91. [*In re Bozanich* (1942) S.C.R. 130, at p 136.]

1.4.22 Notwithstanding these judgments, the situation, from a constitutional point of view, of these provincial statutes is still confusing. While there is substantially similar legislation in respect to preferences in all provinces, creditors in at least three provinces, in order to protect themselves against preferential payments made by their insolvent debtors, must resort to bankruptcy proceedings, while, in the other provinces, there is at least uncertainty as to whether or not the particular provincial Preference Statute is constitutional. Moreover, as the *Fraudulent Preferences Acts* of three provinces have been found to be unconstitutional or inoperative, there is some doubt as to whether certain provisions of the Fraudulent Conveyances Acts may not also be unconstitutional.

1.4.23 *The Extent of Federal Jurisdiction under Section 91 (21):* If the exclusive competence of the Parliament of Canada over each of the classes of subjects enumerated in section 91 is well established, one could still question how broad an interpretation should be given to bankruptcy and insolvency. Although there have been a relatively large number of cases on the question, the Courts have not given any precise definition of these two concepts. This is not in itself surprising, for the courts on constitutional matters tend to avoid abstract or general statements and doctrinal discussions. However, in order to describe the extent of the constitutional grant of power over bankruptcy and insolvency with any precision, it is necessary to summarize the decisions of the courts on this question.

1.4.24 In a decision rendered in 1888 [*Supra*, 1.4.07], the Superior Court of Quebec refused to give a narrow interpretation to the words 'bankruptcy and insolvency'. In that case, it had been contended that the legislative power of the Parliament of Canada does not extend to laws providing for a distribution of an insolvent debtor's estate without a concurrent discharge from his liabilities and that the *Winding Up Act* was therefore unconstitutional. The Court held that the ultimate purposes of bankruptcy and insolvency are distribution and discharge and that Parliament had full discretion to legislate to the extent of its power or within its power. In other words, whether the legislation shall release the debtor from further liability or not is a mere matter of policy. To appreciate the correctness of these views, it should be borne in mind that, under the bankruptcy system of some countries, for instance France, the debtor is not entitled to a discharge, except with the unanimous consent of the creditors.

1.4.25 In *Attorney-General for British Columbia* v *Attorney-General for Canada* (*In Re Farmers' Creditors Arrangement Act*) the Province of British Columbia alleged that the Act does not truly form legislation relating to 'bankruptcy and insolvency' but is an invasion of the sphere of the provincial legislatures in relation to 'Property and Civil Rights in the Province'. In its report, the Judicial Committee of the Privy Council said:

In a normal community it is certain that these conditions (which bring the bankruptcy law into operation) will require revision from time to time. Their Lordships are unable to hold that the statutory conditions of insolvency which enabled a creditor or the debtor to invoke the aid of the bankruptcy laws, or the classes to which these laws applied, were intended to be stereotyped under head 21 of section 91 of the *British North America Act* so as to confine the jurisdiction of the Parliament of Canada to the legislative provisions then existing as regards to the matters. [(1937) 18 C.B.R., 217 at p 222 (P.C.).]

1.4.26 It results, from the position taken by the Privy Council in respect of the constitutionality of the *Farmers' Creditors Arrangement Act*, that as in the United States (*supra* 1.4.06), the concepts of bankruptcy and insolvency are not limited to the connotation they had at the time of the Constitution. As society changes, so does the subject matter in relation to which the Parliament of Canada has exclusive legislative authority under head 21 of section 91 of *The British North America Act, 1867*. Insofar as it does not resort to colourable devices, the discretion committed to the Parliament of Canada is unfettered. It is so wide that, in our opinion, Parliament may validly adopt legislation in prevention of insolvency and bankruptcy such as that proposed *infra* in 3.1.41. As Viscount Simon L.C. once stated:

... to legislate for prevention appears to be on the same base as legislation for cure. [*A.G. Ont.* v *Can. Temperance Federation*, (1946) 2 D.L.R. (A.C.] 193; 85 Can. CC. 225.]

1.4.27 *Courts and Procedure*. The Parliament of Canada is authorized to create courts, not by section 91, but by section 101 of the *British North America Act, 1867*. This section reads as follows:

101 The Parliament of Canada may, notwithstanding anything in this Act, from time to time, provide for the Constitution, Maintenance, and Organization of a General Court of Appeal for Canada, and for the Establishment of any additional Courts for the better Administration of the Laws of Canada

Under this section, the Parliament of Canada, in addition to establishing a General Court of Appeal for Canada, has the authority to create any additional court to ensure the better administration of the laws of Canada. This does not, however, permit Parliament to create a court charged with the settlement of 'disputes' in matters coming under the classes of subjects over which the provincial legislatures have exclusive legislative power. Indeed, it is well established that the words 'laws of Canada' refer solely to the law relating to matters coming under federal legislative authority. [Bora Laskin, *Canadian Constitutional Law*, 3rd ed., Toronto The Carswell Company Ltd., 1966, p 187; Gilles Pepin, *Les Tribunaux administratifs et la constitution*, Montréal, Les Presses de L'Université de Montréal, 1969, pp 325 and 326.] As the subjects of 'bankruptcy and insolvency' come within this authority, there can be no doubt that Parliament can give jurisdiction over this field of law either to an existing federal court, such as the Exchequer Court of Canada, or to any new federal Court it may create to specifically assume this jurisdiction.

1.4.28 In either case, there is the very real question as to whether or not a federal court, in the exercise of its jurisdiction, can incidentally apply provincial law. According to Mr. Justice Laskin in his book, *The Canadian Constitutional Law:*

The recognition in the Exchequer Court of provincial legislation defining substantial law – depends ... on the substantive law declared by Parliament under s 101 of the B.N.A. Act to be applicable therein or, failing such statutory declaration, on the common law (or admiralty law as well) applicable to the assigned jurisdiction. Provincial statute law cannot apply unless there is some federal statutory basis for finding that it was incorporated into federal law for federal purposes. [Bora Laskin, *op. cit.*, p 822.]

1.4.29 It should be noted that section 101 of the B.N.A. Act is not peremptory. It merely empowers Parliament to establish 'from time to time ... any additional courts ...' There is, moreover, no practical necessity to establish new courts, for Parliament can rely on the provincial courts to adjudicate upon all matters arising out of any federal statute. Indeed, it can, in matters coming under its legislative jurisdiction, impose judicial duties not only on provincial courts, but also on any provincial civil servant, any individual or any institution. This was established by the Supreme Court of Canada in *Valin* v *Langlois* (1879) 3 S.C.R. 1, p 37–38; (1879) 5 A.C. 115.] and has been confirmed on several significant occasions, notably in 1903, in *In re Vancini* [(1903–1904) 34 S.C.R. 621, pp 625 and 626.], in which Mr. Justice Sedgewick adopted the following statement made by A.H.F. Lefroy:

The Dominion Parliament can, in matters within its sphere, impose duties upon any subjects of the Dominion, whether they be officials of provincial courts, other officials, or private citizens, and there is nothing in the *British North America Act* to raise a doubt about the power of the Dominion Parliament to impose duties upon existing Provincial Courts or to give them new powers as to matters which do not come within the subjects assigned exclusively to the legislatures of the provinces or to deprive them of jurisdiction over such matters. [A. Lefroy, *The Legislative Powers in Canada*, Toronto, The Toronto Law Book and Publishing Co. Ltd., 1897–98, p 510.]

1.4.30 When the Parliament of Canada wishes the provincial courts to have jurisdiction over issues arising out of federal legislation, it is not necessary that such jurisdiction be specifically conferred upon the provincial courts. *The Bills of Exchange Act* is, for example, silent as to the court which has the jurisdiction to try issues arising out of it. Yet, litigants obtain, from the provincial courts, legal recognition of the rights conferred on them by this Act [Gilles Pepin, *op. cit.*, p 343.]. This is explained by Mr. Justice Laskin as follows:

The abstention of Parliament from setting up federal courts of first instance to try issues falling within federal competence does not leave them at large. It is fully accepted that they may be triable in the provincial courts, either as a matter of entertaining common or decisional law causes of action (whether provincial or federal common or decisional law) or as a matter of exercising jurisdiction arising under federal legislation, whether the legislation explicitly confers it or not. As the Privy Council put it in *Board* v *Board*, (1919) A.C. 956, 48 D.L.R. 13, (1919) 2 W.W.R. 940: 'If the right exists, the presumption is that there is a Court which can enforce it, for no other mode of enforcing it is prescribed, that alone is sufficient to give jurisdiction to the King's Courts of Justice. In order to oust jurisdiction it is necessary in the absence of a special law excluding it altogether to plead that jurisdiction exists in some other Court'. The application of this proposition to provincial courts depends, it is submitted, on whether the provincial Courts have the jurisdiction to adjudicate on the right which is in question. Such jurisdiction has, by and large, been found in pre-confederation powers of such Courts which have a continuing force under s 129 of the B.N.A. Act. Where, after Confederation, it is evident that a provincial Court has no jurisdiction in respect of matters falling within exclusive federal competence, the central question is whether Parliament alone may confer it. Clearly the substantive justiciable matter must be found only on a statute of Parliament or on existing common law which would be subject to Parliament's control. Where a federal statute embraces or declares the right sued upon, it may quite conceivably be held as a matter of construction, or of implicit reference, that provincial courts are envisaged as the agencies of enforcement. [Bora Laskin, *op. cit.*, note 24, p 818.]

1.4.31 It follows from the foregoing that, in matters coming under its jurisdiction, the Parliament of Canada can either establish a system of courts parallel to the provincial courts or accept the principle of the 'communality' of the provincial courts. In respect to the second hypothesis, Parliament has the power to establish the procedure that the provincial courts must follow in the exercise of their federal functions. This principle was, as we have seen, established beyond a doubt by *Cushing* v *Dupuy* in 1880 [See *supra* 1.4.11]

1.4.32 *Conclusion:* As shown in this chapter, the Parliament of Canada has exclusive legislative power over bankruptcy and insolvency and these two subject matters have been broadly interpreted by the courts. Moreover, whenever it is necessary for the effective operation of its legislation in this field, Parliament may deal with matters that would otherwise be within the exclusive legislative competence of the provincial legislatures. By way of conclusion, to the extent that there are legal remedies to the problems related to bankruptcy and insolvency, it is the responsibility of Parliament to look for these remedies and to legislate accordingly, as its legislative authority is supreme for this purpose.

NOTE In *Robinson* v *Countrywide Factors Ltd.*, [1977] 2 W.W.R. 111, 72 D.L.R. (3d) 500, supra p 644, the Supreme Court of Canada held that where the limitation period imposed by the Bankruptcy Act prevented the trustee in bankruptcy from impeaching a preferential transaction under that Act, the trustee could still avail himself of provincial legislation and, in effect, circumvent the limitation period.

19
Alternatives to Bankruptcy

INTRODUCTION

An insolvent consumer debtor may choose to avail himself of the provisions of Part III
of the new Bankruptcy Bill to propose an arrangement with his creditors; a similar
scheme is available to commercial debtors under Part IV of the Bill.

In both cases, a central purpose of the schemes is to provide the debtor with
'breathing-space' to trade or work his way back to a state of solvency. In return for
avoiding the full consequences of bankruptcy, the debtor may commit himself to a
larger payment to creditors (over time) than they perhaps would receive in a bankruptcy. Recalling Leff's analysis of the collection process (Chapter 1), it is useful to
consider when it may be in the interests of a creditor to pursue ordinary individualized
collection remedies, agree to an arrangement between a debtor and his creditors, or
press for bankruptcy. A debtor often faces a similar calculus in choosing between
proposing an arrangement with his creditors or voluntarily entering bankruptcy.

1 TASSÉ REPORT, pp 89–99 (footnotes omitted)

3.1.01 *Arrangements Generally:* Almost all consumer bankruptcies are no asset or nominal
asset cases in which the creditors get nothing. Indeed, for all estates closed in Canada in 1968,
the unsecured creditors, including those that are preferred, received a total dividend of something less than six cents on the dollar. This would indicate that bankruptcy proceedings are
generally of little practical value as a means of collective execution.
3.1.02 For these reasons, it would seem to be, as a rule, to the advantage of all concerned that an
insolvent debtor should voluntarily come to an arrangement with his creditors. On the one hand,
the creditors who would normally receive almost nothing on bankruptcy, as shown above,
should, in this way, receive something. The debtor, on the other hand, can avoid much of the
stigma of bankruptcy and may more readily rehabilitate himself. As a result, the community may
well be saved the hardship, loss and often serious dislocation that may follow from a failure or a
series of failures. It is for these reasons that to reach out and to assist the overburdened debtor in
his difficulties, at the earliest possible moment, is one of the most important functions of the
bankruptcy system.
3.1.03 An arrangement under the *Bankruptcy Act* is different from a composition or extension
agreement that a debtor may make with his creditors outside of the Act. If an arrangement, made
under the Act, is accepted by a majority of creditors and ratified by the court, it binds all of the
creditors, whether it is accepted by them or not. *Supra*, in 1.3.23, a brief outline is given of the
procedure by which a debtor may make a proposal for an arrangement with his creditors.
3.1.04 Provisions permitting an insolvent debtor to make a proposal to his creditors are

designed, among other purposes, to encourage a debtor to pay what he can on his debts over a period of time. If an arrangement is accepted, the debtor will, as a rule, be permitted to retain his property. This often gives him the opportunity to re-organize his affairs and, ultimately, to consolidate his financial position.

3.1.05 A debtor who makes an arrangement with his creditors should, as a rule, pay more to his creditors than they would receive on a bankruptcy. As an arrangement is more demanding, however, not all debtors will choose to try to make an arrangement with their creditors as an alternative to straight bankruptcy. For the small debtor not in business, it may be beyond his endurance to live in reduced circumstances for several years, which an arrangement may require. The debtor in business may have difficulty in obtaining credit and, generally, in carrying on his business by reason of the restrictions often resulting from an arrangement. A debtor may well consider that the risk and hardship involved in the making of an arrangement is greater than any advantage that may accrue to him.

3.1.06 There are a number of reasons, however, that may induce a debtor to make an arrangement with his creditors. For example, the debtor is, as a rule, able to retain assets that he would otherwise forfeit on bankruptcy. These assets have a greater value and economic potential in his hands than if they were to be liquidated for the benefit of his creditors. Moreover, a debtor does not, under an arrangement, suffer the incapacities that he would, under a bankruptcy. This is especially important if, as is recommended *infra*, in 3.2.091 et. seq., these incapacities should become more severe than they are now. It is also proposed to restrict the number of times that a debtor, during a given period, may obtain a release of his debts by way of bankruptcy. For that reason, a debtor may have no other alternative, but to make an arrangement with his creditors, to obtain a release from his debts. Moreover, the small debtor may welcome the opportunity to make an arrangement in order to receive, along the lines proposed *infra*, in 3.1.30 et. seq., the assistance and counselling that will help him to learn to live within his means. The reduced publicity, which should prevail in these cases, and the avoidance of the stigma of bankruptcy should also induce some debtors to seek to make arrangements with their creditors.

3.1.07 Whether or not a debtor succeeds in performing an arrangement, to a great extent, depends upon his character, pride, self-discipline and tenaciousness. For these reasons, arrangements cannot be forced upon insolvent debtors. It must be their free and voluntary choice. They should, however, be encouraged, as much as possible, to make arrangements with their creditors for the payment of their debts.

3.1.08 *Present Facilities For Making Arrangements:* The present *Bankruptcy Act* and other statutes provide a variety of facilities whereby a debtor may make a proposal for an arrangement with his creditors. Except as they relate to small debtors, there are no serious deficiencies in the provisions of the *Bankruptcy Act* relating to arrangements and, in general, it would appear that the legislation functions reasonably well. There are, however, two matters that deserve consideration. These are, firstly, the multiplicity of statutes that, at present, contain provisions relating to arrangements and, secondly, the desirability of providing a procedure permitting a debtor to give notice of his intention to make an arrangement. The need to provide small debtors with facilities to make arrangements adapted to their needs and conditions is discussed *infra*, in 3.1.13 et. seq.

3.1.09 *An Integrated Scheme For Arrangements:* The procedures whereby an insolvent debtor may make a proposal for an arrangement with his creditors are now found in four statutes. All of these procedures should be brought together and placed in the *Bankruptcy Act*. The new procedure should be as flexible as possible so as to permit the greatest variety of arrangements to suit as many situations as possible.

3.1.10 *Notice of Intention:* Too often a debtor does not make a proposal for an arrangement with his creditors until bankruptcy is imminent. As a result, there is often not enough time for the debtor and his advisers to carefully formulate the proposal. While a debtor may be criticized for delaying to make a proposal until the last moment, the legislation should not have the practical effect of forcing him to make a hasty proposal that may be ill-conceived. Neither should it have the effect of putting him in the position where he makes a proposal that is rejected but that might well have been accepted if only the debtor had had a reasonable opportunity to arrange the necessary financing, guarantees and other details.

3.1.11 In order to gain time so as to permit more careful consideration of all the problems and alternatives involved in making a proposal, a debtor, under the present Act, may persuade a friendly creditor to a file a petition for a receiving order. This results in an automatic stay of all proceedings against the debtor by his own creditors. While to the advantage of the debtor, this practice is against the spirit, if not the letter of the law. To prevent this, and in recognition of the fact that it is, in most cases, in the interest of both the creditors and their debtor that a reasonable time be given to a debtor to prepare a proposal free from the pressure of his creditors, a debtor should be authorized to file a notice of his intention to present a proposal for an arrangement.

3.1.12 For a certain period of time after a notice of intention is filed, all proceedings against the debtor should be stayed. Creditors could, however, protect themselves and their interest in the property of the debtor by applying for the appointment of an interim receiver. So that the privilege to file a notice of intention would not be abused, the failure of the debtor to file a petition for a proposal within the time limit after the notice is given, would be regarded as *prima facie* evidence that the debtor has ceased to pay his debts generally as they mature. A petition for a receiving order based on this presumption could then be filed.

3.1.13 *Present Facilities For Small Debtors to Make Arrangements:* Many small debtors not in business need special facilities adapted to their needs and conditions. The opinion was expressed *supra*, in 2.1.13 to 2.1.20, that the plight of the consumer or wage-earner debtor was one of the most important problems that must be faced in the field of bankruptcy today. New and more flexible and effective methods for the relief of the small debtor must be devised. Provisions, which have the practical effect of making it difficult for a small debtor to make an arrangement with his creditors, must be removed. For the purpose of the following paragraphs, the term 'small debtor' will be used to refer to the class of debtors, the largest part of which are wage-earners, but which also includes all those who are not in business.

3.1.14 At present, the provisions of the *Bankruptcy Act* permitting a debtor to make an arrangement with his creditors are not well adapted to the situation of the small debtor. While there is no reason, in principle, why such a debtor could not make a proposal under Part III of the Act, in practice, the costs, and particularly the fees of a private trustee are beyond his means.

3.1.15 Part X of the present Act was enacted in 1966, in recognition of the special problems of the small debtor. This Part provides a simple and inexpensive scheme for the orderly payment of the debts of a debtor who is not in business. The Part was limited, until recently, to debts less than $1,000. There are also other debts, particularly secured debts, that are excluded.

3.1.16 The chief merit of Part X is that, while an order is outstanding, no proceeding, as a rule, may be instituted against the debtor in respect of any debt to which the Part applies. One of the defects of Part X is that it only applies to the debtors residing in the provinces in which the provincial government concerned requests the Part to be proclaimed in force. Until it is proclaimed in force in all provinces, all debtors in Canada do not have the same opportunities for their relief and rehabilitation. There are, in addition, no provisions for summary relief from unconscionable transactions, the valuation of deficiency claims, the cancellation and valuation of executory contracts or for bringing secured creditors within the provision of the Part. Finally, it would seem that creditors, covered by the Part, may petition for a receiving order against the debtor even if he is not in default.

3.1.17 The following statement of the Honourable Daniel R. Cowans, of the United States, poses the problem well not only in terms of the United States, but also of the Canadian circumstances:

A number of debtors, wisely or otherwise, are not willing to concede defeat in their efforts to pay their obligations. Rather than take the easier way out, they claim they desire to devote future income to the payment of their debts even though, in the bankruptcy, they would be excused from doing so. Indeed, many who go through straight bankruptcy profess a most solemn intention to pay their debts in spite of their discharge. Actually, they seldom do so. Unquestionably in some cases the intention was not expressed in sincerity. In many other cases however, the failure is due to the lack of a sufficiently firm determination. In some of these and in still others there is a lack of sufficient knowledge of money management. No one familiar with debtor-creditor problems would deny that millions of persons do not understand financial matters well enough to live within their income. Some persons believe that such debtors should be made to suffer as an aid to learning. At the other extreme is the view that they must be let alone because the debtor's freedom from worry is a more important objective for society than the payment of debts.

3.1.18 It should be recognized that many small debtors sincerely want to pay their debts in full and, if this cannot be done, they want to pay as much as they can as an alternative to bankruptcy. While debtors should be encouraged to pay their debts, for the reasons mentioned earlier, *supra* 3.1.06, they should not, however, be put in the position of being forced to pay them by being denied the right to voluntarily enter bankruptcy.

3.1.19 The path of the small debtor who wants to make a voluntary arrangement with his creditors must be made easier. He should be encouraged both to frame a feasible arrangement for his own circumstances and, then, carry it out to its completion. At the same time, the power of creditors to reject arrangements must be limited. Other obstacles placed by creditors in the way of a debtor wishing to make an arrangement should be removed. For the small debtor, the opportunity to make a fresh start through an arrangement is, for example, largely illusory if much of his property which he requires to maintain a minimum standard of living may be repossessed by his creditors.

3.1.20 The provisions now contained in the *Bankruptcy Act*, permitting a small debtor to make an arrangement with his creditors, should be extended. The system must be comprehensive, just and equitable to both debtors and creditors. We believe that there are, in this respect, two types of need for those not in business who wish to make an arrangement with their creditors. Firstly, there are those debtors who need only time to pay all of their debts in full. A procedure permitting them to make an extension agreement binding upon all their creditors should be available. Secondly, there is the need of those debtors who cannot pay their debts in full, but who do not want to go into bankruptcy. For these debtors, there should be available a simple and inexpensive procedure permitting them to make a composition with their creditors.

3.1.21 *Arrangements For Small Debtors by Way of an Extension:* For the reasons already mentioned, there should be a simple procedure largely modelled on the present Part x, whereby a small debtor could make an extension agreement with all of his creditors, whether secured or unsecured, except a mortgagee or vendor of immoveable property. Under our proposed procedure, any insolvent debtor, whose principal income is derived from wages, salary or commissions and who does not, on his own account, carry on business, would have the right to make an application for a consolidation order. An extension agreement or consolidation of debts would be made and be binding upon all creditors of the debtor, unless the amounts that the debtor can reasonably expect to pay are not sufficient to reimburse, within three years, all of his debts with interest calculated at the rate of 5%. This period of time is as long as one can reasonably expect most debtors and their families to accept the discipline of the financial restrictions imposed by an arrangement. A creditor would be permitted to object to the consolidation order in respect of the amount listed as being owed to him or another creditor, the amounts fixed for periodical payment by the debtor and the times of payment of such amounts. On the filing of a petition, all proceedings against the debtor would be stayed until the petition is either withdrawn or dismissed or, if a consolidation order is made, until it is subsequently set aside by the court. There would be no meeting of creditors, but any creditor, whether secured or unsecured, would have the right to apply to the court for the annulment of the order, provided he exercises it within thirty days after the date of the making of the order and he shows to the court that the order is not in the best interest of all the creditors or constitutes an abuse that amounts to fraud with respect to particular creditors. The annulment of the consolidation order would, in such a case, result in the automatic bankruptcy of the debtor.

3.1.22 Such a system would be fair and equitable and would have the merit of being both simple and inexpensive. It would be available only to a debtor who can be expected to pay all of his debts within three years. As a debtor would not be allowed to come under this plan unless it can be reasonably expected that he will fulfill his obligations, the creditors would normally fare better under a consolidation order than in a bankruptcy.

3.1.23 *Arrangements For Small Debtors by Way of Composition:* With respect to small debtors, we see the need for another scheme. The plan already described would be for the debtor who wants to pay his creditors in full and has the means and capacity to do so within a period not longer than three years. The other plan, which we now discuss and recommend, would be for the debtor who wants to pay his debts, but cannot reasonably be expected to be able to pay them in full within three years. This plan would differ from an extension agreement and present Part x, in that the debtor at the end of the plan would receive a release of the balance of his debts. However, the principal difference, between present Part x and the new scheme we recommend, is that there would be a positive approach to the rehabilitation of the debtor. This would compare to the approach taken by the court in respect of the rehabilitation of a person convicted of a crime through the facilities of the probation service. The small debtor who cannot pay or has not the desire or incentive to commit himself to an arrangement that may extend over many months could go into bankruptcy. Of the three alternatives, however, only bankruptcy could be forced on a debtor.

3.1.24 Under the plan, there would be an immediate stay of all proceedings against the debtor as soon as he proposes an arrangement. This stay would continue during the term of the arrangement. At the end of the term, which could not be longer than three years, the debtor would receive a release from the balance of his debts.

3.1.25 In the recommendations made for the plan permitting a debtor to make an arrangement by way of an extension, there is no provision for a meeting of creditors, as the debtor would be proposing to pay his creditors in full. In the case of an arrangement by way of a composition, we are of the opinion that a meeting of creditors should be called. The creditors would there have the opportunity of learning, at first hand, the nature of the proposed arrangement and better able to assess the good faith and capacities of the debtor. The creditors would be in a position to weigh what they could expect to receive under the arrangement with what they would receive under an immediate bankruptcy. All creditors, except those whose claims are postponed, would then have the right to accept or reject the plan proposed. If a majority of the creditors at the meeting accept the plan, all creditors would be bound by it, including those whose claims are postponed. If a quorum is not present at the meeting, the arrangement would be deemed to have been accepted. The ratification of the court would not be required, but a creditor could, within ten days, apply to the court for an order annulling the arrangement where it is not in the best interest of all creditors or constitutes an abuse that amounts to fraud with respect to particular creditors. The annulment of the arrangement would, in such a case, result in the automatic bankruptcy of the debtor.

3.1.26 *Provisions Applicable to all Arrangements by Small Debtors:* The default of the small debtor would result in the summary setting aside of the arrangement and the creditors would then have the right to enforce their claim by any means available, including bankruptcy. There is a need, however, to provide for some flexibility in the operation of an arrangement by a small debtor. He may be faced with an emergency that prevents him from complying with the arrangement. For that reason, there should be a provision allowing the debtor, under certain conditions, to suspend his payments and to make up, after the term contemplated for the arrangement has expired, the payments he has missed. An attitude that would interpret the spirit of the plan as a contract to pay fixed periodic sums for a fixed term of time, without any provision for a variation in the plan where circumstances have changed, would defeat the aim of the plan.

3.1.27 We are of the opinion that there should be a real attempt, through an arrangement, to help the debtor to learn money management and to resist the many pressures that can lead to recurring financial difficulties and insecurity. In almost every community, there are agencies providing advice on the preparation of a family budget and financial guidance and counselling. It would be essential that every step be taken to ensure that debtors under a plan fully use these services. Because of the major role these agencies could have in the financial rehabilitation of the debtor, the government should be prepared to assist them and, where they do not exist, to provide the service directly to these small debtors.

3.1.28 Periodically, the debtor should be required to review the operation of his arrangement. To gain experience in the proper handling of money, he could, for example, be permitted to retain the payments payable under the arrangement and, under supervision, pay the dividends due to his creditors pursuant to the arrangement. In this way, it could be hoped that the debtor would acquire some experience in the management of money and, thereby, be able to, at least, recognize and avoid the circumstances that, in the future, could again lead him to financial disaster.

3.1.29 *Provisions Applicable to all Arrangements:* The difference between a debtor succeeding or failing in the making or the performance of an arrangement may well depend upon whether or not the debtor has been the victim of a single harsh, onerous or unconscionable transaction. The debt incurred in, or the continuing burden of, a particular transaction may make it difficult for him to come to an arrangement with his other creditors and to perform it, if one is accepted. Creditors may also be reluctant to accept an arrangement, if another creditor is permitted to keep an advantage obtained by harsh and unconscionable conduct. In other cases, they may have doubt that the debtor can carry out the arrangement, if he must continue to assume the liability of an onerous lease or contract. It is, therefore, important that, for all debtors, in all types of arrangements, there be summary procedures to provide relief against harsh and unconscionable transactions and for the disclaimer of executory contracts or leases.

3.1.30 The contract, which may be too onerous to the debtor, may be a commercial contract required to be performed over a period of time. In the case of a manufacturer, for example, it may be that, through miscalculation, each unit is produced by him at a loss, making the operation unprofitable. To the wage-earner, this may be a contract to purchase food for a home freezer, in an excessive amount or price, over a period of time, or an agreement to take a long series of dance lessons. To a businessman, a lease may be too onerous, if the arrangement he proposes to make contemplates his closing down certain facilities and his reducing the scope of his operations, in order to do business at a profit. For the debtor not in business, it may be advisable for him to move from a luxurious to a more modest dwelling. In all these cases, the debtor should, with suitable safeguards, be permitted to disclaim the contract or lease, and we so recommend. If, however, the other party minimizes his loss, a claim for damages should be provable in the arrangement.

3.1.31 In all the provinces of Canada, there are Unconscionable Transactions Relief Acts that permit the courts to intervene and grant relief where the cost of a loan is excessive, harsh and unconscionable. Although all the statutes are similar to each other, only a minority of them, however, apply to both vendor and lender credit transactions. Under all the statutes, the procedure to obtain relief is costly in time and money. For the purposes of an arrangement, the relief available may have little practical value, if the arrangement is completed, or well on the way to being completed, before final judgment is obtained. We accordingly recommend that there be a summary procedure that would permit the simple, speedy review of vendor and lender credit transactions, where the cost of the credit is excessive or the transaction is otherwise harsh and unconscionable.

3.1.32 *The Treatment of Secured Creditors:* We have referred, *supra* in 2.1.24 to 2.1.29, to the growth of secured financing, in recent decades, not only on the part of commercial debtors, but of consumers as well. We have also mentioned, *supra* in 2.1.06, the fact that used goods in the hands of a trustee, and, for the matter, in the hands of a secured creditor on repossession, have only a fraction of the value they had while in the hands of the debtor. An important question that arises is what should be the position of secured creditors under the various plans for an arrangement proposed in this Report. The question also arises as to how these creditors should be treated when, at the time the arrangement is made, they have repossessed their security, but the debt has not been entirely paid.

3.1.33 Under the general plan for an arrangement, supra in 3.1.08 and 3.1.09, which, we expect, should continue, in practice, to apply mostly, if not only, to commercial debtors, the secured creditor would keep his right, under his contract, to repossess or liquidate his security, notwithstanding the filing of a petition for, or the making of, an arrangement by the debtor. However, unless the debtor is otherwise in default, the mere fact that a debtor has become insolvent or bankrupt or has filed a petition for an arrangement, should not permit the creditor to accelerate the payments under the contract or to repossess or liquidate the security, notwithstanding any provision contained in the contract or any statutory rule to the contrary. The provisions regarding the evaluation of deficiency claims, which are described *infra* in 3.1.39, would, however, apply where the secured creditor exercises his right to repossess or has already exercised it, at the time of the filing of the petition for an arrangement.

3.1.34 Different considerations, however, arise in the case of arrangements by small debtors by way of extension or composition. Most small debtors, who find themselves in financial trouble, do not own, free from encumbrance, the property they need to maintain a decent standard of living. The car they need for work, their stove, refrigerator, furniture and often clothing, are being bought on time and are not owned outright, or else have been pledged as security for a loan to obtain relief from a previous financial crisis. Very often, it is the desperate effort of these debtors to keep up their payment on these secured debts that makes it impossible for them to pay any reasonable amount on their unsecured debts. When this occurs, the pressure put by the unsecured creditors upon the debtor is often more than the debtor can resist. As a result of a garnishee or a physical or mental breakdown, induced by the worry over his condition, he may lose his job. With the loss of his wages, he can no longer pay his secured creditors. When the creditors repossess their security, the situation of the debtor becomes still more desperate.

3.1.35 The legislative changes recommended *supra* in 3.1.33 should also apply in the case of arrangements by small debtors by way of extension or composition. Further restrictions should be imposed on the rights of a creditor having a security on a movable and on those of an unpaid vendor of movables, in the case of arrangements by small debtors. We believe that, under an extension arrangement, a creditor should not be permitted to exercise any right he may have under a security on a movable, unless the security was given during the sixty days prior to the filing of the petition for an arrangement and less than two-thirds of the amount owing has been paid. In order to provide for an adequate safeguard against abuses on the part of debtors, in these circumstances, the secured creditor should be given the right to choose, within a certain delay, between filing a claim under the plan or maintaining his rights under the contract. These restrictions should not prove detrimental to these creditors as, under such an arrangement, all creditors are expected to be paid in full.

3.1.36 Still other considerations apply in the case of an arrangement by way of a composition by a small debtor as, under such an arrangement, the debtor does not comtemplate paying his debts in full. In such circumstances, the secured creditor should be given the right to choose, within a certain delay, between filing a claim under the plan or maintaining his rights under the contract, in every case where the debtor has not already paid two-thirds of the amount owing.

3.1.37 The other question that remains to be discussed relates to the secured creditor who, before a petition for an arrangement has been filed, has already exercised his right to repossession, and is allowed to file a claim for the balance of his debt under the arrangement, as recommended *supra* in 3.1.33.

3.1.38 In these cases, the normal procedure would apply and, the credit grantor, where allowed under the relevant law, would have the right to seize the security, sell it and apply the proceeds of the realization against the balance of the debt. Under such procedure, any surplus is returned to the debtor, but, when the amount realized in insufficient to satisfy the debt, a claim may be made against the debtor for the deficiency between the amount owing and the proceeds of the realization of the security. When the re-sale of the security is not carried out with due care or the credit grantor is not diligent in obtaining the best price for the security seized, the deficiency claim against the debtor will be larger than what it should be. In many cases, the repossession and liquidation of the security result in a double loss to the debtor. He loses the property that is repossessed and he may stand to lose a good part of the loan or purchase price, if there is little realized on the re-sale.

3.1.39 To protect the debtor from the improvident foreclosure sale, we recommend that, in these cases, there be a summary procedure to adjust the value of the deficiency claim of a creditor to the amount it would have been, if the creditor had used reasonable diligence and prudence in the liquidation of the security.

3.1.40 Finally, in some cases, the debtor may have immovables that he should be allowed to keep in order to facilitate an arrangement with his creditors. To provide temporary relief, in these cases, we recommend that there should be a procedure permitting the temporary suspension of the principal payments on immovable property, any amount not paid during the period of the suspension, however, to be made up by the debtor, when the period of suspension is lifted.

3.1.41 *Moratorium*: The final recommendation that we make to assist insolvent debtors to satisfy their debts, other than by bankruptcy, is that the Governor in Council should have the authority to proclaim a moratorium for any specified region of the country or designated industry, whereby all proceedings against any debtor covered by the moratorium, unless otherwise permitted, would be stayed. When there is a severe drought, earthquake, fire, crop failure or other act of God or some serious financial failure, disaster or set-back that may adversely affect an entire community or region, those affected by the disaster may well need an opportunity to adjust to it and reorganize their affairs. A moratorium staying, for a short period of time, all proceedings against those affected may well be sufficient for them to avoid more difficult financial problems as, they may, after the moratorium is lifted, be able to meet their liabilities as they become due and, in this way, avoid personal bankruptcy. Although the term of the moratorium should not exceed a few months, perhaps six months at the most, there should be some safeguard against possible abuse and hardship, for example, by permitting a creditor to apply to the court to have the moratorium lifted in respect of a particular debt, if the balance of convenience and hardship indicates that it is just to do so.

3.1.42 *Bankruptcy*: Although it is desirable that all debtors should try to pay their due debts, without resorting to bankruptcy, there are some who cannot or will not pay their debts. For these debtors, there is a need for bankruptcy. In the following chapter, our recommendations, in this regard, will be discussed.

2 ARRANGEMENTS FOR THE CONSUMER DEBTOR

The Bankruptcy Bill (S-14)

2. (1) In this Act,
'consumer debtor' means
   (*a*) an individual who is insolvent but does not include such an individual where he has debts determined in accordance with subsection (2) exceeding twenty thousand dollars or such other amounts as may be prescribed; or
   (*b*) an individual who is a bankrupt and who prior to becoming a bankrupt was an individual referred to in paragraph *a*;
   (2) For the purpose of determining the amount of the debts of a consumer debtor
   (*a*) no account shall be taken of debts secured by real property, where such property constitutes the principal residence of the debtor;
   (*b*) only the amount of debts declared by the debtor at the time of filing a request for a proposed arrangement pursuant to section 65 shall be taken into account notwithstanding any other debts that are disclosed after such filing; and
   (*c*) where, pursuant to subsection 65(2), an administrator prepares a proposed arrangement with respect to individuals who are married to one another, a debt owed to one creditor by both individuals shall be taken into account only once.

PART III ARRANGEMENTS FOR THE CONSUMER DEBTOR

Interpretation

63. In this Part,
'date of the proposed arrangement' means the date inscribed as the date of filing pursuant to subsection 68(1);
'debtor' means a consumer debtor.

Filing of Proposed Arrangements

64. (1) Subject to subsection (2), any debtor may file a proposed arrangement in respect of himself, whereby he undertakes to pay a stated portion of the claims that are admissible under this Part or to pay them in full.

(2) A debtor who is a bankrupt may file a proposed arrangement in respect of himself

(*a*) if he did not become a bankrupt as a result of an annulment of an arrangement under this Part or Part IV; or

(*b*) if the first meeting of creditors under Part V has not been held.

65. (1) Every debtor who intends to file a proposed arrangement in respect of himself shall

(*a*) file a request in prescribed form with the administrator in the locality of the debtor;

(*b*) give all the information necessary to prepare the proposed arrangement to the administrator; and

(*c*) give all assistance in his power to the administrator in the preparation of the proposed arrangement.

(2) Where individuals are married to one another and both of them request the administrator to prepare a proposed arrangement in respect of them as if they were one debtor, the administrator may do so.

Duties of Debtor

67. Without restricting the generality of subsection 65(1), every debtor who files a request pursuant to paragraph 65(1)*a* shall

(*a*) disclose to the administrator such information as is necessary for the administrator to take into consideration the matters set out in section 69;

(*b*) disclose to the administrator the property of the debtor and any property that he holds in trust, the particulars of his debts, the names and addresses of his creditors, the security interest, if any, held by each of them and such other information as may be required by the administrator;

(*c*) disclose to the administrator any property transferred by the debtor, other than by way of gift, within one year preceding the filing of the request and how and to whom and for what consideration any part thereof was transferred, except property that was transferred in the ordinary course of affairs of the debtor or used for reasonable expenses;

(*d*) disclose to the administrator any property transferred by the debtor by way of gift within five years preceding the filing of the request;

(*e*) where required by the administrator, attend for examination under oath before the administrator;

(*f*) attend any meeting of creditors and give such information concerning his property and affairs as the creditors may reasonably require;

(*g*) where required by the administrator, examine as to their correctness the proofs of claim filed; and

(*h*) keep the administrator advised of his address until the arrangement is fully performed or annulled.

Duties of Administrator

68. (1) Where the administrator is satisfied that a debtor who files a request pursuant to paragraph 65(1)(*a*) is entitled to make an arrangement and that he can reasonably be expected, within the term of the arrangement, to earn more income or receive more property than will be necessary to support him and his dependants, the administrator shall prepare a proposed arrangement on behalf of the debtor and, when the debtor indicates he is in agreement with the proposed arrangement, inscribe on the proposed arrangement a date of filing.

69. Where the administrator prepares a proposed arrangement, he shall take into consideration
  (*a*) the circumstances and family responsibility of the debtor; and
  (*b*) the property and expected future earnings and property of the debtor.

Contents of Proposed Arrangement

70. A proposed arrangement
  (*a*) shall be in prescribed form and set out sufficient information concerning the property, income, debts and expenses of the debtor and such other material information with respect to the debtor as may be required to enable the creditors to make a reasoned decision in respect of the proposed arrangement;
  (*b*) shall state the time and the amounts to be paid to the administrator by the debtor and
    (i) the portion of the debts that the debtor proposed to pay, or
    (ii) the total amount that the debtor is to pay irrespective of the amount of claims filed together with a statement that, on the basis of the claims known at the time of preparing the proposed arrangement, the creditors should receive a stated amount or a stated portion of their claims;
  (*c*) may provide for the payment of claims for less than a specified amount in advance of the payment of other claims; and
  (*d*) may include any other provision not inconsistent with this Part.

Stay of Proceedings

71. (1) Subject to subsections (2) and (5), no creditor who would have an admissible claim pursuant to section 76 if an arrangement were made may, from the date of the proposed arrangement, exercise a remedy against the debtor or his property or institute or continue a proceeding for the recovery of a debt from the debtor until
  (*a*) the proposed arrangement is withdrawn or rejected; or
  (*b*) the court, on application, so allows, in which case the remedy may be exercised or the proceeding may be instituted or continued subject to such terms and conditions as the court may impose.

(2) Subsection (1) does not operate to prevent a creditor from exercising a remedy against a debtor or his property or from instituting or continuing a proceeding with respect to any of the following:
  (*a*) any right the creditor may have as a secured creditor to realize or otherwise deal with the property subject to the security interest of such creditor where such security interest is in property that is perishable or likely to depreciate rapidly in value;
  (*b*) any acts that are required by law to be performed to render a transfer effective against third parties, to prevent a security interest from being terminated, or to permit perfection of a security interest or other right by legal action, registration or otherwise;
  (*c*) any right the creditor may have as a secured creditor to collect, take possession of, or take conservatory measures with respect to, any property subject to his security interest;
  (*d*) any right in addition to the rights set out in paragraphs (*a*) to (*c*) and (*e*) the creditor may have as a secured creditor to realize or otherwise deal with the property subject to his security interest but only to the extent that the secured creditor realizes or otherwise deals with such property in a manner consistent with the continued operation of the debtor's business; and
  (*e*) any acts that are required to permit the completion or closing of any contractual obligation made in good faith and without knowledge of the filing of a notice of intention or a

proposed arrangement if, on receipt of knowledge of such filing, the creditor notifies the administrator of the contractual obligation and gives him full particulars thereof.

(6) Notwithstanding any other Act of Parliament or of the legislature of a province or any agreement governing the rights of a creditor or a class of creditors, no person may realize or otherwise deal with property of a debtor, terminate a lease or other agreement, or claim any accelerated payment under a lease or other agreement by reason only of the insolvency of a debtor or by reason of any proceeding taken under this Act where

(*a*) a notice of intention referred to in subsection 66(1) is filed;

(*b*) a proposed arrangement is filed; or

(*c*) an arrangement has been made under this Part in respect of the debtor and the debtor is not in default thereunder.

Documents to be Sent

72. The administrator shall, within five days after the date of the proposed arrangement, send to every known creditor of the debtor

(*a*) a copy of the proposed arrangement;

(*b*) a proof of claim in prescribed form; and

(*c*) a notice, in prescribed form, stating that no meeting of creditors will be called unless creditors having more than fifty per cent in value of the claims admissible pursuant to section 76 request the administrator to call a meeting of creditors by sending to him, within twenty-five days of the date of the proposed arrangement,

  (i) a notice, in writing, requesting the administrator to call a meeting of creditors, and

  (ii) completed proofs of claim in prescribed form.

Meetings of Creditors

73. (1) Where creditors having more than fifty per cent in value of the claims admissible pursuant to section 76 request the administrator to call a meeting of creditors, the administrator shall call a meeting of the creditors of the debtor to be held not later than forty-five days from the date of the proposed arrangement.

(5) A debtor may withdraw a proposed arrangement at any time prior to the acceptance or deemed acceptance of the proposed arrangement.

(6) Where, one-half hour after the time appointed for a meeting of creditors under this section, a quorum is not present, the proposed arrangement is deemed to have been accepted by the creditors.

(9) Where the administrator is not requested to call a meeting of creditors pursuant to subsection (1), the proposed arrangement is deemed to be accepted by the creditors.

(10) Where, pursuant to this section, a proposed arrangement is withdrawn, rejected, deemed to be rejected or amended the administrator shall forthwith send to every known creditor a notice in the prescribed form.

(11) A proposed arrangement that is accepted or deemed to be accepted by the creditors is an arrangement under this Part.

General

76. Subject to sections 77, 78 and 79, a claim is admissible in an arrangement made under this Part for any debt

(*a*) to which the debtor is subject at the date of the proposed arrangement; and

(*b*) where the debtor is a bankrupt, from which he has been released by the effect of the bankruptcy order.

77. (1) Subject to subsection (2), no claim is admissible under an arrangement made under this Part where the claim is secured by real property.

(2) Where at the date of the proposed arrangement the value of the real property of the debtor subject to a security interest is less than the total amount owing under the security interest in the property, the secured creditor has an admissible claim for any difference between the amount owing under his security interest in the property and the amount he would receive if the real property were sold for an amount equal to the value of the real property.

78. (1) No claim is admissible under an arrangement made under this Part where the claim is for a debt secured by personal property if

(*a*) less than two-thirds of the amount of the original contractual obligation has been paid; and

(*b*) the creditor, by giving the prescribed notice within twenty-five days of the date of the proposed arrangement, elects not to participate in the arrangement and to rely on any right he may have to realize or otherwise deal with the property.

(2) Notwithstanding subsection (1), where less than two-thirds of a contractual obligation referred to in paragraph (*a*) of that subsection has been paid, a claim for the amount owing is admissible under an arrangement made under this Part if, within the six months preceding the date of the proposed arrangement, the debtor entered into a contract with the creditor whereby a former debt to the creditor was extinguished and

(*a*) the amount outstanding on such former debt at the date of the contract was included as all or part of the amount payable to the creditor under such contract; or

(*b*) the personal property given to secure the former claim forms part of the property that is subject to the security interest under such contract.

(3) Where pursuant to paragraph (1)(*b*) a secured creditor elects not to participate in an arrangement, the only remedy that the creditor may exercise, in case of default by the debtor, is any right such creditor may have to repossess the personal property or to realize it, unless

(*a*) the proposed arrangement is withdrawn or rejected; or

(*b*) the arrangement is annulled.

(4) Where a secured creditor who elects not to participate in an arrangement exercises any right to repossess or to realize the personal property given to secure his claim before the proposed arrangement is withdrawn or rejected or the arrangement is annulled, the debtor is released from the total amount of that claim.

79. (1) Notwithstanding anything in this Act, no claim is admissible for, and no debtor who makes an arrangement is released from,

(*a*) a fine or penalty imposed by a court;

(*b*) a debt arising out of a recognizance or bail bond; or

(*c*) a liability to pay maintenance and support in respect of another person for a period subsequent to the date of the proposed arrangement.

(2) Notwithstanding anything in this Act, a claim is admissible for, but no debtor who makes an arrangement is released from, any debt arising out of fraud where the debtor has been convicted of such fraud under the *Criminal Code*.

80. (1) Where a claim of a secured creditor is not admissible under an arrangement made under this Part, the administrator may, notwithstanding anything in this Part, require, by giving the prescribed notice, the secured creditor to file with the administrator a proof of security interest together with a valuation made by the secured creditor of the property subject to the security interest.

(2) On application, a court may postpone any right a secured creditor may have to realize or otherwise deal with property subject to a security interest on such terms and conditions and for

such period of time as the court thinks fit, if such postponement does not materially adversely affect the secured creditor.

Disallowance of Proofs

84. (1) The administrator may require a creditor to supply further evidence to substantiate a proof of claim or proof of security interest.

(2) The administrator may disallow, in whole or in part, any claim other than a claim in respect of a security interest.

(3) Without limiting the generality of subsection 2, where the cost of money borrowed by a debtor is excessive or the terms of a transaction are harsh or unconscionable, the administrator may disallow any claim in respect of the money borrowed to the extent that the loan is unenforceable or may be reduced under any Act of Parliament or of the legislature of a province governing harsh or unconscionable transactions.

85. Where a proposed arrangement is accepted or deemed to be accepted, the debtor is released, to the extent provided for in the arrangement, from the debts for which a claim is admissible under section 76 and to which he was subject at the date of the proposed arrangement and, if he is a bankrupt, from the debts from which he had been released by the effect of the bankruptcy order.

86. (1) An arrangement made under this Part is binding on the debtor and every creditor of the debtor who has an admissible claim and operates

(*a*) to dismiss any petition that is pending in respect of the debtor; and

(*b*) where the debtor is a bankrupt, to annul the bankruptcy order and to revest in the debtor all the property that vested in the trustee by the effect of the bankruptcy order unless the terms of the arrangement otherwise provide and to revive the debts of the debtor that were discharged by the bankruptcy order.

(2) Where, pursuant to subsection (1), a petition is dismissed or a bankruptcy order is annulled, a claim for costs or remuneration arising out of the bankruptcy proceedings is admissible under this Part.

87. (1) The administrator shall exercise such supervision over and give such advice to a debtor who files a request under section 65 as the administrator thinks may be helpful to assist the debtor to rehabilitate himself financially and to carry out his financial obligations.

88. A debtor in respect of whom an arrangement is made under this Part shall, during the term of the arrangement,

(*a*) disclose to the administrator, on request, any material change in his assets and debts; and

(*b*) execute such instruments and generally do such acts or things in relation to his property as may be ordered by the court or reasonably required by the administrator

89. Where a creditor who is bound by an arrangement requests information in addition to the statement referred to in paragraph 92(1)(*b*), the administrator shall report to any such creditor

(*a*) the terms of the arrangement; and

(*b*) the manner in which the debtor is performing his obligations under the arrangement.

90. (1) An assignment of existing or future wages, made by a debtor before the date of the proposed arrangement in respect of himself is of no effect in respect of wages that become receivable after the date of the proposed arrangement.

(2) In order to ensure compliance with the terms of a proposed arrangement the administrator may, at any time after the date of the proposed arrangement, require of, and take from, the debtor an assignment of any amount payable to the debtor, including wages, that may become payable in the future, but no such assignment can, unless the debtor otherwise agrees, be for an

amount greater than is due and payable pursuant to the terms of the proposed arrangement.

(3) An assignment made pursuant to subsection (2) is of no effect against a person owing the amount payable until a notice of the assignment is served on that person.

(4) This section ceases to apply where the proposed arrangement is rejected or deemed to be rejected by the creditors.

91. (1) The administrator may issue a certificate in prescribed form in respect of an arrangement and he may cause the certificate to be filed in any place where a certificate of judgment or writ of execution may be filed.

(2) A certificate filed pursuant to subsection 1 shall, subject to the rights of secured creditors in existence at the time of the filing of the certificate,

(a) operate as a certificate of judgment or writ of execution when so filed; and

(b) be a charge on the property of the debtor.

92. (1) The administrator shall, at least once every six months,

(a) distribute rateably among the creditors the moneys received by him for the purposes of the arrangement in accordance with the terms thereof; and

(b) send to each creditor whose claim has not been disallowed a statement indicating the manner in which the debtor is performing his obligations under the arrangement.

(2) Notwithstanding paragraph (1)(a), the administrator is not required to pay a dividend of less than ten dollars or such greater amount as may be prescribed except in the case of a final dividend.

94. (1) The release by this Part of a debtor in respect of a debt does not affect the liability of a person who was, in respect of the debt, a partner or a guarantor or jointly and severally bound with the debtor unless, and to the extent that, such person is released by this Part.

(2) No person shall bring an action against a debtor to obtain payment or satisfaction in respect of a debt from which the debtor has been released by this Part notwithstanding

(a) the giving by the debtor of

(i) an express or implied agreement to pay the debt,

(ii) an express or implied promise to pay the debt, or

(iii) an express or implied acknowledgement that the debt is owing; or

(b) the giving of any new consideration to the debtor.

(3) Where, after a debtor is released in respect of a debt by this Part, a person becomes indebted to the debtor, such person shall not claim as a set-off the amount of any debt in respect of which the debtor has been released by this Part.

(4) No employer shall dismiss, suspend, lay-off or otherwise discipline a debtor on the ground that

(a) a proposed arrangement is to be or has been filed in respect of the debtor;

(b) an arrangement has been made in respect of the debtor; or

(c) the debtor has made an assignment of wages pursuant to subsection 90(2) that is enforceable against the employer.

(5) No public utility may alter its service, refuse service or otherwise discriminate against a debtor or his estate on the ground that

(a) a proposed arrangement is to be or has been filed to respect of the debtor;

(b) an arrangement has been made in respect of the debtor; or

(c) a debt owed to the utility for services rendered to the debtor prior to the date of the proposed arrangement in respect of the debtor has not been paid.

(6) Subsection 5 does not preclude a public utility from discontinuing service if the debtor does not pay for services rendered subsequent to the date of the proposed arrangement.

Term of Arrangement

95. (1) Subject to subsection (2), an arrangement made under this Part shall be for a term not exceeding three years.

(2) Subject to subsection (3), where the administrator is of the opinion that a debtor cannot reasonably be expected to fulfil the obligations imposed on him by an arrangement made under this Part, the administrator may vary the term, the amounts to be paid or the times of payment set out in the arrangement but not so as to extend the term beyond four years from the date of the proposed arrangement.

Annulment of Arrangement

96. (1) On application and on such notice to the administrator as may be prescribed, the court may annul an arrangement made under this Part where it constitutes a fraud with respect to a particular creditor and, on such an annulment, the debtor is deemed to have filed a petition in respect of himself under subsection 135(1) that is in accordance with paragraphs 134(1)(*a*) and (*b*) and the administrator shall forthwith make a bankruptcy order in respect of the debtor.

(2) On application and on such notice to the administrator as may be prescribed, the court may annul an arrangement made under this Part where the debtor defaults

    (*a*) in fulfilling his duties under this Act; or

    (*b*) in complying with the terms of the arrangement, an order of the court or a direction of the administrator.

(3) Unless the administrator varies an arrangement pursuant to subsection 95(2) the arrangement is deemed to be annulled

    (*a*) where the payments to be made under the arrangement are payable on a monthly or shorter basis, on the day the debtor is in default in his payments in an amount equal to the total of three months payments; or

    (*b*) where the payments to be made under the arrangement are on a basis other than that referred to in paragraph (*a*), ten days after such payments become payable and are not paid.

(4) When an arrangement made under this Part is annulled

    (*a*) the administrator shall, within ten days of the annulment, send a notice in prescribed form to the debtor and the creditors bound by the arrangement;

    (*b*) the debtor is not, without leave of the court, entitled to further relief under this Part or Part IV while any debt for which a claim was admitted in the arrangement is unpaid;

    (*c*) the rights of the creditors are revived for the amount of their claims less any dividend received except where the arrangement is annulled under subsection (1); and

    (*d*) the administrator shall distribute to the creditors bound by the arrangement the moneys received by him and not yet distributed, unless a bankruptcy order is made with respect to the debtor prior to the distribution, in which case the administrator shall remit such moneys to the trustee of the estate for distribution to the creditors of the estate in bankruptcy.

Right to File Petition

97. (1) Any creditor who is bound by an arrangement and who is entitled to file a petition in respect of an insolvent debtor pursuant to section 136 or 137 may, within thirty days of a notice sent by the administrator pursuant to subsection 73(10) or 95(10) or paragraph 96(4)(*a*), file with the administrator a petition in respect of a debtor where

    (*a*) a proposed arrangement with respect to such debtor is withdrawn, rejected or deemed to be rejected pursuant to section 73;

    (*b*) an arrangement is rejected or deemed to be rejected pursuant to section 95;

    (*c*) the court annuls an arrangement with respect to the debtor pursuant to subsection 96(2); or

    (*d*) such arrangement is deemed to have been annulled under subsection 96(3).

3 COMMERCIAL ARRANGEMENTS

The Bankruptcy Bill, (S-14)

Proposed Arrangements

    100. (1) Subject to subsection (2), a proposed arrangement may be filed in respect of

    (*a*) an estate of a bankrupt;

    (*b*) a debtor who is insolvent; or

    (*c*) an insurance company, as defined in section 332, where the filing is authorized by a superintendent of insurance referred to in that section and the insurance company is insolvent.

    (2) A proposed arrangement may not be filed in respect of

    (*a*) a bank or other corporation if any of the deposits held by such bank or corporation are insured by the Canada Deposit Insurance Corporation or are insured or guaranteed under a provincial enactment that provides depositors with protection against the loss of moneys on deposit with financial institutions; or

    (*b*) a credit union, within the meaning of subsection 137(6) of the *Income Tax Act*.

    (3) Subject to subsection (2), a proposed arrangement or an amendment thereto may be filed

    (*a*) by a bankrupt or a debtor referred to in subsection (1);

    (*b*) by the trustee of an estate;

    (*c*) where a corporation is in the process of being liquidated or dissolved and the corporation is insolvent, by the liquidator of the corporation;

    (*d*) in respect of an estate of a bankrupt, by any person who has, in respect of the bankruptcy, an admissible claim that has not been disallowed;

    (*e*) where a corporation is bankrupt,

      (i) by a receiver of the corporation whether or not he is so authorized in the instrument under which he is appointed, or

      (ii) by the trustee under a trust indenture for a holder or any class of holders of a debt obligation issued by the corporation or a predecessor of the corporation; or

    (*f*) where a corporation is insolvent, with the permission of the court,

      (i) by a receiver of the corporation whether or not he is so authorized in the instrument under which he is appointed, or

      (ii) by the trustee under a trust indenture for a holder or any class of holders of a debt obligation issued by the corporation or a predecessor of the corporation.

    101. (1) Before a debtor who is not a bankrupt files a proposed arrangement, he may file a notice of intention in prescribed form with the administrator in the locality of the debtor stating therein

    (*a*) his intention to file a proposed arrangement; and

    (*b*) the name of the trustee who has agreed in writing to act as the trustee under the arrangement and a copy of such agreement shall be filed with the notice of intention.

    (2) Unless the court, on application, otherwise orders, where a notice of intention is filed pursuant to subsection (1), no creditor of the debtor may exercise a remedy against the debtor or

his property or institute or continue a proceeding for the recovery of a claim for a period of ten days from the date of filing the notice.

(3) Notwithstanding subsection (2), a creditor who, without knowledge of the filing of a notice of intention, exercises a remedy against a debtor or his property or institutes or continues a proceeding for the recovery of a claim is not guilty of an offence under this Act or the *Criminal Code* by reason only of his exercising the remedy or instituting or continuing the proceeding.

(4) Where a third party who has no knowledge of the filing of a notice of intention by a debtor acquires property of that debtor from a creditor who exercised a remedy against the debtor or his property, the acquisition is not invalid by reason of the exercise of the remedy by the creditor.

(5) Unless the court otherwise orders, where a debtor does not file a proposed arrangement under subsection 102(1) within ten days of the filing of a notice of intention pursuant to subsection (1)

   (*a*) if a petition (hereinafter in this section referred to as the 'first petition') had been filed before the notice of intention was filed, the debtor is deemed to have filed a petition in respect of himself under subsection 135(1) on the day the first petition was filed; and

   (*b*) if a petition had not been filed before the notice of intention was filed, the debtor is deemed to have filed a petition in respect of himself under subsection 135(1) on the day the notice of intention was filed with the administrator.

(6) Where a petition in respect of a debtor is deemed to be filed under subsection (5), the administrator shall, unless the court, on application, otherwise orders, forthwith make a bankruptcy order in respect of the debtor and appoint as trustee the trustee named in the first petition or, if no first petition has been filed, the trustee named in the notice of intention and that trustee shall, within five days of the date of bankruptcy, call the meeting of creditors required by section 203.

(7) Subsection (2) does not apply where a notice of intention is filed within six months of the filing of any preceding notice of intention.

102. (1) Proceedings for an arrangement shall be instituted by filing with the administrator in the locality of the debtor

   (*a*) a proposed arrangement in prescribed form setting out the terms thereof; and

   (*b*) a statement, in prescribed form or in a form as near thereto as circumstances permit, of the assets and liabilities of the debtor certified as being correct to the belief and knowledge of the person filing the proposed arrangement.

...

(7) Where a proposed arrangement has been filed with respect to a debtor, no creditor of the debtor having a claim admissible under section 111 may exercise a remedy against the debtor or his property or institute or continue a proceeding for the recovery of the claim in respect of the debtor or his property,

   (*a*) subject to subsection (8), until the proposed arrangement is withdrawn, the creditors reject the proposed arrangement, or an arrangement is made; or

   (*b*) unless the court so allows, in which case the remedy may be exercised or the proceeding may be instituted or continued subject to such terms and conditions as the court may impose.

(8) Subsection 101(2) and subsection (7) do not operate to prevent a creditor from exercising a remedy against a debtor or his property or from instituting or continuing a proceeding with respect to

   (*a*) any right the creditor may have as a secured creditor to realize or otherwise deal with the property subject to the security interest of such creditor where such security interest is in property that is perishable or likely to depreciate rapidly in value;

(*b*) any acts that are required by law to be performed to render a transfer effective against third parties, to prevent a security interest from being terminated, or to permit perfection of a security interest or other right by legal action, registration or otherwise;

(*c*) any right the creditor may have as a secured creditor to collect, take possession of, or take conservatory measures with respect to, any property subject to his security interest;

(*d*) any right in addition to the rights set out in paragraphs (*a*) to (*c*) and (*e*) to (*f*) the creditor may have as a secured creditor to realize or otherwise deal with the property subject to his security interest but only to the extent that the secured creditor realizes or otherwise deals with such property in a manner consistent with the continued operation of the debtor's business;

(*e*) any acts that are required to permit the completion or closing of any contractual obligation made in good faith and without knowledge of the filing of a notice of intention or a proposed arrangement if, on receipt of knowledge of such filing, the creditor notifies the trustee named in the notice or proposed arrangement of the contractual obligation and gives him full particulars thereof; and

(*f*) the sale of assets of the debtor by a secured creditor where the sale is to be by way of auction or tender and the sale has been advertised.

(9) Notwithstanding any other Act of Parliament or of the legislature of a province or any agreement, no person may terminate a lease or other agreement, or claim any accelerated payment under a lease or other agreement by reason only of the insolvency of a debtor or by reason of any proceeding taken in consequence thereof where

(*a*) a notice of intention is filed;

(*b*) a proposed arrangement is filed; or

(*c*) an arrangement under this Part is being performed with respect to the debtor.

103. (1) For the purpose of this section, 'partly performed contract' means a contract for the purchase, sale, supply or lease of personal property or services in respect of which delivery of the personal property or performance of the services or payment in full of the consideration is not made at the time the contract is executed, but does not include a lease of personal property that creates a security interest within the meaning of subsection 3(1).

(2) Where a proposed arrangement is filed in respect of a lessor under a contract relating to a lease of goods, the proposed arrangement shall not contain a provision referred to in subsection (3) in respect of the contract.

(3) Subject to the consent of any secured creditor who has an interest in the partly performed contract, where a debtor in respect of whom a proposed arrangement is filed is a party to a partly performed contract, the proposed arrangement may contain a provision repudiating the contract.

(4) Where a proposed arrangement contains a provision referred to in subsection (3), the other party may, by notice in writing to the trustee named in the proposed arrangement, accept the repudiation at any time before the proposed arrangement is approved by the court.

(5) A repudiation, pursuant to this section, of a partly performed contract is effective on the day

(*a*) the trustee named in the proposed arrangement receives a notice under subsection (4), or

(*b*) the proposed arrangement is approved by a court under section 117, whichever is the earlier.

(6) Where an arrangement provides for the repudiation of a partly performed contract, the other party to the partly performed contract has an admissible claim under the arrangement for the amount of any loss, as determined under section 248, that he suffers by reason of the repudiation.

(7) Where a proposed arrangement in respect of a debtor provides for the repudiation of a partly performed contract, the other party to the contract, whether or not he accepts the repudiation pursuant to subsection (4), is deemed for the purpose of voting on the proposed arrangement to be a creditor whose claim is materially and adversely affected.

(8) For the purpose of determining the number of votes that a creditor referred to in subsection (7) is entitled to cast at a meeting of creditors, the partly performed contract proposed to be repudiated under subsection 3 is deemed to have been repudiated on the day the proposed arrangement was filed with the administrator.

(9) The other party to a partly performed contract that is proposed to be repudiated under subsection (3) is not a member of a separate class by reason only of the proposed repudiation.

104. (1) Where a debtor in respect of whom a proposed arrangement is filed is a lessee under a lease of real property, the proposed arrangement may contain a provision repudiating the lease.

(2) Subject to subsection (9), the effective date of repudiation of a lease, pursuant to this section, is the later of

(a) the day the proposed arrangement containing a provision repudiating the lease is approved by a court under section 117, and

(b) any day respecting the proposed repudiation set out in the proposed arrangement that is not more than three months later than the day referred to in paragraph (a).

(3) The repudiation of a lease under subsection (1) operates to determine, as of the effective date of repudiation established under subsection (2), the rights, duties and liabilities of the lessee in respect of the lease repudiated and, subject to subsections (12) and (13), discharges the lessee from liability in respect of the lease repudiated.

(4) For the purpose of voting on the proposed arrangement, a lessor who is party to a lease that is proposed to be repudiated under subsection (1) is deemed to be a creditor with an admissible claim that is materially and adversely affected.

(5) For the purpose of determining the number of votes that a lessor referred to in subsection (4) may cast at any meeting of creditors, the claim of the lessor is deemed to be for the amount he would have been entitled to claim as determined under subsection (11), if the effective date of repudiation of the lease had been the date of filing the proposed arrangement.

(6) The lessor under a lease that is proposed to be repudiated under subsection (1) is not a member of a separate class by reason only of the proposed repudiation.

(7) Where a lessee referred to in subsection (1) had, before he filed a proposed arrangement, sublet the whole or any part of the leased property or granted a security interest in the leased property, the trustee shall serve on the sub-lessee or secured creditor, as the case may be, concurrently with sending copies of the proposed arrangement to creditors under subsection 109(2), a copy of the proposed arrangement and a concise statement of the rights of the sub-lessee or secured creditor under this section.

(8) Notwithstanding the repudiation of a lease pursuant to this section, a sub-lessee or secured creditor who is served with the documents referred to in subsection (7) may, not later than fifteen days after the proposed arrangement is approved by the court under section 117, elect on the effective date of repudiation of the lease to stand in the same position with the lessor as if he were a direct lessee from the lessor, but a sub-lessee or secured creditor who so elects is subject

(a) to the same obligations, except in respect of rent, as the lessee was subject to under the lease as of the date the proposed arrangement was filed; and

(b) in respect of rent, to pay to the lessor

(i) the same rent the sub-lessee paid to the lessee, if such rent is greater than that payable by the lessee to the lessor, or

(ii) the same rent the lessee paid to the lessor with respect to the premises leased by the sub-lessee, if that rent is greater than that payable by the sub-lessee to the lessee.

(9) Where a lessee who repudiates a lease pursuant to this section had granted a sublease of, or security interest in, the leased property before he filed the proposed arrangement, the effective date of repudiation of the lease set out in the proposed arrangement shall be a day not earlier than the sixteenth day following the day on which the court approves the proposed arrangement under section 117.

(10) Where a sub-lessee or secured creditor who is served with the documents referred to in subsection (7) does not make an election under subsection (8), the sublease of, or security interest in, the leased property terminates on the effective date of repudiation of the lease determined under subsection 2.

(11) Subject to subsection (12), a lessor shall not make a claim for accelerated rent or for damages arising out of a repudiation of a lease pursuant to this section.

(12) A lessor may, where the lease is repudiated pursuant to this section, claim the lesser of

(a) the amount of the rent for the remaining term of the lease, and

(b) six months rent under the lease or such greater amount as is approved in the arrangement, and, where he does so, there shall be deducted from the claim

(c) the balance of any deposit given to the lessor by the lessee for any purpose;

(d) any amount received by the lessor as accelerated rent;

(e) any rent paid in advance by the lessee; and

(f) the value of any security interest taken by or granted to the lessor in respect of rent or other moneys due under the lease.

(13) Subject to subsection 102(9), nothing in this section affects the right of a lessor to terminate a lease of real property proposed to be repudiated under subsection (1) for any reason other than the proposed repudiation.

(14) Where a bankruptcy order is made in respect of a debtor who has made a proposed arrangement that includes a repudiation of a lease of real property pursuant to this section, the claim of the lessor against the estate of the debtor shall be determined in accordance with subsection 197(24).

(15) In this section, 'lessor' includes a landlord and 'lessee' includes a tenant.

105. (1) There shall be set out in every proposed arrangement the terms thereof, including

(a) the name of the trustee who has agreed to be the trustee under the arrangement;

(b) details of payments including the names of the persons receiving the payments made or proposed to be made by the debtor or the person filing the proposed arrangement or any person on behalf of the debtor or such person for services rendered in connection with

   (i) the preparation and presentation of the proposed arrangement, and

   (ii) the carrying out of the proposed arrangement;

(c) the provision made for the payment of

   (i) the expenses and remuneration of any interim receiver, and

   (ii) the costs and disbursements incidental to the preparation and presentation of the proposed arrangement and the carrying out of the arrangement;

(d) the nature and timing of proposed payments including payments by way of an issue of securities proposed to be made by the debtor to the trustee and to the creditors whose claims would be affected by the arrangement;

(e) where the debtor is a corporation, details of any provisions that affect the rights of shareholders of the corporation and any provisions that relate to raising of additional capital including the details of

   (i) any securities proposed to be issued as a term of the arrangement, and

(ii) the persons to whom the securities will be issued and the consideration therefor; and

(*f*) the name of any guarantor of the proposed arrangement.

(2) There shall be set out in a proposed arrangement or annexed to the proposed arrangement

(*a*) an agreement with a trustee referred to in paragraph (1)(*a*);

(*b*) any agreement of a guarantor referred to in paragraph (1)(*f*);

(*c*) a list of all creditors of the debtor and their addresses, subdivided to indicate

(i) the claims of each creditor whose claim is not affected by the arrangement, and

(ii) the claims of creditors, individually or by class of claims, whose claims are affected by the arrangement and, as far as it is possible for the person filing the proposed arrangement to determine, how the arrangement will affect each claim or class of claims; and

(*d*) a statement in prescribed form of the assets and liabilities of the debtor.

(3) Every trustee, solicitor and accountant shall disclose any agreement as to fees and the amount of any retainer or deposit that he receives in respect of services to an estate.

(4) Section 37 does not apply in respect of an arrangement under this Part unless

(*a*) the debtor or a majority of creditors voting as a single class at a meeting of creditors request the registrar to tax the accounts referred to in that section; or

(*b*) the arrangement sets out the total amount that the debtor is to pay irrespective of the claims filed.

(5) A person who guarantees the carrying out of a proposed arrangement is bound to fulfil his obligations under the guarantee, notwithstanding

(*a*) the withdrawal under subsection 102(3) of the notice of intention relating to the proposed arrangement, the proposed arrangement or the arrangement;

(*b*) any misrepresentation by the debtor named in the arrangement to the creditors or the guarantor; or

(*c*) any default by the debtor in carrying out the arrangement.

106. (1) Any provision that is reasonable in the circumstances and not inconsistent with this Part and Part VI may be included in a proposed arrangement.

(2) Notwithstanding subsection (1), a proposed arrangement may provide

(*a*) for the payment of the admissible claims of a class or part of a class of unsecured creditors at a level of priority other than the level of priority determined pursuant to section 265; and

(*b*) for the payment of the claims of a class or part of a class of secured creditors at a level of priority other than the level of priority determined by the law applicable to the security interests held by the class or part of the class.

(3) Where a term of a proposed arrangement provides

(*a*) that claims of a class or part of a class of unsecured creditors shall rank at a lower level of priority than the level determined pursuant to section 265, or

(*b*) that claims of a class or part of a class of secured creditors shall rank at a lower level of priority than the level of priority determined by the law applicable to the security instrument held by the class,

the creditors in the class so affected are entitled to vote separately in respect of that term and such term is accepted by the creditors so affected if at least two-thirds of the votes cast by the class is in favour of acceptance of the term.

(4) Where a proposed arrangement provides that a person who has a security interest in property of a debtor is not to be affected by the arrangement, the trustee is not entitled to require such person to file a proof thereof under subsection 255(1).

(5) A person who has a security interest in property of the debtor may file a proof of claim in

an arrangement but such proof of claim must be filed at least five days prior to the first meeting of creditors.

(6) Where a proposed arrangement so provides, sections 168 to 185 apply with such modifications as the circumstances require.

(7) For the purposes of subsection (6),

(*a*) any reference in sections 168 to 185 to the date of filing a petition shall be construed as a reference to the earlier of filing a notice of intention and the filing of a proposed arrangement; and

(*b*) any reference in sections 168 to 185 to a bankrupt shall be construed as a reference to the debtor in respect of whom the proposed arrangement is filed.

108. (1) The trustee named in a proposed arrangement shall make an appraisal of the property and a reasonable investigation of the affairs of the debtor sufficient to enable him to report to the creditors

(*a*) the financial situation of the debtor;

(*b*) whether or not any agreement purporting to give a security interest to a creditor is a valid agreement;

(*c*) whether or not the debtor made a transfer

　(i) that is material,

　(ii) that is a dividend, or

　(iii) that is a redemption or purchase of shares

that a court could review or set aside under sections 168 to 185 if a bankruptcy order had been made in respect of the debtor on the date on which a notice of intention or the proposed arrangement is filed, whichever date is the earlier;

(*d*) the causes of the insolvency of the debtor; and

(*e*) any other material facts required to enable a creditor to make a reasoned decision to accept or not to accept the proposed arrangement.

(2) The court, on application of the trustee, may order any person to produce any documents in his possession or under his control or disclose any other information that he may have that the court considers relevant and desirable in connection with the appraisal of the property and the investigation of the affairs of the debtor undertaken pursuant to subsection (1).

109. (1) The first meeting of creditors whose claims are to be affected by an arrangement shall be held within thirty days from the date of filing the proposed arrangement with the administrator on such day and at such place as the trustee and administrator agree to.

(2) The trustee named in the proposed arrangement shall forthwith call the first meeting of creditors by sending to the administrator, the debtor and each creditor at his latest known address

(*a*) a notice setting forth

　(i) the date, time and place of the meeting, and

　(ii) such other information as may be prescribed;

(*b*) a copy of the proposed arrangement and the documents referred to in subsection 105(2);

(*c*) a form of proof of claim in prescribed form; and

(*d*) a proxy and a mail ballot in prescribed form.

(3) In addition to the documents referred to in subsection (2), the trustee shall, at least ten days prior to the date of the meeting, send

(*a*) to every creditor and to the administrator a copy of the report on the result of the investigation made pursuant to subsection 108(1); and

(*b*) to every creditor any amendment to the proposed arrangement the trustee had filed with the administrator.

(4) Where the terms of a proposed arrangement may materially adversely affect the rights of a

shareholder of a debtor corporation, the trustee may apply to the court for directions as to whether the notice referred to in paragraph (2)(*a*), the copy of the proposed arrangement or any other information should be sent to the shareholder.

110. (1) At the first meeting of creditors held pursuant to section 109, the creditors shall consider the affairs of the debtor, including the report on the result of the investigation made pursuant to subsection 108(1), and

(*a*) accept or reject the proposed arrangement sent pursuant to subsection 109(2) and any amendment sent pursuant to paragraph 109(3)(*b*); or

(*b*) accept the proposed arrangement with such amendments as they agree to where such amendments provide all creditors whose claims are to be affected by the arrangement with benefits equal to or more advantageous than those provided in the proposed arrangement.

(3) Where there is no quorum for the first meeting of creditors or where there are insufficient votes cast in favour of acceptance of the proposed arrangement, the proposed arrangement is, unless the chairman of the meeting adjourns it for reasonable cause, deemed to be rejected.

(4) Where, at the first meeting of creditors,

(*a*) the person filing a proposed arrangement,

(*b*) any guarantor of the proposed arrangement, and

(*c*) the majority of the creditors, voting as one class, who are affected by the arrangement and who are present or represented at the meeting

agree to the adjournment of the meeting, the Chairman shall adjourn the meeting.

111. Where a claim of a creditor is to be affected in whole or in part by an arrangement, he has an admissible claim to that extent under the arrangement.

112. (1) Where a person filing a proposed arrangement does not apply to a court under section 99 to determine the appropriate classes of claims of creditors, the chairman of the first meeting of creditors held pursuant to section 109 shall determine whether there is more than one class of claims of creditors and, if so, the class in which each claim is included in accordance with subsection 290(3).

(2) A person who is aggrieved by a decision of a chairman made under subsection (1) may apply to a court under subsection 99(3), and on such application the court may uphold, or modify the decision of the chairman.

(3) A proposed arrangement is accepted by the creditors whose claims are affected thereby where at least two-thirds of the votes cast by the creditors included in each class of claims is in favour of acceptance of the proposed arrangement.

113. (1) A creditor who is related to the debtor may vote against but not for the acceptance of the proposed arrangement.

(2) A creditor who has any claim set out in subsection 265(6) may not vote in respect of that claim on the proposed arrangement.

(3) Notwithstanding subsection 293(3), where the trustee named in a proposed arrangement is a creditor, the trustee shall not vote as a creditor on the proposed arrangement.

114. (1) Where a proposed arrangement is deemed to be rejected under subsection 110(3) or where, at their first meeting, the creditors whose claims are to be affected by an arrangement do not accept the proposed arrangement,

(*a*) if a petition had not been filed before the proposed arrangement was filed or before a notice of intention was filed, a petition in respect of the debtor is deemed to have been filed

(i) on the day the proposed arrangement was filed with the administrator, or

(ii) where the proposed arrangement was preceded by a notice of intention, on the day such notice was filed with the administrator;

(*b*) the chairman of the meeting shall, if the proposed arrangement was intended to affect all classes of claims of unsecured creditors, forthwith hold a meeting of the creditors present which meeting is deemed to be a meeting called pursuant to section 203; and

(*c*) if the proposed arrangement was not intended to affect all classes of claims of unsecured creditors, the trustee named in the proposed arrangement shall, within five days, call the meeting of creditors required by section 203.

(2) Subsection (1) does not apply to a proposed arrangement that affects only the claims of secured creditors.

(3) Where a petition in respect of a debtor is deemed to be filed under subsection (1), the administrator shall forthwith make a bankruptcy order in respect of the debtor and appoint as trustee

(*a*) a trustee whom he shall, as far as possible, select by reference to the wishes of the most interested creditors, if ascertainable at that time; or

(*b*) the trustee named in the proposed arrangement that the creditors did not accept.

(4) Where a petition in respect of a debtor was filed before a proposed arrangement was filed and, at their first meeting, the creditors whose claims are to be affected by the arrangement do not accept the proposed arrangement, the administrator shall forthwith make a bankruptcy order in respect of the debtor and appoint as trustee

(*a*) a trustee whom he shall, as far as possible, select by reference to the wishes of the most interested creditors if ascertainable at that time, or

(*b*) the trustee named in the proposed arrangement that the creditors did not accept,

and the trustee so appointed shall,

(*c*) if the proposed arrangement was intended to affect all classes of claims of unsecured creditors, forthwith hold a meeting of the creditors present which meeting is deemed to be a meeting called pursuant to section 203; and

(*d*) if the proposed arrangement was not intended to affect all classes of claims of unsecured creditors, within five days, call the meeting of creditors required by section 203.

116. Where a proposed arrangement is accepted by the creditors, the trustee shall,

(*a*) within thirty days of the acceptance, apply to the court for approval of the proposed arrangement;

(*b*) not less than ten days before the date of the hearing for approval, file with the court and forward to the administrator a copy of the proposed arrangement as accepted by the creditors;

(*c*) prepare a report on the proposed arrangement in prescribed form and file a copy thereof with the court and with the administrator not less than ten days before the hearing under subsection 117(1); and

(*d*) at least ten days prior to the hearing of the application, send a notice of the time and place of the hearing to all creditors whose claims are affected by the proposed arrangement.

117. (1) The court shall, before approving a proposed arrangement, consider the report of the trustee referred to in paragraph 116(*c*), and may hear the trustee and any interested party who wishes to be heard and request any further evidence it considers necessary.

(2) On an application for approval of a proposed arrangement, a court may

(*a*) make any amendment to the proposed arrangement that, in the opinion of the court, does not materially and adversely affect the claims of any creditor or class of creditors, the shareholders; or

(*b*) make a material amendment to the proposed arrangement and require re-submission of the proposed arrangement as amended to such creditors and shareholders as the court may direct.

(3) The court shall

(*a*) approve a proposed arrangement;

(*b*) refuse to approve a proposed arrangement; or

(*c*) order, subject to such conditions as it thinks fit to impose, re-submission to the creditors of a proposed arrangement.

(4) The court may refuse to approve a proposed arrangement

(*a*) where the proposed arrangement does not comply in a material way with section 105;

(*b*) where the proposed arrangement is not feasible or its terms are not reasonable or not calculated to benefit the creditors generally;

(*c*) where the effect of a proposed repudiation of a partly performed contract under section 103 is to discriminate unfairly against another party to the contract or the effect of a proposed repudiation of a lease of real property under section 104 is to discriminate unfairly against the lessor or a sub-lessee of, or a secured creditor having a security interest in, the leased property; or

(*d*) where the debtor is a corporation, if the proposed arrangement is not just and equitable in the interests of the shareholders.

(5) For the purposes of paragraph (4)(*c*), the court, in determining whether a proposed repudiation referred to in that paragraph discriminates unfairly, shall take into consideration the full present value of the partly performed contract or lease obligation and the position of the other party to the contract or the lessor, as the case may be, if a bankruptcy order were made instead of an arrangement.

(6) Where the court approves a proposed arrangement in respect of a bankrupt, the approval by the court operates to annul the bankruptcy order and to revest in the debtor or in such other person as the court may approve all the right, title and interest of the trustee in the property of the debtor, unless the terms of the arrangement otherwise provide.

(7) A proposed arrangement that is approved by the court is an arrangement made under this Part.

118. The court, on approving a proposed arrangement, may make such orders as may be necessary to give effect to the arrangement.

119. (1) Where the court refuses to approve a proposed arrangement,

(*a*) if a petition had not been filed before the proposed arrangement was filed or before a notice of intention was filed, a petition in respect of the debtor is deemed to have been filed

   (i) on the day the proposed arrangement was filed with the administrator, or

   (ii) where the proposed arrangement was preceded by a notice of intention, on the day such notice was filed with the administrator;

(*b*) the court shall immediately make a bankruptcy order in respect of the debtor and appoint as trustee

   (i) a trustee whom the court shall, as far as possible, select by reference to the wishes of the most interested creditors if ascertainable at that time, or

   (ii) the trustee named in the proposed arrangement; and

(*c*) the trustee appointed under paragraph (*b*) shall, within five days after the refusal of the court to approve the proposed arrangement

   (i) file a report in prescribed form with the administrator, and

   (ii) call the meeting of creditors required by section 203.

(2) Where the court refuses to approve a proposed arrangement and a petition had been filed

before the proposed arrangement was filed or before a notice of intention was filed,

    (*a*) the court shall immediately make a bankruptcy order in respect of the debtor and shall appoint as trustee

        (i) a trustee whom the court shall, as far as possible, select by reference to the wishes of the most interested creditors if ascertainable at that time, or

        (ii) the trustee named in the proposed arrangement;

and the trustee so appointed shall, within five days of the date of bankruptcy, call the meeting of creditors required by section 203; and

    (*b*) the trustee named in the proposed arrangement shall, within five days after the refusal of the court to approve the proposed arrangement, file a report in prescribed form with the administrator.

    (3) Subsection (1) does not apply to a proposed arrangement that affects only the claims of secured creditors.

Court Formulated Arrangements

    120. (1) Subject to subsection (2), where the debts of a debtor, including secured debts, exceed one million dollars and a proposed arrangement is filed in respect of the debtor

    (*a*) that is not accepted by the creditors, or

    (*b*) that the court refuses to approve,

the court, on application and on five days notice of the application to the debtor, the creditors, the trustee and the Superintendent, may endeavour to formulate a proposed arrangement acceptable to the creditors and the debtor.

    (2) The court may decline to endeavour to formulate a proposed arrangement in any case where the court does not consider that it can do so in a manner that is just and equitable to the creditors generally or it is of the opinion that the application has not been made in good faith.

    (3) A proposed arrangement formulated by the court shall have regard to

    (*a*) the interest of any person in the property of the debtor;

    (*b*) the provisions of section 105 in so far as they are applicable; and

    (*c*) the possible effect, if an arrangement is not made, on

        (i) employees and suppliers of the debtor, and

        (ii) the community in which the debtor is located or does business.

    (*d*) the feasibility of financing the arrangement and the future viability of the business.

    121. Where the court endeavours to formulate a proposed arrangement, the court shall appoint a trustee to assist the court to formulate the proposed arrangement and to carry it out if it is accepted.

    122. Where the court appoints a trustee under section 121, it may require the trustee

    (*a*) to investigate and report to the court on the conduct, property, liabilities and financial condition of the debtor, any act of the debtor, the operation of the business of the debtor and the desirability of the continuance thereof and any other matter relevant to the formulation of a proposed arrangement by the court;

    (*b*) to give notice to the administrator and any other person that such person may, within a time specified in the notice, submit representations regarding the formulation of the proposed arrangement; and

    (*c*) to perform such other duties to assist the court to formulate the proposed arrangement and to carry it out if it is accepted.

    123. (1) Where an application is filed with the court pursuant to subsection 120(1), no creditor of the debtor having a claim admissible under section 111 may exercise a remedy against the debtor or his property or institute or continue a proceeding for the recovery of the claim

(*a*) until the proposed arrangement is approved or otherwise disposed of; or

(*b*) unless the court so allows, in which case the remedy may be exercised or the proceeding may be instituted or continued subject to such terms and conditions as the court may impose.

(2) Subsection (1) does not operate to prevent a creditor from exercising a remedy or from instituting or continuing a proceeding with respect to any of the following:

(*a*) any right the creditor may have as a secured creditor to realize or otherwise deal with the property subject to the security interest of such creditor where such security interest is in property that is perishable or likely to depreciate rapidly in value;

(*b*) any acts that are required by law to be performed to render a transfer effective against third parties, to prevent a security interest from being terminated, or to permit perfection of a security interest or other right by legal action, registration or otherwise;

(*c*) any right the creditor may have as a secured creditor to collect, take possession of, or take conservatory measures with respect to, any property subject to his security interest;

(*d*) any right in addition to the rights set out in paragraphs (*a*) to (*c*) and (*e*) and (*f*) the creditor may have as a secured creditor to realize or otherwise deal with the property subject to his security interest but only to the extent that the secured creditor realizes or otherwise deals with such property in a manner consistent with the continued operation of the debtor's business;

(*e*) any acts that are required to permit the completion or closing of any contractual obligation made in good faith and without knowledge of the filing of a notice of intention or a proposed arrangement if, on receipt of knowledge of such filing, the creditor notifies the trustee of the contractual obligation and gives him full particulars thereof; and

(*f*) the sale of assets of the debtor by a secured creditor where the sale is to be by way of auction or tender and the sale has been advertised.

124. (1) Where the court formulates a proposed arrangement, the trustee appointed by the court shall call a meeting of the creditors whose claims are to be affected by the proposed arrangement and submit the proposed arrangement to them.

(2) A meeting of creditors referred to in subsection (1) shall be held in the manner directed by the court.

(3) The creditors may, by resolution, accept, amend or reject a proposed arrangement formulated by the court.

(4) Where a proposed arrangement formulated by the court is accepted by all classes of creditors whose claims are to be affected by the arrangement, the court is deemed to have approved the proposed arrangement.

(5) Where a proposed arrangement formulated by the court is amended or rejected by the creditors or any class of creditors whose claims are to be affected by the arrangement, the court may, after hearing and considering any objections by any interested person,

(*a*) approve the proposed arrangement as formulated;

(*b*) amend the proposed arrangement and approve it as amended; or

(*c*) withdraw the proposed arrangement.

(6) A proposed arrangement deemed to be approved by the court under subsection (4) or approved by the court under subsection 5 is an arrangement made under this Part.

126. (1) A claim of a creditor shall be determined

(*a*) where an arrangement is made in respect of a bankrupt, as of the date of bankruptcy, and

(*b*) where an arrangement is made in respect of a person who is not a bankrupt, as of the date of filing a notice of intention or, if no such notice is filed, as of the date of filing the proposed arrangement.

(2) An arrangement is binding on the debtor and every creditor of the debtor in respect of any admissible claim that the creditor has under section 111.

128. (1) Subject to subsection (2), all moneys payable under the arrangement shall be paid to the trustee and be applied by him in accordance with the terms of the arrangement.

(2) An arrangement may provide that payments to creditors other than unsecured creditors need not be made through the trustee.

(3) Where an arrangement provides for the distribution of property in the nature of promissory notes or other evidence of indebtedness by or on behalf of the debtor or, where the debtor is a corporation, of securities of the corporation, such property shall be applied in the manner referred to in subsection (1) as nearly as may be.

(4) Unless a debtor consents thereto in writing, no arrangement imposes on the debtor any obligation to take any action or make any payment that he would not be required to take or make if the arrangement were not made.

129. (1) An arrangement is fully performed where all the money and property to which persons are entitled under its terms have been transferred to such persons.

(2) Where an arrangement is fully performed, the trustee shall give a certificate in prescribed form to the debtor and to the administrator.

(3) On full performance of an arrangement, the debtor is released to the extent set out in the arrangement from any debt for which a claim is admissible under section 111.

(4) Where a proposed arrangement provides that a claim of a secured creditor is not to be affected by the arrangement, the debtor is not released from the claim, unless the creditor files a proof of claim or proof of security interest.

130. Where the debtor or any guarantor of the debtor defaults, for thirty days or more, in the performance of any obligation imposed by the terms of an arrangement, the trustee shall forthwith send notice of the default to the administrator and each creditor who proved a claim in the arrangement and whose claim remains unpaid.

131. (1) Where default occurs or is expected to occur in the performance of an arrangement or where it appears to the court that the arrangement cannot continue without injustice or undue delay or that the approval of the proposed arrangement by the court was obtained by fraud, the court may, on application and with such notice to all interested persons as the court may direct,

(a) vary the terms of the arrangement to facilitate its performance; or

(b) annul the arrangement.

(2) Where, pursuant to subsection (1), the court varies the terms of an arrangement or annuls an arrangement, the trustee shall forthwith send notice of the variation or annulment to the administrator and to each creditor who proved a claim in the arrangement.

(3) An order made under subsection (1) does not affect the validity of any transfer of property or payment made, or anything done under the arrangement.

132. (1) Where the court annuls an arrangement, the debtor is deemed to have filed a petition on the date of the annulment order and

(a) the court shall forthwith

(i) make a bankruptcy order in respect of the debtor, and

(ii) appoint as trustee in the bankruptcy of the debtor

(A) a trustee whom the court shall, as far as possible, select by reference to the wishes of the most interested creditors if ascertainable at that time, or

(B) the trustee under the arrangement; and

(*b*) the trustee appointed pursuant to paragraph (*a*) shall, within five days of the annulment order,

   (i) file a report in the prescribed form with the administrator, and

   (ii) call the meeting of the creditors required by section 203.

(2) Subsection (1) does not apply to an arrangement that affects only claims of secured creditors.

(3) Notwithstanding subsection (1), for the purposes of sections 168 to 185, where an arrangement is annulled, the debtor is deemed to have filed a petition on the earlier of

(*a*) the date of filing a notice of intention, and

(*b*) the date of filing a proposed arrangement

unless the arrangement otherwise provides in respect of a transfer reported pursuant to paragraph 108(1)(*c*).

NOTE *Re Alberta Western Wholesale Lumber Ltd.* (1961) 27 D.L.R. (2d) 598 (B.C.S.C.), discusses the criteria that the Court looks at in considering a proposal by an insolvent person. The proposal must be approved by the creditor, and then approved by the Court, pursuant to s 41 of the Act. In the *Alberta Western Wholesale* case, the company was petitioned into bankruptcy by its largest creditor, Canadian Collieries Resources. While the petition was pending, the debtor made a petition which was drafted by Canadian Collieries. The proposal provided for payment of creditors' claims in full over a 5 year period without interest, or alternatively, for immediate payment at 35 cents on the dollar, on approval of the proposal by the Court. The bulk of the creditors endorsed the proposal. On approval, Canadian Collieries was to purchase all shares of the debtor. The Trustee recommended approval of the proposal, and an application was brought under s 41 to secure Court approval.

The Court approved the scheme. Ruttan J held that in spite of the trustee's endorsement and the creditors approval, it was the duty of the Court to protect the creditors if need be against their reckless enthusiasm, but on the evidence, the proposal was couched in reasonable terms. Although Canadian Collieries gained control of the bankrupt company, this would be of benefit to all of the creditors. Mere acquisition of the shares gave control, but did not automatically increase their value. Of course Canadian Collieries hoped to gain from its operation of the debtor company, but this could only follow payment in full of the unsecured creditors under the proposal. Thus, there was no economic immorality involved, as the proposal improved the position of all classes of creditors.

Comment on *Re Alberta Western Wholesale* (1961), 2 C.B.R. (N.S.) 162.

After a proposal has been approved by the creditor, it is to be submitted to the Court for approval. Section 41(1) of the Act provides that the Court shall consider the report of the trustee and may hear such further evidence as it deems advisable in deciding whether or not to approve the proposal.

Section 41(2) raises two questions for the Court to consider on an application for approval of a proposal. (1) Are the terms of the proposal reasonable? (2) Are the terms of the proposal calculated to benefit the general body of creditors? In determining whether or not to approve the proposal, the Court must consider not only the wishes and interests of creditors, but the conduct of the debtor and the interests of the public and future creditors and the requirements of commercial morality.

It is always the problem when a proposal has been carried by the vote of one or two large creditors, especially when the majority of creditors do not see fit to attend a meeting of creditors or appoint a proxy or send a voting letter to the trustee. If the majority of creditors neglect to pursue their own interests by attending the meeting of creditors the Court will, of necessity, find it quite difficult to protect them unless in very clear cases.

Of course in most cases a proposal is the 'brain-child' of a trustee, but in such cases it is for the creditors to determine whether the proposal is calculated to benefit them. If it appears to the majority of the creditors that the proposal is not to their benefit it is very easy for them to defeat the proposal at the creditors' meeting, considering that a proposal will only be carried if it has been approved by a majority number and three-quarters in value of the creditors with proof of claims present, personally or by proxy, and voting on the resolution at the meeting.

In re The Man With The Axe Ltd. (1961), 2 C.B.R. (N.S.) 8 (Man. Q.B.)

31st January 1961. MONNIN J.: The Court is moved for the approval of a proposal filed by the debtor on 19th December 1960, which was approved by a large majority of the creditors at a meeting held to consider it on 5th January 1961.

I have before me the proposal; the trustee's report dated 18th January 1961; his supplementary report filed yesterday morning, and a number of voluminous affidavits filed either on the first motion or filed yesterday.

The majority of the creditors favour the proposal which will give them 30 cents on the dollar, whilst an assignment in bankruptcy, if it is to come, will only bring them between 3 and 10 cents on the dollar. They are content to take 30 cents on the dollar rather than risk a very small dividend which might otherwise be forthcoming. On a dollar and cents basis their attitude is quite understandable. The minority shareholders do not wish to accept 30 cents, and are prepared to take the risk of getting much less, but they desire to bring to the Court's attention the conduct of the debtor, and they have done so in the material filed and with the help of the trustee's report.

As has been said by other very able judges, it is my duty to take into consideration not only the wishes and interest of the creditors (majority and minority creditors) but the conduct of the debtor, the interest of the public and future creditors, the moral standpoint or, in other words, the requirements of commercial morality.

The conduct of the debtor is not satisfactory. On the contrary, it deserves condemnation. It is not because others have done certain things in the past that those actions are no longer blameworthy. The debtor failed for a few weeks to disclose to its creditors and the trustee, who also occupied the position of interim receiver, that stock-in-trade valued at $32,000 had been stored away in a warehouse, obviously to protect the interests of Mr. Clesby. I am unable to find in this conduct the innocence that counsel would like me to find. This fact was not disclosed to the trustee until shortly after 16th December 1960. By it Mr. Clesby, a guarantor, was temporarily given a preference, and the overdraft at the bank was reduced during that period.

The debtor knew for many months prior to the filing of the proposal that it was insolvent and not meeting its obligations. Its financial statement as of 31st January 1960, was erroneous, so much so that its auditors disclaimed responsibility for its contents. Inventory was valued at retail price instead of cost price as in the past. Obviously this was done to deceive those into whose hands the balance sheet would eventually fall, and to show a good financial position when in fact it was weak and crumbling.

Weekly salaries, raised some months before, were paid to persons who performed no work for the debtor. $28,990 was paid to Marantz & Sons Limited between May and November, 1960, when actually no purchases were made from that firm during the year 1960. Mr. Frank Marantz, the main shareholder of Marantz & Sons, is a shareholder of the debtor, a co-guarantor, and was in receipt of a weekly salary, though in his affidavit he admitted that he took no active part in the day-to-day management of the debtor's affairs.

The loss in the ten months previous to the proposal has not been satisfactorily explained. The debtor had no control over its cash position. The affidavits of 16th December and 19th December 1960, show cash on hand in the amount of $25,000, a round figure like all other figures in these two statements, while in fact it was $20,144.81.

The assets of the debtor are not of a value equal to 50 cents on the dollar on the amount of its unsecured liabilities. As I said previously, the debtor has continued to trade long after knowing itself to be insolvent, even to the point of selling its stock at a loss in order to get cash in the till.

The debtor's entire course of conduct shows extreme levity in management. The 1960 financial statement was false. The first statement of assets and liabilities as of 25th November 1960, sworn to on 19th December 1960, is all in round figures and turned out to be wrong in many respects. The course of conduct indicates poor business management as well as serious lack of morality in business.

To approve this proposal the Court would have to close its eyes to all the facts disclosed, and it would only approve it in order to give all the creditors 30 cents in the dollar and permit all of them to secure the most that they can expect.

Although the creditors would be financially better off if the proposal were accepted the Court's approbation in this case would be tantamount to condonation and acquiescence in the debtor's conduct, and could even be considered by others as encouragement to proceed in the same fashion.

The proposal is not in the public interest. Pursuant to s 34(3) and, in the exercise of my discretion, well knowing the consequences to all, I refuse to allow the proposal. Creditors who indiscriminately advance lines of credit must face the consequences of their foolhardiness.

The trustee is entitled to his costs against the debtor, as well as those of his counsel throughout the entire proceedings, including the motion for examination of certain persons, which was disposed of last week. If the parties cannot agree I may be spoken to and will dispose of it then.

Debtor, guarantors, and individual shareholders of the debtor corporation will have no costs of this motion.

With respect to the motion for an order for the examination under oath before the Registrar of four named persons, those who argued that the Court had jurisdiction to dispose of the matter will have their costs against the debtor up until the matter of jurisdiction was disposed of by me on 21st January 1961, in the afternoon. Thereafter since success was divided and, except as previously stated, I allow no costs to the representatives of the minority or majority creditors.

Comment on *In re The Man With The Axe Ltd.* (1961), 2 C.B.R. (N.S.) 11

This decision goes a long way towards discouraging proposals made by dishonest debtors. The judgment shows that there are sufficient safeguards in the Act to prevent the approval of proposals which would offend the public interest or the requirements of commercial morality.

Unfortunately, in cases where the creditors are offered somewhat more than they could expect on an assignment, or what the debtor makes them believe they might receive, they gladly approve the proposal and usually no creditor makes the effort to appear in Court to oppose it. Of course it is not sufficient for a creditor to oppose the proposal without submitting to the Court sufficient evidence why it should not be approved. In this case the objecting creditors through

their counsel, submitted to the Court a considerable amount of evidence as a result of which the
Court had no difficulty in concluding that it should refuse the proposal.

This decision shows very clearly that the Bankruptcy Act is not always at fault; sometimes the
creditors are the ones who should accept the sole blame for their misfortunes because they do
not go to the trouble of protecting their interest.

4 THE LIMITATIONS OF THE ALTERNATIVE TO BANKRUPTCY

In spite of the arrangement and proposal schemes, the overwhelming majority of
insolvent debtors choose bankruptcy. The following article attempts to explain why
American debtors have chosen the personal bankruptcy route.

THE GROWING POPULARITY OF PERSONAL BANKRUPTCY

[Reproduced from 14 June 1971 edition of Moneysworth, a consumer newsletter published in
the U.S.A.]

If you're a $10,000-a-year man, taking home $665 monthly and with $550 in living expenses and
$335 in debt payments (for car, credit charges, past medical bills, etc.), you're a prime prospect
for personal bankruptcy – even though you probably never thought about it. Simple arithmetic
shows that you are sinking $220 deeper into debt each month. And the rule-of-thumb is that if
you can't pay off your debts (excepting a mortgage) within two or three years, you're a potential
bankrupt.

Lately, more and more people are discovering the advantages of personal bankruptcy.
According to *The New York Times*, the number of individuals – as opposed to businesses – filing
for bankruptcy has reached 'alarming' proportions. Last year, 178,202 people went bankrupt –
ten times the number of businesses. This year, according to Prof. Marvin S. Kayne, of
Berkeley's School of Law and one of the nation's top experts, the figures will exceed 200,000.

REASONS Bankruptcy is on the increase, first, because the moral stigma attached to going
bankrupt has all but vanished. Nowadays people even seem to admire a sophisticated consumer
who can turn the bankruptcy law to personal advantage. 'Increasingly, the people who take the
bankruptcy route are not innocent victims of misfortune, but slick operators,' says *The Wall
Street Journal*.

Second, the weakened state of the economy has left many people overextended on credit.
Suddenly, there are no fat dividend checks, no overtime pay, and, in many cases, no jobs – but
installment payments still have to be met.

Finally, there's the increasing sophistication of the consumer. More and more people are
college graduates and, as Leonard G. Rose, president of National Account System, the nation's
largest collection agency, states 'It certainly doesn't help that more and more books are being
written these days on how to avoid paying your bills'.

WHAT IS PERSONAL BANKRUPTCY? How does it work? To begin with, personal bankruptcy is
a Constitutionally-guaranteed right, intended to give every citizen who becomes hopelessly
mired in debt a chance to make a fresh start.

Essentially, what a person filing for bankruptcy does is to file a statement in Federal court
declaring that his debts exceed his assets. He lists his debts and assets and the court (through an
official called a 'referee') decides how much of his assets to divvy among his creditors. The

bankrupt is then declared absolved of all financial obligations that existed at the time he filed, and the creditors absorb the loss.

The entire procedure is so simple and painless that many people have made a career of building up indebtedness and shucking it periodically via bankruptcy (once every six years is the most often the law will allow). Indeed, the statistics show that at least 20% of all people who file for bankruptcy do so more than once.

Moreover, the law permits you to keep most of the things needed to maintain life with a modicum of dignity: Your income (which is not attachable once you have declared bankruptcy), your home, furniture, TV, appliances, car (up to a certain value), credit union and pension balances, and savings accounts (up to $1,000). The property you may keep varies from state to state, but a California referee is quoted in *The Boom of Going Bust: The Growing Scandal in Personal Bankruptcy*, by George Sullivan, as saying: 'A person here can go through bankruptcy and still come out with $20,000 to $30,000 worth of property, including an automobile, television, a homesteaded house, appliances, and clothing.'

OTHER ADVANTAGES Surprisingly, you may end up with a better credit rating than before you filed. Rudolph Severa, head of the Credit Bureau of Greater New York, says that people who have gone into bankruptcy particularly for reasons like prolonged illness do not necessarily have their credit rating impaired. Much more important than a history of bankruptcy, says he, is the person's earning capacity, education level, etc. Prof. Kayne states that 'Believe it or not, your credit rating may even be better after filing. Before you filed, you were a bad credit risk. After filing, since you cannot file again for six years, you are debt-free and credit managers consider you a good risk.'

If you're conscience-stricken over your inability to repay accumulated debts, bankruptcy may even give you a spiritual lift. Carlton ('Cookie') Gilchrist, a football player with the Denver Broncos, after shedding a huge indebtedness, said, 'It made me feel free, like a man possessed of great strength – like my career was just starting.'

DISADVANTAGES You should know about them, too. First, you will have to pay certain debts even if you do go bankrupt. Mainly, these are alimony, child support, all taxes not more than three years old, and 'secured' loans (those where the creditor can take back whatever it was you bought).

Second, utilities may be reluctant to provide you with gas, electricity, water, or phone service in the future. That's why some habitual bankrupts make sure that they pay their utility bills, no matter what.

Third, some employers automatically fire any employee who files for bankruptcy – even though it's illegal to do so.

Fourth, if you need a license to practice – as in plumbing or electrical work – in some states you may lose your license, though probably only temporarily.

HOW TO FILE If you should decide to go bankrupt, first and foremost hire a lawyer. He will charge you about $250 (plus $50 for court fees); but the money will be well spent (and you can get a lawyer from a legal aid society for next to nothing). The lawyer will:

* Take care of all paperwork. You will then be required to make just one brief court appearance. This will be followed by a six-month waiting period during which your creditors are informed of your bankruptcy (and, meanwhile, any new assets – or liabilities – you acquire are completely unaffected by the bankruptcy).

* Show you how to legally keep money or property you might otherwise lose. For example, if you have an income tax refund coming, you will lose it unless your lawyer tells you when to collect it and what to buy with it (e.g. clothes, food, a house, a mortgage prepayment, etc.). Or

he might advise you to convert cash or stocks into life insurance premiums or credit union or Federal savings and loan deposits, which cannot be touched by anyone but yourself.

  * Negotiate with your creditors. Creditors – even those who are secured – seldom want their merchandise back, it is used and extremely difficult to resell at full value. A lawyer, according to Prof. Kayne, 'can perform bargaining miracles. You might find, for example, that if you owe $1,500 on a car at $75 a month, with bankruptcy filed the creditor will accept $750 at $37.50. The lawyer can thus cut your debt in half and save you the car!'

  * Steer you clear of other pitfalls. For example, Sidney Sherwin, a New York bankruptcy attorney and author of *How to Get Out of Debt Painlessly*, tells of a woman who went to her bankruptcy hearing dressed in a Black Diamond mink coat. Though she argued that it was her only coat, her creditors went home with it.

  * Make sure you list all your debts. If you don't, you're still liable for those you don't list. *The Wall Street Journal* reports the case of a Bogalusa, Louisiana, boilerroom helper named Terrence Keene who 'just laughed' when the Home Finance Service Company filed suit against him to collect a $586 personal loan. 'I had already gone bankrupt on that loan,' Keene is quoted as saying, 'and I was sure I was safe.' But it turned out that Keene had failed to include the loan on the list of obligations he submitted to court, and Home Finance won a judgment for $586 plus $400 in legal costs, despite Keene's bankruptcy.

  YOUR NAME IS PROTECTED Finally, if you're worried about gossip by neighbors resulting from publicity, forget it. The only time newspapers report personal bankruptcies is when celebrities are involved – as in the case of Eddie Fisher, Mickey Rooney, and Lammot du Pont Copeland (who is in the process of shedding a cool $63-million).

  The moral of the story is this: If celebrities can go bankrupt, and if the Penn Central and Rolls-Royce can, so can you.

20

Beginning the Process

INTRODUCTION

The materials in this chapter trace through the initiation and administration of a bankruptcy. The structure and jurisdiction of the bankruptcy courts are described and rules governing which debtors and creditors fall within the ambit of the bankruptcy process outlined. Special rules governing the status as debtors of infants, farmers and fishermen, deceased estates, partnerships and corporations and their officers are set out. The materials go on to describe the two principal methods by which bankruptcy may be initiated: voluntarily (through petition by a debtor), or involuntarily (through petition by a creditor), and two supplemental routes via the breakdown of a consumer or commercial arrangement. The chapter concludes with a statement of the powers of a trustee in bankruptcy and two accounts from trustees in bankruptcy as to practical problems commonly encountered in the administration of bankruptcy estates.

I THE BANKRUPTCY COURT

a / Structure and Jurisdiction

i Tassé Report, pp 163–7 (footnotes omitted)

3.7.01 There has been no consistency in Canadian legislation in designating the courts that have jurisdiction over bankruptcy and insolvency. Courts that have been given jurisdiction, at one time or another, have included the Superior Courts of the provinces, County and District Courts, the Court of Probate in Nova Scotia and provincial Boards of Review.

3.7.02 A legacy of this legislative tinkering is a certain amount of confusion concerning the exact jurisdiction of the courts and of their officers. This confusion originated with the creation of the new Bankruptcy Courts in 1919 and in their hasty abolition in 1922.

3.7.03 To better understand how this confusion originated and developed, it is helpful to consider the following sections of the 1919 Act which relate to the jurisdiction and procedure of the courts:

   63. (1) The following named courts *are constituted Courts of Bankruptcy and invested ... with such jurisdiction at law and in equity* as will enable them to exercise original, auxiliary and ancillary jurisdiction in bankruptcy and in other proceedings authorized by this Act ...

   (3) The courts in this subsection named *are constituted Appeal Courts of Bankruptcy ...*

   64. (3) ... *all the powers and jurisdiction in bankruptcy* and otherwise conferred by this Act *may and shall be exercised by or under the direction of one of the judges of the court* upon which such powers and jurisdiction are so conferred, *and the Minister of Justice shall from time to time assign a judge or judges of such court for that purpose ...*

65. (1) The registrars of the several courts exercising bankruptcy jurisdiction under this Act shall have the powers and jurisdiction in this section mentioned ...

(2) In this Act, unless the context otherwise requires or implies, the expression, ... (ee) 'registrar' includes any other officer who performs duties like those of a registrar, ...

3.7.04 In 1922, the Ontario Court of Appeal, expressed the view that, in enacting a bankruptcy statute, Parliament would be competent to entrust its administration to provincial courts and judges, but it did question, as it was put by Chief Justice Meredith, whether Parliament had 'authority to create a Dominion court and to man it with the provincial courts and judges'.

3.7.05 Parliament reacted quickly by deleting the words 'are constituted Courts of Bankruptcy'. The amending statute also provided that the designation of judges to assume primary responsibility for the administration of the Act should reside in the several provincial Chief Justices and not as theretofore, in the Minister of Justice. No other changes have been made since. The curious result is that, although the provincial Superior Courts now have jurisdiction in bankruptcy, the apparatus of the former federal bankruptcy court still remains. This explains most of the present confusion surrounding the bankruptcy and insolvency jurisdiction of the courts.

3.7.06 Section 140 of the Bankruptcy Act is a good example of how confusing the provisions of the Bankruptcy Act concerning the Courts can be. It purports to vest jurisdiction in bankruptcy in the several provincial Superior Courts. If the section were deleted, there would be no change in the result. Superior Courts have jurisdiction in respect to all federal statutes, unless a federal statute stipulates to the contrary. The problems resulting from the vesting of the provincial courts with 'such jurisdiction at law and in equity as will enable them to exercise original, auxiliary and ancillary jurisdiction in bankruptcy' has been discussed *supra* in 2.3.11.

3.7.07 Section 142 is another section that, in the context of the present Act, is largely meaningless. It purports to give the Chief Justice of the Superior Courts the right to assign bankruptcy work to judges. The several Chief Justices have this power apart from the statute. To provide that the judgment of a single judge shall be deemed to be the judgment of the court is again saying no more than what would be the law without the section. Subsection 2, which purports to preserve and maintain, in all Superior Court judges, jurisdiction in bankruptcy, does not seem to add any greater authority to section 140, which gives the bankruptcy jurisdiction to the Superior Courts in the first place. As we have seen in the preceding paragraph, this jurisdiction would have vested in these courts and their judges, even if nothing had been said in the Act.

3.7.08 Section 144(1), which provides that every court shall have a seal, and section 144(4), which provides that the court shall hold periodic sittings, had a real meaning in the context of the 1919 Act when the new Courts of Bankruptcy were created. These sections, under the present Act, have no meaning, as the courts having jurisdiction are the Superior Courts which have their own seals and their own provisions for holding periodical sittings.

3.7.09 The office and function of the registrar under the present Act are particularly anomalous. During the period when there was a federal Court of Bankruptcy, i.e., 1919–1920, the registrar fulfilled a useful and necessary function. A court was constituted, judges were designated, but there were no clerks or other necessary officers. To remedy this, 'the Chief Justice of each court upon which such powers and jurisdiction are so conferred' was empowered to 'appoint ... such registrars, clerks, and other officers in bankruptcy as he deems necessary ...'. This in itself was not particularly clear. There was no provision for designating one of the judges of the Court of Bankruptcy as Chief Justice, but the intention, no doubt, was to refer to the Chief Justices of the several provincial Superior Courts which were 'constituted Courts of Bankruptcy'. Although it remained in the discretion of the Chief Justice to appoint a registrar, the Act conferred upon the latter a number of specific powers, the exercise of which were deemed to be the orders or acts of the court.

3.7.10 Once the Court of Bankruptcy was abolished, there was no necessity for continuing the practice of appointing 'registrars, clerks and other officers in bankruptcy'. All necessary functions and duties, which did not require to be exercised by a judge, could be performed by the other regular Superior Court officers.

3.7.11 Although there is some doubt as to whether or not the registrar is a provincial or federal judicial officer, Parliament has the power to impose duties upon provincial court officials in regard to matters within its legislative field. It would seem however, to be the safest conclusion that registrars, both under the 1919 Act, when there was a federal Bankruptcy Court, and under the present Act, are federally appointed officers with a limited jurisdiction under the *Bankruptcy Act*. Although they may be at the same time and for other purposes, provincial court officers, their jurisdiction as registrars flows, not from any appointment as officers of the provincial Superior Courts, but from their appointment by the Chief Justices under the authority delegated to them by the *Bankruptcy Act*.

3.7.12 In 1936, the Ontario Court of Appeal held that registrars were not judges. In 1949, however, new powers have been given to the registrars. Since then, the Act also provides that the powers and jurisdiction of registrars may be exercised by judges, that a registrar may refer any matter ordinarily in his jurisdiction to a judge for disposition, and that a judge may direct that any matter before a registrar be brought before him for hearing. The Ontario Court of Appeal implied that the strongest ground for holding a registrar to be a judge was the provision that 'any order made or act done by such registrars in the exercise of the said powers and jurisdiction shall be deemed the order or act of the court', and that this was not a sufficient reason for holding the registrar to be a judge. With the very much extended judicial powers of a registrar, there is reason to doubt whether the courts would today come to the same conclusion. Certainly, the doubt remains as to whether or not registrars are junior federal judges acting within the framework of the provincial Superior Courts. In our opinion, it is not desirable to perpetuate this untidy and confusing situation.

3.7.13 A decision must also be made as to which court should have jurisdiction. When this decision is made, the entire jurisdiction over bankruptcy and insolvency should be given to that court. The courts that might reasonably be considered in this connection are the provincial Superior Courts, and the Exchequer Court, which would become the Federal Court of Canada, if Bill C-192, read for the first time in the House of Commons on March 2, 1970, becomes law. The chief advantage in designating the Exchequer Court as the court having jurisdiction in bankruptcy is that it would assist in creating a greater uniformity of law than now exists when there is only the occasional appeal to the Supreme Court of Canada and not too many to the provincial Courts of Appeal. This advantage, however, would be more than largely offset by the numerous problems and uncertainty that would result for the litigants having to decide, with respect to many matters, whether the Superior Court of their province, or the Exchequer Court, has jurisdiction. Similar difficulties arise under the present Act, as the rules of procedure prescribed by and under the Act must be followed when the Superior Court is sitting in bankruptcy. To vest the Exchequer Court with jurisdiction in bankruptcy would only compound a difficult situation, as bankruptcy often involves problems of property and civil rights and no federal court, other than the Supreme Court of Canada, could exercise general jurisdiction over the matters coming within the exclusive legislative authority of the provinces. In our opinion, the disadvantage in giving jurisdiction to the Exchequer Court, in preference to the provincial Superior Courts would outweigh the advantages.

3.7.14 As the office of registrar is somewhat of an anomaly, we see no need why this should be perpetuated. In this respect, it should be recalled that the workload of the court will be considerably reduced if our recommendations relating to the discharge of trustees and the passing of the accounts of trustees, lawyers and others are accepted. We, therefore, recommend that the office be abolished. This is not to say that there will be no officers such as clerks, masters, prothonotaries, or other court officials, to assist the court in the discharge of its responsibilities. We believe, however, that the decision as to whether administrative support is required should be made by each provincial authority, having regard to the normal practice of the courts in other matters. It should be open to these authorities to designate the functions to be performed by officers other than judges, in all matters not specifically assigned to a judge by the Bankruptcy Act.

ii The Bankruptcy Bill (s-14)

2. (1) In this Act,
'court' means
  (a) in the Provinces of Newfoundland, Nova Scotia and Ontario, the trial division or branch of the Supreme Court of the Province,
  (b) in the Provinces of British Columbia and Prince Edward Island, the Supreme Court of the Province,
  (c) in the Provinces of Alberta, Manitoba, New Brunswick and Saskatchewan, the Court of Queen's Bench for the Province,
  (d) in the Province of Quebec, the Superior Court of the Province, and
  (e) in the Yukon Territory and the Northwest Territories, the Supreme Court thereof;

381. (1) Every court has original jurisdiction in bankruptcy and in other proceedings, except proceedings under Part x, instituted under this Act during their respective terms and in vacation and in chambers.

(2) The several courts of appeal throughout Canada, within their respective jurisdictions, have jurisdiction to hear and determine appeals from the court.

(3) The lieutenant governor in council of each province shall appoint and assign such registrars or deputy registrars as he considers necessary for the transaction or disposal of matters in respect of which power or jurisdiction is given to a registrar by this Act and may limit the power or jurisdiction of any such registrar or deputy registrar.

(4) The Chief Justice of the court, and in the Province of Quebec the Chief Justice or the Associate Chief Justice in the district to which he was appointed, may, if in his opinion it is advisable or necessary for the good administration of this Act, nominate or assign one or more judges of the court to exercise judicial powers and jurisdiction conferred by this Act that may be exercised by a single judge, and the judgment, decision or order of a judge so nominated or assigned shall be deemed to be the judgment, decision or order of the court, and a reference in this Act to the court applies to any judge so exercising the powers and jurisdiction of the court.

(5) Nothing in this section diminishes or affects the powers or jurisdiction of the court or of any judge thereof not so specially nominated or assigned.

382. The Minister may, with the concurrence of the Minister of Justice, if in his opinion it is advisable or necessary for the proper administration of this Act, authorize any judge of a county court to exercise any or all of the powers and jurisdiction of the court or of a judge thereof, subject to any limitation or condition, and any judge so authorized shall be deemed to be a judge of the court and references to the court or to the judge of the court apply to such judge according to the terms of his authority.

383. The practice and procedure of the court, including the practice in chambers and the holding of examinations, shall be its ordinary procedure in civil proceedings, unless the practice or procedure is inconsistent with this Act or such regulations respecting practice and procedure and the holding of examinations as may be prescribed.

384. A judge may exercise in chambers the whole or any part of the jurisdiction conferred on him by this Act or the regulations.

385. A judge may refer any matter within the jurisdiction conferred on him by this Act or the regulations to a registrar.

386. Where the court, on application, may make an order under this Act, any interested person including an administrator may apply to the court unless the Act states expressly who may apply.

387. (1) In any proceedings under this Act, the proceedings may be instituted in a summary manner by petition, originating notice of motion, or otherwise as the rules of the court provide, and subject to any order respecting notice to interested parties or costs, or any other order the court thinks fit.

(2) Every order of a court may be enforced as if it were a judgment of the court.

388. (1) The court may, on satisfactory proof that the affairs of the bankrupt can be more economically administered within another judicial district within Canada or for other sufficient cause, transfer any pending proceeding to another judicial district in Canada.

(2) No proceeding under this Act shall be invalidated by reason of its having been instituted, taken or carried on in the wrong judicial district but the court may, at any time, transfer a proceeding to the proper judicial district.

iii *Re M. B. Greer and Company* (1953), 33 C.B.R. 69 (S.C.O.)

SMILY J.: This is an application on behalf of the trustee for an order setting aside as against the trustee a mortgage made by the above-named debtor, dated August 30, 1951, for $6,054.90, and registered in the Registry Office for the Registry Division of the City of London on September 7, 1951 as no. 56558, on the ground that the mortgage is null and void under the provisions of *The Fraudulent Conveyances Act*, R.S.O. 1950, c 148, *The Assignments and Preferences Act*, R.S.O. 1950, c 26, and s 60 of *The Bankruptcy Act*, 1949, 2nd Sess. (Can.), c 7.

It is alleged that at the time the mortgage was granted by the debtor to Webster Industries Limited the debtor had approximately 25 creditors to whom he owed approximately $16,500, including the amount of $6,504.90 owing to Webster Industries Limited, the exact amount of the mortgage; that no merchandise had been supplied to the debtor by Webster Industries Limited after December 1950; and that no present or future consideration was given by Webster Industries Limited either in cash or in goods supplied in return for the granting of the mortgage, and that the mortgage secured only the past indebtedness of the debtor to Webster Industries Limited.

One of the questions raised on this application is whether the mortgage is a settlement. In my opinion it is not a settlement. It certainly does not have the attributes that I have always considered to be associated with a settlement. Under the present statute there is no definition of 'settlement', as there was in the former *Bankruptcy Act*, R.S.C. 1927, c 11, which might be said to include a mortgage of this kind.

The main question probably is as to the procedure to be followed where the trustee attacks a mortgage given to a creditor of the debtor, and whether he may proceed in the Bankruptcy Court in the bankruptcy proceedings, or whether he must proceed by action.

Mr. Justice Middleton, in *Bartley's Trustee* v *Hill* (1921), 1 C.B.R. 477, 50 O.L.R. 321, 61 D.L.R. 473, 3 Can. Abr. 563, pointed out in effect that *The Bankruptcy Act* was framed for the purpose and with the intention of avoiding large incidental expense in the administration of the estates of insolvents. I think that is the purport of his statement. In that case an action was instituted by an authorized assignee under an assignment from an insolvent debtor to set aside a previous assignment by the debtor for the benefit of his creditors, adopting the form of assignment authorized under the Ontario statute. Middleton J. said, at p 479: '... assuming that the authorized trustee is really convinced of the necessity of removing this filmy cloud from his title, his proper remedy is found in an application under Rule 120 [now Rule 101, B. & G. 332], which provides for a summary application by the trustee to set aside any conveyance which is void under the Act as against his title. It is clear that the plaintiff has mistaken his remedy, and the action is entirely misconceived; and I, therefore, dismiss it, with costs to be paid by the trustee to the defendant.'

It has been my understanding, generally speaking, that all matters relating to the bankruptcy or connected with the bankrupt's property may be dealt with in the bankruptcy proceedings in the Bankruptcy Court, unless proceedings are taken against a stranger to the bankruptcy, as in the case of *In re Lofsky*, 28 C.B.R. 164, [1948] O.R. 782, [1947] 4 D.L.R. 374, 1947 Can. Abr. 29. I do not think that a creditor of the bankrupt, who has taken a mortgage from the debtor as security for his claim, could be considered a stranger to the bankruptcy.

At all events, having regard to the provisions of the present Act as mentioned above, and Rule 101, I am of opinion that the transfer of property by way of mortgage, such as is here attacked, may be dealt with in the Bankruptcy Court in bankruptcy proceedings, that is, summary application under Rule 101.

I think, therefore, that there should be an issue directed to try the question whether this mortgage was a fraudulent conveyance as against the creditors, and should be set aside. The trustee will be the plaintiff, and there will be pleadings and the rights of production and discovery.

COMMENT
By Lloyd W. Houlden, B.A., LL.B. of the Ontario Bar

It is clear that a question which is purely one of property and civil rights cannot be decided in a Bankruptcy Court. It is also clear that a bankruptcy matter may infringe on property and civil rights and yet be within the jurisdiction of the Bankruptcy Court. It is a difficult problem to decide where the dividing line lies between the two types of questions.

In deciding this issue, there seems to be two separate phases which must be considered. First, the Court must decide against whom the action is being brought. In that connection, it seems clear from the cases that if the action is being brought against a third party, or a stranger to the bankruptcy, that the Bankruptcy Court will not take jurisdiction: *Re Maple Leaf Fruit Co.*, 30 C.B.R. 23, [1949] 3 D.L.R. 426, 1949 Can. Abr. 26; *Re Reynolds*, 10 C.B.R. 127, 62 O.L.R. 360,

[1928] 3 D.L.R. 562, 3 Can. Abr. 514. In the present case, the action was being brought against a creditor, and on this ground the Bankruptcy Court had no difficulty in finding that there was jurisdiction.

The second phase of the question is the matter of what remedy the Court will allow to be claimed in the bankruptcy proceedings. If the remedies being sought are those given by *The Bankruptcy Act*, for example, an action to declare a transaction a preference or a settlement, there is no doubt that there is jurisdiction. The *Rousseau* case which is referred to by Mr. Justice Smily seemed to indicate that even although the action was to be maintained against a creditor, that if the remedy were not given by *The Bankruptcy Act*, that it could not properly be taken in the Bankruptcy Court. The problem arose squarely in the *Greer* case because the learned Judge indicates that the mortgage was not a settlement and therefore the remedies which were claimed were not those given by *The Bankruptcy Act*, but by provincial statutes dealing with property and civil rights. The *Rousseau* approach was rejected by the learned Judge in the case at hand, and his view seems to be that because of s 166 and s 41(6) of the present *Bankruptcy Act*, the Bankruptcy Court can take jurisdiction in this type of action even although the remedy is not one provided by *The Bankruptcy Act*. It is to be noted, however, that he refers to the provisions of *Bankruptcy Rule* 101 which seems to contemplate the type of proceedings that were brought in this action. *Quaere* whether the Court would go so far as to say that because an action is brought against a person who is not a stranger or third party to the bankruptcy, jurisdiction therefore followed to decide the matter in issue regardless of the remedy which was sought.

b / Locality

i The Bankruptcy Bill (s-14)

2. (1) In this Act,
'locality of the debtor' means, in respect of the filing of a proposed arrangement with the administrator or the filing of a petition under subsection 135(1), the bankruptcy district in which, and in all other cases, the judicial district that is the principal place in which
- (*a*) the debtor carried on business in Canada at any time during the year immediately preceding the filing of the petition or proposed arrangement,
- (*b*) the debtor resided in Canada at any time during the year immediately preceding the filing of the petition or proposed arrangement if during that period he did not carry on business in Canada,
- (*c*) the property of the debtor is situated or his debts are payable at the date of filing the petition or proposed arrangement, if during the year immediately preceding the filing of the petition or proposed arrangement the debtor did not carry on business or reside in Canada, or
- (*d*) the registered office or head office of the debtor is situated in Canada, if the debtor is a corporation;

134. (1) A petition shall be
- (*a*) in prescribed form;
- (*b*) verified by the petitioner or by a person duly authorized on his behalf who has personal knowledge of the facts alleged in the petition; and
- (*c*) except for a petition pursuant to subsection 135(1), filed with the court in the locality of the debtor and served on the debtor.

(2) Where a petition is filed with the court, the person filing the petition shall send forthwith a copy of the petition to the administrator in the locality of the debtor.

(3) No petition shall be withdrawn except with leave of the court.

135. (1) A debtor who is insolvent may file a petition in respect of himself, which petition shall be filed with the administrator in the locality of the debtor.

(2) Where a petition filed pursuant to subsection (1) is in accordance with paragraphs 134(1)(*a*) and (*b*), the administrator shall forthwith make a bankruptcy order.

ii *In Re Rotenberg* (1941), 22 C.B.R. 433 (S.C.O.)

LENNOX, ESQ., Asst. Master, Acting Registrar in Bankruptcy: This is a motion for an order rescinding the receiving order made herein by the Registrar in Bankruptcy on July 29, 1941, and was heard by me in the Registrar's absence.

On July 18, 1941, an informal meeting of creditors was held in the office of the debtor's solicitor in Toronto. On the same day a petition in bankruptcy was filed in Montreal, apparently as a result of the information disclosed at the meeting. No decision was reached by the creditors on this day, and the meeting adjourned to July 25. In the meantime, the Montreal bailiff was unable to serve the debtor at his place of business in that city, or find any trace of him in Montreal, and certified as to this under date of July 21 when the petitioning creditor obtained an order for substituted service of the petition by leaving a certified copy in the mail box and with the janitor on the premises. On July 23 the local credit manager in Toronto of the creditor telephoned the debtor and advised him of the petition.

On July 25 the adjourned meeting was unable to effect a compromise, and on this day a second petition was filed in Toronto, and served on July 26. On July 28 the debtor consented to a receiving order, and upon this consent a receiving order was made on July 29. On the same day the Deputy Registrar at Montreal appointed an interim receiver, and on the return of the petition on July 31 made a final receiving order.

On these facts Mr. Sankey submits that the local order should be rescinded or stayed under the provisions of sec. 164 [9 C.B.R. 318]. Mr. Gale, on the other hand, submits that the proper procedure is to apply to a Judge under the provisions of Rule 12 [9 C.B.R. 351]. I am unable to agree with the latter contention. Rule 12 is designed to meet a situation where a single petition has been presented in the wrong locality. Here there are competing petitions. Upon a proper application for rescission being made an officer of the Court is bound to consider whether, in view of subsequent material, the order is a proper one; and as a final analysis, having regard to the provisions of sec. 2 (*y*) [9 C.B.R. 22], which forum will best serve the interest of the estate and the body of the creditors as a whole.

The order was unquestionably properly made on the material then before the Registrar. The applicant rests his argument mainly on the theory that in the light of the debtor's consent, the local proceedings are irregular and an abuse of the process of the Court. I am referred to *In re Lalonde* (1924), 4 C.B.R. 416, 55 O.L.R. 279, 3 Can. Abr. 308, 375, in which the Court has, in effect, ruled that any action on the part of a debtor taken subsequent to the launching of a petition against him, either by making an assignment, or consenting to a later petition, should be taken as a consent to the original proceedings, on the ground that the action of the debtor is to be taken as an attempt to direct the administration of his affairs by making his own choice of custodian. These cases were decided at a time when trustees in Bankruptcy were not required to be licensed. The situation is now somewhat different; but that feature need not be considered here.

The ruling is based on the supposition that the debtor could not have been prompted by any sound or proper motive. In the present case the debtor is vitally interested, as will be disclosed later, as to where his affairs should be administered, as between the city in which he resides, or has his abode, and a point hundreds of miles distant. Many demands may be made on his time, and in view of this circumstance it cannot fairly be said it is a case of choosing between custodians.

There is no evidence that the local petitioning creditor attended the informal meetings and so was aware of the proceedings in Quebec. He refers to these meetings in his petition, but his affidavit of verification qualifies certain of his statements as based on inquiries, information and belief. The material in support of the application raises implications against him, as well as the debtor. On the other hand, it is not explained on what material the applicant saw fit to apply for an order for substituted service of this petition, an order of last recourse, when their Toronto representative was able to contact the debtor two days later. It is further not disclosed whether they were aware of the local receiving order when they applied for and obtained an order appointing an interim receiver, and if they were aware of this, what the purpose or necessity of the order was, or how it could be implemented.

Courts in Bankruptcy are auxiliary to each other, and this situation having developed, and there being no evidence of any irregularity rendering the proceedings in this Court a nullity, I consider it my duty to consider where the proceedings may be carried on most effectively and expeditiously, (tested in the light of sec. 2(y)) and if the balance rests with Quebec, to stay the proceedings here; or if, on the material, any uncertainty should still exist, then to decide in favour of Quebec as being the jurisdiction in which the first petition was presented.

The petition shall be presented to the Court having jurisdiction in the locality of the debtor: sec. 4(5) [9 C.B.R. 31]. The 'locality of a debtor' is defined by sec. 2(y)(i)(ii)(iii) [9 C.B.R. 22] as follows:

(y) 'locality of a debtor', whether a bankrupt or assignor, means

(i) the principal place where the debtor has carried on business during the year immediately preceding the date of the presentation against him of a bankruptcy petition or the making by him of an authorized assignment;

(ii) the place where the debtor has resided during the year immediately preceding the date of the presentation against him of a bankruptcy petition or the making by him of an authorized assignment; or

(iii) in cases not coming within (i) or (ii), the place where the greater portion of the property of such debtor is situate.

My understanding of the foregoing conditions is that clause (i) is the primary consideration; it weighs the direct interests of the creditors; and clause (ii) which directly considers the convenience of the debtor, and indirectly the interest of the creditors, in respect of the cost of securing the debtor's attendance, only comes into play when (i) is not conclusive.

I have been referred to many authorities containing broad principles of law but they, in my opinion, are of little assistance. We are not dealing with a technical question, but a practical question of expediency, and each particular case must be considered in the light of its own particular facts. Lord Loreburn L.C. in *De Beers Consolidated Mines Ltd.* v *Howe*, [1906] A.C. 455, at p 458, 75 L.J.K.B. 858, said: '... the real business is carried on where the central ... control actually abides'. But that was a taxation case, and consequently the decision turned on technical considerations. The central control of the debtor's business is unquestionably in Toronto, and the practical angle of this is that those who are qualified to testify as to his records and accounts, and concerning the detail of his business are resident in Toronto or the vicinity. Otherwise there is little satisfactory evidence, upon which to make a decision, under this clause. It appears that in amount of their claims, the creditors are fairly equally divided between the two jurisdictions; in the matter of numbers there is considerable doubt. The question of the collection of accounts receivable is, of course, an important factor. The debtor's sworn statement that the greater portion of these are owing in this jurisdiction is not, in itself, sufficiently definite. But the fact that this business was commenced in Toronto eight years ago, and that the Montreal branch has been only operating for four years, lends weight to the assertion.

From the foregoing consideration there appears to be a balance, if not a preponderance, of convenience in favour of carrying on proceedings in this jurisdiction. But if there should be a doubt, this is outweighed by a consideration of clause (ii). The material discloses that the debtor has resided in Toronto for the past twenty years, where he has carried on this business for the past eight years, and only commenced operating in Montreal owing to trade union difficulties in Toronto. If there was any reason to discredit his sworn statement, this would be largely offset by the Montreal bailiff's certificate, which states that he was unable to find any ordinary place of residence belonging to the debtor in Montreal.

If, indeed, the debtor has spent most of his time in Montreal in the past few years, it is still not the place of his abode, and his business having ceased, he has no apparent reason to spend more time there: *In re Tobin* (1930), 12 C.B.R. 55, 3 Can. Abr. 351, as follows, at p 58:

... it would require a very clear text to take the liquidation of an insolvent estate away from the Province where the debtor has his domicile, his principal establishment, his electoral status, where he is liable to pay taxes and where his succession, when he dies, will devolve.

Cited with approval by Mr. Justice Urquhart in *Re Solloway*, 19 C.B.R. 350, [1938] O.W.N. 373, 1938 Can. Abr. 44, is a strong statement of policy in such matters.

A person's conduct may best be reviewed in the community in which he resides, and according to the standards of such community. But I am not resting my decision on abstract considerations. As I have already indicated, if these proceedings are removed from this jurisdiction the debtor may be seriously prejudiced in earning a livelihood due to demands being made for attendance in Montreal; and otherwise even though the consideration of other factors may not be conclusive, such information as is available indicates that proceedings should be continued in Ontario.

For these reasons the application will be dismissed. The respondents are entitled to costs out of the assets of the estate forthwith after taxation.

2 DEBTORS AND CREDITORS IN BANKRUPTCY

a / The Debtor: Tassé Report, pp 101–3 (footnotes omitted)

3.2.002 The Debtor: Before a debtor, under the present Act, may voluntarily become bankrupt, his liabilities to his creditors provable as claims under the Act must amount to at least one thousand dollars. This has been the law since 1949. Prior to that, the provable claims had to amount to at least five hundred dollars. Other countries have not the same concern with the amount of debt a debtor must have before voluntarily resorting to bankruptcy. In England, all a debtor must establish is that he 'is unable to pay his debts'. The Australian Act is silent regarding the amount of debt owed by the debtor. In the United States, a voluntary petition may be filed without any consideration of the amount owed.

3.2.003 Before a debtor may be petitioned into bankruptcy, his debts owing to the petitioning creditor or creditors must amount to one thousand dollars or more. This compares with fifty pounds in England, five hundred dollars in Australia and one thousand dollars in the United States. In France, only a debtor who is in business may be put into bankruptcy and no minimum amount of debt is required.

3.2.004 Representations have been made that the minimum amount of debt a debtor must have before he may become bankrupt should be increased to two, three or five thousand dollars and that wage earners, or those who are not in business, should not be permitted to resort to bankruptcy. Both suggestions reflect a concern that some persons take an undue advantage of the *Bankruptcy Act* or that it should be more difficult for a wage earner to resort to bankruptcy.

3.2.005 Taken by itself, the amount of a person's debts is not particularly meaningful. It only becomes meaningful when the debts are compared with the person's assets. A person may, for example, have $1,000 of debts and assets worth $999 and be legally insolvent. It could be suggested that a person should not be forced into bankruptcy unless he had a deficit between his assets and liabilities of at least one thousand dollars. This would be difficult to ascertain as there could always be honest differences of opinion over the value of assets. It would, in addition, not take into consideration the case of the debtor who might have a surplus of his assets over his liabilities but, for lack of liquidity, could be quite unable to pay his debts as they fall due.

3.2.006 The time is past when bankruptcy was regarded as the privilege of only a certain class of debtors, such as merchants or traders. When credit is equally available to all, bankruptcy should be equally available to all debtors. The burden of debt is just as real and as great, if not greater, to the wage earner as the man in business. That a debtor should have a minimum amount of debt to voluntarily become bankrupt would discriminate against the small debtor. To increase the amount of debt required before a debtor could voluntarily become bankrupt, would be to further the discrimination. It would, at the same time, be somewhat absurd to have to say to the small debtor, who wanted the relief that bankruptcy could give, that he does not owe enough and to go away and incur additional debt before he could avail himself of the bankruptcy process.

3.2.007 It may be argued that, if a debtor cannot, or will not, pay his debts, bankruptcy, as a form of execution, should be available to a creditor no matter how much the debt may be. It was understandable, when bankruptcy was almost criminal in character and the penalties against a bankrupt were harsh, that the law would require a creditor to prove that the debtor owed to him a certain minimum debt before the debtor could be forced into bankruptcy. Now that many of the harshest sanctions against an insolvent debtor have been removed or ameliorated, bankruptcy is no more drastic than most other creditor rights. It is not unreasonable, however, as a condition precedent to a creditor choosing bankruptcy over any other method of execution, to continue to require him to have a substantial claim against the debtor. Such a condition has the effect of reducing the number of creditors who can, without joining others, initiate bankruptcy proceedings. This is especially the case with small debtors, as the number of their creditors with a claim of $1,000 is generally much smaller than is the case of other debtors. This seems desirable, however, as no useful purpose could be served by allowing creditors with only small claims to force the small debtors in bankruptcy. On the other hand, it would not seem reasonable to increase the amount of claim a creditor must have before he may force a debtor into bankruptcy. This might mean, in some cases, that liquidation would be postponed while the debtor became further financially involved with less assets subsequently being available to the creditors.

3.2.008 For these reasons, there should be, in our opinion, no minimum amount of debt that a debtor must have to become voluntarily bankrupt. In the case of an involuntary bankruptcy, the amount of debt that must be owed to the petitioning creditor or creditors should remain at one thousand dollars.

b / Special Classes of Debtors

i Infants

NOTE In the English case of *In re a Debtor: Commissioners of Customs and Excise* v *The Debtor*, [1950] 1 Ch. 282, the infant had been a partner in a small manufacturing venture. Both she and her partner were liable under the Finance (no. 2) Act, 1940, for purchase tax. When £284 of purchase tax was unpaid, the Commissioners of Customs and Excise applied for a receiving order against both partners. The Registrar in Bankruptcy made an order against the adult partner, but refused to make one against the infant, holding that he had no jurisdiction to do so.

The English Court of Appeal held that in this business the infant could be adjudicated bankrupt. The Act under which she owed the tax created no exemption for infants and there was therefore a binding and owing debt. Thus it could be a basis for a petition for a receiving order. Where prior confusion stemmed from, the Court decided, was the fact that, under common law, and in particular under the Infants Relief Act, 1874, there were few debts that were binding upon infants. If the debt was not binding, bankruptcy could not occur. However, if the debt is binding notwithstanding the infancy of the debtor, then that infancy is not a bar to bankruptcy.

ii Farmers and Fishermen: Tassé Report, p 103

3.2.009 Under the present Act, an individual engaged solely in fishing, farming or the tillage of the soil or who works for wages, salary, commission or hire at a rate of compensation not exceeding twenty-five hundred dollars per year and who does not, on his own account, carry on business, cannot be forced into bankruptcy, by reason of section 25 of the present Act. The protection that this section purports to give is, in fact, illusory. The property of these debtors that, by virtue of this section, cannot be seized through the bankruptcy process may be seized through other methods of execution. If, however, by provincial law, the property of these debtors is exempt from seizure, the same would apply in bankruptcy, as the property that is exempt from vesting in the trustee is the property that by provincial law is exempt from seizure.
3.2.010 An undischarged bankrupt is required, by the effect of section 157, to disclose the fact that he is an undischarged bankrupt whenever he seeks to obtain credit for a purpose other than necessaries of life. Creditors are prevented, by the effect of section 25, from forcing into bankruptcy farmers, fishermen, and the other persons mentioned therein. It follows that the obligation imposed by section 157 and the possible credit restrictions that its compliance would normally entail cannot be extended to these persons, unless they voluntarily file an assignment in bankruptcy. As a result, it may be argued that section 25 has been designed to protect, in this way, these persons.
3.2.001 In the new *Bankruptcy Act* that we are proposing, the provision equivalent to the present section 157 would apply only to debtors who have been dishonest or held responsible for their bankruptcy and to no others. As a result, farmers and fishermen with clean hands would enjoy the same protection as under the present Act, even if the creditors are permitted to exercise against them, as well as against the other debtors, the collective means of execution devised by the Bankruptcy Act. For this reason, there would be no justification, in the proposed Act, for a provision comparable to section 25.

The Bankruptcy Bill (S-14)

139. Sections 136 to 138 do not apply to an individual debtor who derives all or substantially all of his income from farming or fishing.

See below, p 775, for sections 136–8

NOTE In *Re Gartrell* (1923), 3 C.B.R. 874 (Sask. K.B.), affirmed (1923–4), 4 C.B.R. 103 (Sask. C.A.), a businessman who suddenly took up farming after committing an act of bankruptcy was not permitted to take advantage of the exemption. *Re Gartrell* was followed in *Re Doerbecker*, [1941] 3 D.L.R. 776 (S.C.O.).
QUESTION What is the policy of the exemption for farmers? Is it to protect them from bankruptcy for debts incurred on the farm, or is it to protect them as a class from being forced off the land by bankruptcy? Does *Gartrell* apply this policy correctly?

A farming corporation cannot be exempted from a petition. The word 'individual' as used in s 30 [now s 139] of the Act means 'natural person', as distinct from a corporation: *Re Witchekan Lake Farms Ltd.*, [1975] 1 W.W.R. 471, 50 D.L.R. (3d) 314 (Sask. C.A.).

iii The Deceased Debtor: The Bankruptcy Bill (S-14)

GENERAL

410. (1) For the purposes of this Act, except where otherwise expressly provided in this Act, a person and
   (*a*) on his death, his heirs, executors, administrators or other legal representative, or
   (*b*) on his being found to be mentally incompetent or incapable of handling his own affairs, his committee or other legal representative
are deemed to be one and the same person and the acts or omissions of the one are deemed to be the acts or omissions of the other.

(2) Subsection (1) does not apply where a person who dies or is found to be mentally incompetent or incapable of handling his own affairs is accused of an offence under Part X.

(3) Where a debtor in respect of whom a petition or a proposed arrangement has been filed dies, the proceedings thereunder shall, unless the court otherwise orders, be continued as if he were alive or as if a legal representative had been appointed in respect of him and the court may, for the purpose of the proceedings, appoint a person to administer the estate during the proceedings.

iv Partnership: The Bankruptcy Bill (S-14), ss 154; 164–6

154. (1) The court may make a bankruptcy order on proof of
   (*a*) the facts alleged in the petition;
   (*b*) the service of the petition on the debtor; and
   (*c*) the sending of the petition to the administrator in the locality of the debtor.

(2) Where a bankruptcy order is made in respect of a partnership, no member of the partnership is, or shall be deemed to be, a bankrupt as a result of such bankruptcy order.

(3) Notwithstanding the dissolution of a partnership, a bankruptcy order may be made in respect of it at any time before the final liquidation and distribution of the assets of the partnership.

(4) Where bankruptcy orders are made against all the partners of a partnership other than the limited partners, if any, the court may make a bankruptcy order in respect of the partnership.

164. (1) Where a bankruptcy order is made in respect of a partnership, the court, on application, may determine whether the partnership property is sufficient to pay the costs of administration and the claims proved in the bankruptcy and where it finds a deficiency may

(a) order that a judgment for the amount of such deficiency be entered in favour of the trustee of the estate of the partnership against

(i) one or more of the general partners who is not a bankrupt, or

(ii) any limited partner to the extent that he is found to be liable for the claims proved in the bankruptcy;

(b) fix a time within which the amount of the judgment under paragraph (a) shall be paid; and

(c) until the estate of the partnership is fully administered, stay proceedings, other than proceedings under this Act, against any member of the partnership in respect of claims in respect of debts for which the partner and partnership are jointly liable.

(2) Where a bankruptcy order is made in respect of a member of a partnership or a partnership, the court that has jurisdiction over the member or partnership may, for the purposes of this Act, assume jurisdiction over all the members of the partnership and the partnership and may consolidate the proceedings or any of them on such terms as the court thinks fit.

(3) The trustee shall keep separate accounts of the property of a partnership and the property of each member of the partnership who is a bankrupt.

(4) The costs of administration shall be paid from the estate of the partnership and each of the partners who is a bankrupt in such proportions as the registrar decides when he passes the final statement of accounts of the trustee.

165. (1) Where a partnership is a bankrupt, the property of the partnership shall be applied in the first instance in payment of the debts of the partnership, and the separate property of each partner shall be applied in the first instance in payment of his separate debts.

(2) Where a partnership is a bankrupt, the trustee of the bankrupt partnership may file a claim against the estate of each partner for the amount of any debts of the partnership.

(3) Where there is a surplus after paying the debts of a partner in respect of his separate property, the surplus is deemed to be part of the property of the partnership.

(4) Where there is a surplus in respect of the property of a partnership, such surplus is deemed to be a part of the separate property of each partner in proportion to his right and interest in the property of the partnership.

166. (1) Where a member of a partnership becomes a bankrupt, the court, on application of the trustee and after notice to the other members of the partnership, may

(a) authorize the trustee to institute or continue any proceeding on behalf of the partnership; and

(b) direct that the other members

(i) receive their proper share of the benefits derived from the proceeding, or

(ii) be indemnified against costs, if they do not claim any benefit from the proceeding.

(2) Where, pursuant to subsection (1), authority to institute or continue a proceeding is given to the trustee, any release of the claim to which the proceeding relates that is given by the members of the partnership without the concurrence of the trustee at any time after the trustee has given the members notice of an application to the court to institute or continue the proceeding is unenforceable against the trustee.

(3) This section applies to persons who are jointly and severally liable as if they were partners.

Re Squires Bros., [1922] 3 C.B.R. 191 (Sask. K.B.).

MACLEAN, J. On March 23, 1922, Charles E. Squires, one of the two partners in the firm of Squires Bros., of Domremy, Saskatchewan, purported to make on behalf of his firm an assignment under *The Bankruptcy Act*, 1919, ch. 36, in favour of the Canadian Credit Men's Trust Association, Limited, as authorized trustee. The trustee proceeded to wind up the partnership business and did sell the assets. The other partner, William Squires, was, about this time, absent from Domremy for a few weeks, and was not apprised of the assignment, nor was he aware of the activities of the trustee until after the partnership assets had been sold. Immediately upon William Squires ascertaining what had transpired, he notified the trustee and protested against any further dealings with the affairs of the firm. The trustee now brings this application for directions. A notice of motion was served on all the interested parties. A great many questions are asked by the trustee, but they all depend on the validity of the assignment, and the intention of this application is to bring up the question in this summary way.

Counsel for the trustee relies upon sec. 85 (as amended, 1921, ch. 17) of *The Bankruptcy Act*, [1 C.B.R. 581] which reads as follows:

> For all or any of the purposes of this Act, an incorporated company may act by any of its officers or employees authorized in that behalf, a firm may act by any of its members, and a lunatic may act by his committee or curator or by the guardian or curator of his property.

It is contended on behalf of the trustee that as the section quoted expressly provides that the officer or employee acting for an incorporated company must be authorized in that behalf, and as no such provision is stated in respect to a member by whom a firm acts, the lack of definite or any authority by a firm to one of its members to make an assignment will not affect the validity of that assignment. In my opinion the section quoted merely outlines procedure in making an assignment and does not purport to, and could not, change the substantive law affecting partnerships. A member of a partnership may bind himself and his partners upon all contracts made in the course of the ordinary scope of the partnership business. An assignment such as the one in question is not within the ordinary scope of the partnership business, but practically amounts to a suspension of business and a dissolution of the partnership itself. The law on this point is very fully and forcibly stated by Draper, C.J. in *Cameron v Stevenson* (1862) 12 U.C.C.P. 389. It is clear, therefore, that in the absence of authority from or subsequent ratification by William Squires the assignment cannot be considered the assignment of the firm.

The evidence before me is to the effect that William Squires did not authorize his partner, Charles E. Squires, to make the assignment. An affidavit, filed on behalf of the trustee, alleges, that what Charles E. Squires stated to the trustee at the time was that his brother William would have no objection if he, Charles E. Squires, made an assignment on behalf of the firm. It is clear from the affidavit of William E. Squires himself and the affidavit filed on behalf of the trustee that Charles E. Squires had no authority to make the assignment and that he did not represent to the trustee that he had such authority. It is also clear, from the affidavit of William Squires, that there has been no ratification by himself of the act of his brother in making the assignment.

Counsel for the trustee argues that the words in reference to a firm in the section of *The Bankruptcy Act* above quoted should be strictly construed, and that by implication a member of the firm need not be specially authorized as is required of an officer or employee of an incorporated company. The strict interpretation of the words in question is that a firm may, by one of its members, make an assignment. What is really contended for by counsel is an interpretation to the effect that a member may make an assignment for his firm – something totally different to a firm acting by one of its members.

In my opinion the assignment is invalid. In view of that it is unnecessary to deal with any of the questions raised, excepting the second question, which in substance is whether the assignment may be treated as the assignment of Charles E. Squires himself and whether his assets pass to the trustee. It is true that if the assignment were a valid one the separate assets of Charles E. Squires would pass to the assignee as well as his interest in the firm, and if Charles E. Squires had made a personal assignment his interest in the partnership would also pass to the trustee and the ultimate result might be the same in either case. But he clearly did not intend to make a personal assignment, or he would have done so, and it is not difficult to conceive numerous instances where a partner might be ready to enter into an assignment by the firm and yet not be willing to make a personal assignment.

It seems to me that an authorized assignment under *The Bankruptcy Act* must be the voluntary act of the assignor, and must show expressly and not by implication his intention to assign. An authorized assignment cannot be construed out of a document which the party executing it intended for some other purpose, even though the execution of that document might, in itself, constitute an act of bankruptcy. The assignment in question does not constitute an assignment under the Act by Charles E. Squires. William Squires will have his costs against the trustee.

QUESTION If a partner can create binding debts that lead to a petition against the firm, why not let him assign the firm into bankruptcy? Would *Re Squire Bros.* still be valid under the new Bankruptcy Bill?

v The Corporation: Tassé Report, pp 57–8; 108–9; 127–8 (footnotes omitted)

2.1.30 *The Limited Liability Corporation*: A corporation is a legal entity separate and distinct from its shareholders. As a rule, it is only the corporation that is bound by the action done in its name or on its behalf, and not its shareholders, directors or officers. The abuse of this rule has posed serious problems in bankruptcy administration.

2.1.31 The *Bankruptcy Act* treats corporations in almost all respects as if they were individuals. There are only a very few sections of the Act that deal with the special circumstances of corporations. Section 118, for example, specifies who must perform the duties of a bankrupt, where the bankrupt is a corporation, and section 162 imposes a penal liability upon officers of a corporation and others who authorize, condone or participate in the commission of an offence. Special rules have also been devised to reach the individuals who control corporations, where dividends have been paid, or shares redeemed, while the corporation was insolvent. Under company legislation, liability is also usually imposed upon directors for the payment of arrears of wages to employees.

2.1.32 In many respects, the *Bankruptcy Act* is ineffective in the case of limited liability corporations. Sanctions against undischarged bankrupts, for example, are meaningless, where the debtor is a corporation. The device of the limited liability corporation is often used to make a mockery of the provisions of the *Bankruptcy Act* designed to keep out of business the dishonest or incompetent businessman. To use the words of Senator David A. Croll, 'more and more businesses have clothed themselves in corporate garments which have neither bodies to be kicked nor souls to be damned.'

2.1.33 In actual practice, there is little apparent difference between an individual in business, in his own right, and an individual who does business through a limited liability company of which he is the beneficial owner of all of its shares. There is, however, a very real difference when a bankruptcy occurs. In the one case, the individual is required to surrender all of his property that is not exempt from seizure. He may also be refused a discharge or have a discharge granted subject to conditions. This may effectively keep him out of business for some time. In the other case, the individual, on the bankruptcy of his company, may keep all of his own personal property. The company, alone, is required to surrender its property and it is, as a rule, immaterial to the individual whether or not the company is given a discharge. The inconvenience caused to this individual often lasts no longer than it takes to incorporate a new company. The use of a limited company in such a manner can often put the law in disrepute.

2.1.34 The corporate veil has been frequently pierced in company, combines and taxing statutes. Sometimes, this has not been easy to accomplish, but one should not be discouraged, as an English judge once said: 'the legislature can forge a sledge-hammer capable of cracking open the corporate shell.' A principle that commends itself was contained, some years ago, in the following dictum in the reasons for judgment of a case tried in the United States: 'When the notion of legal entity is used to defeat public convenience, justify wrong, protect fraud or defend crime, the law will regard the corporation as an association of persons.'

3.2.024 *Persons Abusing the 'Corporate Veil'*. A primary purpose of the *Bankruptcy Act* is to prevent fraud and to encourage commercial morality. This can only be achieved if the debtor is subject to the control of the court. Where the debtor is a corporation, the corporate entity may have to be disregarded, so that the economic realities behind the legal facade may be taken into account in exercising control over those who acted on behalf of the corporation. In order to prevent a dishonest or incompetent debtor from returning to business, it will be recommended *infra*, in 3.2.097 that the incapacities of a bankrupt be increased and extended over a longer period of time. This could be largely ineffective in preventing fraud and promoting commercial morality, if the flesh and blood individuals who were responsible for corporate decisions cannot be reached, so that the incapacities imposed upon individual debtors could be imposed upon them. In England, the court may restrain those convicted of certain offences involving fraud from acting as directors or taking part in the management of companies for a period not exceeding five years. We make a recommendation in this respect, *infra*, in 3.2.096.

3.2.025 When bankruptcy occurs, however, much damage may already have been done and the question arises as to whether some liability should not, in some circumstances, personally attach to the directors or officers of the bankrupt corporation. There are precedents for setting aside the corporate veil where it has been abused and creditors have suffered. The English *Companies Act*, for example, provides that if, in the course of the winding up of a company, it appears that any business of the company has been carried on with intent to defraud creditors or for any fraudulent purpose, the court may declare that persons who were knowingly parties to the fraud shall be personally responsible, without any limitation of liability, for all or any of the debts or other liabilities of the company. The French *Code de Commerce* similarly provides that

... peut être déclaré personnellement en règlement judiciare ou liquidation des biens tout dirigeant de droit ou de fait, apparent ou occulte, rémunéré ou non, qui a:
– sous le couvert de la personne morale masquant ses agissements, fait des actes de commerce dans un intérêt personnel;
– ou disposé des biens sociaux comme des siens propres;
– ou poursuivi abusivement, dans son intérêt personnel, une exploitation déficitaire qui ne pouvait conduire qu'à la cessation des paiements de la personne morale.

3.2.026 We recommend that, where a person carries on business through the means of a limited liability corporation that he, or persons related to him, control and, that becomes bankrupt, the court should have, in specific circumstances such as those described *infra* in 3.2.027, the power to order that person to pay to the estate in bankruptcy of the corporation an amount being the equivalent to the deficiency between the assets and liabilities of the corporation at the time of bankruptcy. Such person should, however, be allowed to limit his liability by proving that the loss suffered by the creditors and resulting from his misconduct was less than such deficiency.

3.2.027 We believe that the recommendation contained in the preceding paragraph should apply where the person referred to therein,

i has made, in his own interest or in the interest of a person related to him, a transaction that cannot reasonably be considered to have been entered into in the interest of the corporation;

ii mingled his own property with that of the corporation or dealt with the property of the corporation as if it were his own, or

iii was, in any way, responsible for the corporation conducting its business with a view to defrauding its creditors or for any other fraudulent purposes.

The recommendation should also apply where the corporation continued to do business resulting in some benefit or advantage to the person, or persons related to him, that controlled the corporation, when they knew or should have known that the corporation was insolvent and that there was no reasonable expectation that it would soon become solvent.

3.2.095 We have expressed the view, *supra* (2.1.30 et seq.), that the present *Bankruptcy Act* has not sufficiently kept pace with the manner in which business is conducted through the use of the limited liability corporation. Not only is it most difficult to reach the controlling agents of a bankrupt corporation, but the sanctions that apply in the case of an individual bankrupt and the status of a bankrupt are largely meaningless in the case of a corporation. For these reasons, it is important that some procedure be devised so that the grossly incompetent or dishonest businessman who had been trading through the device of a corporation could be kept out of business, as if he had been trading under his own name.

3.2.096 For these reasons, we recommend that the legal status of a bankrupt should apply not only to all individual bankrupts, but also to such directors or officers (including those who, in fact, control the affairs of the corporation) of a corporation who are, for example, either primarily responsible for the bankruptcy of a corporation or who have substantially aggravated its insolvency. In the latter case, the status of a bankrupt would extend to an officer or director of a bankrupt corporation only on the order of the court. The effect of bankruptcy attaching to the property of a bankrupt would not, in such a case, extend to this type of bankrupt, except in the circumstances described supra in 3.2.024 to 3.2.027.

The Bankruptcy Bill (s-14)

2. (1) In this Act,
'agent' means

(a) in respect of a corporation, a director or an officer thereof or any person who is related to the corporation or who has, directly or indirectly, *de facto* control of the corporation... but does not include an interim receiver, trustee or receiver.

188. (1) Where a bankruptcy order is made in respect of a corporation, the directors and former directors of the corporation are jointly and severally liable to employees of the corporation

(a) for all wages payable at the date of bankruptcy to the employees not exceeding two thousand dollars for each such employee for services performed for the corporation; and (*b*) for any amount that had become due and payable by the corporation prior to the date of bankruptcy as pension and other health and welfare plan contributions in respect of the employees of the corporation, other than employees related to the corporation or an agent or former agent of the corporation, to the amount of five hundred dollars in respect of each such employee,

while they are or were such directors.

(2) A director or former director is not liable under subsection (1) unless a proof of claim for wages has been filed within six months after the date of bankruptcy and has not been disallowed.

(3) A director or former director is not liable under subsection (1) if he relies in good faith on

(*a*) financial statements of the corporation represented to him by an officer of the corporation or in a written report of the auditor of the corporation fairly to reflect the financial condition of the corporation; or

(*b*) a report of a lawyer, accountant, engineer, appraiser or other person whose profession lends credibility to a statement made by him.

(4) Where a director or former director pays wages referred to in subsection (1) for which an employee has an admissible claim in the bankruptcy of the corporation, the director or former director is entitled to any priority that the employee would have been entitled to and, where a judgment has been obtained, he is entitled to an assignment of the judgment.

(5) A director or former director who has satisfied a claim for wages under this section is entitled to contribution from the other directors or former directors who are liable for the wages.

(6) For the purposes of this section, 'corporation' means a body corporate incorporated to carry on business.

(7) In this section, 'former director' means any person who was a director of a corporation at any time within the two years immediately preceding the date of filing of a petition in respect of the corporation.

189. (1) Subject to section 192, an agent or former agent is liable for any deficiency in the estate of a person for whom he acts as agent where that person becomes a bankrupt and the agent or former agent, in his own pecuniary interest or the pecuniary interest of someone related to him other than the person who became a bankrupt, caused the person when the person was insolvent

(*a*) to carry on business in a manner that, at that time, was contrary to the pecuniary interest of the person;

(*b*) to enter into a transaction that, at the time of the transaction, was contrary to the pecuniary interest of the person to enter;

(*c*) to refrain from carrying on business in a manner that, at the time, was in the pecuniary interest of the person to carry on;

(*d*) to refrain from entering into a transaction that, at the time, would have been considered to be in the pecuniary interest of the person;

(*e*) to continue a business by resorting to sales below cost to the detriment of the creditors, ruinous borrowings or similar acts in circumstances where it was not reasonable to expect that bankruptcy could be prevented and where those acts would aggravate the insolvency of the person; or

(*f*) to conduct a business with a view to impeding, defrauding, obstructing or delaying the creditors of the business generally.

(2) Where, on application of the trustee, it is proved that an agent or former agent is liable for a deficiency in the estate of the person for whom he was acting as agent, the court may, subject to subsection (3), give judgment to the trustee for the amount of the deficiency.

(3) An agent or former agent is not liable for a deficiency in the estate of the person for whom

he acted as agent where it is proved that
    (*a*) at any time after the agent or former agent caused such person to take any of the actions set out in subsection (1), the person was solvent; or
    (*b*) such agent or former agent relied in good faith on
        (i) where the person is an individual, financial statements of the person represented to him by the person or in a written report of the auditor of the person fairly to reflect the financial condition of the person,
        (ii) where the person is a corporation, financial statements of the corporation represented to him by an officer of the corporation or in a written report of the auditor of the corporation fairly to reflect the financial condition of the corporation, or
        (iii) a report of a solicitor, accountant, appraiser or other person whose profession lends credibility to a statement made by him.

190. Where an agent or former agent fails to keep accounts in a manner that permits the trustee to distinguish the property of the agent or former agent from that of the person for whom he acts or acted as agent and such person subsequently becomes a bankrupt, the agent or former agent, subject to section 192, is liable for the deficiency in the estate and, on application of the trustee and on establishing the amount of the deficiency, the court shall give judgment to the trustee for that amount.

191. Where, under sections 190 and 191, an agent or former agent is liable for the amount of the deficiency in an estate, the liability of the agent or former agent is reduced if and to the extent that it is proved that the amount of the loss or damage caused to the estate by the agent or former agent is smaller than the amount of the deficiency.

372. (1) Where a corporation is guilty of an offence under this Act, any agent or former agent of the corporation who directed, authorized, assented to, acquiesced in or participated in the commission of the offence is a party to and guilty of the offence and is liable on conviction to the punishment provided for the offence whether or not the corporation is prosecuted or convicted therefor.

c / The Creditor: Tassé Report, pp 103–5 (footnotes omitted)

3.2.012 *Who May Petition?*: Under the present *Bankruptcy Act*, only a creditor may petition the court for a receiving order against a debtor. This reflects a philosophy that bankruptcy is essentially a private matter between the creditors and their debtor. Very often, however, the creditors are unaware of the insolvency of their debtor at an early stage. This results in lengthening the critical period, before bankruptcy, during which the assets of a debtor available for distribution among his creditors may decrease. 'It is of the very essence of every wise and judicious bankrupt law, not only to provide for the fair, equal and speedy distribution of the estate of the insolvent, but to step in and arrest his downward course to ruin, so as to save for the creditors as much of the estate as possible. ...'

3.2.013 Often the creditor may not be the first to know that his debtor is insolvent. Frequently, the first to know that a debtor is in financial difficulties is a department or agency of government that exercises some regulatory or supervisory authority over the affairs of a debtor, such as a Department of Insurance or a Securities Commission. Where such a department or agency of government exercises such an authority, it is to protect the public from the possibility of fraud and to promote its confidence in the regulated enterprise. The public, however, may have a misconception of the role of these agencies and may be lulled into a false sense of security. Many people are, for example, under the impression that, if such a government department or agency has good grounds to believe that a regulated enterprise is insolvent or is about to become insolvent, it will petition for a bankruptcy order in respect of the enterprise. In a statement made in December of 1966, following the collapse of Prudential Finance Corporation, the Attorney-General of the Province of Ontario, the Honourable A.A. Wishart, questioned the adequacy of the *Bankruptcy Act* and the *Criminal Code* and suggested that the impact of the collapse might have been less severe, had the law been adequate. The criticism made by Mr. Wishart was to the effect that the *Bankruptcy Act* did not permit a government to take any action when it comes to its knowledge that a company may be in some financial difficulties, unless, of course, the government is a creditor.

3.2.014 For these reasons, we recommend that any agency or department of government, whether federal or provincial, that exercises a regulatory or supervisory authority over the financial affairs of a debtor, should be given the means of initiating bankruptcy proceedings whenever this would be necessary for the protection of the public interest. There are at least three precedents for such legislation.

The Canada Deposit Insurance Corporation Act, for example, provides in section 29 that:

(1) Where, in the opinion of the (Canada Deposit Insurance) corporation, a member institution is or is about to become insolvent, the corporation may, for the protection of the public interest, initiate and take any measures or proceedings that a creditor of the member institution may initiate or take under law to preserve the assets of the member institution, to have it wound-up or petition for a receiving order under the *Bankruptcy Act.*

(2) For the purpose of this section, the corporation shall be deemed to be a creditor of a member institution notwithstanding that the deposit insurance in respect thereof has been cancelled.

Subsection 2 of section 161 of Part III (dealing with Insurance Companies) of the *Winding-Up Act* reads as follows:

(2) When any company is deemed to be insolvent under the provisions of this Act, or of any other act of the Parliament of Canada, the Attorney-General of Canada, on the request of the Minister (of Finance), may apply to the court for an order that the company be wound up.

A further and recent precedent may be found in the *Bill for an Act Respecting Investment Companies*. Subsection 1 of section 25 of this Bill provides that, under specific circumstances,

... the Attorney-General for Canada may apply to a court of competent jurisdiction for a receiving order under the *Bankruptcy Act* and a receiving order may be made against such company as if it had committed an act of bankruptcy.

3.2.015 We also recommend that the Superintendent of Bankruptcy, for the reason outlined *infra*, 3.4.22, should have the power, in the limited circumstances there described, to initiate bankruptcy proceedings.

3 COMMENCEMENT OF PROCEEDINGS

a / Voluntarily: The Bankruptcy Bill (s-14)

4. For the purposes of this Act, a person is insolvent where

(*a*) the property of the person, if it were realized at a fair value, would be insufficient to pay all his certain and liquidated debts whether or not the debts are due; or

(*b*) the person has ceased to pay his certain and liquidated debts generally as they become due.

134. (1) A petition shall be

(*a*) in prescribed form;

(*b*) verified by the petitioner or by a person duly authorized on his behalf who has personal knowledge of the facts alleged in the petition; and

(*c*) except for a petition pursuant to subsection 135(1), filed with the court in the locality of the debtor and served on the debtor.

(2) Where a petition is filed with the court, the person filing the petition shall send forthwith a copy of the petition to the administrator in the locality of the debtor.

(3) No petition shall be withdrawn except with leave of the court.

135. (1) A debtor who is insolvent may file a petition in respect of himself, which petition shall be filed with the administrator in the locality of the debtor.

(2) Where a petition filed pursuant to subsection (1) is in accordance with paragraphs 134(1)(*a*) and (*b*), the administrator shall forthwith make a bankruptcy order.

b / Involuntarily: The Bankruptcy Bill (s-14)

136. One or more unsecured creditors of a debtor may file a petition in respect of the debtor where, at the date of the filing, the debtor

(*a*) is insolvent; and

(*b*) is indebted to the petitioner or petitioners in an aggregate amount of at least one thousand dollars and the debt or each of the debts, as the case may be, would, if a bankruptcy order were made, be an admissible claim in the bankruptcy.

137. (1) Where a secured creditor

(*a*) undertakes to give up his security interest for the benefit of the unsecured creditors in the event of the making of a bankruptcy order against a debtor, or

(*b*) gives the particulars of his security interest and an estimate of its value,

he may be admitted as a petitioning creditor in the same manner as if he were an unsecured creditor, but, where the secured creditor gives the particulars of his security interest and an estimate of its value, he shall not be admitted as a petitioning creditor for more than the amount by which the debt owing to him exceeds the estimated value of the property subject to the security interest.

(2) Where a bankruptcy order is made, and a secured creditor has been admitted as a petitioning creditor pursuant to subsection 1, the trustee may direct the secured creditor to execute any power of attorney, conveyance, deed or instrument that may be required to give full effect to the undertaking given by that creditor pursuant to paragraph (1)(*a*).

138. Where a department or agency of the Government of Canada or of a province exercises a regulatory or supervisory function in respect of the financial condition of a debtor and the debtor is insolvent, the Attorney General of Canada or the attorney general of the province, as the case may be, may file a petition in respect of the debtor

(*a*) on his own initiative, where he is the head of the department or is responsible for the agency before Parliament or the legislature; or

(*b*) at the request of the minister who, for Canada or the province, is head of the department or is responsible for the agency before Parliament or the legislature.

c / Via the Breakdown of an Arrangement

i The Consumer Debtor: The Bankruptcy Bill (s-14)

96. (1) On application and on such notice to the administrator as may be prescribed, the court may annul an arrangement made under this Part where it constitutes a fraud with respect to a particular creditor and, on such an annulment, the debtor is deemed to have filed a petition in respect of himself under subsection 135(1) that is in accordance with paragraphs 134(1)(*a*) and (*b*) and the administrator shall forthwith make a bankruptcy order in respect of the debtor.

(2) On application and on such notice to the administrator as may be prescribed, the court may annul an arrangement made under this Part where the debtor defaults

    (*a*) in fulfilling his duties under this Act; or

    (*b*) in complying with the terms of the arrangement, an order of the court or a direction of the administrator.

97. (1) Any creditor who is bound by an arrangement and who is entitled to file a petition in respect of an insolvent debtor pursuant to section 136 or 137 may, within thirty days of a notice sent by the administrator pursuant to subsection 73(10) or 95(10) or paragraph 96(4)(*a*), file with the administrator a petition in respect of a debtor where

    (*a*) a proposed arrangement with respect to such debtor is withdrawn, rejected or deemed to be rejected pursuant to section 73;

    (*b*) an arrangement is rejected or deemed to be rejected pursuant to section 95;

    (*c*) the court annuls an arrangement with respect to the debtor pursuant to subsection 96(2); or

    (*d*) such arrangement is deemed to have been annulled under subsection 96(3).

(2) Where a petition filed with the administrator pursuant to subsection (1) is in accordance with paragraphs 134(1)(*a*) and (*b*), the administrator shall, if a trustee is willing to act, forthwith make a bankruptcy order.

ii The Commercial Debtor: The Bankruptcy Bill (s-14)

114. (1) Where a proposed arrangement is deemed to be rejected under subsection 110(3) or where, at their first meeting, the creditors whose claims are to be affected by an arrangement do not accept the proposed arrangement,

    (*a*) if a petition had not been filed before the proposed arrangement was filed or before a notice of intention was filed, a petition in respect of the debtor is deemed to have been filed

      (i) on the day the proposed arrangement was filed with the administrator, or

      (ii) where the proposed arrangement was preceded by a notice of intention, on the day such notice was filed with the administrator;

    (*b*) the chairman of the meeting shall, if the proposed arrangement was intended to affect all classes of claims of unsecured creditors, forthwith hold a meeting of the creditors present which meeting is deemed to be a meeting called pursuant to section 203; and

    (*c*) if the proposed arrangement was not intended to affect all classes of claims of unsecured creditors, the trustee named in the proposed arrangement shall, within five days, call the meeting of creditors required by section 203.

(2) Subsection (1) does not apply to a proposed arrangement that affects only the claims of secured creditors.

(3) Where a petition in respect of a debtor is deemed to be filed under subsection (1), the

administrator shall forthwith make a bankruptcy order in respect of the debtor and appoint as trustee

   (*a*) a trustee whom he shall, as far as possible, select by reference to the wishes of the most interested creditors, if ascertainable at that time; or

   (*b*) the trustee named in the proposed arrangement that the creditors did not accept.

(4) Where a petition in respect of a debtor was filed before a proposed arrangement was filed and, at their first meeting, the creditors whose claims are to be affected by the arrangement do not accept the proposed arrangement, the administrator shall forthwith make a bankruptcy order in respect of the debtor and appoint as trustee

   (*a*) a trustee whom he shall, as far as possible, select by reference to the wishes of the most interested creditors if ascertainable at that time, or

   (*b*) the trustee named in the proposed arrangement that the creditors did not accept, and the trustee so appointed shall,

   (*c*) if the proposed arrangement was intended to affect all classes of claims of unsecured creditors, forthwith hold a meeting of the creditors present which meeting is deemed to be a meeting called pursuant to section 203; and

   (*d*) if the proposed arrangement was not intended to affect all classes of claims of unsecured creditors, within five days, call the meeting of creditors required by section 203.

4 ACTS OF BANKRUPTCY

a / Tassé Report, pp 105–7 (footnotes omitted)

3.2.016 *Acts of Bankruptcy*: Traditionally, the conduct of the debtor, and not financial embarrassment, was the essential element of an involuntary bankruptcy. The status of bankruptcy commenced with an act by the debtor, such as flight from the country or a withdrawal from the market place. As bankruptcy was originally largely criminal or quasi-criminal in character, it was felt that a debtor should not be forced into bankruptcy, unless he had done something to merit such treatment. As one writer explained:

The objective of the medieval law was to deal with the debtor who had done something that was legally culpable. Gradually the element of culpability became secondary and the mere fact that something, not necessarily culpable, had been done, that an act had been committed, became the essence of bankruptcy. The objective of the modern law is radically different. Instead of primarily dealing with the legal phenomenon involved in the debtor's *conduct*, it seeks to regulate the economic situation that arises out of the debtor's financial *condition*.

More recently, Professor J.A. MacLachlan, who is regarded as one of the most prominent of modern scholars of bankruptcy in the United States, said:

It has become increasingly apparent in modern times, however, that these so called acts (of bankruptcy) are merely statutory conditions precedent to the maintenance of an involuntary petition, and have no necessary relation to the metaphysical concept of an act done by the bankrupt or omitted by him in default of the discharge of some duty within his power to perform.

'Acts of bankruptcy' are now recognized as 'nothing but the reflexes of an insolvent man.' The failure to found bankruptcy upon the fact of insolvency rather than upon the commission of an act, has resulted in 'a weakening of the bankruptcy law in relation to its important function of doing equity between creditors.' The necessity of having to prove an 'act of bankruptcy' often delays bankruptcy until the debtor has become more deeply in debt, with the result that the creditors receive less.

3.2.017 The inadequacy of a system based on 'acts of bankruptcy' has long been apparent and attempts have been made to circumvent them. In England, 'acts of bankruptcy' do not apply to corporations, which may be wound up if the corporation is 'unable to pay its debts'. Moreover, a judgment creditor of an individual may, pursuant to the *Bankruptcy Act*, serve a notice upon the debtor to pay the amount owing in seven days. Failure to comply with the notice constitutes an 'act of bankruptcy'. This has the effect of almost dispensing with the use of other 'acts of bankruptcy' by judgment creditors. In Canada, under the *Winding-Up Act*, there is no provision for 'acts of bankruptcy'; a company is deemed insolvent 'if it is unable to pay its debts as they become due.' This definition was used as a model for a new 'act of bankruptcy', first introduced into the *Bankruptcy Act* in 1922, which provided that 'a debtor commits an act of bankruptcy ... if he ceases to meet his liabilities generally as they become due.' It has become the 'act of bankruptcy' most frequently used by a petitioning creditor in Canada.

3.2.018 The traditional concern over the conduct of a debtor was not matched by a similar concern as to whether or not the debtor was insolvent. These concepts have evolved to such an extent that

insolvency, using that term in the widest sense, is a primary consideration in determining who shall and who shall not be subjected to the peculiar effects of the bankruptcy process. Thus it has been frequently observed that our modern law of bankruptcy is essentially a law of insolvency.

Indeed, the ultimate concern of a creditor is not so much whether the debtor is or is not insolvent from a balance sheet point of view, but whether or not the debtor has ceased to pay his debts generally as they mature. Various events or criteria should be available as tests or presumptions that the debtor has, in fact, ceased or is about to cease to pay his debts generally as they mature and that would make the debtor amenable to the bankruptcy process.

3.2.019 It is, for these reasons, recommended that a petitioning creditor should be entitled to a receiving order if he can show, in any manner, with or without the aid of the presumptions hereafter referred to, that the debtor has ceased to pay his debts generally as they mature. Certain events, such as the debtor making a general assignment of his property for the benefit of his creditors, should constitute a conclusive presumption that the debtor has, in fact, ceased to pay his debts generally as they mature. Other events or facts, such as the debtor absconding without known provisions for the due and prompt payment of any of his debts, should be regarded as *prima facie* evidence that the debtor has ceased to pay his debts generally as they mature, thus throwing upon the debtor the burden of proving that he has not ceased paying his debts generally.

3.2.020 *Bankruptcy Notice: The Bankruptcy Acts* of England and Australia have a procedure for the service of a bankruptcy notice. A creditor, after having obtained a final judgment against a debtor, may serve on him a bankruptcy notice demanding payment of the debt. If the debtor does not, within a stipulated time limit after service, comply with the notice, he commits an 'act of bankruptcy.'

3.2.021 *The Winding-Up Act* has also a provision similar to a bankruptcy notice. A company is deemed, under that Act, to be unable to pay its debts as they become due, whenever a creditor, to whom the company is indebted in a sum exceeding two hundred dollars or more, serves a demand requiring the company to pay the sum due and the company has, for ninety days, in the case of a bank, and, for sixty days, in all other cases, neglected to pay such sum or to secure or compound for the same to the satisfaction of the creditor.

3.2.022 In the 1962 Report of the Committee appointed to review the bankruptcy law of Australia, it was said:

When, as is the case in Australia, a large number of bankruptcy notices are issued and relatively few become the basis of creditors' petitions, it is a reasonable inference that the service of bankruptcy notices on debtors has led to beneficial results to creditors, obviating further proceedings in bankruptcy. If, of course, a creditor used the procedure of a bankruptcy notice to obtain an unjust preference, (the fraudulent preference section of the Act) could be availed of, in the event of the debtor becoming a bankrupt, to set aside the preference. The service of a bankruptcy notice on a debtor also has advantages to the debtor. For example, it gives the debtor the opportunity of establishing that he does not owe the debt claimed by the creditor to be due to him or of proving that he has secured or compounded for the debt.

3.2.023 A bankruptcy notice is intended to be not so much a procedure for the recovery of a debt, although it may have this effect, but a procedure whereby a conclusive presumption of insolvency is created to facilitate setting the machinery of bankruptcy into motion. We are of the opinion that, having regard to the fact that the greatest depreciation of a debtor's assets takes place in the critical period immediately prior to bankruptcy, it is highly desirable that bankruptcy should quickly follow where a debtor has ceased to pay his debts as they mature. The bankruptcy notice may serve a useful function in permitting a presumption of insolvency to be quickly established where the creditor has a judgment against the debtor. To a considerable degree, it is expected that the bankruptcy notice will replace the present 'act of bankruptcy' whereby a sheriff makes a *nulla bona* return to a writ of execution, which, if our recommendations concerning 'acts of bankruptcy' are accepted, would constitute a presumption that the debtor has ceased to pay his debts generally as they mature. The disadvantage in the use of the present 'act of bankruptcy' in respect of a *nulla bona* return is that a busy sheriff may take a month or more before he can ascertain whether or not the debtor has property to satisfy the judgment and, if not, make a *nulla bona* return.

5 JUDICIAL DISCRETION

a / The Bankruptcy Bill (s-14)

152. Where proceedings under a petition are stayed pursuant to subsection 151(1) or (2) or are not being prosecuted with reasonable diligence, the court may, by reason of the delay or for any other sufficient cause, dismiss the petition or, subject to section 137, substitute or admit on such terms as it thinks fit any other creditor as a petitioner.

153. (1) Where a petition is filed in respect of more than one debtor, the court may dismiss the petition as to one or more of them, without prejudice to the effect of the petition as against any other debtor.

(2) The court may dismiss a petition where it

(*a*) is not satisfied with the proof of the facts alleged in the petition or of the service of the petition;

(*b*) is satisfied by the debtor that he is solvent; or

(*c*) is satisfied that for other sufficient cause a bankruptcy order should not be made.

b / *In Re Gillingham Estate* (1955), 35 C.B.R. 10 (S.C.O.)

SMILY J. (orally): In this petition, on behalf of the Attorney-General of Canada, it is stated that the estate of the deceased Gilford Stanley Gillingham is indebted to the Attorney-General of Canada in the sum of $3,217.30. I understand that this is not disputed, although it is contended on behalf of some of the creditors that a debt does not arise until after the death of the deceased.

The acts of bankruptcy relied upon by the petition are: 'That on or about October 5, 1954, it [the estate] gave notice to the following creditors [and the petition then sets out the list of creditors] that it had suspended or that it was about to suspend payment of its debts; (b) that on or about October 5, 1954, it ceased to meet its liabilities generally as they became due.' What is relied upon in support of that statement is that the executrix of the estate launched an application before the Court for an order determining whether the claim of the Crown should be preferred over the other creditors or whether it should be paid *pari passu* and without preference or priority pursuant to s 48(1) of *The Trustee Act,* R.S.O. 1950, c 400. As material on that application an affidavit was made by the executrix pointing out that the assets of the estate consisted of $3,445.39, on deposit in the Bank of Toronto, in the city of Toronto; and that there were outstanding accounts remaining to be paid, which were set out, including the debt of the Attorney-General of Canada, the total being $4,319.43. Then this further statement by the executrix: 'I am anxious to settle and pay all of the outstanding creditors to the extent of the assets of the estate, but am unable to ascertain who ranks in priority.'

It will at once appear that the matter is a simple one so far as the administration of the estate is concerned and so far as the material before the Court shows, namely, the question of paying those creditors from the amount of cash that is payable of that amount and in accordance with whatever priorities properly exist. It was said by the late Mr. Justice Middleton quite early in the days of the application of the bankruptcy law in Ontario, which was shortly following the enactment of *The Bankruptcy Act* of 1919, that one of the purposes of *The Bankruptcy Act* was to enable the assets of a debtor to be economically and expeditiously distributed among the creditors. If a receiving order is made in this matter it will involve the appointment of a trustee, advertising for debts, meetings of creditors, the expenses of the trustee, his fees, and his disbursements, and I cannot see how it is going to enable the assets of the debtor to be more economically and expeditiously distributed among these creditors than if that were done by the executrix. In fact, it would seem to me that it clearly would not be as economical and, possibly, not as expeditious.

There are really three questions to be decided. One is whether the acts of bankruptcy, as set out in the petition, have been established. Another is whether the estate of a deceased debtor is within the provisions of *The Bankruptcy Act* unless it is shown that an act of bankruptcy was committed by the debtor during his lifetime. It is contended on behalf of the opposing creditors particularly, that the provisions of *The Bankruptcy Act* do not cover, and do not apply to, the estate of a deceased person where the alleged act of bankruptcy took place after the death of the debtor, that s 22(1), being a new section in *The Bankruptcy Act* of 1949, does not go back any farther and applies only where an act of bankruptcy has been committed by the debtor during his lifetime.

Then there is the further question whether, assuming that the Act does apply, and that the Crown, or the petitioner, has established the acts of bankruptcy, the Court should, under the provisions of s 21(7), dismiss the petition for the reason, as I have more or less indicated, that it would not be to the advantage of the creditors to make the order, but rather that the assets of the debtor can be more economically and expeditiously distributed among the creditors by leaving the estate in the hands of the executrix rather than through the process of bankruptcy proceedings and that therefore the interest of the creditors would be better served, that is, the creditors in general at any rate, would be better served by dismissing the petition.

I may say that I am of the opinion that the discretion of the Court should be exercised in the direction of dismissing the petition for the reason above mentioned, that the creditors would be as well, if not better, served by not putting the estate to the expense of bankruptcy proceedings but rather allowing the distribution of the assets of the estate among the creditors to be made by the executrix. There is nothing to indicate that this will not be done in this case in a satisfactory manner in accordance with the law.

That being so, I am not called upon to deal with the other two questions. However, I think I should make this comment, and that is that I am at least doubtful whether the evidence establishes acts of bankruptcy as set out in the petition, in other words, whether the material establishes, within the provisions of *The Bankruptcy Act,* that notice was given to the creditors, or the Attorney-General of Canada, or the Crown, that the executrix 'had suspended or was about to suspend payment of its [the estate's] debts', or that the executrix has ceased to meet the liabilities of the estate generally as they become due. That is not what the affidavit says, nor do I think is it the effect of the affidavit. The executrix does not say she will not pay the outstanding accounts, but rather that she is anxious, so far as she is able, to pay the debts of the estate but is unable to ascertain who ranks in priority.

Then as to the other question. I am not called upon to decide that in view of the position I have taken, but my present view is that the provisions of *The Bankruptcy Act*, including s 22(1) and the definitions of 'debtor' and 'person' are sufficient to apply to the estate of a deceased debtor even though the act of bankruptcy does not take place until after the decease of the debtor. As I say, I am not called upon to decide that, and I am not addressing myself to it. That is my present view. I am inclined to favour the judgments of the Court, some of which have been mentioned, to the effect that the interpretation sections of *The Bankruptcy Act* so apply to the estate of a deceased debtor, but, as I say, I am not deciding that point.

The petition will accordingly be dismissed. I think the costs of the debtor should be paid by the petitioning creditors. I do not think the costs of the executrix should be saddled on the estate. It seems to me they should follow the event. However, I do not think any order should be made as to the costs of the opposing creditors.

NOTE In *Re St. Joseph's Co-operative Association Ltd.* (1950), 30 C.B.R. 157 (S.C.O.), Urquhart J dismissed a petition for bankruptcy where although the debtor was technically insolvent, if the order were made the preferred creditors would receive only a part of their claims and the unsecured creditors nothing at all. If the debtor, on the other hand, were allowed to continue with his business, then there was at least a possibility of a profit being made. Further, the debtor's business was construction and the Court felt that every social encouragement should be given to new home construction.

6 FUNCTIONS OF TRUSTEES

a / The Bankruptcy Bill (S-14)

198. When a trustee is appointed, he shall forthwith inform himself of the property and liabilities of the bankrupt and the names and addresses of the creditors.

199. (1) The trustee shall forthwith take possession of all the property of the bankrupt that vests in the trustee pursuant to the bankruptcy order, other than property in the possession of a secured creditor that the secured creditor is entitled to have in his possession pursuant to a security interest.

(2) For the purpose of acquiring or retaining possession of the property of the estate, the trustee has power to act as a trustee anywhere.

(3) No person is entitled to withhold the records of a bankrupt or the estate from the trustee or claim any lien on such records.

200. The trustee is entitled to have access to all records relating to the property or affairs of a bankrupt other than records required for the purposes of a prosecution under this or any other Act of Parliament.

201. (1) After a bankruptcy order is made, the trustee shall forthwith make an inventory, in prescribed form, of the property of the bankrupt and of the property held in trust by the bankrupt, in so far as it may be ascertained, as of the date of bankruptcy.

(2) Where, after making the inventory referred to in subsection (1), the trustee learns of any additional property of the bankrupt as of the date of bankruptcy or of any property that had not been included in the inventory and that subsequently vests in the trustee, the trustee shall amend the inventory to include the additional property.

(3) Where the trustee makes an inventory pursuant to subsection (1) or an amendment pursuant to subsection (2), the bankrupt shall give all the assistance in his power to the trustee.

(4) The trustee shall send a copy of the original inventory and any amendment thereto to the bankrupt and, on request, to the administrator.

202. (1) The trustee may, where necessary in the interest of the estate, before the first meeting of creditors,

(a) take conservatory measures and summarily dispose, in a commercially reasonable manner, of property that is perishable or likely to depreciate rapidly in value;

(b) insure any insurable property of the estate for such amount and against such hazards as he considers advisable;

(c) obtain such legal advice and take such judicial proceedings or other appropriate actions as he considers necessary for the recovery or protection of the property of the estate;

(d) with the permission of the court, incur obligations, borrow money and give a security interest on the property of the estate in amounts and on terms authorized by the court;

(e) carry on the business of the bankrupt; and

(f) with the permission of the court, exercise any of the powers set out in subsection 204(1) that are not set out in paragraphs (a) to (e).

(2) Where an administrator is trustee of an estate and incurs obligations or borrows money pursuant to paragraph (1)(d), Her Majesty in right of Canada or of a province is not liable for the fulfilment of the obligation or the repayment of the money borrowed.

(3) A trustee is not required to insure property of the debtor in which the estate has no interest of value or to take conservatory measures in respect of such property but, where the trustee decides not to insure such property or take conservatory measures in respect thereof, he shall forthwith notify any person who has an interest in such property of his decision.

203. (1) The trustee shall call the first meeting of the creditors of an estate and it shall be held within thirty days of the date of bankruptcy.

(2) The trustee shall send the prescribed notice of the first meeting of creditors to the bankrupt and to each known creditor and be accompanied by

(a) a list of the known creditors expected to claim fifty dollars or more and the estimated amount of each such claim together with the addresses of such creditors;

(b) a form of proof of claim; and

(*c*) a proxy and a mail ballot in prescribed form.

(3) If, within one-half hour after the time appointed for the first meeting of creditors, there is no quorum, the meeting is deemed to have been held.

204. (1) After the first meeting of creditors, the trustee may, with the permission of the board of inspectors, in relation to the administration of the estate,

(*a*) insure any insurable property of the estate for such amount and against such hazards as he considers necessary;

(*b*) carry on the business of the bankrupt to the extent he considers necessary for the beneficial disposal or liquidation or dissolution of the business;

(*c*) obtain such advice or assistance as he considers necessary;

(*d*) employ the bankrupt

   (i) to manage the estate,

   (ii) to carry on the business of the bankrupt, or

   (iii) to aid in any other respect

   and make a reasonable allowance out of the estate to the bankrupt as consideration for his services;

(*e*) institute or continue any proceeding;

(*f*) refer any dispute to arbitration;

(*g*) compromise and settle any claim made by or against the estate;

(*h*) subject to section 198, elect to retain any property for the whole or part of the unexpired term of a lease of such property or to assign, surrender or disclaim any interest of a bankrupt as lessee in a lease of, or other temporary interest in, any property;

(*i*) lease any property;

(*j*) incur obligations, borrow money or give security interests on any property of the estate;

(*k*) sell all or any part of the property of the estate by way of

   (i) tender in such manner as may be prescribed,

   (ii) public auction, or

   (iii) private contract;

(*l*) by quit claim or deed, divest himself of all or part of the property of the estate in favour of the debtor;

(*m*) accept, with or without terms or conditions, an undertaking to pay a sum of money at a future time as consideration or part of the consideration for the sale of any property of the estate;

(*n*) divide in its existing form among the creditors, according to its estimated value, any property of the estate that from its peculiar nature or other special circumstances cannot be readily or advantageously sold; and

(*o*) return to the bankrupt any property of the estate that the trustee finds he cannot realize or otherwise dispose of.

(2) For the purposes of subsection (1), the permission of the board of inspectors may be general or specific.

(3) The failure of the trustee to obtain the permission of the board of inspectors required by this Act does not affect the validity of a transfer where

(*a*) the transfer was for valuable consideration; and

(*b*) the other party acted in good faith and without knowledge of the failure to obtain permission.

205. (1) Where the trustee incurs obligations and borrows money pursuant to sections 202 and 204, such obligations shall be discharged and such money shall be repaid out of the estate in accordance with the agreement under which the obligation was incurred or the money was borrowed before any distribution is made in accordance with the applicable order of priority set out in this Act.

(2) Where an administrator is trustee of an estate and incurs obligations or borrows money pursuant to sections 202 and 204, Her Majesty in right of Canada or of a province is not liable for the fulfilment of the obligation or the repayment of the money borrowed.

206. Where the trustee sells property of an estate by tender and does not comply with the prescribed procedures in respect of such sales, the trustee is personally liable for any damages to the estate arising out of the failure to comply, but such failure does not affect the validity of a sale if

(*a*) the transfer was for valuable consideration; and

(*b*) the other party acted in good faith and without knowledge of the failure to comply with the regulations.

207. (1) The trustee need not carry on the business of the bankrupt where

(*a*) the realizable value of the property is, in his opinion, insufficient to protect the trustee fully against possible loss occasioned by so doing; and

(*b*) the creditors or the board of inspectors, after the trustee so requests, neglect or refuse to secure the trustee against possible loss occasioned by so doing.

(2) All debts incurred and credit received in carrying on the business of a bankrupt are, unless the contrary is proved, deemed to be debts incurred and credit received by the estate and not debts incurred and credit received by the trustee.

(3) For the purpose of giving a security interest under the *Bank Act*, the trustee, where he carries on the business of the bankrupt, is deemed to be a person engaged in the class of business previously carried on by the bankrupt.

208. (1) The trustee is not required to make any tax or other return that the bankrupt was required to make in respect of the time prior to the date of bankruptcy.

(2) Where the trustee makes any tax or other return that the bankrupt was required to make, the bankrupt shall give all assistance in his power to the trustee.

209. (1) Where a creditor requests the trustee to institute or continue a proceeding that, in the opinion of the creditor, would benefit the estate and the trustee refuses or neglects to do so, the creditor may obtain from the court an order

(*a*) authorizing him to institute or continue the proceeding

   (i) in his own name,

   (ii) at his own expense, and

   (iii) on such notice to the trustee and on such other terms and conditions as the court may direct; and

(*b*) requiring the trustee to transfer to the creditor any right or title of the trustee to, or interest in, the proceedings and its subject-matter, including any records related thereto.

(2) Where, before the court makes an order under subsection 1, the trustee signifies to the court his readiness to institute or continue the proceeding for the benefit of the estate, the court shall fix the time within which the trustee shall do so and, if the proceeding is instituted or continued by him within the time so fixed, any benefit derived belongs to the estate.

(3) Where a proceeding instituted or continued by a creditor pursuant to subsection 1 is successful,

(*a*) any benefit derived belongs exclusively to the creditor and such other creditors who joined with him in the proceeding to the extent of their total claims and costs;

(*b*) each claim of the creditor and the other creditors who joined with him in the proceeding is reduced accordingly; and (*c*) any surplus belongs to the estate and is payable to the trustee or, where the court so directs, the debtor.

210. (1) When an estate is fully administered, the trustee shall forthwith file a final statement of accounts of the estate with the registrar.

(2) Where the term of office of a trustee terminates before the estate is fully administered, the trustee or his legal personal representative shall, within thirty days from such termination, file a statement of accounts of the estate with the registrar for the period that the trustee administered the estate.

(3) For the purposes of subsection 1, when, in the opinion of the registrar, all the property of an estate that may be realized without needlessly protracting the administration is realized, the estate is deemed to be fully administered.

(4) The trustee shall send a copy of the statement of accounts filed with the registrar pursuant to subsection 1 or a summary thereof to every creditor who proved a claim, every inspector, the debtor and the administrator.

(5) A statement of accounts filed with the registrar pursuant to subsection 1 shall be in prescribed form.

b / Herbert G. Gordon, c.a., 'Operation of a Business in Bankruptcy' (1961), 2 c.b.r. (N.S.) 107.

A person or a corporation can become bankrupt either voluntarily, through making an assignment under the Bankruptcy Act, or involuntarily, through a petition being filed by a creditor or creditors, and a receiving order being made by the court. When a receiving order is issued against an insolvent debtor, the name of the trustee requested by the petitioning creditor is inserted by the Official Receiver. In the case of an assignment, the name of the trustee suggested by the solicitor for the debtor is inserted. The trustee so named proceeds with the administration of the estate until the first meeting of creditors, at which time the latter may confirm his appointment, or by special resolution may appoint or substitute another licensed trustee.

The trustee of a bankrupt business usually follows the routine set down in the Bankruptcy Act. He takes possession of the books and records, completes an inventory, verifies the bankrupt's statement of affairs, advises all known creditors of the bankruptcy, and attends the first meeting of creditors. After his confirmation as trustee and the election of inspectors, he proceeds with the realization of the assets of the bankrupt. Generally speaking, the assets of the bankrupt are sold by tender or auction sale, or in any other manner which, in the opinion of the trustee and the inspectors, realizes the maximum amount for the creditors.

Occasionally, a situation arises where it appears to the trustee to be advantageous, from the standpoint of the creditors in general, that the business be temporarily carried on in order to realize the maximum amount from the assets available. When this occurs, s 8(7) of the Bankruptcy Act provides that 'the trustee may, when necessary in the interest of the estate, carry on the business of the bankrupt until a date fixed for the first meeting of creditors'. Following the first meeting of creditors and the election of inspectors, s 10(1) of the Bankruptcy Act provides that 'the trustee with the permission of the inspectors may carry on the business of the bankrupt so far as it may be necessary for the beneficial administration of the estate'. When the trustee is considering continuing operations until the creditors meet, it is advisable for him to consult two or three of the largest creditors. If those creditors are agreeable to his proposal, he can then discuss it with the court and obtain the court's approval.

COOPERATION OF EMPLOYEES

Before making a decision, the trustee must also consult with the management and the key personnel of the bankrupt. Since he is considering entering into the operation of a business with which he is probably not too familiar, it is important that he secure their full cooperation. It will be principally on their calculations that he decides to terminate or to carry on temporarily. Under most circumstances, he is unable to make an immediate decision and will generally ask the employees to return to the premises a day or two after he has taken possession. The employees are naturally concerned as to the payment of their arrears of wages and holiday pay, as well as their immediate future employment. The trustee can gather them at a meeting and assure them that those who wish to continue until the operations have been completed will be paid any wages accruing during the period of his operation. He should also tell them that claims for unpaid wages at the time of the bankruptcy are given priority under the Bankruptcy Act over all other claims of preferred or unsecured creditors, and that payment of their claims will be made by him as quickly as possible. In most cases, the employees are willing to cooperate.

The decision to carry on operations generally arises where perishable assets are involved or, more frequently, where a substantial portion of the inventory consists of semi-processed goods. For example, if at the time of bankruptcy a clothing manufacturer had dress or suiting materials already cut to fill orders on hand, the expenditure of a moderate amount could convert these materials into finished garments. Thus they are more readily disposable than materials which have not been cut for a specific purpose.

DECISION OF BANK

In many bankruptcies the trustee finds that the stock-in-trade has been pledged to the bank as security under s 88 of the Bank Act. Since the bank then owns the inventory, it decides as to whether or not the business should be continued. In most cases it will decide to carry on operations as it can realize more from its security if the inventory can be converted to finished goods than if it is in a raw or semi-processed state. The bank can engage the trustee as its agent to complete the inventories, but if he accepts the position, he does so entirely beyond his capacity as trustee in the bankruptcy. Under these conditions, the problem of financing the operations is minimized as the bank will advance necessary funds without further security.

If, however, the inventories are not assigned to a bank, the trustee must make the arrangements for financing through the bank. If such financing must take place before the first meeting of the creditors and the appointment of inspectors, the trustee should consult with the court. The Bankruptcy Act provides that 'with the permission of the court, an interim receiver or trustee, prior to the appointment of inspectors, may make necessary or advisable advances, incur obligations, borrow money and give security on the property of the debtor in such amounts and upon such terms and upon such property as may be authorized by the court, and such advances, obligations or money borrowed shall be repaid out of the property of the debtor in priority to the claims of the creditors'.

Following the appointment of inspectors, the trustee should ask their approval of actions taken prior to their appointment, and must also receive their permission to carry on the business, so far as it may be necessary for the beneficial administration of the estate. Permission must also be received from the inspectors for any further borrowing of money or pledging of property of the bankrupt estate.

SAVING PERISHABLE INVENTORY

Occasionally the trustee is faced with a decision of carrying on a business where perishable property is involved. The writer was once appointed trustee of a canning company during the peak of the canning season. At that time the company had in its receiving sheds a considerable quantity of pears and peaches which had been received from farmers under contract. Truckers were constantly arriving at the warehouse with further additional fruit which had been contracted for by the company, and deliveries were expected to continue for a period of three or four weeks. The bankrupt had a quantity of tins and labels on hand as well as barrels of maraschino cherries, cubed pineapple, sliced oranges, etc. Arrangements were made with the can manufacturer for the delivery of additional cans on a C.O.D. basis, and the bank agreed to provide funds for the payment of all necessary expenses. Thousands of tins of fruit cocktail were prepared until the pineapple, cherry and orange stock had been completely used up, and production was then shifted over to the canning of pears and peaches. The fruit growers were unable to make arrangements at that late date to deliver their produce to any other canning factory. As a result, they would have suffered very severe losses if production had been halted and would have made substantial claims against the bankrupt company. Since the staff was available, and orders were already on hand for the sale of a large percentage of the production, operations were continued until the contract of the deliveries had been completed.

During the course of operations additional orders are often received which necessitate the purchase of additional materials. The natural tendency of the staff is to advise the trustee to accept the new orders as an extended operational period means an additional term of employment. The trustee must review the situation thoroughly before accepting or refusing an order, keeping in mind that the company probably arrived at a state of bankruptcy because of poor management, and the decisions of the staff in the present circumstances are questionable.

SAVING A GOOD BUSINESS

Occasionally, the continuation of operations by the trustee will facilitate the sale of the business as a going concern. A long-established business which finds itself in financial difficulties through unusual circumstances can very often be salvaged by the introduction of new capital and new management. Recently an incorporated company of this nature found it necessary to make an assignment due to an extremely heavy loss incurred as a result of a serious blunder on a large contract. The previous history of the firm had been good, but due to lack of working capital the profits had been moderate and the surpluses retained did not materially increase the working capital.

During the course of the trusteeship, a third party made an investigation and judged that the business could be put on a paying basis with the introduction of new capital and a modification of the manufacturing process. As a result, the previous shareholders transferred their shares over to the new principal, and a further meeting of creditors was called. A proposal was offered to the creditors which provided for a settlement of 50 cents on the dollar over a period of 18 months. This was substantially more than would have been paid if the trustee had completed liquidation and distribution. Following the creditors' acceptance, the bankruptcy proceedings were annulled and the proposal approved by the court. With a very substantial loss carry-forward available, the company retained a corresponding amount of future profits on a tax-free basis, and the funds thus retained assisted in settling the claims of the unsecured creditors under the proposal.

DUTIES OF TRUSTEE

All operations, of course, are carried on under the guidance of either the trustee or his representatives and care must be taken that the interests of the creditors are protected at all times. Since the trustee is operating the business, he should make sure that, in addition to the usual insurance coverage for fire, theft, automotive fleet, etc., comprehensive liability insurance is secured to cover any claims arising during the course of his operations.

It is necessary that the trustee maintain a complete and accurate record of his receipts and disbursements during the period of operation. On winding up the affairs of the bankrupt, he must present a complete statement of receipts and disbursements, for approval by the inspectors, the Registrar, and the Superintendent of Bankruptcy.

The decision of the trustee to recommend continuation of operations should not be made without cautious deliberation. Success can only be achieved by cooperation from the bank, management and employees as well as from suppliers of material which will be required in future operations. In the beginning, the trustee will no doubt be offered the whole-hearted support of the creditors and inspectors, but experience has proven that in a short time the guidance and enthusiasm of the inspectors gradually diminish, due to the pressure of other matters and the trustee ends up playing a 'lone hand'. If the result of operations does not measure up to the optimistic hopes of the creditors, the trustee is always criticized. Nevertheless, a satisfactory operation providing dividends in excess of those realizable on a quick disposal of assets is a recommendation of his abilities. As well as being a gratifying experience to him, it is usually productive of a fee in excess of that he would receive on a wind-up operation.

c / W. A. Farlinger, C.A., 'Bankruptcy – A Trustee Speaks Out' (1972), 13 C.B.R. (N.S.) 105.

In Canada, the public eye has been focused the past few years on commercial insolvencies. Much publicity has been attracted by certain 'fraudulent' bankruptcies and more recently by a few large insolvencies that involved a large number of public investors. This publicity has brought numerous issues into the spotlight of public attention. Many of the issues currently being discussed are of major significance to chartered accountants.

The role of the trustee in bankruptcy has not attracted as much public attention recently as other issues that are of interest to accountants. However, the performance of trustees continues to be a matter of serious concern to creditors, lending institutions, lawyers and others involved in insolvency situations from time to time.

With the amendments made to the Bankruptcy Act in 1966 (these amendments adopted almost verbatim the recommendations in the CICA brief), there has been a substantial increase in the staff of the Superintendent of Bankruptcy, much stricter supervision of trustees followed, and some trustees have not had their licences renewed. The vast majority of trustees in bankruptcy are competent, honest and experienced businessmen, well qualified to enter into the complicated business dealings required to liquidate a business to the best possible advantage. Nevertheless, one frequently hears complaints about them. Most trustees in bankruptcy are chartered accountants and many firms of practising accountants do work in the insolvency area. It is felt that there is a lack of understanding of the nature and extent of work done by trustees.

[The criticisms that are most frequently made of trustees in bankruptcy include:]

THE RESULTS OF LIQUIDATION ARE DISAPPOINTING

This complaint arises in almost every bankruptcy. Trustees are frequently blamed for doing an unimaginative liquidation job which appears to creditors to merely take the form of an auction sale at distress prices. The results of this auction sale are compared by creditors with the most recent financial statement prepared by the debtor. It is not unusual in the case of insolvent companies to find that values for inventories and accounts receivable as recorded on financial statements have been overstated; also, liabilities are frequently understated. Trustees find that a significant proportion of insolvent companies have financial statements that have not been audited or, alternatively, have audit reports with significant qualifications. Accordingly, financial statements on which creditors have been relying are often incorrect. Under such circumstances, creditors may be comparing the end results of the liquidation with figures that bear no relation to the facts.

The liquidation process itself usually involves a loss in realization below those figures that would be appropriate for the valuation of assets on a going-concern basis. But this is not always the case. Fixed assets for example, may realize a good deal more than the book figures, as might marketable securities.

Inventories, however, pose a difficult problem for the liquidator. In some cases, it is possible to sell the inventories to customers in the ordinary course of business and the normal mark-up may be obtained. After allowing for selling and administration costs, the net yield in these cases might approximate cost or even higher. It is not always possible to sell inventories on a going-concern basis, although this is often done for a limited period.

Purchasers usually view inventories in a bankruptcy with some scepticism and the price they will pay is affected by the fact that there is no warranty and the goods are sold on an as-is basis. In the case under review, some inventory was sold at full retail price to customers prior to the bulk sale. Because credit could not be extended to the majority of the company's customers, most of the inventory was put up for tender and the price obtained resulted in a loss on book values of 25 cents on the dollar in one category of the inventory, and 48 cents on the dollar in the case of the other.

Reference has already been made to the almost inevitable deterioration in accounts receivable that takes place in most bankruptcies. It is very difficult to estimate the amount of deterioration attributable to the bankruptcy in this specific case because there was no accurate way of estimating the proper going-concern value of the accounts receivable. It is likely, however, that in a business of this type the deterioration due to the liquidation itself would amount to 25% of a fair going-concern value of the accounts receivable.

In a liquidation situation, it is a truism that a business should produce more if it is sold as a going-concern. In the example in hand, every effort was made to sell the business and all these attempts met with failure because there really was no worthwhile business to sell. However, this was by no means clear at the outset.

The main point to be made is that the most significant factor in creditor disappointment in the results of liquidation stems from the fact that the original financial information given to creditors by the debtor is usually incorrect.

THE WINDING-UP TAKES TOO LONG

In the case under discussion, the estate was open for four years. This type of lengthy administration appears most upsetting to many creditors. Trustees do make interim distributions and essentially all of the money in hand is paid out to creditors as it accumulates. In spite of this, credit managers appear to be very anxious to have the bankruptcy wound up quickly. It may be that the very mention of the debtor company holds bad memories for credit managers that they would like to file away.

There are many factors that delay the winding-up of estates. Final clearances from government taxing authorities and rebates of taxes are difficult and slow to achieve. Settlement of creditors' claims, particularly where contingent or damage claims are involved, can be very time-consuming and slow in settlement. Liquidation inevitably produces lawsuits, and lawsuits prosecuted to their completion take extended periods. In most bankruptcies the estate cannot be properly wound up in less than two or three years.

TRUSTEES DO NOT KEEP CREDITORS INFORMED

Some companies appear to have a policy that requires the credit manager to receive reports at stated intervals on all bankruptcies. There are cases where these policies are completely inflexible and the credit manager contacts the trustee in bankruptcy every few months, regardless of the size of his claim. Such rigid rules serve no purpose other than to waste the time of credit people and the trustee.

It is clear, however, that trustees do not always keep creditors currently informed. It seems reasonable that creditors might expect a quarterly report from the trustee in estates where there is some substantial activity. Where lengthy lawsuits are involved and there is no change in the estate, it would not seem to make much sense to report more frequently than once a year unless new developments occur. In the case in hand, the trustee held two general meetings of creditors and sent out interim reports to creditors on seven occasions during the administration of the estate. From time to time, creditors object to trustees acting in a dual capacity. It can be argued that there might be a conflict of interest where the trustee is also acting as the agent of a secured creditor and where the creditor's secured position is challenged. In a limited number of situations, this point may have some validity, although it is invariably a question of law as to whether or not a creditor's security is valid against a trustee in bankruptcy. It is the responsibility of the solicitor to the estate to give a legal opinion as to the status of secured creditors and, where doubt exists, the matter is judicially determined. The trustee must always follow the practice of realizing the maximum amount from the assets for benefit of whatever party is finally determined to be entitled to the proceeds.

The practice of having one liquidator in charge of the whole liquidation is much more efficient; it reduces costs, and facilitates the sale of the business as a going-concern in situations where this is feasible.

In the case under examination, the trustee acted as agent for the bank which held security in the accounts receivable and that portion of the inventory which was under warehouse control. The trustee was able to borrow from the bank at the outset to keep the business in operation, while sale possibilities were being pursued. The various matters were so inter-related that it would have been difficult and much more expensive for two different liquidators to do the job.

LIQUIDATION COSTS TOO HIGH

It is likely that most creditors gauge the amount of work done by the trustee from the few times they come in contact with him during the course of the administration of the estate. The majority of staff involved in this type of work is of a senior or specialized category, and students-in-accounts are seldom used in trustee work. In the case under review, the trustee's staff spent approximately 500 days and its total remuneration as trustee and as agent for the bank amounted to $30,000. It is probable that in most bankruptcies, trustees receive fees which, if reduced to an hourly basis, would provide about the same recovery as that received by other specialists practising public accounting.

The work of a trustee in bankruptcy is difficult, to say the least. It seems that the trustee is always called into a problem on the Friday afternoon preceding a long week-end. Frequently, his work is carried out in an atmosphere where emotions are high and certain phases of the work must be completed under great pressure of time. In most circumstances, it is a foregone conclusion that his clients will be disappointed in the dollar result of his efforts. In some cases, he may even be the logical party for credit managers to use as an excuse for their own errors in judgment. Frequently, however, trustees do achieve real personal satisfaction from their efforts in working out a going-concern reorganization in which everyone benefits. Few trustees can complain that life is ever dull.

d / Carrying On the Bankrupt's Business

i The Bankruptcy Bill (s-14), s 204(1)(b) (set out above, p. 783)

ii *Potato Distribution Inc.* v *Eastern Trust Co.* (1955), 35 C.B.R. 161 (P.E.I. C.A.)

TWEEDY J. This is an appeal from a judgment of my Lord the Chief Justice, upon an application by Potato Distributors Incorporated for an order declaring a certain contract to be frustrated and void by reason of the bankruptcy of the debtor, or in the alternative, for an order that the trustee in bankruptcy disclaim the said contract as onerous.

The learned Chief Justice refused the application and as to the alternative order sought he held it clearly could not be considered upon the application before him as the above appellant was only a contractor and not a creditor at that time.

Since then, however, Russell Hammill and Russell Ching, two creditors of the debtor, have been added as intervenants. Some objection was made to this procedure, but for the purpose of this appeal it was agreed that the appeal be considered as properly before the Court and that the appeal should be heard and determined upon its merits.

The contract in question is dated April 9, 1955, and is between the debtor of the one part and the appellant of the other part and is for sale and delivery by the debtor to the appellant in each of the years, 1955, 1956, and 1957, of 25,000 bags of certified Number One Canada A Grade Sebago Seed Potatoes and also 1,750 bags of certified Number One Canada A Grade Small Sebago Seed Potatoes, ship's tackle at Summerside, Charlottetown or Souris in Prince Edward Island.

The date of delivery of said potatoes in each of the said three years was to be during the months of November and December, and the price agreed to be paid by the purchaser appellant to the debtor was $1.75 United States funds per 100 pound bag.

On August 25, 1955, a receiving order was made against the debtor and the respondent was appointed trustee in bankruptcy. No potatoes have been delivered under the contract.

The grounds of appeal are as follows:

1 From the very nature of bankruptcy, performance of a three-year contract by the trustee is inapt.

2 More especially is this so where, as in the present case, performance of the contract involves gambling on the potato market.

3 *The Bankruptcy Act* does not contemplate carrying on the business of the bankrupt by the trustees where that business is of a highly speculative nature.

4 Carrying on business by the trustee must be confined to such business as will promote a reasonably speedy winding up of the estate.

5 The undertaking given by the trustee in the present case would be worthless in certain circumstances, and His Lordship therefore erred in refusing the appellant's application upon such an undertaking.

The argument was devoted mainly to s 10(1)(c) of *The Bankruptcy Act*, 1949, 2nd Sess. (Can.), c 7, which reads as follows:

The trustee may, with the permission of the inspectors, do all or any of the following things:
...
(c) carry on the business of the bankrupt so far as may be necessary for the beneficial administration of the estate.

It was contended by the appellant that the completion of the contract by the trustee is the carrying on of the business of the debtor; business that is not necessary for the beneficial administration of the estate.

Dealing now with the main question whether or not by carrying out this contract the trustee is carrying on business not necessary for the beneficial administration of the estate.
[Tweedy J then discussed several previous authorities]

After carefully considering all the above cases and the other cases cited, I cannot reach the conclusion that the trustee in this case is carrying on business of the bankrupt that is not necessary for the beneficial administration of the estate.

The potato business of the bankrupt was only one branch of many other lines of business carried on by it. Among others mentioned were plumbing, feed business, hardware business and many others.

All the trustee is trying to do by carrying out this contract is to endeavour to mitigate the liabilities as much as possible and not try to make a profit.

As so often pointed out, *The Bankruptcy Act* was passed for two main objects: 1. To secure the creditors the best result, *i.e.*, an economical administration, and 2. To enable an honest bankrupt to obtain a discharge and to make a fresh start.

It is not as though the trustee were entering upon some new project. Here he is trying to do the best possible, guided by the views of his inspectors for the creditors as a body and not for any one group.

I am of the opinion, therefore, that the learned Chief Justice was right in refusing to grant an order declaring the contract to be frustrated and void subject to the express undertaking given by the trustee that no distribution of assets would be made among the creditors until after the date of the completion of the three-year contract with the appellant, and that the assets of the bankrupt in the hands of the trustee would be answerable to the appellant for any damages arising from a breach of the contract.

[The appeal was dismissed. MacGuigan J concurred in the result.]

QUESTION Given the wording of s 204(1)(*b*) of the new Bankruptcy Bill, what would be the result of the *Potato Distribution* case if it were decided now?

e / Redirecting the Bankrupt's Mail

The Bankruptcy Bill (s-14), ss 212–13

212. (1) The trustee may, by sending a notice in prescribed form to the Canada Post Office, request that any mail addressed to a bankrupt that is directed to the places mentioned in the notice shall be redirected or sent by the Canada Post Office, to the trustee or such other person as the trustee may designate.

(2) Where the bankrupt is an individual, the notice referred to in subsection (1) is operative only during the ninety days immediately following the date of bankruptcy unless the court, on application, extends such period of time on such terms as it thinks fit.

(3) Unless the court otherwise orders, this section does not apply to a consumer bankrupt.

213. (1) When mail of a bankrupt is redirected or sent pursuant to section 212, the trustee or the person to whom the mail is redirected or sent

(*a*) may open that mail; and

(*b*) where the bankrupt is an individual, shall forthwith send to the bankrupt all mail that is not required for the purposes of this Act.

(2) On application of the bankrupt, the court may make such order as it thinks fit to preserve the confidentiality of that part of any mail referred to in subsection (1) that is solely of a personal nature.

(3) Where it is no longer useful for the purposes of this Act to have mail redirected or sent pursuant to section 212, the trustee shall forthwith instruct the Canada Post Office, to disregard the notice given pursuant to that section.

21

The Property of the Bankrupt

INTRODUCTION

The materials in this chapter deal first with the question of what property vests in a debtor's trustee in bankruptcy on the making of a bankruptcy order and the exemptions to which a debtor is entitled. The chapter goes on to consider special rules governing after-acquired property (property acquired by the debtor during the course of the bankruptcy) and especially after-acquired wages; rights of action to which the debtor might be entitled; property held by the debtor on defeasible conditions; and the court's residual discretion to exclude from the bankrupt estate property otherwise available to the trustee on behalf of the creditors.

The second part of the chapter focuses on rules of which the trustee may avail himself to upset transactions into which the bankrupt may have entered prior to bankruptcy under which he has divested himself of property that might otherwise have been available to the creditors in the bankruptcy. These transactions fall into three broad classes: reviewable, non-arms-length, transactions; gifts; and preferential treatment of particular creditors. These rules raise difficult questions as to how creditors and debtors associated with failing or faltering businesses should conduct their relationships when bankruptcy has not yet occurred (and of course may not occur).

I PROPERTY VESTING IN THE TRUSTEE

a / Tassé Report, pp 109–10

3.2.028 When bankruptcy occurs, the property of the debtor available for distribution among his creditors automatically vests in the trustee. It is then the responsibility of the trustee to identify this property, wherever and in whose possession it may be, and thereafter to take possession of it and protect it. The property is thereafter liquidated and the proceeds thereof distributed among the creditors in full settlement of their claims.

3.2.029 *Property that Vests:* Under the present Act, the property of a bankrupt that is exempt from execution or seizure under the laws of the province within which the property is situated and in which the bankrupt resides and the property that is held by the bankrupt in trust for another person do not vest in his estate in bankruptcy. Apart from these exceptions, all the property owned by the debtor, at the date of his bankruptcy, and all that acquired by him before his discharge is divisible among his creditors. A very wide definition of property is contained in the Act, which includes money, goods, land, property of any description and things in action.

3.2.030 The property of a debtor that is validly held by a secured creditor, either by way of a charge or by way of a conveyance subject to a right of redemption, does not vest in the trustee, but the equity of redemption does pass to the trustee.

3.2.031 *Exemptions:* As bankruptcy is a method of collective execution, to which is added a release of debts, it is only just and equitable that a bankrupt should not be able to withhold, from his creditors, property of any substantial value. A debtor may, however, obtain a release of his debts by way of an arrangement instead of through bankruptcy. If he is able to propose an arrangement that is acceptable to his creditors, it is not unreasonable that he should, in those circumstances, be entitled to retain his property. Indeed, the right of a debtor to retain his property, if he makes an arrangement, can be a strong incentive for him to make one. We are of the opinion that this is not an undesirable incentive as, in most cases, creditors will receive more through an arrangement than they would through the liquidation of the property by way of bankruptcy. Moreover, to the extent that the amount of property that is exempt from vesting in a trustee is increased, this has the effect of decreasing a debtor's incentive to make an arrangement.

3.2.032 In this context, it is difficult to justify the present provisions of the *Bankruptcy Act* with respect to exemptions. As the exemptions are established by the provinces, they vary from one to the other. As a result, there is not, across Canada, a uniform law of bankruptcy with respect to the property that is available for distribution among the creditors of a bankrupt.

3.2.033 Exemption laws have been devised by the provinces in the exercise of their legislative powers to deal with matters coming within their jurisdiction. It should not necessarily be taken for granted that these exemption laws are equally appropriate in the context of bankruptcy. For example, to increase the amount of property of a debtor that is exempt from seizure has different implications depending on whether or not there is a bankruptcy. Outside of bankruptcy, the result could be that it will be more difficult for a creditor to execute upon his judgment. It may take longer for him to collect what is owed to him. He is not, however, required, in the end, to take less than what is owed to him. It is a different matter in bankruptcy. As the amount of the property of a debtor exempt from seizure is increased, there is a corresponding decrease in what is available for the creditors. The debtor will, as a rule, obtain a release of his debts irrespective of the amount his creditors have received. There comes a time when it is unjust, insofar as the creditors are concerned, to release the debts of a bankrupt without having regard to the amount of the property that he can retain. It would not be unreasonable, under these circumstances, to require a debtor to decide between keeping his exempt property and not obtaining a release of his debts or giving up some of his exempt property and obtaining a release of his debts.

3.2.034 Some bankruptcy statutes, such as those of England and Australia, contain a list of the property exempt from seizure. There is no constitutional reason why the same approach could not be taken in Canada. We are of the opinion, however, that it is preferable to leave to the provinces the responsibility for deciding what property should be exempt from seizure. In such a large country as Canada, the economies of the various regions may dictate different considerations for deciding what property should be exempt from seizure. However, the release of debts that a debtor receives in bankruptcy and the conditions under which it can be obtained are within the power of the Parliament of Canada to legislate, as they pertain to the subject matter of bankruptcy and insolvency. For these reasons, we recommend that all debtors should have the choice of retaining in bankruptcy all of their property that is exempt from seizure by the laws of the province in which they reside. A debtor, however, would only be entitled to a release of his debts, if the exempt property that is retained has a value not greater than, for example, $1,000, which would be increased by $300 for each of his dependents up to the maximum of $3,000. Such a scheme would provide for a variation, across the country, in the kind of property that is exempt. However, the value of exempt property that a bankrupt could keep, while at the same time obtaining a release from his debts, would be uniform across the country.

b / The Bankruptcy Bill (s-14)

158. (1) When a bankruptcy order is made, all the property of the bankrupt at that date vests, subject to the rights of secured creditors, in the trustee, except, in the case of an individual who is a bankrupt,

(*a*) the real property of the bankrupt that is exempt from execution or seizure under the law of the province or jurisdiction in which it is situated;

(*b*) the personal property of the bankrupt that is exempt from execution or seizure under the law of the province or jurisdiction in which the bankrupt was resident during the year immediately preceding the filing of the petition or the greatest part of that year;

(*c*) rights under an insurance contract not exempt under paragraph (*b*) that provides for a cash surrender value where, within thirty days after the trustee ascertains the net cash surrender value of the contract, he notifies the debtor of the net cash surrender value and the debtor or any other person pays an amount equal to the net cash surrender value to the trustee;

(*d*) where a person is disabled, amounts payable to that person under an insurance contract, a retirement income fund, a retirement savings plan or a pension fund or plan; and

(*e*) a deferred profit-sharing plan, a retirement income fund or a retirement savings plan registered under the *Income Tax Act* up to an amount prescribed or determined in the prescribed manner.

(2) In determining the net cash surrender value of an insurance contract pursuant to paragraph (1)(*c*), any loan against the contract shall be deducted from the cash surrender value.

(3) Where the insurer normally pays a cash sum on the surrender of an insurance contract that does not provide for a cash surrender value,

(*a*) paragraph (1)(*c*) applies as if the contract contained a provision for a cash surrender value; and

(*b*) the cash sum is deemed to be the cash surrender value.

(4) The trustee may, with the permission of the inspectors, accept in full payment of the rights under an insurance contract referred to in paragraph (1)(*c*) the loan value of such contract.

(5) For the purposes of this section, 'insurance contract' includes a contract to provide for the payment of an annuity.

159. (1) Subject to subsection (2), where a bankruptcy order is made in respect of a debtor who holds property in trust for another, the bankruptcy trustee has, subject to any instrument creating the trust and any other applicable law, all the rights, powers and duties in respect of the property so held that the debtor had immediately prior to the making of the bankruptcy order and the trustee shall distribute that property

(*a*) in accordance with the terms of the trust; or

(*b*) if he cannot comply with the terms of the trust, in accordance with such directions as the court, on application, may give.

(2) Where the court, on application, thinks that the bankruptcy trustee is not the appropriate person to be the trustee of property that the bankrupt held in trust for another, the court may appoint another person to be the trustee of that property.

(3) The court, on application, may determine the portion, if any, of a trust referred to in subsection (1) that may be used to pay the costs of the trustee in administering the trust.

2 AFTER-ACQUIRED PROPERTY

a / Tassé Report, pp 114–15 (footnotes omitted)

3.2.047 The provisions for the vesting of after-acquired property have always been in the *Bankruptcy Act* and, as such, may be considered to be sanctified by tradition. It is questionable, however, whether the concept is valid in a modern bankruptcy system. Certainly, in practice, the value of the provisions is doubtful. All indications are that the percentage of after-acquired property realized in bankruptcy is negligible. As a matter of practice, only an individual will have after-acquired property, and this takes the form of either the sizeable part of his wages or, in the rare case, of property that he inherits. In situations where a bankrupt can foresee acquiring property of some value, the provisions may, in actual life, be easily circumvented. As all trustees do not show the same concern for after-acquired property, debtors are not treated the same throughout the country. In any event, when a trustee intervenes to claim the property, the cost of realizing after-acquired property is high. Perhaps the real purpose of the after-acquired property provisions is to punish the bankrupt. A bankrupt who has committed a bankruptcy offence may be denied an immediate and unconditional discharge. The threat of the possibility that a discharge may be refused and delayed and that, during that time, all his after-acquired property will be subject to seizure by the trustee, was no doubt considered to be a deterrent to a debtor tempted to commit a bankruptcy offence. We think, however, that it is ill advised to use the threat of refusing or postponing a discharge as a penalty or sanction against a bankrupt. The concept of seizing and distributing a debtor's property and releasing his debts should be kept separate from the incapacities attached to bankruptcy. We recommend, for instance, *infra* in 3.2.096 et seq., that certain bankrupts be prevented from returning to business for a certain period of time. At all times, however, bankrupts should be in a position to obtain gainful employment without the threat of the seizure of his after-acquired property. Otherwise, some debtors may choose to remain idle or to conceal, through various means, whatever property they may acquire.

3.2.048 For these reasons, we recommend that after-acquired property should not vest in the trustee, except in the case of property that a bankrupt acquires by inheritance within six months after bankruptcy; also, if a debtor within a certain period of time after his bankruptcy acquires great wealth, he should be called upon to share it with his creditors. These two exceptions are discussed in the following paragraphs.

3.2.049 *Property Acquired by Inheritance*: The first exception to the rule recommended above concerns property acquired by inheritance after bankruptcy. There is a similar exception in the United States *Bankruptcy Act*. The reason for it is explained as follows by Professor J.A. MacLachlan:

… it offends common sense, if not common decency, to permit a debtor to go into bankruptcy as his wealthy ancestor reclines upon his deathbed, and procure a discharge from his debts after coming into wealth on the morn after petition in bankruptcy.

3.2.050 *Bankrupt Becoming Prosperous*: The second exception to the rule that after-acquired property should not vest in the trustee concerns the case of the debtor who, within a period, such as three years or so after the date of his bankruptcy, acquires great wealth. In such circumstances, the court should be able to order the debtor to pay such moneys to, or consent to such judgment in favour of, the trustee, as it may direct. This proposed provision is not intended to interfere with the economic rehabilitation of the debtor. It is desirable that, as soon as possible, he should acquire steady and well paid employment and that he be in a position to support himself and his dependents in reasonable comfort. Nothing should be done to discourage a former bankrupt from accumulating savings and building up an estate. If, however, the debtor should, within three years or so after his bankruptcy, acquire great wealth, it is only just that he should share his good fortune with his creditors. In the United States, where after-acquired property does not vest in the trustee and there is no such provision as we here propose, the Act can, in isolated circumstances, be held in disrespect. The movie star may go bankrupt today and sign a lucrative contract tomorrow. A prize-fighter, on the eve of a championship bout, may similarly voluntarily become bankrupt to prevent his creditors from sharing his expected good fortune. This kind of abuse would not be possible if our recommendation, in this regard, were implemented.

b / The Bankruptcy Bill (s-14)

160. (1) Where a bankruptcy order is made in respect of an individual and the individual, before he ceases to be a bankrupt in accordance with subsection 231(1),
- (*a*) earns an income at a rate in excess of five hundred dollars a month or such greater amount as may be prescribed, or
- (*b*) acquires property or earns income in excess of that necessary to maintain a reasonable standard of living.

the court, on application, may make an order vesting in the trustee the whole or part of such income or such property.

(2) In making an order pursuant to subsection (1), the court shall take into consideration
- (*a*) the personal situation, family responsibilities and financial commitments of the individual concerned;
- (*b*) the dividends paid or forecast to be paid out of the estate;
- (*c*) any relevant circumstances referred to in section 215; and
- (*d*) any applicable provincial law dealing with the exemption of property from execution or

seizure.

(3) For the purpose of subsection (1), the world 'income' means taxable income of the individual, for a taxation year as determined under the *Income Tax Act*.

c / *Re Chemesco Construction Co.*, [1960] o.w.n. 516 (s.c.)

SMILY, J., at the conclusion of the argument delivered judgment in the following terms:

In determining what would be a proper amount for the debtors to be allowed respectively for the maintenance of themselves and their families on the one hand, or the proper amount which the trustee for the creditors is entitled to have deducted from their salaries, for the benefit of the creditors on the other hand, I of course must take everything into consideration.

On the evidence which is before me, and I do not disregard the remarks in the *Tod* case, [1934] s.c.r. 230 to which I referred in my reasons for judgment noted [1960] o.w.n. 371, and by which I am judging it such amount should allow for, in the words of the reasons for judgment

A fair and reasonable amount required for the maintenance of himself and family according to their condition in life ... the Court ought not to cut down the bankrupt's means of livelihood too closely, but ought to leave a liberal margin for his support.

However, I do not think it was ever intended, or that the *Tod* case suggests, that the interests of the estate creditors should be entirely disregarded. I think when the Supreme Court said

The general rule is that the bankrupt is entitled to a fair and reasonable amount required for the maintenance of himself and family according to their condition in life.

It was not necessarily the amount they saw fit to expend but the amount which was required for the maintenance of the debtor and his family. And I think it would not be unfair to say, that requirement is not entirely unrelated to the condition of the debtors with respect to their obligations.

The Bankruptcy Act, R.S.C. 1952, c 14, of course provides that any after-acquired property is part of the estate and is that to which the trustee is entitled for the benefit of creditors, and salary earned, subject to the limitation providing for the maintenance of the debtor and his family, is after acquired property, also having regard to the Wages Act and provisions with respect to the seizable portions of the salary.

I think when one looks at the *Tod* case, it is apparent that the Court must not cut the income allowance to the debtor for maintenance and support to the bone, that some margin should be left over and above what would be a minimum. I think the debtors are entitled to live with some relation to their standing in life, but as I have intimated the test should not be what they consider they should have for their maintenance without any regard to the creditors whatsoever.

I must take into account that the estimates of the expenditures required by the debtors for the maintenance of themselves and their families are to a substantial extent just estimates, and I do not think from the evidence I can necessarily say that the amounts which have been spent – and it is suggested should be spent – are necessary amounts to be spent under the circumstances, amounts which the debtors are entitled to spend, even if one considers their standing in the community.

I think the debtors in this position with respect to their after acquired property and salary before their discharge should keep their expenditures to a reasonable amount, having regard as I have said to the rights of the creditors.

I am not suggesting that they are obliged to skimp and save to the last cent in any way, or that their allowances should be a minimum; rather there should be some amount over what is absolutely necessary in the circumstances. In other words the allowances should be reasonable and fair to all concerned, liberal if you like but within reason.

I think on the evidence which has been given and having regard to that evidence, taking everything into account, the debtors can and should be able to spare something from their salaries as part of their after acquired property up until the time of their discharge.

d / *Re Colthart*, [1945] 1 D.L.R. 193 (S.C.O.)

URQUHART J.: This is an application by the trustee on behalf of certain creditors who joined together under s 69 of the *Bankruptcy Act* (the trustee having declined to do so on behalf of the creditors generally) for an order directing the debtor to pay out of his earnings a certain sum in excess of necessary requirements for the benefit of the applicant creditors.

The debtor was in the building business in Windsor, Ontario, prior to April 28, 1942 when he was adjudged a bankrupt. He alleges that his bankruptcy was the result of his underestimating two building contracts in which he was engaged at the time. Seeing that he could not continue he asked his main creditors to accept a compromise to enable him to continue but they refused.

He seeks to derive some merit from the fact of their refusal and also from the fact that he had dealt with them for some years in large sums and that their present claims are small in comparison to the total of the business which they derived from him. I have been listening to this argument for several years. The debtor argues in the case of one creditor that as he has given it $20,000 worth of business over a previous period of time and their claim is only $2,000, that they should forget about the claim and be generous. Nothing could be more fallacious than this species of reasoning.

It was a bad failure and the trustee has very little in its hands to go on. In fact recoveries will scarcely equal disbursements, if they will do that, which I doubt. The creditors therefore will get nothing unless I make the order applied for.

Most of the defence of the debtor in his affidavit consists of history and other irrelevant matters. As to the earnings and situation of the debtor, both sides are in virtual agreement.

The debtor is employed presently at the Canadian Bridge Co. Ltd. in Walkerville which is known to me to be an excellent concern and one which is doing and is capable of doing a large business. So far as I can gather he is a war worker doing physical labour and is being paid at the rate of $1.09 an hour. His gross earnings for one year up to June 15, 1944, were $2,785.18, according to the company's letter. The letter adds:

'Since he is on an hourly rate and our operations have recently been curtailed, there is a possibility that the amount earned may be reduced for a similar period ahead.'

I do not think I could take into account the suggestion contained in the last paragraph as to my way of thinking there is no prospect of an immediate termination of the war in Europe and it is more than likely that this company, which has always enjoyed a large share of such business as is going, will continue to be busy for a considerable time.

The debtor says that he is in bad health, but no independent evidence or doctor's certificate of such is given and I do not pay much attention to his statement in that regard. He seems to be able to satisfy his employers. He is 52 years of age and supports only his wife in an apartment for which he pays $45 per month. This apartment is in an excellent district and is much beyond what a bankrupt debtor in Windsor and an ordinary labourer should indulge in. I know of plenty of houses in Windsor quite suitable which rent for considerably less. Rents in Windsor owing to too early freezing did not rise much beyond those of the depression period and I would assume that the apartment occupied by the debtor cannot be justified considering his station in life as an ordinary war worker and the fact that he has been a bankrupt for more than two years.

Little or nothing can be done now to remedy this situation as the housing shortage in Windsor is known to me to be very acute. I only mention the matter because it indicates in the debtor a lack of appreciation of his condition and a lack of regard for his creditors. Such an attitude is shown throughout the material. For example, the creditors suggest that he told one or more of them that he had withdrawn from the business $300. on the occasion of his son's wedding in Toledo recently; and that in 1941 he had used $1,000 of the moneys of the business to pay off a mortgage owed by his wife on certain of her property. The debtor of course denies both that he did these things and that he told anyone that he did ... A good deal in the material indicates that his wife may have private means. The earnings of the debtor during a yearly period were $2,785.18 gross. These are subject to certain deductions, income tax, unemployment insurance, hospitalization and the like, which leave a net during the period of $2,227.70 or an equivalent of $42.84 per week to provide for the living expenses of the debtor and his wife.

Counsel for the creditors suggests that he could well afford to pay the excess over $30 per week. While on the other hand counsel for the debtor says that he could not pay more than $10 per month even if an order were made.

The main defence of the debtor is that the Court has no power to order and will not order a wage earner, whose earnings are based on an hourly rate to make periodical payments to his creditors. The point has not come up squarely in any of the Canadian cases.
[Urquhart J discussed *Clarkson* v *Tod* [1934] 2 D.L.R. 316 (S.C.C.) which held that an order may be made in respect of salary. He then extended that principle to wage-earners as well as salaried employees.]

The debtor, though actually earning wages, is not a 'wage-earner' as defined by the Act. Section 2(*ll*) defines a wage-earner as 'one who works for wages, salary, commission or hire at a rate of compensation not exceeding fifteen hundred dollars per year, and who does not on his own account carry on business.'

A 'wage-earner' cannot be put into bankruptcy (see s 7), but there is nothing in the Act which exempts him from any other part.

The usual order should go, but the question remains, what amount should be paid by the debtor to his creditors.

The general rule in the these cases is that the debtor is entitled to the fair and reasonable amount required for the maintenance of himself and family according to their condition in life. As Lord Esher says in *Re Shine, Ex p. Shine*, [1892] 1 Q.B. 522 at p 532: 'I think the Court ought not to cut down the bankrupt's means of livelihood too closely, but ought to leave a liberal margin for his support.'

The present case approximates that of Plamandon above mentioned, except that Plamandon was more moderate in the amount he paid for rent, which was in my opinion more in keeping with his status as a war worker. Plamandon being newly married had also the prospect of a family. I ordered him to pay $30 per month.

In the present case, in view of the rent which the debtor is paying, I can hardly make so great an order, but I am taking into account the saving on insurance premiums and all other circumstances set forth above and dealt with in the argument. I can see no reason why out of his earnings the debtor could not pay approximately $25 per month to his creditors. Taking his net earnings of $2,227.70, they are roughly $185 per month. The order will therefore go that the debtor will pay to the trustee for the creditors concerned, the excess over $160 per month, and as he has expressed the wish to pay any amount ordered in half-monthly instalments, the order may provide for such. First payment to be made on next pay day (date to be ascertained and put in order). The order may follow the form used in the case of Plamandon. The application having been resisted, the debtor will pay the costs of the applicant hereof, fixed at $30, which may be added to the debt of the creditors. When the debt of the creditors interested as well as the above costs and the costs and remuneration of the trustee are satisfied, this order shall cease to have effect, as other creditors are not interested in the result.
Order accordingly.

3 RIGHTS OF ACTION

Ritenburg v *Crown Trust Co.* (1962), 33 D.L.R. (2d) 498 (Alta. S.C.)

RILEY, J.: Clause 10 of the agreed statement of facts reveals that Messrs. O'Connor and O'Connor made a payment of $5,675.76 to Crown Trust Company on behalf of the applicant on May 15th, 1957. The said amount of $5,675.76 was paid pursuant to the following statement:

Judgment recovered by Ritenburg for damages for personal injuries arising out of a motor vehicle accident	$6,274.51
Monies collected by O'Connor & O'Connor on account of mortgage by one Ralph Mathews to Ritenburg	2,401.25
	8,675.76
Less fees of O'Connor & O'Connor	3,000.00
Paid Crown Trust Company	$5,675.76

It is admitted on behalf of the applicant that he was not entitled to retain the monies collected from Ralph Mathews, being payments on account of a certain mortgage in the amount of $2,401.25. It follows therefore that the amount being claimed from the Trustee, Crown Trust Co. by the applicant is for the sum of $3,274.51 since the Trustee is entitled to retain the said sum of $2,401.25 out of the $5,675.76 presently held by it.

The question for determination therefore is whether the monies recovered by the applicant by way of compensation for pain and suffering and personal injuries are attachable by the Trustee as 'property' within the meaning of the *Bankruptcy Act* for distribution among the applicant's creditors.

The definition of property in the *Bankruptcy Act*, R.S.C. 1952, c 14 is found in s 2(*o*):

2. (*o*) 'Property' includes money, goods, things in action, land, and every description of property, whether real or personal, movable or immovable, legal or equitable, and whether situate in Canada or elsewhere and includes obligations, easements and every description of estate, interest and profit, present or future, vested or contingent, in, arising out of, or incident to property.

Section 39 of the *Bankruptcy Act* provides:

39. The property of a bankrupt divisible amongst his creditors shall not comprise
(*a*) property held by the bankrupt in trust for any other person,
(*b*) any property that as against the bankrupt is exempt from execution or seizure under the laws of the province within which the property is situate and within which the bankrupt resides,
but it shall comprise
(*c*) all property wherever situate of the bankrupt at the date of his bankruptcy or that may be acquired by or devolve on him before his discharge, and
(*d*) such powers in or over or in respect of the property as might have been exercised by the bankrupt for his own benefit.

The English law on this point is paraphrased in 2 Hals., 3rd ed., at pp. 401–2, para. 805:

All rights of action which relate directly to the bankrupt's property and can be turned into assets for the payment of debts pass to the trustee, but where a cause of action arises from the bodily or mental suffering or personal inconvenience of the bankrupt, or from injury to his person or reputation, then the right of action remains with the bankrupt.

Paragraph 3 of the Agreed Statement of Facts states that Ritenburg recovered a judgment of $8,000 as compensation for pain and suffering, medical expenses, loss of employment, and permanent partial disability. Paragraphs 7 and 8 reveal that Ritenburg recovered the sum of $6,274.57 from the Unsatisfied Judgment Fund of the Province of Alberta on account of the said judgment.

In *Drake* v *Beckham* (1843), 11 M. & W. 315 at p 319, 152 E.R. 823, Lord Denham, C.J., stated:

There is no doubt that a right of action for an injury to the body or feelings of a trader, arising from a tort, indpendent of contract, does not pass to his assignees ... In all those cases the primary cause of action, if of a nature, properly speaking, personal, and the right to maintain it, would die with the bankrupt.

The respondent urges that there was a judgment debt of the applicant existing at the time of bankruptcy, and not a personal right of action. It seems to me to be illogical, unjust and inequitable to say that rights of action personal to the bankrupt never pass to the Trustee, but the fruits thereof do. In point of fact such an argument runs contrary to the decision of *Re Hollister*, quoted *supra*.

It is, of course, patent that an unappealed order is a 'speaking order', but in this case the Court did not purport to decide the rights of the parties '*inter se*' but merely made an interim preservation order.

4 That in any event the monies were paid over to the trustees under a mistake of law and were not recoverable by the debtor except in the discretion of the Court, and that this is not a case where the discretion of the Court should be exercised in favour of the bankrupt. The monies were not, of course, paid over under any mistake of law but were paid over pursuant to the Court order of June 28, 1954. Were it a matter of my discretion I would exercise the same in favour of the bankrupt.

In the result I reject the respondent's arguments and direct that the respondent pay to the applicant the sum of $3,274.51 out of the funds presently held by it, less the costs awarded to the Trustee. There will be, of course, no costs of the applicant because the matters herein should have been raised some seven years ago. The Trustee is allowed the sum of $300 plus its reasonable disbursements in respect of this application.

Ritenburg v *Crown Trust* was applied in *Re Brodie*, [1969] 1 O.R. 285, which involved damages received in the settlement of a motor vehicle action.

QUESTION Why should tort damages for loss of earnings be exempt from the bankruptcy when wages are not?

4 DEFEASIBLE INTERESTS

In *Re Burroughs-Fowler*, [1916] 2 Ch. 251

PETERSON J. In this case I am required to solve a puzzle which arises out of a clause relating to a protected life interest under a marriage settlement dated March 24, 1905. Under that settlement W. J. Fowler (who afterwards took the name of Burroughs-Fowler), on the occasion of his marriage with his then intended wife, settled certain property belonging to him. The property was conveyed to the trustees in trust for conversion and investment of the proceeds, and the trust premises were to be held by the trustees upon the following trusts: [His Lordship read the trusts above set out and continued:] The marriage took place a few days after the execution of the settlement, and on May 13, 1915, the husband was adjudicated bankrupt. The trustee in bankruptcy has entered into negotiations for the sale of the bankrupt's interest under the settlement, and the question which has arisen is what is the interest which has vested in the trustee and of which the trustee is now able to dispose.

Now the limitation until the settlor is declared bankrupt is void as against the trustee in bankruptcy, and therefore, so far as the trustee in bankruptcy is concerned, the words relating to the bankruptcy and insolvency of the settlor must be treated as if they were omitted altogether from the clause. But on the other hand the provision as to bankruptcy and insolvency is not void as between the husband and the wife; for it was decided in *In re Johnson* ([1904] 1 K.B. 134) that, while the provision for the cessation of the life interest on bankruptcy was void as against the trustee in bankruptcy, it was effective for the purpose of producing a forfeiture as between the person who had the protected life interest and the persons interested in remainder. What, then, is the result? It is said that the result may be that the trustee in bankruptcy will be in a position to dispose of more than was vested in the bankrupt himself. That would be so in any case, because, so far as the trustee is concerned, the provisions for terminating the protected life interest upon bankruptcy are void. It seems to me that the true view is that, so far as the trustee in bankruptcy is concerned, the provisions as to bankruptcy and insolvency must be treated as excluded from the settlement, and the trustee is therefore in a position to deal with the interest of the husband under the settlement, whatever it may be, as if those provisions were excluded. So far, however, as the wife is concerned the forfeiture by reason of the bankruptcy has already taken place, and, therefore, it is no longer possible for the husband hereafter to do or suffer something which would determine his interest. The result is that the trustee in bankruptcy is in possession of the life interest of the bankrupt, which is now incapable of being affected by any subsequent forfeiture.

5 RESIDUAL DISCRETION

In Re Thellusson, [1919] 2 K.B. 735

July 31. WARRINGTON L.J. read the following judgment: The question in this appeal is whether the circumstances of this case justify the exercise by the Court of the jurisdiction it has often asserted of directing its officer – in this case a trustee in bankruptcy – to pursue a line of conduct which an honest man actuated by motives of morality and justice would pursue, although not compellable thereto by legal process.

The facts are these. The appellant Mr. Abdy, an officer in the army, became acquainted with the debtor, a retired naval captain, in October, 1918. In the middle of November the debtor asked the appellant if he would lend him 1000*l.* to enable him to discharge a pressing debt. The appellant consulted his solicitor and found that he could only raise the money by insuring his life and mortgaging the policy. He thereupon stipulated that the debtor must agree to repay not only the 1000*l.* but the expenses of effecting the policy, including the premium. Pending the effecting of the insurance the appellant paid 100*l.* to the debtor on account by means of a promissory note guaranteed by his solicitor, and the transaction was completed on January 3, 1919, by the advance of the further sum of 900*l.* to the debtor on his signing an agreement of that day by which he bound himself to pay to the appellant the sum of 1272*l.* on July 3, 1919, with interest at 6 per cent. The 272*l.* was the amount of the premium and expenses above referred to.

The 900*l.* was paid to the debtor's bankers. Out of it they paid themselves the amount of an overdraft due to them, leaving a balance of 764*l.* 0*s.* 5*d.* in their hands.

It subsequently appeared that unknown to the appellant and his solicitor and (as was said by the debtor) to him also a receiving order had been made against him on January 2. The appellant and his solicitor were also ignorant of the facts that the debtor had committed an act of bankruptcy and that a petition had been presented, though these latter facts must of course have been known to the debtor.

The appellant states that had he known that a receiving order had been made he would not have paid the 900*l*. to the debtor, and there is every reason to accept this statement.

The Official Receiver, as trustee in bankruptcy, having required the bank to pay him the 764*l*. 0*s*. 5*d*., and having received it from them the appellant applied by motion to the Court in Bankruptcy that the loan transaction be declared void, and/or rescinded and that the Official Receiver do repay to the appellant the 764*l*. 0*s*. 5*d*. above mentioned. This money was in fact at the time of the application still in the hands of the Official Receiver.

On May 12, 1919, Horridge J., sitting in Bankruptcy, dismissed the appellant's motion with costs; hence this appeal. Before Horridge J. it was contended that the loan transaction ought to be set aside on the ground of common mistake or mistake of fact as to something affecting the subject-matter of the contract, but it was also contended that even if there was no legal right in the appellant to rescind the transaction and so recover the money it would not under the circumstances be in accordance with strict notions of honesty and justice for the Official Receiver to retain it, and the Court ought in exercising control over its officer to order him to do that which a strictly honest man would do – namely, to repay the 764*l*. 0*s*. 5*d*. to the appellant.

Horridge J. arrived at a conclusion adverse to the appellant on his legal claim, and, on his appeal to the Court's discretionary jurisdiction, was of opinion, for reasons which do not clearly appear from his judgment, that the case was not one in which the Court ought to interfere with the legal title. Before this Court the legal claim was hardly pressed, and, without going so far as to say it could not succeed, I will assume that it ought not to do so. The question then arises whether the Court ought to exercise the discretionary jurisdiction over its officer to which I have referred.

The first matter to be determined is what are the limits of the jurisdiction. The first case in which the jurisdiction in question appears to have been exercised in the case of a trustee in bankruptcy is *Ex parte James*. (1) In that case an execution creditor acting under what proved to be a mistaken view of the law voluntarily paid the proceeds of his execution to the trustee in bankruptcy of the debtor. On an application by the execution creditor for repayment by the trustee, the Court ordered the trustee to repay notwithstanding that he could not by law be compelled so to do. The ground of the decision is thus stated by James L.J.: 'A trustee in bankruptcy is an officer of the Court ... The Court, then, finding that he has in his hands money which in equity belongs to some one else, ought to set an example to the world by paying it to the person really entitled to it. In my opinion the Court of Bankruptcy ought to be as honest as other people.'

We have here a trustee in bankruptcy in possession of money of the bankrupt which he knows was lent to him by Mr. Abdy in ignorance of the fact that on the day before the payment a receiving order had been made and which would not have been so lent if the facts had been known to the lender. I think under such circumstances an honest man would on ascertaining the facts at once repay the money, and, in my opinion, the trustee must be ordered to pay the 764*l*. 0*s*. 5*d*. accordingly.

The debtor is not before us except so far as the trustee represents him. If there are any rights or obligations arising out of the loan transaction which, notwithstanding the bankruptcy, remained vested in or binding on the debtor these will not be affected by our order, save, of course, so far as they may be affected by the repayment of the 764*l*. 0*s*. 5*d*.

I think the applicant is entitled to the costs of this appeal, but, inasmuch as the trustee was entitled to have the decision of the Court in the matter, there should be no costs in the Court below.

ATKIN, L.J. read the following judgment: ... We were pressed in argument with the contention put before the Court in *In re Tyler* (2) that 'great difficulties will arise in the administration of bankruptcy if the Court is to decide according to what it considers high-minded without regard to law or equity.' I think that these difficulties are exaggerated. But while one may agree that opinions as to rules of honesty differ, the difficulty of recognizing honesty when she appears, affords no inadequate reason for discarding her altogether. The advantages of maintaining a high standard of commercial morality in my judgment far outweigh the suggested inconveniences of administration. If I may repeat the words of Lord Esher the proposition strikes me as a good, a righteous and a wholesome one, and I eagerly desire to adopt it.

The application to the facts of this case, if relatively of small importance, does not appear to me to present much difficulty. Assume that the debtor knew the facts when he received the money can it be suggested that a high-minded man would have completed the transaction and received the money? He would know that the object of the transaction was defeated, that the money would go straight into the possession of the Official Receiver, and that the sweeping away of his assets in bankruptcy would make it impossible for him to comply with his convenant to repay. Can it be said that any different rule of conduct should have guided him when a day or two later he discovered the true facts? If he ought as a just man then to have restored the money, then so ought the officer of the Court who receives the money from him. It is said that the same position will always arise where money or goods are handed over in a mistaken belief as to the recipient's financial position. I do not agree. The important fact here is that the whole of the recipient's assets had been taken from his control by operation of law. The mere uncertainty that arises while a man is left with full disposing power of his available assets, such as they are, presents a different problem which can be considered when it arises.
Appeal allowed.

QUESTIONS Why should the proximity in time of the loan to the date of bankruptcy affect the distribution of the estate? It may be that other creditors had advanced their money to discharge other debts or for other bona fide purposes. Why should this creditor gain a priority over them?

6 ANTECEDENT TRANSACTIONS

The Bankruptcy Bill (s-14)

7. (1) For the purposes of this Act,
(*a*) it is a question of fact whether persons not related to each other were, at a particular time, dealing with each other at arm's length; and
(*b*) persons related to each other are deemed not to deal with each other at arm's length.
(2) For the purposes of this Act, individuals are related to each other
(*a*) where one is married to the other; or
(*b*) where one is connected with the other by blood relationship, marriage or adoption,
   (i) in direct line, or
   (ii) in collateral line to the degree existing between brothers and sisters, whether they have the same parents or only the same father or mother.

(3) For the purposes of this Act,

(*a*) 'adoption' includes *de facto* adoption;

(*b*) 'blood relationship' includes an illegitimate relationship;

(*c*) two individuals of the opposite sex are deemed to be married to one another where they live together as husband and wife; and

(*d*) an individual is deemed to have the same relationship by marriage to the relatives of his spouse during the existence of the marriage and thereafter as his spouse has by blood relationship.

8. (1) For the purposes of this section,

(*a*) a person or group of persons controls a corporation where the person or group
   (i) holds more than fifty per cent of the issued shares of the corporation having full voting rights under all circumstances, or
   (ii) holds fifty per cent of the issued shares of the corporation having full voting rights under all circumstances and the person or a member of the group is entitled to cast a deciding vote at a meeting of shareholders;

(*b*) 'related group' means a group of persons each member of which is related to every other member of the group;

(*c*) 'unrelated group' means a group of persons that is not a related group; and

(*d*) a person who has a contractual right, either immediately or in the future and either absolutely or contingently to, or to acquire, shares of a corporation or to control the voting rights attached to shares of a corporation, shall be deemed to have the same position in relation to the control of the corporation as if he owned the shares.

(2) Paragraph (1)(*d*) does not apply where the right of the person to, or to acquire, shares of a corporation or to control the voting rights attached to shares of a corporation is not exercisable until the death of an individual designated in the contract.

(3) Paragraph (1)(*d*) does not apply where

(*a*) the corporation is a party to a contract with another person and the contract provides that on the fulfilment of a condition or the happening of an event that it is reasonable to expect will be fulfilled or will happen,
   (i) the other person ceases to have an interest in shares of the corporation, and
   (ii) the shares are acquired by a person with whom the other person deals at arm's length; and

(*b*) the chief purpose for which a person has an interest in shares of the corporation is as a result of a security interest in respect of
   (i) a loan made by the person, the whole or any part of which is outstanding, or
   (ii) any shares issued by the corporation that are held by the person and that are, under the contract, required to be redeemed by the corporation or purchased by another person with whom the vendor of the shares deals at arm's length.

(4) Where a corporation is controlled by a person, it is related to

(*a*) the person who controls it; and

(*b*) any person related to the person who controls it.

(5) Where a corporation is controlled by a related group, it is related to

(*a*) each member of the group; and

(*b*) any person related to a member of the group.

(6) Where a corporation is controlled by an unrelated group, it is related to any person

(*a*) who, being a member of the group, is related to each other member; or

(*b*) who, not being a member of the group, is related to each member of the group.

(7) Without restricting the generality of subsections (4) to (6), two corporations are related to each other

    (*a*) where they are related to the same person or controlled by the same person or group; or

    (*b*) where one corporation is controlled by an unrelated group and the other corporation is controlled by another unrelated group and each member of one group is a member of or related to at least one member of the other group.

7 GIFTS AND REVIEWABLE TRANSACTIONS

a / Tassé Report, pp 115–16 (footnotes omitted)

3.2.051 *Fraudulent Conveyances and Reviewable Transactions*: A debtor must be just to his creditors before he can rightfully be generous with his property for the benefit of others. For most of the common law jurisdictions of the world, this principle was first embodied in the *Fraudulent Conveyances Act* of 1571, which declared that conveyances made with intent to defeat, hinder, delay or defraud creditors were 'clearly and utterly void, frustrated and of no effect.' Most, if not all, of the common law provinces have a *Fraudulent Conveyances Act* and an *Assignment and Preferences Act*, both of which relate to fraudulent conveyances. The *Civil Code* of Quebec also has provisions with respect to the avoidance of contracts and payments made in fraud of creditors. Finally, sections 60, 61 and 62 of the *Bankruptcy Act* avoid certain settlements of property, if the settler subsequently becomes bankrupt.

3.2.052 The constitutionality of the provincial *Fraudulent Conveyances Acts* and *Fraudulent Preferences Act* has been discussed *supra* in 1.4.16 et seq. As trustees frequently rely upon the *Fraudulent Conveyances Acts* and the *Civil Code*, it would be unfortunate if they were deprived of the kind of remedy provided by this legislation.

3.2.053 In 1966, the *Bankruptcy Act* was amended by the addition of provisions allowing for the review of certain transactions involving, for example, related persons. A similar technique is used in income tax matters. Through this technique, a transaction made between persons not dealing at arms' length, within twelve months prior to bankruptcy, may be reviewed. If, in the transaction, the debtor gave conspicuously more than he received, then judgment may be given for the difference. The onus is on the party who benefited from the transaction to show that it was fair. Section 67B also provides that, where a corporation, within twelve months of bankruptcy, has redeemed shares or granted a dividend, when the corporation was insolvent, or that rendered the corporation insolvent, recovery may be made against the directors or against certain shareholders of the bankrupt corporation. The onus is on the recipient to show that, immediately after the receipt of the benefit, the company was not insolvent.

3.2.054 The sections regarding reviewable transactions relate only to those transactions where the debtor and the creditor are not dealing with each other at arms' length. Admittedly, these are the situations where there is the greatest temptation for a debtor to be generous with his property. The provisions, by shifting the onus of proof, have been useful in controlling many situations where transactions were technically legal, but were commercially immoral. However, the field covered by the provincial *Fraudulent Conveyances Acts* or the *Civil Code* is wider than the one covered by the *Bankruptcy Act*. In our opinion, the *Bankruptcy Act* should cover the entire field of fraudulent conveyances, so as to make available, in the case of an estate administered under the *Bankruptcy Act*, the relief provided by the *Fraudulent Conveyances Acts* and Articles 1032–1040 of the *Civil Code*, and we so recommend.

b / The Bankruptcy Bill (s-14)

10. (3) Notwithstanding any other Act of Parliament or any Act of a legislature of a province, where a bankruptcy order or an arrangement is made in respect of a debtor, no person may

(*a*) take or continue any proceeding to review or set aside a transfer to or from the debtor on the grounds that such transfer is a fraudulent preference or conveyance except in accordance with sections 168 to 185 and section 246; and

(*b*) if the debtor is a corporation, take or continue any proceeding

(i) to review or set aside a dividend payment, share redemption or share purchase effected by the corporation except in accordance with section 170, or

(ii) to compel directors or former directors of the corporation to pay any arrears of wages, except in accordance with section 188.

168. Where a person makes a gift and subsequently becomes a bankrupt, the court, on application of the trustee may set aside the gift

(*a*) where the interest of the donor in the gift does not pass irrevocably at least six months before the date the petition is filed;

(*b*) where the donor and donee are not at arm's length and the interest of the donor does not pass irrevocably at least one year before the date the petition is filed; or

(*c*) where, at the time the interest of the donor passes irrevocably, the donor is insolvent or unable to pay his debts without the aid of the property comprised in the gift.

169. (1) Where persons who are at arm's length enter into a transfer and one of the persons subsequently becomes a bankrupt, the court, on application of the trustee, may review the transfer where it was entered into

(*a*) less than three months before the date of filing the petition and otherwise than in the normal course of affairs; or

(*b*) less than six years before the date of filing the petition and with the intent, known to both parties, to impede, obstruct, delay or defraud a creditor.

(2) Where persons who are not at arm's length enter into a transfer and subsequently one of the persons becomes a bankrupt, the court, on application of the trustee, may review the transfer where it was entered into less than six years before the date of filing the petition.

(3) In making an application under this section, the trustee may estimate what, in his opinion, was the fair value of the consideration of each party to the transfer and the values on which the court may make a finding pursuant to subsection (4) shall be the values estimated by the trustee unless other values are proved.

(4) Where, in reviewing a transfer pursuant to this section, the court finds that one consideration was conspicuously greater in fair value than the other to the detriment of the party who subsequently became a bankrupt, the court may

(*a*) determine the amount of the difference in the fair values and give judgment for an amount not exceeding the amount of the difference to the trustee against the other party;

(*b*) determine the amount of the difference in the fair values and reduce the claim of the other party against the estate by an amount not exceeding the amount of the difference; or

(*c*) make an order declaring the transfer to be void and restoring each party to the transfer in so far as possible to the state that he was in immediately prior to the transfer.

(5) Where, in reviewing a transfer pursuant to this section, the court finds that the effect of the transfer was to impede, obstruct, delay or defraud the creditors or any of them, the court may set aside the transfer and restore each party to the transfer in so far as possible to the state that he was in immediately prior to the transfer.

170. (1) Where, less than one year before the date of filing of a petition in respect of a corporation that subsequently becomes a bankrupt, the corporation paid a dividend other than a share dividend or redeemed or purchased any of its shares when the corporation was insolvent or where such payment, redemption or purchase of shares would render the corporation insolvent, the court may, on application of the trustee, give judgment to the trustee for the amount of the dividend paid to, or shares redeemed or purchased from, a shareholder,

    (*a*) if the shareholder is at arm's length with the corporation and each of its directors, against the directors jointly and severally, without prejudice to any right that a director may have to recover from the shareholder the amount the director has paid to the trustee; or

    (*b*) if the shareholder is not at arm's length with either the corporation or one of its directors, against the shareholder and also against the directors but, in respect of the directors jointly and severally, without prejudice to any right that a director may have to recover from the shareholder the amount the director has paid to the trustee.

(2) A director is not liable under this section for the amount of a dividend paid to, or shares redeemed or purchased from, a shareholder where,

    (*a*) such director votes against or dissents from the declaration or payment of the dividend or the redemption or purchase of shares and, in voting against or dissenting, he complies with the requirements of the law governing the operation of the corporation; or

    (*b*) such director relies in good faith on

        (i) financial statements of the corporation represented to him by an officer of the corporation or in a written report of the auditor of the corporation fairly to reflect the financial condition of the corporation, or

        (ii) a report of a solicitor, accountant, appraiser or other person whose profession lends credibility to a statement made by him.

171. Where a debtor transfers the bulk of his non-exempt property by way of trust or otherwise for the general benefit of his creditors and subsequently becomes a bankrupt, the court may, on application of the trustee, set aside the transfer except where the transfer was by way of an arrangement.

c / *Re Bozanich*, [1942] 2 D.L.R. 145 (S.C.C.)

SIR LYMAN P. DUFF C.J.C.: The material facts are stated in the respondents' factum, as follows:

'The debtor, George Bozanich, operated a small retail grocery and meat market in the City of Windsor, under the name and style of "Goodwill Market" from January 1936 until July, 1939, when he discontinued business. On October 21st, 1939, he made an authorized assignment under the bankruptcy Act. The appellant company is a wholesale grocery firm with which the debtor had substantial dealings from the commencement of the business until April, 1939.

'On April 5th, 1939, the debtor executed a chattel mortgage in favour of the appellant to secure the sum of $900.00, the amount of a long past due indebtedness owing by the debtor to the appellant company. The chattel mortgage covered most of the debtor's store fixtures other than his cash register and it is alleged that the said fixtures at the time of the chattel mortgage and also at the time of the subsequent assignment constituted by far the greater part of the debtor's realizable assets.

'At the same time the appellant also took from the debtor a so-called lien note on the cash register as security for the sum of $361.45.

'Upon bankruptcy occurring the appellant claimed to be a secured creditor by virtue of both the chattel mortgage and the lien note, and the respondent, the trustee in bankruptcy, attacked the validity of both securities in a motion instituted in the Supreme Court of Ontario (in bankruptcy) heard before the Honourable Mr. Justice Urquhart on April 1st, 1940.

'The learned Bankruptcy Judge directed the trial of an issue before the Senior Judge of the County Court of the County of Essex to determine the validity of the questioned securities. The trustee was made plaintiff in the issue and the present appellant was made defendant and the trial Judge was directed to find as to the validity of the chattel mortgage and the lien note and to find for or against the right of the appellant company to rank as a secured creditor under either or both of the said documents.

'On the trial of this issue the lien note was set aside and there has been no appeal from this decision. The County Court Judge, however, reported that the chattel mortgage was valid and effectual as against the trustee in bankruptcy and that it did not constitute a "settlement" within the meaning of Section 60 of The Bankruptcy Act.

'An appeal was taken by the trustee in bankruptcy from the finding of the trial Judge with respect to the chattel mortgage and on this appeal the Honourable Mr. Justice Urquhart held that the chattel mortgage did constitute a "settlement" under the provisions of the said section of the Bankruptcy Act and ordered a new trial before the County Court Judge on this basis, directing also that both parties might adduce further evidence.

'The trial Judge having failed to make any finding as to good faith and valuable consideration within the meaning of Section 60 subection 3(b) of The Bankruptcy Act, and the learned Bankruptcy Judge finding himself unable to determine this question on appeal, the new trial was directed for the purpose of deciding this question and it was directed that the onus of establishing good faith and valuable consideration would be on the creditor, the present appellant.

'From the decision of the Bankruptcy Judge an appeal was taken by the present appellant to the Court of Appeal for the Province of Ontario on the ground that the finding that the chattel mortgage was a "settlement" was erroneous, and that in any event the decision of the trial judge amounted to a finding of good faith and valuable consideration. The trustee cross-appealed from the portion of the judgment of the Bankruptcy Judge directing a new trial on the ground that the onus being on the creditor to establish good faith and valuable consideration, the failure of the trial judge to find affirmatively in favour of the creditor on these points was sufficient to entitle the trustee to the relief sought.

'The appeal and cross-appeal came on for hearing on December 9th, 1940, before the Honourable Mr. Justice Riddell, Acting Chief Justice, the Honourable Mr. Justice Henderson and the Honourable Mr. Justice Gillanders. On December 21st, 1940, the majority of the Court delivered judgment dismissing the appeal and the cross-appeal and confirming the decision of the Bankruptcy Judge that the chattel mortgage was a "settlement" within the meaning of the Bankruptcy Act, Section 60, and also the directions of the Bankruptcy Judge for a new trial. The Honourable Mr. Justice Henderson dissented from the judgment and would have allowed the appeal and restored the report of the trial judge on the ground that the transaction was not a "settlement".'

The question raised by the appeal concerns the interpretation of ss 60 to 62 inclusive and s 64 of the *Bankruptcy Act*, which are under the caption 'Settlement and Preferences'. Sections 60, 61 and 62 were enacted in 1919 and s 64 in the following year. These were, in substance, re-enactments of ss 42 and 44 of the English *Bankruptcy Act* of 1914 [c 59].

The controversy turns upon the effect of s 62(3) which is in these words: 'For the purpose of this section and sections sixty and sixty-one "settlement" shall include any conveyance or transfer of property.'

It is contended that by force of this section the ordinary meaning of 'settlement' is extended in such a manner as to bring within its scope any conveyance or transfer of property. The corresponding provision in the English *Bankruptcy Act*, which was found in the Act of 1869 [c 71], was the subject of discussion and decision before the enactment of the Canadian *Bankruptcy Act* of 1919 [c 36]; and it may, I think, properly be said that in 1919 when these provisions were adopted by Parliament it was the settled law in England that, although in the form of definition these words purport to enlarge the meaning of the term 'settlement', they must, by reason of the context, be restricted in their scope. Broadly speaking, the settled principle in England is that this clause has not the effect of bringing within the scope of the term 'settlement', as used in the sections corresponding to ss 60, 61 and 62 of our Act, transactions which have none of the essential elements of a 'settlement', as that term is commonly understood.

In the treatise on Bankruptcy and Insolvency in the 2nd edition of Halsbury [vol. 2, para. 487] by Lord Justice Luxmoore it is stated that the term 'settlement' 'implies an intention that the property shall be retained or preserved for the benefit of the donee in such a form that it can be traced'. This construction was well settled in the year 1919 when the relative provisions of the English statute were enacted as part of the bankruptcy law of this country. It is proper to assume that it was the statute as it had been construed by the English Courts and applied in the administration of bankruptcy law in England that Parliament intended to adopt.

I pass now to s 64 which deals with transactions between an insolvent person and his creditor. The history of the law relating to such transactions is familiar. At common law there is nothing to prevent a debtor preferring one creditor to another. The statute, 13 Eliz., c 5, did not prohibit such transactions. This common law privilege is obviously opposed to the fundamental principle of bankruptcy law – the equitable distribution of assets among all entitled to share, and the law of fraudulent preference was originally developed by the Courts on the basis of the principles of the *Bankruptcy Acts*. The principle of s 64 was first formulated by statute in s 92 of the *Bankruptcy Act* of 1869. In Canada in most of the Provinces there were, prior to the *Bankruptcy Act*, statutory enactments making voidable transfers of property by an insolvent made with the intention of giving a particular creditor an 'unjust preference'.

When ss 61 and 62 of the *Bankruptcy Act* are read together with s 64 and these enactments are considered in light of the history of the law in relation to preferences, I find it impossible to convince myself that such a transaction as that with which we are now concerned falls within the intendment of 'settlement', as employed in those sections. It belongs, I think, to the class of transactions, the validity of which is to be determined by the application of s 64.

I may add that in my opinion the provisions of R.S.O. 1927, c 162, in relation to preferences are superseded by s 64 of the *Bankruptcy Act*, and that the authority of the Ontario Legislature to enact such legislation is, in consequence of the enactment of s 64, suspended in virtue of the concluding paragraph of s 91 [of the *B.N.A. Act*].

The appeal should be allowed and the report of His Honour, Judge Coughlin, restored with costs throughout.

Whether, therefore, 'settlement' is or not a technical expression, it is apparent that, in the mind of the legislator, the use of the word 'settlement' was intended to connote a particular kind of gift or grant excluding the others. Both ss 60 and 62, since over a quarter of a century, had been in the English Act in similar language; and the Canadian *Bankruptcy Act* borrowed them from the English statute. The construction of the word had been settled in England for some appreciable time and it had there acquired an established meaning.

It need not be stated that all conveyances or transfers of property are not settlements; nor can it be said that a settlement is a settlement because it happens to be a conveyance or a transfer.

Without attempting to give a definition of the word – and more particularly of that word as used in s 60 – it seems to me sufficient for the purpose of interpreting the section to adopt a passage of Cave J., in the case of *Re Player, Ex p. Harvey* (1885), 15 Q.B.D. 682 at pp 686–7: 'One must look at the whole of the language of the section in applying that definition and consider what is meant by 'settlement.' Although 'settlement,' by the 3rd subsection 'shall for the purposes of this section include any conveyance or transfer of property,' yet I think the view of my brother Mathew is well founded, and that a settlement in the ordinary sense of the word is intended. The transaction must be in the nature of a settlement, though it may be effected by a conveyance or transfer. The end and purpose of the thing must be a settlement, that is, a disposition of property to be held for the enjoyment of some other person.' This view was concurred in by Mathew and Wills JJ.

In the *Player* case, a gift of money to a son, made for the purpose of enabling him to commence business on his own account, was held not to be a 'settlement of property' within the meaning of the section of the English *Bankruptcy Act*, which renders such settlements void in certain specified cases as against the Trustee in Bankruptcy of the settlor.

In the case of *Re Vansittart, Ex p. Brown*, [1893] 1 Q.B. 181, upon an application under the section in the English Act (again, it should be noted, expressed in identical language with ss 60 and 62(3) of the Canadian Act) to avoid a gift of valuable jewelry by the bankrupt, it appeared that such jewelry had been given by him as a present to his wife within two years of his bankruptcy. It was held that, to bring a transfer of personal property within the section, it must be manifest, from the nature and circumstances of the case, that it was the object of the transferor that the subject-matter of the transfer should permanently remain the property of the transferee; and, in the premises, it must be taken that the bankrupt contemplated the retention by his wife of the present which he had given her. In that case, Vaughan Williams J. approved the construction of Cave J. in the *Player* case; and, applying it to the facts in the case then before him, he found that the donor contemplated the retention by his wife of the present which he gave her, and accordingly held the gift void against the trustee in bankruptcy.

Again, the Court of Appeal, in the case of *Re Plummer* ([1900] 2 Q.B.790 – Lord Alverstone M.R., Rigby and Collins L.JJ.) approved of the principle stated in *Re Vansittart, Ex p. Brown* and *Re Player, Ex p. Harvey* and held that the mere fact that some business had been acquired by the son partly by means of money obtained from or paid by the father was not sufficient to make the transaction a 'settlement' within the section. 'Settlement', in the English *Bankruptcy Act*, was held to mean such a conveyance or transfer by the donor as contemplates the retention of the property by the donee, either in its original form or in such a form that it can be traced, and does not extend to a conveyance or transfer of property which cannot be traced, as, for instance, where there is a gift of money to be employed in a business or in the purchase of a business and the money is so employed or spent, the business itself not being settled.

In his judgment, Rigby L.J., referred to what Cave J., had said (as above reproduced) in the *Player* case and observed (p 808): 'I do not think that that judgment has been impeached by any of the later authorities that have been referred to.'

Collins L.J., expressing the same view, said (p 180): 'It is impossible, in my opinion, to treat such a transaction as the subject-matter of a "settlement" within the section.'

It seems that the word 'settlement' used in the *Bankruptcy Act* does not embrace the set of circumstances constituting the facts of the case at bar. I doubt whether an arrangement with a creditor may ever be considered a settlement; and I would incline to the opinion that, generally speaking, 'settlement' involves the idea of a clear gift, or that type of cases where provision is made for a trust of some sort. It should not be taken to include an ordinary business transaction between a debtor and a creditor.

The transaction in the case at bar was one to secure a past and future indebtedness. The chattel mortgage in question was given in the course of an ordinary commercial transaction. The mortgagor settled nothing on the mortgagee.

Subsection (3) of s 62 provides that 'settlement' shall include any conveyance or transfer of property; but the section which declares the transaction void against the trustee is s 60. That section uses the word 'settlement'. It follows that 'conveyance or transfer', in s 62(3) must be qualified by the word 'settlement' in s 60. The mere fact that the transaction is said to include any conveyance or transfer does not make the transaction a settlement. The transactions which are declared void under s 60 are such conveyances and transfers as come within the meaning of the word in s 60.

As pointed out by Henderson J.A., the necessary elements of a settlement were found in the *Trenwith* case; but they are not to be found in the case now under review, where the transaction does not include any of the elements which one must find present in a settlement.

The Act, as broad as it is, allows of a clear distinction between settlements though effected by a conveyance or transfer of property and conveyances or transfers of property not in the nature of a settlement.

In the circumstances of the present case, I think the appeal ought to be allowed and the decision of the County Court Judge restored with costs throughout.

CROCKET J., concurs with RINFRET J.
DAVIS and KERWIN JJ., concur with SIR LYMAN P. DUFF C.J.C.
Appeal allowed.

8 FRAUDULENT PREFERENCES

a / Tassé Report, pp 116–18 (footnotes omitted)

3.2.055 *Fraudulent Preferences*: The payment by an insolvent person of a pre-existing debt is a preference. It is objectionable as it diminishes his assets to the detriment of his other creditors. The law against preferences prevents the race from being to the swift and promotes a more equitable distribution of the assets of the debtor. It, at the same time, makes it much less attractive for a creditor to negotiate preferential arrangements with insolvent debtors and indirectly encourages a higher level of commercial morality and greater confidence in the credit system.

3.2.056 The present law relating to preferences draws a line three months before the date of bankruptcy, in the normal case, or twelve months, where the parties are related, and creates an insulated period of time during which creditors cannot, by their efforts at collecting, through the use of pressure or otherwise, secure an advantage over the other creditors. In effect, the race by the creditors for the assets of the debtor is stopped three months or twelve months, as the case may be, before bankruptcy. The creditors who receive more than their share in the three or twelve month period are required to surrender it.

3.2.057 Useful as the provisions are, they have led to much litigation. The most troublesome feature is the necessity to show the intent of the debtor to give a preference. In some provinces, the courts have held that the intent of the creditor to receive a preference must also be established. This is known as the requirement of a 'double intent'. In 1949, an attempt was made to remove from the Act the necessity of determining the intent of the debtor or creditor. This would have greatly facilitated the use of the provisions. Unfortunately, the proposed amendment was not contained in the final draft of the Bill for the 1949 Act. The result has been twenty more years of litigation.

3.2.058 The law of preferences was developed before methods of financing through the security of inventory and receivables were widely used. The present law, now, defeats the purpose of legislation such as the new Ontario *Personal Property Security Act*, which is based upon Article 9 of the *Uniform Commercial Code* of the United States. Under this type of legislation, a security may attach to a shifting quantity and quality of property sometimes described as a 'moving stream'. New goods may be substituted for old goods. Goods may change as they are processed or manufactured into different goods. These, in turn, may be converted into receivables. The scheme of the legislation is that the proceeds from the inventory of the debtor and the replacement inventory come under the umbrella of a floating charge. As soon as inventory is sold and converted into receivables or new inventory is acquired, the security interest attaches to the receivables and inventory. When the security interest attaches to new property, there is necessarily a pre-existing debt. For this reason, the inclusion of new property in the security in this manner is a preference, and, if it has occurred within three months of bankruptcy, it could be set aside as fraudulent.

3.2.059 Section 88 of the *Bank Act*, whereby a floating charge over inventory and receivables may be created, presents a similar difficulty. However, section 169 of the *Bankruptcy Act*, which exempts the rights and privileges conferred on banks from the operation of the *Bankruptcy Act*, prevents property vesting in banks within the suspect period prior to bankruptcy from being set aside as a fraudulent preference. In our view, there is no logical or commercial reason why the law in this respect should be different in the case of a bank and all other creditors.

3.2.060. In our opinion, the law of preferences, as it is contained in the *Bankruptcy Act*, is basically sound and it has the same over-riding importance that it has always had in the bankruptcy system and the commerical community. We recommend, however, that it should be modified so as to provide a more comprehensive and equitable system. When a preference is given within the suspect period, intention should be irrelevant. No creditor should, for any reason, improve his position, at the expense of the other creditors, within the suspect period immediately prior to bankruptcy. The proof of the intent to give a preference should, however, be sufficient to impeach the preference given outside the suspect period. Furthermore, the law of preferences should, in our view, apply equally to banks and other creditors; it should, however, be such as to protect securities given under Section 88 of the *Bank Act* and new Personal Security Legislation, so that the intent and purposes of such legislation would not be defeated.

b / The Bankruptcy Bill (s-14)

172. The court, on application of the trustee, may set aside a transfer that is a preference in favour of a creditor at arm's length with the debtor where
   (*a*) the transfer was made less than three months before the date of filing of a petition;
   (*b*) the debtor was insolvent at the time of the transfer; and
   (*c*) the transfer was made with the intent of the debtor to give a preference.

173. (1) The court, on application of the trustee, may set aside a transfer that is a preference in favour of a creditor who is not at arm's length with the debtor where it is proved that
   (*a*) the transfer was made less than three years before the date of filing of a petition;
   (*b*) the debtor was insolvent at the time of the transfer; and
   (*c*) the transfer was made with the intent of the debtor to give a preference.

(2) For the purposes of subsection (1), a transfer to a creditor made more than forty-five days and less than one year before the filing of the petition is deemed to have been made with the intent of the debtor to give a preference unless the creditor proves that the transfer was made in the normal course of affairs of the debtor in relation to the creditor.

(3) For the purposes of subsection (1), a transfer to a creditor made less than forty-five days prior to the date of filing of the petition is deemed to have been made with the intent of the debtor to give a preference unless the creditor proves that the transfer was made

(*a*) in the normal course of affairs of the debtor in relation to the creditor; and

(*b*) in satisfaction of a debt incurred within thirty days of the transfer.

174. (1) Where a debtor whose debts are guaranteed makes a transfer that has the effect of releasing the guarantor in whole or in part from the guarantee and the debtor subsequently becomes a bankrupt, the transfer is deemed to be a preference given by the debtor to the guarantor and the guarantor is deemed to be a creditor who has received a benefit to the extent to which he was released from the guarantee by the transfer and, on application of the trustee, the court may, if the preference is one that may be set aside by it under section 172 or 173, order the guarantor to pay to the trustee an amount equal to the benefit whether or not the transfer that had the effect of releasing the guarantor may be set aside by the court under this Part.

(2) For the purposes of this section, 'guarantor' includes a person who, at the date of the transfer, was the partner of the debtor or was jointly and severally bound with him.

175. (1) Where the court, pursuant to this Part, sets aside a transfer, the court may make an order

(*a*) empowering the trustee to recover the property or the value thereof from the person to whom the bankrupt transferred the property or, subject to subsection (2), from any other person to whom the property has been transferred;

(*b*) assigning to the trustee the rights of the creditor in property subject to a security interest that is set aside pursuant to this Part;

(*c*) subrogating the trustee to the rights of the transferor to compel payment or satisfaction where the consideration payable for or on a transfer of property or any part thereof remains unsatisfied;

(*d*) restoring in so far as possible each party to the transfer to the state that he was in immediately prior to the making of the transfer; or

(*e*) vesting in the trustee any rights or powers required by the trustee for the benefit of the estate.

(2) Subsection (1) does not apply where any person to whom property has been transferred paid or gave in good faith adequate valuable consideration for the property and any recourse of the trustee is solely against the person party to the transfer with the bankrupt.

176. In determining the amount of a preference, there shall be

(*a*) deducted therefrom the value of any transfer to the debtor made subsequent to the preference by the creditor who benefits from the preference; and

(*b*) added thereto the value of any transfer or new security interest given by the debtor to the creditor subsequent to the preference.

177. (1) Where a person has released or returned to a debtor property previously transferred by the debtor in a transfer that is not a preference and the debtor substitutes other property for the property released or returned, the substitution is a transfer that is not a preference except to the extent that the value of the substituted property as of the date at which the person agrees to accept the substituted property for the property released or returned exceeds the value of the property released or returned.

(2) For the purposes of subsection (1), the release or return and substitution of property need not take place simultaneously where the release or return is made in contemplation of the substitution and the substitution is made within a reasonable time after the release or return.

178. (1) Where a debtor makes an accelerated payment of premiums or a payment to pay up an insurance policy pursuant to an insurance contract in respect of which a beneficiary has been designated, the court may, on application of the trustee, set aside the payment if it is made by the debtor out of his property less than twelve months before a petition is filed in respect of him or when he is insolvent.

(2) Where the court is satisfied that a payment may be set aside under subsection 1, the court shall order that

(*a*) the proportion of the premium paid, or

(*b*) the amount of the payment to pay up the insurance policy made

by the debtor for coverage for the period commencing from the date of the application to the court be paid to the trustee by the insurer less

(*c*) the amount of any claim paid under the insurance contract prior to the date of the application to the court; and

(*d*) any amount of the premium repaid prior to the date of the application to the court.

(3) Subsection (1) does not apply where a debtor makes an accelerated payment of premiums or a payment to pay up an insurance contract in respect of which a beneficiary has been designated, if the beneficiary gave, in good faith, adequate valuable consideration for the designation as beneficiary.

(4) For the purposes of this section, 'insurance contract' includes a contract to provide for the payment of an annuity.

179. A transfer, payment of dividend or redemption or purchase of shares may not be set aside or be subject to review pursuant to sections 168 to 178 where it is proved that, at any time after the transfer, payment of dividend or redemption or purchase of shares was made and before the date of bankruptcy, the person who subsequently became a bankrupt was solvent.

180. (1) Where a donee of a gift that is set aside pursuant to section 168 surrenders voluntarily or as a result of a judicial proceeding the gift or the value of the gift to the trustee in the bankruptcy of the donor, the donee has an admissible claim in the bankruptcy of the donor for the value of the gift.

(2) Where a party to a transfer that is reviewable under section 169 surrenders voluntarily or as a result of a judicial proceeding an amount equal to the difference between the consideration that he received and the consideration that he gave, he has an admissible claim for the amount surrendered in the bankruptcy of the other party.

(3) Where a creditor surrenders to the trustee voluntarily or as a result of a judicial proceeding property that the creditor obtained as a result of a preference, the creditor has an admissible claim for the value of the property in the bankruptcy of the person who transferred the property.

(4) A person who has an admissible claim under subsections (1) to (3) shall not set-off any debt payable to the estate against the admissible claim.

181. (1) A transfer, payment of dividend or redemption or purchase of shares that occurs between the date of filing of a petition and the date of bankruptcy may be set aside or reviewed in like manner as if it has occurred immediately prior to the filing of the petition.

(2) Where a bankruptcy order is made in respect of the estate of a deceased person, the provisions of this Part apply to any transfer made by the deceased person as if a petition had been filed in respect of the deceased person immediately before his death.

182. Where a transfer has the effect of giving a preference to a creditor, evidence that the transfer was made under pressure is not receivable to substantiate such transfer and the debtor may not avail himself of such evidence to support such transfer.

183. For the purposes of sections 168 to 182, where registration is required to make a transfer effective against third parties and such transfer is not registered within thirty days after it is made the transfer is deemed to have been made

   (*a*) where the transfer was registered prior to the filing of a petition, at the time it was registered; or

   (*b*) where the transfer was not registered prior to the filing of a petition, immediately prior to such filing.

184. No person may institute a proceeding to obtain a remedy under sections 168 to 182 after three years from the date of bankruptcy.

185. A dividend or any other transfer of assets made pursuant to an arrangement may not be set aside as a preference under this Part.

c / Duncan and Honsburger, *Bankruptcy In Canada* (3rd ed. 1961), pp 469–71; 479; 484 (Footnotes omitted)

1 *What is a fraudulent preference is determined by the words of the section.*
Apart from the law of bankruptcy a conveyance to a creditor with a view to giving him a preference is unimpeachable both at common law and under *The Statute of Elizabeth I.*

The purpose of the section is not to interfere with the rights of a creditor who has merely obtained a benefit but to protect the body of creditors who have suffered a wrong through the application of the debtor's property in a fraudulent preference. The right must be invoked by one who suffers a real and actual prejudice and not by one who alleges an eventual prejudice.

2 *Transactions within the section.*
A *Must be of debtor's own property.* To fall within the section the transaction must be with reference to the property of the debtor, and not that of a creditor, or of a third party, such as a promoter who had purchased goods for the company prior to its incorporation, or of a person for whom the debtor is a trustee. Consequently when money is advanced for a specific purpose clothed with a trust, and the object for which it was advanced fails, there will be no fraudulent preference if the money is returned to the person who advanced it.

It is no fraudulent preference for a debtor to refuse to accept goods consigned to him even when this enables the consignor to exercise his right of *stoppage in transitu*; but if the debtor voluntarily returns goods which he has already accepted and which have become his, there will be a fraudulent preference.

B *Conveyances, transfers, or charges.*

i *Return of goods.* One of the most common forms of transaction is the return of goods to the creditor. Such return can not be objected to when the creditor has the right under local law to a dissolution of sale by reason of non-payment of price. It has been held that the delivery under such conditions to the creditor of other goods of a similar description can be supported. Similarly goods may be returned when they were received on condition that the debtor should have the right to return them if not sold during the Christmas season. But the transfer of goods to a creditor within the three month's period when the creditor did not sell the goods to the debtor and at the time of the transfer the creditor knew the debtor to be insolvent will be set aside as fraudulent and void as against the trustee.

In many cases the transaction has been upheld, in others it has been disallowed, the different results depending on the 'view' with which the transaction was entered into and on the knowledge of the creditor, actual or presumed, of the insolvency of the debtor ...

When a debtor returns goods to his vendor within three months of his bankruptcy the onus is on the creditor to prove that the transfer is not fraudulent.

...

3 *Evidence of other 'view'*

...

B *Charge or mortgage given in pursuance of previous agreement.* Where it is shown that a charge given to a creditor was in pursuance of an agreement to give a security, the agreement having been entered into prior to the commencement of the three months' period, this will generally avail to rebut the presumption of intent to prefer. ...

G *Payment to a secured creditor.* A payment to a secured creditor, e.g. a creditor who has a lien on the property of the debtor, is not within the section, at least where the payment does not exceed the value of the security.

d / The Question of Intent

i The Bankruptcy Bill (s-14), ss 172–3 (See p 815 above)

ii *Re B.C. Boat Sales Ltd.; Casson v Redisco of Canada Ltd.* (1962), 35 D.L.R. (2d) 557 (B.C.C.A.)

APPEAL from a judgment of McInnes, J., 31 D.L.R. (2d) 123, dismissing a motion to declare a chattel mortgage void as a fraudulent preference. Reversed.

NORRIS, J.A.: The facts in this matter are stated in the judgment of my brother Wilson. For the reasons given by him, I am satisfied that on the footing that it is necessary to consider the intention of the debtor alone in order to establish fraud under s 64(1) of the *Bankruptcy Act*, R.S.C. 1952, c 14, the chattel mortgage which was the subject-matter of these proceedings is void as against the Trustee in Bankruptcy.

As to the creditor who obtained the benefit of the chattel mortgage, I am satisfied that it is not necessary in this case to consider his intent and, with respect, I am of the opinion that the judgment of Ruttan, J., in *Re Blenkarn Planer Ltd.* (1958), 14 D.L.R. (2d) 719, 37 C.B.R. 147, and of Winter, J., in *Earle Sons & Co. v Crane* (1959), 20 D.L.R. (2d) 468, 44 M.P.R. 71, 38 C.B.R. 115 *sub nom. Re Mills & Mills, Earle Sons & Co. v Crane*, on this question are correct.

In my respectful opinion this Court is not bound by the judgment in *Benallack v Bank of B.N.A.* (1905), 36 S.C.R. 120, and cases which followed it because the *Bankruptcy Act* was not under consideration in that case nor was it in effect. The statute which is under consideration in the present appeal renders the *Benallack* judgment inapplicable here:

A because s 64(1) states that a document such as the one before us on this appeal is to 'be deemed fraudulent and void *as against the trustee in the bankruptcy*', and

B because the *Bankruptcy Act* in its terms throughout puts the Trustee in relation to the debtor and the debtor giving such a preference in relation to the creditor receiving it, generally in such a position before the law, that it is clear that the Courts in a case such as the one before us are concerned only with the intent of the debtor.

In my respectful opinion, the *Bankruptcy Act* constitutes a code enacted since the judgment in *Benallack v Bank of B.N.A., supra*, and:

A in relation to the position as between the trustee and the debtor, the position of a creditor, apart from his declared rights under the statute, is now merely an incident to the rights of the trustee in relation to the debtor;

B   in relation to the position between the debtor and creditors generally, the position of the creditors is radically changed by the provisions interposing the receiver in bankruptcy and the trustee in that relationship.

The result of the enactment of this code with the changes mentioned is that the law as decided in the *Benallack* case (which was a decision on a statute in very limited terms) no longer applies to a transaction such as that before us.

While the learned trial Judge did not make reference to *Benallack v Bank of B.N.A.*, he did say [31-D.L.R. (2d) 123 at p 124]:

In my view, the law is now clear there must be the double standard. In other words, there must be the intent on the part of both the bankrupt and the party receiving the benefit.

and it is implicit in those words that he followed that judgment. For the reasons stated I am unable, with respect, to agree with him.

TYSOE, J.A.: The relevant facts and the evidence relating to them have been fully canvassed by my brother Wilson in his reasons for judgment. I respectfully agree with his interpretation of the evidence.

With every deference to the learned Judge below [31 D.L.R. (2d) 123], in my opinion the evidence establishes, not only that B.C. Boat Sales Ltd. was on September 9, 1960, when it made the payment of $440.99 to its creditor, the respondent, and on September 16, 1960, when it gave the chattel mortgage to that creditor, insolvent, but also that the payment was made and the chattel mortgage was *given by the debtor and accepted by the creditor* 'with a view to giving such creditor a preference over the other creditors' within the meaning of s 64 of the *Bankruptcy Act*; also that both the payment and the chattel mortgage had that effect.

With respect, I am impelled to the conclusion that the respondent creditor has not satisfied the onus which is upon it of rebutting the presumption which is set up by s-s (2) of s 64.

In my view, therefore, we have here a fraudulent preference and, as the debtor became bankrupt within three months after September 9, 1960, the payment and the chattel mortgage are void as against the appellant Trustee in Bankruptcy.

Argument was addressed to us on the subject of whether intent to prefer on the part of both the bankrupt and the creditor is necessary to constitute a fraudulent preference. Having formed the opinion that there was such double intent here, I do not have to decide this question. I would like to say, however, that I am impressed by what was said on this subject by Ruttan, J., in *Re Blenkarn Planer Ltd.*, 14 D.L.R. (2d) 719, 37 C.B.R. 147, and by Winter, J., in *Earle Sons & Co. v Crane*, 20 D.L.R. (2d) 468, 44 M.P.R. 71, 38 C.B.R. 115 *sub nom. Re Mills & Mills, Earle Sons & Co. v Crane*, and were it not for the judgment in *Benallack v Bank of B.N.A.* (1905), 36 S.C.R. 120, I would conclude that s 64 refers only to the intention of the debtor. If I were free to follow my own powers of reasoning and my own opinion resulting therefrom, I should say that to hold that there is no fraudulent preference unless there is intent on the part of the creditor as well as the debtor requires reading into the section something which is not there. But I am bound by the authority of the Supreme Court of Canada – it is my duty to follow it. In the *Benallack* case the Court was dealing with an Ordinance of the Yukon Territory, but the wording of that Ordinance is so closely similar to that of s-s (1) of s 64 of the *Bankruptcy Act* that I cannot say the judgment and the rule enunciated therein does not apply to the said s 64 I feel I should follow the *Benallack* case until the question of whether concurrent intent is required to constitute a fraudulent preference within the meaning of that section is dealt with by the Supreme Court of Canada.

I would allow the appeal.

WILSON, J.A.: Once certain facts are established the burden of proof is on the creditor who supports the transaction and not on the Trustee in Bankruptcy who resists it.

In order to shift the onus of proof to the creditor the trustee must prove:

1 That the conveyance and payment impugned were made to the creditor within three months of the bankruptcy. This has been clearly shown.
2 That the transactions had the effect of giving the creditor a preference. I do not understand the existence of this fact to be seriously disputed by the creditor, and indeed, on the evidence, it could not be.

Therefore the onus of proof is shifted and that onus requires the creditor to rebut the presumption thus established. The presumption is that the transactions were made with a view to giving the creditor a preference.

Under other circumstances I might be impelled to decide whether or not it was necessary, in order to refute the presumption for the creditor to clear both himself and the debtor of an intention to prefer or only to clear the debtor of such an intent; to decide whether or not I must follow the judgment of the Supreme Court of Canada in *Benallack* v *Bank of B.N.A.* (1905), 36 S.C.R. 120, or might accept the reasoning of Ruttan, J., in *Re Blenkarn Planer Ltd.*, 14 D.L.R. (2d) 719, 37 C.B.R. 147, and of Winter, J., in *Earle Sons & Co.* v *Crane*, 20 D.L.R. (2d) 468, 44 M.P.R. 71, 38 C.B.R. 115 *sub nom. Re Mills & Mills, Earle Sons & Co.* v *Crane*. Since I am convinced that the evidence in the present case does not clear either debtor or creditor of complicity in the intent to prefer, but rather establishes that intent as held by both of them, I need not enter into that field but can follow the prudent course set by Duff, J., as he then was, in *Salter & Arnold, Ltd.* v *Dominion Bank*, [1926] 3 D.L.R. 684, [1926] S.C.R. 621, 7 C.B.R. 639, and by Cartwright, J., in *Velensky, Velensky & Budovitch* v *Can. Credit Men's Trust Ass'n Ltd.*, 22 D.L.R. (2d) 689, [1960] S.C.R. 385, 38 C.B.R. 162 *sub nom. Re Bernard Motors Ltd., Velensky & Budovitch* v *Can. Credit Men's Trust Ass'n Ltd.* In each of these cases the learned Judges of the Supreme Court of Canada found they were not required to decide the point of law I have mentioned and left it at large, at least for the Supreme Court of Canada, not necessarily for lower Courts. I must say I was greatly impressed by the reasoning of Ruttan, J., and of Winter, J., but I do not, with respect, feel that either one of them really came to grips with the *Benallack* decision. However, my view of the facts in the present case does not require me to grasp that particular nettle.

I proceed to discuss the evidence and the inferences which should be drawn from it. I deal first with certain matters of fact that seem clearly established.

1 The impugned transactions had the effect of giving the creditor preference.
2 The debtor was insolvent.
3 The debtor, at the relevant times, knew it was insolvent.

Again, Moore said that he would carry on if he could raise more capital. He could not raise more capital, and he knew he could not. Therefore he knew that his company could not carry on. This refutes the argument that he thought that the extension of time given by the chattel mortgage, which gave him no new capital, would enable his company to carry on and survive, and, indeed, his other evidence, already cited, refutes it. I refer here to *Re Piette*, 1 C.B.R. (N.S.) 1, [1960] Rev. Leg. 156, which holds that it is no answer to say that the debtor could have carried on if he could have got a loan.

Martin was branch manager of the creditor company. He has denied any knowledge of the insolvency at the time of the impugned transactions of the debtor company and any 'view' to secure a preference. I extract these facts from his evidence.

On September 13, 1960, he drew up a schedule (ex. 1) showing an overdue indebtedness to his company of $5,347.82, the amount secured by the chattel mortgage after deducting a certain payment made to the creditor on September 9th by means of cheques payable to the debtor and endorsed over and given to the creditor. Most of this remaining indebtedness represented monies paid to the debtor under contracts which made those payments the property of the creditor. The monies paid had been converted to the debtor's use. For six months prior to the bankruptcy the creditor was continually requesting payment of overdue accounts. Cheques issued to the creditor for overdue accounts had been returned unpaid by the debtor's bank. The creditor had on one occasion gone so far as to attach to goods of the debtor covered by chattel mortgage notices of seizure. The creditor knew that the debtor's banker had reduced its line of credit. The creditor, put on enquiry, had made no proper enquiries. The creditor knew there were always 'a goodly number of people who had not been paid'. The creditor knew that the debtor's book accounts were assigned to its bank. The fact that the debtor paid $449.99 to the creditor on September 9, 1960, not in cash or by its own cheque but by cheques made out to the debtor and endorsed over to the creditor 'excited its suspicions'. The fact that in August or September the creditor could not get 'current financial information' about the debtor also excited its suspicions. The creditor knew that the debtor was in the period in question slowing down in its payments and was suspicious. 'They (the debtor) appeared to be getting tighter and tighter for money.' ... It is no answer to say that the debtor could have carried on if he could have got a loan (*Re Piette, supra*). Therefore, since the debtor had told the creditor that he needed and could not obtain additional money, the creditor was put on warning that the debtor could not carry on without it and that, therefore, it was bankrupt. Then I refer again to the lack of enquiry by Martin, and I say that these facts establish that the creditor knew that the debtor was not just insolvent but bankrupt. From this it follows that the creditor also knew that the taking of the money and the conveyance must give him a preference. I think the creditor has not disproved the intent.

Reverting to the intention of the debtor, I cite this passage from *Re Progressive Farmers' Co., Ex p. Brown Bros. & Burnstead Ltd.*, (1923), 3 C.B.R. 702 at p 706, *per* Tweedie, J.:

it may be argued that the dominant motive of the debtor was to secure an extension, but he knew he could not secure an extension without giving a preference, and therefore, his primary purpose was to give that preference so that as an instance thereof, he could obtain an extension of time, ...

And I draw attention to the fact, undoubtedly known to both debtor and creditor, that these were, at a time of insolvency, transactions out of the ordinary course of business.

I would allow the appeal.

Appeal allowed.

iii *Re Shaughnessy Super Market and Codville Company Ltd.* (1963), 37 D.L.R. (2d) 524 (Man. Q.B.)

NITIKMAN, J.: This is a motion by the Canadian Credit Men's Trust Association Limited, Trustee of the estate of Melvin Ostrowsky and Mike Cyndroski, trading as Shaughnessy Super Market, a bankrupt, for an order declaring that payment by the said bankrupts to Codville

Company Limited of $8,000 was for the purpose of maintaining a fraudulent preference in respect of the other creditors of the estate of the said bankrupts and requiring the said Codville Co. to repay the sum of $8,000 to the Trustee in Bankruptcy, and for a further order declaring a certain chattel mortgage made by the bankrupts in favour of Codville Co. was a fraudulent preference in respect of the other creditors of the estate of the said bankrupts and requiring the said Codville Co. to deliver to the Trustee in Bankruptcy a discharge of the said chattel mortgage.

Melvin Ostrowsky and Mike Cyndroski (hereinafter referred to as the debtors) purchased the Shaughnessy Super Market, a retail grocery store located at 1333 Manitoba Ave., Winnipeg, from one William Rudyk in 1958. It was what is commonly referred to as an I.G.A. store, and while no written agreement was entered into between the Codville Co. (hereinafter referred to as Codville) and the debtors (although it appears to have been intended that such a written agreement would be entered into between them), in effect the understanding was that the major purchases of merchandise would be made from or through the medium of Codville, and this in fact was the case.

The purchase-price of the business and fixtures was $14,500, and of the stock-in-trade approximately $7,000. This was paid by the debtors assuming a lien on certain equipment in favour of Peoples Co-op Ltd., for $3,500, repayable with interest at 5% at the rate of $75 per month; $11,000 by a loan from 'I.A.C.' [Industrial Acceptance Corporation], through what was believed to be a conditional sales contract (but which was, at the date of the bankruptcy, discovered to be not a conditional sales contract) and a promissory note, both of which were guaranteed by Codville, repayable at $225 per month, and the balance of the purchase-price in cash.

To raise the cash payment the debtors borrowed $4,800 from the father of the debtor Ostrowsky and $2,800 from other sources, so it can be seen that there was little if any actual cash investment by the debtors themselves – hardly a satisfactory arrangement for the operation of a highly competitive type of business – and it is small wonder that, with the indebtedness and finance charges to be liquidated, the debtors soon found themselves in financial difficulties.

By the autumn of 1959 the debtors owed Codville for merchandise purchased approximately $12,000. (This was in addition to the amount Codville had guaranteed under the promissory note for $11,000 to I.A.C.) The debtors had given Codville a series of post-dated cheques and some of these, from time to time, had been returned 'N.S.F.'. Codville began pressing for payment in full, threatening otherwise to take proceedings to close the business. In November, 1959, the debtors were advised by telephone that Codville would no longer supply them with merchandise and they would have to arrange for other sources of supply, and on or about November 10, 1959, Codville commenced an action in the Court of Queen's Bench, Winnipeg, against the debtors for recovery of $12,345.70, the price of goods sold and delivered by Codville at the request and on the credit of the debtors.

Following this action the debtors had to purchase merchandise on a day-to-day basis from various wholesalers, paying cash for their purchases, but they were able to make several rather substantial purchases from Weidman Brothers Limited on credit, for which amount Weidman Bros. Ltd. became unsecured creditors on the bankruptcy.

The debtors, however, still hoped to be able to continue in business – it was a forlorn hope to be sure, but one in which the debtors seemingly indulged with misplaced confidence – and in order to settle the lawsuit and prevent, as the debtors believed, the closing of their business, they arranged to return to Codville merchandise valued at approximately $800; to pay Codville $8,000 in cash; and to execute and deliver to Codville a chattel mortgage for $3,367.65, repayable at the rate of $100 per month, to include principal and interest at 8%, given on the security of the fixtures in the store premises. In order to raise the $8,000, the debtors borrowed $2,700 from Public Finance Corporation Ltd. on the security of two automobiles belonging to them; $1,250 from Modern Dairies Ltd. on the security of a boat, motor and trailer owned by one of them; and $4,400 from one Fred Shaw on the security of a chattel mortgage to be registered against the fixtures and stock-in-trade of the business of the debtors. The chattel mortgage to Shaw was registered on February 18, 1960, and the chattel mortgage to Codville was registered on March 28, 1960, the Codville chattel mortgage being made subject to the Shaw chattel mortgage, both being subject to the lien in favour of I.A.C. aforementioned, which lien, as already mentioned, it afterwards transpired was not in fact a lien contract at all but merely a promissory note. Accordingly, Shaw's mortgage became a first mortgage and Codville's a second. However, it was admitted on the hearing that in any event the security was only sufficient to indemnify the Shaw mortgage, so the question of the chattel mortgage to Codville becomes academic for all practical purposes.

On receipt by Codville of the $8,000, Codville paid off the indebtedness of the debtors to I.A.C. which Codville had guaranteed and became an unsecured creditor of the debtors for the amount that it so paid.

Arrangements for settling the Queen's Bench action and payment over of the $8,000, as well as delivery of the executed chattel mortgage to Codville by the debtors, were agreed upon between the parties on or about January 22, 1960; but the monies were not actually paid over until March 11, 1960, on which date the debtors also delivered to Codville the chattel mortgage for $3,367.65.

That the settlement was agreed upon on or about January 22nd is evidenced by a letter dated March 2, 1960 from Codville's solicitors to the solicitors for the debtors, which is to the following effect:

The stock-in-trade taken back by the Codville Company Limited is valued at $878.05; we enclose photographic copies of the inventory sheets, fully balanced and extended, and we believe that your clients will have a copy thereof.

The original claim of The Codville Company was $12345.70; from this should be deducted the $878.05 for stock, and a further $100.00 for the sign, leaving a net balance due to the plaintiff of $11367.65.

Of this latter amount, you will be sending us $8000.00 in cash, and this leaves a figure of $3367.65 to be secured by way of a promissory note and chattel mortgage.

In addition, we are to receive $100.00 on account of our taxable costs herein.

Please, therefore, let us have the sum of $8000.00 by return mail, together with our costs of $100.00 – our disbursements, to date, amount of $62.25. As we have already reminded you in our letter of February 16th, we were to receive this $8000.00 *within ten days from the date of our arrangement, and this was about a month ago.*

In addition, please draw your forms of Chattel Mortgage and promissory note sending a copy of each to us right away for approval as to form, so that we may get this entire matter cleaned up without further delay. We shall expect your reply by return mail, with the monies you promised us a long time ago. (Italics mine.)

Moreover, in his evidence Melvin Ostrowsky admitted that the agreement for settlement was made in the latter part of January and stated that the debtors had turned the money over to their solicitors some two or three weeks before March. Whether this money included the amount borrowed from Shaw or was merely the amounted raised on the security of the automobiles and boat, motor and trailer is not clear. Ostrowsky further stated: 'The purpose of making payment was to get Codville off our back and continue to stay in business.'

Codville alleges that the reason the monies were not paid over to it until March 11th was because of certain delays experienced by its solicitors in attempting to close out the agreement with the debtors' solicitors, resulting in the letter of March 2, 1960, quoted above, being written. I make no comment as to the reason for this delay, as the letter speaks for itself, but I have no doubt, and I find, that the agreement for settlement was made on or about January 22, 1960.

The hopes of the debtors of being able to continue in business did not materialize and the debtors made an authorized assignment in bankruptcy on May 5, 1960.

It was admitted by all parties at the hearing that on March 11, 1960, the debtors were insolvent within the meaning of the *Bankruptcy Act*, R.S.C. 1952, c 14, and the evidence establishes that they were in fact insolvent for some considerable time prior to that date.

I find that on March 11, 1960, the debtors knew they were insolvent and I further find that Codville knew on March 11, 1960, and for some considerable time before then, that the debtors were insolvent. While Codville has not been shown to have known where all of the money for the original purchase came from, it certainly knew of the indebtedness to I.A.C. and Peoples Co-op. Moreover it had, for a very protracted period, access to the debtor's books. One Frank Toomer, an accountant recommended by I.G.A., audited the books of the debtors. He took weekly statements of accounts and removed the books for examination. The books reflected the complete business operation, and the statements of account or invoices rendered the debtors from Codville included debits for Toomer's attendances for auditing the books. Moreover, the evidence discloses that on a number of occasions cheques issued by the debtors to Codville were, as earlier mentioned, returned by the bank on which they were drawn marked 'N.S.F.'. This was particularly the case in the autumn of 1959 and undoubtedly was one of the reasons leading to the issue of the statement of claim by Codville against the debtors. The situation by March 11th had deteriorated even further and I am satisfied from a consideration of the above that Codville, on March 11th, and for a considerable period prior to that date, knew that the debtors were in fact insolvent.

In view of my finding that on the date of the payment of the $8,000 by the debtors to the creditor both debtors and creditor were aware the debtors were insolvent, it is not necessary for me to decide whether, in order to constitute a fraudulent preference, not only the debtors but the creditor too had knowledge of the debtors' insolvency. I nevertheless point out that there still remains considerable divergence of opinion on this point.

Some of the cases which have held that knowledge on the part of both debtor and creditor of the formers' insolvency is essential are: *Re Bartle* (1941), 22 C.B.R. 260; *Re Bell* (1922), 67 D.L.R. 66, 32 Man. R. 9, 2 C.B.R. 271 (C.A.); *Re Webb* (1921), 64 D.L.R. 633, 51 O.L.R. 5, 2 C.B.R. 16; *Re Demry & Demry, Trustee* v *Holland*, [1924] 4 D.L.R. 1275, 34 Man. R. 534, 5 C.B.R. 293 (C.A.); *Re Aboud*, [1941] 1 D.L.R. 801, 22 C.B.R. 121 at p 126; *Re Trafalgar Motors* (1952), 33 C.B.R. 87 at p 88.

Cases which have held that knowledge on the part of the debtor of his insolvency is sufficient are: *Earle Sons & Co.* v *Crane* (1959), 20 D.L.R. (2d) 468, 44 M.P.R. 71, 38 C.B.R. 115 *sub nom. Re Mills & Mills, etc.*; *Burns* v *Royal Bank of Canada, Burns* v *Graham* (1922), 69 D.L.R. 608, 51 O.L.R. 564, 2 C.B.R. 241; *Re Blenkarn Planer Ltd.* (1958), 14 D.L.R. (2d) 719, 26 W.W.R. 168, 37 C.B.R. 147; *Velensky, Velensky & Budovitch* v *Can. Credit Men's Trust Ass'n Ltd.*, 22 D.L.R. [2d] 689, [1960] S.C.R. 385, 38 C.B.R. 162 *sub nom. Re Bernard Motors Ltd., etc.*, in which Cartwright, J., makes no finding as to whether or not concurrent intent is necessary (see p 694

D.L.R., p 390 S.C.R., p 167 C.B.R.), and I adopt the language of Wilson, J.A., in *Re B.C. Boat Sales Ltd., Casson* v *Redisco of Canada Ltd.* (1962), 35 D.L.R. (2d) 557 at p 564, 39 W.W.R. 411 at p 419, where he says:

... I need not enter into that field but can follow the prudent course set by Duff, J., as he then was, in *Salter & Arnold, Ltd.* v *Dominion Bank*, [1926] 3 D.L.R. 684, [1926] S.C.R. 621, 7 C.B.R. 639 (affirming [1925] 1 D.L.R. 401, [1925] 1 W.W.R. 207, 34 Man. R. 565, 5 C.B.R. 416), and by Cartwright, J., in *Velensky, Velensky & Budovitch* v *Can. Credit Men's Trust Ass'n Ltd.* 22 D.L.R. (2d) 689, [1960] S.C.R. 385, 38 C.B.R. 162 *sub nom. Re Bernard Motors Ltd., Velensky & Budovitch* v *Can. Credit Men's Trust Ass'n Ltd.* In each of these cases the learned Judges of the Supreme Court of Canada found they were not required to decide the point of law I have mentioned and left it at large, at least for the Supreme Court of Canada, not necessarily for lower Courts.

I find, however, that the motion of the trustee fails on two other grounds:

The first ground is that while the payment of $8,000 was made on March 11, 1960, the agreement for the payment was actually concluded on January 22nd, more than three months prior to the bankruptcy, and it is that earlier date which governs.

See also *Re Blenkarn Planter Ltd.* (1958), 14 D.L.R. (2d) 719, 26 W.W.R. 168, 37 C.B.R. 147, the [C.B.R.] headnote of which reads in part as follows:

A creditor lent the debtor a large sum of money, taking in exchange a promissory note. Later he lent him a further sum of money, and at the insistence of the creditor a chattel mortgage was prepared which was subsequently redrafted and not finally executed until within three months of the bankruptcy. On an application by the trustee to set aside the chattel mortgage as a fraudulent preference, *held*, since the chattel mortgage had been executed pursuant to the previous agreement to give security for the loan, which agreement had been entered into prior to the commencement of the three months' period, this was sufficient to rebut the presumption of an intention to prefer.

The facts in the within case are, in many respects, parallel and I would, accordingly, find that there was no intent to prefer on the part of either the debtors or the creditor.

I come now to the second ground on which I have concluded that the action of the Trustee must fail.

If then we are to assume that the payment to Codville was within the three months' period of the bankruptcy (and I have found against this), then, in any event, the payment is only deemed a fraudulent preference if it is made with a view to giving such creditor a preference over other creditors and not otherwise.

In the within case I have no hesitation in finding that there was no such view on the part of the debtors. Their view was not to prefer Codville over other creditors; their only purpose was to compromise a lawsuit and to continue in business. The debtors were not actuated by any feelings of friendship towards Codville. Their acts were purely self-serving. They were genuinely convinced that unless they made settlement with Codville their business would be closed up.

In cross-examination Ostrowsky stated that their purpose in making the payment was to get Codville 'off our back and continue to stay in business'. I believe Ostrowsky and accept this evidence as a true reason for the payment. The debtors wanted desperately to continue in business. They hoped that by arranging for discontinuance of the lawsuit they would be able to remain in business and perhaps yet make a success of it. It was not to be, as events were soon to prove, but I am satisfied the debtors honestly believed that with the statement of claim satisfied they would be able to arrange their finances in such a way that they would be able to carry on. No doubt that is why they refused to agree to pay the balance of $3,367.65 indebtedness to Codville, secured by the second chattel mortgage, at the rate of $500 a month, and insisted on the monthly payments being only $100. Their sole purpose was to benefit themselves.

As Killam, c.j., said in *Codville* v *Fraser* (1902), 14 Man. r. 12 at p 24:

If the debtor's account is to be taken as correct, it appears to me that there could not properly be any other inference than that his dominant motive was to make an arrangement for continuing the business. As we can see the case now, this was practically hopeless; but parties in his position do not usually recognize this so clearly as it appears afterwards to others.

I find as a fact that the payment of $8,000 to Codville, and the receipt by Codville of the money, did not constitute a fraudulent preference and that the same applies to the chattel mortgage.

The motion by the Trustee is dismissed.

Costs of the Codville Co., as well as those of the Trustee, will be paid out of the estate. Motion dismissed.

QUESTION In the two foregoing cases, had you been retained to advise the creditors prior to the transactions in question, how would you have advised them to proceed? Are the law's expectations of creditors realistic in this context?

NOTE The question of whether or not concurrent intent is necessary to find a fraudulent preference may finally have been resolved. The Supreme Court of Canada in *Hudson* v *Benallack* (below) (1975), 59 D.L.R. (3d) 1, reversing (1974), 41 D.L.R. (3d) 624 (Alberta s.c.a.d.) has held that it is not necessary to find a concurrent intent of the debtor and creditor in order to set aside a payment as a fraudulent preference. No intent is required on the part of the creditor to receive the preference. Only the intention of the debtor is relevant.

Further, the wording of ss 172–3 of the new Bankruptcy Bill is much more specific than the old Act; the new Act requires that the transfer be made 'with the intent of the debtor to give a preference' while the old Act required only 'a view to giving such creditor a preference'.

iv *Hudson* v *Benallack* (1975), 59 D.L.R. (3d) 1 (S.C.C.)

The judgment of the Court was delivered by DICKSON, J.:

I

This appeal raises a question of statutory construction which, one should think, would not cause difficulty, but which has indeed given rise to an abundance of conflicting legal opinion and a thoroughly obfuscated state of the law. The question is whether the words 'with a view to giving such creditor a preference' contained in s 73 (1) of the *Bankruptcy Act*, R.S.C. 1970, c B-3, require only an intention on the part of the insolvent debtor to prefer or a concurrent intent on the part of both debtor and creditor.

Any conveyance or transfer of property or payment made by an insolvent person in favour of any creditor with a view to giving such creditor a preference over other creditors is deemed fraudulent and void as against the trustee in bankruptcy if the insolvent person becomes bankrupt within three months thereafter or within 12 months where the insolvent person and the preferred creditor are related persons.

II

In the present case the transaction impugned is the assignment on March 1, 1972, by G. S. & D. Construction Ltd. to the respondents, John Alexander Benallack and Lillian M. Benallack, of the assignor's interest, as purchaser, in an agreement for sale of certain lands in the City of Calgary. The consideration for the assignment was stated to be $15,250. At the time the assignor company was indebted to the assignees in the amount of $15,000 with interest and this indebtedness was used to offset the purchase price of the assignor's interest in the agreement of sale. All of the issued shares of G. S. & D. Construction Ltd. were owned by George Bayard Benallack and Shirley Edna May Benallack, the son and daughter-in-law respectively of the respondents. G. S. & D. Construction Ltd. made an assignment in bankruptcy on June 27, 1972, within the 12-month period mentioned in s 74 of the Act, and the appellant Hudson was named as trustee. The learned Chambers Judge, Cullen, J., made a number of findings, of which the following are of moment:

1 On March 1, 1972, the date of the assignment, the bankrupt company was an insolvent person within the meaning of the *Bankruptcy Act*;
2 The bankrupt and the respondents were related persons within the meaning of the Act and s 74 applied;
3 The respondents received a preference over other creditors as a result of the assignment;
4 The bankrupt intended to give the respondents a preference over its other creditors.

Cullen, J., held against the need for concurrent intent and declared the assignment to be void as against the trustee in bankruptcy. The Appellate Division of the Supreme Court of Alberta reversed [41 D.L.R. (3d) 624, [1974] 1 W.W.R. 548]. 459, reviewed many of the authorities and concluded that the principle enunciated in *Benallack v Bank of British North America* was not applicable to s 73 of the *Bankruptcy Act* and that the Court need have regard only to the intent or view of the debtor. McIntyre, J.A. (Robertson and Taggart, JJ.A., concurring), made this observation in the course of his reasons for judgment (at p 755 D.L.R., p 465 W.W.R.):

It would then seem that the law on this subject is well settled. However, one cannot review the many cases decided on this point without sensing that the Judges in Canada, including appellate Judges, have grown restive under the need to apply the concurrence of intent principle from the *Benallack* case to the construction of s 73 of the *Bankruptcy Act*.

Mr. Justice McDermid, with whom Mr. Justice Prowse concurred, considered the Supreme Court of Canada decision in *Benallack v Bank of British North America* (1905), 36 S.C.R. 120, to be binding, although Mr. Justice McDermid was of the opinion that if he had been originally considering the proper interpretation of s 73, he would not have read into the section the secondary meaning that the creditor as well as the debtor must have the view of giving the creditor a preference over other creditors. Mr. Justice Clement concurred in the judgment of

McDermid, J.A., but he did not share the opinion of Mr. Justice McDermid as to the proper construction of s 73.

III

On the question whether proof of concurrent intent on the part of the debtor and creditor must be shown before the transaction can be set aside, there is, as I have indicated, a wide divergence of opinion. There are many decisions in which it has been held that concurrent intent must be proved; others in which it has been held that the Court is concerned only with the intent of the debtor; and still others in which the point has been left unresolved.

In the jurisprudence of British Columbia one finds such cases as *Re Blenkarn Planer Ltd.* (1958), 14 D.L.R. (2d) 719, 26 W.W.R. 168, 37 C.B.R. 147 (B.C.S.C.), in which Mr. Justice Ruttan held, *obiter*, that the view of the debtor alone is to be considered. In *Re Totem Painting Co. Ltd.* (1960), 32 W.W.R. 143, I C.B.R. (N.S.) 38 (B.C.S.C.), Mr. Justice Wilson apparently was of the opinion that the intention of the creditor was of importance. In *Re B.C. Boat Sales Ltd.* (1962), 35 D.L.R. (2d) 557, 39 W.W.R. 411, 4 C.B.R. (N.S.) 168 (B.C.C.A.), two of the Judges held the evidence established a double intent and it was therefore unnecessary to decide whether s 64 (now s 73) of the Act called for consideration of the creditor's intent. Norris, J.A., strongly supported the position that the intent of the person receiving the benefit is irrelevant. Wilson, C.J.S.C., reached the same conclusion in *Re Pacific Belting Co. Ltd.* (1971), 14 C.B.R. (N.S.) 233 (B.C.S.C.), followed in *Re Lock Enterprises Ltd.* (1971), 16 C.B.R. (N.S.) 83 (B.C.S.C.). The British Columbia Court of Appeal in the recent case of *Flor-Lay Services Ltd.* v *Stewart* (1974), 51 D.L.R. (3d) 749, [1975] 2 W.W.R. 459, reviewed many of the authorities and concluded that the principle enunciated in *Benallack* v *Bank of British North America* was not applicable to s 73 of the *Bankruptcy Act* and that the Court need have regard only to the intent or view of the debtor. McIntyre, J.A. (Robertson and Taggart, JJ.A., concurring), made this observation in the course of his reasons for judgment (at p 755 D.L.R., p 465 W.W.R.):

It would then seem that the law on this subject is well settled. However, one cannot review the many cases decided on this point without sensing that the Judges in Canada, including appellate Judges, have grown restive under the need to apply the concurrence of intent principle from the *Benallack* case to the construction of s 73 of the *Bankruptcy Act*.

IV

Although the Courts of the country appear divided, more or less evenly, on the need for a concurrent intent before invalidating a transaction, the textbook writers and commentators do not evidence such divergence of opinion. The editors of Duncan & Honsberger, *Bankruptcy in Canada*, 3rd ed. (1961), p 485, point out that s 64 (now s 73) makes no reference to the view of the creditor and that the cases in England and in the other Dominions on corresponding sections in Bankruptcy Acts contain no references to the view of the creditor, the view of the debtor alone being considered. The editors of Houlden & Morawetz, *Bankruptcy Law of Canada*, Cumulative Supplement, 1974, p 83, say:

In view of the plain meaning of Sec. 73, the concurrent intent of both debtor and creditor is not necessary to show a fraudulent preference. The intention of the debtor alone is to be considered.

and in Bradford & Greenberg's *Canadian Bankruptcy Act*, 3rd ed., p 163, the authors cite 'an intention on the part of the debtor to prefer' as one of the two circumstances constituting a fraudulent preference. See also 2 C.E.D. (Ont. 3d), pp 15–334: 'The intention of the debtor alone is to be considered', and *Comment* in (1959), 37 C.B.R. 153, and *Notes on Section 64 of The Bankruptcy Act* by Professor Réginald Savoie in (1967), 9 C.B.R. (N.S.) 1.

v

If this Court is free to decide the issue of concurrent intent untrammelled by earlier decisions, there would seem to be at least three reasons why we should not engraft upon s 73 of the *Bankruptcy Act* an additional concept, that of concurrent intent: first, the policy of the *Bankruptcy Act*; second, the history of the Act; third, the language of s 73.

The object of the bankruptcy law is to ensure the division of the property of the debtor ratably among all his creditors in the event of his bankruptcy. Section 112 of the Act provides that, subject to the Act, all claims proved in the bankruptcy shall be paid *pari passu*. The Act is intended to put all creditors upon an equal footing. Generally, until a debtor is insolvent or has an act of bankruptcy in contemplation, he is quite free to deal with his property as he wills and he may prefer one creditor over another but, upon becoming insolvent, he can no longer do any act out of the ordinary course of business which has the effect of preferring a particular creditor over other creditors. If one creditor receives a preference over other creditors as a result of the debtor acting intentionally and in fraud of the law, this defeats the equality of the bankruptcy laws.

The cognizance of the creditor or its absence should be irrelevant. One can sympathize with the rationale of concurrent intent, which is the desire to protect an innocent creditor who accepts payment of a debt in good faith, but it is hard to reconcile this point of view with the language of the statute, with the history of bankruptcy legislation, and with the right of other innocent creditors to equal protection.

I have concluded that a finding of concurrent intent is not necessary in order to set aside a payment as a fraudulent preference under s 73 of the *Bankruptcy Act*. I do not believe that the decision of this Court in *Benallack* v *Bank of British North America* is authoritative in interpreting s 73 of the *Bankruptcy Act*. However similar may be the wording, I do not think that a phrase in a provincial or territorial Ordinance of three paragraphs dealing with preferential assignments and having a particular legislative history and jurisprudence should govern the language of a federal Act of some 213 sections dealing with bankruptcy and having an entirely different legislative history and jurisprudence.

One must recall that fraudulent preference statutes and fraudulent conveyance statutes outside of the bankruptcy laws have generally contained a section exempting from the application of the statute any assignment or payment or *bona fide* sale of goods made in the ordinary course of trade to innocent purchasers. Such saving provisions are contained in our provincial fraudulent preference statutes and in each of the cases relied on in the 1905 *Benallack* judgment a similar statute was under consideration. These statutes required consideration of the knowledge or *bona fides* of the creditor. Under the law relating to bankruptcy the rule has been different, as the English authorities cited earlier in these reasons will confirm.

I am further of the view that s 3 of the Yukon Ordinance plays the same role in the interpretation of the Ordinance as the proviso to s 92 of the English Act of 1869 played in *Butcher* v *Stead*, requiring consideration of the knowledge and intent and privity of the creditor; but there is no counterpart of s 3 of the Ordinance to be found in s 73(1) of the *Bankruptcy Act*. Section 75(1) of the Act, which protects certain transactions, is the only section in which the *bona fides* of the creditor emerges. Section 75(1) is very limited in scope. It is expressly made 'Subject to the foregoing provisions of this Act ... with respect to the avoidance of certain settlements and preferences ...' and only comes into operation when s 73(1) does not apply. Section 75(1) in express terms calls for double intent whereas s 73(1) does not.

Our duty is to construe the language of s 73 of the *Bankruptcy Act* within the ambit and policy of that Act; if we go to the words of the statute we find that what is to be considered as fraudulent and void is:

> **73.** (1) Every conveyance ... of property [*i.e.*, the assignment in favour of respondents] ... made by any insolvent person [*i.e.*, G. S. & D. Construction Ltd.] in favour of any creditor [*i.e.*, the respondents] ... with a view to giving such creditor a preference ...

It seems to me plain from the quoted words that the view, the only view, with which s 73(1) of the Act is concerned is that of the insolvent person making the conveyance and we should not be diverted to any other conclusion by reliance upon a case in which a different statute in different language was construed. Whether or not a conveyance or payment is a fraudulent preference depends entirely on the intention of the debtor. The trial Judge has found against the respondents on this point.

I would allow the appeal, set aside the judgment of the Appeal Division and restore the judgment of Cullen, J., with costs throughout.
Appeal allowed.

9 TRANSACTIONS IN LAND

The Bankruptcy Bill (s-14)

> **276.** Notwithstanding anything in this Act, a transfer of property,
> (*a*) by a transferor after a bankruptcy order or other vesting order affecting such property has been made in respect of the transferor, or
> (*b*) by a trustee after
>   (i) a bankruptcy order affecting such property has been annulled,
>   (ii) a new trustee has been substituted for him, or
>   (iii) a quit claim or a disclaimer affecting such property has been filed pursuant to this Act,
> made to, or in favour of, a transferee who was in good faith and gave adequate valuable consideration for the property is as valid and effective as if the bankruptcy order or other vesting order, the annulment, the substitution of a new trustee, the quit claim or disclaimer had not been made, unless such order, annulment, substitution, quit claim or disclaimer or a caveat or caution had been registered against the property in the proper office prior to the registration of the transfer.

NOTE AND QUESTION This section overturns a common law rule exemplified by *Ex Parte Rabbidge, In Re Pooley*, (1878) 8 Ch. 367 (C.A.). There, a bankrupt contracted to sell a leasehold interest. A deposit was paid before the receiving order, but the balance was not paid until after. Although the purchaser had not known of the bankruptcy, the Court held that title had passed to the trustee who could not be compelled to assign it to the purchaser. What would have been the result if full payment had been made before the receiving order, but no formal conveyance had taken place?

10 PROTECTED TRANSACTIONS

The Bankruptcy Bill (s-14)

175. (1) Where the court, pursuant to this Part, sets aside a transfer, the court may make an order,

(*a*) empowering the trustee to recover the property or the value thereof from the person to whom the bankrupt transferred the property or, subject to subsection (2), from any other person to whom the property has been transferred;

(*b*) assigning to the trustee the rights of the creditor in property subject to a security interest that is set aside pursuant to this Part;

(*c*) subrogating the trustee to the rights of the transferor to compel payment or satisfaction where the consideration payable for or on a transfer of property or any part thereof remains unsatisfied;

(*d*) restoring in so far as possible each party to the transfer to the state that he was in immediately prior to the making of the transfer; or

(*e*) vesting in the trustee any rights or powers required by the trustee for the benefit of the estate.

(2) Subsection 1 does not apply where any person to whom property has been transferred paid or gave in good faith adequate valuable consideration for the property and any recourse of the trustee is solely against the person party to the transfer with the bankrupt.

22
Distributing the Estate and Discharge

The materials in this chapter deal broadly with the question of what claims creditors may legally prove in a bankruptcy, and the priority rules in the Bankruptcy Bill governing the order in which claims are to be paid by the trustee when distributing the bankrupt's estate among the creditors. The special, and largely insulated, status of the secured creditor is also outlined.

The chapter concludes by setting out the process of a debtor's discharge from bankruptcy and its effects on his property, his debts, and his personal status.

I PROVABLE CLAIMS

a / Tassé Report, p 119 (footnote omitted)

3.2.064 *Contingent Claims*: Under the present Act, all debts and liabilities, present or future, to which a bankrupt is subject at the date of the bankruptcy or to which he may become subject before the date of the bankruptcy may be proved in the bankruptcy. A contingent or unliquidated claim may also be proved if it is previously valued by the court. If the court refuses to value the claim, the holder of the claim may not prove it in the bankruptcy. As it cannot be proved, it is not released on the discharge of the bankrupt. Through no fault of the bankrupt, what could be the single largest claim against him may not be released. On his discharge, he will not be able to satisfy it and may be forced to go into bankruptcy a second time to obtain the release of a claim to which he was subject at the date of his first bankruptcy. There would, of course, be no problem if the court would always value a contingent or unliquidated claim. However, in many cases, the courts have refused to summarily value these claims. Judges have said that it was difficult to value the claims with any degree of certainty short of a full trial where all the evidence available in respect to both liability and damages was adduced. While respectful of the position taken by the courts in this matter, we are of the opinion that it does not sufficiently regard the relative positions of the claimant and the bankrupt. If the claim is not valued, the debtor is faced with what might be an impossible burden of debt after his bankruptcy. On the other hand, as a practical matter, there would be relatively little difference to the amount of the dividend a creditor receives for his injuries or damages arising out of a contingent or unliquidated claim, if the claim was not valued with complete exactitude, having regard to the fact that the dividend, on the average, would be about four cents on the dollar. Thus, the dividend the creditor would receive, if the claim was valued at \$20,000, would be \$800 and if, it was valued at \$15,000, it would be \$600. The difference of \$200 on the dividend that could be available to the creditor, in such a case, should not stand in the way of the possibility that a debtor may be discharged with an unreleased debt of $15,000 or $20,000. Judges are often called upon to make similar valuations where there is often little evidence and a wide discretion, such as the valuation for pain and suffering or the amount of maintenance to be paid to support a wife or child. J.A. MacLachlan, in discussing the problem of the valuation of contingent claims, has said:

Modern developments have facilitated the fair estimation of claims. Actuarial and analogous statistical data have been accumulated in various fields and the development of the casualty and surety business has been helpful. If the problem be approached with the basic principle in mind that an approximate valuation is much better than none, a reasonable value of some contingencies may be found in terms of the cost of insuring against them ...

It is therefore our recommendation that all contingent or unliquidated claims, to which a bankrupt is subject at the date of his bankruptcy, should be provable claims and that, in all cases, the court should be required to summarily value the same.

b / The Bankruptcy Bill (s-14)

157. When a bankruptcy order is made in respect of a debtor, a claim is admissible in the bankruptcy for any debt to which the debtor is subject at the date of bankruptcy.

248. (1) The trustee shall, for the purposes of this Act, value any admissible claim that is contingent or unliquidated.

(2) Where the components of a claim do not rank equally in the applicable order of priority set out in this Act, the trustee shall value each component that is contingent or unliquidated.

(3) Where, pursuant to subsection (1) or (2), the trustee values a claim, he shall give notice of the valuation to the creditor who filed the proof of claim.

(4) Where a creditor has a claim that is contingent or unliquidated, the trustee may apply to the court for valuation of the claim for the purpose of determining the number of votes that the creditor is entitled to cast at a meeting of creditors referred to in the application.

(5) Notwithstanding section 400, no appeal to the court of appeal lies from a decision of the court under subsection (4).

(6) Notwithstanding section 286, where the court has valued a claim pursuant to subsection (4), the chairman of the meeting of creditors in respect of which the claim was valued may not disallow the claim for the purpose of voting at the meeting.

254. (1) A creditor is not entitled to receive a dividend in respect of a claim unless a proof of claim or proof of security interest in prescribed form is filed with the trustee and the claim is not disallowed.

(2) A proof of claim or proof of security interest may be filed by a creditor, a person authorized by the creditor or any other person who, in the opinion of the trustee, has the proper knowledge of the claim or security interest.

2 SCHEME OF DISTRIBUTION

a / Tassé Report, pp 120–4 (footnotes omitted)

3.2.065 It is often said that a fundamental purpose of bankruptcy is the equal distribution of the property of a debtor among his creditors. In fact, all creditors are not treated the same. Not less than ten classes of claimants are given a statutory priority to payment of dividends. However, all creditors, within the same class, are treated alike.

3.2.066 There are many reasons for the failure of the bankruptcy system to save a fair share of the assets of an insolvent debtor for the ordinary unsecured creditors. We have alluded to some of them *supra* in 2.2.07 and 2.2.08. Perhaps the most visible of these reasons is that too many classes of creditors are paid in priority to others.

3.2.067 In our opinion, the priority on distribution given to several classes of creditors cannot be justified. In some cases, the present priority should be abolished. In other cases, it should be modified. This will result in a more equitable distribution of the property of an insolvent debtor among his creditors. Moreover, although the overall increase in dividends to the ordinary creditors might not be great, this should promote greater confidence in the entire bankruptcy system and result in an increased interest of creditors in the administration of estates. It may also discourage expensive litigation, occasionally resorted to at the instance of the ordinary creditors who have little, if anything, to lose and all to gain, while the cost, in effect, is being borne by priority creditors. In the following paragraphs, we discuss whether each of the priorities under the present Act is justified.

3.2.068 *Funeral and Testamentary Expenses*: Payable as a first priority are the reasonable funeral and testamentary expenses incurred by the legal personal representative of the deceased bankrupt. The reference to 'a deceased bankrupt' can only be to a debtor who has died after he became bankrupt. It cannot refer to a debtor whose estate becomes bankrupt after his death, as the estate cannot be referred to as a 'deceased bankrupt'. This creates the anomalous result that a claim for funeral expenses, which existed as of the date of bankruptcy of an insolvent estate, is not given a priority, while a claim for funeral expenses, which was not even in existence at the date of the bankruptcy of the debtor, ranks as a first priority. Furthermore, this is a strange result since such a claim, having necessarily occurred after the bankruptcy, is not 'provable in bankruptcy' and, for that reason, should not normally qualify for a dividend.

3.2.069 If a debtor who is not a bankrupt dies and his estate is subsequently put into bankruptcy, there is no reason why the funeral director should not equally share the available assets with other creditors including the nurse, the physician and others who attended to him prior to his death. Similarly, under a system where a bankrupt is permitted to retain his after-acquired property, there is no reason why the creditors, at the date of the bankruptcy, should be asked to take less, in order to permit a creditor whose claim arose after the date of bankruptcy, whether it be for funeral expenses or otherwise, to share in the distribution of the property of the debtor available at the date of bankruptcy. Perhaps some may argue that to abolish the priority for funeral expenses will make it more difficult to arrange for the burial of an insolvent or a bankrupt who may then have to be buried in a paupers' grave or at public expense. At worse, however, this would be no different from the many other cases of debtors dying insolvent. Moreover, if the deceased was a bankrupt, he could have, on his death, a small estate consisting of the property that he accumulated after his bankruptcy. This estate could be used to pay the funeral expenses. On balance, we have come to the conclusion that the priority given for funeral and testamentary expenses should be abolished.

3.2.070 *Costs of Administration*: The costs of administration, including the expenses and fees of the trustee and legal costs, are the second priority for payment of dividends under the present Act. In our opinion, it is only appropriate that these costs should be paid, and continue to be paid, in priority to all other costs.

3.2.071 *The Superintendent's Levy*: The third priority is the levy payable to the Superintendent of Bankruptcy to defray the expenses of his administration and supervision. At present, the levy varies, from two per cent of the first million dollars paid by the trustee for any purpose other than costs, to one-tenth of one per cent of the amount in excess of two million dollars. Some may argue that the cost of administering a public statute, such as the *Bankruptcy Act*, should be borne by the tax-paying public at large. In a large measure, the levy may, however, be considered as a payment to the Superintendent for his part in the administration of an estate. The point may well be made then that the government is, in effect, stepping in to fill the vacuum resulting from the creditors no longer taking any real and continuing interest in the control of the administration of bankruptcy estates. On balance, we have come to the conclusion that the levy should continue to be paid immediately after the other costs of administration, in priority to the other creditors.

3.2.072 *Wages*: The fourth priority concerns claims for wages, salaries, commissions or compensation of any clerk, servant, travelling salesman, labourer or workman, for services rendered during three months next preceding the bankruptcy, to the extent of five hundred dollars. It has been said that the purpose of the priority was 'to favour those who could not be expected to know anything of the credit of their employer'. The three-month period does seem to be ample time as the employee knows that he is not being paid and 'should not mislead creditors indefinitely by working at their expense, when the bankrupt becomes such "slow pay" as to indicate that he is failing.' In our opinion, it is reasonable to restrict the period to three months, but we recommend that the dollar amount be increased to one thousand dollars, to take into account the decreased value of the dollar.

3.2.073 *Municipal Taxes*: The fifth priority relates to municipal taxes owing by the bankrupt, where such taxes are not secured by real property, but only to the extent of the bankrupt's interest in the properties in respect of which the taxes were imposed. We see no reason why a municipality should be treated differently from any other creditor. A municipality has the means to protect itself in the same way as do other creditors and it should not be in the position to, in effect, require the creditors of a bankrupt taxpayer to pay the taxes that the taxpayer did not pay. For these reasons, we recommend that the priority for municipal taxes be abolished.

3.2.074 *Landlord's Claim for Rent*: The landlord's claim for arrears of rent, for a period of three months next preceding the bankruptcy, and accelerated rent, for a period not exceeding three months after the bankruptcy if entitled thereto under the lease, constitutes the sixth priority. The total amount so payable is not, however, to exceed the realization from the property on the premises under the lease. It is not obvious why a landlord is permitted to hold back taking proceedings against a failing tenant and then be permitted to recoup himself at the expense of the other creditors. It might be said, however, that it is in the interest of a debtor, who has some hope of rehabilitating himself short of bankruptcy, that his landlord should not take proceedings to terminate the lease at the first opportunity. On balance, we are of the opinion that a good case can be made for retaining the priority of the landlord for three months rent in arrears next preceding the bankruptcy, but the priority for three months accelerated rent cannot be justified and we recommend that it be abolished.

3.2.075 *Crown Priority*: The last priority, but the priority under which the largest amounts are paid, is that of the Crown. The history of the Crown priority goes back a long time. In *Magna Carta*, it was said that : 'The King's debtor dying, the King shall be first paid'. At common law, the Crown had a prerogative right to be paid first. The Crown continued to assert its prerogative after the enactment of the first Bankruptcy Acts, on the ground that a statute could not bind the Crown. Eventually, the application of the *Bankruptcy Act* was extended to the Crown, but it continued to assert the necessity of a priority in its favour, on the ground that the Crown was invariably, certainly in respect of taxes, an unwilling creditor and could not choose its debtor. For these reasons it was in the public interest and necessary for the protection of the public treasury that it be paid first.

3.2.076 It is, we believe, important to re-examine the public policy in respect of the Crown priority. It must be determined whether such a priority is justified in a modern society. Certainly, it is not necessary for the financial stability of the government. The argument that the Crown cannot choose its own debtor has some relevance in claims for taxes, but none, as regards contractual claims. In this respect, it should be pointed out that individuals claiming damages do not choose their debtors either; and yet, they do not benefit by a priority of rank. One wonders whether, in our economy of easy credit, the businessman has always the economic freedom to choose his debtor or whether he is not bound, to a certain point, to give credit to the same extent as do his closest competitors. It could even be argued that the government should rank after ordinary creditors, as the public treasury is, in fact, in a better position than anyone to bear the inevitable losses. The government can, in effect, divide the burden of tax left unpaid by the bankrupt among all the tax paying public. It would be more logical for the government to do this, than to take advantage of the bankruptcy of an insolvent taxpayer to reimburse itself, at the expense of the creditors who have already suffered losses. Certainly, there can be no rational explanation for the government to attempt to obtain payment of the tax due by a bankrupt from his creditors. Such a proposition offends one's sense of natural justice.

3.2.077 Whatever the logic or lack of logic there is in the priority of the Crown, the cumulative impact of the priority has substantially increased since the Second World War. Crown priorities have grown in three dimensions: (1) the rates of existing or old taxes have been increased; (2) there have been many new kinds of taxes; and (3) the Crown has become extensively engaged in business, particularly through the use of Crown corporations to which the Crown priority has been held, in many cases, to apply. The apathy of creditors to take part in the administration of an estate in bankruptcy can very well be explained by reason of the Crown priority. Very often, for the creditors to involve themselves in the administration of estates is equivalent to their volunteering as agents of the public treasury.

3.2.078 Professor J.A. MacLachlan, in his usual forthright manner and perhaps with some exaggeration, very harshly criticized the priority of the Government of the United States under its *Bankruptcy Act*, in these words:

The unprecedented multiplicity and magnitude of tax claims is greatly aggravated by their priority ... They strike the commercial community where it is weak by further impairing the financial condition of creditors who have had the misfortune of extending credit to a bankrupt. Unless governments can stop proliferating taxes to lavish largesse on politically favoured groups and to give public credit to those unworthy of private credit, bankruptcy may become just another device for paying official salaries. Dividends of priority creditors and to general creditors in bankruptcy have been less than 5¢ per capita per annum in relation to the national population, so the revenue at stake is chicken feed, but the commercial repercussions of accentuating bankruptcy frustrations may be disproportionate.

3.2.079 In our opinion, the priority of the Crown in our modern society cannot be justified and we recommend that it be abolished.

3.2.080 *Postponement of Certain Claims*: We point out *supra*, in 2.1.12, that, as there are good and bad debtors, so there are good and bad creditors. 'Equality is equity' is a concept as old as bankruptcy, the same as its corollary that creditors, as a rule, should be paid *pari passu*. The discussion in the preceding paragraphs, however, serves to demonstrate that the law prefers some creditors to others. But, from the general body of ordinary creditors who would normally rank together *pari passu*, the law identifies certain creditors the payment of whose claims is postponed until the claims of all other creditors have been satisfied. Such is the case, for example, of the claim of a creditor who, prior to bankruptcy, has entered with the debtor into an improper transaction otherwise than at arm's length. There are other cases, not now mentioned in the Act, that, in our opinion, deserve the same treatment. Such is the case, for example, of the claim of a creditor resulting from the operation of a penal clause under a contract, where no damages have in fact been proven. The same treatment should be given to a claim in respect of which a wilfully false statement or a wilful misrepresentation has been made to the trustee or to the court. Similarly, the same rule should apply to claims with respect to which a voidable preference was given, unless the preference was disclosed to the trustee not more than two weeks after the creditor became aware of the bankruptcy.

b / The Bankruptcy Bill (s-14)

265. (1) Every person who is entitled to make a claim in a bankruptcy or under an arrangement or to make a claim for administrative costs payable out of an estate is either a secured creditor or an unsecured creditor and unsecured creditors are
   (*a*) preferred;
   (*b*) ordinary; or
   (*c*) deferred.
(2) A claim of a secured creditor is specifically referred to
   (*a*) in respect of a consumer arrangement, in sections 77 and 78;
   (*b*) in respect of a consumer bankruptcy, in subsections 163(3) to (12);
   (*c*) in respect of a commercial arrangement, in subsections 101(2) and 102(8) and section 123; and
   (*d*) in respect of a bankruptcy other than a consumer bankruptcy, in sections 149 and 150 and sections 249 to 253.
(3) Each paragraph of subsections (4) and (6) designates a class of claims, and each subparagraph of those subsections designates a subclass of claims.
(4) Preferred creditors are those whose claims arise in respect of:
   (*a*) the debts or other obligations incurred by the interim receiver pursuant to paragraph 280(1)(*c*) or by the trustee in carrying on the business of the debtor;
   (*b*) in the circumstances set out in section 272,
     (i) the costs of distress, or
     (ii) the bill of costs of the solicitor, including the fees of the sheriff and the land registration fees, with respect to the creditor who, before the date of filing the petition or proposed arrangement, has first had a sheriff seize any property of the debtor but only to the amount of the proceeds from the realization of the property;
   (*c*) legal costs, other expenses and fees in the following order:
     (i) legal costs for collections,
     (ii) legal costs of an interim receivership,
     (iii) fees and expenses of an interim receiver,
     (iv) legal costs incurred by a petitioning creditor up to the making of a bankruptcy order,
     (v) where a proposed arrangement is rejected by the creditors or where the court does

      not approve a proposed arrangement and the court finds that the costs incurred were of benefit to the creditors in the ensuing bankruptcy, legal costs, expenses and fees of the trustee reasonably incurred in good faith on behalf of the debtor from the date of filing a notice of intention referred to in subsection 101(1) to the date of bankruptcy or, if no such notice was filed, the date of filing the proposed arrangement to the date of bankruptcy,

   (vi) legal costs awarded against the estate that are incurred after the making of the bankruptcy order or the filing of a proposed arrangement,

   (vii) legal costs and the expenses of administration excluding the costs described in subparagraphs (i) to (vi) and subparagraph (viii), and

   (viii) fees of the trustee;

(*d*) where an arrangement is annulled, the claims and legal costs, other expenses and fees in the following order:

   (i) legal costs and other expenses reasonably incurred in good faith by the trustee, and

   (ii) the fees of the trustee;

(*e*) claims for wages for any amount that had become due and payable by an employer prior to the date of bankruptcy or the date of filing of the proposed arrangement,

   (i) other than any amount for which the employer is liable as pension and other health and welfare plan contributions, except wages of an employee or a salesman related to the debtor or an agent or a former agent of the debtor, to the amount of two thousand dollars, together with, in the case of a salesman, disbursements properly incurred by him in respect of the business of the debtor to the amount of six hundred dollars, and

   (ii) as pension and other employee benefit plan contributions in respect of the debtor's employees or salesmen, except employees or salesmen related to the debtor or an agent or a former agent of the debtor, to the amount of five hundred dollars in respect of each such employee or salesman;

(*f*) where an arrangement is annulled, claims for debts incurred for the purposes of carrying on the business of the debtor between the date of the proposed arrangement and the date on which the arrangement was annulled

   (i) if the debts were incurred by the interim receiver or trustee in accordance with the arrangement, and

   (ii) if the arrangement provided that new creditors were to have a priority;

(*g*) claims of a lessor of real property for arrears of rent for a period of three months immediately preceding the date of bankruptcy or date of filing of the proposed arrangement but the total amount so payable shall not exceed the net realization from the property on the premises under lease;

(*h*) subject, in the case of an arrangement under Part IV, to subsection 104(11), claims of a lessor of real property under subsection 197(23) but no such claim may be made for an amount exceeding the net amount realized from the disposal of the property on the premises under lease; and

(*i*) claims of Her Majesy in right of Canada or of a province where the debtor collected moneys that he is required by statute

   (i) to collect on behalf of Her Majesty, and

   (ii) to hold separate and apart from his own moneys,

and the moneys are deemed by such statute to be held in trust for Her Majesty but no such claim shall exceed an amount equal to the amount of any cash on hand or in a bank or other depository at the date of bankruptcy or date of filing the proposed arrangement.

(5) Ordinary creditors are

(*a*) those whose claims are not referred to in subsections (4) and (6); and

(*b*) those whose claims are for an amount, in respect of claims referred to in those subsections, in excess of the amounts permitted by those subsections but they are ordinary creditors only in respect of the amount of that excess.

(6) Deferred creditors are those whose claims arise in respect of the following:

(*a*) interest on all claims at the rate of five per cent per annum or such higher rates as may be prescribed from the date of bankruptcy; and

(*b*) claims

    (i) for damages resulting from a loss of profit,

    (ii) arising out of a gift,

    (iii) made pursuant to subsection 180(1) or (2),

    (iv) under a contract, where the contract provides an indemnity or penalty to the extent that the amount of the indemnity or penalty, or its value, exceeds the amount or value of any actual damages suffered, and

    (v) of creditors that are subordinated by contract to the payment of ordinary creditors referred to in subsection (5).

(7) Where a person referred to in subsection (5) has a claim for a debt that at the date of bankruptcy or filing of a proposed arrangement is not payable or is or becomes payable by reason only of the bankruptcy or insolvency of the debtor, the amount of the claim is the present value of the debt determined in the prescribed manner.

(8) No claim of an ordinary creditor shall be paid until all claims of preferred creditors have been paid in full.

(9) No claim of a deferred creditor shall be paid until all claims of preferred creditors and ordinary creditors have been paid in full.

(10) The classes and subclasses of claims set out in subsections (4), (6), (14) and (15) are ranked in order of priority.

(11) No claim in a class of claims shall be paid until all claims in each class having higher rank in the category have been paid in full, and no claim in a subclass of claims shall be paid until all claims in each subclass having higher rank in the class have been paid in full.

(12) Except where it is expressly stated otherwise

(*a*) in subsection (4) or (6),

(*b*) in subsection (14), in the case of bankruptcy of a bank,

(*c*) in subsection (15), in the case of bankruptcy of a financial institution, or

(*d*) in an order of priority under Part VIII, in the case of bankruptcy of an insurance company, all claims in a class or subclass rank equally without preference among themselves and, where the assets of the estate are not sufficient to pay in full the claims included in a class or subclass, such claims shall be paid rateably.

(13) Where there is more than one part to a claim, the parts of the claim may be included in different classes or different subclasses

(*a*) in subsections (4) to (6);

(*b*) where the bankrupt is a bank, in the order of priority under subsection (14); or

(*c*) where the bankrupt is a financial institution, in the order of priority under subsection (15); or

(*d*) where the bankrupt is an insurance company, in an order of priority for an insurance company under Part VIII.

(14) Notwithstanding subsections (4) to (6), the claims of persons having claims admissible in a bankruptcy of a bank and claims for administrative costs payable out of the estate of the bank are payable in the following order of priority:

(*a*) the debts or obligations incurred by the interim receiver or trustee in carrying on the business of the bank;

(*b*) the costs of administration in the order of priority referred to in paragraphs (4)(*b*) and (*c*);

(*c*) the payment of the notes issued by the bank, intended for circulation in a country outside Canada and then outstanding, exclusive of those in respect of which payment has been made as contemplated by subsection 73(3) of the *Bank Act*;

(*d*) the payment of any amount due to Her Majesty in right of Canada, in trust or otherwise, except indebtedness evidenced by bank debentures;

(*e*) the payment of any amount due to Her Majesty in right of a province, in trust or otherwise, except indebtedness evidenced by bank debentures;

(*f*) the deposit liabilities of the bank;

(*g*) the indebtedness evidenced by a bank debenture subject to the prior payment in full of such other liabilities of the bank as are mentioned in that debenture or in any document under which it was issued;

(*h*) the claims of all other creditors in the order of priority set out in paragraphs (4)(*d*) to (*h*), subsection (5) and paragraph (6)(*a*), to the extent that they are not included in the prior liabilities referred to in paragraph (*g*);

(*i*) the claims of creditors that are subordinated by contract to the payment of ordinary creditors referred to in subsection (5); and

(*j*) the amount of any penalties for which the bank is liable.

(15) Notwithstanding subsections (4) to (6), the claims of persons having claims admissible in a bankruptcy of a financial institution and claims for administrative costs payable out of the estate of a financial institution arise in respect of the following:

(*a*) the debts or obligations incurred by the interim receiver or trustee in carrying on the business of the financial institution;

(*b*) the costs of administration in the order of priority referred to in paragraphs (4)(*b*) and (*c*);

(*c*) the payment of any amount due to Her Majesty in right of Canada, in trust or otherwise;

(*d*) the payment of any amount due to Her Majesty in right of a province, in trust or otherwise;

(*e*) the deposit liabilities of a financial institution and any payment made to a financial institution for investment;

(*f*) the claims of all other creditors in the order of priority set out in paragraphs (4)(*d*) to (*h*), subsection (5) and paragraph (6)(*a*);

(*g*) the claims of creditors that are subordinated by contract to the payment of ordinary creditors referred to in subsection (5);

(*h*) penalties for which the financial institution is liable.

(16) For the purposes of this section 'financial institution' means a credit union, caisse populaire, trust company, loan company, mutual fund, investment contract company, or any like institution other than a bank that accepts deposits or payments from the public for investment.

c / Wage Priorities

i The Bankruptcy Bill (s-14), s 265(4)(e) (p 839 above)

ii The Employment Standards Act, s.o. 1974, c 112

15. Every employer shall be deemed to hold vacation pay accruing due to an employee in

trust for the employee whether or not the amount therefor has in fact been kept separate and apart by the employer and the vacation pay becomes a lien and charge upon the assets of the employer that in the ordinary course of business would be entered in books of account whether so entered or not.

iii *Re Dairy Maid Chocolates Ltd.* (1973), 17 C.B.R. (N.S.) 270 (S.C.O.)

HOULDEN J. (orally): This is an application by the trustee acting in re the proposal of the above-named debtor for an order that the claim of the Director of Employment Standards on behalf of employees of the above-named debtor is not a valid trust claim. As the constitutional validity of The Employment Standards Act, R.S.O. 1970, c 147, is being questioned in this application, notice of the proceedings has been given to the Attorney General for Canada and the Attorney General for Ontario. The Attorney General for Canada has not seen fit to appear on the return of the motion.

The facts are not in dispute. On 24th March 1972 the debtor lodged a proposal with the trustee. The proposal was accepted by creditors and in due course approved by the Court. The proposal provided that all the assets of the debtor were to be sold and the proceeds paid to the trustee for distribution in accordance with the terms of the proposal.

The Director of Employment Standards filed with the trustee a proof of claim dated 26th May 1972 in the amount of $7,244.30. The claim is for vacation pay owing to various employees of the debtor company. It was filed as a trust claim pursuant to s 47(*a*) of the Bankruptcy Act, R.S.C. 1970, c B-3. Section 47(*a*) provides that the property of a bankrupt divisible amongst his creditors shall not comprise property held by the bankrupt in trust for any other person. By virtue of s 46 of the Bankruptcy Act, s 47(*a*) also applies in the case of a proposal.

The claim is made pursuant to s 8(2) of The Employment Standards Act which reads as follows:

8. (2) Every employer shall be deemed to hold vacation pay accruing due to an employee in trust for the employee and for payment of the vacation pay over in the manner and at the time provided under this Act and the regulations, and the amount shall be a charge upon the assets of the employer or his estate in his hands or the hands of a trustee and shall have priority over all other claims.

The basis of calculation of the amount which is deemed to be accruing due under s 8(2) is set out in s 30 of The Employment Standards Act. It provides:

30. Where an employee has not been given a vacation with pay pursuant to section 27 or the employment of an employee is terminated for any cause or by operation of law, the employee shall be paid,

    (*a*) an amount equal to 2 per cent of the total pay of the employee in the first twelve months of employment or any part thereof; and

    (*b*) an amount equal to 4 per cent of the total pay of the employee in each succeeding twelve months of employment, or any part thereof.

Counsel for the respondent and for the Attorney General were content that a period should be put after the words 'in his hands' in s 8(2). They frankly conceded that in the case of an insolvency, there was no power in the provincial legislature to give priority over other claims or to create a trust on property in the hands of a trustee.

If a period is put in the suggested place and the section is treated as being severable, I believe it creates a valid trust on property coming into the hands of the trustee. It seems to me that under the section, as an employee renders services to an employer, vacation pay is deemed to accrue due. The amount of such vacation pay constitutes a trust fund which is a charge for the amount owing upon the assets of the employer.

In this case, there were substantial assets in the hands of the employer. Counsel for the trustee admitted that the filing of the proposal terminated the employment of the employee. Sections 8(2) and 30 are, therefore, applicable and when the trustee received the property of the debtor, it was subject to the trust created by s 8(2).

Counsel for the trustee admitted that it is within the legislative competence of the Province of Ontario to create a trust; however, he submitted that by creation of this trust, the province was attempting to create a different scheme of distribution than that provided by the Bankruptcy Act and, therefore, the legislation was ultra vires. I do not believe this is so. The creation of the trust is in no way related to bankruptcy. By s 30 of The Employment Standards Act, the charge became effective not on bankruptcy, but on termination of employment for any cause or by operation of law. Bankruptcy would come within the words 'by operation of law'.

It is true that the creation of the trust does affect the amount of property available for distribution to creditors, but this does not make it invalid. The same point was argued in *John M. M. Troup Ltd.* v *Royal Bank of Canada*, [1962] S.C.R. 487 at 494, 3 C.B.R. (N.S.) 224, 34 D.L.R. (2d) 556, in connection with the trust created by s 3(1) of The Mechanics' Lien Act, R.S.O. 1950, c 227, as amended, and Judson J. in the Supreme Court of Canada rejected it in these words:

As to bankruptcy, the creation of a trust by s 3(1) does affect the amount of property divisible among the creditors but so does any other trust validly created.

The provincial legislature has the right to create a valid trust, and in my opinion, it has done so in s 8(2) of The Employment Standards Act. By s 47(a) of the Bankruptcy Act, such trust property does not form part of the property of the bankrupt. The claim is, therefore, a valid charge on the property of the debtor in the hands of the trustee.

The present case is unlike *Re Deslauriers Const. Products Ltd.*, [1970] 3 O.R. 599, 14 C.B.R. (N.S.) 197 (sub nom. *A.G. Can.* v *Perlmutter*), 13 D.L.R. (3d) 551 (C.A.), in that the trust is enforceable only in respect of *assets of the employer* that were in existence at the date of the termination of the employment. It does not purport to create a charge on assets of the bankrupt estate. It is also different from *Re Moore; Moore Trustee* v *The Queen* (1957), 42 M.P.R. 86, 37 C.B.R. 112, 15 D.L.R. (2d) 681 (N.B. C.A.), in that the charge is created on the assets of the employer in the hands of the employer not on property in the hands of the trustee. The property which passes to the trustee in bankruptcy or the trustee under the proposal is subject to the charge created by the trust when the trustee receives it.

There will, therefore, be an order that the claim of the Director is a valid trust claim within s 47(a) of the Bankruptcy Act and shall be paid out of the assets of the debtor in the hands of the trustee. Counsel for the respondent and for the Attorney General are not asking for costs. There will, therefore, be no order as to costs save and except that the costs of the trustee shall be paid out of the assets of the estate.

COMMENT
by David E. Baird

This decision is the latest illustration of how provincial and federal legislation have made a mockery of the priority provisions set out in s 107 of the Bankruptcy Act, R.S.C. 1970, c B-3.

Prior to 1949, the Bankruptcy Act made no attempt to legislate in respect of provincial or federal taxes or any lien or charge created by the taxing statutes: the Bankruptcy Act, 1919, c 36, s 51(6). As may have been expected each level of government attempted to legislate that its indebtedness was entitled to the highest priority and in almost every bankrupt estate it was necessary to obtain a court ruling on the respective priorities of the claims for public utilities, municipal, provincial and federal taxes.

When the Bankruptcy Act was revised in 1949 [1949 (Can.), c 7], Parliament attempted to remedy the confusion as provision was made for the respective priorities of business tax, provincial and federal taxes: the Bankruptcy Act, s 107. Priority was also given to wage earners and to the landlord for arrears of rent. The provincial and even the federal draftsmen, realized that the Bankruptcy Act of 1949 left two large loopholes. The first is that the distribution under s 107 of the Bankruptcy Act is subject to the rights of secured creditors and secondly that by virtue of s 47(*a*) of the Bankruptcy Act, property held by the bankrupt in trust for others does not vest in the trustee in bankruptcy. With these two opportunities available, provincial legislatures have regularly subverted the priorities set out in the Bankruptcy Act. In the case of *Re Clemenshaw; Workmen's Compensation Board* v *Canadian Credit Men's Trust Assn.* (1962), 4 C.B.R. (N.S.) 238, 40 W.W.R. 199, 36 D.L.R. (2d) 244, the British Columbia Court of Appeal held that the Workmen's Compensation Board was a secured creditor as defined by s 2(*r*) of the Bankruptcy Act. Section 48 of The Workmen's Compensation Act, R.S.B.C. 1960, c 413, provided that an amount due to the Board by an employer constituted a lien in favour of the Board payable in priority over all liens, charges or mortgages of any person. Similar legislation is found in many provincial statutes. For example in Ontario such provisions are found in the following statutes: The Corporations Tax Act, R.S.O. 1970, c 91, s 94(1), and The Retail Sales Tax Act, R.S.O. 1970, c 415, s 18.

What is the effect of this proliferation of paramount liens? It is clear that in creating a lien in priority over all other claims for a particular tax, the legislature has given no consideration to social priorities. Should a claim for retail sales tax have priority over the amount owing to an employee for wages? Should an amount owing for public utilities have priority over the landlord's claim for arrears of rent? In Ontario the legislature has granted the highest priority to various taxes but has made a lesser attempt to protect the position of the unpaid workman for arrears of wages: see The Employment Standards Act, R.S.O. 1970, c 147, s 8(1). This section gives a person with unpaid wages priority only over preferred, ordinary or general creditors of the employer.

Even Parliament has not hesitated in reversing or superseding the priorities created by s 107 of the Bankruptcy Act. It has used the loophole dealing with trust property. In the case of *Re Deslauriers Const. Products Ltd.*, [1970] 3 O.R. 599, 14 C.B.R. (N.S.) 197 (sub nom. *A.G. Can.* v *Perlmutter*), 13 D.L.R. (3d) 551 (C.A.), the provisions of the Canada Pension Plan, 1964–65 (Can.), c 51, ss 22(1), 24(3) and 24(4), creating a trust were upheld. In the Canada Pension Plan, Parliament was not content to provide that moneys actually deducted were to be held in trust but went so far as to create a fictional trust. Whether or not any money was actually deducted and whether or not any deductions could be traced, an amount equal to the amount that should have been deducted is deemed to be payable as trust funds out of any property owned by the bankrupt. Under s 107 of the Bankruptcy Act, the amounts owing for Canada Pension Plan deductions would have been preferred claims. However, it appears that Parliament for some reason considered that pension plan deductions should be paid in priority to all other preferred creditors including employees.

This insidious attempt to quietly and ruthlessly supersede the priorities set out in s 107 of the

Bankruptcy Act is illustrated by this case. The legislature attempted in a very cumbersome fashion to make indebtedness for vacation pay both a secured claim and the basis for a trust. Why it was necessary to rely on both loopholes in the Bankruptcy Act is not clear. The right of a provincial legislature to create trusts and thus, circumvent the priorities in the Bankruptcy Act was upheld by the Supreme Court of Canada in the case of *John M. M. Troup Ltd.* v *Royal Bank of Canada*, [1962] S.C.R. 487, 3 C.B.R. (N.S.) 224, 34 D.L.R. (2d) 556. The provinces' right to legislate is found under head (13) of s 92 of the B.N.A. Act, 1867, which deals with property and civil rights.

The danger created by provincial and federal statutes creating trusts and secured creditors without any co-ordination or consideration of the general social needs of the community was recognized by the Study Committee on Bankruptcy and Insolvency Legislation, Canada 1970, and it recommended that the right of governments to create deemed trusts or to create secured creditors be abolished. See s 2.043 and s 2.044 of the report. The following footnote in the report illustrates the committee's views on the artificial creation of deemed trusts:

The following observation, although made in reference to the by-laws of a corporation, seems not to be inappropriate to the discussion of a 'deemed trust', whereby the concept of a trust is changed into something altogether different. 'To deem ... that a thing happened when not only it is known that it did not happen, but it is positively known that precisely the opposite of it happened, is a conception to my mind if applied to a subject matter such as that of art. 93, amounts to a complete absurdity.' *Robert Batcheller & Sons, Ltd.* v *Batcheller*, [1945] Ch. 169 at 176, [1945] 1 All E.R. 522 at 530 per Romer J. One also recalls the words of Humpty Dumpty 'when I use the word' he said in rather a scornful tone, 'it means just what I choose it to mean – neither more nor less.' Through the Looking-Glass and what Alice in Wonderland Found There, Lewis CARROLL.

The learned Judge in this case was bound by decisions of higher courts but to hold that money owing from A to B could in any sense be deemed to have been held in trust by A for B clearly breaches all the normal concepts of a trust. The normal attribute of a trust is that some property or asset in existence is held by A for B. In the case of vacation pay there is no asset in existence but rather an obligation to pay at a future date. There is not even a nominal or obligatory deduction as in the case of the Canada Pension Plan deductions since the amount owing for vacation pay is a percentage of the employee's regular wages and is paid in addition to the gross wages of the employee. To apply the concept of a trust to such an indebtedness is an absurd departure from normal legal principles characterizing a trust. In all other instances where statutory trusts have been created, there is a receipt of property or a deduction. In this instance, the legislature has stretched the concept of trust to the absurd solely for the purpose of circumventing the priorities of s 107 of the Bankruptcy Act.

In most statutes where liens or deemed trusts are created no procedure is set up to cover the method of realizing on property subject to the lien or deemed trust. No provision is made in The Employment Standards Act to pay the reasonable costs of liquidation or even to provide for a method of liquidation. It appears that the various legislatures and Parliament expect the trustee in bankruptcy to follow the procedures available in the Bankruptcy Act for the purpose of converting the property into cash but then are prepared to demand the proceeds without provision for trustee's fees and expenses.

This appears to have been the intention of the legislature when enacting s 8(2) of The Employment Standards Act since a claim for three months' vacation pay would already have priority under s 107(1)(*d*) of the Bankruptcy Act subject only to the costs of administration.

Greschuk J. of the Supreme Court of Alberta in the case of *Re Bates Electric Ltd.*, ante, p 253, has recognized the paramountcy of the provisions of the Bankruptcy Act in dealing with the realization and distribution of the assets of a bankrupt. It is unfortunate that provincial governments have not recognized the need in society for one statute regulating the method of distributing the assets of an insolvent person. It is even more difficult to understand why the federal government has been prepared to permit the constant mockery of the Bankruptcy Act by its own legislation.

3 SECURED CREDITORS

a / Tassé Report, p 111

3.2.035 *Secured Creditors:* Under the present Act, the secured creditors do not come for most purposes within the provisions of the Act and their security does not vest in the trustee. They can, as a rule, proceed with the seizure and liquidation of their security in the same manner in which they could if there had not been a bankruptcy.

3.2.036 The position of secured creditors, under the various plans for an arrangement recommended in this Report, has been discussed *supra*, in 3.1.32 to 3.1.40. We do not believe that the rights of the secured creditors should vary depending on whether the debtor succeeds in making an arrangement or has been placed in bankruptcy. To give a privileged position to the secured creditor in the case of the bankruptcy of the debtor would, in many cases, constitute an invitation to the secured creditor to use all means available to him to defeat the attempts of the debtor to make an arrangement.

3.2.037 In the case of the bankruptcy of any debtor, we recommend a number of changes in the treatment of the secured creditor or an unpaid vendor. The first one relates to a clause that is frequently found in a variety of contracts whereby a debtor is deemed to be in default merely on becoming insolvent or bankrupt. We believe that, so long as the debtor has not defaulted in the payments due under the contract, the creditor or vendor should not be permitted to either have the remaining payments on the debt accelerated or to realize on the security or property, and we so recommend. If this recommendation were implemented, the debtor would be in a better position to effect an arrangement with his creditors or, this failing, the trustee would be in a better position to sell the business of the debtor as a going concern.

3.2.038 Secondly, a secured creditor should not be allowed, in any case, to repossess or realize his security, whether on movable or immovable property, without having first proven the validity and value of his security, and given the trustee the opportunity to attack the security, to redeem it, or to pay any arrears on the debt.

3.2.039 We finally recommend that, in all cases where there would have been repossession or realization of movable or immovable property, either before or after bankruptcy, the summary procedure recommended *supra* in 3.1.39, to adjust the value of any deficiency claim that may remain to the amount it would have been, if the creditor had used reasonable diligence and prudence in the liquidation of the security, should apply.

3.2.040 In the case of the bankruptcy of a 'small debtor', we recommend that there be no other change in the treatment of creditors having a security on immovable property. However, we recommend that the creditor having a security on movables be prevented from realizing or repossessing the security where the debtor has paid two-thirds of the amount owing. If less than two-thirds of the amount owing is paid, the secured creditor should be given the right to choose, within a certain delay, between filing a claim in the bankruptcy or maintaining his rights under the contract. Where the creditor chooses to maintain his rights under the contract or in the cases where he has already exercised them before the bankruptcy, his claim for any balance of the debt should be postponed until the claims of all other creditors are paid in full. In order for the system to be effective, these restrictions should also be imposed on the rights of an unpaid vendor of movables.

b / The Bankruptcy Bill (s-14)

137. (1) Where a secured creditor
(*a*) undertakes to give up his security interest for the benefit of the unsecured creditors in the event of the making of a bankruptcy order against a debtor, or
(*b*) gives the particulars of his security interest and an estimate of its value,
he may be admitted as a petitioning creditor in the same manner as if he were an unsecured creditor, but, where the secured creditor gives the particulars of his security interest and an estimate of its value, he shall not be admitted as a petitioning creditor for more than the amount by which the debt owing to him exceeds the estimated value of the property subject to the security interest.

(2) Where a bankruptcy order is made, and a secured creditor has been admitted as a petitioning creditor pursuant to subsection (1), the trustee may direct the secured creditor to execute any power of attorney, conveyance, deed or instrument that may be required to give full effect to the undertaking given by that creditor pursuant to paragraph (1)(*a*).

149. (1) Subject to subsection (2), where a bankruptcy order has been made in respect of a debtor, a secured creditor shall not, unless he is authorized in writing by the trustee or the court, on application, otherwise orders, exercise any right he may have to realize or otherwise deal with property of the debtor subject to the security interest of such creditor until
(*a*) ten days after a proof of security interest in prescribed form has been filed with the trustee, or
(*b*) ten days after the date of the first meeting of creditors,
whichever is the later.

(2) Subsection (1) does not operate to prevent a creditor from exercising a remedy against a debtor or his property or from instituting or continuing a proceeding with respect to any of the following:
(*a*) any right the creditor may have as a secured creditor to realize or otherwise deal with the property subject to the security interest of such creditor where such security interest is in property that is perishable or likely to depreciate rapidly in value;
(*b*) any acts that are required by law to be performed to render a transfer effective against third parties, to prevent a security interest from being terminated, or to permit perfection of a security interest or other right by legal action, registration or otherwise;
(*c*) any right the creditor may have as a secured creditor to collect, take possession of, or take conservatory measures with respect to, any property subject to his security interest;
(*d*) any right in addition to the rights set out in paragraphs (*a*) to (*c*) and (*e*) and (*f*) the creditor may have as a secured creditor to realize or otherwise deal with the property subject to his security interest but only to the extent that the secured creditor realizes or otherwise deals with such property in a manner consistent with the continued operation of the debtor's business;
(*e*) any acts that are required to permit the completion or closing of any contractual obliga-

tion made, in good faith, and without knowledge of the making of the bankruptcy order if, on receipt of knowledge of the making of the bankruptcy order, the creditor notifies the trustee of the contractual obligation and gives him full particulars thereof; and

(*f*) the sale of assets of the debtor by a secured creditor where the sale is to be by way of auction or tender and the sale has been advertised.

(3) A court shall not order a secured creditor to desist from proceeding with a sale referred to in paragraph (2)(*f*) unless the applicant for the order undertakes to compensate the secured creditor in full for the costs incurred with respect to the sale.

150. (1) Where the security agreement does not restrict the right of a debtor to transfer property subject to a security interest, the trustee may transfer any such property of the estate without the consent of the secured creditor and subject to such security interest.

(2) Subject to subsection (3), the trustee may, notwithstanding anything in an agreement, transfer any property of an estate that is subject to a security interest, without the consent of the secured creditor and subject to such security interest.

(3) Where, pursuant to subsection (2), a trustee intends to transfer property subject to a security interest, he shall send to the secured creditor a notice in writing of his intention to do so at least fifteen days prior to the date of the transfer and, unless within such period the secured creditor sends to the trustee a notice in writing objecting to such transfer on the grounds that it would materially and adversely affect him, the trustee may transfer such property pursuant to that subsection.

(4) Where, pursuant to subsection (3), a secured creditor sends a notice of objection to a transfer, the trustee may apply to the court for an order permitting him to transfer property referred to in the notice of objection and the court may, if it is satisfied that such transfer will not materially and adversely affect the secured creditor, make such an order and impose such conditions on the transfer as it thinks fit.

249. A claim for a secured debt is admissible as an unsecured claim

(*a*) if the security interest is assigned to the trustee for the general benefit of the creditors, for the whole amount of the debt; or

(*b*) if the security interest is not so assigned, unless an enactment of the legislature of a province otherwise provides, for the balance due to the secured creditor after deducting from the debt

(i) the value of the property subject to the security interest, as determined pursuant to this Act, at the date of bankruptcy or the date of filing the proposed arrangement, or

(ii) the net proceeds from the realization of the property subject to the security interest.

250. (1) Where a bankruptcy order or an arrangement is made in respect of a debtor, if a secured creditor is entitled to realize or otherwise deal with property of the debtor that is subject to a security interest, the trustee who is vested with or who has control of the records and property of the debtor shall, unless a court, on application, otherwise orders, give access to the relevant records and give possession of the property subject to the security interest to the secured creditor.

(2) A secured creditor who proposes to realize or otherwise deal with property of a debtor referred to in subsection (1) that is subject to a security interest shall, before doing so, advise the trustee of the proposed method of realizing or otherwise dealing with the property of the bankrupt.

(3) A secured creditor who exercises any right he may have to realize or otherwise deal with property of a debtor referred to in subsection (1) that is subject to a security interest shall

(*a*) act honestly and in good faith;

(*b*) realize or otherwise deal with the property in a timely and commercially reasonable manner; and

(*c*) forthwith report to the trustee the conservatory measures taken, the method and results of any realization and any other dealings in respect of the property.

(4) Where a bankruptcy order or an arrangement is made in respect of a debtor, a secured creditor who exercises any right he may have to realize or otherwise deal with property of the debtor that is subject to a security interest

(*a*) shall, if the proceeds exceed the amount of the debt, forthwith forward the excess to the trustee; and

(*b*) is liable to the estate for any damages that the estate suffers if he fails to act in accordance with subsection (3).

251. (1) Until a secured creditor realizes property subject to a security interest, a trustee may, by notice in writing to the secured creditor, elect to

(*a*) redeem the property subject to the security interest; or

(*b*) require the property subject to the security interest to be realized.

(2) A secured creditor may, by notice in writing served on the trustee, require the trustee to elect whether or not he will redeem the property subject to a security interest of such creditor or require it to be realized.

(3). Where a trustee is served with a notice from a secured creditor pursuant to subsection (2), the trustee shall, if he

(*a*) elects to redeem the property subject to the security interest of the secured creditor, or

(*b*) elects to require such property to be realized,

cause a notice in writing to that effect to be served on the secured creditor not later than twenty days after receipt of the notice from the secured creditor.

(4) Where, pursuant to subsection (1) or (3), a trustee signifies, by notice in writing, to a secured creditor that he elects to redeem the property subject to the security interest of such creditor, he shall pay forthwith to the secured creditor the lesser of

(*a*) the amount of the secured debt; and

(*b*) the value of the property subject to the security interest as determined pursuant to paragraph 256(2)(*b*).

(5) Where the trustee is served with a notice from a secured creditor pursuant to subsection (2) and disputes the validity of the security interest of the secured creditor, the trustee shall forthwith pay to a third party agreed to by the secured creditor to hold in escrow the lesser of

(*a*) the amount of the secured debt; and

(*b*) the value of the property subject to the security interest as determined pursuant to paragraph 256(2)(*b*).

(6) Subject to subsection (8), where, pursuant to subsection (1) or (3), a trustee signifies, by notice in writing, to a secured creditor that he elects to require the property subject to the security interest of such creditor to be realized, the secured creditor shall proceed to realize the property in accordance with subsections 250(3) and (4).

(7) Where a sale of assets of the debtor by a secured creditor is by way of auction, the secured creditor or the trustee acting on behalf of the estate may bid or purchase.

(8) Where, pursuant to subsection (6), the trustee signifies to a secured creditor that he elects to require the property subject to the security interest of the secured creditor to be realized, the court, on application of the secured creditor, may postpone the realization for such period of time as the court thinks fit.

(9) Where the trustee makes no election under subsection (1) or (3) or, having made an

election under subsection (1) or (3), fails to comply with subsection (4),

- (*a*) he is no longer entitled to redeem the property subject to the security interest or to require the property to be realized;
- (*b*) if any interest in the property subject to the security interest vested in the trustee, the interest thereupon vests in the secured creditor,
- (*c*) the debt owing to the secured creditor is reduced by the amount at which the secured creditor assessed the value of the property subject to his security interest in the proof of security interest sent to the trustee under subsection 256(2); and
- (*d*) he is no longer entitled to inspect the property subject to the security interest.

(10) Subject to subsection (9), every secured creditor shall give the trustee a reasonable opportunity to inspect the property subject to the security interest that he holds and, if, after the date of bankruptcy or after an arrangement is made, the secured creditor realizes the property subject to the security interest before the trustee has had an opportunity to inspect the property, the secured creditor unless a court, on application otherwise orders

- (*a*) is not entitled, where the proceeds of the realization are less than the amount of the debt, to file a proof of claim for the deficiency;
- (*b*) shall provide to the trustee an accounting of the proceeds of the realization; and
- (*c*) shall, if the proceeds of the realization exceed the amount of the debt, forthwith forward the excess to the trustee.

252. The court, on application, may postpone any right a secured creditor may have to realize or otherwise deal with property of a debtor that is subject to a security interest on such terms and conditions and for such period of time as the court thinks fit, if such postponement does not materially adversely affect the secured creditor.

253. (1) Where a secured creditor has a right to realize or otherwise deal with the property of the debtor that is subject to a security interest, the court may, on application,

- (*a*) review and fix the fees and disbursements incurred in realizing or otherwise dealing with the property subject to the security interest; and
- (*b*) subject to subsection (2), give directions
    - (i) as to the period of time to be given to the trustee to inspect the property pursuant to subsection 251(10), and
    - (ii) as to the method of realizing or otherwise dealing with the property subject to the security interest.

(2) The court shall not give directions pursuant to paragraph (1)(*b*) if the creditor who holds a security interest on property satisfies the court that

- (*a*) the directions would materially and adversely affect him; or
- (*b*) the amount that might reasonably be expected from a realization in a commercially reasonable manner of the property subject to the security interest would not be sufficient to pay the debt owed pursuant to the security agreement.

4 EFFECT OF BANKRUPTCY ON THE PERSON

a / Tassé Report, pp 126–8 (footnotes omitted)

3.2.091 Under the present Act, the status of a bankrupt commences when a receiving order by the Court is made or an assignment is filed with the official receiver. It terminates when the debtor obtains his discharge. While a debtor has the status of a bankrupt, he suffers a number of incapacities. *The British North America Act* provides, for example, that 'The place of a Senator shall become vacant ... if he is adjudged bankrupt or insolvent, or applies for the benefit of any law relating to insolvent debtors, or becomes "a public defaulter".' Most corporations Acts prohibit a bankrupt from being a director. It is offence, under the *Bankruptcy Act* for a bankrupt to engage in trade or business without disclosing to all persons with whom he enters into a business transaction that he is an undischarged bankrupt. Similarly, it is an offence for a bankrupt to obtain credit for a purpose other than the supply of necessaries for himself and his family to the extent of five hundred dollars or more, from any person, without informing that person that he is an undischarged bankrupt.

3.2.092 By giving a special status to the bankrupt, it is possible for the business community to identify him and avoid extending credit to him. The good debtor, who has been honest and unfortunate, can, in most cases, expect an early discharge. The bad type of debtor, under the present Act, may be either refused a discharge or granted one under conditions during which the status of a bankrupt will continue.

3.2.093 There are, however, a number of weaknesses in the present system. In the case of an honest, but incompetent debtor, the court hearing an application for discharge may conclude that, while the bankrupt is honest and, for that reason, deserves an opportunity for a new start in life, he should not be granted a discharge too early because he has proved himself to be incompetent. In other cases, the discharge may depend upon the attitude of the creditors. If the creditors wish to harass the debtor, they can make it difficult for him to obtain an early discharge. Moreover, courts have a wide discretion in deciding whether a discharge should be granted, which is not uniformly exercised. In some areas, the courts are much more generous in granting discharges than they are in others. And even in the same area, some judges may well approach the question of discharge differently from others. To attach a condition for the payment of a sum of money to a discharge, in some cases, has the effect of condemning a debtor to bankruptcy indefinitely, unless the court should subsequently agree to set aside or modify the condition.

3.2.094 While the making of a receiving order against, or an assignment by, any person, except a corporation, operates as an application for discharge, some debtors ask that the application be waived or, else, some trustees automatically ask the debtor for a waiver, in order to avoid the responsibility of making the application. In other cases, the discharge is refused because the bankrupt is unable to attend or to afford the cost of retaining counsel to attend on his behalf, on the return of the application for his discharge. While it is impossible to ascertain how many undischarged bankrupts there are in the country, their number must be great. We are of the opinion that this is not a healthy condition for either the debtors concerned or the commercial community, whose members may not know whether they are dealing with an undischarged bankrupt.

3.2.095 We have expressed the view, *supra* (2.1.30 et seq.), that the present *Bankruptcy Act* has not sufficiently kept pace with the manner in which business is conducted through the use of the limited liability corporation. Not only is it most difficult to reach the controlling agents of a bankrupt corporation, but the sanctions that apply in the case of an individual bankrupt and the status of a bankrupt are largely meaningless in the case of a corporation. For these reasons, it is important that some procedure be devised so that the grossly incompetent or dishonest businessman who had been trading through the device of a corporation could be kept out of business, as if he had been trading under his own name.

3.2.096 For these reasons, we recommend that the legal status of a bankrupt should apply not only to all individual bankrupts, but also to such directors or officers (including those who, in fact, control the affairs of the corporation) of a corporation who are, for example, either primarily responsible for the bankruptcy of a corporation or who have substantially aggravated its insolvency. In the latter case, the status of a bankrupt would extend to an officer or director of a bankrupt corporation only on the order of the court. The effect of bankruptcy attaching to the property of a bankrupt would not, in such a case, extend to this type of bankrupt, except in the circumstances described supra in 3.2.024 to 3.2.027.

3.2.097 The status of a bankrupt, in all cases, would continue for five years after the date of bankruptcy. To make it more difficult, if not impossible, for the bad type of debtor from being in a position to renew the methods he formerly adopted to the detriment of the business community, no contract in respect of which credit is extended by or to the bankrupt in the course of his carrying on a business would be enforceable. Any bankrupt could, however, at any time, but more than one month after the making of a bankruptcy order, apply to the court for a certificate terminating his status of a bankrupt. A certificate could be granted only if the bankrupt establishes that his bankruptcy was caused by circumstances beyond his control, that his insolvency was not substantially aggravated by his fault and that the public interest does not require him to be further prevented from entering into and carrying on a business.

3.2.098 In our view, the present concept of the status of a bankrupt has largely failed to accomplish what was intended because there was no clear distinction made between the effect of bankruptcy on the person of the debtor and the effect on his property. The recommendations that we make in regard to after-acquired property (*supra*, 3.2.046 to 3.2.050), and the discharge of the debtor and the release of his debts (*supra*, 3.2.087 and 3.2.088) are all based on that distinction, as are the recommendations contained in the preceding two paragraphs.

b / The Bankruptcy Bill (s-14)

224. Where a caveat is filed in respect of an agent or former agent of a bankrupt, such agent or former agent shall not, without leave of the court, until the caveat ceases to be in force

(*a*) be a director or an officer of, or manage a corporation; and

(*b*) directly or indirectly, engage in or carry on any trade or business without disclosing the existence of the caveat to all persons with whom he incurs debts in the course of carrying on such trade or business.

225. (1) Subject to subsections (2) and (3), a bankrupt who enters into a contract whereby he extends credit, directly or indirectly, immediately or at a future date, in the course of carrying on a business does not have the capacity

(*a*) to enforce the contract; or

(*b*) to transfer the contract or any rights thereunder.

(2) Where a bankrupt transfers for value a contract whereby he extended credit and the transferee does not know that the transferor is bankrupt at the time of the transfer, the transferee may enforce the contract or transfer the contract or any rights thereunder.

(3) Where a bankrupt enters into a contract whereby he extends credit, a trustee in any subsequent bankruptcy of the bankrupt may enforce the contract or transfer the contract or any rights thereunder.

(4) For the purposes of this section, 'bankrupt' includes an agent or former agent of a bankrupt against whom a caveat has been filed during the period the caveat is in force.

226. Where a person under the laws of another country has or had a status comparable to that of a bankrupt under the bankruptcy or insolvency laws of that other country and less than five years have elapsed from the commencement of that status, such person is subject to sections 225, 227 and 370 but is not entitled to obtain a certificate pursuant to section 222.

227. A person who is a bankrupt is not qualified to be a director or an officer of a corporation.

230. Where, in respect of a bankrupt,

(*a*) a bankruptcy order had been made within five years prior to the filing of the petition for the current bankruptcy order, and

(*b*) in the opinion of the court, his bankruptcy is an abuse of the bankruptcy process to the detriment of the creditors of the estate,

the court may, on application made not late than thirty days after the day fixed for the first meeting of the creditors, revive all debts from which the debtor had been released by either of those bankruptcy orders.

5 DISCHARGE: THE TRUSTEE

a / Tassé Report, pp 157–8

3.6.36 *Discharge of Interim Receivers, Receivers and Trustees*: Under the present Act, when a trustee has had his accounts passed, he may apply to the court for a discharge. The discharge has the effect of relieving the trustee from all liability in respect of any act done or default made by him in the administration of the estate in relation to his conduct as trustee. We believe that the discharge of the trustee should be automatic upon the passing of his accounts and we so recommend. The same rule should apply to interim receivers and receivers.

b / The Bankruptcy Bill (s-14)

46. (1) On the passing of the final statement of accounts of an interim receiver, the interim receiver is discharged from all liability that he incurred to any person for whose benefit he administered the estate.

(*a*) in respect of any act done or default made while acting in that capacity; or

(*b*) in relation to his conduct as interim receiver.

(2) On the passing of the final statement of accounts of an estate, the trustee is discharged from all liability he incurred to any person for whose benefit he administered the estate,

(*a*) in respect of any act done or default made in the administration of the estate; or

(*b*) in relation to his conduct as trustee.

(3) A discharge pursuant to subsection (1) or (2) may, on application, be revoked by a judge on proof that the discharge was obtained by fraud or by the omission of some material fact or that the trustee has committed a breach of his fiduciary duty.

(4) On the passing of the final statement of accounts of an interim receiver or of an estate, the interim receiver or the trustee, as the case may be, shall forthwith send a notice of discharge in prescribed form to the administrator.

6 DISCHARGE: THE BANKRUPT

a / Tassé Report, pp 125–6 (footnotes omitted)

3.2.084 The concept of the conditional discharge and the less than complete release of debts, in a large measure, reflect the former quasi-criminal character of bankruptcy. It, in effect, operates as a penalty or a sanction against the bankrupt.

3.2.085 We are of the opinion that much of the rehabilitative effect of his discharge and release from debts is lost, when a bankrupt is left with substantial debts after his discharge. Indeed, in some cases, it may almost be regarded as a mockery of the bankruptcy system to take all of the seizable property of a debtor, distribute it among the creditors and then leave the debtor to cope with some of his largest creditors from whose debts he has not been released. If the *Bankruptcy Act* is not entirely commercial legislation at its present stage of development, it certainly is no longer criminal legislation. If the conduct of a debtor is criminal, the penalties or sanctions imposed against him should be those of the criminal law. The bankruptcy process should be used only to impose settlements upon the conflicting claims between a debtor and his creditors and claims between the creditors themselves. This is not to say that commercial morality is not to be encouraged. This, however, in our opinion, may be done more effectively by extending the restrictions inherent in the status of a bankrupt than by penalizing the bankrupt by not releasing him from his debts.

3.2.086 Almost two hundred years ago, Lord Mansfield said that '... all the debts of a bankrupt are due in conscience, notwithstanding he has obtained his certificate; and there is no honest man who does not discharge them, if he afterwards has it in his power to do so'. Certainly, many bankrupts would not dispute this, although, admittedly, the possibility of repaying any substantial payment on the debts from which they have been released is, in the case of most bankrupts, no more than wishful thinking on their part. It is, nonetheless, an ambition that should not be discouraged. Unfortunately, some creditors take advantage of debtors, in this regard, often in their most vulnerable moment, when their pride and self-respect have been seriously hurt in having to resort to, or being forced into, bankruptcy. For example, they may trick the debtor into paying, by one way or another, debts from which he has been released. A debtor may also be pressed into agreeing, as a condition for a creditor not opposing the application for the discharge, that it would not release the debtor from a claim of a particular creditor. Moreover, a creditor may persuade the debtor to make a payment on account of a debt from which he has been released or otherwise acknowledge that he is bound or will pay it, in order that the claim against him may be legally revived.

3.2.087 We recommend, in the first place, that the debtor be released from all claims that may be proved against an estate, except a fine or penalty imposed by a court and the dividend a creditor would have been entitled to receive on any claim not disclosed to the trustee where such creditor had no notice of the bankruptcy. While this may not strictly be within the terms of our study, we suggest that consideration be given to the problem of the debtor against whom a fine or penalty has been imposed. While the debtor would not be released from such a debt through the bankruptcy process, we believe that consideration should be given to granting to some other agency, such as the Parole Board, the authority to make an order releasing him from such a debt. Someone who has committed a crime, perhaps early in life, who has been convicted and imprisoned and who has nothing to repay the fine or penalty imposed upon him should not have to face, for his lifetime, the burden of a debt that would, in effect, make it impossible for him to ever financially rehabilitate himself.

3.2.088 We recommend, in the second place, that the release of a debtor from his debts should be unconditional and take effect as of the date of bankruptcy. We further recommend that the release of debts should have the effect of extinguishing the liability of the debtor to pay the debt and that any express or implied promise to revive such liability be unenforceable.

3.2.089 We do not want to discourage a debtor from attempting to repay his debts after his discharge. Our only concern is that a debtor should not be put in the position where he may be tricked into paying a discharged debt. Whether or not a debtor wishes to make payments on account of a debt from which he has been released should be a voluntary decision on his part and the law should protect the debtor in this regard.

3.2.090 Past experience has shown that the temptation is great, on the part of some debtors, to abuse the bankruptcy process as an easy way to get rid of their legitimate creditors. While some debtors, in our modern society, can, not long after a bankruptcy, get again into the situation where bankruptcy is the only remedy to their problems, some procedure must be devised to protect creditors against the abuses of the unscrupulous ones. For these reasons, we recommend that the court should have the power to annul a release of debts resulting from a bankruptcy that has occurred less than five years after another bankruptcy, in any case where the debtor has, in effect, abused the bankruptcy process to the detriment of his creditors.

b / The Bankruptcy Bill (s-14)

214. (1) At any time after a person becomes a bankrupt, the administrator may, where he thinks fit, and shall, where he is so directed by the Superintendent, make or cause to be made an inquiry of the bankrupt as to
  (*a*) the causes and the circumstances of the bankruptcy;
  (*b*) any fact that may have contributed to the insolvency of the bankrupt;
  (*c*) the manner in which the bankrupt prior to the date of bankruptcy transferred any property or conducted a business; and
  (*d*) any matter for which an agent or former agent may be liable pursuant to section 189 or 190.

(2) When the administrator makes or causes an inquiry to be made under subsection 1, the bankrupt shall
  (*a*) attend, at such time and place as may be fixed, for examination under oath by the administrator; and
  (*b*) produce, on demand, any relevant record that he has in his possession.

215. Without limiting the generality of paragraph 214(1)(*a*), the administrator may inquire into all or any of the following:
  (*a*) the incurring by the bankrupt of an unjustifiable expense by the taking or continuing of a frivolous or vexatious proceeding;
  (*b*) any act done or omitted by the bankrupt with a view to defeating or delaying the creditors generally;
  (*c*) the commission by the bankrupt of an offence under this Act or any other Act where there are reasonable grounds for believing that such an offence has been committed, either before or after the date of bankruptcy, in connection with the property that vested or should have vested in the trustee;
  (*d*) the failure by the bankrupt to keep and preserve
    (i) the usual and proper records for a business of the type or size carried on by the bankrupt, or
    (ii) records that are sufficient to disclose the transactions and financial position of the business during the three years immediately preceding the date of bankruptcy;
  (*e*) the continuation of a business by the bankrupt where it was continued
    (i) by resorting to sales below cost to the detriment of the creditors, ruinous borrowings or similar acts, and
    (ii) in circumstances where bankruptcy could not reasonably be expected to be prevented;

(*f*) a material deficiency of assets of the bankrupt to meet the liabilities that is not satisfactorily accounted for;

(*g*) a material loss of specific assets of the bankrupt that is not satisfactorily accounted for;

(*h*) any gambling, wagering, gross incompetence or carelessness, extravagant expenses or rash speculation by the bankrupt that caused the bankruptcy or substantially aggravated his insolvency;

(*i*) the entering into or the carrying on of a business by the bankrupt with property obtained on credit where the credit was obtained by the use, in any manner whatever, of a materially false statement in writing respecting the financial condition of the business; and

(*j*) the likelihood that the bankrupt will acquire property or earn income in excess of that necessary to maintain a reasonable standard of living.

216. (1) Where an administrator thinks fit for the purposes of an inquiry pursuant to section 214, he may

(*a*) require any person to produce any record of the bankrupt that is relevant to the inquiry; or

(*b*) by appointment, examine under oath before the court or an officer thereof any person who the administrator thinks may have information that is revelant to the inquiry.

(2) A trustee who has information that he believes relates to any matter set out in sections 214 and 215 that is connected with a bankruptcy in which he is the trustee shall forthwith transmit the information to the administrator and may request the adminstrator to file, pursuant to subsection 217(1), a caveat against an individual who is a bankrupt, or pursuant to subsection 218(1), a caveat against any agent or former agent of a bankrupt.

(3) Where a creditor of an estate whose claim is not disallowed has information that he believes relates to any matter set out in sections 214 and 215 that is connected with the bankruptcy, he may transmit the information to the adminstrator and request him to investigate such matters and to file, pursuant to subsection 217(1), a caveat against an individual who is a bankrupt, or, pursuant to subsection 218(1), a caveat against any agent or former agent of a bankrupt.

217. (1) Where an administrator has reason to believe that any of the circumstances set out in section 215 apply to an individual who is a bankrupt, the administrator may, within six months from the date of bankruptcy, file a caveat in prescribed form with the Superintendent.

(2) Where an administrator files a caveat pursuant to subsection (1), he shall send a notice of the filing to the bankrupt at his latest known address.

218. (1) Where an administrator has reason to believe that

(*a*) any of the circumstances set out in section 215 (*a*) to (*i*) may be imputed to an agent or former agent of a bankrupt, or

(*b*) an agent or former agent of a bankrupt may be liable for any matter pursuant to section 189 or 190,

the administrator may, within one year from the date of bankruptcy of the bankrupt, file a caveat in prescribed form with the Superintendent.

(2) Where an administrator files a caveat pursuant to subsection (1), he shall send a notice of the filing to the agent or former agent at his latest known address.

219. (1) Where, after being requested to file a caveat pursuant to subsection 216(2) or (3), the administrator does not do so, the person who made the request may, after sending the prescribed notice to the administrator, apply to the court for an order directing the administrator to file a caveat as requested.

(2) Where, pursuant to subsection (1), a trustee applies to the court, he shall send notice of the application to the administrator at least forty days prior to the hearing of the application.

(3) Where, pursuant to subsection (1), a creditor applies to the court, he shall send notice of the application to the administrator and to the trustee at least forty days prior to the hearing of the application.

(4) Every person who, pursuant to subsection (1), applies to the court for an order directing the administrator to file a caveat in respect of a bankrupt or an agent or former agent of a bankrupt shall, at least forty days prior to the hearing of the application, serve a copy of the application on the bankrupt or agent or former agent.

(5) The administrator and the trustee of the estate shall, at least twenty days prior to the date of the hearing of an application pursuant to subsection (1), file with the court and serve on the bankrupt or the agent or former agent of the bankrupt, as the case may be,

(a) a notice to the effect that they have no representations to make; or

(b) a report as to

(i) the causes of the bankruptcy,

(ii) in the case of a bankrupt, any of the circumstances set out in section 215 that may be attributed to the bankrupt, and

(iii) in the case of an agent or former agent of a bankrupt, the circumstances set out in section 215 that may be imputed to the agent or former agent and any matter set out in section 189 or 190 for which the agent or former agent may be liable.

(6) For the purposes of this section, the report of the administrator and the trustee filed under subsection (5) is, in the absence of evidence to the contrary, proof of the statements contained therein.

(7) Where a bankrupt or an agent or former agent of a bankrupt intends to dispute any statement contained in an application filed in respect of him pursuant to subsection (1) or in a report filed in respect of him pursuant to subsection (5), he shall, at least ten days before the date of the hearing, send to the applicant, the administrator and the trustee a notice in writing specifying the statements that he proposes to dispute.

(8) After the hearing of an application filed pursuant to subsection (1), the court may order the administrator to file a caveat with the Superintendent if the court is of the opinion that

(a) in the case of a bankrupt, any of the circumstances set out in section 215 may be attributed to him; and

(b) in the case of an agent or former agent of a bankrupt, any of the circumstances set out in section 215 may be attributed to him or he may be liable in respect of any matter set out in section 189 or 190.

(9) Subject to subsection (10) and section 222, where the court makes an order pursuant to subsection (8), the caveat shall remain in force for a period of five years or such shorter period as the court may determine in its order.

(10) The court, on application, may shorten the period during which a caveat is to remain in force.

(11) No costs shall be awarded to a creditor on an application made pursuant to subsection (1).

220. Where, six months after an individual becomes a bankrupt,

(a) the administrator has not filed a caveat pursuant to subsection 217(1),

(b) the court has not ordered the filing of a caveat pursuant to paragraph 219(8)(a), and

(c) no application under subsection 219(1) is pending before the court,
the administrator shall, on application of the individual, issue a certificate of discharge.

(2) When the period during which a caveat in respect of an individual is to remain in force expires, the administrator shall, on application of the individual, issue a certificate of discharge.

221. (1) Where a caveat is filed pursuant to subsection 217(1), 218(1) or 219(8), the person in respect of whom the caveat was filed may apply to the court for a certificate of discharge.

(2) Where, pursuant to subsection (1), a person in respect of whom a caveat was filed applies for a certificate of discharge, he shall give the administrator, the trustee and any creditor who appeared on an application under subsection 219(1) notice of the application at least forty days prior to the hearing thereof and the administrator shall, at least twenty days prior to the hearing, file with the court and serve on the applicant for the certificate

(*a*) a notice to the effect that he has no representations to make; or

(*b*) a report as to

    (i) the causes of the bankruptcy,

    (ii) in the case of a bankrupt, any of the circumstances set out in section 215 that may be attributed to the bankrupt, and

    (iii) in the case of an agent or former agent of a bankrupt, the circumstances set out in section 215 that may be attributed to the agent or former agent and any matter set out in section 189 or 190 for which the agent or former agent may be liable.

(3) For the purposes of this section, the report of the administrator filed under subsection (2) is, in the absence of evidence to the contrary, proof of the statements contained therein.

(4) Where an applicant for a certificate of discharge intends to dispute any statement contained in the report of the administrator filed under subsection (2), the applicant shall, at least ten days before the date of the hearing, send a notice in writing to the administrator specifying the statements that he proposes to dispute.

(5) At the hearing of an application for a certificate of discharge under this section

(*a*) the administrator or a creditor, in person or through his representative or counsel, may

    (i) examine the bankrupt or any agent or former agent of the bankrupt as to any matter set out or any material omission in the report filed with the court pursuant to subsection (2),

    (ii) rebut any evidence that is submitted against the report, and

    (iii) present any submission in support of the report;

(*b*) the applicant for the certificate shall be given full opportunity to be heard; and

(*c*) the court may consider any further evidence or material that it thinks relevant.

222. Where a bankrupt or an agent or former agent of a bankrupt applies to the court for a certificate of discharge, the court may

(*a*) order the administrator to issue the certificate if the court is of the opinion that

    (i) in the case of a bankrupt, none of the circumstances set out in section 215 may be attributed, in a material way, to him, or

    (ii) in the case of an agent or former agent of a bankrupt, none of the circumstances set out in section 215 may be attributed in a material way, to him and he is not liable in respect of any matter set out in section 189 or 190; or

(*b*) shorten the period during which a caveat issued in respect of the bankrupt, agent or former agent is to remain in force.

223. A certificate of discharge shall be in prescribed form.

231. (1) An individual who is a bankrupt ceases to be a bankrupt when

(*a*) six months have elapsed from the date of bankruptcy and the administrator has not filed a caveat pursuant to section 217;

(*b*) the administrator issues a certificate pursuant to a court order made under section 222 or pursuant to section 232;

(*c*) the bankruptcy order is annulled pursuant to subsection 86(1) or 117(6) or section 392;

(*d*) a caveat has been filed and five years have elapsed from the date of bankruptcy; or (*e*) where the court, pursuant to subsection 219(9) or (10) or section 222, specifies a shorter period than five years, such shorter period has elapsed.

(2) A corporation that is a bankrupt ceases to be a bankrupt when

(*a*) the administrator issues a certificate pursuant to section 232; or

(*b*) the bankruptcy order is annulled pursuant to subsection 117(6) or section 392.

(3) Where a caveat is filed in respect of an agent or former agent of a bankrupt, the caveat ceases to have any effect when

(*a*) the administrator issues a certificate pursuant to section 232 in respect of the bankrupt for whom the agent or former agent acted as agent;

(*b*) the court annuls the bankruptcy order in respect of the bankrupt for whom the agent or former agent acted as agent;

(*c*) the administrator issues a certificate pursuant to a court order made under section 222;

(*d*) five years have elapsed from the date of bankruptcy; or

(*e*) where the court, pursuant to subsection 219(9) or (10) or section 222 specifies a shorter period than five years, such shorter period has elapsed.

232. When all claims admitted in a bankruptcy are fully paid, the administrator shall, on application of any interested person, issue a certificate to that effect.

233. Where a person ceases to be a bankrupt, any statutory disqualification or incapacity by reason of the bankruptcy ceases.

234. Where a certificate of discharge under this Act is tendered by or on behalf of a debtor to the sheriff, prothonotary, bailiff or other officer in charge of issuing or executing writs of execution or seizure, such persons shall release to the debtor or other person tendering the certificate of discharge any writ of seizure or execution issued against the debtor or his property prior to the date of his bankruptcy.

c / *Re Buell* (1954), 35 C.B.R. 53 (S.C.O.)

SMILY J.: This is an application for the discharge of the debtor. It is opposed by the Minister of Highways for the Province of Ontario. The report of the trustee shows that the debtor made an assignment for the general benefit of his creditors on April 28, 1954, and that in his statement of affairs the debtor showed assets valued at $19.71, consisting of cash on hand of $9.71 and realty of $10. The realty consisted of some vacant land in the Province of Prince Edward Island in which the debtor appeared to have an equity, and from which the trustee realized $25. The total amount shown in the trustee's report as realized from the assets of the debtor was $134.71, which included $100 received as retainer on the trustee's fees. The liabilities of the debtor were shown in the statement of affairs as $4,943.87 to unsecured creditors, the same being Chester and Irene Carr, with a claim of $4,243.87, and Donald A. Flock with a claim of $700. The claim of the Carrs is for the amount of a judgment rendered in The Supreme Court of Ontario on January 20, 1954, against the debtor for damages arising out of a motor car accident, and costs. The claim of Mr. Flock is apparently for his services as solicitor in the proceedings in which the judgment was rendered as aforesaid.

At the time of the assignment the debtor was employed at hourly wages amounting to approximately $55 a week. Subsequent to the judgment and prior to the assignment he had an equity in a motor car which he sold for $100. The debtor is 27 years of age and married; he has no family. Nothing was paid by the debtor on account of the judgment, except by way of a set-off for the amount which he obtained under the judgment for divided negligence, amounting to $190, and on May 13, 1954, an order was made under the provisions of *The Highway Traffic Act*, R.S.O.

1950, c 167, for payment of the judgment by the Minister of Highways out of the unsatisfied judgment fund, and pursuant to the provisions of that Act the judgment was assigned to the Minister of Highways on May 18, 1954.

Counsel for the debtor objected to the Minister's being represented on the hearing of the application for discharge, on the ground that the Minister of Highways was not a 'creditor' within the meaning of *The Bankruptcy Act*, R.S.C. 1952, c 14. I do not agree with this contention, but at any rate counsel for the Minister of Highways could be heard as *amicus curiae*.

There is no question but that the debtor made his assignment for the purpose of getting rid of the judgment against him, having apparently in view that if this was done by an unconditional discharge under *The Bankruptcy Act* and a certificate granted under s 132 to the effect that the bankruptcy was caused by misfortune, without any misconduct on his part, he might be able to have his driver's licence and right to have a motor vehicle permit restored. His driver's licence had been cancelled under the provisions of *The Highway Traffic Act* as a result of his failure to pay the judgment mentioned. If this were so, the result, of course, would be to nullify the effect of the provisions of *The Highway Traffic Act*.

Whether or not this would be a proper ground to refuse the discharge, I am of the opinion, as I said in *Re Palach*, 33 C.B.R. 227, [1953] O.W.N. 563, [1953] 4 D.L.R. 79, 1953. Can. Abr. 42, that *The Bankruptcy Act* was never intended to enable a judgment debtor promptly to get rid of a judgment for damages, and, I might add, with no other purpose to serve than the convenience and comfort of the debtor. It is not suggested that lack of a driver's licence or motor vehicle permit would harass or prevent or even hinder him from earning a livelihood. However, to clear up any misunderstanding there might be of what was said in the *Palach* case, let me state here that I did not intend to imply that *The Bankruptcy Act* was not available to an insolvent person who was not engaged in business. This is indicated in that judgment where I said that the dismissal of the application for discharge would be without prejudice to a further application 'if it should happen that the debtors are, or one of them is, desirous of going into business, or some other reason arises to justify reconsideration under *The Bankruptcy Act*'.

I think it is a fair statement to say that originally bankruptcy and insolvency legislation was designed to enable the assets of an honest debtor to be equitably distributed among his creditors, and to enable him to have a livelihood, in business or otherwise, which he might have difficulty in doing unless he was freed of the burden of his debts, and, with respect to a debtor who was not engaged in business but who had been imprisoned for non-payment of his debts, that he might be released from imprisonment. Bankruptcy laws are now of wider application and provide for the right of persons who are not engaged in business to make assignments of their property to trustees for distribution amongst their creditors and for discharge from further liability with respect to their debts, subject of course, to certain rules and conditions. But, as has been said, *The Bankruptcy Act* should not be regarded as a clearing-house for the liquidation of debts solely, irrespective of the circumstances in which they were incurred. As to the position of the debtor, if it is a case of a person being so weighed down by his debts as to be incapable of properly earning a living or of performing the ordinary duties of citizenship, including the support of a wife and family, that is one thing; but where the only object to be served is the comfort and convenience of the debtor and his being freed from the necessity for using his earning-capacity or any property he may acquire or be able to acquire in the future for the discharge or partial discharge of his debts, it is quite another.

It appears from the examination of the debtor as a judgment debtor that he has some prospects of receiving an inheritance from his mother. In *In re Jobin* (1932), 13 C.B.R. 532, 3 Can. Abr. 1337, Sedgewick J. said:

... it is stated that the debtor may reasonably expect benefit from her father as his heir or as a devisee under his will.

The bankrupt does not desire or intend to go into business again, but she desires to be free to take whatever benefit might accrue to her from her father or his estate.

I see no reason why the Court should do anything to assist her in receiving money and being free to spend that money for herself and not in payment of her just debts.

Of course the debtor may not receive this inheritance, but I think some further time should elapse and some other circumstance should be shown before it can be said that it would be unreasonable to expect that any payment could be made by the debtor on this debt, either out of earnings or out of after-acquired property, or that the necessities of the case justified the giving of consideration to the granting of a conditional or absolute discharge. I do not think it is desirable at this time to make an order for periodical payments on account of the judgment debt. The trustee's report states that the debtor was at the date of the report unemployed, and it would be difficult to determine what amounts should be paid. In this connection it may be noted that the debtor did not take advantage of the provisions of s 90 of *The Highway Traffic Act* by applying for the privilege of paying the judgment in instalments.

Having regard to the matters to which I have already referred, I think it preferable that the application for discharge should be dismissed, without prejudice to a further application if the circumstances make it reasonable that the question of a discharge, conditional or absolute, be reconsidered.

The application will accordingly be dismissed.

d / *Re Palach and Palach*, [1955] 4 D.L.R. 204 (S.C.O.)

SMILY, J. (orally): This matter has given me considerable concern. As counsel for the Minister of Highways has intimated, there are, no doubt, many situations of this kind, where there are judgments against people of little or no means, which would make it difficult for them to pay the judgments, although in many cases they could probably make some payments on account, but that situation can be unsatisfactory. In *Re Shackleton, Ex p. Shackleton* (1889), 6 Morr. 304 at pp 307–8, Cave J. said on a similar application, or at least when settling the question of imposing a condition on a debtor before granting discharge: 'In deciding that question the Court ought to have regard to public morality and to the interests of the public generally, and unless the Court finds a man in receipt of income derived from his earnings or otherwise which is more than sufficient to keep his family in the enjoyment of the ordinary necessities of life according to their station, or unless it is satisfied that he is likely to succeed to property, it is not a wise thing to grant an order subject to a condition affecting after-acquired property. The Court ought to be careful to see it does not by a condition of that sort do away with the motive which a man has for exertion to work in his calling which is a good thing for the public interest generally. If such a burden is put on a man that he can have no hope of bettering his position he will not make the effort, and few men are more easily discouraged than that class of men who become bankrupt.'

Whether what he said would apply entirely to conditions at the present time, I think there is something to it, and it is worthy of consideration. On the other hand, as I have said in *Re Buell*, [1955], 4 D.L.R. 137, O.W.N. 421 the *Bankruptcy Act*, R.S.C. 1952, c 14, should not be regarded solely as a clearing-house for the liquidation of debts, irrespective of the circumstances in which they were incurred.

As to the position of the debtor, if it is a case of a person being so weighed down by debts as to become unable to earn a living or perform the ordinary duties of citizenship, including the support of a wife and family, that is one thing, but where the only object to be served is the comfort and convenience of the debtor and his being freed from the necessity of using his own capacity or any property he may acquire or may be able to acquire in future for the discharge or partial discharge of his debts it is quite another. In *Re Buell, supra*, it appeared that there was the possibility of the debtor's inheriting property from his mother, but that might not take place until some time in the distant future.

As I say, the matter has given me considerable concern because of the number of cases that no doubt exist, since there might be a tendency of debtors to consider that they were entitled to obtain a discharge of a judgment against them for damages in motor car cases, or in other cases, as a matter of course, simply by going through bankruptcy proceedings *pro forma*, which would not be a satisfactory condition of affairs. Such debtors would not feel that there was any necessity for them to make the effort to make some payment on the judgment, but on the other hand a situation may arise from time to time where a debtor is prevented by such a judgment from properly earning his living or if not prevented, then, in the spirit of the case to which I have referred, discouraged from working to earn his living and provide for his family and from performing the ordinary duties of citizenship, and matters of that nature, such as supporting a wife and family.

I think that every such case must be dealt with on its own merits, and cannot be taken as a general pattern other than what I have enunciated in my previous judgments – that the *Bankruptcy Act* must not be considered to be a clearing-house solely for the liquidation of debts.

Now in this case material has been filed to indicate that this debtor at the present time is making a relatively small weekly wage amounting to $21.60. He has a wife and three children. It would seem obvious that with that wage he would not be able to provide properly for his wife and children and have anything left over to pay on this judgment. He may have a larger wage in the spring, but it is not very encouraging for a man, an ordinary labourer, to have to liquidate or try to liquidate a judgment of such an amount by payments from what money he can spare from his wages after providing properly for his wife and children. He has an opportunity to go into farming. I think farming in this country is a very desirable and essential occupation. It is well known that there is tendency for persons to leave the farm and come to the city for work, and the occupation of farming is not too popular. I think that it could almost be said that anything that would encourage the taking up of farming is desirable, and it may be that if this debtor is able to carry out this plan he will be successful in it and able to make proper provision for his wife and family and also possibly to do something toward this obligation, which is undoubtedly an obligation.

I have in mind that this might be an appropriate case in which to make an order on condition, but the condition must be such as not to discourage this debtor from carrying out the condition and from performing useful labour and looking after the duties of citizenship, to use the words previously referred to, including the proper provision for his wife and family. I, therefore, propose to make an order of discharge on condition that the debtor will consent to a judgment for $1,000 in favour of this judgment creditor, and that execution is not to issue or other proceedings to be taken under the judgment without leave of the Court. While counsel for the Minister of Highways has indicated that it is not the practice to garnishee wages, and I am quite sure that the Department would not do anything unduly embarrassing to this debtor, yet I think that in circumstances of this kind some protection should be given to the debtor so that he will not be subject to any process until he has had an opportunity of establishing himself and making some reasonable provision for taking care of this judgment. If it is found that even the judgment for $1,000 will prevent him from carrying out his duties of citizenship, I repeat those words, a

further application can be made, but I would think that would not be too difficult or hard a condition to be imposed. The order should be made in each of these applications, judgment was obtained against both Mr. and Mrs. Palach.
Order for conditional discharge.

In the following case, as a condition of discharge, the Court ordered the bankrupt to pay one-half of an outstanding judgment. His principal creditor had obtained the judgment against him for injuries caused by the wilful and wanton misconduct of the bankrupt. The Court would not allow the bankrupt to use his financial predicament as a device for avoiding his obligations.

e / *Kozack* v *Richter* (1973), 36 D.L.R. (3d) 612 (S.C.C.)

PIGEON, J.: This is an appeal, by special leave of this Court, from a judgment of the Court of Appeal of Saskatchewan varying the order made by a Judge of the Court of Queen's Bench on respondent's application for discharge under the *Bankruptcy Act*, R.S.C. 1970, C B-3. This order has suspended the discharge for a period of three months only. In the Court of Appeal, it was directed that respondent be required to consent to judgement being entered against him in the sum of $1,800 payable without interest by monthly payments of $50 starting February 1, 1970.

Respondent's debt towards the appellant arises out of an automobile accident. She was a gratuitous passenger in his car when she suffered serious head injuries in a collision with a train at a grade crossing in the City of Regina. Red lights were flashing and a warning bell was ringing and respondent was found fully responsible by reason of 'wilful and wanton misconduct'. Damages were assessed by MacPherson, J., at $12,909.03 plus costs taxed at $1,194. Respondent's appeal from this judgment was unanimously dismissed. Thereupon, he made an assignment under the *Bankruptcy Act* and, in due course, applied for discharge.

The net result of the order appealed from is obviously that the appellant will recover nothing. With respect, I cannot agree that this is in conformity with the proper principles to be applied in the exercise of the discretion vested in the Courts by the provisions of the *Bankruptcy Act* respecting discharge.

In the present case, respondent's bankruptcy was precipitated by his condemnation to pay damages to the appellant. This being due to a finding of 'wilful and wanton misconduct' on his part, certainly his financial predicament cannot be said to have arisen 'from circumstances for which he cannot justly be held responsible'. The Courts below did not ignore this provision. However, the sanction meted out in the first instance was purely nominal. In the Court of Appeal, respondent was in effect ordered to make payments that would hardly cover more than appellant's costs in the trial Court and in the Court of Appeal. Although respondent is a wage-earner with a large family in very modest circumstances, I cannot agree that the proper application of the provisions above quoted should result in a plaintiff making no recovery for personal injuries caused by gross negligence. It would mean that motorists in respondent's situation would be able to tell such a claimant: 'There is no use suing me, if you lose you will have to pay the costs, if you win I will make an assignment in bankruptcy and you will get nothing.'

Counsel for the appellant has referred us to a number of cases dealing with analogous situations on applications for discharge. Among recent cases, the following may be noted: *Rice and Rice* v *Copeland et al.* (1965), 51 D.L.R. (2d) 147, 51 W.W.R. 227, 7 C.B.R. (N.S.) 288, in which the bankruptcy was similarly precipitated by a claim for damages arising out of a car

accident which was said to be due to driving in an intoxicated condition. Dickson J. (as he then
was), ordered the bankrupts to pay as a condition of their discharge 25% of their unsecured
liabilities. He said at pp 151–2:

In *Re McIntosh* (1958), 16 D.L.R. (2d) 207, 26 W.W.R. 541, 37 C.B.R. 212, Williams, C.J.Q.B.,
agreed with the judgment of Smily, J., in *Re Buell*, [1955] 4 D.L.R. 137, [1955] O.W.N. 421, 35
C.B.R. 53, that although the *Bankruptcy Act* is available to an insolvent not engaged in business,
the Act was never intended to enable a judgment debtor to get rid of a judgment for damages and
with no other purpose to serve than the convenience and comfort of the debtor.

In *Re Sederoff v Vigneault* (1942), 23 C.B.R. 228, [1942] 1 Que. K.B. 44, the debtor had gone
into bankruptcy to escape payment of a judgment in damages arising out of an automobile
collision. The bankruptcy Judge, in the exercise of his discretion, suspended the discharge until
the debtor had paid 50 cents in the dollar, on the amount of his unsecured liabilities. The Court of
Appeal refused to interfere.

In the present case, I would not increase the amount of the monthly payments fixed by the
Court of Appeal, but I would increase the sum to be paid to approximate 50% of the total debt to
the appellant without interest.

For those reasons, I would allow the appeal with costs and vary the judgment of the Court of
Appeal by increasing to $7,200 plus the costs in this Court, the amount of the judgment to be
satisfied by the respondent as a condition of his discharge.
Appeal allowed.

[Martland, Ritchie and Spence JJ concurred. Abbot J dissented on the ground that the judicial
discretion exercised by the Courts below was not unreasonable.]

f / *Re Bowerman* (1966), 9 C.B.R. (N.S.) 261 (S.C.O.)

21st December 1966. McDermott J.: This was an application by the bankrupt, Derek John
Bowerman, for discharge from bankruptcy, originally heard in part on 29th November 1966,
when the same counsel and creditor were present, and on that date adjourned to 15th December
1966 for the purpose of the bankrupt producing further financial statements as to income,
business expenditure, and costs of living for a 3 month period ending 30th November 1966, to be
presented to the Court.

At the conclusion of the submissions made in this matter, I indicated that judgment would be
given fairly early in the forthcoming week, with very little in the way of reasons, as the motion
was well and thoroughly argued and presented in every facet by all counsel present and the one
creditor appearing in person.

In the result, the judgment of the Court is that, whereas proof has been made of the following
facts under s 130 of the Bankruptcy Act, namely:

'(*c*) the bankrupt has continued to [contract liabilities] after knowing himself to be insolvent;

'(*e*) the bankrupt has brought on, contributed to, his bankruptcy by rash and hazardous
speculations …

'(*m*) the bankrupt has failed to perform [one of] the duties imposed on him under this Act' in
that he failed to deliver all his property to the trustee,

The bankrupt's discharge be suspended for nine months and that he be discharged on and
from 21st September 1967, subject to the following conditions:

The bankrupt shall pay the sum of $500 per month to the trustee for the general benefit of the creditors, for a period of 48 months, the first payment to be made on 1st January 1967.

The figures hereinafter outlined are not the exact figures given to the Court but are rounded to generally the amount of money owing to creditors who have proven, or are moneys already collected by the trustee or to be collected.

The amount owing to the preferred creditor, Department of National Revenue, for income tax as at the date of bankruptcy, was approximately $25,400; the amounts owing to the main unsecured creditors were approximately:

Dr. Lou Kane $11,000
The Toronto-Dominion Bank $ 4,200
Larry William Beaupre $25,000

In addition to this are the costs of the general administration of the estate by the trustee, including legal expenses and other disbursements.

It appears from statements presented to the Court on behalf of the bankrupt that the expected amount of gross income of the bankrupt, who is a physician, an eye specialist, is $5,400 per month, against which must be charged average monthly business expenses of about $1,900, and all other living expenses consisting of income tax, maintenance of first wife and two children, and maintenance of present wife, food, rent, clothing, premiums on adequate life insurance, public utilities for living quarters, medical and dental expense, pension fund contribution, transportation and other normal expenditures, being the miscellaneous requirements of a married man in the medical profession, who must maintain a position equivalent to his qualifications and the expectations of his patients; all of which run without much doubt, to approximately $3,000 per month.

Deducting these outlays from his gross income, would leave about $500 per month to enable the trustee to make some adequate distribution in favour of ordinary creditors, in addition to the one preferred creditor, namely, The Department of National Revenue to which there is owing as a proved claim approximately $25,400.

The trustee outlined in his report that he had realized some $11,228 including the cash surrender value of the insurance carried by the bankrupt, and including quite substantial accounts receivable. To this there is the expectation of adding, eventually, a half share in the equity of a parcel of real estate in England, which is mortgaged, and in which the total equity is about $9,000 Canadian funds, or say $4,000 for a one-half interest, this being the property in which the former wife of the bankrupt and his two infant children reside.

Taken into consideration also, is the possible prosecution by The Toronto-Dominion Bank against the bankrupt for fraud in connection with his original application for a loan, unsecured, of some $8,700 against which the bankrupt has repaid about $4,500 at the date of bankruptcy.

The debt of $11,000 owing to Dr. Lou Kane is the balance owing on the purchase of the medical practice in Oshawa, Ontario, originally purchased at about $42,000, which might well be considered an inflated value. The indebtedness of Larry William Beaupre arose out of a most intricate, strange, risky stock-purchasing venture, entered into by the bankrupt and the creditor, which resulted eventually in no gain or profit, but in a judgment being given to the creditor (who incidentally if the scheme had worked out was in a position to make about 33% on his investment of cash, within a space of one year), after the debtor's consent, when judgment was entered into in the amount of approximately $25,000, which no doubt hastened the act of the bankruptcy in filing an assignment in bankruptcy some ten days later.

Looking at the present recovery by the trustee, the possible prosecution against the bankrupt, and the most substantial income received now by the bankrupt in a gross figure, and taking from it the necessary outlays referred to, it does not appear that it would cripple the bankrupt in being required to pay $500 per month to the trustee, for a period of 4 years, to enable some distribution eventually to be made to the ordinary creditors, in addition to full payment of the preferred creditor.

The bankrupt doctor is 38 years of age, has had little vacation in recent years, and has been loaded with problems financial, domestic and otherwise, which perhaps have aged him ten years more than would be the case if he had not become so entangled in so many unhappy contracts.

However, I visualize that if these moneys are paid, including the first payment of $500 being made on 1st January 1967, the full preferred claim for income tax will be taken care of before long, and if the real estate in England is eventually realized upon there may be some recovery in the neighbourhood of 30 cents to 40 cents on the dollar (taking into consideration the present realization by the trustee) for distribution amongst the ordinary creditors.

The costs of the trustee and of the creditors The Toronto-Dominion Bank and The Department of National Revenue shall all be paid out of the moneys to be received from the monthly payments to be paid by the bankrupt, those of the trustee on a solicitor and client basis, and those of the two creditors represented on this application on a party and party basis.

COMMENT

When deciding as to whether a discharge of a bankrupt should be granted subject to a condition that he has to make certain payments for the benefit of his creditors, the general principle seems to be that any condition which the Court imposes should not be oppressive or interfere with the debtor maintaining his family and himself in accordance with their requirements and necessities, having regard to their station in life. On the other hand, the Court cannot entirely ignore the rights of the creditors and the obligation of the debtor to them. (See *In re Lambert* (1962), 3 C.B.R. (N.S.) 216, 3 Can. Abr. (2nd) 3352).

It would seem that the principles which guide the Court when ordering payments to the trustee, for the benefit of the creditors, as a condition of the discharge of the bankrupt, are similar to those applicable to payments to be made by the debtor to his creditors, out of his salary, while he is in bankruptcy. However, the decision which faces the Court in ordering a conditional discharge is far more difficult than when ordering payments out of after-acquired property during bankruptcy. In the latter case it can be established how much the debtor earns and what he needs for the support of himself and his family, but, after some bankrupts obtain their discharge, they may find themselves suddenly in receipt of a higher income than during bankruptcy – a fact which is, of course, unknown to the Court when the order for the conditional discharge is being made. In such a case, an application can be made by the trustee pursuant to the provisions of s 144(5) of the Bankruptcy Act to vary the former order of conditional discharge. On the other hand, if the debtor suffers a financial set-back after his discharge from bankruptcy, he may likewise apply, under s 144(5) of the Act to have the order varied.

In the instant case the debtor had a very large income and the Court felt that, even after making payments for the maintenance of his family and himself and payment of income tax, there would be at least $500 per month available for the benefit of his creditors. Accordingly, an order was made providing for the payment by the debtor to the trustee, for the benefit of the creditors of such a sum of money 'which would not cripple the bankrupt'.

See *Re Kaplan* (1975), 19 C.B.R. (N.S.) 287 (S.C.O.), where a conditional discharge was given to a lawyer in order that he could pay off his debts in a more effective fashion by practicing law.

Before the Court will make an order requiring the bankrupt to make payments to his creditors on a discharge, the Court must be satisfied that the bankrupt has sufficient earnings properly to maintain himself and his family and leave a surplus for creditors. *Re Rainville* (1972), 17 C.B.R. (N.S.) 99 (S.C.O.) is a recent case reiterating this well-settled judicial dictum. However, where the debts owed are so large that any payments made by the bankrupt could not be of any conceivable use to the creditors he should not be required, as a condition for his discharge, to make payments to his creditors: *Re Wortsman* (1972), 17 C.B.R. (N.S.) 209 (S.C.O.).

Where a husband and wife owe joint debts and they both work to support the family, orders against their respective salaries should not be made unless it is established that their combined salaries are in excess of what is needed for the support of themselves and their family. The need should be measured in accordance with what is reasonable in the circumstances and the status of life the family occupies: *Re Sweitzer and Sweitzer* (1974), 19 C.B.R. (N.S.) 85 (Sask. Q.B.).

g / *Re Provost* (1974), 19 C.B.R. (N.S.) 95 (Sask. Q.B.), discusses the principles which the court considers in an application for an absolute discharge. The applicant was a young school teacher. Most of his liabilities were the result of loans made to him to enable him to pay for tuition and other necessary expenses while attending university. He claimed that he was entitled to a discharge because he needed all of his salary to maintain himself and his family. Bayda J was not sympathetic to his plight:

Perhaps the most salient fact which emerges from the circumstances before me relates to the reason for the granting of the loans by the two credit unions. I have not been called upon to decide whether a loan granted by a financial institution to pay the borrower's living expenses while attending a university as well as other costs associated with gaining an education constitutes a 'debt or liability for goods supplied as necessaries of life' within the meaning of s 148(1)(*g*) of the Act, and I do not do so. I do think, however, that such a loan ranks on a moral level as high as a debt for necessaries or alimony, a liability under a maintenance or affiliation order, and a debt arising out of fraud or dishonesty – in short, those classes of debts and liabilities in respect of which an order of discharge does not (by the operation of s 148(1) of the Act) release the bankrupt. It strikes me as being grossly unfair for a person to be able to go to a financial institution and say 'I have no assets but take a chance on me anyway and lend me some money for my education; when I have my new professional status (my new "asset") I will pay you back out of earnings' and then on getting his education says to his creditor, with impunity, 'I am not making as much money as I expected and I am not able to comfortably pay you now, so, I am asking you to forego the debt and if you do not, I will make an assignment in bankruptcy and cancel it out'. Judicial approbation of such an attitude could result in a serious undermining of the current system of student loans.

Is there anything in the applicant's present circumstances which makes it just for him to take this position? He is a healthy 30-year-old man, with a small family. He earns a gross monthly salary of $825.83, an amount which is reputedly higher than the income received by the average Canadian family and practically $3,000 more than that received by the average Saskatchewan family. From his salary, there is deducted $50.22 superannuation and $138 for income tax (a portion of which may be refundable) and approximately $18 for STF dues, unemployment insurance fees and similar items. He nets $620.12 per month. In his affidavit he deposes that this entire amount is expended for support and maintenance of himself and his family 'on a modest scale'. I do not question the truthfulness of this statement but I find it difficult to accept that a person earning as much as this applicant is not in a position to assume any debt load whatever. To grant the applicant an absolute discharge would be to cater to his convenience and comfort and nothing more. To expunge his debts with no further effort from him would be in these circumstances unjust.

h / In *Re Hawkins* (1977) 23 C.B.R. (N.S.) 78 (S.C.O.), Ferron, Registrar was extremely critical of the statements contained in the bankrupt's affidavit of earnings. As a measure of the court's disapproval of the bankrupt's behaviour and lack of responsibility in compiling the affidavit, the discharge was suspended for a three-year period:

There is an item in the statement annexed to the affidavit indicating that the bankrupt spends $126 each month for 'social gifts and Christmas gifts'. Now that indicates that the bankrupt pours out some $1,500 a year on gifts. This is a generous and prodigious sum when one considers that the trustee was not able to recover any assets whatsoever in the bankrupt's estate and that the bankrupt left in his wake $10,753.63 in debts. As I will indicate later in these reasons, the debtor will have to extend his bounty of gifts to his creditors.

There appears in the bankrupt's affidavit an item for prescriptions, and the bankrupt deposes that he pays $25 a month for the preparation of prescriptions. The amount is not significant but the item points up the extent of the lack of preparation for the hearing and the negligence in the preparation of the affidavit. A cursory glance at the bundle of cheques and drugstore receipts indicates that very few of the items mentioned in the receipts have anything to do with doctor's prescriptions. Several of the receipts clearly indicate that the charge is made for cigarettes. Such is an indication of the time and effort expended in the preparation of this matter on the application to this court.

7 WHAT IS NOT COVERED BY A DISCHARGE

a / Tassé Report, p 124

3.2.081 *Discharge of the Debtor and Release of Debts:* We discuss *infra*, in 3.2.091 et seq., at some length, the concept of the status of a bankrupt. For the purpose of the discussion here, it is sufficient to point out that under the present Act a bankrupt is not entitled to a discharge as of right. The court may either grant or refuse an absolute order of discharge, suspend the operation of the order or grant it subject to terms or conditions.

3.2.082 The effect of the discharge is to release the bankrupt of all claims provable in his bankruptcy, except:

A a fine or penalty imposed by a court or a debt arising out of a recognizance or bail bond;

B any debt or liability for alimony;

C any debt under a maintenance or affiliation order or under an agreement for maintenance and support of a spouse or child living apart from the bankrupt;

D any debt arising out of fraud, embezzlement, misappropriation or defalcation while the bankrupt was acting in a fiduciary capacity;

E any debt or liability for obtaining property by false pretenses or fraudulent misrepresentation;

F liability for the dividend that a creditor would have been entitled to receive on any provable claim not disclosed to the trustee, unless such creditor had notice or knowledge of the bankruptcy and failed to take reasonable action to prove his claim; or

G any debt or liability for goods supplied as necessaries of life, the court having power to make such order for payment thereof as it deems just or expedient.

3.2.083 The effect of not releasing the bankrupt from certain debts on discharge is to give a privileged position to the creditors concerned. They have the right to share in the property of the debtor, at the date of his bankruptcy, as well as the right to claim against the property he acquires after his discharge.

b / The Bankruptcy Bill (s-14)

244. (1) Notwithstanding anything in this Act, no claim is admissible for, and no bankrupt or person who makes an arrangement is released from,
   (*a*) a fine or penalty imposed by any court;
   (*b*) a debt arising out of a recognizance or bail bond; or
   (*c*) a liability to pay maintenance and support in respect of another person for a period subsequent to the date of bankruptcy or the filing of the proposed arrangement.
   (2) Notwithstanding anything in this Act, a claim is admissible for, but no bankrupt or person who makes an arrangement is released from, any debt arising out of fraud where the debtor has been convicted of such fraud under the *Criminal Code*.

c / *Seaboard Securities Canadian Ltd.* v *Durand et ux.* (1969), 13 C.B.R. (N.S.) 276 (Sask. Dist. Ct.)

5th June 1969. McCLELLAND D.C.J. The plaintiff sues the defendants, who are husband and wife, to recover the balance owing on a promissory note dated 7th January 1966.

The facts are not seriously in dispute. The promissory note sued on was in the principal sum of $1,539.48, and was to cover a present advance, less an insurance premium, and a balance of a little over $1,000 owing on a previous note. The previous note in turn covered two earlier loans on which cash had been advanced. Other than accrued interest and insurance premiums, no so-called 'service charges' or advance interest was included in the amount of the promissory note sued on.

While the present manager of the plaintiff company was not in charge when the loans recited above were made, there is no doubt as to the correctness of his evidence. The portion of the male defendant's examination for discovery entered by the plaintiff makes it clear that this defendant understood the transaction and does not dispute the amount or terms of the promissory note.

The male defendant made an assignment in bankruptcy on 9th January 1967, and the trustee in the said bankruptcy was discharged on 10th July 1967. Apparently no conditions had been attached to the male defendant's discharge.

It is clear from the questions and answers of the male defendant in his examination for discovery entered as evidence that when the male defendant made application for the loan covered by the promissory note in question, he gave only a partially correct statement of his other indebtedness. He declared three accounts totalling about $1,980 but concealed the existence of at least four other accounts totalling some $2,800. He admitted that he did not disclose these debts because he feared that his loan application might not be approved if the existence of these debts were known. He had at first endeavoured to pass off his deception as a more or less innocent act, not being a statement under oath, and a deception which he believed could easily have been discovered had the plaintiff troubled to make a thorough investigation. The deception had been brought to light in his examination before the trustee in bankruptcy, but there is no evidence that it was called to the attention of Sirois J. who granted the order for discharge.

Counsel for the male defendant argues that the plaintiff's claim having been included in the bankrupt's liabilities, and the bankrupt having been discharged by the Bankruptcy Court, this Court has no jurisdiction to deal with the matter.

Section 135(1) (*e*) of the Bankruptcy Act, R.S.C. 1952, c 14, reads as follows:

135. (1) An order of discharge does not release the bankrupt from ...

(*e*) any debt or liability for obtaining property by false pretences or fraudulent misrepresentation.

Counsel for the plaintiff quoted an abundance of cases to show that s 135 applies to allow actions to be brought against the bankrupt after his discharge: See *Caron* v *Household Finance Corpn. of Can.*, [1960] Que. S.C. 317, 37 C.B.R. 210; *Beneficial Finance* v *Durward* (1961), 2 C.B.R. (N.S.) 173; *Beneficial Finance Corpn.* v *Anderson*, [1964] 1 O.R. 260, 5 C.B.R. (N.S.) 177. Other reported and unreported cases to the same point were also cited. In addition, counsel for the plaintiff cited *Rice* v *Copeland* (1965), 51 W.W.R. 227, 7 C.B.R. (N.S.) 288, a decision of the Queen's Bench of Manitoba in Bankruptcy, wherein Dickson J. is quoted as follows at p 230:

Household Finance Corporation of Canada filed notice of intention to oppose the application of the bankrupts for discharge on the ground that the moneys obtained by Rice from Household Finance on or about July 12, 1963, were obtained by him by fraud in that he fraudulently misrepresented his financial condition in his application for a loan from Household Finance Corporation.

However, the law is clear that the court should not on an application by a bankrupt for his discharge, enter upon an inquiry as to whether the bankrupt has been guilty of fraud: *In re Kemper* [1961] O.W.N. 288, 2 C.B.R. (N.S.) 130. The bankruptcy court with its summary procedures is not the proper forum to determine a charge of such gravity and complexity. In *Household Finance Corporation of Canada* v *Gratton* (1960) 1 C.B.R. (N.S.) 172 (Que.), the creditor brought a separate action in the ordinary courts for the purpose of asserting its claim that the debtor in procuring two loans had mentioned only a portion of his liabilities. It appears to me that this is the proper course for Household Finance Corporation to follow in this case if it wishes to establish its claim for fraud. An order of discharge does not release the bankrupt from any debt or liability arising out of fraud: The Bankruptcy Act, sec. 135(1)(*d*). See also *In re McCue and McKay* (1962) 3 C.B.R. (N.S.) 212 (Ont.).

I am satisfied from the evidence that the male defendant's representations were fraudulent within the meaning of s 135(1)(*e*), and that the loan of 7th January 1966 would not have been made had the male defendant declared his full indebtedness.

On argument as to whether the male defendant should be required to pay the full amount of the plaintiff's claim, or simply the amount which was advanced in cash over the amount then owing when it was proved the false representation was made, counsel for the plaintiff cited *Beneficial Finance Corpn.* v *Anderson, supra*, at p 179, where Macdonnell Co. Ct. J. adopted the reasoning of an American judge in similar circumstances:

In reliance upon the defendants' false representation, the plaintiff surrendered an existing obligation, with the right to its immediate enforcement, and entered into a new contract maturing in twenty months, advancing additional cash as well. This constituted a new transaction and resulted in a separate obligation independent of the former debt; and the debt thus incurred created a new and distinct liability for the entire balance due on the note within the intendment of section 17 of the Bankruptcy Act.

The *Anderson* case has been quoted with approval in several of the reported and unreported cases cited.

The amount due under the said promissory note at 1st November 1966, was $1,303.44. To this must be added interest at the rate of two per cent. per month on the unpaid balances to date of judgment. Both defendants are liable for this amount and judgment shall issue accordingly.

As to costs, the female defendant entered an appearance but no defence. The male defendant shall be assessed the costs of the whole action, but as against the female defendant costs up to entering judgment for default of defence.

d / *Beneficial Finance* v *Durward* (1961), 2 C.B.R. (N.S.) 173 (Ont. Co. Ct.)

29th May 1961. WEAVER Co. Ct. J.: This is an action upon a promissory note, for the balance due thereon with interest. The defendant alleges that the debt, being provable in the bankruptcy of the debtor, has been released by the order of discharge.

On or about the 12th October 1959, the defendant made what is known as a 'pay later application' to the Union Travel Service, to enable his wife to travel by steamer to Britain departing on the 17th October 1959.

He was referred by the Union Travel Service to the plaintiff with an application which he had made out on the Travel Service form, which supplied certain information. Upon receipt of the form, with the information thereon, the manager of the plaintiff company made enquiries of the references set out thereon, namely the Ontario Motor League, which was the employer of the defendant, the Bank of Commerce, which was given as his bank, the Household Finance Company, and Allen's Stores, which were given as creditors. Having satisfied himself of the stability of the employment of the defendant, of the fact that he had a small bank account, and no loan at the Canadian Bank of Commerce, and having verified the amount of the loan at Household Finance, and of the debt owing to Allen's Stores, the manager had the defendant come in the next day and fill out an application and financial statement on the plaintiff's form. The manager went over this form with the defendant, and pointed out that he had to list all his creditors. The defendant filled out the application form showing $900 owing to 'Household', and $145 owing to Allen's Stores, totalled at $1,045. The loan was then granted to the defendant and he and his wife executed the promissory note and a chattel mortgage. This latter was not filed in the County Court, and, therefore, was not good against the creditors of the defendant.

A cheque was issued to the defendant and the Union Travel Service jointly.

The defendant made two payments on the note, and in the month of March, 1960, made an assignment in bankruptcy. It appears that in the bankruptcy he showed that he had debts amounting to some $7,000. The plaintiff did not prove in the bankruptcy.

The defendant was discharged from bankruptcy on the 26th October 1960.

At the trial, it was shown that he had a loan with Corpus Christi Parish Credit Union, on which nearly $1,700 was owing at the date of the Beneficial loan, and a further loan of $425 on a note to the Toronto-Dominion Bank, at the Queen and Kenilworth Branch.

The manager of the plaintiff company swore that he would not have granted the loan had the defendant listed these two debts in his application and financial statement. The defendant excused the omission on the grounds that his debt to the Corpus Christi Parish Credit Union was guaranteed by two relatives, and, therefore, he did not regard that he owed it. He also said that although he had listed the Bank of Commerce on the Union Travel application, he had mentioned verbally the Toronto-Dominion Bank, as a place where he had an account, and he thought the manager would find out from the bank about his loan there.

The finance company manager swore in reply that the only bank mentioned to him was the Canadian Bank of Commerce, and he said that he cleared with the Adelaide Street branch of that bank, which was closest to the place of employment of the defendant for any small loans and discovered that there were none.

The plaintiff brought this action relying upon s 135(1)(*e*) of the Bankruptcy Act, which reads:

An order of discharge does not release the bankrupt from ...
   (*e*) any debt or liability for obtaining property by false pretences or fraudulent misrepresentation.

I was referred by counsel to the classic authority, *Derry* v *Peek* (1889), 14 App. Cas. 337, and particularly to the judgment of Lord Herschell, at p 374. I might say that this action was one by a subscriber to shares in a railway company, against the directors of the company for deceit in the statement offering the shares to the public. Lord Herschell says: 'First, in order to sustain an action of deceit, there must be proof of fraud, and nothing short of that will suffice. Secondly, fraud is proved when it is shewn that a false representation has been made, (1) knowingly, or (2) without belief in its truth, or (3) recklessly, careless whether it be true or false ... To prevent a false statement being fraudulent there must, I think, always be an honest belief in its truth. And this probably covers the whole ground, for one who knowingly alleges that which is false, has obviously no such honest belief. Thirdly, if fraud be proved, the motive of the person guilty of it is immaterial. It matters not that there is no intention to cheat or injure the person to whom the statement was made'.

While this is not actually an action for deceit, yet there is a certain analogy between the necessary proof of fraud, or misrepresentation required to maintain the action of deceit, and that required in order to have the benefit of s 135(1)(*e*) of the Bankruptcy Act.

I think that the case at bar is on all fours with one recently reported in the Superior Court in Bankruptcy in Quebec, namely: *Household Finance Corpn.* v *Gratton* (1960), 1 C.B.R. (N.S.) 172. In that case the debtor, in procuring two loans, complied with the lender's requirements including a statement of his outstanding liabilities, which, however, mentioned only a portion of them. The Court held that the debtor, having declared only a portion, the amounts received by him were obtained under false pretences, and therefore the debts for these loans were not released by his discharge.

The defendant raised the question of jurisdiction invoking s 140 of the Bankruptcy Act, which gives jursidiction in bankruptcy matters to the Supreme Court of Ontario. However, Mr. Justice Logie in *Re Wilson* (1930), 38 O.W.N. 240, 11 C.B.R. 425, 3 Can. Abr. 1341, held that a creditor's right of action arises upon the discharge of the debtor, and there is no necessity to set aside the discharge. An ordinary action brought in the Supreme Court and not in bankruptcy is regular and may be proceeded with. This case I think is on all fours with that.

I, therefore, hold that this loan has not been released by the order of discharge, the plaintiff has brought the action in the proper Court, which Court has jurisdiction, and is, therefore, entitled to judgment for the claim and costs.

The balance of claim has been proven at $338.14, interest thereon to the 15th December 1960, amounts to $69.53, further interest to the 17th May, the date of hearing, is $32.32.

Judgment will, therefore go for $440.09. The plaintiff will be entitled to a counsel fee of $25.

QUESTION Will the two foregoing cases still be good law under the new Bankruptcy Bill?

Table of Cases

A page number in italics indicates that the text of the case or a portion thereof is reproduced. A page number in roman type indicates that the case is merely referred to or mentioned.

Index